EIGHTH EDITION

GUIDE TO NEW ENGLAND & CANADIAN MARITIME MARINAS

Powered by Datastract™

Beth Adams-Smith

Contributing Writers:
George Boase, Peter Quandt & Brian Mehler

Editors: Richard Y. Smith & Beth Adams-Smith

Atlantic Cruising Club at Jerawyn Publishing **www.AtlanticCruisingClub.com**

Atlantic Cruising Club's Guide to New England & Canadian Maritime Marinas

EIGHTH EDITION

ISBN 978-0-9759687-2-7
Library of Congress Catalog Number (PCN) 2011905607

Front Cover Photo: Newport, RI harbor front taken from Goat Island by Q.T. Luong, terragalleria.com.

Back Cover Photos: Camden, ME Windjammer Festival — Beth Adams-Smith;
Boston Waterboat Marina backed by Marriott Long Wharf, Boston, MA — Peter Quandt; Nantucket Boat Basin aerial — NBB;
"Savannah" at Wentworth by the Sea Marina — WBTSM; Royal Nova Scotia Yacht Squadron, Halifax, NS — Beth Adams-Smith.

Executed Cover Design — Jessica Gibbon, Spark Design
Initial Cover Design — Rob Johnson
Book Design & Layout — Jessica Gibbon, Spark Design
Photo Retouching — Karina Tkach
Cartography — Jeremy Strain
Data Acquisition — Andrea Piccolo, Tyler Norris Goode, Sarah Newgaard
Programming — Thomas Tustin
Fact Checking — Anca Maierean & MicroCalls BPO
Inputting & Proofing — Tyler Norris Goode
Printer — Walsworth Publishing Company, Marceline, MO

The publishers and editors of the Eighth Edition of *Atlantic Cruising Club's Guide to New England & Canadian Maritime Marinas* have made reasonable efforts to ensure that the information contained herein is accurate and complete. The information in the Marina Reports is gathered and updated from marina questionnaires, personal site visits, telephone contacts, interviews, marina literature, reader comments and other sources. However, Atlantic Cruising Club at Jerawyn Publishing and the publishers and editors make no representation or warranty regarding accuracy and completeness. The perspectives expressed are solely those of the authors and do not represent, in any way, the opinions of any advertisers or sponsors.

None of the information contained herein, including chart schematics, latitude/longitude and reported water depths, is intended for use in navigation and may not be relied upon for such purposes. Readers should consult current NOAA charts and Notices to Mariners.

Ratings and reviews are, by their nature, subjective and subject to change at any time. They are not intended to be statements of fact. The Atlantic Cruising Club at Jerawyn Publishing and the publisher and editors disclaim any responsibility for errors or omissions and do not assume any liability for claims or damages that might arise from use or publication of the *Guide*.

Bulk purchase discounts are available to yacht clubs, rendezvous organizers, boat manufacturers and other nautical groups for any of the Atlantic Cruising Club's Guides to Marinas. Please contact Guide@AtlanticCruisingClub.com or call 888-967-0994.

Atlantic Cruising Club's Guide to New England & Canadian Maritime Marinas is written, compiled, edited and published by:

Atlantic Cruising Club at Jerawyn Publishing
PO Box 978; Rye, New York 10580

www.AtlanticCruisingClub.com

Table of Contents

To ensure objectivity, ACC neither solicits nor accepts marina advertising, and there is absolutely no charge to marinas or boating facilities for their inclusion in the *Atlantic Cruising Club's Guides to Marinas.* ACC reviewers have personally visited every marina included in this Guide — often two or three times.

New England & the Canadian Maritimes — *Bays, Rivers, Sounds and Gulfs*

With the 8th Edition, the *Atlantic Cruising Club's Guide to New England Marinas* has been completely revised and re-researched and is now ACC's *Guide to New England & Canadian Maritime Marinas*. Recognizing that more and more of us are looking for new destinations, unique adventures, and less-touristed ports of call, ACC headed further Downeast to New Brunswick and the St. John River and threaded through the islands of Passamaquoddy Bay to Nova Scotia. We went further up rivers, explored more islands, added another seventy marinas, thousands more images, and went to full-color throughout. And, in keeping with the Atlantic Cruising Club's digital heritage, the enclosed *Guide* on DVD makes all of this information fully searchable on a Windows PC — with more than 6,000 photos "that tell the real story." The digital *Guide* has also been integrated into some electronic charting programs. Following are a few favorite highlights of this 750-plus miles of fascinating coastline:

NOVA SCOTIA

Along Nova Scotia's south shore, it's Maine fifty years ago. Small charming towns and villages with active yacht and boating clubs, some still community-run, are oriented to the sea. Spend a lay-day or two at an upscale resort, dock at a famous bakery café. Don't miss Chester, the regional sailing center, or the sweet little village of Mahone Bay. Seafaring and shipbuilding history is alive in Lunenburg, a world heritage site, with a colorful skyline that is even more picturesque from the cockpit of a boat — especially when moored among some of the Fisheries Museum's barques and schooners.

Dock in downtown Halifax, one of the world's finest harbors, among celebrated ship museums, to take advantage of its impressive big city amenities: fine dining, performing arts, good provisioning, top hotels and 400 years of history. Or make camp at one of the more distant but venerable and welcoming yacht clubs — like the elegant Royal Nova Scotia Yacht Squadron in Halifax Harbour's Northwest Arm. Along Nova Scotia's western shore, Yarmouth and Digby provide a base to explore the province's Acadian culture, outstanding whale watching, Bay of Fundy tide swings and the Evangeline Trail.

NEW BRUNSWICK

By sheer happenstance, on one of several research trips along the St. John River, we followed the Points East Flotilla through the Reversing Falls — the ferocious tidal rip that has challenged mariners for centuries — and observed first-hand the sheer delight as crews on boat after boat saw how benign the Falls are when transited at the right moment. Within an easy walk of the downtown Saint John dock, where boats stage for the trip through the Falls, New Brunswick's largest city promises sidewalk cafes, a provincial museum, indoor malls, walking tours and a fabulous year-round artisnal food market.

Once in the river, the world falls away; it could be a century earlier when steamboats plied the waterway stopping at the big granite wharfs — preserved today by the St. John River Society. It's a 65-mile run upriver to burgeoning Fredericton, the capital of New Brunswick, with several museums, good restaurants and a top-notch farmers' market. Along the way, stop at popular Gagetown for galleries, provisions and socializing, and take a detour up one of the deep, unspoiled, beautiful glacial reaches — Grand Lakes or Grand Bay. Along the Bay of Fundy, St. Andrews, oozing genteel, 19th century charm, is a must stop as is Campobello where the dockage is on the Canadian side but the real attraction, FDR's summer home, is on U.S. soil. For another stopped-in-time experience, rugged, remote Grand Manan Island, a mere six miles offshore, beckons with a promise of adventure, birding and quiet.

DOWNEAST MAINE & MOUNT DESERT ISLAND

The untamed stretch of coast from Passamaquoddy Bay to Frenchman's Bay is sparsely settled with little in the way of transient dockage or moorings; nevertheless, it entices cruisers. Artsy Eastport's handsome brick downtown offers the region's commercial center, shops, galleries, good food, good dockage and marine supplies. Down home Jonesport, more upscale Winterport and old-moneyed Sorrento are each welcome ports along this long, often inhospitable shore.

Tourists have been flocking to Bar Harbor, on the Mount Desert side of Frenchman's Bay, since the 1800's — and the flocking hasn't slowed. The most-touristed spot on the island, it maintains much of its original elegance amid the hucksterism of attraction kiosks and whale watch boats. It's a main entry point into the spectacular, 73-square mile Acadia National Park. The other Mount Desert harbors are more low-key and all delightful — from the Brahmin stronghold of Northeast Harbor, to "quiet side" Southwest Harbor, the birthplace of Hinckley Yachts, to deep Somes Sound fjord and off-the-beaten-path working Bass Harbor. To get away from it all, don't miss the Cranberry Islands — old Maine with just enough civilization.

PENOBSCOT BAY

When boaters talk about "cruising Maine," Penobscot Bay is usually what they mean — for good reason. Despite a blanket of lobster pots as far as the eye can see, this is still cruising at its best. The storybook islands along Eggemoggin Reach, Fox Islands Thorofare, Merchants Row — mast-straight evergreens melting into pink granite shores — each demand a stop: Frenchboro on Long Island, Burnt Coat Harbor on Swan's Island, family-centered North Haven, working Carver's Harbor on Vinalhaven, Stonington on Deer Isle. Some of the mainland harbors, like blue-blood Blue Hill and Dark Harbor, or historic Castine, are little changed in a century. Others, like Rockland and Belfast, have transformed themselves from industrial fishing ports into compelling, cultural destinations. Still others like flourishing Camden and Rockport were as prosperous and affluent when Edith Wharton was a child as they are today.

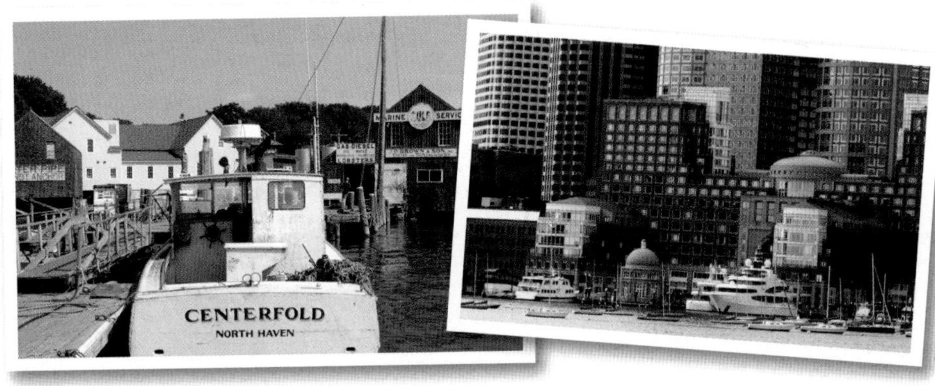

BOOTHBAY HARBOR REGION

Starting south of Rockland, the coastline changes dramatically; the St. George, Medomak, and Damariscotta Rivers create long tendrils of land with isolated, remote harbors, like archetypal Port Clyde, sprinkled along the ocean tip — a marked contrast to the bustling towns at the navigable river heads along Route One. Boothbay Harbor is the exception — one of Maine's biggest tourist magnets, it's neither isolated nor remote. Wall-to-wall, mostly recreational, docks edge the pretty, protected basin. Working wharfs, that berth a productive fishing fleet, balance the ubiquitous gift shops with a dose of reality. Onshore B&Bs occupy impeccably restored homes, restaurants of every stripe keep the populace well-fed, and, cheek by jowl along the lovely, leafy lanes, shops sell kitsch alongside galleries showing serious artists.

THE MID-COAST RIVERS, PORTLAND & THE BEACHES

South of Boothbay, the Sheepscot, Kennebec, Royal and Harraseeket Rivers carve more deep rivulets into the increasingly populated mainland. Pristine harbors, first-class resort marinas, and compelling inland destinations like Wiscasset, Bath and Freeport, provide boaters another good reason to make the scenic slog upriver. About seven NM north of Portland Harbor, Chebeague Island promises an entertaining, and more convenient, stop.

Lively Portland, Maine's largest city, is delightfully manageable with a grown-up, post 60's vibe — check out the Eastern Prom, cobblestone Old Port, the museums, the Sea Dogs and, perhaps most important, a world-class culinary scene. In Portland Harbor, a spectrum of marinas provides a choice of downtown Old Port or out-of-the-fray, across-the-harbor slips and moorings. Its nearest islands, Peaks and Diamond, are a short ferry or private yacht ride away and offer a calm, remote ambiance within shouting distance of the city attractions. Heading south, the Kennebunk and York River marinas give easy access to their affluent, appealing, up-the-river villages with a lay-day worth of activities including their well-known ocean-front beaches, Dock Square, tolley tours, house museums and presidential summer digs.

PISCATAQUA RIVER to BOSTON

The Piscataqua is flanked on the north by Kittery, ME with protected coves and stretches of brand-name outlet stores and on the south by emerging, energetic Portsmouth, NH — with the Strawbery Banke outdoor museum, a vital restaurant community, and no-sales-tax shopping. Pull up to docks right downtown along the swift river or in placid Little Harbor at Wentworth by the Sea for some spa pampering at an historic landmark hotel – with shuttle access to this big little city.

A little further south, the Merrimack River leads to engaging Newburyport. Once home to wealthy sea captains, today it's an historic, likable village with good services, restaurants and wonderful verdant strolls past antique mansions and restored commercial buildings — and there are eight marinas in town, upriver, across the river — everywhere. Closer to Boston, the North Shore towns vacillate between hard-working gritty ports and wealthy bedroom communities. Tourism has spiffed up Gloucester, which gets less commercial and more picturesque with each passing year. Rockport, Marblehead and Manchester ooze graciousness and well-spent money. Beverly and Salem share a harbor but are totally different species. Look past the witch kitsch to really appreciate Salem's rich maritime heritage and outstanding museum. The Boston Harbor Islands, remarkable in their existence as a National Park, are required stops if only to be amazed at what committed citizens and a serious harbor clean-up has wrought amidst one of the most populated areas on the East Coast. Welcoming, working-class Winthrop lies on the outskirts of Boston Harbor across from Logan Int'l while the inner harbor is served by superb marinas in downtown Boston's Wharf District or Charlestown. The city is an open air history museum; the docks along Harborwalk are just steps from Faneuil Hall, the Freedom Trail, Aquarium, Old Ironsides and so much more.

SOUTH SHORE & CAPE COD

Cohasset, Scituate, and Duxbury harbors are buzzing in the "summah" with the usual influx of third generation seasonal residents — most of whom are passionate boaters. Proximity to the Stellwagen Bank makes Green Harbor a draw for anglers, as is Plymouth — but there the similarity ends. Plymouth is a nonstop paean to the pilgrims; tourists flock to the historic sites and living history museums — and all slips and moorings have a view of Mayflower II.

The Cape begins or ends with Provincetown — a place totally unto itself that you either love or leave. It's fun, crowded, hyper — with wonderful restaurants, lots of eco activities and cultural venues plus miles of one of the planet's most spectacular beaches. It's the perfect companion to unspoiled, highly literate Wellfleet. For a quick overnight, Sesuit Harbor's just off the Bay with a river full of slips — or wait until the Cape Cod Canal's northeast entrance. Sandwich Marina used to be just a staging stop until we discovered that less than a mile inland, the oldest village on the Cape (C.1639) is well worth the walk.

Continued on the next page

On the south shore, long, narrow Falmouth Harbor was a luxury seaside destination in the 19th century; now crowded with yachts and ferries, it's lost some luxe but it's still very popular — four marinas welcome transients. Pretty, wealthy Oyster Harbor, in one of the Cape's most secluded, private villages, counterpoints bustling, Kennedy-centric Hyannis — the peninsula's main megayacht-friendly transportation hub. A bit off the boating path, active year-round fishing communities add more salt to the summer influx in Bass Harbor, Saugatuck and Chatham.

BUZZARDS BAY

The Canal spills into Buzzards Bay, one of the most diverse cruising grounds in New England. Onset Bay offers an easy stop for recouping and a stroll through the quirky, gentrifying Victorian town. Beautiful Sippican Harbor and tiny Marion, the quintessential New England village on its shore, is a must stop for sailors and those with a passion for vintage houses and gorgeous yachts. Red Brook berths a high-octane, active marina balanced by an adjacent low-key, classic boatyard, while Fiddlers Cove is about perfect amenities and beautiful Quisset Harbor boasts natural surroundings and lovely Downeast sailboats. For those with a passion for the sea, Woods Hole is a must. Four international oceanographic institutes make their home here; summer-furloughed scientists and Vineyard-focused tourists make an interesting mash-up. Across the bay, New Bedford mixes heavy duty shipyards and the 34-acre New Bedford Whaling National Historical Park — both fascinating to most mariners.

THE ISLANDS

At the foot of Buzzard's Bay, Cuttyhunk, the largest of the Elizabeth Islands, offers 580 acres of unspoiled quiet, with very little to do to tax visitors — bring a good book, food, wine and hiking shoes. Across Vineyard Sound, the westernmost of Martha's Vineyard's four harbors, Menemsha, a working fishing village that doesn't kowtow to tourism, acts a bit like an airlock between Cuttyhunk and the down-island villages. Vineyard Haven has emerged as a major center of wooden boat building — with schooners raising their sails on a regular basis, the harborscape is often dazzling. For two months every summer, Oak Bluffs sheds its Methodist Camp "Victorian gingerbread cottage" heritage and explodes into a lively party lure for young people. Conservative, well-to-do Edgartown, the island's most eastern harbor, reincarnated a once prosperous whaling town into a recreational sailing capital — preserving a remarkable collection of neoclassical sea captains' houses and protecting Chappaquiddick Island's wildlife reserves.

Twenty NM to the east, The Gray Lady, Nantucket Town, is a registered historic district. The whole 54-square mile island is a National Historic Landmark — in some ways that says it all. Once the whaling capital of the world, today, it is a perfectly maintained, stopped-in-time, mid-19th century village; it is quaint, maybe achingly so, and charismatic — catering to a wealthy summer populace and every prosperous yacht on the East coast.

THE SAKONNET RIVER & NEWPORT AREA

The Sakonnet River's wild and craggy shoreline slowly gives way to the tranquility of the Tiverton basin — home to well-protected marinas within pond-like water. Much of the land in between is devoted to gentrified estates, farms and open spaces — which encourages very little commercial river traffic. In the middle of Narragansett Bay, Jamestown's slogan "a bridge apart, a world away" couldn't be more spot on. Quiet and casual, with none of the crowds and bustle of its neighbor across the East Passage, it nonetheless has a plethora of places to eat and shop plus nine square miles of lovely rural byways and maritime attractions. If it's not quiet enough, there's a water taxi to Rose Island Light — where you can be the Keeper for a day, a night or a week. Had enough quiet? The water taxi continues on to Newport!

A world-class harbor and once a major shipping center, Newport lost out to New York in the early 19th century. Fortunately, the Gilded Age brought new life to the City by the Sea when super-wealthy industrialists built their cottages along Bellevue Avenue and became enamored of racing yachts. Today, that legacy remains the heart of the tourist trade. Marinas catering to megayachts and well-heeled boats of all stripes line the harbor front. The Museum of Yachting tells the story, and restaurants, nightlife, shops and crowds abound. Reserve a front-row, Center Harbor mooring and watch the colorful show.

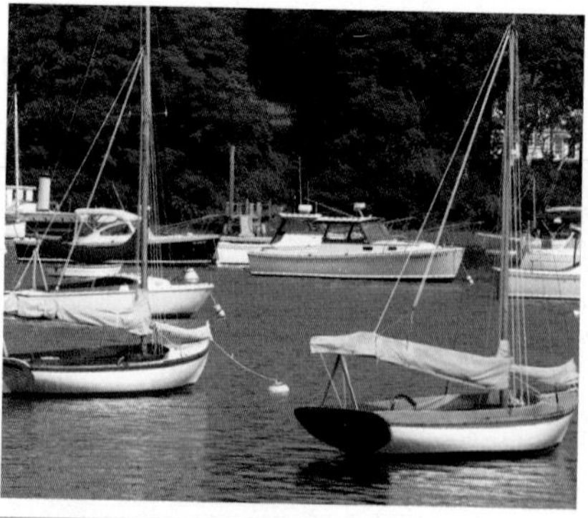

NARRAGANSETT BAY — THE EAST PASSAGE

Sailing north from Newport, two major boatyard-marinas cater to refits or new construction of the high-tech racing yachts of tomorrow. Quietly elegant, all-American Bristol is awash in exquisitely restored buildings, galleries, shops and houses, living history museums and the Holy Grail of classic yachting — the Herreshoff Marine Museum. Further north, prosperous Barrington sports old waterfront houses and some Gilded Age mansions. Its funky neighbor Warren provides a commercial balance. As the Bay gives way to the Providence River, the prize is the proximity to the renaissance city at its head. Providence has emerged as an exciting, vibrant, culinary and arts mecca with an enormous historic district, the famous Waterfires on the river — and even gondolas.

NARRAGANSETT BAY — THE WEST PASSAGE

The quieter West Passage begins in Dutch Harbor — the western shore of Conanicut Island with easy access to Jamestown — and continues north to delightful, relatively quiet Wickford, with a plethora of unique shops, the largest historic district in the country and dockage in Wickford Cove and Mill Basin. Further north, Greenwich Bay, abuzz with boating activity, harbors eight transient-friendly marinas, a state park, beaches and all manner of water-borne recreation.

Arguably New England and the Canadian Maritimes offer the best cruising experiences in the world. And it would be even better if the season were a little longer. So the challenge we all face each season is to pick and choose among this plethora of riches. Hopefully, this Guide will help meet that challenge.

Beth Adams-Smith, Rye, N.Y.

Overview Map of the Nineteen Sub-Regions

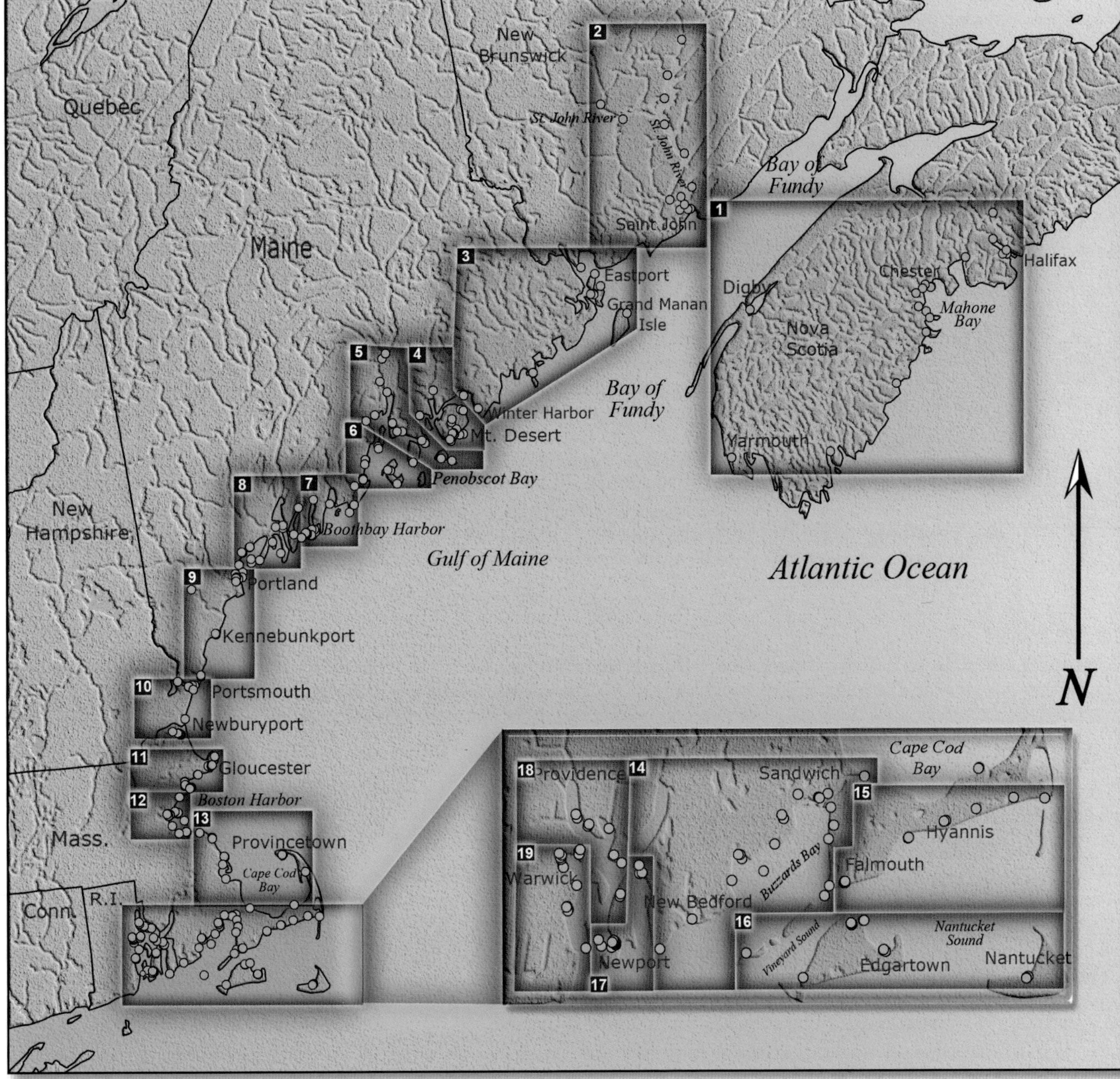

Atlantic Cruising Club's Ratings

The Bell Ratings generally reflect the services and amenities available for the captain and crew rather than the services available for the boat. By their nature, ratings are subjective and may also reflect certain biases of the writers, editors, and other reviewers. It is important to note that a five-bell marina will not always be a boater's best choice. There tends to be a correlation between higher bell ratings and higher overnight transient rates. Many of the resort-type amenities available at four- and five-bell marinas may be of little interest to boaters arriving late in the day and planning an early start the next morning. Similarly, a facility which has a one- or two-bell rating, good security, convenient transportation and a service-oriented staff, may be the best place to "leave the boat" for a period of time between legs of a longer cruise.

The Boatyard Ratings, on the other hand, are less subjective. They simply indicate the extent of the boatyard services and the size of yachts that the facility can manage. To receive a boatyard rating at all (one-travelift), a facility must have a haul-out mechanism — a travelift or marine railway (or, in some cases, a heavy-duty crane or forklift) plus, at a minimum, a standard array of basic boatyard services. To receive a two-travelift rating, a facility will generally have haul-out capacity in excess of 70 tons and a full complement of all possible boatyard services, including Awlgrip facilities. Yards that are primarily dry-stack storage operations are not given boatyard designations.

The MegaYacht Ratings are also less subjective. They indicate a marina's ability to accommodate mega or super yachts (boats with LOAs over 100 ft.) and describe the facilities available. A one-megayacht rating indicates face or slip dockage for vessels over 100 feet with at least 10 ft. of depth. A two-megayacht rating generally indicates a full complement of big boat services, including 100 amp or 200 amp service, three phase, high-rise floating docks and a knowledgeable staff that understands the special needs of larger vessels.

The Sunset Rating is the most subjective rating of all. This symbol indicates remarkable places with special appeal — like a pristine, untouched mooring field with no other facilities in sight, a marina that is, itself, so exquisitely turned out that it is truly beautiful, a view from the docks of a skyline or distant vista that is simply breathtaking, above and beyond services or amenities that are more than the basic rating would suggest, or a marina that offers the possibility of a unique experience. A Sunset means that, in our view, there is more here than the first two ratings can convey — and only you can determine if the additional notation is valid for you and your crew. We'd be very interested in hearing your collective views.

The Bell Ratings

Outlined below are some of the facilities and amenities one might generally find at a marina or boating facility within a given Bell-Rating category. Please note that some marinas within a particular category may not have all of the facilities listed here and some may have more. (The word "Marina" is used generically here, and throughout the *Guide*, to denote all types of marina facilities, including mooring fields and single, unattended piers.)

One Bell: The marina comfortably accommodates vessels over 25 feet in length, accepts overnight transients at docks or on moorings, and generally has heads. These are the "basic requirements" for ACC inclusion. Most facilities that are strictly mooring fields with a dinghy dock or basic docks with limited or no power pedestals or other services fall into this category.

Two Bells: In addition to meeting the basic ACC requirements, the marina generally has docks with power pedestals or a mooring field served by a launch (or a "dinghy loaner"). It has a dedicated marina staff, offers docking assistance, an internet connection, and monitors the VHF. There are heads, showers, and, perhaps, a laundry. It likely has dock carts, a picnic area, and grills.

Three Bells: With attractive facilities, the marina significantly exceeds basic requirements in many physical and operational categories. In addition to the two-bell services, there will usually be a restaurant on-site or adjacent. A pool, beach, or major recreational amenity, (i.e. a sport fishing center, a museum or sightseeing venue, a nature preserve, a significant "downtown") may also be nearby. The marina usually offers docking assistance and other customer-oriented services, a ships' store, cable TV, Wi-Fi, and, hopefully, a pump-out facility.

Four Bells: Worth changing course to visit, the marina significantly exceeds requirements in most physical and operational categories and offers above average service in well-appointed, appealing, and thoughtfully turned-out facilities. In addition to the three-bell services described above, it will have a restaurant on-site, as well as a pool or beach and other desirable amenities like tennis courts, sport fishing charter, or historic or scenic sites. The marina will generally offer concierge services and have a particularly inviting environment.

Five Bells: A "destination" facility, the marina is worth a special trip. It has truly superior facilities, services, and atmosphere. A five-bell marina is located in a luxurious, impeccably maintained environment and provides absolutely everything a cruising boater might reasonably expect, perhaps even room service to the boat. It offers all that is promised in a four-bell marina, plus outstanding quality in every respect.

Bell ratings reflect both subjective judgment and objective criteria. The ratings are intended to reflect the overall boater experience and are significantly impacted by a marina's setting and general ambiance. Maritime museums are usually given a Sunset Rating to indicate that they offer nautical buffs more than just services. Ratings are also geographically specific and reflect the general level of available services in a given region. In other words, a five-bell marina in Florida (with a year-round season) will usually offer more services and facilities than a five-bell marina in Maine with a shorter season.

A Tour of a Marina Report

Photos: *One for each marina in the printed Marina Report, up to 25 in full color on the enclosed DVD and on the website. Most were taken by ACC personnel during periodic visits. They are intended to provide a noncommercial, visual sense of each facility.*

Ratings: *Bells (1 – 5) reflect the quality of on-site marina facilities plus location, recreation, dining, lodgings, etc. Travelifts (1 - 2) indicate the extent of the boatyard services. MegaYachts (1 - 2) describe a marina's capacity for accommodating vessels 100 feet and larger. A Sunset denotes a place with Special Appeal — be it unique, beautiful, culturally interesting, unspoiled, a maritime center, a major attraction or in the heart of the town or city.*

Icons: *Ten icons denote Fuel, Pump-out, Certified Clean Marinas, Internet/Wi-Fi, Restaurant, Provisioning, Golf, Swimming, Catamaran Dockage & SportFish Focus*

Top Section: *Facts, facts and more facts, including VHF channels, phone numbers, e-mail/ website addresses, number of slips, moorings, power options (rates for all), and much more. The format of this section is identical for every Marina Report for easy reference and comparison.*

Navigational Information
Lat: 44°12.506' **Long:** 069°03.641' **Tide:** 10 ft. **Current:** n/a **Chart:** 13305
Rep. Depths (*MLW*): Entry 15 ft. **Fuel Dock** 10 ft. **Max Slip/Moor** 13 ft./50 ft.
Access: Penobscot Bay to Camden Harbor

Marina Facilities *(In Season/Off Season)*
Fuel: *Renneco* - Gasoline, Diesel
Slips: 60 Total, 20 Transient **Max LOA:** 150 ft. **Max Beam:** 30 ft.
Rate *(per ft.)*: **Day** $2.75* **Week** n/a **Month** n/a
Power: 30 amp $15, **50 amp** $30, **100 amp** n/a, **200 amp** n/a
Cable TV: No **Dockside Phone:** No
Dock Type: Fixed, Floating, Long Fingers, Alongside, Wood
Moorings: 59 Total, 54 Transient **Launch:** Yes (Free**), Dinghy Dock
Rate: Day $42 **Week** $250 **Month** Inq.
Heads: 5 Toilet(s), 3 Shower(s)
Internet: Yes *(Wi-Fi, Free)* **Laundry:** 3 Washer(s), 3 Dryer(s)
Pump-Out: Full Service, 1 Central **Fee:** Free **Closed Heads:** Yes

Marina Operations
Owner/Manager: Shane Flynn **Dockmaster:** Amy Armstrong
In-Season: May-Sept, 7am-5pm **Off-Season:** Sept-Apr, 7am-3:30pm
After-Hours Arrival: Call ahead. Tie up at fuel dock and check in in the am
Reservations: Yes, Recommended **Credit Cards:** Visa/MC
Discounts: None
Pets: Welcome, Dog Walk Area **Handicap Access:** Yes, Heads, Docks

Wayfarer Marine

Wayfarer Marine

59 Sea Street; Camden, ME 04843

Tel: (207) 236-4378 **VHF: Monitor** Ch. 71 **Talk** Ch. 71
Fax: (207) 236-2371 **Alternate Tel:** (207) 236-4378
Email: info@wayfarermarine.com **Web:** wayfarermarine.com
Nearest Town: Camden *(0.5 mi.)* **Tourist Info:** (207) 236-4404

Marina Services and Boat Supplies
Services - Docking Assistance, Concierge, Boaters' Lounge, Trash Pick-Up, Dock Carts **Communication -** Mail & Package Hold, Fax in/out *($2/pp)*, FedEx, UPS, Express Mail *(Sat Del)* **Supplies - OnSite:** Ice *(Block, Cube)*, Ships' Store, CNG **Under 1 mi:** Propane *(Willey 236-3256)*

Boatyard Services
OnSite: Travelift *(110T)*, Crane *(25T)*, Hydraulic Trailer *(80T, 35T)*, Launching Ramp, Engine mechanic *(gas, diesel)*, Electrical Repairs, Electronic Sales, Electronics Repairs, Hull Repairs, Rigger, Canvas Work, Bottom Cleaning, Brightwork, Air Conditioning, Refrigeration, Compound, Wash & Wax, Interior Cleaning, Propeller Repairs, Woodworking, Life Raft Service, Yacht Interiors, Metal Fabrication, Painting, Awlgrip, Total Refits **OnCall:** Divers **Dealer for:** Westerbeke. **Member:** ABBRA, ABYC, Other Certifications: Nautor's Swan, Oyster Yachts **Yard Rates:** $45-75/hr., Haul & Launch $12.50-14.50/ft., Power Wash $2/ft., Bottom Paint $65/hr. **Storage:** On-Land $45/ft. Inside $8-8.75/sq.ft. Heated $13/sq.ft.

Restaurants and Accommodations
OnSite: Lite Fare *(Marina Market 7am-4pm)* **Near:** Inn/B&B *(Hawthorn 236-8842, $150-300)* **Under 1 mi:** Restaurant *(Peter Ott's 236-4032, D $17-29, Tavern $8-18)*, *(Waterfront 236-3747, L $9-21, D $8-26)*, *(Vincent's at Whitehall Inn 236-3891, D $10-28, Fine Dining)*, *(Cappy's 236-2254, L & D $8-23)*, *(Lobster Pound 789-5550, L $4-18, D $13-26)*, Lite Fare *(Camden Deli 236-8343, B $3-7, L & D $6-8)*, Pizzeria *(Camden House 230-2464)*

Recreation and Entertainment
OnSite: Picnic Area, Grills **Near:** Playground, Tennis Courts, Cultural Attract *(Camden Civic Theater 236-2281; Camden Opera 236-7693)* **Under 1 mi:** Movie Theater *(Bay View 236-8722)*, Video Rental *(Harbor 236-9596)*, Museum *(Conway Homestead 236-2257)* **1-3 mi:** Pool *(YMCA 236-3375 $10/5 & Fitness Ctr)*, Golf Course *(Goose River 236-8488)*

Provisioning and General Services
OnSite: Provisioning Service *(1st Mate Services 841-SAIL)*, Wine/Beer, Laundry *(1st Mate Concierge)* **Near:** Bank/ATM, Library *(Camden 236-3440)* **Under 1 mi:** Convenience Store *(Village Variety 236-2085)*, Market *(French & Brawn 236-3361,)*, Supermarket *(Hannaford 236-8577)*, Gourmet Shop *(Zesty 485-0815)*, Delicatessen *(Camden Deli 236-8343)*, Health Food *(Nature's Choice 236-8280)*, Liquor Store *(Rite Aid 236-4546)*, Bakery, Farmers' Market *(Wed 3:30-6, Sat 9-noon Knox Mill Pkg Lot)*, Post Office, Catholic Church, Protestant Church, Beauty Salon, Dry Cleaners, Bookstore *(Owl & Turtle 236-4769; Sherman's 236-2223)*, Pharmacy *(Rite Aid 236-4546)*, Hardware Store *(Rankins 236-3275)*, Department Store *(Reny's)*

Transportation
OnSite: Courtesy Car/Van, Water Taxi *(Free for Wayfarer guests $5/RT MemDay-LabDay)* **OnCall:** Bikes *(Bikesenjava 596-1004)*, Rental Car *(National 800/698-8424, USave 236-2320)*, Taxi *(Joe's 975-3560)*, Airport Limo *(Schooner Bay 594-5000, Mid-Coast 236-2424)* **Near:** Local Bus **Airport:** Rockland/Bangor Int'l. *(12 mi./45 mi.)*

Medical Services
911 Service **Near:** Chiropractor *(Johnstone 236-3416)* **Under 1 mi:** Doctor *(Hope 236-2201)*, Dentist *(Day 236-8891)*, Holistic Services *(Sanctuary Spa 236-3338 Massage $75/60 min.)* **Hospital:** Penobscot Bay 596-8000 *(4 mi.)*

6. ME - WESTERN PENOBSCOT BAY

Setting -- Wayfarer Marine sprawls along the length of Camden Harbor's north shore. A mammoth blue travelift and small red dockhouse roost above fuel and dinghy floats on the eastern point overlooking the expansive mooring field. On the upland, a string of large white buildings give way to dark red boat sheds near the schooner berths at the harbor head. Sprinkled along the boardwalk, amidst flower-filled planters, swooping bat-wing awnings shelter wooden picnic tables. Side-tie docks float below berthing vessels rafted two or three deep. Every perch offers breathtaking views of the harbor, village and Camden Hills.

Marina Notes -- *Dockage: $4.25/ft. slips. Up to 16 ft. beam $2.75/ft side-tie & rafted; over 16 ft. beam $4/ft. Over 80 ft or 20 ft. beam $6/ft.. Harbor floats: $55/nt. "WMC" #s 1-21 to starboard, #s 30-67 to port. 5 "big boat" moorings to 70 ft. LOAs. 1500 linear ft. dockage & 20 slips. **Launch free to guests, others $5/RT - Mon-Sat 7am-8pm, Sun 8am-8pm. Founded 1963, new owner 2008. Purchased Harbor Head Marina with 39 slips. Major service yard - 9 climate controlled processing bays (including 2 150 ft. x 35 ft.). Inside heated & unheated storage. New 10,000 square foot heated storage building on 8.5 acres. Hauls yachts to 110 tons, drafts to 14 feet. Sweet yard tug "Barbie D." Well-stocked ships' store Mon-Fri 7am-3:30pm. Useful courtesy car. Pleasant Boaters' Lounge with coffee, TV, Wi-Fi Hot Spot, tables & chairs. Bathhouse: Inviting tiled heads with glass-door showers.

Notable -- Over the past 200 years, there have been seven boatyards on this "quiet side" of the harbor; Wayfarer is steeped in Camden history. The launch offers easy access to the picturesque town's extensive services and amenities. Alternatively, dinghy to the Town Landing or walk the half mile around the head.

PHOTOS ON DVD: 25

CAMDEN HARBOR 116

Marina Name: *300 marinas and marine facilities are included in the New England & Canadian Maritimes volume.*

Sub-Regions: *The New England & Canadian Maritimes volume includes 19 sub-regions. For quick reference, these sub-region tabs are visible on the outside page edges. In each sub-region, Marina Reports are ordered North to South, mouth to source.*

Middle Section: *What's available, where and how to find it. Marine Services & Boat Supplies, Boatyard Services (including rates), Restaurants and Accommodations, Recreation and Entertainment, Provisioning and General Services, Transportation and Medical Services, all classified by distance — On-Site, Nearby, Within 1 mile, 1-3 miles or distance beyond 3 miles. Names, phone numbers, price ranges, and more.*

Photos on DVD: *Indicates the number of photos of this facility that are on the DVD.*

Bottom Section: The *"Setting" commentary portrays a sense of the marina's surroundings and location. "Marina Notes" provides important and useful facts about the marina and its operations that may not have been covered in either of the earlier sections. "Notable" addresses what is special, unique or noteworthy about this facility or its immediate environs — from special events or services, nearby attractions to interesting side trips and/or local lore.*

Harbor: *Harbor or body of water on which the marina resides including a river, creek, bay or sound.*

The Marina Reports

In this *Guide*, individual Marina Reports are presented in a one-page, easy-reference format to make it as user-friendly as possible. On the DVD, as well as on the website, additional pages contain up to 24 additional images that expand to full-screen or as a full-screen slide show.

In addition to the Ratings described on page 8, ten Icons highlight services and facilities that are most important to cruising boaters.

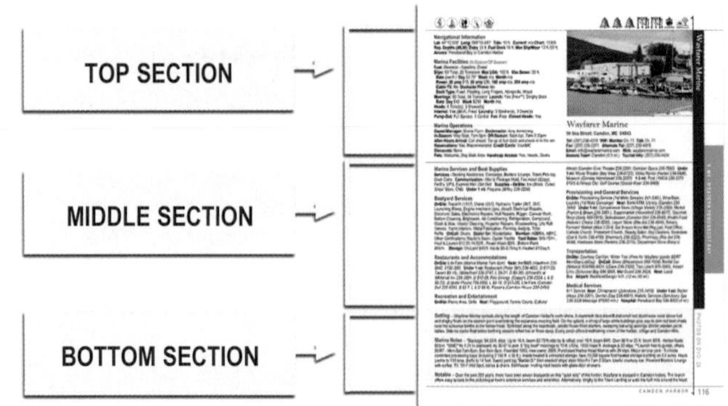

Services Icons: 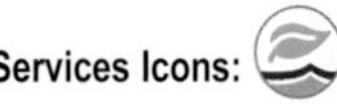 for Certified Clean Marina – CCM,  for Pump-Out,  for Internet, for Fuel, for Restaurant,  for Provisioning nearby,  for Catamaran docks,  for Sportfish Charters,  for Pool/Beach and  for Golf within a mile.

Each Report provides over 300 items of information, grouped into the following sections and categories:

TOP SECTION

Name
Address

Primary & Toll-Free Phone Numbers
Alternate Phone — After-Hours
Fax Number

VHF channels — Talk & Monitor
E-mail Address
Web URL

Nearest Town (distance)
Tourist Office Phone Number

Navigational Information

Harbor (*bottom of page*)
Latitude/Longitude

Tidal Range & Maximum Current
Chart Number

Access — General Directions
MLW Depths *(reported by the marinas)*

Entry & Fuel Dock Depths
Deepest Slip/Mooring

Marina Facilities (In Season/Off Season)

Fuel: Availability and Brand
Diesel or Gasoline
Slip-Side or OnCall Fueling
High-Speed Pumps
Maximum Boat LOA & Beam
Slips: Number of Total/Transient
Rates: Daily, Weekly, Monthly
Power (Availability & Rates):
30amp, 50 amp, 100 amp, 200 amp
Cable TV: Availability, Terms, Rates
Dockside Phone: Terms, Rates

Dock Type
Fixed or Floating
Alongside/Side-Tie
Short or Long Fingers, Pilings
Dock Material
Wood, Concrete, Vinyl,
Aluminum or Composite
Moorings: Total/Transient
Rates: Daily, Weekly, Monthly
Launch Service — Terms and Fees
Dinghy Dock — Terms and Fees

Heads:
Number of Toilets
Number of Showers
Dressing Rooms
Hair Dryers & Other Amenities
Laundry:
Number of Washers & Dryers
Irons and Ironing Boards
Book Exchange
Internet Access/Wi-Fi:
Type, Location & Fees

Services to Anchored Boats
Pump-out Availability & Fees
On-Site or OnCall
Full Service or Self Service
Number of Central Stations
Number of Portable Stations
In-Slip Dedicated Units
Pump-Out Boats
Closed Head Requirements
All Pump-Out facilities are also listed on www.AtlanticCruisingClub.com.

The number of transient slips or moorings does not necessarily indicate that they are dedicated transient. Many facilities rent open slips or moorings when their seasonal tenants are not in port. The number is the facility's guesstimate of general availability at any given time. In-Season and Off-Season rates are listed as $2.50/1.75. The seasonal dates/hours are outlined in "Marina Operations." If rates are complicated, then the daily rate for a 40-foot boat is used, followed by an asterisk; the rate structure is explained in "Marina Notes."

If there is side-tie dockage, rather than individual slips, then the number used is based on face-dock feet divided by an average 40 foot boat length, followed by another asterisk. Dock Type is listed as "Alongside" and the specifics are detailed in "Marina Notes." The lack of finger piers may signal "Stern-To, Med-Mooring." The availability of 300 amp, European Voltage and 3-Phase is listed under "Marina Services and Boat Supplies." Internet Access specifies the presence of Wi-Fi as well as the locations of broadband or dial-up dataports — plus the fees.

Marina Operations

Marina Owner/Manager
Dockmaster/Harbormaster
Dates & Hours of Operation

After Hours Arrival Procedure
Reservation Policies
Pets: Welcome?
Dog Walk Area, Kennel

Discount Programs
Boat-US, Marina Life, Safe/Sea
Dockage Fuel & Repair Discounts
Handicap Accessibility

Credit Cards Accepted:
Visa, MasterCard, Discover,
Diners Club, American Express

For municipal facilities, the Harbormaster is listed under "Marina Owner/Manager" followed by "(Harbormaster)" after his/her name. Dates and Hours for both in-season and off-season indicate the time frames for the In-season/Off-season rates.

MIDDLE SECTION

Most of the information in this section is classified by "Proximity" — the distance from the marina to the service or facility, as follows:

On-Site — at the marina
OnCall — pick-up, delivery or slipside service
Nearby — up to approximately 4/10 of a mile — a very easy walking distance
Within 1 mile — a reasonable, though more strenuous, walking distance
1 – 3 miles — a comfortable biking distance, a major hike or a cab ride
3+ miles — a taxi, courtesy car or rental car distance — generally included is the approximate distance from the marina

(FYI: In this section, telephone area codes are included only if they are different from the area codes in the marina's contact information.)

Marina Services and Boat Supplies

General Services:
Docking Assistance
Dock Carts
Trash Pick-up
Security — Type & Hours
Concierge Services
Room Service to the Boat
Boaters' Lounge

Megayacht Facilities:
Additional Power Options:
300 Amps
Three-Phase
European Voltage
Crew Lounge
Catamaran Dockage
SportFish Focus

Communications:
Mail and Package Hold
Courier Services
FedEx. Airborne, UPS
Express Mail, Saturday Delivery
Phone Messages
Fax In and Out — Fees
Pay Phones

Supplies: (Listed by Proximity)
Ice — Block, Cubes, Shaved
Ships' Stores — Local Chandlery
West Marine, Other Marine
Discount Stores
Bait & Tackle
Live Bait
Propane & CNG

Under Services are additional power options beyond the basic amperage covered in the "Marina Facilities" section. Communications includes couriers that service the marina's area; this does not imply that the marina will manage the process (unless concierge services are offered). Assume that dealing with couriers will be up to the individual boater. MegaYacht Facilities (denoted by a Rating symbol) means a marina accommodates at least 100 feet LOA and may offer higher amperage power options. Listed here, and in Marina Notes, are the additional power options beyond those listed in Marina Facilities. Under Supplies are, among many other items, resources for galley fuel. As those who rely on CNG know, it is becoming harder and harder to find. (Please share any sources you discover with your fellow boaters.)

Boatyard Services

Nearest Boatyard (If not on-site):
Travelift (including tonnage)
Railway
Forklift
Crane
Hydraulic Trailer
Launching Ramp
Engine Mechanics — Gas & Diesel
Electrical Repairs
Electronic Sales
Electronic Repairs
Propeller Repairs

Air Conditioning
Refrigeration
Rigger
Sail Loft
Canvas Work
Upholstery
Yacht Interiors
Brightwork
Painting
Awlgrip (or similar finish)
Woodworking
Hull Repairs

Metal Fabrication
Divers
Bottom Cleaning
Compound, Wash & Wax
Inflatable Repairs
Life Raft Service
Interior Cleaning
Yacht Design
Yacht Building
Total Refits
Yacht Broker
Dealer For: (Boats, Engines, Parts)

Yard Rates:
General Hourly Rate
Haul & Launch (Blocking included)
Power Wash
Bottom Paint (Paint included?)
Boat Storage Rates:
On Land (Inside/Outside)
In the Water
Memberships & Certifications:
ABBRA — No. of Cert. Techs.
ABYC — No. of Cert. Techs.
Other Certifications

If the facility does not have a boatyard on-site, then the name and telephone number of the nearest boatyard is provided. In most cases, the services listed as "Nearby" or "Within 1 mile" will be found at that facility. "Dealer For" lists the manufacturers that the Boatyard services and its Authorized Dealerships. "Memberships and Certifications" refers to the two maritime trade organizations (ABBRA — American Boat Builders & Repairers Association and ABYC — American Boat and Yacht Council) which have programs that train and certify boatyard craftspeople and technicians. Several of the other professional maritime organizations and many manufacturers also offer rigorous training and certification on their particular product lines. These are included under "Other Certifications."

Restaurants and Accommodations

Restaurants
Seafood Shacks
Raw Bars

Snack Bars
Coffee Shops
Lite Fare

Fast Food
Pizzeria
Hotels

Motels
Inns/B&Bs
Cottages/Condos

Since food is a major component of cruising, considerable attention has been given to both restaurants and provisioning resources. Eateries of all kinds are included (with phone numbers); full-service restaurants are listed simply as Restaurants. If delivery is available it is either noted or the establishment is listed as "OnCall." An attempt has been made to provide a variety of dining options and, whenever possible, to include the meals served Breakfast, Lunch, Dinner, Sunday Brunch (B, L, and/or D) plus the price range for entrées at each meal. If the menu is Prix Fixe (table d'hôte — one price for 3 - 4 courses), this is indicated in the commentary. On rare occasions, if a restaurant has received very high marks from a variety of reviewers, that will be noted, too. If we are aware of a children's menu, the listing will indicate "Kids' Menu." Often the hours of on-site restaurants are included in "Marina Notes" or "Notable."

Price ranges have been gathered from menus, websites, site visits, marina notes and phone calls. Although these change over time, the range should give you an idea of the general price point. In large cities, the list generally consists of a handful of the closest restaurants — we expect that you will supplement this with a local restaurant guide. In small towns, the list provided may be "exhaustive" — these may be all there are, and they may not be close.

Frequently, the need for local off-boat overnight accommodations arises — either for guests, crew changes, or just because it's time for a real shower or a few more amenities or a bed that doesn't rock. We have attempted to list a variety of local lodgings and, whenever possible, have included the room rate, too. The rates listed generally cover a 12-month range. So, if you are cruising in high season, expect the high end of the range. If the lodgings are part of the marina, then there is often a "package deal" of some sort for marina guests wishing to come ashore. We have asked the question about "package deals" and included the answers in "Marina Notes."

Recreation and Entertainment

Pools (heated or not)
Beach
Picnic Areas & Grills
Children's Playground
Dive Shop
Volleyball
Tennis Courts
Golf Course
Fitness Center
Jogging Paths
Horseback Riding
Hike/Bike Paths
Bowling
Sport Fishing Charter
Party Boat
Movie Theater
Video Rentals
Video Arcade
Park
Museum
Galleries
Cultural Attractions
Sightseeing
Special Events

What there is to do, once you're tied up and cleaned up, is often a driving force in choosing a harbor or a particular marina. If you are choosing a facility to spend a lay-day or escape foul weather, the potential land-based activities become even more important. We have created a list of the possible major types of recreation and entertainment activities and have organized them, again, by proximity; if they are more easily reached by dinghy we note that, too.

A public golf course is almost always listed unless it is farther than 25 miles. Boat Rentals include kayaks, canoes and small boats. Party Boats are sometimes known as "head boats." Museums cover the gamut from art and maritime to historic houses and districts to anthropological and environmental. Cultural Attractions can range from local craft ateliers to aquariums to live theaters to all manner of musical concerts. Sightseeing can range from whale watching to historical walking tours. Special Events usually covers the major once-a-year local tourist extravaganzas — and almost all require significant advance planning (often these also appear in the "Notable" section). Galleries, both fine art and crafts, are listed under Entertainment rather than General Services, since we view them more as opportunities for enlightenment than the shops that they really are. Admission prices are provided for both Adults and Children, when available, and are listed with the Adult price first, followed by the Children's price, i.e., $15/7. Occasionally, there is a family package price, which is also listed. Most entertainment and recreation facilities also offer Student and Senior Citizen pricing and other discounts; unfortunately, we don't have space to note them, but we do provide a phone number, so call and ask.

Provisioning and General Services

Complete Provisioning Service
Convenience Store
Supermarket — usually major chain
Market — smaller, local store
Gourmet Shop
Delicatessen
Health Food Store
Wine/Beer Purveyor
Liquor/Package Store
Bakery
Farmers' Markets
Green Grocer
Fishmonger
Lobster Pound
Crab House
Bank/ATMs
Post Office
Library
Houses Of Worship
Catholic Church
Protestant Church
Synagogue
Mosque
Beauty Salon
Barber Shop
Dry Cleaners
Laundry — Full Service
Bookstore
Pharmacy
Newsstand
Hardware Store
Florist
Retail Shops
Department Store
Copy Shops
Buying Club

As noted previously, we think that most boaters travel on their stomachs, so knowing how to find local provisioning resources is very important. In addition, there is a fairly constant need for all kinds of services and supplies. When delivery is available for any of the provisioning resources or services, we've either noted that in the commentary or listed it as "OnCall."

For major provisioning runs, we have tried to identify the closest outlet for a regional supermarket chain. If a smaller, but fairly well supplied, market is close by, we include it as well as the more distant chain supermarket. Most people, we've discovered, really prefer to find interesting, local purveyors, so the presence of a Farmers' Market is noted. Usually, these are one or two-day-a-week events, so the exact days, times and locations are included. To differentiate Farmers' Markets from produce markets and farm stands, the latter are listed as Green Grocers. We've also tried to locate full Provisioning Services that will "do it all" and deliver dockside. And Fishmonger is just another name for fish sellers — these could be regular fish markets or directly "off-the-boat."

In the "General Services" category, we've included the nearest libraries because they can be wonderful sources of all kinds of "local knowledge," and can provide a welcome port on a foul weather day. They also usually have children's programs during the "season" and, with growing frequency, offer data ports or public Internet access on their own PCs. The Laundry in this section should not to be confused with the washers and dryers at the marina. Laundries are usually combination "do it for you" drop-off and self-service operations — and are frequently near restaurants or recreation or entertainment venues.

Transportation

Courtesy Car or Van
Bikes
Water Taxi
Rental Car — Local and Nat'l
Taxi
Local Bus
Intercity Bus
Rail — Amtrak & Commuter
Ferry Service
Airport Limo
Airport — Regional & Nat'l

Once most cruisers hit land, they are on foot (except for those fortunate souls with sufficient on-board storage to travel with folding bikes). So transportation, in all its guises, becomes a very important consideration. We've divided transportation into two categories — getting around while in port and the longer-range issue of getting to and from the boat. If the marina or boatyard provides some form of courtesy car or van service, it's noted first. These services can include unlimited use of a car (very rare), scheduled use of a car (often 2 hours), an on-demand "chauffeured" van service, a scheduled van service, or a marina manager or employee willing to drive you to "town" at a mutually convenient time. The guests' use of this service is sometimes completely unrestricted; other times, it is reserved exclusively for provisioning or restaurant trips. If the details of this arrangement are simple, they are explained in the commentary; if complicated, they are explained in the "Marina Notes." Courtesy cars and/or vans are one of the most volatile of the marina services so, if this is important to you, call ahead to confirm that it's still available and to ask about the terms.

The Airport Limo services are either individual car services or vans. Rail covers Amtrak as well as commuter services that connect to a city, an Amtrak stop, or an airport. Local Buses also include the seasonal trolleys that are becoming more common (and extraordinarily useful) in more tourist-oriented ports. Local, regional and inter-city ferry services are listed. Rates, when included, are usually for both Adults and Children, and indicate if one-way or round-trip; they are listed with the Adult price first, followed by the Children's price, i.e., $25/17RT. Note that there are usually Senior Citizen and Student prices, but space has precluded their inclusion. Don't forget to ask.

For those of us cruising the coast less than full time, the logistics of going back and forth to the boat is often the stuff of nightmares. Rental cars have a variety of uses — local touring or long distance (back to where you left your car, to the airport, or back home). We list local rental car agencies (for day rents), and regional ones (like Enterprise). We tend not to list the national ones (where pick-up and drop-off may be restricted to airports or downtown locations) because these are obvious and often very difficult to get to. Because Enterprise delivers and picks up — remembering that you have to return the driver to his/her office — we always include the nearest Enterprise office, if one exists, as "OnCall." (If another agency advertises pick-up/delivery, that information is included as "OnCall," too).

Note that some franchise auto rentals, because the outlets are locally or regionally owned, seem to have a wide range of "drop-off" policies. Sometimes, if the region is large enough, it is possible to pick the car up at the current marina and drive to the marina where you left your own car, and leave the rental right there. When available, this service is just great. Call and check. The Airport listing often includes both the nearest regional and the nearest international. Because, as noted, long-distance, one-way car rentals are often based at airport locations, a marina's distance from an airport takes on a larger meaning than just catching a plane.

Medical Services

911 Service	Dentist	Holistic Service	Ambulance	Hospital
Doctor	Chiropractor	Veterinarian	Optician	

The data in this section is provided for informational purposes only and does not imply any recommendation. ACC is simply listing the nearest practitioner in each category. The first listing is the availability of 911 service; this service is surprisingly not ubiquitous — so it is important to know if dialing 911 will "work" in a given area. In the listings for Doctors, preference is given to walk-in clinics, then group practices and then general practitioners or internists. Dentists, Chiropractors, Veterinarians, and Holistic Services are also chosen in a similar fashion. A single practitioner is listed only if a "group" is not nearby. Holistic services will generally list massage therapists or full-service spas, but may also include acupuncturists, energy healers, and yoga classes when we find them. Hospital is usually the nearest major facility; if this is very far away and we are aware of a satellite, that will be noted — especially if there are no physicians nearby.

BOTTOM SECTION

Setting

This section provides a description of the location, environment, and ambiance of each marina, boatyard or mooring field, including its views both landside and waterside, and any easily identifiable landmarks.

Marina Notes

Marina-specific information not included in the middle and top sections is detailed here. The source for this data includes interviews with marina staff, marina literature, marina comments provided to ACC, and surveyor/reviewer observations during site visits. If the rate structure is too complicated to detail in the "Facilities" section, a thorough explanation will be included here, preceded by an asterisk. Anything that is noteworthy about the facility is described in this paragraph — including history, background, recent changes, damage, renovations, new facilities, new management and general marina atmosphere. If there is a restaurant or some form of lodging on-site, it is noted here, including any special deals for marina guests. If the marine services are part of a resort or a private yacht club with extensive recreation facilities, the level of access to those facilities is also detailed here or in "Notable." The facilities and services available to the visiting cruiser are also reflected in the rating. Certified Clean Marinas are indicated by CCM (see www.AtlanticCruisingClub.com for a complete description and a listing of all Certified Clean Marinas in this volume). "Bathhouse:" includes a description and commentary on heads and showers (noting, if they are, for instance, below par for the rating or particularly nice).

Notable

This section focuses on what is special or unique about each facility — additional items of interest related to the marina itself or the surrounding area. Details on special events, nearby attractions, the local community, ways of "getting around," the best beaches, special things to do, or other noteworthy facilities and/or services are listed here. Occasionally, there's also an elaboration on the on-site or nearby restaurants, amenities, or accommodations. Or, perhaps the marina is near an airport, in a secure basin, the owner lives on-site, or the rates are low — any or all of which might make this a good place to leave the boat for a while.

For a complete explanation of the Data Gathering and Review Process, please see "About Atlantic Cruising Club" on www.AtlanticCruisingClub.com.

The Digital Guide on DVD

The enclosed DVD contains the *Atlantic Cruising Club's Digital Guide to New England & Canadian Maritime Marinas*; it includes all of the data and Marina Reports that are in this print version with more than 5,000 color photographs, all searchable on over 100 datafields.

- **Installation** — Simply insert the enclosed DVD into your computer's DVD drive. The installation program starts automatically. If it doesn't, click "Start/Run" and enter "d://setup.exe" (assuming your DVD drive is "d"). Or, select "Explore" or "My Computer," click on the DVD drive, then "setup.exe." During the installation process, you are asked to choose how many of the three components you wish to copy to your hard drive — this affects the amount of hard disk space the program uses. If you have the hard disk capacity, it is best to install all three components. The program will run somewhat faster, and you will not need to have the DVD always at hand.

- **The Digital Guide is built around four screens:**

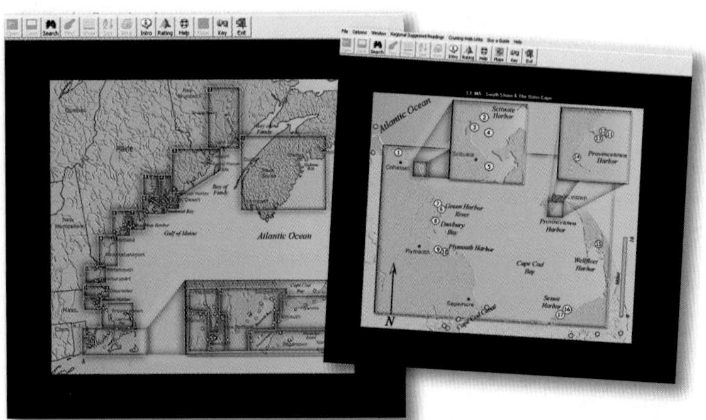

Region and Sub-Region Maps — Click on the "Maps" button to view a map of the New England and Canadian Maritime Region with each of the 19 sub-regions outlined. Click on one of the outlines to access the map for that particular Sub-Region. The locations of each of the marinas in that geographic area are displayed on the map. The location "points" and the marina names are "hot." Click on them to display the Marina Report for that marina. If you would prefer to add additional criteria to a marina search (or to skip the graphics interface entirely), the "search" button on the New England and Canadian Maritime Regional map screen and on each of the Sub-Region map screens takes you directly to the Marina Search screen.

Marina Search Settings — This screen permits the user to enter up to 100 different search criteria — either singly or in combination. You may search for a particular marina by name (or part of a name), for all of the marinas in a particular geographic region, city, or body of water, for marinas able to accommodate your vessel's LOA and draft, etc., etc., etc. If you arrived at this screen from one of the Sub-Region maps, then that Sub-Region is already entered in the "Location Search" box. You may add more sub-regions using the "Select Sub-Region" button. Once you have set the criteria for your search, click the "Find Marinas" button at the bottom of the screen (or the "Find" button in the toolbar). The search result (the number of marinas meeting your criteria) is indicated in the "Marinas Found" field. At this point, either refine your search to generate more or fewer marina choices or click the "Show Marinas" button to proceed to the next screen.

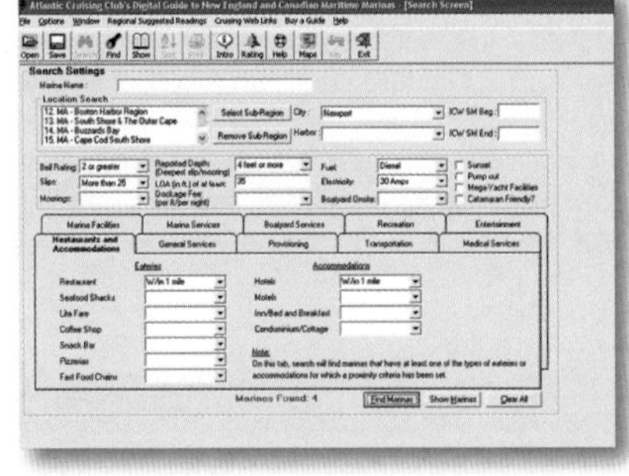

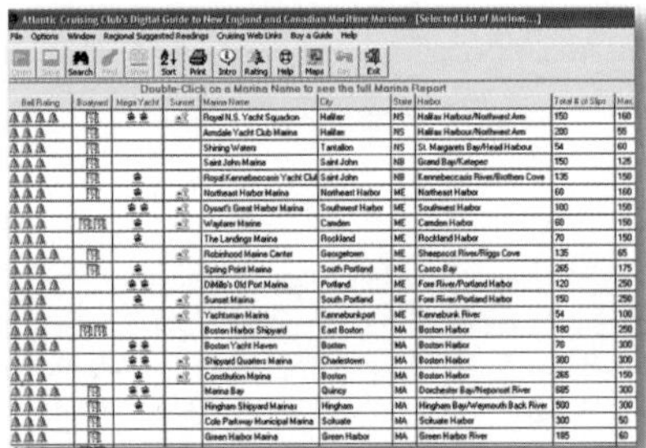

List of Selected Marinas — All of the marinas that meet your criteria are displayed on this screen. Next to each Marina Name are several items of information, including: Bell, Boatyard, MegaYacht, and Sunset Ratings, city, state, and harbor. If, during the search, you set a criterion for "Slips," "Moorings," "LOA" or "Dockage Fee," a column for each selection also appears in the "List of Selected Marinas." The List may be sorted either geographically (default) or alphabetically. To view a full Marina Report for any of the marinas on the List, simply double-click on its name.

Marina Report — The Marina Reports in *ACC's Digital Guide* are identical to the Marina Reports in this printed version of the *Guide* but with some enhancements: The Reports are interactive and each contains up to to 25 additional full color marina photos. The Marina Reports Screen also lists the names of the other marinas that met your most recent search criteria. Clicking on one of those marina names displays its Marina Report. Finally, there is a box in the lower left hand corner of the Marina Report for you to enter your comments and observations about a given marina. This data is stored within the program and becomes part of the record for that marina. You can also print Marina Reports (and your comments, if you wish) using the Print command.

Note: ***For proper operation of the Digital Guide, Internet Explorer must be installed on your computer. Each regional volume of the ACC Guides will automatically install into a separate, clearly labeled folder. They will operate independently.***

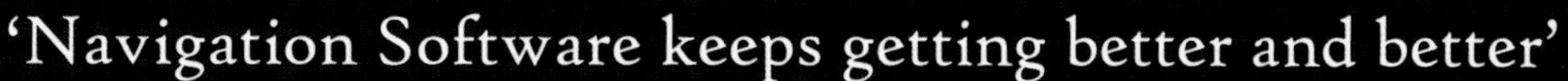

Atlantic Cruising Club Guides Now Available in Coastal Explorer

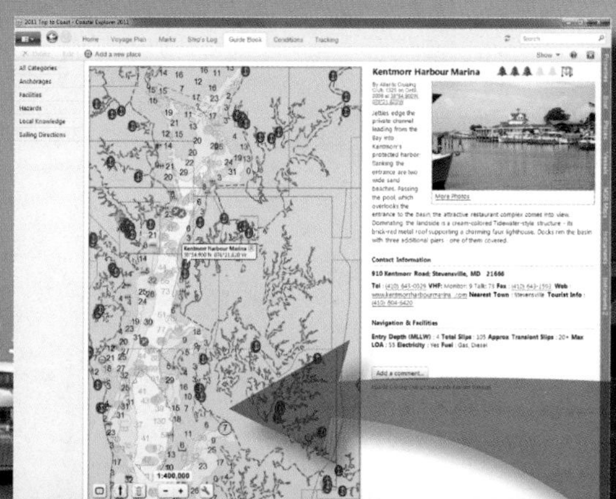

Basic information included for free

Kentmorr Harbour Marina

Complete Marina information available with purchase of an Atlantic Cruising Club Guide

Coastal Explorer is full featured PC based navigation software for desktop or laptop computers. Coastal Explorer displays an icon precisely showing the vessel's location on the chart when connected to a GPS. Virtually any NMEA instrument data can be displayed on the screen. Radar overlay is available with purchase of compatible hardware. Coastal Explorer includes free charts for United States waters, the complete Coast Pilot, tides and tidal currents, weather and a gazetteer with over 4 million searchable place names. The software is designed to provide all the information needed to safely get from one place to another. Coastal Explorer includes basic Atlantic Cruising Club marina information for free and complete marina data is supported upon purchase of this and other Atlantic Cruising Club Guides.

COASTAL EXPLORER

Visit www.rosepointnav.com for more information

The Atlantic Cruising Club's Website

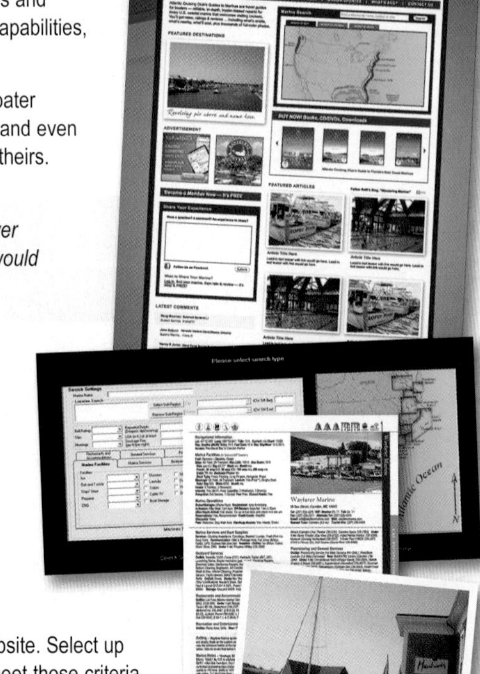

www.AtlanticCruisingClub.com has been serving boaters since 1999, and, after years of upgrades and enhancements, ACC decided it was time for a total rebuild to handle the enhanced marina search capabilities, massive photo files, a library of fresh content and all of the new bells and whistles.

In the works (or live by the time you read this): slide shows and video, easy downloads, personal boater pages, immediate marina updates, integration into digital charts like Rose Point's Coastal Explorer, and even more interactivity — including better ways to share your opinions with your fellow boaters and hear theirs.

We welcome your constructive comments as more and more features are added. Nothing is ever finished in cyberspace, so if you don't like a particular function or it doesn't work the way you would like it to, please tell us. Unlike a book that is set in stone, web development is never ending ...

Marina Search — Find a Marina: The all-new ACC website houses the complete 1,800-marina database which underlies the comprehensive *Atlantic Cruising Club's* regional *Guides to Marinas*. There are several ways for boaters to use the website to find the *right* marina:

- **Map/Chart or Geographic Interface:** Beginning with a map of North America, a boater can "drill down" through increasingly more detailed maps — choosing either the graphical or the Google map interface. It's all point & click simple. Pass the cursor over the numbered button and the marina name appears; click and the complete full color Marina Report is displayed — with up to 25 photos.
- **Marina Search Interface:** The tabbed Marina Search screen on the DVD is also on the website. Select up to 100 search criteria — either singly or in any combination — for a list of all marinas that meet those criteria.
- **Search by Index —** Drill down through the states/provinces, regions, harbors/rivers/bays to the list of marinas. Click on one to display the Marina Report.
- **Search by Name —** Just type in the name of a marina, state/province, city, or harbor, river or bay for a quick list of all of the relevant marinas. The pre-populated search function will assist your search. Click on a name for the Marina Report.

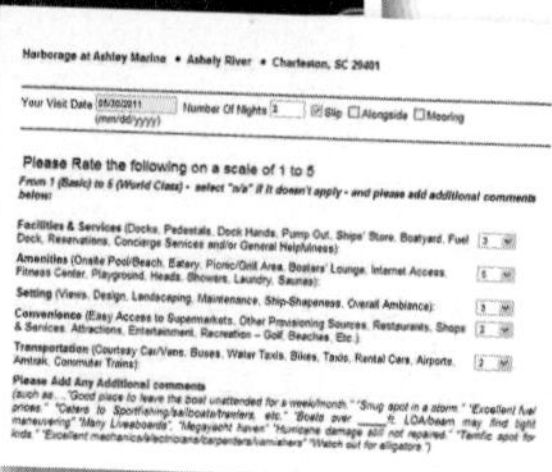

Cruiser Comments: A section on each online Marina Report allows boaters to share their experiences. At the top of each online Marina Report are the words, "Add a comment/Read Other Comments." Please check in often to rate and review the marinas you've visited, comment on ACC's ratings and reviews — and read what other boaters have left.

Marina Updates: The Reports in the *Atlantic Cruising Club's Guide to New England & Canadian Maritime Marinas* are current when published, but marinas are in a fairly constant state of evolution. ACC updates the Marina Reports as facts change and posts the new information or the revised Marina Reports on the ACC website.

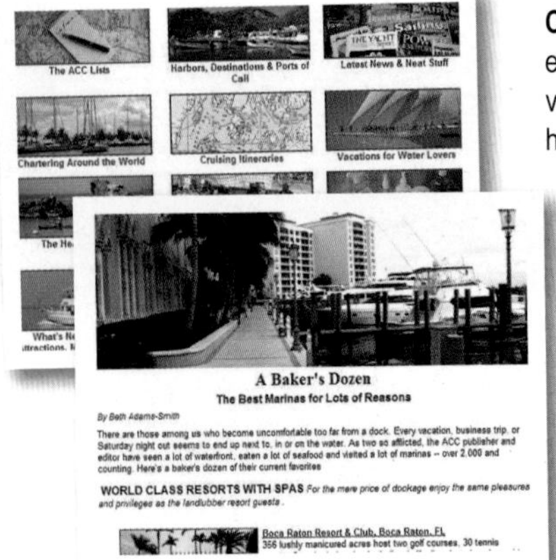

Cruising Info, Boating Lifestyle and Destination Articles: ACC writers and reviewers share their experiences in articles on the do-not-miss and the below-the-radar regions and harbors, cruise itineraries, vacations for boaters (on and off boats), provisioning, cruising lifestyles, chartering around the world, healthy/green boating, the healthy boater and a members' favorite — the ACC "Best of" Lists.

Suggested Reading: For every region, there is an extensive reference list of books that cruisers might find interesting — with photos of the covers, ACC's reviews, pricing, and direct links for purchases. Additional recommendations are always welcome.

Cruising Links: These are hot URLs to resources on the web that ACC has found particularly useful. Recommendations are also always welcome.

Click the links to "like" Atlantic Cruising Club on FaceBook, "follow" ACC on Twitter and read Beth's Blog WanderingMariner.com.

A complimentary six-month Silver Membership is included with the purchase of this *Guide*. Select "Join Now," then "Silver," then follow the instructions.

ATLANTIC CRUISING CLUB'S

GUIDE TO NEW ENGLAND & CANADIAN MARITIME MARINAS

THE MARINA REPORTS

EIGHTH EDITION

Geographic Listing of Marinas

Continued on the next page

Continued on the next page

Marina Name	*Harbor*	*City, State*	*Page No.*
9. MAINE — CASCO BAY, PORTLAND & THE BEACHES, continued			
Portland Yacht Services	Fore River/Portland Harbor	Portland, ME	176
DiMillo's Old Port Marina	Fore River/Portland Harbor	Portland, ME	177
Sunset Marina	Fore River/Portland Harbor	South Portland, ME	178
South Port Marine	Fore River/Portland Harbor	South Portland, ME	179
Chick's Marina	Kennebunk River	Kennebunkport, ME	180
Kennebunkport Marina	Kennebunk River	Kennebunkport, ME	181
Yachtsman Marina	Kennebunk River	Kennebunkport, ME	182
York Town Docks & Moorings	York Harbor	York Harbor, ME	183
Donnell's Dockage	York Harbor	York Harbor, ME	184
10. MAINE / NEW HAMPSHIRE / MASSACHUSETTS — PISCATAQUA TO MERRIMACK RIVERS			**185**
Kittery Point Town Wharf	Piscataqua River/Pepperrell Cove	Kittery, ME	186
Kittery Point Yacht Yard	Piscataqua River/Kittery Point	Kittery, ME	187
Prescott Park Municipal Dock	Piscataqua River	Portsmouth, NH	188
Badgers Island East	Piscataqua River	Kittery, ME	189
The Marina at Harbour Place	Piscataqua River	Portsmouth, NH	190
Badgers Island Marina	Piscataqua River	Kittery, ME	191
Great Bay Marine	Piscataqua River	Portsmouth, NH	192
Wentworth by the Sea Marina	Little Harbor	New Castle, NH	193
Hampton River Marina	Hampton Harbor	Hampton, NH	194
Newburyport Harbor Marina	Merrimack River	Newburyport, MA	195
Newburyport Waterfront Park	Merrimack River	Newburyport, MA	196
Hilton's Marina	Merrimack River	Newburyport, MA	197
Windward Yacht Yard	Merrimack River	Newburyport, MA	198
Cove Marina	Merrimack River	Salisbury, MA	199
Newburyport Boat Basin	Merrimack River	Newburyport, MA	200
Merri-Mar Yacht Basin	Merrimack River	Newburyport, MA	201
Marina at Hatter's Point	Merrimack River	Amesbury, MA	202
11. MASSACHUSETTS — NORTH SHORE			**203**
Rockport Harbor	Rockport Harbor	Rockport, MA	204
Cape Ann's Marina Resort	Annisquam River/Blynman Canal	Gloucester, MA	205
Gloucester Harbor Moorings	Gloucester Harbor	Gloucester, MA	206
Madfish Grille	Gloucester Harbor/Smith Cove	Gloucester, MA	207
East Gloucester Marine	Gloucester Harbor	Gloucester, MA	208
Brown's Yacht Yard	Gloucester Harbor	Gloucester, MA	209
Pier 7/Enos Marine	Gloucester Harbor/Cripple Cove	Gloucester, MA	210
Crocker's Boat Yard	Manchester Harbor	Manchester, MA	211
Manchester Marine	Manchester Harbor	Manchester, MA	212
Beverly Port Marina	Danvers River/Beverly Channel	Beverly, MA	213
Glover Wharf Municipal Marina	Danvers River/Beverly Channel	Beverly, MA	214
Brewer Hawthorne Cove Marina	Salem Harbor	Salem, MA	215
Pickering Wharf Marina	Salem Harbor	Salem, MA	216
Salem Water Taxi	Salem Harbor	Salem, MA	217
Fred J. Dion Yacht Yard	Salem Harbor	Salem, MA	218
Corinthian Yacht Club	Marblehead Harbor	Marblehead, MA	219
Tucker's Wharf Municipal Docks	Marblehead harbor	Marblehead, MA	220
Boston Yacht Club	Marblehead Harbor	Marblehead, MA	221
Dolphin Yacht Club	Marblehead Harbor	Marblehead, MA	222

Continued on the next page

Marina Name	Harbor	City, State	Page No.
14. MASSACHUSETTS — BUZZARDS BAY, continued			
Earl's Marina	Nasketucket Bay	Fairhaven, MA	276
Fairhaven Shipyard & Marina	Acushnet R./New Bedford Harbor	Fairhaven, MA	277
Acushnet River Safe Boating Marina	Acushnet R./New Bedford Harbor	Fairhaven, MA	278
Pope's Island Marina	Acushnet R./New Bedford Harbor	New Bedford, MA	279
New Bedford Yacht Club	Apponagansett Harbor	South Dartmouth, MA	280
F. L. Tripp & Sons, Inc.	Westport Harbor	Westport Point, MA	281
15. MASSACHUSETTS — CAPE COD SOUTH SHORE			**283**
Falmouth Marine Yachting Center	Falmouth Harbor	Falmouth, MA	284
MacDougalls' Cape Cod Marine	Falmouth Harbor	Falmouth, MA	285
Falmouth Harbor Town Marina	Falmouth Harbor	Falmouth, MA	286
East Marine	Falmouth Harbor	Falmouth, MA	287
Oyster Harbors Yacht Basin	West Bay/Osterville Crosby Basin	Osterville, MA	288
Crosby Yacht Yard	West Bay/Osterville Crosby Basin	Osterville, MA	289
Hyannis Marina	Lewis Bay/Hyannis Harbor	Hyannis, MA	290
Bismore Park Bulkhead	Lewis Bay/Hyannis Harbor	Hyannis, MA	291
Bass River Marina	Bass River	West Dennis, MA	292
Saquatucket Harbor Marina	Saquatucket Harbor/Harwich Port	Harwich, MA	293
Chatham Harbormaster Moorings	Stage Harbor	Chatham, MA	294
Stage Harbor Marine	Stage Harbor	Chatham, MA	295
16. MASSACHUSETTS — THE ISLANDS			**297**
Cuttyhunk Town Marina	Cuttyhunk Pond	Cuttyhunk, MA	298
Menemsha Harbor	Menemsha Harbor	Chilmark, MA	299
Tisbury Wharf	Vineyard Haven Harbor	Vineyard Haven, MA	300
Vineyard Haven Marina	Vineyard Haven Harbor	Vineyard Haven, MA	301
Black Dog Wharf	Vineyard Haven Harbor	Vineyard Haven, MA	302
Owen Park Town Dock	Vineyard Haven Harbor	Vineyard Haven, MA	303
Oak Bluffs Marina	Oak Bluffs Harbor	Oak Bluffs, MA	304
Dockside Market Place & Marina	Oak Bluffs Harbor	Oak Bluffs, MA	305
North Wharf Moorings	Edgartown Harbor	Edgartown, MA	306
Mad Max Marina	Edgartown Harbor	Edgartown, MA	307
Harborside Inn	Edgartown Harbor	Edgartown, MA	308
Nantucket Moorings	Nantucket Harbor	Nantucket, MA	309
Nantucket Boat Basin	Nantucket Harbor	Nantucket, MA	310
17. RHODE ISLAND — SAKONNET RIVER & NEWPORT HARBOR			**313**
Sakonnet Point Marina	Sakonnet River/Sakonnet Harbor	Little Compton, RI	314
Pirate Cove Marina	Sakonnet River	Portsmouth, RI	315
Standish Boat Yard	Sakonnet River	Tiverton, RI	316
Brewer Sakonnet Marina	Sakonnet River	Portsmouth, RI	317
Jamestown Boat Yard	East Passage	Jamestown, RI	318
Conanicut Marina	East Passage	Jamestown, RI	319
Newport Moorings	Newport Harbor	Newport, RI	320
West Wind Marina	Newport Harbor	Newport, RI	321
Casey's Marina	Newport Harbor	Newport, RI	322
Newport Marina	Newport Harbor	Newport, RI	323
Brown & Howard Wharf Marina	Newport Harbor	Newport, RI	324
Marina at Forty 1 Degrees North	Newport Harbor	Newport, RI	325

Continued on the next page

Photography Credits

In addition to the images provided by the marinas to supplement those taken at the time of ACC's visits, the following photographers and agencies were generous in providing further images that helped tell the story: Bath, ME Chamber of Commerce; Billy Black, Newport, RI; Max Bossman, Martha's Vineyard; Camden-Rockport-Lincolnville Chamber of Commerce; Mark Chester, Woods Hole, MA; Dan Cutrona, Falmouth, MA; William P. DeSousa-Mauk, DeMa Public Relations, Cape Cod; Cape Cod Chamber of Commerce & CVB; Flightline Photography, Portsmouth, NH; Michael Galvin, Nantucket Chamber Of Commerce; Louisa Gold, Martha's Vineyard; Hobson Photos, Bath, ME; Jonathan Latcham, Quissett, MA; Amazing Maine by Carol Latta, Camden, ME; Tom Leach, Saquatucket, MA; Matt Levin, Camden, ME; Martha's Vineyard Chamber of Commerce; Brian Morris, Chatham, MA; John Phelan, Marion, MA; Greater Newburyport Chamber of Commerce & Industry; Marc Peltzer, Martha's Vineyard; Plymouth County Convention & Visitors Bureau; Greater Portsmouth Chamber of Commerce; Amy Rader, Quissett, Falmouth, Woods Hole, MA; Paul Rifkin, Osterville, Cotuit, MA; Robinson PhotoArt, Bath, ME; Bob Schellhammer, Martha's Vineyard; Peter Simon, Martha's Vineyard; David Welch, Martha's Vineyard; John McQuarrie, Lunenburg, NS.

Preface Photos: *Aerial of Oyster Harbor, Osterville, MA — Paul Rifkin; S/V Blue Nose II, Lunenburg, NS; Working Fleet, North Harbor, Grand Manan Island, NB; Dockside Restaurant, Northeast Harbor, ME; J.O. Brown, North Haven, ME — all 4 Beth Adams-Smith; Rowe's Wharf, Boston, MA — Peter Quandt; Black Dog Tavern, Vineyard Haven, MA — Martha's Vineyard Chamber of Commerce/Betsy Corsiglia; Sailboats in Quisset Harbor, MA — Amy Rader.*

1. NS – Southern & Western Shores

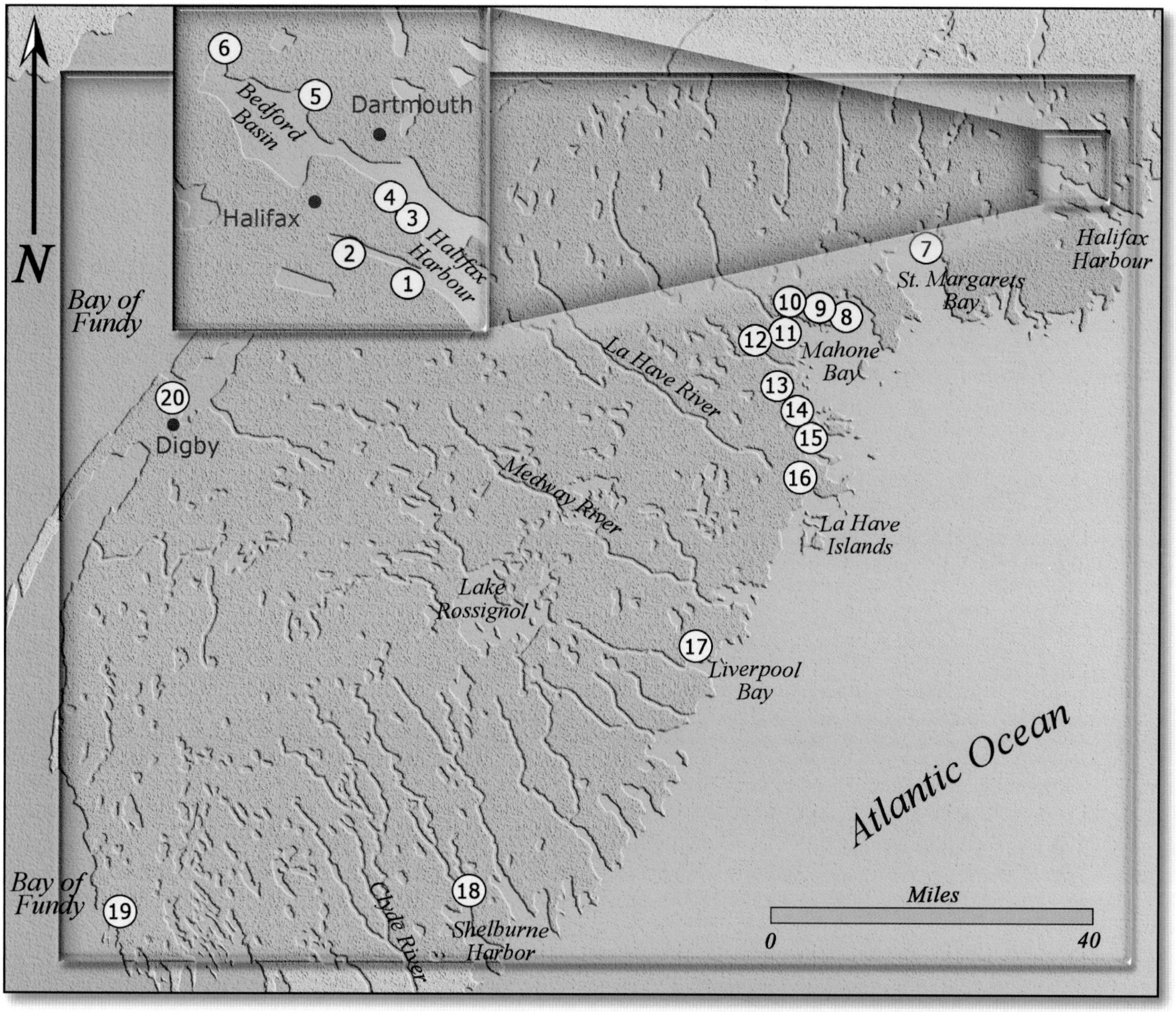

MAP	MARINA	HARBOR	PAGE
1	Royal N.S. Yacht Squadron	Halifax Harbour	28
2	Armdale Yacht Club Marina	Halifax Harbour	29
3	Maritime Museum of the Atlantic	Halifax Harbour	30
4	Halifax Marina — Harbourwalk	Halifax Harbour	31
5	Dartmouth Yacht Club	Bedford Basin	32
6	Bedford Basin Yacht Club	Bedford Basin	33
7	Shining Waters	St. Margarets Bay	34
8	The Rope Loft Marina	Mahone Bay	35
9	Chester Yacht Club	Mahone Bay	36
10	South Shore Marine	Mahone Bay	37
11	Gold River Marina	Mahone Bay	38
12	Atlantica Marina Oak Island	Mahone Bay	39
13	Mahone Bay Civic Marina	Mahone Harbour	40
14	Lunenburg Yacht Club	Mahone Bay	41
15	Lunenburg Historic Waterfront	Lunenburg Harbour	42
16	LaHave Bakery & Outfitters	LaHave River Entry	43
17	Brooklyn Marina	Liverpool Bay	44
18	Shelburne Harbour Yacht Club	Shelburne Harbour	45
19	Killam Brothers Marina	Yarmouth Harbour	46
20	R.W.N.S.Y.S. & Digby Marina	Annapolis Basin	47

RATINGS:  1-5 for Marina Facilities & Amenities,  1-2 for Boatyard Services,  1-2 for MegaYacht Facilities, for Something Special.

SERVICES:  for CCM – Certified Clean Marina,  for Pump-Out,  for Internet,  for Fuel,  for Restaurant, for Provisioning nearby,  for Catamaran-friendly,  for SportFish Charter, for Pool/Beach, and for Golf within a mile. *For an explanation of ACC's Ratings, see page 8.*

Royal N.S. Yacht Squadron

376 Purcells Cove Road; Halifax, NS B38-1C7

Tel: (902) 477-2595 **VHF: Monitor** Ch. 68 **Talk** n/a
Fax: (902) 477-6298 **Alternate Tel:** n/a
Email: dockmaster@rnsys.com **Web:** www.rnsys.com
Nearest Town: Halifax *(5 mi.)* **Tourist Info:** (902) 490-4000

Navigational Information

Lat: 44°37.169' **Long:** 063°34.498' **Tide:** 5.5 ft. **Current:** .5 kt. **Chart:** 4202
Rep. Depths (*MLW*): Entry 12 ft. **Fuel Dock** 12 ft. **Max Slip/Moor** 20 ft./55 ft.
Access: Halifax Harbour to Northwest Arm past Point Plesant

Marina Facilities *(In Season/Off Season)*

Fuel: Gasoline, Diesel
Slips: 150 Total, 15 Transient **Max LOA:** 160 ft. **Max Beam:** n/a
Rate *(per ft.)*: **Day** $1.80* **Week** n/a **Month** n/a
Power: 30 amp $5, **50 amp** $10, **100 amp** $20, **200 amp** $30
Cable TV: No **Dockside Phone:** No
Dock Type: Fixed, Floating, Long Fingers, Alongside, Wood
Moorings: 70 Total, 15 Transient **Launch:** Yes (Comp.), Dinghy Dock
Rate: Day $40-75 **Week** n/a **Month** n/a
Heads: 5 Toilet(s), 3 Shower(s)
Internet: Yes *(Wi-Fi, Free)* **Laundry:** 1 Washer(s), 1 Dryer(s)
Pump-Out: OnSite **Fee:** $20 **Closed Heads:** Yes

Marina Operations

Owner/Manager: Wayne Blundell **Dockmaster:** Same
In-Season: May-Oct, 8am-10pm** **Off-Season:** Nov-Apr, 8am-4pm
After-Hours Arrival: Call 902-477-2595
Reservations: Yes, preferred **Credit Cards:** Visa/MC
Discounts: None
Pets: Welcome, Dog Walk Area **Handicap Access:** Yes

Marina Services and Boat Supplies

Services - Docking Assistance, Security *(10pm-6am)*, Trash Pick-Up, Dock Carts, Megayacht Facilities, 3 Phase **Communication -** FedEx, UPS **Supplies - OnSite:** Ice *(Block, Cube)* **1-3 mi:** Ships' Store **3+ mi:** Propane *(Walkers 454-0291, 6 mi)*

Boatyard Services

OnSite: Railway *(30T)*, Crane *(Jib 5T, Spar 1,500 lb.)*, Hydraulic Trailer *(20T)*, Launching Ramp **OnCall:** Engine mechanic *(gas, diesel)*, Electrical Repairs, Electronic Sales, Electronics Repairs, Hull Repairs, Rigger, Sail Loft, Canvas Work, Divers, Bottom Cleaning, Brightwork, Air Conditioning, Interior Cleaning, Propeller Repairs, Woodworking, Inflatable Repairs, Upholstery, Yacht Interiors, Metal Fabrication, Painting, Awlgrip

Restaurants and Accommodations

OnSite: Restaurant *(Club Dining Room Reservations req, jacket & tie. Tue-Sat 11am-9pm. Sun 11am-4pm. Brunch buffet Sat, Brunch menu Sun), (Wardroom Reserv. Not Req.)*, Snack Bar *(Pool Canteen seasonal - sandwiches, salads, ice cream, drinks)* **1-3 mi:** Restaurant *(Lakeside Grill at Chocolate Lake 477-5611), (Mandarin Kitchen 477-5696), (Armview Diner 455-4395, B $6-12, L $6-18, D $6-23, Upscale, 50's Diner Kids' $4-6)*, Coffee Shop *(Tim Horton's)*, Pizzeria *(Euro 479-7979, Del.)*, Hotel *(Best Western Chocolate Lake 477-5611, $135-180)* **3+ mi:** Restaurant *(Doraku 425-8888, 5 mi.), (Bish World Cuisine 425-7993, D $20-27, 6 mi.), (da Maurizio 423-0859, D $11-35, 6 mi.)*, Hotel *(The Westin Nova Scotian 421-1000, 6 mi.), (The Halliburton 420-0658, $145-350, 6 mi.), (Lord Nelson Hotel 423-6331, $140-260, 5 mi.)*

Recreation and Entertainment

OnSite: Heated Pool *(1 salt & 1 fresh, MidJun-LateSep)*, Playground, Tennis Courts, Special Events *(Biennial Marblehead to Halifax Race - July)* **1-3 mi:** Picnic Area, Grills, Dive Shop, Fitness Center *(The Tower 420-5555)*, Hike/Bike Trails, Bowling *(Bowlarama 479-2695)*, Movie Theater, Video Rental *(Blockbuster 423-4550)*, Park, Sightseeing *(Tristar 483-8211)* **3+ mi:** Golf Course *(Eaglequest Grandview 435-3767, 20 mi.)*, Museum *(5 mi.)*

Provisioning and General Services

OnCall: Provisioning Service **1-3 mi:** Convenience Store, Supermarket, Gourmet Shop *(Just Us! Cafe 423-0856)*, Delicatessen, Wine/Beer, Liquor Store *(Premier Wine & Spirits 435-6945)*, Bakery, Green Grocer, Bank/ATM, Post Office, Library, Beauty Salon, Barber Shop, Dry Cleaners, Laundry, Bookstore, Pharmacy *(Sobeys 492-4501)*, Newsstand, Hardware Store *(Canadian Tire 477-5608)*, Florist, Clothing Store, Copies Etc. *(Winwick 453-2900)* **3+ mi:** Farmers' Market *(Halifax Seapot Market 492-4043, 6 mi.)*, Catholic Church *(5 mi.)*, Protestant Church *(5 mi.)*, Synagogue *(5 mi.)*

Transportation

OnCall: Rental Car *(Enterprise 446-4388)*, Taxi *(Yellow 420-000; Casino 429-4000)*, Airport Limo *(Airporter 873-2091)* **Near:** Local Bus, InterCity Bus **Airport:** Halifax Stanfield Int'l *(30 mi.)*

Medical Services

911 Service **OnCall:** Ambulance **1-3 mi:** Dentist *(Dalhousie 494-2101)*, Chiropractor *(Active 429-2225)* **3+ mi:** Doctor *(QEII Clinic 473-7072, 5.5 mi.)*, Holistic Services *(LC Acupuncture & Naturopathy Clinic 492-8839, 5 mi.)*, Veterinarian *(Halifax 422-8595, 5 mi.)* **Hospital:** QEII 473-7072 *(5 mi.)*

Setting -- Tucked into the northwest arm of Halifax Harbour, just past Point Pleasant Park to starboard, RNSYS's extensive facilities sprawl along the port shore. Perched on the rocks, the blue and white dockmaster's office is backed by the boatyard and Spar Loft. A curved airy dining room highlights the charming stone and rose stucco post-WW II clubhouse. A double-peaked dining pavilion sits right at the water's edge, and a large swimming pool overlooks the harbor.

Marina Notes -- *$1.80/ft. regular dock, $3.70/ft. mega-yachts on fixed wharf or heavy floating docks. Heavy Mooring $75/day, Regular $40/day. **Peak Season 8am-11pm, May-Jun/Oct-Nov 8am-8pm, Off Season 8am-4;30pm. 3-phase. Moorings 1200-4000 lb. cement block. Established 1837 as Halifax Y.C.- oldest yacht club in N.A. Home to biennial Marblehead-Halifax Ocean Race - estab.1905. 150 slips - 160 ft. LOA, 80 moorings - 75 ft. LOA with launch service. Haulout, Winter Storage. Fuel, Pump-out. 2 large pools (kiddie pool). Bathhouse: Pleasant club-quality heads, painted wooden dividers, dressing rooms.

Notable -- The 900-member Club has an international membership that focuses primarily on sailing. The Clubhouse has two main dining spaces - a formal first floor dining room which spills out onto a waterside patio and the spectacular, but casual, all-windows, half-round Wardroom which features a pub menu. The Squadron's many rooms and buildings provide engaging venues for social events or a club cruise evening - the Dining Room (30), the Wardroom (60), the Spar Shed (which transforms into elegant space for 250), two smaller second-floor board rooms and, further up-harbor, Saraguay House, a striking contemporary overlooking the Northwest Arm which can manage groups up to 150 in four spaces. Downtown Halifax is 15 minutes by cab - $15.

PHOTOS ON DVD: 25

Navigational Information
Lat: 44°37.590' **Long:** 063°36.470' **Tide:** 5.5 ft. **Current:** .5 kt. **Chart:** 4202
Rep. Depths (*MLW*): Entry 20 ft. **Fuel Dock** 20 ft. **Max Slip/Moor** 25 ft./40 ft.
Access: Halifax Harbour to Northwest Arm to Head

Marina Facilities *(In Season/Off Season)*
Fuel: Gasoline, Diesel, High-Speed Pumps, On Call Delivery
Slips: 200 Total, 2 Transient **Max LOA:** 55 ft. **Max Beam:** 16 ft.
Rate *(per ft.)*: **Day** $1.50 **Week** n/a **Month** n/a
Power: 30 amp Incl., **50 amp** n/a, **100 amp** n/a, **200 amp** n/a
Cable TV: No **Dockside Phone:** No
Dock Type: Floating, Alongside, Wood
Moorings: 35 Total, 10 Transient **Launch:** Yes (Comp.), Dinghy Dock
Rate: Day $25 **Week** n/a **Month** n/a
Heads: 4 Toilet(s), 2 Shower(s)
Internet: Yes *(Wi-Fi, Vista Care/Fat Port, Sub.)* **Laundry:** None
Pump-Out: No **Fee:** n/a **Closed Heads:** Yes

Marina Operations
Owner/Manager: Christine Bray **Dockmaster:** Same
In-Season: April-Nov, 8:30am-10pm **Off-Season:** Dec-Mar, Closed
After-Hours Arrival: Call in advance
Reservations: Yes **Credit Cards:** Visa/MC
Discounts: None
Pets: Welcome **Handicap Access:** No

Armdale Yacht Club Marina

PO Box 2210; 75 Burgee Run; Halifax, NS B3L 4T7

Tel: (902) 477-4617 **VHF: Monitor** Ch. 68 **Talk** Ch. 68
Fax: (902) 477-0148 **Alternate Tel:** n/a
Email: office@armdaleyachtclub.ns.ca **Web:** www.armdaleyachtclub.ns.ca
Nearest Town: Halifax *(5 mi.)* **Tourist Info:** (902) 490-4000

Marina Services and Boat Supplies
Services - Boaters' Lounge, Security, Trash Pick-Up, Dock Carts **Communication -** Mail & Package Hold, FedEx, UPS **Supplies - OnSite:** Ice *(Cube)* **Near:** Marine Discount Store *(The Binnacle 423-6464)* **1-3 mi:** Ships' Store *(The Binnacle 423-6464)*, Bait/Tackle *(Fishing Fever 454-2244)*, Propane *(Walkers 454-0291)*

Boatyard Services
OnSite: Railway *(20T - max 40 ft. LOA, 20 ft. beam)*, Launching Ramp **OnCall:** Electrical Repairs *(Paul Shipley)* **Under 1 mi:** Canvas Work *(DRH 475-3295)*.

Restaurants and Accommodations
OnSite: Restaurant *(Armdale Yacht Club 477-4617, L $7-10, D $10-15, Lunch Mon-Fri 11:30am-2:30pm, Dinner Wed-Sat 5:30-9:30pm, Brunch Sat & Sun 10-3pm)* **Under 1 mi:** Coffee Shop *(Tim Hortons)*, Pizzeria *(Euro Pizza 479-7979, Delivers)* **1-3 mi:** Restaurant *(Armview 455-4395, B $6-12, L $6-18, D $6-23, Kids' $4-6, Upscale 50's Diner)*, Seafood Shack *(Phil's Seafood 431-3474)*, Fast Food *(Subway, McDs)*, Hotel *(Atlantic Inn 423-1161, $105-215)*, *(Lord Nelson 423-6331, $140-260)*, *(Best Western Chocolate Lake 477-5611, $135-180)*, Inn/B&B *(Welcome Inn 446-6500, $95-175)*, Condo/Cottage *(Le Cabines Du Portage 224-2822)*

Recreation and Entertainment
Near: Park *(Deadmen's Island; Sir Sanford Fleming)* **Under 1 mi:** Fitness Center *(Balance Naturopathic Health Centre 425-4848)*, Bowling *(Bowlarama 455-1519)* **1-3 mi:** Pool *(Spryfield Wave Pool)*, Golf Course *(Old Ashburn 443-8260)*, Boat Rentals *(Tall Ship Silva 429-9463)*, Movie Theater *(Empire 422-2022)*, Video Rental *(Blockbuster 423-4550)* **3+ mi:** Hike/Bike Trails *(Point Pleasant Park, 4 mi.)*, Museum *(Natural History 424-7353; Maritime Museum 424-7490, 5 mi.)*, Tours *(Ambassatours Gray Line 800-565-7173; Harbour Hopper 490-8687, 5 mi.)*, Sightseeing *(Citadel, 4 mi.)*

Provisioning and General Services
Under 1 mi: Supermarket *(Sobey's 454-7416)*, Liquor Store *(West End Mall 453-0128, Nova Scotia 423-7126)*, Laundry *(Olympic 422-5571; Bayers Rd. 455-7223)*, Pharmacy *(Sobey's 454-7416; Lawton's 453-8847)*, Hardware Store *(Canadian Tire 422-4598)* **1-3 mi:** Health Food *(Planet Organic 425-7400)*, Bakery *(Smith's Bakery and Cafe 429-1393)*, Farmers' Market *(Halifax 492-4043 - Lower Water St.)*, Library *(Halifax North 490-5723)*, Beauty Salon *(Cutans 477-4000)*, Barber Shop *(Phat's 423-6596)*, Dry Cleaners *(Same Day 832-1599)*, Florist *(Flower Trends)*, Retail Shops *(Halifax Shopping Centre 454-8666 - 150 stores; Walmart 454-7990)*

Transportation
OnCall: Rental Car *(Enterprise 446-4388)*, Taxi *(Yellow 420-0000; Casino 429-6666)*, Airport Limo *(Airporter 873-2091)* **Near:** Local Bus *(Metro Transit 490-4000)* **3+ mi:** Ferry Service *(Metro Transit-Waterfront, 5 mi.)* **Airport:** Halifax Int'l *(18 mi.)*

Medical Services
911 Service **Under 1 mi:** Doctor *(Atlantic Medical Clinic 455-4333)*, Dentist *(West End 453-2100)*, Holistic Services *(Balance Naturopathic 425-4848)* **1-3 mi:** Veterinarian *(Spryfield 477-4040)* **Hospital:** QEII 473-7072 *(3 mi.)*

Setting -- Tucked almost to the head of Halifax Harbour's Northwest Arm, past the Royal Nova Scotia Yacht Squadron and the ten-story Dingle Tower to port, the Armdale Yacht Club covers all of Melville Island. Ten docks surround the island as if spokes on a wheel. Perched on the hill, the white two-story clubhouse features an all-window dining room that opens onto a dining porch - both have spectacular views of the docks and down the Northwest Arm.

Marina Notes -- *Fuel Dock & Launch Hours. Ofice Hours: 9am-noon & 1pm-4pm. Transients mostly on north dock near Race House. Subscription Wi-Fi available. Laptops automatically find Vista Care, a service of Fat Port (866-328-7678). Launch tender until dusk. Gray, single-story Sail Training Center overlooks backside docks. Slipway/cradle haul out for dry storage. Active sailing program. Less than a half mile walk, The Binnacle sells everything boaty - it's worth the trip. Bathhouse: Functional, all-tile heads, metal dividers, vanity with inset sinks. Accessible at back entrance from 9am to dining room closing.

Notable -- AYC is built on the grounds of a 17thC military prison - look for the old cell block. A short walk south, Sir Sanford Fleming Memorial Park is home to the famous Dingle Memorial Tower which was erected in 1912 to honor parliamentary governments throughout the Commonwealth. Climb to the top for spectacular views of the Northwest Arm, laze on the small life-guarded beach or walk the two trails that wind through 95 acres of salt marsh, heath barrens and forest. West End Mall is about 2.5 KM and the Halifax Shopping Center is just beyond. The #15 Bus stops about every hour in front of AYC. To get to downtown Halifax or Spring Garden Road, a major shopping street, take the #15 to main Mumford Rd. transfer terminals, then change to the #1 (runs every 15 minutes).

PHOTOS ON DVD: 15

Maritime Museum of the Atlantic

1675 Lower Water Street; Halifax, NS B3J 1S3

Tel: (902) 424-7490 **VHF: Monitor** n/a **Talk** n/a
Fax: (902) 424-0612 **Alternate Tel:** (902) 424-7491
Email: readsa@gov.ns.ca **Web:** http://museum.gov.ns.ca/mma
Nearest Town: Halifax **Tourist Info:** (902) 490-4000

Navigational Information

Lat: 44°38.560' **Long:** 633°41.900' **Tide:** 6.5 ft. **Current:** n/a **Chart:** 4237
Rep. Depths (*MLW*): Entry 32 ft. **Fuel Dock** n/a **Max Slip/Moor** 10 ft./-
Access: Georges Is. north 0.5 mi. to west side of Halifax Harbour

Marina Facilities *(In Season/Off Season)*

Fuel: *4ReFuel - 835-6608/888-473-3835* - On Call Delivery
Slips: 14 Total, 14 Transient **Max LOA:** 160 ft. **Max Beam:** 32 ft.
Rate *(per ft.)*: **Day** $1.60* **Week** n/a **Month** n/a
Power: 30 amp n/a, **50 amp** n/a, **100 amp** n/a, **200 amp** n/a
Cable TV: No **Dockside Phone:** No
Dock Type: Fixed, Alongside, Wood
Moorings: 0 Total, 0 Transient **Launch:** n/a
Rate: Day n/a **Week** n/a **Month** n/a
Heads: None
Internet: No **Laundry:** None
Pump-Out: No **Fee:** n/a **Closed Heads:** Yes

Marina Operations

Owner/Manager: Maritime Museum/WDCL **Dockmaster:** Stephen Read
In-Season: Year Round, 9am-5pm** **Off-Season:** n/a
After-Hours Arrival: Check-in at Museum Main Desk the next morning
Reservations: Yes, Preferred **Credit Cards:** Visa/MC, Dscvr, Amex
Discounts: None
Pets: Welcome **Handicap Access:** No

Marina Services and Boat Supplies

Services - Security *(24/7)* **Communication -** Pay Phone, FedEx, DHL, UPS, Express Mail **Supplies - Near:** Ships' Store *(Sea Gulf 481-1661)* **1-3 mi:** Bait/Tackle *(Fishing Fever 454-2244)*, Propane *(Walkers 454-0291)*

Boatyard Services

Nearest Yard: Dartmouth Yacht Club (902) 468-6050

Restaurants and Accommodations

Near: Restaurant *(Murphy's at the Cable Wharf 420-1015, L $12-18, D $12-25)*, *(Blue Nose II 425-5092, D $10-20)*, *(Bicycle Thief 425-7993, D $26-39)*, *(daMaurizio 423-0859, D $11-33, an old Brewery)*, *(Sweet Basil 425-2133, L $8-16, D $14-24)*, *(McKelvie's Delishes Fishes 421-6161, L $9-15, D $17-33, early bird $14-18, 4-6pm)*, *(Great Wall 422-6153, L & D $7-14,)*, *(Ryan Duffy's Steak & Seafood 421-1116, B $8-15, L $10-21, D $26-45, Brunch $10-12, Kids' $7-12)*, *(Old Triangle Irish Ale House 492-4900, L & D $10-18, Kids $6)*, Snack Bar *(Queen's Wharf Market Kiosks Incl. Cow's Ice Cream)*, Lite Fare *(Dragon King 431-8588, Take-out $7-13, Buffet $11+)*, *(Captain's Catch 422-8459, Fish & Chips)*, *(Dill Pickle 422-4088, Fresh & Healthy)*, Pizzeria *(Sicilian 423-5555, Del.)*, *(Venus 425-8882)*, Hotel *(Radisson 429-7233, $105-250)*, *(Lord Nelson 423-6331, $180-300)*

Recreation and Entertainment

OnSite: For Kids *(Theodore Tugboat plus Digby the Cable Ship, Barrington Barge & 20 more)*, Museum *(Maritime of the Museum $4.75-8.75/$2.75-5.25)*, Tours *(Harbour Hopper 490-8687 $26/15; McNab Island Ferry Nature Tours 465-4563 $12/10)*, Special Events *(Ferry Boat Tales, Wed-Fri, 2pm)* **Near:** Fitness Center *(Vital Yoga 429-7285; Push 423-7874)*, Jogging Paths, Cultural Attract *(Neptune Theater 429-7070)* **Under 1 mi:** Pool *(Centennial 490-7219 $4/3)*, Movie Theater *(Empire-8 422-2022)*, Video Rental *(Blockbuster)*, Sightseeing *(Citadel Nat'l Historic Site 426-5080 $7.80-11.79/$3.90-5.80)* **1-3 mi:** Golf Course *(Sherwood G & C 275-3267)*

Provisioning and General Services

OnSite: Library *(Mon-Fri by app't 424-7890 - 5,000 books, 20,000 photos, shipping registers from 1700s)*, Retail Shops *(Marine Heritage Store 423-9787)* **Near:** Market *(Taishan Asian 406-8828)*, Delicatessen *(Pete's Frootique & Deli 425-5700)*, Health Food *(Home Grown Organics 492-1412)*, Bank/ATM, Catholic Church, Protestant Church, Beauty Salon *(Moda Capelli 423-2406)*, Bookstore *(Reads 423-6980)*, Pharmacy *(Lawton 429-3261)* **Under 1 mi:** Supermarket *(Sobey's 422-9884; Atlantic Superstore 492-3240)*, Farmers' Market *(Halifax Seaport at Pier 20 492-4043)*, Fishmonger *(Seaport Farmers' Market)*, Laundry *(Kwick 429-2023)*

Transportation

OnCall: Taxi *(Yellow 420-0000)*, Airport Limo *(Halifax 448-9288)* **Near:** Bikes *(I Love Bikes 719-4325)*, Rental Car *(Budget 492-7500, Avis 492-2847)*, Local Bus *(Metro Trransit)*, InterCity Bus *(Acadian 800-567-5151)*, Rail *(VIA Rail)*, Ferry Service *(to Dartmouth)* **Airport:** Halifax Int'l *(20 mi.)*

Medical Services

911 Service **OnCall:** Ambulance **Near:** Doctor *(Lo 429-7910; Grant 425-5440)*, Dentist *(Bishop's Landing 423-4193)*, Chiropractor *(Maritime 492-2102)*, Holistic Services *(Tomalty Homeopathy 446-5800; Qing Li Chinese Therapy 440-5200)*, Optician *(Vogue 492-1234)* **1-3 mi:** Veterinarian *(Woodbury 455-7297)* **Hospital:** QE II 473-2700 *(1 mi.)*

Setting -- Located in the center of Halifax's bustling waterfront, the museum's wharves offer alongside tie-up for private recreational vessels. Berthing among the collection of historic vessels can be a voyage highlight if you don't mind being an exhibit. Sprawled along the head of the wharves, a fascinating maritime collection is housed in boat sheds and exhibition buildings - the most striking of which is the modern, ship-like Devonian Wing. All of Halifax is a stone's throw.

Marina Notes -- *$1.50/ft. under 60 ft., $2/ft. over 60 ft. Side-tie dockage - 3 jetty faces 180 ft. in length. **Mon-Fri only. Wharves open to public 24/7. Comp. day & evening dockage. Managed by WDCL. Must confirm $1 million liability insurance. On-call boat supplies & repair services (Premier 444-3625). Museum Hours: May-Oct Mon, Wed-Sun 9:30-5:30, Tue 9:30-8pm (May & Oct Sun 1-5:30); Nov-Apr Tue 9:30-8pm, Wed-Sat 9:30-5, Sun 1-5. Small Craft Gallery available for club cruise events ($1000) - dinner for 90, reception for 250. Bathhouse: Heads - Bishop's Landing, Visitor Info Centre, Ferry Terminal, Museum

Notable -- Canada's largest maritime museum is at the center of the three-km long boardwalk that runs from Pier 21 to Casino Nova Scotia. Onsite is the 1913, 180-foot steam-powered hydrographic survey ship CSS "Acadia" and, in summer, the HMCS "Sackville," a World War II Flower-class corvette and, when the reconstruction has been completed, "Bluenose III" part time. Within the museum buildings are 30,000 artifacts from 1850 to today, Navy Gallery, Days of Sail, Age of Steam, Shipwreck Treasures, On the Rocks local shipwreck database, Titanic & Halifax, plus 20 of the 70 small craft collection boats are displayed in the boat sheds. Visit the restored 1880s William Robertson & Son ship chandlery and watch the ongoing restoration of the 1937 C Class sloop "Whim."

PHOTOS ON DVD: 25

Navigational Information
Lat: 44°38.582' **Long:** 063°34.111' **Tide:** 6.5 ft. **Current:** n/a **Chart:** 4237
Rep. Depths (*MLW*): Entry 20 ft. **Fuel Dock** n/a **Max Slip/Moor** 20 ft./-
Access: Georges Is. north 0.5 mi. to west side of Halifax Harbour

Marina Facilities *(In Season/Off Season)*
Fuel: *4refuel* - On Call Delivery
Slips: 80 Total, 25 Transient **Max LOA:** 292 ft. **Max Beam:** n/a
Rate *(per ft.)*: **Day** $1.50/1.00* **Week** n/a **Month** n/a
Power: 30 amp Incl., **50 amp** Incl., **100 amp** **Incl., **200 amp** n/a
Cable TV: No **Dockside Phone:** No
Dock Type: Fixed, Floating, Alongside, Wood
Moorings: 0 Total, 0 Transient **Launch:** n/a
Rate: Day n/a **Week** n/a **Month** n/a
Heads: None
Internet: Yes *(Wi-Fi, Free)* **Laundry:** None
Pump-Out: No **Fee:** n/a **Closed Heads:** Yes

Marina Operations
Owner/Manager: Waterfront Development **Dockmaster:** Adam Langley
In-Season: May-Aug, 7am-7pm **Off-Season:** Dec-Mar, Varies
After-Hours Arrival: Contact Security by Phone (902) 471-5070
Reservations: Yes, Preferred **Credit Cards:** Visa/MC, Amex
Discounts: None
Pets: Welcome, Dog Walk Area **Handicap Access:** Yes

Halifax Marinas - Harbourwalk

The Cable Wharf, 1751 Lower Water Street; Halifax, B3J 1S5

Tel: (902) 229-2628 **VHF: Monitor** Ch. 68 **Talk** Ch. 68
Fax: (902) 422-7582 **Alternate Tel:** (902) 422-5115
Email: marina@wdcl.ca **Web:** www.my-waterfront.ca
Nearest Town: Halifax **Tourist Info:** (902) 490-4000

Halifax Marinas - Halifax Harbourwalk

1. NS - SOUTHERN & WESTERN SHORES

Marina Services and Boat Supplies
Services - Docking Assistance, Security *(24/7, Staffed)*, Trash Pick-Up **Communication -** Pay Phone, FedEx, UPS **Supplies - OnCall:** Ships' Store *(Premier 489-7253)* **1-3 mi:** Bait/Tackle *(Fishing Fever 454-2244)*, Propane *(Walkers 454-0291)*

Boatyard Services
Nearest Yard: Dartmouth Yacht Club (902) 468-6050

Restaurants and Accommodations
OnSite: Snack Bar *(Queens Wharf Market kiosks incl. Cow's ic cream)* **Near:** Restaurant *(Murphy's at the Cable Wharf 420-1015, L $12-18, D $12-25, 11:30am-10pm)*, *(Blue Nose II 425-5092, D $10-20)*, *(Montreal Grill & Diner 425-5900)*, *(Brussell's 446-4700, L $8-24, D $8-27)*, Coffee Shop *(Uncommon Grounds 431-3101)*, Pizzeria *(Sicilian 423-5555, Del.)*, Hotel *(Radisson 429-7233)*, *(Delta Barrington 429-7410)*, *(Four Points 423-4444)*, *(Halifax Marriott 421-1700, Harbourfront)* **Under 1 mi:** Restaurant *(Hamachi 425-7711, B 15, L 20, D 30)*, *(Bicycle Thief 425-7993, D $26-39)*

Recreation and Entertainment
OnSite: Playground, Jogging Paths *(Harborwalk)* **Near:** Fitness Center *(Vital Yoga 429-7285; Push 423-7874)*, Fishing Charter, Party Boat *(Murphy's 420-1015 $55/39)*, Tours *(Murphy's Tours 420-1015: "Haligonian III" Whale Watch $36/20, "Mar" Pirate Tall Ship $15/10, $24/17, Harbour Hopper $26/15, Theodore Tugboat $20/15)*, Cultural Attract *(Neptune Theater 429-7070)*, Sightseeing *("Harbour Queen" Historical Harbour Tour 420-1015 $18-25/$15-17)* **Under 1 mi:** Pool *(Centennial 490-7219 $4/3)*, Movie Theater *(Empire 423-4860)*, Video Rental *(Blockbuster 422-7365)* **1-3 mi:** Beach *(McNabs Is.)*, Golf Course *(Sherwood 275-3267)*, Park *(Pt. Pleasant)*, Museum *(AGNS, N.S.Natural History 424-7353; Maritime Museum of the Atlantic 424-7490)*, Galleries *(Art Gallery of Nova Scotia 424-7542)*, Special Events *(Halifax Jazz Fest - Jul; Busker Fest - Aug.)*

Provisioning and General Services
OnCall: Provisioning Service *(Premier Marine Services 489-7253)* **Near:** Bank/ATM, Post Office, Library *(Halifax 490-5700)*, Bookstore *(Doull 429-1652)*, Newsstand **Under 1 mi:** Convenience Store, Supermarket *(Sobey's 422-9884)*, Health Food *(Sobey's 422-9884)*, Wine/Beer *(Bishop's Cellar 490-2675)*, Farmers' Market *(Pier 20, Seaport Mkt. 492-4043 - Wed, Fri, Sat, Sun, estab 1750)*, Green Grocer *(Pete's Frootique 835-4997)*, Fishmonger *(Halifax Seaport Mkt)*, Beauty Salon, Barber Shop, Dry Cleaners, Laundry, Pharmacy, Hardware Store *(Canadian Tire 422-4598)*, Copies Etc. **1-3 mi:** Liquor Store *(NSLC 424-3754)*, Synagogue

Transportation
OnSite: Bikes *(I Love Bikes 719-4325)* **OnCall:** Taxi *(Yellow 420-0000)*, Airport Limo *(Halifax 448-9288)* **Near:** Rental Car *(Budget 492-7500; Avis 492-2847)*, Local Bus *(Metro Transit)*, InterCity Bus *(Acadian 800-567-5151)*, Rail *(VIA Rail)*, Ferry Service *(Metro Transit Dartmouth-Halifax Harbour 490-4000)* **Airport:** Halifax Int'l *(25 mi)*

Medical Services
911 Service **OnCall:** Ambulance **Under 1 mi:** Doctor *(IWK Health Centre 470-8888)*, Dentist *(Scotia Dental 423-8161)*, Chiropractor *(Maritime Chiropractic Clinic 492-2102)* **1-3 mi:** Veterinarian *(Full Circle Vet Alternative 461-0951)* **Hospital:** Nova Scotia 464-3114 *(1 mi.)*

Setting -- In the shadow of historic Halifax's striking skyline, where glass skyscrapers rub shoulders with restored 19th century boat sheds, yachts can share wharf space with historic vessels and tour boats - from the schooner "Mar" to "Theodore Tugboat." A kilometer of dockage on nine wharfs march along Harbourwalk. In the thick of the action, Queen's Wharf docks lie directly south alongside Cable Wharf which supports a huge, easy-to-spot barn-red restaurant

Marina Notes -- *Over 60 ft. LOA $2/ft./1.50. All side-tie. Free day docks. **Power & water hook-ups avail. Fees for power 2012+. Services vary by wharf. Owned/operated by Waterfront Development Corporation & N.S. Province. One km of public berths incl. 1,000 ft of floating docks. Cable Wharf (south side) 280 ft. floating; Tall Ships Quay 350 ft. seawall, Cunard Boardwalk 200 ft. seawall, South Battery Marina 386 ft. floating, Summit Seawall 124 ft. floating, Salter Boardwalk 246 ft. seawall, Sackville Jetty (south side) 280 ft. floating, Museum 90 ft. floating, Queen's Wharf North (south side) 175 ft. wharf, Bishop's Landing - floats for smaller boats. On-call boat supplies & repair services (Premier 444-3625). Bathhouse: Bishop's Landing, Visitor Info Centre & Ferry Terminal

Notable -- Colorful kiosks sprinkled along lively Harbourwalk offer food, beverages, tours, artworks and crafts, while an occassional busker draws a crowd. Top notch restaurants, world-class hotels, theaters, museums, performing arts and all manner of shops are within feet of any berth as is the Maritime Museum of the Atlantic. Cable Wharf is action central for the Halifax waterfront; almost every water tour leaves from there or a nearby wharf. Barn-red Murphy's Restaurant sprawls along the entire Cable Wharf putting diners literally on the water with spectacular views. Visit Pier 20 for the fabulous Seaport market.

PHOTOS ON DVD: 25

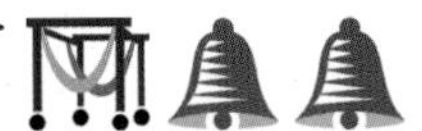   

Dartmouth Yacht Club

697 Windmill Rd.; Dartmouth, NS B3B 1B7

Tel: (902) 468-6050 **VHF: Monitor** Ch. 68 **Talk** Ch. 68
Fax: (902) 468-0385 **Alternate Tel:** n/a
Email: dyc@ns.sympatico.ca **Web:** www.DYC.NS.CA
Nearest Town: Dartmouth *(3.5 mi.)* **Tourist Info:** (902) 490-4000

Navigational Information

Lat: 44°51.926' **Long:** 063°36.674' **Tide:** 8 ft. **Current:** n/a **Chart:** 4201
Rep. Depths (*MLW*): Entry 15 ft. **Fuel Dock** 6 ft. **Max Slip/Moor** 15 ft./40 ft.
Access: Eastern shore Bedford Basin, 1.25 mi. NW of MacKay Bridge

Marina Facilities *(In Season/Off Season)*

Fuel: Gasoline, Diesel
Slips: 195 Total, 5 Transient **Max LOA:** 44 ft. **Max Beam:** 16 ft.
Rate *(per ft.)*: **Day** $1.00* **Week** n/a **Month** n/a
Power: 30 amp Incl., **50 amp** n/a, **100 amp** n/a, **200 amp** n/a
Cable TV: No **Dockside Phone:** No
Dock Type: Floating, Long Fingers, Wood
Moorings: 50 Total, 5 Transient **Launch:** Yes (Comp.), Dinghy Dock
Rate: Day $16 **Week** n/a **Month** n/a
Heads: 4 Toilet(s), 4 Shower(s) *(dressing rooms)*
Internet: Yes **Laundry:** None
Pump-Out: OnSite, Full Service **Fee:** $15 **Closed Heads:** Yes

Marina Operations

Owner/Manager: Dan Gallina **Dockmaster:** Same
In-Season: May 15-Sep 15, 8am-9pm **Off-Season:** Apr-May, Sep-Oct, 8-5
After-Hours Arrival: Call in advance.
Reservations: Yes, Preferred **Credit Cards:** Visa/MC
Discounts: None
Pets: Welcome **Handicap Access:** Yes, Heads, Docks

Marina Services and Boat Supplies

Services - Security *(Swipe-Card Gate)*, Trash Pick-Up **Communication -** FedEx, UPS **Supplies - OnSite:** Ice *(Cube)* **Near:** Ships' Store

Boatyard Services

OnSite: Travelift *(30T-max beam 16 ft.)*, Launching Ramp *($25)*, Engine mechanic *(gas, diesel)*, Electrical Repairs **Under 1 mi:** Electronic Sales, Hull Repairs, Rigger, Sail Loft, Canvas Work, Painting, Awlgrip. **Yard Rates:** Haul & Launch $26/ft., Power Wash $25 **Storage:** In-Water $2.10/sq.ft., On-Land $2.10/sq.ft.

Restaurants and Accommodations

Near: Restaurant *(Old Port Pub & Grill 404-7678)*, *(Brewdebakers Tap & Grill 468-1059)*, Fast Food *(McD's, Tim Hortons, Subway, Wendy's, BK)*, Lite Fare *(Linda's Cafe 468-1344)*, Pizzeria *(Panini's Deli & Pizzeria 404-9999)*, Motel *(Burnside 468-7117, very basic)* **1-3 mi:** Hotel *(Best Western Dartmouth 463-2000)*, *(Comfort Inn 463-9900)*, *(Country Inn & Suites 465-4000)*, *(Ramada 468-8888)* **3+ mi:** Restaurant *(Ducky's on the Waterfront 464-3825, B $6-11, L $8-15, D $19-22, 3.5 mi.)*

Recreation and Entertainment

3+ mi: Cultural Attract *(Theater at Alderney Landing 461-4698, 3.5 mi.)*, Galleries *(Alderney Landing 461-4698, 3.5 mi.)*

Provisioning and General Services

Near: Wine/Beer *(Moosehead Cold Beer 468-2337)*, Laundry *(C&G 468-4995)*, Copies Etc. *(Harbour City 468-5080)* **Under 1 mi:** Bank/ATM *(Bank of NS)*, Hardware Store *(Lumber Mart 468-7772; Payzant 468-3500)* **1-3 mi:** Convenience Store *(Ultramar 464-9843)*, Supermarket *(Sobey's 463-2910; Bay-Lee 469-0550)*, Liquor Store *(N.S. 461-2441)*, Farmers' Market *(Alderney Landing - Sat. 8-1 461-4698)*, Catholic Church, Protestant Church, Library *(Dartmouth North 866-0124)*, Beauty Salon *(Tony & Son 463-0854)*, Barber Shop, Pharmacy *(Lawton 481-7112)*, Retail Shops *(Shannon Park Shopping Ctr - 1.5 mi.)*

Transportation

OnCall: Rental Car *(Enterprise 469-1689)*, Taxi *(Bob's 434-2200; Blue Bell 465-5555)*, Airport Limo *(Atlas 877-0087; A-1 Prestige 456-4274)* **Near:** Local Bus *(Metro Transit 490-4000 - Rte. 51)* **3+ mi:** Ferry Service *(Aldernay Ferry to Halifax, every 30 mins. $2.25/1.50, 3.5 mi.)* **Airport:** Halifax Int'l *(25 mi.)*

Medical Services

911 Service **1-3 mi:** Doctor *(Liliane 468-2774)*, Dentist *(Burnside 468-2361)*, Veterinarian *(Harbour Cities 463-7610)* **3+ mi:** Chiropractor *(Aldernay 464-2225, 4 mi.)* **Hospital:** Dartmouth 465-8300 *(4.5 mi.)*

PHOTOS ON DVD: 22

Setting -- On Bedford Basin's eastern shore, DYS's network of quality docks is nestled into Wright's Cove - surrounded by highlands and protected by Navy Island. Five acres host a modest clubhouse with porch, a lawn sprinked with umbrella-topped tables, and a dry storage area serviced by a travelift.

Marina Notes -- *Flat rate - $37/day. Established in 1962. Cozy boaters' lounge with wood stove, bar, TV and tables. Fri, Sat & Sun. Indoor bar hours in season: Mon & Thu 4pm-10pm, Wed & Fri 4pm-11pm, Sat 11am-10pm, Sun 11am-7pm. DYC also owns the southern half of Navy Island. Plans for new three-story contemporary clubhouse. Only pump-out in Halifax Harbour. Swipe-card gates; a card is required except during office hours Mon-Fri 8am-4:30pm or when bar is open. An independent onsite firm offers services for marine engines and hulls. Travelift $13/ft. Bathhouse: comfortable, all-tile sparkling heads. Note: Enter the cove at the north end of the island - south of Rent Point.

Notable -- Club cruises will find event accommodations for up to 100 ($70-350 fee) for a dinner or a BBQ on the patio. Kitchen Door Catering (476-6729) is up the street. About a mile. Burnside Industrial Park is home to many useful services and supplies. Two supermarkets are about 1.5 miles. Ferry Terminal Park at the Dartmouth City Waterfront is about 3.5 miles south on Windmill Road. Take the ferry across to Halifax or explore the boardwalk and Alderney Landing (where the original settlers landed in 1750) which hosts the Saturday Farmers' Market, Sunday Crafts Fair, an arts gallery, a theater, shops, eateries and a visitors' center. Nearby is the World Peace Pavilion and the bronze propeller from the icebreaker Sir John A. MacDonald. Festivals are also held here.

Navigational Information
Lat: 44°43.355' **Long:** 063°39.513' **Tide:** 8 ft. **Current:** n/a **Chart:** 4201
Rep. Depths (*MLW*): Entry n/a **Fuel Dock** n/a **Max Slip/Moor** -/-
Access: Halifax Harbour to Bedford Basin, about 0.5 mi. north of H48

Marina Facilities *(In Season/Off Season)*
Fuel: No
Slips: 43 Total, 3 Transient **Max LOA:** 35 ft. **Max Beam:** n/a
Rate *(per ft.)*: **Day** $1.00 **Week** n/a **Month** n/a
Power: 30 amp Incl., **50 amp** n/a, **100 amp** n/a, **200 amp** n/a
Cable TV: No **Dockside Phone:** No
Dock Type: Floating, Long Fingers, Alongside, Wood
Moorings: 40 Total, 4 Transient **Launch:** Yes (Comp.)
Rate: Day $20 **Week** $140 **Month** n/a
Heads: 5 Toilet(s), 2 Shower(s)
Internet: Yes *(Wi-Fi, Free)* **Laundry:** None
Pump-Out: No **Fee:** n/a **Closed Heads:** Yes

Marina Operations
Owner/Manager: Eric Shields **Dockmaster:** Same
In-Season: May-Oct, 9am-9pm **Off-Season:** n/a
After-Hours Arrival: n/a
Reservations: Yes, Required **Credit Cards:** Visa/MC
Discounts: None
Pets: Welcome **Handicap Access:** Yes

Bedford Basin Yacht Club

Bedford Basin Yacht Club

377 Shore Drive; Bedford, NS B4A 2C7

Tel: (902) 835-3729 **VHF: Monitor** Ch. 68 **Talk** Ch. 68
Fax: (902) 835-2047 **Alternate Tel:** n/a
Email: bbyc@ns.sympatico.ca **Web:** www.bbyc.ns.ca
Nearest Town: Bedford *(0 mi.)* **Tourist Info:** (902) 490-4000

Marina Services and Boat Supplies
Services - Security *(24 hrs., Cameras)*, Trash Pick-Up **Communication -** FedEx, UPS **Supplies - OnSite:** Ice *(Cube)* **1-3 mi:** Ships' Store *(Bowsprit Marina 443-0533)*, Propane *(Wilsons 444-4246)*

Restaurants and Accommodations
OnSite: Lite Fare *(Club Dining Room Twice weekly BBQs.)* **Near:** Restaurant *(May Garden Chinese 832-2226)*, *(The Cellar Bar & Grill 835-1592, L & D $11-20, Italian, pizza, pasta, calamari - fireplaces & patio)*, *(Sunnyside 835-7204, Casual, family)*, Lite Fare *(Cora's Breakfast and Lunch 832-5252)*, Pizzeria *(Tomivinos 835-7777)* **Under 1 mi:** Restaurant *(Il Mercato Trattoria 832-4531, L $13-15, D $13-22)*, *(Finbar's Irish Pub 832-2917, L & D $10-17 casual, Wknd brunch $9-20)*, *(Steamy's 446-8855)*, *(Thai Garden 835-8335)*, *(True North Diner 832-1950, L $4-10, D $5-11, Exp lunch $9, B Sat & Sun)*, Coffee Shop *(Tim Horton)*, Fast Food *(Subway, McD's, The Wedge, The Chickenburger)*, Pizzeria *(Jessy's Pizza 835-4444)*, *(On the Wedge 835-3864)*, Motel *(Maritime 835-8307)*, *(Stardust 472-3316)* **1-3 mi:** Motel *(Esquire 835-3367)*, Hotel *(Comfort Inn 443-0303)*

Recreation and Entertainment
Near: Heated Pool *(Lions Park)*, Picnic Area, Playground, Jogging Paths **Under 1 mi:** Fitness Center *(Nubody's 835-6696)*, Museum *(Atlantic Canada Aviation 873-3773)* **1-3 mi:** Boat Rentals *(Passage Privateers 406-8687)*, Bowling *(Super Bowl 864-6400)*, Video Rental *(Mainway 494-5070)* **3+ mi:** Golf Course *(Glen Arbour 835-4653, 5 mi.)*

Provisioning and General Services
Near: Protestant Church **Under 1 mi:** Supermarket *(Atlantic 832-3117; Pete's Frootique 835-4997)*, Gourmet Shop, Health Food *(Healthy Selection 832-7511)*, Catholic Church, Library *(Halifax Reg. 490-5740)*, Dry Cleaners *(Same Day 832-1599)*, Pharmacy *(Drugstore 835-3086; Lawtons 835-3393)*, Newsstand, Department Store *(Canadian Tire, Winners, Walmart)* **1-3 mi:** Delicatessen *(Sackville Deli 864-1600)*, Wine/Beer *(Moosehead Cold Beer 468-2337)*, Laundry *(Mill Cove 835-0553)*, Copies Etc. *(The Print Shop 865-1651)* **3+ mi:** Hardware Store *(Home Depot 457-3480, 6 mi.)*

Transportation
OnCall: Rental Car *(Enterprise 252-3313)*, Taxi *(Belair 483-4591)*, Airport Limo *(4 Hire 497-4655)* **Airport:** Halifax Int'l *(12 mi.)*

Medical Services
911 Service **OnCall:** Ambulance **Under 1 mi:** Doctor *(Mayflower Med 835-1628)*, Dentist *(Granville 835-6554)*, Holistic Services *(Leigh 446-3825; Summit Day Spa 835-6888; Serendipity Spa)*, Optician *(Harken Optical)* **1-3 mi:** Veterinarian *(Sunnyview 835-2223)* **Hospital:** Cobequid Community 869-6101 *(2.5 mi.)*

Setting -- On the western shore of placid Bedford Bay, at the head of Bedford Basin, BBYC's small, contemporary two-and-a-half story gray-sided clubhouse stands on the shore overlooking three main docks and a large mooring field. Brightly painted Adirondack-style chairs are scattered about the waterfront veranda. The surrounding shoreline is dotted with upscale homes.

Marina Notes -- Established in 1953. Wednesday & Friday night BBQs. For club cruises, BBYC is set up to manage events of varying sizes. 5 ton electric hoist, spar crane. Winter storage for 100 boats with electric & water. Large mooring field with launch/tender service - all day until dusk. Hosts regattas throughout the summer - including welll-known ARK in July. An active Adult Learn-to-Sail program. Bathhouse: All tile with curtained separate shower enclosure, metal stall dividers.

Notable -- Because Bedford seldoms sees the fog that rolls into Halifax, it is often called Sunnyside or Sunny Cove. The clubhouse's expansive second floor deck, with transparent wind screen, is set up to enjoy that sunshine. It promises long views across the whole bay - which are even better from the third floor crow's nest- Lion's Park is closeby with two heated outdoor pools, basketball court, and playground. Several casual eateries are an easy walk and about half a mile is Sunnyside Mall with Canadian Tire, Lawtons, Pete's Frootique and about 60 other shops. And what you don't find there will be at Bedford Place Mall just beyond. Reportedly Bedford, a Halifax commuter suburb, has one of the highest per capita incomes in Canada - the lovely homes make for a pleasant walk.

PHOTOS ON DVD: 22

Shining Waters

148 Nautical Way; Tantallon, NS B3Z 2P3

Tel: (902) 826-3625 **VHF: Monitor** Ch. 16 **Talk** Ch. 15*
Fax: (902) 826-3626 **Alternate Tel:** n/a
Email: marina@shiningwaters.ca **Web:** www.shiningwaters.ca
Nearest Town: Halifax *(15 mi.)* **Tourist Info:** (902) 490-4000

Navigational Information

Lat: 44°39.450' **Long:** 063°54.767' **Tide:** 6 ft. **Current:** n/a **Chart:** 4386
Rep. Depths (*MLW*): Entry 15 ft. **Fuel Dock** 15 ft. **Max Slip/Moor** 15 ft./-
Access: St. Margaret's Bay to eastern shore of Head Harbour

Marina Facilities *(In Season/Off Season)*

Fuel: Gasoline, Diesel
Slips: 54 Total, 10 Transient **Max LOA:** 60 ft. **Max Beam:** n/a
Rate *(per ft.)*: **Day** $2.00 **Week** $275 **Month** $950
Power: 30 amp Incl., **50 amp** n/a, **100 amp** n/a, **200 amp** n/a
Cable TV: No **Dockside Phone:** No
Dock Type: Floating, Long Fingers, Alongside, Concrete, Wood
Moorings: 28 Total, 2 Transient **Launch:** None, Dinghy Dock
Rate: Day $40 **Week** n/a **Month** n/a
Heads: 2 Toilet(s), 2 Shower(s)
Internet: Yes *(Wi-Fi, Free)* **Laundry:** 1 Washer(s), 1 Dryer(s)
Pump-Out: OnSite, Full Service, 1 Port **Fee:** $30 **Closed Heads:** Yes

Marina Operations

Owner/Manager: Blair Patey **Dockmaster:** Andrea Levy
In-Season: Sprng, Sum, Fall, 8am-9pm **Off-Season:** Winter, 9am-5pm
After-Hours Arrival: Call in advance
Reservations: Yes, Preferred **Credit Cards:** Visa/MC, Interac
Discounts: None
Pets: Welcome **Handicap Access:** Yes, Heads, Docks

Marina Services and Boat Supplies

Services - Docking Assistance, Trash Pick-Up, Dock Carts **Communication -** Fax in/out, FedEx, DHL, UPS *(Sat Del)* **Supplies - OnSite:** Ice *(Cube)*, Ships' Store

Boatyard Services

OnSite: Travelift *(20T)*, Forklift, Hydraulic Trailer, Launching Ramp, Engine mechanic *(gas, diesel)*, Electrical Repairs, Electronic Sales, Electronics Repairs, Hull Repairs, Rigger, Compound, Wash & Wax, Inflatable Repairs, Painting **OnCall:** Interior Cleaning **Near:** Sail Loft, Canvas Work, Propeller Repairs, Upholstery. **3+ mi:** Life Raft Service *(20 mi.)*. **Dealer for:** Caribe, Walker Bay Genesis & Kaiyan Inflatables; Nissan & Tohatsu Outboards, Furno Electronics, Yanmar, Mercruiser. **Yard Rates:** $40-65/hr., Haul & Launch $9.50/ft. *(blocking $54/stand)*, Power Wash $1.80/ft., Bottom Paint $12/ft. **Storage:** On-Land $1.75-3/sq.ft.

Restaurants and Accommodations

OnSite: Restaurant *(Shining Waters 826-3625, L $10-16, D $19-34, Snacks $6-11, Sun brunch buffet $19, Wed - Mariners 4-course Lobster supper $29-43)*, Fast Food *(Subway)* **OnCall:** Pizzeria *(Recardo's 275-5688)* **1-3 mi:** Inn/B&B *(Rum Hollow Seaside Inn 826-7683, $100-160)* **3+ mi:** Lite Fare *(Mariposa Natural Market & Cafe 820-3350, 3.5 mi., Veg-friendly), (The Java Factory Cafe 820-5282, 3.5 mi.)*

Recreation and Entertainment

OnSite: Picnic Area, Boat Rentals *(Sun Sea Kayaks 850-7732 $20-30/hr., $70-90/day; Four Winds Charter 492-0022, 2-hr cruises $25/20, 3-hr. Nature & Whale Watch $35/20)*, Tours *(Sun Sea 4 hr. Kayak Tour $65, 2.5 hr. Sunset Tour $45, 3-4 hr Hiking Tours $40-45 plus training courses.)* **Near:** Jogging Paths **1-3 mi:** Beach *(Queensland Beach on Boutiliers Point - 15 min. by dinghy, also Mink Island)* **3+ mi:** Golf Course *(Glen Arbour 835-4653, 11 mi.)*, Museum *(Ivan's Childhood Home 823-2386, 12 mi.)*, Sightseeing *(Peggy's Cove, 12 mi.)*, Galleries *(6 mi.)*

Provisioning and General Services

Under 1 mi: Post Office **1-3 mi:** Convenience Store, Bakery *(White Sails 826-1966)*, Hardware Store, Buying Club **3+ mi:** Supermarket *(Sobey's 826-3180, 5 mi.)*, Gourmet Shop *(Acadian Maple 826-2312, 3.5 mi.)*, Health Food *(Mariposa Natural 820-3350, 3.5 mi.)*, Liquor Store *(NSCL, 5 mi.)*, Bank/ATM *(Scotia Bank 826-2124, 4 mi.)*, Catholic Church *(St. Margarets, Glen Margaret, 6 mi.)*, Protestant Church *(St. Nicholas 826-1156, 4 mi.)*, Library *(Upper Tantallon 826-3330 - Internet, 5 mi.)*, Pharmacy *(Sobeys, 5 mi.)*

Transportation

OnCall: Taxi *(Aero - 10 mi.)* **Airport:** Halifax Int'l *(35 mi.)*

Medical Services

911 Service **OnCall:** Ambulance **Near:** Optician **1-3 mi:** Doctor *(Pair O' Docs 826-9387)*, Dentist *(St. Margaret's 826-2151)*, Veterinarian *(Tantallon 826-9344)* **Hospital:** QEII Health Center 473-2700 *(25 mi.)*

Setting -- In Head Harbour at the northeast corner of St. Margaret's Bay, ten acres with 1,200 feet of water frontage on Mackerel Point are home to the relatively recent Shining Waters marina. A spectacular, bow-front, all-glass, two-story contemporary building hosts the large ships' store, restaurant, event spaces and bathhouse. Just beyond the travelift bay, tables are scattered across the picnic lawn and an inviting hammock is tucked into the trees. Views from the second floor deck are across the docks to the mooring field to the mouth of the bay. The surrounding countryside is fairly undeveloped and very pretty.

Marina Notes -- *Channel Varies. Floating mixed-material docks - concrete squares set within wide wooden frames. Fuel dock Mon-Wed 9-5, Thu-Fri 9-8, Sat 9-6, Sun 9-4. Large ships store supplements its significant inventory with catalog shopping. 20-ton travelift manages up to 250 dry storage boats. Periodic events open to transients from "Newfie" Jigg dinners to Lobster bakes to Caribbean feasts. Mooring field serviced by dinghy dock. Bathhouse: Very attractive, modern gray granite tiles, black vanities with teal trim, fiberglass shower stalls with glass doors. Note: Enter Head Harbour between Indian Pt. & Croucher Is.

Notable -- The marina's 8,000-square foot building hosts a restaurant with innovative local cuisine provided by Chef Chris Burton (Tue-Sun, noon-9pm). 30 to 250 guests can be accommodated for a variety of catered special events - perfect for club cruises (buffets $32-44/pp + tax/grat). An onsite kayak company leases kayaks by the hour or the day, offers tours and an extensive roster of training programs. Also onsite Four Winds Charter offers two and three-hour whale watching and nature tours (and can be charted for special events). The closest town is Tantallon but most services are 5 miles away in Upper Tantallon.

Navigational Information
Lat: 44°32.252' **Long:** 064°14.368' **Tide:** 6 ft. **Current:** 0 kt. **Chart:** 4381
Rep. Depths (*MLW*): Entry 30 ft. **Fuel Dock** n/a **Max Slip/Moor** 16 ft./30 ft.
Access: Mahone Bay, Pass Quarker Is to port, then to starbd at Freda's Pt.

Marina Facilities *(In Season/Off Season)*
Fuel: No
Slips: 20 Total, 6 Transient **Max LOA:** 42 ft. **Max Beam:** 14 ft.
Rate *(per ft.)*: **Day** $1.50* **Week** n/a **Month** n/a
Power: 30 amp Incl., **50 amp** n/a, **100 amp** n/a, **200 amp** n/a
Cable TV: No **Dockside Phone:** No
Dock Type: Floating, Long Fingers, Alongside
Moorings: 3 Total, 3 Transient **Launch:** No, Dinghy Dock
Rate: Day $0.75/ft. **Week** n/a **Month** n/a
Heads: 1 Toilet(s), 1 Shower(s) *(dressing rooms)*
Internet: Yes *(Wi-Fi, Free)* **Laundry:** None
Pump-Out: No **Fee:** n/a **Closed Heads:** Yes

Marina Operations
Owner/Manager: Elaine Tough **Dockmaster:** Derek Delamere
In-Season: May-Oct, 11am-10pm **Off-Season:** Oct-Dec, Noon-9pm
After-Hours Arrival: Call in Advance
Reservations: Yes, Preferred **Credit Cards:** Visa/MC, Dscvr, Amex
Discounts: None
Pets: Welcome, Dog Walk Area **Handicap Access:** No

The Rope Loft Marina

PO Box 518; 36 Water Street; Chester, NS B0J 1J0

Tel: (902) 275-3430 **VHF: Monitor** Ch. 68 **Talk** Ch. 68
Fax: (902) 275-4220 **Alternate Tel:** (902) 275-4220
Email: wedine@ropeloft.com **Web:** www.ropeloft.com
Nearest Town: Chester **Tourist Info:** (902) 275-4616

Marina Services and Boat Supplies
Services - Security *(24/7, Owner Lives on Premises)*, Trash Pick-Up **Communication -** Mail & Package Hold, Fax in/out *(N/C)*, FedEx, UPS **Supplies - OnSite:** Ice *(Cube)* **Near:** Ships' Store *(Chester Marine Shop 277-1182)*, Propane

Boatyard Services
OnSite: Launching Ramp, Electrical Repairs, Electronic Sales, Electronics Repairs, Divers, Bottom Cleaning, Air Conditioning, Refrigeration, Woodworking **Nearest Yard:** South Shore Marine (902) 275-3711

Restaurants and Accommodations
OnSite: Restaurant *(Rope Loft 275-3430, B $8, L $8-16, D $12-22, Lobster $32+ Fri. nite Roast beef, Brunch Sat & Sun only, Kids' Menu)* **Near:** Restaurant *(Carta 275-5131)*, *(Nicki's Inn 275-4342, D $16-28)*, Lite Fare *(Kiwi Cafe 275-1492, B $3-13, L $6-18, Dinner Fri. only)*, *(Fo'c'sle Tavern 275-1408, L & D $8-9 Sandwiches & salads)*, *(Chester Organics 273-3663, Veg-friendly)*, Inn/B&B *(Mecklenburgh Inn 275-4638, $95-155)*, *(Nicki's 275-4342, $120-150)* **Under 1 mi:** Restaurant *(Big Reds 275-3777)*, Coffee Shop *(Tim Horton's)*, Fast Food *(McDs, Subway)*, Inn/B&B *(Hawthorne 277-1759, $85-135)* **1-3 mi:** Restaurant *(Windjammer 275-3714)*, Motel *(Windjammer 275-3567, $70+)* **3+ mi:** Condo/Cottage *(Celtic Cottages 275-1391, $100, 4 mi.)*

Recreation and Entertainment
Near: Pool *(Lido Tidal Pool)*, Beach, Playground, Tennis Courts, Fitness Center *(Take Thirty 275-3255)*, Hike/Bike Trails, Movie Theater *(Chester Playhouse 275-3933 - Concerts. live theater)*, Video Rental *(Chester Variety 275-3400)*, Tours *(Boat Tours)*, Sightseeing *(Chester)*, Galleries *(Jim Smith Pottery 275-3272, Warp & Woof 275-4795)*, Special Events *(VIC 275-4616; Chester Race Week, mid-Aug)* **1-3 mi:** Picnic Area, Grills, Golf Course *(Chester GC 275-4543)*

Provisioning and General Services
Near: Convenience Store *(Chester Variety Chester Variety 275-3400, Hammonds Kwik Mart)*, Delicatessen *(Julien's)*, Health Food *(Chester Organics 273-3663; Kiwi Too 275-2570)*, Liquor Store *(NSLC)*, Bakery *(Julien's 275-2324)*, Bank/ATM, Post Office, Catholic Church, Protestant Church, Library *(Zee Valle)*, Beauty Salon *(Vadal's 275-3793)*, Dry Cleaners, Pharmacy *(Pharmsave 275-3518)*, Newsstand, Copies Etc. *(Chester Variety)* **Under 1 mi:** Supermarket *(Save Easy 275-3262)*, Laundry *(LN Video & Laundromat 275-4960)*, Hardware Store *(Chester Home 275-4839)*, Florist *(Flowers, Flowers 275-5707)* **3+ mi:** Farmers' Market *(Hubbard's Red Barn Sat 8-noon, Sun 10-2, 15 mi.)*

Transportation
Near: Ferry Service *(Chester-Tancook Island 275-3221 $5)* **Airport:** Halifax Int'l *(60 mi.)*

Medical Services
911 Service **Near:** Dentist *(Chester Dental 275-3828)* **Under 1 mi:** Doctor *(Chester Family 275-5625)* **1-3 mi:** Chiropractor *(Chester Health 275-5900)* **3+ mi:** Veterinarian *(Evans, 6 mi.)* **Hospital:** Bridgewater *(30 mi.)*

Setting -- From Chester Harbour, cruise into narrow Front Harbour. Just past the Ferry Wharf, Rope Loft sits right in the middle of the village of Chester and everything is walkable. Two spacious dining porches - railed with transparent wind-screens - front the two-story natural shingled building. Gaily colored umbrellas protect the diners. The first-floor porch wraps around to a protected cocktail deck that spills out onto the floating docks that parallel the shore.

Marina Notes -- *120 linear feet of dockage. Owned by Derek Delamere, an active sailor, who is a fount of information. Rope Loft serves a wide variety of casual cuisine in four locations: the first floor pub, the first floor porch, the second floor dining room or out on the second floor deck that overlooks the docks, mooring field and out to the Harbour. Lunch, dinner and weekend brunch. Small sections of floating wooden docks strung together. Pump-out at Municipal Dock. Bathhouse: Restaurant heads only. Chester Rink at top of the hill has showers. Note: Dockage available at public ferry wharf - not south side.

Notable -- Just seaward of Rope Loft's dock, the L-shaped ferry dock is home to the 82-foot "William S. Ernst" that transports passengers to Big Tancook and Little Tancook. A 45-minute, 5-mile trip from Government Wharf, there are four runs weekdays and two on the weekend. Settled by French Hugenots in the 1800s, these two sparsely settled islands boast 100 and 35 residents each. Big Tancook has a small museum and a cafe. Established in 1759, Chester has been home to pirates, rum runners and privateers, but today it's an old moneyed seaside resort with elegant homes and a casual, unpretentious vibe. The tiny, charming business district is surrounded by lovely, leafy lanes that demand to be strolled. And boaters have the very best views of the waterfront mansions.

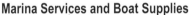

PHOTOS ON DVD: 23

Chester Yacht Club

PO Box 290; 21 South Street; Chester, NS B0J 1J0

Tel: (902) 275-3747 **VHF: Monitor** Ch. 16 **Talk** Ch. 68
Fax: (902) 275-2525 **Alternate Tel:** n/a
Email: cycsteward@eastlink.ca **Web:** www.cyc.ns.ca
Nearest Town: Chester **Tourist Info:** (902) 275-4616

Navigational Information

Lat: 44°32.154' **Long:** 064°14.536' **Tide:** 7 ft. **Current:** 6 kt. **Chart:** 431
Rep. Depths (*MLW*): Entry 30 ft. **Fuel Dock** n/a **Max Slip/Moor** -/16 ft.
Access: Mahone Bay due north of Big Tancook Island

Marina Facilities *(In Season/Off Season)*

Fuel: No
Slips: 0 Total, 0 Transient **Max LOA:** 60 ft. **Max Beam:** n/a
Rate *(per ft.)*: **Day** n/a **Week** n/a **Month** n/a
Power: 30 amp n/a, **50 amp** n/a, **100 amp** n/a, **200 amp** n/a
Cable TV: No **Dockside Phone:** No
Dock Type: Fixed, Floating, Wood
Moorings: 45 Total, 10 Transient **Launch:** No, Dinghy Dock
Rate: Day $20 **Week** $140 **Month** n/a
Heads: 3 Toilet(s)
Internet: No **Laundry:** None
Pump-Out: No **Fee:** n/a **Closed Heads:** Yes

Marina Operations

Owner/Manager: Yacht Club **Dockmaster:** Kim Johnson
In-Season: Jul-Aug, noon-8pm **Off-Season:** Jun, Sep, Oct, Varies
After-Hours Arrival: Call in advance for instructions
Reservations: Yes, Preferred **Credit Cards:** Visa/MC
Discounts: None
Pets: No **Handicap Access:** No

Marina Services and Boat Supplies

Communication - FedEx, UPS **Supplies - OnSite:** Ice *(Cube)* **Near:** Ships' Store *(Chester Marine 277-1182)*, Propane

Boatyard Services

OnSite: Crane, Launching Ramp **Near:** Electrical Repairs, Electronic Sales, Electronics Repairs, Divers, Bottom Cleaning, Air Conditioning, Refrigeration. **Nearest Yard:** South Shore Marine - 5 mi. (902) 275-3711

Restaurants and Accommodations

Near: Restaurant *(Rope Loft 275-3430, B $8, L $8-16, D $12-22, Breakfast wknds only; Night Life)*, *(Carta 275-5131)*, *(Nicki's Inn 275-4342, D $16-28)*, Lite Fare *(Kiwi Cafe 275-1492, B $3-13, L $6-18, Dinner Only)*, *(Fo'c'sle Tavern 275-1408, L & D $8-9, Chester's Nightlife hangout)*, *(Chester Organics 273-3663, Veg-friendly)*, Inn/B&B *(Mecklenburgh Inn 275-4638, $95-155)*, *(Nicki's 275-4342, $120-150)*, *(Hawthorne 277-1759, $85-135)* **Under 1 mi:** Coffee Shop *(Tim Hortons)*, Fast Food *(McD's, Subway)*, Pizzeria *(Recardos 275-5688, Delivers)* **1-3 mi:** Restaurant *(Windjammer 275-3714)*, Motel *(Windjammer 275-3567, $70+)*

Recreation and Entertainment

OnSite: Beach *(tiny pebble beach)* **Near:** Pool *(Lido Tidal Pool)*, Playground, Tennis Courts *(Chester Tennis Club 275-4535)*, Jogging Paths, Hike/Bike Trails, Video Rental *(Chester Variety 275-3400)*, Park *(Parade Square, Lordly Park)*, Museum *(Lordly Manor 275-3826 1806 Georgian demonstrates 19thC upper class life; Zoe Velle)*, Tours *(Tancook Island Ferry)*, Cultural Attract *(Chester Playhouse 275-3933 - Concerts, Live Theater)*, Sightseeing *(Self-Guided Walking Tours - Visitors' Center)*, Galleries *(Amicus 275-2496, Chester Arts Centre 275-5789)*, Special Events *(Race Week - Mid-Aug)* **Under 1 mi:** Fitness Center *(Mangled Mamas Gym 275-3801)* **1-3 mi:** Golf Course *(Chester GC 275-4543)*

Provisioning and General Services

Near: Convenience Store *(Chester Variety 275-3400)*, Health Food *(Kiwi Too 275-2570, Chester Organics 273-3663)*, Wine/Beer *(NSLC)*, Liquor Store *(NSLC 275-3242)*, Bakery *(Julien's 275-2324)*, Bank/ATM *(Scotia)*, Post Office, Catholic Church, Protestant Church, Library *(Zoe Valle)*, Beauty Salon *(Vadals 275-3793)*, Bookstore *(Wayward Used)*, Florist *(Flowers, Flowers 275-5707)*, Retail Shops, Copies Etc. *(Chester Variety)* **Under 1 mi:** Supermarket *(Hammonds Save Easy 275-3262)*, Laundry *(LN Video & Laundromat 275-4960)*, Pharmacy *(Chester Pharmasave 275-3518)*, Hardware Store *(Chester Home 275-4839)*

Transportation

Near: Ferry Service *(Tancook Island $5 RT)* **Airport:** Halifax Int', *(60 mi.)*

Medical Services

911 Service **OnCall:** Ambulance **Near:** Doctor *(Jaymore 275-3529)*, Dentist *(Andrea 275-3828)* **1-3 mi:** Chiropractor *(Chester Health 275-5900)*, Veterinarian *(Chester Basin 275-3551)* **Hospital:** South Shore Reg. *(30 mi.)*

Setting -- From Mahone Bay, leave 135 foot high Freda's Point at the tip of The Peninsula to port as you enter Chester Harbour. CYC's 3-story pretty white clapboardclubhouse topped by a brick-red roof is easy to spot on the western shore. A covered veranda steps down onto a brick patio furnished with red painted Adirondack-style chairs - all with an expansive view of the harbour. A floating dinghy dock services the mooring field.

Marina Notes -- Chester is the heart of sail racing in Nova Scotia, and its 3,000 residents throughly enjoy ensuring it stays that way. Chester Yacht Club is home base for Chester Race Week -approximately 150 boats each year make it Canada's biggest keelboat regatta, the oldest in NA. Bluenose Championship also held here. Weekly IOD and Bluenose racing. Active junior sailing program - Optis, Micros & 420s. Bar and bar snacks only. Butch Heisler (275-2216) manages Back Harbour mooring field. Pump-out at Municipal Dock Bathhouse: Heads only, no showers

Notable -- Watch the races from Parade Square, a grassy patch with a band stand and war memorials, just above CYC. Across the narrow neck on Victoria Street, The Lido, a public saltwater tidal pool that fills at high tide, and adjacent Kings Wharf are popular spots at sunset. To discover Chester, pick up a walking tour from Visitor Information in the 1901 train station. The little village is awash in unique, locally owned, shops, galleries and all manner of historic buildings. Chester Theater runs a summer festival with live theater, concerts, dance, stand-up comedy. Take the ferry to Tancook Island - or take the boat and pick up a mooring. Walk the picturesque lanes, stop for a bite at the small cafe that serves great fish 'n chips and buy some famous Tancook sauerkraut.

PHOTOS ON DVD: 25

Navigational Information

Lat: 44°33.450' **Long:** 064°17.150' **Tide:** 5 ft. **Current:** n/a **Chart:** 4381
Rep. Depths (*MLW*): Entry 40 ft. **Fuel Dock** 9 ft. **Max Slip/Moor** -/40 ft.
Access: Hawker Pt. between Marriot's Cove & Chester Basin

Marina Facilities *(In Season/Off Season)*

Fuel: Gasoline, Diesel
Slips: 0 Total, 0 Transient **Max LOA:** 50 ft. **Max Beam:** n/a
Rate *(per ft.)*: **Day** n/a **Week** n/a **Month** n/a
Power: 30 amp Incl., **50 amp** n/a, **100 amp** n/a, **200 amp** n/a
Cable TV: No **Dockside Phone:** No
Dock Type: n/a
Moorings: 95 Total, 12 Transient **Launch:** Yes (Comp.), Dinghy Dock
Rate: Day $25 **Week** $175 **Month** $295
Heads: 3 Toilet(s), 2 Shower(s)
Internet: Yes *(Wi-Fi, Free)* **Laundry:** 1 Washer(s), 1 Dryer(s)
Pump-Out: No **Fee:** n/a **Closed Heads:** Yes

Marina Operations

Owner/Manager: Shawn Mulrooney **Dockmaster:** Same
In-Season: Mar-Dec, 8am-5pm **Off-Season:** Jan-Feb, Closed
After-Hours Arrival: Mooring balls without white jugs attached to hawsers
Reservations: Yes, Preferred **Credit Cards:** Visa/MC, Debit, Cash
Discounts: None
Pets: Welcome **Handicap Access:** Yes

South Shore Marine

PO Box 316; 130 Marina Rd; Chester, NS B0J1J0

Tel: (902) 275-3711 **VHF: Monitor** Ch. 16 **Talk** Ch. 68
Fax: (902) 275-2416 **Alternate Tel:** n/a
Email: southshoremarine@eastlink.ca **Web:** www.southshoremarine.ca
Nearest Town: Chester *(3.5 mi.)* **Tourist Info:** (902) 624-6151

Marina Services and Boat Supplies

Communication - Pay Phone, FedEx, UPS **Supplies - OnSite:** Ice *(Block)*, Ships' Store *(Large stock marine supplies, clothing, gifts)* **OnCall:** Ice *(Shaved)* **1-3 mi:** Bait/Tackle

Boatyard Services

OnSite: Travelift *(20T - 44 ft. x 14 ft.)*, Crane, Engine mechanic *(gas)*, Hull Repairs, Rigger, Brightwork, Compound, Wash & Wax, Painting, Awlgrip, Total Refits **OnCall:** Electrical Repairs, Electronic Sales, Electronics Repairs, Divers, Bottom Cleaning, Woodworking **1-3 mi:** Canvas Work, Metal Fabrication. **Dealer for:** Transat Marine, Western Marine, Stright-Mackay, Mermaid Marine. **Yard Rates:** $32-50/hr., Haul & Launch $7/ft., Power Wash $2/ft., Bottom Paint $32/hr. **Storage:** In-Water $1.50/sq.ft., On-Land $2/sq.ft., Inside $3/sq.ft.

Restaurants and Accommodations

1-3 mi: Restaurant *(Rope Loft 275-3430, L $8-16, D $12-22, cafe with beautiful view of the harbor, Wknd brunch 11am-1pm)*, *(The Kiwi Cafe 275-1492, L & D $7-15)*, *(Windjammer 275-3714, L $4-12, D $7.25-25, Seafood, Canadian, Lebanese, Kids' $6 Veg-friendly)*, *(Nicki's Inn 275-4342, L $10-14, D $16-28)*, Seafood Shack *(Seaside Shanty Restaurant 275-2246, L $8-18, D $10-22, Kids' $3-5 - in Chester Basin)*, Coffee Shop *(Tim Hortons 275-3733)*, Lite Fare *(Fo'c'sle Tavern 27-514-08 , L & D $8-9, Favorite local tavern with pub fare)*, Pizzeria *(Duke Street)*, Motel *(The Windjammer Motel 275-3567, $70+)*, Inn/B&B *(Mecklenburgh Inn 275-4638, $95-155)*, *(Nicki's Inn 275-4342, $120-150)*

Recreation and Entertainment

Near: Picnic Area, Grills, Video Rental *(Cow Store)* **1-3 mi:** Beach *(Freda's)*, Park *(Church Memorial 275-4628)*, Cultural Attract *(Chester Playhouse 275-3933)*, Sightseeing *(Tancook Island Ferry 424-8687)* **3+ mi:** Golf Course *(Chester G.C. 275-4543, 4 mi)*

Provisioning and General Services

Under 1 mi: Convenience Store *(Charlotte's Maritime Market 275-2441)* **1-3 mi:** Market, Supermarket *(Chester Save Easy 275-3262; Chester Basin Value Foods)*, Liquor Store *(NSLC 275-3242)*, Bakery *(Julien's 275-2324)*, Green Grocer *(Pumpkin Patch Farm Stand - 2 mi.)*, Bank/ATM *(Chester Basin)*, Post Office *(Chester Basin)*, Protestant Church, Beauty Salon *(Between Friends 275-2017)*, Barber Shop, Pharmacy *(Chester Pharmasave 275-3518)*, Hardware Store *(Chester Home 275-4839)*, Florist *(Flowers, Flowers)* **3+ mi:** Fishmonger *(The Fish Store in Gold River 627-3474, 3.5 mi.)*, Bookstore *(The Biscuit Eater Books and Cafe 624-2665, 10 mi.)*

Transportation

OnCall: Taxi *(Bond's 275-7402)* **1-3 mi:** Ferry Service *(Tancook Ferry $5 RT)* **Airport:** Halifax Int'l *(60 mi.)*

Medical Services

911 Service **OnCall:** Ambulance **1-3 mi:** Doctor *(Chester Family 275-5625)*, Dentist *(Chester Clinic 275-3828)*, Holistic Services *(Chester Harbour Yoga & Massage 273-9642)*, Veterinarian *(Chester Basin 275-3551)*
Hospital: South Shore Regional - Bridgewater 543-8065 *(20 mi.)*

Setting -- A classic barn-red colonial, perched on a hill above Steven's Cove, houses the Loft Chandlery, amenities, office and the former restaurant space - all with panoramic views of the expansive mooring field that lies in the lee of Hawker Point. Also onshore is a full-service boat yard, work sheds, haulout bay and on the hard storage. The pristine views are of nearby Shaw Island, more distant Marvin's Island and across this neck of Mahone Bay.

Marina Notes -- Founded by the McCurdys in the '70s. Shawn Mulrooney took the helm in 2010. The Loft chandlery. Moorings only - bright orange ball (1500 lb cement slabs, three 2000 lb). Complimentary launch service Mon-Fri 8-4:30, Sat & Sun 9-6 - marina dinghy left for after hours. Dockage for loading & unloading but not overnight. Full-service yacht yard - haul-out, engine repairs, awlgrip painting system, keel/hull repairs, winter storage (44 ft X 14 ft). Closest pump-out Chester Wharf. Bathhouse: Basic full baths plus laundry. Note: Shoal extends far out from Hawkers Pt.

Notable -- The well-equipped Loft Chandlery has most anything a boater might need, as might be expected from the group who founded The Binnacle in Halifax. Inventory includes Harken & Schaeffer hardware, a large selection of rope, halyards, docklines, fenders, Interlux paint & varnish, and cleaning supplies - all nicely merchandised. The charming village of Chester is just three miles southeast (services are listed above as 1-3 miles) and the little burg of Chester Basin is 1.7 miles west. Dock at the public wharf, past Marvin's Island at the head of the Chester Basin. There's 50 feet of face dock and 5 foot depth; most of the village amenities are nearby.

PHOTOS ON DVD: 20

Gold River Marina

242 Demont Road; Chester Basin, NS B05 1K0

Tel: (902) 275-1322 **VHF: Monitor** n/a **Talk** n/a
Fax: (902) 275-1376 **Alternate Tel:** n/a
Email: Use Form on Website **Web:** www.goldrivermarina.com
Nearest Town: Chester *(7 mi.)* **Tourist Info:** (902) 624-6151

Navigational Information

Lat: 44°32.490' **Long:** 064°18.570' **Tide:** 5 ft. **Current:** n/a **Chart:** 4381
Rep. Depths (*MLW*): Entry 8 ft. **Fuel Dock** 6 ft. **Max Slip/Moor** 7 ft./10 ft.
Access: Northwest corner of Mahone Bay in the mouth of Gold River

Marina Facilities *(In Season/Off Season)*

Fuel: *Ultramar* - Gasoline, Diesel
Slips: 45 Total, 4 Transient **Max LOA:** 40 ft. **Max Beam:** 13 ft.
Rate *(per ft.)*: **Day** $1.85* **Week** $25 **Month** $40
Power: 30 amp Incl., **50 amp** n/a, **100 amp** n/a, **200 amp** n/a
Cable TV: No **Dockside Phone:** No
Dock Type: Floating, Long Fingers, Wood
Moorings: 5 Total, 1 Transient **Launch:** n/a, Dinghy Dock
Rate: Day $50 **Week** $150 **Month** $300
Heads: 3 Toilet(s), 3 Shower(s) *(dressing rooms)*, Book Exchange
Internet: Yes *(Wi-Fi, Free)* **Laundry:** 1 Washer(s), 1 Dryer(s)
Pump-Out: No **Fee:** n/a **Closed Heads:** Yes

Marina Operations

Owner/Manager: Leigh Robertson **Dockmaster:** Darrin Swinimer
In-Season: Apr 15-Nov 15, 8:30am-4:30pm **Off-Season:** n/a
After-Hours Arrival: n/a
Reservations: Yes, Preferred **Credit Cards:** Visa/MC, Cash, Interac
Discounts: None
Pets: No **Handicap Access:** No

Marina Services and Boat Supplies

Communication - FedEx, UPS **Supplies - OnSite:** Ice *(Block, Cube)*, Ships' Store **1-3 mi:** Propane *(Kaizers 275-2544)*

Boatyard Services

OnSite: Railway *(50T)*, Engine mechanic *(gas, diesel)*, Electronics Repairs *(Baetech 237-8345)*, Hull Repairs *(Benoits)*, Sail Loft *(Stevens 634-9338)*, Brightwork, Woodworking, Painting, Awlgrip *(Benoits)*, Total Refits **OnCall:** Electrical Repairs, Electronic Sales, Canvas Work, Bottom Cleaning, Air Conditioning, Propeller Repairs, Life Raft Service, Yacht Interiors, Metal Fabrication **Under 1 mi:** Launching Ramp. **1-3 mi:** Inflatable Repairs. **Yard Rates:** $60/hr., Haul & Launch $9.50/ft., Power Wash $2.50/ft. **Storage:** On-Land $0.40/ft./mo., Inside $1.10/ft./mo.

Restaurants and Accommodations

Under 1 mi: Condo/Cottage *(Celtic Cottages 275-1391)* **1-3 mi:** Restaurant *(Seaside Shanty L & D $8-22)*, Lite Fare *(Mo's Grill & Dining room 627-1053)*, Inn/B&B *(Sword & Anchor 275-2478, 8 ensuite guest rooms $100-115, a family suite $150, plus a guest House $250-300)* **3+ mi:** Fast Food *(Subway, Tim Hortons 7 mi.)*, Lite Fare *(F'o'csle Tavern 275-1408, 7 mi., L & D $8-10)*, Motel *(Windjammer 275-3567, $70-90, 7 mi.)*, Hotel *(Oak Island Resort 627-2600, $100-3000, 5 mi.)*, Inn/B&B *(Mecklenburgh Inn 275-4638, $80-150, 7 mi.)*

Recreation and Entertainment

OnSite: Picnic Area, Grills *(Fire Pit, too)* **Near:** Beach *(Wild Rose Park - across the river by dinghy)*, Park *(Wild Rose)*, Special Events *(Annual Mackerel Snappers Picnic - Rose Park - July.Western Shore Fire Department Fun Day & Firework display - Aug)* **3+ mi:** Tennis Courts *(7 mi.)*, Golf Course *(Chester Golf Club 275-4702, 7 mi.)*, Video Rental *(Chester Save Easy, 7 mi.)*

Provisioning and General Services

Near: Convenience Store *(Mohammed Sodey's Riverview 627-2974)*, Fishmonger *(ELP - dinghy across river)* **Under 1 mi:** Market *(Chester Basin Value Foods 275-2122)*, Pharmacy *(McDougall's Pharmasave 857-1743)* **1-3 mi:** Green Grocer, Bank/ATM, Post Office, Library *(Halifax Regional)*, Beauty Salon, Barber Shop, Newsstand, Retail Shops **3+ mi:** Supermarket *(Chester Save Easy; FoodChopper, 6 mi.)*, Health Food *(Chester Organics, 6 mi.)*, Wine/Beer *(6 mi.)*, Liquor Store *(6 mi.)*, Farmers' Market *(Chester, Mahone Bay, Lunenburg & Hubbards, 6 mi.)*, Lobster Pound *(At Chester Save Easy, 6 mi.)*, Hardware Store *(Chester Home 275-4839, 6 mi.)*

Transportation

OnCall: Rental Car *(Enterprise 527-5909)*, Taxi *(Chester 277-2727)* **Airport:** Halifax Int'l *(65 mi.)*

Medical Services

911 Service **OnCall:** Ambulance **1-3 mi:** Veterinarian *(Chester Basin)* **3+ mi:** Doctor *(Chester Family 275-5625, 6 mi.)*, Dentist *(Andrea 275-3828, 10 mi.)*, Chiropractor *(Rusaw 275-5900, 10 mi.)*, Holistic Services *(Physiotherapist 275-5086, 6 mi.)* **Hospital:** South Shore Regional *(30 mi.)*

PHOTOS ON DVD: 24

Setting -- In a quiet spot at the mouth of Gold River, two main floating docks flank the travelift bay. They parallel the shoreline, one wrapping around a small peninsula; each hosts a single row of slips on its outboard face. Three ramps lead to the upland. On shore, it's mostly pure boatyard - with the counterpoint of an expansive, nicely maintained boaters' deck with picnic tables and a grill that overlooks the docks and river. The original pale blue edifices of Gold Water Marine are the main work sheds supplemented by a new, large megadome for inside storage surrounded by the dry storage areas.

Marina Notes -- *Daily flat rate $75. Former site of Gold Water Marine. Gold River hosts a roster of "Preferred Service Providers," ostensibly onsite, that offer particular expertises. Most are listed under BY services. On the hard storage for up to 200 boats. Modified 20-ton railway pulls small day boats and good size yachts - including cats. Marina staff may arrange rides for transient boaters. Bathhouse: In front of main building. Quite nice, recent full baths with painted walls, lots of hooks, molded fiberglass shower stall with sliding glass door. Pleasant laundry room. Note: Markers often not in place until after lobster season.

Notable -- Settled in 1760, the community of Chester Basin, population 2000, is truly rural Nova Scotia; the center of the village is about a mile and a half from the docks.There you will find a lovely, upscale bed and breakfast, convenience store, pharmacy, gas station, grocery, post office, animal hospital, a church and a quaint old cemetery. Keep an eye out for antique and craft shops and art galleries. Across the river, narrow Wild Rose Park edges 1,500 feet of shoreline. Tie up at the wharf to enjoy the beach (with changing rooms & showers), picnic tables, and a view of Capt. Kidd's Oak Island. Summer is also mackerel season.

Navigational Information
Lat: 44°31.330' **Long:** 064°18.340' **Tide:** 6 ft. **Current:** 0 kt. **Chart:** 4381
Rep. Depths (*MLW*): Entry 12 ft. **Fuel Dock** 12 ft. **Max Slip/Moor** 10 ft./18 ft.
Access: Mahone Bay to Northeast corner

Marina Facilities *(In Season/Off Season)*
Fuel: Gasoline
Slips: 41 Total, 3 Transient **Max LOA:** 40 ft. **Max Beam:** 14 ft.
Rate *(per ft.)*: **Day** $1.90* **Week** $420 **Month** $1200
Power: 30 amp Incl., **50 amp** n/a, **100 amp** n/a, **200 amp** n/a
Cable TV: No **Dockside Phone:** No
Dock Type: Floating, Long Fingers, Alongside, Wood
Moorings: 4 Total, 4 Transient **Launch:** No, Dinghy Dock
Rate: Day $50 **Week** $280 **Month** $1200
Heads: 2 Toilet(s), 2 Shower(s) *(dressing rooms)*
Internet: Yes *(Wi-Fi in Lobby**)* **Laundry:** 2 Washer(s), 2 Dryer(s)
Pump-Out: No **Fee:** n/a **Closed Heads:** Yes

Marina Operations
Owner/Manager: Wynand "Dutch" Baerken **Dockmaster:** Same
In-Season: May 15 -Oct 15, 9am-5/6pm **Off-Season:** Oct 16-May 14, Closed
After-Hours Arrival: Contact Guest services at the Resort
Reservations: Yes, Preferred **Credit Cards:** Visa/MC, Amex
Discounts: None
Pets: Welcome **Handicap Access:** Yes, Heads, Docks

Atlantica Oak Island Marina

PO Box 6; 36 Treasure Drive; Western Shore, NS B0J 3Md

Tel: (902) 627-3340 **VHF: Monitor** n/a **Talk** n/a
Fax: (902) 627-1162 **Alternate Tel:** n/a
Email: wbaerken@yahoo.com **Web:** www.atlanticaoakisland.com
Nearest Town: Mahone Bay *(8 mi.)* **Tourist Info:** (902) 624-6151

Marina Services and Boat Supplies
Services - Docking Assistance, Trash Pick-Up, Dock Carts
Communication - FedEx, UPS **Supplies - OnSite:** Ice *(Cube)* **OnCall:** Ships' Store *(Chester Marine Services 277-1182)* **1-3 mi:** Propane *(Petro Canada - fill or exchange; Galen's, Bridgewater 543-9539 6 mi.)*, CNG *(Ultra Mar exchange - public wharf)*

Boatyard Services
OnSite: Launching Ramp **OnCall:** Engine mechanic *(gas, diesel)*, Electrical Repairs, Bottom Cleaning, Refrigeration **Nearest Yard:** Gold River (902) 275-1322

Restaurants and Accommodations
OnSite: Restaurant *(La Vista Dining Room B $9-12, L $8-13, D $18-23, Kids' $6. Breakfast 7-11am, Lunch 11am-2pm, Dinner 5-9pm)*, Lite Fare *(Fireside Lounge L & D $7-12)*, Hotel *(Oak Island $80-300)* **3+ mi:** Restaurant *(Seaside Shanty 275-2246, 4 mi.)*, *(Windjammer 275-3567, 7.5 mi.)*, Motel *(Windjammer 275-3567, 7.5 mi.)*

Recreation and Entertainment
OnSite: Heated Pool *(2 - indoor & outdoor)*, Spa *(Jacuzzi & hot tub)*, Beach, Picnic Area, Playground, Tennis Courts, Fitness Center *(Very complete)*, Boat Rentals *(Kayak Shack 627-3340 $25-35/hr, $85-115/day)*, Fishing Charter *(Kayak Shack)*, For Kids *(Mini Golf)*, Tours *(Miss Adventure Boat Tours 627-3340 $45; Sea 'N Seals Eco Tours 634-8495 $35/15)*
Near: Jogging Paths **3+ mi:** Golf Course *(Osprey Ridge 543-6666, 15 mi.)*, Museum *(Settlers' 624-6263 Mon-Sat 10am-5pm, Sun 1-5pm, Free, 5.5 mi.)*, Cultural Attract *(Chester Playhouse 275-3933, 5 mi.)*

Provisioning and General Services
OnSite: Bank/ATM, Post Office, Beauty Salon, Barber Shop **Near:** Green Grocer *(Glyda's Fruits & Veg 627-2090)* **Under 1 mi:** Hardware Store *(Terry Zwicker 627-2358)* **1-3 mi:** Fishmonger *(Fish & Lobster 627-3474)*, Laundry **3+ mi:** Supermarket *(Bridgewater Superstore 543-1809, 18 mi.)*, Liquor Store *(Mahone Bay 624-8300, 6.5 mi.)*, Farmers' Market *(Mahone Bay 7 days, 6.5 mi.)*, Catholic Church *(8 mi.)*, Protestant Church *(8 mi.)*, Dry Cleaners *(8 mi.)*, Pharmacy *(Chester 275-3518, Pharmasave 275-5681, 8 mi.)*, Florist *(Flowers, Flowers 275-5707, 8 mi.)*

Transportation
OnSite: Bikes *(Kayak Shack 627-3340 $25/half day, $40/day)* **OnCall:** Rental Car *(Enterprise 527-5909 - from Bridgewater)*, Taxi *(Ocean View 527-8251 - from Lunenburg)* **Airport:** Halifax Int'l *(50 mi.)*

Medical Services
911 Service **OnSite:** Holistic Services *(Oak Island Spa - 1 hr. Massage $80)* **OnCall:** Ambulance **3+ mi:** Doctor *(Chester Clinic 275-3529, 12 mi.)*, Dentist *(Chester Family 275-5184, 4 mi.)*, Chiropractor *(Bridgewater 543-1660, 13 mi.)*, Veterinarian *(Chester Basin 275-3551, 3.5 mi.)* **Hospital:** South Shore Regional 543-4603 *(13 mi.)*

PHOTOS ON DVD: 25

Setting -- Tucked into a basin created by rip rap breakwaters at the head of Mahone Bay, are the slips and mooring field of this small, full-service resort and spa. Onshore Atlantica Hotel's three-story, gray-sided contemporary buildings sprawl along a ridge overlooking the bay and the resort facilities - pool, tennis court, mini-golf, playground and bathhouse. In the main are an indoor pool, fitness center, full-service spa and salon and two restaurants.

Marina Notes -- *All Flat Rates: $75/night. **Computer in Dockhouse, Wi-Fi in Lobby. New set of Condos built on the left in the area that used to be a repair facility. Resort owned and being developed by Ken Roe. Water gets shallow in right hand side of basin. Expansion of docks on hold temporarily. Guest of marina is guest of hotel (but cannot sign). Slips & alongside dockage. Gas only. $10 discount for marina guests at resort hotel. For supplies, head to Mahone Bay (6 mi.), Chester (10 mi.), Chester Basin (3.5 mi.). Bathhouse: Full baths with fiberglass & glass shower stalls, ceramic tile floors. Airy laundry with sink & folding counter. Note: Only pump-outs are at Mahone Bay Civic Marina & Chester Municipal Dock.

Notable -- Atlantica Hotel's third floor dining spaces LaVista, Fireside Lounge and an al fresco deck all boast panoramic views. Onshore accommodations include 105 guestrooms, 13 cottages and 2 waterside condos. A spa, salon and fitness center feature full menu of massages, body therapies and salon services. The indoor pool has a jacuzzi and hot tub in a windowed bay. Club cruises will find 13,000 square feet of meeting and event space. Since 1795, the famous Oak Island Money Pit has confounded treasure seekers. It's not open to the public, but boaters can cruise by the reported home of Capt. Kidd's loot.

Mahone Bay Civic Marina

PO Box 609; Lighthouse Rte.; Mahone Bay, NS BOJ 2EO

Tel: (902) 624-0117 **VHF: Monitor** Ch. 68 **Talk** Ch. 68
Fax: (902) 531-2362 **Alternate Tel:** n/a
Email: n/a **Web:** www.mahonebaycivicmarina.ca
Nearest Town: Mahone Bay **Tourist Info:** (902) 624-6151

Navigational Information

Lat: 44°26.817' **Long:** 064°22.467' **Tide:** 6 ft. **Current:** 2 kt. **Chart:** 4381
Rep. Depths (*MLW*): Entry 10 ft. **Fuel Dock** n/a **Max Slip/Moor** 6 ft./8 ft.
Access: Pass between Andres & Eisenhauers Points

Marina Facilities *(In Season/Off Season)*

Fuel: No
Slips: 10 Total, 3 Transient **Max LOA:** 75 ft. **Max Beam:** n/a
Rate *(per ft.)*: **Day** $0.85* **Week** n/a **Month** n/a
Power: 30 amp $4, **50 amp** n/a, **100 amp** n/a, **200 amp** n/a
Cable TV: No **Dockside Phone:** No
Dock Type: Fixed, Floating, Long Fingers, Alongside, Wood
Moorings: 40 Total, 5 Transient **Launch:** Yes ($1/pp/1-way), Dinghy Dock
Rate: Day $23* **Week** $100 **Month** $235
Heads: 4 Toilet(s), 1 Shower(s)
Internet: Yes *(Wi-Fi, Free)* **Laundry:** None
Pump-Out: OnSite, Full Service **Fee:** $10 **Closed Heads:** No

Marina Operations

Owner/Manager: Dave Devenne **Dockmaster:** Bob Douglas
In-Season: Jul-LabDay, 9-9** **Off-Season:** May-Jun; Sep-Oct, 9-5
After-Hours Arrival: Call in advance
Reservations: Yes **Credit Cards:** Visa/MC, Debit
Discounts: None
Pets: Welcome, Dog Walk Area **Handicap Access:** Yes, Heads

Marina Services and Boat Supplies

Services - Docking Assistance, Trash Pick-Up, Dock Carts
Communication - Phone Messages, FedEx, UPS **Supplies - OnSite:** Ice *(Cube)* **Under 1 mi:** Propane *(Irving)*, CNG

Boatyard Services

OnSite: Launching Ramp *($5)* **OnCall:** Sail Loft, Canvas Work, Brightwork, Propeller Repairs, Woodworking, Inflatable Repairs, Yacht Interiors, Metal Fabrication **3+ mi:** Electronics Repairs *(6 mi)*. **Nearest Yard:** Mahone Bay Boatworks (902) 212-2266

Restaurants and Accommodations

Near: Restaurant *(Mug & Anchor Pub 624-6378, Live entertainment, Blues Band Night. 2nd floor Brewpub with waterside deck.)*, *(Gazebo Cafe 624-6484, L $8-20, D $15-22, Inside or waterfront gazebo)*, *(Innlet Cafe 624-6363, L & D $12-22, waterview stone dining patio 11:30am-9pm)*, *(Cheesecake Gallery, Bistro & Wine Bar 624-0579)*, Lite Fare *(Biscuit Eater 624-book, Wi-Fi)*, Pizzeria *(Bayside 624-1253)*, Inn/B&B *(Mahone Bay 624-6388, $95-135)*, *(Hearts Desire 624-8470)*, *(Three Thistles 624-0517, $90-125, & Apts.)*

Recreation and Entertainment

OnSite: Special Events *(Mahone Bay Classic Boat Fest - last wknd July)* **Near:** Pool *(Mahone Bay Town Pool)*, Playground, Tennis Courts, Fitness Center *(Mahone Bay Centre 624-0890)*, Boat Rentals *(East Coast Outfitters - kayaks - 852-2567)*, Hike/Bike Trails *(Waterside route perfect for biking)*, Fishing Charter, Video Rental *(Irving Retail)*, Museum *(Mahone Bay Settlers 624-6263, Free Mon-Sat 9am-5pm, Sun 1-5pm)*, Tours *(South Shore 543-5107 $35/15)*, Cultural Attract *(Music at the Three Churches Summer Concerts 531-2248 $20)*, Sightseeing *(Self-Guided Walking Tours - see the Visitors' Center 165 Edgewater St.)*, Galleries *(Dozens of craft shops & galleries, including The Moorings 624-6208, Amos Pewter 624-9457 - demonstrations)* **1-3 mi:** Beach *(Westhaven's Beach - Mader's Cove Rd.)*

Provisioning and General Services

Near: Convenience Store, Supermarket *(Mahone Bay Save-Easy 624-8044)*, Gourmet Shop *(Joanne's Market 624-6305, wonderful "to go")*, Delicatessen, Wine/Beer, Liquor Store *(NSLC 624-8300)*, Bakery *(Joanne's)*, Farmers' Market *(Every Friday orning)*, Green Grocer *(Joanne's Market, local, organic)*, Bank/ATM *(Bank of Montreal)*, Post Office, Protestant Church, Laundry *(531-3325)*, Bookstore *(Biscuit Eaters 624-book)*, Pharmacy *(Kinburn Pharmasave 624-8347)*, Retail Shops *(Suttles & Seawinds 624-8375 - original store of small, upscale NS boutique chain; Quality Quilts 624-6177)*, Copies Etc. **1-3 mi:** Hardware Store *(Nova Scotia Building Supplies 624-8328)* **3+ mi:** Library *(Bridgewater, 15 mi.)*, Department Store *(Walmart, 15 mi.)*

Transportation

Near: Bikes *(East Coast Outfitters 852-2567)*, Water Taxi, Local Bus *(Once a day)* **1-3 mi:** Taxi **3+ mi:** Rental Car *(15 mi.)* **Airport:** Halifax Int'l *(70 mi.)*

Medical Services

911 Service **OnCall:** Ambulance **Near:** Doctor, Chiropractor *(South Shore 624-6443)*, Veterinarian *(South Shore 624-9736)* **3+ mi:** Dentist *(Lunenburg 634-8880, 5.5 mi.)* **Hospital:** South Shore Regional 543-4603 *(9 mi.)*

Setting -- Wend your way among some of Mahone Bay's hundreds of islands to the western shore where the Civic Marina's modest docks and large mooring field provide immediate access to this pretty village. A small colonial style clapboard building in shades of teal and brick houses the amenities and a nearby gray shingled structure the dockmaster. The marina is literally on South Main Street, aka the Lighhouse Route, and all of Mahone Bay is a very short walk.

Marina Notes -- *Berths Flat rate: Under 30 ft. $25, 35 ft. $30, 40 ft. $35, 50 ft. $40, Over 50 ft. $45. During Classic Boat Fest Moorings flat fee for 4-day weekend $100. **All marine service available July-Labor Day but docks and moorings are available from Mid-May through Mid-October. Closed Mid-October to Mid-May. Day runs 24 hrs noon to noon. Operated by the Mahone Bay Wooden Boat Society - Dave Devenne, Chair. Not for Profit, self-supported, volunteer organization with an agreement with Town of Mahone Bay that rents them the land for a $1/annual fee. Uses mostly local summer help. Dinghy float east of town wharf. Repairs at Truman Boat. Nearest haulout South Shore & Gold River. ABC Marine in Lunenburg for parts and repairs. Nearest fuel one mile at Irving. Bathhouse: Good quality municipal issue cinderblock walls, cement floor - in a pretty teal & brick building. Showers $3.

Notable -- Established in 1754, Mahone Bay defines the word "picturesque." The village edges an arm of the Bay where three 19th century churches famously sit along the head - their spires piercing the sky and their images reflected in the often placid water. Restored Italianate, Gothic and Classic Revival buildings line leafy lanes, many occupied by B&Bs, galleries, museums and local specialty stores. Favorite pastime are shopping, gallery hopping and kayaking.

Navigational Information
Lat: 44°24.683' **Long:** 064°19.367' **Tide:** 6 ft. **Current:** 1 kt. **Chart:** 4320
Rep. Depths (*MLW*): Entry 30 ft. **Fuel Dock** 10 ft. **Max Slip/Moor** 18 ft./20 ft.
Access: Mahone Bay Fairway to Prince Inlet - SW tip Herman's Is.

Marina Facilities *(In Season/Off Season)*
Fuel: *Ultramar* - Gasoline, Diesel
Slips: 40 Total, 4 Transient **Max LOA:** 42 ft. **Max Beam:** 10 ft.
Rate *(per ft.)*: **Day** $1.25* **Week** $325 **Month** $800
Power: 30 amp Incl., **50 amp** n/a, **100 amp** n/a, **200 amp** n/a
Cable TV: No **Dockside Phone:** No
Dock Type: Floating, Long Fingers, Alongside, Wood
Moorings: 100 Total, 10 Transient **Launch:** Yes (Incl.), Dinghy Dock
Rate: Day $35 **Week** $150 **Month** $400
Heads: 4 Toilet(s), 2 Shower(s) *(dressing rooms)*
Internet: No **Laundry:** None
Pump-Out: No **Fee:** n/a **Closed Heads:** Yes

Marina Operations
Owner/Manager: Faye Pickrem **Dockmaster:** Greg Mills
In-Season: Jun-Aug, 10am-9pm** **Off-Season:** May & Sep, Noon-6pm
After-Hours Arrival: Call ahead for Mooring or Berth ID #
Reservations: Yes, Preferred **Credit Cards:** Visa/MC
Discounts: None
Pets: Welcome, Dog Walk Area **Handicap Access:** Yes, Heads, Docks

Lunenburg Yacht Club

PO Box 820; 734 Herman's Island Rd.; Lunenburg, NS B0J 2C0

Tel: (902) 634-3745 **VHF: Monitor** Ch. 16 **Talk** Ch. 68
Fax: n/a **Alternate Tel:** n/a
Email: manager@lyc.ns.ca **Web:** www.lyc.ns.ca
Nearest Town: Lunenburg *(5 mi.)* **Tourist Info:** (902) 624-6151

Marina Services and Boat Supplies
Services - Docking Assistance, Boaters' Lounge, Trash Pick-Up, Dock Carts **Communication -** Pay Phone, FedEx, UPS, Express Mail **Supplies - OnSite:** Ice *(Cube)* **3+ mi:** Ships' Store *(Boat Locker 640-3202, 5 mi.)*, Propane *(Irvings Lunenburg/Mahone Bay, 5 mi./6 mi.)*

Boatyard Services
OnSite: Launching Ramp **OnCall:** Engine mechanic *(gas, diesel)*, Electrical Repairs, Electronic Sales, Electronics Repairs, Hull Repairs, Rigger, Sail Loft, Canvas Work, Divers, Bottom Cleaning, Brightwork, Air Conditioning, Refrigeration, Compound, Wash & Wax, Interior Cleaning, Propeller Repairs, Woodworking, Inflatable Repairs, Life Raft Service, Upholstery, Metal Fabrication **Nearest Yard:** South Shore Marina (902) 275-3711

Restaurants and Accommodations
OnSite: Restaurant *(LYC Galley & Bar)* **OnCall:** Pizzeria *(J3s 634-9999)* **1-3 mi:** Condo/Cottage *(Prince's Inlet Retreat 634-4224, $115-175, 2-bedroom cottages with kitchens)* **3+ mi:** Restaurant *(The Dockside Lobster and Seafood 634-3005, 5 mi.)*, *(Tin Fish 640-4040, 5 mi., L & D $8-24)*, *(Innlet Cafe 624-6363, 5 mi., L & D $12-22)*, *(Gazebo Cafe 624-6484, L $8-20, D $15-22, 5 mi.)*, *(Old Fish Factory 634-3333, L $8-20, D $14-36, 5 mi., part of Fisheries Museum - ice cream, too.)*, Hotel *(Lunenburg Arms 640-4040, $110-270, 5.5 mi., & Spa!)*, Inn/B&B *(Mahone Bay 624-6388, $105-135, 5 mi.)*, *(Three Thistles 624-0517, $90-125, 5 mi., & Apts.)*

Recreation and Entertainment
OnSite: Picnic Area, Grills **OnCall:** Dive Shop **Near:** Jogging Paths, Hike/Bike Trails **Under 1 mi:** Golf Course *(Bluenose G. C. 634-4260)* **1-3 mi:** Beach *(Mahone Bay islands by dinghy)* **3+ mi:** Tennis Courts *(Lunenburg 634-9288, 5 mi.)*, Fitness Center *(Ship Shape 634-3132, 5 mi.)*, Museum *(Fisheries Museum of the Atlantic in Lunenburg 634-4794 $10/3 Shipbuilding, rum-running, marine biology & Bluenose II, 5 mi.)*, Cultural Attract *(Lunenburg cultural heritage site, 5 mi.)*, Sightseeing *(Ovens Natural Park $8/4 sea caves, panning for gold, inflatable boats, 13 mi.)*

Provisioning and General Services
3+ mi: Supermarket *(Mahone Bay Save-Easy 624-8044, 5 mi.)*, Liquor Store *(Mahone Bay NSLC 624-8300, 5 mi.)*, Pharmacy *(Kinburn Pharmasave 624-8347, 5 mi.)*, Hardware Store *(Lunenburg 634-4301, 5 mi.)*, Department Store *(Walmart, 12 mi.)*

Transportation
OnCall: Rental Car *(Enterprise Bridgewater 527-5909, 12 mi.)*, Taxi *(HR 634-4478)*, Airport Limo *(Try Town 521-0855)* **3+ mi:** Bikes *(Bike Barn 634-3426, 5 mi.)* **Airport:** Halifax Int'l. *(70 mi.)*

Medical Services
911 Service **OnCall:** Ambulance **3+ mi:** Doctor *(Beaton 634-7226, 5 mi.)*, Holistic Services *(South Shore Massage 634-3073, 5 mi.)*, Veterinarian *(Seaside 634-3561, 5 mi.)* **Hospital:** Fisherman's Mem 634-8801 *(5 mi.)*

Setting -- The yacht club is set on the southwest tip of Herman's Island in Prince Inlet, which is connected to the mainland by a short causeway bridge. The single story, black-shingled clubhouse sits on a small rise overlooking the top-quality floating docks and the mooring field beyond. On the veranda, bright red umbrellas shade comfortable tables and chairs. For most of the summer a blue-and-white striped tent graces the nicely landscaped lawn for outdoor dining and events. Activities center around the gray-clapboard Capt. Douglas Mosher Sail Training Center - which also berths one of the bathhouses.

Marina Notes -- *Flat rate, $55.nt. **Complex Dock Hours (Inq.) 60 ft. side-tie on Fuel dock. Galley Lunch & dinner July/Aug Noon-2pm & 5-8 pm wkly, 10am-8/9pm wknds. Off-season shorter hrs. Kids' Learn To Sail Program 634-7245. Add'l BY services - Yacht Shop 634-4331 & BWs 640-5252. Bathhouse: Two sets. Clubhouse - Modest, club-quality heads, tile floor, skirted vanities, flowers. Sail Training Center - sparkling, all tile, shower curtains, dressing rooms.

Notable -- A bit off the beaten path - but still near two top tourism villages - LYC offers a bit of quiet in an unspoiled, serene part of the bay. Small club cruises will find a warm welcome and the clubhouse can accommodate a midday or evening event. Despite the address, LYC is actually midway between the villages of Mahone Bay and Lunenburg. It's five miles to Lunenburg proper - the picturesque UNESCO World Heritage site steeped in maritime tradition - and five and a half miles to Mahone Bay - a charming, sweet village. Nothing is within walking distance, but consider a dinghy cruise of Prince Inlet for wildlife viewing. A taxi services the club and Enterprise rent-a-car will pick up. For a little time off the boat, Prince's Inet Retreat is about a mile and a half down the road.

PHOTOS ON DVD: 20

Lunenburg Historic Waterfront

280 Montague St.; Lunenburg, NS BOJ 2C0

Tel: (902) 640-3202 **VHF: Monitor** Ch. 68 **Talk** Ch. 68
Fax: (902) 640-3203 **Alternate Tel:** (902) 634-4794
Email: doug@boatlocker.ca **Web:** my-waterfront.ca
Nearest Town: Lunenburg **Tourist Info:** (902) 634-8100

Navigational Information

Lat: 44°22.190' **Long:** 064°18.160' **Tide:** 6 ft. **Current:** n/a **Chart:** 4328
Rep. Depths (*MLW*): Entry 19 ft. **Fuel Dock** n/a **Max Slip/Moor** 12 ft./15 ft.
Access: Enter Lunenburg Hbr bet. Battery Pt. & Kaulbach Head to north side

Marina Facilities *(In Season/Off Season)*

Fuel: *Bailly's 634-4487* - Gasoline, Diesel, On Call Delivery
Slips: 12 Total, 12 Transient **Max LOA:** 80 ft. **Max Beam:** n/a
Rate *(per ft.)*: **Day** $1.00* **Week** n/a **Month** n/a
Power: 30 amp Incl., **50 amp** Incl., **100 amp** n/a, **200 amp** n/a
Cable TV: No **Dockside Phone:** No
Dock Type: Floating, Long Fingers, Short Fingers, Wood
Moorings: 8 Total, 8 Transient **Launch:** No, Dinghy Dock
Rate: Day $20 **Week** n/a **Month** n/a
Heads: 2 Toilet(s), 2 Shower(s)
Internet: No **Laundry:** None
Pump-Out: Full Service **Fee:** Free **Closed Heads:** Yes

Marina Operations

Owner/Manager: WDCL/Fisheries Museum **Dockmaster:** Doug Phlip
In-Season: Year Round, 9am-5pm **Off-Season:** n/a
After-Hours Arrival: Call in advance
Reservations: Yes **Credit Cards:** Visa/MC, Interac
Discounts: None
Pets: Welcome, Dog Walk Area **Handicap Access:** No

Marina Services and Boat Supplies

Services - Docking Assistance, Security *(24/7, Night Watchman)*, Trash Pick-Up **Communication -** FedEx, UPS, Express Mail **Supplies - OnSite:** Ice *(Block, Cube)*, Ships' Store *(Boat Locker 640-3202)*, Propane *(Irving Oil 543-5804 - Exch)*

Boatyard Services

OnCall: Engine mechanic *(gas, diesel)*, Electrical Repairs, Electronics Repairs, Hull Repairs, Rigger, Sail Loft, Canvas Work, Divers, Bottom Cleaning, Propeller Repairs, Woodworking, Life Raft Service, Upholstery, Metal Fabrication **Near:** Railway *(10T)*, Forklift. **Under 1 mi:** Travelift, Launching Ramp *(Lunenburg Foundry)*. **Nearest Yard:** Lunenberg Foundry Shipyard (902) 640-3333

Restaurants and Accommodations

Near: Restaurant *(Magnolia's Grill 634-3287, L & D $9-25 - '50s diner)*, *(Old Fish Factory 634-3333, L $8-20, D $15-35)*, *(Grand Banker 634-3300, L & D $10-20, Wknd Brunch $12)*, *(Rum Runner 634-8778, L $8-12, D $15-32)*, *(Fleur de Sel 640-2121, D $24-36)*, *(Big Red's 634-3554)*, *(Trattoria della Nonna 640-3112, L & D $12-25 Fine Italian)*, Fast Food *(Subway)*, Pizzeria *(J3 634-9999, delivers)* **Under 1 mi:** Restaurant *(The Knot Pub 634-3334, L & D $7-17 - far end of town)*, *(Tin Fish 640-4040, D $10-27, Live music wknds)*, Coffee Shop *(Tim Horton's)*, Hotel *(Lunenburg Arms 640-4040, $113-300)*, *(Rum Runner 634-9200, $70-170)*, Inn/B&B *(Pelham House 634-7113, $95-110)*, *(Smugglers' Cove 634-7500, $90-170)*, *(1826 Maplebird 634-3863, $90-120)*, *(Brigantine 634-3300, $80-140)*

Recreation and Entertainment

Near: Heated Pool *(Lunenburg 634-4499)*, Playground, Fitness Center *(Ship Shape 634-3132)*, Fishing Charter *(Lunenburg Ocean Adventures 634-4833; Heritage Fishing Tours 640-3535)*, Museum *(Lunenberg Fisheries Museum of the Atlantic 634-4794; Knaut-Rhuland House 634-3498)*, Tours *(Lunenburg Whale Watching 527-7175)*, Special Events *(Lunenburg Folk Fest 634-3180 1st Wknd Aug)* **Under 1 mi:** Tennis Courts *(Lunenburg 634-9192; 634-9288)*, Sightseeing *(Eric Croft Walk Tour $15/10)*, Galleries *(Over 20 incl. Houston North 634-8869 - Inuit Folk Art)* **1-3 mi:** Golf Course *(Bluenose 634-4260 semi-private)*, Bowling *(Bluenose 634-8344)*

Provisioning and General Services

Near: Delicatessen *(Salt Shaker 640-3434 Lunch $7-13)*, Library *(South Shore 634-8008)*, Pharmacy *(Fulton's 634-8652)* **Under 1 mi:** Supermarket *(Foodland 634-8218)*, Liquor Store, Farmers' Market *(Thurs 8-noon, Comm. Centre - Victoria & Green Sts.)*, Fishmonger *(Lunenburg 634-3470)*, Bookstore *(Elizabeth's 634-8149)* **1-3 mi:** Convenience Store *(Mike's Qwik Way 634-3307; Circle K 634-3641)*, Market *(Save Easy 634-375)*, Laundry *(Water Mkt 634-4755)*, Hardware Store *(Lunenburg 634-4301)*

Transportation

OnCall: Rental Car *(Enterprise 527-5909)*, Taxi *(Oceanview 527-8251; Mercer 529-0232)* **Airport:** Halifax Int'l *(70 mi.)*

Medical Services

911 Service **Near:** Chiropractor *(Flavin's 640-3100)* **Under 1 mi:** Doctor *(Pelham 634-4454)* **1-3 mi:** Dentist *(Lunenburg 634-8880)*, Veterinarian *(Seaside 634-3561)* **Hospital:** Fisherman's Mem 634-8801 *(1.4 mi.)*

Setting -- On the north side of Lunenburg Harbour, historic brick-red buildings back sturdy, century-old wharves that march along the harbor-front. The famed Fisheries Museum anchors the harbor and the UNESCO Heritage site that surrounds it. Transient berths are available at the museum wharves on the eastern end and at the Historic Zwicker Visitors Dock which now hosts 120 feet of new floats a bit west - and a small mooring field lies in the middle of the harbor.

Marina Notes -- *Two separate facilities offer dockage: Zwicker Docks & Mooring Field managed by Doug Phlip, Lunenburg Boat Locker (See Contact #s above, cell 902-277-1414, www.boatlocker.ca) - 120 ft. floating dockage - $25/nt. to 30 ft. & $0.75/ft add'l for LOA over 30 ft. plus 8 moorings - $20/nt.). And Fisheries Museum of the Atlantic (902-634-4794; fax 902-634-9587, museum.gov.ns.ca\fma,), 240 ft. side-tie wharf - $1/ft. Mooring field just off Town Dock - "BL" on balls & "Boat Locker" on bridle. Public dinghy docks at Fisheries Museum & Zwicker Wharf. Bathhouse: Vinyl shower stalls, colorful curtains.

Notable -- The Fisheries Museum of the Atlantic berths and Zwicker Visitors Docks are part of the Lunenburg UNESCO Heritage Site. The reconstruction of unbeatable, 1921 schooner "Bluenose," being built by a team of three Lunenburg companies,attracts mariners from around the world. The best way to see "Old Town" is on foot. Founded in 1753, it was laid out on the 18thC British Grid pattern and is little changed in over 250 years. Eric Croft's hour-and-a-half tour leaves from the kiosk across from the Museum at 10am, 2 & 9pm. Or do it yourself following the Interpretive Panels throughout the town. Architecture fans will be in heaven: Second Empire, Saltbox, revised Gothic, Queen Anne, coupled with the famous five-sided Scottish dormer known as the Lunenburg Bump.

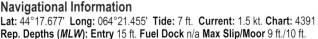

Navigational Information
Lat: 44°17.677' **Long:** 064°21.455' **Tide:** 7 ft. **Current:** 1.5 kt. **Chart:** 4391
Rep. Depths (*MLW*): **Entry** 15 ft. **Fuel Dock** n/a **Max Slip/Moor** 9 ft./10 ft.
Access: Nova Scotia South Coast 15 NM west of Lunenburg Bay

Marina Facilities *(In Season/Off Season)*
Fuel: On Call Delivery
Slips: 5 Total, 5 Transient **Max LOA:** 50 ft. **Max Beam:** n/a
Rate *(per ft.)*: **Day** $0.50* **Week** n/a **Month** n/a
Power: 30 amp Incl., **50 amp** n/a, **100 amp** n/a, **200 amp** n/a
Cable TV: No **Dockside Phone:** No
Dock Type: Fixed, Floating, Alongside, Wood
Moorings: 1 Total, 1 Transient **Launch:** None, Dinghy Dock
Rate: Day $7 **Week** Inq. **Month** n/a
Heads: 2 Toilet(s), 1 Shower(s), Book Exchange
Internet: No **Laundry:** 1 Washer(s), 1 Dryer(s), Iron Board
Pump-Out: No **Fee:** n/a **Closed Heads:** No

Marina Operations
Owner/Manager: Gael Watson **Dockmaster:** Same
In-Season: MidJun-Oct, 8:30am-5:30pm **Off-Season:** Nov-MidJun, 9am-5pm
After-Hours Arrival: Dock, then check-in in the morning
Reservations: Yes **Credit Cards:** Visa/MC, Debit Card
Discounts: None
Pets: Welcome, Dog Walk Area **Handicap Access:** Yes, Docks

LaHave Bakery & Outfitters

PO Box 40; 3421 Rt 331; LaHave, NS BOR 1C0

Tel: (902) 688-2908 **VHF: Monitor** n/a **Talk** n/a
Fax: (902) 688-1083 **Alternate Tel:** (902) 688-2908
Email: n/a **Web:** n/a
Nearest Town: Bridgewater *(12 mi.)* **Tourist Info:** n/a

Marina Services and Boat Supplies
Services - Trash Pick-Up **Communication -** FedEx, UPS **Supplies - OnCall:** Ice *(Cube)* **3+ mi:** Ships' Store *(Covey Island Boatworks 766-4226, 4 mi.)*, Marine Discount Store *(Yacht Shop 634-4331, 9 mi.)*, Propane *(8 mi.)*, CNG *(8 mi.)*

Boatyard Services
OnSite: Travelift *(75T)*, Railway *(200 tons)*, Brightwork, Woodworking *(LaHave Mairne Woodworking - interiors, deck furnishings, refits, cabinetry)*, Yacht Interiors **OnCall:** Engine mechanic *(gas, diesel)*, Electrical Repairs, Electronic Sales, Electronics Repairs, Hull Repairs, Canvas Work, Divers, Bottom Cleaning, Air Conditioning, Refrigeration, Compound, Wash & Wax

Restaurants and Accommodations
OnSite: Lite Fare *(LaHave Bakery 688-2908, L $5-7, Everything from scratch, some produce from owner's garden)* **3+ mi:** Restaurant *(Two Chefs Indian Restaurant 543-9661, 5 mi.)*, *(Magnolia's Grill 634-3287, 7 mi., L & D $8-25)*, *(Fleur de Sel 640-2121, D $24-36, 6 mi., Open Apr-Oct)*, *(Dockside Lobster and Seafood Restaurant 634-3005, 4 mi.)*, Hotel *(Lunenburg Arms Hotel 640-4040, 4 mi.)*, Inn/B&B *(Fairview Inn 543-2233, 8 mi.)*, *(Smugglers Cove Inn 634-7500, 4 mi.)*

Recreation and Entertainment
OnSite: Galleries *(LaHave Crafts Co-Op - wide variety of quality products from 30 local artisans)* **Under 1 mi:** Museum *(Fort Point 688-1632)* **1-3 mi:** Beach *(Crescent Beach, Rissers Beach)*, Fitness Center, Park *(Rissers Beach Provincial Park)* **3+ mi:** Tennis Courts *(Lunenburg Tennis Club 634-9192, 5 mi.)*, Golf Course *(Olde Town G.C. 527-0211, 7 mi.)*

Provisioning and General Services
OnSite: Bakery *(LaHave Bakery 688-2908 "traditional breads from locally grown, fresh-milled grains")*, Farmers' Market *(Seasonal, Sat 9am-1pm)* **Near:** Post Office **1-3 mi:** Fishmonger *(JT's Seafood 677-2877)*, Pharmacy *(Drugstore 634-3126)*, Hardware Store *(Lunenburg 634-4301)* **3+ mi:** Convenience Store *(Mike's Kwik Way- 634-3307, 9 mi.)*, Library *(South Shore Regional 634-8008, 4 mi.)*

Transportation
OnCall: Rental Car *(Enterprise 527-5909; Avis 543-1787 - 8 mi.)*, Taxi *(PC Cab 634-8201)*, Airport Limo *(PC Cab 634-8201)* **Near:** InterCity Bus *(Trius Lines - the South Shore from Yarmouth to Halifax 877-566-1567)*, Ferry Service *(LaHave - East LaHave Ferry)* **Airport:** Halifax Int'l *(85 mi.)*

Medical Services
911 Service **OnCall:** Ambulance **3+ mi:** Doctor *(Lunenburg Medical-Dental Centre 634-8880, 7 mi.)*, Dentist *(Lunenburg 634-8880, 7 mi.)*, Chiropractor *(Associate 543-2131, 9 mi.)*, Holistic Services *(Seameadow Massage Therapy 827-2222, 5 mi.)*, Veterinarian *(Seaside 634-3561, 6 mi.)* **Hospital:** South Shore Regional 543-4603 *(10 mi.)*

Setting -- Three-quarters of a mile up the LaHave River, two docks jut out from the western shore below the large, historic clapboard and red-shingled building that houses the LaHave Bakery. An old, sturdy stationary wharf competes with the baby blue floating dock - in settled weather, the latter usually wins the transient boaters. Brightly colored Adirondack-style double chairs and picnic tables grace a grassy patch and sit on the wharf's outer edge.

Marina Notes -- *150 ft. side-tie. Power 110 cord. BY services Lunenburg Shipyard (640-3333). A "Way-Port" for vessels cruising South Shore. Bathhouse: Brightly painted modest heads; separate shower room - metal stall with curtain. Casual laundry room ($1.50 wash, $2 dry). Note: 300 ft. north, LaHave Seafood's 75 ft X 50 Ft. wharf welcomes transients when fishing trawlers away (688-2773), LaHave R. Y.C. (688-3177) for moorings ($30) & fuel.

Notable -- An historic turn-of-the-last-century maritime center was reinvented as the LaHave Bakery, famous throughout Atlantic Canada. The Cafe serves lunch - soups, sandwiches, savories and pastries - and carries basic provisions. During the summer, Saturday morning sees a farmers market from 9am-1pm and a permanent Craft Co-Op where 30 local artisans display their work. The big red building is also home to Homegrown Skateboards and LaHave Marine Woodworking, which specializes in classic small boats and quality yacht joinery. The nearby Fort Point Museum, housed in a replica of an early lighthouse, memorializes the area's history from 1632 when French Viceroy de Razilly landed at Fort Point to establish LaHave as the capital of New France and was accompanied by the Capuchin Fathers who founded Canada's first school. Wander the French Garden, apple trees and Champlain roses.

Brooklyn Marina

100 Shore Road; Brooklyn, NS B0J 1H0

Tel: (902) 354-4028 **VHF: Monitor** Ch. 16 **Talk** Ch. 68
Fax: n/a **Alternate Tel:** n/a
Email: info@brooklynmarina.ca **Web:** www.brooklynmarina.ca
Nearest Town: Liverpool *(3 mi.)* **Tourist Info:** (902) 354-5741

Navigational Information

Lat: 44°03.000' **Long:** 064°41.000' **Tide:** 6 ft. **Current:** 2 kt. **Chart:** 4379
Rep. Depths (*MLW*): Entry 50 ft. **Fuel Dock** 6 ft. **Max Slip/Moor** 8 ft./10 ft.
Access: Liverpool Bay to UM50, NE past Bowater Mersey wharf to port

Marina Facilities *(In Season/Off Season)*

Fuel: Gasoline, Diesel
Slips: 30 Total, 3 Transient **Max LOA:** 45 ft. **Max Beam:** 16 ft.
Rate *(per ft.)*: **Day** $1.00* **Week** n/a **Month** n/a
Power: 30 amp Incl., **50 amp** n/a, **100 amp** n/a, **200 amp** n/a
Cable TV: No **Dockside Phone:** No
Dock Type: Floating, Wood
Moorings: 4 Total, 3 Transient **Launch:** n/a, Dinghy Dock
Rate: Day $20?* **Week** n/a **Month** n/a
Heads: 2 Toilet(s), 1 Shower(s)
Internet: Yes *(Wi-Fi, Free)* **Laundry:** None
Pump-Out: No **Fee:** n/a **Closed Heads:** No

Marina Operations

Owner/Manager: David & Claire Godfrey, Directors **Dockmaster:** Same
In-Season: May-Oct, 8am-8pm **Off-Season:** Nov-Apr, Closed
After-Hours Arrival: Tie Up and check in in morning
Reservations: No **Credit Cards:** Cash only
Discounts: None
Pets: Welcome, Dog Walk Area **Handicap Access:** No

Marina Services and Boat Supplies

Services - Docking Assistance, Boaters' Lounge, Trash Pick-Up, Dock Carts **Communication -** FedEx, DHL, UPS **Supplies - OnSite:** Ice *(Cube)* **3+ mi:** Ships' Store *(Nodding Marine 543-7994, 24 mi.)*

Boatyard Services

OnSite: Launching Ramp **Nearest Yard:** Steel & Engine Products (902) 354-3483

Restaurants and Accommodations

OnSite: Snack Bar *(Canteena B $2.50-4, L $1-5, Daily 11am-7pm, Sat 8am-7pm, Sun brunch 11am-2pm)* **OnCall:** Pizzeria *(Liverpool Pizzeria 354-2422)* **Near:** Hotel *(Best Western Liverpool 354-2377)* **Under 1 mi:** Coffee Shop *(Tim Hortons)*, Motel *(Transcotia 354-3494)* **1-3 mi:** Restaurant *(Lanes 354-3456, B $8.50-11, L $5-16, D $5-26)*, Coffee Shop *(Woodpile Carvings and Cafe 354-4495)*, Fast Food *(McD, KFC, Subway)*, Inn/B&B *(Lanes Privateer 354-3456, $75-135)* **3+ mi:** Restaurant *(Golden Pond - Oriental 354-5186, L $6-24, D $9-24, 5 mi)*

Recreation and Entertainment

OnSite: Playground, Special Events *(Queens County Seafest, last week Aug)* **Near:** Sightseeing *(Coffin Island Lighthouse - Circa 1811, one of the first in region - cruise by on your way to/from the marina)* **Under 1 mi:** Movie Theater *(Astor Theatre 354-5250 - also live entertainment)*, Galleries *(Watercolors & Woodcarvings 354-3774 in Brooklyn; ADJA 354-4167; Artists' Loft 354-3772; Mersey River Crafts 646-1159; Savage 354-5431)* **1-3 mi:** Tennis Courts *(Liverpool 356-3003)*, Golf Course *(White Point 683-2485)*, Fitness Center *(Queens 354-2308)*, Bowling *(Liverpool 354-3212)*, Park *(Fort Point Lighthouse 354-5260)*, Museum *(Rossignol Cultural Center 354-3067 $4/3; Queens County 354-4058 $3; Hank Snow Country Music Centre 354-4675 $3; Sherman Hines Photography 354-2667 $4/3)*, Tours *(Self-Guided Liverpool walking tour of the many grand homes and buildings built by Privateers)*, Cultural Attract *(Liverpool International Theatre Festival, May 2014)* **3+ mi:** Horseback Riding *(Medway Pines Stables 677-2390, 8 mi.)*

Provisioning and General Services

Near: Protestant Church **1-3 mi:** Supermarket *(Sobeys 354-4225 ; Atlantic SuperStore 354-5776)*, Liquor Store *(NSLC 354-4197)*, Bakery *(Piping Hot 356-3434)*, Bank/ATM *(ScotiaBank 354-3431)*, Library *(South Shore 354-5270)*, Beauty Salon *(Hairworx 354-5665)*, Barber Shop *(Ron's 354-2090)*, Pharmacy *(Pharmachoice 354-7101)*, Department Store *(Liverpool Value Plus 354-4717)* **3+ mi:** Farmers' Market *(Medway 677-2884 daily, 6 mi)*

Transportation

OnSite: Bikes *(Donation)* **OnCall:** Taxi *(BJs 354-2973; Grezaud 354-5585; Taxi 1 354-4268)* **Airport:** Halifax Int'l *(100 mi.)*

Medical Services

911 Service **1-3 mi:** Doctor *(Morash 354-5204)*, Chiropractor *(Liverpool Chiropractic & Massage Therapy 354-3644)*, Holistic Services *(Ocean Spa at White Point 354-2711)*, Optician *(Liverpool Eyecare 354-3312)* **3+ mi:** Dentist *(Kingston Family 765-6769, 6 mi.)*, Veterinarian *(Nova Vet 354-4531, 5 mi.)* **Hospital:** Queens General 354-3436 *(2 mi.)*

Setting -- Tucked into a quiet cove off Liverpool Bay, Brooklyn Marina's small network of floating docks is protected by a breakwater and fishing pier. On shore two buildings house a boaters' lounge, bathhouse and a snack bar. Part of the Queens Recreational Boating Association's waterfront park, it extends along the shore to the pretty greensward highlighted by a large red-roofed gazebo that hosts concerts and community events - backed by a photogenic classic white clapboard church. Unfortunately, the dominating view over the water is the Bowater-Mersey Pulp Mill, a fixture since 1929 and a bit of an eyesore.

Marina Notes -- *No set prices. Make a donation based on market. Totally volunteer organization. Owned by QRBA (Queen's Recreational Boating Association). Canteena, a snack bar window with picnic tables, offers simple breakfast Sat, extensive brunch menu Sun, lunch daily (wraps, burgers, mini-pizzas, hot dogs & sausage dogs) plus snacks, ice cream, beverages, & basic sundries. Volunteers often offer rides & help with arrangements. Tues & Thurs are sailing nights. Bathhouse: Bright white tile walls, glass-door shower stall - generally not open at night, but could be arranged.

Notable -- The privateer brig ship "The Rover" was built on marina grounds in 1799-1800 for a local merchant. Founded in 1759, compact, historic Liverpool, on the Mersey River, was the notorious Port of Privateers (government-sanctioned pirates). With average ship's plunder at $1 million, Liverpool became a wealthy town - celebrated every July with Privateer Days. Rossignol Cultural Center exhibits Outhouses, instigated by famed photogrepher Sherman Hines' photos, as well as folk art, wildlife art, Mikmaq history. Six other museums tell the Liverpool story - including native son's Hank Snow's Music Centre.

PHOTOS ON DVD: 25

Navigational Information
Lat: 43°45.294' **Long:** 065°19.213' **Tide:** 6 ft. **Current:** 1 kt. **Chart:** 442
Rep. Depths (*MLW*): Entry 12 ft. **Fuel Dock** 12 ft. **Max Slip/Moor** 12 ft./20 ft.
Access: Past Sandy Pt. Light, bear rt past Gov't Wharf to red bldg to starboard

Marina Facilities *(In Season/Off Season)*
Fuel: *Esso* - Gasoline, Diesel
Slips: 46 Total, 6-8 Transient **Max LOA:** 90 ft. **Max Beam:** n/a
Rate *(per ft.)*: **Day** $1.00* **Week** $5 **Month** n/a
Power: 30 amp $4/7**, **50 amp** n/a, **100 amp** n/a, **200 amp** n/a
Cable TV: No **Dockside Phone:** No
Dock Type: Floating, Short Fingers, Alongside, Wood
Moorings: 12 Total, 9 Transient **Launch:** No, Dinghy Dock ($3/day)
Rate: Day $15 **Week** $75 **Month** $200
Heads: 5 Toilet(s), 2 Shower(s) *(dressing rooms)*, Book Exchange
Internet: Yes *(Wi-Fi, $3)* **Laundry:** 1 Washer(s), 1 Dryer(s)
Pump-Out: No **Fee:** n/a **Closed Heads:** Yes

Marina Operations
Owner/Manager: Jason Smith **Dockmaster:** Same
In-Season: May-Oct, 8am-8pm*** **Off-Season:** Nov-Apr, Closed
After-Hours Arrival: Report in in the morning
Reservations: Yes, Preferred **Credit Cards:** Visa/MC, Debit, CAsh
Discounts: None
Pets: Welcome, Dog Walk Area **Handicap Access:** Yes, Heads, Docks

Shelburne Harbour Yacht Club

PO Box 1437; 107 Water Street; Shelburne, NS B0T 1W0

Tel: (902) 875-4757 **VHF: Monitor** Ch. 16 **Talk** Ch. 72
Fax: (902) 875-2280 **Alternate Tel:** n/a
Email: yachtclub@ns.aliantzinc **Web:** www.shyc.ca
Nearest Town: Shelburne **Tourist Info:** (902) 354-5741

Marina Services and Boat Supplies
Services - Docking Assistance, Concierge, Boaters' Lounge, Trash Pick-Up, Dock Carts **Communication -** Pay Phone, FedEx, DHL, UPS **Supplies - OnSite:** Ice *(Block, Cube)* **Near:** Ships' Store *(NAPA 875-2522)* **Under 1 mi:** Propane *(Irving 875-3033)*

Boatyard Services
OnCall: Forklift, Crane, Engine mechanic *(gas, diesel)*, Electrical Repairs, Electronics Repairs **Near:** Hydraulic Trailer, Divers, Bottom Cleaning, Brightwork, Air Conditioning, Refrigeration. **Under 1 mi:** Hull Repairs. **1-3 mi:** Travelift *(30T)*, Propeller Repairs, Woodworking, Metal Fabrication.
Nearest Yard: Shelburne Ship Repair (902) 875-8100

Restaurants and Accommodations
OnSite: Lite Fare *(SHYC L $6-18, D $12-18, Lunch Tue-Fri, Dinner Fri only - delivered by local eateries: Charlotte Lane, Sea Dog & Bean Dock)* **Near:** Restaurant *(Charlotte Lane 875-3314, L $8-30, D $17-30, Swiss owner-chef, seafood)*, *(Sea Dog 875-2862, B $7-10, L $8-18, D $17-28)*, *(Lothar's Café 875-3697, L $7-15, D $15-26)*, *(Loung's 875-1300)*, Lite Fare *(Loyalist Inn 875-3333, B $8-10)*, *(Bean Dock 875-1302)*, *(Mr. Fish 875-3474, L $7-10, fish & chips shack, picnic tables)*, *(Shelburne Café L $3.50-17, 8am-7pm)*, Pizzeria *(A-1 Piero 875-1222, Del.)*, Inn/B&B *(Cooper's 875-4656, $100-185)*, *(Loyalist 875-5333, $65-90)* **Under 1 mi:** Fast Food *(Scotia Lunch, Subway, Tim Hortons)*, Inn/B&B *(Millstones 875-4525, $90-140)*

Recreation and Entertainment
OnSite: Cultural Attract *(Osprey Arts Centre 875-2359 - 190 seat theater, 60 events yearly)* **Near:** Picnic Area, Jogging Paths, Boat Rentals *(Sea Dog Kayaks 875-1131)*, Museum *(The Dory Shop $3; Shelburne County, Ross-Thomson House & Store, Muir-Cox Shipyard 875-3219, $3 each, all 4 $8)*, Tours *(MV Brown Eyed Girl 409-9640 Three tours $25/10 to $35/15)*, Sightseeing *(Harbour Tours 875-6521)*, Galleries *(Tottie's Crafts 875-2584 local artisans; Coastline)*, Special Events *(Lobster Fest - Jun; Loyalist Landing - May)* **Under 1 mi:** Beach, Hike/Bike Trails, Bowling, Video Rental *(Video Focus 875-4699)* **1-3 mi:** Park *(Islands Provincial 875-4304 Directly across harbour - dinghy or 1.2 mi. hike on railway rte.)* **3+ mi:** Golf Course *(River Hills 637-2415, 12 mi.)*

Provisioning and General Services
Near: Market *(Lyle's)*, Farmers' Market *(Sat 8-11am, Loyalist Plaza 875-2753)*, Bank/ATM *(CIBC Water St.)*, Protestant Church, Beauty Salon *(Glee's 875-2274)*, Laundry, Bookstore *(Whirligig 875-1117)*, Pharmacy *(TLC Pharmasave 875-4852)* **Under 1 mi:** Convenience Store *(Maria's 875-1906)*, Supermarket *(Sobeys 875-2458)*, Wine/Beer, Liquor Store *(NSLC 875-2462)*, Bakery, Post Office, Catholic Church, Library *(875-3615 Internet)*, Dry Cleaners, Hardware Store *(Woodworkers 875-3900; TimbrMart 875-7300)*, Florist *(Advivas 875-2101)*, Retail Shops *(Shelburne Mall)*

Transportation
Under 1 mi: Rental Car *(Rent-A-Wreck 875-3200)* **Airport:** Yarmouth Int'l/Halifax Int'l *(60 mi./130 mi.)*

Medical Services
911 Service **Near:** Dentist *(Roseway 875-4441)*, Chiropractor *(875-1472)* **Under 1 mi:** Doctor *(S.W. Health 875-3011)* **1-3 mi:** Veterinarian *(Jordan Branch 875-4033)* **Hospital:** Roseway 875-3011 *(1.5 mi.)*

Setting -- About two miles north of Sand Point in deepwater Shelburne Harbour, a rock breakwater protects the impeccable SHYC floating docks at the edge of the Historic Waterfront District - part of the Muir-Cox Shipyard Museum Complex. Decks wrap the the club's two-story barn red clapboard building providing views across the marina, mooring field and down the lake-like harbour - the third largest natural harbor in the world.

Marina Notes -- *$25 min. **Power 15A $4 & 30A $7. ***Until 10pm Fri. Founded 1903. Best fuel prices. Bar but no kitchen services - daily lunch & Friday night dinner provided by local restaurants - order ahead and it is served at your table. Restarted dinghy sailing in the harbor; one of the largest Albacore sailing fleets in the world. Anchor & use YC facilities $3/pp. Bathhouse: Full baths, vinyl tile floor, painted walls, vanity, flowers, molded fiberglass shower stalls wtih curtains. Small laundry. Note: Additional dockage at public wharf. Boatyard services at Shelburne Ship Repair - revived with an infusion of $8.8 million.

Notable -- SHYC shares space in what was once Harley S. Cox and Sons' large vessel building with the Osprey Arts Centre &Theatre, Shelburne Harbour Marina Assoc. and Shelburne Sailing School. Sprinkled among the mix of real antiques and re-creations left behind by Hollywood are three other museums. The Dory Shop, the last of 7 boat factories, gives demonstrations among its interpretive exhibits and replicas of 1780 rowing boats. Shelburne County Museum covers the Loyalist period when 10,000 refugees arrived from Maine. And the 1785 Ross-Thompson store is a preserved Loyalist shop. Once one of N.A.'s largest shipbuilding centers, Shelburne is also credited with birthing the private yacht. Salmon aquaculture re-started the economy; watch for the yellow buoys.

PHOTOS ON DVD: 25

Killam Brothers Marina

PO Box; 400 Main Street; Yarmouth, NS B5A 1G2

Tel: (902) 740-1380 **VHF: Monitor** Ch. 16 **Talk** Ch. 16
Fax: (902) 742-1230 **Alternate Tel:** n/a
Email: waterfront@yarmouth-town.com **Web:** n/a
Nearest Town: Yarmouth **Tourist Info:** (877) 552-4040

Navigational Information

Lat: 43°50.181' **Long:** 066°07.372' **Tide:** 15.5 ft. **Current:** n/a **Chart:** 4245C
Rep. Depths (*MLW*): Entry 20 ft. **Fuel Dock** 12 ft. **Max Slip/Moor** 14 ft./14 ft.
Access: Bunker Is. Light, Channel 1.5 mi to Inner Harbor

Marina Facilities *(In Season/Off Season)*

Fuel: Gasoline, Diesel
Slips: 30 Total, 24 Transient **Max LOA:** 220 ft. **Max Beam:** 30 ft.
Rate *(per ft.)*: **Day** $0.80* **Week** n/a **Month** n/a
Power: 30 amp Incl, **50 amp** Incl, **100 amp** Incl, **200 amp** Incl
Cable TV: No **Dockside Phone:** No
Dock Type: Floating, Short Fingers, Alongside, Wood
Moorings: 9 Total, 7 Transient **Launch:** Yes (Free), Dinghy Dock
Rate: Day $20 **Week** n/a **Month** $100
Heads: 8 Toilet(s), 6 Shower(s) *(dressing rooms)*
Internet: Yes *(Wi-Fi, Free)* **Laundry:** 2 Washer(s), 2 Dryer(s)
Pump-Out: No **Fee:** n/a **Closed Heads:** Yes

Marina Operations

Owner/Manager: Jim Corning **Dockmaster:** Paul Pothier
In-Season: May 1-Oct 15, 8am-5pm **Off-Season:** Oct 16-Apr 30, Closed
After-Hours Arrival: Call in advance
Reservations: Yes **Credit Cards:** Visa/MC, Dscvr, Din, Amex, Tex
Discounts: None
Pets: Welcome, Dog Walk Area **Handicap Access:** Yes, Heads, Docks

Marina Services and Boat Supplies

Services - Docking Assistance, Trash Pick-Up, Dock Carts, 3 Phase **Communication -** FedEx, UPS, Express Mail **Supplies - OnSite:** Ships' Store **Near:** Ice *(Cube)* **1-3 mi:** Bait/Tackle *(Broph's 745-0581)*

Boatyard Services

Nearest Yard: A.F. Theriault & Son (902) 645-2327

Restaurants and Accommodations

OnSite: Restaurant *(Rudder's Brew Pub 742-7311, L $7.50-22, D $7.50-28, Wknd entertainment. Unique barrel gravity flow brewery - hand crafts dark ales, light & wheat beers)*, Lite Fare *(Rudder's Seafood Waterfont Express L & D $3-16. Boiled Lobster to go $13)* **OnCall:** Pizzeria *(Jake's 742-8882)* **Near:** Restaurant *(Ship's Bell at Rodd Colony Harbour 742-9194)*, *(Chez Bruno 742-0031, L $3-24, D $11-29)*, Coffee Shop *(Tom Hortons)*, Lite Fare *(Haley's Lounge Nightly entertainment, pub menu)*, Pizzeria *(Greco Donair 742-6666)*, Hotel *(Rodd-Grand 742-2446, $90-150)*, Inn/B&B *(McKinnon-Cann House Historic Inn 742-9900, $120-160)* **Under 1 mi:** Inn/B&B *(Harbour's Edge 742-2387, $135-150)* **1-3 mi:** Restaurant *(Jo-Annes Quick & Tasty 742-6606, L $3-12, D $8-18)*

Recreation and Entertainment

OnSite: Picnic Area, Cultural Attract *(Kilam Bros Coal Shed outdoor stage - 2-3 concerts each wknd - best seat is on the boat)*, Special Events *(Waterfront Fest & Boat Parade of Lights - June)* **Near:** Hike/Bike Trails, Park *(Frost - beautifully cultivated greenswad tumbles to the sea)*, Sightseeing *(Self-guided walking tour - Queen Anne, Classic Revival, Italianate, Georgian architecture - business district & residential Collins Heritage Conservation District)*, Galleries *(Yarmouth Arts Regional Centre 742-8150)* **Under 1 mi:** Pool *(YMCA 742-7181)*, Playground, Tennis Courts, Golf Course *(Yarmouth 742-2161)*, Fitness Center *(YMCA)*, Bowling *(Brunswick Lanes 742-2186)*, Video Rental *(Movie Gallery 742-5862)*, Museum *(Yarmouth County 742-5539 $5/2; Fire Fighters 742-5525 $4/2)* **1-3 mi:** Movie Theater *(Empire 742-7819)*, Tours *(Famous Cape Forchu Lighthouse)*

Provisioning and General Services

Near: Convenience Store *(Digby 245-4048)*, Health Food *(Yarmouth Natural Foods 742-2336)*, Wine/Beer, Bank/ATM, Post Office, Catholic Church, Protestant Church, Library *(742-2486)*, Beauty Salon, Barber Shop, Laundry, Bookstore *(Lam's Used 742-2149)*, Pharmacy *(Pharmasave 742-7825)*, Retail Shops *(Tooie's Country Store 742-6968)* **Under 1 mi:** Supermarket *(Sobey's 742-2882)*, Liquor Store *(NSLC 742-6711)*, Bakery *(Old World Bakery & Deli 742-2181)*, Fishmonger, Dry Cleaners, Department Store, Buying Club, Copies Etc. *(Ellis Print 742-8831)* **1-3 mi:** Hardware Store *(Canadian Tire 749-1600)*

Transportation

OnCall: Taxi *(Campbell's 742-6101; Cloud Nine 742-3992)* **1-3 mi:** Rental Car *(Avis 742-3323; Budget 742-9500)* **Airport:** Yarmouth Int'l *(3 mi.)*

Medical Services

911 Service **Near:** Holistic Services *(Maritime Natural Healing 645-3357)* **Under 1 mi:** Doctor *(Harbour South 742-8333)*, Chiropractor *(Harbourview 742-2097)*, Veterinarian *(Parade Street 742-3108)* **1-3 mi:** Dentist *(Yarmouth 742-3355)* **Hospital:** Yarmouth Reg. 742-3541 *(1 mi.)*

Setting -- Yarmouth's municipal slips and megayacht-capable face dock sprawl along the attractively landscaped waterfront - backed by the colorfully planted town square with a bandstand gazebo and the Killam Bros. Coal Shed outdoor stage. Doctors' Island, home to flocks of cormorants and shore birds, protects the pink mooring balls and docks. Onshore an antique, red-trimmed, three-story gray colonial houses the office and amenities; the adjacent yellow two-story Rudder's Restaurant & Brew Pub, built in 1867 as part of Young's Wharf, sports a waterside dining deck. Yarmouth's pretty downtown is a block away.

Marina Notes -- *Flat rate: $31.50 up to 40 ft., $40 41-50 ft., $50 51-60 ft. 61-70 ft. $60 Max LOA at slips plus up to 70 ft. alongside. Owned/Operated by City of Yarmouth. Relatively recent sturdy floating docks plus newly installed majorside-tie dock - all with heavy cleats. Manages Parker-Eakin docks as well. Plus 9 moorings tied to 1,000 lb blocks. Wave attenuator reduces swell. Port of entry to Nova Scotia. Bathhouse: Pleasant take on standard municipal butter yellow painted cinderblock heads with brick red cement floors. Locked showers with curtains & dressing rooms. Also laundry in shower room.

Notable -- The Kilam Brothers Coal Shed outdoor stage hosts concerts from rock and roll to classical music on long weekends (Fridays, Saturdays, and Sundays) draws crowds of 200-300. The red & green Rudder's Waterfront Express serves lobster and sandwiches to go. Upscale, pine-paneled Rudder's features two dining rooms and three event spaces - 80 for a sit-down or 120 for cocktails. Yarmouth's architecturally interesting Main Street offers most any service or supplies boaters might need. The Cat Ferry to/from Maine has been suspended; alternatives are under discussion.

PHOTOS ON DVD: 25

Navigational Information
Lat: 44°37.532' **Long:** 065°45.300' **Tide:** 28 ft. **Current:** n/a **Chart:** n/a
Rep. Depths (*MLW*): Entry 10 ft. **Fuel Dock** n/a **Max Slip/Moor** 10 ft./-
Access: Bay of Funday to Grand Manan Channel

Marina Facilities *(In Season/Off Season)*
Fuel: No
Slips: 40 Total, 8 Transient **Max LOA:** 75 ft. **Max Beam:** n/a
Rate *(per ft.)*: **Day** $1.25* **Week** n/a **Month** n/a
Power: 30 amp Incl., **50 amp** Incl., **100 amp** n/a, **200 amp** n/a
Cable TV: No **Dockside Phone:** No
Dock Type: Floating, Long Fingers, Alongside, Wood
Moorings: 0 Total, 0 Transient **Launch:** n/a, Dinghy Dock
Rate: Day n/a **Week** n/a **Month** n/a
Heads: 2 Toilet(s), 1 Shower(s) *(dressing rooms)*, Book Exchange
Internet: Yes *(Wi-Fi, Free)* **Laundry:** 1 Washer(s), 1 Dryer(s)
Pump-Out: No **Fee:** n/a **Closed Heads:** No

Marina Operations
Owner/Manager: Jeff Sutherland (hrbmstr) **Dockmaster:** Darryl Jelfs
In-Season: Mid-Apr-Mid-Oct, 9am-9pm **Off-Season:** Mid-Oct-Mid-Apr, Close
After-Hours Arrival: Call in advance to arrange
Reservations: Yes, Preferred **Credit Cards:** Visa/MC, Din, Amex
Discounts: None
Pets: Welcome, Dog Walk Area **Handicap Access:** No

R.W.N.S.Y.S. & Digby Marina

PO Box 2384; 100 Water Street; Digby, NS B0V 1AD
Tel: (902) 245-1867 **VHF: Monitor** Ch. 12 **Talk** Ch. 12
Fax: (902) 245-2194 **Alternate Tel:** (902) 247-5352
Email: digbyharbour@ns.aliantzinc.ca **Web:** www.rwnsyc.ca/marina
Nearest Town: Digby **Tourist Info:** (902) 834-2226

Marina Services and Boat Supplies
Services - Docking Assistance, Trash Pick-Up **Communication -** Fax in/out *($2)*, FedEx, DHL, UPS **Supplies - OnSite:** Ice *(Cube)* **Near:** Ships' Store *(Tidal BY 245-5663)*, Bait/Tackle *(Digby Marine 245-2655)* **Under 1 mi:** Propane *(Royal 245-5928)*, CNG *(Royal)*

Boatyard Services
OnCall: Divers, Refrigeration **Near:** Travelift *(20T)*, Railway, Electronic Sales, Electronics Repairs, Hull Repairs. **Nearest Yard:** Tidal Marine 245-5663 & Larche (902) 245-2171

Restaurants and Accommodations
OnSite: Restaurant *(Captain's Cabin 245-4868, L&D $8-13)*, *(House of Wong 245-4125)*, *(Shoreline 245-6667, B $4-5, L $6-13, D $9-25, Kids' $4-9)*, Seafood Shack *(O'Neils Royal Fundy Fish Market & Cafe 245-5411, $6-14)* **Near:** Restaurant *(Dockside 245-4950, L & D $10-20, Munchies $8-16 Deck, Dock)*, *(Fundy 245-4950, L $9-15, D $16-34, Deck, glass solarium)*, *(Boardwalk Cafe 245-5497, L&D $5-10)*, Lite Fare *(Club 98 245-4950, DJ wknds, Pool Tables)*, Pizzeria *(Ricacardo Del.)*, Motel *(Shoreline Suites 245-5110, $65+)*, *(Dockside Suites 245-4950, $119-139)*, *(Boardwalk Suites 245-5497)*, Inn/B&B *(Thistle Down 245-4490)* **Under 1 mi:** Restaurant *(Churchill's at Digby Pines L $10-16, D $10-36, Grande Lounge $7-17)*, Fast Food *(Subway, McD's, KFC, DQs, Tim Hortons)*, Hotel *(Digby Pines Resort 245-2511, $125-200+, 85 rooms, 31 cottages)*

Recreation and Entertainment
OnCall: Sightseeing *(Kathleen's Experiences 834-2024 - Digby Neck or Annapolis Valley $50 half day; Thurs $15 RT to Briar Island; BI Whale & SeaBird 839-2995 $49-58)* **Near:** Beach, Boat Rentals *(Dockside Kayaks 245-4950 half-day $50-65)*, Video Rental *(Grabbamovie 245-1978)*, Park, Museum *(Admiral Digby 245-6322 Mon-Sat, 9am-5pm)*, Tours *("Passage Provider" Whale Watch 245-4950 $48/36)* **Under 1 mi:** Playground, Tennis Courts **1-3 mi:** Golf Course *(Digby Pines, Stanley Thompson design)*, Bowling *(Wilson's 245-4444)*

Provisioning and General Services
Near: Convenience Store *(Digby 245-4080)*, Bakery *(Robin's)*, Fishmonger *(O'Neill's 245-5411)*, Bank/ATM, Post Office, Catholic Church, Protestant Church *(1878 Trinity Anglican built by shipwrights)*, Beauty Salon *(Salon by Sea 245-4907)*, Bookstore *(Signature 245-2349)*, Florist *(Harbour Rose 245-5080)* **Under 1 mi:** Supermarket *(Sobey's 245-6183)*, Liquor Store *(NS 245-4411)*, Library *(245-2163, Internet)*, Pharmacy *(Shoppers 245-4722)*, Hardware Store *(Canadian Tire 245-2527; Wilson's 245-4731)* **1-3 mi:** Department Store *(Atlantic Superstore, Walmart)*

Transportation
OnCall: Rental Car *(Enterprise 245-5936)*, Taxi *(Basin 245-4408; Digby 245-6162; Admiral 245-4542)*, Airport Limo *(Kathleen's 834-2024)* **Near:** InterCity Bus *(Acadian 422-1500 to Halifax)* **3+ mi:** Ferry Service *(to Saint John, NB, 3 mi.)* **Airport:** Digby/Halifax Int'l *(4 mi./145 mi.)*

Medical Services
911 Service **OnCall:** Ambulance **Near:** Dentist *(Haslam 245- 3535)*, Chiropractor *(Alliance 245-2427)*, Veterinarian *(Bay View 245-5205)* **Under 1 mi:** Doctor *(Lafkovici 245-6611)* **1-3 mi:** Holistic Services *(Pines Resort Day Spa 245-7726, Massage $95/hr)* **Hospital:** Digby 245-2501 *(1 mi.)*

Setting -- On Annapolis Basin's western shore, the quality docks are tucked into the corner of the harbor - protected by the "E" shaped commercial wharf that berths scallop draggers and fishing trawlers. The gangway leads through the Yacht Club's wooden gate to pretty Admiral's Walk which runs along the water to Memorial Park - a greensward complete with cannons. A row of eateries, sporting big windows and waterfront decks, and village shops overlook the boats.

Marina Notes -- *Flat rate: 25-39 ft.11" $50, 40-50 ft. $60, Group rates. Max 42 ft. LOA & 12 ft beam in slips. Up to 50 ft. at T-head. Over 50 ft. & megayachts at Commercial Wharf with new floats $75-100 - call. Private moorings possible; ample anchorage for larger vessels (all facilities avail.). Developed by town in collaboration with RWNSYS. Clubhouse on 2nd floor of gaily painted building at top of gangway. Features heads, a bar area, pool table & lovely deck overlooking the harbor. Bandstand hosts free concerts Wed 7-9pm (Celtic, blues & country). Bathhouse: Simple - 2 heads one shower.

Notable -- Digby, still a small fishing village, is home to the largest inshore scallop fleet on the eastern seaboard; it's also whale watch heaven. Sweet, Georgian-style Admiral Digby Museum's two floors of period rooms explore the town's heritage. Visit lovely Digby Pines Resort , a 1929 Norman-style chateau, for a night off the boat, a spa day or 18 holes at a one of Canada's top courses. Two must-do lay days: breath-taking Brier Island, at the tip of Digby Neck, is worth the two ferries and 40 miles. Take a tour or rent a car for incredible views, whale and sea bird watching. Nova Scotia's original captial, Annapolis Royal (C.1605), lies 18 miles at the basin's head. The village's historic district includes 150 heritage properties - see them with Tour Annapolis Royal (532-303, $7/3).

PHOTOS ON DVD: 25

2. NB – St. John River

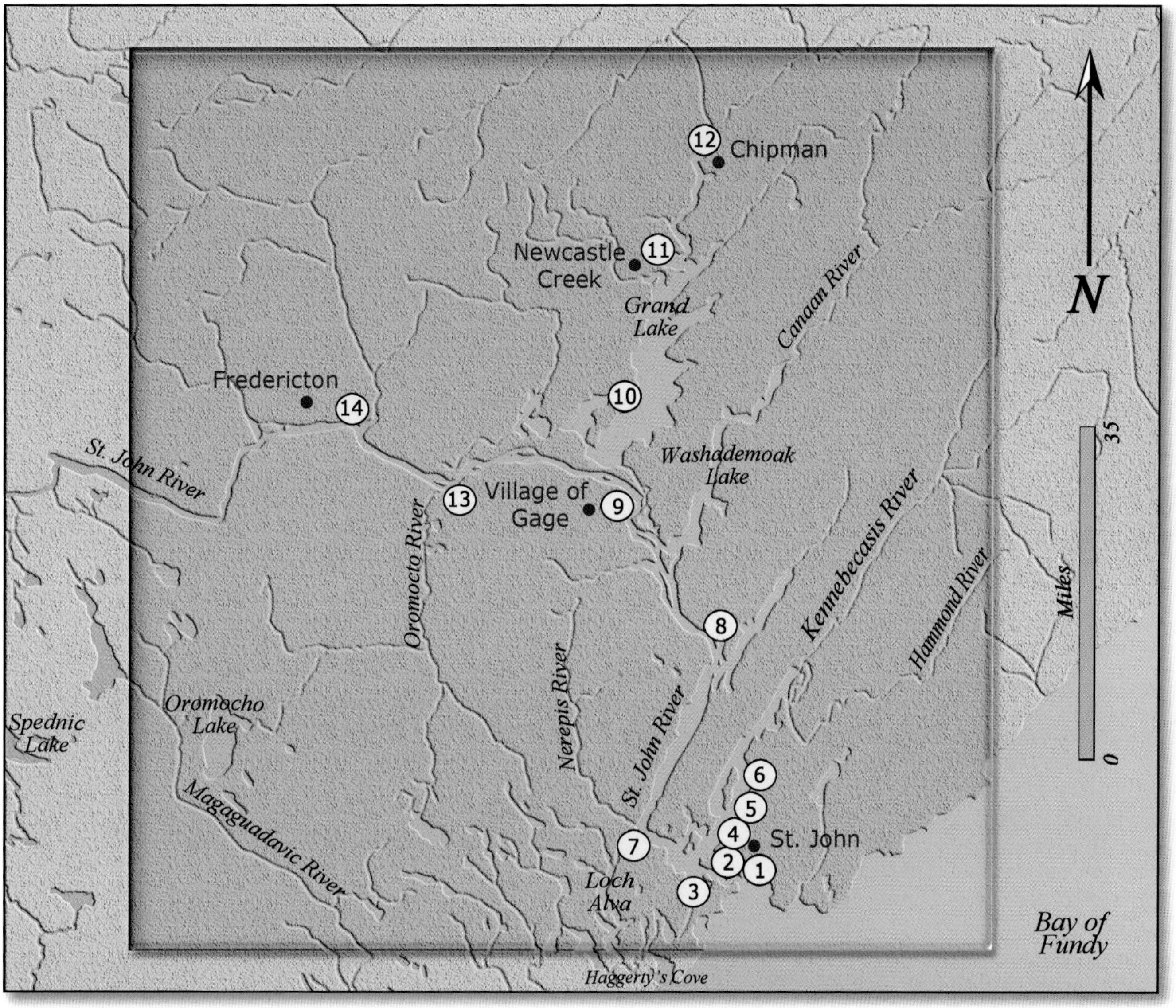

MAP	MARINA	HARBOR	PAGE
1	**Market Slip Docks**	*Saint John Harbour*	*50*
2	**Saint John Power Boat Club**	*Marble Cove*	*51*
3	**Saint John Marina**	*Grand Bay*	*52*
4	**Brundage Point River Centre**	*Grand Bay*	*53*
5	**Royal Kennebeccasis Yacht Club**	*Kennebecasis River*	*54*
6	**Renforth Boat Club**	*Kennebecasis River*	*55*
7	**Rothesay Yacht Club**	*Kennebecasis Bay*	*56*
8	**Evandale Resort & Marina**	*St. John River*	*57*
9	**Gagetown Marina & Wharf**	*Gagetown Creek*	*58*
10	**Fredericton Yacht Club**	*Grand Lake*	*59*
11	**Newcastle Creek Yacht Club**	*Grand Lake*	*60*
12	**Village of Chipman Marina**	*Grand Lake*	*61*
13	**Oromocto Marina**	*Oromocto River*	*62*
14	**Regent Street Wharf & Moorings**	*St. John River*	*63*

RATINGS: 1-5 for Marina Facilities & Amenities,  1-2 for Boatyard Services,  1-2 for MegaYacht Facilities,  for Something Special.

SERVICES: for CCM – Certified Clean Marina,  for Pump-Out,   for Internet,  for Fuel,  for Restaurant,  for Provisioning nearby,  for Catamaran-friendly,  for SportFish Charter,  for Pool/Beach, and  for Golf within a mile. *For an explanation of ACC's Ratings, see page 8.*

Market Slip Docks

One Market Square; Saint John, NB E2L 4Z6

Tel: (506) 649-6066 **VHF: Monitor** Ch. 16 **Talk** n/a
Fax: n/a **Alternate Tel:** (506) 636-4982
Email: theresa.ellefsen@sjwaterfront.com **Web:** sjwaterfront.com
Nearest Town: Saint John **Tourist Info:** (506) 658-2855

Navigational Information
Lat: 45°16.372' **Long:** 066°03.797' **Tide:** 27 ft. **Current:** n/a **Chart:** 4117
Rep. Depths (*MLW*): Entry 24 ft. **Fuel Dock** n/a **Max Slip/Moor** 6 ft./-
Access: Entrance channel to east of Partridge Is., 333 deg. to range markers

Marina Facilities *(In Season/Off Season)*
Fuel: No
Slips: 8 Total, 8 Transient **Max LOA:** 125 ft. **Max Beam:** n/a
Rate *(per ft.)*: **Day** $0* **Week** n/a **Month** n/a
Power: 30 amp n/a, **50 amp** n/a, **100 amp** n/a, **200 amp** n/a
Cable TV: No **Dockside Phone:** No
Dock Type: Floating, Alongside, Wood
Moorings: 0 Total, 0 Transient **Launch:** n/a
Rate: Day n/a **Week** n/a **Month** n/a
Heads: None
Internet: Yes *(Wi-Fi Hilton Lobby)* **Laundry:** None
Pump-Out: No **Fee:** n/a **Closed Heads:** No

Marina Operations
Owner/Manager: Saint John Dev. **Dockmaster:** Andy Somerville (Hrbrmstr)
In-Season: May 26-Oct 14, 7am-dusk **Off-Season:** Oct 15-May 25, Closed
After-Hours Arrival: Contact Harbormaster Ch. 16 or 506-636-4982
Reservations: No - 1st come, 1st served **Credit Cards:** n/a
Discounts: None
Pets: Welcome **Handicap Access:** No

Marina Services and Boat Supplies
Communication - FedEx, UPS **Supplies - Near:** Ice *(Cube)* **1-3 mi:** Ships' Store *(Dykeman's Marine 506-634-1852)*

Boatyard Services
Nearest Yard: Saint John Marina (506) 738-8484

Restaurants and Accommodations
OnSite: Restaurant *(Brigantine Lounge 693-8484, L $8.50-$17, D $8.50-33, Hilton)*, Lite Fare *(Turn of the Tides 693-8484, B $5-17, Hilton - a la carte or $17 buffet 6:30-11am)*, Hotel *(Hilton Saint John 693-8484, $115-150, Day Use rate $50 or 50% of lowest rate - use of a room & all hotel amenities until 6pm)* **OnCall:** Pizzeria *(Pizza Hut)* **Near:** Restaurant *(Lemongrass Thai Fare 657-8424, D $11-25)*, *(Saint John Ale House 657-2337, D $17-27, Pub $9-20)*, *(Opera Bistro 642-2222, L $10-14, D $14-33, 3-course Tasting $38)*, *(Grannan's Seafood Restaurant 648-2323, L $10-16, D $17-43)*, *(Saint John Ale House 657-2337, L&D $9-25)*, Raw Bar *(Billy's Seafood Co. 672-3474)*, Coffee Shop *(Tim Hortons)*, Fast Food *(McDs, Subway)*, Lite Fare *(Extreme Pita 652-1122)*, *(Peppers Pub 657-8424, $11-25)*, Pizzeria *(Julius Pizza 634-0988)*, Hotel *(Delta 648-1981)*, *(Chipman Hill Suites 693-1171, $50-300)*, Inn/B&B *(Mahogony Manor 636-8000, $100-110)*

Recreation and Entertainment
OnSite: Pool *(Hilton Day Rate - or at nearby Canada Games Aquatic Centre)*, Jogging Paths *(Harbour Passage Pathway)* **Near:** Fitness Center *(Canada Games Aquatic Centre 658-4715 $7.50/5 per day)*, Park, Museum *(New Brunswick 643-2300; Jewish Historical 657-4790)*, Cultural Attract *(Imperial Theater)*, Sightseeing *(Reversing Falls Jet 888-634-8987; Historic Saint John 658-4700)*, Galleries *(Handworks 652-9787; Isaac Antiques 652-3222)*, Special Events *(Canada Day, Salty Jam Music Festival, New Brunswick Day, Fundy Fog Fest)* **1-3 mi:** Golf Course *(Rockwood Park 634-0090)*, Boat Rentals *(DMK Marine 635-4150)*, Bowling *(Fairview 652-8480)* **3+ mi:** Movie Theater *(Empire Theatres 657-3456, 3.5 mi.)*

Provisioning and General Services
Near: Convenience Store *(Union St. 693-1215)*, Market *(City Market, Brunswick Square, 7 days - rings a bell to mark opening & closing)*, Wine/Beer, Liquor Store *(NB)*, Bakery *(Treats 633-7620)*, Farmers' Market *(City Market)*, Bank/ATM, Post Office, Catholic Church, Protestant Church, Synagogue, Library *(Saint John 643-7220 - Internet)*, Beauty Salon *(Element 5 642-7725)*, Bookstore *(Coles -658-9114)*, Pharmacy *(Lawton's 634-1422)*, Florist, Retail Shops *(Market Sq; Brunswick Sq.)* **Under 1 mi:** Laundry *(City 634-1488)* **1-3 mi:** Supermarket *(Sobeys Lansdowne 652-4470)*, Hardware Store *(Canadian Tire 634-2606)*, Buying Club *(Atlantic Superstore)* **3+ mi:** Department Store *(Walmart 634-8036, 4 mi.)*

Transportation
OnCall: Rental Car *(Enterprise 693-8688; Avis 634-7750)*, Taxi *(Vet's 658-2020)* **Near:** Ferry Service *(Princess of Acadia to Digby, NS)* **Under 1 mi:** Local Bus *(Handi-Bus 648-0609)* **Airport:** Saint John *(8.5 mi.)*

Medical Services
911 Service **Near:** Holistic Services *(Element 5 Day Spa 642-6422; Salkey 693-0722)* **Under 1 mi:** Doctor *(Lawtons 634-1422)*, Dentist *(MacDonald 649-5131)*, Chiropractor *(Sheppard 635-8182)* **1-3 mi:** Veterinarian *(Saint John 633-4191)* **Hospital:** Saint John Regional 648-6000 *(3.5 mi.)*

Setting -- Two red and white lighthouses flank the rectangular basin just off Saint John Harbour where a U-shaped side-tie floating dock sits in the shadow of the Hilton Hotel. Up the ramp, sidewalk cafes march up the hill and well-used volleyball courts overlook the docks. Market Square is almost adjacent. Harbour Passage Pathway starts here and rims the waterfront, inviting a delightful stroll or jog. All of Uptown Saint John is an easy walk.

Marina Notes -- *Free. 320 feet alongside dockage. Owned by Saint John Development, Managed by Market Square 658-3600. Gates open 7am, locked at dusk - get key from Market Square. MLW depths 3-6.6 ft. - clearly marked on dock. Max Stay 24 hrs w/out permission. Longer stays usually granted. (125 ft. yacht moored here 5 days). 3 dock sections: 120 ft., 100 ft. & 100 ft. No security. Long steel gangway becomes steps to manage low tide. Most boats stage here to wait for slack tide at Reversing Falls before entering St. John River; 20-minute window for optimal passage. Call 658-2855 for info. Good video shows how the falls works. Bathhouse: Hilton $50 Day-Use fee - Room, Fitness Center, pool, heads & showers or Canada Games Aquatic Center $7.50/5.

Notable -- Saint John is Canada's oldest incorporated city. Guided tours cover the historic district, Reversing Falls, Imperial Theatre, and the compelling New Brunswick and Jewish Historical Museums. A block from the docks, Market and Brunswick Square have 60+ shops and services connected by a pedway system - including the Provincial Museum, main library, convention center, shops and CanPark office. A few blocks up the hill, City Market is a spectacular provisioning resource with produce, seafood, meats, all manner of prepared foods and maritime crafts. Fire boats welcome cruise ships with a water show.

PHOTOS ON DVD: 25

Navigational Information
Lat: 45°16.406' **Long:** 066°05.081' **Tide:** 2 ft. **Current:** 6 kt. **Chart:** 4141
Rep. Depths (*MLW*): Entry 6 ft. **Fuel Dock** 6 ft. **Max Slip/Moor** 6 ft./-
Access: Thru Reversing Falls E 2 small islands + 40° starboard

Marina Facilities *(In Season/Off Season)*
Fuel: Slip-Side Fueling, Gasoline, Diesel, On Call Delivery
Slips: 60 Total, 5 Transient **Max LOA:** 50 ft. **Max Beam:** 17 ft.
Rate *(per ft.)*: **Day** $0.50* **Week** n/a **Month** n/a
Power: 30 amp 30, **50 amp** 30, **100 amp** n/a, **200 amp** n/a
Cable TV: No **Dockside Phone:** Yes
Dock Type: Floating, Long Fingers, Alongside, Wood, Aluminum
Moorings: 0 Total, 0 Transient **Launch:** n/a, Dinghy Dock
Rate: Day n/a **Week** n/a **Month** n/a
Heads: 4 Toilet(s), 1 Shower(s), Book Exchange
Internet: Yes *(Wi-Fi, Free)* **Laundry:** 1 Washer(s), 1 Dryer(s)
Pump-Out: No **Fee:** n/a **Closed Heads:** No

Marina Operations
Owner/Manager: Kevin Downes **Dockmaster:** Scott Gilbert
In-Season: May-Nov, 8am-9pm **Off-Season:** Nov-May, 9am-5pm
After-Hours Arrival: Security on hand
Reservations: Yes, Preferred **Credit Cards:** Cash only
Discounts: None
Pets: Welcome, Dog Walk Area **Handicap Access:** No

Saint John Power Boat Club

PO Box 1072; 100 Kennedy Street; Saint John, NB E2K 1C4
Tel: (506) 642-5233 **VHF: Monitor** Ch.16 **Talk** Ch.68
Fax: n/a **Alternate Tel:** (506) 642-5233
Email: suitsus1@hotmail.com **Web:** n/a
Nearest Town: Saint John **Tourist Info:** (506) 658-2855

Marina Services and Boat Supplies
Services - Docking Assistance, Boaters' Lounge, Security *(24 hrs.)*, Trash Pick-Up, Dock Carts **Communication -** Pay Phone, FedEx, DHL, UPS, Express Mail **Supplies - OnSite:** Ice *(Block, Cube)* **Under 1 mi:** Ships' Store *(Dykeman's 634-1852)*, Marine Discount Store *(Millidgeville Marine 633-1454)* **1-3 mi:** Propane *(Salesse Heating 333-7051)*

Boatyard Services
OnSite: Travelift *(20 T)*, Railway *(20 T)*, Engine mechanic *(gas, diesel)*, Electrical Repairs, Electronic Sales, Hull Repairs, Canvas Work, Brightwork, Air Conditioning, Refrigeration, Compound, Wash & Wax, Propeller Repairs, Woodworking, Inflatable Repairs

Restaurants and Accommodations
Near: Restaurant *(Reversing Falls 635-1999, B $3-10, L $5-10, D $10-20)*, Hotel *(Killam Furnished Suites 650-9558, $395-495 Weekly)* **Under 1 mi:** Restaurant *(Bamboo East 634-1661, L & D $8-15)*, Hotel *(Holiday Inn Express Hotel & Suites 642-2622, $117-139)* **1-3 mi:** Restaurant *(Billy's Seafood 672-3474)*, *(Bolilerworks 693-3663)*, *(Church Street Steakhouse 648-2373)*, Seafood Shack *(Grannan's Seafood 634-1555)*, Coffee Shop *(Tim Hortons 693-0090)*, Fast Food *(McD's, Wendy's)*, Hotel *(Hilton 693-8484, $109-199)*, *(Chipman Hill Suites 693-1171, $49-299)*, *(Delta 648-1981)*, *(Chateau Saint John 644-4444)*

Recreation and Entertainment
OnSite: Picnic Area *(on the deck)*, Grills, Fitness Center, Hike/Bike Trails **Near:** Playground *(Bridge St. Park)*, Movie Theater *(Empire Theatres 657-3456)*, Video Arcade, Park *(Bridge St.)*, Sightseeing *(Freedom Tours 800-561-2324)* **Under 1 mi:** Museum *(New Brunswick 643-2300)* **1-3 mi:** Heated Pool *(Saint John Aquatic Center)*, Boat Rentals *(Reversing Falls Jet Boat Ride 634-8987)*, Bowling *(Fairview Bowling Lanes 652-8480)*, Tours *(Reversing Falls Jet Boat Ride 634-8987)* **3+ mi:** Golf Course *(Rockwood Park 634-0090 , 5 mi.)*

Provisioning and General Services
Near: Convenience Store *(Smart Choice 635-5855)*, Market *(Millidgeville Market Superstore 658-6054)*, Health Food *(Bulk Barn 634-0910)*, Wine/Beer, Liquor Store *(NB 633-3940)*, Bakery, Bank/ATM, Post Office, Catholic Church, Protestant Church, Synagogue, Beauty Salon, Barber Shop, Dry Cleaners, Pharmacy *(Drugstore 658-6094)*, Newsstand, Hardware Store *(Dykeman's 634-1852)*, Florist *(Lancaster 635-1040)*, Department Store *(Dollarama 674-1687)*, Mosque **Under 1 mi:** Supermarket *(Sobey's 652-4470)*, Library *(Saint John 643-7220)*

Transportation
OnSite: Rental Car *(Discount 633-4440, delivery)*, Local Bus *(Saint John Transit 658-4700)* **1-3 mi:** Taxi *(Royal Taxi 652-5050)* **Airport:** Saint John Municipal 638-5555 *(9 mi.)*

Medical Services
911 Service **OnCall:** Ambulance **Near:** Doctor *(Comeau 634-6870)* **Under 1 mi:** Dentist *(Scichilone 634-2911)* **1-3 mi:** Chiropractor *(Atlantic Laser & Sheppard 635-8182)*, Holistic Services *(Total Balance Massage Therapy 649-5155)*, Veterinarian *(Saint John 633-4191)* **Hospital:** Saint John Regional 648-6000 *(1 mi.)*

Setting -- St. John Power Boat Club is tucked into the northeast corner of well-protected Marble Cove - a blaze on a boulder marks the entrance. At the head of the U-shaped, aging wood docks, a small blue-trimmed, two-story white clubhouse sports second floor dormers and a deck; a blue awning lettered "Saint John Power Boat Club" shades the windows. Trees block some of the industrial views out to the river. A green trailer houses the dockmaster's home office.

Marina Notes -- *Flat Rate $20 for overnight. Founded 1911. Casual, affordable, close to (actually within) downtown Saint John. Membership not necessary. One side of basin has stern-to slips without finger piers, opposite are side-tie wharves. A fuel dock is at the basin head. Dedicated visitors' dockage for boats staging for slack tide at Reversing Falls. Helpful guidance & advice provided. Large dry storage area and boatyard with 20 ton travelift and 20 ton railway (draft to 5 ft., beam to 15 ft.) plus designated work floats. Security on site 24/7 - key-coded gate. Clubhouse for functions only. Very safe storm harbor. Bathhouse: Basic, women's 2nd floor, clubhouse, faux pine paneling, 2 heads. Men's on 3rd floor. Planned renovation 2011/12.

Notable -- Cathedral-ceilinged 3rd floor event room would work well for a club cruise event - a small deck looks over the marina to the river. Good staging location for leaving the St. John River. For specific information on the nearby Reversing Falls call 658-2937. Grocery stores and downtown Saint John is about a mile away with shops, restaurants, museums, walking tours, the fabulous market and festivals all season long. Canada Day Celebrations kick off the summer season. Salty Jam music festival is the 2nd weekend in July; New Brunswick Day is the first week in August followed by Fundy Fest the third week.

2. NB - ST. JOHN RIVER
PHOTOS ON DVD: 20

Saint John Marina

2050 Westfield Rd.; Saint John, NB E2M 6H2

Tel: (506) 738-8484 **VHF: Monitor** Ch.16 **Talk** Ch.68
Fax: (506) 738-2007 **Alternate Tel:** n/a
Email: saintjohnmarina@rogers.com **Web:** saintjohnmarina.ca
Nearest Town: Grandbay *(3 mi.)* **Tourist Info:** (506) 658-2855

Navigational Information
Lat: 45°16.769' **Long:** 066°09.256' **Tide:** 4 ft. **Current:** 0.5 kt.. **Chart:** 4141
Rep. Depths (*MLW*): Entry 8 ft. **Fuel Dock** n/a **Max Slip/Moor** 12 ft./-
Access: Riverside of Reversing Falls - buoyed channel to breakwater

Marina Facilities *(In Season/Off Season)*
Fuel: *Irving* - Slip-Side Fueling, Gasoline, Diesel
Slips: 150 Total, 20 Transient **Max LOA:** 125 ft. **Max Beam:** 14 ft.
Rate *(per ft.)*: **Day** $1.50* **Week** $50 **Month** $200
Power: 30 amp $5, **50 amp** n/a, **100 amp** n/a, **200 amp** n/a
Cable TV: No **Dockside Phone:** Yes, Switchboard, 4 line(s)
Dock Type: Floating, Long Fingers, Pilings, Wood, Aluminum
Moorings: 0 Total, 0 Transient **Launch:** n/a, Dinghy Dock
Rate: Day n/a **Week** n/a **Month** n/a
Heads: 4 Toilet(s), 2 Shower(s) *(dressing rooms)*
Internet: Yes *(Wi-Fi - Lounge, Restaurant)* **Laundry:** 1 Washer(s), 1 Dryer(s)
Pump-Out: OnSite, Full Service **Fee:** $15 **Closed Heads:** No

Marina Operations
Owner/Manager: Bill Brown **Dockmaster:** Sarah Williams
In-Season: May-Oct, 9am-4pm **Off-Season:** Nov-Dec, 10am-1pm
After-Hours Arrival: Call prior to arrival
Reservations: Yes, Preferred **Credit Cards:** Visa/MC
Discounts: None
Pets: Welcome, Dog Walk Area **Handicap Access:** Yes, Heads, Docks

Marina Services and Boat Supplies
Services - Boaters' Lounge, Trash Pick-Up **Communication -** Mail & Package Hold, Phone Messages, Fax in/out *($2)*, FedEx, DHL, UPS, Express Mail **Supplies - OnSite:** Ice *(Cube)*, Ships' Store **1-3 mi:** Ice *(Block)*, Propane *(Co-op 738-8421)*

Boatyard Services
OnSite: Crane *(38T)*, Hydraulic Trailer *(9T)*, Launching Ramp *($10)*, Engine mechanic *(gas, diesel)*, Electrical Repairs, Electronic Sales, Electronics Repairs, Hull Repairs, Rigger, Woodworking, Painting, Awlgrip, Total Refits **3+ mi:** Sail Loft *(Doyle-Scot Sails 635-0414, 7 mi.)*, Propeller Repairs *(9 mi.)*, Life Raft Service *(Sea Pro 633-0070, 9 mi.)*, Metal Fabrication *(Mike Hussey 757-8925, 7 mi.)*. **Dealer for:** Mermaid Marine. **Yard Rates:** $65/hr., Haul & Launch $6.50/ft. **Storage:** On-Land $1.50/ft./mo.

Restaurants and Accommodations
OnSite: Restaurant *(Port Side Pub & Grill 738-8484, L & D $4-16.50, Kids' $5-6. Casual dining in Lower Deck Lounge & special events in Upper Deck space)* **OnCall:** Restaurant *(Wok Taste 738-1178, L & D $5-9)*, Pizzeria *(Pizza Delight 738-8496, delivers)* **3+ mi:** Restaurant *(Reversing Falls 635-1999, B $3-10, L $5-10, D $10-20, 6 mi.)*, Coffee Shop *(Tim Hortons 738-2571, 3.5 mi., $3-6)*, Hotel *(Hilton 693-8484, $109-199, 5 mi.)*, *(Delta 648-1981, 5 mi.)*, *(Country Inn 635-0400, 4 mi.)*, *(Comfort Inn 674-1873, $110-128, 5 mi.)*

Recreation and Entertainment
OnSite: Tours *(Voyageur II Riverboat built in Carlys, LA $25/20 2-hr. cruise, 3rd Sun of Month)* **1-3 mi:** Fitness Center *(Human Performance 738-8299)*, Bowling *(Grand Bay 738-8476)*, Video Rental, Cultural Attract *(Concerts at Unity Park, Grand Bay, Wed 7-8pm)* **3+ mi:** Beach *(5 mi.)*, Golf Course *(Westfield 757-2250, 6 mi.)*, Boat Rentals *(Go Fundy Events 672-0770, 6 mi.)*, Movie Theater *(Empire Theater 657-3456, 5 mi.)*, Museum *(N.B Museum 643-2300, 5 mi.)*

Provisioning and General Services
OnSite: Bank/ATM, Copies Etc. **Under 1 mi:** Catholic Church, Protestant Church **1-3 mi:** Convenience Store *(Grand Bay)*, Wine/Beer *(Grand Bay)*, Liquor Store *(Noloc - Grand Bay 738-3990)*, Farmers' Market *(Sun 9am-1pm, Brundage Point River Centre, Grand Bay)*, Post Office *(Grand Bay)*, Beauty Salon *(Grand Bay)*, Barber Shop, Dry Cleaners, Laundry, Pharmacy *(Guardian 738-8406)*, Hardware Store *(Home 738-8436)* **3+ mi:** Supermarket *(Atlantic Superstore 648-1320; Sobey 674-1460, 5 mi.)*, Health Food *(Bulk Barn, 5 mi.)*, Library *(West Branch 643-7260 , 6 mi.)*, Florist *(5 mi.)*, Retail Shops *(Lancaster Mall 635-1107 - 25 stores, 5 mi.)*, Department Store *(Zellers 635-1818, 5 mi.)*, Buying Club *(Costco, 6 mi.)*

Transportation
OnCall: Rental Car *(Enterprise 693-8688)*, Taxi *(Coastal 635-1144)*, Airport Limo *(H M S 529-3371)* **3+ mi:** Ferry Service *(Princess Acadia to Digby, NS, 7 mi.)* **Airport:** Saint John *(25 mi.)*

Medical Services
911 Service **1-3 mi:** Doctor *(Garland 635-8881)*, Dentist *(Cummings 672-3184)*, Chiropractor *(Bayside 738-8811)* **3+ mi:** Veterinarian *(Saint John 633-4191 , 3.5 mi.)* **Hospital:** Saint John Reg. 648-6000 *(10 mi.)*

Setting -- On the river side of the Reversing Falls where the St. John meets Grand Bay, a rocky breakwater protects Saint John Marina's 125 berths on the east side. On the upland, gray wooden picnic tables surround an all-glass enclosed gazebo with pale blue roof. Behind that, brick red railings lead to a large outdoor deck off the second-floor Upper Deck event space that tops the office and Lower Deck Lounge below.

Marina Notes -- *Weekly, monthly flat rates. $25 min. Founded 1980. New 10 ft. wide docks with 30 ft. finger piers. Closed Jan-Apr. Accommodates up to 125 ft LOA. Dedicated Visitors' dock space. Fuel station with gas, diesel & pump-out. Reserve in advance. Dockhands help with lines. Full-service boatyard. Two marine shops - fiberglass & mechanical. Pool table in first floor lounge. Bathhouse: Off lounge. Simple ceramic tile floors, faux tile walls, fiberglass shower enclosure. Laundry. Note: Two wrecks at NW end of breakwater.

Notable -- Saint John Marina's authentic, recently renovated Mississippi River Boat, the double-decker, stern wheeler "Voyageur II," accommodates 100 passengers for cruises along the St. John and Kennebeccasis Rivers - and is also available for private 2-3 hour cruises with a meal. The newly renovated Lower Deck Lounge, a 75-seat Bar & Grill, offers casual dining inside or on the lawn. The 200-seat Upper Deck Lounge banquet facility opens out onto a 30 by 60 foot deck that overlooks the marina - perfect for a club cruise (see their website for menus). Just three miles north, Grand Bay and the Brundage Point River Centre feature a number of community events - country music concerts, Friday night outdoor films, Artists in Motion special events and Dragon Boat races.

Brundage Point River Centre

PO Box 3001; 4 Ferry Road; Grandbay-Westfield, NB ESK 4V3

Tel: (506) 738-6406 **VHF: Monitor** n/a **Talk** n/a
Fax: (506) 738-6407 **Alternate Tel:** n/a
Email: dcoles@towngbw.ca **Web:** www.town.grandbay-westfield.nb.ca
Nearest Town: Grand Bay-Westfield **Tourist Info:** (506) 658-2855

Navigational Information

Lat: 45°20.858' **Long:** 066°13.373' **Tide:** 3 ft. **Current:** 3 kt. **Chart:** 4141
Rep. Depths (*MLW*): Entry 20 ft. **Fuel Dock** n/a **Max Slip/Moor** -/20 ft.
Access: St John River Just south of Westfield Ferry

Marina Facilities *(In Season/Off Season)*

Fuel: No
Slips: 0 Total, 0 Transient **Max LOA:** 50 ft. **Max Beam:** n/a
Rate *(per ft.)*: **Day** n/a **Week** n/a **Month** n/a
Power: 30 amp n/a, **50 amp** n/a, **100 amp** n/a, **200 amp** n/a
Cable TV: No **Dockside Phone:** No
Dock Type: Floating, Alongside
Moorings: 5 Total, 5 Transient **Launch:** No, Dinghy Dock
Rate: Day Free **Week** n/a **Month** n/a
Heads: 6 Toilet(s)
Internet: Yes *(Wi-Fi, Free)* **Laundry:** None
Pump-Out: No **Fee:** n/a **Closed Heads:** No

Marina Operations

Owner/Manager: Dan Coles **Dockmaster:** Same
In-Season: Jun-LabDay, 8:30am-8:30pm **Off-Season:** Sep-May, *9am-6pm
After-Hours Arrival: Call ahead to inquire about availability
Reservations: No **Credit Cards:** n/a
Discounts: None
Pets: Welcome, Dog Walk Area **Handicap Access:** Yes, Heads, Docks

Marina Services and Boat Supplies

Services - Trash Pick-Up **Communication -** FedEx, UPS, Express Mail
Supplies - 3+ mi: Ships' Store *(Pier Side Marine 738-2194, 4 mi.)*

Boatyard Services

Nearest Yard: Saint John Marina (506) 738-8484

Restaurants and Accommodations

Near: Lite Fare *(Westfield Country Store 757-2511, B $2.75-4.30, L $2-7.50, B & L - Limited menu but all home-made)* **1-3 mi:** Restaurant *(Wong's Chinese)*, *(Jack's Country Kitchen 757-1881)*, Coffee Shop *(Tim Horton's)*, Lite Fare *(Scholten's Take Out)*, *(Aromas Food Court 738-2051)*, Pizzeria *(Pizza Delight 738-8496)*, *(Pizza Shack 738-1122, Del.)* **3+ mi:** Hotel *(Comfort Inn 674-1873, 5 mi.)*, *(Country Inn & Suites 635-0400, 5 mi.)*, *(Delta 648-1981, 5 mi.)*

Recreation and Entertainment

OnSite: Beach *(Also Crystal Beach at campground on other side of ferry landing)*, Picnic Area, Movie Theater *(Outdoor Movie Night 738-6406 Fri 7pm)*, Special Events *(Canada Day; Artists in Motion, Late Sep)* **Near:** Playground *(school)*, Jogging Paths, Hike/Bike Trails *(Eight-mile Heritage Trail lineal park links the river towns - interpretive signs, kiosks, shelters, benches)*, Video Rental *(Westfield Country Store)*, Cultural Attract *(Concerts Unity Park, Grand Bay, Wed 7-8pm)* **1-3 mi:** Tennis Courts *(Englewood)*, Golf Course *(Westfield Golf & Country Club 757-2250)*, Fitness Center *(at the River Valley Community Centre & Curves at Sobey Plaza 757-8255)*, Bowling, For Kids *(River Valley Community Centre Arena and Rink 738-8222 - public sessions)*, Park, Museum *(Mount Hope Farm Historic Site 757-8608)*

Provisioning and General Services

OnSite: Farmers' Market *(Sun 9am-1pm - most weeks, but call to be sure)* **Near:** Convenience Store *(Westfield Country Store 757-2511)*, Catholic Church, Protestant Church **Under 1 mi:** Meat Market *(Morris Meats 738-3301)* **1-3 mi:** Market *(Pumpkin Patch 738-8841)*, Supermarket *(Sobey 738-2353)*, Wine/Beer *(Wine & Stein 738-8085)*, Liquor Store *(Grand Bay 738-3990)*, Bakery *(Village Square 738-8202)*, Bank/ATM *(Irving)*, Post Office, Beauty Salon *(Cutting Edge 738-8412)*, Barber Shop *(Big Mike's 738-9185)*, Hardware Store *(Home 738-8436)*, Florist *(River Valley 738-3249)* **3+ mi:** Dry Cleaners *(3 mi.)*, Pharmacy *(Guardian 738-8406, 3 mi.)*

Transportation

OnSite: Ferry Service *(Westfield Cable Ferry to Hardings Point on Kingston Peninsula)* **OnCall:** Rental Car *(Enterprise 693-8688 - from Saint John)*, Taxi *(Coastal 635-1144)* **Airport:** Saint John *(30 mi.)*

Medical Services

911 Service **Under 1 mi:** Doctor *(Medical Center 738-8426)* **1-3 mi:** Dentist *(Grand Bay Family Dental 738-8449)*, Chiropractor *(Bay Side 738-8811)*, Holistic Services *(Trinity Therapeutic Massage 651-5188; RH Acupuncture 738-9165)*, Veterinarian *(River Valley 738-3306)* **Hospital:** Saint John Regional 648-6000 *(30 mi.)*

Setting -- On the south side of the river, a smart French-blue bow-shaped contemporary building perches on a short rise overlooking nicely landscaped grounds, a single floating dock and small mooring field beyond. A cupola tops the bright blue metal roof and hanging baskets highlight the Brundage Point River Centre's attractive home. A waterside picnic table invites a casual meal. The Grand Bay ferry terminal is adjacent.

Marina Notes -- *Off-season open just Mon-Fri. Five moorings on 2,000 lb cement block, orange balls. One night free. Floating dock for dinghies and short term (3 hr.) dockage 4.5 ft. MLW. Attractive, water-front event space available - up to 64 seated, casual seating for 100, stand-up 150. Special rate for fleet captains & club cruises. $40 to rent space including fully equipped kitchen with all dishes & glassware. Must leave everything as found. Several Caterers in Grand Bay-Westfield. Bathhouse: Fresh & new. Composite wood floors, painted walls, bright blue muni-style dividers. No showers or laundry.

Notable -- For a fun side trip, the virtually onsite Westfield cable ferry crosses the river on demand; on the far side in Harding's Point on Kingston Peninsula is a convenience store, campground and beach. Westfield Country Store and restaurant is an easy walk from the River Centre. The well-supplied market also serves up DVD rentals, fireworks and casual food for breakfast and lunch (burgers, sandwiches, fish & chips, Sun-Thur 9am-3pm, Fri 9am-4pm & Sat 7am-3pm). A little under three miles, Village Square features a bakery, bowling, Home Hardware, barber shop, and Pumpkin Patch grocery. The town of Grand Bay-Westfield is 2.7 miles as is the River Valley Community Centre Arena & Ice Rink - all linked by the Heritage Trail. Start at Unity Park.

PHOTOS ON DVD: 23

Royal Kennebeccasis Yacht Club

1042 Millidge Avenue; Saint John, NB E2K 2P6

Tel: (506) 632-0186 **VHF: Monitor** n/a **Talk** n/a
Fax: (506) 652-3323 **Alternate Tel:** n/a
Email: rkyc1@nbnet.nb.ca **Web:** www.rkyc.nb.ca
Nearest Town: Saint John *(3.5 mi.)* **Tourist Info:** (506) 658-2855

Navigational Information
Lat: 42°18.229' **Long:** 066°06.216' **Tide:** 3 ft. **Current:** 1.5 kt. **Chart:** 4141
Rep. Depths (*MLW*): Entry 10 ft. **Fuel Dock** 8 ft. **Max Slip/Moor** 10 ft./25 ft.
Access: I mile from Reversing Falls

Marina Facilities *(In Season/Off Season)*
Fuel: *Irving* - Slip-Side Fueling, Gasoline, Diesel, High-Speed Pumps
Slips: 135 Total, 10 Transient **Max LOA:** 150 ft. **Max Beam:** 30 ft.
Rate *(per ft.)*: **Day** $1.25* **Week** $300 **Month** Inq.
Power: 30 amp $15**, **50 amp** n/a, **100 amp** n/a, **200 amp** n/a
Cable TV: No **Dockside Phone:** Yes
Dock Type: Floating, Long Fingers, Alongside, Wood
Moorings: 20 Total, 20 Transient **Launch:** n/a, Dinghy Dock
Rate: Day $25 **Week** $125 **Month** n/a
Heads: 6 Toilet(s), 3 Shower(s)
Internet: Yes *(Wi-Fi, Free)* **Laundry:** None
Pump-Out: OnSite, Full Service **Fee:** $10 **Closed Heads:** Yes

Marina Operations
Owner/Manager: Gary Arthurs **Dockmaster:** Same
In-Season: June-August, 10am-8pm **Off-Season:** Sept-Oct, 9am-3pm
After-Hours Arrival: Pick up mooring
Reservations: No **Credit Cards:** Visa/MC
Discounts: None
Pets: Welcome, Dog Walk Area **Handicap Access:** Yes, Heads, Docks

Marina Services and Boat Supplies
Services - Docking Assistance, Boaters' Lounge, Crew Lounge, Security *(Night Time)*, Trash Pick-Up, Dock Carts **Communication -** Mail & Package Hold, Phone Messages, FedEx, DHL, UPS, Express Mail *(Sat Del)* **Supplies - Near:** Ships' Store *(Millidgeville Marine 633-1454)* **3+ mi:** Propane *(Salesse Heating 333-7051, 6.5 km.)*

Boatyard Services
OnSite: Railway *(22T)*, Crane *(28T)*, Launching Ramp, Compound, Wash & Wax **OnCall:** Engine mechanic *(gas, diesel)*, Electrical Repairs, Electronics Repairs, Hull Repairs, Rigger, Sail Loft, Canvas Work, Divers, Bottom Cleaning, Brightwork, Air Conditioning, Refrigeration, Propeller Repairs, Woodworking, Inflatable Repairs, Upholstery, Metal Fabrication **Yard Rates:** Haul & Launch $7/ft.

Restaurants and Accommodations
OnSite: Restaurant *(RKYC D $16.50-23, Thursday night buffet)* **Under 1 mi:** Restaurant *(Thai Hut 657-2726)*, Coffee Shop *(Tim Hortons 658-6133)*, Fast Food *(Wendy's, McDs)* **1-3 mi:** Restaurant *(Reversing Falls Restaurant 635-1999, B $3-10, L $5-10, D $10-20)*, *(Grannan's Seafood 634-1555)*, *(Billy's Seafood 672-3474)*, *(S.J.Ale House 657-2337)*, *(Vito's 634-3900)*, *(Church Street Steakhouse 648-2373)*, *(Copper Penny 633-1100, L $3-5, D $5-15, Pizzas, subs, burgers, entrees, Delivers!)*, Hotel *(Holiday Inn Express 642-2622, $117-139)*, *(Killam Furnished Suites 650-9558, $395-495, weekly)*, *(Hilton 693-8484, $109-199)*, *(Chipman Hill Suites 693-1171, $49-299)*, *(Chateau Saint John 644-4444)*, *(Delta 648-1981)*

Recreation and Entertainment
OnSite: Picnic Area, Grills **1-3 mi:** Beach *(by Boat - Tucker Park)*, Tennis Courts, Golf Course *(Rockwood Park 634-0090)*, Jogging Paths *(Rockwood)*, Horseback Riding *(Rockwood)*, Bowling *(Fairview 652-8480)*, Video Rental *(Movie Tyme 634-1265)*, Museum *(New Brunswick 643-2300)* **3+ mi:** Movie Theater *(Empire 847-7469, 7.5 mi.)*

Provisioning and General Services
Under 1 mi: Convenience Store, Market *(Golden Leaf)*, Bank/ATM, Post Office, Beauty Salon *(Hickey Sisters 214-8222; Silhouette Day Spa 672-2772)*, Barber Shop, Pharmacy *(Pharmasave 658-6094)* **1-3 mi:** Supermarket *(Millidgeville Superstore 658-6054)*, Delicatessen *(Raymond's 642-2859)*, Catholic Church, Protestant Church, Library *(Saint John 643-7220)*, Laundry *(Landstowne Place)*, Hardware Store *(Dykeman's 634-1852)*, Florist, Department Store *(Dollarama 753-2769)* **3+ mi:** Gourmet Shop *(Lancaster 635-1040 , 4 mi.)*, Health Food *(Bulk Barn 634-0910 , 6.5 mi.)*, Farmers' Market *(Sant John City Market 763-3490 - daily , 3.5 mi.)*

Transportation
OnCall: Bikes *(Reversing Falls 634-8987)*, Rental Car *(Enterprise 633-4901)*, Taxi *(Royal 652-5050)* **Near:** Local Bus *(S.J. Transit 658-4700)* **Airport:** Saint John 638-5558 *(18 mi.)*

Medical Services
911 Service **Under 1 mi:** Dentist *(Millidge Place 634-0221)* **1-3 mi:** Doctor *(Saint John Reg. 648-6000)*, Chiropractor *(Hayhoe Naturopathy 652-1778)*, Holistic Services *(Dalling Massage 633-0561)*, Veterinarian *(Saint John Animal 633-4191)* **Hospital:** Saint John Reg. 648-6000 *(3 mi.)*

Setting -- At the mouth of the Kennebecasis River, just off Grand Bay, RKYC sits in the center of Brothers Cove between Indian and Goat Islands. An L-shaped earthen rock berm protects three main docks with wood floating piers managed by a small dockhouse. Haul-out, fuel and learn-to-sail docks are on the north side. The gracious glass-fronted, two-story white clubhouse sports a lookout tower and attractively decorated interior that overlooks the marina.

Marina Notes -- *Flat rate $50. **15A only. Founded 1898. Wait at basinentrance; attendant directs boaters to a mooring or berth & provides orientation. Fuel dock Mon-Fri 11am-8pm, Sat & Sun 9am-6pm. "A" dock slips on one side & dinghy dockage on the other; "B" dock slips on both sides; "C" dock slips on one side & alongside dockage on other. First six slips have finger piers, then it's stern-to. Leash pets. Interior recently renovated - attractive lounge area, windowed dining room. bar. Pool table & large function room upstairs. Active Junior Sailing Programs. Sponsors Historic Coronation Cup for J35s. Bathhouse: Inside - main clubhouse, two modest heads, fiberglass stall showers, small dressing rooms & sink. Italian tile floors. Outside - two heads, 1 shower open 24/7

Notable -- Fifty-six steps lead to the lookout tower's spectacular views across the cove to the islands. Wing chairs snuggle around the fireplace in the recently renovated clubhouse and, adjacent to the bar, a sea of blue and gold barrel chairs invite cocktails or TV viewing. Tables sprawl along the window wall of the dining room. Upstairs are a pool table and large function room - perfect for club cruises.Transients are welcome at all club events, including informal Spar Shed parties. Fast food joints are walking distance; a bus stop within 50 yards provides easy access to laundry, stores, more eateries and Saint John.

PHOTOS ON DVD: 25

Navigational Information
Lat: 45°21.355' **Long:** 066°00.844' **Tide:** 2 ft. **Current:** n/a **Chart:** 4141
Rep. Depths (*MLW*): **Entry** 12 ft. **Fuel Dock** n/a **Max Slip/Moor** 18 ft./18 ft.
Access: Upriver from Reversing Falls on the Kenebecasis

Marina Facilities *(In Season/Off Season)*
Fuel: No
Slips: 5 Total, 0 Transient **Max LOA:** 100 ft. **Max Beam:** n/a
Rate *(per ft.)*: **Day** n/a **Week** n/a **Month** n/a
Power: 30 amp n/a, **50 amp** n/a, **100 amp** n/a, **200 amp** n/a
Cable TV: No **Dockside Phone:** Yes
Dock Type: Fixed, Concrete
Moorings: 55 Total, 2 Transient **Launch:** No, Dinghy Dock
Rate: Day $20 **Week** n/a **Month** n/a
Heads: 1 Toilet(s)
Internet: No **Laundry:** None
Pump-Out: No **Fee:** n/a **Closed Heads:** Yes

Marina Operations
Owner/Manager: Rheal Guimond, Comm **Dockmaster:** Eric Phinney, Hrbms
In-Season: May-Oct, Varies **Off-Season:** Nov-Apr, Closed
After-Hours Arrival: Call in advance
Reservations: No **Credit Cards:** Cash only
Discounts: None
Pets: Welcome **Handicap Access:** Yes

Renforth Boat Club

PO Box 363; 149 James Renforth Drive; Saint John, NB E2L 4L9

Tel: (506) 847-1724 **VHF: Monitor** n/a **Talk** n/a
Fax: n/a **Alternate Tel:** n/a
Email: gsteeves@nbnet.nb.ca **Web:** www3.nbnet.nb.ca/gsteeves/RBC.html
Nearest Town: Rothesay *(3 mi.)* **Tourist Info:** (506) 658-2855

Marina Services and Boat Supplies
Services - Boaters' Lounge **Supplies - 1-3 mi:** Ships' Store *(Seamasters 633-0070)*, Propane *(Alternatives 633-1500)* **3+ mi:** Bait/Tackle *(Bass Tackle Plus 847-1287, 4 mi.)*

Boatyard Services
OnSite: Launching Ramp **Nearest Yard:** Saint John Marina (506) 738-8484

Restaurants and Accommodations
1-3 mi: Restaurant *(Shadow Lawn Inn 847-7539)*, *(Orient Express 847-2288)*, *(Commons Creperie 847-8480)*, Coffee Shop *(Tim Hortons 847-4160)*, *(Red Whale Café 849-1158)*, Fast Food *(KFC, McDs, A&W, DQ, Subways)*, Motel *(Park Plaza 633-4100)*, *(Best Western 657-9966)*, Hotel *(Hampton Inn 647-4600)*, Inn/B&B *(Shadow Lawn Inn 847-7539)*

Recreation and Entertainment
OnSite: Picnic Area, Playground, Park *(Rotary)*, Special Events *(Dragon Boat Festival Late Aug)* **Near:** Beach, Tennis Courts *(McGuire Community Park)*, Jogging Paths, Hike/Bike Trails **Under 1 mi:** Golf Course *(Riverside C.C. 847-7545)* **3+ mi:** Bowling *(Kennebecasis Valley 849-2275, 4 mi.)*, Fishing Charter *(Bass Tackle Plus 847-1287, 4 mi.)*, Movie Theater *(Empire 847-7469, 4 mi.)*, Video Rental *(Block Buster 633-1806, 4 mi.)*

Provisioning and General Services
Under 1 mi: Convenience Store *(Circle K 847-4110)* **1-3 mi:** Supermarket *(Bulk Barn 634-0910)*, Health Food *(Bulk Barn)*, Wine/Beer *(Wine Kitz 847-2739)*, Liquor Store *(NB Liquor 847-6110)*, Library *(East Branch Library 643-7250)*, Bookstore *(Benjamin's - children)*, Pharmacy *(Kennebecasis 847-7581)*, Department Store *(Zellers 633-7540)* **3+ mi:** Bank/ATM *(4 mi.)*, Post Office *(4 mi.)*, Catholic Church *(4 mi.)*, Hardware Store *(Kent 648-1000; Home Depot 632-9440, 4 mi.)*

Transportation
OnCall: Rental Car *(Enterprise 633-4901; Budget 633-3434 - 4 mi. , Enerprise?)*, Taxi *(Diamond 648-8888)* **Airport:** Saint John *(12 mi.)*

Medical Services
911 Service **1-3 mi:** Doctor *(Alexander 849-0099)*, Dentist *(Bonner 633-1086)*, Chiropractor *(Rothesay 847-7263)* **3+ mi:** Holistic Services *(Harmony Hands Massage 849-4263, 4 mi.)*, Veterinarian *(Fairvale 847-7519, 4 mi.)* **Hospital:** KV Medical Clinic 849-2273 *(4 mi.)*

Setting -- A modest natural-color, clapboard-sided clubhouse sits on the shore overlooking the mooring field and Kennebecasis River beyond. The new "L-shaped" 180-foot concrete public wharf sits between it and the adjacent Renforth Rotary Park - with picnic tables, a red and white lighthouse and playground. The Boat Club's dinghy float is directly in front of the clubhouse next to the boat launch.

Marina Notes -- Run by volunteers. Harbormaster Eric Phinney (849-1770) - also rector of St. James the Less Church (846-7696). Nearest fuel is 0.8 mi. south at Torryburn Mainway Circle K Convenience Store. Wi-Fi possible. Single-room clubhouse hosts tables, chairs, a small kitchen, stereo and wood stove. Recently rebuilt 12-foot wide launching ramp. Small craft marine railway. Bathhouse: A single head inside the clubhouse. No shower.

Notable -- Immediately adjacent to the Renforth Boat Club, a crisp candy-cane lighthouse is the visual focus of pretty Renforth Rotary Park and the new Town of Rothesay public concrete wharf - which features a designated swimming area along the north face. Flowers spill out of large planters providing a riot of color. Overlooking the water, a half dozen benches dot the short boardwalk and two picnic tables sit on a cement patio. A creative playground is centered in a swath of carefully tended lawn. Two town tennis courts are just up the street at the McGuire Community Center and a tenth of a mile further, J.M. Fitzgerald Memorial Field is home to a baseball diamond and basketball courts. A perfect location for a hike or a more liesurely stroll; there are beautiful houses along the river. Rothesay's town hall is 4 miles to the north - RBC is in the old Renforth area of Rothesay.

PHOTOS ON DVD: 14

Rothesay Yacht Club

8 Wharf Road; Rothesay, NB E2E 5X1

Tel: (506) 847-7245 **VHF: Monitor** n/a **Talk** n/a
Fax: n/a **Alternate Tel:** n/a
Email: rycmanager@hotmail.com **Web:** rothesayyachtclub.com
Nearest Town: Rothesay *(1.5 mi.)* **Tourist Info:** (506) 658-2855

Navigational Information
Lat: 45°23.611' **Long:** 066°00.997' **Tide:** 3-4 ft. **Current:** n/a **Chart:** 4141
Rep. Depths (*MLW*): Entry 12 ft. **Fuel Dock** n/a **Max Slip/Moor** 10 ft./12 ft.
Access: 7.5 nautical miles NE of Grand Bay near the mouth of the St. John R.

Marina Facilities *(In Season/Off Season)*
Fuel: No
Slips: 100 Total, 3 Transient **Max LOA:** 40 ft. **Max Beam:** 16 ft.
Rate *(per ft.)*: **Day** $0.50* **Week** n/a **Month** $180
Power: 30 amp Incl., **50 amp** n/a, **100 amp** n/a, **200 amp** n/a
Cable TV: No **Dockside Phone:** No
Dock Type: Floating, Alongside, Wood
Moorings: 86 Total, 3 Transient **Launch:** No, Dinghy Dock
Rate: Day $10 **Week** n/a **Month** n/a
Heads: 2 Toilet(s)
Internet: Yes *(Wi-Fi, Free)* **Laundry:** None
Pump-Out: OnSite, Full Service **Fee:** Free **Closed Heads:** No

Marina Operations
Owner/Manager: Denise Snow **Dockmaster:** Mike Dow
In-Season: VicDay-LabDay, 9am-9pm **Off-Season:** Oct-May, 9am-5pm
After-Hours Arrival: Call in advance
Reservations: Yes, Preferred **Credit Cards:** Cash
Discounts: None
Pets: Welcome **Handicap Access:** No

Marina Services and Boat Supplies
Services - Trash Pick-Up, Dock Carts **Communication -** FedEx, UPS **Supplies - OnSite:** Ice *(Block)* **3+ mi:** Ships' Store *(Dykman's Hardware, Milledge Marine, 10 mi.)*

Boatyard Services
OnSite: Crane *(Mast Stepper $25/hr.)*, Launching Ramp *($25)* **Nearest Yard:** RKYC - 9 mi. (506) 632-0186

Restaurants and Accommodations
Near: Restaurant *(Shadow Lawn Inn 847-7539)*, *(Vito's Dining Room & Lounge 847-4400)*, *(Commons Creperie 847-8480)*, Coffee Shop *(Tim Hortons 847-4160)*, *(Red Whale Café 849-1158)*, Pizzeria *(Pizza Delight 849-1199)*, Inn/B&B *(Shadow Lawn)* **Under 1 mi:** Restaurant *(China Coast 847-4448)*, Fast Food *(KFC, McD's, DQ, A&W, Subway KFC, McDs)* **1-3 mi:** Restaurant *(Orient Express 847-2288)*, *(King Pie 216-0052)*, Pizzeria *(Pomodori 847-9663)*, *(Angelo's 849-9090)*, Motel *(Amsterdam Inn 849-8050)* **3+ mi:** Motel *(Amsterdam Inn 849-8050, 4 mi.)*, Hotel *(Hampton Inn 647-4600, 7 mi.)*, *(Hilton Saint John 693-8484, 7 mi.)*

Recreation and Entertainment
OnSite: Grills *(BBQ Hut)* **Near:** Beach *(Long Island)*, Playground *(Rothesay Commons - basketball, too)*, Jogging Paths *(Rothesay Commons)*, Hike/Bike Trails *(Stroll the neighborhood - spectacular vintage waterfront houses)*, Park *(Rothesday Commons)*, Special Events *(NB fine Craft Fest 2nd wk July, St. John Dragon Boat Festival Aug)* **Under 1 mi:** Bowling *(Kennebecasis Valley 849-2275)*, Video Rental *(Blockbuster 849-1118)* **1-3 mi:** Golf Course *(Riverside C.C. 847-7545)*, Movie Theater *(Empire)*

Provisioning and General Services
Near: Bank/ATM *(Scotia Bank)*, Post Office, Protestant Church, Beauty Salon, Barber Shop, Bookstore *(Benjamin's Children's Books 848-1234)* **Under 1 mi:** Catholic Church, Laundry, Pharmacy *(Guardian)* **1-3 mi:** Convenience Store *(Circle K 847-2027)*, Supermarket *(Sobey's 847-5697)*, Hardware Store *(Kent Bldg Supplies)*, Department Store *(Super Store)* **3+ mi:** Liquor Store *(Quispansis, 3 mi.)*

Transportation
OnCall: Taxi *(Valley 849-9000; Independent 848-2323)* **Near:** Local Bus *(to Hampton or to Saint John)* **3+ mi:** Rental Car *(Discount Car & Truck Rental 633-3434, 7 mi.)* **Airport:** Saint John Airport 638-5558 *(10 mi.)*

Medical Services
911 Service **Near:** Doctor *(KV Medical Clinic 849-2273)*, Veterinarian *(Kennebecasis Valley 849-1137)* **Under 1 mi:** Chiropractor *(Rothesay 847-7263)*, Holistic Services *(Harmony Massage 849-4263)* **1-3 mi:** Dentist *(Pettingill 847-2813)* **Hospital:** Saint John Regional 648-6000 *(10 mi.)*

Setting -- Seven and a half miles north of Grand Bay, Rothesay sits across from Ministers Face Long Island beyond Mather Island. A new barrier protects the harbor. Landside, a gray shingled Cape Cod trimmed in blue is topped by a black roof with RYC in big white letters. It's surrounded by trees and a nicely landscaped, shrubbed lawn dotted with white picnic tables. A side deck overlooks the earth berm and docks.

Marina Notes -- *$20/1st 25 ft. , then $0.50/ft.$180/mo. flat rate. Founded 1907. Call when entering Grand Bay. Phones & radio not always monitored, so leave message. 130 full-time members and 40 associates. New long finger has been added to the existing rectangular stone breakwater to completely protect the docks and mooring field - even from the southwest. 150 feet of dedicated side-tie transient dockage on the new floating wharf adjacent to the new earthen barrier. Max LOA 50 ft. on moorings. Anchoring permitted for larger vessels. Mooring holders can pull in to dock while going to town for provisions. Clubhouse has a full kitchen available for club cruises and other events. Catamaran dockage available. Bathhouse: Fairly new, wood vanities, wallpaper borders inside clubhouse. Note: Beware of cable ferry at the river's end past the mooring field.

Notable -- A dragon boat makes its home here. It competes locally and is used by a number of teams for practice. Weekly sailboat races open to all - ask for a handbook and a handicap. RYC also sponsors junior sail regattas. Long Island makes a good dinghy destination - a century ago this tree-covered isle was all pasture. Today there are hiking trails and on the far side several beaches. A paddlewheeler used to stop in the "gut" - between Long and Mathers Islands.

Navigational Information
Lat: 45°35.270' **Long:** 066°01.490' **Tide:** 2 ft. **Current:** 1.5 kt. **Chart:** 4141
Rep. Depths (*MLW*): Entry 25 ft. **Fuel Dock** 25 ft. **Max Slip/Moor** 25 ft./30 ft.
Access: Up river from Reversing Falls past Kennecabasis River

Marina Facilities *(In Season/Off Season)*
Fuel: *PetroCanada* - Slip-Side Fueling, Gasoline, Diesel
Slips: 30 Total, 30 Transient **Max LOA:** 100 ft. **Max Beam:** 30 ft.
Rate *(per ft.)*: **Day** $1.00* **Week** n/a **Month** n/a
Power: 30 amp n/a, **50 amp** n/a, **100 amp** n/a, **200 amp** n/a
Cable TV: No **Dockside Phone:** No
Dock Type: Floating, Alongside, Composition
Moorings: 3 Total, 3 Transient **Launch:** n/a, Dinghy Dock
Rate: Day $20 **Week** n/a **Month** n/a
Heads: 6 Toilet(s), 4 Shower(s) *(dressing rooms)*
Internet: Yes *(Wi-Fi, Free)* **Laundry:** None
Pump-Out: No **Fee:** n/a **Closed Heads:** Yes

Marina Operations
Owner/Manager: Robert Olsen **Dockmaster:** Same
In-Season: May-Oct, 9am-9pm **Off-Season:** Nov-Apr, Closed
After-Hours Arrival: Call in advance
Reservations: No **Credit Cards:** Visa/MC
Discounts: None
Pets: Welcome, Dog Walk Area **Handicap Access:** Yes, Heads

Evandale Resort Marina

3500 Route 124; Evansdale, NB E5M 2G8

Tel: (506) 468-2222 **VHF: Monitor** n/a **Talk** n/a
Fax: (506) 468-1899 **Alternate Tel:** (506) 647-3380
Email: evandalebob@gmail.com **Web:** n/a
Nearest Town: Saint John *(38 mi.)* **Tourist Info:** (506) 658-2855

Marina Services and Boat Supplies
Services - Docking Assistance, Trash Pick-Up **Communication -** Mail & Package Hold, Fax in/out *($1/pg)*, FedEx, UPS, Express Mail **Supplies - OnSite:** Ice *(Cube)*, Ships' Store, Bait/Tackle, Live Bait *(worms)*

Boatyard Services
Nearest Yard: Loyalist Boat Works (506) 738-1850

Restaurants and Accommodations
OnSite: Restaurant *(Evandale Dining Room 468-2222, B $6, L $10, D $12, Break 9-11am in Main dining room, Lounge & Patio. Sunday Dinner Buffet 4-8:30pm)*, Lite Fare *(Evandale Lounge Apps, Fish & Chips, Pot Pies, BBQ - Served in Lounge & Patio)*, Hotel *(Evandale Resort 468-8222, $139-199, 6 ensuite rooms)*

Recreation and Entertainment
OnSite: Heated Pool *(30 ft. by 50 ft.)*, Picnic Area **Near:** Jogging Paths

1-3 mi: Beach **3+ mi:** Golf Course *(Springfield Valley Golf Course 485-8843, 12 mi.)*, Park *(Oak Point Provincial, 7 mi.)*

Provisioning and General Services
OnSite: Convenience Store, Bakery, Bank/ATM **3+ mi:** Market *(Hache HP 783-3737; Ducey's 485-5942, 6 mi.)*, Wine/Beer *(Belle Isle Vineyards 485-8846, 5 mi.)*, Liquor Store *(Norton One-Stop 839-1919, 20 mi.)*, Post Office *(6.5 mi.)*, Catholic Church *(3.5 mi.)*, Protestant Church *(3.5 mi.)*, Pharmacy *(Grand Bay Guardian 738-8406, 23 mi.)*

Transportation
OnSite: Water Taxi *($60/hr.)* **Near:** Ferry Service *(Rte 102 across to Rte 124, year round)* **Airport:** Fredericton/Saint John *(48 mi./50 mi.)*

Medical Services
911 Service **OnCall:** Ambulance **Hospital:** Saint John 648-6000 *(40 mi.)*

Setting -- Three sets of floating paralell docks lie along the river's southern shore connected to the picturesque resort by a long boardwalk. Twenty-five lush green acres surround the sprawling three-story, butter yellow 1889 Victorian Inn - one of the last of the historic St. John Riverboat Hotels. Three dining rooms overlook the eating and sun decks, screened porch, heated pool, a rarity in these parts, as well as the unspoiled riverscape and ferry dock beyond.

Marina Notes -- *700 linear ft. side-tie dockage plus 3 moorings. Recent, upscale floating composite docks. Originally built in 1889 by John O. VanWart as the Hotel VanWart to serve steamboat & rail passengers - tracks once ran in front of hotel. Most recently Eveleigh Hotel. Acquired by current owners Bob & Al Olsen in 2008. Extensive and ongoing restorations and additions maintain the country charm - with much more to come. New innkeepers and young team getting the kinks out. Summer-time alfresco kitchen services lounge & 2500 square foot deck. Convenience store in poolhouse along with amenities. Bathhouse: Changing rooms, new heads & showers and coin-op laundry in poolhouse.

Notable -- Since there is nothing nearby and no way to get to what is further away, Evandale is, happily, a destination marina that invites a lay day or at least a long morning or afternoon. The 25,000 square foot resort features three dinng areas that seat 110 as well as a lounge that seats 60 (Fleet Captains take note). Adjacent to the pool, a large deck hosts umbrella-topped tables for alfresco dining and lounge chairs. For a night ashore, six comfortable ensuite guest rooms, some with jacuzzis, are furnished in Victorian East Lake and other traditional styles. The 18-car Evandale ferry runs a half mile across the river 24/7.

PHOTOS ON DVD: 20

Gagetown Marina & Wharf

50 Front Street; Village of Gagetown, NB E5M 1A1

Tel: (506) 488-1992; (877) 488-1992 **VHF: Monitor** Ch.68 **Talk** Ch.16
Fax: (506) 488-3415 **Alternate Tel:** (506) 261-2309
Email: nancy@gagetownmarina.ca **Web:** gagetownmarina.com
Nearest Town: Fredericton *(15 mi.)* **Tourist Info:** (506) 488-6006

Navigational Information

Lat: 45°46.600' **Long:** 066°08.500' **Tide:** 2 ft. **Current:** 1 kt. **Chart:** 4141
Rep. Depths (*MLW*): Entry 25 ft. **Fuel Dock** 15 ft. **Max Slip/Moor** 20 ft./20 ft.
Access: 0.9 mi north of Gagetown Light

Marina Facilities *(In Season/Off Season)*

Fuel: Slip-Side Fueling, Gasoline, Diesel
Slips: 30 Total, 5 Transient **Max LOA:** 50 ft. **Max Beam:** n/a
Rate *(per ft.)*: **Day** $1.25* **Week** n/a **Month** n/a
Power: 30 amp Incl***, **50 amp** n/a, **100 amp** n/a, **200 amp** n/a
Cable TV: No **Dockside Phone:** No
Dock Type: Floating, Alongside, Wood
Moorings: 24 Total, 10 Transient **Launch:** No, Dinghy Dock
Rate: Day $25 **Week** n/a **Month** $525
Heads: 4 Toilet(s), 2 Shower(s) *(dressing rooms)*, Book Exchange
Internet: Yes *(Wi-Fi - Docks & Pub, Free)* **Laundry:** 3 Washer(s), 3 Dryer(s)
Pump-Out: Full Service, 1 Central **Fee:** $10** **Closed Heads:** Yes

Marina Operations

Owner/Manager: Nancy McQuade Webb **Dockmaster:** Same
In-Season: Mid-May-Oct, 9am-9pm **Off-Season:** Nov-Mid-May, Closed
After-Hours Arrival: After 8pm, tie up at the fuel dock. Go to the Pub
Reservations: Yes, Preferred **Credit Cards:** Visa/MC, Amex, Irving, Debit
Discounts: None
Pets: Welcome, Dog Walk Area **Handicap Access:** No

Marina Services and Boat Supplies

Services - Docking Assistance, Trash Pick-Up, Dock Carts **Communication -** Pay Phone, FedEx, UPS, Express Mail **Supplies - OnSite:** Ice *(Block, Cube)*, Ships' Store *(Village Boatique 488-6006 - plus catalog orders)*, Live Bait, Propane *(arge tanks at Irving)*

Boatyard Services

OnCall: Engine mechanic *(gas, diesel)*, Air Conditioning, Refrigeration **Near:** Launching Ramp.

Restaurants and Accommodations

OnSite: Restaurant *(The Old Boot Pub/Dockside 488-3441, B $4-7, L $6-14, D $6-14)*, Lite Fare *(Dockside Bar)*, Pizzeria *(The Old Boot Pub)* **Near:** Restaurant *(Creek View 488-9806)*, Inn/B&B *(Step-Aside 488-1808, $60-80, 5 rooms in an 1880s riverside house - includes full breakfast)*, *(Doctor's Hill 3 rooms)* **Under 1 mi:** Condo/Cottage *(Ferryland Adventures 488-3263, $100-150, 3 units overlooking St. John River)*

Recreation and Entertainment

OnSite: Picnic Area, Grills, Boat Rentals *(Kayaks $15/hr., $45/half day, $75/day & Canoes $10/hr, $30/half day, $50/day)*, Hike/Bike Trails **Near:** Playground *(school)*, Fishing Charter *(Parks Lake)*, Video Rental *(gas station across street)*, Park *(Rotary Park Landing & Mount Ararat Wildlife Management Area - across the Creek on Gagetown Island - canoe/kayak destination)*, Museum *(James McNichol & Wm. H. Needham Orange Lodge 488-8884 Sat noon-5pm; Queens County Hist. Soc.- Tilley House & Queens County Court House 488-2483 - both 7 days 10am-5pm MidJun-MidSep)*, Cultural Attract *(A Celebration of Birds 488-1888 Naturalist Club events - 263 species of birds sighted w/in 9 mi. of Gagetown)*, Sightseeing *(Just stroll the village - stop by St. John Anglican Church)*, Galleries *(44 Front St - 488-8193 - 30 artists exhibit; G.A.S. Community fine arts & crafts; Greig Pottery 488-2074; Grimcross Crafts artisans & craftsmen 7 days, June-Oct; Juggler's Cove Pottery & Fine Arts - 488-2574 - 7 days; Loomcrofters 488-2400; O'Hara's)*, Special Events *(Queens County Fair, Mid-Sep; Spring into summer Fest mid-Jun; Gagetown Jubilee 3rd week Jun)*

Provisioning and General Services

OnSite: Bank/ATM, Hardware Store *(Ships' Store)*, Retail Shops *(Village Boatique - clothing, local arts & crafts, t-shirts & boat supplies)*, Copies Etc. **Near:** Market *(Nan's Country Store 488-2553)*, Supermarket *(K&W 488-6328 groceries & liquor)*, Wine/Beer, Liquor Store *(Nan's)*, Meat Market *(Irving)*, Post Office, Catholic Church, Protestant Church, Beauty Salon *(Mani-Pedi at Spa)* **Under 1 mi:** Green Grocer *(Cameron's Orchard - U-Pick 488-2895 Mid-Aug-Dec; Charlotte's Family Orchard U-pick 488-2630 - both apples, pears, plums, veggies)* **1-3 mi:** Farmers' Market *(July & Aug every day - Jemseg)*

Transportation

OnSite: Courtesy Car/Van *(Marina car - replace gas)* **OnCall:** Rental Car *(Enterprise 459-4100)* **Under 1 mi:** Ferry Service *(Cable Ferry to Lower Jemseg - 800-561-4063- 24 hrs. Free)* **Airport:** Fredericton *(20 mi.)*

Medical Services

911 Service **Near:** Holistic Services *(Blue Lotus Spa, massages)* **Under 1 mi:** Doctor *(Haines)* **Hospital:** Oromocto 357-4700 *(22 mi.)*

Setting -- Just off the St. John River, the marina's docks sprawl along Gagetown Creek with alongside tie-ups on both sides of an 875-foot floating dock. The Dockside Bar, an alfresco patio, overlooks the water, backed by the The Old Boot Pub a bit further up the bank. Across the creek is pristine Gagetown Island and a block inland, the small, pretty, arts-centered village clusters along Front Street and Tilley Road.

Marina Notes -- *830 ft. side-tie dockage. Flat Rate to 50 ft. 21-30 ft. $35, 31-40 ft. $50, 41-50 ft. $60, Over 50 ft, $60 + $1/ft.. Docks/Moorings: any 10 nights for price of 7. **Free to marina guests. ***15A &30A. 50A only if seasonal tenant away. Owner Nancy MacQuade Webb continually upgrades amenities. Reservations recommended - prime stop plus many seasonals. Expect help with lines. Included in transient fees: private showers, water, power, waste disposal, pump-out, and Wi-Fi on the docks & in the pub. No repair personnel on staff; talented residents usually available plus many services are on-call. Fun events held frequently at the pub. Bathhouse: Recent half & full baths with glass shower doors - immediately south under "Grimross Crafts" sign.

Notable -- A popular gathering spot, The Old Boot Pub bar is actually a 22-foot long boat. The Village Boatique serves up marine supplies, fudge, logoed clothing, all manner of gifts - and is the village tourism center. K&W is a remarkably well-supplied supermarket. Stroll the village. Engaging Gagetown is a magnet for artists - galleries feature the work of local artisans and fine artists. Queens County Historical Society maintains provincial and national historic sites. Across the creek, Mount Ararat Wildlife area beckons kayakers. A short walk out of town are two U-pick farms. Major services are in Fredericton/Oromocto.

Navigational Information
Lat: 45°55.182' **Long:** 066°05.944' **Tide:** n/a **Current:** n/a **Chart:** 4142
Rep. Depths (*MLW*): Entry 40 ft. **Fuel Dock** n/a **Max Slip/Moor** -/12 ft.
Access: Jemsburg to Grand Lake to Douglas Harbour

Marina Facilities *(In Season/Off Season)*
Fuel: No
Slips: 0 Total, 0 Transient **Max LOA:** 50 ft. **Max Beam:** n/a
Rate *(per ft.)*: **Day** n/a **Week** n/a **Month** n/a
Power: 30 amp n/a, **50 amp** n/a, **100 amp** n/a, **200 amp** n/a
Cable TV: No **Dockside Phone:** Yes
Dock Type: n/a
Moorings: 35 Total, 8 Transient **Launch:** No, Dinghy Dock
Rate: Day $10 **Week** n/a **Month** n/a
Heads: 2 Toilet(s), 2 Shower(s), Book Exchange
Internet: No **Laundry:** None
Pump-Out: OnSite, Self Service **Fee:** Free **Closed Heads:** Yes

Marina Operations
Owner/Manager: Fredericton Yacht Club **Dockmaster:** Sterling Keays
In-Season: Jun-Sep, Dawn to Dusk **Off-Season:** Oct-May, Closed
After-Hours Arrival: Anchor or use club mooring
Reservations: No **Credit Cards:** Cash only - pay at Hunter's One-Stop
Discounts: None
Pets: Welcome, Dog Walk Area **Handicap Access:** No

Fredericton Yacht Club

PO Box 25; Fredericton, NB* E3B 4Y2

Tel: (506) 457-6282 **VHF: Monitor** Ch.16 **Talk** Ch.68
Fax: (506) 457-6054 **Alternate Tel:** n/a
Email: info@fyc.ca **Web:** www.fyc.ca
Nearest Town: Minto *(15 mi.)* **Tourist Info:** (506) 433-6602

Marina Services and Boat Supplies
Supplies - Near: Ice *(Cube)*

Boatyard Services
OnSite: Launching Ramp

Restaurants and Accommodations
Near: Lite Fare *(Hunter's One-Stop Take-Away L & D $2.50-8.25 Burgers, Sandwiches, Platters)*

Provisioning and General Services
Near: Convenience Store *(Hunter's One-Stop-General Store 385-2292)*, Wine/Beer *(Hunter's)*, Liquor Store *(Hunter's-One-Stop)*, Laundry *(Hunter's One-Stop 8am-10pm)*, Newsstand **3+ mi:** Supermarket *(Minto Foodland 327-3024, 14 mi.)*, Library *(Minto 327-3220, 13 mi.)*

Transportation
OnCall: Taxi *(Minto 327-3246 - 15 mi.)* **Airport:** Fredericton International *(15 mi.)*

Medical Services
911 Service **OnCall:** Ambulance **Hospital:** Minto 327-7800 *(13 mi.)*

Setting -- Tucked into small, quiet Douglas Harbour off Grand Lake, Fredericton Yacht Club has made this outpost its primary moorage. The dinghy float provides access to the mooring field across the harbour on the far side of the channel - known as The Bedroom. A small, tan, clapboard-sided single-room building serves as a utilitarian clubhouse. FYC also owns the 120-foot concrete historic wharf; the surroundings are gloriously untouched and pristine.

Marina Notes -- *Contact info for the main clubhouse in Fredericton. Physically the facility is on Rte. 690 at McGowans Corner in Douglas Harbour. Formerly Douglas Harbour Marina on Grand Lake once owned by Hunter's One-Stop. Pretty much totally "self-serve." For a key to the clubhouse, pump-out and amenities, visitors walk or dinghy to Hunter's One-Stop Convenience Store. The "Clubhouse" contains two picnic tables, assorted chairs and a book exchange. Bathhouse: Two recent full baths - vanity sink and fiberglass shower stall. Laundry with three washers & three dryers at Hunter's One-Stop.

Notable -- Douglas Harbour is a Grand Lake Meadows Interpretive Site. Its 3100 hectacres form a unique warm, dry microclimate that berths several unique species, including Bur Oak, Silver Maple and Butternut trees, as well as large populations of rare Yellow Rail, Black Tern and Wilson's Phalarope. It's a critical part of the St. John River Wetlands - the largest freshwater habitat in the Maritimes. Nearby Hunter's One-Stop General Store sells gas, groceries, wine, beer, spirits and ice - there is literally nothing else near. Turn right at the head of the driveway or dinghy up the channel - a rickety small boat floating dock provides easy access to Hunter's. The well-supplied market also sports a little take-out stand and a covered picnic pavilion.

PHOTOS ON DVD: 16

Newcastle Creek Yacht Club

4028 Rte 690 - The Wharf Road; Newcastle Creek, NB E4B 2K7

Tel: (506) 327-6708 **VHF: Monitor** Ch. 63 **Talk** Ch. 63
Fax: n/a **Alternate Tel:** (506) 327-6708
Email: jdebouver@nbpoiner.com **Web:** www.ncyc.webs.com
Nearest Town: Minto *(3 mi.)* **Tourist Info:** (506) 433-6602

Navigational Information

Lat: 46°03.428' **Long:** 066°00.450' **Tide:** n/a **Current:** n/a **Chart:** 4142
Rep. Depths (*MLW*): Entry 20 ft. **Fuel Dock** n/a **Max Slip/Moor** 12 ft./20 ft.
Access: Jemseg River to Grand Lake

Marina Facilities *(In Season/Off Season)*

Fuel: No
Slips: 25 Total, 2 Transient **Max LOA:** 65 ft. **Max Beam:** 15 ft.
Rate *(per ft.)*: **Day** $1.00 **Week** n/a **Month** n/a
Power: 30 amp Incl., **50 amp** n/a, **100 amp** n/a, **200 amp** n/a
Cable TV: No **Dockside Phone:** No
Dock Type: Floating, Long Fingers, Alongside, Wood
Moorings: 4 Total, 0 Transient **Launch:** No, Dinghy Dock
Rate: Day n/a **Week** n/a **Month** n/a
Heads: 1 Toilet(s)
Internet: No **Laundry:** None
Pump-Out: OnSite, Self Service, 1 Central **Fee:** Free **Closed Heads:** Yes

Marina Operations

Owner/Manager: Jason Debouver **Dockmaster:** Tim Thornton
In-Season: May-Nov, 9am-Dusk **Off-Season:** Dec-Apr, Closed
After-Hours Arrival: Call in Advance
Reservations: Yes, Preferred **Credit Cards:** Cash only
Discounts: None
Pets: Welcome, Dog Walk Area **Handicap Access:** No

Marina Services and Boat Supplies

Services - Boaters' Lounge, Security *(24 hrs., camera)*, Trash Pick-Up **Communication -** Pay Phone (1) **Supplies - 1-3 mi:** Ships' Store *(DiCarlo's Home Hardware 327-3308)*, Propane *(Corbin's Irving 327-4227)*

Boatyard Services

OnSite: Engine mechanic *(gas)* **Under 1 mi:** Hydraulic Trailer *(15T)*, Engine mechanic *(diesel)*. **1-3 mi:** Electrical Repairs *(Upton Marine Services)*, Electronics Repairs *(Upton)*, Air Conditioning *(Miller AC & Heating)*, Refrigeration *(Miller)*, Metal Fabrication *(Minto Machine Shop)*.

Restaurants and Accommodations

1-3 mi: Restaurant *(Silver Dragon 327-1188)*, *(Omega 327-3759)*, *(MacFarlane's 327-3639)*, *(Maciver's Family 327-8982)*, Coffee Shop *(Tim Hortons)*, Lite Fare *(Myjaken's Take-Out 327-9098)*, Pizzeria *(Twins 327-4477, delivers)* **3+ mi:** Motel *(Ashdon Place 327-8805, 5 mi.)*

Recreation and Entertainment

OnSite: Picnic Area **Near:** Jogging Paths, Park **1-3 mi:** Pool, Playground, Tennis Courts, Golf Course *(Ridgeview Greens Golf & CC 327-3535 - 9 holes and a casual eatery)*, Video Rental, Museum *(Minto Museum 327-4573/ 327-9083 - in restored train depot with a caboose; NB Internment Camp Museum 327-3573 $1.50/free Mon-Fri 10am-5pm, Sat & Sun noon-5pm)*, Cultural Attract *(Minto Sports & Country Music Walls of Fame - 452-2992, Minto Library)*, Special Events *(July 1st Summer Fest)*

Provisioning and General Services

1-3 mi: Convenience Store *(Corbin's 327-6861)*, Supermarket *(Dunbar's Save Easy 327-3320 & Minto Foodland 327-3024)*, Wine/Beer, Liquor Store, Bank/ATM *(Scotia Bank)*, Post Office, Catholic Church, Protestant Church, Library *(Minto 327-3220 - internet access)*, Beauty Salon, Laundry, Pharmacy *(Shoppers Drug Mart 327-3396)*, Hardware Store *(DiCarlo's Home 327-3308)*, Florist *(Daamen's 327-3379)*, Retail Shops, Department Store *(Great Canadian 327-8383)*

Transportation

OnCall: Taxi *(Dad's 327-3337)* **Airport:** Chipman Airport *(15 mi.)*

Medical Services

911 Service **OnCall:** Ambulance **1-3 mi:** Doctor *(Haynes 327-3347; Morrissy 327-3309)*, Dentist *(Minto 327-3980)*, Veterinarian *(Country Vet 327-4466)* **Hospital:** Oromocto Public 357-4700 *(30 mi.)*

Setting -- In the shadow of the Grand Lake Generating Station on McMann Point, NCYC is on the site of an original 120-foot concrete steamship wharf that sits in the center of a small cove off East Grand Lake. A single pier parallels the wharf and shore with stern-to slips on both sides. Additional dockage is alongside the historic wharf. The generating station's conspicuous red-and-white banded chimney - topped by red aircraft lights - makes it hard to miss.

Marina Notes -- NCYC, formerly Grand Lake Boaters, founded in 1997. At New Castle Creek Marina. Private Club - enthusiastically welcomes visitors. Volunteer-run so telephone frequently isn't answered and contact is difficult or impossible. Use website or plan on just "showing up." Free pump-out onsite. Floating piers are laid from the concrete wharf which is 120 ft. long by 50 ft. wide. Nearest Fuel (gas & diesel) 3 miles at either Corbin's Irving (327-4227) or Shell (327-4334) in Minton. Bathouse: Single Porta-Pottie.

Notable -- The family-oriented membership is devoted to restoring old working boats - converting them to lovely recreational vessels. It's worth a stop just to admire the fleet. The adjacent Grand Lakes Generating Station created energy from coal mined nearby from 1931 until 2010 (coal mining started here in the 1600s). All services and supplies are three miles away packed into Minto's four-block business district. At the library, on the municipal building's second floor, the Minto Sports Wall of Fame and the Minto Country Music Wall of Fame honor more than 50 regional country musicians and athletes. The Minto Museum, housed in the old train station, focuses on mining and railroading, and the fascinating 2,000 square foot NB Internment Camp Museum features 600 artifacts.

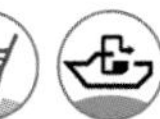

Navigational Information
Lat: 46°10.370' **Long:** 065°32.550' **Tide:** n/a **Current:** n/a **Chart:** 4142
Rep. Depths (*MLW*): Entry 10 ft. **Fuel Dock** n/a **Max Slip/Moor** 8 ft./-
Access: East end of Grand Lake up Salmon River

Marina Facilities *(In Season/Off Season)*
Fuel: No
Slips: 10 Total, 10 Transient **Max LOA:** 40 ft. **Max Beam:** 10 ft.
Rate *(per ft.)*: **Day** $0* **Week** n/a **Month** n/a
Power: 30 amp n/a, **50 amp** n/a, **100 amp** n/a, **200 amp** n/a
Cable TV: No **Dockside Phone:** No
Dock Type: Floating, Alongside, Wood
Moorings: 0 Total, 0 Transient **Launch:** n/a
Rate: Day n/a **Week** n/a **Month** n/a
Heads: 2 Toilet(s)
Internet: No **Laundry:** 1 Washer(s), 1 Dryer(s)
Pump-Out: OnSite, Full Service **Fee:** Free **Closed Heads:** No

Marina Operations
Owner/Manager: Village of Chipman **Dockmaster:** Mark Glenn
In-Season: July-Sep 15, 9am-9pm **Off-Season:** Sep 16-Jun, Closed
After-Hours Arrival: None
Reservations: No **Credit Cards:** Cash only
Discounts: None
Pets: Welcome, Dog Walk Area **Handicap Access:** No

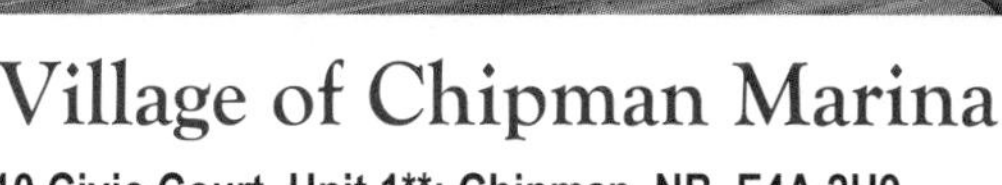

Village of Chipman Marina

10 Civic Court, Unit 1; Chipman, NB E4A 2H9**

Tel: (506) 339-6604 **VHF: Monitor** n/a **Talk** n/a
Fax: (506) 339-6197 **Alternate Tel:** n/a
Email: villchip@nbnet.nb.ca **Web:** www.chipmannb.com
Nearest Town: Chipman **Tourist Info:** (506) 339-6601

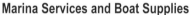

Marina Services and Boat Supplies
Services - Trash Pick-Up, Dock Carts **Communication -** FedEx, UPS
Supplies - Near: Ice *(Block, Cube)*, Ships' Store *(Napa 339-6642)*, Propane *(Irving 339-6673)*

Boatyard Services
OnSite: Launching Ramp **Near:** Yacht Interiors *(Hoyt's 339-6665)*.

Restaurants and Accommodations
Near: Restaurant *(Queens County Inn - Restaurant & Lounge 339-6677, across bridge)*, Lite Fare *(Karen's Take-Out 339-5826)*, *(M & R Take-Out 339-6222)*, *(Greco Express 339-5826)*, *(Dee's Diner & Takout 339-5587)* **Under 1 mi:** Motel *(Cozy Pines 339-6810)*, Inn/B&B *(Queens County 339-6677)*

Recreation and Entertainment
OnSite: Picnic Area, Grills, Playground *(also at Hamilton Baird Park)*, Museum *(Village of Chipman - in Railway Car)* **Near:** Hike/Bike Trails *(The Nature Trail connects Main Street & Wegesegum Lane)*, Video Rental, Park *(Chipman Woodlands; Hamilton Baird Park)*, Special Events *(Chipman Summer Fest)* **Under 1 mi:** Beach *(Hamilton Baird Park)*, Tennis Courts *(Hamilton Baird)*, Boat Rentals *(Kayaks)*, Bowling *(Chipman Bowl-A-Rama - arcade, canteen & pool tables)*, Volleyball *(Hamilton Baird)*, Video Arcade *(Bowl-A-Rama)* **1-3 mi:** Horseback Riding *(Russ Rasmussen 339-5697)* **3+ mi:** Golf Course *(Ridgeview Greens Golf & CC 327-3535 - 9 holes and a casual eatery, 12 mi.)*

Provisioning and General Services
Near: Convenience Store *(Doherty's Kwik-Way; Irving Mainway; Wilson's)*, Supermarket *(Chipman Save Easy 339-5855; Value Foods 339-8888)*, Wine/Beer, Liquor Store *(NB Liquor at Irving Mainway)*, Green Grocer *(Slocum's Produce 362-5544 Jul-Sep)*, Bank/ATM *(Scotia 339-1820)*, Post Office, Catholic Church *(St. Andrews)*, Protestant Church *(St. Augustine Anglican)*, Library *(Chipman 339-5852, Internet Access)*, Beauty Salon *(Beth's 339-5252; Clipper's 339-6625)*, Barber Shop, Pharmacy *(Shoppers Drug Mart 339-6686)*, Newsstand, Hardware Store *(Napa Auto Parts 339-6642)*, Florist *(Chipman 339-6073)*

Transportation
OnCall: Taxi *(Dad's -327-3337 - from Minto)* **Near:** InterCity Bus *(Acadian Bus Service 458-6000 to/from Fredericton)* **Airport:** Fredericton/Chipman *(55 mi./1 mi.)*

Medical Services
911 Service **OnCall:** Ambulance **Near:** Doctor *(Chipman Health Centre 339-7650)*, Holistic Services *(Relief Massage Therapy)* **3+ mi:** Dentist *(Flemming 327-3980, 9 mi.)*, Veterinarian *(Country Vet 327-4466, 3.5 mi.)*
Hospital: Oromocto Public 357-4700 *(50 mi.)*

Setting -- These modest docks, situated in the small village of Chipman, provide a destination for the scenic trip up the Salmon River from the head of Grand Lake. Just shy of the Route 10 bridge, a single boardwalk leads from two floating parallel, side-tie docks to a casual park. A bandstand, a pair of picnic pavilions and the bathhouse - all topped by pyramidal roofs - overlook the river; an antique railway car houses the Chipman Museum. The village is a block away.

Marina Notes -- *400 feet side-tie Free dockage. **Contact address is Village Hall - not marina address which is on Main Street close to King St. No power. Nearest fuel (gas & diesel) - 4 miles at local service station. Bathhouse: Two basic heads - no showers in gray clapboard building. Washer & Dryer.

Notable -- The Village of Chipman is an industrial timber town (J.D. Irving Woodlands and Grand Lake Timber) that has worked hard to expand its amenities to create a pleasant, attractive environment - with lots of parks, an arena with a ballfield and good supplies and services. The timber companies have both created the industrial climate and contributed generously to changing it. The Chipman Museum, housed in an antique railroad car, tells the story of Chipman through memorabilia collected from the local citizenry. Irving's Grand Lake Timber and J.D. Irving Woodlands are close to the docks. Acres of felled trees sprawl along the roadway. A pretty park lies between the mill and road. Chipman rewards the long cruise up river with bountiful provisioning sources - several convenience stores, two supermarkets and farm-fresh seasonal produce. Along Main Street, a very short walk from the docks, there's also a Napa hardware store, hair salons, a few casual eateries and an ice cream shop. The small, well-supplied library offers computers with internet access.

Oromocto Boat Club & Marina

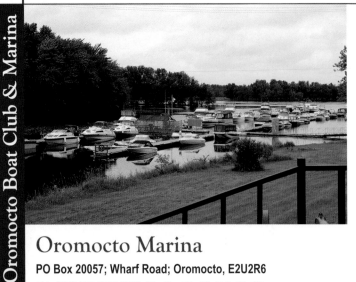

Oromocto Marina

PO Box 20057; Wharf Road; Oromocto, E2U2R6

Tel: (506) 357-7374 **VHF: Monitor** Ch. 68 **Talk** Ch. 28
Fax: (506) 454-3396 **Alternate Tel:** (506) 454-2577
Email: marilynblais@live.ca **Web:** www.oromoctoboatclub.ca
Nearest Town: Oromocto **Tourist Info:** (506) 446-5010

Navigational Information

Lat: 45°51.125' **Long:** 066°28.360' **Tide:** 0 ft. **Current:** n/a **Chart:** 4142
Rep. Depths (*MLW*): Entry 9 ft. **Fuel Dock** 6 ft. **Max Slip/Moor** 17 ft./-
Access: Intersection of St. John River & Oromocto River

Marina Facilities *(In Season/Off Season)*

Fuel: *Regular & Hi-Test* - Gasoline
Slips: 110 Total, 10 Transient **Max LOA:** 60 ft. **Max Beam:** n/a
Rate *(per ft.)*: **Day** $1.00* **Week** n/a **Month** n/a
Power: 30 amp Incl.**, **50 amp** n/a, **100 amp** n/a, **200 amp** n/a
Cable TV: No **Dockside Phone:** No
Dock Type: Floating, Long Fingers, Wood
Moorings: 0 Total, 0 Transient **Launch:** n/a, Dinghy Dock
Rate: Day n/a **Week** n/a **Month** n/a
Heads: 2 Toilet(s), 2 Shower(s)
Internet: Yes *(Wi-Fi, Free)* **Laundry:** 1 Washer(s), 1 Dryer(s)
Pump-Out: Full Service, 1 Central **Fee:** Free **Closed Heads:** Yes

Marina Operations

Owner/Manager: Town of Oromocto **Dockmaster:** Rene Desaulniers
In-Season: Jun-Oct 15, 10am-9pm **Off-Season:** Oct 16-May, Closed
After-Hours Arrival: Call Ch. 68
Reservations: Yes, Preferred **Credit Cards:** Cash Only
Discounts: None
Pets: Welcome, Dog Walk Area **Handicap Access:** Yes

Marina Services and Boat Supplies

Services - Docking Assistance, Security *(Security Cameras)*, Trash Pick-Up, Dock Carts **Communication -** FedEx, UPS, Express Mail **Supplies - OnSite:** Ice *(Block, Cube)* **1-3 mi:** Propane *(Canadien Tire 357-3304)* **3+ mi:** Marine Discount Store *(Phil's Auto 446-6135, 3 mi.)*

Boatyard Services

Near: Launching Ramp. **3+ mi:** Electronic Sales *(Phil's Auto & Recreation 446-6135, 3 mi.)*.

Restaurants and Accommodations

Near: Restaurant *(Dragon Boat Restaurant 357-8282, L $7-14, D $7-14)*, Coffee Shop *(Tim Hortons 357-9699, B $3-6, L $3-6, D $3-6)*, Fast Food *(KFC, McD's, A&W)*, Pizzeria *(Pizza Delight 357-3359)* **1-3 mi:** Restaurant *(Jungle Jim's Eatery 623-5467, L $6-10, D $7-16)*, *(Brookside Restaurant 776-8383, L $5-20, D $5-20)*, Motel *(Days Inn Oromocto 357-5657, $105-230)* **3+ mi:** Hotel *(Crowne Plaza Fredericton Lord Beaverbrook 455-3371, $142-369, 12 mi.)*

Recreation and Entertainment

OnSite: Picnic Area *(BBQ dockside)*, Playground, Jogging Paths, Park *(Sir Douglas Hazen)*, Special Events *(Pioneer Days, 1st wknd July)* **Near:** Fitness Center *(Curves)*, Boat Rentals *(Eco-Logical Adventures 357-6868. Kayaks $15/hr., $30 half-day, $50 full day. Canoes & double kayaks $20/hr., $40 half-day, $60/Full Day. Sailboat $25/hr., $100/day)*, Hike/Bike Trails *(Sentier NB Bike Trail 800-526-7070 - Eco-Logical offers bike tours)*, Tours *(Kayak Tours $40/pp min 4)* **1-3 mi:** Golf Course *(Gage Golf 357-9343, military 18-hole course open to public)*, Movie Theater *(Base Theater 446-3613)*, Museum *(CFB Gagetown Military Museum 422-1304)*

Provisioning and General Services

Near: Supermarket *(Atlantic Superstore)*, Wine/Beer, Farmers' Market *(Sat, 9am-3pm, Hazen Park - small with limited food & crafts)*, Bank/ATM *(ScotiaBank, Royal Bank)*, Post Office, Catholic Church, Protestant Church, Beauty Salon, Barber Shop, Pharmacy *(Shoppers Drug Mart 357-5566)*, Newsstand, Retail Shops *(Oromocto Mall incl. Giant Tiger, Dollarama)*, Department Store *(Bargain Shop 446-4844)*, Buying Club *(SuperStore)* **Under 1 mi:** Library *(Oromocto 357-3329)*, Hardware Store *(Canadien Tire)*, Copies Etc. *(Pharmachoice 357-9808)* **3+ mi:** Laundry *(4 mi.)*

Transportation

OnCall: Rental Car *(Enterprise 459-4100; National 446-4105)* **Near:** Bikes *(Eco-Logical 357-6868 $5/hr.)*, Taxi *(Town Taxi Oromocto 357-3341)* **Airport:** Greater Fredericton 460-0920 *(6 mi.)*

Medical Services

911 Service **OnCall:** Ambulance **Near:** Doctor *(Fraser 357-8060)*, Chiropractor *(Oromocto Family 357-8803)* **Under 1 mi:** Holistic Services *(Carlisle Professional Massage Therapy 446-5088)* **1-3 mi:** Dentist *(Oromocto Dental Centre 446-3300)*, Veterinarian *(Oromocto Vet. Hospital 357-8880)* **Hospital:** Oromocto Public 357-4700 *(0.6 mi.)*

Setting -- At the mouth of Oromocto River between Thatch Island and Hazen Park, this busy marina shares the quiet waterway with multitudes of kayakers. Landside, the well-manicured park features sheltered picnic tables on concrete platforms, a bandstand, a replica log fort and wooden benches tucked under trees. Across the river, livestock roam on unspoiled, grassy Thatch Island lending a bucolic ambiance to the marina.

Marina Notes -- *Flat rate $35 to 42 ft., add'l fee over 42 ft. Rates under review - call to confirm. **15A & 30A power. Owned by Town of Oromocto. Recently expanded & renovated. 1200 ft. face docks. Pump-out on separate floating dock south of main docks. Gasoline available onsite. Covered BBQs with tables on dock. Welcome package with info about marina & town services provided. Free Wi-Fi. Water treatment plant up river. Bathhouse: Public heads in the brown block building. Private fiberglass showers and heads just for marina guests plus free stacked washer/dryer in the replica log fort (24/7).

Notable -- Sir Douglas Hazen Park is the site of Pioneer Day, summer concerts and canoe & kayak rentals. Eco-Logical Adventures is the go-to place for all manner of water and biking sports - lessons, rentals & tours. A path leads to Deer Park, which sports many trails that wind through wetlands, oOr explore further up river in the dinghy or kayak. Less than a 5-minute walk, the community center hosts a weekly market, and a shopping mall includes a supermarket, pharmacy, hardware store, bakery, restaurants and retail shops. Oromocto is one of Canada's "model" towns. It is also home to Canada's Forces Base (CFB) Gagetown, one of the largest military bases in the commonwealth - which also berths the open-to-the-public Military Museum and golf course.

2. NB - ST. JOHN RIVER

PHOTOS ON DVD: 21

Navigational Information

Lat: 45°57.805' **Long:** 066°38.137' **Tide:** 1.5 ft. **Current:** 5 kt. **Chart:** 4142
Rep. Depths (*MLW*): **Entry** 10 ft. **Fuel Dock** n/a **Max Slip/Moor** 10 ft./12 ft.
Access: St. John River head of navigation

Marina Facilities *(In Season/Off Season)*

Fuel: Gasoline
Slips: 50 Total, 10 Transient **Max LOA:** 50 ft. **Max Beam:** 20 ft.
Rate *(per ft.)*: **Day** $1.50* **Week** n/a **Month** n/a
Power: 30 amp Incl., **50 amp** n/a, **100 amp** n/a, **200 amp** n/a
Cable TV: No **Dockside Phone:** No
Dock Type: Floating, Alongside, Wood
Moorings: 24 Total, 4 Transient **Launch:** No, Dinghy Dock
Rate: Day $20 **Week** n/a **Month** n/a
Heads: 4 Toilet(s), 4 Shower(s) *(dressing rooms)*
Internet: Yes *(Wi-Fi, Free)* **Laundry:** None
Pump-Out: OnSite, Full Service **Fee:** $10 **Closed Heads:** Yes

Marina Operations

Owner/Manager: Reid Shepard (Cmmdr) **Dockmaster:** Students
In-Season: Jul-Aug, 10am-10pm* **Off-Season:** May, Jun, Sep, weekends
After-Hours Arrival: Call in Advance**
Reservations: Yes **Credit Cards:** Visa/MC
Discounts: None
Pets: Welcome, Dog Walk Area **Handicap Access:** Yes, Docks

Regent Street Wharf & Moorings

PO Box 154; 161-527 Beaverbrook Ct.; Fredericton, NB E3B 1X6

Tel: (506) 455-1445 **VHF: Monitor** Ch.68 **Talk** n/a
Fax: (506) 450-8183 **Alternate Tel:** (506) 461-6703
Email: info@capitalcityboatclub.com **Web:** www.capitalcityboatclub.com
Nearest Town: Fredericton **Tourist Info:** (506) 460-2410

Marina Services and Boat Supplies

Services - Docking Assistance, Security *(Locked gate)*, Trash Pick-Up, Dock Carts **Communication -** Pay Phone, FedEx, UPS **Supplies - OnSite:** Ice *(Block)* **Near:** Propane *(King St Mainway 458-9690)*

Boatyard Services

OnSite: Launching Ramp

Restaurants and Accommodations

OnSite: Restaurant *(Maverick Room D $22-34, upscale, white tablecloth, off Terrace)*, *(The Terrace B $6.50-12, L $10-19, D $16-28, Breakfast buffet $7-11)*, Hotel *(Lord Beaverbrook Crown Plaza 45-533-71 , $142-369)* **Near:** Restaurant *(Snooty Fox 474-1199, B $5, L $7-17, D $7-17, rooftop patio)*, *(Caribbean Flavas 45-912-30 , L $7-13, D $7-20)*, *(Mexicali Rosa's 451-0686, L $5-10, D $10-25)*, *(The Diplomat 24 hrs., upscale)*, *(Brewbaker's 459-0067, L $11-14, D $11-37)*, *(James Joynce Irish Pub L & D $8-12)*, *(Blue Door 455-2583, L $11-14, D $11-37, Superb)*, *(McGuire's Landing)*, *(El Burrito Loco Outside dining)*, Lite Fare *(Crumbs)*, *(Mei's Chinese Takeout 454-2177, L & D $7-15)*, *(Cora's B & L)*, Pizzeria *(Pizza Delight 453-1400, Delivers)* **Under 1 mi:** Hotel *(Delta Fredericton 457-7000, $189-850)*, Inn/B&B *(Carriage House Inn 452-9924, $99-125)*

Recreation and Entertainment

OnSite: Heated Pool *(Lord Bevaerbrook Crown Plaza)*, Spa, Picnic Area, Tennis Courts *(Lord Beaverbrook)*, Fitness Center *(Lord Beaverbrook 5:30am-11pm)*, Tours *(River Trails Bike Tours. Tue-Sat 11am & 4:30pm $8+)* **Near:** Playground, Boat Rentals *(Aquatic Rowing Club - kayaks & canoes)*, Video Rental *(Jumbo 457-2267)*, Museum *(York Sunbury Hist. Society 455-6041; Science East 457-2340)*, Cultural Attract *(Concerts Officers Sq. Tue & Thu 7:30, Lighthouse Sun 3pm, Fri 7:30)*, Sightseeing *(Guided Heritage Walking Tours, City Hall 10am, Free)*, Galleries *(Beaverbrook Art Gallery 458-8545)* **1-3 mi:** Golf Course *(Kingswood)*, Bowling *(Bowl-A-Drome 472-2361)*, Movie Theater *(Empire 458-9704)*

Provisioning and General Services

OnSite: Beauty Salon *(Arabesque 450-3339)* **Near:** Supermarket *(Sobey's)*, Delicatessen *(M & T 458-9068)*, Health Food *(True Food Organics 459-4333)*, Wine/Beer, Liquor Store *(The Superstore)*, Bakery, Farmers' Market *(Sat 6am-1pm, Boyce 451-1815)*, Fishmonger *(Victory 458-8480)*, Bank/ATM, Post Office, Catholic Church, Protestant Church, Synagogue, Library *(Fredericton 460-2800)*, Barber Shop, Dry Cleaners, Laundry, Bookstore *(Westminster 454-1442)*, Pharmacy *(Ross 458-9951)*, Hardware Store *(Simms 454-4663)*, Copies Etc. *(Inkadoo 455-0033)*

Transportation

OnSite: Bikes *(River Trails $7/hr., $25/day)* **OnCall:** Taxi *(Trius 454-4444)* **Near:** Rental Car *(Avis, Hertz)*, Local Bus *(Fredericton Trans. 460-2200 Kings Place Mall, Yacht Club)*, InterCity Bus *(Acadien - to Moncton, Saint John, Halifax)* **Airport:** Fredericton *(8 mi.)*

Medical Services

911 Service **OnSite:** Holistic Services *(Salon Arabesque Spa 450-3339; Lifesong Yoga & Wellness Centre 455-2444 - about a mile)* **Near:** Doctor *(Randall 459-3622)*, Dentist *(Wilson 452-7695)* **Under 1 mi:** Optician *(Vogue)*, Veterinarian *(South Paw 454-2224)* **1-3 mi:** Chiropractor *(Lilly Family 472-7000)* **Hospital:** Everett-Chalmers 452-5400 *(1 mi.)*

Setting -- Located on the St. John River, the Regent Street dock - a single, long, side-tie float - sprawls along a pretty waterfront park in the midst of the delightful, historic capital city of Fredericton. The amenities, snack bar, and rentals are housed in an imposing red and white faux lighthouse that overlooks the docks and the river. The Lord Beaverbrook Crown Plaza is immediately adjacent and welcomes boaters to its facilities.

Marina Notes -- *Side-tie dockage. 15 & 30 Amp power included. **No reservations for Canada Day, N.B. Day, Labour Day. Add'l Contact tel: 461-6714. 250 ft. dedicated guest dockage. Old RR Bridge (now pedestrian trail) creates max air draft of 27 ft. Two free moorings seaward of bridge for sailboats; dinghy to marina. Whole city wired for Wi-Fi - Fred Zone. Lord Beaverbrook is considered onsite - more heads & showers, an indoor pool, a fitness center, a little lounge bar, an upscale reatuaurant - very short walk from docks. Bathhouse: Lovely heads; all tile & granite decorated in sage green & butter yellow.

Notable -- Historic Ffedericton, the capital of New Brunswick, is a two-minute walk. There's lots to do, a fun vibe and a great mix - leafy streets, college students, history, culture and good eating - from top notch Blue Door to a variety of ethnic and casual restaurants. The bar scene is at Nicky Z's and 20/20 - all nearby. Free events abound - concerts in Officers Square (Tue & Thu 7:30pm) and Under the Stars Classic Movie Series at Barracks Square (Sun 9pm). The Lighthouse Deck features Thursday night yoga and live bands (Sunday 3pm & Friday 7:30). The fabulous W.W. Boyce Farmers market is a must with almost 90 vendors indoors and out. Provision the boat, take out some prepared meals, then linger over breakfast or lunch while enjoying the local scene.

2. NB - ST. JOHN RIVER

PHOTOS ON DVD: 25

ATLANTIC CRUISING CLUB'S Guides to Marinas

The Most Comprehensive *Boater-Biased* Marina Information Available.

Full-Page Reports Include Complete Facility and "What's Nearby" Details *plus* Ratings, Reviews, Rates and Thousands of Photos.

ACC's Guide to New England & Canadian Maritime Marinas – 8th Ed. Expanded & Revised
Halifax, NS to Wickford, RI • **$39.95**

ACC's Guide to Long Island Sound Marinas
Block Island, RI to Cape May, NJ • **$24.95**

ACC's Guide to Chesapeake Bay Marinas
C&D Canal, DE to Hampton Roads, VA • **$32.95**

ACC's Guide to Mid-Atlantic/ICW Marinas
Hampton, VA to St. Marys, GA • **$39.95**

ACC's Guide to Florida's East Coast Marinas
Fernandina, FL to Key West, FL • **$29.95**

ACC's Guide to Florida's West Coast Marinas
Everglades City, FL to Pensacola, FL • **$34.95**

ACC's Guide to Pacific Northwest Marinas
Campbell River, BC to Brookings, OR • **$29.95**

Complimentary Silver-Level Website Membership with each Guide

These are Boater-Biased Consumers' Guides. To insure total editorial objectivity, ACC does not solicit or accept advertising or any other form of remuneration from the marinas that it covers in its Guides.

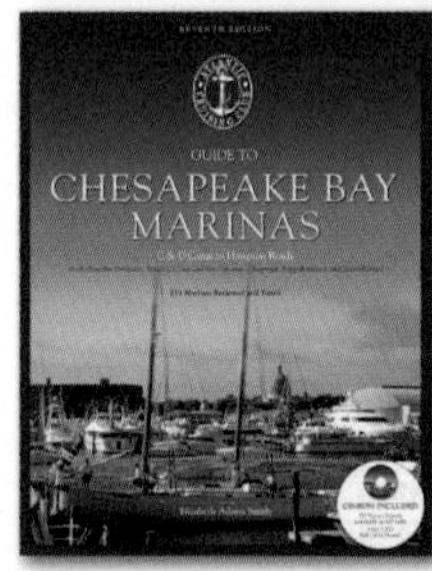

Every Guide Includes an Interactive Digital ACC Guide on CD/DVD-ROM

3. NB/ME – Passamaquoddy Bay & Downeast Maine

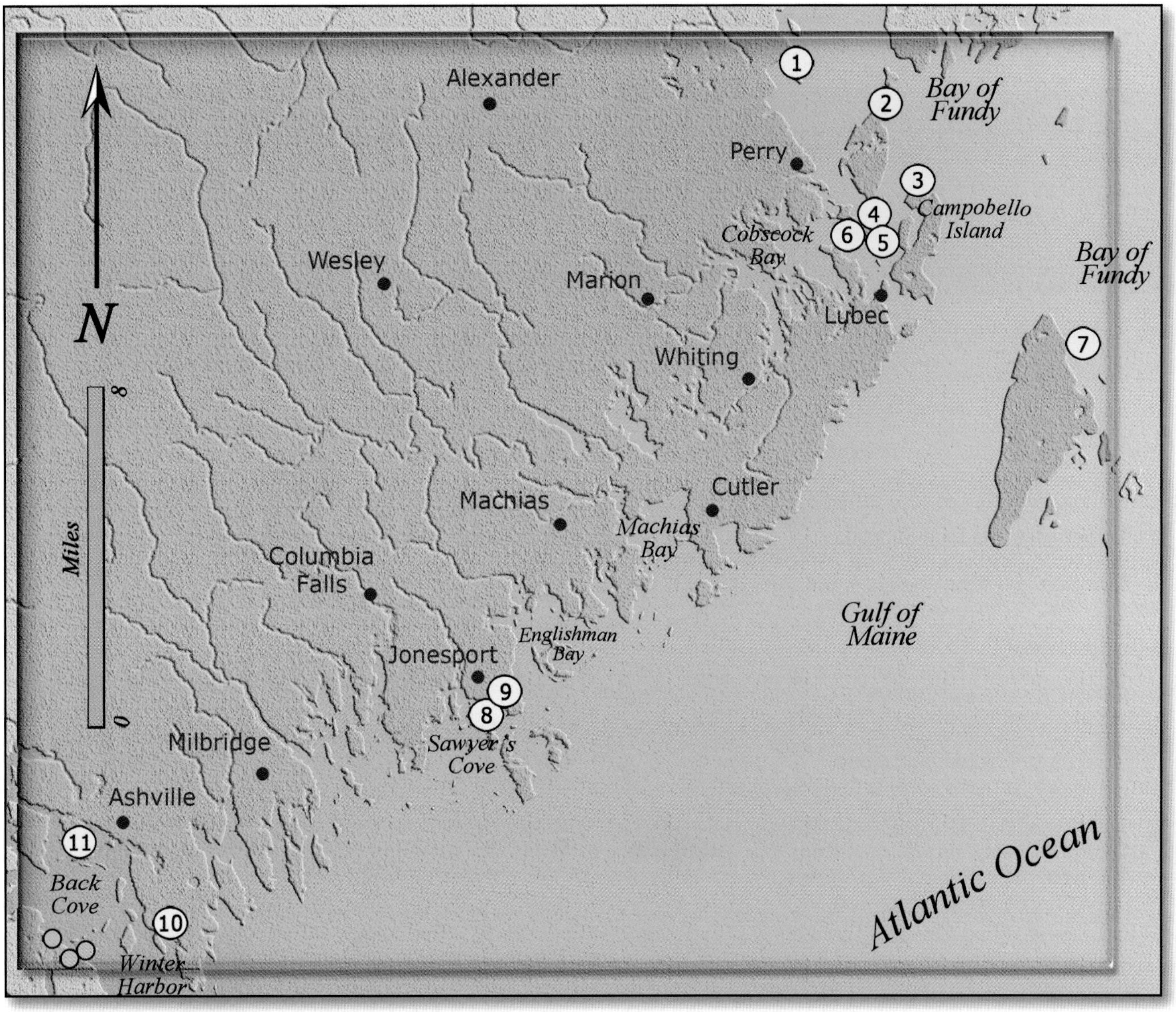

MAP	MARINA	HARBOR	PAGE
1	**St. Andrews Market Wharf**	*St. Andrews Harbour*	66
2	**Deer Island Wharves**	*Passamaquoddy Bay*	67
3	**S.E. Newman & Sons Head Harbour Marina**	*Head Harbour*	68
4	**Eastport Lobster & Fuel**	*Friar Roads*	69
5	**Eastport Breakwater**	*Friar Roads*	70
6	**Moose Island Marine**	*Head Harbor Passage*	71
7	**Grand Manan Harbour Authority**	*North Head*	72
8	**Jonesport Municipal Marina**	*Mossabec Reach*	73
9	**Jonesport Shipyard**	*Moosabec Reach*	74
10	**Winter Harbor Marina**	*Winter Harbor*	75
11	**West Cove Boat Yard**	*Sorrento Harbor*	76

RATINGS: 1-5 for Marina Facilities & Amenities,  1-2 for Boatyard Services,  1-2 for MegaYacht Facilities,  for Something Special.

SERVICES: for CCM – Certified Clean Marina,  for Pump-Out, for Internet,  for Fuel,  for Restaurant,  for Provisioning nearby, for Catamaran-friendly,  for SportFish Charter,  for Pool/Beach, and  for Golf within a mile. *For an explanation of ACC's Ratings, see page 8.*

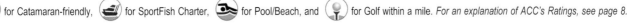

St. Andrews Market Wharf

212 Water Street; St. Andrews, NB E5B 1B4

Tel: (506) 529-5170 **VHF: Monitor** Ch. 16 **Talk** Ch.78
Fax: (506) 529-5183 **Alternate Tel:** (506) 529-5120
Email: wharf@townofstandrews.ca **Web:** townofstandrews.ca
Nearest Town: St. Andrews **Tourist Info:** (506) 529-3556

Navigational Information
Lat: 45°04.160' **Long:** 067°03.160' **Tide:** 26 ft. **Current:** n/a **Chart:** 4331
Rep. Depths (*MLW*): Entry 13 ft. **Fuel Dock** n/a **Max Slip/Moor** 10 ft./14 ft.
Access: Passamaquoddy Bay to St. Andrews Harbour

Marina Facilities *(In Season/Off Season)*
Fuel: No
Slips: 15 Total, 2 Transient **Max LOA:** 90 ft. **Max Beam:** n/a
Rate *(per ft.)*: **Day** $2.00* **Week** n/a **Month** n/a
Power: 30 amp n/a, **50 amp** n/a, **100 amp** n/a, **200 amp** n/a
Cable TV: No **Dockside Phone:** Yes
Dock Type: Fixed, Floating, Alongside, Concrete, Wood
Moorings: 40 Total, 18 Transient **Launch:** Until 7pm (Comp.), Dinghy Dock
Rate: Day $25 **Week** n/a **Month** n/a
Heads: 6 Toilet(s)
Internet: No **Laundry:** None
Pump-Out: OnSite, Full Service **Fee:** $10 **Closed Heads:** No

Marina Operations
Owner/Manager: Town of St. Andrews **Dockmaster:** H.W. (BB) Chamberlain
In-Season: May 15-Oct 15, 7am-6pm **Off-Season:** Oct 16-May 14, Inq.
After-Hours Arrival: Call in Advance
Reservations: Yes, Preferred **Credit Cards:** Cash only
Discounts: None
Pets: Welcome, Dog Walk Area **Handicap Access:** Yes, Heads, Docks

Marina Services and Boat Supplies
Services - Docking Assistance, Security *(20 hrs., staff, camera)*, Trash Pick-Up **Communication -** Phone Messages, Fax in/out, FedEx, UPS
Supplies - Near: Ice *(Block, Cube)*, Ships' Store *(J. Anderson 529-1985)*

Boatyard Services
OnCall: Rigger, Metal Fabrication **Near:** Launching Ramp, Engine mechanic *(gas, diesel)*, Electrical Repairs, Divers *(Navy Island 529-4555)*.
Nearest Yard: Moose Island Marine (207) 853-4513

Restaurants and Accommodations
Near: Restaurant *(The Gables 529-3440, B $4-7, L & D $8-25)*, *(Inn on Frederick 529-2603)*, *(Europa 529-3818, B $7-12, D $18-29)*, *(Kennedy Inn 52-988-44 , L $7-14, D $7-30)*, *(Harbour Front 529-4887)*, *(Elaine's Chowder House 529-4496)*, *(Lobster Bay 529-4840)*, Pizzeria *(Olde Tyme 529-8800, Italian specialties)*, Motel *(St Andrews 529-4571, $80-230)*, Inn/B&B *(Europa 529-3818, $95-165)*, *(Mulberry 529-4948, $95-120)*, *(Treadwell 529-1011, $99+)* **Under 1 mi:** Restaurant *(Library Lounge & Dining Room 529-8823, Algonquin)*, *(Veranda Algonquin)*, Lite Fare *(Kingsbrae Garden Cafe 529-3335, L $8-14.50, 10am-6pm)*, *(Right Whale Pub 529-8823, Algonquin)*, Hotel *(Fairmount Algonquin 529-8823, $120-480, Recent $10 million addition - impeccable, charming)*, Inn/B&B *(Kingsbrae Arms Relais & Chateaux 529-1897, $395-995, ulitmate luxury)*

Recreation and Entertainment
Near: Picnic Area, Playground *(Robert S. Leathers Design)*, Dive Shop *(Navy Island 529-4555)*, Fitness Center, Hike/Bike Trails *(Two Meadows)*, Fishing Charter, Movie Theater *(W.C. O'Neill Arena 529-4347 Summer)*, Video Rental, Museum *(Ross Memorial 529-5124 - 19th Century N.B. furniture)*, Sightseeing *(Whale Watch: Island Quest 529-9885; Tall Ship 529-8116; Quoddy Link 529-2600; Fundy Tide Runners 529-4481)*, Galleries *(Dozens)* **Under 1 mi:** Beach *(Tidal Pool at Katy's Cove 529-3433)*, Tennis Courts *(Harriet St.)*, Golf Course *(Algonquin G.C. 529-7142)*, Park *(Kingsbrae 529-4875 $12/9)*, Cultural Attract *(Huntsman Aquarium Touch Pool 529-1200; Atlantic Salmon Interpret. Centre 529-1384 $4.50/2.50)* **1-3 mi:** Tours *(Ministers Island 529-5081 $12/10)*

Provisioning and General Services
Near: Convenience Store *(Cummings 529-8816)*, Supermarket *(St. Andrews Save Easy 529-3831)*, Health Food *(Sweet Harvest Market & Cafe 529-6249)*, Wine/Beer, Liquor Store *(Alcohol NB 529-6250)*, Fishmonger *(Lobster Market 529-3190)*, Bank/ATM, Post Office, Catholic Church, Protestant Church, Library *(Ross Mem. - Internet)*, Beauty Salon, Barber Shop, Laundry *(Kiwanis Camping 8am-10pm)*, Pharmacy *(Cockburn's 529-3113)*, Hardware Store *(St. Andrews 529-3158)*, Florist *(Gardens by the Sea)*, Department Store *(Great Canadian 529-4746)*

Transportation
OnCall: Rental Car *(Enterprise 529-5518; HMS 529-3101)*, Taxi *(529-3371)*, Airport Limo *(HMS 529-3101)* **Airport:** Fredericton/Saint John Int'l. *(90 mi./60 mi.)*

Medical Services
911 Service **Near:** Doctor *(Health Centre 529-9120)*, Dentist *(Imrie 529-8381)* **Under 1 mi:** Holistic Services *(Fairmont Algonquin Spa)*, Veterinarian *(St Andrews 529-3036)* **Hospital:** St. Stephens 465-4444 *(18 mi.)*

Setting -- Below the imposing, drive-on Market Wharf, long gangplanks lead up from the floating docks. The Wharfinger's office overlooks the mooring field and directs the active commercial traffic. At the wharf head, a tourism office and activity kiosks cluster in theAdventure Centre and Market Square; a few steps beyond, the exquisite village of St. Andrews-by-the-Sea's National Historic District hosts a wealth of activities, attractions, restaurants, shops and galleries.

Marina Notes -- *Slips rarely available. Mooring #1 for megayachts. Radio Wharfinger; a boat will lead you to your mooring or slip - required for vessels larger than 45 ft. Optional launch service until 7pm. Active working harbor - Fishermen leave 6 am. Anchorage avail for up to 220 ft boats. Limited slips, dinghy dockage, and launch. Mostly commercial vessels in berths. Bathhouse: Heads in St. Andrews Town Hall - red brick building at head of wharf. Showers & Laundry at Kiwanis campground (10 min walk east; free for the boaters 529-3439). Inquire about rides. Note: To clear in call CANPASS 888-226-7277.

Notable -- Stroll Water Street at the head of the wharf; 100 to 200-year-old buildings house shops, galleries, studios, inns and restaurants. Founded in 1783 by Loyalists fleeing the U.S., most of the original houses were barged down the Calais River and re-assembled. In the 19th C., St. Andrews-by-the-Sea grew from ship building to a premier summer colony when the spectacular landmark Fairmont Algonquin Hotel was built in 1889. Two marine centers interpret the fascinating interdial area and four whale watch tours take you there. Visit 27-acre Kingsbrae Horticultural Garden and Ross Memorial museum highlighting 19th C. New Brunswick furnishings. At low tide, drive across the ocean floor to railway magnate Sir William Van Horne's 495-acre estate on Minister's Island.

Navigational Information

Lat: 45°01.151' **Long:** 066°56.702' **Tide:** 25 ft. **Current:** n/a **Chart:** 4331
Rep. Depths (*MLW*): Entry 20 ft. **Fuel Dock** n/a **Max Slip/Moor** 9 ft./-
Access: n/a

Marina Facilities *(In Season/Off Season)*

Fuel: No
Slips: 30 Total, 5 Transient **Max LOA:** 75 ft. **Max Beam:** n/a
Rate *(per ft.)*: **Day** $0* **Week** n/a **Month** n/a
Power: 30 amp n/a, **50 amp** n/a, **100 amp** n/a, **200 amp** n/a
Cable TV: No **Dockside Phone:** No
Dock Type: Fixed, Floating, Alongside, Wood
Moorings: 0 Total, 0 Transient **Launch:** n/a
Rate: Day n/a **Week** n/a **Month** n/a
Heads: None
Internet: No **Laundry:** None
Pump-Out: No **Fee:** n/a **Closed Heads:** No

Marina Operations

Owner/Manager: Donny Stuart, Harbormaster **Dockmaster:** Same
In-Season: Year Round, 9am-5pm **Off-Season:** n/a
After-Hours Arrival: Contact Harbourmaster
Reservations: No **Credit Cards:** n/a
Discounts: None
Pets: Welcome **Handicap Access:** No

Deer Island Wharves

Deer Island, NB E5V-1N3

Tel: (506) 747-2117 **VHF: Monitor** n/a **Talk** n/a
Fax: n/a **Alternate Tel:** n/a
Email: cline@nbnet.nb.ca **Web:** www.deerisland.nb.ca
Nearest Town: Lord's Cove, Fairhaven **Tourist Info:** (506) 747-2034

Marina Services and Boat Supplies

Supplies - Near: Ships' Store *(Welch Store - Fairhaven)*

Boatyard Services

Nearest Yard: Moose Island Marine (207) 853-4513

Restaurants and Accommodations

Near: Restaurant *(45th Parallel 747-2231, L & D $6-22 Fairhaven overlooking Western Passage)*, Motel *(45th Parallel 747-2222, 10 units - Fairhaven - half way between equator & north pole)*, Inn/B&B *(Deer Island Inn 747-1998, $75-85, Lord's Cove)* **Under 1 mi:** Restaurant *(Fisherman's Cove Café 747-2089, 1 mi. from Stuart Town)*, Lite Fare *(Spirit of the Island 747-1010, Stuart Town)*, Inn/B&B *(Harbour Island Inn 747-0995, Turn of Last Century on 30 acres - Lord's Cove)*, Condo/Cottage *(Sunset Beach Cottage & Suites 747-2972, $80, Fairhaven)*, *(Bayview Cottage 747-0002, Lord's Cove)* **1-3 mi:** Condo/Cottage *(Richardson Lookout Cottages 747-2286, $85, Richardson)*

Recreation and Entertainment

Near: Video Rental *(Welch Store - Fairhaven)*, Galleries *(Boat Shop Art Gallery 747-2310, Island Baskets 747-2310, Atlantic Mill Island Art, paintings, buoys, shells and rocks - all in Leonardsville; Six Acre Studio 747-1188; Fireball Gallery 747-2009 Lord's Cove)* **Under 1 mi:** Sightseeing *(Lambert's Outer Island Tours 747-2426 - small group 2-hour Whale Watching for Minkes, Finback & Humpbacks $50/pp on 22.5 ft. day cruiser)* **1-3 mi:** Playground *(Deer Island)*, Dive Shop *(NB Divers & Guided Divers 292-5111 - Deer Island Point is a popular spot)*, Boat Rentals *(Seascape Kayak Tours 747-1884)*, Hike/Bike Trails *(Big Meadow Marsh, Eagle Hill Trail, & Deer Island Point for birding - eagles & osprey)*, Park *(Deer Island Point 747-2423 - camping too)*

Provisioning and General Services

Near: Market *(Welch Store 747-2254 - post office, groceries, gas - Fairhaven)*, Lobster Pound *(Youngs 747-1999 near Richardson)*, Post Office *(Leonardville)*, Bookstore *(Dandelion Books and Crafts - Stuart Town)*, Hardware Store *(Welch - Fairhaven)* **Under 1 mi:** Convenience Store *(Bella's Country Store 747-2439 - snacks, gifts, soft-serve ice cream, gourmet coffee)*, Bank/ATM *(Credit Union - Stuart Town)* **1-3 mi:** Crabs/Waterman *(Cheesecake Crabs - may deliver)*, Protestant Church *(Barriston Church - Stuart Town)*, Library

Transportation

Under 1 mi: Ferry Service *(to Campobello $16, Eastport $13 - both Summer season only, to Letete $13 - year round 6am-10:30pm)* **Airport:** Eastport Muni *(12 mi.)*

Medical Services

911 Service **OnCall:** Ambulance **1-3 mi:** Doctor *(Deer Island Health Center 747-4150 Mon-Fri, physician 1 day a week)* **Hospital:** Centre de Santé de Fundy 456-4200 *(20 mi.)*

Setting -- The smallest of the Fundy Isles, Deer Island's eastern Bay of Fundy shore and western Passamaquoddy Bay shore are lined with coves and harbors. Six public wharves, including Stuart Town, Lord's Cove, Leonardville and Fairhaven provide recreational vessel tie-ups among the commercial boats. Fishing - catching, raising and processing - still dominates the rhythms and character of the small, largely untouristed villages.

Marina Notes -- *Free dockage. Lat/Long for Lord's Cove. Stuart Town Wharf 4701.083, 6656.300, Leonardville Wharf 4458.283, 5657.183. Fairhaven Wharf. 4457.85, 6700.466. Complimentary side-tie and berths are available on a first come, first serve basis. Power, when available, is often 10 & 15A. Dock quality varies - Lord's Cove has beautiful, harwood floating docks also Canadian Port of Entry. The middle section "what's nearby" has been annotated to indicate which wharf that particular service is near. Bathouse: Some Porta Potties.

Notable -- Stuart Town, Lord's Cove, Richardson and Lambertsville all cluster together at the north end of the 3 mile by 10 mile island. Leonardville overlooks the West Isles on the the rugged eastern side and Fairhaven sprawls along the sunny west side. Watch for herring and sardine weirs - similar to those that have been here since the 1870s, the more recent lobster pounds that harken back to the '20s and the newest, salmon aquaculture pens at the mouth of Lord's Cove. At the southern tip, 40-acre Deer Island Point Park features trails, beaches, a ferry landing and the best view of "Old Sow" - Fundy currents and eddies swirl between Deer Island Point and Eastport three hours on either side of high tide to create the largest tidal whirlpool in the western hemisphere.

PHOTOS ON DVD: 25

S.E. Newman & Sons

2455 Route 774; Wilsons Beach, NB E5E 1K3

Tel: (506) 752-2620 **VHF: Monitor** n/a **Talk** n/a
Fax: (506) 752-5067 **Alternate Tel:** (506) 752-2300
Email: Stephen@senewmanboats.com **Web:** senewmanboats.com
Nearest Town: Lubec, ME *(6 mi.)* **Tourist Info:** (506) 752-7043

Navigational Information

Lat: 44°56.628' **Long:** 066°55.199' **Tide:** 28 ft. **Current:** 3 kt. **Chart:** n/a
Rep. Depths (*MLW*): Entry 20 ft. **Fuel Dock** n/a **Max Slip/Moor** 20 ft./-
Access: Half mile past East Quoddy LIghthouse in Head Harbour

Marina Facilities *(In Season/Off Season)*

Fuel: No
Slips: 30 Total, 10 Transient **Max LOA:** 60 ft. **Max Beam:** n/a
Rate *(per ft.)*: **Day** $1.00* **Week** n/a **Month** n/a
Power: 30 amp Incl., **50 amp** n/a, **100 amp** n/a, **200 amp** n/a
Cable TV: No **Dockside Phone:** No
Dock Type: Floating, Alongside, Aluminum
Moorings: 0 Total, 0 Transient **Launch:** n/a
Rate: Day n/a **Week** n/a **Month** n/a
Heads: 1 Toilet(s)
Internet: No **Laundry:** None
Pump-Out: No **Fee:** n/a **Closed Heads:** No

Marina Operations

Owner/Manager: Stephen E. Newman **Dockmaster:** Norman Brown
In-Season: May-Oct, 8am-6pm **Off-Season:** Nov-Apr, Closed
After-Hours Arrival: Call (506) 754-2300
Reservations: Yes, Preferred **Credit Cards:** Visa/MC, Cash
Discounts: None
Pets: Welcome, Dog Walk Area **Handicap Access:** No

Marina Services and Boat Supplies

Services - Docking Assistance, Trash Pick-Up **Communication -** Fax in/out, FedEx, UPS **Supplies - 3+ mi:** Ice *(Cube)*

Boatyard Services

OnSite: Travelift *(40T)*, Launching Ramp, Electrical Repairs, Hull Repairs, Divers, Bottom Cleaning, Woodworking

Restaurants and Accommodations

Under 1 mi: Condo/Cottage *(Brown's Waterfront Homestead 752-2059, $150, $900/week - Wilsons Beach overlooking the Bay - owned by Newmans), (Pollock Cove Cottages 752-2300, $95-225, 10 sweet little cottages overlooking Passamaquoddy Bay - owned by Newmans)* **1-3 mi:** Restaurant *(Family Fisheries 752-2470, eat inside, on the deck or take-out. Local seafood, lobster - cooked or live, kids play area)* **3+ mi:** Restaurant *(Herring Cove Clubhouse/Restaurant 5 mi)*, Inn/B&B *(Lupine Lodge 752-2555, $85-200, 5 mi., 1915 lodge), (Owen House 752-2977, $110-210, 5 mi., Historic waterfront Inn)*

Recreation and Entertainment

Near: Sightseeing *(Island Cruises Whale Watching 752-1107 Daily 10am, 1pm & 4pm; East Quoddy Lighthouse - also called Head Harbour Light)* **3+ mi:** Beach *(6 mi.)*, Picnic Area *(Friar's Head - adjacent to Roosevelt Estate, 6 mi.)*, Golf Course *(Herring Cove Golf Course 752-7041, 6 mi.)*, Hike/Bike Trails *(Roosevelt Park - 10 miles of trails - nine from 0.6 mi to 2.4 mi., 6 mi.)*, Park *(Roosevelt Campobello International Park 752-2922 Free. Year Round half hour before sunrise & after sunset, 6 mi.)*, Tours *(Roosevelt Cottage 752-2922 Free, 9am-5pm ET. Take the tour, stroll the garden, visit the other four cottages & outbuildings, 6 mi.)*

Provisioning and General Services

OnSite: Copies Etc. **Under 1 mi:** Fishmonger *(Family Fisheries 752-2470 - 7 days - clams. shrimp, chowder, lobsters live or cooked over a wood fire)*, Retail Shops *(Pollock Cove Gift Shop - wide variety of crafts, clothing, books, guides attractively merchandised in a beautiful space with spectacular views)* **1-3 mi:** Post Office *(Wilson Beach)*, Protestant Church **3+ mi:** Market *(Co-Op Store, 5 mi.)*, Supermarket *(Campobello Valu-Foods 752-2667, 6 mi.)*, Wine/Beer *(Co-Op, 5 mi.)*, Liquor Store *(Co-Op, 5 mi.)*, Bank/ATM *(5 mi.)*, Catholic Church *(5 mi.)*, Library *(Campobello 752-7082 , 5 mi.)*, Beauty Salon *(Oasis Salon, 5 mi.)*, Pharmacy *(Coop Store; Rexall Guardian Herring Cove 752-1811, 5 mi.)*, Hardware Store *(Boyd Bros Home Hardware Building Centre 755-1500, 3.5 mi..)*

Transportation

OnSite: Courtesy Car/Van **3+ mi:** Ferry Service *(to Deer Island, 10 mi.)*
Airport: Bangor, ME/Saint John, NB *(100 mi./120 mi.)*

Medical Services

911 Service **OnCall:** Ambulance **3+ mi:** Doctor *(Campobello Medical Center, 7 mi.)* **Hospital:** Downeast Community - Michias 255-2500 *(40 mi.)*

Setting -- Cruising toward Head Harbour, watch for Minke, Finback, Humpback and North Atlantic Right whales as well as seals, harbour porpoises, eagles and sea birds with a spectacular view of the most-photographed lighthouse in North America - East Quoddy Light. Sheltered Head Harbour is bustling with working boats. On the upland a long gray shed houses the S.E. Newman boat building operation and at its feet, a single L-shaped floating dock parallels the shore berthing a couple dozen slips on one side and a face dock on the other. Bright yellow railings punch through the fog.

Marina Notes -- *Flat Rate: Under 30 ft. $25, 30-40 ft. $30, 40-60 ft. $45. 320 ft. of side-tie face dock. Former salmon farming operation converted to marina - repurposed floating docks and ramps, grated surface. Builders of "Northern Bay" sport fishing boats - high end, superbly finished 25-36 ft. Owner drives boaters for supplies at mutually convenient times. Only Canadian Customs check-in for boats on Island - Call CBSA 888-226-7277. Bathhouse: Basic head.

Notable -- Island Cruises' 37 -oot "Mister Matthew," a traditional twenty-passenger Bay of Fundy fishing boat, has been whale watching out of Head Harbour since 1995. Paul's Variety is 1.25 miles from the docks. About five miles away Campobello Center has a supermaket, pharmacy, ATM and liquor store. Visiting Roosevelt Campobello International Park is a highlight of cruising this region. Anchor off the estate in Friar Bay (just east of Friar's Head) and dinghy into the beach (the docks are reserved for the Fundy Tide Runner, a tour boat out of St. Andrews). An interpretive deck is just above the beach and FDR's iconic green-roofed, red-shingled "cottage" is a short walk up the path; the impressive Visitor Centre is adjacent. Questions about coming ashore? Contact the ranger.

    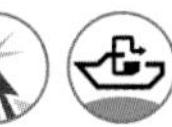 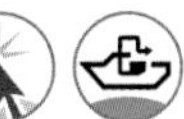 

Navigational Information

Lat: 44°54.561' **Long:** 066°59.091' **Tide:** 24 ft. **Current:** 4 kt. **Chart:** 13394
Rep. Depths (*MLW*): Entry 100 ft. **Fuel Dock** 18 ft. **Max Slip/Moor** 30 ft./-
Access: Head Harbor passage south to Friar Roads

Marina Facilities *(In Season/Off Season)*

Fuel: Gasoline, Diesel
Slips: 10 Total, 10 Transient **Max LOA:** 80 ft. **Max Beam:** n/a
Rate *(per ft.)*: **Day** $1.50 **Week** n/a **Month** n/a
Power: 30 amp 110V, **50 amp** n/a, **100 amp** n/a, **200 amp** n/a
Cable TV: No **Dockside Phone:** No
Dock Type: Floating, Alongside, Wood
Moorings: 6 Total, 6 Transient **Launch:** No
Rate: Day $25 **Week** n/a **Month** n/a
Heads: 6 Toilet(s), 2 Shower(s) *(dressing rooms)*
Internet: Yes *(Wi-Fi, Free)* **Laundry:** 1 Washer(s), 1 Dryer(s)
Pump-Out: OnCall **Fee:** Free **Closed Heads:** No

Marina Operations

Owner/Manager: Bob Del Papa **Dockmaster:** Same
In-Season: May 15-Oct 15 **Off-Season:** Oct 16-May 14, Closed
After-Hours Arrival: Call a week in advance for moorings
Reservations: Yes **Credit Cards:** Visa/MC, Dscvr
Discounts: None
Pets: Welcome **Handicap Access:** No

Eastport Lobster & Fuel

167 Water Street; Eastport, ME 04631

Tel: (207) 853-9559 **VHF: Monitor** Ch. 10 **Talk** Ch. 10
Fax: n/a **Alternate Tel:** (207) 853-4700
Email: barharborbob@hotmail.com **Web:** eastportchowderhouse.com
Nearest Town: Eastport *(0.2 mi.)* **Tourist Info:** (207) 853-4644

Marina Services and Boat Supplies

Services - Docking Assistance, Trash Pick-Up **Communication -** FedEx, UPS, Express Mail **Supplies - OnSite:** Ice *(Block, Cube)* **Near:** Ships' Store *(Moose Island Marine 853-6058; S.L. Wadsworth 853-4343)* **Under 1 mi:** Propane *(Dead River Co 853-4202)*

Boatyard Services

Nearest Yard: Moose Island Marine (207) 853-6058

Restaurants and Accommodations

OnSite: Restaurant *(Eastport Chowder House 853-4700, L $9-17, D $13-20, Kids' Menu. Lunch 11am-4pm)* **Near:** Restaurant *(Pickled Herring 853-2323, D $13-25, Fine Dining)*, *(Rose Garden Cafe 853-9598)*, *(Waco Diner 853-4046, B $3-9, L $6-30, D $6-30)*, *(Happy Crab 853-9400, L & D $10-18, Free Wi-Fi)*, Snack Bar *(Rosie's Hot Dogs)*, Lite Fare *(Blue Iris 853-2440, B $3-6, L $4-12)*, Pizzeria *(Bank Square Pizza & Deli 853-2709)*, Motel *(Motel East 853-4747, $105-120, private balconies overlooking bay)*, *(Milliken 853-2955, $75-85)*, Inn/B&B *(Kilby 853-0989, $60-80)*, *(Chadbourne 853-2727, $110-140)*, *(Weston 853-2907, $80-90)*

Recreation and Entertainment

OnCall: Dive Shop *(Moose Island)* **Near:** Picnic Area, Playground *(school)*, Party Boat *(Quoddy Dam 853-2500 - 35 passengers, 8am-12 noon)*, Video Rental *(Shady Pines Cabins)*, Museum *(Tides Institute & Museum of Art 853-4047; Barracks Museum 327-1246)*, Tours *(Summer-Keys Ferry to Lubec, Wed. 6:30pm $15 - concerts begin at 7:30pm; 84 ft. Sylvina W. Beal Windjammer Whale Watching 1:30-4:30pm, $37/20; 93 ft. Halie & Mathew Schooner 853-2500)*, Cultural Attract *(Concerts at Tides Institutes; Eastport Arts Center 853-4650)*, Sightseeing *(National Historic Waterfront District - Main St. Program)*, Galleries *(Crow Tracks, Dancing Dogs Pottery & Art, Eastport Gallery - crafts)*, Special Events *(4th of July; Pirate Fest - Sep; Salmon Fest - LabDay)* **Under 1 mi:** Tennis Courts **3+ mi:** Golf Course *(St. Croix Country Club in Calais 454-8875, 25 mi.)*

Provisioning and General Services

OnSite: Fishmonger, Lobster Pound **OnCall:** Provisioning Service *(Jeff Sterling, Maritime Marine Services 288-1093)* **Near:** Delicatessen *(Bank Square 853-2709)*, Wine/Beer, Liquor Store, Farmers' Market *(Thur 10am-noon, Winter & Washington Sts.)*, Bank/ATM, Post Office *(Stone building - post office above US Customs)*, Catholic Church, Protestant Church, Library *(Peavey Mem. 853-4021)*, Beauty Salon, Barber Shop, Laundry, Pharmacy *(Harvey & Wilson 853-4061)*, Hardware Store *(Wadsworth 853-4343)*, Florist *(Lewis 853-4466)* **Under 1 mi:** Supermarket *(R & M IGA 853-4050)*

Transportation

OnSite: Courtesy Car/Van *(Provisioning runs)* **OnCall:** Rental Car *(Pratt 454-0600)*, Taxi *(from Calais)* **Near:** Bikes *(The Wharf 733-4400)*, Water Taxi *("To & Fro" to Lubec 733-4400 $16/RT)*, Ferry Service *(Deer Island)*
Airport: Eastport/Bangor Int'l *(1 mi./125 mi.)*

Medical Services

911 Service **OnCall:** Ambulance **Near:** Doctor *(Eastport Healthcare 853-6001)*, Dentist *(Eastport Healthcare)*, Holistic Services *(Artful Touch 853-2763)* **3+ mi:** Veterinarian *(Little River 853-0671, 7 mi.)* **Hospital:** Calais Regional Medical Center 454-0978 *(25 mi.)*

Setting -- In a pretty cove along Friar Roads, less than a quarter mile north of Eastport's breakwater and just south of the ferry landing, floating docks lie along a massive wharf that hosts the Chowder House Restaurant and Eastport Lobster & Fuel. Decks edge the popular two-story restaurant and a low-slung gray-shingled building houses the "Lobster Room". An al fresco bar creates a festive, party atmosphere. Downtown Eastport is a short walk.

Marina Notes -- Only fuel in region - last/first in U.S. Open Year-round. Services fishing fleet, USCG, Border Patrol, etc. Provides provisioning transport for boaters. The Cannery, first eatery on site, opened 1968 - two owners, a decade each. In 1996, Eastport Lobster & Fish Co. purchased property, operated restaurant & lobster pound until '02. Management passed to Robert Del Papa; renamed it Eastport Chowder House. Serious facility improvements began - dining deck '06, fuel operation '08, docks & heads '09. US Customs 853-4313. Bathhouse: Recent small gray building at rear of property. Simple but fresh. Coin-op fiberglass shower stalls with curtains. Washer/dryer in each space. Open to all transient boaters.

Notable -- The walls of windows in the 225-seat Chowder House Restaurant's airy pine-paneled dining rooms overlook the wharf. A pool table and arcade games are adjacent to the bar (Happy Hour 4 to 6 pm, Mondays to Fridays). Stop by The Lobster Room to learn how the crustaceans are caught - and to see a left-handed lobster. During the late 19th and early 20th centuries, the sardine industry was the life blood of Eastport. Martin's Dock, Eastport's first sardine canning operation started on this site in the 1870s. By the 1960s, the fish packing business had begun to devolve and the cannery closed its doors.

Eastport Breakwater

PO Box 278; 3 Madison Street; Eastport, ME 04631

Tel: (207) 853-4614 **VHF: Monitor** Ch. 16 **Talk** Ch. 16
Fax: (207) 853-9584 **Alternate Tel:** n/a
Email: director@portofeastport.org **Web:** portofeastport.org
Nearest Town: Eastport **Tourist Info:** (207) 853-4644

Navigational Information

Lat: 44°54.230' **Long:** 066°59.100' **Tide:** 24 ft. **Current:** 4 kt. **Chart:** 13394
Rep. Depths (*MLW*): Entry 100 ft. **Fuel Dock** n/a **Max Slip/Moor** 40 ft./50 ft.
Access: Head Harbor passage south to Friar Roads

Marina Facilities *(In Season/Off Season)*

Fuel: No
Slips: 50 Total, 15 Transient **Max LOA:** 400 ft. **Max Beam:** n/a
Rate *(per ft.)*: **Day** $2.00/$0.50* **Week** n/a **Month** n/a
Power: 30 amp $3, **50 amp** $6, **100 amp** n/a, **200 amp** n/a
Cable TV: No **Dockside Phone:** No
Dock Type: Floating, Alongside, Wood
Moorings: 2 Total, 2 Transient **Launch:** n/a
Rate: Day Inq. **Week** n/a **Month** n/a
Heads: 2 Toilet(s)
Internet: No **Laundry:** None
Pump-Out: No **Fee:** n/a **Closed Heads:** No

Marina Operations

Owner/Manager: Christopher Gardner **Dockmaster:** Charlie Leppin
In-Season: Jun-Sep, 8am-5pm **Off-Season:** Oct-May, 8am-5pm
After-Hours Arrival: Call Office - phone forwarded to cell
Reservations: Yes, Preferred **Credit Cards:** Visa/MC
Discounts: None
Pets: Welcome **Handicap Access:** No

Marina Services and Boat Supplies

Services - Docking Assistance, Trash Pick-Up, Dock Carts **Communication -** Mail & Package Hold, Fax in/out, FedEx, DHL, UPS, Express Mail **Supplies - Near:** Ice *(Cube)*, Ships' Store *(Moose Island Marine 853-6058; S.L. Wadsworth 853-4343)* **Under 1 mi:** Propane *(Dead River Co 853-4202)*

Boatyard Services

Nearest Yard: Moose Island Marine (207) 853-6058

Restaurants and Accommodations

OnSite: Snack Bar *(Rosie's Hot Dogs)* **Near:** Restaurant *(Happy Crab 853-9400, B, L & D $10-18, Free Wi-Fi)*, *(Waco Diner 853-4046, B $3-9, L & D $6-30)*, *(Eastport Chowder House 853-4700, L $7-52, D $13-52)*, *(Pickled Herring 853-2323, D $13-25, Fine Dining, local, fresh, 8 draft beers)*, *(Rose Garden Cafe 853-9598)*, Lite Fare *(Blue Iris 853-2440, B $3-6, L $4-12)*, Pizzeria *(Bank Square Pizza & Deli 853-2709)*, Motel *(Motel East 853-4747, $105-120, private balconies overlooking bay)*, Hotel *(Milliken 853-2955, $75-85)*, Inn/B&B *(Kilby 800-853-4557, $60-80)*, *(Chadbourne 853-2727, $110-140)*, *(Weston 853-2907, $80-90)*

Recreation and Entertainment

OnSite: Picnic Area, Party Boat *(Quoddy Dam 853-2500 - 35 passengers, 8am-12 noon)* **OnCall:** Dive Shop *(Moose Island)* **Near:** Playground *(school)*, Video Rental *(Shady Pines Cabins)*, Museum *(Tides Institute & Museum of Art 853-4047; Barracks Museum)*, Tours *(Summer-Keys Ferry to Lubec, Wed. 6:30pm $15 - concerts begin at 7:30pm; 84 ft. Sylvina W. Beal Windjammer Whale Watching 1:30-4:30pm, $37/20; 93 ft. Halie & Matthew Schooner 853-2500)*, Cultural Attract *(Tides Institutes; Eastport Arts Center 853-4650)*, Sightseeing *(National Historic Waterfront District - Main St. Program)*, Galleries *(Crow Tracks, Dancing Dogs Pottery & Art, Eastport Gallery - crafts)* **Under 1 mi:** Tennis Courts **3+ mi:** Golf Course *(St. Croix Country Club in Calais 454-8875, 25 mi.)*

Provisioning and General Services

OnSite: Copies Etc. *(office)* **OnCall:** Provisioning Service *(Jeff Sterling, Maritime Marine Services 288-1093)* **Near:** Delicatessen *(Bank Square 853-2709)*, Wine/Beer, Liquor Store, Farmers' Market *(Thurs 10am-noon, Winter & Washington Sts.)*, Fishmonger *(Quoddy Bay/Chowder House)*, Lobster Pound *(Eastport 853-9559; Quoddy Bay 853-6640)*, Bank/ATM *(Bangor Savings)*, Post Office *(Stone building - post office above US Customs)*, Catholic Church, Protestant Church, Library *(Peavey Mem. 853-4021)*, Beauty Salon, Barber Shop, Laundry, Hardware Store *(Wadsworth 853-4343)*, Florist *(Lewis 853-4466)* **Under 1 mi:** Supermarket *(R & M IGA 853-4050)* **1-3 mi:** Pharmacy *(Guardian 752-1811)*

Transportation

OnCall: Taxi *(from Calais)* **Near:** Bikes *(The Wharf 733-4400)*, Water Taxi *("To & Fro" to Lubec 733-4400 $16/RT)*, Ferry Service *(to Deer Island)* **Airport:** Eastport/Bangor Int'l *(1 mi./125 mi.)*

Medical Services

911 Service **OnCall:** Ambulance **Near:** Doctor *(Eastport Healthcare 853-6001)*, Dentist *(Eastport Healthcare)* **3+ mi:** Veterinarian *(Little River 853-0671, 7 mi.)* **Hospital:** Calais Regional Medical Center 454-7521 *(25 mi.)*

Setting -- The scenic Eastport Breakwater is a massive L-shaped drive-on wharf that protects a network of interior floating docks. Long steel ramps creak 28 feet up and down twice a day. Water Street parallels the docks displaying the rear of 18th and 19th century Victorian, Federal and Greek Revival houses and commercial buildings restored to berth galleries, arts centers, shops and restaurants. The imposing white two-story Coast Guard Station overlooks the wharf.

Marina Notes -- *Over 65 ft LOA $3/ft. Power $25 110A, $50 220. Mostly side-tie floating & lighted dockage. Transients dock on north side of fishing pier, larger vessels to 200 ft. on south side of floating docks with 12 ft. mlw. Megayachts tie up on eastern face of breakwater (Need long power cords). 120 ft. new pier. 24 hr Coast Guard Facility onsite. Port of Entry - Efficent customs clear-in. Wi-Fi coming soon. Harbormaster in small red building a block inland. Picnic tables on a deck above docks. Fuel at Eastport Lobster & Fuel. Bathhouse: 2 porta potties. But 0.2 mi. north, Chowder House heads & showers open to all.

Notable -- Moose Island's beautifully unspoiled easternmost U.S. city (with the second deepest harbor) delivers 300 foot depths and offshore fishing conditions ten minutes from the dock. The fewer than 2,000 residents support an impressive arts scene. Eastport Arts Center houses nine organizations in an 1837 church - including Word of Mouth coffee house, Northern Lights film society, Dance Eastport, ArtsBloom fine arts workshop, Eastport Strings, Passamaquoddy Bay Symphony, a Gallery, Concert Series, and Stage East Community Theater. In a restored 1887 historic building, the collections of the Tides Institute and Museum of Art focus on visual arts, as well as architecture, history and Passamaquoddy and Micmac crafts.

PHOTOS ON DVD: 25

  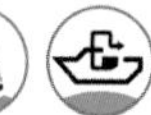

Navigational Information

Lat: 44°54.543' **Long:** 067°00.531' **Tide:** 20 ft. **Current:** 5 kt. **Chart:** 13394
Rep. Depths (*MLW*): Entry 10 ft. **Fuel Dock** n/a **Max Slip/Moor** -/10 ft.
Access: Enter through Head Harbor Passage to Eastport/Deep Cove

Marina Facilities *(In Season/Off Season)*

Fuel: *A.B. Ramsdell 853-4321* - On Call Delivery
Slips: 9 Total, 1 Transient **Max LOA:** 50 ft. **Max Beam:** n/a
Rate *(per ft.)*: **Day** $0.75* **Week** n/a **Month** n/a
Power: 30 amp n/a, **50 amp** n/a, **100 amp** n/a, **200 amp** n/a
Cable TV: No **Dockside Phone:** No
Dock Type: Floating, Alongside, Wood
Moorings: 15 Total, 3 Transient **Launch:** No, Dinghy Dock ($5/day)
Rate: Day $15 **Week** $80 **Month** $200
Heads: 1 Toilet(s), 1 Shower(s)
Internet: No **Laundry:** None
Pump-Out: OnCall, Full Service **Fee:** $50 **Closed Heads:** No

Marina Operations

Owner/Manager: S. Dean Pike **Dockmaster:** Same
In-Season: May-Sep, 8am-5pm **Off-Season:** Oct-Apr, 8am-4:30 M-F
After-Hours Arrival: Call store & leave message
Reservations: Yes, Preferred **Credit Cards:** Visa/MC, Amex
Discounts: None
Pets: Welcome **Handicap Access:** No

Moose Island Marine

PO Box 105; 5 Sullivan Street; Eastport, ME**

Tel: (207) 853-6058 **VHF: Monitor** Ch. 16 **Talk** Ch. 11
Fax: (207) 853-6235 **Alternate Tel:** n/a
Email: mooseislandmarine@verizon.net **Web:** mooseislandmarine.com
Nearest Town: Eastport *(1.8 mi.)* **Tourist Info:** (207) 853-4644

Marina Services and Boat Supplies

Services - Trash Pick-Up **Communication -** Mail & Package Hold, Fax in/out *($1/pp)*, FedEx, UPS, Express Mail **Supplies - OnSite:** Ice *(Block)*, Bait/Tackle **OnCall:** Ships' Store *(Moose Island Marine)* **Near:** Ice *(Cube)* **1-3 mi:** Propane *(Dead River 853-4202)*

Boatyard Services

OnSite: Travelift *(50T - to 80 ft.)*, Hydraulic Trailer *(3T)*, Launching Ramp, Engine mechanic *(gas, diesel)*, Electrical Repairs, Electronic Sales, Electronics Repairs, Hull Repairs, Brightwork, Compound, Wash & Wax, Interior Cleaning, Woodworking **OnCall:** Upholstery, Yacht Design *(Moose Is. Design 853-9515)* **Dealer for:** Volvo Penta. Tohatsu, Maritime Skiff, Karavan. **Member:** ABYC - 2 Certified Tech(s) **Yard Rates:** $45-58/hr., Haul & Launch $135/hr. - Min. 1.75 hrs.. *(blocking $25/hr.)* **Storage:** On-Land Indoor $0.63/sq.ft.mo. & Outside $2/ft./mo.

Restaurants and Accommodations

1-3 mi: Restaurant *(Waco Diner 853-4046, B $3-9, L & D $6-30)*, *(Eastport Chowder House 853-4700, L $7-52, D $13-52)*, *(Happy Crab 853-9400, B, L & D $10-18)*, *(Pickled Herring 853-2323, D $13-25, Fine Dining)*, Lite Fare *(Blue Iris 853-2440, B $3-6, L $4-12)*, Pizzeria *(Bank Square Pizza & Deli 853-2709)*, Motel *(Motel East 853-4747, $105-120)*, Inn/B&B *(Chadbourne 853-2727, $110-140)*, *(Milliken 853-2955, $75-85)*

Recreation and Entertainment

OnSite: Dive Shop *(Downeast Diving 263-8251)* **Near:** Picnic Area **Under 1 mi:** Tennis Courts **1-3 mi:** Party Boat *(Quoddy Dam 853-2500 - 35 passengers, 8am-12 noon)*, Video Rental, Park, Museum *(Tides Institute & Museum of Art 853-4047; Barracks 327-1246)*, Tours *(Summer-Keys Ferry to Lubec, Wed. 6:30pm $15; 84 ft. Sylvina W. Beal Windjammer Whale Watching 1:30-4:30pm, $37/20; 93 ft. Halie & Matthew 853-2500)*, Cultural Attract *(Eastport Arts Center 853-4650 - Word of Mouth coffee house, Northern Lights films, Dance Eastport, ArtsBloom, Eastport Strings, Passamaquoddy Bay Symphony, Gallery, Concerts, Stage East Com. Theater 853-7314)*, Sightseeing *(Nat'l Historic Wtfrnt District)*, Galleries *(Crow Tracks, Dancing Dogs Pottery, Eastport Crafts)*, Special Events *(Maine Salmon Fest - week after LabDay)*

Provisioning and General Services

OnCall: Provisioning Service *(Maritme Marine 853-9400)* **Under 1 mi:** Supermarket *(R & M IGA 853-4050)* **1-3 mi:** Delicatessen *(Bank Square 853-2709)*, Wine/Beer, Liquor Store, Farmers' Market *(Thurs 10am-noon, Winter & Washington Sts.)*, Lobster Pound *(Eastport 853-9559; Quoddy Bay 853-6640)*, Bank/ATM, Post Office, Catholic Church, Protestant Church, Library *(Peavey 853-4021 Internet)*, Beauty Salon *(Harborside Clipper)*, Laundry, Bookstore, Pharmacy *(Rite Aid 853-4061)*, Hardware Store *(Wadsworth 853-4343)*, Florist *(Mainely 853-4374)*

Transportation

OnSite: Courtesy Car/Van **1-3 mi:** Bikes *(The Wharf 733-4400)*, Water Taxi *(To & Fro to Lubec 733-4400 $16/RT)*, Rental Car *(Pratt 454-0600)* **Airport:** Eastport/Bangor *(0.1 mi./125 mi.)*

Medical Services

911 Service **1-3 mi:** Doctor *(Eastport Health 853-6001 + Dentist)*, Holistic Services *(Artful Touch 853-2763)* **Hospital:** Calais Reg. 664-0978 *(25 mi.)*

Setting -- Tucked into Deep Cove on the back side of Moose Island, Moose Island Marine is wedged between Eastport Municipal Airport and the Shackford Head State Park peninsula. The seaward end of the drive-on concrete wharf is flanked by the travelift bay and launch ramp and surrounded by side-tie and stern-to floating quality wood docks. The neatly laid out, protected mooring field lies beyond. Marine Technology Center Boat School is adjacent.

Marina Notes -- *Max length on docks 35 ft.LOA - stress on pilings due to tide swing is too great for larger boats. Only short term tenants on docks. Moorings calculated at 100 lbs per foot. All granite: 5500 lb, 4500 lb, & 3500 lb. **Address is Moose Island Chandler in village - docks are 1.7 mi across island. Fabulous ships' store with two floors of anything you might need - delivers to docks. Staff drives boaters to town on mutually convenient schedule. $5/per pkg for hold. 5 acre boatyard, with 12,000 sq. ft. indoor storage (max to 50 ft.) Leases and manages travelift from adjacent Boat School. School has a grant to put water and power on docks - stay tuned. Bathhouse: Heated, cement floor, metal shower stall, open 24/7.

Notable -- Moosehead Marine has a symbiotic relationship with the virtually onsite Boat School an affiliate of Husson University. Dean Pike taught boat building there for three decades. 4.5 miles north. Pleasant Point, Perry is one of the Passamaquoddy Tribe's two homes (796-2301). Legend says that People of the Dawn have lived here for at least 600 generations. Pleasant Point Council (known as Sipayik) has about 2,000 tribal members. Known for the fine workmanship of their baskets, jewelry, wood-carved items, and canoes; the artisans sell their work at shops on the reservation.

PHOTOS ON DVD: 25

Grand Manan Harbour Authority

PO Box 907; Grand Manan, NB E5G 4M1

Tel: (506) 662-8482 **VHF: Monitor** n/a **Talk** n/a
Fax: n/a **Alternate Tel:** (506) 660-0490
Email: gmfa@nb.aibn.com **Web:** www.grandmanannb.com
Nearest Town: North Head **Tourist Info:** (506) 662-3442

Navigational Information

Lat: 44°45.800' **Long:** 066°44.717' **Tide:** 28 ft. **Current:** 3 kt. **Chart:** 4115
Rep. Depths (*MLW*): Entry 30 ft. **Fuel Dock** n/a **Max Slip/Moor** 15 ft./25 ft.
Access: n/a

Marina Facilities *(In Season/Off Season)*

Fuel: *From Irving By Truck 662-3433* - Gasoline, Diesel, On Call Delivery
Slips: 30 Total, 1 Transient **Max LOA:** 60 ft. **Max Beam:** n/a
Rate *(per ft.)*: **Day** $1.25* **Week** $75 **Month** $250
Power: 30 amp n/a, **50 amp** n/a, **100 amp** n/a, **200 amp** n/a
Cable TV: No **Dockside Phone:** No
Dock Type: Floating, Wood
Moorings: 16 Total, 16 Transient **Launch:** None
Rate: Day n/a **Week** n/a **Month** n/a
Heads: None
Internet: No **Laundry:** None
Pump-Out: No **Fee:** n/a **Closed Heads:** No

Marina Operations

Owner/Manager: GMHA **Dockmaster:** Phil Ellis (Acting Harbormaster)
In-Season: Year Round, 24/7 **Off-Season:** n/a
After-Hours Arrival: n/a
Reservations: No **Credit Cards:** Cash Only
Discounts: None
Pets: Welcome **Handicap Access:** No

Marina Services and Boat Supplies

Services - Trash Pick-Up **Communication -** Pay Phone **Supplies - Near:** Ice *(Cube)* **3+ mi:** Ships' Store *(Island Home Hardware 662-8441, 6 mi.)*

Boatyard Services

3+ mi: Travelift *(150T, 9 mi.)*. **Nearest Yard:** Fundy Marine Service Centre (506) 662-8481

Restaurants and Accommodations

Near: Restaurant *(Inn at Whale Cove 662-3181, D $22-28), (Marathon Inn 662-8488), (Shore Crest 662-3216, B, L & D), (Sailor's Landing 662-9620, B, L & D 6:30am-9pm), (Galloways 662-8871)*, Lite Fare *(Compass Road 662-8570, B & L), (Back Porch Cafe 662-8994)*, Inn/B&B *(Compass Rose 662-8570, $89-139), (Marathon Inn 662-8488, $80-130, 28 rooms, Pool, Wi-Fi), (Manan Island Inn 662-8624, $80-100, 9 rooms), (Shore Crest 662-3216, $65-120)*, Condo/Cottage *(Whale Cove 662-3181, $125-160)*

Recreation and Entertainment

OnSite: Tours *(Whales-n-Sails Adventures 662-1999 $65/45 - 60 ft. "Elsie Menota" 11:30 & 4pm; Sea Watch Tours 662-8552 10 mi. in Seal Cove - Machias Seal Island - Landing Permits - Puffins $85/45, Pelagic Bird, Whale Watching $63/43)* **Near:** Playground *(Alexandria Park)*, Tennis Courts, Boat Rentals *(Adventure High Kayak Tours 662-3563 - 3 hrs $60-75)*, Hike/Bike Trails *(Maintained Trail System- maps at tourism office & shops. Hike to Swallow Tail Light. Bike to White Head Island via the free ferry)*, Video Rental *(Fundy House 662-8341)*, Galleries *(GM 662-3293)*, Special Events *(Rotary Fest - 1st week Aug; Canada Day)* **Under 1 mi:** Golf Course *(Brookside Golf Course 662-3253 - club rentals, adjacent 18-Hole Mini-Golf $7/5)*, Park *(Hole-in-the-Wall 662-3152 ,$4/Free. Camping too)*, Cultural Attract *(G.M. Whale & Seabird Research Station 662-3804 a marine history museum)* **3+ mi:** Museum *(Grand Manan 662-3524 at Grand Harbour - Visitor Center, Moses Memorial Bird Collection, a Fresnel lens, geology, archeology, natural history & the G.M. Fishing Industry, 6 mi.)*, Sightseeing *(Atlantic Air Charters 662-8525, 8 mi.)*

Provisioning and General Services

Near: Farmers' Market *(Sat am, late June to Sept. Organic produce, crafts, baked goods, preserves)*, Fishmonger *(Flagg Dulse 662-3660 Nori & Dulse)*, Bank/ATM *(Bank of Nova Scotia)*, Post Office *(Also Canadian Customs 662-3232)*, Protestant Church, Laundry *(Hole-in-the-Wall Park & 6 mi. south at Grand Harbour)* **Under 1 mi:** Convenience Store *(Grand Isle Drugs 662-3439)*, Bakery *(North Head 662-8862 Tue-Sat, 6am-6pm)*, Pharmacy *(Grand Isle 662-3439)* **3+ mi:** Supermarket *(Atlantic Save Easy 662 8152, 4 mi.)*, Wine/Beer *(3.5 mi.)*, Liquor Store *(3.5 mi.)*, Green Grocer *(Harbour View Garden - organic 662-8681, 5 mi.)*, Catholic Church *(6 mi.)*, Library *(662-7099, 6 mi.)*, Hardware Store *(Island Home, Grand Harbour, 6 mi.)*

Transportation

OnCall: Taxi *(Leighton Spicer 662-3708/662-4904)* **Near:** Bikes *(Adventure High 662-3563 $22/day)*, Ferry Service *(To Blacks Harbour 642-0520 - 90 min crossing $11/5.40)* **Airport:** Atlantic Charters 662-8525 *(7 mi.)*

Medical Services

911 Service **Under 1 mi:** Doctor *(Quayyum & Parveen 662-3193)*, Dentist *(Van Worthern 662-3287)* **3+ mi:** Ambulance *(Atlantic Air Ambulance 662-8525, 7 mi.)* **Hospital:** Grand Manan 662-4060 *(1 mi.)*

Setting -- Fifteen-mile long Grand Manan lies six miles off the mainland. Man-made North Head, the most interesting harbor for pleasure craft, is on the northeast corner around Fish Head's Swallowtail Light tucked into Flaggs Cove. Protected by a breakwater, car ferries dock at the first wharf; crayon-colored seiners and draggers berth at the second. Ingalls Head near Grand Harbour is less inviting, but Seal Cove, almost at the tip, ofers good depth and protection.

Marina Notes -- *Flat rate - Under 35 ft $30. Over 35 ft $50. 16 privately owned moorings, use at own discretion. Floating dockage likely requires rafting off fishing boats. 14 to 28 ft. tide minimized in harbor. Most "middle section" info for North Head. Services & facilities in Grand Harbour (7 mi. by road) or Seal Cove (about 13 mi.) noted. CanPass Port of Entry. Haulout at Lee Lambert's Fundy Marine. Bathhouse: heads & showers at Hole-In-The-Wall 662-3152.

Notable -- If a whale-watching trip is on the agenda, this is the place. Whales-n-Sails Adventures' marine biologist Laurie Murison leads trips twice daily on a comfortable, 46-passenger vessel that promises whale sightings - including Humpbacks, Finback, Minke, the rare North Atlantic Right Whale plus harbour porpoise, Atlantic white-sided dolphins and tons of unique sea birds. With almost 300 bird species on Grand Manan, it is a birders' paradise. The entrance to 300 acre Hole-in-the-Wall park and campground is 0.6 mi. from the docks. Ten-minute hike through coastal forest leads to the iconic natural rock arch. Nearly 20 trails riddle the island, covering 40 miles. Fishing supports Grand Manan - lobstering, seining herring & sardines from the weirs, handlining and gill netting and scallop dragging. Lobsters from Maine & all Atlantic provinces are held here in one of the world's largest lobster pounds. Sea vegetables are big business.

Navigational Information

Lat: 44°31.862' **Long:** 067°35.674' **Tide:** 11.5 ft. **Current:** 2 kt. **Chart:** 1332
Rep. Depths (*MLW*): Entry 6 ft. **Fuel Dock** n/a **Max Slip/Moor** 4 ft./8 ft.
Access: Moosabec Reach to town breakwater

Marina Facilities *(In Season/Off Season)*

Fuel: *Look Lobster - 300 yds.* - Gasoline, Diesel
Slips: 10 Total, 2 Transient **Max LOA:** 40 ft. **Max Beam:** n/a
Rate *(per ft.)*: **Day** $0* **Week** n/a **Month** n/a
Power: 30 amp n/a, **50 amp** n/a, **100 amp** n/a, **200 amp** n/a
Cable TV: No **Dockside Phone:** No
Dock Type: Floating, Alongside, Wood
Moorings: 0 Total, 0 Transient **Launch:** n/a, Dinghy Dock
Rate: Day n/a **Week** n/a **Month** n/a
Heads: 1 Toilet(s)
Internet: No **Laundry:** None
Pump-Out: No **Fee:** n/a **Closed Heads:** No

Marina Operations

Owner/Manager: Russell Batson (Harbormaster) **Dockmaster:** Same
In-Season: Year Round, 24/7 hrs. **Off-Season:** n/a
After-Hours Arrival: Tie Up at Eastern Float
Reservations: No **Credit Cards:** n/a
Discounts: None
Pets: Welcome, Dog Walk Area **Handicap Access:** No

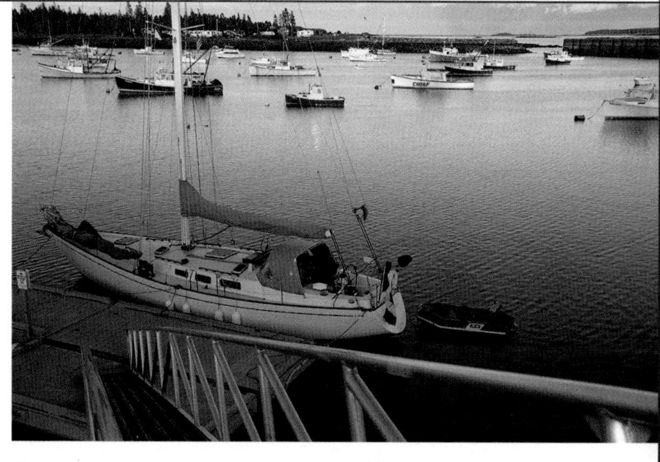

Jonesport Municipal Marina

1 Batson's Point; Jonesport, ME 04649

Tel: (207) 497-5931 **VHF: Monitor** Ch. 16 **Talk** Ch. 03
Fax: n/a **Alternate Tel:** (207) 497-5926
Email: n/a **Web:** n/a
Nearest Town: Jonesport **Tourist Info:** (207) 963-2547

Marina Services and Boat Supplies

Communication - UPS, Express Mail **Supplies - Near:** Ice *(Block, Cube)*, Ships' Store *(T.A. King 497-2274)*, Bait/Tackle *(Jonesport Fishing Supply 497-9665)*, Propane

Boatyard Services

OnSite: Launching Ramp **OnCall:** Divers, Bottom Cleaning **Near:** Hydraulic Trailer, Hull Repairs, Rigger, Canvas Work, Brightwork, Propeller Repairs, Woodworking. **Under 1 mi:** Metal Fabrication. **Nearest Yard:** Jonesport Shipyard (207) 497-2701

Restaurants and Accommodations

Near: Restaurant *(Tall Barney's 497-2403, B $3-7, L $5-15, D $7-17, B-Lobster Omlette $19, D- Surf & Turf $25)*, Pizzeria *(Jonesport 497-2187)*, Inn/B&B *(Harbor House 497-5417)*, Condo/Cottage *(Blue Nose Cottage on Sawyer Cove 497-2701)*

Recreation and Entertainment

OnSite: Party Boat **Near:** Video Rental *(Mossabec Video 497-2662)*, Tours *(Laura Fish Coastal Cruises on her tour boat "Aaron Thomas" 598-7473; Learn about Lobstering with Capt Paul Ferriero on the "Honey B")*, Galleries *(Harbor House Antiques 497-5417; Nelson's Decoys, Downeast Gallery & Puffin Art Gallery - 3 in one - 497-3488, Moospecke Antiques 497-2457; Jonesport Nautical Antiques & Nautical Art 800-996-5655; Pierce Kettering 497-2874)* **1-3 mi:** Tennis Courts *(Municipal)* **3+ mi:** Hike/Bike Trails *(Great Wass Island - 5-mile loop hike or scheduled guided hikes with Dan Grenier, Maine Preserves Manager. Contact maine_events@tnc.org, 4.5 mi.)*, Park *(Nature Conservancy's Great Wass Island 729-5181- by car or dinghy from Beal's Island, 4 mi.)*, Sightseeing *(Maine Central Model Railroad - 900 ft. HO display 497-2255, Helen & Buz Beal, free but donation appreciated, 4 mi.)*

Provisioning and General Services

Near: Convenience Store, Market *(Jonesport IGA 497-2189)*, Wine/Beer, Green Grocer *(Tall Barney's - cold cuts too)*, Meat Market, Bank/ATM, Post Office, Library, Laundry, Hardware Store *(Church's True Value 497-2778; T.A. King 497-2274)*, Department Store **Under 1 mi:** Liquor Store

Transportation

Airport: Bangor Int'l *(65 mi.)*

Medical Services

911 Service **OnCall:** Ambulance **Near:** Doctor *(Jonesport Medical Center 497-5614)*, Dentist *(Jonesport Medical Center)* **3+ mi:** Veterinarian *(Machias 255-8200, 20 mi.)* **Hospital:** Downeast Community in Machias 255-3356 *(20 mi.)*

Setting -- Along Moosabec Reach, at the mouth of Sawyer Cove, a dramatic, 1200-foot corrugated steel-and-concrete breakwater protects the Jonesport wharf and mooring field. Brightly colored lobster trawlers mix with recreational vessels in the placid inner harbor. A long boardwalk connects the floats to the small village where a pretty white steeple peeks above the foliage and a handful of galleries, a casual restaurant, and some shops dot the quiet main street.

Marina Notes -- *Dockage free to visiting boaters. Recreational boat on northern dock. Fuel - gas & diesel - 300 yards at Look Lobster (497-2353). The number listed rings in the Harbormaster's house; his name is Russell Batson. Call after 5pm. Walking distance to boatyard services at Jonesport Shipyard up the Cove. Wander down to Moosabec Variety to watch the community jigsaw puzzlers. Bathhouse: 1 Porta-Pottie. Laundry in village.

Notable -- Unspoiled, untouristed Maine is hard to come by - but it is alive and well in Jonesport. A quintessential lobstering village on a peninsula that extends 12 miles. Hike the five-mile loop trail in the 1579-acre Nature Conservancy's Great Wass Island Preserve - where bald eagles, eiders, osprey, mergansers circle above large stands of Jack Pine, the largest in Maine, coastal plateau bogs with 10,000 years worth of sphagnum moss that give rise to rare plants like beachhead iris, bakeapple, marsh felwort, deer-hair sedge, dragon's mouth orchid and bird eye primrose that manage to survive in this harsh climate of wind, salt spray and fog. On June 12, 1775, in the first naval battle of the Revolution, the British armed sloop "Margaretta" surrendered to local Mainers in Machias Bay. According to local lore, she was eventually chased up Sawyers Cove and burned by the British - her bones still lie there under the mud.

Jonesport Shipyard

PO Box 214; 285 Main Street; Jonesport, ME 04649

Tel: (207) 497-2701 **VHF: Monitor** Ch. 16 **Talk** Ch. 9
Fax: (207) 497-2701 **Alternate Tel:** n/a
Email: jshipyard@mgemaine.com **Web:** n/a
Nearest Town: Jonesport **Tourist Info:** (207) 963-2547

Navigational Information

Lat: 44°32.041' **Long:** 067°35.478' **Tide:** 11.5 ft. **Current:** 3 kt. **Chart:** 1332
Rep. Depths (*MLW*): Entry 8 ft. **Fuel Dock** n/a **Max Slip/Moor** -/7 ft.
Access: Moosabec Reach to breakwater then north 800 ft. to moorings

Marina Facilities *(In Season/Off Season)*

Fuel: No
Slips: 0 Total, 0 Transient **Max LOA:** 45 ft. **Max Beam:** n/a
Rate *(per ft.)*: **Day** n/a **Week** n/a **Month** n/a
Power: 30 amp n/a, **50 amp** n/a, **100 amp** n/a, **200 amp** n/a
Cable TV: No **Dockside Phone:** No
Dock Type: n/a
Moorings: 5 Total, 5 Transient **Launch:** No, Dinghy Dock
Rate: Day $20 **Week** $140/45 **Month** $380/150
Heads: 2 Toilet(s), 4 Shower(s), Book Exchange
Internet: Yes *(Wi-Fi, Free)* **Laundry:** 2 Washer(s), 3 Dryer(s)
Pump-Out: Full Service, 1 Central **Fee:** $65/hr by appt **Closed Heads:** Yes

Marina Operations

Owner/Manager: Patricia Noreen **Dockmaster:** Same
In-Season: Year Round, 8am-4:30pm **Off-Season:** n/a
After-Hours Arrival: Pick Up a mooring; Check in next morning
Reservations: Yes **Credit Cards:** Visa/MC, Amex
Discounts: None
Pets: Welcome, Dog Walk Area **Handicap Access:** No

Marina Services and Boat Supplies

Services - Security *(24 hrs., Owners Live On-Site)*, Trash Pick-Up, Dock Carts **Communication -** Mail & Package Hold, Fax in/out *($1/pp)*, UPS, Express Mail **Supplies - OnSite:** Ships' Store *(T.A. King 497-2274)* **Near:** Ice *(Block, Cube)* **Under 1 mi:** Marine Discount Store *(Hamilton 497-2778)*, Propane *(Taking 497-2274)*

Boatyard Services

OnSite: Hydraulic Trailer *(30T)*, Launching Ramp, Engine mechanic *(gas, diesel)*, Hull Repairs, Rigger, Brightwork, Compound, Wash & Wax, Propeller Repairs, Woodworking, Yacht Interiors **OnCall:** Divers **Near:** Canvas Work *(Downeast 497-2251)*. **Yard Rates:** $58/hr., Bottom Paint $53/hr. **Storage:** On-Land $3.25/ft./mo; Inside $7.50/sq.ft./season

Restaurants and Accommodations

OnSite: Condo/Cottage *(Bluenose Cottage 497-2701, $850/wk)* **Near:** Coffee Shop *(Mossabec Great Crab Rolls)*, Pizzeria *(Jonesport 497-2187, L & D $10-12 No Del.)*, Inn/B&B *(Harbor House 497-5417)* **Under 1 mi:** Restaurant *(Tall Barney 497-2403, B $3-7, L $5-15, D $7-17, B-Lobster Omlette $19, D- Surf & Turf $25)*

Recreation and Entertainment

OnSite: Picnic Area **Near:** Beach, Video Rental *(Mossabec Video 497-2662)*, Museum *(Sardine Museum 497-2961)*, Tours, Sightseeing *(Laura Fish Coastal Cruises on her tour boat "Aaron Thomas" 598-7473; Learn about Lobstering with Capt Paul Ferriero on the "Honey B.")*, Galleries *(Harbor House Antiques 497-5417; Nelson's Decoys, Downeast Gallery & Puffin Art Gallery - 3 in one - 497-3488, Moospecke Antiques 497-2457; Jonesport Nautical Antiques & Nautical Art 497-5655; Pierce Kettering 497-2874)*, Special Events *(4th of July)* **Under 1 mi:** Tennis Courts **3+ mi:** Park *(Nature Conservancy's Great Wass Island 729-5181- by car or dinghy via Beal's Island, 4 mi.)*

Provisioning and General Services

Near: Convenience Store *(Mossabec)*, Wine/Beer, Lobster Pound, Protestant Church, Hardware Store *(T.A. King 497-2274; Church True Value 497-2778)* **Under 1 mi:** Market *(IGA)*, Liquor Store *(Stewarts Grocery)*, Bakery, Green Grocer *(Tall Barney's - cold cuts too)*, Bank/ATM, Post Office, Library *(Peabody Memorial Internet)*, Department Store

Transportation

OnSite: Courtesy Car/Van *(Owners can sometimes help)* **Airport:** Machias/Bar Harbor *(20 mi./50 mi.)*

Medical Services

911 Service **OnCall:** Ambulance **1-3 mi:** Doctor *(Weisberger 497-5614)* **3+ mi:** Chiropractor *(Knowles, 20 mi.)*, Veterinarian *(Machias 255-8200, 20 mi.)* **Hospital:** Downeast Community in Machias 255-3356 *(20 mi.)*

Setting -- Tucked into quiet, serene Sawyer Cove, past the working harbor, Jonesport Shipyard hides a full-service repair facility a short walk from the sweet old Maine lobster village. Picnic tables and fireplaces sit on a grassy knoll overlooking the mooring field and dinghy dock - with spectacular views out the cove to the crayon colored lobster boats floating inside the breakwater. The Jonesport peninsula pokes six miles into the ocean so it's an easy cruise in and out.

Marina Notes -- Moorings & dinghy dock. Fuel quarter mile at Looks - Dysarts Gas & Diesel. Wi-Fi - available on moorings with external antenna, otherwise in Laundry Room. Quality boat repairs & restorations. Large boatshed, on hard storage, well-equipped ships' store. Bathhouse: Immaculate, yellow and blue walls trimmed with nicely executed varnished wood joinery. Fiberglass shower stalls. Large, bright, airy laundry room with book exchange, Wi-Fi, wood trim.

Notable -- Head back on the water to understand more about this unique, unspoiled corner of the world. Cruise with Laura Fish on her tour boat "Aaron Thomas." Learn all about Lobstering with Capt Paul Ferriero on the "Honey B." Sadly, the famous Norton's "The Chief" boat trip to 15-acre Machias Seal Island for a close up view of the Atlantic Puffins no longer operates. Nearest access to Machias is with Sea Watch Tours, Grand Manan Island, NB or Bold Coast Charters, Cutler, ME. The spectacular 3500 Puffin summer nesting colony - the largest on the Maine Coast - also attracts Razorbills, Common Murres, Guillemots, Eiders, Gannets, Shearwaters, Storm-Petrels, Cormorant, Auks, Loons, Black Ducks, Grebes, Eagles. and Arctic Terns. Jonesport's Fourth of July is a multi-day event with a parade, pipers, community dinners, competitions and the famous "Fastest Lobster Boat in the World" race through Moosabec Reach.

Navigational Information
Lat: 44°23.350' **Long:** 068°04.850' **Tide:** 15 ft. **Current:** n/a **Chart:** 13322
Rep. Depths (*MLW*): Entry 10 ft. **Fuel Dock** n/a **Max Slip/Moor** 6 ft./-
Access: Round Grindstone Neck, past entr. to Sand Cove into Henry Cove

Marina Facilities *(In Season/Off Season)*
Fuel: Diesel
Slips: 0 Total, 0 Transient **Max LOA:** 60 ft. **Max Beam:** n/a
Rate *(per ft.)*: **Day** n/a **Week** n/a **Month** n/a
Power: 30 amp n/a, **50 amp** n/a, **100 amp** n/a, **200 amp** n/a
Cable TV: No **Dockside Phone:** No
Dock Type: n/a
Moorings: 10 Total, 10 Transient **Launch:** None, Dinghy Dock
Rate: Day $25 **Week** $150 **Month** n/a
Heads: 2 Toilet(s)
Internet: No **Laundry:** None
Pump-Out: OnSite, Full Service **Fee:** Free **Closed Heads:** No

Marina Operations
Owner/Manager: Warren Pettegrow **Dockmaster:** Same
In-Season: May-Oct, 9am-6pm **Off-Season:** Nov-Apr, Closed
After-Hours Arrival: Call in advance for instructions
Reservations: Yes **Credit Cards:** Visa/MC, Cash or checks only
Discounts: None
Pets: No **Handicap Access:** No

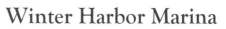

Winter Harbor Marina

88 Sargent Street; Winter Harbor, ME 04693

Tel: (207) 963-7449 **VHF: Monitor** n/a **Talk** n/a
Fax: n/a **Alternate Tel:** n/a
Email: n/a **Web:** n/a
Nearest Town: Winter Harbor *(0.5 mi.)* **Tourist Info:** (207) 963-7658

Marina Services and Boat Supplies
Services - Trash Pick-Up **Communication -** FedEx, UPS, Express Mail **Supplies - Under 1 mi:** Ice *(Cube)* **3+ mi:** Ships' Store *(U S Bells 963-7184, 5 mi.)*

Boatyard Services
OnSite: Hydraulic Trailer, Engine mechanic *(gas, diesel)*

Restaurants and Accommodations
Near: Condo/Cottage *(Mainstay Cottages)* **Under 1 mi:** Restaurant *(Chase's 963-7171, B, L & D $5-12 - and take-out)*, *(Fisherman's Inn 963-5585, L $13-30, D $17-29, Not fine dining, but good local food since 1947)*, Lite Fare *(HarborGirl Emporium and Cafe 963-5900, eat-in, take-out 11am-9pm, Free Wi-Fi)*, Inn/B&B *(Oceanside Meadows Inn 963-5557, $119-209, 1860s beach front sea captain's home on 200 acres of forest & meadow)* **1-3 mi:** Motel *(Pines Motel & Cottages 96-322-96 , $55-70)* **3+ mi:** Restaurant *(Nautica Pub 963-7916, 4 mi., L & D $4-7)*, Hotel *(Elsa's 963-7571, $105-165, 4 mi.)*

Recreation and Entertainment
Near: Hike/Bike Trails *(11.5 mile loop from Winter Harbor around Schoodic Point section of Acadia National Park or short hikes from Blueberry Hill Parking Area - via Island Explorer)*, Special Events *(Winter Harbor Lobster Festival - 2nd Sat Aug -Lobsters, Breakfasts, Craft Fair, Parade; Schoodic Arts Fest - Aug 963-2569)* **Under 1 mi:** Bowling *(Turner Mem. 963-5559)*, Cultural Attract *(Schoodic Arts for All 963-2569 Year-round concerts, dance, theater, film, fine art, and Last Friday of Month Coffee House - all at newly restored 1904 Hammond Hall)*, Galleries *(Maloué 963 2193, Little Field 963-6005, Whitmer Hammond Antiques 963-7542, Winter Harbor Anqiues - Work 963-7900, Blair Art Glass 963-2664, whopaints 963-2076)* **1-3 mi:** Golf Course *(Grindstone Neck G.C. 963-7760 open to public)* **3+ mi:** Tours *(Bartlett Maine Estate Winery 546-2408, 7 mi.)*

Provisioning and General Services
Near: Supermarket *(IGA)*, Gourmet Shop *(J.M. Gerrish Provisions 963-2727)*, Wine/Beer *(J.M. Gerrish)*, Farmers' Market *(Tue, 9am-noon, 546-2395 Newman & Main Sts.)* **Under 1 mi:** Fishmonger *(Grindstone Neck 963-7347 - Smoked seafood)*, Lobster Pound *(Winter Harbor Lobster Co-Op 963-5857)*, Post Office, Protestant Church, Library *(Winter Harbor 963-7556 - wonderful stone & shingle 19th C. building)*, Newsstand, Retail Shops *(Winter Harbor 5 & 10 963-7927 - whatever you need: souvenirs, copies, fax, photo developing, newspapers)*, Department Store *(Winterharbor Five & Ten 963-7927)*, Copies Etc. *(5 & 10)* **3+ mi:** Delicatessen *(Downeast Deli 963-2700, 4.5 mi.)*, Hardware Store *(Anderson Marine 422-3542, 7 mi.)*

Transportation
OnSite: Local Bus *(Island Explorer 288-2984 - to Schoodic Point section of Acadia National Park plus Birch Harbor & Prospect Harbor - June 23-Aug 31)*, Ferry Service *(Bar Harbor 288-2984 $29.50/19.50 RT- June 23 - Aug 31, 8:30, 10:30am, 1, 3, 5pm. Bikes $6)* **OnCall:** Rental Car *(Enterprise 664-2662 - Ellsworth)* **Airport:** Bar Harbor 667-7329 *(31 mi.)*

Medical Services
911 Service **Under 1 mi:** Doctor *(Newman 963-2001)* **Hospital:** Maine Coast Memorial 664-5311 *(7 mi.)*

Setting -- On the west side of Winter Harbor, past Sand Cove (home of Winter Harbor Yacht Club) and Inner Harbor (home to the lobster fleet), Winter Harbor Marine lies midway along the east side of Henry Cove. At the head of the cove, the small, pretty village of Winter Harbor promises a lively arts scene with galleries, studios, concerts and exhibits along with restaurants and provisions that serve the summer colony and the lobstering community.

Marina Notes -- The Bar Harbor Ferry that berths here is the primary business - and very convenient. Mooring field is open to the south and southwest. Winter Harbor Yacht Club (963-2275) in Sand Cove (wide open) also welcomes visiting boaters on their moorings (with launch service) or, on rare occassion, their floats. The village is a half mile from the marina and one mile from the Y.C. Bathhouse: 2 Basic heads

Notable -- Schoodic Arts for All art center hosts art exhibits, concerts, and performances throughout the summer months in recently restored 1904 Hammond Hall. The famous Lobster Festival includes lobster boat races with 13 classes, over 80 craft exhibitors, lobster dinner, road races, and the parade. Hike out to exclusive Grindstone Neck, the beautiful old summer colony that was founded during the heyday of railroads and steamships. The onsite Bar Harbor ferry not only makes Bar Harbor a quick hop across Frenchman's Bay, but also brings the fabulous Island Explorer to the door making all of the 2100-acre Schoodick Peninsula section of Acadia Nat'l Park accessible to on-foot boaters. A 12-mile shoreline loop is perfect for those with bikes aboard. Alternatively take the Island Explorer to Schoodick Gatehouse at the Education & Research Center (site of the U.S. Navy base closed in 2002) for maps and hiking advice.

PHOTOS ON DVD: 25

West Cove Boat Yard

PO Box 383; 41 Waukeag Avenue; Sorrento, ME 04677

Tel: (207) 422-3137 **VHF: Monitor** n/a **Talk** n/a
Fax: (207) 422-3137 **Alternate Tel:** (207) 610-4568
Email: Christopher@westcoveboatyard.com **Web:** westcoveboatyard.com
Nearest Town: Ellsworth *(14 mi.)* **Tourist Info:** (207) 963-7658

Navigational Information

Lat: 44°28.525' **Long:** 068°10.933' **Tide:** 11 ft. **Current:** 1 kt. **Chart:** 13318
Rep. Depths (*MLW*): Entry 12 ft. **Fuel Dock** n/a **Max Slip/Moor** -/7 ft.
Access: Frenchman Bay to Northern Part of Sorrento "Boot"

Marina Facilities *(In Season/Off Season)*

Fuel: No
Slips: 0 Total, 0 Transient **Max LOA:** 50 ft. **Max Beam:** n/a
Rate *(per ft.)*: **Day** n/a **Week** n/a **Month** n/a
Power: 30 amp n/a, **50 amp** n/a, **100 amp** n/a, **200 amp** n/a
Cable TV: No **Dockside Phone:** No
Dock Type: n/a
Moorings: 6 Total, 6 Transient **Launch:** None, Dinghy Dock
Rate: Day $35 **Week** n/a **Month** n/a
Heads: None
Internet: Yes *(Wi-Fi, Free)* **Laundry:** None
Pump-Out: No **Fee:** n/a **Closed Heads:** No

Marina Operations

Owner/Manager: Christopher LaRiviere **Dockmaster:** Louis Sutherland
In-Season: Year Round, 7:30am-4pm M-F **Off-Season:** n/a
After-Hours Arrival: None
Reservations: No **Credit Cards:** Cash/Check
Discounts: None
Pets: Welcome **Handicap Access:** No

Marina Services and Boat Supplies

Services - Trash Pick-Up **Communication -** FedEx, UPS **Supplies - OnSite:** Ships' Store *(Limited)*

Boatyard Services

OnSite: Forklift *(5T)*, Crane *(15T)*, Hydraulic Trailer *(15T)*, Launching Ramp, Engine mechanic *(gas, diesel)*, Electrical Repairs, Electronics Repairs, Hull Repairs, Rigger, Divers, Bottom Cleaning, Brightwork, Compound, Wash & Wax, Interior Cleaning *($35/hr.)*, Propeller Repairs, Woodworking, Yacht Interiors, Metal Fabrication, Painting, Total Refits **Yard Rates:** $45-75/hr, Haul & Launch $8-10/ft./1-way, Power Wash $3/ft., Bottom Paint $15/ft.. **Storage:** On-Land Out $60/ft., In $60/ft/season

Restaurants and Accommodations

Under 1 mi: Inn/B&B *(Bass Cove Farm 422-3564)* **3+ mi:** Restaurant *(Chester Pike's Galley 422-2059, 5 mi., Sullivan - B, L & D - blueberry pancakes, seafood specials)*

Recreation and Entertainment

OnSite: Boat Rentals *(15 ft. whaler $350/wk.; 23 ft. C&C $700/wk.)* **Near:** Tennis Courts *(& Croquet Courts)*, Movie Theater *(Library)*, Sightseeing *(79-acre Preble Island - home to roosting eagles)*, Galleries *(Lynn Stone 415-789-8077 - unique wearable art made from seaglass, beachstones and sterling)* **Under 1 mi:** Pool *(Sorrento Salt Water)*, Golf Course *(Blink Bonnie Golf Links - 422-3930 Public, 9 holes, covering 5,553 yards)*

Provisioning and General Services

Near: Lobster Pound *(Sorrento Lobster, 422-9082)*, Post Office *(across form Town Dock)*, Protestant Church *(Church of the Redeemer - Episcopal)*, Library *(Seasonal - National Register of Historic Places)* **3+ mi:** Convenience Store *(Young's Market, 5 mi.)*, Supermarket *(Dunbars, Sullivan, 7 mi.)*, Pharmacy *(Ellsworth, 20 mi.)*, Hardware Store *(Anderson Marine 422-3542 Goldsboro, 7 mi.)*

Transportation

OnCall: Rental Car *(Enterprise 664-2662 - Ellsworth)*, Taxi *(Cell Kell 667-7306 - Ellsworth)* **Airport:** Bar Harbor/Bangor *(23 mi./60 mi.)*

Medical Services

911 Service **OnCall:** Ambulance **Under 1 mi:** Dentist *(Sorrento Dental 422-3770)* **3+ mi:** Doctor *(Crowley, Hanson, Nabozny, Pentin 963-4066, 9 mi.)*, Chiropractor *(Croft 963-7154, 9 mi.)*, Veterinarian *(Schoodic Animal Hosp 422-9999, 3 mi.)* **Hospital:** Maine Coast Mem., Ellsworth plus Life Flight Helipad in town *(23 mi.)*

Setting -- Around Bean Point, West Cove's small, protected mooring field is tucked into Back Cove - surrounded by evergreens standing on a rock-bound ledge. On shore, the modest boatyard facility belies the old Maine craftsmanship happening within or the lovely summer community that surrounds it.

Marina Notes -- On some charts this is Black Cove. Moorings attached to granite blocks in mud. Three heated service bays for boats to 50 Ft. LOA plus 20,000 Square Feet of indoor storage - for boats to 60 ft. Manages 150 boats. West Cove can arrange access to the private Sorrento Swimming Pool. Hurricane Hole. Sorrento Yacht Club has three guest moorings; inquire at their office in the library. Bathhouse: None - heads at Town Dock.

Notable -- At the tip of Waukeag Neck, Sorrento is one of the Gouldsboro Penninsula's quiet, elegant, stopped-in-time summer colonies. In 1889, Maine Central's Boston & Mount Desert Limited along with steamship service spurred resort development which included the large Hotel Sorrento. The hotel burned long ago, train and steamship service ceased and the resort collapsed.Today the gorgeous old turn-of-the-last-century style "cottages" are still here and impeccably maintained. The Town Dock, in the main harbor a tenth of a mile walk across the peninsula, is near the little village center - with the gray-shingled post office, church and seasonal 1892 shingled Victorian Sorrento Public Library, trimmed in yellow and rimmed with porches. The tide fills the private Sorrento Swimming Pool off Nautilus Road (a little over half a mile) that is managed by the Village Improvement Association - along with tennis, croquet, golf, sailing and a day camp. Sorrento Lobster's large commercial pound is wedged into a small cove beyond the main harbor between Preble Island and the neck.

4. ME – Mount Desert Region

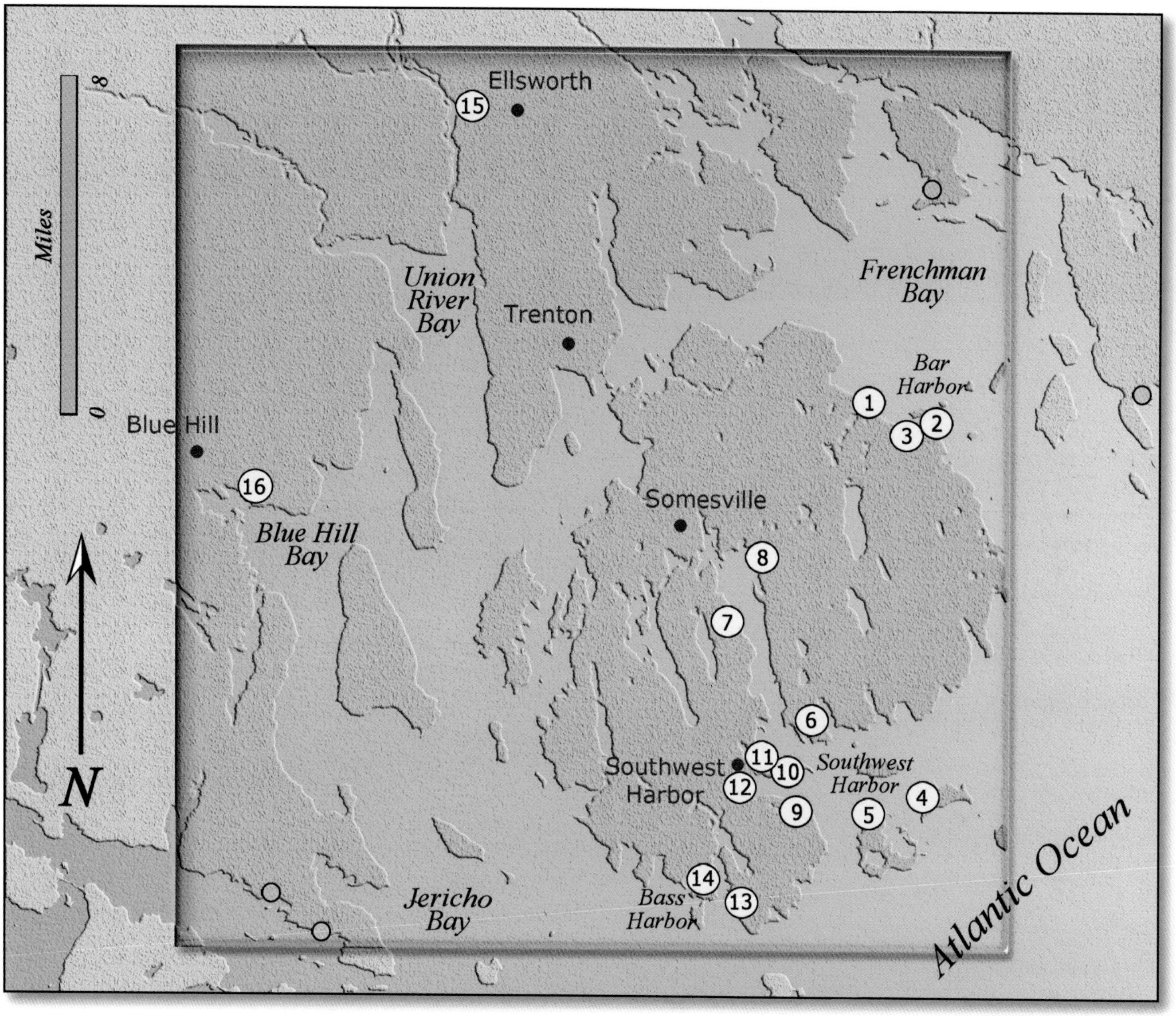

Miles 0 8
N
Ellsworth
Union River Bay
Trenton
Frenchman Bay
Bar Harbor
Blue Hill
Blue Hill Bay
Somesville
Southwest Harbor
Southwest Harbor
Jericho Bay
Bass Harbor
Atlantic Ocean

MAP	MARINA	HARBOR	PAGE
1	**Bar Harbor Regency Resort**	*Frenchman Bay*	78
2	**Bar Harbor Municipal Marina**	*Frenchman Bay/Bar Harbor*	79
3	**The Harborside Hotel & Marina**	*Frenchman Bay/Bar Harbor*	80
4	**Islesford Dock Restaurant**	*Little Cranberry Harbor*	81
5	**Cranberry Island Moorings**	*Spurling's Cove*	82
6	**Northeast Harbor Marina**	*Northeast Harbor*	83
7	**John Williams Boat Company**	*Somes Sound*	84
8	**Henry R. Abel & Co. Yacht Yard**	*Somes Sound*	85
9	**Hinckley Service Yacht Yard**	*Southwest Harbor*	86
10	**Beal's Lobster Pier**	*Southwest Harbor*	87
11	**Southwest Boat Marine**	*Southwest Harbor*	88
12	**Dysart's Great Harbor Marina**	*Southwest Harbor*	89
13	**Morris Yachts**	*Bass Harbor*	90
14	**Up Harbor Marine**	*Bass Harbor*	91
15	**Ellsworth Harbor Park**	*Blue Hill Bay/Union River*	92
16	**Kollegewidgwok Yacht Club**	*Blue Hill Bay*	93

RATINGS: 1-5 for Marina Facilities & Amenities,  1-2 for Boatyard Services,  1-2 for MegaYacht Facilities,  for Something Special.

SERVICES:  for CCM – Certified Clean Marina,  for Pump-Out, for Internet,  for Fuel, for Restaurant,  for Provisioning nearby,  for Catamaran-friendly,  for SportFish Charter,  for Pool/Beach, and  for Golf within a mile. *For an explanation of ACC's Ratings, see page 8.*

Bar Harbor Regency Resort

123 Eden Street; Bar Harbor, ME 04609

Tel: (207) 266-5857; (800) 234-6835 **VHF: Monitor** n/a **Talk** n/a
Fax: (207) 288-3089 **Alternate Tel:** (800) 234-6835
Email: n/a **Web:** bhregency@yahoo.com
Nearest Town: Bar Harbor *(1.2 mi.)* **Tourist Info:** (207) 288-5103

Navigational Information

Lat: 44°24.003' **Long:** 068°13.514' **Tide:** 13 ft. **Current:** 2 kt. **Chart:** 13302
Rep. Depths (*MLW*): Entry 20 ft. **Fuel Dock** n/a **Max Slip/Moor** 12 ft./-
Access: North side of Bar Harbor bar in Frenchman Bay

Marina Facilities *(In Season/Off Season)*

Fuel: No
Slips: 4 Total, 4 Transient **Max LOA:** 200 ft. **Max Beam:** n/a
Rate *(per ft.)*: **Day** $3.00 **Week** Inq. **Month** Inq.
Power: 30 amp Incl., **50 amp** Incl., **100 amp** Incl., **200 amp** n/a
Cable TV: No **Dockside Phone:** No
Dock Type: Floating, Pilings, Alongside, Wood
Moorings: 0 Total, 0 Transient **Launch:** n/a
Rate: Day n/a **Week** n/a **Month** n/a
Heads: 2 Toilet(s), 1 Shower(s) *(dressing rooms)*, Hair Dryers, Sauna
Internet: Yes *(Lobby)* **Laundry:** 42 Washer(s), 4 Dryer(s), Iron, Iron Board
Pump-Out: No **Fee:** n/a **Closed Heads:** No

Marina Operations

Owner/Manager: Eben Salvatore **Dockmaster:** Debbie Jordan
In-Season: Late May-Oct. 12 **Off-Season:** Oct-May, Closed
After-Hours Arrival: Call ahead, then see front desk at the hotel
Reservations: Yes, Required **Credit Cards:** Visa/MC, Dscvr, Din, Amex
Discounts: None
Pets: Welcome **Handicap Access:** Yes, Heads, Docks

Marina Services and Boat Supplies

Services - Docking Assistance, Concierge, Boaters' Lounge **Communication -** Mail & Package Hold, Phone Messages, Fax in/out, FedEx, DHL, UPS, Express Mail *(Sat Del)* **Supplies - 1-3 mi:** Ice *(Block, Cube)*, Bait/Tackle *(Kyle's Ketch 288-8211)*, Propane *(Clark Coal 288-3309, Burwaldo's 288-5515, Maine Street Market)*

Boatyard Services

Nearest Yard: Hinckley Yacht Yard, SW Harbor (207) 244-5572

Restaurants and Accommodations

OnSite: Restaurant *(Edenfield 288-9723, B $10, D $8-34)*, Seafood Shack *(Stewmans Lobster Pound 288-9723, L & D $7-23, Kids' $5-6 - Lobster Market Price)*, Snack Bar *(Tiki Bar L $5-12, at the pool)*, Hotel *(Bar Harbor Regency 288-9723, $150-360)* **Near:** Restaurant *(Looking Glass B $7-11, D $10-33, Blue Nose Inn)*, Motel *(Days Inn 288-3321, $99-185)*, Hotel *(Bar Harbor Hotel - Blue Nose Inn 288-3453, $145-300)*, *(Bayview 288-5861, $150-250)* **Under 1 mi:** Restaurant *(The Club 288-5033, D $50)*

Recreation and Entertainment

OnSite: Heated Pool, Spa, Picnic Area, Grills, Playground, Tennis Courts *(Lighted)*, Fitness Center, Jogging Paths *(ocean front)* **Near:** Museum *(Dorr Natural History 288-5395, $3.50/1, Mon-Sat 10-5; Abbe Native American 288-3519 & 1904 Ledgelawn 288-4596 - 1 mi.)*, Galleries *(Blum Art at COA 288-5015)*, Special Events *(Blessing of Fleet - Jun; Village Green concerts Mon, Thurs 8pm; Music Fests - Jul; Jazz Fest - Aug)* **Under 1 mi:** Movie Theater *(Criterion 288-3441)*, Park *(Acadia National Park 288-3338)* **1-3 mi:** Golf Course *(Kebo Valley 288-3000)*, Boat Rentals *(Sea Kayak Tours 800-347-0940)*, Video Rental *(Arnold's 288-4145)*, Video Arcade, Cultural Attract *(Oceanarium & Lobster Hatchery 288-5005)*, Sightseeing *(Bar Harbor AtlantiCat Whale Watch 288-2386 - 3 trips/day $58/28/8)*

Provisioning and General Services

OnSite: Convenience Store, Lobster Pound, Newsstand, Copies Etc. **Under 1 mi:** Post Office, Catholic Church, Protestant Church, Beauty Salon, Dry Cleaners, Hardware Store *(Paradis True Value 288-4995)* **1-3 mi:** Supermarket *(Hannaford 288-5680)*, Delicatessen *(Cottage Street 288-3010)*, Health Food *(A&B Naturals 288-8480)*, Wine/Beer, Liquor Store *(Bayside 288-2772)*, Bakery *(Morning Glory 288-3041)*, Farmers' Market *(Sun 10-1, 223-2293 YMCA)*, Fishmonger *(Parsons 288-4736)*, Library *(Jesup Mem 288-4245)*, Bookstore *(Sherman's 288-3161)*, Pharmacy *(Rite Aid 288-2222)*

Transportation

OnSite: Local Bus *(Island Explorer 288-4573)* **OnCall:** Rental Car *(Enterprise 667-1217)*, Taxi *(At Your Service 288-9222)* **Near:** Ferry Service *(Bay Ferry 888-249-7245)* **1-3 mi:** Bikes *(Bar Harbor Bicycle 288-3886)* **Airport:** Bar Harbor/Bangor Int'l. *(9 mi./50 mi.)*

Medical Services

911 Service **OnCall:** Ambulance **Under 1 mi:** Veterinarian *(Acadia 288-5733)* **1-3 mi:** Doctor *(Family Health Ctr 288-5606)*, Dentist *(High Street 288-4754)*, Chiropractor *(Gerrish 288-3980)*, Holistic Services *(Acadia Massage 288-3899)* **Hospital:** M.D.I. Health Center 288-5081 *(1.5 mi.)*

Setting -- Directly on Frenchman Bay, north of the Bar Harbor bar, Regency Sunspree's manicured lawns and gardens roll to the water where a lighted wharf, dotted with umbrella-topped picnic tables, leads to a single floating dock with a long T-head. The well appointed resort fans out on either side of the fixed pier. Stewman's Lobster Pound with two outdoor seating areas sits at the head. An outdoor snake-shaped pool with Tiki hut overlooks the Bay - backed by an arc of balconied three-story hotel buildings housing 278 richly decorated rooms and an elegant brick-and-stone half-timbered event facility.

Marina Notes -- 200 ft. Floating dock with 140 ft. T-head. Uprotected. All the facilities available to marina guests - including the water-view heated pool and hot tub, concierge service, two restaurants, waterside lobster pound, exercise room, sauna, 2 lighted tennis courts, oceanfront jogging path, putting green, day/evening child care and junior program. Bar Harbor Resorts also owns Harborside. Bathhouse: Located on lower level; head, shower & sauna. Laundry.

Notable -- Pick up the Island Explorer at the front door (free shuttle bus every 15 min.) to visit downtown Bar Harbor's shops, restaurants and galleries, 41,000 acre Acadia National Park, Northeast or Southwest Harbors or Somes Sound. Adjacent is The Cat, a high-speed ferry to Yarmouth, Nova Scotia. The College of the Atlantic's waterfront campus is 0.1 mi. - a perfect strolling/picnicking destination. Its Natural History Museum is housed in the original Acadia Nat'l Park headquarters. COA is also home to the Allied Whale Marine Mammal Lab. Acadia Nat'l Park's new Visitors' Center (8am-6pm Jun-Aug, 8am-4:30pm off season) in downtown Bar Harbor and the Kebo Valley Golf Club are a little over a mile away.

Navigational Information
Lat: 44°23.523' **Long:** 068°12.193' **Tide:** 10 ft. **Current:** 2 kt. **Chart:** 13318
Rep. Depths (*MLW*): Entry 40 ft. **Fuel Dock** 8 ft. **Max Slip/Moor** 12 ft./60 ft.
Access: Frenchman Bay through entrance buoys east of Municipal Pier

Marina Facilities *(In Season/Off Season)*
Fuel: *At Harbor Place* - Slip-Side Fueling, Gasoline, Diesel
Slips: 8 Total, 8* Transient **Max LOA:** 185 ft. **Max Beam:** n/a
Rate *(per ft.)*: **Day** $3.00 **Week** n/a **Month** n/a
Power: 30 amp $6, **50 amp** $12, **100 amp** $20, **200 amp** $40
Cable TV: No **Dockside Phone:** No
Dock Type: Floating, Alongside, Wood
Moorings: 15 Total, 15 Transient **Launch:** None, Dinghy Dock
Rate: Day $30 **Week** n/a **Month** n/a
Heads: 7 Toilet(s)
Internet: Yes *(Harbormaster's Office)* **Laundry:** 2 Washer(s), 2 Dryer(s)
Pump-Out: Full Service **Fee:** Free **Closed Heads:** Yes

Marina Operations
Owner/Manager: Charles A. Phippen (Harbormaster) **Dockmaster:** Same
In-Season: Jul-Aug, 7:30am-9pm **Off-Season:** Sep-Jun, 8am-5pm
After-Hours Arrival: Call before arrival or anchor outside the harbor
Reservations: Yes, Preferred, Slips Only** **Credit Cards:** Visa/MC
Discounts: None
Pets: Welcome, Dog Walk Area **Handicap Access:** Yes, Heads, Docks

Bar Harbor Municipal Marina

1 Town Pier; Bar Harbor, ME 04609

Tel: (207) 288-5571 **VHF: Monitor** Ch. 16, 9 **Talk** Ch. 68
Fax: (207) 288-1034 **Alternate Tel:** (207) 288-3391
Email: bhhmaster@barharbormaine.gov **Web:** www.BarHarborMaine.com
Nearest Town: Bar Harbor *(0 mi.)* **Tourist Info:** (207) 288-5103

Marina Services and Boat Supplies
Services - Docking Assistance, Security *(24 Hrs., Video)*, Trash Pick-Up, Megayacht Facilities, 3 Phase **Communication -** Pay Phone, FedEx, DHL, UPS, Express Mail **Supplies - Near:** Ice *(Cube)*, Bait/Tackle, Propane *(Maine Street Market)* **1-3 mi:** Live Bait *(Kyle's Ketch 288-8211)*

Boatyard Services
OnSite: Launching Ramp **OnCall:** Divers **Nearest Yard:** Morris Yachts - NEH (207) 276-5300

Restaurants and Accommodations
Near: Restaurant *(Maggie's 288-9007, L $16-34)*, *(Galyn's 288-9706, L $6-11, D $16-22)*, *(Reading Room 288-3351, B $3-10, L $7-19, D $19-28, Bar Harbor Inn)*, *(Michelle's 288-2138, D $26-39, Fine Dining, Ivy Manor)*, *(Fish House 288-3070, L $8-29, D $13-29, Kids $4-7)*, *(Cafe This Way 288-4483, D $14-24, Breakfast)*, Lite Fare *(Morning Glory Bakery 288-3041, 7am-7pm)*, *(Jordan's 288-3586, B $3-7, L $3-9, 5am-2pm, Breakfast all day)*, Pizzeria *(Epi Sub & Pizza 288-5853)*, *(Rosalie's 288-5666)*, Hotel *(Bar Harbor Inn 288-3351, $99-379)*, *(Harborside 288-5033, $99-1500)*, Inn/B&B *(Ullikana B&B 288-9552, $140-250)*

Recreation and Entertainment
OnSite: Beach, Picnic Area, Tours *(Oli's Trolley 288-9899 1 hr. $15/10 & 2.5-hr. $29/15)* **Near:** Pool *("Y" 288-3511)*, Fitness Center *(YMCA)*, Boat Rentals *(Aquaterra Sea Kayaks 288-0007)*, Hike/Bike Trails, Fishing Charter, Movie Theater *(Criterion 288-3441)*, Video Rental *(Arnold's 288-4145)*, Park, Museum *(Abbe Downtown - Native American 288-3519 $6/2; Bar Harbor Historical Society 288-0000)*, Cultural Attract *(Bar Harbor Music Fest 288-5744)*, Sightseeing *(BH Whale Watch 288-2386 $58/28; Lulu Lobster Tour 963-2341 $30/17 - simply fabulous)* **1-3 mi:** Golf Course *(Kebo Valley G.C. 288-5000)*

Provisioning and General Services
Near: Convenience Store *(Maine St. Market 288-8185)*, Supermarket *(Hannaford 288-5680)*, Health Food *(A&B Naturals 288-8480)*, Wine/Beer *(House 288-1200)*, Liquor Store *(Bayside 288-2772)*, Farmers' Market *(Sun 10-1, YMCA)*, Lobster Pound *(Stewmans 288-0342)*, Bank/ATM, Post Office, Catholic Church, Protestant Church, Library *(Jesup 288-4245)*, Beauty Salon, Barber Shop, Laundry, Bookstore *(Sherman's 288-3161)*, Pharmacy *(West End 288-3318)*, Hardware Store *(True Value 288-4995)*

Transportation
OnSite: Bikes *(Aquaterra 288-0007; Acadia 288-9605)* **OnCall:** Rental Car *(Enterprise 667-1217 18 mi.)*, Taxi *(AAA 288-8294)* **Near:** Local Bus *(Island Explorer 288-4573, Free. 8 routes cover all of Acadia Nat'l Park)*, Ferry Service *(Bay Ferry to Winter Harbor 244-7312 $30/20 RT)* **Airport:** Bar Harbor/Bangor Int'l. *(9 mi./50 mi.)*

Medical Services
911 Service **OnCall:** Ambulance **Near:** Holistic Services *(Spa at Bar Harbor Inn 288-3351 $90/50 min)*, Veterinarian *(Acadia 288-5733)* **Under 1 mi:** Doctor *(Family Health 288-5606)*, Dentist *(High St. 288-4754)* **Hospital:** M.D.I. Health Center 288-5081 *(0.5 mi.)*

Setting -- Protected by Bar Island and the Porcupines, Bar Harbor's parking-lot size granite municipal wharf pokes into the harbor and expansive mooring field. The pier's north side is abuzz with commercial vessels, ventures and a tender float, while the south side's two long floating docks berth large pleasure craft with views of stately Bar Harbor Inn's rolling lawns. The brown-shingled single-story harbormaster's office overhangs the water and buckets of flowers and green wooden benches edge the brick walkways. All of bustling, flower-bedecked Bar Harbor is a stone's throw.

Marina Notes -- *Two 96-foot long side-tie floating docks, each with gangways. Day fee $1.50/ft. **No reservations for moorings just slips - call far ahead for Jul/Aug. Power: 100A, 200A - single & 3-phase. Water fee $30/day. Moorings: granite blocks - 1 17,000 lb., 3 8-9,000 lbs, Rest 5,000 lb. Pleasure boat dinghy dock. Call when entering harbor, a dockhand will assist to mooring. Pump out & fuel next door at Harbor Place; cruise ship tenders frequently tie up these docks. Bathhouse: Municipal-style public toilets at dock, 7am-9pm. Nearest showers at YMCA 288-3511 (0.5 mi,) $9/5 or $16/Family for pool & fitness, too.

Notable -- Bar Harbor is a pretty but very touristed resort town. Expect crowds. Many excursions leave from adjacent Harbor Place, including whale, seal watching, & kayaking. The .75-mile-long Shore Path, with spectacular views of Frenchman Bay, heads south from here past lovely Agamont Park and the elegant Bar Harbor Inn - the 4-masted schooner Margaret Todd, the ferry to Winter Harbor, departs from its pier. Or walk right up the hill; shops and restaurants line Cottage, Main, Mt. Desert and Worcester Streets ('til 9pm.). Or stroll north toward the mansions - at low tide walk across the bar to Bar Island.

PHOTOS ON DVD: 25

The Harborside Hotel & Marina

55 West Street; Bar Harbor, ME 04609

Tel: (207) 288-8329; (800) 328-5033 **VHF: Monitor** Ch. No **Talk** n/a
Fax: (207) 288-3089 **Alternate Tel:** (207) 266-5857
Email: djordan@barharborresorts.com **Web:** www.theharborsidehotel.com
Nearest Town: Bar Harbor **Tourist Info:** (207) 288-5103

Navigational Information

Lat: 44°23.490' **Long:** 068°12.337' **Tide:** 11 ft. **Current:** 0 kt. **Chart:** 13323
Rep. Depths (*MLW*): Entry 10 ft. **Fuel Dock** n/a **Max Slip/Moor** 10 ft./-
Access: Green can 7 into Bar Harbor, then turn to starboard

Marina Facilities *(In Season/Off Season)*

Fuel: No
Slips: 20 Total, 20 Transient **Max LOA:** 165 ft. **Max Beam:** 60 ft.
Rate *(per ft.)*: **Day** $3.50* **Week** Inq. **Month** Inq.
Power: 30 amp Inq., **50 amp** Inq., **100 amp** Inq., **200 amp** n/a
Cable TV: No **Dockside Phone:** No
Dock Type: Floating, Long Fingers, Alongside, Wood
Moorings: 0 Total, 0 Transient **Launch:** n/a, Dinghy Dock
Rate: Day n/a **Week** n/a **Month** n/a
Heads: 3 Toilet(s), 3 Shower(s)
Internet: Yes *(Biz. Center)* **Laundry:** 6 Washer(s), 6 Dryer(s), Iron
Pump-Out: OnSite, Full Service **Fee:** Free **Closed Heads:** Yes

Marina Operations

Owner/Manager: Eben Salvatore **Dockmaster:** Debbie Jordan
In-Season: May-Oct **Off-Season:** n/a
After-Hours Arrival: Call hotel front desk
Reservations: Yes, Preferred **Credit Cards:** Visa/MC, Dscvr, Amex
Discounts: None
Pets: Welcome, Dog Walk Area **Handicap Access:** Yes

Marina Services and Boat Supplies

Services - Docking Assistance, Room Service to the Boat, Security *(Closed ramp)*, Dock Carts, Megayacht Facilities, 3 Phase **Communication -** Pay Phone (2), FedEx, DHL, UPS, Express Mail *(Sat Del)* **Supplies - Near:** Ice *(Block, Cube)*, Bait/Tackle, Propane *(Maine Street Market)*

Boatyard Services

OnCall: Rigger, Canvas Work, Divers, Bottom Cleaning **Nearest Yard:** Morris Yachts - NEH (207) 276-5300

Restaurants and Accommodations

OnSite: Restaurant *(Bar Harbor's The Club 288-9568, D $20-30, Tues-Sun 5-10)*, *(La Bella Vista 288-5033, B $8-14, L $7-24, D $15-32)*, Lite Fare *(Vanderbilt Lounge - Drinks & Apps 5-11pm)*, *(Pool Splash Bar)*, Hotel *(Harborside $140-850)*, *(Bar Harbor Club 288-3348, $150-400)* **Near:** Restaurant *(Reading Room at Bar Harbor Inn 288-3351, B $3-10, L $7-19, D $19-28)*, *(Havana 288-2822, D $12-28)*, *(Maggie's 288-9007, D $15-24)*, *(Stewman's Lobster Pound 288-0346, L & D $7-23, Kids'$5-6)*, *(Geddy's Pub 288-5077, L $7-17, D $8-26, plus pizzas)*, *(West Street 288-5242, L $7-23, D $12-27, Kids $5-8, Early bird 11am-6pm $12-15, lobster $16)*, *(Lompoc Cafe 288-9392, L $7-9, D $13-17.50, Kids $4.50-6.50, 15 beers on tap, live music)*, *(Mache Bistro 288-0447, D $16-21)*, Lite Fare *(Jordan's 288-3586, B $3-7, L $3-9)*, Hotel *(Bar Harbor Inn 288-3351, $85-350)*, Inn/B&B *(Ivy Manor Inn 288-2138, $95-350)*, *(Maples Inn 288-3443, $60-150)*

Recreation and Entertainment

OnSite: Heated Pool, Spa, Tennis Courts, Fitness Center, Tours *(Lulu Lobster 288-3136 $30/17)* **Near:** Beach, Picnic Area, Boat Rentals *(Aquaterra Kayaks 288-0007, 2 hr. tour $37)*, Movie Theater *(Criterion 288-3441)*, Video Rental *(Arnold's 288-4145)*, Museum *(Abbe Native American 288-2179 $6/2)*, Cultural Attract *(B.H. Music Fest 288-5744)*, Sightseeing *(Bar Harbor Whale Watch AtlantiCat 288-2386 - 3 trips $58/28)* **1-3 mi:** Golf Course *(Kebo Valley 288-5000)*

Provisioning and General Services

OnSite: Bank/ATM **Near:** Convenience Store *(Maine Street Market 288-8185)*, Supermarket *(Hannaford 288-5680)*, Wine/Beer *(Bayside 288-2772)*, Liquor Store, Farmers' Market *(Sun 10-1, YMCA)*, Lobster Pound *(Maine 288-0188)*, Post Office, Catholic Church, Protestant Church, Library *(Jesup Mem. 288-4245)*, Laundry *(Bar Harbor 288-9064)*, Bookstore *(Sherman's 288-3161)*, Pharmacy *(West End 288-3318)*, Newsstand, Hardware Store *(Bar Harbor 288-5567; True Value 288-4995)*

Transportation

OnCall: Rental Car *(Enterprise 667-1217)*, Taxi *(AAA 288-8294)* **Near:** Bikes *(Aquaterra 288-0007, Acadia 288-9605)*, Local Bus *(Island Explorer 288-4573, Free)*, Ferry Service *(Bay Ferry to Winter Harbor 244-7312 $30/20 RT)* **Airport:** Bar Harbor/Bangor Int'l *(9 mi./50 mi.)*

Medical Services

911 Service **OnSite:** Holistic Services *(Bar Harbor Club Spa 288-5251 - Massage $100/50 min)* **OnCall:** Ambulance **Near:** Doctor *(High St. Health Center 288-5119)*, Dentist *(High St. 288-4754)*, Veterinarian *(Acadia 288-5733)* **Hospital:** MDI Health Center 288-5081 *(0.5 mi.)*

PHOTOS ON DVD: 25

Setting -- Tucked into the western end of Bar Harbor, luxurious Harborside is snug against the Bar Island bar and well-protected by the Porcupines. High quality dock berth sailboats, megayachts and water excursions - backed by the hotel's easily recognized, half-timbered, English Tudor architecture and long, three-story balconied buildings. Lushly planted flower beds outline patios sprinkled with umbrella-topped tables and an expansive undulating pool.

Marina Notes -- *900 linear feet with three fingers. Formerly Golden Anchor. Same ownership as Bar Harbor Regency Sunspree. Multi-year, multi-million dollar renovation 2001-03 in conjunction with adjacent Bar Harbor Club. Reservations suggested. All hotel services available to marina guests: pool, hot tub, fitness room, Wi-Fi plus dining, tennis and spa amenities at adjacent Bar Harbor Club. 187 guest rooms and suites - balconies overlook the Bay. Aptly named Bella Vista Restaurant offers dining inside or topside on the open air deck --with same view. Bathhouse: Heads & Showers lower level off Fitness Center.

Notable -- The Harborside complex traces its heritage to the early 1900's. A string of tiny shops, nicknamed "Peanut Row," was destroyed in the 1947 fire. The Golden Anchor was built here during Bar Harbor's restoration. Adjacent, Tudor-style Bar Harbor Club was originally built by J.P. Morgan in the 30's as a private playground for the town's wealthiest summer folk. Today, a luxurious new spa, exercise room, tennis courts, waterside pool, elegant dining room and boutique are set in the impeccably restored structure surrounded by beautifully landscaped grounds. Top-rated Lulu's Lobster Tour, knowledgeably narrated by Capt. John Nicolai, berths here, and Bar Harbor Whale Watch docks nearby. At Bridge & West Streets the path to Acadia's Bar Island is accessible at low tide.

Navigational Information

Lat: 44°15.600' **Long:** 068°14.123' **Tide:** 11 ft. **Current:** n/a **Chart:** 13318
Rep. Depths (*MLW*): Entry 20 ft. **Fuel Dock** 12 ft. **Max Slip/Moor** -/60 ft.
Access: Gilley Thorofare to Cranberry Harbor

Marina Facilities *(In Season/Off Season)*

Fuel: *Fishermen's Co-op* - Gasoline, Diesel
Slips: 0 Total, 0 Transient **Max LOA:** 40 ft. **Max Beam:** n/a
Rate *(per ft.)*: **Day** n/a **Week** n/a **Month** n/a
Power: 30 amp n/a, **50 amp** n/a, **100 amp** n/a, **200 amp** n/a
Cable TV: No **Dockside Phone:** No
Dock Type: Floating, Wood
Moorings: 10 Total, 10 Transient **Launch:** No, Dinghy Dock
Rate: Day $20* **Week** n/a **Month** Inq.
Heads: 4 Toilet(s), Book Exchange
Internet: No **Laundry:** None
Pump-Out: No **Fee:** n/a **Closed Heads:** Yes

Marina Operations

Owner/Manager: Daniel S. Lief **Dockmaster:** Same
In-Season: MidJun-MidSep, 9a-11p **Off-Season:** MidSep-MidJun, Closed
After-Hours Arrival: Contact restaurant (207) 244-7494
Reservations: Yes **Credit Cards:** Visa/MC, Dscvr
Discounts: None
Pets: Welcome **Handicap Access:** Yes, Heads

Islesford Dock Restaurant

Islesford, ME 04646

Tel: (207) 244-7494 **VHF: Monitor** Ch. 9 **Talk** Ch. 9
Fax: n/a **Alternate Tel:** n/a
Email: cynthia@ubuntufund.org **Web:** www.islesford.com
Nearest Town: Southwest Harbor *(3 mi.)* **Tourist Info:** (207) 244-9264

Marina Services and Boat Supplies

Communication - Fax in/out **Supplies - Near:** Ice *(Cube)* **1-3 mi:** Ships' Store **3+ mi:** Propane *(Dead River 244-3131 on mainland, 6 mi.)*, CNG *(Hinckley 244-7100 or Morris Yacht 244-5511, 3 mi.)*

Boatyard Services

OnSite: Launching Ramp **OnCall:** Engine mechanic *(gas, diesel)* **Nearest Yard:** Cranberry Island BY, 1 mi. (207) 244-7316

Restaurants and Accommodations

OnSite: Restaurant *(Islesford Dock Restaurant L $6-16, D $9-29, Sunday Br. $5-$15. Lunch 11-3 - except Mon. Dinner 5-9, 7 nights, also small plates $6-14)* **Near:** Condo/Cottage *(Vintage Island Home 917-251-8776, Formerly Braided Rugs Inn - 3 nt. min.)*, *(A dozen plus see islesford.com)*

Recreation and Entertainment

OnSite: Beach *(Sand)*, Picnic Area, Galleries *(Islesford Dock Gallery, Marion Baker's Islesford Pottery 244-9108; Sue Hill's Winters Work. Short walk inland - Islesford Artists Gallery 244-3145 - MidJun-LabDay 10am-4pm, shows work of both summer & year-round residents; Island Girl Sea Glass)* **Near:** Playground, Jogging Paths, Boat Rentals *(Little Cranberry Island Kayak Rentals 244-5854)*, Hike/Bike Trails, Fishing Charter *(Capt. Edgar Blank 266-4353 - tours, towing & minor repairs)*, Park *(Acadia National Park 288-3338)*, Museum *(Acadia Nat'l Park's Islesford Historical Museum 244-9224 - Free - collection depicts the life and history of the Cranberry Islands and its people -- ship models, nav aids, toys, photos, etc. Open from Jun 15-Sep, 9am-Noon & 2:30-3:30pm)*, Cultural Attract *(Three day Painting Workshops 244-7494 Sept. $350)*, Sightseeing *(Capt. Stefanie Alley's Lobster Boat Tours 244-7466 - 1 hr for 6 people $75)*

Provisioning and General Services

Near: Lobster Pound *(Cranberry Isles Fishermen's Co-op 244-5438 or Thomas Lobster Company 244-5876 www.thomaslobster.com - phone or Internet orders only)*, Post Office *(Mon-Friday 7:30am-3:30pm, Sat 7:30am-9am, 10:30am -1pm)*, Catholic Church, Protestant Church, Library *(Islesford Library 244-9565 - Internet. Check out Julie's Garden)*, Retail Shops *(Winter's Work - www.winterswork.com, a craft shop - displays include work by author/illustrator Ashley Bryan; Island Girl Seaglass & Gift Shop)*

Transportation

OnSite: Water Taxi *(John Dwelley's "Delight" 244-5724 $55-70; Cadillac 244-0575 $45-100)* **OnCall:** Ferry Service *(Beal & Bunker 244-3575 $24/12 RT to Northeast Harbor; Cranberry Cove 244-5882 $24/16 RT to Southwest Harbor)* **1-3 mi:** Local Bus *(Island Explorer but every ferry stop is an Explorer stop. Line 7 stops at Cranberry Cove ferry landing in Southwest Harbor; lines 5 & 6 stop at Beal & Bunker ferry landing in Northeast Harbor)* **Airport:** Bar Harbor/Bangor Int'l. *(18 mi./55 mi. ferry or water taxi)*

Medical Services

911 Service **OnCall:** Ambulance *(EMT on island)* **3+ mi:** Doctor *(S.W. Harbor, 3 mi.)* **Hospital:** Mount Desert Island 288-8439 via ferry/car or Life Flight Helicopter *(10 mi.)*

Setting -- Between Hadlock Point and Sand Beach, three weathered wood buildings perch on pilings above the water in Hadlock Cove. Two floating day docks, connected by a small bridge, edge the pilings below popular Islesford Dock Restaurant. A gangway leads to a long open deck with entrances to the restaurant and crafts ateliers and galleries; a canvas-topped eating deck overlooks the harbor. Portside Acadia Park's Islesford Historical Society's Georgian brick home features a manicured picnic area. Starboard the ferry and mailboat docks lie beyond the blue Cranberry Isles Fisherman Co-op.

Marina Notes -- *3 of 10 moorings managed by restaurant. 5 owned by town, yacht club or are memorial moorings (free) & 2 are $20/nt private rentals. Since 1993, Owners Dan & Cynthia Lief onsite from 7am-12am 7 days (mid-Jun to early Sep) - provide info on all moorings (no one left without one). Ice & water. Fuel 10am-noon Mon-Sat (cash only). General Store closed. Adjacent Little Cranberry Y.C. supports active summer program. Mechanics near but boatyards 3 miles away (Hinckley's or Morris). Bathhouse: Heads only - Islesford Park Dept. Last door at far end of rest. & gray bldg to left of Museum.

Notable -- The Lief's eclectic menu features local seafood, organic meat, their own home-grown vegetables & herbs lobster from the o-op and nothing fried. It's a bustling happy place with a nightly guest list as diverse as the food. (An intense, short season recommends advance reservations.) Winter's Work, right on the dock, displays Islesford's year-round residents' "off-season" hand work. Next door, Isleford Pottery's active studio shows create a diverse gallery. A five-minute walk inland to Danny and Katy Fernald's glorious Isleford Artists showing 25 local artists; then stop by the warm, inviting library in Neighborhood House.

PHOTOS ON DVD: 25

Cranberry Island Moorings

PO Box 56; Cranberry Isles*, ME 04625

Tel: (207) 244-0575 **VHF: Monitor** n/a **Talk** n/a
Fax: n/a **Alternate Tel:** (207) 244-4475
Email: n/a **Web:** cranberryisles.com
Nearest Town: Southwest Harbor *(3 mi.)* **Tourist Info:** (207) 244-9264

Navigational Information

Lat: 44°15.556' **Long:** 068°16.105' **Tide:** 12 ft. **Current:** n/a **Chart:** 13318
Rep. Depths (*MLW*): Entry 55 ft. **Fuel Dock** n/a **Max Slip/Moor** -/35 ft.
Access: Western Way to Spurling's Cove

Marina Facilities *(In Season/Off Season)*

Fuel: No
Slips: 0 Total, 0 Transient **Max LOA:** 60 ft. **Max Beam:** n/a
Rate *(per ft.)*: **Day** n/a **Week** n/a **Month** n/a
Power: 30 amp n/a, **50 amp** n/a, **100 amp** n/a, **200 amp** n/a
Cable TV: No **Dockside Phone:** No
Dock Type: Floating, Wood
Moorings: 3 Total, 3 Transient **Launch:** No, Dinghy Dock
Rate: Day $20 **Week** n/a **Month** n/a
Heads: 2 Toilet(s)
Internet: Yes *(Wi-Fi at Library, Free)* **Laundry:** None
Pump-Out: No **Fee:** n/a **Closed Heads:** Yes

Marina Operations

Owner/Manager: Norman Sanborn (Harbormaster) **Dockmaster:** Same
In-Season: May 15-Oct 15 **Off-Season:** Oct 16-May 14, Closed
After-Hours Arrival: n/a
Reservations: No **Credit Cards:** Cash only
Discounts: None
Pets: Welcome **Handicap Access:** No

Marina Services and Boat Supplies

Supplies - 1-3 mi: Ships' Store *(Hinckley Ships' Store 244-7100 - ferry)* **3+ mi:** Propane *(Dead River Co. 244-3131 - ferry , 4 mi.)*

Boatyard Services

Near: Travelift *(30T)*, Railway, Forklift, Engine mechanic *(gas, diesel)*, Electrical Repairs, Hull Repairs, Canvas Work, Brightwork, Propeller Repairs, Woodworking, Metal Fabrication, Painting, Awlgrip, Total Refits, Yacht Design, Yacht Building, Yacht Broker. **Nearest Yard:** Newman & Gray (207) 244-0575

Restaurants and Accommodations

OnSite: Lite Fare *(Seawich Café 244-0622, in General Store)* **Near:** Lite Fare *(Hitty's Café 244-7845, L $3.50-8, at Cranberry House, last week in May to second wknd Oct 10am-4pm daily. Free Wi-Fi.)*, Condo/Cottage *(Many Rental Houses almost all are weekly)*

Recreation and Entertainment

Near: Tennis Courts *(next to Cranberry House)*, Jogging Paths, Hike/Bike Trails *(One mile easy trail to Whistler's Cove, facing the Western Way - starts behind Cranberry House)*, Movie Theater *(Tues, Thurs & Sat 7:30pm at Cranberry House - Apr-Oct, Thurs Mid-Jun-Mid-Sep only)*, Museum *(Preble-Marr Historical 244-7800, Free - Jun-Sep 10am-4pm Eight display panels describe GCI's history; docent answers questions about current island life.Small video library with large screen TV)*, Cultural Attract *(Concerts, Workshops, Classes, Lectures at Cranberry House - opened in '08; Heliker-LaHotan Foundation)*, Sightseeing *(Self-guided island tour - see map on DVD)*, Galleries *(The Whale's Rib 244-5153 Local art, gifts & jewelry; Peter Eldredge Fine Art, Sculpture, & Trompe l'Oeil)*, Special Events *(GCI Historical Society's Home, Art & Garden Tour $25 - eight stops. Wed in Mid-Aug)* **Under 1 mi:** Beach *(Whistler Cove sand beach)*

Provisioning and General Services

OnSite: Market *(Cranberry General Store 244-0622 right at the dock - Action Central - front porch serves as the boaters' lounge. - new management '09.)*, Post Office **Near:** Protestant Church *(Congregational)*, Library *(244-7358 Public head. MidJun-Aug Mon-Fri 10am-3pm, Early Jun & Sep Mon, Wed & Fri, Winter Tue & Thur 9am-1:30pm. 5 online computers, color copier, fax plus Free- 24/7 Wi-Fi inside and outside.)*, Retail Shops *(Island Girl Seaglass MemDay-ColDay and Gift Shop)* **3+ mi:** Pharmacy *(Carroll Drug Store 244-5588 - by ferry , 5 mi.)*, Hardware Store *(McEachern & Hutchins 244-7243 - by ferry, 5 mi.)*

Transportation

OnSite: Ferry Service *(Beal & Bunker 244-3575 to Northeast Harbor; Cranberry Cove 244-5882 to Southwest Harbor)* **OnCall:** Water Taxi *(Cadillac 244-0575; Delight 244-5724)* **1-3 mi:** Local Bus *(Island Explorer bus line 7 stops at Cranberry Cove ferry landing in Southwest Harbor; lines 5 & 6 stop at Beal & Bunker ferry landing in Northeast Harbor)* **Airport:** Bar Harbor 667-7329 - by ferry *(15 mi.)*

Medical Services

911 Service **OnCall:** Ambulance *(Emergency contact Lorraine Bracy - day 460-6696)* **Hospital:** M.D.I. 288-8439 - by ferry *(12 mi)*

PHOTOS ON DVD: 25

Setting -- Just two miles from bustling Southwest Harbor, quiet, remote Great Cranberry Island feels light years away. On the north end, the G.C.I. mooring field lies in the curve of Spurling Cove. Along the shore are the Newman & Gray Boatyard, two barn-red buildings and the General Store - with a popular front porch. Ferries land at the large float and a smaller one serves dinghies and skiffs. Above, the long fixed wharf connects to the upland.

Marina Notes -- *Address & Alt Tel no: Town of Cranberry Isles (Denise McCormick, Clerk). Main phone: Harbormaster. Guest moorings: white with blue stripe - outer mooring field in middle of harbor. Max stay three days. Longer stays? Ask about private mooring. Be aware of ferries. Fuel pump up-island - easier fuel at Islesford. Newman & Gray Boatyard ($57/hr.): 30T travelift, boat sheds to 50 ft. In The Pool, Barbara Stainton's Cranberry Island Boatyard builds Western Way boats . Wi-Fi at library 1/2-mile inland. Bathhouse: Public toilets near the dock, in Cranberry House & in Library.

Notable -- A quarter mile inland, Cranberry House, the cultural center of the island, includes the Preble-Marr Historical Museum. Summer resident author Rachel Field (1894-1942) set her classic children's book "Hitty, Her First Hundred Years." on G.C.I. - the center features a collection of Hitty dolls from all over the world. Further upland is the library and community center. Overlooking "The Pool" are Cranberry Island B.Y. and the pretty Heliker-LaHotan Foundation complex. The legacy of artists John Heliker and Robert LaHotan, it offers a 3-4 week residency program for established painters and sculptors. The studios are open to the public at the end of each session. About 38 hardy souls live here year round and another 350 or so arrive for the summer.

   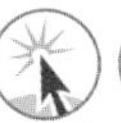  

Navigational Information

Lat: 44°17.673' **Long:** 068°17.123' **Tide:** 12 ft. **Current:** n/a **Chart:** 13318
Rep. Depths (*MLW*): Entry 30 ft. **Fuel Dock** 20 ft. **Max Slip/Moor** 12 ft./20 ft.
Access: Gulf of Maine to Eastern Way to Northeast Harbor

Marina Facilities *(In Season/Off Season)*

Fuel: *Clifton Dock - Ch.9 (276-5308)* - Gasoline, Diesel
Slips: 60 Total, 15 Transient **Max LOA:** 160 ft. **Max Beam:** n/a
Rate *(per ft.)*: **Day** $2.50* **Week** Inq. **Month** Inq.
Power: 30 amp $10, **50 amp** $20, **100 amp** $40, **200 amp** $80
Cable TV: Yes, $5/night **Dockside Phone:** Yes, $5
Dock Type: Floating, Long Fingers, Short Fingers, Pilings
Moorings: 60 Total, 60 Transient **Launch:** None, Dinghy Dock
Rate: Day $35* **Week** Inq. **Month** Inq.
Heads: 6 Toilet(s), 7 Shower(s), Hair Dryers
Internet: Yes *(Wi-Fi, Free)* **Laundry:** None
Pump-Out: OnSite, Full Service, 1 Central **Fee:** $5 **Closed Heads:** Yes

Marina Operations

Owner/Manager: Shawn Murphy (Harbormaster) **Dockmaster:** Same
In-Season: May 15-Oct 1, 24 hrs. **Off-Season:** Oct-May 14, 8am-4pm
After-Hours Arrival: Call for instructions
Reservations: Yes, Recommended** **Credit Cards:** Visa/MC
Discounts: None
Pets: Welcome, Dog Walk Area **Handicap Access:** Yes, Heads

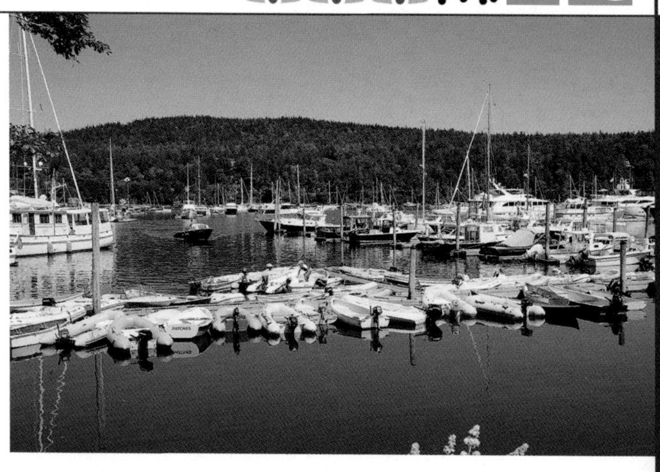

Northeast Harbor Marina

PO Box 237; 41 Harbor Drive; Northeast Harbor, ME 04662

Tel: (207) 276-5737 **VHF: Monitor** Ch. 9/16 **Talk** Ch. 68
Fax: (207) 276-5741 **Alternate Tel:** n/a
Email: harbormaster@mtdesert.org **Web:** mountdesert.org
Nearest Town: Northeast Harbor *(0.1 mi.)* **Tourist Info:** (207) 276-5040

Marina Services and Boat Supplies

Services - Docking Assistance, Boaters' Lounge, Dock Carts, Megayacht Facilities **Communication -** Pay Phone (4), FedEx, UPS, Express Mail **Supplies - OnSite:** Ice *(Block, Cube)* **Near:** Ships' Store *(F.T. Brown 276-3329)*, Bait/Tackle **Under 1 mi:** Propane *(Coastal Energy 276-5201)* **1-3 mi:** West Marine *(At Dysart's - by water)*, CNG *(Hinckley's 244-7100 - by water)*

Boatyard Services

OnSite: Travelift *(25T)*, Launching Ramp *($5)*, Engine mechanic *(gas, diesel)*, Electrical Repairs, Electronics Repairs, Hull Repairs, Rigger, Divers, Bottom Cleaning **OnCall:** Crane, Sail Loft, Inflatable Repairs

Restaurants and Accommodations

OnSite: Restaurant *(Main Sail at Kimball Terrace 276-5857, B $4-7, L $6-17, D $10-19, terrace overlooks docks)* **Near:** Restaurant *(Colonel's Rest. & Bakery 276-5147, B plus L & D $8-25)*, *(Docksider 276-3965, L $3-18, D $3-18)*, *(Red Bird Provisions 276-3006, L $13-20, D $24-34)*, Lite Fare *(Full Belli Deli 276-4299, L & D $7-20)*, Hotel *(Kimball Terrace 276-3883, $70-205)*, Inn/B&B *(Grey Rock 276-9360, $155-375)*, *(Colonel Suites 288-4775, $130-200)* **Under 1 mi:** Restaurant *(Asticou Inn Restaurant 276-3344, L $16-22, D $16-22, dinghy landing)*, Inn/B&B *(Maison Suisse 276-5423, $135-205)*, *(Asticou 800-258-3373, $250-350, Dinghy Landing)* **1-3 mi:** Restaurant *(Jordan Pond House in Acadia 276-3316, L $8.50-18, D $10.25-19, afternoon tea, popovers $8.25-9.50)*

Recreation and Entertainment

OnSite: Picnic Area *(overlooking harbor)*, Tennis Courts *($10/hr.)* **Near:** Video Rental *(McGrath Variety 276-5548)*, Park *(Acadia)*, Museum *(Great Harbor Maritime 276-5262)*, Galleries *(Island Artisans, Shaw Jewelry, Northeast Fine Art, Wingspread, Smart Studio)* **Under 1 mi:** Golf Course *(Northeast Harbor GC 276-5335 - founded 1895, $85)*, Hike/Bike Trails *(Eliot Mountain Trail from Thuya Garden)*, Sightseeing *(Acadia Carriage Trails, Thuya & Asticou Gardens, Sea Princess' naturalist-led tours 276-5352)*

Provisioning and General Services

Near: Convenience Store, Supermarket *(Pine Tree 276-3335 - delivers to docks)*, Wine/Beer *(Pine Tree)*, Liquor Store *(Pine Tree; Liquor Locker 244-3788 - delivers)*, Bakery *(The Colonel's 276-5147 bakery, wine, pizza - delivers)*, Farmers' Market *(Thu 9am-Noon 546-2395, Kimball Terrace)*, Bank/ATM, Post Office, Catholic Church, Library *(276-3333)*, Beauty Salon, Laundry *(Shirt Off Your Back 276-5611)*, Bookstore *(Wikhegan 276-5079; McGrath Variety 276-5548)*, Newsstand, Hardware Store *(F.T. Brown Ace 276-3329)*, Retail Shops *(Kimball, Romantic Room, Holmes, Local Color)*

Transportation

OnSite: Local Bus *(Island Explorer 288-4573, 667-5796, Free)*, Ferry Service *(Beal & Bunker's to Cranberry Isles 244-3575 RT $24/6)* **OnCall:** Water Taxi *(MDI 244-7312)*, Airport Limo *(Airport & Harbor 667-5995)* **Near:** Bikes *(Island 276-5611)* **Airport:** Bar Harbor/Bangor Int'l. *(12 mi./50 mi.)*

Medical Services

911 Service **Near:** Doctor *(Northeast Harbor Clinic 276-3331 8:30am-12:15pm)*, Holistic Services *(Bella's Spa 276-3638 $105/50 min massage; Greenbaum Massage 276-4057)* **3+ mi:** Chiropractor *(Gerrish 288-3980, 6 mi.)* **Hospital:** M.D.I. 288-8439 *(7 mi.)*

Setting -- Even in the fog, beautiful Northeast Harbor manages to deliver that elusive Downeast experience. When the mist lifts, the views across the harbor are of Bald Peak Mountain and exquisite Asticou Inn. Impeccably maintained yachts line the ship-shape floating docks and dot the mooring field. Behind the small gray harbormaster's office, the Memorial Park's expansive lawn tumbles down the hill. The Yachtsmen's Building perches above the dinghy dock.

Marina Notes -- *Up to 49 ft. $2.50, 50-59 ft. $3, 60 ft. + $3.50/ft. Moorings: 20-29 ft. $25/nt., 30-39 ft. $30, 40-49 ft. $35, 50 ft.+ $45. Green buoys, numbers indicate max LOA. Rafting permitted. **Limited transient slip reservations (Fax start Jan 1) - mostly T-heads, often rafted 2-3 deep. Moorings not reservable; arrive 11am (check in by VHF once in harbor). Yachtsmen's Building at C of C - heads, reading room, coffee, tea, computer (hi-speed), helpful staff. No launch; use northern-most dinghy docks. Morris Yachts' full service B.Y. onsite (244-5511). At harbor entrance, Clifton Fuel Dock - 50 lb. block ice & manual pump-out. Bathhouse: 24 hrs. Knotty pine, fiberglass shower stalls (8 quarters/4.5 min), great handicap bath. Sundries, towels $2-6. Add'l. heads on dock.

Notable -- The quintessential "Old Maine" village, a short walk up the hill, promises a few casual eateries, a couple excellent restaurants, good provisioning, galleries, enticing shops and low-key activities that cater to its very private, moneyed summer residents. A little out of the tourist bustle, yet the Island Explorer makes Acadia National Park and the neighboring villages easily accessible. The Asticou Terraces, including Azalea and Thuya Gardens and Thuya Lodge, march up the mountain across the Harbor; a convenient dinghy dock sits at the base. Excursions leave from the docks, including ferries to the Cranberries.

PHOTOS ON DVD: 25

John Williams Boat Company

PO Box 80; 17 Shipwright Lane; Mount Desert, ME 04660

Tel: (207) 244-7854 **VHF: Monitor** n/a **Talk** n/a
Fax: (207) 244-9912 **Alternate Tel:** n/a
Email: info@jwboatco.com **Web:** www.jwboatco.com
Nearest Town: Southwest Harbor *(5 mi.)* **Tourist Info:** (207) 276-5040

Navigational Information

Lat: 44°20.159' **Long:** 068°19.122' **Tide:** 12 ft. **Current:** 1 kt. **Chart:** 13318
Rep. Depths (*MLW*): Entry 35 ft. **Fuel Dock** n/a **Max Slip/Moor** 35 ft./140 ft.
Access: Southwest Harbor to Somes Sound, two-thirds up on west shore

Marina Facilities *(In Season/Off Season)*

Fuel: No
Slips: 0 Total, 0 Transient **Max LOA:** n/a **Max Beam:** n/a
Rate *(per ft.)*: **Day** n/a **Week** n/a **Month** n/a
Power: 30 amp n/a, **50 amp** n/a, **100 amp** n/a, **200 amp** n/a
Cable TV: No **Dockside Phone:** No
Dock Type: Fixed, Floating, Wood
Moorings: 20 Total, 5 Transient **Launch:** No
Rate: Day $25 **Week** $150 **Month** $500
Heads: 1 Toilet(s)
Internet: Yes *(Wi-Fi, Free)* **Laundry:** None
Pump-Out: No **Fee:** n/a **Closed Heads:** No

Marina Operations

Owner/Manager: Jock Williams **Dockmaster:** Jaime Weir
In-Season: Year Round, 8am-4pm **Off-Season:** n/a
After-Hours Arrival: Take any available mooring
Reservations: No **Credit Cards:** Visa/MC
Discounts: None
Pets: Welcome **Handicap Access:** No

Marina Services and Boat Supplies

Services - Docking Assistance **Communication -** Mail & Package Hold, Phone Messages, Fax in/out, FedEx, UPS, Express Mail **Supplies - 1-3 mi:** Propane *(Somesville One-Stop)* **3+ mi:** Ice *(Block, Cube)*, West Marine *(5 mi.)*, Bait/Tackle *(5 mi.)*

Boatyard Services

OnSite: Travelift *(30T)*, Crane *(14T Hydraulic w/ 60 ft. boom)*, Launching Ramp, Engine mechanic *(gas, diesel)*, Electrical Repairs, Hull Repairs, Rigger, Bottom Cleaning, Brightwork, Compound, Wash & Wax, Interior Cleaning, Propeller Repairs, Woodworking, Inflatable Repairs, Metal Fabrication, Painting, Awlgrip, Total Refits, Yacht Design, Yacht Building, Yacht Broker **OnCall:** Electronic Sales, Electronics Repairs, Sail Loft, Canvas Work, Divers, Air Conditioning, Refrigeration, Upholstery **Member:** ABBRA - 2 Certified Tech(s), ABYC - 2 Certified Tech(s) **Yard Rates:** $50-65/hr., Haul & Launch $105/use + labor, Power Wash $35/hr.+ labor **Storage:** On-Land Outside $50/ft, Inside $75/ft, Heated $115/ft.

Restaurants and Accommodations

1-3 mi: Seafood Shack *(Abel's Lobster Pound 276-5827, L $11-33, D $18-56, Across Somes Sound by dinghy)* **3+ mi:** Restaurant *(DeMuro's Top of the Hill 244-0033, D $10-28, 4 mi, Most entrees in teens, Kids $7, 5-6pm $8-11; Full dinner with wine/beer $17)*, Fast Food *(Subway 3.5 mi, One-Stop)*

Recreation and Entertainment

OnSite: Sightseeing *(Old Quarry - a picturesque "quarry lake" - the site of an early 20thC quarry that provided pink granite for national landmark buildings)* **Near:** Boat Rentals *(Canoes at Somes Sound View Campground 244-3890)*, Park *(Acadia National Park 288-3338)* **1-3 mi:** Beach *(Echo Lake)* **3+ mi:** Playground *(Somes, basketball court too, 3 mi.)*, Tennis Courts *(4 mi.)*, Golf Course *(Causeway Club 244-3780, 4 mi.)*, Museum *(Mount Desert Island Historical Society, Somesville Museum Tue-Sat 10am-5pm, $1/free, 3 mi.)*, Cultural Attract *(Acadia Repertory Theatre, Somesville Masonic Hall 244-7260; Somesville Footbridge - honors MDI's first settlers, 3 mi.)*, Galleries *(A.J. Higgins Antiques, 3 mi.)*

Provisioning and General Services

3+ mi: Convenience Store *(Somesville One-Stop 244-5504 - well-equipped small market, 3.5 mi.)*, Supermarket *(Southwest Food Mart, 5 mi.)*, Wine/Beer *(Somesville, 3.5 mi.)*, Liquor Store *(Somesville One-Stop, 3.5 mi.)*, Bank/ATM *(3.5 mi.)*, Post Office *(3 mi.)*, Protestant Church *(pies every Wesnesday, 3 mi.)*, Library *(Somesville Library Wed 1-6pm, Sat 9am-2pm, 3 mi.)*, Beauty Salon *(Sally's Hair 244-4495, 3.5 mi.)*

Transportation

OnCall: Rental Car *(Enterprise 664-2662 - from Trenton)* **Near:** Local Bus *(Acadia Island Explorer 288-4573, www.exploreacadia.com)* **Airport:** Bar Harbor/Bangor Int'l. *(20 mi./55 mi.)*

Medical Services

911 Service **OnCall:** Ambulance **3+ mi:** Doctor *(Southwest Harbor Clinics, 5 mi.)* **Hospital:** Mount Desert 288-5081 *(10 mi.)*

Setting -- About two-thirds up the western shore of deep, clear Somes Sound fjord, the John Williams Company sits below the old Hall Quarry. It's easily identifiable by the pretty downeast craft floating in its mooring field or cradled in its travelift. The views from their docks are reminiscent of pre-touristed Maine. It's quiet, truly beautiful, and relatively unspoiled. Walk inland, and the remoteness is the same.

Marina Notes -- Quarry purchased in 1970's. JWBC built on site. Full-service boatyard & custom boat builder here ever since. Home of Stanley Yachts, a series of classic pleasure motor yachts and work boats 26 - 44 ft. Focuses on combining the best of wood and fiberglass construction. Full repair & restoration services plus facilities for storing 35 boats indoor and 125 outside. Private float dockage for large vessels by reservation. Bathhouse: 1 head.

Notable -- Hike to the top of the quarry for a look at the pink granite used in the Franklin Mint and N.Y. Public Library - and the quarry pool left behind by the excavation. This area of Mt. Desert and Acadia is fairly isolated with few services or facilities. However, the free Island Explorer's #7 Southwest Harbor bus stops nearby. Dinghy (or bus) to Somes Harbor at the head of the Sound; dock on the west side at private Somesville Landing (vistors & donations welcome). Or anchor out in 20-25 ft. and dinghy in. Walk to the main road and turn left for the village and the library and museum, or right for the One-Stop and bank. Two miles south, MDI's most popular beach, Echo Lake Beach, makes a good hiking or bus destination - lifeguards, warm water, real sand and life guards make it a kids must. It's about 3/4 mile from the docks to Rte 102 (Island Explorer bus stop) and then about one mile south.

Navigational Information
Lat: 44°21.360' **Long:** 068°18.440' **Tide:** 10 ft. **Current:** 3 kt. **Chart:** 13318
Rep. Depths (*MLW*): Entry 60 ft. **Fuel Dock** n/a **Max Slip/Moor** 25 ft./60 ft.
Access: Southwest Harbor to upper Somes Sound, eastern shore

Marina Facilities *(In Season/Off Season)*
Fuel: No
Slips: 9 Total, 3 Transient **Max LOA:** 80 ft. **Max Beam:** 20 ft.
Rate *(per ft.)*: **Day** $2.00* **Week** Inq. **Month** Inq.
Power: 30 amp Incl., **50 amp** Incl., **100 amp** Incl., **200 amp** n/a
Cable TV: No **Dockside Phone:** No
Dock Type: Floating, Long Fingers, Alongside, Wood
Moorings: 33 Total, 18 Transient **Launch:** Yes, workboat, Dinghy Dock
Rate: Day $30 **Week** $140 **Month** n/a
Heads: 2 Toilet(s)
Internet: No **Laundry:** None
Pump-Out: OnCall, Full Service, 1 Port **Fee:** $5 **Closed Heads:** No

Marina Operations
Owner/Manager: Frank Gott **Dockmaster:** Same
In-Season: May-Oct 1, 6am-3pm **Off-Season:** n/a
After-Hours Arrival: Pick up red ball mooring
Reservations: Yes, Preferred **Credit Cards:** Visa/MC
Discounts: None
Pets: Welcome **Handicap Access:** Yes, Heads

Henry R. Abel & Co. Yacht Yard

P.O.Box 184; Abels Lane at Rte 198; Mount Desert, ME 04660**

Tel: (207) 276-5057 **VHF: Monitor** n/a **Talk** n/a
Fax: (207) 276-9831 **Alternate Tel:** n/a
Email: henryrabelyacht.com **Web:** n/a
Nearest Town: Somesville *(2 mi.)* **Tourist Info:** (207) 276-5040

Marina Services and Boat Supplies
Services - Security *(Marina employees)*, Trash Pick-Up, Dock Carts, 3 Phase **Communication -** Mail & Package Hold, Fax in/out, FedEx, UPS, Express Mail **Supplies - 1-3 mi:** Marine Discount Store *(Hamilton Marine)*, Propane *(Somesville One-Stop)* **3+ mi:** Ships' Store *(5 mi.)*, West Marine *(7 mi.)*, Boat/US *(7 mi.)*, CNG *(Hinckley 244-5525, 7 mi.)*

Boatyard Services
OnSite: Travelift *(50T & 30T)*, Forklift, Crane, Engine mechanic *(gas, diesel)*, Hull Repairs, Rigger, Divers, Bottom Cleaning, Brightwork, Compound, Wash & Wax, Interior Cleaning, Woodworking, Yacht Broker **OnCall:** Electrical Repairs, Electronic Sales, Electronics Repairs, Painting, Awlgrip **Yard Rates:** $58/hr., Haul & Launch $280, Power Wash $35/hr. **Storage:** On-Land Outside $26/ft., Inside $79/ft. & $4/sq.ft.

Restaurants and Accommodations
OnSite: Seafood Shack *(Abel's Lobster Pound 276-5827, L $11-33, D $18-56, 7 days 12-9pm Lobster Roll $21, Lobster Dinners $28-56, 1.5 lb Lobster dinner $35, Reef & Beef $43)* **1-3 mi:** Fast Food *(Subway)*

Recreation and Entertainment
OnSite: Beach, Picnic Area **Near:** Jogging Paths **Under 1 mi:** Hike/Bike Trails *(Acadia's Giant Slide Trailhead, 0.6 mi. south on Rte 3/198. Leads to 1,373 ft. Sargent Mountain. Moderate difficulty 4.4 mi. RT)*, Park *(Acadia National Park 288-3338)* **1-3 mi:** Museum *(Mount Desert Island Historical Society's 1892 Sound School House Museum, $1/free. Mon-Sat, 10am-5pm)*, Cultural Attract *(Acadia Repertory Theatre at Somesville Masonic Hall 244-7260; Somesville Footbridge - honors MDI's first settlers)*

Provisioning and General Services
OnSite: Lobster Pound **1-3 mi:** Convenience Store *(Somesville One-Stop - well equipped small market)*, Wine/Beer, Liquor Store *(Somesville One-Stop)*, Bakery, Bank/ATM, Post Office, Catholic Church, Protestant Church *(Somesville Union Meeting House 244-9260)*, Library *(Somesville Library Wed 1-6pm, Sat 9am-2pm)*, Beauty Salon *(Sally's Hair 244-4495)* **3+ mi:** Supermarket *(Shop N Save, 10 mi.)*

Transportation
Near: Local Bus *(Acadia Island Explorer 288-4573, Free. Brown Mountain #6 route. Links Bar Harbor & Northeast Harbor via Eagle Lake Road & Rt. 198. 7 RT's a day connect in Somesville to #7 Southwest Harbor bus)* **Airport:** Bar Harbor/Bangor Int'l. *(20 mi./50 mi.)*

Medical Services
911 Service **OnCall:** Ambulance **Hospital:** Mt. Desert Is. 288-5081 *(8 mi.)*

Setting -- Near the head of Somes Sound, on the eastern shore, a sizeable mooring field surrounds a string of sturdy floats that berth downeast cruising yachts. A break in the wall of spruce rising above the granite ledge reveals a tidy, well-maintained yacht yard - a pair of bright-blue travelifts backed by neat brick-red boat sheds. Adjacent to the yard, famous Abel's Lobster Pound peeks through the trees. Picnic tables sprinkle the lawn below the attractive two-story flagstone, glass and shingle restaurant. The outdoor dining deck looks out over the mooring field, picnic grove and outdoor covered wood-fired boiler below.

Marina Notes -- *If you eat at Abels, dockage free during the meal and $1.50/ft. overnight. Moorings balls mostly orange over granite blocks up to 15,000 lbs. - some white ones on smaller stones. Workboat serves as Launch. Prefer max LOA of 50 ft. on moorings. Up to 100A 3-phase on docks. 30 + year-old full-service boatyard, extensive facilities and personal service. Most staff custom boat builders. Restaurant reservations useful; no special treatment for boaters. Bathhouse: the restaurant heads are shared by boaters. Note: to dinghy to Somesville, dock at private Somesville Landing (visitors & donations welcome).

Notable -- Family-owned Abel's Lobster Pound is a Mount Desert insitution (July-LabDay Noon- 9pm, Late June 5-8:30pm). Eat at shore-side picnic tables, in the window-walled knotty pine dining rooms or on the second-floor deck. Dining Room reservations are a rigid 6pm, 6:30, 8, and 8:30pm, 7 days. Picnic table service is flexible; eat anytime. Most supplies and services are about 7 miles away. But a 2-mile walk, Island Explorer or dinghy ride to picturesque Somesville will net a lovely stroll. Turn left at the light past the museum, footbridge, library, church, and Masonic Hall. Turn right for a few shops and the One-Stop.

PHOTOS ON DVD: 18

Hinckley Service Yacht Yard

PO Box 699; 130 Shore Road; Manset, ME 04679

Tel: (207) 244-5572; (888) hin-ckle **VHF: Monitor** Ch. 10 **Talk** Ch. 10
Fax: (207) 244-9433 **Alternate Tel:** (207) 244-5531
Email: pfrederick@hinckleyyachts.com **Web:** n/a
Nearest Town: Southwest Harbor *(1.5 mi.)* **Tourist Info:** (207) 244-9264

Navigational Information

Lat: 44°16.081' **Long:** 068°18.378' **Tide:** 12 ft. **Current:** n/a **Chart:** 13318
Rep. Depths (*MLW*): Entry 12 ft. **Fuel Dock** 12 ft. **Max Slip/Moor** 40 ft./-
Access: Gulf of Maine to Eastern Way to Southwest Harbor

Marina Facilities *(In Season/Off Season)*

Fuel: Diesel
Slips: 0 Total, 0 Transient **Max LOA:** 120 ft. **Max Beam:** n/a
Rate *(per ft.)*: **Day** $0 **Week** n/a **Month** n/a
Power: 30 amp n/a, **50 amp** n/a, **100 amp** n/a, **200 amp** n/a
Cable TV: No **Dockside Phone:** No
Dock Type: Floating, Alongside, Wood
Moorings: 70 Total, 65 Transient **Launch:** Yes (Incl.), Dinghy Dock
Rate: Day $35 **Week** $125 **Month** Inq.
Heads: 2 Toilet(s), 3 Shower(s)
Internet: No **Laundry:** 2 Washer(s), 2 Dryer(s)
Pump-Out: OnSite, Full Service, 1 Central **Fee:** $5 **Closed Heads:** No

Marina Operations

Owner/Manager: Paul Frederick **Dockmaster:** Nick Madeira
In-Season: Apr-Nov, 7am-5pm **Off-Season:** Dec-Mar, 9am-4pm
After-Hours Arrival: Pick up a mooring. Hinckley pennant indicates reserved
Reservations: Yes **Credit Cards:** Visa/MC, Amex
Discounts: None
Pets: Welcome **Handicap Access:** No

Marina Services and Boat Supplies

Services - Docking Assistance, Trash Pick-Up, Dock Carts **Communication -** Pay Phone, FedEx, UPS, Express Mail **Supplies - OnSite:** Ice *(Cube)*, Ships' Store, Propane, CNG **Under 1 mi:** West Marine *(at Dysarts)*, Marine Discount Store *(Rockland Boat 244-7870)*

Boatyard Services

OnSite: Travelift *(35, 70 & 160T)*, Forklift, Crane *(20T)*, Hydraulic Trailer *(25T Boss)*, Engine mechanic *(gas, diesel)*, Electrical Repairs, Electronic Sales, Electronics Repairs, Hull Repairs, Rigger, Canvas Work, Bottom Cleaning, Brightwork, Air Conditioning, Refrigeration, Compound, Wash & Wax, Interior Cleaning, Woodworking, Upholstery, Yacht Interiors, Metal Fabrication, Painting, Awlgrip, Total Refits, Yacht Design, Yacht Building, Yacht Broker **OnCall:** Divers, Inflatable Repairs, Life Raft Service **Yard Rates:** $40-75/hr., Haul & Launch $9-16/ft., Power Wash $3-4/ft., Bottom Paint $50/hr. **Storage:** On-Land Outside $40-45/ft. Inside $90/ft.

Restaurants and Accommodations

Near: Restaurant *(The Moorings 244-7070, L $4-11, D $13-19)*, Inn/B&B *(The Moorings Inn 244-5523, $75-195, adjacent, Cottages $95-245)* **Under 1 mi:** Restaurant *(XYZ Restaurant & Gallery 244-5221, D $16-18, Mexican)*, Seafood Shack *(Captain's Galley at Beal's Lobster Pound 244-3202, L $3-10, D $3-30, by dinghy)*, Pizzeria *(Little Notch 244-3357)*, Inn/B&B *(Penury Hall 244-7102)*, Condo/Cottage *(Acadia Cabins 244-5388, $105-140)* **1-3 mi:** Restaurant *(Red Sky 244-0476, D $19-29)*, *(Fiddler's Green 244-9416, D $16-28)*, *(Cafe Dry Dock 244-5842, L $8-13, D $9-23)*, Fast Food *(Maine Pizza & Sub Shop 244-0078)*, Lite Fare *(Breakfast at Grumpy's 244-1082, B $4-10, L $4-13)*, Motel *(Seawall 244-3020, $65-120)*

Recreation and Entertainment

Near: Jogging Paths, Boat Rentals *(Mansell 244-5625)*, Video Rental *(Southwest 244-9825)*, Park **1-3 mi:** Fitness Center *(Harbor House 244-3713, $10)*, Museum *(Wendell Gilley 244-7555)*, Cultural Attract *(SW Harbor Oceanarium 244-7330)* **3+ mi:** Tennis Courts *(Causeway, 4 mi.)*, Golf Course *(Causeway Club 244-3780, 4 mi.)*

Provisioning and General Services

Under 1 mi: Market *(Sawyer's 244-3315 - delivers to dock)*, Delicatessen *(Double J 244-5544)*, Wine/Beer *(Sawyer's)*, Liquor Store *(Sawyer's - also Liquor Locker 244-3788)*, Fishmonger *(Fish Truck - corner of Rte 102)*, Protestant Church **1-3 mi:** Supermarket *(Gott's 244-3431)*, Health Food *(Burdocks 244-0108)*, Bakery *(Little Notch 244-4043)*, Farmers' Market *(Fri. 9am-1pm 546-2395 St. John Divine Pkg Lot)*, Bank/ATM, Post Office, Catholic Church, Library *(SWH 244-7065, Internet)*, Beauty Salon, Dry Cleaners, Laundry *(Village Washtub 244-0220)*, Bookstore *(Rue Cottage 244-5542)*, Pharmacy *(Carroll 244-5588)*, Newsstand *(Tom Cat)*, Hardware Store *(McEachern & Hutchins 244-5567)*

Transportation

OnSite: Courtesy Car/Van *(By reservation)* **OnCall:** Water Taxi, Rental Car *(Enterprise 667-1217)* **Near:** Local Bus *(Island Explorer 667-5796)*, Ferry Service *(Cranberry Cove 460-1981 $24/16 RT)* **1-3 mi:** Bikes *(Southwest Cycle 244-5856)* **Airport:** Bar Harbor/Bangor Int'l. *(23 mi./50 mi.)*

Medical Services

911 Service **Near:** Dentist, Chiropractor, Ambulance **1-3 mi:** Doctor *(SW Harbor Medical 244-5513)* **Hospital:** Mt. Desert Island 288-5081 *(18 mi.)*

Setting -- At the entrance to Southwest Harbor, a vast mooring field, occupied by a diverse rainbow of beautiful Hinckley yachts, seems to dance attendance on the ship-shape two-acre village of blue-trimmed, gray-shingled buildings on shore. A string of floats leads to the fixed wharf that abuts a massive travelift bay, providing access to the upland. To the east, another long pier sports a row of blue umbrella-topped tables that leads to The Moorings restaurant and Inn.

Marina Notes -- Since 1928, the original Hinckley boatyard. Hauling capacity to 150T. 70 moorings to 120 ft. LOA. Very limited dock space. Pump-out - Mon-Fri, 7am-5pm, Sat & Sun 9-3 Hinckley logo on white mooring balls; green Hinckley flag indicates mooring reserved. Launch service during biz hours; limited on-call after hours. Loaner dinghies for mooring runs. Courtesy car by reservation. CNG available. Hinckley name/logo clothing and gifts in Ships' Store. Inquire about shed tours: see Hinckleys being built. Seasonal moorings $1,250. Nearest fuel at Beal's. Six additional moorings - Town of SW Harbor; Dennis Dever, Harbormaster (Ch. 9, 16, 244-7913). Bathhouse: Two-story salt box at head of dock. Lower floor. Surprisingly modest, 2 individual shower rooms, composite floors, fiberglass stalls. Separate toilets. Washers, dryers, vending machines.

Notable -- For dinner or a night ashore, the Moorings Restaurant, and separately owned Moorings Inn, are nearly surrounded by the Hinckley operation. The village of Southwest Harbor has maintained its quiet-side vibe but still has a plethora of enticing dining and provisioning options. The Island Explorer stops nearby (providing access to all of Acadia Nat'l Park) or dinghy up harbor to Dysart's or Upper Town Dock, or take the ferry to the Cranberry Islands.

PHOTOS ON DVD: 25

Navigational Information

Lat: 44°16.536' **Long:** 068°18.835' **Tide:** 10 ft. **Current:** 2 kt. **Chart:** 13318
Rep. Depths (*MLW*): Entry 30 ft. **Fuel Dock** 20 ft. **Max Slip/Moor** -/30 ft.
Access: On the East Shore of Southwest Harbor next to Coast Guard Station

Marina Facilities *(In Season/Off Season)*

Fuel: *Citgo* - Slip-Side Fueling, Gasoline, Diesel, High-Speed Pumps
Slips: 0 Total, 0 Transient **Max LOA:** 100 ft. **Max Beam:** 20 ft.
Rate *(per ft.)*: **Day** n/a **Week** n/a **Month** n/a
Power: 30 amp n/a, **50 amp** n/a, **100 amp** n/a, **200 amp** n/a
Cable TV: No **Dockside Phone:** No
Dock Type: Fixed, Floating, Wood
Moorings: 4 Total, 4 Transient **Launch:** None, Dinghy Dock
Rate: Day $30/20 **Week** $150/100 **Month** Inq.
Heads: 3 Toilet(s)
Internet: No **Laundry:** None
Pump-Out: No **Fee:** n/a **Closed Heads:** No

Marina Operations

Owner/Manager: Sam Beal **Dockmaster:** Larry Dykes
In-Season: Jun-Sep, 7am-5pm **Off-Season:** Oct-May, 7am-4pm
After-Hours Arrival: n/a
Reservations: No **Credit Cards:** Visa/MC, Amex
Discounts: None
Pets: Welcome **Handicap Access:** Yes, Heads

Beal's Lobster Pier

PO Box; 182 Clark Point Road; Southwest Harbor, ME 04679

Tel: (207) 244-3202; (800) 245-7178 **VHF: Monitor** Ch. 88 **Talk** Ch. 88
Fax: (207) 244-9479 **Alternate Tel:** n/a
Email: bealslobster@roadrunner.com **Web:** www.bealslobsterpier.net
Nearest Town: Southwest Harbor *(0.7 mi.)* **Tourist Info:** (207) 224-9264

Marina Services and Boat Supplies

Services - Docking Assistance, Trash Pick-Up **Communication -** Fax in/out *($5)*, FedEx **Supplies - OnSite:** Ice *(Block, Cube, Shaved)* **Under 1 mi:** West Marine **1-3 mi:** Ships' Store *(Hinckley 244-7100)*, Propane *(Dead River 244-9835)*, CNG *(Hinckley 244-5572)*

Boatyard Services

OnSite: Forklift **OnCall:** Sail Loft, Canvas Work, Bottom Cleaning, Brightwork, Interior Cleaning **Near:** Railway, Crane, Launching Ramp, Engine mechanic *(gas, diesel)*, Electrical Repairs, Hull Repairs, Divers, Woodworking, Painting. **Nearest Yard:** Southwest Boat (207) 244-5525

Restaurants and Accommodations

OnSite: Seafood Shack *(The Captain's Galley at Beal's 244-3202, L $3-10, D $3-30, Inside & outside, all tables overlook the harbor)* **Near:** Restaurant *(Xanthus at Claremont L $11-18, D $24-27, Prix Fixe $29, Small Plates $8-15, Lunch at Boat House)*, Hotel *(Claremont 244-5036, $155-$310)*, Inn/B&B *(Lindenwood Inn 244-5335, $95-255)*, *(Harbour Cottage Inn 244-5738, $165-255)*, *(Clark Point Inn 244-9828, $95-245)*, *(Cranberry Hill 244-5007, $110-155)* **Under 1 mi:** Restaurant *(Eat-A-Pita Café 244-4344, B $4-6, L $5-7, D $14-21)*, *(Dry Dock Café 244-5842, B $7, L $6-11, D $10-16)*, *(Red Sky 244-0476, D $19-29)*, *(Chow Maine Café 669-4142, B $6, L $10, D $12)*, *(Fiddler's Green 244-9416, D $19-29)*, Pizzeria *(Little Notch 244-3357)*

Recreation and Entertainment

OnSite: Picnic Area, Boat Rentals *(Harbor Boat Rentals, 17' Boston Whaler, 22' Mako 244-0557)*, Fishing Charter *(Masako Queen Deep Sea Fishing - "S/V Vagabond" 244-5385 - 1/2 & 3/4 Days)* **Near:** Playground, Dive Shop, Museum *(Wendell Gilley 244-7555, $5/2 Tue-Sun, 10am-4pm Art of bird carving)* **Under 1 mi:** Beach, Park *(Acadia Nat'l)*, Tours *(Maine State Kayaks 244-9500, $45/4 hr. tour)* **1-3 mi:** Tennis Courts *(Causeway Club)*, Golf Course *(Causeway Club 244-3780)*, Sightseeing *(Mt. Desert Is,)*

Provisioning and General Services

OnSite: Lobster Pound **OnCall:** Delicatessen *(Double J Grocery & Deli 244-5544)* **Near:** Bank/ATM, Protestant Church, Newsstand **Under 1 mi:** Market *(Sawyer's 244-3315 gourmet, organic, delivers to boats)*, Gourmet Shop, Wine/Beer *(Sawyer's)*, Bakery, Farmers' Market *(Fri. 9am-1pm 546-2395 St. John Divine Pkg Lot)*, Post Office, Library *(Southwest Harbor 244-7065, Internet)*, Beauty Salon, Barber Shop, Pharmacy *(Carroll 244-5588)*, Hardware Store *(McEachern & Hutchins 244-5567)*, Retail Shops **1-3 mi:** Convenience Store *(Gott's 244-3431)*, Supermarket *(SW Food Mart)*, Liquor Store *(Sawyer's; Liquor Locker 244-3788, delivers)*, Catholic Church *(by water)*, Laundry *(Village Wash 244-0220)*

Transportation

OnCall: Rental Car *(Enterprise 667-1217)* **Near:** Bikes *(Southwest Cycle 244-5856)*, Local Bus *(Acadia Island Explorer 288-4573, Free)*, Ferry Service *(Cranberry Cove to Cranberry Islands 460-1981 $24/16 RT)* **Airport:** Bar Harbor/Bangor Int'l. *(21 mi./50 mi.)*

Medical Services

911 Service **Near:** Doctor *(Southwest Harbor Med Center 244-5513)*, Ambulance **Under 1 mi:** Dentist **1-3 mi:** Holistic Services *(Greenbaum Massage 276-4057)*, Veterinarian *(SW Harbor Vet Clinic 244-3336)*
Hospital: Mount Desert Island 288-5081 *(14 mi.)*

Setting -- Beal's is on the working side of Southwest Harbor, on Clark Point next to the U.S. Coast Guard station and town dock - its mooring field nestled among the fishing fleet. On shore, an attractive, very long, natural shingled two-story newish structure stretches out over the wharf. The lobstering operation occupies the water end and Captain's Galley the remainder - with windows overlooking the harbor. A large float manages dinghies, fuel and deliveries.

Marina Notes -- Beal family facility since 1930. Restaurant & wholesale lobster operation first; transient boating facility second. Suzanne Beal Madeira & Pete Madeira have run Captain's Galley since 2005. The "short stay" dock is shared with the lobster fleet. Four moorings - no launch service, bring your dinghy. Overnight slips not available. Water, gas, diesel, ice, and some marine hardware. Heated indoor winter storage $100/ft. Additional moorings from Southwest Harbor Town Moorings - Harbormaster 244-7913. Bathhouse: Heads shared with restaurant.

Notable -- While the amenities are limited, mooring among the fishing fleet is a true down-east experience in a busy, working seaside community. Enjoy fresh boiled lobster and other seafood specialties in the rough at picnic tables on the pier. Captain's serves the crustaceans starting at 9am - your lobster and go-withs are packed into your net bag and dropped into the boiler. A few blocks walk west, the renowned Wendell Gilley Gallery celebrates water fowl carving with exhibits and workshops. Acadia Island Explorer's Rte 7 bus also stops at the museum. Take it east to Bass Harbor or west to Bar Harbor - or anywhere in between. Walk a bit further into Southwest Harbor - a delightful low-key village with some lovely restaurants, services, and shops.

PHOTOS ON DVD: 20

Southwest Boat Marine Services

PO Box 260; 168 Clark Point Road; Southwest Harbor, ME 04679
Tel: (207) 244-5525 **VHF: Monitor** Ch. 16 **Talk** Ch. 8
Fax: (207) 667-4013 **Alternate Tel:** (207) 326-8548
Email: southwestboat@hypernet.com **Web:** www.southwestboat.com
Nearest Town: Southwest Harbor *(0.6 mi.)* **Tourist Info:** (207) 244-9264

Navigational Information

Lat: 44°16.565' **Long:** 068°18.827' **Tide:** 10 ft. **Current:** 2 kt. **Chart:** 13318
Rep. Depths (*MLW*): Entry 20 ft. **Fuel Dock** n/a **Max Slip/Moor** 15 ft./20 ft.
Access: Penobscot Bay to Southwest Harbor, eastern shore

Marina Facilities *(In Season/Off Season)*

Fuel: No
Slips: 15 Total, 5 Transient **Max LOA:** 100 ft. **Max Beam:** n/a
Rate *(per ft.)*: **Day** $1.00/Inq. **Week** $5 **Month** $15
Power: 30 amp Incl., **50 amp** Incl., **100 amp** n/a, **200 amp** n/a
Cable TV: No **Dockside Phone:** No
Dock Type: Fixed, Floating, Short Fingers, Pilings, Alongside, Wood
Moorings: 3 Total, 3 Transient **Launch:** Yes (Free), Dinghy Dock
Rate: Day $20 **Week** $100 **Month** $250
Heads: 1 Toilet(s), 1 Shower(s)
Internet: No **Laundry:** None
Pump-Out: OnSite, Full Service, 1 Central **Fee:** Free **Closed Heads:** No

Marina Operations

Owner/Manager: Jeff Berzinis **Dockmaster:** Same
In-Season: Year-Round, 9am-5pm **Off-Season:** n/a
After-Hours Arrival: Call in advance and then tie up in an available slip
Reservations: Yes, Preferred **Credit Cards:** Visa/MC
Discounts: None
Pets: Welcome **Handicap Access:** No

Marina Services and Boat Supplies

Services - Docking Assistance, Trash Pick-Up, Dock Carts **Communication -** Pay Phone, FedEx, DHL, UPS, Express Mail **Supplies - OnSite:** Ice *(Shaved)* **Near:** Ice *(Block, Cube)*, Ships' Store *(Rockland Boat 594-8181)*, West Marine *(at Dysart's)* **Under 1 mi:** Bait/Tackle **1-3 mi:** Propane *(Hinckley's 244-5572)*, CNG *(Hinckley's)*

Boatyard Services

OnSite: Railway *(250 ft.)*, Crane *(25T)*, Divers *(Underwater hull inspection)*, Bottom Cleaning, Metal Fabrication **OnCall:** Engine mechanic *(gas, diesel)*, Electrical Repairs *(Village Electronics 244-7323)*, Electronic Sales *(Village Electronics)*, Rigger, Sail Loft, Air Conditioning, Refrigeration, Compound, Wash & Wax, Interior Cleaning, Propeller Repairs

Restaurants and Accommodations

Near: Restaurant *(Xanthus at Claremont 244-5036, L $11-18, D $24-27, Lunch in Boat House)*, Seafood Shack *(The Captain's Galley at Beal's Lobster Pier 244-3202, L $3-10, D $3-30, Inside & outside, all tables overlook the harbor)*, Hotel *(Claremount 244-5036, $155-310)*, Inn/B&B *(Harbor Cottage Inn 244-5738, $165-255)*, *(Clark Point Inn 244-9828, $95-245)* **Under 1 mi:** Restaurant *(Moorings Restaurant 244-7070, across the harbor)*, *(Red Sky 244-0476, D $19-29)*, *(Dry Dock Café 244-5842, B $7, L $6-11, D $10-16)*, *(Fiddler's Green 244-9416, D $19-29)*, *(Eat-A-Pita Café 244-4344, B $4-6, L $5-7, D $14-21)*, Pizzeria *(Little Notch 244-3357)*

Recreation and Entertainment

Near: Jogging Paths, Boat Rentals *(Mansell 244-5625)*, Park, Museum *(Wendell Gilley 244-7555 $5/2)* **Under 1 mi:** Beach, Tours *(Maine State Kayaks 244-9500, $45/4 hr. tour)*, Sightseeing *(Acadia National Park 288-3338)* **1-3 mi:** Tennis Courts, Golf Course *(Causeway Club 244-3780)* **3+ mi:** Horseback Riding *(Seal Cove Riding Stable 276-3622, 4 mi.)*

Provisioning and General Services

Near: Lobster Pound *(Beal's 244-3202)* **Under 1 mi:** Convenience Store, Market *(Sawyer's Market 244-3315, Southwest Foodmart 244-5601 both deliver)*, Supermarket *(Carroll's IGA; Gotts 244-3431)*, Delicatessen *(Double J Grocery & Deli 244-5544)*, Wine/Beer *(Sawyer's)*, Liquor Store *(Sawyer's; Liquor Locker 244-3788, delivers)*, Bank/ATM, Post Office, Protestant Church, Library *(Southwest Harbor PL 244-7065, Internet)*, Beauty Salon *(Sargasso 244-4034)*, Barber Shop, Laundry, Pharmacy *(Carroll 244-5588)*, Hardware Store *(McEachern & Hutchins 244-5567)*, Florist *(West Side 244-3540)*

Transportation

OnSite: Water Taxi **OnCall:** Rental Car *(Enterprise 667-1217)* **Near:** Bikes *(Southwest Cycle 244-5856)*, Local Bus *(Island Explorer 288-4573)*, Ferry Service *(Cranberry Island 460-1981 $24/16 RT)* **Airport:** Bar Harbor/Bangor Int'l. *(21 mi./50 mi.)*

Medical Services

911 Service **OnCall:** Ambulance **Near:** Doctor *(SW Harbor Med Center 244-5513)* **Under 1 mi:** Dentist **1-3 mi:** Holistic Services *(Greenbaum Massage 276-4057)*, Veterinarian *(SW Harbor 244-3336)* **Hospital:** Mt. Desert Island 288-5081 *(14 mi.)*

PHOTOS ON DVD: 18

Setting -- Adjacent to the Coast Guard station, next to Beal's, Southwest Boat is on the north side of the harbor where the local fishing fleet gathers. A long, barn-roofed, natural-shingled work shed sits on the "L-shaped" stationary wharf that protects the floating docks. This venerable boat yard puts pleasure craft in the heart of the working, bustling harbor. For those who love all things "boat," watching the dance as the lobstermen go about their business is compelling.

Marina Notes -- Founded in 1937 when Henry Hinckley & Lennox Sargent bought the Chester Clements Yard. Later purchased by the Berzinis & Sawyers. Since 1998 owned & managed by Audrey & Jeff Berzinis.Today Southwest Boat offers year-round dockage, moorings & inside storage for vessels to 100 ft. 25 ton crane, a 250 foot railway. Specialize in steel boat repair; on-site machine shop provides welding, metal fabrication. Diver for underwater hull inspections. Towing and salvage. Island 65 foot, 50 ton barge service. Water taxi. Can arrange for most repair services. No fuel. Downeast Diesel & Marine (244-5145) down the road. Additional moorings from Southwest Harbor Town - Harbormaster 244-7913. Bathhouse: One Porta Potty.

Notable -- Southwest Boat owns three barges - 65 ft. "Neptune" (60 tons), 59 ft. "Triton" (30 tons) and smaller "Pluto" - that provide critical transport services to the islands and support for marine construction, moorings, and salvage work - all very fascinating. In addition, MDI Community Sailing Center bases here (with their fleet of Optis) as does the "Aids to Navigation" team of the U.S. Coast Guard. The lively village of Southwest Harbor is an easy walk, with endless activities: shopping, restaurants, and local festivals. The free Island Explorer covers all of Acadia - take Rte 7 west to Bar Harbor and east to Bass Harbor.

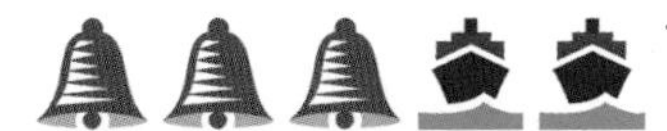

Navigational Information

Lat: 44°16.430' **Long:** 068°19.340' **Tide:** 12 ft. **Current:** 2 kt. **Chart:** 13318
Rep. Depths (*MLW*): Entry 12 ft. **Fuel Dock** 5 ft. **Max Slip/Moor** 12 ft./-
Access: Gulf of Maine to Eastern Way to Southwest Harbor

Marina Facilities *(In Season/Off Season)*

Fuel: Diesel, High-Speed Pumps
Slips: 100 Total, 25 Transient **Max LOA:** 150 ft. **Max Beam:** n/a
Rate *(per ft.)*: **Day** $2.95* **Week** Inq. **Month** Inq.
Power: 30 amp $15, **50 amp** $25, **100 amp** $40, **200 amp** n/a
Cable TV: No **Dockside Phone:** No
Dock Type: Floating, Long Fingers, Short Fingers, Alongside, Concrete
Moorings: 0 Total, 0 Transient **Launch:** n/a, Dinghy Dock (Inq.)
Rate: Day n/a **Week** n/a **Month** n/a
Heads: 14 Toilet(s), 7 Shower(s) *(dressing rooms)*, Book Exchange
Internet: Yes *(Wi-Fi, Free)* **Laundry:** 2 Washer(s), 2 Dryer(s)
Pump-Out: OnSite, Full Service, 1 Central **Fee:** Free **Closed Heads:** No

Marina Operations

Owner/Manager: Micah & Jane Peabody **Dockmaster:** Micah Peabody
In-Season: May-Oct, 6am-9pm **Off-Season:** Nov-Apr, 7:30am-4:30pm
After-Hours Arrival: Call ahead for instructions
Reservations: Yes, Preferred **Credit Cards:** Visa/MC
Discounts: Boat/US **Dockage:** n/a **Fuel:** n/a **Repair:** n/a
Pets: Welcome, Dog Walk Area **Handicap Access:** Yes, Heads, Docks

Dysart's Great Harbor Marina

PO Box 1503; 11 Apple Lane; Southwest Harbor, ME 04679

Tel: (207) 244-0117 **VHF: Monitor** Ch. 9 **Talk** Ch. 8
Fax: (207) 244-7526 **Alternate Tel:** (207) 944-4826
Email: info@dysartsmarina.com **Web:** www.dysartsmarina.com
Nearest Town: Southwest Harbor *(0.5 mi.)* **Tourist Info:** (207) 244-9264

Marina Services and Boat Supplies

Services - Docking Assistance, Concierge, Boaters' Lounge, Dock Carts, 3 Phase **Communication -** Pay Phone, FedEx, DHL, UPS, Express Mail **Supplies - OnSite:** Ice *(Block, Cube)*, West Marine *(244-0300)* **Near:** Ships' Store *(Hamilton Marine 244-7870)*, Bait/Tackle **Under 1 mi:** Propane *(Acadia 244-9664)*, CNG *(Hinckley)*

Boatyard Services

OnSite: Forklift, Electronic Sales, Sail Loft, Canvas Work, Divers, Bottom Cleaning, Brightwork, Compound, Wash & Wax, Interior Cleaning, Propeller Repairs, Woodworking, Inflatable Repairs, Upholstery **OnCall:** Engine mechanic *(gas, diesel)*, Electrical Repairs, Electronics Repairs, Hull Repairs, Rigger, Air Conditioning, Refrigeration, Yacht Interiors, Metal Fabrication, Yacht Design, Yacht Broker **Nearest Yard:** Hinckley (207) 244-5572

Restaurants and Accommodations

OnSite: Restaurant *(Gilley's Head of the Harbor 244-5222, $3-20, new management, pizza & subs)*, Lite Fare *(Breakfast at Grumpy 244-1082, B $4-10, L $4-13)* **Near:** Restaurant *(Red Sky 244-0476, D $19-29)*, *(Café Dry Dock 244-5842, L $8-13, D $9-23)*, *(Eat-A-Pita & Café 2 244-4344, B $4-6, L $5-7, D $15-26)*, *(Fiddler's Green 244-9416, L $6-17, D $19-29)*, Lite Fare *(Quietside Cafe & Ice Cream)*, Pizzeria *(Little Notch 244-3357)*, Motel *(Acadia Cabins 244-5388, $80-100)*, Inn/B&B *(The Kingsleigh 244-5302, $110-305)*, *(Dry Dock Inn 244-5842, $75-200)*, *(Inn at Southwest 244-3835, $110-190)* **Under 1 mi:** Restaurant *(The Claremont 244-5036, L $11-18, D $18-24, Prix Fixe $29)*, *(Harbor Cottage Inn 244-5738)*, Seafood Shack *(Captain's Galley at Beal's 244-3202, L $3-10, D $3-30)*, *(Captain's Galley at Beal's 244-3202, L&D $3-30)*, Inn/B&B *(Lindenwood 244-5335, $75-250)*

Recreation and Entertainment

OnSite: Picnic Area, Grills *(Lobster Steamers too)*, Boat Rentals *(Hinckley Yacht Charters)*, Fishing Charter **OnCall:** Dive Shop **Near:** Pool, Beach, Playground, Tennis Courts, Fitness Center *(Harbor House 244-3713, $10)*, Jogging Paths, Video Rental **Under 1 mi:** Golf Course *(Causeway C.C. 244-3780)*, Museum *(Wendell Gilley 244-7555 $5/2)* **1-3 mi:** Tours *(Maine State Kayaks 244-9500, $45/4 hr. tour)*

Provisioning and General Services

OnSite: Lobster Pound **Near:** Market *(Sawyer's 244-3315, Del)*, Supermarket *(Gotts 244-3431; SW Food Mart 244-5601 3 mi. Del.)*, Wine/Beer *(Sawyer's)*, Liquor Store *(Liquor Locker 244-3788, Del.)*, Bakery *(Little Notch)*, Bank/ATM, Post Office, Protestant Church, Library, Beauty Salon, Pharmacy *(Carroll 244-5588)*, Hardware Store *(McEachern & Hutchins 244-5567)* **Under 1 mi:** Farmers' Market *(Fri. 9-1, St. John)*, Florist *(Westside 244-3540 Del.)* **1-3 mi:** Laundry *(Plaza 244-0234 Del.)*

Transportation

OnSite: Courtesy Car/Van **OnCall:** Bikes *(Southwest Cycle 244-5856)*, Rental Car *(Enterprise 667-1217)*, Airport Limo *(Airport Taxi 667-5995)* **Near:** Local Bus *(Island Explorer)* **Under 1 mi:** Ferry Service *(Cranberry Island)* **Airport:** Bar Harbor/Bangor Int'l. *(21 mi./50 mi.)*

Medical Services

911 Service **Near:** Doctor *(SW Harbor Med. Ctr 244-5513)* **Under 1 mi:** Holistic Services *(South Harbor Massage 244-3168)* **1-3 mi:** Dentist *(C.S. Mallor 288-5333)*, Veterinarian *(SW Harbor 244-3336)* **3+ mi:** Chiropractor *(Knowle's 244-5870, 3.5 mi.)* **Hospital:** Mt. Desert Is. 288-5081 *(14 mi.)*

Setting -- Dysart's sits at the head of Southwest Harbor - just downhill from "downtown" - with views the entire length of the harbor. Three main docks sport slips on one side and a side-tie face on the other - perfect for the large vessels and megayachts that gather here. At the top of the gangway, a summer tent, for barbecues and picnics, is backed by the blue-trimmed gray-shingled dockmasters' office. Further upland, one finds a long two-story gray building with a deck, a few nautically oriented shops and the bathhouse. Most other services are an easy walk into town.

Marina Notes -- *Under 50' $2.95/ft, 50'-64' $3.20/ft., 64'-180' $3.50/ft. Built by Dysart family 1990. Still owned/operated by Dysarts (original partnership with Hinckley - called Great Harbor). Ongoing upgrades. Hail once in harbor abeam of Coast Guard Station. New docks for vessels to 150 ft. with 100A, 3-phase power. Some dockage stern-to. Midday check-out. Concierge services & courtesy car (Peabodys lend work truck). Extensive boatyard services. Dockside grills & lobster steamers. Off-season, commercial fishing boats dock here. Bathhouse: Tile & cinderblock full baths at end main building. Large, airy laundry.

Notable -- Dysart's is a magnet for larger vessels, a popular destination for club cruises, rendezvous, and other special events; they also hosts weekly themed dock parties, too. Two restaurants are just up the hill, and almost every provisioner delivers right to the boat (Sawyer's, Beal's, SW Food, Liquor Locker, etc.). Prretty little Southwest Harbor is a third mile walk with more eateries, shops and services. The free Island Explorer's Route 7 heads south to Bernard and Bass Harbor and runs north along Somes Sound to Bar Harbor where all routes converge - making all of Acadia National Park's 46,856 acres easily accessible.

PHOTOS ON DVD: 25

Morris Yachts

PO Box 395; 53 Granville Road; Bass Harbor, ME 04653

Tel: (207) 244-5511 **VHF: Monitor** Ch. 9 **Talk** Ch. 68
Fax: (207) 244-9726 **Alternate Tel:** n/a
Email: service@morrisyachts.com **Web:** www.morrisyachts.com
Nearest Town: Southwest Harbor *(3.2 mi.)* **Tourist Info:** (207) 244-9264

Navigational Information

Lat: 44°14.046' **Long:** 068°20.835' **Tide:** 12 ft. **Current:** 1 kt. **Chart:** 13318
Rep. Depths (*MLW*): Entry 20 ft. **Fuel Dock** 20 ft. **Max Slip/Moor** -/30 ft.
Access: Eastern Blue Hill Bay to Bass Harbor on Mount Desert Island

Marina Facilities *(In Season/Off Season)*

Fuel: *Texaco* - Slip-Side Fueling, Diesel
Slips: 0 Total, 0 Transient **Max LOA:** 50 ft. **Max Beam:** 15 ft.
Rate *(per ft.)*: **Day** $0 **Week** n/a **Month** n/a
Power: 30 amp n/a, **50 amp** n/a, **100 amp** n/a, **200 amp** n/a
Cable TV: No **Dockside Phone:** No
Dock Type: n/a
Moorings: 32 Total, 16 Transient **Launch:** None, Dinghy Dock
Rate: Day $30 **Week** $150 **Month** n/a
Heads: 3 Toilet(s), 3 Shower(s) *(dressing rooms)*
Internet: Yes *(Office, Free)* **Laundry:** 1 Washer(s), 1 Dryer(s)
Pump-Out: Full Service **Fee:** $50 **Closed Heads:** No

Marina Operations

Owner/Manager: Chris Murray **Dockmaster:** Mark Tubbs
In-Season: Year Round, 8am-5pm **Off-Season:** n/a
After-Hours Arrival: All major holidays
Reservations: Yes, Required **Credit Cards:** Visa/MC
Discounts: None
Pets: Welcome, Dog Walk Area **Handicap Access:** No

Marina Services and Boat Supplies

Services - Docking Assistance, Security *(24 Hrs.)* **Communication -** Mail & Package Hold, Phone Messages, Fax in/out, FedEx, DHL, UPS, Express Mail **Supplies - OnSite:** Ice *(Block, Cube)* **OnCall:** Propane, CNG **1-3 mi:** Ships' Store, West Marine *(244-0300)*

Boatyard Services

OnSite: Travelift *(50T)*, Engine mechanic *(gas, diesel)*, Electrical Repairs, Electronic Sales, Electronics Repairs, Hull Repairs, Rigger, Divers, Bottom Cleaning, Brightwork, Air Conditioning, Refrigeration, Compound, Wash & Wax, Interior Cleaning, Woodworking, Metal Fabrication, Painting, Awlgrip, Total Refits, Yacht Broker **OnCall:** Sail Loft, Canvas Work, Propeller Repairs, Upholstery **Dealer for:** Morris, Yanmar, Raytheon, Panda. **Member:** ABBRA, ABYC - 3 Certified Tech(s) **Yard Rates:** $42-75/hr., Haul & Launch $10-12/ft., Power Wash $2-3/ft., Bottom Paint $18/ft. *(paint incl.)* **Storage:** On-Land Out: $50/ft. In: $7.50/ft. Heated $11.50-13/sq.ft.

Restaurants and Accommodations

OnCall: Pizzeria *(Little Notch 244-3357)* **Near:** Seafood Shack *(Seafood Ketch 244-7463, L $6-17, D $16-28, 11am-9pm)*, *(Maine-Ly Delights 244-3656, L & D $3-12.50 Great lobster roll. 11am-9pm Across from Ferry)*, *(Thurston's Lobster Pound 244-7600, L $3-10.50, D $20-28, Self-serve - Lobsters $9-10/lb. plus "dinner" $6-12. Dinghy across harbor 11am-8:30pm)*, Inn/B&B *(Bass Harbor 244-5157, $75-130, Restored 1870 house)* **Under 1 mi:** Condo/Cottage *(Bass Harbor Cottages & Inn 244-3460, $60-175)* **1-3 mi:** Inn/B&B *(Ann's Point 244-9595, $235-285)* **3+ mi:** Restaurant *(Sips Wine Bar 244-4550, 3.5 mi., 2 oz sip or a 5 oz glass)*, Motel *(Seawall 244-3020, $65-120, 3.5mi., Particularly nice motel - helpful, gracious owners)*

Recreation and Entertainment

Near: Beach, Jogging Paths, Hike/Bike Trails, Park *(Acadia Nat'l)* **Under 1 mi:** Galleries *(Antique shops in Bernard, up the hill to Ravenswood for Ship Models)* **1-3 mi:** Video Rental, Museum *(Bass Harbor Head Light 1.4 mi. - grounds open 9am-Sunset)*, Sightseeing *(Acadia - Seawall Campground)* **3+ mi:** Tennis Courts *(Causeway, 5 mi.)*, Golf Course *(Causeway Club 244-3780, 5 mi.)*

Provisioning and General Services

Near: Fishmonger, Lobster Pound **Under 1 mi:** Post Office, Library **1-3 mi:** Convenience Store *(Gott's 244-3431, pizza too; McKinley 244-9750)*, Bank/ATM, Protestant Church, Hardware Store *(McEachern & Hutchins 244-5567)* **3+ mi:** Market *(Sawyer's 244-3315 - delivers, 3.3 mi.)*, Supermarket *(Southwest Food Mart 244-5601 Del, 4.3 mi.)*, Wine/Beer *(Sawyer's Specialties 244-3315 Del., 3.3 mi.)*, Liquor Store *(Liquor Locker 244-3788 Del., 5 mi.)*, Bakery *(Little Notch, 3.3 mi.)*, Farmers' Market *(Fri. 9am-1pm 546-2395 St. John, 3.5 mi.)*, Catholic Church *(3.5 mi.)*, Beauty Salon *(Sargasso 244-4034, 3.5 mi.)*, Pharmacy *(Carroll 244-5588, 3.5 mi.)*

Transportation

OnCall: Rental Car *(Hertz 667-5017)*, Taxi *(Airport & Harbor 667-5995)* **Near:** Local Bus *(Island Explorer - Rte 7 Free island-wide bus service)*, Ferry Service *(Swan's Island & Frenchboro)* **Airport:** Bar Harbor *(15 mi.)*

Medical Services

911 Service **1-3 mi:** Doctor *(Walk-in Clinic 244-5630)*, Veterinarian *(SWH 244-3336)*, Ambulance **Hospital:** MDI 288-5081 *(18 mi.)*

PHOTOS ON DVD: 25

Setting -- Past the Bass Harbor Head Light, in the Outer Harbor, a shedding, brown-shingled two-story building balances on an ancient stone wharf; it sports a white sign lettered Morris Service. Two new docks float on either end - tied to the wharf by sturdy gangplanks. A complex of nicely restored antique buildings counterpoint the large forest green state-of-the art service sheds that march up the hill. The water view is deceptive - this is an impressive operation.

Marina Notes -- CCM. Family owned service yard. Morris Yachts founded in 1972. Service yard & brokerage moved to Bass Harbor in 1999. Custom production/manufacturing facility moved off island to Trenton. New 50-ton travelift, widened & lengthened haul-out bay, increased storage, upgraded painting services - two, AwlGrip bays. 38,000 sq. ft. indoor storage, half heated. Parts Dept (7:30am-4pm, 8am-noon Sat.). Mooring field straddles the fairway. No overnight transient docks in Outer Harbor; Morris maintains dockage at Up Harbor Marine. Dinghy dockage at Morris & town dock. For town moorings, Bass Harbor harbormaster, David Schlafer 244-4564, Ch.16. Bathhouse: Three full baths, washer/dryer in brown-shingled building up hill.

Notable -- This is the quietest part of MDI's quiet side. The views are spectacular and dramatic; yet the hustle, bustle and activities are a free Island Explorer ride away - it turns around here but stops next door at the Frenchboro/ Swan's Island ferry terminal. Route 7 zips around to Bernard and then all the way to Bar Harbor - stop anywhere in between. Or haul your bikes aboard the ferry for a day's adventure on Swan's Island or a longer stay on Frenchboro. For well-priced seafood, Maine-ly Delights is across the road. For a hike, the Bass Harbor Light is a worthy destination. Or tour Bernard; dinghy up harbor to the town dock.

Navigational Information

Lat: 44°14.483' **Long:** 068°21.166' **Tide:** 11 ft. **Current:** 5 kt. **Chart:** 13316
Rep. Depths (*MLW*): Entry 10 ft. **Fuel Dock** n/a **Max Slip/Moor** 10 ft./-
Access: Blue Hill Bay past Bass Harbor Head Light into Inner Harbor - to port

Marina Facilities *(In Season/Off Season)*

Fuel: No
Slips: 20 Total, 3 Transient **Max LOA:** 50 ft. **Max Beam:** 14 ft.
Rate *(per ft.)*: **Day** $1.50* **Week** n/a **Month** $80
Power: 30 amp $8, **50 amp** n/a, **100 amp** n/a, **200 amp** n/a
Cable TV: No **Dockside Phone:** No
Dock Type: Floating, Alongside, Wood
Moorings: 0 Total, 0 Transient **Launch:** n/a
Rate: Day n/a **Week** n/a **Month** n/a
Heads: 2 Toilet(s), 2 Shower(s) *(dressing rooms)*, Book Exchange
Internet: Yes *(Wi-Fi, Free)* **Laundry:** 1 Washer(s), 1 Dryer(s)
Pump-Out: Full Service, 1 Central **Fee:** $10 **Closed Heads:** Yes

Marina Operations

Owner/Manager: Carlton Johnson **Dockmaster:** Same
In-Season: May 15 - Oct 15, 9am-5pm **Off-Season:** Oct 16-May 14, Closed
After-Hours Arrival: Call in advance
Reservations: Yes, Preferred **Credit Cards:** Visa/MC
Discounts: None
Pets: Welcome, Dog Walk Area **Handicap Access:** Yes, Heads, Docks

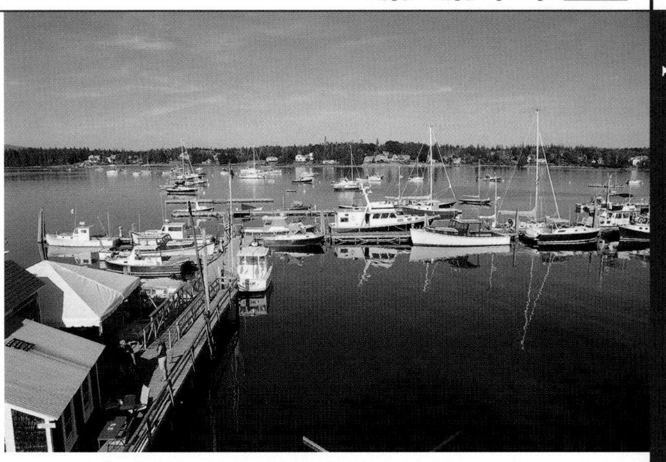

Up Harbor Marine

PO Box 148; Columbia Ave.; Bernard, ME 04612

Tel: (207) 266-0270 **VHF: Monitor** n/a **Talk** n/a
Fax: n/a **Alternate Tel:** n/a
Email: cjohnson077@roadrunner.com **Web:** upharbormarine.com
Nearest Town: Bernard *(0.5 mi.)* **Tourist Info:** (207) 244-9264

Marina Services and Boat Supplies

Services - Docking Assistance, Boaters' Lounge, Trash Pick-Up, Dock Carts **Communication -** FedEx, UPS, Express Mail **Supplies - OnSite:** Ice *(Cube)* **1-3 mi:** Ships' Store, Propane *(Hinckley 244-5572)*, CNG *(Hinckley)* **3+ mi:** West Marine *(244-0300, 3.2 mi.)*

Boatyard Services

OnSite: Railway, Electrical Repairs, Electronics Repairs, Hull Repairs, Rigger, Divers, Brightwork, Refrigeration, Compound, Wash & Wax, Interior Cleaning, Propeller Repairs, Woodworking, Inflatable Repairs **OnCall:** Engine mechanic *(gas, diesel)*, Sail Loft, Canvas Work, Upholstery, Metal Fabrication **Yard Rates:** $50/hr.

Restaurants and Accommodations

Near: Seafood Shack *(Thurston's Lobster Pound 244-7600, L $3-10.50, D $20-28, Self-serve a la carte - Lobsters $9-10/lb. then add "dinner" $6-12. 11am-8:30pm)*, *(Maine-Ly Delights 244-3656, L & D $3-12.50 11am-9pm Dinghy to Morris Yachts. Across from Ferry)*, *(Seafood Ketch 244-7463, L $6-17, D $16-28, 11am-9pm. Dinghy to their dock.)* **1-3 mi:** Lite Fare *(Gott's Takeout & Del 244-3431)*, Inn/B&B *(Ann's Point 244-9595, $235-285, Exquisite 4-suite B&B, 700 ft. water frontage)*, *(Bass Harbor 244-5157, $75-130)*, Condo/Cottage *(Bass Harbor Cottages & Inn 244-3460, $60-175, Or dinghy directly across the harbor)* **3+ mi:** Motel *(Seawall 244-3020, $65-120, 5 mi., An out-of-the-ordinary motel - personal & helpful)*

Recreation and Entertainment

Near: Jogging Paths, Hike/Bike Trails *(Ship Harbor trail, sign posted with historical & geological information; Wonderland trail leads to pebble beaches and tidal pools)*, Galleries *(A Half dozen incl: Old Red Store Antiques 244-0240; Antique Wicker 244-3983; A. Jones)* **Under 1 mi:** Tours *(Island Cruises to Frenchboro 244-5785 - Morning Lunch $27/17, Afternoon Nature $23/17)* **1-3 mi:** Playground, Sightseeing *(Bass Harbor Marsh - Many sea birds. Navigable by kayak or canoe. Spectacular sunsets behind Western Mountains)* **3+ mi:** Tennis Courts *(Causeway, 5 mi.)*, Golf Course *(Causeway G. C. 244-3780, 5 mi.)*

Provisioning and General Services

Near: Lobster Pound *(Thurston)* **Under 1 mi:** Post Office *(244-5150)*, Library *(Bass Harbor 244-3798)* **1-3 mi:** Convenience Store *(McKinley Market 244-9750; Gott's 244-3431, pizza too)*, Bank/ATM, Hardware Store *(McEachern & Hutchins 244-5567)* **3+ mi:** Market *(Sawyer's 244-3315 Del, 3.5 mi.)*, Supermarket *(Southwest Food Mart 244-5601, 5 mi.)*, Liquor Store *(Sawyer's Del, 3.5 mi.)*, Bakery *(Little Notch, 3.5 mi.)*, Farmers' Market *(Fri. 9am-1pm 546-2395 St. John Divine, 3.5 mi.)*, Catholic Church *(4 mi.)*, Protestant Church *(3.5 mi.)*, Pharmacy *(Caroll 244-5588, 4 mi.)*

Transportation

OnCall: Rental Car *(Hertz 667-5017, delivers, 15 mi.)*, Airport Limo *(Airport & Harbor Car 667-5995)* **Near:** Local Bus *(Island Explorer - Rte 7)* **1-3 mi:** Ferry Service *(Swan's Island & Frenchboro)*

Medical Services

911 Service **OnCall:** Ambulance **3+ mi:** Doctor *(Community Health Ctr 244-5630, 4.5 mi.)*, Veterinarian *(SWH 244-3336, 4 mi.)* **Hospital:** MDI 288-5081 *(18 mi.)*

Setting -- Cruise past the Bass Harbor Head Light, Morris Yachts, the Swan's Island Ferry terminal, the large brick cannery turned condo and into the Inner Harbor. Aptly named Up Harbor Marine is on the south shore - just past two-story Thurston's Lobster Pound - easily recognized by the bright yellow roofs that top the screened porch wedding-caked dining rooms. In front of the marina are two long parallel face docks - one connected to a large, sturdy wharf that supports the single-story weathered brown-shingled clubhouse. Adjacent is a narrow two-story contemporary boathouse separated by the haul-out railway.

Marina Notes -- The Bass Harbor Yacht Club makes its home here as does a small-scale community sailing center with six boats. Full-service boat yard facilities with a small railway. Well constructed floating wood docks in excellent condition, quality pedestals. Outer-most dock not connected to main wharf. Spoil island just off last dock, has a beach and camping. Bathhouse: Two inviting spacious full bathrooms with tile floors, pastel beadboard wainscotting, fiberglass shower stalls and welcome chair. Large, airy laundry room.

Notable -- Bass Harbor homes the largest lobster fleet on the island which helps Bernard maintain its laidback working community ambiance. But it has a sweet little fishing village vibe with shops clearly catering to affluent summer residents with delightful Port in A Storm bookstore and a half dozen antique shops and galleries. Thurston's Lobster Pound, reportedly the best on MDI, is a bit pricier (albeit still self-serve) and a bit nicer than others. The screened porch dining rooms - topped by bright yellow canvas - are built on a wharf overlooking the fleet. For hikers, Bernard offers two excellent trails Ship Harbor and Wonderland.

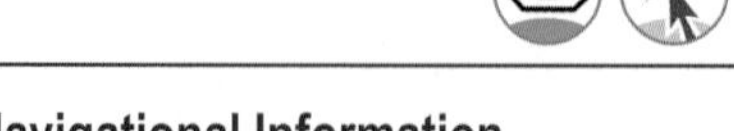

Ellsworth Harbor Park

PO Box 586; One City Hall Plaza; Ellsworth, ME 04605

Tel: (207) 667-6311 **VHF: Monitor** Ch. 9/16 **Talk** Ch. 9
Fax: n/a **Alternate Tel:** n/a
Email: mainerandy@hotmail.com **Web:** cityofellsworthme.org
Nearest Town: Ellsworth *(0.6 mi.)* **Tourist Info:** (207) 288-5103

Navigational Information

Lat: 44°32.116' **Long:** 068°25.266' **Tide:** 10 ft. **Current:** 2 kt. **Chart:** n/a
Rep. Depths (*MLW*): Entry 6 ft. **Fuel Dock** 6 ft. **Max Slip/Moor** 6 ft./6 ft.
Access: North 3 miles up Union River

Marina Facilities *(In Season/Off Season)*

Fuel: *Citgo* - Gasoline
Slips: 17 Total, 5 Transient **Max LOA:** 50 ft. **Max Beam:** n/a
Rate *(per ft.)*: **Day** $1.25* **Week** n/a **Month** n/a
Power: 30 amp Incl., **50 amp** Incl., **100 amp** n/a, **200 amp** n/a
Cable TV: No **Dockside Phone:** No
Dock Type: Floating, Alongside, Concrete
Moorings: 40 Total, 2 Transient **Launch:** No, Dinghy Dock
Rate: Day $20 **Week** n/a **Month** n/a
Heads: 2 Toilet(s)
Internet: Yes *(Wi-Fi, Free)* **Laundry:** None
Pump-Out: OnSite, Self Service **Fee:** Free **Closed Heads:** Yes

Marina Operations

Owner/Manager: Randy Heckman (Hrbmstr) **Dockmaster:** Same
In-Season: May 15 - Oct 15, 8am-5pm **Off-Season:** Oct 16 - May 14, Closed
After-Hours Arrival: Call in Advance
Reservations: Yes, Preferred **Credit Cards:** Visa/MC, Dscvr
Discounts: None
Pets: Welcome, Dog Walk Area **Handicap Access:** Yes, Heads, Docks

Marina Services and Boat Supplies

Communication - FedEx, UPS, Express Mail **Supplies - Near:** Ice *(Cube)*, Propane *(Dear River 667-4681)* **Under 1 mi:** Ice *(Block)*, Ships' Store *(Chase Leavitt 667-9390 charts, etc)*

Boatyard Services

OnSite: Launching Ramp **Nearest Yard:** Webber's Cove (207) 374-2841

Restaurants and Accommodations

OnSite: Snack Bar *(Scoops Ice Cream & More Take-Out from converted rail car)* **Near:** Restaurant *(Jasper's 667-5318, D $6-24)*, Fast Food *(Wendy's, KFC, Friendly's, Subway, McDs)*, Motel *(Comfort Inn 667-1345)*, *(Jasper's 667-5318, $53-116)* **Under 1 mi:** Restaurant *(Mex 667-4494)*, *(Finn's Irish Pub 667-2808, Inside - 1932 Jerry O'Mahoney Dining Car)*, *(Simone's 667-1007)*, *(Bangkok 667-1324)*, *(Cleonice Mediterranean Bistro 664-7554, L $6-10, D $19-24, Small Plates: $13-17, Tapas $3-10)*, *(Riverside Cafe 667-7220)*, Seafood Shack *(Union River Lobster Pot 667-5077, overlooking the river)*, Coffee Shop *(The Maine Grind 667-0011)*, Pizzeria *(Charlie's 667-3189)*, Motel *(Ramada 667-9341)*, *(Eagles' Lodge 667-3311)*

Recreation and Entertainment

OnSite: Picnic Area, Special Events *(Shakespeare in the Park - mid Aug; Ellsworth Antique Show, mid-Aug)* **Under 1 mi:** Tennis Courts *(Ellsworth Tennis Ctr. 664-0400)*, Fitness Center *(Downeast Family YMCA 667-3086 - $8/3 day)*, Bowling *(Eastward 667-9228)*, Movie Theater *(Grand 1st run features & Maine Coast Cinema 667-3251)*, Museum *(Woodlawn, The Black Family House 667-8671 $10/3 - workshops, exhibits, tours of 1827 brick mansion)*, Cultural Attract *(Grand Auditorium 667-5911)*, Galleries *(Antique shops)* **1-3 mi:** Golf Course *(Bucksport 469-7612 - 9 holes)* **3+ mi:** Park *(Acadia, 15 mi.)*

Provisioning and General Services

Near: Supermarket *(Shaw's 667-2293; Hannaford's 667-5300 - 0.8 mi.)*, Beauty Salon *(Tracey's)*, Laundry *(Downeast 667-8129)*, Pharmacy *(Shaw's 667-2293)* **Under 1 mi:** Convenience Store *(Mike's 667-4444)*, Health Food *(John Edwards 667-9377- well-stocked, oldest in Maine)*, Wine/Beer *(Wine Gallery 667-9377; Hannaford's 667-5300)*, Farmers' Market *(Sat 9:30-noon, 192 Main St; Mon & Thu 2-5:30pm 245 E. Main St.)*, Bank/ATM, Post Office, Catholic Church, Protestant Church, Library *(Ellsworth 667-6363 - Wi-Fi 24/7 - Federalist 1817 riverfront)*, Dry Cleaners *(Gold Star 667-3551)*, Bookstore *(Options 667-8200)*, Florist *(Bud Connection 288-5300)*, Retail Shops *(Maine Coast Mall 667-9905 & Downtown Main Street)* **1-3 mi:** Hardware Store *(Home Depot 667-1986)*, Department Store *(Walmart 667-6780)*

Transportation

OnCall: Rental Car *(Enterprise 667-1217 - 0.3 mi.)*, Taxi *(Cell Kell 667-7306)*, Airport Limo *(Crystal 667-4121)* **Near:** Local Bus *(Downeast 667-3727 - 4 RT M-F to Bar Harbor $5; to Blue Hill & Stonington)* **Under 1 mi:** Bikes *(Bar Harbor Bike Shop)* **Airport:** Bar Harbor/Bangor *(9 mi./30 mi.)*

Medical Services

911 Service **OnCall:** Ambulance **Near:** Doctor *(Risser 664-5311)*, Dentist *(Caddoo 667-5744)*, Chiropractor *(Coastal Maine 669-4028)* **Under 1 mi:** Holistic Services *(Pampered Pleasures Day Spa 667-6606 - Massage $65/60 min.)*, Optician *(Pierson 667-8879)*, Veterinarian *(Small Animal Clinic 667-2341)* **Hospital:** Maine Coast Mem 664-5311 *(1.1 mi.)*

Setting -- At the northeast end of Union River Bay, just north of Mill Cove, the Union River's well marked channel leads three miles rom the last red buoy to eclectic, bustling Ellsworth. The river's undeveloped, wooded shoreline belies the lively energetic city beyond the trees. The mooring field consumes much of the turning basin; a relatively new concrete floating dock extends to an old granite wharf courtesy of a full-race arched gangway. At the top is a gas pump. Onshore are a large gazebo, picnic shelters and picnic tables scattered about the greensward. The harbormaster makes camp in a small log cabin.

Marina Notes -- *130 linear feet of double-side dockage. 4 hrs. dockside complimentary. Overnight $1.25/ft. Channel dredged 2004 - min. 5 ft mlw, but closer to 7 ft. (mind the channel buoys). Bathhouse: Gray-shingled Cape Cod - standard municipal heads.

Notable -- Ellsworth is the commercial and shopping center of Mount Desert & Hancock County - witness the mile of outlets - including L.L. Bean - and malls along Rts. 1/3 (0.8 mile east of the docks). But there is also the lively, historic quite charming downtown along Main St. between Rte 1A and the river (0.6 mile north of the docks) where a few good restaurants, coffee spots and unique shops reside in 1930's-era buildings that literally rose from the ashes after a fire wiped out the town in 1933. Notable is the recently restored Art Deco Grand Auditorium where something's happening 330 days a year - concerts, fim, theater, dance, events, The Met & summer theater camp - and the abundance of antique shops. Just across the river, stunning "Woodlawn," Col. John Black's House is now a museum that depicts life during the booming timber days, furnished exactly as it was when the family lived there - with formal gardens and rolling lawns.

  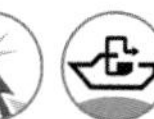 

Navigational Information
Lat: 44°24.453' **Long:** 068°33.723' **Tide:** 10 ft. **Current:** n/a **Chart:** 13316
Rep. Depths (*MLW*): Entry 17 ft. **Fuel Dock** 10 ft. **Max Slip/Moor** -/24 ft.
Access: R N 6 into Outer Harbor - only facility on eastern shore

Marina Facilities *(In Season/Off Season)*
Fuel: Gasoline, Diesel
Slips: 0 Total, 0 Transient **Max LOA:** n/a **Max Beam:** n/a
Rate *(per ft.)*: **Day** n/a **Week** n/a **Month** n/a
Power: 30 amp n/a, **50 amp** n/a, **100 amp** n/a, **200 amp** n/a
Cable TV: No **Dockside Phone:** No
Dock Type: n/a
Moorings: 36 Total, 6 Transient **Launch:** Yes (Free), Dinghy Dock
Rate: Day $25 **Week** n/a **Month** n/a
Heads: 2 Toilet(s), Book Exchange
Internet: Yes *(Wi-Fi, Free)* **Laundry:** None
Pump-Out: OnSite, Self Service **Fee:** $20 **Closed Heads:** Yes

Marina Operations
Owner/Manager: David Danielson **Dockmaster:** Same
In-Season: Jun-Sep 15, 8am-5:45pm **Off-Season:** Sep 16-May, Closed
After-Hours Arrival: Pick up an open mooring
Reservations: No, first come **Credit Cards:** Cash or Check only
Discounts: None
Pets: Welcome **Handicap Access:** No

Kollegewidgwok Yacht Club

PO Box 368; East Blue Hill Road; Blue Hill, ME 04614

Tel: (207) 374-5581 **VHF: Monitor** Ch. 9 **Talk** Ch. 78
Fax: n/a **Alternate Tel:** n/a
Email: kycbluehillme@gmail.com **Web:** www.kollegewidgwokyc.com
Nearest Town: Blue Hill *(1.7 mi.)* **Tourist Info:** (207) 374-2281

Marina Services and Boat Supplies
Services - Boaters' Lounge, Dock Carts **Communication -** Pay Phone (1), UPS **Supplies - OnSite:** Ice *(Block, Cube)*

Boatyard Services
Under 1 mi: Railway *(and 10T trailer for boats to 30 ft.)*, Engine mechanic *(gas, diesel)*. **Nearest Yard:** Webber's Cove Yacht Yard (207) 374-2841

Restaurants and Accommodations
1-3 mi: Restaurant *(Arborvine 374-2119, D $27-30, exquisite fine dining)*, *(Marlintin's Grill L $4-13, D $4-13, not in Village, 0.5 mi. from town)*, Seafood Shack *(Fishnet 374-5240, L $5-8, D $9-16, only 1.4 mi.)*, Lite Fare *(B.H. Hearth Bakery & Pizzeria 610-9090, Delivers)*, *(B.H. Co-op 374-2165, L $3-9)*, *(Barncastle 374-2300, 3-8pm. to 9pm Fri & Sat $6-18, pizzas, sandwiches, salads - lovely)*, *(Bird Watchers Cafe 374-3740, B & L $2-6)*, Pizzeria *(Yannis 374-9999)*, Inn/B&B *(Blue Hill Inn 374-2844, $140-260, picks up)*, *(Blue Hill Farm 374-5166, $90-110)*, *(Barncastle 374-2300, $100-185)*

Recreation and Entertainment
OnCall: Boat Rentals *(Rocky Coast Outfitters 374-8866 - kayaks, canoes, free delivery)* **Near:** Jogging Paths **1-3 mi:** Picnic Area *(Blue Hill Town)*, Grills, Playground, Tennis Courts, Fitness Center *(Blue Hill Yoga Ctr. 374-2004)*, Museum *(Parson Fisher House 374-2459, Mon-Sat 2-5pm $2/free, home of Renaissance man Jonathan Fisher - the Thos. Jefferson of Maine; 1815 Holt House houses Blue Hill Historical Society)*, Cultural Attract *(Kneisel Hall Chamber Festival - July-MidAug, Fri eves & Sun afternoons 374-2811, the "Cradle of Chamber Music Teaching in America"; Bagaduce Music Lending Library 374-5454 - one of the largest collections of sheet music in the world)*, Sightseeing *(Blue Hill Tower)*, Galleries *(Artisans, Parker Point Road)*, Special Events *(Blue Hill Fair - LabDay weekend; Pan New England Steelband Fest - May)* **3+ mi:** Hike/Bike Trails *(Osgood or Blue Hill Mountains, 3 mi.)*

Provisioning and General Services
1-3 mi: Market *(Merrill & Hinckley 374-2821 - delivers)*, Supermarket *(Tradewinds)*, Gourmet Shop *(Moveable Feast 374-2441 - catering business, not shop)*, Health Food *(B.H. Food Co-op 374-8999)*, Wine/Beer *(B.H. Wine Shop 374-2161)*, Liquor Store *(Merrill & Hinckley)*, Bakery *(B.H. Hearth Bakery 610-9090, Baker's Café 374-5018)*, Farmers' Market *(Sat 9-11:30am Fairgrounds; Wed 3-5pm Cong Church)*, Bank/ATM, Post Office, Protestant Church, Library *(B.H. 374-5515 - Internet)*, Laundry *(B.H. Laundry 7am-9pm 374-2777)*, Bookstore *(B.H. Books 374-5632, North Light Books 374-5422)*, Pharmacy *(Rite Aid - 0.5 mi. beyond town)*, Hardware Store, Florist *(Fairwinds 374-5621)*

Transportation
OnCall: Bikes *(Rocky Coast Outfitters 374-8866 and The Activity Center)*, Taxi *(Eddie's Island 367-5503; Peninsula 374 -3510)*, Airport Limo *(Airport Harbor Taxi 288-9222)* **Airport:** Bangor Int'l. *(40 mi.)*

Medical Services
911 Service **OnCall:** Ambulance **1-3 mi:** Veterinarian *(Maine Coast 374-2385)* **Hospital:** Blue Hill Mem 374-2836 - near dinghy landing *(1.7 mi.)*

Setting -- On the eastern shore of Blue Hill's Outer Harbor, KYC's small, contemporary gray club house, new sailing building, and active floats are immediately visible. The mooring field seems to fill the harbor; the surrounding shoreline is unspoiled, quite beautiful and spotted with lovely old, perfectly maintained, Maine "cottages." About a mile and a half by road or dinghy, creative, energetic Blue Hill is clearly devoted to the arts in all its manifestations.

Marina Notes -- Moorings available on first come basis. Launch service 8am-5:45pm. Cozy knotty pine club house with large fireplace. Wi-Fi in clubhouse & entire mooring field. Private Y.C. welcomes all visiting boaters. Cruising Club of America station. Dumpster in parking lot. 30 min. max on dock (no overnights on floats.). Water for tanks only (50 gal. max). Facility rental for Y.C. cruises $900. KSEA (Kollegewidgwok Sailing & Education Association) teaches all Blue Hill Peninsula children - regardless of club membership. Webber Cove B. Y. in Inner Harbor - moorings, BY services (thin water). Pronunciation? Try KOLL-edg-e-widg-e--wok. Translation from Abenaki: salt fresh rapids or mixed rapids. Bathhouse: 2 knotty pine heads.

Notable -- The dearth of taxis limits travel into Blue Hill Village to foot, dinghy, or the kindness of strangers or restaurants (1.4 miles to Co-op & FishNet; 1.85 mi. to village center). Blue Hill is home to many artists and artisans, including three renowned pottery studios: Rackliffe's 374-2297 and Mark Bell 374-5881. Thriving musical organizations include Kneisel Hall and Bagaduce Music Library. Blue Hill-based community Steel band Flash! in the Pans has ignited an all-age pans explosion; they play at B.H. Town Park. Kids will also enjoy the eco-cruises, walks & workshops at MERI Center for Marine Studies.

PHOTOS ON DVD: 25

5. ME – Eastern Penobscot Bay

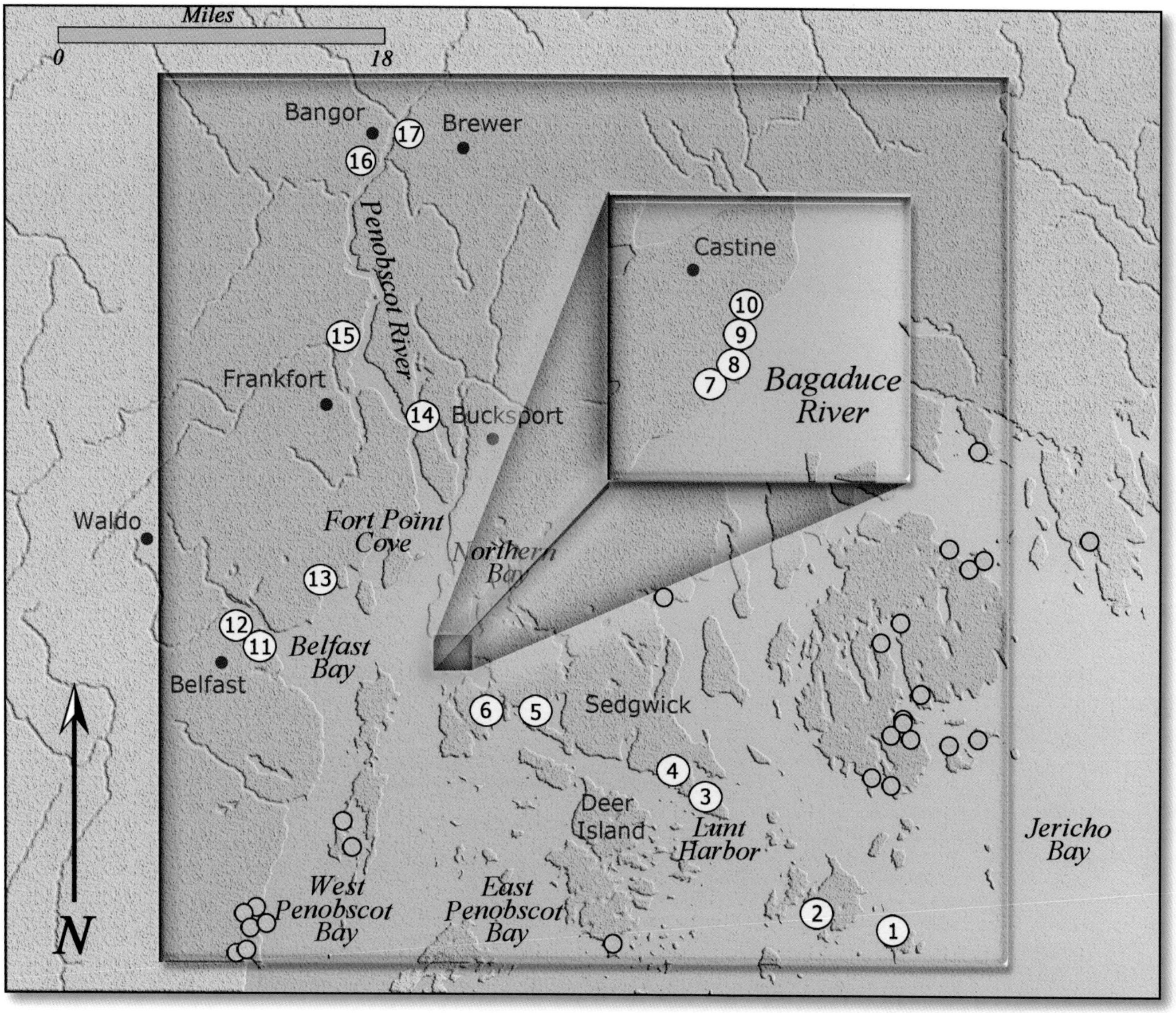

MAP	MARINA	HARBOR	PAGE
1	Lunt & Lunt	*Lunt Harbor*	96
2	Burnt Coat Harbor Moorings	*Burnt Coat Harbor*	97
3	Wooden Boat School	*Eggemoggin Reach/Great Cove*	98
4	Brooklin Boat Yard	*Eggemoggin Reach/Center Harbor*	99
5	Buck's Harbor Marine	*Eggemoggin Reach/Buck's Harbor*	100
6	Seal Cove Boatyard	*Horseshoe Cove*	101
7	Castine Town Dock	*Bagaduce River*	102
8	Dennett's Wharf	*Bagaduce River*	103
9	Eaton's Boatyard	*Bagaduce River*	104
10	Castine Yacht Club	*Bagaduce River*	105
11	Belfast City Landing	*Passagassawakeag River*	106
12	Belfast Boatyard	*Passagassawakeag River*	107
13	Searsport Landing	*Searsport Harbor*	108
14	Bucksport Marina	*Penobscot River*	109
15	Winterport Marina	*Penobscot River*	110
16	Hamlin's Marina	*Penobscot River*	111
17	Bangor Landing Waterfront Park	*Penobscot River*	112

RATINGS: 1-5 for Marina Facilities & Amenities,  1-2 for Boatyard Services,  1-2 for MegaYacht Facilities,  for Something Special.

SERVICES: for CCM – Certified Clean Marina,  for Pump-Out, for Internet,  for Fuel, for Restaurant,  for Provisioning nearby, for Catamaran-friendly,  for SportFish Charter,  for Pool/Beach, and for Golf within a mile. *For an explanation of ACC's Ratings, see page 8.*

Lunt & Lunt

Frenchboro, Long Island, ME

Tel: (207) 334-2902 **VHF: Monitor** Ch. 80 **Talk** Ch. 80
Fax: n/a **Alternate Tel:** (207) 334-2922
Email: docksidedeli@live.com **Web:** www.luntlobsters.com
Nearest Town: Frenchboro **Tourist Info:** n/a

Navigational Information

Lat: 44°07.265' **Long:** 068°21.817' **Tide:** 10 ft. **Current:** n/a **Chart:** 13313
Rep. Depths (*MLW*): Entry 35 ft. **Fuel Dock** n/a **Max Slip/Moor** -/12 ft.
Access: Blue Hill Bay to Long Island, north end

Marina Facilities *(In Season/Off Season)*

Fuel: Gasoline, Diesel
Slips: 0 Total, 0 Transient **Max LOA:** n/a **Max Beam:** n/a
Rate *(per ft.)*: **Day** n/a **Week** n/a **Month** n/a
Power: 30 amp n/a, **50 amp** n/a, **100 amp** n/a, **200 amp** n/a
Cable TV: No **Dockside Phone:** No
Dock Type: n/a
Moorings: 15 Total, 15 Transient **Launch:** No, Dinghy Dock
Rate: Day $25 **Week** n/a **Month** n/a
Heads: 1 Toilet(s)
Internet: Yes *(Wi-Fi - on Dock & Wharf, Free)* **Laundry:** None
Pump-Out: No **Fee:** n/a **Closed Heads:** Yes

Marina Operations

Owner/Manager: Dean Lunt **Dockmaster:** Kristi Lunt
In-Season: June-Sep, 8am-8pm **Off-Season:** Oct-May, Closed
After-Hours Arrival: Call in advance to inquire
Reservations: No **Credit Cards:** Visa/MC, Dscvr
Discounts: None
Pets: Welcome **Handicap Access:** No

Marina Services and Boat Supplies

Supplies - OnSite: Ice *(Block, Cube)*

Restaurants and Accommodations

OnSite: Seafood Shack *(Lunt's Dockside Deli 334-2902, Mon-Sat 7am-7pm, Sun Noon-7pm, light breakfast. Full menu begins 11am)* **Near:** Seafood Shack *(Frenchboro Offshore Store 334-2943, Take-out - Lobster rolls, lobsters, desserts, chowders, Mon-Fri 9am-8pm, Sat & Sun 7am-8pm)*, Condo/Cottage *(Harbor House Cottage 334-2991, $400/3days, $800/wk)*

Recreation and Entertainment

OnSite: Fishing Charter *(Zachery D. Lunt 334-2902 - 32 ft. "Sandi" or the 38 ft. "Zachary Nathaniel")*, Sightseeing *(Capt. Zach's Lobster & Fishing Tour 334-2902 $25/15 - Max 6 people. 90-minute tour aboard 32 ft "Sandi" or the 38 ft. "Zachary Nathaniel")* **Near:** Beach *(Gooseberry Point, Eastern, Little and many more)*, Playground, Hike/Bike Trails *(10 miles of trails through Frenchboro Preserve - maps available at the museum. Periodic field trips are offered by MCHT.)*, Movie Theater *("Drive-In" Movie, Friday nights at the Firehouse - dress warmly, bring blankets & chairs)*, Tours *(Island Cruises from Bass Harbor 244-5785 - Morning lunch cruise $27/17, Afternoon nature cruise $23/17)*, Galleries *(Historical Society's Gift Shop 334-2924 - sells crafts from local artisans)*, Special Events *(Frenchboro Lobster Dinner, 2nd Sat in Aug, $25 incl. Ferry; 4th of July - all day event)*

Provisioning and General Services

OnSite: Lobster Pound *(Lunt & Lunt)* **Near:** Convenience Store *(Offshore Store - small inventory of basic items)*, Bakery *(Frenchboro Bakery & Island Candy Shop 460-2099)*, Protestant Church *(Long Island Congregational Church, a center of island life, deisgned & built by Alexander MacDonald in 1890, adjacent parsonage built 1904)*, Library *(Frenchboro 334-2924 - In museum building. Open 24/7/365 but with limited staffing)*, Retail Shops *(Offshore Store)*

Transportation

Near: Ferry Service *(Maine State Ferry to Bass Harbor 244-3254 $17.25/9.25 Fri 2 trips, Wed, Thur, Sun 1 trip. 50-min crossing.)*

Medical Services

No 911 Service **OnCall:** Ambulance *(Fire Department EMTs)*

Setting -- On the north shore of Outer Long Island in Blue Hill Bay, peaceful, remote Lunt Harbor is filled with active working boats and, in season, a good handful of pleasure craft. In the southwest corner, a rambling complex of single-story gray buildings perchs on the Lunt & Lunt Lobster company wharf. The Dockside Deli occupies most of them with a covered picnic pavilion and more tables on the wharf. A gangway leads to the lobster and dinghy float.

Marina Notes -- Founded as S.L. Lunt Lobsters in 1951 by Dick and Vivian Lunt. Lunt family has operated a fishing business here since 1820 - first cod, then in the 1900s, lobster. The Deli opened in 1987.with lobsters live, cooked, in rolls plus steamers, scallops, pie & famous peanut butter cups. Moorings - granite blocks in 10-12 feet. (Lunt Buoys un-marked; most private buoys labeled). Pick one up; pay at Deli. Yacht Club cruises, rendezvous & other special events graciously accommodated. No trash receptacles - take to mainland. 65 year-round residents; 100 in summer. Bathhouse: Head shared with Deli.

Notable -- 170-year-old Frenchboro, clustered around Lunt Harbor, lies about eight miles from the coast of Mount Desert. 967 of the island's acres, including 5.6 miles of shoreline, are protected by the Frenchboro Preserve owned by the Maine Coast Heritage Trust. Ten miles of rustic hiking trails pass in and out of private and Preserve land. Above the Fire Pond, the Historical Society's Museum, founded by Vivian Davis Lunt in the '70's, displays historical island artifacts and the work of local artisans.The 2nd weekend in August, "The Dinner" attracts 4/500 friends and visitors who eat lobster and "go-withs" in the field next to the church (replenishing the church coffers). Zach Lunt's Lobster Tour demonstrates the art of lobstering while lifting the hood on the business of lobstering.

Navigational Information

Lat: 44°08.558' **Long:** 068°26.941' **Tide:** 10 ft. **Current:** n/a **Chart:** 13313
Rep. Depths (*MLW*): Entry 15 ft. **Fuel Dock** 9 ft. **Max Slip/Moor** -/15 ft.
Access: Past Hockamock Head Light, first facility to port

Marina Facilities *(In Season/Off Season)*

Fuel: *at Fishermen's Co-op or Steamboat Wharf* - Gasoline, Diesel
Slips: 0 Total, 0 Transient **Max LOA:** n/a **Max Beam:** n/a
Rate *(per ft.)*: **Day** n/a **Week** n/a **Month** n/a
Power: 30 amp n/a, **50 amp** n/a, **100 amp** n/a, **200 amp** n/a
Cable TV: No **Dockside Phone:** No
Dock Type: n/a
Moorings: 30 Total, 30 Transient **Launch:** No, Dinghy Dock
Rate: Day $20 **Week** Inq. **Month** Inq.
Heads: 2 Toilet(s)
Internet: Yes *(Wi-Fi - at new library, Free)* **Laundry:** None
Pump-Out: No **Fee:** n/a **Closed Heads:** Yes

Marina Operations

Owner/Manager: Kevin Staples **Dockmaster:** Same
In-Season: Jul-Sep, 11am-7pm **Off-Season:** Oct-Jun, Closed
After-Hours Arrival: Pick up an empty mooring and check-in in the morning
Reservations: No, except for pre-paid groups **Credit Cards:** Cash/Check onl
Discounts: None
Pets: Welcome **Handicap Access:** No

Burnt Coat Harbor Moorings

317 Atlantic Road; Swan's Island, ME 04685

Tel: (207) 526-4201 **VHF: Monitor** Ch. 68 **Talk** n/a
Fax: n/a **Alternate Tel:** (207) 526-4323
Email: boathouse@midmaine.com **Web:** n/a
Nearest Town: Swan's Island Village *(1 mi.)* **Tourist Info:** (207) 244-9624

Marina Services and Boat Supplies

Communication - Pay Phone (1) **Supplies - Near:** Ice *(Block, Cube)*, Ships' Store *(Limited supplies at Fishermen's Co-op)*

Boatyard Services

OnSite: Divers, Propeller Repairs **Near:** Engine mechanic *(gas, diesel)*.

Restaurants and Accommodations

OnSite: Restaurant *(Debbie Staple's Boat House & Gift Shop 526-4201, L $2-16, D $6-18, Seasonal - grilled & fried, sandwiches & platters, hard ice cream)* **Near:** Seafood Shack *(Underwater Taxi 526-4204, Take-out Lobsters - also fish, steamers, crab & chowders - take out or picnic tables)* **1-3 mi:** Coffee Shop *(Island Bake Shoppe B & L, 7am-2pm Mon-Sat)*, Lite Fare *(Carrying Place 526-4043, Take-out 11am-7pm, 7 days Seafood, chicken, burgers, fries, sodas, hot & cold sandwiches, pizza)*, Motel *(Harbor Watch'Inn 526-4563, $75-120, In Minturn - 2.5 mi. around harbor or dinghy across)*, Inn/B&B *(Carter House 266-0958, $60-65)*

Recreation and Entertainment

OnCall: Tours *(Lobster boat tours "Averill Marie" 526-4563 - To Stonington & Isle au Haut - Wed 10:30am, To Stonington - Sat 4pm.)* **Near:** Hike/Bike Trails *(Hike up Goose Pond Mt. or Big Mt. Island - riddled with trails, see map on DVD.)*, Sightseeing *(Walk to the 1872 lighthouse at Hockamock Head - now part of a Swan's Island park - take a picnic)*, Galleries *(The Boathouse - Wide selection of quality crafts from local artisans)* **Under 1 mi:** Beach *(2 in walking distance or dinghy to Fine Sand Beach in Toothacher Cove or across to Minturn Town Landing and head inland for warmer water of Quarry Pond)*, Special Events *(Sweet Chariot Music Festival - a 3-night early Aug folk festival - in the Harbor & at Oddfellows Hall)* **1-3 mi:** Museum *(S.I. Lobster & Marine Museum 526-4282 - in Capt. Henry Lee House. Small, but interesting antique fishing equipment, nav. systems, etc. Located just above the Ferry Landing in Mackerel Cove Mon, Wed, Sun 11am-4pm, Natural History Museum next door.)*

Provisioning and General Services

Near: Convenience Store *(Boathouse - limited provisions)*, Fishmonger *(UnderWater Taxi 526-4204)*, Lobster Pound *(Swan's Island Co-Op 526-4327 or Kent's Wharf 526-4186 on western shore; Underwater Taxi on eastern shore)*, Retail Shops *(Gift shop at Boathouse & My Place Gifts noon-4pm, 6 days)* **Under 1 mi:** Library *(Burned down 2008. Rebuilt 2010 w/ $398,000 Fed. stimulus grant. Restoring historical collection via "Swan's Island Memory Project." Wi-Fi space w/ $50,000 King Foundation grant)* **1-3 mi:** Market *(Carrying Place on Sand Beach Rd. 526-4043 Basic necessities plus ice cream, baked goods, fresh produce, newspapers)*, Bakery *(Island Bake Shoppe near Ferry Landing)*, Post Office *(526-4194 1.3 mi.)*, Protestant Church, Laundry *(Atlantic Laundromat 526-4478)*

Transportation

3+ mi: Ferry Service *(Capt. Henry Lee Ferry to Bass Harbor from Mackerel Cove, RT $16.50/9.50, 6 trips/day 526-4273 or 244-3254, 3.5 mi.)*

Medical Services

No 911 Service **OnCall:** Ambulance *(EMTs & Ferry docks on SI overnight for emergencies)* **Near:** Doctor *(Bi-weekly physician viisits, weekly RN visits)* **Hospital:** Mount Desert 288-8439 *(by ferry)*

Setting -- A bit of old Maine, this quintessential working harbor is the perfect antidote to the quaint, touristed mainland. Secluded, remote Burnt Coat is bounded on the west by Swan's Island village, on the east by Minturn, and on the south by Harbor Island. Some of the island's 7,000 hilly acres provide protection for the picture postcard mooring field - but it berths boats for about 40 full-time lobstermen and more part-time ones, so come dawn......

Marina Notes -- Transient moorings - green balls - individually owned by Swan's Island lobstermen & managed by Kevin Staples, a local lobsterman turned entrepreneur (50/50 split). Before 1pm, fuel available at Swan's Island Fishermen's Co-op (526-4327), on the western shore below red buildings, or at Swan's Island Steamboat Wharf, Ch.68, (526-4186) - water, ice & lobsters. No trash disposal or pumpout service. But - Kevin lends his car for an island tour, delivers lobster dinners to the boat or picks up fogged-in boaters. Bathhouse: Single Porta Potty across from restaurant. Note: Sep & Oct large lobster pen in harbor.

Notable -- The Swan's Island community (350 year-rounders swelling to a thousand in summer) works hard at preserving a fragile way of life. But whatever was here last year may not be here next - it's a continuing dance. Kevin & Debbie Staples have operated the Boathouse - the large, natural sided, 2-story building perched on the western shore - in various iterations for 15 years. Now a family business, the restaurant has been renovated and its offerings increased - with a half-dozen family members pitching in. Their daughters run the gift shop - hand-blown glass, exquisite shawls, pottery, fine art, books and their own seaglass jewelry. Across the harbor, UnderWater Taxi sells prepared seafood, fresh fish & live lobsters as does the Fishermans Co-Op. S.I. is dry - BYO!

PHOTOS ON DVD: 25

Wooden Boat School

PO Box 196; Naskeag Point Road; Brooklin, ME 04616

Tel: (207) 359-4651 **VHF: Monitor** Ch. 16 **Talk** Ch. 68
Fax: (207) 359-8920 **Alternate Tel:** n/a
Email: rich@woodenboat.com **Web:** www.woodenboat.com
Nearest Town: Brooklin *(1.5 mi.)* **Tourist Info:** (207) 374-3242

Navigational Information

Lat: 44°14.822' **Long:** 068°33.376' **Tide:** 10 ft. **Current:** n/a **Chart:** 13316
Rep. Depths (*MLW*): Entry 12 ft. **Fuel Dock** n/a **Max Slip/Moor** -/10 ft.
Access: Eggemoggin Reach to just north of Babson Island

Marina Facilities *(In Season/Off Season)*

Fuel: No
Slips: 0 Total, 0 Transient **Max LOA:** 50 ft. **Max Beam:** n/a
Rate *(per ft.)*: **Day** n/a **Week** n/a **Month** n/a
Power: 30 amp n/a, **50 amp** n/a, **100 amp** n/a, **200 amp** n/a
Cable TV: No **Dockside Phone:** No
Dock Type: n/a
Moorings: 8 Total, 8 Transient **Launch:** None, Dinghy Dock
Rate: Day $15 **Week** $105 **Month** n/a
Heads: 2 Toilet(s)
Internet: No **Laundry:** None
Pump-Out: No **Fee:** n/a **Closed Heads:** No

Marina Operations

Owner/Manager: Rich Hilsinger (Director) **Dockmaster:** Jon Wilson
In-Season: Jun-Oct, 8am-5pm **Off-Season:** Nov-May, Closed
After-Hours Arrival: Call in advance
Reservations: No **Credit Cards:** Cash Only
Discounts: None
Pets: Welcome **Handicap Access:** No

Marina Services and Boat Supplies

Supplies - Under 1 mi: Ice *(Block, Cube, Shaved)*, Ships' Store *(Wooden Boat Store - New, airy large contemporary. Clothing, books, models, woodworking tools, toys, marine supplies)*, Propane

Boatyard Services

Nearest Yard: Brooklin Boat Yard (207) 359-2236

Restaurants and Accommodations

OnSite: Inn/B&B *(Boat School Student Housing $275, per week)* **1-3 mi:** Restaurant *(Lookout 359-2188, D $18-28)*, *(The Brooklin Inn 359-2777, D $16-28, Loster MP. Sun brunch $10-12 - moorings too.)*, *(The Irish Pub 359-2777, D $16, Lighter fare at Brooklin Inn)*, Inn/B&B *(The Brooklin Inn 359-2777, $95-125, 5 rooms w/ private baths)*, *(Dragon Flye Inn 266-3331, $120-195, Aug only)*

Recreation and Entertainment

OnSite: Tours *(Wooden Boat School 8am-5pm, Mon-Sat, Jun-Oct; also kayak tours)* **1-3 mi:** Beach *(Naskeag Point)*, Picnic Area, Galleries *(Curry, Streeter & Snyder Studios. And Benjamin Mendlowitz's spectacular marine photographs at Noah Publications 359-2131 - Calendar of Wooden Boat)* **3+ mi:** Golf Course *(Pine Ridge Golf Center 359-6788, 12 mi.)*

Provisioning and General Services

OnSite: Bookstore *(Wooden Boat Store - also in town - Noah Publications 359-213, books on wooden boats, including those of designer Joel White)*, Clothing Store *(Wooden Boat Store)* **Under 1 mi:** Wine/Beer, Post Office, Protestant Church, Newsstand **1-3 mi:** Convenience Store *(Brooklin General Store 359-8817, 5:30am-7pm 1.5 mi.)*, Gourmet Shop *(Betsy's Sunflower 359-5030, next to General Store)*, Library *(Friend Memorial 359-2276 Internet. Tue-Sat 10am-6pm)*, Retail Shops *(Betsy's Sunflower 359-5030, kitchen, garden, boating & home goods)* **3+ mi:** Supermarket *(Blue Hill Market 374-5137, 11 mi.)*

Transportation

OnSite: Airport Limo *(Shuttle to Bangor Int'l)* **Airport:** Bangor Int'l. *(50 mi.)*

Medical Services

911 Service **OnCall:** Ambulance **3+ mi:** Doctor *(12 mi.)*, Dentist *(12 mi.)*
Hospital: Blue Hill Memorial 374-2836 *(12 mi.)*

Setting -- Built on the site of an early 20th C. cannery, this 64-acre waterfront estate overlooks Eggemoggin Reach. The offices of the Wooden Boat School are in a beautifully restored large white brick manor house. Old brick stables have been redesigned to house the active school programs. At the head of the substantial main pier, a green-trimmed stone and shingle two-story boathouse sports an inviting front porch and dramatic fieldstone fireplace -- a large dinghy dock floats at its foot. Picnic tables overlook the mooring field - many in a large pavilion that shelters classes, picnics and events.

Marina Notes -- Moorings tied to large granite blocks, several for larger yachts. No reservations. Home of "Wooden Boat Magazine" & "Professional Boatbuilder - also manages annual Wooden Boat Show at Mystic Seaport, CT. Contemporary shingled, beautifully merchandised Wooden Boat Store on property. Extensive maritime research library in the manor house (research librarians avail Tues & Wed, independent research other days by appt.). School tuition ranges from $500-1,150 plus $275/week room or $100/week mooring or campsite, and $175/week board. Bathhouse: Camper site heads & showers.

Notable -- Each year, over 600 students, professionals and amateurs, attend a variety of concurrent, one and two-week-long courses on boat building, seamanship, and marine arts. Visiting the school is fascinating - ask about tours. The two-story boathouse hosts classes and staff housing; student houses are nearby. The tiny town of Brooklin is a 1.5 mile walk or bike ride; you'll find two inns, a fine-dining restaurant, Irish pub, cafe, general store, gourmet kitchen shop and a library with a garden dedicated to Brooklin resident E.B. White. A 2.5-mile hike the other way leads to Naskeag Point's small beach and picnic area.

Navigational Information
Lat: 44°15.781' **Long:** 068°34.790' **Tide:** 12 ft. **Current:** 0 kt. **Chart:** 13316
Rep. Depths (*MLW*): Entry 16 ft. **Fuel Dock** n/a **Max Slip/Moor** 6 ft./25 ft.
Access: Eggemoggin Reach to Center Harbor

Marina Facilities *(In Season/Off Season)*
Fuel: No
Slips: 0 Total, 0 Transient **Max LOA:** 75 ft. **Max Beam:** n/a
Rate *(per ft.)*: **Day** $0 **Week** n/a **Month** n/a
Power: 30 amp n/a, **50 amp** n/a, **100 amp** n/a, **200 amp** n/a
Cable TV: No **Dockside Phone:** No
Dock Type: Floating, Long Fingers, Alongside
Moorings: 80 Total, 8 Transient **Launch:** No, Dinghy Dock
Rate: Day $25 **Week** $75-150* **Month** $175-400
Heads: 1 Toilet(s)
Internet: No **Laundry:** None
Pump-Out: No **Fee:** n/a **Closed Heads:** No

Marina Operations
Owner/Manager: Frank Hull **Dockmaster:** Same
In-Season: Year-Round, 7am-3:30pm Mon-Fri **Off-Season:** n/a
After-Hours Arrival: Call in advance
Reservations: Yes **Credit Cards:** Cash or check only
Discounts: None
Pets: Welcome **Handicap Access:** No

Brooklin Boat Yard

PO Box 143; 44 Center Harbor Road; Brooklin, ME 04616

Tel: (207) 359-2236 **VHF: Monitor** n/a **Talk** n/a
Fax: (207) 359-8871 **Alternate Tel:** n/a
Email: boatyard@brooklinboatyard.com **Web:** www.brooklinboatyard.com
Nearest Town: Brooklin *(0.5 mi.)* **Tourist Info:** (207) 374-3242

Marina Services and Boat Supplies
Services - Trash Pick-Up **Communication -** Mail & Package Hold, Fax in/out *($1/p)* **Supplies - Under 1 mi:** Ice *(Cube)*, Ships' Store *(Brooklin Marine Supply 359-5030)* **3+ mi:** Propane *(12 mi.)*

Boatyard Services
OnSite: Travelift *(80T)*, Forklift, Hydraulic Trailer *(20T)*, Launching Ramp, Engine mechanic *(gas, diesel)*, Electrical Repairs, Hull Repairs, Rigger, Bottom Cleaning, Brightwork, Air Conditioning, Refrigeration, Compound, Wash & Wax, Interior Cleaning, Propeller Repairs, Woodworking, Metal Fabrication, Painting, Awlgrip, Total Refits, Yacht Design, Yacht Building, Yacht Broker **Near:** Divers *(various)*. **Under 1 mi:** Sail Loft, Canvas Work. **1-3 mi:** Upholstery. **Dealer for:** Westerbeke. **Member:** ABBRA, ABYC - 1 Certified Tech(s) **Yard Rates:** $42-62/hr., Haul & Launch $7-8.50/ft., Power Wash $2/ft., Bottom Paint $55/hr. **Storage:** On-Land Out $6.75/ft; In $8.25sq/ft; Heated $11.25sq/ft

Restaurants and Accommodations
Under 1 mi: Motel *(The Lookout Inn & Restaurant 359-2188, $115-155, room includes breakfast, weekly cottage rentals for $1022-1400, pets welcome cottage), (Reach Lodge 359-5532, $150, includes continental breakfast)*, Inn/B&B *(DragonFlye Inn 359-8080, $120-195, Aug only)* **1-3 mi:** Restaurant *(The Lookout Inn & Restaurant 359-2188, D $18-28, may close on Saturdays for weddings, call ahead), (The Brooklin Inn 359-2777, D $16-28, Brunch $10-12)*, Lite Fare *(The Irish Pub D $16, at the Brooklin Inn)*, Inn/B&B *(Brooklin Inn 359-2777, $95-125)*

Recreation and Entertainment
Near: Beach **Under 1 mi:** Special Events *(Music & Arts Fest at Flye Point - last wknd June; 4th July - parade, races & games)* **1-3 mi:** Video Rental, Galleries *(Blossom Studio, Balombini, Naskeag Gallery, Hooked Rugs, Curry, Streeter, Snyder, Salt Air Primitives)* **3+ mi:** Golf Course *(11 mi.)*

Provisioning and General Services
1-3 mi: Convenience Store *(Brooklin General Store 359-8817, 5:30am-7pm)*, Gourmet Shop *(Betsy's Sunflower 359-5030, next to General Store)*, Wine/Beer, Fishmonger *(Brooklin General)*, Post Office, Library *(Friend Memorial 359-2276 - Garden dedicated to Brooklin resident E.B. White)*, Bookstore *(Wooden Boat School Store 359-4651; Noah Publications 359-2131- wooden boat books, including classic "Wood, Water and Light" & Calendar of Wooden Boats)*, Newsstand, Retail Shops *(Clothing, books, models, wood-working tools, toys, marine supplies; Betsy's Sunflower 359-5030, kitchen, garden, boating & home goods)* **3+ mi:** Supermarket *(Blue Hill Market 374-5137, 11 mi.)*, Bank/ATM *(11 mi.)*

Transportation
Airport: Bangor Int'l. *(50 mi.)*

Medical Services
911 Service **3+ mi:** Doctor *(11 mi.)*, Dentist *(11 mi.)* **Hospital:** Blue Hill Memorial 374-2836 *(11 mi.)*

Setting -- Just off Eggemoggin Reach, Center Harbor seems to be the spiritual and actual home of the contemporary wooden boat movement. The mooring field is filled with the products of Brooklin's boat builders -- from prams to offshore yachts. The shoreline is dominated by a towering three-story, weathered shingled boat shed. a large travelift and a small village of work sheds. At the foot of the long fixed wharf, a floating deep-water dinghy dock berths a flotilla of wooden dinks. For those who appreciate a sleek downeast sheer and are enamored with this romantic craft, Brooklin is a destination.

Marina Notes -- *Small Mooring under 150 lbs. $25/day, $75/wk, $175/mo., Large Mooringover 150 lbs. $25/day, $150/wk., $400/mo. Founded 1960. This is strictly a boatyard with moorings. Deepwater dinghy dock. 16,000 sq. ft. inside storage. Main shed accommodates boats to 120 ft. 60-man crew. World-wide reputation for designing, building, restoring custom wooden yachts - power and sail. Also provides extensive maintenance and repair services. Modest parts department - catalog overnight. Ask about a brief tour of the sheds - it's an impressive operation. Bathhouse: Pleasant head, 2nd floor main shed.

Notable -- A half-mile walk, the tiny village of Brooklin (population 850) is home to the Brooklin Inn, Restaurant & Pub, library, post office, the well-supplied Brooklin General Store (fish & lobster, too), a marine chandler, Betsy's Sunflower and a half dozen galleries. On the other side of town, The Wooden Boat School (see Marina Report) teaches boat-building skills and publishes WoodenBoat Magazine. Marine photographer Benjamin Mendlowitz's Noah Publications publishes a series of books on wooden boats. And nearby Bridges Point Boat Yard, builds Joel White's classic-looking (fiberglass) sloop.

Buck's Harbor Marine

PO Box; 684 Coastal Road; South Brooksville, ME 04617

Tel: (207) 326-8839 **VHF: Monitor** Ch. 9/16 **Talk** Ch. 10
Fax: (207) 326-8855 **Alternate Tel:** (207) 348-5253
Email: bucksharbor@bucksharbor.com **Web:** www.bucksharbor.com
Nearest Town: Blue Hill *(11 mi.)* **Tourist Info:** (207) 374-2281

Navigational Information

Lat: 44°20.014' **Long:** 068°43.602' **Tide:** 12 ft. **Current:** n/a **Chart:** 13309
Rep. Depths (*MLW*): Entry 35 ft. **Fuel Dock** 21 ft. **Max Slip/Moor** -/20 ft.
Access: Penobscot Bay to head of Eggemoggin Reach; use east entrance

Marina Facilities *(In Season/Off Season)*

Fuel: *89 Oct. Gas & Low-sulfur Marine Diesel* - Gasoline, Diesel
Slips: 3 Total, 3 Transient **Max LOA:** 160 ft. **Max Beam:** n/a
Rate *(per ft.)*: **Day** $2.00* **Week** n/a **Month** n/a
Power: 30 amp Incl., **50 amp** Incl., **100 amp** n/a, **200 amp** n/a
Cable TV: No **Dockside Phone:** No
Dock Type: Floating, Alongside, Concrete, Wood, Aluminum, Composition
Moorings: 26 Total, 26 Transient **Launch:** By arrangement, Dinghy Dock
Rate: Day $35 **Week** $162 **Month** Inq.
Heads: 2 Toilet(s), 3 Shower(s) *(dressing rooms)*, Book Exchange
Internet: Yes *(Wi-Fi, Free)* **Laundry:** 1 Washer(s), 1 Dryer(s)
Pump-Out: OnSite, Full Service **Fee:** Inq. **Closed Heads:** Yes

Marina Operations

Owner/Manager: Jerry & Lois Kirschenbaum **Dockmaster:** Same
In-Season: Jul-Aug, 8am-7pm **Off-Season:** Sept-Oct, 9am-5pm
After-Hours Arrival: Call ahead for instructions
Reservations: Yes Preferred **Credit Cards:** Visa/MC, Dscvr, Tex
Discounts: None
Pets: Welcome **Handicap Access:** Yes, Docks

Marina Services and Boat Supplies

Services - Docking Assistance, Concierge, Trash Pick-Up, Dock Carts **Communication -** Pay Phone, FedEx, UPS **Supplies - OnSite:** Ice *(Block, Cube)*, Ships' Store *(Good basic ships' supplies, overnight parts delivery, cruising guides)*, Bait/Tackle

Boatyard Services

OnSite: Crane *(2T)* **OnCall:** Engine mechanic *(gas, diesel)*, Electrical Repairs, Electronic Sales, Electronics Repairs, Rigger, Sail Loft, Canvas Work, Divers, Bottom Cleaning, Interior Cleaning, Propeller Repairs **Near:** Launching Ramp. **Nearest Yard:** Seal Cove Boat Yard (207) 326-4422

Restaurants and Accommodations

Near: Restaurant *(Buck's Comfort Food Downeast 326-8839, D $17-24, Upscale, white tablecloth. 5:30-8:30pm, 7 days in season, off-season closed Mon. Ch. 9, 10)*, Snack Bar *(Buck's Harbor Market 326-8683, 7am-7pm Summer, 7am-6pm Fall, open to 1 on Sun. Pizza too)* **1-3 mi:** Restaurant *(Oakland House 359-8521)* **3+ mi:** Inn/B&B *(Oakland House 359-8521, $145-270, 4 mi., 1907 seaside lodge & 15 cottages; $400-4,000/wk)*

Recreation and Entertainment

OnSite: Boat Rentals *(12 Sail & Power bareboat charters - 38-41 ft. cruising sailboats $1750-29950/wk, 32-43 ft. GB trawlers $1300-4350/wk, day sailers, picnic launch - reduced rates off-season)* **Near:** Tennis Courts *(Buck's Harbor Yacht Club)* **1-3 mi:** Sightseeing *(Tour tiny Sow's Ear Winery 326-4649 Tue-Sat 10am-5pm - for a tasting of wine and cider made from local, organic fruit)*

Provisioning and General Services

OnSite: Convenience Store *(Ice cream, beer/wine, cheese, oysters, hats, shirts, crafts & gifts)*, Gourmet Shop *(Key Lime Pies!)*, Wine/Beer, Lobster Pound *(lobster pen right under the dock - always available)*, Bookstore *(Good selection, incl. "Safe Boat" and other nautical works by co-owner Jerry Kirschenbaum & Robert McCloskey's children's books)*, Retail Shops *(Gourmet foods, gifts, toys, macramé & fancy knotware, plus books, magazines, newspapers, shirts, hats)* **Near:** Market *(Buck's Harbor Market 326-8683, now moving to gourmet with Jonathan Chase at helm)*, Delicatessen, Bakery, Farmers' Market *(Thur 9-11am So. Brooksville)*, Fishmonger, Post Office, Protestant Church, Newsstand, Copies Etc. *(Buck's Harbor Market)* **1-3 mi:** Library **3+ mi:** Supermarket *(Merrill & Hinckley 374-2821 in Blue Hill, 12 mi.)*

Transportation

OnSite: Courtesy Car/Van *(Staff will help if mutually convenient)* **Airport:** Bar Harbor/Bangor Int'l. *(27mi./55mi.)*

Medical Services

911 Service **OnCall:** Ambulance **Hospital:** Blue Hill Memorial *(12 mi.)*

Setting -- Protected through 340 degrees by Harbor Island, deep, beautiful Buck's Harbor sits at the head of Eggemoggin Reach near the tiny village of Brooksville. Perched on an historic 1814 granite pier, the small turquoise-trimmed white office building and two tall white fuel tanks, backed by a barn-roofed shed, pop against the spruce-covered hill. A floating dock leads to a large wood deck with picnic tables and Adirondack chairs overlooking the mooring field.

Marina Notes -- *Very limited transient dockage. Near-future reconfiguration will create ten slips. Founded 1810, acquired by Kirschenbaums 1994. Green, numbered mooring balls (mushroom anchors & granite blocks) - 1 for 100 ft., 3 for 60-70 ft. 22 for smaller yachts (wait for assignment). Up to 60 boat flotillas accommodated on moorings - need to raft. Two work boats equipped with 1,000 lb & 8,000 lb lift capacities maintain moorings. Operates 12-boat charter fleet. Bases 10 lobster boats. Buck's Harbor Yacht Club for guest moorings (326-9265), tennis courts, club house, Bathhouse: Small white building with hunter green doors - behind fuel tanks - impeccable blue tile & knotty pine full baths plus laundry. On the dock - fun, enclosed outdoor shower stalls with awesome views.

Notable -- For a perfect dinner, there's a lobster pound under the wharf and home-made Bahamian Key lime pies in the store - reserve on the VHF. Boaters head to Buck's Market for gourmet provisions, wine, take-out along with groceries, fresh baked bread, newspapers, and a deli. Next door, Chef Jonathan Chase offers a fine-dining locavore experience at Buck's restaurant with an electic, market-based menu - inside or on the deck. Buck's Harbor, in the heart of blueberry country, is the setting for Robert McCloskey's beloved children's books "One Morning in Maine" and "Blueberries for Sal." Blue Hill is a twenty-minute drive.

Navigational Information
Lat: 44°20.340' **Long:** 068°46.166' **Tide:** 9 ft. **Current:** 1 kt. **Chart:** 13316
Rep. Depths (*MLW*): Entry 14 ft. **Fuel Dock** n/a **Max Slip/Moor** -/9 ft.
Access: East Penobscot Bay to Horseshoe Cove

Marina Facilities *(In Season/Off Season)*
Fuel: No
Slips: 0 Total, 0 Transient **Max LOA:** 60 ft. **Max Beam:** n/a
Rate *(per ft.)*: **Day** n/a **Week** n/a **Month** n/a
Power: 30 amp n/a, **50 amp** n/a, **100 amp** n/a, **200 amp** n/a
Cable TV: No **Dockside Phone:** No
Dock Type: n/a
Moorings: 20 Total, 10 Transient **Launch:** No, Dinghy Dock
Rate: Day $20 **Week** n/a **Month** n/a
Heads: None
Internet: No **Laundry:** None
Pump-Out: No **Fee:** n/a **Closed Heads:** Yes

Marina Operations
Owner/Manager: Bob Vaughan **Dockmaster:** Same
In-Season: Year Round, 7am-3:30pm **Off-Season:** n/a
After-Hours Arrival: Call in Advance or Check in Next morning
Reservations: No **Credit Cards:** Cash or Check only
Discounts: None
Pets: Welcome **Handicap Access:** No

Seal Cove Boatyard

124 Horseshoe Cove Rd.; Harborside, ME 04642

Tel: (207) 326-4422 **VHF: Monitor** Ch. 9/16 **Talk** Ch. 68
Fax: (207) 326-4411 **Alternate Tel:** n/a
Email: sealcoveboatyard@gmail.com **Web:** sealcoveboatyard.com
Nearest Town: Brooksville *(7 mi.)* **Tourist Info:** (207) 374-3242

Marina Services and Boat Supplies
Services - Trash Pick-Up **Communication -** Fax in/out, FedEx, UPS **Supplies - OnSite:** Ships' Store **3+ mi:** Propane *(Gray Plumbing & Heating 326-4788, 6 mi.)*

Boatyard Services
OnSite: Travelift *(38.5T)*, Railway, Hydraulic Trailer, Engine mechanic *(gas, diesel)*, Electrical Repairs, Electronics Repairs, Hull Repairs, Brightwork, Air Conditioning, Refrigeration, Compound, Wash & Wax, Woodworking, Painting, Total Refits *(extensive services)*

Restaurants and Accommodations
1-3 mi: Hotel *(Hiram Blake Cottages 326-4951, $600-1450)* **3+ mi:** Restaurant *(Buck's 326-8683, 5 mi., Fine dining in So. Brooksville at Jonathan Chase's locavore establishment)*

Recreation and Entertainment
1-3 mi: Park *(Holbrooke Sanctuary - main entrance 2 mi. Coastal & inland hiking trails in an undeveloped, wild, remote peninsula. Trail maps and Bird check list at sanctuary)* **3+ mi:** Golf Course *(Bar Harbor Golf Course 667-7505, 35 mi.)*

Provisioning and General Services
3+ mi: Market *(Buck's Harbor Market 326-8683 - gourmet prepared foods, wine, produce, and most neccessities Buck's Harbor Market 326-8683 Buck's Harbor Market 326-8683 , 5 mi.)*, Supermarket *(Merrill & Hinckley in Blue Hill 374-2821, 11 mi.)*, Wine/Beer *(Buck's Harbor, 5 mi.)*, Green Grocer *(Mon-Sat 1-5pm, Four Season Farm Stand - 609 Weir Cove Rd., 4 mi.)*, Library *(Brooksville 326-4560, 7 mi.)*, Pharmacy *(Rite Aid 374-3565, 15 mi.)*, Hardware Store *(Rose Building Products 374-5645, 15 mi.)*

Transportation
Airport: Bar Harbor/Bangor *(38 mi./50mi)*

Medical Services
911 Service **OnCall:** Ambulance **3+ mi:** Doctor *(Blue Hill Family Medicine 374-2311, 16 mi.)* **Hospital:** Blue Hill Memorial Hospital 374-2836 *(16 mi.)*

Setting -- Deep into narrow, tidal Horseshoe Cove, Seal Cove Boatyard's 24 brick red sheds and outside storage sprawl across 6 acres. Their mooring field dots the length of the cove - above and below the boatyard. The narrow slash of blue is hugged by walls of spruce and at lower tides, great scrapes of gravel are visible above the water. A travelift bay and two railways make clear the real focus here.

Marina Notes -- Owned and managed by Vaughan Family since 1936. 500 lb. to 5000 lb. granite block moorings. Pick up a mooring and contact the yard - don't attempt to navigate the cove beyond moorings without local knowledge. Water available on float. Dinghy from mooring to BY float. New 38.5 ton travelift - counter balanced fendering protects hull. Cradles for storage then railway for launch. Three work bays (one 65 ft.) hot-water heated & humidified for traditional varnish apps. Latest HVLP spray tech. Stores over 210 boats to 55 ft. 55,000 sq. ft. of inside, dirt-floor storage - to maintain humidity. Bathhouse: None

Notable -- Explore the upper reaches of the river very carefully in the dinghy - ask the Vaughans for advice. Two miles from the boatyard, 1230-acre wild, undeveloped Holbrook Island Sanctuary, the original source of tall pines for the ships built in Castine, is only accessible by boat. There's a free mooring near the dinghy float (with a donation box) and two more in Tom Cod Cove (all three marked "HIS Guest"). Pick up a trail map at the office - six one-way marked trails range from 0.2 mi to 0.5 mile. The island has been left to return to its natural state. Four miles by road, the Four Season Farm Stand sells the harvest from gardening authors Eliot Coleman and Barbara Damrosch's experimental market garden; Damrosch also writes Washington Post's column "A Cooks Garden."

Castine Town Dock

PO Box 204; Emerson Hall, Court Street; Castine, ME 04421

Tel: (207) 266-7711 **VHF: Monitor** Ch. 16 **Talk** Ch. 9
Fax: (207) 326-9465 **Alternate Tel:** (207) 326-4502
Email: townoffice@castine.me.us **Web:** www.castine.me.us
Nearest Town: Bucksport *(14 mi.)* **Tourist Info:** (207) 469-6818

Navigational Information

Lat: 44°23.221' **Long:** 068°47.803' **Tide:** 11 ft. **Current:** 3 kt. **Chart:** 13302
Rep. Depths (*MLW*): Entry 50 ft. **Fuel Dock** n/a **Max Slip/Moor** 20 ft./70 ft.
Access: East Penobscot Bay to RW bell "CH". Head 075° up river

Marina Facilities *(In Season/Off Season)*

Fuel: No
Slips: 7 Total, 7 Transient **Max LOA:** 80 ft. **Max Beam:** n/a
Rate *(per ft.)*: **Day** $2.00* **Week** Inq. **Month** Inq.
Power: 30 amp Incl., **50 amp** n/a, **100 amp** n/a, **200 amp** n/a
Cable TV: No **Dockside Phone:** No
Dock Type: Floating, Alongside, Wood
Moorings: 2 Total, 2** Transient **Launch:** No, Dinghy Dock
Rate: Day Inq. **Week** n/a **Month** n/a
Heads: 2 Toilet(s), Book Exchange
Internet: No **Laundry:** None
Pump-Out: OnSite, Self Service **Fee:** Free **Closed Heads:** No

Marina Operations

Owner/Manager: Ben Gray (Hrbrmstr) **Dockmaster:** Owen Read
In-Season: Jun 15-Sep 15, 8am-7pm **Off-Season:** Sep 16-Jun 14, On call
After-Hours Arrival: Check with harbormaster in the morning
Reservations: No **Credit Cards:** Check or cash only
Discounts: None
Pets: Welcome, Dog Walk Area **Handicap Access:** Yes, Heads, Docks

Marina Services and Boat Supplies

Services - Docking Assistance, Security *(Campus Security)*, 3 Phase **Communication -** Pay Phone (1), FedEx, UPS, Express Mail *(Sat Del)* **Supplies - Near:** Ice *(Block, Cube)*, Ships' Store *(Four Flags 326-8526)* **1-3 mi:** Live Bait *(South by Northeast 326-2067)* **3+ mi:** Propane *(Gary's Fuel 326-8808, 6.5 mi.)*

Boatyard Services

OnSite: Launching Ramp **OnCall:** Divers **Near:** Engine mechanic *(gas, diesel)*, Hull Repairs, Rigger, Bottom Cleaning, Brightwork, Compound, Wash & Wax, Interior Cleaning, Propeller Repairs, Woodworking, Inflatable Repairs. **Nearest Yard:** Eaton's Boat Yard (207) 326-8579

Restaurants and Accommodations

OnSite: Restaurant *(Reef Pub 326-4040, D $9-16.50, Tacos on Tues, pizza to go)*, Snack Bar *(The Breeze 326-9034, L $2.50-14, fried clams, scallops, shrimp, baskets, burgers, ice cream, May-Oct 11am-4pm)* **Near:** Restaurant *(Stella's 326-9710, D $12-25, New Orleans food & live jazz/blues - above Bah's Bakehouse)*, *(Pentagoet Inn 326-8616, D $18-28)*, *(Dennett's Wharf 326-9045, L & D $8-25 - & pizza. Kids $6)*, Lite Fare *(Bah's Bakehouse B $2-7, L $4-7, 7am-7pm)*, Inn/B&B *(Castine Inn 326-4365, $95-275, Boaters' showers, laundry & sauna - arrange in advance)*, *(Pentagoet Inn 326-8616, $140-285)* **Under 1 mi:** Restaurant *(Commodore Room at Manor Inn 326-4861, D $17-27, dinner 6-8pm, Picks up and returns to docks)*, Inn/B&B *(The Manor Inn 326-4861, $115-275, Picks up at dock; Pet friendly, extra $25)*

Recreation and Entertainment

OnSite: Picnic Area, Boat Rentals *(Castine Kayak Adventures 866-3506 $45-60/day)*, Sightseeing *(MV "State of Maine" offers guided tours)* **Near:** Pool *(Maine Maritime Academy 326-4311)*, Playground, Tennis Courts, Hike/Bike Trails, Park *(Ft. Madison; Ft. George; Dyces Head Light)*, Tours *(Castine Historical Society 326-4118 - fascinating self-guided walking tour)*, Special Events *(Retired Skippers' Race, Aug; Band concerts)* **Under 1 mi:** Beach *(Backshore Beach)*, Golf Course *(Castine G.C. 326-8844)*, Museum *(Wilson Museum Complex 326-9247 - named one of 10 last great places in New England. Includes 1665 John Perkins House Sun & Wed 2-5pm)*

Provisioning and General Services

Near: Convenience Store *(Variety)*, Market *(T & C Grocery 326-4818)*, Wine/Beer, Liquor Store *(T & C)*, Bakery *(Bah's Bake House)*, Farmers' Market *(Thu 9am-11:30am, 326-1014)*, Lobster Pound *(Eaton's Boatyard)*, Bank/ATM, Post Office, Catholic Church, Protestant Church *(Episcopal, Congregational, Unitarian)*, Library *(Witherle Memorial 326-4375, Internet)*, Bookstore *(Compass Rose 326-9366)*, Newsstand

Transportation

OnCall: Taxi *(Don's 236-4762)*, Airport Limo *(Mid-Coast 236-2424)* **Near:** Bikes *(Castine Kayak Adventures 866-3506 $20/day)* **Airport:** Bar Harbor/Bangor Int'l. *(29/30 mi.)*

Medical Services

911 Service **Near:** Doctor *(Castine Community Health Services 326-4348)*, Dentist *(Ciano 326-9500)*, Ambulance **Hospital:** Blue Hill Memorial 374-2836 *(15 mi.)*

Setting -- Approaching Castine along the Bagaduce River, the M.V. State of Maine, Maine Maritime Academy's training ship, dominates the view. Just past the ship, the Castine Town Dock floats at the foot of the large Main Street Wharf - the center of this charming, historic town. Picnic tables and a small green and white pavilion share the wharf with The Breeze snack bar. Main Street, lined with stately elms, eclectic local shops and grand old inns, marches up the hill.

Marina Notes -- *"Town Dock" 140 ft. floating face docks at the foot of two gangplanks. "Acadia Dock" for pick-up & drop off only. Inside face for dinghy dockage. Max 2 hrs. free daytime tie-up (9-5). Overnight starts 3pm, check-out 9am. Max LOA 80 ft. **Town's 2 moorings designated for schooners or mega-yachts. Data ports at library. Bathhouse: Cement floor, uninviting municipal heads on wharf. Lovely private showers ($7 incl. towel & soap) at Castine Inn.

Notable -- Founded in 1613 as Fort Pentagoet, Castine's four hundred years living under five "flags": Native American, British, Dutch, French and U.S - permeate the town. The whole village is on the National Register of Historic Places - so a walk becomes an historic tour (free maps at the Chamber of Commerce). Walk along Perkins Street to the Wilson Museum, Perkins House, blacksmith shop and out to Fort Madison, where grassy earthworks tell the story of both British occupaitons. The looming 499-foot State of Maine offers free 30-minute guided tours (326-4311, 326-2420). The 4-year Maine Maritime Academy is located a few blocks north on the site of British Barracks (pool open to the public). Dinner & dancing with local musicians at Manor Inn. Friday nights at 6pm, free band concerts are held on the grounds of the Wilson Museum - raining? concerts move to Main Street Church. Bring blankets and a picnic.

Navigational Information

Lat: 44°23.283' **Long:** 068°47.748' **Tide:** 12 ft. **Current:** 3 kt. **Chart:** 13302
Rep. Depths (*MLW*): Entry 12 ft. **Fuel Dock** n/a **Max Slip/Moor** 12 ft./-
Access: Penobscot Bay to Castine Harbor, look for large yellow awning

Marina Facilities *(In Season/Off Season)*

Fuel: No
Slips: 3 Total, * Transient **Max LOA:** 110 ft. **Max Beam:** 15 ft.
Rate *(per ft.)*: **Day** $2.75* **Week** n/a **Month** n/a
Power: 30 amp n/a, **50 amp** n/a, **100 amp** n/a, **200 amp** n/a
Cable TV: No **Dockside Phone:** No
Dock Type: Floating, Alongside, Wood
Moorings: 1 Total, 1* Transient **Launch:** No, Dinghy Dock
Rate: Day $30 **Week** n/a **Month** n/a
Heads: 3 Toilet(s)
Internet: No **Laundry:** None
Pump-Out: No **Fee:** n/a **Closed Heads:** No

Marina Operations

Owner/Manager: Paul Brouillard **Dockmaster:** Same
In-Season: May-Oct 15, 11am-11pm **Off-Season:** Oct 16-Apr, Closed**
After-Hours Arrival: Tie up, and check in in the morning
Reservations: Yes, mooring only **Credit Cards:** Visa/MC, Dscvr
Discounts: None
Pets: Welcome **Handicap Access:** Yes, Heads, Docks

Dennett's Wharf

PO Box 215; 15 Sea Street; Castine, ME 04421

Tel: (207) 326-9045 **VHF: Monitor** n/a **Talk** n/a
Fax: (207) 326-9045 **Alternate Tel:** n/a
Email: info@dennettswharf.net **Web:** www.dennettswharf.net
Nearest Town: Bucksport *(14 mi.)* **Tourist Info:** (207) 469-6818

Marina Services and Boat Supplies

Communication - Pay Phone (2), FedEx, UPS, Express Mail *(Sat Del)*
Supplies - OnSite: Ice *(Cube)* **Near:** Ice *(Block)*, Ships' Store *(Eaton's 326-4727, Four Flags 326-8526)* **3+ mi:** Bait/Tackle *(South by Northeast 326-2067, 3.5 mi.)*, Propane *(Gary's Fuel 326-8808, 6.5 mi.)*

Boatyard Services

Near: Hydraulic Trailer, Launching Ramp, Engine mechanic *(gas, diesel)*, Electrical Repairs, Divers, Brightwork, Propeller Repairs, Woodworking, Inflatable Repairs. **Nearest Yard:** Eaton's Boatyard (207) 326-8579

Restaurants and Accommodations

OnSite: Restaurant *(Dennett's Wharf & Oyster Bar 326-9045, L & D $8-25 - & pizza. Kids $6. Couple dozen beers on tap. All wines $7/glass $28/bottle)* **Near:** Restaurant *(The Reef 326-4040, D $9-16.50)*, Snack Bar *(The Breeze L $2.50-14)*, Lite Fare *(Compass Rose)*, *(Bah's Bakehouse 326-9510, B $2-7, L $4-8, 7am-7pm)*, Inn/B&B *(Pentagoet Inn 326-8616, $140-285)*, *(Castine Inn 326-4365, $95-275, Boaters' showers $7, laundry)* **Under 1 mi:** Restaurant *(Commodore Room at The Manor Inn 326-4861, D $15-26, Picks up at docks and returns after dinner)*, Inn/B&B *(The Manor Inn 326-4861, $115-275, Pet-friendly, extra $25)*

Recreation and Entertainment

OnSite: Boat Rentals *(Castine Kayak Adventures tours & rentals 866-3506 Half day tour $55, 2 hr. sunset $40)* **Near:** Pool *(Maine Maritime Academy 326-4311)*, Picnic Area, Playground *(Perkins School)*, Dive Shop, Tennis Courts, Hike/Bike Trails *(Witherle Woods - 185 acres 4.2-mile trail network)*, Video Rental *(Witherle Memorial Library 326-4375)*, Cultural Attract *(Castine Historical Society 326-4118 Sat 10-4, Sun 1-4)*, Sightseeing *(State of Maine 326-4311 and all of Castine)*, Galleries *(Castine Historical Handworks 326-4460 traditional craftsmanship)* **Under 1 mi:** Beach *(Backshore Beach)*, Golf Course *(Castine Golf Club 326-8844)*, Park, Museum *(Wilson Museum 326-9247 Tue-Sun 2-5pm; Perkins House, Blacksmith Shop, Hearse House Wed & Sun 2-5pm)*

Provisioning and General Services

OnSite: Fishmonger **Near:** Market *(T & C Grocery 326-4818, wine, liquor)*, Gourmet Shop, Delicatessen, Wine/Beer, Liquor Store, Bakery *(Bah's Bakehouse 326-9510 7am-5pm)*, Farmers' Market *(Thu 9am-11:30am 326-1014)*, Lobster Pound *(Eaton's Boatyard 326-8579)*, Bank/ATM, Post Office, Catholic Church, Protestant Church, Library *(Witherle Memorial 326-4375, Internet Mon 4-8pm, Tue-Fri 11am-5pm, Sat 11am-2pm)*, Bookstore *(Compass Rose 326-9366 gift shop, bookstore & café)*, Newsstand, Retail Shops *(Four Flags 326-8526 nautical gear, gifts, Vera Bradley colorful print bags, housewares)*

Transportation

OnCall: Rental Car *(Enterprise 800-325-8007 from Ellsworth 30 mi.)*, Taxi *(Don's 236-4762)* **Near:** Bikes *(Castine Kayak Adventures 866-3506 $20/day)* **Airport:** Bar Harbor/Bangor Int'l. *(29mi./30mi.)*

Medical Services

911 Service **Near:** Doctor *(Community Health Services 326-4348)*, Dentist *(Ciano 326-9500)*, Holistic Services *(Blue Moon Massage 326-4983)*, Ambulance **Hospital:** Blue Hill Memorial 374-2836 *(15 mi.)*

Setting -- Just past Castine Town Docks, a brick red metal roof tops the renovated gray shingled Dennett's Wharf that hovers on pilings over the river. Blue and green umbrellas protect al fresco picnic tables on the large deck which are backed by the bright yellow tent - signed "Dennett's Wharf." You can't miss it! Side-tie floats wrap two sides of this water-side seafood restaurant in a building that dates back to the early 1800s - a short hop from Castine's Main Street.

Marina Notes -- *120 linear ft. of dockage for day tie-ups, occassional overnight & dinghy dockage. Only one mooring. Family-owned. Restaurant lounge & portion of the deck serve as boaters' lounges. Interesting cruise event option: 3 seating areas: indoor (35+ people), outside under an enclosed canopy (65+ people), and an open deck. Rotating selection of about 20 on-tap beers ($2.75-$6.50). Flat rate wines $7/glass, $28/bottle. Display depicts the history of Dennett's. Live entertainment on weekends. Castine Kayak Adventures kayak tours & rentals plus bikes. Data ports at the library a few blocks away. Bathhouse: Heads shared with restaurant. Small, well kept just inside fish market area. Nearby inn offers showers for a fee.

Notable -- Originally a sail and rigging loft, Dennett's became, with the advent of steam vessels, a landing wharf for visitors from Boston, Washington and New York. It was also home to one of the first "9 pin" bowling lanes -- which has been excavated and beautifully restored; one of the lanes functions as the bar. The Historic District is at the back door. A leg-stretching hike parallels the shore - with Walking Tour map in hand, head along Water Street to Perkins - past a dozen waterfront 18th & 19th C. houses and museums to Ft. Madisonn and then 1828 Dyces Head Lighthouse - at the mouth of the Bagaduce.

PHOTOS ON DVD: 22

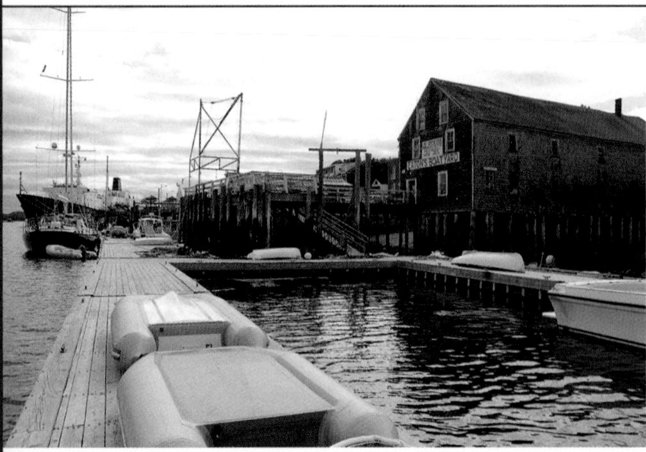

Eaton's Boatyard

PO Box 123; Sea Street; Castine, ME 04421

Tel: (207) 326-8579 **VHF: Monitor** Ch. 9 **Talk** Ch. 9
Fax: (207) 326-4727 **Alternate Tel:** n/a
Email: eatons@hypernet.com **Web:** n/a
Nearest Town: Bucksport *(14 mi.)* **Tourist Info:** (207) 469-6818

Navigational Information

Lat: 44°23.291' **Long:** 068°47.742' **Tide:** 12 ft. **Current:** 3 kt. **Chart:** 13309
Rep. Depths (*MLW*): Entry 12 ft. **Fuel Dock** 11 ft. **Max Slip/Moor** 11 ft./50 ft.
Access: Penobscot Bay to Castine Harbor, 5th set of docks to port

Marina Facilities *(In Season/Off Season)*

Fuel: Gasoline, Diesel
Slips: 8 Total, 2* Transient **Max LOA:** 200 ft. **Max Beam:** n/a
Rate *(per ft.)*: **Day** $2.75 **Week** n/a **Month** n/a
Power: 30 amp $3, **50 amp** $6, **100 amp** $12, **200 amp** n/a
Cable TV: No **Dockside Phone:** No
Dock Type: Floating
Moorings: 10 Total, 10 Transient **Launch:** No, Dinghy Dock
Rate: Day $25 **Week** Inq. **Month** Inq.
Heads: None
Internet: No **Laundry:** None
Pump-Out: No **Fee:** n/a **Closed Heads:** No

Marina Operations

Owner/Manager: Kenny Eaton **Dockmaster:** Suzanne Eaton
In-Season: Summer, 6am-Dusk **Off-Season:** Fall-Win-Sprg, 7am-4pm
After-Hours Arrival: Call ahead, then tie up and check in in the morning
Reservations: Yes **Credit Cards:** Cash only
Discounts: None
Pets: Welcome **Handicap Access:** No

Marina Services and Boat Supplies

Services - Docking Assistance, Concierge **Communication -** Pay Phone (1), FedEx, UPS, Express Mail **Supplies - OnSite:** Ice *(Block, Cube)*, Ships' Store **Under 1 mi:** Propane *(Gary's Fuel Service 326-8808)* **3+ mi:** Bait/Tackle *(South by Northeast 326-2067, 3.5 mi.)*

Boatyard Services

OnSite: Forklift, Hydraulic Trailer *(20T, 44 ft.)*, Electrical Repairs, Electronics Repairs, Hull Repairs, Rigger, Bottom Cleaning, Brightwork, Compound, Wash & Wax, Interior Cleaning, Painting, Yacht Broker **OnCall:** Engine mechanic *(gas, diesel)*, Electronic Sales, Canvas Work, Divers, Refrigeration, Upholstery, Metal Fabrication **Near:** Launching Ramp. **Yard Rates:** $45/hr., Haul & Launch $10/ft. *(blocking $1/ft.)*, Power Wash $2.80/ft., Bottom Paint $45/hr. **Storage:** On-Land Inside $4/ft./mo. Outside $2/ft./mo.

Restaurants and Accommodations

Near: Restaurant *(Dennett's Wharf 326-9045, L & D $8-25 & pizza. Kids $6)*, *(Stella's 326-9710, above Bah's Bakehouse - New Orleans food & live jazz/blues)*, *(Pentagoet Inn 326-8616, D $18-28)*, Snack Bar *(The Breeze 326-9200, L $2.50-14, May-Oct 11am-4pm)*, Lite Fare *(Bah's Bakehouse 326-9510, B $3-7, L $3-7, D $3-10, 7am-7pm)*, Inn/B&B *(Pentagoet Inn 326-8616, $140-285)*, *(The Castine Inn 326-4365, $95-275, Showers $7 & Laundry for boaters)* **Under 1 mi:** Restaurant *(Commodore Room at Manor Inn 326-4861, D $17-27, 6-8pm, call for pick-up)*, Inn/B&B *(Manor Inn 326-4861, $115-275, Pet friendly $25)*, Condo/Cottage *(Castine Cottages 326-8003)*

Recreation and Entertainment

Near: Playground *(Perkins School)*, Boat Rentals *(Castine Kayak Adventures 866-3506 $45-60/day)*, Park, Tours *(Self-Guided Historic District Walking Tour)*, Cultural Attract *(Castine Historical Society 326-4118; John Perkins House)* **Under 1 mi:** Pool *(Maine Maritime Academy 326-4311, Town Pool at Backshore Beach)*, Tennis Courts *(Castine G.C.)*, Golf Course *(Castine Golf Club 326-8844)*, Video Rental, Museum *(Wilson Museum 326-8753)*, Sightseeing *(Maine Maritime Academy 464-6565)* **1-3 mi:** Beach *(Backshore Beach)*

Provisioning and General Services

OnSite: Lobster Pound *(Will even cook 'em)* **Near:** Convenience Store, Market *(T & C Grocery 326-4818)*, Gourmet Shop, Delicatessen, Wine/Beer *(T & C)*, Liquor Store, Farmers' Market *(Thu 9am-11:30am)*, Bank/ATM, Post Office, Library *(Witherle Memorial 326-4375, Internet access)*, Bookstore *(Compass Rose 326-9366; Maine Maritime 326-4983)*, Newsstand, Florist **Under 1 mi:** Bakery *(Bah's Bakehouse 326-9510)*, Catholic Church

Transportation

OnSite: Water Taxi *(Bagaduce)* **OnCall:** Taxi *(Don's 236-4762)* **Near:** Bikes *(Castine Kayak 866-3506 $20/day)* **3+ mi:** Rental Car *(Penguin 338-6111, 14 mi.)* **Airport:** Bar Harbor/Bangor Int'l. *(29 mi./30 mi.)*

Medical Services

911 Service **OnCall:** Ambulance **Near:** Doctor *(Castine Community Health Services 326-4348)*, Dentist *(Ciano 326-9500)* **Hospital:** Blue Hill Memorial 374-2836 *(15 mi.)*

PHOTOS ON DVD: 23

Setting -- Just past Dennett's Wharf, this 1927 classic, family-run, down-home Maine boatyard is easily identified by its big weathered shingled shed built on a massive wharf over the Bagaduce. A U-shaped dock floats on each side linked by a single long face dock. A sturdy gangway leads to the large deck sprinkled with gear, hoses and picnic tables. While rustic Eaton's primary focus is providing yard services, any needed amenity is a very short walk.

Marina Notes -- * 280 running ft. of dock face for transients - accommodates 12-15 boats with rafting. 100A service. Fuel discounts on volume purchases. Only full-service boatyard in Castine. Currently operated by the fourth generation - father and daughter. On-site 44 ft./20T trailer. 32,000 sq. ft. of inside storage. Limited amenities for the boater. Eating on the boat? Eaton's will provide live lobsters - and even cook them! Manor Inn will pick up and deliver to the docks. Internet access is at the library. Bathhouse: None. Note: Lovely Castine Inn, a short walk up the hill, offers very nice showers for boaters ($7 incl. soap & towels) - just check in at the front desk. Sauna by advance arrangement.

Notable -- Bagaduce Boating Co. (run by one of the Eaton daughters) offers harbor tours from the dock in a classic 1950's 30-foot boat built right onsite ($20/hr., $35/18 two hrs.- six passenger limit; children 10-16 half price, under 10 free). Dennett's Wharf is right next door for great people-watching and lunch or dinner. A little farther west is the Maine Maritime Academy's 499 ft. State of Maine training ship (tours available). Four hundred years of history welcome you to this picturesque village filled with intriguing sites and diverse activities. It's a walking town; pick up a copy of the excellent tour map at any local shop.

Navigational Information

Lat: 44°23.444' **Long:** 068°47.680' **Tide:** 11 ft. **Current:** 3 kt. **Chart:** 13309
Rep. Depths (*MLW*): Entry 50 ft. **Fuel Dock** n/a **Max Slip/Moor** 15 ft./70 ft.
Access: East Penobscot Bay to Castine Harbor

Marina Facilities *(In Season/Off Season)*

Fuel: No
Slips: 15 Total, 5 Transient **Max LOA:** 90 ft. **Max Beam:** n/a
Rate *(per ft.)*: **Day** $1.00* **Week** n/a **Month** n/a
Power: 30 amp n/a, **50 amp** n/a, **100 amp** n/a, **200 amp** n/a
Cable TV: No **Dockside Phone:** No
Dock Type: Floating, Wood
Moorings: 5 Total, 5 Transient **Launch:** None, Dinghy Dock
Rate: Day $35* **Week** n/a **Month** n/a
Heads: 3 Toilet(s), 2 Shower(s) *(dressing rooms)*
Internet: No **Laundry:** None
Pump-Out: No **Fee:** n/a **Closed Heads:** No

Marina Operations

Owner/Manager: Tom Pedersen **Dockmaster:** Debbie Rogers
In-Season: Jun15-Sep30, 8am-10pm **Off-Season:** Oct1-Jun 14, Closed
After-Hours Arrival: Sign-in book on 1st Floor
Reservations: No **Credit Cards:** Cash or check only
Discounts: None
Pets: Welcome **Handicap Access:** No

Castine Yacht Club

PO Box 34; 63 Water Street; Castine, ME 04421

Tel: (207) 326-9231 **VHF: Monitor** Ch. 9 **Talk** Ch. 10
Fax: n/a **Alternate Tel:** (207) 326-4521
Email: rogsmu@netsense.net **Web:** www.castineyachtclub.org
Nearest Town: Bucksport *(14 mi.)* **Tourist Info:** (207) 469-6818

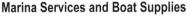

Marina Services and Boat Supplies

Services - Docking Assistance, Boaters' Lounge, Trash Pick-Up, Dock Carts **Communication -** Mail & Package Hold, FedEx, UPS, Express Mail **Supplies - OnSite:** Ice *(Cube)* **Near:** Ice *(Block)*, Ships' Store *(Eaton's 326-8879; Four Flags 326-8526)* **3+ mi:** Marine Discount Store *(Hamilton Marine 800-639-2715, 20 mi.)*, Propane *(Gary's Fuel 326-8808, 6.5 mi.)*

Boatyard Services

Near: Hull Repairs, Rigger. **Nearest Yard:** Eaton's (207) 326-8579

Restaurants and Accommodations

Near: Restaurant *(The Reef 326-4040, D $9-16.50)*, *(Stella's 326-9710, D $12-25, Above Bah's Bakehouse - New Orleans food & live jazz/blues)*, *(Dennett's Wharf 326-9045, L & D $8-25 -& pizza. Kids' $6)*, Snack Bar *(The Breeze L $2.50-14, May-Oct 11am-4pm)*, Coffee Shop *(Bah's Bakehouse 326-9510, B $2-7, L $4-8, 7am-7pm, Wi-Fi)*, Lite Fare *(Compass Rose 326-9366)*, *(Castine Variety 326-0690, $5-17, ice cream parlor, pizza Mon-Thur 7am-7pm, Fri & Sat 7am-8pm, Sun 8am-5pm)*, Inn/B&B *(Castine Inn 326-4365, $95-275, Boaters' showers $7, Laundry)* **Under 1 mi:** Restaurant *(Pentagoet Inn 326-8616, D $10-20)*, Inn/B&B *(Pentagoet 326-8616, $140-285)*, Condo/Cottage *(Castine Cottages 326-8003)* **1-3 mi:** Restaurant *(Commodore Room at The Manor Inn 326-4861, D $15-26, Will pick up at club and return)*, Inn/B&B *(The Manor Inn 326-4861, $115-275)*

Recreation and Entertainment

OnSite: Picnic Area, Grills, Tours *(Kayak Tours - Tues Jul & Aug $15 non-members)* **Near:** Playground *(Adams School)*, Boat Rentals *(Castine Kayak Aventures 866-3506)*, Video Rental, Park, Sightseeing *(State of Maine training ship, Castine Historical Society 326-4118)*, Galleries *(Castine Historical Handworks 326-4460 traditional craftsmanship)* **Under 1 mi:** Pool *(Maine Maritime Academy 326-4311; Backshore Beach Tidal Town Pool)*, Beach *(Backshore Beach)*, Tennis Courts *(Castine G.C.)*, Golf Course *(Castine Golf Club 326-8844)*, Museum *(Wilson Museum 326-9247 Tue-Sun 2-5pm; Perkins House, Blacksmith Shop, Hearse House Wed & Sun 2-5pm; Castine Historical Society 326-4118 Sat 10-4, Sun 1-4.)* **1-3 mi:** Hike/Bike Trails *(Witherle Woods - 185 acres 4.2-mile trail network)*

Provisioning and General Services

Near: Market *(T & C Grocery 326-4818 wine, liquor)*, Delicatessen *(Bah's 326-9510)*, Wine/Beer, Liquor Store, Bakery *(Bah's, Wi-Fi)*, Farmers' Market *(Thu 9-11:30am 326-1014)*, Green Grocer, Lobster Pound, Bank/ATM, Post Office *(1814)*, Catholic Church, Protestant Church, Library *(Witherle Memorial 326-4375, Mon 4-8pm, Tue-Fri 11am-5pm, Sat 11am-2pm - Wi-Fi Internet 24/7)*, Bookstore *(Compass Rose 326-9366 gift shop, bookstore & café; Maine Maritime 326-9333)*, Newsstand, Retail Shops *(Four Flags 326-8526 nautical gear, gifts, Vera Bradley colorful print bags, housewares)*

Transportation

OnCall: Taxi *(Don's 236-4762)* **Near:** Bikes *(Castine Kayak Adventures 866-3506 $20/day)* **Airport:** Bar Harbor/Bangor Int'l. *(29 mi./30 mi.)*

Medical Services

911 Service **OnCall:** Ambulance **Near:** Doctor *(Community Health Services 326-4348)*, Dentist *(Ciano 326-9500)*, Holistic Services *(Blue Moon Massage 326-4983)* **Hospital:** Blue Hill Memorial 374-2836 *(15 mi.)*

Setting -- The fourth facility in Castine, lovely, quiet CYC is a short walk from town - the most scenic and residential choice. A network of floats surround the long stationary boardwalk that leads to the 2-story, gray-sided, contemporary clubhouse topped by a pyramidal roof. The inviting second floor porch, usually populated by welcoming members, enjoys views of the unspoiled far shore, kids racing their dinghies, or the action down river closer to town.

Marina Notes -- *Overnight dockage on westerly four floats. Contribution $30 for boats under 30 ft. LOA, plus $1/ft over 30 ft. Must leave by 9am. No power. Five guest moorings $25, over 45 ft $35. Mooring labled "CYC GUEST # 1", etc. Yachts with LOAs over 35 ft, use #3 & #5. Max 24 hrs. Daytime Dockage - 9am-6pm, unattended max 60 minutes. Private yacht club welcomes visitors. Trash disposal under street-side entrance. $1/per bag. Blue bin for returnable bottles. Active junior sailing club. Tuesday night lectures. Phone for local calls or CC. Bring a dinghy. Bathhouse: Inviting full baths $3/shower.

Notable -- Castine is a walking town with lots of history -- it's lived under five flags and was originally called Ft. Pentagoet. Pick up a copy of the excellent walking tour at any local shop. Kayak and bike rentals near Dennett's are a short walk away, as are the museums, parks, and restored Georgian and Federalist houses. Just two blocks away, off Court Street, is a beautiful square with the historic 19th C. Witherle Library (with data ports), Abbott and Adams Schools, Whitney House and other early 19thC houses. On the other side of town, Wilson Museum (326-8753) features a pre-Revolutionary War house. Smith Cove, less than a mile away on the other side of the river, is a good hurricane hole or anchorage area. The Manor Inn transports boaters for dinner/lodging.

PHOTOS ON DVD: 23

Belfast City Landing

131 Church Street; Belfast, ME 04915

Tel: (207) 338-1142 **VHF: Monitor** Ch. 9 **Talk** Ch. 9
Fax: (207) 338-6222 **Alternate Tel:** n/a
Email: harbormaster@acadia.net **Web:** www.cityofbelfast.org
Nearest Town: Belfast **Tourist Info:** (207) 338-5900

Navigational Information

Lat: 44°25.736' **Long:** 069°00.235' **Tide:** 10 ft. **Current:** 3 kt. **Chart:** 13309
Rep. Depths (*MLW*): Entry 13 ft. **Fuel Dock** 12 ft. **Max Slip/Moor** 15 ft./20 ft.
Access: Belfast Bay to Passagassawakeag River

Marina Facilities *(In Season/Off Season)*

Fuel: *Irving* - Slip-Side Fueling, Gasoline, Diesel, High-Speed Pumps
Slips: 25 Total, 25 Transient **Max LOA:** 140 ft. **Max Beam:** 25 ft.
Rate *(per ft.)*: **Day** $1.75/Inq. **Week** Inq. **Month** Inq.
Power: 30 amp $5, **50 amp** $10, **100 amp** $20, **200 amp** n/a
Cable TV: No **Dockside Phone:** No
Dock Type: Fixed, Floating, Long Fingers, Short Fingers, Pilings, Wood
Moorings: 350 Total, 25 Transient **Launch:** No, Dinghy Dock
Rate: Day $25 **Week** n/a **Month** n/a
Heads: 6 Toilet(s), 4 Shower(s), Book Exchange
Internet: Yes *(Wi-Fi, Free)* **Laundry:** None
Pump-Out: Full Service, 1 Central **Fee:** $5 **Closed Heads:** Yes

Marina Operations

Owner/Manager: Katherine Messier (Harbormaster) **Dockmaster:** Same
In-Season: May-Oct, 7am-6pm **Off-Season:** Nov-Apr, 7am-4pm
After-Hours Arrival: Check in the next morning.
Reservations: Yes, Recommended **Credit Cards:** Visa/MC
Discounts: None
Pets: Welcome, Dog Walk Area **Handicap Access:** Yes, Heads, Docks

Marina Services and Boat Supplies

Services - Docking Assistance, Security *(Local Police Dept.)*, Trash Pick-Up, Dock Carts **Communication -** Pay Phone (2), FedEx, UPS, Express Mail *(Sat Del)* **Supplies - OnSite:** Ice *(Block, Cube)* **Near:** Ships' Store, Propane *(Consumer Fuel 338-2000)* **3+ mi:** Marine Discount Store *(Hamilton Marine 548-6302, 6 mi.)*

Boatyard Services

OnSite: Launching Ramp **Nearest Yard:** Belfast B.Y. (207) 338-5098

Restaurants and Accommodations

OnSite: Restaurant *(Weathervane 338-1774, L $4-8, D $5-16, Twin lobster deal)* **Near:** Restaurant *(Dockside Family Restaurant 338-6889, L $10, D $10)*, *(Chase's Daily 338-0555, Vegetarian)*, *(Darby's Pub 338-2339, L $4-11, D $7-16)*, *(Thai Bhurapar 338-3899, L $8-9, D $10-17)*, *(Dudley's Diner 338-0555)*, Seafood Shack *(Young's Lobster Pound 338-1160, Dinghy across harbor - BYOB)*, Lite Fare *(Lookout Grill 338-8900, $5-10, pizza)*, *(Belfast Co-op)*, *(Three Tides 338-1707, Tapas $3-11, Marshall Wharf beers on tap)*, *(Bay Wrap 338-9757, L $4-6)*, Pizzeria *(Alexia's 338-9676)*, Inn/B&B *(Alden House 338-2151, $90-130)*, *(White House 338-1901, $100-160)*, *(Jeweled Turret 338-2304, $95-150)*

Recreation and Entertainment

OnSite: Beach, Picnic Area, Boat Rentals *(Water Walkers Kayak 338-6424 $20-50/day)* **Near:** Pool *(City Park)*, Heated Pool *(Indoor - Y 338-4598)*, Grills, Playground, Tennis Courts *(City Park)*, Movie Theater *(Colonial 338-1930)*, Video Rental *(Opera House 338-3405)*, Park, Museum *(Belfast Museum 338-9229 Thu- Mon 11am-4pm)*, Tours *(Water Walkers Kayak 338-6424 2-hr. Harbor Tour $35, 3-hr. Sears Island $45)*, Cultural Attract *(Belfast Maskers 338-9668)*, Sightseeing *(Museum in the Streets - self-guided tour)*, Special Events *(Thurs - Concerts at Heritage Park; Gallery Walk - all open to 9pm; Street Fest monthly Fri; Maine Celtic Fest, Wooden Boat Building)* **3+ mi:** Golf Course *(Northport 338-2270, 4 mi.)*

Provisioning and General Services

Near: Convenience Store, Market *(Co-Op 338-2532)*, Gourmet Shop, Health Food *(Green Store 338-4045, Co-Op 338-2532 - organic produce & meat, bulk grains, prepared foods)*, Wine/Beer *(Co-Op)*, Bakery *(Weaver's 338-3540)*, Farmers' Market *(Fri 9am-1pm, Front Street)*, Lobster Pound *(Young's - by dinghy)*, Bank/ATM, Post Office *(also Customs Office)*, Catholic Church, Library *(338-3884, Internet)*, Beauty Salon, Barber Shop, Dry Cleaners *(Em Bee)*, Laundry *(Belfast Laundromat)*, Hardware Store *(Trustworthy 338-1094)*, Florist *(Wild Flower 338-1230)*, Copies Etc. *(County Copy 338-5411)* **Under 1 mi:** Supermarket *(Hannaford 338-5377)*, Protestant Church, Pharmacy *(Rite Aid 338-4411)* **1-3 mi:** Liquor Store *(Hannaford)*, Department Store *(Reny's 338-4588)*

Transportation

OnCall: Rental Car *(Pooler's 338-6111)* **Near:** Water Taxi, Taxi *(Bay 338-1993)* **Under 1 mi:** InterCity Bus *(Concord Trailways 800-639-3317)*
Airport: Bangor Int'l. *(30 mi.)*

Medical Services

911 Service **Near:** Doctor *(Hagney 38-4244)*, Dentist *(Matthew 338-0700)*, Chiropractor *(Community 338-6463)*, Holistic Services *(Spring Tree Therapies 338-2223)* **Hospital:** Waldo County 930-2500 *(1 mi.)*

PHOTOS ON DVD: 25

Setting -- At the mouth of the Passagassawakeag River, the City Landing is the first facility to starboard - the floating docks and wide launching ramp tuck in between Heritage Park and the Weathervane restaurant. The active dinghy dock services a sprawling mooring field. And on the pier, the hospitable harbor master's gray dockhouse sports ruffled curtains and an ad hoc tourism office. A block up the hill, is an appealing, and underrated, little Victorian city.

Marina Notes -- Two dinghy docks: inner dock near main gangway & off Heritage Park. No launch service. Daytime dockage - 1st hr. free, 2-8 hrs. $0.20/ft./hr. Face docks 110 ft. & 120 ft. Yachts to 140 ft. 360 moorings, 25 reserved for transients (including 18 owned by Belfast BY, but managed by BCL) - with up to 2 ton granite block anchors. Protected but can get rolly in S/SE breeze. 40-passenger "American Star" & "American Glory" cruise ships dock here weekly. Penobscot Bay Tractor Tug Co. berths two handsome tugs just north. Two adjacent scenic public parks - Waterfront Heritage Park and Belfast City Park. Bathhouse: A bit up the hill. New '07. Cinderblock, municipal-style heads open to all. Key-coded showers a step up.

Notable -- Belfast, founded in 1773, has taken itself through a successful renaissance from a commercial town with a polluted harbor to a bustling, arts-filled tourist destination, restored to its mid-19th C. splendor (with clean water!) Blocks of Federal-style and Greek Revival houses have earned it National Historic Registry status. A revitalized brick Victorian business district has attracted innovative shops, restaurants, a movie theater, theatrical troupe, markets and a plethora of arts and artisan galleries. It's a "walking" town - follow the "Museum in the Streets" signs. Fish the harbor for Atlantic Mackerel and Striped Bass.

Navigational Information
Lat: 44°25.742' **Long:** 069°00.280' **Tide:** 10 ft. **Current:** 3 kt. **Chart:** 13309
Rep. Depths (*MLW*): Entry 21 ft. **Fuel Dock** n/a **Max Slip/Moor** 21 ft./16 ft.
Access: Belfast Bay to port side of Passagassawakeag River

Marina Facilities *(In Season/Off Season)*
Fuel: *City Landing* - Slip-Side Fueling, Gasoline, Diesel
Slips: 12 Total, 2 Transient **Max LOA:** 65 ft. **Max Beam:** 14 ft.
Rate *(per ft.)*: **Day** $1.65 **Week** n/a **Month** n/a
Power: 30 amp Incl., **50 amp** n/a, **100 amp** n/a, **200 amp** n/a
Cable TV: No **Dockside Phone:** No
Dock Type: Fixed, Floating, Long Fingers, Wood
Moorings: 18 Total, 18 Transient **Launch:** None, Dinghy Dock
Rate: Day $30* **Week** n/a **Month** n/a
Heads: 1 Toilet(s)
Internet: Yes *(Wi-Fi, Inq.)* **Laundry:** None
Pump-Out: No **Fee:** n/a **Closed Heads:** Yes

Marina Operations
Owner/Manager: Alex Turner/Howie Soule **Dockmaster:** Same**
In-Season: Year-Round, Mon-Fri 7:30am-4pm **Off-Season:** n/a
After-Hours Arrival: Check in with harbormaster if no reservation 338-1142
Reservations: Yes, Preferred **Credit Cards:** Cash or check
Discounts: None
Pets: Welcome, Dog Walk Area **Handicap Access:** No

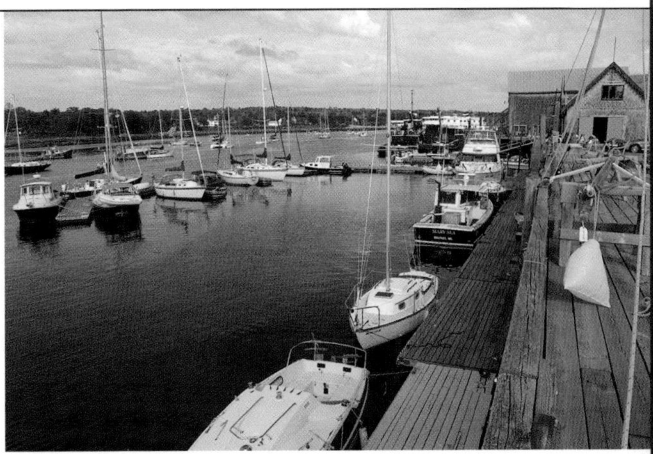

Belfast Boatyard

PO Box 142; 41 Front Street; Belfast, ME 04915

Tel: (207) 338-5098 **VHF: Monitor** Ch. 16 **Talk** n/a
Fax: (207) 338-6440 **Alternate Tel:** (207) 338-5098
Email: howie@belfastboatyard.com **Web:** belfastboatyard.com
Nearest Town: Belfast **Tourist Info:** (207) 338-5900

Marina Services and Boat Supplies
Services - Docking Assistance, Security *(8 Hrs.)*, Trash Pick-Up, Dock Carts **Communication -** Mail & Package Hold, Phone Messages, Fax in/out, FedEx, DHL, UPS, Express Mail **Supplies - OnSite:** Ships' Store **Near:** Ice *(Block, Cube)*, Propane *(Consumer Fuel 338-2000)*

Boatyard Services
OnSite: Travelift *(30T)*, Railway, Crane, Hydraulic Trailer *(25T)*, Engine mechanic *(gas, diesel)*, Electrical Repairs, Electronic Sales, Electronics Repairs, Hull Repairs, Rigger, Sail Loft, Divers, Bottom Cleaning, Brightwork, Air Conditioning, Refrigeration, Compound, Wash & Wax, Interior Cleaning, Propeller Repairs, Woodworking, Inflatable Repairs, Upholstery, Yacht Interiors, Painting **Yard Rates:** $52/hr., Haul & Launch $175 flat, Power Wash $1.25/ft. **Storage:** On-Land $22.50/ft.

Restaurants and Accommodations
OnSite: Lite Fare *(Three Tides 338-1707, Tapas $3-11, Marshall Wharf beers. Tue-Sat 4pm-?)*, *(Look Out 338-8900, $5-10 & Pizza, Billiards)* **Near:** Restaurant *(Chase's Daily 338-0555, Vegetarian. Special Fri dinner)*, *(Thai Bhurapar 338-3833, L $8-9, D $8-17)*, *(Dockside 338-6889)*, *(Weathervane 338-1774, L $4-7, D $5-12)*, *(Darby's Pub 338-2339, L $4-11, D $7-18)*, Seafood Shack *(Young's Lobster Pound 338-3498, Dinghy across harbor, BYOB)*, Lite Fare *(Dudley's Diner 338-1884)*, Pizzeria *(Alexia's 338-9676)*, Inn/B&B *(Jeweled Turret Inn 338-2304, $65-80)*, *(The White House 338-1901, $100-165)*

Recreation and Entertainment
OnSite: Cultural Attract *(Belfast Maskers 338-9668)* **Near:** Pool *(City Park 338-1661)*, Picnic Area *(City Park)*, Grills, Playground, Tennis Courts *(City Park)*, Boat Rentals *(Water Walkers Kayaks 338-6424 $20-50/day)*, Hike/Bike Trails *(Skateboard Park)*, Movie Theater *(Colonial 338-1930)*, Video Rental *(Opera House 338-3405)*, Park, Sightseeing *(Museum in the Streets)*, Special Events *(Heritage Park concerts Thu. 5-7pm; Gallery Walk - open to 9pm; Arts in the Park, 2nd wknd July)* **3+ mi:** Golf Course *(Northport G.C. 338-2270, 4 mi.)*

Provisioning and General Services
OnSite: Wine/Beer *(Marshall Wharf Brewery)* **Near:** Market *(Belfast Co-Op 338-2532)*, Health Food *(Green Store 338-4045, Belfast Co-Op)*, Bakery *(Weavers 338-3540)*, Farmers' Market *(Fri 9am-1pm Front Street)*, Lobster Pound *(Young's - dinghy)*, Bank/ATM, Post Office, Catholic Church, Protestant Church, Library *(338-3884, Internet access)*, Beauty Salon, Barber Shop, Dry Cleaners, Laundry, Hardware Store *(Trustworthy 338-1094)*, Florist *(Wild Flowers 338-1230)*, Copies Etc. *(Belfast Office 338-1010)* **Under 1 mi:** Supermarket *(Hannaford 338-5377)*, Pharmacy *(Rite Aid 338-4411)* **1-3 mi:** Department Store *(Reny's)*

Transportation
OnCall: Taxi *(Bay 338-1993)* **Near:** Bikes *(Belfast 338-0008)*, Rental Car *(Poolers 338-6111)* **Airport:** Bangor Int'l. *(30 mi.)*

Medical Services
911 Service **Near:** Doctor *(Naturopath - Hagney 338-4244)*, Dentist *(Mathew 338-0700)*, Chiropractor *(Community Chiro 338-6463)*, Holistic Services *(Spring Tree 338-2223)*, Veterinarian *(Belfast 338-3260)* **Hospital:** Waldo County 338-2500 *(1 mi.)*

Setting -- Past City Landing and the brace of red tugboats, Belfast Boatyard's quality docks - a combination of slips and long stretches of side-tie - float beneath Marshall Wharf. The busy boatyard spills out onto the docks and shares the wharf with several buildings that house a variety of activities including Three Tides, Marshall Wharf Brewery, Lookout Pub, and Belfast Masker's Theater. Revitalized, energetic and hospitable Belfast is a stone's throw away.

Marina Notes -- *Owns 18 of the 25 transient moorings managed by City Landing. Founded 1980. Added new docks to the north and offers six floating docks with slips. **Belfast harbormaster Kathy Messier serves as after-hours "dockmaster." Full-service yard with a combined 9 decades of experience. Specializes in repairs and restorations of awlgrip fiberglass hulls & anything for wooden vessels. Maineport Towboats berths two handsome tugs next door. Bathhouse: Very basic head. Use City Landing bathhouse or showers & sauna at Belfast Dance Studios 338-5380 (yoga & movement classes.)

Notable -- The official "Boater's Lounge" is Rollies Café just up the hill; but onsite Lookout Pub's pair of pool tables might be a close second. Three Tides, perched high above the docks, serves tapas with one of 13 Marshall Wharf brews on tap. Belfast Maskers' summer theater performs in the rejuvenated B & M Railway Station theater or at Steamboat Landing Park. Walk the restored Rte. 1 footbridge for the view, the fishing (Atlantic Mackerel or Striped Bass) or all the way accross to Young's Lobster Pond (about 1.2 mi.). In the 19th C. Belfast was home to 11 shipbuilders - pick up the Historic Tour or just walk the "Museum in the Streets." There's also a skateboard park, ice cream parlor, new basketball and tennis courts, a pool and a kayak company that offers guided tours.

PHOTOS ON DVD: 25

Searsport Landing

PO Box 498; 5 Church St.*; Searsport, ME 04974

Tel: (207) 548-2722 **VHF: Monitor** Ch. 9/10 **Talk** Ch. 71/78
Fax: n/a **Alternate Tel:** (207) 548-2529
Email: n/a **Web:** www.searsportme.net
Nearest Town: Belfast *(5 mi.)* **Tourist Info:** (207) 338-5900

Navigational Information

Lat: 44°27.179' **Long:** 068°55.508' **Tide:** 10 ft. **Current:** n/a **Chart:** 13309
Rep. Depths (*MLW*): Entry 11 ft. **Fuel Dock** n/a **Max Slip/Moor** -/11 ft.
Access: Penobscot Bay to Searsport Harbor

Marina Facilities *(In Season/Off Season)*

Fuel: No
Slips: 0 Total, 0 Transient **Max LOA:** 70 ft. **Max Beam:** n/a
Rate *(per ft.)*: **Day** n/a **Week** n/a **Month** n/a
Power: 30 amp n/a, **50 amp** n/a, **100 amp** n/a, **200 amp** n/a
Cable TV: No **Dockside Phone:** No
Dock Type: Floating, Alongside
Moorings: 60 Total, 3 Transient **Launch:** No, Dinghy Dock
Rate: Day $10-20* **Week** n/a **Month** n/a
Heads: 1 Toilet(s)
Internet: No **Laundry:** None
Pump-Out: No **Fee:** n/a **Closed Heads:** No

Marina Operations

Owner/Manager: Wayne Hamilton (Harbormaster) **Dockmaster:** Same
In-Season: Year-Round, 9am-5pm **Off-Season:** n/a
After-Hours Arrival: Call in advance
Reservations: Yes **Credit Cards:** n/a
Discounts: None
Pets: Welcome, Dog Walk Area **Handicap Access:** No

Marina Services and Boat Supplies

Communication - FedEx, UPS, Express Mail **Supplies - Near:** Ice *(Cube)* **Under 1 mi:** Marine Discount Store *(Hamilton Marine 548-6302 - 8am-5pm, 7 days - biggest chandlery in New England; family operation with harbormaster at the helm)* **1-3 mi:** Propane *(Hydes 474-3030)*

Boatyard Services

Nearest Yard: Belfast Boat Yard (207) 338-5098

Restaurants and Accommodations

OnSite: Snack Bar *(Poppy's Wiener Wagon)* **Near:** Restaurant *(Rollie's Bar & Grill 548-2900)*, Coffee Shop *(Coastal Coffee 548-2400, 7:30am-3:30pm)*, Motel *(Baits 548-7299)*, *(Yardarm 548-2404)*, Inn/B&B *(Watchtide by the Sea 548-6575)*, *(Carriage House Inn 548-2167)*, *(Elm Cottage B&B 548-2941, Vegetarian)*, *(Sea Captain's Inn 548-0919)* **Under 1 mi:** Restaurant *(The Brick House 548-6550, 10am-Mid, 7 Days)*, Snack Bar *(Cook's Crossing Ice Cream)*, Fast Food *(Blimpies 548-2728)* **1-3 mi:** Restaurant *(Rhumb Line 548-2600, Fine dining, dinner only)*, *(Angler's 548-2405, L & D $5-21 Kids $4-5. Take-out too)*

Recreation and Entertainment

OnSite: Picnic Area, Grills **Near:** Beach *(Mosmann Park)*, Playground *(Mosman)*, Video Rental *(Tozier's)*, Museum *(Penobscot Marine Museum; Searsport Historical Society)*, Tours *(Museums in the Street - follow the informative panels)*, Galleries *(18 antique shops, artisan studio & fine arts galleries - Searsport Antique Mall - 70 dealers; Hillmans; By the Bay 548-0920; Downeast 548-2393, Gaul's 548-0232; Primrose Farm 548-6019, Pumpkin Patch 548-6047; Thomas J. Jewett, Hobby Horse 548-2981)* **1-3 mi:** Hike/Bike Trails *(930-acre uninhabited Sears Island, connected to the mainland by a causeway. Managed by Maine Coast Heritage Trust and the MDOT. Mile-long car-free road & numerous trails. Beautiful beaches, spectacular views)*

Provisioning and General Services

Near: Market *(Tozier's 548-6220 - very well-supplied)*, Liquor Store *(Tozier's)*, Bank/ATM *(Bangor Savings)*, Protestant Church, Library *(Carver Memorial 548-2303 Internet, Maritime collection, Mon-Fri 10am-5pm, Sat 10am-1pm)*, Beauty Salon *(Angela Austin)*, Bookstore *(Left Bank Books 548-6400 Mon-Sat 9am-6pm, Sun 10am-5pm; Penobscot Books 548-6490)* **Under 1 mi:** Convenience Store *(Steamboat Mobil 548-2728 Dunkin' Donuts, Blimpie)*, Laundry *(Fillmore's Washtub 548-2412)* **3+ mi:** Supermarket *(Hannaford's 338-5377, 6.5 mi.)*, Catholic Church *(4 mi.)*, Hardware Store *(Jerry's 338-0409, 3.5 mi.)*

Transportation

OnCall: Airport Limo *(Mid-Coast 236-2424)* **Under 1 mi:** InterCity Bus *(Concord Trailways 945-4000 - at Steamboat Mobil - daily trips via Rte 1 to Portland/Boston/Logan/Bangor)* **Airport:** Bangor Int'l *(30 mi.)*

Medical Services

911 Service **OnCall:** Ambulance **Near:** Dentist *(Baldus 548-6161)*, Chiropractor *(Oceanside 338-1153)* **Under 1 mi:** Doctor *(Searsport Health Center 548-2475)* **1-3 mi:** Veterinarian *(Searsport 548-2924)* **Hospital:** Waldo County General 338-2500 *(8.5 mi.)*

PHOTOS ON DVD: 25

Setting -- Searsport is the second deepest harbor in Maine. The mooring field surrounds a "Y"-shaped 70 ft. fishing pier that extends from a granite rock wharf with finger floats for dinghy dockage or temporary tie-up for loading and unloading. The upland is mostly parking lot with a grassy picnic area and a dark yellow hot-dog trailer. From the landing, it is 0.2 mile up Steamboat Avenue to Route 1 - the beginning of the historic village and Penobscot Marine Museum.

Marina Notes -- *Fee is a suggested donation. **Town hall. Physical address of dock is foot of Steamboat Ave. Depth at floating dock 4.5 ft. mlw. One float is handicap-accessible. Water &15A power. Town transient mooring is #1, Penobscot Marine Museum Mooring (#55) - takes up to 70 ft. yacht. Make reservations for all moorings with Harbormaster. Open to south and southwest. To make a mooring reservation, or discuss any other issues, contact very helpful Wayne Hamilton, Searsport Harbormaster, at 207-548-2722 or on VHF channels 9, 10, 71 or 78. Bathhouse: Porta Potty.

Notable -- Shipping and ship building were very big business and, in 1889, 77 sea captains lived here. Today, it is home to an enticing maritime musuem, a plethora of antique shops, galleries and B&Bs - many in former sea captain's homes. A easy walk from the dock, the Penobscot Marine Museum's 13 buildings create a 19th C. seafaring village with exhibits depicting the region's rich maritime and ship-building heritage. From Wabanaki canoes to full-rigged Cape Horners and Square-rigged down-easters, the museum explores the power of the boat. There's also an impressive gallery of maritime paintings (penobscotmarinemuseum.org). On the north side of Mill Pond, four-acre Mosman Park offers a saltwater beach, picnic area, playground, and ball field.

Navigational Information

Lat: 44°34.314' **Long:** 068°47.813' **Tide:** 11 ft. **Current:** 9 kt. **Chart:** 13309
Rep. Depths (*MLW*): Entry 16 ft. **Fuel Dock** 5 ft. **Max Slip/Moor** 26 ft./-
Access: Penobscot River to southern end of Verona Island

Marina Facilities *(In Season/Off Season)*

Fuel: Gasoline, On Call Delivery
Slips: 50 Total, 6 Transient **Max LOA:** 60 ft. **Max Beam:** n/a
Rate *(per ft.)*: **Day** $1.75/$1.50 **Week** Inq. **Month** $10**
Power: 30 amp $3, **50 amp** $5, **100 amp** n/a, **200 amp** n/a
Cable TV: No **Dockside Phone:** No
Dock Type: Floating, Long Fingers, Short Fingers, Wood
Moorings: 0 Total, 0 Transient **Launch:** n/a, Dinghy Dock
Rate: Day n/a **Week** n/a **Month** n/a
Heads: 1 Toilet(s), 1 Shower(s) *(dressing rooms)*
Internet: No **Laundry:** None
Pump-Out: OnSite, Self Service **Fee:** Free **Closed Heads:** Yes

Marina Operations

Owner/Manager: Steve York **Dockmaster:** Same
In-Season: MemDay-LabDay, 9am-5pm** **Off-Season:** May, Sep, Oct, 9am-5
After-Hours Arrival: Call in advance and pre-pay
Reservations: Yes, Preferred **Credit Cards:** Visa/MC, Dscvr, Amex
Discounts: None
Pets: No **Handicap Access:** Yes, Docks

Bucksport Marina

88 Main Street; Bucksport, ME 04416

Tel: (207) 469-5902; (800) 499-5840 **VHF: Monitor** Ch. 9 **Talk** Ch. 9
Fax: (207) 989-5842 **Alternate Tel:** (207) 989-5840
Email: syork@portharbormarine.com **Web:** www.portharbormarine.com
Nearest Town: Bucksport **Tourist Info:** (207) 469-6818

Marina Services and Boat Supplies

Services - Docking Assistance, Security, Dock Carts **Communication -** FedEx, UPS, Express Mail **Supplies - OnSite:** Ice *(Block, Cube)*, Ships' Store **Near:** Propane *(Ace Hardware)*

Boatyard Services

OnSite: Engine mechanic *(gas, diesel)*, Electrical Repairs, Propeller Repairs, Inflatable Repairs, Total Refits **OnCall:** Rigger, Divers, Bottom Cleaning, Brightwork **Near:** Compound, Wash & Wax, Interior Cleaning, Metal Fabrication. **Nearest Yard:** Port Harbor Marine - 15 mi. (207) 989-5840 **Member:** ABBRA

Restaurants and Accommodations

OnCall: Pizzeria *(House of Pizza 469-7511, 11am-9pm)* **Near:** Restaurant *(McLeod's Restaurant & Pub 469-3963, L $5-15, D $9-20, Tue-Sat 11:30am-2pm, 5-9pm, Sun 11:30-2pm)*, *(Ming's Chinese Garden)*, Snack Bar *(Wahl's Dairy Port ice cream)*, Fast Food *(McDs, Subway)*, Motel *(BW Fort Knox Inn 469-3113, $85-140, Part of the old Jed Prouty Inn)* **Under 1 mi:** Restaurant *(Sea Breeze 469-0249, B $4-7, L $4-21, 5am-2pm. Burgers, sandwiches, seafood, comfort food, pizza. Dinner Fri. Across river on way to Fort)*, Lite Fare *(Wo's BBQ Grill 469-2500, $2-19 across bridge, 11am-8pm)*, Motel *(Bucksport Motor Inn 469-3111, $59-109)*

Recreation and Entertainment

OnSite: Picnic Area, Grills, Jogging Paths, Hike/Bike Trails, Park *(Chamberlain Freedom, Free concerts at Gazebo, Sat.)*, Museum *(Bucksport Hist. Society 469-2464)* **Near:** Movie Theater *(The 1916 Alamo 469-6910 across the street - current films & classics from Northeast Historic Film's moving-image archive)*, Sightseeing *(Versa Paper Mill 469-1700, free tours Mon, Wed, Fri, Jun-Aug, 10am-3pm, 12 yrs & older)*, Special Events *(Bay Fest - Last wknd July - Hourly buses to Fort)* **Under 1 mi:** Fishing Charter, Cultural Attract *(Penobscot Narrow Observatory & Ft. Knox State Park 469-7719 $5/3, Daily 9am-Sunset)* **1-3 mi:** Golf Course *(Bucksport G.C. 469-7612)*, Fitness Center *(Isaac Farrar Mansion YWCA 941-2808)*, Bowling *(Bucksport 469-6686)*

Provisioning and General Services

Near: Convenience Store *(Tozier's Bucksport Variety 469-2753)*, Farmers' Market *(Thu 9am-3pm)*, Bank/ATM, Post Office, Catholic Church, Library, Beauty Salon *(Shear Elegance 469-3707, Studio 83 469-2140)*, Barber Shop, Dry Cleaners, Laundry, Bookstore *(Bookstacks 469-8992 - wi-fi, too!)*, Pharmacy *(Community 469-7030)*, Florist *(Sheehan's 469-3999)* **Under 1 mi:** Supermarket *(Hannafords/Shop N Save 469-3282)*, Wine/Beer, Liquor Store *(Rite Aid 469-2925)*, Hardware Store *(True Value 469-2451; Napa Auto)*

Transportation

OnCall: Rental Car *(Enterprise 800-325-8007)*, Airport Limo **Under 1 mi:** Bikes **Airport:** Bangor Int'l. *(16 mi.)*

Medical Services

911 Service **OnCall:** Holistic Services *(In Good Hands Massage 469-1119)*, Ambulance **Near:** Doctor *(Bucksport Family Medicine)*, Dentist **Under 1 mi:** Chiropractor, Veterinarian *(Bucksport Vet 469-3614)* **Hospital:** Eastern Maine Med. Center 973-7000 *(16 mi.)*

Setting -- Just beyond the spectacular Penobscot Narrows Bridge, this small facility sits amidst Chamberlain Freedom Park, a mile-long promenade that edges the river - from the Verona-Bucksport bridge all the way to massive Versa Paper's Bucksport mill - and is dotted with benches and picnic tables. Three quality floating docks link to a main pier that parallels the shore. A small blue dockhouse manages the operation. Directly across the harbor are the "unmissable" Penobscot Narrows Bridge & Observatory, Fort Knox Historic Site and the old Waldo-Hancock Bridge. It's just steps to Bucksport's Main Street.

Marina Notes -- *In-season hrs. 9am-5pm, Thurs-Mon; Off-season 9am-5pm, Fri-Mon. Mailing address: 23 Main Rd; Holden, ME 04429. Founded 2001. 70 ft. gas dock (diesel on call), pump-out. Well-stocked marine store. Permanent neon palm trees. Pets not permitted. Decade-long $35-50 million Penobscot Landing project to revitalize the waterfront. Bathhouse: Side of building, newly renovated, all-tile full baths. Note: 12 Army Corp rental moorings from Bucksport Marine Services 469-6300. Town Dock 260 ft. with dinghy floats (1 hr.) & side-tie dockage, 15 ft. mlw for vessels over 80 ft. (Heads on Town Dock)

Notable -- On the Fort Knox Campus, the spectacular Penobscot Narrows Observatory sits 42 stories above the river at the top of the cable-stay bridge. Timed tickets are issued for the speedy elevator ride. The surrounding 125-acre Fort Knox, Historic Site looks like a 5-sided medieval castle with massive 20-foot high granite walls. Built in 1844 to guard approaches to Bangor on the Penobscot River, it is the most-visited historic site in Maine. Kids love the maze of deep underground tunnels, caves, tours and demonstrations. Bring flashlights for the Long Alley tunnel and gun powder room. Picnic on the grounds.

PHOTOS ON DVD: 25

  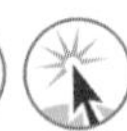   

Winterport Marina

PO Box 130; 49 Water Street; Winterport, ME 04496

Tel: (207) 223-8885 **VHF: Monitor** Ch. 9,16 **Talk** Ch. 10
Fax: (888) 401-2662 **Alternate Tel:** n/a
Email: info@winterportmarine.com **Web:** www.winterportmarine.com
Nearest Town: Winterport *(0.2 mi.)* **Tourist Info:** (207) 947-0307

Navigational Information

Lat: 44°38.194' **Long:** 068°50.446' **Tide:** 10 ft. **Current:** 5 kt. **Chart:** 13309
Rep. Depths (*MLW*): Entry 15 ft. **Fuel Dock** 15 ft. **Max Slip/Moor** 15 ft./25 ft.
Access: 12 miles north of Penobscot Bay

Marina Facilities *(In Season/Off Season)*

Fuel: Gasoline, Diesel
Slips: 16 Total, 6 Transient **Max LOA:** 50 ft. **Max Beam:** n/a
Rate *(per ft.)*: **Day** $1.75 **Week** $8.5 **Month** $20
Power: 30 amp $5, **50 amp** $5, **100 amp** n/a, **200 amp** n/a
Cable TV: No **Dockside Phone:** No
Dock Type: Floating, Alongside, Wood
Moorings: 4 Total, 2 Transient **Launch:** n/a, Dinghy Dock
Rate: Day $20 **Week** $80 **Month** $200
Heads: 1 Toilet(s), 1 Shower(s)
Internet: Yes *(Wi-Fi, Free)* **Laundry:** 1 Washer(s), 1 Dryer(s)
Pump-Out: OnSite, 1 Port **Fee:** $10 **Closed Heads:** Yes

Marina Operations

Owner/Manager: Eric Bratcher **Dockmaster:** Same
In-Season: Year-Round, 8am-4pm **Off-Season:** n/a
After-Hours Arrival: Call ahead
Reservations: No **Credit Cards:** Visa/MC, Dscvr, Amex
Discounts: Boat/US **Dockage:** 25% **Fuel:** n/a **Repair:** 15%
Pets: Welcome, Dog Walk Area **Handicap Access:** No

Marina Services and Boat Supplies

Services - Docking Assistance, Trash Pick-Up **Communication -** Mail & Package Hold, Fax in/out *($2)*, FedEx, DHL, UPS, Express Mail **Supplies - OnSite:** Ships' Store *(Overnight delivery)* **Under 1 mi:** Ice *(Block, Cube)* **1-3 mi:** Propane

Boatyard Services

OnSite: Crane, Hydraulic Trailer *(20 T)*, Launching Ramp *($5)*, Engine mechanic *(gas, diesel)*, Electrical Repairs, Electronics Repairs, Hull Repairs, Rigger, Brightwork, Woodworking, Painting, Total Refits **OnCall:** Sail Loft, Canvas Work, Propeller Repairs, Metal Fabrication **Yard Rates:** $55/hr., Haul & Launch $5/ft. + labor, Power Wash $45 + labor **Storage:** On-Land Outside $3/ft./month; Inside $5/ft./mo.

Restaurants and Accommodations

Near: Restaurant *(My Fork Bar and Grill 223-4003)*, *(Rosie's Diner 223-5003, B $3-7, L $3-7, D $7-16)*, Pizzeria *(Winterport Pizza 223-4902)*, Inn/B&B *(Mermaid Cove Inn 223-5992, $65-125, 1836 Sea Captain's home)*, *(Old Winterport Commercial House 223-5854 22-358-54 , $65-90, 1833 inn & stagecoach stop)*

Recreation and Entertainment

Near: Museum *(Winterport Historical Association - 1864 building)*, Galleries *(Anderson Gallery at Winterport Winery 223-4500 shows local artists; Old Winterport Commercial Antiques 223-5854; Mermaid Cove Antiques & Gift Shop 223-5992)* **3+ mi:** Golf Course *(Streamside Golf Course 223-9009 , 7 mi.)*, Movie Theater *(Alamo Theatre 469-6910 , 13 mi.)*

Provisioning and General Services

Near: Farmers' Market *(Deerfield/Fisher Farm 223-4803; Organic farm straight up Elm St.; Hillcrest Orchard 223-4416)*, Green Grocer *(Parker Produce)*, Beauty Salon *(Riverside Hair Designs 299-2978; Angel Hair Studio, 223-4754)*, Laundry *(Bob's 735-4237)* **Under 1 mi:** Convenience Store *(On the Go 223-3906)*, Delicatessen *(Freshies Deli 223-3906)*, Wine/Beer *(Winterport Winery & Penobscot Bay Brewing 223-4500)*, Liquor Store, Bank/ATM *(ATM)*, Catholic Church, Protestant Church, Library *(Winterport Memorial 223-5540)* **1-3 mi:** Post Office **3+ mi:** Supermarket *(Hannaford's 862-5444 , 9 mi.)*, Pharmacy *(Rite Aid 862-4900 , 8 mi.)*, Hardware Store *(True Value 862-4444, 8 mi.)*

Transportation

Airport: Bangor Int'l *(12 mi.)*

Medical Services

911 Service **Under 1 mi:** Doctor *(Winterport Family Medicine 223-5074)*, Holistic Services *(Creative Bodywork 223-4131)*, Optician *(Winterport Family Eye Care 223-5555)*, Ambulance **1-3 mi:** Veterinarian *(Ridge Runner Veterinary Services 223-2596)* **Hospital:** Mayo Regional 564-4479 *(11 mi.)*

PHOTOS ON DVD: 25

Setting -- About halfway between Penobscot Bay and Bangor, Winterport Marine's 980 linear feet of side-tie floating dock paralells the shore and its mooring balls float just offshore. A gangway leads to the office in a weathered-shingle boat shed - surrounded by a rustic, working boat yard and on-the-hard storage. The stretch of dense, uninterrupted pine and spruce that rises from the far river bank is delightfully un-developed. Winterport is a very short walk.

Marina Notes -- Internet access available. Travelift awaits a travelift bay. Meantime, a large hydraulic trailer launches boats. Gas & Diesel plus Pump-out available. Full-service boatyard. Handles boats to 40 ft. incl. multi-hulls. 2900 sq. ft. heated work space and 20,000 sq. ft. indoor storage. Marine supplies delivered next day. Dockworks, builder of ramps and floats onsite. Wi-Fi available. Launch ramp. Bathhouse: Rustic full bath.

Notable -- Settled in 1766, the small river town of Winterport was the head of navigation during winter months because the river remained ice-free to here. When the Upper Penobscot froze, goods would be hauled overland to Winterport for shipping downriver - creating a vibrant economy, a ship building center and home to many sea captains. The Panic of 1857 turned the tide but left behind a small historic district including the exquisite 1833 Union Meeting House and Winterport Historical Association Museum. Antique shops, galleries, atleliers, eateries and B&Bs occupy beautifully restored early 19th C. buildings - many on the National Register of Historic Places. Several farm stands are in the village, which seems clearly on the upswing as more buildings are reclaimed. Winterport Winery and Penobscot Bay Brewing are an easy walk. Taste their fruit wines, hand-crafted beers and new ice cream - and visit the onsite Anderson Gallery.

Navigational Information
Lat: 44°45.934' **Long:** 068°47.769' **Tide:** 10 ft. **Current:** n/a **Chart:** 13309
Rep. Depths (*MLW*): Entry 20 ft. **Fuel Dock** n/a **Max Slip/Moor** 8 ft./-
Access: Penobscot Bay 17 miles up Penobscot River

Marina Facilities *(In Season/Off Season)*
Fuel: Gasoline, Diesel
Slips: 28 Total, 3 Transient **Max LOA:** 40 ft. **Max Beam:** n/a
Rate *(per ft.)*: **Day** $1.50 **Week** n/a **Month** n/a
Power: 30 amp Incl., **50 amp** n/a, **100 amp** n/a, **200 amp** n/a
Cable TV: No **Dockside Phone:** No
Dock Type: Floating, Long Fingers, Wood
Moorings: 5 Total, 5 Transient **Launch:** No, Dinghy Dock
Rate: Day $25 **Week** n/a **Month** n/a
Heads: 2 Toilet(s)
Internet: Yes *(Computer, Free)* **Laundry:** None
Pump-Out: OnSite, Self Service **Fee:** Free **Closed Heads:** Yes

Marina Operations
Owner/Manager: Dan Higgins **Dockmaster:** Same
In-Season: Year Round, 8am-5pm** **Off-Season:** n/a
After-Hours Arrival: Call in Advance
Reservations: Yes, Required **Credit Cards:** Visa/MC, Dscvr, Amex
Discounts: None
Pets: Welcome **Handicap Access:** No

Hamlin's Marina

100 Marina Road; Hampden, ME 04444

Tel: (207) 941-8619 **VHF: Monitor** Ch. 16 **Talk** Ch. 9
Fax: (207) 941-8628 **Alternate Tel:** n/a
Email: mhansen@hamlinsmarina.com **Web:** hamlinsmarina.com
Nearest Town: Bangor *(3 mi.)* **Tourist Info:** (207) 947-0307

Marina Services and Boat Supplies
Services - Docking Assistance, Trash Pick-Up, Dock Carts **Communication -** FedEx, UPS, Express Mail **Supplies - OnSite:** Ice *(Cube)*, Ships' Store **Under 1 mi:** Propane *(Foster Energy 947-5336)* **1-3 mi:** Bait/Tackle *(Van Raymond Outfitters 989-6001)*

Boatyard Services
OnSite: Hydraulic Trailer, Launching Ramp, Engine mechanic *(gas, diesel)*, Electrical Repairs, Electronic Sales, Electronics Repairs, Hull Repairs, Rigger, Compound, Wash & Wax, Propeller Repairs, Woodworking, Metal Fabrication, Painting, Awlgrip **OnCall:** Sail Loft, Canvas Work, Inflatable Repairs, Life Raft Service **Dealer for:** Yamaha and Honda outboards, Volvo Gas & Diesel, Mercruiser, Indmar I/Os & Inboards, Eastern, MasterCraft, Rinker, Stingray, Polarkraft, Hurricane, Godfrey. **Yard Rates:** $65-105, Haul & Launch $225 *(blocking incl.)*, Power Wash $1.50/ft. **Storage:** On-Land Inside: $29-52/ft., Outside $19-42/ft.

Restaurants and Accommodations
OnSite: Restaurant *(Dana's Grill at Dockside 990-3307, L & D $2-13 - burgers, sandwiches, lobster rolls, crab rolls, wraps, fried chicken - most $5-8)* **Near:** Snack Bar *(R & K Variety 942-8355, Take-out, pizza, sandwiches, salads, burgers)*, Pizzeria *(Pat's 947-6488, a Bangor landmark)* **1-3 mi:** Restaurant *(Perri House 941-0112)*, *(Geaghan's Pub 945-3730, B $4-10, D $5-19, Irish specials)*, Motel *(Fireside Inn & Suites 942-1234, $80-120, next to Hollywood Slots)*, *(Hollywood Slots 877-779-7771)*

Recreation and Entertainment
OnSite: Special Events *(Last Sat. Jun - River Rodeo)* **1-3 mi:** Tennis Courts *(Bangor Tennis 942-4836)*, Golf Course *(Bangor Municipal G.C. 941-0232; Pine Hill G.C. 989-3824)*, Video Rental *(Edge 990-2002)*, Museum *(Cole Land Transportation 990-3600 $6/Free - 9am-5pm, 7 days - over 200 antique vehicles of virtually every stripe from snow removal equipment to 10 fire trucks 1910-1948.)*, Cultural Attract *(Penobscot Theater 947-6618 Live theater at Bangor Opera House - a local institution since 1973)* **3+ mi:** Bowling *(Family Fun 942-6701, 4.5 mi.)*, Movie Theater *(Movie Magic 941-9419, 4 mi.)*

Provisioning and General Services
Near: Convenience Store *(R & K Variety 942-8355)*, Hardware Store *(Stern's Lumber 942-0222)*, Retail Shops *(Turner Sporting Goods 941-0801)* **Under 1 mi:** Wine/Beer, Bank/ATM, Catholic Church, Protestant Church **1-3 mi:** Supermarket *(Shaws-Osco 942-9441)*, Post Office, Synagogue, Library *(Edythe Dyer/Hampden 862-3550 Internet)*, Laundry *(Hampden 862-9995)*, Pharmacy *(Shaw's Osco 942-9441)*, Florist *(Hampden 862-3018)* **3+ mi:** Department Store *(Walmart Supercenter 989-5068, 6 mi.)*

Transportation
OnCall: Taxi *(Dick's 942-6403)* **Near:** Rental Car *(Rent-A-Wreck 942-4600)*, InterCity Bus **Airport:** Bangor Int'l *(6 mi.)*

Medical Services
911 Service **OnCall:** Ambulance **Near:** Doctor *(Osteopathic Center 945-5400)*, Chiropractor *(Baker Family 945-4321)* **1-3 mi:** Dentist *(Hampden Family 862-2600)*, Veterinarian *(Farren 862-4825)* **Hospital:** Saint Joseph's Hospital 907-1000 *(4 mi.)*

Setting -- Hamlin's single dock floats below a full-service marine center. Attractive teak-stained clapboard contemporary buildings house the fuel pumps, ships store and snack bar surrounded by a nicely kept lawn sprinkled with picnic tables. The boatyard, storage and boat sales part of the operation are in the rear - a long, multi-bay boat shed opens onto expansive on-the-hard storage. The view across the river is an untouched wall of green.

Marina Notes -- **Closed Sunday. Formerly called Turtle Head Marina. 28 slips with power. Fuel - gas & diesel. Mostly seasonal dockage. Full boatyard services. Certified for most engines. Specializes in Gelcoat repair and awlgrip. Major focus on the sale of 30 ft. and under power boats. Manages larger vessels for dry storage - including cats. Home base for PenBay Explorers Cruising Club - power boat owners who daytrip in company throughout Penobscot Bay. Annual event - River Rodeo with live music, high-flying wakeboarding & waterski demonstrations. Bathhouse: Recent heads.

Notable -- Dana's Grill is basically a take-out window that serves a covered patio filled with comfortable tables and chairs. Additional picnic-style tables are on the lawn overlooking the water. The fare includes well-priced lobster and crab rolls, fried chicken, wraps, burgers and ice cream - and daily specials. A small gaggle of useful services are a short walk on US 1A. The Penobscot River's water quality has greatly improved over the past 30 years as industrial pollution was reduced to comply with the Clean Water Act. Now, in an unprecedented collaboration designed to revive the native fisheries, the Penobscot River Restoration Project is attempting to restore species of sea-run fish by removing two upriver dams.

PHOTOS ON DVD: 15

Bangor Landing Waterfront Park

88 Front Street; Bangor, ME 04401

Tel: (207) 947-5251 **VHF: Monitor** Ch. 16/9 **Talk** Ch. 9
Fax: (207) 992-4194 **Alternate Tel:** (207) 992-4248
Email: harbor.master@bangormaine.gov **Web:** n/a
Nearest Town: Bangor **Tourist Info:** (207) 947-0307

Navigational Information

Lat: 44°47.470' **Long:** 068°45.430' **Tide:** 12 ft. **Current:** 4 kt. **Chart:** 13309
Rep. Depths (*MLW*): Entry 16 ft. **Fuel Dock** n/a **Max Slip/Moor** 14 ft./14 ft.
Access: Follow well marked channel up river 20 mi. from Bucksport

Marina Facilities *(In Season/Off Season)*

Fuel: No
Slips: 30 Total, 15 Transient **Max LOA:** 200 ft. **Max Beam:** n/a
Rate *(per ft.)*: **Day** $1.30* **Week** Inq. **Month** Inq.
Power: 30 amp Incl., **50 amp** Incl., **100 amp** n/a, **200 amp** n/a
Cable TV: No **Dockside Phone:** No
Dock Type: Floating, Alongside, Wood, Aluminum
Moorings: 6 Total, 6 Transient **Launch:** No, Dinghy Dock
Rate: Day $20 **Week** n/a **Month** n/a
Heads: 2 Toilet(s), 1 Shower(s)
Internet: No **Laundry:** None
Pump-Out: Self Service, 2 Central **Fee:** Free **Closed Heads:** No

Marina Operations

Owner/Manager: Gerald Ledwith (Hbrmstr) **Dockmaster:** Same
In-Season: May 15-Oct 15 **Off-Season:** Oct 16-May14*
After-Hours Arrival: Tie-up and check in in morning
Reservations: Yes, Preferred **Credit Cards:** Cash or check
Discounts: None
Pets: Welcome, Dog Walk Area **Handicap Access:** Yes

Marina Services and Boat Supplies

Services - Trash Pick-Up **Communication -** FedEx, UPS, Express Mail **Supplies - Near:** Ice *(Cube)*, Propane *(U-Haul; Dead River 989-2770)* **Under 1 mi:** Bait/Tackle *(Eddie's 947-1648)* **3+ mi:** Ships' Store *(Port Harbor Marine 989-5840; Hamlin's Marina 941-8619 2 mi.; Waterfront Marine 942-7026 1.5 mi., 4 mi.)*

Boatyard Services

Nearest Yard: Hamlin's Marina (207) 941-8619

Restaurants and Accommodations

OnSite: Restaurant *(Sea Dog Brewing Co 947-8004, L & D $8-23, Mon-Fri 11am-1am, Sat & Sun 7am-1am)* **Near:** Restaurant *(The Reverend Noble Pub 942-9339, 4pm-1am)*, *(City Slickers Tex-Mex 941-0010)*, *(Thistle's 945-5480, L $9-12, D $10-26, Fine dining with Latin touch)*, *(Taste of India 945-6865, L $7, D $11-14, Lunch buffet)*, *(Muddy Rudder 989-5389, L $6-10, D $15-20, Walk across bridge)*, Fast Food *(McD's)*, Hotel *(Charles Inn 992-2820 992-2820, $79-149, Art gallery)*, Inn/B&B *(Fiddlehead Inn 989-1854, $95, Vegetarian, across river)* **1-3 mi:** Restaurant *(Hollywood Slots Epic Buffet)*, Motel *(Village Green 989-3330, $60)*

Recreation and Entertainment

OnSite: Hike/Bike Trails, Park *(Waterfront)*, Special Events *(American Folk Fest, last wknd Aug; Hollywood Slots Waterfront Concert Series - big names)* **Near:** Video Rental *(Edge 990-2002)*, Museum *(Maine Discovery Museum 262-7200 $7/7 Largest in N.E. - 3 floors of kid-focused exhibits; Bangor Center of History 942-1900 $3/Free)*, Cultural Attract *(Penobscot Theater 947-6618 at Bangor Opera House)*, Sightseeing *(Historic District Walking Tour)* **Under 1 mi:** Fitness Center *("Y" 941-2808)* **1-3 mi:** Tennis Courts *(Bangor 942-4836)*, Golf Course *(Bangor Muni. 941-0232)*, Bowling *(Bangor-Brewer 989-3798)*, Movie Theater *(Hoyts 942-1303)*

Provisioning and General Services

Near: Supermarket *(Shaw's-Osco: Bangor 942-9441)*, Liquor Store *(Shaw's)*, Bank/ATM, Beauty Salon *(Bella 945-6230)*, Dry Cleaners, Laundry, Bookstore *(Briar Patch 941-0255 for kids - and more along Central St.; Borders at Bangor Mall)*, Pharmacy *(Miller Drug 947-8369)*, Hardware Store *(Aubuchon Hardware)* **Under 1 mi:** Wine/Beer *(State Street Wine Cellar 262-9500)*, Farmers' Market *(Sat 9am-1pm 326-4741 Sunnyside Greenhouse near Bangor Auditorium)*, Library *(Bangor 947-8336 Internet)*, Barber Shop **1-3 mi:** Delicatessen *(Freshies Deli 942-3670)*, Post Office, Catholic Church, Protestant Church, Synagogue, Department Store *(Walmart 989-5068)*, Copies Etc. *(Staples 947-9225)* **3+ mi:** Health Food *(Natural Living Center 990-2646 , 4.5 mi.)*

Transportation

OnCall: Rental Car *(Enterprise 942-2772)*, Taxi *(Dick's 942-6403)* **Near:** Local Bus *(BAT 992-4670 9 routes to all surrounding towns, mall, university - Main hub near docks)*, InterCity Bus *(Concord to Portland, Boston, Logan)* **1-3 mi:** Bikes *(Pat's 989-2900)* **Airport:** Bangor Int'l *(3.5 mi.)*

Medical Services

911 Service **Near:** Doctor *(Twin City Fam 989-2326)*, Chiropractor *(Northeast 990-5711)* **Under 1 mi:** Dentist *(Twin City 945-6036)*, Holistic Services *(Jiva Massage at Central Yoga 735-7447)* **1-3 mi:** Veterinarian *(Brewer 989-6531)* **Hospital:** Eastern Maine Med. Ctr 973-7000 *(1.5 mi.)*

Setting -- Sprawled along the Penobscot's west bank, Bangor Landing's five floats are backed by Waterfront Park - a grassy promenade dotted with benches and picnic tables. Gangways lead from the modest wood floats to the Park. Onsite Sea Dog Brewery restaurant, a rehabilitated shoe factory, offers inside dining in large wood-paneled rooms or outside on the veranda overlooking the docks.

Marina Notes -- Five sets of docks - Landing #5, the first approached, for visiting cruise ships including American Cruise Line's 215-foot long "American Eagle." Landing #4 for seasonal dockage. Landing #2 & #3 for transient dockage, and Landing #1 - closest to downtown for dinghy dockage.The entire stretch from the 22 ft. high Union Street Bridge to the the City's Bass Park Complex near I-395's 78-foot bridge are part of a long-term redevelopment plan. *Off Season contact info: Tel: (207) 992-4248, Fax: (207) 992-4194, Email: engineering@bangormaine.gov. Bathhouse: modest heads in small gray house in park.

Notable -- At the end of August, the dockside American Folk Festival promises four stages and dozens of food and craft vendors. Once the busiest lumber port in the world, Bangor's 19th C. boomtown era left behind a treasure-trove of historic buildings. A four-block walk, pretty Market Square's Mobius sculpture is surrounded by sidewalk cafes and local shops housed in restored buildings. Nearby Main Street, hosts the fabulous Maine Discovery Museum and Penobscot Theater. Hike a mile north to the Broadway Historic District to see the lumber barons' 19th-century mansions or over to West Broadway to Stephen King's red-turreted Victorian with spider web gates. Getting anywhere is easy - the BAT bus hub is a couple blocks. Hollywood Slots Casino & Raceway is closeby.

6. ME – Western Penobscot Bay

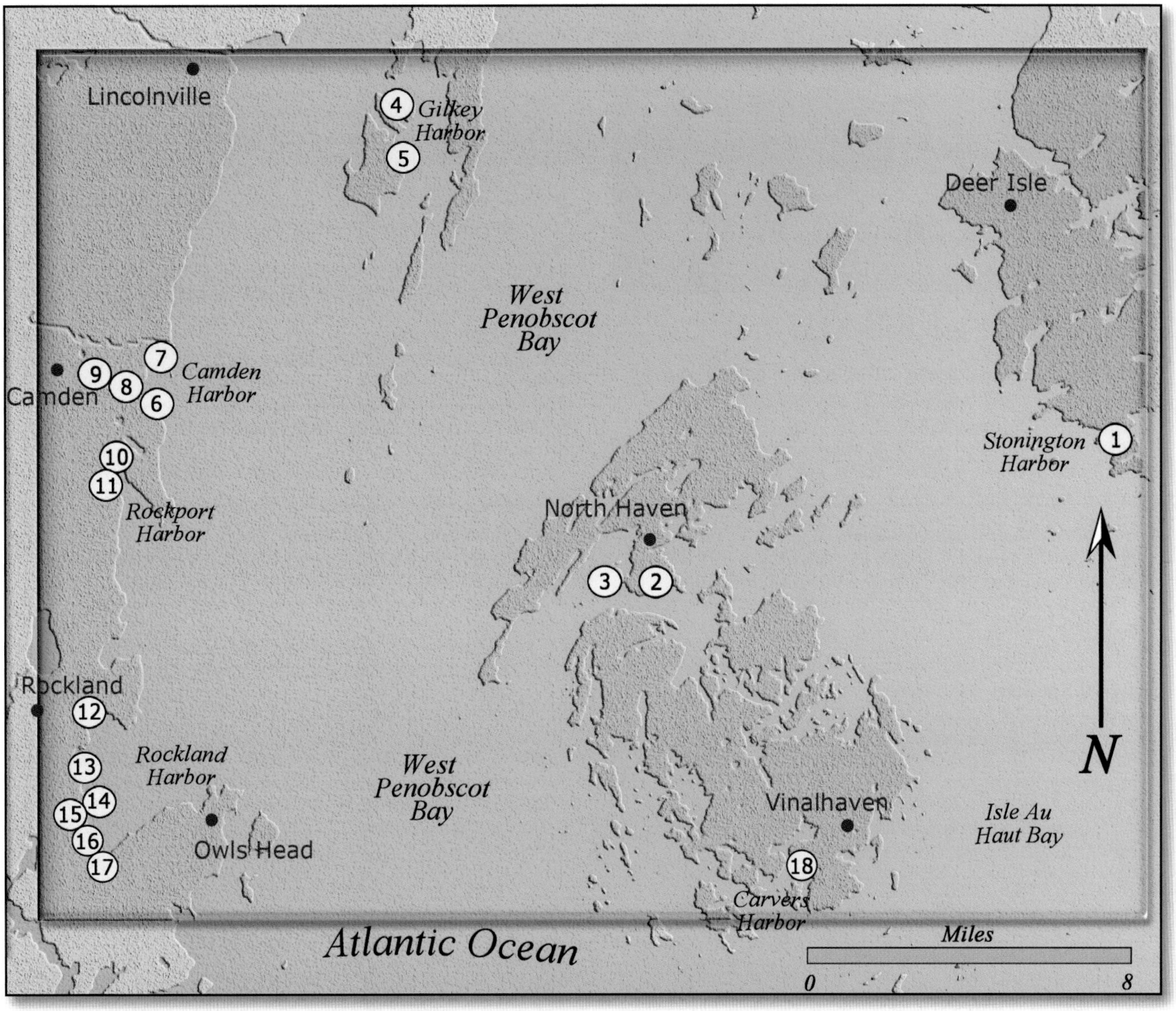

MAP	MARINA	HARBOR	PAGE	MAP	MARINA	HARBOR	PAGE
1	**Billings Diesel and Marine**	*Stonington Harbor*	*114*	10	**Rockport Marine Park**	*Rockport Harbor*	*123*
2	**J.O. Brown & Sons**	*Fox Islands Thorofare*	*115*	11	**Rockport Marine**	*Rockport Harbor*	*124*
3	**Thayers Y-Knot Boatyard**	*Southern Harbor*	*116*	12	**Knight Marine Service**	*Rockland Harbor*	*125*
4	**Warren Island State Park**	*Gilkey Harbor*	*117*	13	**Beggar's Wharf**	*Rockland Harbor*	*126*
5	**Dark Harbor Boat Yard**	*Gilkey Harbor*	*118*	14	**Journey's End Marina**	*Rockland Harbor*	*127*
6	**Camden Yacht Club**	*Camden Harbor*	*119*	15	**The Landings Marina**	*Rockland Harbor*	*128*
7	**Wayfarer Marine**	*Camden Harbor*	*120*	16	**Rockland Public Landing**	*Rockland Harbor*	*129*
8	**Willey Wharf**	*Camden Harbor*	*121*	17	**Trident Yacht Basin**	*Rockland Harbor*	*130*
9	**Camden Town Dock**	*Camden Harbor*	*122*	18	**Vinalhaven's Carvers Harbor**	*Carvers Harbor*	*131*

RATINGS: 1-5 for Marina Facilities & Amenities,  1-2 for Boatyard Services,  1-2 for MegaYacht Facilities,  for Something Special.

SERVICES: for CCM – Certified Clean Marina,  for Pump-Out,  for Internet, for Fuel,  for Restaurant, for Provisioning nearby, for Catamaran-friendly,  for SportFish Charter,  for Pool/Beach, and for Golf within a mile. *For an explanation of ACC's Ratings, see page 8.*

Billings Diesel and Marine

PO Box 67; Moose Island Road; Stonington, ME 04681

Tel: (207) 367-2328 **VHF: Monitor** Ch. 16 **Talk** Ch. 10
Fax: (207) 367-5925 **Alternate Tel:** n/a
Email: office@billingsmarine.com **Web:** billingsmarine.com
Nearest Town: Stonington *(0.75 mi.)* **Tourist Info:** (207) 348-6124

Navigational Information

Lat: 44°08.902' **Long:** 068°40.736' **Tide:** 10 ft. **Current:** n/a **Chart:** 13313
Rep. Depths (*MLW*): Entry 20 ft. **Fuel Dock** 12 ft. **Max Slip/Moor** 12 ft./12 ft.
Access: Penobscot Bay to Deer Isle Thorofare to Allen Cove

Marina Facilities *(In Season/Off Season)*

Fuel: Gasoline, Diesel
Slips: 25 Total, 15 Transient **Max LOA:** 150 ft. **Max Beam:** 25 ft.
Rate *(per ft.)*: **Day** $2.00* **Week** n/a **Month** n/a
Power: 30 amp Incl., **50 amp** Incl., **100 amp** Incl., **200 amp** Incl.
Cable TV: No **Dockside Phone:** No
Dock Type: Fixed, Floating, Short Fingers, Pilings
Moorings: 20 Total, 10 Transient **Launch:** No, Dinghy Dock
Rate: Day $30 **Week** $150 **Month** n/a
Heads: 2 Toilet(s), 2 Shower(s)
Internet: Yes *(Wi-Fi, Free)* **Laundry:** 1 Washer(s), 1 Dryer(s)
Pump-Out: Full Service, 1 Central **Fee:** $5 **Closed Heads:** Yes

Marina Operations

Owner/Manager: Peter Grindle **Dockmaster:** Same
In-Season: Year-Round, 7am-3:30pm* **Off-Season:** n/a
After-Hours Arrival: Call ahead for instructions
Reservations: Yes, Preferred **Credit Cards:** Visa/MC
Discounts: None
Pets: Welcome, Dog Walk Area **Handicap Access:** No

Marina Services and Boat Supplies

Services - Docking Assistance, Security *(24 Hrs., watchman)*, Dock Carts, 3 Phase **Communication -** Pay Phone (2), FedEx, DHL, UPS, Express Mail **Supplies - OnSite:** Ice *(Block, Cube)*, Ships' Store *(Thousands of items; also New England Marine 367-2692)* **3+ mi:** Propane *(Percy Brown 348-2247, 5.5 mi.)*

Boatyard Services

OnSite: Travelift *(35T)*, Railway *(3 to 275T)*, Forklift, Crane *(2)*, Hydraulic Trailer *(2 Brownell)*, Engine mechanic *(gas, diesel)*, Electrical Repairs *(Blackmore 367-2703)*, Hull Repairs, Rigger, Bottom Cleaning, Brightwork, Air Conditioning, Refrigeration, Compound, Wash & Wax, Propeller Repairs, Woodworking, Metal Fabrication, Painting, Awlgrip, Total Refits **OnCall:** Electronic Sales, Electronics Repairs, Divers **Dealer for:** Westerbeke, Caterpillar, Allison, Cummins, Volvo, Detroit, Z-F, Lugger, Yanmar. **Member:** ABYC **Yard Rates:** $50-80/hr., Haul & Launch $9/ft., Power Wash $2ft., Bottom Paint $55/hr. + paint **Storage:** In-Water $0.35/sq.ft./mo., On-Land Inside $0.85 sq.ft./mo. Outside $0.50/sq.ft./mo.

Restaurants and Accommodations

Under 1 mi: Restaurant *(The Seasons 367-2600)*, *(The Fisherman's Friend 367-2442, L $6-13, D $6-20)*, Lite Fare *(Susie Q's 367-2415)*, *(Harbor Café 367-5099, B $2-5, L $2-10)*, Pizzeria *(Harbor View Store)*, Motel *(Boyce's 367-2421, $50-135)*, Inn/B&B *(Inn on the Harbor 367-2420, $85-225, Free marina pick-up, lovely, panoramic waterfront views, right in town)*, *(Près du Port 367-5007, $85)* **1-3 mi:** Restaurant *(Cockatoo Portuguese 348-2300, L $8-19, D $14-35)*, Lite Fare *(Lily's Café 367-5936, L $6-11)*

Recreation and Entertainment

Near: Boat Rentals *(Old Quarry Kayak & Canoe 367-8977)* **Under 1 mi:** Park *(Acadia Nat'l Park - Isle au Haut Ferry $14/$5)*, Museum *(Deer Isle Granite 367-6331)*, Cultural Attract *(Opera House Arts 367-2788)*, Sightseeing *(Everett Knowlton's miniature village on East Main)*, Galleries *(Six incl. D. Mortenson's)*, Special Events *(Deer Isle Jazz Festival - end of July)* **3+ mi:** Golf Course *(Island C.C. 348-2379 $33-40 18 holes, 10 mi.)*

Provisioning and General Services

OnSite: Lobster Pound *(or Stonington Co-Op 800-315-6625 1.5 mi.)* **Near:** Bank/ATM, Post Office **Under 1 mi:** Convenience Store *(Burnt Cove 367-2681)*, Market *(Harbor View Store)*, Supermarket *(Bartletts 367-2386)*, Wine/Beer *(The Seasons 367-6348)*, Bakery *(Susie Q's 367-2415)*, Fishmonger *(North Atlantic 367-2459)*, Catholic Church, Protestant Church, Library *(Stonington 367-5926)*, Beauty Salon *(Coastal Hair 367-6344)*, Bookstore *(Dockside 367-2652)*, Pharmacy *(Island 367-6333)*, Hardware Store *(V & S Variety 367-5570; NAPA 367-5959)* **1-3 mi:** Farmers' Market *(Fri 10am-Noon Comm. Ctr.)*

Transportation

OnCall: Taxi *(Eddie's Island 367-5503)*, Airport Limo *(Tranportation Matters 348-2674, $95 to Bangor Airport)* **Under 1 mi:** Bikes, Ferry Service *(Isle au Haut 367-5193, $36/19 RT rent a bike on island $25)* **Airport:** Knox County/Bangor *(30/48 mi.)*

Medical Services

911 Service **1-3 mi:** Doctor *(Island Medical Center 367-2311)*, Dentist *(Island Medical Cntr)* **Hospital:** Blue Hill Memorial 374-2836 *(20 mi.)*

Setting -- Billings Diesel is perched on the edge of Moose Island, with spectacular views up Deer Island Thorofare. Landside, the docks are integrated into a very extensive and well-maintained boatyard. It is a comfortable one-mile walk to the bustling village of Stonington, a quintessential Maine village with a strong lobster and fishing economy that welcomes, but does not cater to, tourists.

Marina Notes -- *Mon-Fri 7am-3:30pm, Sat 9am-noon. Marina staffed weekends during season. 11 massive granite block moorings to 50 ft. LOA. 200 V, 3-phase. Travelift to 35 tons, 3 railways (2 under cover) hauls to 275T, up to 150 ft. LOA. Nine storage sheds, plus yard service sheds, incl. full woodworking. Services both recreational & commercial vessels (slightly higher rates for pleasure craft). Harlan Billings 24/7 towing $125/hr 367-6559. Extensive parts inventory; well-stocked ships' store. Bathhouse: Rustic full baths, fiberglass stalls, rubber flooring. Cranky washer/dryer.

Notable -- Restaurants, charming B&Bs, galleries, provisioning sources and a museum are a one-mile walk into the village. Or dinghy to the public town dock on the starboard side below the blue building near Fisherman's Friend and the lobsterman statue. Wild and beautiful Isle au Haut, in Acadia National Park, is a 14 mi./45 min. ferry ride from Atlantic Ave Hardware Dock. The ferries go to the town of Isle au Haut and to Duck Harbor, which is in the park (5 RTs a day). Or take your "big boat" to Duck Harbor. Home to "Lobster Chronicle" author Linda Greenlaw, the island boasts 500 ft. hills, densely forested shores, and pebble beaches. No services; the only places to stay are five lean-to's or The Keeper's House, a truly unique, off-the-grid experience (367-2261) $294-335 AP.

PHOTOS ON DVD: 25

Navigational Information
Lat: 44°07.638' **Long:** 068°52.333' **Tide:** 10 ft. **Current:** n/a **Chart:** 13305
Rep. Depths (*MLW*): Entry 15 ft. **Fuel Dock** 6 ft. **Max Slip/Moor** -/30 ft.
Access: Penobscot Bay to Fox Islands Thorofare

Marina Facilities *(In Season/Off Season)*
Fuel: *E10 Gasohol - 10% ethanol* - Gasoline, Diesel
Slips: 0 Total, 0 Transient **Max LOA:** 42 ft. **Max Beam:** n/a
Rate *(per ft.)*: **Day** $0 **Week** n/a **Month** n/a
Power: 30 amp n/a, **50 amp** n/a, **100 amp** n/a, **200 amp** n/a
Cable TV: No **Dockside Phone:** No
Dock Type: Fixed, Short Fingers, Alongside, Concrete
Moorings: 12 Total, 12 Transient **Launch:** Maybe ($3pp), Dinghy Dock
Rate: Day $20 **Week** $100 **Month** Inq.
Heads: 1 Toilet(s), 2 Shower(s)
Internet: No **Laundry:** 2 Washer(s), 2 Dryer(s)
Pump-Out: No **Fee:** n/a **Closed Heads:** Yes

Marina Operations
Owner/Manager: Foy W. Brown **Dockmaster:** Same
In-Season: May-Sep, 7am-5pm* **Off-Season:** Oct-Apr, Closed
After-Hours Arrival: Call ahead; pick up mooring and check-in in the am
Reservations: First come, first served. Be early **Credit Cards:** Visa/MC
Discounts: None
Pets: Welcome **Handicap Access:** No

J.O. Brown & Sons

PO Box 525; 1 Boatyard Rd.; North Haven, ME 04853

Tel: (207) 867-4621 **VHF: Monitor** Ch. 16 **Talk** Ch. 9
Fax: (207) 867-4757 **Alternate Tel:** (207) 867-2282
Email: jobrown@midcoast.com **Web:** n/a
Nearest Town: Rockland *(10 mi.)* **Tourist Info:** (207) 276-5040

Marina Services and Boat Supplies
Communication - Pay Phone, FedEx, UPS, Express Mail **Supplies - OnSite:** Ice *(Block)*, Ships' Store **Near:** Ice *(Cube)*

Boatyard Services
OnSite: Travelift *(30T)*, Engine mechanic *(gas, diesel)*, Hull Repairs, Divers, Bottom Cleaning **OnCall:** Electronics Repairs *(Phil Des Lauriers 867-2227)* **Yard Rates:** Inq.

Restaurants and Accommodations
OnSite: Restaurant *(Brown's Coal Wharf Restaurant 867-4739, L $7-12, D $15-25, 6 days during summer, 6pm-9pm, Cash only)* **Near:** Restaurant *(Nebo Lodge 867-2007, D $16-23)*, *(Coopers Landing 867-2060, L & D $4-16 open daily July & Aug 11am-9pm)*, Snack Bar *(Waterman's Community Center 6:30am-4pm Wi-Fi)*, Inn/B&B *(Nebo Lodge 867-2007, $100-250, Opened in '06 by Island women. Simply lovely.)* **Under 1 mi:** Lite Fare *(North Haven Grocery 867-2233)*, Inn/B&B *(Our Place Inn 867-4998, $75-125, 19thC.Inn, cottages & 3-story "lighthouse")*

Recreation and Entertainment
OnSite: Sightseeing *(The parade of sailboats cruisng along Fox Islands Thorofare)* **Near:** Jogging Paths, Hike/Bike Trails *(27 miles of roads)*, Movie Theater *(Waterman's Community Center 867-2100 Fri nights)*, Cultural Attract *(Waterman's Community Center - 134-seat state-of-the-art theater, concerts, art exhibits, theater/dance productions, presentations, films, summer camps, workshops)*, Galleries *(Eric Hopkins 867-2229, North Haven 867-4444, Calderwood Hall 867-2265, Carrier Ceramics 867-4410)* **Under 1 mi:** Golf Course *(North Haven Golf 867-2054)*, Museum *(North Haven Historical Society 867-4752 Tue-Thu 1:30-4pm)*

Provisioning and General Services
OnSite: Lobster Pound *(also Bubba Gumps 542-5484)*, Laundry, Hardware Store **OnCall:** Supermarket *(Shaw's Supermarket in Rockland - 594-8615 via Penobscot Island Air 596-7500. They offer pack-up & delivery service. Fee depends on order size)*, Oysterman *(Adam Campbell 867-4453 N.H. Oysters)*, Pharmacy *(Rite Aid in Rockland 596-0036 Phone orders)* **Near:** Provisioning Service *(H. J. Blakes 867-2060 call ahead & order will be waiting for you.)*, Wine/Beer, Farmers' Market *(Sat 9-11am, Ballfield)*, Post Office, Catholic Church, Protestant Church *(Episcopal & Baptist services)*, Library *(North Haven 867-9797 Mon-Sat noon-4pm)*, Retail Shops *(Calderwood Crafts, North Island Fiber, WindWillow Gifts)* **Under 1 mi:** Market *(North Haven Grocery 867-2233)*

Transportation
OnSite: Water Taxi *(Shuttle across harbor to Vinalhaven $3/pp 1-way, $5 RT)* **Near:** Bikes *(Nebo Lodge 867-2007; Our Place 867-4998)*, Ferry Service *(to Rockland 596-2202/867-4441, $26 per car, $9 per person)* **Airport:** North Haven/Knox County/Bangor - Penobscot Island Air 596-7500 Scheduled flights to Rockland $55/pp + charter *(2 mi./15 mi./45 mi.)*

Medical Services
911 Service **OnCall:** Doctor *(North Haven Clinic 867-2021 Mon-Fri, 8am-1pm)*, Holistic Services, Ambulance **Hospital:** Penobscot Bay Medical Center 596-8000 *(16 mi. via ferry)*

Setting -- Located in beautiful North Haven village, just east of the ferry dock, this down-home, classic boatyard promises a bit of iconic "old Maine." Just east of the ferry landing, an aging reddish brown clapboard boat shed sporting a large white "J.O. Brown & Son" sign, sits on granite pilings at the head of two rustic docks flanking a travelift bay. Miscellaneous equipment and assorted buildings cluster around the wharf. The picture postcard harbor is abuzz with activity.

Marina Notes -- *Closed Sun. Moorings east of ferry dock "JOB" or "X." July & Aug grab one before 4pm. Gas, diesel, town water. Founded in 1888, when James Osman Brown built 4 North Haven dinghies. 5th generation Browns at the helm. Most BY services - including wooden boating building using band saw installed in 1900. Incredible array of parts & supplies. Additional dinghy dock at Town Landing. Bathhouse: in former store. Rustic showers & heads on 1st floor - locked, need key. Laundry in basement ($5). Closed when BY closed. Note: Moorings possible from private North Haven Casino Y.C. ("NHC") 867-4497.

Notable -- In the 1880s, the island was discovered by Bostonians - and later New Yorkers - looking for a simpler summer lifestyle that included good dinghy racing. Collaborating with William Weld, J.O. Brown added a gaff-rig to an earlier design, birthing the North Haven, the oldest continually raced class in the US. Waterman's Community Center, down the street, competes with Brown's as action central for island life - a gallery, coffee shop, theater and community room with an active year-round schedule of events for the whole family - Friday night movies, summer theater, concerts, lectures, workshops, exhibits and more. Stroll the village, including Eric Hopkin's Gallery or out toward Southern Harbor. Or dinghy across to Perry Creek.

PHOTOS ON DVD: 25

Thayers Y-Knot Boatyard

Thayers Y-Knot Boatyard

668a Main Street; North Haven, ME 04853

Tel: (207) 867-4701 **VHF: Monitor** Ch. 16 **Talk** Ch. 77
Fax: (207) 867-4702 **Alternate Tel:** n/a
Email: thayeryknot@ad.com **Web:** n/a
Nearest Town: North Haven *(0.75 mi.)* **Tourist Info:** (207) 276-5040

Navigational Information
Lat: 44°07.944' **Long:** 068°53.475' **Tide:** 10 ft. **Current:** 2 kt. **Chart:** 13305
Rep. Depths (*MLW*): Entry 14 ft. **Fuel Dock** n/a **Max Slip/Moor** -/12 ft.
Access: Browns Head Light, Sugarloaves, Fox Ear spindle to ctr of harbor

Marina Facilities *(In Season/Off Season)*
Fuel: No
Slips: 0 Total, 0 Transient **Max LOA:** 50 ft. **Max Beam:** 16 ft.
Rate *(per ft.)*: **Day** n/a **Week** n/a **Month** n/a
Power: 30 amp n/a, **50 amp** n/a, **100 amp** n/a, **200 amp** n/a
Cable TV: No **Dockside Phone:** No
Dock Type: Floating, Wood
Moorings: 30 Total, 2 Transient **Launch:** No, Dinghy Dock
Rate: Day $25 **Week** Inq. **Month** Inq.
Heads: 1 Toilet(s), 1 Shower(s)
Internet: No **Laundry:** None
Pump-Out: No **Fee:** n/a **Closed Heads:** No

Marina Operations
Owner/Manager: Collette Marves Haskell **Dockmaster:** Same
In-Season: May-Sep, 7am-5pm **Off-Season:** Oct-Apr, 7am-3:30pm
After-Hours Arrival: Call in advance
Reservations: Yes, Preferred **Credit Cards:** Visa/MC
Discounts: None
Pets: Welcome **Handicap Access:** No

Marina Services and Boat Supplies
Communication - FedEx, UPS **Supplies - OnSite:** Ships' Store **Near:** Ice *(Block, Cube)* **Under 1 mi:** Propane *(Rex Crockett 867-2215)*

Boatyard Services
OnSite: Travelift *(50T)*, Railway, Crane *(20T)*, Launching Ramp, Engine mechanic *(gas, diesel)*, Electrical Repairs, Electronic Sales, Electronics Repairs, Hull Repairs, Rigger, Bottom Cleaning, Brightwork, Air Conditioning, Compound, Wash & Wax, Interior Cleaning, Woodworking, Inflatable Repairs, Metal Fabrication, Awlgrip, Total Refits, Yacht Building **OnCall:** Divers **Member:** ABBRA, Other Certifications: Diesel Mechanic, Awlgrip Application **Yard Rates:** $50/hr., Haul & Launch $5/ft., Power Wash $25 **Storage:** On-Land Outside/Inside $5-10/ft./mo.; $35-55/season

Restaurants and Accommodations
Near: Lite Fare *(North Haven Grocery 867-2233)* **Under 1 mi:** Restaurant *(Brown's Coal Wharf 867-4739, L $7-12, D $15-25, Mon-Sat Jul-Aug, 6-9, Fri & Sat 'til ColDay. Cash only)*, *(Coopers Landing 867-2060, L & D $4-16 July & Aug 11am-9pm)*, *(Nebo Lodge 867-2007, D $16-23)*, Snack Bar *(Waterman's Community 6:30am-4pm Wi-Fi)*, Inn/B&B *(Our Place 867-4998, $75-125, 19th C. Farmhouse, cottages, 3-story "lighthouse")*, *(Nebo Lodge 867-2007, $100-250, Local & green - contruction, furnishings, art, food)*

Recreation and Entertainment
Near: Jogging Paths, Hike/Bike Trails, Museum *(North Haven Historical Society 867-4752 Tue-Thu 1:30-4pm)* **Under 1 mi:** Playground, Golf Course *(North Haven 867-2054)*, Movie Theater *(Waterman's Community Center 867-2100 Fri nights)*, Cultural Attract *(Waterman's Comm. Center - 134-seat theater, concerts, art exhibits, theater/dance productions, presentations, films, summer camps, workshops)*, Galleries *(Eric Hopkins 867-2229, North Haven 867-4444, Calderwood Hall 867-2265, Carrier Ceramics 867-4410)*

Provisioning and General Services
OnCall: Supermarket *(Shaw's Supermarket in Rockland - 594-8615 via Penobscot Island Air 596-7500.)*, Oysterman *(Adam Campbell 867-4453 N.H. Oysters)*, Pharmacy *(Rockland Rite Aid 596-0036)* **Near:** Market *(North Haven Grocery 867-2233)* **Under 1 mi:** Provisioning Service *(Coopers Landing 867-2060 call ahead & order will be waiting for you.)*, Wine/Beer, Farmers' Market *(Sat 9-11am, Ballfield)*, Lobster Pound *(J.O. Brown 867-4621; Bubba Gumps 542-5484)*, Post Office, Catholic Church, Protestant Church *(Episcopal & Baptist)*, Library *(North Haven 867-9797 Mon-Sat noon-4pm)*, Laundry *(Brown's)*, Hardware Store *(Brown's)*, Retail Shops *(Calderwood Crafts, North Island Fiber, WindWillow Gifts)*

Transportation
Under 1 mi: Bikes *(Nebo Lodge 867-2007; Our Place 867-4998)*, Water Taxi *(Brown's Shuttle across harbor to Vinalhaven $3/pp 1-way, $5 RT)*, Ferry Service *(to Rockland 596-2202/867-4441, $26 per car, $9/pp)* **Airport:** North Haven/Knox County/Bangor - Penobscot Island Air 596-7500 Scheduled flights to Rockland $55/pp + charter *(2 mi./15 mi./45 mi.)*

Medical Services
911 Service **OnCall:** Ambulance **Under 1 mi:** Doctor *(North Haven Clinic 867-2021 Mon-Fri, 8am-1pm)* **Hospital:** Penobscot Bay Medical Center 596-8000 *(16 mi. via ferry)*

Setting -- In Southern Harbor, at the head of the red and green-staked channel, Thayer's float and travel lift bay lead to an expansive ship-shape boatyard. A small barn-red dockhouse and a grassy plot with a picnic table overlook the quiet, serene harbor. Further up the rutted dirt road, small out buildings, two open boat storage sheds and an enomous gray work building are interspersed with on-the-hard storage areas. The village center is a three-quarter mile walk.

Marina Notes -- Family owned and operated since the early '70s. Moorings in Southern Harbor (also Pulpit Harbor and the Thorofare). Channel to dock with water & power - dredged to 3.5 ft mlw. Extensive services for the boat; few amenities for the boater. Specializes in high quality repairs & restorations - fiberglass, repowering, awlgripping, electronic installations. Fuel at J.O. Brown (can arrange 5 gals delivered). Bathhouse: Newly renovated full bath. In paint shop, top of stairs, back of offices. Note: Head straight into the center of harbor - but not one hour before or after low tide.

Notable -- A quieter, more protected alternative to the Thorofare, Southern Harbor boasts some exquisite views - memorialized in many of Eric Hopkins' paintings (his gallery is in the village). Nearby are North Haven Grocery and coffee shop, the Historical Society's museum (docented by octagenarian Lewis Haskell) and the smallest K-12 community school in New England. The village is an easy, very pretty walk. Stop by the amazing Waterman's Community Center - something's happening almost every day in summer - or just for a cup of tea. Peruse the galleries. Book a special dinner at beautiful, historic 1912 Nebo Lodge - restored by a group of island women, now owned/managed with great aplomb by Maine's Congresswoman Chellie Pingree and her friends and family.

PHOTOS ON DVD: 21

Navigational Information
Lat: 44°16.395' **Long:** 068°56.627' **Tide:** 10 ft. **Current:** n/a **Chart:** 13305
Rep. Depths (*MLW*): Entry 14 ft. **Fuel Dock** n/a **Max Slip/Moor** -/15 ft.
Access: Gilkey Harbor, Due north 700 Acre Is., next to Spruce Is.

Marina Facilities *(In Season/Off Season)*
Fuel: No
Slips: 0 Total, 0 Transient **Max LOA:** n/a **Max Beam:** n/a
Rate *(per ft.)*: **Day** $0 **Week** n/a **Month** n/a
Power: 30 amp n/a, **50 amp** n/a, **100 amp** n/a, **200 amp** n/a
Cable TV: No **Dockside Phone:** No
Dock Type: Floating, Wood
Moorings: 10 Total, 10 Transient **Launch:** No, Dinghy Dock
Rate: Day $10-20** **Week** n/a **Month** n/a
Heads: 7 Toilet(s)
Internet: No **Laundry:** None
Pump-Out: No **Fee:** n/a **Closed Heads:** Yes

Marina Operations
Owner/Manager: Charlene (Sunshine) Hood **Dockmaster:** Rangers
In-Season: MemDay-Sep15, Dwn-Dsk **Off-Season:** Sep16-MemDay, Clsd
After-Hours Arrival: Not an option
Reservations: Yes, preferred **Credit Cards:** Visa/MC
Discounts: None
Pets: Welcome **Handicap Access:** No

Warren Island State Park

PO Box 105; Lincolnville*, ME 04849

Tel: (207) 941-4014 **VHF: Monitor** n/a **Talk** n/a
Fax: (207) 941-4222 **Alternate Tel:** n/a
Email: charlene_hood@maine.gov **Web:** state.me.us/doc/parks
Nearest Town: Lincolnville *(3 mi.)* **Tourist Info:** (207) 236-4404

Marina Services and Boat Supplies
Services - Dock Carts **Supplies - Under 1 mi:** Ice *(Block, Cube)*, Ships' Store *(Dark Harbor Boat Yard 734-2246)*

Boatyard Services
Near: Launching Ramp *(On Islesboro - half mile)*. **Nearest Yard:** Dark Harbor Boat Yard (207) 734-2246

Restaurants and Accommodations
1-3 mi: Lite Fare *(The Landing 734-0975, by dinghy "gourmet trailer" at the Grindle Pt. Ferry Landing, Tue-Sat 7am-7pm, Sun 8am-2pm)*, *(Dark Harbor Shop 734-8878, by dinghy B & L 8am-7pm - Deli, ice cream, sundries)*, Inn/B&B *(Aunt Laura's 734-8245, $80, 1855 Cape. No meals. Two 2-bed, 2 bath units - Main House or B&B area - also available weekly $700-800/wk.)*

Recreation and Entertainment
OnSite: Beach *(on Cradle Cove and West Penobscot Bay sides)*, Picnic Area *(3 individual areas & 1 large group)*, Grills, Jogging Paths **Near:** Museum *(Dinghy to Grindle Pt. Islesboro Historical Society 734-6733 Sun-Thu, 12:30-4:30pm; Grindle Pt. Lighthouse & Sailor's Memorial Museum at the Ferry Landing 734-2253 Tue-Sun 9am-4:30pm)*, Tours *(Dinghy tour of the Dark Harbor "cottages" on Islesboro)*, Sightseeing *(Dinghy - Gibson's 1926 miniature Norman castle on 700 Acre Is.'s eastern tip. Built for his grandchildren; not open to public but visible from water)* **Under 1 mi:** Tennis Courts *(Tarrantine Tennis Club 734-2241, by dinghy)*, Golf Course *(Tarrantine Golf Club 734-6970, by dinghy)*

Provisioning and General Services
Near: Library *(Alice L. Pendleton Memorial 734-2218 Mon & Wed 10am-Noon, 1:30-4pm - Mini-library at ferry landing - by dinghy)* **1-3 mi:** Convenience Store *(Island Market 734-6672 - famous baked goods, desserts, party platters, picnics, etc. Dinghy to Islesboro - then hike)*, Market *(Durkee's General Store 734-2201 full grocery inventory, plus take-out. Dinghy to Islesboro then hike.)*, Catholic Church *(by dinghy)*, Protestant Church *(by dinghy)*, Bookstore

Transportation
OnCall: Water Taxi *(Tom Daley, Quicksilver 734-8379)*, Rental Car *(Enterprise 800-325-8007 to Lincolnville Beach on mainland)*, Airport Limo *(From Lincolnville mainland Schooner Bay Limo & Taxi 594-5000)* **Near:** Ferry Service *("Margaret Chase Smith" from Grindle Point to Lincolnville Beach $10/pp RT - 9 RTs daily)* **Airport:** Bangor Int'l. - from Lincolnville Beach *(35 mi.)*

Medical Services
No 911 Service **1-3 mi:** Doctor *(Islesboro Health Center 734-2213)*
Hospital: Waldo County 930-2525 - via ferry or water taxi *(9 mi.)*

Setting -- Opposite Grindle Point, beautiful, spruce-covered 70-acre Warren Island State Park features a stationary pier, gangway and float surrounded by nine guest moorings. Onshore are three campsites, two with shelters and fireplaces, large-group areas with seasonal tented picnic areas and individual picnic sites - needle-carpeted trails cut through the woods opening onto sun-dappled clearings. The helpful ranger/manager lives in a small brown cottage.

Marina Notes -- *Phone & fax are Northern Region Bureau of Parks & Lands; 106 Hogan Rd; Bangor, ME 04401. Address for Park's mainland post office box. **Mooring donation requested - usual $10-20. Boat-access only. 12 tenting campsites (8 reservable), 3 Adirondack-style lean-to's plus 3 individual picnic areas. Summer weekend sites reserved soon after Feb. 1 opening. Large group event area used by Y.C. cruises & schooner lobster bakes. Knowledgeable, creative manager Sunshine Hood makes it all work. Bathhouse: 7 compost toilets.

Notable -- Warren Island's earliest recorded dwelling was pre-Revolution. During the 19th century, a half-dozen families lived here - a house foundation is at Picnic Site #1. Then in 1899, William Folwell bought the island and built a $75,000, 15,000-sq. ft, 22-room log cabin with unpeeled spruce logs from the island. In 1919, the house burned to the ground and the property eventually reverted to Islesboro. It was dedicated as a state park in 1967 - the first with boater-only access. Isolated, peaceful and pristine, it offers opportunities for birding, nature photography, fishing, swimming. It's a half-mile dinghy ride to Islesboro's public landing or to the Grindle Pt. ferry dock. In Ames Cove, Tarrantine Yacht Club's docks and dining room may be open to members of reciprocal Y.C.s (734-2281).

Dark Harbor Boat Yard

Main Rd., 700 Acre Island*; Islesboro, ME 04848

Tel: (207) 734-2246 **VHF: Monitor** Ch. 9 **Talk** Ch. 11
Fax: (207) 734-8331 **Alternate Tel:** n/a
Email: info@darkharborboatyard.com **Web:** www.darkharborboatyard.com
Nearest Town: Lincolnville *(3 mi.)* **Tourist Info:** (207) 223-5449

Navigational Information
Lat: 44°15.526' **Long:** 068°56.337' **Tide:** 11 ft. **Current:** n/a **Chart:** 13305
Rep. Depths (*MLW*): Entry 14 ft. **Fuel Dock** 6 ft. **Max Slip/Moor** -/14 ft.
Access: Penobscot Bay to Islesboro to Gilkey Harbor/Cradle Cove

Marina Facilities *(In Season/Off Season)*
Fuel: Gasoline, Diesel
Slips: 0 Total, 0 Transient **Max LOA:** 70 ft. **Max Beam:** n/a
Rate *(per ft.)*: **Day** n/a **Week** n/a **Month** n/a
Power: 30 amp n/a, **50 amp** n/a, **100 amp** n/a, **200 amp** n/a
Cable TV: No **Dockside Phone:** No
Dock Type: Floating, Alongside, Wood
Moorings: 20 Total, 20 Transient **Launch:** None, Dinghy Dock
Rate: Day $25 **Week** Inq. **Month** Inq.
Heads: 1 Toilet(s), 2 Shower(s)
Internet: No **Laundry:** 1 Washer(s), 1 Dryer(s)
Pump-Out: No **Fee:** n/a **Closed Heads:** Yes

Marina Operations
Owner/Manager: John Gorham **Dockmaster:** Same
In-Season: Jul-Aug, 7am-5pm* **Off-Season:** Sep-Jun, 7am-5pm*
After-Hours Arrival: Call ahead
Reservations: Yes, Preferred **Credit Cards:** Visa/MC, Dscvr
Discounts: None
Pets: Welcome **Handicap Access:** No

Marina Services and Boat Supplies
Supplies - OnSite: Ice *(Block, Cube)*, Ships' Store

Boatyard Services
OnSite: Railway *(40T)*, Crane, Hydraulic Trailer, Engine mechanic *(gas, diesel)*, Electrical Repairs, Electronics Repairs, Rigger, Bottom Cleaning, Brightwork, Compound, Wash & Wax, Interior Cleaning, Woodworking, Painting **OnCall:** Hull Repairs, Canvas Work, Divers, Awlgrip **Member:** ABBRA **Yard Rates:** Inq. **Storage:** On-Land inside only

Restaurants and Accommodations
Under 1 mi: Lite Fare *(The Landing 734-0975, a "gourmet trailer" at the Ferry Landing, Tue-Sat 7am-7pm, Sun 8am-2pm)*, *(Dark Harbor Shop 734-8878, B, L 8am-7pm - Deli, ice cream, sundries)*, Inn/B&B *(Aunt Laura's 734-8245, $80, 1855 Cape. No meals. Two 2-bed, 2 bath units - Main House or B&B area -available as weekly rentals. $700-800/wk.)*

Recreation and Entertainment
Near: Beach *(Pendleton Point)*, Tennis Courts *(Tarrantine Tennis Club 734-2241, dinghy)*, Golf Course *(Tarrantine Golf Club 734-6970, dinghy)*, Jogging Paths *(2-3 miles of private roads on 700 Acre or Warren Islands)*, Hike/Bike Trails *(Isleboro's narrow roads not ideal for biking. But if aboard, the island's flat - take care)*, Sightseeing *(Dinghy tour of the Dark Harbor "cottages" and Gibson's 1926 miniature Norman castle on 700 Acre Is.'s eastern tip. Built for his grandchildren; not open to public but visible from water)*

Under 1 mi: Park *(Warren Island State Park 287-3821)*, Museum *(Islesboro Historical Society 734-6733 Sun-Thu, 12:30-4:30pm; Grindle Pt. Lighthouse & Sailor's Memorial Museum at the Ferry Landing 734-2253 Tue-Sun 9am-4:30pm)*

Provisioning and General Services
1-3 mi: Convenience Store *(Durkee's General Store 734-2201 full grocery inventory, plus take-out - by dinghy)*, Market *(Island Market 734-6672, owned by former owners of Blue Heron Rest. "Shake" & "Loony" Mahan's famous baked goods, desserts, party platters, picnics, etc. - by dinghy)*, Wine/Beer, Liquor Store *(Durkee's)*, Post Office *(by dinghy)*, Catholic Church *(by dinghy)*, Protestant Church *(Sunset at Grndle Pt.)*, Library *(Alice L. Pendleton Memorial 734-2218 Mon & Wed 10am-Noon, 1:30-4pm - Mini-library at ferry landing - by dinghy)*, Beauty Salon

Transportation
OnCall: Water Taxi *(Tom Daley, Quicksilver 734-8379)*, Rental Car *(Enterprise 800-325-8007 to Lincolnville Beach)* **Near:** Airport Limo *(From Lincolnville mainland Schooner Bay Limo & Taxi 594-5000)*, Ferry Service *("Margaret Chase Smith" from Grindle Point to Lincolnville Beach $10/pp RT - 9 RTs daily)* **Airport:** Bangor Int'l. from Lincolnville Beach *(35 mi.)*

Medical Services
911 Service **1-3 mi:** Doctor *(Islesboro Health Center 734-2213)* **Hospital:** Waldo County General 930-2525 - via ferry *(9 mi.)*

Setting -- In Gilkey Harbor's Cradle Cove, just past the eastern tip of 700 Acre Island, Dark Harbor's long granite-block pier, huge white fuel tank and three floats are backed by a cluster of structures and boatsheds. At the top of the first ramp, a small dock house overlooks the mooring field, protected by Warren and Spruce Islands. Onshore, flower boxes decorate a small picnic deck that edges the attractive, shingled ships' store and office. Beyond, it's pure boatyard.

Marina Notes -- *Mailing: Box 25, Lincolnville, ME 04849. **Jul-Aug Mon-Thu 7am-5pm, Fri & Sat 9am-4pm, Sun 9am-4pm. Sep-Jun Mon-Thu 7am-5pm, closed Fri-Sun. Reserve Jul & Aug. Moorings - 500 lb.- 2T granite blocks hold 100 ft.+ vessels. Schooners moor here. Yacht club cruises, too. Fuel dock 6 ft. mlw. No trash disposal. Full-service yard. 40-ton railway to 40-ft. boat. Maintains, stores, repairs islanders' boats including Dark Harbor 20 fleet (races Fri & Sat). Gas, diesel, outboard technician. Well-stocked chandlery. Bathhouse: Side of main building. 24 hrs. Two inviting shower rooms (green w/ French blue trim), fiberglass stalls. Laundry. Note: Pendleton Yacht Yard (734-6728) in Islesboro's Ames Cove 3-5 transient moorings & dinghy landing (dry at mlw).

Notable -- Private, bridgeless 700-acre island, just off 14-mile long Islesboro, was the summer home of Charles Dana Gibson (of Gibson Girl fame). DHBY's property is owned by the Gibson family. Isleboro Island homes three communities. Dark Harbor, developed in the late 19th century as a gilded age resort with opulent shingle-style "cottages," remains a private wealthy summer colony - some 6th generation residents. Pripet, at the other end, is a bustling village of fishers and boatbuilders. In between, Islesboro hosts most of the services. Tarrantine Y.C.'s docks may be open to members of reciprocal clubs (734-2281).

Navigational Information
Lat: 44°12.436' **Long:** 069°03.672' **Tide:** 10 ft. **Current:** n/a **Chart:** 13305
Rep. Depths (*MLW*): Entry 15 ft. **Fuel Dock** n/a **Max Slip/Moor** 8 ft./50 ft.
Access: Past Curtis Island to Camden Inner Harbor, first facility to port

Marina Facilities *(In Season/Off Season)*
Fuel: No
Slips: 4 Total, 4 Transient **Max LOA:** 42 ft. **Max Beam:** n/a
Rate *(per ft.)*: **Day** $1.00* **Week** n/a **Month** n/a
Power: 30 amp n/a, **50 amp** n/a, **100 amp** n/a, **200 amp** n/a
Cable TV: No **Dockside Phone:** No
Dock Type: Floating, Alongside, Wood
Moorings: 4 Total, 4 Transient **Launch:** Yes (Free**), Dinghy Dock
Rate: Day $35 **Week** n/a **Month** n/a
Heads: 2 Toilet(s)
Internet: No **Laundry:** None
Pump-Out: OnCall *(Ch. 16)*, Full Service **Fee:** Free **Closed Heads:** Yes

Marina Operations
Owner/Manager: Elaine Booker **Dockmaster:** Barb Goos
In-Season: Jun-Aug, 8am-8pm **Off-Season:** May, Sep, Oct, 8am-4pm
After-Hours Arrival: Call in Advance
Reservations: Yes **Credit Cards:** Cash & check
Discounts: None
Pets: Welcome **Handicap Access:** No

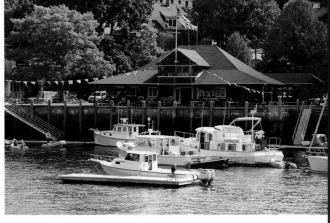

Camden Yacht Club

PO Box 204; 68 Bayview Street; Camden, ME 04843

Tel: (207) 236-3014 **VHF: Monitor** Ch. 68 **Talk** Ch. 68
Fax: n/a **Alternate Tel:** (207) 236-7033
Email: cycdock@midcoast.com **Web:** camdenyachtclub.org
Nearest Town: Camden *(0.3 mi.)* **Tourist Info:** (207) 236-4404

Marina Services and Boat Supplies
Services - Docking Assistance, Boaters' Lounge, Dock Carts **Communication -** FedEx, DHL, UPS, Express Mail *(Sat Del)* **Supplies - OnSite:** Ice *(Block, Cube)* **Near:** Ships' Store *(Wayfarer 236-4378)*, Propane *(P.G.Willey 236-3256)*

Boatyard Services
Nearest Yard: Wayfarer Marine (207) 236-4378

Restaurants and Accommodations
OnSite: Restaurant *(Camden Y.C. Lunch 11:30am-2pm)* **Near:** Restaurant *(Atlantica 236-6011, L $8-14, D $24-29, also lite menu $16-18)*, *(Ephemere & Wine Bar 236-4451, D $18-28, Mon-Sat)*, *(Natalie's 236-7008, D $22-32, Fine Dining)*, *(Francine Bistro 230-0083, D $20-28)*, *(Cappy's Chowder 236-2254, L $7-15, D $10-20, 11am-Mid)*, *(Peter Ott's Steakhouse 236-4032, D $16-22)*, *(The Waterfront 236-3747, L $10-14, D $10-21)*, *(Hartstone Inn 236-4259, D $40, prix fixe. Wed-Sun, 7pm seating, excellent)*, Seafood Shack *(Bay View Lobster 236-2005, L $4-18, D $4-26)*, Snack Bar *(Scott's Place 236-8751, L $2-6)*, Lite Fare *(Camden Deli 236-8343, 6am-10pm great view of falls)*, Hotel *(Camden Harbour Inn 236-4200, $105-255)*, Inn/B&B *(Elms B&B 236-7330, $75-125)*, *(Hartstone Inn $100-190)*, *(Lord Camden 236-4325, $90-210)*, *(The Belmont 236-8053, $85-180)*

Recreation and Entertainment
Near: Beach *(Laite Memorial Park)*, Picnic Area *(Dinghy to Curtis Island)*, Grills, Playground, Tennis Courts, Park *(Laite Memorial)*, Cultural Attract *(Camden Civic Theater 236-2281, Camden Opera House 236-7693)*, Sightseeing *(Camden-Rockport Historical Society's 2.5 mi. tour)*, Special Events *(Schooner Weekend -LabDay)* **Under 1 mi:** Video Rental *(Harbor Video 236-9596)*, Museum *(1780 Old Homestead incl. Conway House/Cramer Museum 236-2257 $5/2 Tue-Fri, 10am-4pm)* **1-3 mi:** Heated Pool *(YMCA 236-3375 $10/5 & Fitness Ctr)*, Fitness Center *(YMCA)* **3+ mi:** Golf Course *(Goose River 236-8488, 4 mi.)*

Provisioning and General Services
OnCall: Provisioning Service *(1st Mate Services at Wayfarer Marine 841-sail)* **Near:** Market *(French & Brawn 236-3611)*, Supermarket *(Hannaford 236-8577)*, Delicatessen *(Camden Deli 236-8343)*, Health Food *(Nature's Choice 236-8280)*, Liquor Store *(Rite Aid)*, Bakery *(Meeting Brook Bookshop & Bakery)*, Farmers' Market *(Wed 3:30-6, Sat 9-noon Knox Mill Pkg Lot)*, Bank/ATM, Post Office, Catholic Church, Protestant Church, Library *(236-3440, Internet)*, Beauty Salon, Barber Shop, Dry Cleaners *(Spotless 236-2530)*, Laundry *(Bishops 236-3339)*, Bookstore *(Owl & Turtle 236-4769; Sherman's 236-2223; Stone Soup 763-3354)*, Pharmacy *(Rite Aid 236-4546)*, Newsstand, Hardware Store *(Rankins 236-3275)*, Florist, Copies Etc. *(Kax Office Services)* **Under 1 mi:** Department Store *(Reny's)*

Transportation
OnCall: Rental Car *(Enterprise 594-9093)*, Taxi *(Joe's 975-3560)*, Airport Limo *(Schooner Bay 594-5000, Mid-Coast 236-2424)* **1-3 mi:** Bikes *(Maine Sport 236-7120 $20/dy)* **Airport:** Rockland/Bangor Int'l. *(12 mi./45 mi.)*

Medical Services
911 Service **Near:** Doctor *(Hope 236-2201)*, Dentist *(Day 236-8891)*, Chiropractor *(Johnstone 236-3416)*, Holistic Services *(Sanctuary 236-3338 Massage $75/60 min.)* **Hospital:** Penobscot Bay 596-8000 *(4 mi.)*

Setting -- At the mouth of Camden's Inner Harbor, historic Camden Yacht Club is the first facility to port. The deep red, John Calvin Stevens Shingle-Style club house - topped by a small-screened dormer - is surrounded on three sides by covered patios and spacious, nicely manicured lawn. The smaller, matching red building houses the dockmaster's office, boaters' lounge and storage sheds. The views are simply spectacular. The dance of the schooners and stunning down-east yachts maneuvering through the bustling Inner Harbor backed by the Camden Hills. Look south to the Outer Harbor mooring field and Pen Bay.

Marina Notes -- *Flat Rate $40 for Side Tie dockage. 42 ft. max LOA for Inner Harbor Float. **Launch: Free to guests on moorings or inner harbor floats. Others $2 one-way or $3RT/pp - 8am-8pm, 3rd wk Jun-Aug, until 6pm shoulder season. Founded 1906. Property donated by Cyrus H.K. Curtis. Clubhouse, on National Register of Historic Places, designed by Maine's most famous architect in 1911. Closed MidOct-MidApr. No power on limited-tie-up docks. Private Y.C. Moorings & floats open to all yachtsmen. Lunch served in clubhouse, guests welcome. Bathhouse: Lovely, recently renovated knotty-pine heads, no showers.

Notable -- This side of the harbor is closer to "downtown." CYC is within easy walking distance of all the delights of Camden, but a little out of the way of the summer tourist crowds with a quieter ambiance. Camden Hills State Park, 3rd largest in the state, is about 2 miles north $2/.50 - with lots of hiking and picnicking possibilities, including a climb to the top of Mt. Battie (1 hr. RT). Camden-Rockport Historical Society publishes a walking/biking map available at the C of C building. Six schooners, from 42 to 123 feet, home berth in Camden Harbor - some offer 2-4 hour harbor cruises and others 2-6 day excursions.

PHOTOS ON DVD: 25

Wayfarer Marine

Wayfarer Marine

59 Sea Street; Camden, ME 04843

Tel: (207) 236-4378 **VHF: Monitor** Ch. 71 **Talk** Ch. 71
Fax: (207) 236-2371 **Alternate Tel:** (207) 236-4378
Email: info@wayfarermarine.com **Web:** wayfarermarine.com
Nearest Town: Camden *(0.5 mi.)* **Tourist Info:** (207) 236-4404

Navigational Information

Lat: 44°12.506' **Long:** 069°03.641' **Tide:** 10 ft. **Current:** n/a **Chart:** 13305
Rep. Depths (*MLW*): Entry 15 ft. **Fuel Dock** 10 ft. **Max Slip/Moor** 12 ft./50 ft.
Access: Penobscot Bay to Camden Harbor

Marina Facilities *(In Season/Off Season)*

Fuel: *Renneco* - Gasoline, Diesel
Slips: 60 Total, 20 Transient **Max LOA:** 150 ft. **Max Beam:** 30 ft.
Rate *(per ft.)*: **Day** $2.75* **Week** n/a **Month** n/a
Power: 30 amp $15, **50 amp** $30, **100 amp** n/a, **200 amp** n/a
Cable TV: No **Dockside Phone:** No
Dock Type: Fixed, Floating, Long Fingers, Alongside, Wood
Moorings: 59 Total, 54 Transient **Launch:** Yes (Free**), Dinghy Dock
Rate: Day $42 **Week** $250 **Month** Inq.
Heads: 5 Toilet(s), 3 Shower(s)
Internet: Yes *(Wi-Fi, Free)* **Laundry:** 3 Washer(s), 3 Dryer(s)
Pump-Out: Full Service, 1 Central **Fee:** Free **Closed Heads:** Yes

Marina Operations

Owner/Manager: Shane Flynn **Dockmaster:** Ben Cashen
In-Season: May-Sept, 7am-5pm **Off-Season:** Sept-Apr, 7am-3:30pm
After-Hours Arrival: Call ahead. Tie up at fuel dock and check in in the am
Reservations: Yes, Recommended **Credit Cards:** Visa/MC
Discounts: None
Pets: Welcome, Dog Walk Area **Handicap Access:** Yes, Heads, Docks

Marina Services and Boat Supplies

Services - Docking Assistance, Concierge, Boaters' Lounge, Trash Pick-Up, Dock Carts **Communication -** Mail & Package Hold, Fax in/out *($2/pp)*, FedEx, UPS, Express Mail *(Sat Del)* **Supplies - OnSite:** Ice *(Block, Cube)*, Ships' Store, CNG **Under 1 mi:** Propane *(Willey 236-3256)*

Boatyard Services

OnSite: Travelift *(110T)*, Crane *(25T)*, Hydraulic Trailer *(80T, 35T)*, Launching Ramp, Engine mechanic *(gas, diesel)*, Electrical Repairs, Electronic Sales, Electronics Repairs, Hull Repairs, Rigger, Canvas Work, Bottom Cleaning, Brightwork, Air Conditioning, Refrigeration, Compound, Wash & Wax, Interior Cleaning, Propeller Repairs, Woodworking, Life Raft Service, Yacht Interiors, Metal Fabrication, Painting, Awlgrip, Total Refits **OnCall:** Divers **Dealer for:** Westerbeke. **Member:** ABBRA, ABYC, Other Certifications: Nautor's Swan, Oyster Yachts **Yard Rates:** $45-75/hr., Haul & Launch $12.50-14.50/ft., Power Wash $2/ft., Bottom Paint $65/hr. **Storage:** On-Land $45/ft. Inside $8-8.75/sq.ft. Heated $13/sq.ft.

Restaurants and Accommodations

OnSite: Lite Fare *(Marina Market 7am-4pm)* **Near:** Inn/B&B *(Hawthorn 236-8842, $150-300)* **Under 1 mi:** Restaurant *(Peter Ott's 236-4032, D $17-29, Tavern $8-18), (Waterfront 236-3747, L $9-21, D $8-26), (Vincent's at Whitehall Inn 236-3891, D $10-28, Fine Dining), (Cappy's 236-2254, L & D $8-23), (Lobster Pound 789-5550, L $4-18, D $13-26)*, Lite Fare *(Camden Deli 236-8343, B $3-7, L & D $6-8)*, Pizzeria *(Camden House 230-2464)*

Recreation and Entertainment

OnSite: Picnic Area, Grills **Near:** Playground, Tennis Courts, Cultural Attract *(Camden Civic Theater 236-2281; Camden Opera 236-7693)* **Under 1 mi:** Video Rental *(Harbor 236-9596)*, Museum *(Conway Homestead 236-2257)* **1-3 mi:** Pool *(YMCA 236-3375 $10/5 & Fitness Ctr)*, Golf Course *(Goose River 236-8488)*

Provisioning and General Services

OnSite: Provisioning Service *(1st Mate Services 841-SAIL)*, Wine/Beer, Laundry *(1st Mate Concierge)* **Near:** Bank/ATM, Library *(Camden 236-3440)* **Under 1 mi:** Convenience Store *(Village Variety 236-2085)*, Market *(French & Brawn 236-3361,)*, Supermarket *(Hannaford 236-8577)*, Gourmet Shop *(Zesty 485-0815)*, Delicatessen *(Camden Deli 236-8343)*, Health Food *(Nature's Choice 236-8280)*, Liquor Store *(Rite Aid 236-4546)*, Bakery, Farmers' Market *(Wed 3:30-6, Sat 9-noon Knox Mill Pkg Lot)*, Post Office, Catholic Church, Protestant Church, Beauty Salon, Dry Cleaners, Bookstore *(Owl & Turtle 236-4769; Sherman's 236-2223)*, Pharmacy *(Rite Aid 236-4546)*, Hardware Store *(Rankins 236-3275)*, Department Store *(Reny's)*

Transportation

OnSite: Courtesy Car/Van, Water Taxi *(Free for Wayfarer guests $5/RT MemDay-LabDay)* **OnCall:** Bikes *(Bikes 'n' Janke 596-1004)*, Rental Car *(National 800-698-8424, USave 236-2320)*, Taxi *(Joe's 975-3560)*, Airport Limo *(Schooner Bay 594-5000, Mid-Coast 236-2424)* **Near:** Local Bus **Airport:** Rockland/Bangor Int'l. *(12 mi./45 mi.)*

Medical Services

911 Service **Near:** Chiropractor *(Johnstone 236-3416)* **Under 1 mi:** Doctor *(Hope 236-2201)*, Dentist *(Day 236-8891)*, Holistic Services *(Sanctuary Spa 236-3338 Massage $75/60 min.)* **Hospital:** Penobscot Bay 596-8000 *(4 mi.)*

Setting -- Wayfarer Marine sprawls along the length of Camden Harbor's north shore. A mammoth blue travelift and small red dockhouse roost above fuel and dinghy floats on the eastern point overlooking the expansive mooring field. On the upland, a string of large white buildings give way to dark red boat sheds near the schooner berths at the harbor head. Sprinkled along the boardwalk, amidst flower-filled planters, swooping bat-wing awnings shelter wooden picnic tables. Side-tie docks float below berthing vessels rafted two or three deep. Every perch offers breathtaking views of the harbor, village and Camden Hills.

Marina Notes -- CCM *Dockage: $4.25/ft. slips. Up to 16 ft. beam $2.75/ft side-tie & rafted; over 16 ft. beam $4/ft. Over 80 ft or 20 ft. beam $6/ft.. Harbor floats: $55/nt. "WMC" #s 1-21 to starboard, #s 30-67 to port. 5 "big boat" moorings to 70 ft. LOAs. 1500 linear ft. dockage & 20 slips. **Launch free to guests, others $5/RT - Mon-Sat 7am-8pm, Sun 8am-8pm. Founded 1963, new owner 2008. Purchased Harbor Head Marina with 39 slips. Major service yard - 9 climate controlled processing bays (including 2 150 ft. x 35 ft.). Inside heated & unheated storage. New 10,000 square foot heated storage building on 8.5 acres. Hauls yachts to 110 tons, drafts to 14 feet. Sweet yard tug "Barbie D." Well-stocked ships' store Mon-Fri 7am-3:30pm. Useful courtesy car. Pleasant Boaters' lounge with coffee, TV, Wi-Fi Hot Spot, tables & chairs. Bathhouse: Inviting tiled heads with glass-door showers.

Notable -- Over the past 200 years, there have been seven boatyards on this "quiet side" of the harbor; Wayfarer is steeped in Camden history. The launch offers easy access to the picturesque town's extensive services and amenities. Alternatively, dinghy to the Town Landing or walk the half mile around the head.

PHOTOS ON DVD: 25

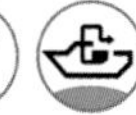

Navigational Information

Lat: 44°12.516' **Long:** 069°03.783' **Tide:** 9 ft. **Current:** n/a **Chart:** 13305
Rep. Depths (*MLW*): Entry 15 ft. **Fuel Dock** 10 ft. **Max Slip/Moor** 10 ft./72 ft.
Access: Camden Outer Harbor to west side of Inner harbor

Marina Facilities *(In Season/Off Season)*

Fuel: Slip-Side Fueling, Gasoline, Diesel
Slips: 6 Total, 6 Transient **Max LOA:** 80 ft. **Max Beam:** 24 ft.
Rate *(per ft.)*: **Day** $4.00* **Week** n/a **Month** n/a
Power: 30 amp $15, **50 amp** $30, **100 amp** $50, **200 amp** n/a
Cable TV: No **Dockside Phone:** No
Dock Type: Floating, Alongside
Moorings: 9 Total, 9 Transient **Launch:** No, Dinghy Dock
Rate: Day $30-50 **Week** n/a **Month** n/a
Heads: 1 Toilet(s), 1 Shower(s)
Internet: No **Laundry:** None
Pump-Out: OnCall, Full Service, 1 Port **Fee:** Free **Closed Heads:** Yes

Marina Operations

Owner/Manager: Wight Family **Dockmaster:** Same
In-Season: May-Sep, 7am-5pm **Off-Season:** Oct-Apr, 7am-5pm
After-Hours Arrival: Call in advance
Reservations: Yes, Preferred **Credit Cards:** Visa/MC, Dscvr
Discounts: None
Pets: Welcome **Handicap Access:** No

Willey Wharf

PO Box 24; 24 Bay View Street; Camden, ME 04840

Tel: (207) 236-3256 **VHF: Monitor** n/a **Talk** n/a
Fax: n/a **Alternate Tel:** (207) 236-7316
Email: n/a **Web:** n/a
Nearest Town: Camden **Tourist Info:** (207) 236-4404

Marina Services and Boat Supplies

Services - Docking Assistance, Trash Pick-Up **Communication -** Mail & Package Hold, Phone Messages, FedEx, UPS, Express Mail **Supplies - OnSite:** Propane **Near:** Ice *(Cube)*, Ships' Store *(Wayfarer Marine 236-4378)* **3+ mi:** Marine Discount Store *(Hamilton Marine, Searsport 548-6302, Rockland 594-8181, 8 mi.)*

Boatyard Services

OnCall: Divers, Bottom Cleaning **Nearest Yard:** Wayfarer Marine (207) 236-4378

Restaurants and Accommodations

Near: Restaurant *(Cuzzy's 236-3272)*, *(Bayview Lobster 236-2005, L $4-18, D $4-26)*, *(Waterfront 236-3747, L $7-14, D $10-22)*, *(Francine Bistro 230-0083, D $20-28)*, *(Ephemere 236-4451, D $18-27)*, *(Natalie's 236-7008, D $22-32, French & No. Italian, fine dining)*, *(Atlantica 236-6011, L $8-14, D $24-29)*, *(Cedar Crest 236-7722, B, L, D)*, Lite Fare *(Boynton-McKay 236-2465)*, *(McMahon's Knox Grill 236-4431, To Go - Lunches-Dinners for 4 $17-40)*, Inn/B&B *(Camden Harbor Inn 236-4200, $105-255)*, *(Lord Camden 236-4325, $90-220)*, *(Windward House 236-9656, $100-280)*, *(Camden River 236-0500, $160-210)*

Recreation and Entertainment

Near: Beach *(Laite Memorial Park)*, Picnic Area, Grills, Playground, Tennis Courts, Boat Rentals *(Maine Sport Outfitters Kayak tours 236-8797 - 2hr harbor $35, 4 hr. $75)*, Video Rental *(Harbor 236-9596)*, Park *(Camden Harbor at Megunticook River)*, Tours *(Windjammer 2-hr. Trips- Appledore 236-8353, Olad 236-2323, Surprise 236-4687, Lazy Jack 230-0602)*, Cultural Attract *(Camden Civic Theater 236-2281, Camden Opera House 236-3353)*, Galleries **Under 1 mi:** Heated Pool *(YMCA 236-3375 $10/5 day pass)*, Fitness Center, Museum *(1780 Old Homestead incl. Conway House/Cramer Museum 236-2257 $5/4 Mon-Thu, 10am-4pm)* **3+ mi:** Golf Course *(Goose River 236-8488, 4 mi.)*

Provisioning and General Services

Near: Market *(French & Brawn 236-3361)*, Delicatessen *(Camden Deli 236-8343)*, Health Food, Wine/Beer, Liquor Store *(Rite Aid)*, Bakery *(Cappy's; Meetingbrook 236-6808)*, Farmers' Market *(Wed 3:30-6, Sat 9-noon Knox Mill Pkg Lot)*, Bank/ATM, Post Office, Catholic Church, Protestant Church, Library *(236-3440, Internet service)*, Beauty Salon, Laundry *(Clean Bee 236-2530)*, Bookstore *(Owl & Turtle 236-4769 - marine section; Sherman's 236-2223; Stone Soup 763-3354)*, Pharmacy *(Rite Aid 236-4546)* **Under 1 mi:** Supermarket *(Hannaford 236-8577)*, Hardware Store *(Rankins 236-3275)*, Department Store *(Reny's)*

Transportation

OnCall: Bikes *(Ragged Mountain 236-6664)*, Rental Car *(Enterprise 594-9093, USave 236-2320)*, Taxi *(Joe's 975-3560)*, Airport Limo *(Schooner Bay 594-5000, Mid-Coast 236-2424)*, InterCity Bus *(Concord - Bangor-Boston)* **Airport:** Rockland/Bangor Int'l. *(12 mi./45 mi.)*

Medical Services

911 Service **Near:** Doctor *(Hope 236-2201)*, Dentist *(Day 236-8891)*, Chiropractor *(Johnstone 236-3416)*, Holistic Services *(Sanctuary 236-3338 Massage $75/60 min.; Stimson, massage therapist 691-5191)*, Optician *(Lary 236-3429)* **Hospital:** Penobscot Bay 596-8000 *(4 mi.)*

Setting -- Between Camden Yacht Club and Camden Town Dock, Willey Wharf's dockage looks out over one of the prettiest harbors on the East Coast. Views are the schooner docks backed by the Camden Hills or across the mooring field to the Outer Harbor. Sturdy gangways lead from recent, high-quality floats to the large stationary wharf with power posts, tanks, and gas and diesel pumps. It's a short walk to this charming town's tourist center.

Marina Notes -- *Offers floating slips & side-tie docks with rub rails to 80 ft LOA yachts. Power to 200A, Single Phase, three & four prong. Plus 9 moorings in Outer Harbor - 1 to 100 ft. LOA, 8 to 40 ft. LOA and Inner Harbor floating dock just off fixed dock. No launch. Dinghy dock at foot of fixed dock (Wayfarer's water taxi $2 1-way, $3 RT). Primarily a fuel oil, wholesale gasoline & diesel, and propane company - in business since 1899 starting with coal and wood. (Pronounced "Willie") Office at head of docks - no services once office closes. Bathhouse: 1 basic head with shower.

Notable -- Elegant, lovely Camden is a smorgasboard of quintessential Maine experiences. Five spectacular schooners make their home here, offering two-hour to six-day trips; when in port, they're an integral part of the scenery. Walk the streets and alley ways, past the impeccably restored Victorian Opera House, Olmstead-designed Camden Harbor Park and Fletcher Steel's 1929 Amphitheater to the 1927 library above. Camden-Rockport Historical Society publishes a walking/biking tour map of historic sites. Or bike to Beauchamp Point, past Aldemere Farm's oreo-cookie-belted Galloway cows, to Calderwood Lane to Vesper Hill Children's Chapel. Or climb to the top of Mt. Battie; sit on the rock where Camden-native Edna St. Vincent Millay found much of her inspiration.

PHOTOS ON DVD: 25

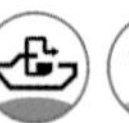

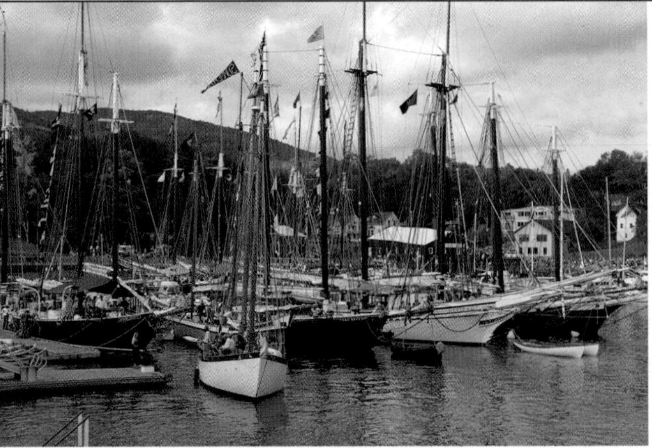

Camden Town Dock

PO Box 1207; Elm Street; Camden, ME 04843

Tel: (207) 236-7969 **VHF: Monitor** Ch. 16 **Talk** Ch. 11
Fax: n/a **Alternate Tel:** n/a
Email: n/a **Web:** n/a
Nearest Town: Camden **Tourist Info:** (207) 236-4404

Navigational Information
Lat: 44°12.549' **Long:** 069°03.792' **Tide:** 10 ft. **Current:** n/a **Chart:** 13305
Rep. Depths (*MLW*): Entry 15 ft. **Fuel Dock** n/a **Max Slip/Moor** 10 ft./-
Access: Penobscot Bay, past Curtis Island to Camden Harbor

Marina Facilities *(In Season/Off Season)*
Fuel: Gasoline, Diesel
Slips: 10 Total, 10 Transient **Max LOA:** 120 ft. **Max Beam:** 40 ft.
Rate *(per ft.)*: **Day** $2.00/Inq.* **Week** Inq. **Month** Inq.
Power: 30 amp $10, **50 amp** $15, **100 amp** $30, **200 amp** n/a
Cable TV: No **Dockside Phone:** No
Dock Type: Floating, Short Fingers, Alongside, Wood
Moorings: 0 Total, 0 Transient **Launch:** Yes, Ch.71 ($5/RT), Dinghy Dock
Rate: Day n/a **Week** n/a **Month** n/a
Heads: 5 Toilet(s)
Internet: No **Laundry:** None
Pump-Out: OnCall *(Ch. 15)*, Full Service **Fee:** Free **Closed Heads:** Yes

Marina Operations
Owner/Manager: Steve Pixley (Hrbmstr) **Dockmaster:** Scott Entwistle
In-Season: Jun 15-Oct 15, 7am-7pm **Off-Season:** Oct 16-Jun 14, 8am-3pm
After-Hours Arrival: Call (207) 236-7969 for instructions
Reservations: Yes, Preferred **Credit Cards:** Cash and check
Discounts: None
Pets: Welcome, Dog Walk Area **Handicap Access:** Yes, Heads

Marina Services and Boat Supplies
Services - Docking Assistance **Communication -** Pay Phone (4), FedEx, DHL, UPS, Express Mail *(Sat Del)* **Supplies - Near:** Ice *(Cube)*, Ships' Store *(Wayfarer Marine 236-4378)*, Propane *(Willey Wharf 236-7969)*, CNG *(Willey Wharf)* **3+ mi:** Marine Discount Store *(Hamilton Marine, Searsport 548-6302, Rockland 594-8181, 8 mi.)*

Boatyard Services
Near: Travelift *(135T)*. **Nearest Yard:** Wayfarer Marine (207) 236-4378

Restaurants and Accommodations
OnSite: Restaurant *(Atlantica 236-6011, L $8-14, D $24-29)*, *(Bay View Lobster 236-2005, L $4-18, D $4-26)*, Snack Bar *(Skips)* **Near:** Restaurant *(Thai Kitchen 236-9799)*, *(Natalie's 236-7008, D $22-32, Stylish ambiance, French-Northern Italian)*, *(Paulina's Way 230-0555, D $18-22, Wood-fired pizza $15-24)*, *(Mikado Sushi 236-4477, D $8-30)*, *(Village 236-3232)*, *(Peter Otts Steakhouse 236-4032, D $16-22)*, *(Cappy's Chowder House 236-2254, L $6-15, D $10-20)*, *(Waterfront 236-3747, L $7-14, D $10-22)*, *(Hartstone Inn 236-4259, D $40, Prix fixe, Wed-Sun, 7pm)*, Snack Bar *(Bagel Café 236-2661)*, Pizzeria *(Zaddik's 236-6540, $6-15 del.)*, Hotel *(BW Camden River 236-0500, $160-210)*, *(Camden Harbor Inn 236-4200, $105-255)*, Inn/B&B *(Lord Camden 236-4325, $90-220)*, *(Windward House 236-9656, $100-280)*, *(Whitestone $105-195)* **Under 1 mi:** Inn/B&B *(Norumbega 236-4646, $160-525, Unique, delightful 1886 stone Castle)*

Recreation and Entertainment
Near: Beach *(Laite Memorial Park)*, Picnic Area, Grills, Playground, Tennis Courts, Video Rental *(Harbor 236-9596)*, Park *(Camden Harbor at Megunticook River)*, Tours *(Windjammer 2-hr. Trips- Appledore 236-8353, Olad 236-2323, Surprise 236-4687, Lazy Jack 230-0602)*, Cultural Attract *(Camden Civic Theater 236-2281, Camden Opera House 236-3353)*, Sightseeing *(Camden-Rockport Historical Society's 2.5 mi. walking tour)* **Under 1 mi:** Museum *(1780 Old Homestead incl. Conway House/Cramer Museum 236-2257 $5/4 Mon-Thu, 10-4)* **1-3 mi:** Heated Pool *(YMCA 236-3375 $10/5 day pass)*, Fitness Center *(YMCA)* **3+ mi:** Golf Course *(Goose River 236-8488, 4 mi.)*

Provisioning and General Services
OnSite: Gourmet Shop *(Zesty 485-0815)* **Near:** Market *(French & Brawn 236-3361)*, Delicatessen *(Camden Deli 236-8343)*, Liquor Store *(Rite Aid)*, Bakery *(Cappy's; Meetingbrook 236-6808)*, Farmers' Market *(Wed 3:30-6pm, Sat 9am-noon Knox Mill Pkg Lot)*, Lobster Pound, Bank/ATM, Post Office, Catholic Church, Protestant Church, Library *(236-3440, Internet service)*, Beauty Salon, Barber Shop, Laundry, Bookstore *(Owl and Turtle 236-4769; Sherman's 236-2223; Stone Soup 763-3354)*, Pharmacy *(Rite Aid 236-4546)*, Florist **Under 1 mi:** Supermarket *(Hannaford 236-8577)*, Hardware Store *(Rankins 236-3275)*, Department Store *(Reny's)*

Transportation
OnCall: Rental Car *(Enterprise 594-9093)*, Taxi *(Mid Coast Limo 236-2424)* **Near:** InterCity Bus *(Concord to Boston)* **Airport:** Knox County/Bangor Int'l. *(6 mi./45 mi.)*

Medical Services
911 Service **Near:** Doctor, Dentist, Chiropractor *(Johnstone 236-3456)*, Holistic Services, Ambulance **Hospital:** Penobscot Bay 596-8000 *(4 mi.)*

Setting -- In the southwestern corner of Camden Harbor, the Town Dock lies in the heart of the action - just 200 feet from the village center. The crowded harbor berths a mix of pleasure craft, schooners, and tour boats; in summer, the upland is standing-room-only as well. Wedged in among the seasonal docks, the town offers eight smaller slips, two megayacht sized tie-ups and a public "U" shaped dinghy float. Up the gangway, next to the harbormaster's small yellow house, two restaurants spill out onto the boardwalk - which is dotted with green benches, flower boxes and the occasional busker. A bit futher inalnd are heads, a Welcome Center and Harbor Dogs snack shack. Next door, one of the Megunticook River's several waterfalls bisects pretty Camden Harbor Park.

Marina Notes -- *Under 40 ft. $2/ ft., 40-60 ft. $3/ft., Over 60 ft. $3.50/ft. 30, 50 &100Amp. Very busy July & August. Call for slip assignment when abeam of red & green buoy marked 5 mph. Ideal for 30 - 40' boats; only two spots for 100 ft+ yachts. A harbor monitor delivers packages to boat. Federal gov dredged to 10 ft. mlw. Harbor redesigned with wider channel, new docks. Pumpout boat (Ch. 15) Bathhouse: Public heads. Showers & laundry at Wayfarers. Showers also at YMCA - 1 mi. south. Note: Flow of boat traffic in harbor is counter-clockwise. Free dinghy dockage 2-3 hrs. - serves whole mooring field.

Notable -- This delightful tourist mecca is beautifully maintained and the town dock is no exception. Within easy walking distance are dozens of restaurants, services, shops, attractions, galleries, inns plus a plethora of high-quality cultural offerings, beautiful parks and public buildings supported by a sophisticated year-round population. Try to get away from the harbor (Mt. Beattie, Laite Park, bike tour); the crowds subside and the region's true beauty emerges.

   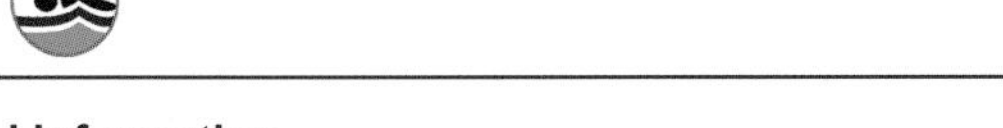

Navigational Information
Lat: 44°11.152' **Long:** 069°04.416' **Tide:** 9 ft. **Current:** n/a **Chart:** 13305
Rep. Depths (*MLW*): Entry 10 ft. **Fuel Dock** n/a **Max Slip/Moor** 10 ft./50 ft.
Access: Penobscot Bay to the northwest end of Rockport Harbor

Marina Facilities *(In Season/Off Season)*
Fuel: No
Slips: 7 Total, 2 Transient **Max LOA:** 100 ft. **Max Beam:** n/a
Rate *(per ft.)*: **Day** $2.00 **Week** n/a **Month** n/a
Power: 30 amp n/a, **50 amp** n/a, **100 amp** n/a, **200 amp** n/a
Cable TV: No **Dockside Phone:** No
Dock Type: Floating, Alongside, Composition
Moorings: 30 Total, 5 Transient **Launch:** None, Dinghy Dock
Rate: Day $25 **Week** n/a **Month** n/a
Heads: 2 Toilet(s), 2 Shower(s)
Internet: No **Laundry:** 2 Washer(s), 2 Dryer(s)
Pump-Out: OnCall, Full Service **Fee:** Free **Closed Heads:** Yes

Marina Operations
Owner/Manager: Abbie Leonard (Hrbrmstr) **Dockmaster:** Same
In-Season: Jun-Sep, 7am-7pm **Off-Season:** Oct-May, Varies
After-Hours Arrival: Call in advance
Reservations: Yes **Credit Cards:** Cash or Check
Discounts: None
Pets: Welcome, Dog Walk Area **Handicap Access:** No

Rockport Marine Park

Pascal Ave.; Rockport, ME 04856

Tel: (207) 236-0676 **VHF: Monitor** Ch. 16 **Talk** Ch. 78
Fax: (207) 230-0112 **Alternate Tel:** n/a
Email: harbormaster@town.rockport.me.us **Web:** town.rockport.me.us
Nearest Town: Rockport *(1 mi.)* **Tourist Info:** (207) 236-4404

Marina Services and Boat Supplies
Services - Docking Assistance, Dock Carts **Communication -** Pay Phone, FedEx, UPS, Express Mail **Supplies - Near:** Ice *(Block, Cube)*, Ships' Store *(Rockport Marine)* **Under 1 mi:** Propane *(Pen-Bay Oil 236-2851)*

Boatyard Services
Nearest Yard: Rockport Marine (207) 236-9651

Restaurants and Accommodations
Near: Restaurant *(Shephards Pie 236-8500, D $9-24)*, Coffee Shop *(RAYR - Expresso Bar 230-7009)*, Lite Fare *(Rockport Corner Shop 236-8361, breakfast)* **Under 1 mi:** Restaurant *(Prism Glass Gallery & Cafe 230-0061, L $6-15, D $15-24, Guggelman-Henner's artwork adorns dining room)*, *(The Helm 236-4337)*, *(Cody's Original Roadhouse 236-3700, L & D $11-19)*, Lite Fare *(3 Dogs Cafe 230-0955, B $3-5, L $8-14, 8am-5:30pm, 'til 4pm Sun Bright, airy space)*, Pizzeria *(Dominos 236-6212, Del.)*, Motel *(Schooner Bay 236-2205, $53-110, Beautiful Grounds. Impeccably maintained. Flowers abound)*, *(Seven Mountains 236-3276)*

Recreation and Entertainment
OnSite: Beach *(water tested weekly)*, Picnic Area, Grills **Near:** Park *(Cramer Park)*, Museum *(Center of Maine Contemporary Art 236-2875 $5/free 20+ shows a season)*, Tours *(65 ft. Schooner Heron 236-8605 3 hrs w/ lunch $55/30, 2.5 hrs $45/20, Sunset Sail w/ hors d'oeuvres $55/30; 74 ft. Timberwind 236-0801 aat Town Landing)*, Cultural Attract *(Rockport Opera House 236-2514 million-dollar renovation 19th-century charm 20th-century conveniences)*, Galleries *(Caldwell 706-4000; Elan 236-4401; Prism Glass 230-0061; Carver Hill 236-0745)* **Under 1 mi:** Heated Pool *("Y" 236-3375 $8/4)*, Playground, Fitness Center *("Y")*, Boat Rentals *(Main Sports Outfitters 236-8797 - Kayak rentals)* **1-3 mi:** Tennis Courts *(Rockport Rec Park 236-9648)*, Golf Course *(Goose River 236-8488, Golfer's Crossing Mini 230-0090)*, Bowling *(Oakland Park 594-7525)*

Provisioning and General Services
Near: Bookstore *(Whelann 236-4795)* **Under 1 mi:** Gourmet Shop *(The Market Basket 236-4371 Specialty foods with serious take out)*, Wine/Beer *(The Market Basket; RAYR - the wine shop)*, Bakery *(Sweet Sensations 230-0955 at 3 Dogs)*, Fishmonger *(Graffam Bros. 236-8391 .5 mi. Lobsters, too)*, Bank/ATM, Post Office, Library *(236-3642)* **1-3 mi:** Supermarket *(Hannaford 236-8577 - 1.2 mi.)*, Health Food *(Fresh Off the Farm 236-3260)*, Farmers' Market, Catholic Church, Protestant Church, Beauty Salon, Pharmacy *(Waltz 230-1053; Hannaford 236-8577)*, Hardware Store *(Rankins 236-3275)*

Transportation
Near: Rental Car *(Enterprise 594-9093, Smith's 236-2320)*, Taxi *(Don's 236-4762; Joe's 975-3560)*, Airport Limo *(Mid-Coast 236-2424)*, InterCity Bus *(Concord-Trailways - Bangor-Boston)* **Under 1 mi:** Bikes *(Maine Sport Outfitters $15/day 800-722-0826)*

Medical Services
911 Service **Under 1 mi:** Doctor *(Midcoast Med 236-2169)*, Dentist *(Olivas 236-4169)*, Chiropractor *(Rockport Fam.)* **1-3 mi:** Veterinarian *(Camden Hosp. for Animals 236-2311)* **Hospital:** Penobscot Bay 596-8000 *(1 mi.)*

Setting -- Along the northwestern shore, lovely Rockport Marine Park's 200-foot floating dock - with side-tie dockage for big boats and inside dinghy tie-ups - parallels the grassy park. Surrounded by flowers, a sculpture honors Andre the seal, who famously served as Rockport's assistant harbormaster, and, snugged against the hillside, the old lime kilns describe a chapter in Rockport's history. The harbormaster's immaculate, green-trimmed, craftsman-style, gray-shingle dockhouse berths offices and the bathhouse. Beautifully maintained by the Rockport Garden Club, the park has become a magnet for the area's artists.

Marina Notes -- Dinghy landings at Town Dock, Rockport Marine, & onsite. Launch ramp. Bathhouse: In dockhouse, stepped-up cinder block. Municipal. Spacious, hunter green heads & showers. Laundry. Note: Across Goose River, Rockport Boat Club welcomes yachters - 1 transient mooring.

Notable -- The most beautiful resident here is the 65 ft. Schooner "Heron," built by Nigel "Twig" Bower at his Camden shop and launched in 2003. She makes three trips daily along Penobscot Bay. For 25 years, Rockport's Assistant Harbormaster was a seal, and the inspiration of the children's book "A Seal Called André: The Two Worlds of a Maine Harbor Seal" by Harry Goodridge (former Rockport Harbormaster) & Lew Dietz. A 1994 Film "André" is available on video. During the 19th century, Rockport played an important role providing lime up & down the East Coast. A fire in the early 1900's combined with the growing popularity of cement killed the industry. In 1970 the Triple Lime Kilns were preserved and displayed with the steam locomotive that hauled limestone from the quarries - and a bell from an 1890 US Lighthouse. For a hike or bike ride, ask for directions to the Vespers Children's Chapel and the Galloway Belted cows.

PHOTOS ON DVD: 25

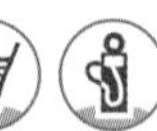

Rockport Marine

PO Box 203; 1 Main Street; Rockport, ME 04856

Tel: (207) 236-9651 **VHF: Monitor** Ch.16 **Talk** Ch. 78A
Fax: (207) 236-0758 **Alternate Tel:** n/a
Email: office@rockportmarine.com **Web:** www.rockportmarine.com
Nearest Town: Rockport **Tourist Info:** (207) 236-4404

Navigational Information
Lat: 44°11.200' **Long:** 069°04.333' **Tide:** 9 ft. **Current:** n/a **Chart:** 13305
Rep. Depths (*MLW*): Entry 10 ft. **Fuel Dock** 10 ft. **Max Slip/Moor** 10 ft./65 ft.
Access: Penobscot Bay to the northeast end of Rockport Harbor

Marina Facilities *(In Season/Off Season)*
Fuel: Gasoline, Diesel
Slips: 5 Total, 5 Transient **Max LOA:** 100 ft. **Max Beam:** n/a
Rate *(per ft.)*: **Day** $2.50 **Week** n/a **Month** n/a
Power: 30 amp Incl., **50 amp** Incl., **100 amp** n/a, **200 amp** n/a
Cable TV: No **Dockside Phone:** No
Dock Type: Floating, Long Fingers, Short Fingers, Pilings, Wood
Moorings: 35 Total, 15 Transient **Launch:** No, Dinghy Dock
Rate: Day $30 **Week** $175 **Month** $600
Heads: None
Internet: Yes *(Wi-Fi, Free)* **Laundry:** None
Pump-Out: OnCall *(Once a week)* **Fee:** Free **Closed Heads:** Yes

Marina Operations
Owner/Manager: T. Allen **Dockmaster:** Same
In-Season: Jun-Sep, 7am-4pm **Off-Season:** May-Oct, 7am-3:30pm
After-Hours Arrival: Help yourself - settle up next morning
Reservations: Yes, Preferred **Credit Cards:** Visa/MC
Discounts: None
Pets: Welcome, Dog Walk Area **Handicap Access:** No

Marina Services and Boat Supplies
Services - Docking Assistance, Dock Carts **Communication -** Mail & Package Hold, Phone Messages, Fax in/out, FedEx, UPS, Express Mail **Supplies - OnSite:** Ice *(Block, Cube)*, Ships' Store **Under 1 mi:** Propane *(Pen-Bay Oil 236-2851)*

Boatyard Services
OnSite: Travelift *(55T)*, Forklift, Crane, Engine mechanic *(gas, diesel)*, Electrical Repairs, Hull Repairs, Rigger, Bottom Cleaning, Brightwork, Compound, Wash & Wax, Interior Cleaning, Woodworking, Yacht Interiors, Metal Fabrication, Painting, Total Refits, Yacht Design, Yacht Building **OnCall:** Hydraulic Trailer, Electronics Repairs *(10 mi.)*, Sail Loft, Divers, Refrigeration, Upholstery, Awlgrip **Near:** Launching Ramp. **Member:** ABBRA **Yard Rates:** $50-70/hr., Haul & Launch $8/ft., Power Wash $25-40, Bottom Paint $55/hr. **Storage:** On-Land In $6/sq.ft./mo. Out $3/sq.ft.

Restaurants and Accommodations
Near: Restaurant *(The Helm 236-4337)*, *(Shephards Pie 236-8500, D $9-24)*, Lite Fare *(3 Dogs Cafe 230-0955, B $3-6, L $8-14, Kids $7)*, *(Rockport Corner Shop B $3-6, L $3-7)* **Under 1 mi:** Restaurant *(Prism Glass Gallery & Cafe 230-0061, L $6-15, D $15-24)*, Pizzeria *(Domino's 236-6212, Del.)*, Motel *(Seven Mountains 236-3276)*, *(Schooner Bay 236-2205)*, *(Country Inn 236-2725)* **1-3 mi:** Restaurant *(Lotus Chinese 236-2133, L $5-7, D $7-16)*

Recreation and Entertainment
OnSite: Tours *(20-passenger "Timberwind" Schooner trips 236-0801 $495 3 days - $936 6 days; "Schooner Heron" Day tours $20-55.)* **Near:** Museum *(Centr for Maine Contemporary Art 236-2875 $5/Free)*, Cultural Attract *(Bay Chamber Concerts)*, Galleries *(Caldwell 706-4000; Elan 236-4401; Prism Glass 230-0061; Carver Hill 230-0034)* **Under 1 mi:** Picnic Area, Playground **1-3 mi:** Heated Pool *(Y" 236-3375 $8/4)*, Golf Course *(Goose River 236-8488)*, Fitness Center *("Y")*, Boat Rentals *(Maine Sport 800-722-0826 kayaks $50/day, canoes $35/day)*, Bowling *(Oakland Park 594-7525)*, Video Rental *(Harbor 236-9596)*

Provisioning and General Services
Near: Delicatessen, Lobster Pound **Under 1 mi:** Convenience Store, Gourmet Shop *(Market Basket 236-4371)*, Wine/Beer *(RAYR)*, Bakery *(Sweet Sensations 230-0955 at 3 Dogs, pies, tortes, cakes, ice cream)*, Bank/ATM, Post Office, Library *(236-3642)*, Florist **1-3 mi:** Supermarket *(Hannaford 236-8577)*, Health Food *(Fresh Off the Farm 236-3260)*, Liquor Store *(Rite Aid 236-4546)*, Farmers' Market, Catholic Church, Protestant Church, Beauty Salon, Bookstore, Pharmacy *(Camden 236-2250)*, Hardware Store *(Rankins 236-3275)*

Transportation
OnCall: Rental Car *(Enterprise 594-9093, Smith's 236- 2320)*, Taxi *(Joe's 975-3560)*, Airport Limo *(Mid-Coast Limousine 236-2424)* **Near:** Water Taxi *(Wildwood 236-6951)* **Under 1 mi:** InterCity Bus *(Concord-Trailways)* **1-3 mi:** Bikes *(Maine Sport Outfitters $15/day 800-722-0826)* **Airport:** Knox County/Bangor Int'l. *(10 mi./46 mi.)*

Medical Services
911 Service **Under 1 mi:** Doctor *(Midcoast Med 236-2169)*, Dentist *(Olivas 236-4169)*, Chiropractor *(Rockport Family 236-8486)* **1-3 mi:** Veterinarian *(Camden 236-2311)* **Hospital:** Penobscot Bay 596-8000 *(1.2 mi.)*

Setting -- At the northeast head of one of the prettiest working harbors in Maine, Rockport Marine's cluster of impeccable brick-colored sheds and offices, backed by a high walll of greenery, is the stuff of picture postcards. Below the matching brick red travelift and granite wharf, a set of floating docks berths a spectacular collection of classic boats. A steep driveway leads up the hill to the tiny town.

Marina Notes -- Well-known for building & restoring fine wooden yachts. Family-owned business since 1962. 40 seasonal storage boats in 5 sheds built specifically for wooden boats - newest with modern climate control system for optimal year-round storage & painting. Minimal transient services - ice, fuel and water. "Rockport Roll" - exposed to the south. Dinghy dockage at Town Landing at head of Harbor, at Marine Park on western side & onsite. Bathhouse: None. Short walk across Goose River to Rockport Marine Park for heads, showers, laundry or to Rockport Boat Club (236-4900).

Notable -- The 70-foot windjammer "Timberwind," Maine's only pilot schooner, moors at the Town Landing between 3-6 day cruises. She maneuvers with sails and an assist from her little yawlboat without benefit of an inboard engine - a pleasure to watch. Lovely homes and beautiful parks perch on the hillside above the harbor. A few shops are "downtown," but most galleries, stores and provisioners are a mile or two in Camden. Across the harbor at Rockport Marine Park, exhibits describe Rockport's heyday as center of the lime industry - along with a statue of Andre, the harbor seal. Drawn by the light and the varied weather conditions, renowned Maine Photographic Workshop bases nearby - offering professional courses on video, film, photography, digital media.

Navigational Information

Lat: 44°06.465' **Long:** 069°06.478' **Tide:** 10 ft. **Current:** n/a **Chart:** 13302
Rep. Depths (*MLW*): Entry 15 ft. **Fuel Dock** 11 ft. **Max Slip/Moor** 11 ft./20 ft.
Access: Western Penobscot Bay, past Owls Head to Rockland Harbor

Marina Facilities *(In Season/Off Season)*

Fuel: *Citgo* - Slip-Side Fueling, Gasoline, Diesel
Slips: 12 Total, 10 Transient **Max LOA:** 80 ft. **Max Beam:** 15.5 ft.
Rate *(per ft.)*: **Day** $3.00/Inq. **Week** n/a **Month** n/a
Power: 30 amp Incl., **50 amp** Incl., **100 amp** n/a, **200 amp** n/a
Cable TV: No **Dockside Phone:** No
Dock Type: Floating, Long Fingers, Alongside, Wood
Moorings: 16 Total, 8 Transient **Launch:** None, Dinghy Dock
Rate: Day $30 **Week** n/a **Month** n/a
Heads: 2 Toilet(s), 2 Shower(s), Hair Dryers
Internet: Yes **Laundry:** 2 Washer(s), 2 Dryer(s), Iron
Pump-Out: No **Fee:** n/a **Closed Heads:** Yes

Marina Operations

Owner/Manager: Celia Knight **Dockmaster:** Erik MacMillan
In-Season: Year-Round, 7:30am-4pm **Off-Season:** June-Sept, 8am-5pm
After-Hours Arrival: Call ahead for instructions
Reservations: Preferred **Credit Cards:** Visa/MC, Dscvr, Amex
Discounts: None
Pets: Welcome **Handicap Access:** No

Knight Marine Service

PO Box 443; 525 Main Street; Rockland, ME 04841

Tel: (207) 594-4068 **VHF: Monitor** Ch. 9 **Talk** Ch. 9
Fax: n/a **Alternate Tel:** (207) 542-1192
Email: celia@knightmarineservice.com **Web:** knightmarineservice.com
Nearest Town: Rockland **Tourist Info:** (207) 596-0376

Marina Services and Boat Supplies

Services - Docking Assistance, Security *(24 hrs.)* **Communication -** Mail & Package Hold, FedEx, DHL, UPS, Express Mail **Supplies - OnSite:** Ice *(Block, Cube)*, Ships' Store **Near:** Marine Discount Store *(Hamilton Marine 594-8181)* **Under 1 mi:** Propane *(Harry French 594-9866)*

Boatyard Services

OnSite: Travelift *(35T)*, Crane, Hydraulic Trailer, Engine mechanic *(gas, diesel)*, Electrical Repairs, Electronics Repairs, Hull Repairs, Rigger, Brightwork, Interior Cleaning, Woodworking, Upholstery, Yacht Interiors, Painting, Awlgrip, Total Refits **OnCall:** Sail Loft, Canvas Work, Divers, Bottom Cleaning, Air Conditioning, Refrigeration, Propeller Repairs **Yard Rates:** $57/hr., Haul & Launch $7/ft., Power Wash $75, Bottom Paint $57/hr. **Storage:** On-Land Outside: $31/ft.* Inside $53/ft.

Restaurants and Accommodations

OnSite: Snack Bar *(Capt. Hornblower Hot dogs, crab rolls, 7-5)* **Near:** Restaurant *(Rockland Café 596-7556, B $3-11, L & D $3-21)*, *(Suzuki's Sushi 596-7447)*, *(In Good Company 593-9110, D $14-20)*, *(Sun Fire Mexican 594-6196)*, *(Black Bull 593-9060)*, *(Lily Bistro 594-4141, D $$18-26)*, *(Waterworks 596-2753, L $4-9, D $8-15)*, Lite Fare *(Brown Bag 596-6372, B & L)*, Motel *(Navigator 594-2131, $65-189)*, Inn/B&B *(Old Granite Inn 594-9036, $100-200)* **Under 1 mi:** Hotel *(Trade Winds 596-6661, $55-300)*, Inn/B&B *(Capt. Lindsey House 596-7950, $136-211)* **1-3 mi:** Hotel *(Samoset Resort 594-2511, $150-620)*

Recreation and Entertainment

Near: Beach, Playground, Museum *(Farnsworth 596-6457 10am-5pm, W & F 'til 8pm $12/free)*, Cultural Attract *(The Strand 594-0070)* **1-3 mi:** Tennis Courts *(Samoset 594-2511)*, Golf Course *(Rockland 594-9322)*

Provisioning and General Services

Near: Convenience Store *(Southend 596-7321)*, Delicatessen, Health Food *(Good Tern 594-8822)*, Wine/Beer *(Wine Seller 594-2621)*, Liquor Store, Bakery *(Willow 596-0564 - early am)*, Lobster Pound *(J&J 594-7223 - Mike)*, Bank/ATM, Post Office, Catholic Church, Protestant Church, Synagogue, Library, Beauty Salon, Barber Shop, Dry Cleaners, Laundry, Bookstore *(Second Reads 594-4123; Rock City 596-6651; Dooryard 594-5080)*, Florist **Under 1 mi:** Supermarket *(Hannaford 594-2173, Shaw's 594-8615 - shops & boxes for pick-up)*, Gourmet Shop *(In Good Company 594-0015)*, Farmers' Market *(Thurs 9am-Noon Harbor Park)*, Pharmacy *(Rite Aid 596-0036)*, Hardware Store *(E.L. Spear 594-5505)*, Department Store *(WalMart 596-0885; JC Penney's)*

Transportation

OnSite: InterCity Bus *(Coastal Trans 596-6605)*, Ferry Service *(North Haven, Vinalhaven)* **OnCall:** Water Taxi *(Two Toots Ch.9, 594-2891, moorings, too)*, Taxi *(Joe's 975-5637)*, Airport Limo *(Schooner Bay 594-5000)* **Near:** Bikes *(Bikesenjava 596-1004 $20/day)* **Airport:** Knox County/Bangor Int'l. *(3 mi./52 mi.)*

Medical Services

911 Service **OnCall:** Ambulance **Near:** Doctor *(Hall 594-9174)*, Dentist, Chiropractor *(Kelly Chiro 594-0000)*, Holistic Services *(Rheal Day Spa 594-5077)* **1-3 mi:** Veterinarian *(Rockland Animal 594-5850)* **Hospital:** Penobscot Bay 596-8000 *(4 mi.)*

Setting -- On the northern channel, hard by the Vinalhaven/North Haven ferry dock in Lermond's Cove, Knight's impeccable dark red buildings pop against the shore. A single-story dock house and office with a blue & white striped awning is backed by several large sheds flanked by two travelifts. In the rear, the ferry terminal infrastucture looms above the car park, dry boat storage and Capt. Hornblower's snack bar. Knight's is in Rockland's historic commercial district.

Marina Notes -- *Storage rates include haul, power wash & launch. Short Haul $7/ft. Founded 1965. Services commercial as well as recreational vessels. A working, well-maintained, yard. Recently upgraded Awlgrip & Alexseal shed with heated floor. Permits do-it-yourself on boats stored in yard. Parking $8 per day. Stores over 175 boats in the winter. Knight's lovingly tended picture-book tug "Celia" no longer works - she's now dock jewelry. Yard helpers - a Chihuahua and Lab. Day dockage $5/hr. Book Exchange. Bathhouse: Linoleum floor, wood walls, hair dryer, towels & glass shower doors. Showers $2. Laundry $5.

Notable -- Knights is located on Main Street, in the midst of Rockland's historic district where shops, restaurants, and galleries are housed in restored Greek Revival, Colonial, Italianate structures - with a dozen restaurants within a few blocks. Rockland hosts more windjammers than any other port in the East. One of several schooner wharfs is just around the cove (Labor Day is Windjammer weekend in Camden). The head of Rockland Harbor's 7/8 mile granite breakwater marks the beginning of the four-mile Harbor Trail that passes by Knight's door. Walk west to Snow Marine Park or east to the Breakwater. Walk to the world-class Farnsworth Art Museum and Wyeth Center. Or hop on a ferry to North Haven, Vinalhaven or Matinicus for the day. There's a festival almost every week.

Beggar's Wharf

9 Wharf Street; Rockland, ME 04841

Tel: (207) 594-8500 **VHF: Monitor** Ch. 9/16 **Talk** Ch. 10
Fax: n/a **Alternate Tel:** (207) 691-3483
Email: mooringsl@beggarswharf.com **Web:** www.beggarswharf.com
Nearest Town: Rockland *(0.3 mi.)* **Tourist Info:** (207) 596-0376

Navigational Information

Lat: 44°06.330' **Long:** 069°06.185' **Tide:** 10 ft. **Current:** n/a **Chart:** 13302
Rep. Depths (*MLW*): Entry 12 ft. **Fuel Dock** n/a **Max Slip/Moor** 4 ft./12 ft.
Access: Penobscot Bay, past lighthouse into north channel to G3

Marina Facilities *(In Season/Off Season)*

Fuel: No
Slips: 8 Total, 0 Transient **Max LOA:** 150 ft. **Max Beam:** n/a
Rate *(per ft.)*: **Day** n/a **Week** n/a **Month** n/a
Power: 30 amp n/a, **50 amp** n/a, **100 amp** n/a, **200 amp** n/a
Cable TV: No **Dockside Phone:** No
Dock Type: Floating, Short Fingers, Alongside, Aluminum
Moorings: 40 Total, 35 Transient **Launch:** Yes but erratic (Incl), Dinghy Dock
Rate: Day $25-45* **Week** $167 **Month** $579
Heads: 4 Toilet(s), 4 Shower(s)
Internet: Yes *(Computers & Wi-Fi, Free)* **Laundry:** None
Pump-Out: OnCall, 1 Port **Fee:** Free **Closed Heads:** No

Marina Operations

Owner/Manager: Bill & Charlie Weidman **Dockmaster:** Same
In-Season: Jul-Aug, 8am-7pm **Off-Season:** Sep-Jun, varies
After-Hours Arrival: Call for instructions
Reservations: Yes **Credit Cards:** Visa/MC
Discounts: None
Pets: Welcome, Dog Walk Area **Handicap Access:** No

Marina Services and Boat Supplies

Services - Docking Assistance, Concierge, Boaters' Lounge, Trash Pick-Up **Communication -** Mail & Package Hold, FedEx, UPS, Express Mail **Supplies - OnSite:** Ice *(Block, Cube)* **Near:** Ships' Store *(Journey's End)*, Marine Discount Store *(Hamilton 594-8181)*, Propane *(Texaco 594-8094)*

Boatyard Services

OnSite: Divers, Bottom Cleaning **Nearest Yard:** Journey's End (207) 594-4444

Restaurants and Accommodations

Near: Restaurant *(Suzuki's Sushi 596-7447, D $13-30)*, *(Lily's Bistro 594-4141, D $18-26)*, *(Black Bull 593-9060)*, *(In Good Company 593-9110, D $14-20, Small plates $3-12)*, *(Rockland Café 596-7556, B $3-11, L & D $3-21)*, *(In Good Company 594-0015, L & D $5-20)*, *(Thai Kitchen L $8-14, D $8-14)*, Snack Bar *(Wasses Hot Dogs & Ice Cream L $1.50-2)*, Lite Fare *(Brown Bag 596-6372, B $4-7, L $4-7)*, *(Brass Compass 596-5960, Bkfst)*, Pizzeria *(Thorndike Creamery 594-4126)*, Inn/B&B *(Capt. Lindsey 596-7950, $136-211)* **Under 1 mi:** Motel *(Navigator 594-2131, $65-189)*, *(Trade Winds 596-6661, $55-300)*, Inn/B&B *(Old Granite 594-9036, $100-200)*

Recreation and Entertainment

OnSite: Picnic Area *(rustic)*, Grills **Near:** Playground, Fitness Center *(Trade Winds, pool. too $7-20/day)*, Museum *(Maine Lighthouse Museum 594-3301 $5/Free; Farnsworth 596-6457 $12/Free. World class collections in 5 buildings focused on Maine - Andrew, Jamie & N.C. Weyths, Louise Nevelson)*, Cultural Attract *(Strand Theatre 594-0070 Film, Concerts)*, Galleries **Under 1 mi:** Beach, Sightseeing *("The Apprenticeship" - teaches wooden boatbuilding)*, Special Events *(Lobster Fest - Early Aug, Blues Fest - Mid July)* **1-3 mi:** Tennis Courts *(Samoset 594-2511)*, Golf Course *(Rockland G.C. 594-9322)*

Provisioning and General Services

OnCall: Laundry *(pick-up/del)* **Near:** Wine/Beer *(Wine Seller 594-2621)*, Bank/ATM, Post Office, Library, Beauty Salon, Barber Shop, Dry Cleaners, Bookstore *(Reading Corner 596-6651; Rock City 594-4123)*, Newsstand, Florist **Under 1 mi:** Supermarket *(Hannaford 594-2173, Shaw's 594-8615 2 mi. fax order & send taxi)*, Gourmet Shop *(Sweets & Meats 594-2070)*, Health Food *(Good Tern Co-op 594-8822)*, Bakery *(Brown Bag, Willow 596-0564)*, Farmers' Market *(Harbor Park Thu 9am-Noon)*, Catholic Church, Protestant Church, Synagogue, Pharmacy *(Rite Aid 596-0036)*, Hardware Store *(E.L. Spear 594-4331)* **1-3 mi:** Liquor Store, Department Store *(JC Penney, WalMart)*, Copies Etc. *(UPS Store 594-4200)*

Transportation

OnCall: Water Taxi *(Two Toots Ch.9, 594-2891 moorings, too)*, Rental Car *(Enterprise 594-9093)*, Taxi *(Joe's 975-5637)*, Airport Limo *(Schooner Bay 594-5000)* **Near:** Bikes *(Bikesenjava 596-1004 $20/day)*, InterCity Bus *(Coastal Trans)* **Under 1 mi:** Ferry Service *(North Haven, Vinalhaven, Matinicus)* **Airport:** Knox Co/Bangor Int'l. *(3 mi./52 mi.)*

Medical Services

911 Service **Near:** Doctor *(Hall 594-9174)*, Optician *(Herbert 594-4171)* **Under 1 mi:** Dentist *(Theriault 594-8353)*, Chiropractor *(Bay 596-6700)*, Holistic Services *(Rheal Day Spa 594-5077)* **1-3 mi:** Veterinarian *(Rockland Animal 594-5850)* **Hospital:** Penobscot Bay 596-8000 *(4 mi.)*

Setting -- Beggar's Wharf is tucked into a long narrow basin between Journey's End wharf to the south and a commercial complex to the north. A long floating dock of re-purposed salmon pens leads to the rustic upland. Within a cluster of several unrestored historic wharf buildings, a shingled two-story building houses the office and boaters' lounge and an outbuilding houses the heads. It is located on the commercial Tillson Wharf peninsula, dominated by the Coast Guard station and a seaweed processing plant, that T-bones to the center of town. Their two mooring fields are conveniently slightly north and right offf their dock.

Marina Notes -- *Mooring fees: Up to 45 ft. $25/nt, $167/wk, $579/mo. 46-65 ft. $35/$223/$698. Over 65 ft. $45/$279/$861. Add $20/nt. during storms if not already a guest. Larger moorings hold up to 225 ft. yacht. 4 ft. at end of dock. Launched in 2001, on the site of the old Rockland Boat Co. property on Wharf Place (Now Hamilton Marine at 20 Park). Sits on half-acre with 100 feet of harbor front. Launch service a bit ad-hoc, not always staffed. Ask for aerial view with mooring fields marked. Bathhouse: Very nice, tiled walls, fiberglass shower stalls ($3), curtains, dressing rooms. In process of completion.

Notable -- Beggar's Wharf offers laundry service, parking (hard to find in Rockland) and a Friday night campfire and fired-up grill - bring your own food. The Lighthouse Museum is nearby on the peninsula; it's about a quarter mile to the gas-lighted Historic District's shops, services and museums. For Wyeth fans, Rockland approaches Nirvana. Over 9,000 Maine-focused pieces in the Farnsworth's 5 buildings. Stop by the Islands Institute, which helps sustain the Maine islands' unique lifestyle. Beggar's Wharf sits in the center of the Rockland Harbor 4-mile Trail - a footpath that connects Snow Marine Park with the Breakwater.

PHOTOS ON DVD: 23

Navigational Information

Lat: 44°06.300' **Long:** 069°06.165' **Tide:** 11 ft. **Current:** n/a **Chart:** 13302
Rep. Depths (*MLW*): Entry 15 ft. **Fuel Dock** 10 ft. **Max Slip/Moor** 15 ft./20 ft.
Access: Main channel - marina is on both sides of Coast Guard station

Marina Facilities *(In Season/Off Season)*

Fuel: *Texaco* - Gasoline, Diesel, High-Speed Pumps
Slips: 85 Total, 20 Transient **Max LOA:** 275 ft. **Max Beam:** n/a
Rate *(per ft.)*: **Day** $2.00/Inq.* **Week** Inq. **Month** Inq.
Power: 30 amp Incl., **50 amp** Incl., **100 amp** n/a, **200 amp** n/a
Cable TV: No **Dockside Phone:** No
Dock Type: Floating, Concrete, Wood
Moorings: 60 Total, 30 Transient **Launch:** n/a
Rate: Day $30 **Week** n/a **Month** n/a
Heads: 6 Toilet(s), 6 Shower(s)
Internet: Yes *(Office)* **Laundry:** None
Pump-Out: OnSite, Self Service, 1 Central **Fee:** $5 **Closed Heads:** No

Marina Operations

Owner/Manager: Mike Davee **Dockmaster:** Same
In-Season: Jul-Sep, 7am-5pm **Off-Season:** Sep-Jul, 8am-5pm
After-Hours Arrival: Call ahead for directions and instructions
Reservations: Yes, Preferred **Credit Cards:** Visa/MC, Dscvr
Discounts: Yes **Dockage:** n/a **Fuel:** Vol **Repair:** n/a
Pets: Welcome **Handicap Access:** No

Journey's End Marina

120 Tillson Avenue; Rockland, ME 04841

Tel: (207) 594-4444 **VHF: Monitor** Ch. 9 **Talk** Ch. 18
Fax: (207) 594-0407 **Alternate Tel:** n/a
Email: oharajem@midcoast.com **Web:** www.journeysendmarina.com
Nearest Town: Rockland *(0.2 mi.)* **Tourist Info:** (207) 596-0376

Marina Services and Boat Supplies

Services - Docking Assistance, Security *(Cameras)*, Dock Carts **Communication -** Pay Phone (1), FedEx, UPS, Express Mail **Supplies - OnSite:** Ice *(Block, Cube, Shaved)*, Ships' Store, Live Bait *(Herring, Red Fish, Pogies)* **Near:** Marine Discount Store *(Hamilton Marine 594-8181)*

Boatyard Services

OnSite: Travelift *(50T)*, Railway *(750T, 1200T)*, Forklift *(30T)*, Crane *(15T)*, Hydraulic Trailer *(25T)*, Engine mechanic *(gas, diesel)*, Electrical Repairs, Electronic Sales, Electronics Repairs, Hull Repairs, Rigger, Bottom Cleaning, Brightwork, Air Conditioning, Refrigeration, Compound, Wash & Wax, Woodworking, Metal Fabrication, Painting, Awlgrip, Total Refits **OnCall:** Sail Loft, Canvas Work, Divers, Interior Cleaning, Propeller Repairs, Upholstery **Dealer for:** Prop Protectors; Yanmar, FTP Ivelo, Deutz, Cummins, ZF. **Member:** ABBRA, ABYC **Yard Rates:** $65-85/hr., Haul & Launch $7.50-8.50/ft., Power Wash $1.50/ft **Storage:** On-Land $39-62/ft.

Restaurants and Accommodations

Near: Restaurant *(Café Miranda 594-2034, D $15-26, Kids $6-10)*, *(Rockland Café 596-7556, B $3-11, L & D $3-21)*, *(Suzuki's Sushi 596-7447, D $13-30)*, *(Landings 596-6573, L & D $7-20)*, *(Lily's Bistro 594-4141, D $18-26)*, *(In Good Company 593-9110, D $14-21)*, *(Rustica 594-0015, L & D $5-20)*, Snack Bar *(Wassaes Dogs)*, Pizzeria *(Thorndike Creamery 594-4126)*, Inn/B&B *(Capt. Lindsey 596-7950, $136-211)* **Under 1 mi:** Motel *(Trade Winds 596-6661, $55-300)*, Inn/B&B *(Old Granite 594-9036, $100-200)*

Recreation and Entertainment

Near: Picnic Area, Playground, Fitness Center *(Trade Winds, pool, too)*, Museum *(Maine Lighthouse 594-3301 $5/Free; Farnsworth 596-6457 $12/Free - over 9,000 Maine-focused items in 5 buildings)*, Cultural Attract *(Strand Theatre 594-0070 Film, Concerts)*, Galleries *(A dozen)*, Special Events *(Fests - Blues - July, Maine Boats, Homes & Harbor and Lobster - Aug)* **1-3 mi:** Tennis Courts, Golf Course *(Rockland Go.C. 594-9322; Samoset Resort 594-2511)*

Provisioning and General Services

Near: Wine/Beer *(Wine Seller 594-2621)*, Bakery *(Atlantic Atlantic 596-0505)*, Farmers' Market *(Harbor Park Thu 9-1)*, Bank/ATM, Post Office, Library, Beauty Salon, Barber Shop, Dry Cleaners, Bookstore *(Reading Corner 596-6651)*, Pharmacy *(Rite Aid 596-0036)*, Newsstand, Florist, Copies Etc. *(Mail Boxes 594-4200)* **Under 1 mi:** Health Food *(Good Tern 594-8822)*, Liquor Store, Catholic Church, Protestant Church, Synagogue, Laundry, Hardware Store *(E. L. Spear 594-4331)* **1-3 mi:** Supermarket *(Hannaford 594-2173)*, Department Store *(WalMart, JC Penney)*

Transportation

OnCall: Water Taxi *(Two Toots Ch. 9)*, Rental Car *(Enterprise 594-9093)*, Taxi *(Joe's 975-5637)*, Airport Limo *(Schooner Bay 594-5000)* **Near:** Bikes *(Bikesenjava 596-1004 $20/day)* **Under 1 mi:** InterCity Bus *(Coastal Trans 800-639-3317)*, Ferry Service **Airport:** Knox/Bangor Int'l. *(3 mi./52 mi.)*

Medical Services

911 Service **OnSite:** Chiropractor *(Demer's Chiro 594-4104)* **Near:** Doctor *(Emery 594-5683)*, Holistic Services *(Synergy Massage 594-2122)*, Optician *(Herbert 594-4171)* **Under 1 mi:** Dentist *(Theriault 594-8353)* **1-3 mi:** Veterinarian *(Rockland 594-5850)* **Hospital:** Pen Bay 596-8000 *(4 mi.)*

Setting -- Rockland Harbor's main channel heads straight for Journey's End, one of the largest and most extensive operations in Mid-Coast Maine. Behind the Coast Guard Station, high-quality wood and composite docks are tucked into this neat, tidy marina's North and South man-made basins. The basins flank the two-story brick office building, low gray sheds and commercial O'Hara's Wharf and Tillson Avenue. Rockland's vibrant downtown is a few blocks away.

Marina Notes -- CCM *$2/ft. under 75 ft., $3.50/ft. over 75 ft. Owned by O'Hara Family for over 100 years, through 4 generations. Orignally a fish factory, today a "mall" of boating services. Transients usually in South basin - deepest slips here. Reservations start in Jan for festival week-ends. $2.5 million dock renovation. All deep water slips. Welcomes club cruises, Fully stocked ships' store. 4 fueling locations, 3 high speed. Automated 24/7 system with key purchase. Extensive BY services. 8 full-time mechanics, plus fiberglass & paint crew. Operates 3 factory trawlers (Bering Sea, Aleutian Is. & Alaska). Ice Factory. Purchased Rockland Harbor B.Y. - largely commercial now but some transient slips.Bathhouse: Wood paneled, very inviting heads & fiberglass shower stalls with fresh curtains ($5) - only open office hours Mon-Fri 8am-5pm, Sat & Sun 8am-4pm.

Notable -- Famed 132-foot, three-masted "Victory Chimes" schooner berths here; she carries 40 passengers (800-745-5651). On Park Drive, the Maine Lighthouse Museum, a paen to lights and their keepers, with the world's largest collecton of fresnal lenses, is within Maine Discovery Visitor's Center (pick up an "Arts Walking Tour"). Stroll a little further to the center of the National Historic Register business district's restaurants, museums, shops, and galleries.

6. ME - WESTERN PENOBSCOT BAY

PHOTOS ON DVD: 25

The Landings Marina

PO Box 1086; 1 Commercial Street; Rockland, ME 04841

Tel: (207) 596-6573 **VHF: Monitor** Ch. 9/16 **Talk** Ch. 11
Fax: (207) 594-4899 **Alternate Tel:** (207) 596-5971
Email: stenmgt@midcoast.com **Web:** n/a
Nearest Town: Rockland *(0.1 mi.)* **Tourist Info:** (207) 596-0376

Navigational Information

Lat: 44°06.116' **Long:** 069°06.428' **Tide:** 10 ft. **Current:** n/a **Chart:** 13302
Rep. Depths (*MLW*): Entry 12 ft. **Fuel Dock** 10 ft. **Max Slip/Moor** 10 ft./40 ft.
Access: Penobscot Bay to Owls Head past breakwater to South Channel

Marina Facilities *(In Season/Off Season)*

Fuel: Slip-Side Fueling, Gasoline, Diesel, On Call Delivery
Slips: 70 Total, 25 Transient **Max LOA:** 150 ft. **Max Beam:** n/a
Rate *(per ft.)*: **Day** $2.20/Inq.* **Week** Inq. **Month** Inq.
Power: 30 amp $10, **50 amp** $15, **100 amp** $30, **200 amp** n/a
Cable TV: No **Dockside Phone:** Yes
Dock Type: Floating, Wood
Moorings: 12 Total, 5 Transient **Launch:** None, Dinghy Dock
Rate: Day $30 **Week** Inq. **Month** n/a
Heads: 4 Toilet(s), 4 Shower(s) *(dressing rooms)*
Internet: No **Laundry:** 2 Washer(s), 2 Dryer(s)
Pump-Out: OnSite, Self Service **Fee:** Free **Closed Heads:** No

Marina Operations

Owner/Manager: Kevin Taylor **Dockmaster:** Same
In-Season: Jun-Sep, 7am-6pm **Off-Season:** Oct-May, Closed
After-Hours Arrival: Tie Up at Fuel dock - Call 596-9171
Reservations: Yes, with Deposit** **Credit Cards:** Visa/MC, Amex
Discounts: None
Pets: Welcome, Dog Walk Area **Handicap Access:** Yes, Heads, Docks

Marina Services and Boat Supplies

Services - Docking Assistance, Security *(24 Hrs.)*, Dock Carts, Megayacht Facilities **Communication -** Pay Phone, FedEx, UPS, Express Mail *(Sat Del)* **Supplies - OnSite:** Ice *(Block, Cube)* **Near:** Marine Discount Store *(Hamilton 594-8181)*, Live Bait, Propane *(Texaco 594-8094)*

Boatyard Services

Nearest Yard: Journey's End (207) 594-4444

Restaurants and Accommodations

OnSite: Restaurant *(The Landing's L $6-20, D $15-24)* **Near:** Restaurant *(Lily's Bistro 594-4141, D $18-26)*, *(Black Bull 593-9060)*, *(Suzuki Sushi 596-7447, D $13-30)*, *(Cafe Miranda 594-2034, D $15-26, Kids $5-10)*, *(Rockland Cafe 596-7556, B $3-11, L & D $3-21)*, Lite Fare *(Brass Compass 596-5960, Breakfast)*, *(Brown Bag B & L $4-7)*, *(Freddie's $2-10)*, Pizzeria *(Thorndike Creamery 594-4126)*, Motel *(Trade Winds 596-6661, $55-300)*, *(Navigator 594-2131, $65-189)*, Inn/B&B *(Capt. Lindsey 596-7950, $136-212)* **Under 1 mi:** Restaurant *(Amalfi 596-0012, L $3-15, D $16-30)* **1-3 mi:** Restaurant *(Primo 596-0770, D $24-42, Top Rated!)*

Recreation and Entertainment

OnSite: Picnic Area, Tours *(Breakwater Kayak 596-6895 Tours - 2 hrs $40, Half-Day $65-85)* **Near:** Heated Pool *(Trade Winds 596-6661)*, Fitness Center *(Trade Winds)*, Park *(Buoy)*, Museum *(Maine Lighthouse 594-3301 $5/Free; Farnsworth 596-6457 $12/Free. 5 buildings focused on Maine, Incl. 3 Weyths)*, Cultural Attract *(The Strand 594-0070 - Films, concerts)*, Sightseeing *(Walking Tour - Map from C of C)*, Galleries *(Main Street)* **Under 1 mi:** Playground *(Merritt Park)*, Dive Shop *(Johnson 594-2916)* **1-3 mi:** Beach *(Birch Point SP)*, Tennis Courts *(Samoset Resort 594-2511)*, Golf Course *(Samoset)*

Provisioning and General Services

Near: Convenience Store *(Rite Aid)*, Market *(Sage)*, Gourmet Shop *(Sweets & Meats 594-2070)*, Wine/Beer *(Wine Seller 594-2621)*, Bakery *(Atlantic 596-0505, Cafe, too)*, Farmers' Market *(Harbor Park Thu 9am-1pm)*, Bank/ATM, Post Office, Library *(Rockland 594-0310 Internet)*, Beauty Salon *(John Paul 594-5055)*, Barber Shop, Bookstore *(Rock City Books & Coffee 594-4123; Reading Corner 596-6651)*, Pharmacy *(Rite Aid 596-0036)*, Newsstand **Under 1 mi:** Health Food *(Good Tern 594-8822)*, Fishmonger, Catholic Church, Protestant Church, Synagogue, Dry Cleaners *(Park St. 594-9393)*, Laundry, Hardware Store *(E. L. Spear 594-4331)*, Florist, Copies Etc. *(UPS 594-4200)* **1-3 mi:** Supermarket *(Hannaford 594-2173, Shaw's 594-8615 shopping service)*, Department Store *(WalMart, JC Penney)*

Transportation

OnCall: Water Taxi *(Two Toots Ch.9, 594-2891)*, Taxi *(Joe's 975-5637)*, Airport Limo *(Schooner Bay 594-5000; Mid-Coast 236-2424)* **Near:** Bikes *(Bikesenjava 596-1004)*, Rental Car *(U-Save 594-2268)* **Under 1 mi:** InterCity Bus *(Concord 800-639-3317)*, Ferry Service *(North Haven, Vinalhaven, Matinicus)* **Airport:** Knox/Bangor Int'l. *(3 mi./52 mi.)*

Medical Services

911 Service **Near:** Doctor *(Hall 594-9174)*, Chiropractor *(Demer's Chiro 594-4104)*, Holistic Services *(Synergy Massage 594-2122)*, Optician *(Herbert 594-4171)* **Under 1 mi:** Dentist *(Theriault 594-8353)*, Veterinarian *(Rockland 594-5850)* **Hospital:** Pen Bay Medical Center 596-8000 *(4 mi.)*

Setting -- On Rockland Harbor's south channel, past the Coast Guard Station and Fish Pier, The Landings sprawls along the shore. Two long floating docks parallel the upland hosting 70 well-maintained slips. A small gray dock house, at the end of the stationary pier, manages the fuel, pump-out and transient slips and leads to a looming brick-red barn housing boat storage and the bathhouse. The large restaurant occupies the rest of the well-shrubbed waterfront - two outdoor dining spaces, a patio under a white tent and a deck topped by a brick-and-blue awning are backed by a gray two-story building with inside dining.

Marina Notes -- *$2.20 to 46 ft., $3.20 over 46 ft., $3.75 over 75 ft. **Reservations - 50% deposit non-refundable if canceled less than 72 hrs in advance. Knox Divers (596-9171) onsite. Full service marina. Pick up point for local marine repair. Upgraded docks - slips plus 210-ft face dock. Expanded parking lot (fee). Reserve early for North Atlantic Blues Fest (early July) & Lobster Fest (early Aug). Bathhouse: Keycoded, located in red barn. Lovely, varnished knotty pine paneled, cream tile floors, gray tile shower enclosures with glass doors, dressing areas (but coin operated!). Bright, airy, climate-controlled. Laundry.

Notable -- The Landings' airy indoor dining room and outdoor dining decks overlook the marina. On the 2nd floor, an attractive function room with large veranda accommodates 60 - perfect for club cruises. Breakwater Kayak offers a variety of local and multi-day tours. A short walk north begins the charming downtown commercial district with famed Farnsworth Museum and Wyeth Center which houses an impressive, Maine-focused art collection. At the south end of Harbor Trail Snow Marine Park's new interactive Coastal Children's Museum wins rave reviews (385-1105 $4.50/pp) - next to Sail, Power & Steam Museum.

PHOTOS ON DVD: 25

Navigational Information
Lat: 44°06.036' **Long:** 069°06.438' **Tide:** 11 ft. **Current:** .5 kt. **Chart:** 13307
Rep. Depths (*MLW*): Entry 14 ft. **Fuel Dock** n/a **Max Slip/Moor** 10 ft./-
Access: Penobscot Bay to Rockland Harbor to end of South Channel

Marina Facilities *(In Season/Off Season)*
Fuel: No
Slips: 15 Total, 15 Transient **Max LOA:** 120 ft. **Max Beam:** 20 ft.
Rate *(per ft.)*: **Day** $2.00/Inq. **Week** Inq. **Month** Inq.
Power: 30 amp Incl., **50 amp** Incl., **100 amp** n/a, **200 amp** n/a
Cable TV: No **Dockside Phone:** No
Dock Type: Floating, Wood
Moorings: 20 Total, 20 Transient **Launch:** None, Dinghy Dock
Rate: Day $30 **Week** $155 **Month** n/a
Heads: 2 Toilet(s), 2 Shower(s) *(dressing rooms)*, Book Exchange
Internet: Yes *(Wi-Fi, Free)* **Laundry:** 1 Washer(s), 1 Dryer(s)
Pump-Out: OnSite, Full Service, 1 Central **Fee:** Free **Closed Heads:** No

Marina Operations
Owner/Manager: Ed Glaser (Harbormaster) **Dockmaster:** Same
In-Season: May 15-Oct 15, 8am-5pm* **Off-Season:** n/a
After-Hours Arrival: n/a
Reservations: No. First come, first served **Credit Cards:** Visa/MC
Discounts: None
Pets: Welcome, Dog Walk Area **Handicap Access:** Yes, Heads

Rockland Public Landing

Harbor Park, Main Street; Rockland, ME 04841

Tel: (207) 594-0314 **VHF: Monitor** Ch. 9 **Talk** Ch. 11
Fax: n/a **Alternate Tel:** n/a
Email: eglaser@ci.rockland.me.us **Web:** www.rocklandharbor.info
Nearest Town: Rockland *(0.2 mi.)* **Tourist Info:** (207) 596-0376

Marina Services and Boat Supplies
Services - Docking Assistance, Concierge, Dock Carts **Communication -** Pay Phone (2), FedEx, DHL, UPS, Express Mail *(Sat Del)* **Supplies - OnSite:** Ice *(Block, Cube)* **Near:** Marine Discount Store *(Hamilton Marine 594-8181)*, Bait/Tackle **1-3 mi:** Propane *(Kalloch 594-5595)*

Boatyard Services
OnCall: Divers **Nearest Yard:** Journey's End (207) 594-4444

Restaurants and Accommodations
OnSite: Lite Fare *(Shell's Southwest Grill 344-4512, $6-8, Take-Out 11am-4pm whole grain, organic)*, *(Time Out Pub 593-9336, Live Music, Blues)* **OnCall:** Pizzeria *(Domino's 594-9494)* **Near:** Restaurant *(In Good Company 594-0015, L & D $5-20)*, *(Park Street Grille 594-4944, L & D $8-19)*, *(The Landings 596-6563, L $6-19, D $7-25)*, *(Trackside Station 594-7500, L & D $6-20)*, *(Brick's 594-5770)*, *(Amalfi on the Water 596-0012, L $7.50-16.50, D $16-30, Sun Br $9-17)*, *(Cafe Miranda 594-2034, L $3-17, D $11-30)*, *(Boat House 596-0600)*, Lite Fare *(Freddie's Take-Out $2-10)*, *(Atlantic Baking 596-0505)*, *(Brass Compass Cafe 596-5960, B & L $3-15)*, Motel *(Trade Winds 596-6661, $55-300)*, *(Navigator 594-2131, $65-189)* **Under 1 mi:** Inn/B&B *(Capt Lindsay Inn 596-7950, $136-211)*, *(Berry Manor Inn 596-7696, $115-275)* **1-3 mi:** Restaurant *(Primo 596-0770, D $24-42)*

Recreation and Entertainment
OnSite: Picnic Area **Near:** Heated Pool *(Trade Winds 594-2123)*, Beach, Playground, Fitness Center *(Trade Winds $7-20)*, Boat Rentals *(Breakwater Kayak 596-6895)*, Museum *(Farnsworth & Wyeth Ctr 596-5789 $12/free; Coastal Children's 385-1105 $4.50 - 0.7 mi.)*, Tours *(Breakwater Kayak 596-6895)*, Cultural Attract *(1923 Strand Theatre 594-0070 - Films, Concerts)*, Galleries **1-3 mi:** Golf Course *(Rockland G.C. 594-9322, Samoset 594-2511)*

Provisioning and General Services
OnSite: Farmers' Market *(Thu 9am-Noon)* **Near:** Convenience Store *(Rite Aid)*, Gourmet Shop *(Sweets & Meats 594-2070)*, Wine/Beer *(Wine Seller 594-2621)*, Liquor Store *(Rite Aid)*, Bakery *(Atlantic 596-0505, Cafe, too)*, Fishmonger *(Live Lobster 594-2682)*, Bank/ATM, Post Office, Protestant Church, Library *(Rockland 596-7532)*, Beauty Salon, Bookstore *(Reading Corner 596-6651)*, Pharmacy *(Rite Aid 596-0036)*, Florist **Under 1 mi:** Health Food *(Good Tern 594-8822)*, Catholic Church, Synagogue, Dry Cleaners *(Park St. 594-9393)*, Laundry **1-3 mi:** Supermarket *(Hannaford 594-2173, Shaw's 594-8615)*, Hardware Store *(E. L. Spear 594-5505)*, Department Store *(WalMart, JC Penney)*, Copies Etc. *(Staples 596-5696)*

Transportation
OnCall: Water Taxi *(Two Toots Ch.9, 594-2891)*, Taxi *(Joe's 975-5637)*, Airport Limo *(Schooner Bay 594-5000)* **Near:** Rental Car *(U-Save 236-2320)* **Under 1 mi:** Bikes *(Bikesenjava 596-1004)*, InterCity Bus *(Concord 800-639-3317)*, Ferry Service *(596-2202 North Haven, Vinalhaven, Matinicus)* **Airport:** Knox County/Bangor Int'l. *(3 mi./55 mi.)*

Medical Services
911 Service **Near:** Doctor *(Vandersloot 596-0991)*, Chiropractor *(Bay Chiro 596-6700)*, Holistic Services *(Synergy Massage 594-2122)*, Optician *(Coppola 594-9555)* **Under 1 mi:** Dentist *(Theriault 594-8353)* **1-3 mi:** Veterinarian *(Rockland 594-5850)* **Hospital:** Pen Bay Med 596-8000 *(4 mi.)*

Setting -- The South Channel's Public Landing sits on the edge of Harbor Park. A large mooring field buffers the network of well-maintained floating slips and side-tie moorage. A small dockhouse perches on the end of the long granite wharf - edged with flying flags - that leads to the upland. The harbormaster's large white building, topped by a cupola, houses the office and bathhouse. Weekly, a cruise ship walls off the main dock's T-head, and the Famers' Market arrives.

Marina Notes -- *Open to 7pm weekends. No reservations. Two hours free docking. Northeast floats designated 20 min. zones. Free Wi-Fi. Dock stewards help tie up. Rockland Yacht Club onsite. Chamber of Commerce moved to Discovery Center on Park Drive. Ask for Harbor & Art Walk guides. Bathhouse: Backside of harbormaster's office. Public heads during day; shower key coded for evening use. Municipal, tile floor, single-curtained fiberglass shower stall.

Notable -- Harbor Park hosts Shell's Southwest Grill's bright orange trailer, picnic tables and several festivals including the North Atlantic Blues Fest in early July and 5-day Maine Lobster Fest in August plus Rockland's primary night spot: Time Out Pub. No longer the industrial port of yesteryear, it's a quick walk to this renaissance town's substantial array of restaurants, chic shops, top museums and fabulous art galleries in the National Registered Historic district. The Farnsworth's compelling Maine-focused collection with a large Wyeth component has created an arts mecca. Four schooner wharfs also berth the largest Windjammer fleet in the U.S. Stroll south along Harbor Walk to beautiful Amalfi on the Water and then on to the new interactive Coastal Children's Museum and Snow Marine Park. Or take a cab to the Owl's Head Transportation Museum. (Famously irreverant Conte's has moved to South Main Street.)

PHOTOS ON DVD: 25

Trident Yacht Basin

60 Ocean St; Rockland, ME 04841

Tel: (207) 596-0082 **VHF: Monitor** Ch. 16 **Talk** Ch. 10
Fax: (207) 236-8098 **Alternate Tel:** n/a
Email: info@tridentyachtbasin.com **Web:** www.tridentyachtbasin.com
Nearest Town: Rockland *(0.7 mi.)* **Tourist Info:** (207) 596-0376

Navigational Information

Lat: 44°05.959' **Long:** 069°06.314' **Tide:** 11 ft. **Current:** .5 kt. **Chart:** 13307
Rep. Depths (*MLW*): Entry 15 ft. **Fuel Dock** n/a **Max Slip/Moor** 15 ft./-
Access: Penobscot Bay to Rockland Harbor Channel

Marina Facilities *(In Season/Off Season)*

Fuel: No
Slips: 45 Total, 20 Transient **Max LOA:** 200 ft. **Max Beam:** 28 ft.
Rate *(per ft.)*: **Day** $2.50 **Week** Inq. **Month** Inq.
Power: 30 amp $5, **50 amp** $8.50, **100 amp** $25, **200 amp** n/a
Cable TV: No **Dockside Phone:** No
Dock Type: Floating, Alongside, Wood, Composition
Moorings: 0 Total, 0 Transient **Launch:** n/a, Dinghy Dock
Rate: Day n/a **Week** n/a **Month** n/a
Heads: 4 Toilet(s), 4 Shower(s) *(dressing rooms)*, Hair Dryers
Internet: Yes *(Wi-Fi, Free)* **Laundry:** 2 Washer(s), 2 Dryer(s)
Pump-Out: Full Service, 1 Central, 1 Port **Fee:** $5 **Closed Heads:** Yes

Marina Operations

Owner/Manager: Yachting Solutions **Dockmaster:** Charles Foote III
In-Season: Jun-Sep, 8am-6pm **Off-Season:** Oct-May, Closed
After-Hours Arrival: Call 207-596-0082
Reservations: Yes, Preferred **Credit Cards:** Visa/MC, Amex
Discounts: None
Pets: Welcome **Handicap Access:** Yes, Heads, Docks

Marina Services and Boat Supplies

Services - Docking Assistance, Security *(24 hrs.)*, Trash Pick-Up, Dock Carts **Communication -** Mail & Package Hold, FedEx, DHL, UPS, Express Mail **Supplies - OnSite:** Ice *(Block, Cube)* **Under 1 mi:** Ships' Store *(Hamilton Marine 594-8181)*, Propane *(Kalloch 594-5595)*

Boatyard Services

OnCall: Engine mechanic *(gas, diesel)*, Electrical Repairs, Electronic Sales, Electronics Repairs, Hull Repairs, Rigger, Sail Loft, Canvas Work, Divers, Brightwork, Air Conditioning, Compound, Wash & Wax, Propeller Repairs, Woodworking **Nearest Yard:** Yachting Solutions (207) 236-8100

Restaurants and Accommodations

OnSite: Restaurant *(Boathouse Rest & Raw Pier 596-0600, Lunch Mon-Sat 11:30am-4pm, Dinner 7 days 5-9pm, Sun Brunch 11am-3pm)*, *(Amalfi-on-the-Water 596-0012, L $7.50-16.50, D $16-36, Sun Brunch $10-21)* **Near:** Restaurant *(Trackside Station 594-7500, L&D $6-20, Kids' $4)*, *(Bricks 594-5770, $5 lunch)*, *(Park Street 594-4944, L&D $8-19)*, Motel *(Navigator 594-2131, $65-189)*, Inn/B&B *(Ripples-Inn at the Harbor 594-5771, $105-260)* **Under 1 mi:** Restaurant *(Cafe Miranda 594-2034, L $3-17, D $11-30)*, *(Landings 596-6563, L $6-19, D $7-25)*, Inn/B&B *(Trinity on the Ocean 596-0071)* **1-3 mi:** Restaurant *(Primo 596-0770, D $25-42, Region's Best)*

Recreation and Entertainment

OnSite: Beach, Picnic Area, Park **Near:** Playground, Hike/Bike Trails, Party Boat **Under 1 mi:** Pool *(Tradewinds 594-2123 - Fitness Center, too $7-20)*, Boat Rentals *(Breakwater Kayak 596-6895)*, Movie Theater *(Strand 594-0070)*, Museum *(Farnsworth & Wyeth 596-5789 $12/Free; Lighhouse 594-3301 $5/Free; Coastal Children's 975-2530 $4.50)*, Cultural Attract *(Strand - concerts)*, Galleries **1-3 mi:** Golf Course *(Rockland G.C. 594-9322, Samoset 594-2511)*

Provisioning and General Services

Near: Convenience Store *(Maritime Farms 594-7750)*, Gourmet Shop *(Sweets & Meats 594-2070 - wine & bakery too.)*, Farmers' Market *(Thu 9am-Noon Harbor Park)*, Protestant Church **Under 1 mi:** Liquor Store *(Rite Aid 596-0036)*, Bank/ATM, Post Office, Catholic Church, Synagogue, Library *(594-0310)*, Beauty Salon, Dry Cleaners *(Park St. 594-9393)*, Laundry, Bookstore *(Reading Corner 596-6651; Rock City 594-4123)*, Pharmacy *(Rite Aid 596-0036)*, Florist **1-3 mi:** Supermarket *(Hannaford 594-2173; Shaw's 594-8615)*, Hardware Store *(E. L. Spear 594-4331)*, Department Store *(WalMart 596-0885)*

Transportation

OnSite: Courtesy Car/Van *(Comp.)*, Bikes *(Comp.)* **OnCall:** Water Taxi, Taxi *(Joe's 975-5637)*, Airport Limo *(Schooner Bay 594-5000)* **Near:** Rental Car *(U-Save 236-2320)* **Under 1 mi:** InterCity Bus *(Coastal Trans 800-639-3317)* **1-3 mi:** Ferry Service *(596-2202 North Haven, Vinalhaven, Mantinicus)* **Airport:** Knox County/Bangor Int'l *(3 mi./55mi.)*

Medical Services

911 Service **OnCall:** Ambulance **Near:** Doctor *(Van Lonkhuyzen & Cohen 701-4400)*, Chiropractor *(Bay 596-6700)*, Holistic Services *(Synergy Massage 594-2122 - 60 min. $75)*, Optician *(Coppola 594-9555)* **1-3 mi:** Veterinarian *(Rockland 594-5850)* **Hospital:** Pen Bay Med 596-8000 *(4 mi.)*

Setting -- The most southern and newest of the Rockland marinas, Trident's deep water, upscale, side-tie floats snake to a large L-shaped stationary pier edged with forest green railings. A gray-shingled dockhouse overseas the operation. Umbrellaed picnic tables dot the wharf and, on the upland, a gray octagonal contemporary houses the office and bathouse. The Boathouse Restaurant's covered deck merges with the pier. Amalfi-on-the-Water is nearly adjacent.

Marina Notes -- CCM. Main Office: Yachting Solutions: 229 Commercial St., Rockport, ME 04856. 2nd Email: Charlie@yachtingsolutions.com. Rockland's newest facility. Former MBNA Headquarter docks. Well-protected, full-service with spectacular harbor views. 400 ft. side-tie dockage. 100A, single-phase service. Complimentary recent Jeep courtesy car. Gated access to docks. Catamaran dockage same rate. Bathhouse: Recent full baths & laundry.

Notable -- Adjacent to the marina's main pier, Boathouse Restaurant's features an open kitchen, spiral staircase and window walls - with an outdoor deck and bar right on the water. A few steps further, highly regarded Amlafi-on-the-Water offers an equally spectacular venue with panoramic harbor views.The four-mile Harbor Trail starts here, rims the entire waterfront and ends at the Rockland Breakwater Light. All of Rockland's impressive attractions are an easy walk - 0.3 miles south to the new Coastal Children's Musuem or 0.7 mile north finds the Farmsworth, Wyeth Center and the Maine Lighthouse Museum. Bike or cab three miles south to the Owls Head Transportation Museum (594-4418, $10/Free) with 150 historic aircraft, automobiles, bicycles, carriages and engines - including a

Navigational Information

Lat: 44°02.761' **Long:** 068°50.062' **Tide:** 9 ft. **Current:** n/a **Chart:** 13305
Rep. Depths (*MLW*): Entry 27 ft. **Fuel Dock** n/a **Max Slip/Moor** -/14 ft.
Access: Southern tip of Vinalhaven to Carvers Harbor

Marina Facilities *(In Season/Off Season)*

Fuel: *Fishermen's Co-op - Emergency only -*
Slips: 0 Total, 0 Transient **Max LOA:** 40 ft. **Max Beam:** n/a
Rate *(per ft.)*: **Day** n/a **Week** n/a **Month** n/a
Power: 30 amp n/a, **50 amp** n/a, **100 amp** n/a, **200 amp** n/a
Cable TV: No **Dockside Phone:** No
Dock Type: n/a
Moorings: 3 Total, 2 Transient **Launch:** No, Dinghy Dock
Rate: Day $20 **Week** n/a **Month** n/a
Heads: None
Internet: No **Laundry:** None
Pump-Out: No **Fee:** n/a **Closed Heads:** Yes

Marina Operations

Owner/Manager: Kevin Hopkins (Harbormaster) **Dockmaster:** n/a
In-Season: May-Oct 1, 8am-7pm **Off-Season:** Closed
After-Hours Arrival: Call in advance
Reservations: Call harbormaster to reserve **Credit Cards:** Cash only
Discounts: None
Pets: Welcome **Handicap Access:** No

Vinalhaven's Carvers Harbor

Vinalhaven, ME

Tel: (207) 863-2151 **VHF: Monitor** Ch. 16 **Talk** Ch. 82
Fax: n/a **Alternate Tel:** n/a
Email: captbub1973@msn.com **Web:** n/a
Nearest Town: Rockland *(13 mi.)* **Tourist Info:** (207) 863-4471

Marina Services and Boat Supplies

Supplies - Near: Ice *(Block, Cube)*, Ships' Store *(Hopkins Boatyard 863-2551)*, Bait/Tackle *(Fisherman's Friend 863-9317 clothes, boots, etc; Island Lobster Supply 863-4807)*, Propane *(Vinalhaven Fuel 863-4441)*

Boatyard Services

Near: Travelift *(30T)*, Engine mechanic *(gas, diesel)*, Electrical Repairs, Hull Repairs, Propeller Repairs, Woodworking. **Nearest Yard:** Hopkins Boat Yard (207) 863-2551

Restaurants and Accommodations

Near: Restaurant *(The Haven 863-4969, dinner only - Tue-Sat 2 seatings 5:30/6 & 7:30/8pm Harborside or 6-9pm Streetside pub)*, *(The Pizza Pit & Island Coffee House 863-4311, B $3-7, L $6-14, D $6-14, B 4-11am, L 11am-2pm, D 4-8pm Pizzas $7-25)*, *(The Sand Bar 863-4500, L & D $5-11 + pizza)*, *(64 Main Street 863-4464, D $17-18, Sun Brunch $6-11, lovely, upscale)*, Seafood Shack *(Harborside 863-2541)*, Lite Fare *(Harbor Gawker 863-9365, Eat In/TakeOut Lobster & burgers)*, *(Surfside on Harbor Wharf 863-2767, B $3-7, L $3-7, D $10-19, B 4-11am. D - Fri-Sun 5-8 only)*, *(O.P. Lyons Local Locally sourced foods, Wi-Fi)*, Motel *(Tidewater 863-4618, $100-295, built over a spillway overlooking the harbor Also the Gathering Place for events)*, Inn/B&B *(Libby House 863-4696, $75-140)* **Under 1 mi:** Inn/B&B *(Payne Homestead 863-9963, $90-145)*, *(Candlepin Cottages 863-2713, $75-110, 4 log cabins, pool, bowling + apartment $140)*

Recreation and Entertainment

Near: Picnic Area *(Grimes Park, Armbrust Hill or out to Lanes Island Preserve)*, Playground *(Armbrust Hill)*, Fitness Center *(Aero Fit 863-2274)*, Boat Rentals *(Canoes & kayaks - Tidewater Motel, $25/day)*, Video Rental *(Boongies 863-2510)*, Park *(Grimes Park, Armbrust Hill)*, Galleries *(Five Elements 863-2262, New Era 863-9351 run by artist Elaine Crossman, proprieter of Tidewater)* **Under 1 mi:** Beach *(Lawson's Quarry 1 mi.; Booths Quarry 1.5 mi.)*, Museum *(Vinalhaven Hist. Society 863-4410 11am-3pm - walking tour brochure)*, Sightseeing *(Granite quarries, Carvers Cemetery, Odd-Fellows Hall, The Galamander)*

Provisioning and General Services

OnCall: Supermarket *(Shaw's in Rockland)* **Near:** Convenience Store *(Fisherman's Friend 863-2140, wine, beer, snacks, clothes & supplies)*, Market *(Carvers Harbor Market 863-4319)*, Wine/Beer *(Island Spirits 863-2192)*, Liquor Store *(Carvers Harbor Market)*, Fishmonger *(Vinalhaven Co-op 863-2263 wholesale - sells retail to walk-ins)*, Lobster Pound *(Harborside 863-2541)*, Post Office *(863-4620)*, Library *(Vinalhaven 863-4401)*, Beauty Salon *(Teasing 863-4161)*, Newsstand *(Paper Store - out-of-town papers, gifts, fax & copy machines)*, Retail Shops *(Harbor Wharf - galleries, gift shops)* **Under 1 mi:** Protestant Church

Transportation

Near: Bikes *(Tidewater Motel $15/day)*, Rental Car *(Tidewater 863-4618)*, Ferry Service *(to Rockland 863-4421 $17.50/8.50 RT)*

Medical Services

911 Service **OnCall:** Ambulance **Near:** Holistic Services *(Island Healing Hands 863-4263)* **Under 1 mi:** Doctor *(Islands Comm. Medical Center 863-4341)*, Dentist *(ICMS 863-2533)* **Hospital:** Penobscot Bay, Rockland 596-8000 *(20 mi. via ferry)*

Setting -- Crowded, commercial Carvers Harbor sends out a large fishing fleet every morning, making it a bit inhospitable to pleasure craft. But this is authentic Maine and worth the hassle. Hopkins Boatyard, in the northwest corner, services working and recreational vessels; a dock floats below its travelift bay that berths dinghies and the occasional overnight transient. Additional dinghy tie-ups are at Town Dock at the harbor head next to the spillway and at Town Wharf. Ashore, the majority of the village businesses - restaurants, provisioners, galleries, interesting shops - are on West Main Street between the two.

Marina Notes -- Overnight dockage possible at float next to the Ferry Wharf - See harbormaster (750-0507), which also has a dinghy dock (two hour tie-up now permitted. Dinghy dock at Town Dock (in parking lot across from IGA). Tie up to rear or sides, not front. (2 hr. limit on front). No trash disposal. Hopkins Boatyard manages most emergency repairs and maintains a small ships' store. Bathhouse: Heads at Town Wharf and Ferry terminal. No showers.

Notable -- Vinalhaven has a long history as a working island - from the massive granite quarry operations that supplied stone to the east coast from 1826 until 1930 to the current thriving lobstering business with arguably the most productive fleet in the world. 1300 year-round residents (tripling in summer) make this the most populated island in the state. But greenways are not neglected. The Nature Conservancy maintains two islands accessible only by dinghy (729-5181) plus 40-acre Lane's Island Preserve across a bridge outside the village. In Skoog Park, Vinalhaven Land Trust (863-2543) posts hiking trail maps. A thriving artist community has been led by Robert Indiana, who restored the curiously interesting 1885 Odd-Fellow's Hall at the edge of town.

PHOTOS ON DVD: 25

7. ME – The Rivers & Boothbay Harbor

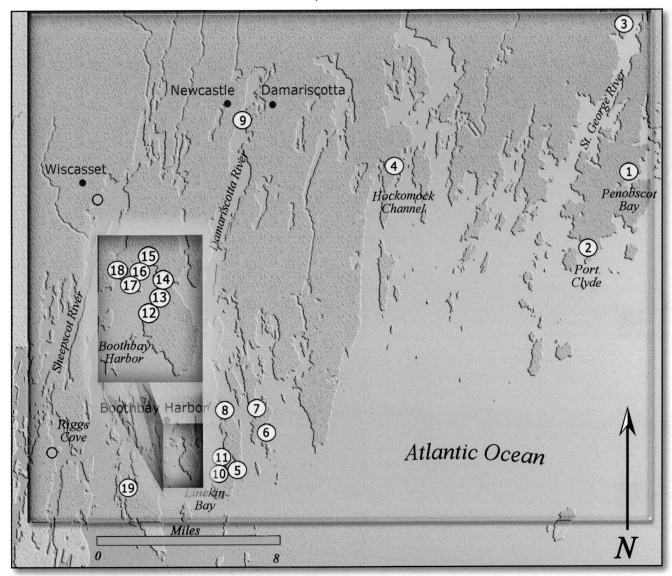

MAP	MARINA	HARBOR	PAGE
1	**Cod End Cookhouse & Marina**	*Tenants Harbor*	134
2	**Port Clyde General Store**	*Port Clyde*	135
3	**Thomaston Town Landing**	*St. George River*	136
4	**Broad Cove Marine Services**	*Medomak River*	137
5	**Spar Shed Marina**	*Damariscotta River*	138
6	**Coveside Marina**	*Damariscotta River*	139
7	**Gamage Shipyard**	*Damariscotta River*	140
8	**Ocean Point Marina**	*Damariscotta River*	141
9	**Schooner Landing**	*Damariscotta River*	142
10	**Smuggler's Cove Inn**	*Linekin Bay*	143
11	**Paul E. Luke**	*Linekin Bay*	144
12	**Carousel Marina**	*Boothbay Harbor*	145
13	**Brown's Wharf Marina**	*Boothbay Harbor*	146
14	**Cap'n Fish's Waterfront Inn**	*Boothbay Harbor*	147
15	**Boothbay Harbor Marina**	*Boothbay Harbor*	148
16	**Tugboat Inn & Marina**	*Boothbay Harbor*	149
17	**Boothbay Harbor Shipyard**	*Boothbay Harbor*	150
18	**Wotton's Wharf**	*Boothbay Harbor*	151
19	**Boothbay Region Boatyard**	*Sheepscot River*	152

RATINGS: 1-5 for Marina Facilities & Amenities,  1-2 for Boatyard Services,  1-2 for MegaYacht Facilities,  for Something Special.

SERVICES: for CCM – Certified Clean Marina,  for Pump-Out, 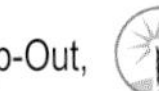 for Internet, 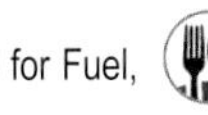 for Fuel, for Restaurant, for Provisioning nearby, for Catamaran-friendly,  for SportFish Charter,  for Pool/Beach, and  for Golf within a mile. *For an explanation of ACC's Ratings, see page 8.*

Cod End Cookhouse & Marina

PO Box 224; 12 Commercial Street; Tenants Harbor, ME 04860

Tel: (207) 372-6782 **VHF: Monitor** Ch. 16, 9 **Talk** Ch. 69
Fax: n/a **Alternate Tel:** n/a
Email: codend@midcoast.com **Web:** www.codend.com
Nearest Town: Rockland *(12 mi.)* **Tourist Info:** (207) 596-0376

Navigational Information

Lat: 43°57.940' **Long:** 069°12.550' **Tide:** 12 ft. **Current:** 1 kt. **Chart:** 13302
Rep. Depths (*MLW*): Entry 15 ft. **Fuel Dock** 10 ft. **Max Slip/Moor** -/15 ft.
Access: Gulf of Maine to Tenants Harbor

Marina Facilities *(In Season/Off Season)*

Fuel: Gasoline, Diesel
Slips: 0 Total, 0 Transient **Max LOA:** n/a **Max Beam:** n/a
Rate *(per ft.)*: **Day** n/a **Week** n/a **Month** n/a
Power: 30 amp n/a, **50 amp** n/a, **100 amp** n/a, **200 amp** n/a
Cable TV: No **Dockside Phone:** No
Dock Type: n/a
Moorings: 14 Total, 14 Transient **Launch:** None
Rate: Day $25 **Week** $160 **Month** $550
Heads: 2 Toilet(s)
Internet: No **Laundry:** None
Pump-Out: No **Fee:** n/a **Closed Heads:** Yes

Marina Operations

Owner/Manager: Susan Miller **Dockmaster:** Same
In-Season: MidJun-MidSep, 8am-6pm **Off-Season:** Sep-May, by chance
After-Hours Arrival: Call for instructions.
Reservations: No **Credit Cards:** Visa/MC, Dscvr
Discounts: Boat/US **Dockage:** Inq. **Fuel:** Inq. **Repair:** n/a
Pets: Welcome, Dog Walk Area **Handicap Access:** Yes

Marina Services and Boat Supplies

Services - Docking Assistance, Trash Pick-Up, Dock Carts **Communication -** Pay Phone, FedEx, UPS, Express Mail *(Sat Del)* **Supplies - OnSite:** Ice *(Block, Cube)*, Ships' Store *(Also at Lyman Morse)* **1-3 mi:** Bait/Tackle *(St George Marine 372-6308)* **3+ mi:** Marine Discount Store *(Hamilton's Rockland, 15 mi.)*

Boatyard Services

Near: Railway, Forklift, Crane, Launching Ramp, Engine mechanic *(gas, diesel)*, Electrical Repairs, Hull Repairs, Rigger, Bottom Cleaning, Brightwork, Compound, Wash & Wax, Woodworking, Inflatable Repairs, Yacht Interiors, Metal Fabrication, Painting, Awlgrip, Total Refits, Yacht Building. **1-3 mi:** Divers. **Nearest Yard:** Lyman Morse (207) 354-6904

Restaurants and Accommodations

OnSite: Seafood Shack *(Cod End Cookhouse 372-8981, L $5-26, D $5-26, 7 days, 11am-8pm July & August - closed after Labor Day. Kids' menu. Delivers to boat.)* **OnCall:** Snack Bar *(Some seasons - delivery boat plies the harbor with muffins, newspapers, trash pick-up etc.)* **Near:** Restaurant *(East Wind Inn 372-6366, B $5-6, D $17-25, B 7:30-11am, D 5:30-9pm, Sun Brunch 11:30am-2pm), (Farmers Restaurant 372-6111, B $5, L $5-16, D $8-16, also delivers, including pizza)*, Lite Fare *(Chandlery L $4-14.50, 11am-3pm), (Schoolhouse Bakery & Coffee Shop 372-9608, M-S 7am-2pm), (Tenants Harbor Market)*, Inn/B&B *(East Wind Inn & Meeting House 372-6366, $99-226, next door)* **1-3 mi:** Snack Bar *(Harpoon 372-6304)* **3+ mi:** Inn/B&B *(Harbor View 372-8162, 4 mi.), (Ocean House 372-6691, 4 mi.)*

Recreation and Entertainment

Near: Playground, Jogging Paths, Volleyball, Galleries *(Nobel Clay Pottery; Pond House Gallery)*, Special Events *(St. George Days)* **Under 1 mi:** Tennis Courts, Museum *(Sarah Orne Jewett Schoolhouse Museum; Olson House)* **1-3 mi:** Beach *(Quarry)*, Dive Shop, Sightseeing *(Marshall Point Lighthouse and Museum 372-6450)* **3+ mi:** Golf Course *(Rockland G.C. 594-9322, 15 mi.)*

Provisioning and General Services

OnSite: Fishmonger *(Cod End Market 372-6782 8am-8pm Lobsters & more; order ahead via radio)* **Near:** Market *(Tenants Harbor General Store 372-6311 Pantry items, wine, beer, a deli, prepared foods & breakfast and lunch)*, Delicatessen, Wine/Beer *(Tenants Harbor)*, Bakery *(Schoolhouse)*, Post Office, Protestant Church, Library *(Jackson Memorial 372-8961)*, Bookstore *(Roseledge Books - 2-6pm daily on the front porch of red cottage)*, Newsstand **1-3 mi:** Farmers' Market **3+ mi:** Liquor Store *(15 mi.)*, Pharmacy *(15 mi.)*

Transportation

OnCall: Rental Car *(Enterprise 594-9093)*, Taxi *(Schooner Bay 594-5000)* **3+ mi:** Ferry Service *(372-8848 Laura B. or Elizabeth Ann to Monhegan Island -- leaves from Port Clyde, 4 mi.)* **Airport:** Knox County/Bangor Int'l. *(12 mi./65 mi.)*

Medical Services

911 Service **OnCall:** Ambulance **3+ mi:** Doctor *(Smith Curtis 273-6400, 11 mi.)*, Chiropractor *(Bay Chiropractic 596-6700, 11 mi.)* **Hospital:** Penobscot Bay 596-8000 *(18 mi.)*

Setting -- Artist Jamie Wyeth's white-washed compound and an abandoned lighthouse mark the entrance to Tenants Harbor - a quintessential Maine fishing village where lobster boats dot the harbor, and lobster traps blanket the long, narrow protected, and oft fog-free harbor. At the northwest head, Cod End's dock floats below a long, sturdy, stationary wharf that leads to the ship-shape, russet-trimmed, shingled Cookhouse and market. The town dock lies just beyond.

Marina Notes -- Owned and operated by the Halls since 1974. Dockside assistance available 7am- 6pm. Float dredged to 10 ft. all sides. Minor repairs and towing available. Harbor density recommends radioing for moorings. Look for the chartreuse/yellow mooring buoys in the southwestern end. Dinghy in to the Cod End Float or the dinghy dock next to the town landing. Moorings also possible from Art's Lobster (372-6265) - red "Rental," Witham's - white balls with blue bands "Rental," or East Wind. Call harbormaster Dave Schmanska (372-6363) for other options. Bathhouse: Heads shared with Cookhouse.

Notable -- The Cookhouse restaurant offers both inside and deck seating at spotless gray picnic tables with views across the harbor - fresh seafood (lobsters, clams, chowders) rolls, baskets, dinner plus desserts; they even deliver prepared food to the boat. Adjacent is a fresh fish market. The lovely, historic East Wind Inn (large white house in photo), next door, serves breakfast, dinner and Sunday brunch in an elegant dining room or "picnic-table" take-out at the Chandlery on their wharf. For a night ashore at the Inn, choose from standard rooms in the main Inn, higher end in the Meeting House (which also accommodates up to 30 for an event), and the best in the Ginny Wheeler House. A pleasant destination hike, Marshall Point Lighthouse & Museum promises spectacular views.

Navigational Information

Lat: 43°55.585' **Long:** 069°15.547' **Tide:** 10 ft. **Current:** n/a **Chart:** 13301
Rep. Depths (*MLW*): Entry 12 ft. **Fuel Dock** 10 ft. **Max Slip/Moor** -/8 ft.
Access: Gulf of Maine to Monhegan Island to Port Clyde

Marina Facilities *(In Season/Off Season)*

Fuel: Gasoline, Diesel
Slips: 0 Total, 0 Transient **Max LOA:** n/a **Max Beam:** n/a
Rate *(per ft.)*: **Day** n/a **Week** n/a **Month** n/a
Power: 30 amp n/a, **50 amp** n/a, **100 amp** n/a, **200 amp** n/a
Cable TV: No **Dockside Phone:** No
Dock Type: Floating
Moorings: 20 Total, 20 Transient **Launch:** Yes, Dinghy Dock
Rate: Day $30 **Week** $150 **Month** Inq.
Heads: 3 Toilet(s), 1 Shower(s)
Internet: No **Laundry:** None
Pump-Out: No **Fee:** n/a **Closed Heads:** Yes

Marina Operations

Owner/Manager: Caroline Volle **Dockmaster:** Same
In-Season: May 26-Oct 15, 6am-7pm **Off-Season:** Oct 16-May 25, 7am-6pm
After-Hours Arrival: Call early in the day
Reservations: Yes, Preferred **Credit Cards:** Visa/MC, Dscvr, Cash
Discounts: None
Pets: Welcome **Handicap Access:** No

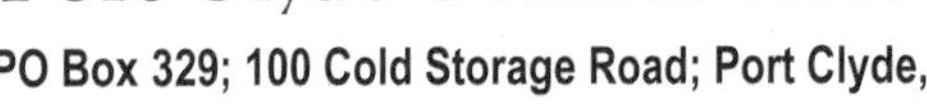

Port Clyde General Store

PO Box 329; 100 Cold Storage Road; Port Clyde, ME 04855

Tel: (207) 372-6543 **VHF: Monitor** Ch. 9 **Talk** Ch. 9
Fax: (207) 372-0634 **Alternate Tel:** n/a
Email: info@lindabeansperfectmaine.com **Web:** See Marina Notes
Nearest Town: Thomaston *(14 mi.)* **Tourist Info:** (207) 596-0376

Marina Services and Boat Supplies

Services - Concierge, Security *(24 hrs., webcams in store & on docks)*, Trash Pick-Up **Communication -** FedEx, UPS, Express Mail **Supplies - OnSite:** Ice *(Block, Cube)*, Ships' Store, Propane **Near:** Live Bait *(St. George Marine)* **Under 1 mi:** Bait/Tackle

Boatyard Services

OnSite: Launching Ramp **OnCall:** Divers **1-3 mi:** Travelift. **Nearest Yard:** Lyman Morse Boatyard (207) 354-6904

Restaurants and Accommodations

OnSite: Seafood Shack *(Dip Net 372-6307, L & D $5-24 - 11:30am-9pm - New Management - Jun-ColDay - deck dining or 16 seats inside)*, Lite Fare *(Port Clyde General Store 372-6543, B $2-6, L $3-8, Breakfast 'til noon, Pizza, too $6-15, 6am-7pm, daily - Linda Bean's Perfect Maine Lobster Roll)* **Near:** Restaurant *(Ocean House BYO)*, *(Harpoon 372-6304, D 5-9pm)*, Snack Bar *(Village Ice Cream Shop)*, Lite Fare *(Barn Cafe Seaside Inn - Tapas)*, Inn/B&B *(Seaside Inn 372-0700, $103-155)*, *(Ocean House 372-6691, $95-145)*, *(Rose Cottage)* **1-3 mi:** Restaurant *(Farmers Restaurant 372-6111, B $5, L & D $5-16)*, Inn/B&B *(Mill Pond House 372-6209, $60-95)* **3+ mi:** Restaurant *(Cod End Cookhouse 372-6782, 4.5 mi., L & D $5-26)*, *(East Wind Inn B $5-6, D $17-25, 4.5 mi., Lunch at Chandlery $4-$15)*

Recreation and Entertainment

OnSite: Picnic Area, Boat Rentals *(Port Clyde Kayaks 372-8100)*, Tours *(Port Clyde Kayaks 372-8100 10am & 2pm, 2.5-4 hrs., $55-70; Mohegan Boat Line Nature & Lighthouse Cruises 372-8848 $24/10.)* **Near:** Playground, Sightseeing *(Monhegan Island 372-8848 - 9 mi. offshore)*, Galleries *(Blue Water Fine Arts; Gallery-by-the-Sea 372-8280; Port Clyde Gallery Tues-Sun 10am-5pm; Seaside Inn; Port Clyde Arts and Crafts Society Thu-Sun 10am-5pm)*, Special Events *(Rock-the-Dock)* **Under 1 mi:** Beach *(Drift-In Beach)*, Museum *(1832 Marshall Point Lighthouse Museum 372-6450 Free & The Olson House 354-0102 - 4 mi.)*, Cultural Attract *(Herring Gut Learning Center - teaches aquaculture & environmental stewardship to at-risk youth)*

Provisioning and General Services

OnSite: Market, Delicatessen, Wine/Beer, Liquor Store, Bakery *(Village Ice Cream & Bakery)*, Lobster Pound *(Linda Bean's huge Lobster Pound - Kids can meet Lobstermen at 6pm)*, Dry Cleaners *(In by 10:30am, Back noon next day)*, Laundry, Bookstore *(Sea Star Shop)*, Newsstand, Retail Shops *("Store Upstairs" 372-6543 - gourmet kitchenware, sewing supplies, gifts, toys, gallery; Port Clyde Kayak - active sportswear)* **Near:** Fishmonger *(Port Clyde Fresh Catch 975-2191)*, Post Office, Protestant Church **1-3 mi:** Supermarket *(Tenants Harbor 372-6311- a modest market)*, Library *(Jackson Mem 372-8961)*, Beauty Salon

Transportation

OnCall: Rental Car *(Enterprise 594-9093)*, Taxi *(Joe's, Rockland)*, Airport Limo *(Schooner Bay, Rockland)* **Near:** Ferry Service *("Laura B." & "Elizabeth Ann" Mailboat to Monhegan Island 372-8848 $30/16 RT)*
Airport: Knox County - Owl's Head/Bangor Int'l. *(17 mi./62 mi.)*

Medical Services

911 Service **3+ mi:** Doctor *(Smith 273-6400, 13 mi.)*, Chiropractor *(Waldoboro 832-6347, 14 mi.)* **Hospital:** Miles Mem. 563-1234 *(20 mi.)*

Setting -- Marshall Point Light, with its unique footbridge, guards Port Clyde's south entrance where picturesque lobster boats are joined by an active groundfishing fleet of well-used, mid-size draggers and pleasure craft on moorings. Floats lead to a set of sturdy wharfs that berth the Monhegan Island Ferry, Town Dock, dining decks with picnic tables and umbrella-shaded cable-spool tables - and the storied, red-trimmed, sage-green Port Clyde General Store.

Marina Notes -- Owned by Linda Bean of L.L. Bean - lindabeansperfectmaine.com. Moorings (white with blue stripe, pink buoy), dinghy dock & "Pilgrim" Flanders Bay 21 launch. Harbor of refuge. Remarkably well-stocked, old-timey, wood-floored general store and lunch counter - groceries, deli, baked goods, meat, fish, lobsters, produce, liquor, wine, beer. Custom provisioning. New "Upstairs" shop. Laundry/drycleaning pick-up. Dip Net eatery now owned by Linda Bean - new menu, new paint. Bathhouse: Single fiberglass shower stall with small linoleum-floored dressing area for boaters. Heads - dockside Porta Potties.

Notable -- At the tip of the St. George peninsula, this rural, vibrant fishing village also sports easels and galleries at every turn. The Olson House is a draw for Andrew Wyeth fans - a series of watercolors and drawings feature the house and its inhabitants. Port Clyde also berths a unique community-supported-fishery, Port Clyde Fresh Catch, that processes seafood for some 350 share-owners (and also sells retail). An easy mile-walk, Marshall Point Lighthouse Museum displays memorabilia from St. George and its lighthouses. The mailboat ferry leaves the wharf for famous Monhegan Island - home to more than 20 artists (including Jamie Wyeth); some with open studios. Six hundred varieties of wildflowers, 200 species of birds, 17 miles of trails make this a naturalist's dream.

PHOTOS ON DVD: 25

Thomaston Town Landing

PO Box 299; Thomaston, ME 04861

Tel: (207) 354-6107 **VHF: Monitor** n/a **Talk** n/a
Fax: (207) 354-2132 **Alternate Tel:** (207) 975-6553
Email: n/a **Web:** town.thomaston.me.us
Nearest Town: Rockland *(5 mi.)* **Tourist Info:** (207) 596-0376

Navigational Information

Lat: 44°04.305' **Long:** 069°10.964' **Tide:** 10 ft. **Current:** 3 kt. **Chart:** 13301
Rep. Depths (*MLW*): Entry 12 ft. **Fuel Dock** n/a **Max Slip/Moor** 7 ft./15 ft.
Access: 10 miles up St. George River from Port Clyde

Marina Facilities *(In Season/Off Season)*

Fuel: No
Slips: 3 Total, 3 Transient **Max LOA:** 80 ft. **Max Beam:** 30 ft.
Rate *(per ft.)*: **Day** $1.00* **Week** $7 **Month** n/a
Power: 30 amp n/a, **50 amp** n/a, **100 amp** n/a, **200 amp** n/a
Cable TV: No **Dockside Phone:** No
Dock Type: Floating, Alongside, Wood
Moorings: 2 Total, 2 Transient **Launch:** No, Dinghy Dock
Rate: Day $20 **Week** $140 **Month** n/a
Heads: 2 Toilet(s)
Internet: No **Laundry:** None
Pump-Out: No **Fee:** n/a **Closed Heads:** Yes

Marina Operations

Owner/Manager: Thomaston **Dockmaster:** Gordon Mank, Jr. (Hrbrmstr)
In-Season: May-Oct, 8am-6pm **Off-Season:** Nov-Apr, Closed
After-Hours Arrival: n/a
Reservations: No **Credit Cards:** Cash or Check only
Discounts: None
Pets: Welcome, Dog Walk Area **Handicap Access:** Yes, Heads, Docks

Marina Services and Boat Supplies

Communication - Mail & Package Hold, FedEx, UPS **Supplies - Under 1 mi:** Ice *(Block, Cube)* **3+ mi:** Marine Discount Store *(Hamilton Marine, Rockland, 6 mi.)*, Propane *(6 mi.)*

Boatyard Services

OnSite: Launching Ramp **OnCall:** Life Raft Service **Near:** Travelift *(110T)*, Engine mechanic *(gas, diesel)*, Electrical Repairs, Electronic Sales, Hull Repairs, Rigger, Divers, Bottom Cleaning, Brightwork, Air Conditioning, Refrigeration, Propeller Repairs, Woodworking, Yacht Interiors, Metal Fabrication, Painting, Awlgrip, Total Refits. **Nearest Yard:** Lyman Morse (207) 354-6904

Restaurants and Accommodations

Near: Restaurant *(Harbor View 354-8173, L $6-12, D $6-27, 11:30am-9pm, 'til 10pm Fri & Sat)* **Under 1 mi:** Restaurant *(Thomaston Cafe 354-8589, B $4-8, L $7.50-14, D $16-25, Break Fri & Sat. 7:30-11, Lunch Mon-Sat 11-2, Dinner Fri & Sat 5:30 +, Sun Brunch 8:30-1:30 $7-9)*, *(Billy's Tavern 354-1177, Lively Irish pub with good pours, live music, all manner of games - center of Thomaston nightlife)*, Pizzeria *(Athens 354-0040)* **1-3 mi:** Hotel *(Hampton Inn & Suites 594-6644)* **3+ mi:** Inn/B&B *(Berry Manor 596-7696, $115-275, 4 mi.)*, *(Weskeag Inn At the Water 596-6676, $90-150, 5 mi.)*

Recreation and Entertainment

OnSite: Picnic Area, Grills **OnCall:** Fishing Charter **Near:** Jogging Paths, Tours *(Museum in the Streets; Thomaston Historical Society 354-2295 Jun-Aug, Tue-Thur 2-4pm, Free)*, Sightseeing *(Knox Street Historic District - Ships' Captains borrowed from every European architectural period)* **Under 1 mi:** Playground, Hike/Bike Trails *(St. George Hiking Trail)*, Park *(Thomaston Athletic Field)*, Museum *(Montpelier - Gen. Henry Knox 354-8062 $7/4 Tue-Sat 10am-3:30pm)*, Galleries *(OP 354-3666 including the Wyeth Archives; Thomaston Place Auctions 354-8141)* **1-3 mi:** Movie Theater *(Flagship Cinema 594-4705)* **3+ mi:** Golf Course *(Rockland G. C. 594-9322, 5 mi.)*

Provisioning and General Services

Near: Convenience Store *(Pik Qwik 354-8223; Waterfront Mkt 354-6114)*, Wine/Beer *(Pik Qwik, Waterfront Market)*, Liquor Store **Under 1 mi:** Market *(Thomaston Grocery 354-2583 - well supplied provisioning stop)*, Bakery *(Thomaston Cafe 354-8589)*, Bank/ATM *(3 banks)*, Post Office *(354-2420)*, Catholic Church, Protestant Church, Library *(Thomaston 354-2453)*, Beauty Salon *(Creative Images 354-2755)*, Barber Shop, Laundry, Bookstore *(Personal 354-8058)*, Newsstand **1-3 mi:** Synagogue, Florist, Retail Shops *(Maine State Prison Showroom 354-9237, daily 9am-5pm - displays over 600 handcrafted, prisoner-made products)* **3+ mi:** Supermarket *(Hannaford Rockland 594-2173, 5 mi.)*, Pharmacy *(5 mi.)*

Transportation

OnCall: Rental Car *(Enterprise, Rockland)*, Taxi *(Hit the Road 230-0095)*, Airport Limo *(Schooner Bay 594-5000)* **Airport:** Knox County *(8 mi.)*

Medical Services

911 Service **OnCall:** Ambulance **Under 1 mi:** Doctor *(Weaver 354-8733; Harshman 354-3545)*, Dentist *(Maine Coast 354-6501)* **3+ mi:** Chiropractor *(Bay 596-6700, 5 mi.)*, Holistic Services *(5 mi.)*, Veterinarian *(Animal Hosp. 594-5850, 5 mi.)* **Hospital:** Pen Bay 596-8000 *(8 mi.)*

Setting -- Ten miles up the St. George River, at the head of navigation, the Town Landing's single float lies just beyond Lyman-Morse's impressive, expansive boatyard facility. Picnic tables sprinkle the lush green knoll sloping to the gangway that leads to the town dock. Just west, a small, red dockhouse marks Harbor View Restaurant's long wharf that leads to the modest red clapboard eatery - with a window-wall dining room and enticing dining deck.

Marina Notes -- *90 linear feet of side-tie dockage plus moorings. Thomaston Boat & Engine Works 594-7013 for diesels; Jeff's Marine 354-2132 for outboards. Immediately adjacent, world-class Lyman-Morse Boatbuilding Co (354-6904) hauls large vessels, builds beautiful craft, & offers boatyard services - including pump-out. Inquire about moorings ($25). Boats being serviced occupy most dockage ($2.50/ft.). Bathhouse: In shingled building at top of ramp.

Notable -- In the park overlooking the landing, a wooden cross commemorates the first English landfall when, in 1605, Capt. George Weymouth sailed up the river seeking possible settlement sites. A colorful sign describes 25 stops on the "Museum in the Streets" walking tour. Follow the sign-posts a half mile north to the center of historic Thomaston - where brick 19th-century buildings stretching along Main Street house locally grown shops, antique galleries and services. In the 1800's, the "Town that Went to Sea" spawned eight ship-building yards that launched ocean-going schooners to transport native lime. A right at the north end of Main leads to "Montpelier," a 1926 re-creation of the 1794 mansion of Revolutionary War hero General Henry Knox, George Washington's first Secretary of War. The original, marked by a stone monument, was near the dock. An original brick outbuilding, housing the Thomaston Historical Society, stands nearby.

PHOTOS ON DVD: 25

    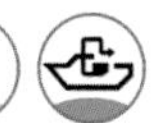 

Navigational Information
Lat: 43°59.549' **Long:** 069°24.466' **Tide:** 9 ft. **Current:** n/a **Chart:** 13301
Rep. Depths (*MLW*): Entry 16 ft. **Fuel Dock** 6 ft. **Max Slip/Moor** 6 ft./30 ft.
Access: Muscongus Sound to Hockomock Channel

Marina Facilities *(In Season/Off Season)*
Fuel: Gasoline, Diesel
Slips: 10 Total, 4 Transient **Max LOA:** 50 ft. **Max Beam:** n/a
Rate *(per ft.)*: **Day** $1.50 **Week** $7 **Month** n/a
Power: 30 amp n/a, **50 amp** n/a, **100 amp** n/a, **200 amp** n/a
Cable TV: No **Dockside Phone:** No
Dock Type: Floating, Wood
Moorings: 6 Total, 6 Transient **Launch:** None, Dinghy Dock
Rate: Day $25 **Week** $70 **Month** Inq.
Heads: 1 Toilet(s)
Internet: Yes *(Wi-Fi DSL, Free)* **Laundry:** 1 Washer(s), 2 Dryer(s)
Pump-Out: OnSite, Full Service, 1 Central **Fee:** $15 **Closed Heads:** Yes

Marina Operations
Owner/Manager: Scott Plummer **Dockmaster:** Same
In-Season: May-Oct, 9am-6pm **Off-Season:** Nov-Apr, Closed
After-Hours Arrival: Call ahead
Reservations: Yes **Credit Cards:** Visa/MC
Discounts: None
Pets: Welcome **Handicap Access:** No

Broad Cove Marine Services

PO Box 208; 374 Medomak Road; Medomak , ME 04551

Tel: (207) 529-5186 **VHF: Monitor** Ch. 9 **Talk** Ch. 6
Fax: (207) 529-4469 **Alternate Tel:** n/a
Email: bcms@tidewater.net **Web:** n/a
Nearest Town: Damariscotta *(10 mi.)* **Tourist Info:** (207) 563-8340

Marina Services and Boat Supplies
Services - Boaters' Lounge, Dock Carts **Communication -** Mail & Package Hold, Phone Messages, Fax in/out *(Free)*, FedEx, DHL, UPS, Express Mail **Supplies - OnSite:** Ice *(Block, Cube)* **3+ mi:** Ships' Store *(15 mi.)*

Boatyard Services
OnSite: Launching Ramp, Rigger, Compound, Wash & Wax **OnCall:** Hydraulic Trailer, Engine mechanic *(gas, diesel)*, Divers, Bottom Cleaning, Propeller Repairs, Woodworking **Yard Rates:** $45/hr., Power Wash $40 **Storage:** On-Land $28/ft.

Restaurants and Accommodations
OnSite: Seafood Shack *(Lobster Shack L & D $5-30)* **3+ mi:** Restaurant *(King Elders Pub & Restaurant 563-6008, 10 mi., Damariscotta)*, *(Anchor Inn 529-5584, 7 mi., Round Pond)*, Pizzeria *(Romeo's Pizza 846-1473, 7 mi.)*, Inn/B&B *(Inn at Round Pond 529-2004, $120-185, 7 mi.)*, Condo/Cottage *(Lake Permaquid Cabins 563-5202, $95/day, $6t00/wk, 7 mi.)*

Provisioning and General Services
OnSite: Convenience Store *(Modest selection part of snack bar)*, Fishmonger, Lobster Pound **1-3 mi:** Post Office *(Bremen 529-5494)*, Protestant Church *(Bremen Union 529-5232)* **3+ mi:** Market *(King Row 529-5380 Round Pond, 7 mi.)*, Supermarket *(Hannaford Damariscotta 563-8131, 10 mi.)*, Farmers' Market *(Damariscotta - Fri & Mon 9am-Noon, 10 mi.)*, Bank/ATM *(10 mi.)*, Pharmacy *(Rite Aid 563-3506, 10 mi.)*, Hardware Store *(Damariscotta 563-3428, 10 mi.)*

Transportation
OnCall: Rental Car *(Enterprise 594-9093 Thomaston, 20 mi.)* **Airport:** Knox County/Portland Jetport *(23 mi./65 mi.)*

Medical Services
911 Service **OnCall:** Ambulance **3+ mi:** Doctor *(Miles Family 563-4780, 10 mi.)*, Dentist *(Beaudoin 832-5181, 9 mi.)*, Chiropractor *(Waldoboro Chiropractic 832-6347, 9 mi.)* **Hospital:** Miles Memorial 563-1234 *(10 mi.)*

Setting -- Three miles north of Round Pond on the Medomak River, an inviting complex of red-roofed, gray buildings perches on the edge of the Hockomock Channel protected by Oar Island. Surrounded by an active lobster operaton, a long float hosts a mix of working boats, recreational craft and dinghies that service the mooring field. Upland is a casual lobster pound with an inviting dining deck overlooking the channel and the comings and goings of the lobster fleet. The surroundings are rural Maine, the views pristine and the "broad cove" beautiful and protected.

Marina Notes -- Downhome, nicely maintained simple facility. Customer-oriented, knowledgeable staff. No power on docks. Wi-Fi, diesel, gas, ice, water, pump-out. Key-coded very casual, very useful Boaters' Lounge with a small sofa and "L-shaped" desk: computer, printer, fax machine & wireless DSL. Call ahead on cell or radio on Ch. 9 or 6 when nearing channel. Dock hands guide boaters in and assign slip or mooring (expect to be part of the lobster fleet). Fuel dock creates heavy powerboat traffic. List of people who can "fix things." Bathhouse: A rustic hallway with recent washer/dryers leads to single basic head.

Notable -- The casual seafood shack features steamed lobster, in every possible size and shell, plus clams, chips, three-bean salad, hot dogs and coffee. Buy lobsters and clams live, cooked to-go, or as a "dinner" consumed on the lovely deck. Those not seafood lovers are out of luck. Broad Cove offers the rare pleasure of nothing - or maybe nothing while doing laundry. Plan to relax, eat, read, and enjoy the scenery and the quiet -- there is nowhere to go and nothing to do. It's nine miles to Waldoboro and ten to Damariscotta, the nearest serious business centers, and seven to the tiny burg of Round Pond.

PHOTOS ON DVD: 19

Spar Shed Marina

PO Box 8381; 9 Spar Shed Lane; East Boothbay, ME 04544

Tel: (207) 633-4389 **VHF: Monitor** n/a **Talk** n/a
Fax: n/a **Alternate Tel:** n/a
Email: sparshed@roadrunner.com **Web:** n/a
Nearest Town: Boothbay *(5 mi.)* **Tourist Info:** (207) 633-7448

Navigational Information
Lat: 43°49.893' **Long:** 069°35.191' **Tide:** 9 ft. **Current:** 2 kt. **Chart:** 13293
Rep. Depths (*MLW*): Entry 6 ft. **Fuel Dock** n/a **Max Slip/Moor** 11 ft./15 ft.
Access: Damariscotta River, Marker 35 to port, and into Little River

Marina Facilities *(In Season/Off Season)*
Fuel: No
Slips: 8 Total, 2 Transient **Max LOA:** 52 ft. **Max Beam:** 15 ft.
Rate *(per ft.)*: **Day** $2.00* **Week** $9 **Month** $22
Power: 30 amp $2, **50 amp** $3, **100 amp** n/a, **200 amp** n/a
Cable TV: No **Dockside Phone:** No
Dock Type: Fixed, Floating, Alongside, Wood
Moorings: 7 Total, 2 Transient **Launch:** n/a, Dinghy Dock
Rate: Day $30 **Week** $180 **Month** $350
Heads: 1 Toilet(s), 1 Shower(s)
Internet: No **Laundry:** None
Pump-Out: No **Fee:** n/a **Closed Heads:** No

Marina Operations
Owner/Manager: George Horn Jr. **Dockmaster:** Same
In-Season: May-Sep, 8am-6pm **Off-Season:** Closed
After-Hours Arrival: Pick up mooring or slip and see manager in morning
Reservations: Preferred **Credit Cards:** Cash/check
Discounts: None
Pets: Welcome, Dog Walk Area **Handicap Access:** No

Marina Services and Boat Supplies
Services - Docking Assistance, Security *(Manager lives on premises)*, Trash Pick-Up **Communication -** Mail & Package Hold, FedEx, DHL, UPS, Express Mail **Supplies - OnCall:** Ice *(Block, Cube)* **1-3 mi:** Ships' Store, West Marine, Bait/Tackle, Propane *(Dead River Oil 633-3144)*, CNG

Boatyard Services
OnSite: Brightwork, Compound, Wash & Wax, Interior Cleaning, Woodworking **OnCall:** Engine mechanic *(gas, diesel)*, Electrical Repairs, Divers, Bottom Cleaning, Air Conditioning, Inflatable Repairs, Upholstery **1-3 mi:** Travelift, Railway, Forklift, Crane, Launching Ramp, Electronic Sales, Hull Repairs, Rigger, Sail Loft, Canvas Work, Metal Fabrication, Painting, Total Refits, Yacht Design. **Nearest Yard:** Ocean Point (207) 633-0773

Restaurants and Accommodations
Near: Motel *(Smuggler's Cove Inn 633-2800, $65-230)* **1-3 mi:** Restaurant *(Ocean Point Inn 633-4200, B $8-15, D $18-30, Kids' $6-10, Dinner Fri-Mon, Tavern Menu nightly $9-17 incl. pizza)*, *(Lobsterman's Wharf 633-3443, L $5-28, D $8-28, 11:30am-6pm Twin lobsters $20, Cheeseburger $5, 3-6pm $13-14.)*, Lite Fare *(East Boothbay General 633-7800, B $3-8.50, L $6-9, Wraps, sandwiches, chowders, muffins, cookies, soft-serve ice cream, pizzas incl. breakfast $8-20)*, Hotel *(Ocean Point Inn 633-4200, $70-220)*, Inn/B&B *(Linekin Bay Resort 633-2494, $110-170/pp, re-opened 2011, 5 lodges, 35 cabins AP - Day & overnight moorings)*, *(Five Gable 633-4551, $140-235)*

Recreation and Entertainment
Near: Jogging Paths, Hike/Bike Trails **1-3 mi:** Beach, Tennis Courts, Galleries *(Studio of Ships 633-4246; Ocean Point Studiio;)* **3+ mi:** Golf Course *(Boothbay Country Club 633-6085, 4 mi.)*, Fitness Center *(YMCA, 5 mi.)*, Museum *(Boothbay Railway Museum, 5 mi.)*

Provisioning and General Services
Near: Lobster Pound *(Little River Lobster 633-2648)* **1-3 mi:** Convenience Store, Market *(East Boothbay General Store 633-7800 - 7 days, Mon-Sat 7am-7pm, Sun 7am-2pm, Newspapers, very well-stocked)*, Wine/Beer *(EBGS)*, Bakery *(EBGS - muffins, cookies, donuts, pies, NY bagels)*, Post Office, Protestant Church **3+ mi:** Supermarket *(Hannaford 366-6465, 5 mi.)*, Bank/ATM *(5 mi.)*, Catholic Church *(6 mi.)*, Library *(Boothbay Harbor Library 633-3112, 5 mi.)*, Laundry *(5 mi.)*, Pharmacy *(Rite Aid 633-7023, 5 mi.)*, Hardware Store *(Poole Brothers Lumber 633-4474, 5 mi.)*

Transportation
OnSite: Bikes *(Free)* **OnCall:** Taxi *(Bobos Coastal 380-4182)* **Airport:** Portland Int'l. *(60 mi.)*

Medical Services
911 Service **OnCall:** Ambulance **3+ mi:** Doctor *(St. Andrews 633-2121, 5 mi.)*, Dentist *(Family 633-4243, 6 mi.)*, Chiropractor *(Boothbay 633-5500, 5.5 mi.)* **Hospital:** St. Andrews 633-7820 *(6.5 mi.)*

Setting -- Just past the split of the Damariscotta and Little Rivers, flying flags identify small, accommodating Spar Shed on the west side of this tranquil hurricane hole. The gray dockhouse, flanked by decks edged with white trellis railings and colorful flower boxes, sits high above the river. Chaise lounges and tables and chairs with yellow umbrellas offer comfortable places to relax and watch osprey and seagulls.

Marina Notes -- Two slips available to visitors, *seasonal rental $65/ft. Reservations preferred, but call on the phone, not the radio. Family owned & operated. Originally Little River Wholesale Lobster Pound (now across the river). A marina since '87. Cone-shaped mooring balls, white with blue stripe "Spar Shed." No launch service, use the dinghy - but will pickup if necessary. Fuel possibly at Lobster Co. Complimentary bicycles (if one assumes the risk). Some basic boatyard services onsite, others can be contracted for - Horns will oversee any work that needs to be done. Cottage adjoining property available for rent (633-6545). Bathhouse: Separate building. Homey nautically themed full bath, yellow wood walls, linoleum floor, shower stall & area rug.

Notable -- A mile and a half south, the 110-year-old Ocean Point Inn, a classic golden-era resort, offers breakfast and dinner along with a stroll along Shore Road with a stop at artist Corinne McIntyre's and potter Fred McIntyre's Ocean Point Studio. Dinghy or hike 2.7 miles north to the tiny, un-touristed village of East Boothbay. A short walk are Smuggler's Cove resort and the historic Paul E. Luke boat building company. A major dinghy adventure (or big boat lunch stop) might be the Nature Conservancy's Damariscove Island, about 2 miles south. Two miles farther is the Island's harbor; at its head is a dinghy landing.

PHOTOS ON DVD: 19

Navigational Information

Lat: 43°50.861' **Long:** 069°33.367' **Tide:** 9 ft. **Current:** n/a **Chart:** 13293
Rep. Depths (*MLW*): Entry 25 ft. **Fuel Dock** n/a **Max Slip/Moor** 12 ft./12 ft.
Access: Damariscotta River to Christmas Cove west shore

Marina Facilities *(In Season/Off Season)*

Fuel: No
Slips: 12 Total, 8 Transient **Max LOA:** 60 ft. **Max Beam:** n/a
Rate *(per ft.)*: **Day** $2.50 **Week** Inq. **Month** Inq.
Power: 30 amp Incl., **50 amp** n/a, **100 amp** n/a, **200 amp** n/a
Cable TV: No **Dockside Phone:** No
Dock Type: Floating, Alongside, Wood
Moorings: 14 Total, 14 Transient **Launch:** Yes, Dinghy Dock
Rate: Day $35 **Week** n/a **Month** n/a
Heads: 3 Toilet(s), 1 Shower(s)
Internet: Yes *(Wi-Fi, Free)* **Laundry:** None
Pump-Out: OnSite, Full Service **Fee:** Free **Closed Heads:** Yes

Marina Operations

Owner/Manager: Amanda Sprague & Joseph Yost **Dockmaster:** Same
In-Season: Jun-Oct, 11am-10pm **Off-Season:** Closed
After-Hours Arrival: Check in at the Inn desk
Reservations: Yes, Preferred **Credit Cards:** Visa/MC
Discounts: None
Pets: Welcome **Handicap Access:** Yes, Heads, Docks

Coveside Marina

98 Coveside Road; South Bristol, ME 04568

Tel: (207) 644-8282 **VHF: Monitor** Ch. 9 **Talk** Ch. 68
Fax: (207) 644-8882 **Alternate Tel:** n/a
Email: info@covesiderestaurant.com **Web:** www.covesiderestaurant.com
Nearest Town: Damariscotta *(14 mi.)* **Tourist Info:** (207) 563-8340

Marina Services and Boat Supplies

Services - Docking Assistance **Communication -** Pay Phone (1), FedEx, UPS **Supplies - OnSite:** Ice *(Block, Cube)* **Under 1 mi:** Ships' Store *(Osier's Wharf 644-8500)*, Bait/Tackle *(Osier's)*

Boatyard Services

Under 1 mi: Travelift *(25T)*, Forklift, Hydraulic Trailer, Launching Ramp, Engine mechanic *(gas, diesel)*, Electrical Repairs, Hull Repairs, Bottom Cleaning, Brightwork, Compound, Wash & Wax, Woodworking, Painting. **1-3 mi:** Electronic Sales, Upholstery. **Nearest Yard:** Gamage Shipyard (207) 644-8181

Restaurants and Accommodations

OnSite: Restaurant *(Burgee Pub & Patio 644-8282, B, L & D $7-23, 7 days Jun-Oct, small plates, sandwiches, rolls, baskets, pastas & bowls + Lobster!)*, *(Coveside Dining Room 644-8282, D $18-28)* **Near:** Inn/B&B *(Unique Yankee B & B 644-1502, $96-140, Panoramic views from observatory, pets welcome)* **Under 1 mi:** Seafood Shack *(Osier's Wharf 644-8500)*, Snack Bar *(Island Grocery ice cream)*, Lite Fare *(Harborside Café 644-8751, B $2-7.50, L $3-9.50, Pizza, too $6.50-14.50)*, Inn/B&B *(Bridge House 644-1478, $115-295, 1 room to 2 bedroom suite)*, *(Sunset B&B 644-8849, $70-160, 2 rooms avail in various configurations)*

Recreation and Entertainment

OnSite: Boat Rentals, Galleries *(Local Artists)* **Near:** Beach, Jogging Paths, Hike/Bike Trails *(bike Rutherford Island)* **Under 1 mi:** Museum *(The Thompson Ice House 644-8551 Wed, Fri, Sat 1-4pm)* **1-3 mi:** Sightseeing *(Witch Island Sanctuary - 18 acres overlook John's Bay, two beaches)* **3+ mi:** Picnic Area *(4 mi.)*, Park *(Pemaquid Beach Park 677-2754, 4 mi.)*

Provisioning and General Services

Under 1 mi: Convenience Store *(Osier's Wharf 644-8500)*, Market *(Harborside 644-8751, Island Grocery 644-8552 Delivers)*, Delicatessen *(marine supplies, seafood and groceries)*, Wine/Beer *(Island Grocery)*, Fishmonger *(Osier's Wharf)*, Lobster Pound *(South Bristol Fishermen's Co-op 644-8224)*, Bank/ATM, Post Office, Protestant Church, Library *(Rutherford 644-1882)*

Transportation

OnSite: Bikes **OnCall:** Rental Car *(Enterprise 882-8393 - Wiscasset 24 mi.)* **Airport:** Portland Int'l. *(70 mi.)*

Medical Services

911 Service **OnCall:** Ambulance **3+ mi:** Doctor *(Rosene 677-3138 - Permaquid, 9 mi.)* **Hospital:** Miles Mem. 563-1234 - Damariscotta *(14 mi.)*

Setting -- On the shore of Christmas Cove, frequently cited as one of the more beautiful gunkholes in Maine, Coveside's restaurant and marina complex is easily identified by its barn-red siding and two dining decks. Two gangways lead from big boat and dinghy floats to the restaurant and amenities. The marina, the cove, as well as lovely Rutherford Island with its old, stately summer cottages have long been magnets for cruisers - filling the harbor with beautiful craft.

Marina Notes -- *Call Ch. 9 for mooring. New owners in 2007: Amanda Sprague & Chef Joseph Yost. Moorings - large white balls with hand-painted black numbers. Use the dink; launch service may be available. Coveside Inn damaged in storm and torn down. Can help with provisioning. Pets O.K. but outside only. Well water for tanks - no boat washing. Pine-paneled hallway gallery for local artists. Bathhouse: Gorgeous new wood-paneled full baths. No laundry.

Notable -- Chef Joseph Yost's Continental menus focus on organic, local produce and seafood. The Burgee Pub & Patio serves lunch and dinner in a cozy, cabin-like atmosphere enhanced by tattered personal signals and burgees that paper the walls and hang from the rafters or at umbrella-topped tables on the comfortable deck with spectacular views of the cove and beyond. Evenings Coveside also offers a more fine-dining experience in its large, pine-paneled, windowed dining room - with just a hint of flags tucked above the rafters. Another deck, with redwood picnic tables covered by a white tent, is ideal for a club cruise - they can seat up to 90 outside and in for special events. Barely a mile west, South Bristol's small group of services surrounds the famous swing bridge over The Gut. Capt. John Smith discovered Christmas Cove on December 25, 1614. By the late 1800's, it was a major N.Y. and Boston steamer destination.

PHOTOS ON DVD: 23

Gamage Shipyard

6 Gamage Drive; South Bristol, ME 04568

Tel: (207) 644-8181 **VHF: Monitor** Ch. 16 **Talk** n/a
Fax: (207) 644-8273 **Alternate Tel:** n/a
Email: gamage@tidewater.net **Web:** www.gamageshipyard.com
Nearest Town: Damariscotta *(15 mi.)* **Tourist Info:** (207) 633-7448

Navigational Information
Lat: 43°51.752' **Long:** 069°33.622' **Tide:** 8 ft. **Current:** 3 kt. **Chart:** 13293
Rep. Depths (*MLW*): Entry 30 ft. **Fuel Dock** n/a **Max Slip/Moor** 14 ft./80 ft.
Access: Damariscotta River north to R6, to The Gut

Marina Facilities *(In Season/Off Season)*
Fuel: Gasoline, Diesel
Slips: 28 Total, 5 Transient **Max LOA:** 60 ft. **Max Beam:** n/a
Rate *(per ft.)*: **Day** $2.00 **Week** n/a **Month** n/a
Power: 30 amp Incl., **50 amp** Incl., **100 amp** n/a, **200 amp** n/a
Cable TV: No **Dockside Phone:** No
Dock Type: Floating, Long Fingers, Alongside, Concrete
Moorings: 16 Total, 4 Transient **Launch:** No, Dinghy Dock
Rate: Day $15 **Week** $8/ft. **Month** n/a
Heads: 1 Toilet(s), 1 Shower(s) *(dressing rooms)*
Internet: Yes *(Wi-Fi, Free)* **Laundry:** None
Pump-Out: No **Fee:** n/a **Closed Heads:** No

Marina Operations
Owner/Manager: Winword Gamage **Dockmaster:** Same
In-Season: Jun-Oct 12, 8am-4:30pm **Off-Season:** Oct 12-May, 8am-4pm
After-Hours Arrival: n/a
Reservations: No. First come, first served **Credit Cards:** Visa/MC
Discounts: None
Pets: Welcome **Handicap Access:** Yes, Docks

Marina Services and Boat Supplies
Services - Docking Assistance, Dock Carts **Communication -** Mail & Package Hold, FedEx, DHL, UPS, Express Mail **Supplies - OnSite:** Ice *(Block, Cube)*, Ships' Store *(Marine Supplies, Ice Cream, Food Items, Beverages, Snacks)*

Boatyard Services
OnSite: Travelift *(25T)*, Forklift, Crane, Engine mechanic *(gas, diesel)*, Electronic Sales, Electronics Repairs, Bottom Cleaning, Brightwork, Compound, Wash & Wax **Yard Rates:** $45/hr., Haul & Launch $5/ft., Power Wash $2/ft. **Storage:** On-Land $11/ft. season

Restaurants and Accommodations
Near: Seafood Shack *(Osier's Wharf 644-8500)*, Snack Bar *(Island Grocery ice cream)*, Lite Fare *(Harborside Café 644-8751, B $2-7.50, L $3-9.50, Pizza, too $6.50-14.50 - Mon-Sat 7am-8pm, Sun 8am-2pm.)*, Inn/B&B *(Bridge House 644-1478, $115-295, 1 room to 2 bedroom suite)* **Under 1 mi:** Restaurant *(Coveside Restaurant 644-8282, D $18-28)*, *(Burgee Pub & Patio at Coveside 644-8282, L & D $7-23, 7 days Jun-Oct, small plates, sandwiches, rolls, baskets, pastas)*, Inn/B&B *(Sunset B & B 644-8849, $70-160, 2 rooms avail in various configurations, kayak rentals too)*, *(Unique Yankee B & B 644-1502, $96-140, Panoramic views of ocean from top deck, pets welcome)*

Recreation and Entertainment
Near: Jogging Paths, Hike/Bike Trails *(Bike Rutherford Island)*, Special Events *(Labor Day River Festival arts & crafts show)* **Under 1 mi:** Museum *(The Thompson Ice House 644-8551 Wed, Fri, Sat 1-4pm - 150-year-old commercial icehouse with video presentation - ice, too!)*, Sightseeing *(Maine Audubon's Witch Island Preserve 781-2330 by dinghy)* **3+ mi:** Beach *(Witch Island Sanctuary, 4 mi.)*, Picnic Area *(Witch Island Sanctuary, 4 mi.)*

Provisioning and General Services
Near: Convenience Store *(Osier's Wharf 644-8500)*, Gourmet Shop, Wine/Beer *(Island Grocery)*, Fishmonger *(Osier's Wharf, outdoor seaside deck seating)*, Lobster Pound *(South Bristol Fishermen's Co-op 644-8224)*, Bank/ATM, Post Office, Protestant Church *(Union Congregational)*, Library *(Rutherford 644-1882)*, Retail Shops *(Cottage Cupboards Antiques)* **Under 1 mi:** Delicatessen *(Harborside Grocery & Deli 644-8751)*

Transportation
OnCall: Rental Car *(Enterprise 882-8393)* **Airport:** Portland Int'l. *(53 mi.)*

Medical Services
911 Service **OnCall:** Ambulance **Hospital:** Miles Memorial 563-1234 Damariscotta *(15 mi.)*

PHOTOS ON DVD: 25

Setting -- Perched on the northwest side of The Gut, which connects the Damariscotta River and John's Bay, Gamage Shipyard's spiffy new facility features concrete floating docks, high-end pedestals and a pretty red-roofed, shingled store and office. Decks surround the one and-a-half-story building - deck chairs on the front porch create a perfect place to watch the green swing bridge as it accommodates the commercial fishing traffic on this busy waterway.

Marina Notes -- Over 150 years old. Recent upgrades: concrete docks, Lighthouse pedestals and a new dockhouse. Depths: fuel dock 11 ft, slips 4-11 ft. Heavy-duty moorings hold boats to 60 ft. Dock house with store, heated winter storage building, updated equipment. 9500 sq. ft. heated space, 4800 sq. ft. unheated space. Outside storage 125 boats. Scheduled - New structure complete with restrooms and laundry facilities will replace dilapidated building. Bathhouse: Single full bathroom with linoleum floor, fiberglass shower stall - separate entrance. Note: Eastern side of swing bridge 55 ft. overhead cables.

Notable -- Originally noted for its work on wooden boats, Gamage now services all types of vessels. Among the many schooners, research vessels and working boats that launched here were Hudson River's Clearwater and Cape Cod's Shenandoah. Around the swing bridge, which crosses the narrow passage known as the Gut, are a cluster of services - including the Island Grocery's new home - a beautiful 21st C. interpretation of a Maine cottage. An easy walk will take you to the beautiful gunkhole, Christmas Cove, and the Coveside Restaurant. Interesting ventures might be the half-mile dinghy ride to Witch Island Sanctuary, or the 4-mile dinghy ride north (with tide on your side) to Menigawum Preserve on 30-acre Stratton Island - trail maps available at the site.

     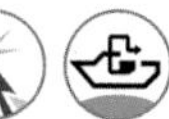 

Navigational Information
Lat: 43°51.900' **Long:** 069°35.070' **Tide:** 9 ft. **Current:** 5 kt. **Chart:** 13293
Rep. Depths (*MLW*): Entry 63 ft. **Fuel Dock** 25 ft. **Max Slip/Moor** 25 ft./63 ft.
Access: Damariscotta River to G7 to East Boothbay

Marina Facilities *(In Season/Off Season)*
Fuel: Slip-Side Fueling, Gasoline, Diesel
Slips: 67 Total, 5 Transient **Max LOA:** 150 ft. **Max Beam:** 50 ft.
Rate *(per ft.)*: **Day** $2.00* **Week** $10/5 **Month** $25/12.50
Power: 30 amp $5, **50 amp** $10, **100 amp** n/a, **200 amp** n/a
Cable TV: Yes, $5 **Dockside Phone:** No
Dock Type: Floating, Long Fingers, Pilings, Alongside, Wood
Moorings: 16 Total, 4 Transient **Launch:** No, Dinghy Dock
Rate: Day $30/15 **Week** $180/90 **Month** $600/300
Heads: 2 Toilet(s), 2 Shower(s)
Internet: Yes *(Wi-Fi, Free)* **Laundry:** 1 Washer(s), 1 Dryer(s)
Pump-Out: OnSite, Self Service, 1 Central **Fee:** Free **Closed Heads:** No

Marina Operations
Owner/Manager: Dan Miller **Dockmaster:** Vicki Lewis
In-Season: May-Oct, 8am-4pm **Off-Season:** Oct-May, 8am-4pm
After-Hours Arrival: Look for slip marked "Transient Available"
Reservations: Yes, Preferred **Credit Cards:** Visa/MC, Dscvr
Discounts: None
Pets: Welcome **Handicap Access:** Yes, Heads, Docks

Ocean Point Marina

176 Ocean Point Road; East Boothbay, ME 04544

Tel: (207) 633-0773 **VHF: Monitor** Ch.9 **Talk** Ch. 18
Fax: (207) 633-3971 **Alternate Tel:** n/a
Email: info@oceanpointmarina.com **Web:** oceanpointmarina.com
Nearest Town: Boothbay Harbor *(3 mi.)* **Tourist Info:** (207) 633-2353

Marina Services and Boat Supplies
Services - Docking Assistance, Security *(24 Hrs., Employees onsite)*, Dock Carts **Communication -** Mail & Package Hold, Phone Messages, FedEx, UPS, Express Mail **Supplies - OnSite:** Ice *(Block, Cube)*, Ships' Store, Bait/Tackle **1-3 mi:** Propane *(Shore Hill 633-4782)*

Boatyard Services
OnSite: Travelift *(35T)*, Forklift, Crane, Hydraulic Trailer, Launching Ramp, Engine mechanic *(gas, diesel)*, Hull Repairs, Rigger, Sail Loft *(Wilson 633-5071)*, Divers, Bottom Cleaning, Brightwork, Air Conditioning, Compound, Wash & Wax, Interior Cleaning, Propeller Repairs, Woodworking, Inflatable Repairs, Painting, Awlgrip, Total Refits, Yacht Broker **OnCall:** Electrical Repairs, Electronics Repairs, Canvas Work *(Creative 633-2056)*, Upholstery, Metal Fabrication *(Mid Coast 633-7553)* **Dealer for:** Mercury, Mercruiser; Quicksilver Inflatables. **Member:** ABBRA, ABYC - 3 Certified Tech(s), Other Certifications: Mercury **Yard Rates:** $35-65/hr., Haul & Launch $8.75-11.75/ft. *(blocking incl.)*, Power Wash $75 Flat, Bottom Paint $6.50-7.50/ft. **Storage:** On-Land Outside: $6.50-7.50/sq.ft; Ins: $9/sq.ft./season

Restaurants and Accommodations
Near: Restaurant *(Lobsterman's Wharf 633-3443, L $5-28, D $8-28, 11:30-6pm Twin lobsters $20, Cheeseburger $5, 3-6pm $13-14)*, Lite Fare *(East Boothbay General Store B $3-8.50, L $6-9)* **Under 1 mi:** Inn/B&B *(Five Gables 633-4551, $130-235, moorings)* **1-3 mi:** Restaurant *(Ocean Point Inn 633-4200, B $8-15, D $18-30, Kids' $6-10, Dinner Fri-Mon, Tavern Menu nightly $9-17 incl. pizza)*, Motel *(Smuggler's Cove 633-2800, $65-230, moorings)*, Hotel *(Ocean Point Inn 633-4200, $70-220)*, Inn/B&B *(Linekin Bay 633-2494, $120-190, moorings)*

Recreation and Entertainment
OnSite: Picnic Area, Grills, Fishing Charter, Party Boat **Near:** Jogging Paths **Under 1 mi:** Galleries *(Wee Scotties Antiques 633-2200; Barlow's Studio of Ships; Anderson Studio; Van Hasslet's)* **1-3 mi:** Beach, Fitness Center *(YMCA)*, Movie Theater *(Harbor 633-0438)*, Video Rental *(Video Loft 633-6509)*, Park *(Levison Preserve)*, Museum *(Boothbay Region Historical Society 633-0820; Boothbay Railway 633-4727 6 mi.)*, Sightseeing *(Ocean Point)* **3+ mi:** Golf Course *(Boothbay C.C. 633-6085, 5 mi.)*

Provisioning and General Services
OnSite: Post Office **Near:** Market *(East Boothbay General 633-7800 - 7 days, Mon-Sat 7am-7pm, Sun 7am-2pm, Newspapers, very well-stocked)*, Gourmet Shop *(EBGS)*, Delicatessen, Wine/Beer *(EBGS)*, Bakery, Protestant Church *(Methodist)* **Under 1 mi:** Convenience Store **1-3 mi:** Supermarket *(Hannaford 633-6465)*, Health Food, Liquor Store, Farmers' Market *(Thur. 9am-noon, Boothbay Mini-Mall)*, Lobster Pound, Bank/ATM, Catholic Church, Library, Beauty Salon, Dry Cleaners, Laundry, Bookstore, Pharmacy *(Rite Aid 633-7023)*, Hardware Store *(Poole Bro. 633-4474)*, Florist, Copies Etc.

Transportation
OnCall: Rental Car *(Enterprise 882-8393)*, Taxi *(Bobo's Coastal 380-4182)*
Airport: Portland Int'l. *(50 mi.)*

Medical Services
911 Service **1-3 mi:** Doctor *(St. Andrews 633-2121)*, Dentist *(Family 633-4243,)*, Chiropractor *(Coastal 633-5511)* **3+ mi:** Veterinarian *(Boothbay 633-3447, 7 mi.)* **Hospital:** St. Andrews 633-7820 *(3 mi.)*

Setting -- About four miles from the Damariscotta's mouth, the extensive dockage and weathered-shingled, two-story offices of Ocean Point are situated in a wide, working cove - with an atmosphere that mixes commercial harbor with untouristed downeast tranquility. East Boothbay is an historic wood-and-steel boat building center and is the birthplace of some extraordinary yachts. Maritime history junkies will find this a worthwhile stop.

Marina Notes -- *Rates up to 60 ft. LOA 61 ft.+ inquire. Formerly C&B Marina, New ownership 2002. Full-service boatyard specializes in Awlgrip & repowering. Two floating docks for vessels to 150 ft., 20-50 ft. beam & 18 ft. draft. Extensively inventoried chandlery (overnight deliveries). Boaters' lounge, with hexagonal picnic tables, coffee dispensary, and rough-hewn log bar, supplants now-closed Norma's Pub. For the first 50 years, site was home to venerable boat builders Goudy & Stevens and Hodgdon Yachts, which moved nearby. Bathhouse: Spacious, attractive new heads, showers & dressing areas.

Notable -- East Boothbay continues as a major shipbuilding center. Hodgdon's Yachts, in East Boothbay since 1816, now builds superyachts using cold-molded wood epoxy (and has a convenient ships' store). Goudy & Stevens, builders of notable yachts like America (original winner of the America's Cup), Sea Star and Cassiar, continues to offer traditional boatyard services. Just next door, Lobsterman's Wharf Restaurant's waterside deck overlooks the docks; a large inside dining room (good for a club cruise event) has expansive views of the harbor. The nearby outstanding East Boothbay General Store offers provisions, take-out, bakery, wine & beer and gourmet foods. Several galleries and studios are hikable, including that of marine artist Earle Barlow.

PHOTOS ON DVD: 20

Schooner Landing

PO Box 1473; 40 Main Street; Damariscotta, ME 04543

Tel: (207) 563-7447 **VHF: Monitor** n/a **Talk** n/a
Fax: (207) 563-5709 **Alternate Tel:** n/a
Email: info@schoonerlandingmaine.com **Web:** schoonerlandingmaine.com
Nearest Town: Damariscotta **Tourist Info:** (207) 563-8340

Navigational Information

Lat: 44°01.955' **Long:** 069°31.974' **Tide:** 9 ft. **Current:** n/a **Chart:** 13293
Rep. Depths (*MLW*): Entry 5 ft. **Fuel Dock** n/a **Max Slip/Moor** 8 ft./-
Access: 14 nm up the Damariscotta River to the Route 1B bridge

Marina Facilities *(In Season/Off Season)*

Fuel: No
Slips: 40 Total, 8 Transient **Max LOA:** 75 ft. **Max Beam:** n/a
Rate *(per ft.)*: **Day** $2.00 **Week** Inq. **Month** $45/ft.
Power: 30 amp Incl., **50 amp** Incl., **100 amp** n/a, **200 amp** n/a
Cable TV: No **Dockside Phone:** No
Dock Type: Floating, Short Fingers, Pilings, Wood
Moorings: 0 Total, 0 Transient **Launch:** n/a
Rate: Day n/a **Week** n/a **Month** n/a
Heads: 2 Toilet(s)
Internet: No **Laundry:** Yes
Pump-Out: No **Fee:** n/a **Closed Heads:** No

Marina Operations

Owner/Manager: Scott Fulsom / Charlie Herrick **Dockmaster:** Same
In-Season: May 15-Oct 31, 9am-1am **Off-Season:** n/a
After-Hours Arrival: Check in at restaurant
Reservations: No **Credit Cards:** Visa/MC, Dscvr, Cash
Discounts: None
Pets: Welcome **Handicap Access:** No

Marina Services and Boat Supplies

Services - Docking Assistance **Communication -** Pay Phone (1), FedEx, DHL, UPS, Express Mail **Supplies - OnSite:** Ice *(Cube)* **Under 1 mi:** Bait/Tackle, Propane **1-3 mi:** Ships' Store *(Clark Auto Parts 563-8128)*

Boatyard Services

OnCall: Engine mechanic *(gas, diesel)*, Electrical Repairs, Electronic Sales, Electronics Repairs, Hull Repairs, Rigger, Sail Loft, Canvas Work, Divers, Bottom Cleaning, Brightwork, Air Conditioning, Refrigeration, Compound, Wash & Wax, Propeller Repairs, Metal Fabrication **Near:** Launching Ramp. **Nearest Yard:** Flowers (207) 563-7404

Restaurants and Accommodations

OnSite: Restaurant *(Schooner Landing 563-7447, L $6-15, D $6-15)* **Near:** Restaurant *(Augustine's Backstreet Landing 563-5666, L $4-14, D $9-22)*, *(King Eiders Pub 563-6008, L $8-18, D $10-23, Kids' $4-7)*, *(Damariscotta River Grill 563-2992, L $5-12, D $17-25, Sun Brunch $6-13)*, *(Zampa's 563-8800, D $11-21, Kids' $6)*, Lite Fare *(Salt Bay Café 563-3302, B $4-9, L $4-20, D $7-25, Veg, too. Kids' $4-6)*, *(The Breakfast Place 563-5434)*, *(Paco's Taco 563-5355, Gluten-free, Veg & Mexican)*, Pizzeria *(Mediterranean Kitchen 563-2882)*, Inn/B&B *(Flying Cloud 563-2484, $85-210)*, *(Oak Gables 563-1476, $150-200)*, *(Tipsy Butler 563-3394, $135-201)*

Recreation and Entertainment

OnSite: Boat Rentals *(Mid-Coast Kayaking 563-5732)*, Fishing Charter *(Damariscotta Charters "Punky's Comet II" 567-3684)* **Near:** Movie Theater *(Lincoln Theater in 1875 Lincoln Hall)*, Park *(skateboard)*, Museum *(Chapman-Hall Tue-Sun 1-5pm $1 - restored 1754 homestead)*, Cultural Attract *(Round Top Center for the Arts 563-1507)*, Galleries *(River Arts in Skidompha; Firehouse; Damariscotta & Sheepscot River Pottery 563-6677)* **Under 1 mi:** Sightseeing *(Salt Bay Trail to Glidden Middens)* **1-3 mi:** Beach, Picnic Area, Grills, Playground, Tennis Courts, Fitness Center *(YMCA 563-3477)* **3+ mi:** Golf Course *(Wawenock 563-3938, 6 mi.)*

Provisioning and General Services

Near: Convenience Store *(Maritime Farms)*, Gourmet Shop, Delicatessen, Wine/Beer, Bakery, Fishmonger *(Fisherman's Catch 563-5888)*, Bank/ATM, Post Office, Catholic Church, Protestant Church, Library *(Skidompha 563-2745 Internet)*, Beauty Salon *(Aaron Michaels 563-2883)*, Barber Shop, Dry Cleaners, Laundry *(Coin-o-Matic)*, Bookstore *(Maine Coast Bookshop & Café 563-3207 - Lincoln Theater)*, Pharmacy *(Rite Aid 563-8489)*, Hardware Store *(Damariscotta 563-3428)*, Florist, Department Store *(Original Reny's 563-5757; Reny's Underground)*, Copies Etc. *(Supplies Unlimited 563-7010)* **Under 1 mi:** Market *(Rising Tide 563-5556. health food, too)*, Supermarket *(Hannaford 563-8131)*, Farmers' Market *(Fri 9am-noon 110 Belvedere Rd; Mon 3-6pm Rising Tide)*, Green Grocer *(Clark's 563-6866)*

Transportation

OnCall: Taxi *(Wicked Good 563-6225)*, Airport Limo *(County 380-7201)* **Airport:** Knox County/Portland Int'l. *(30 mi./60 mi.)*

Medical Services

911 Service **Near:** Doctor *(Soucy 563-6623)*, Dentist *(Mid-Coast 380-6445)*, Chiropractor *(Amato 563-1000)*, Holistic Services *(Gaudreau LMT 563-1441)* **Under 1 mi:** Optician *(Village 563-8879)*, Veterinarian *(Damariscotta 563-3934)* **Hospital:** Miles Memorial 563-1234 *(2 mi.)*

Setting -- At the head of the Damariscotta River, pilings support the Schooner Landing Restaurant complex that looms above the floating docks. Decks, topped with an outdoor bar, tent and umbrellaed tables, surround the bright, glass-fronted eatery providing views down the pretty salt-water estuary - often ripped with swift tidal currents. Oyster beds lie under the infrastructure and docks. Delightful downtown Damariscotta is a stone's throw.

Marina Notes -- Restaurant founded late '60s, marina early '90s. Built over late 18thC. Cottrill's Wharf. Ad-hoc AC requires long power cords. Moorings avail from Harbor Master Paul Bryant (563-3398). Gas & Diesel at Riverside Boat. Inside or deck dining, outside bar, local seafood (7 days 11:30am-9:30pm, Kids' menu). Lively, party atmosphere. Live music in pub Thurs, Fri, Sat nights & Sun afternoon. Happy Hour Mon-Fri 4-6pm. Free oysters 4pm Fri. Pier Party Sun 4-7pm. Game room: pool table, darts, foosball, Golden Tee video golf. Bathhouse: No showers, heads shared with restaurant. Laundromat short walk.

Notable -- Originally a shipbuilding center, Damariscotta - with its Newcastle twin - is now the shopping and financial hub for nearby resort communities. Damariscotta's attractive downtown - lined with brick buildings built after the 1845 fire - promises supplies, services, eateries, galleries and lots to do. Round Top Center for the Arts offers classes, concerts, festivals and exhibits (Mon-Fri 11am-4pm, Sat, Sun noon-4pm). An easy walk across the bridge to Newcastle and the head of the Salt Bay Preserve Heritage Trail; a 3-mile loop skirts Glidden Point to the Glidden Middens. Or dinghy north under the bridge to the 8-acre Whaleback Park, home to more Native American oyster shell mounds. Or dinghy to nearby 506-acre Dodge Point Wildlife Sanctuary (trails and sandy beach).

7. ME - THE RIVERS & BOOTHBAY HARBOR
PHOTOS ON DVD: 23

Navigational Information

Lat: 43°49.870' **Long:** 069°35.556' **Tide:** 12 ft. **Current:** 1 kt. **Chart:** 13293
Rep. Depths (*MLW*): Entry 30 ft. **Fuel Dock** n/a **Max Slip/Moor** -/50 ft.
Access: Gulf of Maine to Linekin Bay

Marina Facilities *(In Season/Off Season)*

Fuel: No
Slips: 0 Total, 0 Transient **Max LOA:** 60 ft. **Max Beam:** n/a
Rate *(per ft.)*: **Day** n/a **Week** n/a **Month** n/a
Power: 30 amp n/a, **50 amp** n/a, **100 amp** n/a, **200 amp** n/a
Cable TV: No **Dockside Phone:** No
Dock Type: Floating, Wood
Moorings: 3 Total, 2 Transient **Launch:** None, Dinghy Dock
Rate: Day $30 **Week** $125 **Month** $600
Heads: 1 Toilet(s), 1 Shower(s) *(dressing rooms)*, Hair Dryers
Internet: Yes *(Wi-Fi, Free)* **Laundry:** None
Pump-Out: No **Fee:** n/a **Closed Heads:** No

Marina Operations

Owner/Manager: Kim Swan and Bill & Karen McFarland **Dockmaster:** Same
In-Season: May 15-ColDay, 8am-11pm **Off-Season:** ColDay-May 15, Closed
After-Hours Arrival: Call ahead
Reservations: Yes, Preferred **Credit Cards:** Visa/MC, Dscvr, Amex
Discounts: None
Pets: Welcome, Dog Walk Area **Handicap Access:** No

Smuggler's Cove Inn

727 Ocean Point Road; East Boothbay, ME 04544

Tel: (207) 633-2800; (800) 633-3008 **VHF: Monitor** n/a **Talk** n/a
Fax: (207) 633-2878 **Alternate Tel:** (207) 380-6496
Email: bill@swanagency.com **Web:** smugglerscovemotel.com
Nearest Town: Boothbay *(4.5 mi.)* **Tourist Info:** (207) 633-2353

Marina Services and Boat Supplies

Services - Boaters' Lounge, Trash Pick-Up **Communication -** Phone Messages, Fax in/out *($2)*, FedEx, DHL, UPS, Express Mail **Supplies - OnSite:** Ice *(Cube)* **Under 1 mi:** Ice *(Block)* **1-3 mi:** Ships' Store, Bait/Tackle, Propane *(General Store)*

Boatyard Services

OnCall: Rigger, Sail Loft *(Wilson 633-5071)*, Canvas Work, Divers, Refrigeration **Near:** Electrical Repairs *(Marine Wiring & Electronics 633-3277)*, Electronic Sales, Electronics Repairs *(Coastal 633-7090)*, Propeller Repairs *(Paul Luke)*, Metal Fabrication. **Under 1 mi:** Travelift. **Nearest Yard:** Paul E. Luke (207) 633-4971

Restaurants and Accommodations

OnSite: Restaurant *(1820 House at Smugglers Cove Inn 633-2800, B $4-9, D $12-25, Salads, Sandwiches to Complete Dinners)*, Motel *(Smuggler's Cove Inn 633-2800, $85-229)* **Under 1 mi:** Restaurant *(Ocean Point Inn 633-4200, B $8-15, D $18-30, Kids' $6-10, Dinner Fri-Mon, Tavern Menu nightly $9-17 incl. pizza)* **1-3 mi:** Restaurant *(Lobsterman's Wharf 633-5481, L $5-28, D $8-28, 11:30am-6pm Twin lobsters $20, Cheeseburger $5, 3-6pm $13-14. Free Dockage)*, Lite Fare *(East Boothbay General 633-7800, B $3-8.50, L $6-9)*, Hotel *(Ocean Point Inn 633-4200, $70-220)*, Inn/B&B *(Five Gables Inn 633-4551, $130-235)*, *(The Inn at Lobsterman's Wharf 633-5481)*, *(Linekin Bay Resort 633-9900, $120-190, Re-Opens 2011)*

Recreation and Entertainment

OnSite: Heated Pool *(84 degrees)*, Beach *(Sandy)* **Near:** Tennis Courts **Under 1 mi:** Horseback Riding, Hike/Bike Trails **1-3 mi:** Fitness Center *("Y" 633-2855)*, Fishing Charter, Movie Theater, Museum *(Boothbay Region Historical Society 633-0820)*, Sightseeing *(Linekin Preserve Hiking Trails 633-4818)* **3+ mi:** Golf Course *(Boothbay Country Club 633-6085, 4 mi.)*, Bowling *(Romar, 5 mi.)*, Cultural Attract *(Opera House 633-6855, 5 mi.)*

Provisioning and General Services

Under 1 mi: Newsstand **1-3 mi:** Provisioning Service, Convenience Store *(East Boothbay General 633-7800 - 7 days, Mon-Sat 7am-7pm, Sun 7am-2pm, Newspapers, very well-stocked)*, Delicatessen *(EBGS)*, Wine/Beer *(EBGS)*, Bakery *(EBGS - muffins, cookies, donuts, pies, NY bagels)*, Bank/ATM, Post Office, Protestant Church, Library *(Boothbay Harbor 633-3112)*, Beauty Salon, Barber Shop, Dry Cleaners, Laundry, Bookstore **3+ mi:** Supermarket *(Hannaford 633-6465, 5 mi.)*, Liquor Store *(Hannaford, 5 mi.)*, Farmers' Market *(5 mi.)*, Fishmonger *(Atlantic Edge 633-2300, 5 mi.)*, Catholic Church *(5 mi.)*, Pharmacy *(Rite Aid 633-7023, 4.5 mi.)*, Hardware Store *(Grovers 633-2694, 6 mi.)*

Transportation

OnCall: Rental Car *(Enterprise 882-8393/Strong's)*, Taxi *(Bobos Coastal 380-4182)*, Airport Limo *(Keys Shuttle 305-289-9997)* **Airport:** Wiscassett/Portland Int'l. *(20 mi./50 mi.)*

Medical Services

911 Service **OnCall:** Ambulance **3+ mi:** Doctor *(St. Andrews 633-2121, 6 mi.)*, Dentist *(Family 633-4243, 5.5 mi.)*, Chiropractor *(Boothbay 633-5500, 5 mi.)*, Veterinarian *(Boothbay 633-3447, 9 mi.)* **Hospital:** St. Andrews 633-7820 *(6 mi.)*

Setting -- The three-acre oceanfront resort lies on the edge of a tranquil, private cove in Linekin Bay. Five two-story, motel-like buildings perch on the attractively landscaped grounds overlooking the heated pool, private sand beach and rocky shore - a small stationary fishing pier with a dinghy float provides access to the protected mooring field. 1820 House Restaurant occupies an authentic early 19thC structure with 21st century window walls. The sunsets from the mooring field and from any place in the resort are outstanding.

Marina Notes -- Est. in 1965 by a health professor from Cornell Medical Center, this complex has been family owned and operated for decades. Bought in '05 by Kim Swan and Bill & Karen McFarland. Renovated in '06 with continual upgrades. 1820 House Restaurant open May 15-Oct 15, 7 days for continental breakfast (7:30-9:30am), Dinner Tue-Sat (6-9pm). Local musicians entertain Fri and Sat. 52 comfortable rooms, most recently renovated with bay-view balconies - one building on piers over the water. "Loaner" dinghy. Bathhouse: A motel room bathroom is dedicated to cruisers.

Notable -- The resort area, originally known as The Upper Elbow, was once an ice farm and, delightfully little has changed since then. The quiet little boat-building community of East Boothbay is 2 miles north, offering a post office, restaurant, two inns, the wonderful East Boothbay General Store, and a taste of the non-touristy part of the Maine coast. A walk south leads to spectacular Ocean Point as well as the 95-acre Linekin Preserve with a 2.5-mile hiking trail along the Damariscotta River. Just a ten-minute ride away from the peace and tranquility of Linekin Bay is bustling, frenzied Boothbay Harbor.

PHOTOS ON DVD: 18

Navigational Information

Lat: 43°50.025' **Long:** 069°35.532' **Tide:** 8 ft. **Current:** 1 kt. **Chart:** 13293
Rep. Depths (*MLW*): Entry 55 ft. **Fuel Dock** n/a **Max Slip/Moor** 12 ft./80 ft.
Access: Gulf of Maine to Linekin Bay - starboard side

Marina Facilities *(In Season/Off Season)*

Fuel: No
Slips: 0 Total, 0 Transient **Max LOA:** 50 ft. **Max Beam:** n/a
Rate *(per ft.)*: **Day** n/a **Week** n/a **Month** n/a
Power: 30 amp n/a, **50 amp** n/a, **100 amp** n/a, **200 amp** n/a
Cable TV: No **Dockside Phone:** No
Dock Type: Floating, Wood
Moorings: 19 Total, 10 Transient **Launch:** No, Dinghy Dock
Rate: Day $15 **Week** $90 **Month** Inq.
Heads: None
Internet: Yes *(Wi-Fi, Free)* **Laundry:** None
Pump-Out: OnCall **Fee:** n/a **Closed Heads:** Yes

Paul E. Luke

15 Luke's Gulch; East Boothbay, ME 04544

Tel: (207) 633-4971 **VHF: Monitor** n/a **Talk** n/a
Fax: (207) 633-3388 **Alternate Tel:** (207) 633-3487
Email: frank@peluke.com **Web:** www.peluke.com
Nearest Town: Boothbay Harbor *(5 mi.)* **Tourist Info:** (207) 633-7448

Marina Operations

Owner/Manager: The Luke Family **Dockmaster:** Frank Luke
In-Season: Year Round, 7am-5pm* **Off-Season:** n/a
After-Hours Arrival: Call in advance
Reservations: Yes **Credit Cards:** Yes
Discounts: None
Pets: Welcome **Handicap Access:** No

Marina Services and Boat Supplies

Communication - FedEx, DHL, UPS, Express Mail **Supplies - 1-3 mi:** Ice *(Cube)*, Propane **3+ mi:** Ships' Store *(5 mi.)*, Bait/Tackle *(5 mi.)*

Boatyard Services

OnSite: Travelift *(35T)*, Engine mechanic *(gas, diesel)*, Hull Repairs, Rigger, Brightwork, Compound, Wash & Wax, Propeller Repairs, Woodworking, Metal Fabrication, Painting, Awlgrip **OnCall:** Electrical Repairs, Electronic Sales, Electronics Repairs, Canvas Work, Divers, Bottom Cleaning, Air Conditioning, Refrigeration, Upholstery, Yacht Interiors **1-3 mi:** Launching Ramp, Sail Loft. **Dealer for:** Luke automatic feathering propellers, soapstone and tile fireplaces, bronze and aluminum ventilators, 12' QT rowboat, and three-piece storm anchors. **Yard Rates:** $52-60/hr., Haul & Launch $13/ft., Power Wash $40 + labor **Storage:** On-Land Inside $8/sq.ft.; Outside $4.75-5.75/sq.ft.

Restaurants and Accommodations

Near: Restaurant *(Smuggler's Cove Inn 633-2800, B $4-9, D $12-25, Salads, Sandwiches to Complete Dinners)*, Motel *(Smuggler's Cove Inn 633-2800, $65-230)* **1-3 mi:** Restaurant *(Ocean Point Inn 633-4200, B $8-15, D $18-30, Kids' $6-10, Dinner Fri-Mon, Tavern Menu nightly $9-17 incl. pizza)*, *(Lobstermen's Wharf 633-4581, L $5-28, D $8-28, 11:30am-6pm Twin lobsters $20, Cheeseburger $5, 3-6pm $13-14. Free Dockage!)*, Lite Fare *(East Boothbay General Store 633-7800, B $3-8.50, L $6-9)*, Inn/B&B *(Linekin Bay Resort 633-2494, $120-190, Re-Opens 2011)*, *(Ocean Point Inn 633-4200, $70-220)*, *(Five Gables 633-4551, $130-235)*

Recreation and Entertainment

OnCall: Party Boat **Near:** Tennis Courts, Jogging Paths, Park *(Barrett Park)* **Under 1 mi:** Hike/Bike Trails **1-3 mi:** Beach, Galleries *(Studio of Ships 633-4246; Ocean Point Studio)* **3+ mi:** Golf Course *(Boothbay Country Club 633-6085, 4 mi.)*, Sightseeing *(Boothbay Region Historical Society 633-0820; Boothbay Railway Museum 633-4727; Coastal Maine Botanical Gardens 633-4333, 5 mi.)*

Provisioning and General Services

1-3 mi: Market *(East Boothbay General Store 633-7800 - 7 days, Mon-Sat 7am-7pm, Sun 7am-2pm, Newspapers, very well-stocked)*, Delicatessen *(EBGS)*, Wine/Beer *(EBGS)*, Liquor Store, Bakery *(EBGS - muffins, cookies, donuts, pies, NY bagels)*, Lobster Pound, Bank/ATM, Post Office, Protestant Church, Newsstand **3+ mi:** Supermarket *(Hannafords 633-6465, 5 mi.)*, Catholic Church *(6 mi.)*, Library *(Boothbay Harbor 633-3112, 5 mi.)*, Bookstore *(5 mi.)*, Pharmacy *(Rite Aid 633-7023, 5 mi.)*, Hardware Store *(Grovers 633-2694, 6 mi.)*

Transportation

OnCall: Taxi *(Bobos Coastal 380-4182)* **Airport:** Wiscassett/Portland Int'l. *(20 mi./60 mi.)*

Medical Services

911 Service **3+ mi:** Doctor *(St. Andrews 633-2121, 6 mi.)*, Dentist *(Family 633-4243, 5.5 mi.)*, Chiropractor *(Boothbay 633-5500, 5 mi.)*, Veterinarian *(Boothbay 633-3447, 9 mi.)* **Hospital:** St. Andrews 633-7820 *(6 mi.)*

Setting -- Just past Smuggler's Cove Inn, the white sheds and docks of the rustic and historic Paul E. Luke boatyard can be seen on the east side of Linekin Bay. The usually quiet mooring field sports panoramic views of the pristine Bay and of the untouristed peninsula's rocky, pine-treed shore.

Marina Notes -- *Open Mon-Fri - on weekends only by chance. Face dock occasionally available for overnight only - inquire (12 ft. mlw). Boatyard services include repowering, Awlgripping, fiberglass deck re-coring, restorations, finishing production hulls. Storage rates include haul, launch & blocking. Known historically for traditional boat building and currently for specialty parts. Yard founded in '39 with two 37 ft. cutters for designer Winthrop Warner. Spectacular wooden yachts for well-known designers like Alden, Sparkman & Stephens, Nielsen, etc. soon followed. Luke now focuses on custom "fittings" and "parts": soapstone, brass and tile boat fireplace stoves, feathering props, 3-piece Luke anchors, dorades, etc. plus an elegant 12 ft. custom rowing dinghy. Bathhouse: None. Note: Add'l Moorings at Linekin Bay Resort in Lewis Cove (633-2492).

Notable -- Maritime history buffs might enjoy Roger Duncan's "Dorothy Elizabeth: Building a Traditional Wooden Schooner" in which Paul E. Luke, Inc., is a prominent player. A 2-mile walk south leads to the Ocean Point Inn & Restaurant, Ocean Point Studio, Lou Landry's Woodworking Studio and further to the point itself for exhilarating views of Maine's rock-bound coast. A 2-mile walk north leads to the small village of East Boothbay. It's also an easy dinghy trip to Barrett Park just north of Lewis Cove.

Navigational Information

Lat: 43°50.650' **Long:** 069°37.605' **Tide:** 9 ft. **Current:** .5 kt. **Chart:** 13296
Rep. Depths (*MLW*): Entry 20 ft. **Fuel Dock** 32 ft. **Max Slip/Moor** 32 ft./55 ft.
Access: 1st marina to starboard located just past USCG R"8"

Marina Facilities *(In Season/Off Season)*

Fuel: *Valvtect* - Gasoline, Diesel, High-Speed Pumps
Slips: 40 Total, 18 Transient **Max LOA:** 200 ft. **Max Beam:** 35 ft.
Rate *(per ft.)*: **Day** $3.00* **Week** $19 **Month** $68
Power: 30 amp $10, **50 amp** $20, **100 amp** n/a, **200 amp** n/a
Cable TV: No **Dockside Phone:** No
Dock Type: Floating, Long Fingers, Alongside, Wood
Moorings: 28 Total, 24 Transient **Launch:** None, Dinghy Dock
Rate: Day $35 **Week** $195 **Month** $740
Heads: 4 Toilet(s), 5 Shower(s), Hair Dryers, Book Exchange
Internet: Yes *(Wi-Fi, Free)* **Laundry:** 2 Washer(s), 2 Dryer(s), Iron
Pump-Out: OnCall **Fee:** Free **Closed Heads:** Yes

Marina Operations

Owner/Manager: Jack Cogswell **Dockmaster:** Sydney McCarthy
In-Season: May 15-Oct 15, 7am-8pm **Off-Season:** Oct 16-May 14, Closed
After-Hours Arrival: Check in at office in morning
Reservations: Yes, Preferred **Credit Cards:** Visa/MC, Dscvr
Discounts: None
Pets: Welcome, Dog Walk Area **Handicap Access:** Yes, Heads, Docks

Carousel Marina

PO Box ; 125 Atlantic Avenue; Boothbay Harbor, ME 04538

Tel: (207) 633-2922 **VHF: Monitor** Ch. 9 **Talk** Ch. 8
Fax: (207) 633-7477 **Alternate Tel:** n/a
Email: carouselmarina@myfairpoint.net **Web:** carouselmarina.com
Nearest Town: Boothbay Harbor *(0.5 mi.)* **Tourist Info:** (207) 633-2353

Marina Services and Boat Supplies

Services - Boaters' Lounge, Security *(24 hrs.)*, Trash Pick-Up, Dock Carts **Communication -** Mail & Package Hold, Phone Messages, Fax in/out, FedEx, DHL, UPS, Express Mail *(Sat Del)* **Supplies - OnSite:** Ice *(Block, Cube)*, Ships' Store, CNG **OnCall:** Propane *(Shore Hills 633-4782)* **Near:** Live Bait **1-3 mi:** Bait/Tackle *(White Anchor 633-3788)*

Boatyard Services

OnSite: Launching Ramp **OnCall:** Engine mechanic *(gas, diesel)*, Electrical Repairs, Rigger, Divers, Bottom Cleaning, Refrigeration **Nearest Yard:** B.H. Shipyard (207) 633-3171

Restaurants and Accommodations

OnSite: Restaurant *(Whale's Tale 633-6644, L $8-17, D $8-29, 11am-4pm, 4-9pm, take-out menu, dockside)*, Motel *(Carousel Marina $125-150, Two waterview rooms)* **Near:** Restaurant *(Rocktide 633-4470, D $10-22, guest docks)*, *(Talay Thai 633-0025)*, *(Brown's Wharf 633-5540, D $15-28)*, *(Lobstermen's Co-op 633-4900, L & D $3-19 + lobster)*, *(Lobster Dock 633-7120)*, Motel *(Captain Fish's 633-6605, $55-120)*, Hotel *(Brown's Wharf 633-5440, $80-160)*, Inn/B&B *(Boothbay Harbor Inn 633-6302, $78-199)* **Under 1 mi:** Restaurant *(Bogie's Hideaway 633-4125, L & D $7-28, Spruce Point)*, *(88 Grandview 633-4125, D $21-29, Spruce Point Inn, Fine Dining)*, Hotel *(Spruce Point 633-4151, $140-360)*

Recreation and Entertainment

OnSite: Picnic Area *(or Barretts Park)*, Grills, Video Rental **Near:** Fishing Charter **Under 1 mi:** Boat Rentals *(Tidal Transit Kayak 633-7140)*, Bowling *(Romar Lane 633-5721- Candlepins)*, Party Boat *(Pier One)*, Park *(Barretts - swimming, pet friendly; Boothbay Harbor Whale)*, Galleries **1-3 mi:** Heated Pool *("Y")*, Playground, Tennis Courts *("Y")*, Golf Course *(Boothbay 633-6366 - private, stay & play pkgs avail.)*, Fitness Center *("Y")*, Movie Theater *(Harbor Theatre 633-0438)*, Video Arcade *(Romar Lanes)*, Museum *(Railway 633-4727)*, Cultural Attract *(Carousel Music Theater 633-5297)*

Provisioning and General Services

OnSite: Copies Etc. **Near:** Lobster Pound *(Lobsterman's Co-op 633-4900)*, Catholic Church **Under 1 mi:** Bakery *(Bakers Way 633-1119)*, Post Office, Protestant Church **1-3 mi:** Convenience Store, Market *(Village 633-0944)*, Supermarket *(Hannaford 633-6465)*, Gourmet Shop *(1820 Vintage House 633-6314)*, Wine/Beer *(Village)*, Liquor Store *(Village)*, Farmers' Market *(Mini Mall, Thu 9am-noon)*, Bank/ATM *(Key Bank)*, Library *(B.H. 633-3112)*, Beauty Salon *(Short Cuts)*, Dry Cleaners *(633-7337)*, Laundry *(B.H. 633-5400)*, Bookstore *(Sherman's 633-7262)*, Pharmacy *(Rite Aid 633-7023)*, Hardware Store *(Grover's 633-2694)*, Florist *(Boothbay 633-2400)*

Transportation

OnSite: Courtesy Car/Van *(1st Come, 1st Served)* **OnCall:** Rental Car *(Strongs 633-4600)*, Taxi *(Tiny's 380-8304; Country Coach 380-7201)* **Near:** Local Bus *(Free trolley 10am-5pm)* **Under 1 mi:** Bikes *(Tidal Transit 633-7140)* **Airport:** Wiscasset/Portland Int'l *(18 mi./62 mi.)*

Medical Services

911 Service **1-3 mi:** Doctor *(Family Care 633-7820)*, Dentist *(Andrews 633-2128)*, Chiropractor *(Boothbay 633-5500)*, Holistic Services *(Spruce Point 633-4152)*, Veterinarian *(Boothbay 633-3447)* **Hospital:** St. Andrews 633-2121, Dock *(2 mi.)*

Setting -- The first marina to starboard, at the gateway to Boothbay Harbor on Spruce Point, Carousel's gray, two-story building, punctuated by colorful plantings and a big yellow "Fuel" sign is surrounded by low-rise, gray, clapboard condos. A red-and-white striped tent shades the fuel dock. Gangways lead from the floating slips to a stationary wharf that hosts the cute red-shuttered dock house. Nearby yellow and navy blue umbrellas top tables outside Whales Tale Restaurant. From the table and the slips are panoramic harbor views coupled with spectacular sunsets.

Marina Notes -- *Over 60 ft. $3.50/ft., $22/ft./wk, $88/ft./mo. Wi-Fi covers mooring field. Marina shuttle. Quantity fuel disc. Established 1965. Named for famous film shot here. Comfortable Captains' lounge - cable TV, DVD-player, continental breakfast, snack bar, book/video library, small kitchen. Chandlery. Ice - 5 lb. cubes, 10 lb. blocks. Whales Tale - inside & patio dining. Motel Rooms - 2 doubles or efficiency with queen (no maid service). Soft drinks & hot dogs at fuel dock. Carousel Yacht Club - pool tables, TV, bar, & event space with fireplace. Bathhouse: Full bathrooms. Laundry, with iron/board, rear of ships' store.

Notable -- Situated on the quiet, east side of Boothbay Harbor, Carousel offers a peaceful respite from the tourist-frenzied downtown area across the harbor - but it's a quick half-mile trek across the footbridge to shops, restaurants and museums. Along the way are more eateries, lobster pounds, inns, motels and shops. Alternatively, there's the marina shuttle and a free trolley to the mall and to several attractions. A mile south, Spruce Point Inn, a "best in the country" sprawling high-end resort, features restaurants, a full-service spa and exquisitely manicured grounds. Don't miss the Maine Coastal Botanical Gardens.

PHOTOS ON DVD: 20

Brown's Wharf Marina

121 Atlantic Avenue; Boothbay Harbor, ME 04538

Tel: (207) 633-5440; (800) 334-8110 **VHF: Monitor** Ch. 9 **Talk** Ch. 68
Fax: (207) 633-2953 **Alternate Tel:** (800) 334-8110
Email: kbrown@brownswharfinn.com **Web:** brownswharfinn.com
Nearest Town: Boothbay Harbor *(0.5 mi.)* **Tourist Info:** (207) 633-2353

Navigational Information

Lat: 43°50.684' **Long:** 069°37.555' **Tide:** 11 ft. **Current:** 0 kt. **Chart:** 13296
Rep. Depths (*MLW*): Entry 20 ft. **Fuel Dock** 20 ft. **Max Slip/Moor** 20 ft./20 ft.
Access: Past McKown Point, second facility on eastern shore

Marina Facilities *(In Season/Off Season)*

Fuel: No
Slips: 50 Total, 15 Transient **Max LOA:** 165 ft. **Max Beam:** n/a
Rate *(per ft.)*: **Day** $2.50/Inq.* **Week** Inq. **Month** Inq.
Power: 30 amp $6, **50 amp** $10, **100 amp** n/a, **200 amp** n/a
Cable TV: Yes **Dockside Phone:** No
Dock Type: Floating, Long Fingers, Alongside, Wood
Moorings: 10 Total, 6 Transient **Launch:** No, Dinghy Dock
Rate: Day $35 & 50* **Week** Inq. **Month** Inq.
Heads: 3 Toilet(s), 2 Shower(s)
Internet: Yes *(Wi-Fi, Free)* **Laundry:** 2 Washer(s), 2 Dryer(s)
Pump-Out: OnSite, Full Service **Fee:** $5 **Closed Heads:** Yes

Marina Operations

Owner/Manager: Ken Brown **Dockmaster:** Timothy Brown
In-Season: May 15-ColDay, 8am-8pm **Off-Season:** Oct-May 14, Closed
After-Hours Arrival: Call in advance
Reservations: Yes for slips** **Credit Cards:** Visa/MC, Dscvr, Amex
Discounts: None
Pets: Welcome **Handicap Access:** No

Marina Services and Boat Supplies

Services - Docking Assistance, Boaters' Lounge, Security *(24 Hrs.)*, Dock Carts **Communication -** Pay Phone (1), FedEx, DHL, UPS, Express Mail *(Sat Del)* **Supplies - OnSite:** Ice *(Block, Cube)* **Near:** Ships' Store *(Carousel Marina next door 633-2922)*, CNG *(Carousel)* **1-3 mi:** Bait/Tackle *(White Anchor 633-3788)*, Propane *(Dead River Co. 633-3144)*

Boatyard Services

OnCall: Divers **Near:** Launching Ramp, Electrical Repairs, Electronics Repairs, Hull Repairs, Rigger, Bottom Cleaning, Brightwork, Refrigeration. **Under 1 mi:** Engine mechanic *(gas, diesel)*. **1-3 mi:** Sail Loft, Canvas Work. **Nearest Yard:** Boothbay Region Boatyard 1 mi. (207) 633-2970

Restaurants and Accommodations

OnSite: Restaurant *(Brown's Wharf Restaurant 633-5440, D $15-28)*, Hotel *(Brown's Wharf 633-5440, $130-240, 70 rooms, efficiencies & cottages $1700/wk)* **Near:** Restaurant *(Windows on the Harbor 633-6302, L & D $9-25, Kids' $4-9)*, *(Rocktide Restaurant 633-4455, D $10-22)*, *(Whale's Tale 633-6644, L $8-17, D $8-29)*, Seafood Shack *(Lobster Dock 633-7120, L & D $3-19 + lobster)*, Motel *(Capn' Fish)*, Hotel *(Boothbay Harbor Inn 633-6302, $90-220)* **Under 1 mi:** Restaurant *(Andrew's Harborside 633-4074, B $3-8.50, L $7.50-13, D $14-29)*, *(Bogie's Hideaway 633-4152, L & D $7-28, Spruce Pt.)*, *(Boat House Bistro 633-7300, L & D $12-32 + tapas)*, *(88 Grandview 633-4152, D $21-29, Spruce Pt. Inn)*, Hotel *(Spruce Point Inn Resort 633-4152, $140-360)* **1-3 mi:** Inn/B&B *(Kenniston Hill 633-2159, $110-150, picks up boaters)*

Recreation and Entertainment

Near: Park **Under 1 mi:** Playground, Bowling *(Romar Lane 633-5721-Candlepins)*, Sightseeing *(Whale Watching)*, Galleries *(Pick up a guide at Head of the Harbor)* **1-3 mi:** Tennis Courts, Golf Course *(Boothbay C.C. 633-6085)*, Fitness Center *(YMCA)*, Movie Theater *(Harbor Theatre 633-0438)*, Video Rental *(Video Loft 633-6509)*, Museum *(Aquarium 633-9559, Boothbay Historical Society 633-0820)*

Provisioning and General Services

Near: Lobster Pound *(Lobstermen's Co-op)*, Catholic Church **Under 1 mi:** Gourmet Shop *(Village Market 633-0944)*, Delicatessen, Wine/Beer, Bank/ATM, Post Office, Protestant Church, Beauty Salon, Barber Shop, Dry Cleaners, Bookstore *(Sherman's 633-7262)*, Hardware Store *(Grovers 633-2694)*, Florist **1-3 mi:** Supermarket *(Hannaford 633-6465)*, Bakery, Farmers' Market *(Mini Mall, Thu 9am-noon)*, Library *(633-3112)*, Laundry, Pharmacy *(Rite Aid 633-7023)*, Retail Shops

Transportation

OnSite: Courtesy Car/Van, Local Bus *(Shoppers Trolleys)* **OnCall:** Rental Car *(Enterprise 882-8393)*, Taxi *(Bobo's 380-4182)* **Under 1 mi:** Ferry Service *(Balmy Days II, Monhegan Isl. 633-2284 Daily 9:30am)* **Airport:** Wiscasset/Portland Int'l. *(15 mi./62 mi.)*

Medical Services

911 Service **OnCall:** Ambulance **Under 1 mi:** Doctor *(Boothbay Whole Health Med 633-3535)*, Dentist, Chiropractor *(Coastal 633-4777)* **1-3 mi:** Veterinarian **Hospital:** St. Andrews 633-2121, has dock *(2 mi.)*

PHOTOS ON DVD: 24

Setting -- Boothbay Harbor's second facility to starboard, flowers and flags highlight Brown's impeccably maintained marina, restaurant and lodging complex. Umbrella-topped tables crowd the front deck of the glass-front, low-slung main building. It's flanked by a small, two-story motel and an expansive three-story hotel edged with balconies. Slips and side-tie docks sprawl along the waterfront below. Views of the bustling harbor are accompanied by the chimes of Our Lady Queen of Peace. On the streetside, the statue of a giant, oil-skinned lobsterman counterpoints the gloriously ubiquitous pots of colorful flowers.

Marina Notes -- *Over 65 ft. $3/ft. Moorings: to 40 ft $35, 41-100 ft. $50 (five rated for boats 80 ft. LOA). **Reservations for slips only, moorings first come, first served. Family owned & operated since 1944. 21 surveillance cameras for 24/7 security. Motel staff 24/7. Offers TV, pump out, Wi-Fi. Fuel. Large ship models decorate restaurant, (breakfast & dinner). Old Salt Shed Lounge section used in early 1700s to store salt. 70 water-view rooms, suites & two cottages. Bathhouse: 1st floor rear of 2-story building. Newly updated heads with wood trim, fiberglass shower stalls, laundry - folding counter, iron & board.

Notable -- All of Boothbay Harbor is easily accessible whether by foot across the narrow bridge, dinghy (town dock) or the free shoppers trolleys; pick up the tourism booklet and a map. Festivals abound - Windjammer days (last week June) Fisherman's Festivals, 4th of July fireworks and Boatbuilder's Day are all celebrations of coastal culture. Kids often enjoy the Fairy House Village (633-4333), whale watching, boat rides, railway museum, aquarium and numerous small beaches within walking distance. Nature lovers will enjoy Boothbay's expanding Botanical Gardens, Land Trust properties and hiking trails.

Navigational Information
Lat: 43°50.879' **Long:** 069°37.466' **Tide:** 11 ft. **Current:** 0 kt. **Chart:** 13296
Rep. Depths (*MLW*): Entry 15 ft. **Fuel Dock** n/a **Max Slip/Moor** 10 ft./10 ft.
Access: Past G9 on the eastern shore of Boothbay Harbor

Marina Facilities *(In Season/Off Season)*
Fuel: No
Slips: 7 Total, 2 Transient **Max LOA:** 155 ft. **Max Beam:** 29 ft.
Rate *(per ft.)*: **Day** $2.50* **Week** Inq. **Month** Inq.
Power: 30 amp $3, **50 amp** $6, **100 amp** n/a, **200 amp** n/a
Cable TV: No **Dockside Phone:** No
Dock Type: Floating, Short Fingers, Alongside, Wood
Moorings: 6 Total, 0 Transient **Launch:** n/a, Dinghy Dock
Rate: Day n/a **Week** n/a **Month** n/a
Heads: 1 Toilet(s)
Internet: No **Laundry:** None
Pump-Out: No **Fee:** n/a **Closed Heads:** Yes

Marina Operations
Owner/Manager: John Fish **Dockmaster:** n/a
In-Season: MidMay-MidOct, 7am-10pm **Off-Season:** Closed
After-Hours Arrival: Check in at Motel desk
Reservations: Yes, Preferred **Credit Cards:** Visa/MC, Amex
Discounts: None
Pets: Welcome **Handicap Access:** No

Cap'n Fish's Waterfront Inn

PO Box 660; 65 Atlantic Avenue; Boothbay Harbor, ME 04538
Tel: (207) 633-6605; (800) 633-0860 **VHF: Monitor** n/a **Talk** n/a
Fax: n/a **Alternate Tel:** n/a
Email: capnfish@roadrunner.com **Web:** www.boothbaywaterfront.com
Nearest Town: Boothbay Harbor *(0.3 mi.)* **Tourist Info:** (207) 633-2353

Marina Services and Boat Supplies
Communication - Pay Phone, DHL, UPS, Express Mail *(Sat Del)* **Supplies - OnSite:** Ice *(Cube)* **Near:** Ships' Store, CNG *(Carousel Marina 633-2922)* **Under 1 mi:** Propane *(Dead River Company 633-3144)* **1-3 mi:** Bait/Tackle *(White Anchor 633-3788)*

Boatyard Services
OnCall: Engine mechanic *(gas, diesel)*, Electrical Repairs, Bottom Cleaning, Brightwork **Nearest Yard:** Boothbay Harbor Shipyard (207) 633-3171

Restaurants and Accommodations
OnSite: Snack Bar *(Dockside Coffee Shop B $3-12, 7:30-9:30am, Tue-Sun, breakfast only)*, Motel *(Cap'n Fish's 633-6605, $75-160)* **Near:** Restaurant *(Brown's Wharf 633-5440, D $15-28)*, *(Boat House Bistro 633-7300, D $12-32, plus tapas)*, *(Andrew's Harborside 633-4074, B $3-8.50, L $7-13, D $14-29)*, *(Whale's Tale 633-6644, L $8-17, D $8-29)*, *(Window's on the Harbor 633-6302, L & D $9-25, Kids $4-9)*, *(Lobster Dock 633-7120, L & D $3-19 + lobster)*, *(Rocktide Restaurant 633-4455, D $10-22)*, *(Boothbay Harbor Inn D.R. B $6-9, D $12-20)*, Pizzeria *(House of Pizza 633-3468)*, Motel *(Rocktide Inn 633-4455, $82-162, docks for guests)*, Hotel *(Boothbay Harbor Inn 633-6302, $90-220)*, *(Brown's Wharf 633-5440, $130-240)*, Condo/Cottage *(Griffin Boat House 633-6300, perched over the water)*

Recreation and Entertainment
Near: Beach, Boat Rentals *(Tidal Transit Ocean Kayak 633-7140)*, Bowling *(Romar Lane 633-5721- Candlepins)*, Sightseeing *(Cap'n Fish's Boat Trips - WhaleWatching)*, Galleries *(Pick up a guide at Head of the Harbor)*, Special Events *(Windjammer Days late June)* **Under 1 mi:** Playground, Fishing Charter, Party Boat **1-3 mi:** Heated Pool *(YMCA 633-2855 $15/day)*, Golf Course *(Boothbay C.C. 633-6085 - private but stay 'n play avail.)*, Fitness Center *(YMCA)*, Movie Theater *(Harbor Theatre 633-0438)*, Video Rental *(Video Loft 633-6509)*, Video Arcade *(Harbor Light 633-3799 in Meadow Mall)*, Museum *(Boothbay Railway 633-4727 $9/5; Boothbay Historical Society 633-0820 633-4727)*, Cultural Attract *(Aquarium 633-9559 $5/3)*

Provisioning and General Services
Near: Lobster Pound *(Fishermen's Co-op)*, Catholic Church **Under 1 mi:** Convenience Store *(Village Market 633-0944)*, Supermarket *(Hannaford 633-6465)*, Gourmet Shop *(Village Market 633-0944)*, Delicatessen, Wine/Beer *(Village)*, Liquor Store *(Village)*, Bakery *(P&P Pastry 633-6511)*, Farmers' Market *(Thu 9am-noon at Mini Mall)*, Bank/ATM, Post Office *(633-3090)*, Protestant Church, Library *(Boothbay Harbor 633-3112)*, Beauty Salon, Dry Cleaners, Laundry, Bookstore *(Sherman's 633-7262)*, Pharmacy *(Rite Aid 633-7023)*, Hardware Store *(Grovers 633-2694)*, Florist, Clothing Store, Retail Shops, Copies Etc. *(Mail Boxes Etc. 633-9991)*

Transportation
OnCall: Rental Car *(Enterprise 882-8393)*, Taxi *(Boothbay Harbor 633-6001)* **Under 1 mi:** Ferry Service *(Balmy Days II, Monhegan Isl. 633-2284 Daily 9:30am)* **Airport:** Wiscasset/Portland Int'l. *(15 m./62 mi.)*

Medical Services
911 Service **OnCall:** Ambulance **Under 1 mi:** Doctor *(Whole Health Med. 633-3535)*, Dentist *(Family Dental 633-4243)*, Chiropractor *(Coastal 633-4777)* **Hospital:** St. Andrews 633-2121, has dock *(1.5 mi.)*

Setting -- Just past McFarland Island, at the entrance to the Inner Harbor, Cap'n Fish's Waterfront Inn & Marina stretches along the starboard shore. A few slips, a long side-tie dock and a dinghy float lie at the foot of the modest complex - connected by an inviting sundeck. Brown-trimmed, tan two-story motel units, a large parking lot and several other tan outbuildings surround the large white marina office. Views across the harbor are of lively downtown Boothbay.

Marina Notes -- *Plus alongside dockage to 155 ft. LOA. Founded in 1972, marina owned & operated by Boothbay native Captain John Fish - also owner of area's largest fleet of sightseeing boats. Moorings seasonal only. Coffee shop open just for breakfast. Small private dock leads down to the water for swimming or fishing. Habor views from 2nd-floor rooms and suite-style motel units - discounted dockage for motel guests. Fuel and pump-out at Carousel Marina. Bathhouse: One head shared with the Dockside Coffee Shop, and no showers.

Notable -- The marina's convenient location on the harbor's "quiet side" puts it an easy eighth of a mile from the footbridge that crosses into the heart of the action. Alternatively, dinghy dockage at the Town Dock just south of Boothbay Harbor Marina (3-hr. max) encourages a water trip across the harbor. Cap'n Fish runs cruises on its 3-vessel fleet, ranging in size from 78 to 100 feet, docked at Pier One on the far side of the bridge: Puffin Nature ($30/15), Whale Watch ($38/25), Lobster Trap Hauling & Seal Watch ($19/10), plus scenic and lighthouse tours (mainewhales.com). Pick up the free Rocktide Trolley to visit the Botanical Gardens, the Aquarium, museums, supermarket, restaurants, galleries and shops. Or take a day trip to Monhegan Island on "Balmy Days" ($30/18).

7. ME - THE RIVERS & BOOTHBAY HARBOR

PHOTOS ON DVD: 23

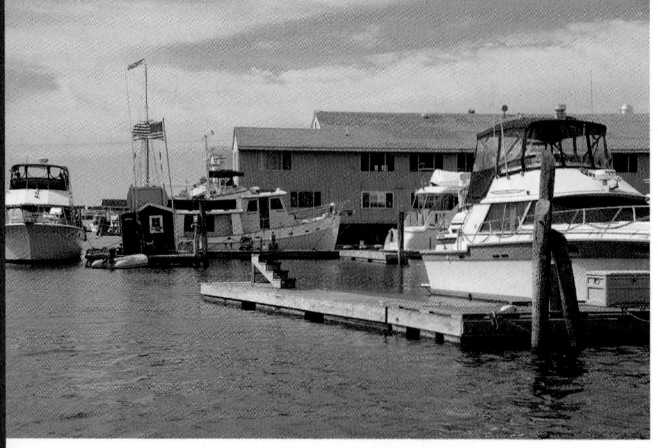

Boothbay Harbor Marina

PO Box 524; Pier One; Boothbay Harbor, ME 04538

Tel: (207) 633-6003 **VHF: Monitor** Ch. 9 **Talk** Ch. 68
Fax: (207) 633-6003 **Alternate Tel:** (941) 773-6997
Email: bbhmarina@aol.com **Web:** boothbayharbormarina.com
Nearest Town: Boothbay Harbor **Tourist Info:** (207) 633-7448

Navigational Information

Lat: 43°51.042' **Long:** 069°37.592' **Tide:** 11 ft. **Current:** 0 kt. **Chart:** 13296
Rep. Depths (*MLW*): Entry 20 ft. **Fuel Dock** n/a **Max Slip/Moor** 20 ft./-
Access: Due North 3/4 mi. past R #8 Buoy 'Tumbler Island'

Marina Facilities *(In Season/Off Season)*

Fuel: No
Slips: 40 Total, 20 Transient **Max LOA:** 150 ft. **Max Beam:** 0 ft.
Rate *(per ft.)*: **Day** $2.50/Inq.* **Week** $13 **Month** 28
Power: 30 amp $5, **50 amp** $7.50, **100 amp** n/a, **200 amp** n/a
Cable TV: Yes Incl. **Dockside Phone:** No
Dock Type: Floating, Short Fingers, Pilings, Alongside, Wood, Composition
Moorings: 1 Total, 1 Transient **Launch:** n/a, Dinghy Dock
Rate: Day $30 **Week** $160 **Month** $485
Heads: 2 Toilet(s), 2 Shower(s)
Internet: Yes *(Wi-Fi, Free)* **Laundry:** 2 Washer(s), 2 Dryer(s)
Pump-Out: OnSite, OnCall **Fee:** $5 **Closed Heads:** No

Marina Operations

Owner/Manager: Judy Engle **Dockmaster:** Same
In-Season: May-Oct 15, 8:30am-5:30pm **Off-Season:** Oct 16-Apr, Closed
After-Hours Arrival: Call (207) 633-6003 or (941) 773-6997
Reservations: Yes, Preferred **Credit Cards:** Visa/MC, Dscvr
Discounts: None
Pets: Welcome **Handicap Access:** Yes, Docks

Marina Services and Boat Supplies

Services - Docking Assistance, Security *(6pm-8am Security gate)*, Trash Pick-Up, Dock Carts **Communication -** Pay Phone (2), FedEx, DHL, UPS, Express Mail *(Sat Del)* **Supplies - Near:** Ice *(Block, Cube)* **Under 1 mi:** Ships' Store *(Marine Supply 633-0709)*, CNG *(Carousel Marina 633-2922)* **1-3 mi:** Bait/Tackle *(White Anchor 633-3788)*

Boatyard Services

OnCall: Divers **Near:** Engine mechanic *(gas, diesel)*, Electrical Repairs, Electronic Sales, Electronics Repairs, Hull Repairs, Rigger, Upholstery, Metal Fabrication. **Nearest Yard:** B.H. Shipyard (207) 633-3171

Restaurants and Accommodations

OnSite: Restaurant *(McSeagull's 633-5900, L $6-18, D $11-28, 7-days Live Entertain.)*, *(Gray's Wharf Waterfront 633-5629, L & D $6-25 Live Music, Billiards)*, Pizzeria *(Pier 1 633-5586, 11am-11pm)* **Near:** Restaurant *(Rocktide 633-4455, D $10-22)*, *(Andrew's Harborside 633-4074, B $3-9, L $7-13, D $14-29)*, *(Boathouse Bistro 633-7300, L $6-14, D $12-32, plus tapas - top rated)*, Seafood Shack *(Fisherman's Wharf 633-5090, L $6-16, D $15-28)*, Motel *(Flagship 633-5094, $70-240)*, Hotel *(Fisherman's Wharf 633-5090)*, *(Boothbay Harbor 633-6302, $90-220)*, Inn/B&B *(Admiral's Quarters & Greenleaf Inn 633-2472, $155-325)*, *(Harbour Towne 633-4300, $70-400)*, *(Harborage 633-4640, $125-255)*

Recreation and Entertainment

Near: Boat Rentals *(Tidal Kayaks 633-7140)*, Bowling *(Romar 633-5721)*, Fishing Charter, Cultural Attract *(Opera House 633.5159)*, Sightseeing *(Cap'n Fish's Excursions 633-3244; Balmy Days to Monhegan Is. 633-2284; B.H. Whalewatch 633-3500)*, Galleries *(Guide at Head of the Harbor)*, Special Events *(Windjammer Days - June)* **Under 1 mi:** Pool *("Y" 633-2855 $15/day)*, Beach *(Barrett Park)*, Playground, Tennis Courts *("Y")*, Fitness Center *("Y")*, Movie Theater *(Harbor 633-5297)*, Video Rental *(Video Loft 633-6509)*, Park *(Barrett)*, Museum *(Boothbay Region Hist.Soc. 633-4727; Boothbay Railway 633-4727 $9/5)* **1-3 mi:** Golf Course *(Boothbay C.C. 633-6085)*, Tours *(Marine Resources Aquarium 633-9674 $5/3)*

Provisioning and General Services

Near: Market *(Village Market 633-0944)*, Delicatessen, Wine/Beer *(Village)*, Liquor Store *(Village)*, Bakery, Fishmonger, Lobster Pound *(Lobstermen's Co-op 633-4900)*, Bank/ATM, Post Office, Protestant Church, Library, Beauty Salon, Dry Cleaners, Laundry, Bookstore *(Sherman's 633-7262)*, Pharmacy *(Rite Aid 633-7023)*, Newsstand, Hardware Store, Florist **Under 1 mi:** Supermarket *(Hannaford 633-6465)*, Farmers' Market *(Thu 9am-noon at Mini Mall)*, Catholic Church, Copies Etc. *(Mail Boxes, Etc. 633-9991)*

Transportation

OnCall: Rental Car *(Enterprise 882-8393)*, Taxi *(Boothbay Harbor 633-6001)* **Near:** Bikes *(Tidal 633-7140)*, Local Bus *(Shopping Trolley)* **Airport:** Wiscasset/Portland Int'l. *(15 mi./60 mi.)*

Medical Services

911 Service **OnCall:** Ambulance **Near:** Dentist *(Family 633-4243)*, Chiropractor *(Coastal 633-4777)* **Under 1 mi:** Doctor *(Andrews Family 633-7820)* **3+ mi:** Veterinarian *(Boothbay 633-3447, 5 mi.)* **Hospital:** St. Andrews 633-2121- has dock *(2 mi.)*

Setting -- Right in the middle of the action, Boothbay Harbor Marina's network of floating docks lie to port at the harbor's navigable head just before the footbridge at Pier One - home to excursion boats and other water activities. Onshore, two bustling restaurants with live entertainment make for festive evenings. Just beyond, the village's colorful, lively shopping district invites a stroll. The views from the outer docks to the mouth of the harbor are dazzling.

Marina Notes -- CCM *Over 70 ft. $3/ft. Dockmaster's little red house at top of ramp. Only downtown marina - expect to enjoy the view from the decks of two onsite eateries (and enjoy their music). Accommodates megayachts & cats on northernmost dock - double 50s. Gated docks locked at all times. Pump-out onsite. Fuel at Carousel's. Bathhouse: Next to land-side entrance. Basic Showers open 24hrs. Coin-Op laundry.

Notable -- Overlooking the marina, McSeagulls restaurant's refurbished dining room overlooks the docks as does its flower-trimmed outdoor deck - shaded by a riot of multi-colored umbrellas. Gray's Wharf next door also offers an alfresco deck, casual indoor dining room and bar. Ticket kiosks for all manner of tours and excursions line the open wood-decked plaza just beyond the marina gates - along with a pub, deli, and pizzeria. It's a few steps up the hill to the center of the most-touristed, but still charming, part of Boothbay Harbor. Restaurants, inns, boutiques, gift shops, fudge & ice cream shops abound. Window-shop, stop at the village green, rent kayaks, re-live the '50s at the candlepin bowling alley - and don't miss the galleries. Walk across the footbridge for breathtaking views down the harbor or the lobster shacks on the far side. The free shoppers trolley loops to the Botanical Gardens, supermaket, musuem, aquarium or mall.

Navigational Information
Lat: 43°50.935' **Long:** 069°37.759' **Tide:** 11 ft. **Current:** 0 kt. **Chart:** 13296
Rep. Depths (*MLW*): Entry 15 ft. **Fuel Dock** n/a **Max Slip/Moor** 15 ft./20 ft.
Access: Past G9 and McFarland Island on the Inner Harbor's western shore

Marina Facilities *(In Season/Off Season)*
Fuel: No
Slips: 30 Total, 13 Transient **Max LOA:** 100 ft. **Max Beam:** n/a
Rate *(per ft.)*: **Day** $2.50/2* **Week** Inq. **Month** Inq.
Power: 30 amp $5, **50 amp** $8, **100 amp** n/a, **200 amp** n/a
Cable TV: Yes Incl. **Dockside Phone:** Yes Hotel office
Dock Type: Floating, Short Fingers, Pilings, Alongside, Wood
Moorings: 15 Total, 10 Transient **Launch:** None, Dinghy Dock
Rate: Day $29/25 **Week** Inq. **Month** Inq.***
Heads: 3 Toilet(s), 2 Shower(s), Hair Dryers, Book Exchange
Internet: Yes *(Wi-Fi, Free)* **Laundry:** 2 Washer(s), 2 Dryer(s), Iron, Iron Board
Pump-Out: OnSite, Full Service **Fee:** $10 **Closed Heads:** No

Marina Operations
Owner/Manager: Bonnie Stover **Dockmaster:** Peter Chase
In-Season: Jun 15-Sep 5, 7am-7pm** **Off-Season:** May-Jun 14&Sep-Oct 15,
After-Hours Arrival: Check in at hotel office
Reservations: Yes, Recommended **Credit Cards:** Visa/MC, Dscvr, Amex
Discounts: None
Pets: Welcome **Handicap Access:** Yes, Heads, Docks

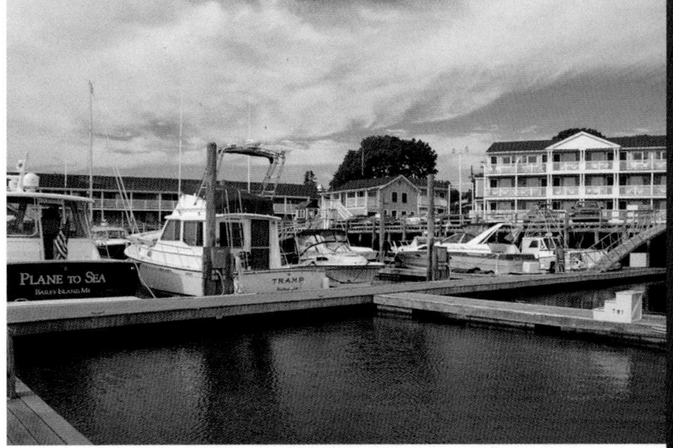

Tugboat Inn & Marina

PO Box 267; 80 Commercial Street; Boothbay Harbor, ME 04538
Tel: (207) 633-4435; (800) 248-2628 **VHF: Monitor** Ch. 9/16 **Talk** Ch. 68
Fax: n/a **Alternate Tel:** (207) 633-4434
Email: info@tugboatinn.com **Web:** www.tugboatinn.com
Nearest Town: Boothbay Harbor *(0.2 mi.)* **Tourist Info:** (207) 633-2353

Marina Services and Boat Supplies
Services - Docking Assistance, Dock Carts **Communication -** Pay Phone, FedEx, UPS, Express Mail *(Sat Del)* **Supplies - OnSite:** Ice *(Block, Cube)* **Near:** Ships' Store, CNG *(Carousel Marina by dinghy)* **Under 1 mi:** Propane *(Dead River 633-3144)*

Boatyard Services
OnCall: Rigger, Divers, Upholstery **Near:** Travelift, Railway, Forklift, Launching Ramp, Engine mechanic *(gas, diesel)*, Electrical Repairs, Electronic Sales, Electronics Repairs, Hull Repairs, Bottom Cleaning, Brightwork, Propeller Repairs, Metal Fabrication. **Nearest Yard:** Boothbay Harbor Shipyard (207) 633-3171

Restaurants and Accommodations
OnSite: Restaurant *(Tugboat 633-4434, L $8-19, D $18-30, Kids' $4-9)*, Lite Fare *(Marina Lounge & Patio Café L&D $8-16)*, Hotel *(Tugboat Inn 633-4434, $85-280, 64 rooms in 5 buildings)* **Near:** Restaurant *(Boathouse Bistro 633-7300, L $6-14, D $12-32), (Fisherman's Wharf Inn 633-5090, L $6-16, D $15-28), (Andrew's Harborside 633-4074, B $3-9, L $6-12, D $14-30)*, Seafood Shack *(Kaler's Crab House 633-5839, L $5-14, D $10-23, Kids' $3-5)*, Lite Fare *(Ebb Tide 633-5692, B $4-7, L $4-13, D $7-13), (Blue Moon Café 633-2200, B $3-9, L $4-10)*, Inn/B&B *(Admiral's Quarters & Greenleaf Inn 633-7346, $155-325), (Capt Sawyers 633-2290, $55-130)*

Recreation and Entertainment
OnSite: Picnic Area, Boat Rentals *(Charger 380-4556 - sailboats, skiffs)*, Fishing Charter *(Charger 380-4556; Sashimi 633-4902; Redhook 633-3807)* **Near:** Bowling *(Romar 633-5721)*, Cultural Attract *(Opera House 633-5159)*, Sightseeing *(Cap'n Fish's Excursions 633-3244; Balmy Days to Monhegan Is. 633-2284; B.H. Whalewatch 633-3500)* **Under 1 mi:** Movie Theater *(Harbor 633-3799)*, Video Rental *(Video Loft 633-6509)*, Museum *(Boothbay Region Hist. Soc. 633-0820; Boothbay Railway 633-4727 $9/5)* **1-3 mi:** Pool *("Y")*, Beach *(Barrett Park)*, Playground *(Barrett Park)*, Tennis Courts *("Y")*, Golf Course *(Boothbay C.C. 633-6085 Stay & Play)*, Fitness Center *("Y")*, Park *(Barrett)*, Tours *(M.R. Aquarium 633-9559 $5/3)*

Provisioning and General Services
Near: Market *(Village Market 633-0944)*, Delicatessen *(Village)*, Wine/Beer *(Village)*, Liquor Store, Bakery, Fishmonger *(Daily Catch)*, Lobster Pound *(Lobster Wharf 633-4900, by dinghy)*, Bank/ATM, Post Office, Protestant Church, Library, Beauty Salon, Barber Shop, Bookstore *(Sherman's 633-7262)*, Newsstand, Hardware Store *(Grovers 633-2694)*, Florist *(Boothbay Greenhouses 633-2400)*, Clothing Store, Retail Shops, Copies Etc. *(Coastal Shipping 633-5515)* **Under 1 mi:** Supermarket *(Hannaford 633-6465)*, Farmers' Market *(Mini Mall Thu 9am-noon)*, Green Grocer, Catholic Church, Dry Cleaners, Laundry, Pharmacy *(Rite Aid 633-7023)*

Transportation
OnCall: Rental Car *(Enterprise 882-8393)*, Taxi *(Coastal 380-4182)* **Near:** Bikes *(Tidal 633-7140)*, Local Bus *(Free shopping trolley)* **Airport:** Wiscasset/Portland Int'l. *(15 mi./60 mi.)*

Medical Services
911 Service **Near:** Chiropractor *(Boothbay 633-5500)* **Under 1 mi:** Doctor *(Andrews Family 633-7820)*, Dentist *(Family 633-4243)* **3+ mi:** Veterinarian *(B.H. 633-3447, 5 mi.)* **Hospital:** St. Andrews 633-2121, has dock *(1 mi.)*

Setting -- Just past McFarland's Island, the picture-perfect Tugboat complex of gray-shingled buildings topped by red roofs lies along along the port side of the Inner Harbor. A small dock house oversees the two sets of high-end, carefully maintained floating slips and side-tie docks flanked by two stationery wharves. Verandas front five two- and three-story structures that house the hotel rooms. A red tugboat marks the entrance to a large window-walled dining room overlooking the docks with a cozy pub on the ground floor. The entire operation is blessed with panoramic views of this active, legendary harbor.

Marina Notes -- *Over 70 ft. LOA $3/ft. **High season- 24 hr. check-in desk. ***$5 fax charge for 1st page. Seasonal Slips $59-63/ft. Moorings $895. Mooring balls "TBI" + "C" & number. If arriving after hours, staff puts "reserved" on buoy. Call for rigging instructions. Greets boats - handles lines, power hook-ups. Picnic tables right on the docks. Yacht club cruise destination. Lovely hotel rooms with A/C and waterfront verandas. Bathhouse: Lower level of main building. Three full baths with "coin-op" fiberglass shower stalls, hair dryers. Pleasant anteroom with comfy white benches. Laundry with folding table.

Notable -- The Tugboat Inn Restaurant is built into the side of The Maine, a 1917 tugboat, and serves lunch (11:30am-2:30pm) and dinner (5:30-9pm) daily. The Marina Lounge & Patio Deck offer lighter fare. At the southern edge of town, Tugboat is a five-minute walk from the bustling village - historic inns, more restaurants, gift shops, galleries, the classic village green and library. Three sport fish charter boats base here. Nature and whale-watch excursions depart from nearby docks - Monhegan Island cruises from Pier 8 and Boothbay Whalewatch from Pier 6. The free trolley makes reaching Hannaford's and aquarium easy.

PHOTOS ON DVD: 25

Boothbay Harbor Shipyard

PO Box 462; 120 Commercial St.; Boothbay Harbor, ME 04538

Tel: (207) 633-3171 **VHF: Monitor** Ch. 9 **Talk** Ch. 68
Fax: (207) 633-3824 **Alternate Tel:** n/a
Email: info@boothbayharborshipyard.com **Web:** See Marina Notes
Nearest Town: Boothbay Harbor *(0.5 mi.)* **Tourist Info:** (207) 633-2353

Navigational Information
Lat: 43°50.941' **Long:** 069°37.951' **Tide:** 11 ft. **Current:** 0 kt. **Chart:** 13296
Rep. Depths (*MLW*): Entry 30 ft. **Fuel Dock** n/a **Max Slip/Moor** -/30 ft.
Access: Leave G9 to starboard, to the west of McFarland Island

Marina Facilities *(In Season/Off Season)*
Fuel: No
Slips: 0 Total, 0 Transient **Max LOA:** 100 ft. **Max Beam:** n/a
Rate *(per ft.)*: **Day** n/a **Week** n/a **Month** n/a
Power: 30 amp n/a, **50 amp** n/a, **100 amp** n/a, **200 amp** n/a
Cable TV: No **Dockside Phone:** No
Dock Type: Floating, Alongside
Moorings: 25 Total, 15 Transient **Launch:** None, Dinghy Dock
Rate: Day $35 **Week** $150 **Month** $450
Heads: None
Internet: No **Laundry:** None
Pump-Out: No **Fee:** n/a **Closed Heads:** No

Marina Operations
Owner/Manager: Joe Jackimovicz **Dockmaster:** Larry Colcord
In-Season: Year-Round, 7am-3:30pm **Off-Season:** n/a
After-Hours Arrival: Pick up a vacant mooring; check in in the morning
Reservations: No **Credit Cards:** Visa/MC, Dscvr
Discounts: None
Pets: Welcome **Handicap Access:** No

Marina Services and Boat Supplies
Services - Dock Carts **Communication -** Mail & Package Hold, Fax in/out, FedEx, UPS, Express Mail **Supplies - Near:** Ice *(Block)*, Ships' Store, Propane *(Dead River 633-3144)* **Under 1 mi:** Ice *(Cube)* **1-3 mi:** Bait/Tackle *(White Anchor 633-3788)*, CNG *(Carousel Marina 633-2922)*

Boatyard Services
OnSite: Travelift, Railway *(700T & 150T)*, Forklift, Crane, Hydraulic Trailer, Engine mechanic *(gas, diesel)*, Electrical Repairs, Electronic Sales, Electronics Repairs, Hull Repairs, Rigger, Bottom Cleaning, Brightwork, Compound, Wash & Wax, Interior Cleaning, Woodworking, Upholstery, Yacht Interiors, Metal Fabrication, Painting, Total Refits, Yacht Design, Yacht Building **OnCall:** Sail Loft, Canvas Work, Divers **Under 1 mi:** Launching Ramp. **1-3 mi:** Propeller Repairs. **Member:** ABYC **Yard Rates:** $65/hr., Haul & Launch $10-12/ft. *(blocking incl.)*, Power Wash $5-8.50/ft. **Storage:** On-Land Out - $4/sq.ft. season, Inside $7/sq. ft. covered

Restaurants and Accommodations
Near: Restaurant *(Boathouse Bistro 633-7300, L $6-14, D $12-32)*, *(Tugboat Inn 633-4434, L $8-19, D $18-30, Kids' $4-9)*, *(Andrew's Harborside 633-4074, B $3-9, L $6-12, D $14-30)*, *(Christopher's Boathouse 633-6565, L $6-10, D $16-27)*, Seafood Shack *(Kaler's Crab House 633-5839, L $5-14, D $10-23, Kids' $3-5)*, Snack Bar *(Dunton's Doghouse Crab rolls, too)*, Lite Fare *(Tugboat Lounge 633-4434, L & D $8-16)*, *(Blue Moon Cafe 633-2200, B $3-9, L $4-10)*, *(Ebb Tide 633-5692, B $5-13, L $7-13)*, Hotel *(Tugboat Inn 633-4434, $85-280)*, Inn/B&B *(Admiral's Quarters & Greenleaf Inn 633-2474, $155-225)*, *(Capt. Sawyers 633-2290, $55-130)*, *(Sur la Mer 633-7400, $140-275, moorings for guests)*, *(Anchorwatch 633-7565, $105-175)*

Recreation and Entertainment
Near: Boat Rentals *(Tidal Transit Kayaks 633-7140)*, Bowling *(Romar)*, Fishing Charter *(Charger 380-4556; Sashimi 633-4902)*, Sightseeing *(Cap'n Fish 633-3244; Balmy Days to Monhegan Is. 633-2284; B.H. Whalewatch 633-3500)* **Under 1 mi:** Tennis Courts *("Y" & BRHS)*, Fitness Center *("Y")*, Movie Theater *(Harbor 633-3799)*, Video Rental *(Video Loft 633-6509)* **1-3 mi:** Beach *(Barrett Park; Hendricks Head)*, Playground, Golf Course *(Boothbay C.C. 633-6085)*, Museum *(Boothbay Railway 633-4727 $9/5)*

Provisioning and General Services
Near: Market *(Village 633-0944)*, Wine/Beer *(Christopher's 633-6565)*, Liquor Store *(Village)*, Bakery *(P&P 633-6511)*, Bank/ATM, Post Office, Protestant Church, Library, Beauty Salon, Bookstore *(Sherman's 633-7262)*, Pharmacy *(Rite Aid 633-7023)*, Hardware Store *(Grovers 633-2694)*, Florist, Copies Etc. *(Coastal 633-5515)* **Under 1 mi:** Supermarket *(Hannaford 633-6465)*, Farmers' Market *(Mini Mall Thu 9am-noon)*, Lobster Pound *(Lobsterman's Co-Op)*, Catholic Church, Dry Cleaners, Laundry

Transportation
OnCall: Rental Car *(Enterprise 882-8393)*, Airport Limo *(Country Coach 380-7201)* **Near:** Bikes, Local Bus *(Free shopping trolley)* **Under 1 mi:** Taxi *(Boothbay Harbor 633-6001; Coastal 380-4182)* **Airport:** Wiscasset/Portland Int'l. *(15 mi./60 mi.)*

Medical Services
911 Service **Near:** Doctor *(Harbor Medical 633-7820)*, Dentist, Chiropractor *(Coastal 669-4434, The Boothbay 633-5500)* **Hospital:** St. Andrews 633-2121- has dock *(1 mi.)*

Setting -- On the harbor's western shore, Boothbay Harbor Shipyard lies just to the west of McFarland Island. Antique yellow buildings dripping with flowers and recently renovated, state-of-the-art gray and dark green work sheds back the single 150-foot sturdy wharf that seems to reach into the mooring field. Classic schooners, private yachts and commercial craft in various stages of repair flank the pier and crowd the upland. Panoramic southern views to the harbor mouth, close proximity to the lively village, and, most of all, the romantic presence of tall ships makes it easy to overlook the lack of any cruiser amenities.

Marina Notes -- Seasonal Moorings $1,000. Founded 1869 as Townsend Marine Railway. Then Sample's in 1941. Sold & renamed B.H.S. in '04. Specializes in design, construction & restoration of wooden vessels. 20 shipwrights, two large shipsaws (6,000 sq. ft. temperature & humidity controlled), two marine railways (700-ton LOAs to 200 ft. & 150-ton LOAs to 90 ft.), carpentry, machine & metal shops. Some heavy moorings accommodate larger yachts (marked "B"). Fuel & Pump-out at Wotton's Wharf. Bathhouse: None. Website: www.boothbayharborshipyard.com.

Notable -- The opportunity to observe the projects du jour - like the recently completed restoration of the 156-foot, 1894 Schooner "Ernestina" or the rebuild of the 1960 replica of 120-foot tall ship "Bounty" is a real treat for most yachters. All the to-do's of downtown Boothbay Harbor are a five-minute walk: shops, restaurants, museums, sightseeing. Look for Bud's Hot Dog cart and Dunton's Doghouse - both Boothbay institutions. Local festivals take place throughout the year, including the Windjammer Days in June with tall ship rigs as far as the eye can see; Boatbuilder's Day early August and fireworks on the 4th of July.

Navigational Information
Lat: 43°51.077' **Long:** 069°38.161' **Tide:** 11 ft. **Current:** 0 kt. **Chart:** n/a
Rep. Depths (*MLW*): Entry 20 ft. **Fuel Dock** 7 ft. **Max Slip/Moor** 16 ft./18 ft.
Access: Due North 0.7 mi. past R#8 buoy "Tumber Is."

Marina Facilities *(In Season/Off Season)*
Fuel: *Bulk only* - Diesel, On Call Delivery
Slips: 10 Total, 10 Transient **Max LOA:** 250 ft. **Max Beam:** 55 ft.
Rate *(per ft.)*: **Day** $2.50* **Week** $15 **Month** n/a
Power: 30 amp $8, **50 amp** $16, **100 amp** $32, **200 amp** n/a
Cable TV: No **Dockside Phone:** No
Dock Type: Floating, Alongside, Wood
Moorings: 8 Total, 8 Transient **Launch:** No, Dinghy Dock
Rate: Day $25 **Week** $175 **Month** n/a
Heads: 3 Toilet(s), 2 Shower(s), Book Exchange
Internet: Yes *(Wi-Fi, ree)* **Laundry:** 1 Washer(s), 1 Dryer(s)
Pump-Out: OnCall *(633-3617)* **Fee:** $5 **Closed Heads:** Yes

Marina Operations
Owner/Manager: Boothbay Region Boatyard **Dockmaster:** Chuck Chaney
In-Season: MemDay-ColDay **Off-Season:** n/a
After-Hours Arrival: Tie up and check-in in the AM
Reservations: Yes, Recommended **Credit Cards:** Visa/MC, Dscvr, Amex
Discounts: None
Pets: Welcome, Dog Walk Area **Handicap Access:** Yes, Heads, Docks

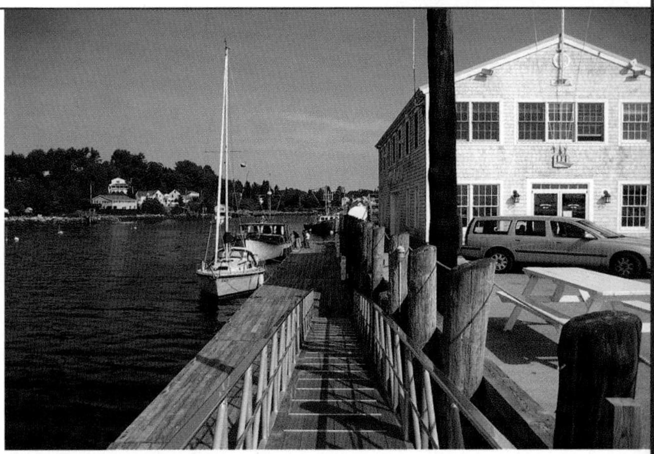

Wotton's Wharf

85 McFarland Point Dr; Boothbay Harbor, ME 04538

Tel: (207) 633-7440 **VHF: Monitor** n/a **Talk** n/a
Fax: n/a **Alternate Tel:** (207) 633-2970
Email: dockmaster@wottonswharf.com **Web:** www.wottonswharf.com
Nearest Town: Boothbay Harbor *(0.5 mi.)* **Tourist Info:** (207) 633-7448

Marina Services and Boat Supplies
Services - Docking Assistance, Security *(24, Cameras)*, Dock Carts, Megayacht Facilities, 3 Phase **Communication -** Mail & Package Hold **Supplies - OnSite:** Ice *(Block, Cube)* **Under 1 mi:** Propane *(Dead River 633-3144)*, CNG *(dinghy to Carousel Marina 633-2922)*

Boatyard Services
OnCall: Forklift, Crane, Engine mechanic *(gas, diesel)*, Electrical Repairs, Rigger, Canvas Work, Divers, Brightwork, Air Conditioning, Compound, Wash & Wax, Woodworking, Yacht Interiors, Painting **Near:** Railway *(500T)*, Launching Ramp, Bottom Cleaning. **1-3 mi:** Travelift *(50T)*, Hydraulic Trailer, Hull Repairs, Inflatable Repairs. **Nearest Yard:** Boothbay Region Boatyard (207) 633-2970

Restaurants and Accommodations
Near: Restaurant *(Tugboat Inn 633-4434, D $9-22)*, *(Kaler's Crab & Lobster House 633-5839, L $5-10, D $12-20)*, Snack Bar *(Dunton's Dogs L $3-10)*, Lite Fare *(Moosehead Coffee & Ice Cream 633-1145)*, Hotel *(Tugboat Inn 633-4434, $85-280)*, Inn/B&B *(Welch House 633-3431, $95-220)*, *(Anchor Watch 633-7565, $105-175)*, *(Topside 633-5404, $125-245)*, *(Sur La Mer 633-7400, $140-275, Moorings)* **Under 1 mi:** Restaurant *(Boathouse Bistro 633-7300, L $6-14, D $12-32)*, *(Andrew's Harborside 633-4074, B $3-9, L $6-12, D $14-30)*, Lite Fare *(Blue Moon 633-2349, B $3-9, L $4-10)*

Recreation and Entertainment
OnSite: Picnic Area **Near:** Hike/Bike Trails *(Boothbay Region Land Trust 633-4818 - Map of 30 miles of trails 137 Townsend Ave.)*, Fishing Charter *(Redhook 633-3807, Charger Charters 380-4556)*, Party Boat, Park, Special Events *(Windjammer wknd - June, Friendship Sloop Days - July)* **Under 1 mi:** Playground, Boat Rentals *(Tidal Transit Kayak 633-7140)*, Bowling *(Romar 633-5721)*, Movie Theater *(Harbor 633-3799)*, Video Rental *(Video Loft 633-6509)*, Sightseeing *(Cap'n Fish's Excursions 633-3244; Balmy Days to Monhegan Is. 633-2264; B.H. Whalewatch 633-3500)*, Galleries **1-3 mi:** Pool *("Y" 633-4816)*, Tennis Courts *("Y")*, Golf Course *(Boothbay C.C. 633-6085)*, Fitness Center *("Y")*, Museum *(Railway 633-4727 $7/3, 9:30am-5pm, Jun-ColDay; Aquarium 633-9559 $5/3)*, Cultural Attract *(Coastal Maine Botanical Gardens 633-4333 $10/5)*

Provisioning and General Services
Under 1 mi: Market *(Village 633-0944)*, Supermarket, Delicatessen, Liquor Store, Farmers' Market *(Mini Mall Thu 9am-noon)*, Lobster Pound, Bank/ATM, Post Office, Protestant Church, Library, Beauty Salon *(Beauty Box 633-3399)*, Dry Cleaners, Laundry, Bookstore *(Sherman's 633-7262)*, Pharmacy *(Rite Aid 633-7023)*, Newsstand, Hardware Store *(Grovers 633-2694)*, Florist, Copies Etc. **1-3 mi:** Catholic Church

Transportation
OnCall: Rental Car *(Enterprise 882-8393)*, Taxi *(Boothbay Harbor 633-3003)* **Near:** Local Bus *(Rocktide Trolley 633-9559)* **Under 1 mi:** Bikes *(Tidal Transit)* **Airport:** Wiscasset/Portland Int'l. *(15 mi./60 mi.)*

Medical Services
911 Service **OnCall:** Ambulance **Under 1 mi:** Dentist *(Family Dental 633-4243)*, Chiropractor *(Boothbay 633-5500)* **1-3 mi:** Doctor *(Andrew's Family Care 633-7820)* **3+ mi:** Veterinarian *(Coastal 633-3447, 5 mi.)* **Hospital:** St. Andrews 633-2121 *(1.5 mi.)*

Setting -- Just inside uncrowded Mill Cove, Wotton's Wharf skims the outer edge of Signal Point's slips. Wotton's long, easy-access, side-tie dock floats west of the wharf in the shadow of the two-story, gray-shingled Cape Cod office building. The fuel station and additional dockage are in the rear. The mooring field starts in the cove and stretches beyond. Spectacular views are of the main harbor dotted with small islands - and inland to the Signal Point's well-maintained grounds and attractive condos.

Marina Notes -- CCM *488 ft. linear side-tie dockage. Owned/managed by Boothbay Region Boatyard. Mega-yacht friendly to LOAs of 250 ft. 30, 50 & 100 amp 3-phase power. Docks protected by Signal Point gate. Free Wi-fi. On-call boatyard services from BRBY. Picnic tables and gas grill on wharf. Bathhouse: 2nd floor - stairs on north side. Newish heads, showers, laundry. Additional head on 1st floor at rear of store. Note: Signal Point no longer accepts transients.

Notable -- Wotton's location outside the inner harbor makes maneuvering easier for larger yachts and offers boaters a reminder of the untouched beauty that first attracted the summer throngs. Yet the kitschy hubbub is a short walk or dinghy ride (tie up for 3 hours at Town Dock, next to Pier Six). Boutiques, galleries (some unexpected gems), water-view restaurants and impeccably restored B & Bs rub shoulders with souvenir hawkers, taffy and T-shirt shops - but it's a mix that works. For more of less-touristed Boothbay, head to the Coastal Maine Botanical Gardens on Barter Island Road. Or to really escape the madding crowds, Boothbay Region Land Trust manages over 1700 acres in 15 preserves with roughly 30 miles of hiking trails and boating access at six islands - pick up a map.

7. ME - THE RIVERS & BOOTHBAY HARBOR
PHOTOS ON DVD: 18

Boothbay Region Boatyard

PO Box 179; 100 Ebenecook Road; West Southport, ME 04576

Tel: (207) 633-2970 **VHF: Monitor** Ch. 9 **Talk** Ch. 68
Fax: (207) 633-7144 **Alternate Tel:** n/a
Email: brb@brby.com **Web:** www.brby.com
Nearest Town: Boothbay Harbor *(5 mi.)* **Tourist Info:** (207) 633-2353

Navigational Information

Lat: 43°49.738' **Long:** 069°40.586' **Tide:** 10 ft. **Current:** n/a **Chart:** 13293
Rep. Depths (*MLW*): Entry 10 ft. **Fuel Dock** 8 ft. **Max Slip/Moor** 8 ft./70 ft.
Access: Sheepscot River past Hendrick's Light to Ebenecook Harbor

Marina Facilities *(In Season/Off Season)*

Fuel: Gasoline, Diesel
Slips: 40 Total, 6 Transient **Max LOA:** 80 ft. **Max Beam:** 16 ft.
Rate *(per ft.)*: **Day** $2.75/lnq. **Week** $15 **Month** $30
Power: 30 amp $8, **50 amp** $16, **100 amp** n/a, **200 amp** n/a
Cable TV: No **Dockside Phone:** No
Dock Type: Floating, Short Fingers, Pilings, Alongside, Wood
Moorings: 40 Total, 6 Transient **Launch:** Yes, Dinghy Dock ($300/season)
Rate: Day $35 **Week** $175 **Month** $500
Heads: 2 Toilet(s), 2 Shower(s), Book Exchange
Internet: Yes *(Wi-Fi)* **Laundry:** 2 Washer(s), 2 Dryer(s)
Pump-Out: Full Service, 1 Central, 8 InSlip **Fee:** $5 **Closed Heads:** Yes

Marina Operations

Owner/Manager: Richard T. Orne **Dockmaster:** Amy Armstrong
In-Season: MemDay-ColDay, 7am-5pm **Off-Season:** Oct-May, 7am-3:30pm
After-Hours Arrival: Call in advance for slip/mooring assignment
Reservations: Yes, Preferred **Credit Cards:** Visa/MC, Dscvr, Amex
Discounts: None
Pets: Welcome, Dog Walk Area **Handicap Access:** Yes, Heads, Docks

Marina Services and Boat Supplies

Services - Docking Assistance, Boaters' Lounge, Dock Carts
Communication - Pay Phone (1), FedEx, DHL, UPS, Express Mail
Supplies - OnSite: Ice *(Block, Cube)*, Ships' Store **1-3 mi:** Propane *(Southport General Store 633-6666)* **3+ mi:** Bait/Tackle *(White Anchor 633-3788, 5 mi.)*

Boatyard Services

OnSite: Travelift *(55T)*, Forklift *(7.5T Negative Lift Taylor)*, Crane *(15T- 60 ft. boom)*, Hydraulic Trailer *(25T Brownell, 20T Hostar)*, Engine mechanic *(gas, diesel)*, Electrical Repairs, Electronic Sales, Electronics Repairs, Hull Repairs, Rigger *(Maloney Marine 633-6788)*, Divers, Brightwork, Air Conditioning, Refrigeration, Compound, Wash & Wax, Interior Cleaning, Woodworking, Painting, Awlgrip, Total Refits, Yacht Broker **OnCall:** Canvas Work, Propeller Repairs, Inflatable Repairs, Upholstery, Metal Fabrication **Dealer for:** OMC, Westerbeke, Yamaha, Lugger, Yanmar, Mercruiser, Northern Lights. **Member:** ABBRA, ABYC - 3 Certified Tech(s), Other Certifications: Yanmar, Northern Lights, Cummins Diesel, Mercruiser, Volvo, Lugger, Westerbeke, Yamaha Outboard **Yard Rates:** $68/hr., Haul & Launch $8/ft. plus labor, Power Wash $35 plus labor **Storage:** On-Land In $11/ft., Heat $14.50/ft. Out $5/ft.

Restaurants and Accommodations

1-3 mi: Seafood Shack *(Robinson's Wharf & Tug's Pub Oyster Bar 633-3830)*, Coffee Shop *(Ship Ahoy 633-5222, 7am-10:30am. Breakfast only. Small boat dockage)*, Lite Fare *(Southport General Store 633-6666)*, Motel *(Ship Ahoy 633-5222, $40-80, 4 motel complexes)*, Hotel *(Oceangate 633-3321, $99-364)* **3+ mi:** Restaurant *(Cape Harbor Grill 633-5242, 3.5 mi.)*, Hotel *(Newagen Seaside Inn 633-5242, $135-285, 3.5 mi.)*

Recreation and Entertainment

OnSite: Picnic Area, Grills **Near:** Jogging Paths, Hike/Bike Trails **Under 1 mi:** Beach **1-3 mi:** Video Rental *(Southport General Store)*, Museum *(Hendricks Hill 633-1102 - 1810 house & boatshop, Tue, Thu, Sat 11am-3pm)* **3+ mi:** Golf Course *(Boothbay Country Club 633-6085, 6 mi.)*, Sightseeing *(Boothbay Harbor, 5 mi.)*

Provisioning and General Services

Under 1 mi: Lobster Pound, Beauty Salon **1-3 mi:** Market *(Southport General Store 633-6666 7am-8pm)*, Wine/Beer *(Southport Gen)*, Fishmonger *(Robinson's Wharf 633-3830 - also wine & microbrews)*, Post Office, Protestant Church **3+ mi:** Supermarket *(Hannaford 633-6465, 5 mi.)*, Liquor Store *(Village Market, 4 mi.)*, Library *(Southport Mem 633-2741, 3.5 mi.)*, Bookstore *(Sherman's 633-7262, 5 mi.)*

Transportation

OnCall: Rental Car *(Enterprise 882-8393)*, Taxi *(Bobo's 380-4182)* **Airport:** Wiscasset/Portland Int'l. *(15 mi./50 mi.)*

Medical Services

911 Service **OnCall:** Ambulance **3+ mi:** Doctor *(St. Andrews Family Care 633-7820, 3.5 mi.)*, Dentist *(Family 633-4243, 5 mi.)*, Veterinarian *(Boothbay 633-3447, 8 mi.)* **Hospital:** St. Andrews 633-2121, has dock *(3.5 mi.)*

Setting -- On rural, richly unspoiled Southport Island, a short way from the mouth of the Sheepscot River, this accommodating, full-service boatyard and marina is tucked into quiet Maddock Cove, the most western of Ebenecook Harbor's three watery fingers. A bevy of freshly painted, gray-shingled buildings overlook the large wharf deck where red-wood, painted picnic tables offer views of the upscale docks and the tranquil mooring field beyond.

Marina Notes -- Staff of over thirty-five full-time craftspeople. One of the most complete facilities on this part of the Maine coast. Also owns Wotton's Wharf in Boothbay Harbor which focuses on megayachts. Well-equipped marine store onsite with hardware, charts, engine parts - next-day service on special orders. Safe and secure harbor. Small, comfortable boaters' lounge. Picnic tables with pleasant view of the harbor. Rates are the same year 'round. Onsite Maloney Marine renowned for rigging. Bathhouse: Tiled floors, roomy heads.

Notable -- BRBY is a very busy boatyard in a very quiet place that's remarkably close - just five miles - to one of the most bustling, touristed regions in all of Maine. A small cluster of services is a little over two miles away and includes the Southport General Store, post office, Robinson's Wharf, and a house museum that preserves early regional life - including boat building. Less than a mile is one of those rare sandy beaches. Or dinghy north to Spectacle Island (owned in part by the Boothbay Region Land Trust) landing on the sandy beach - a popular picnic destination. If bikes are on board, this is a good place to haul them ashore. On your way through Townsend Gut, stop at Robinson's Wharf in Decker's Cove to stock up on seafood or grab a lobster lunch.

8. ME - Mid-Coast Rivers

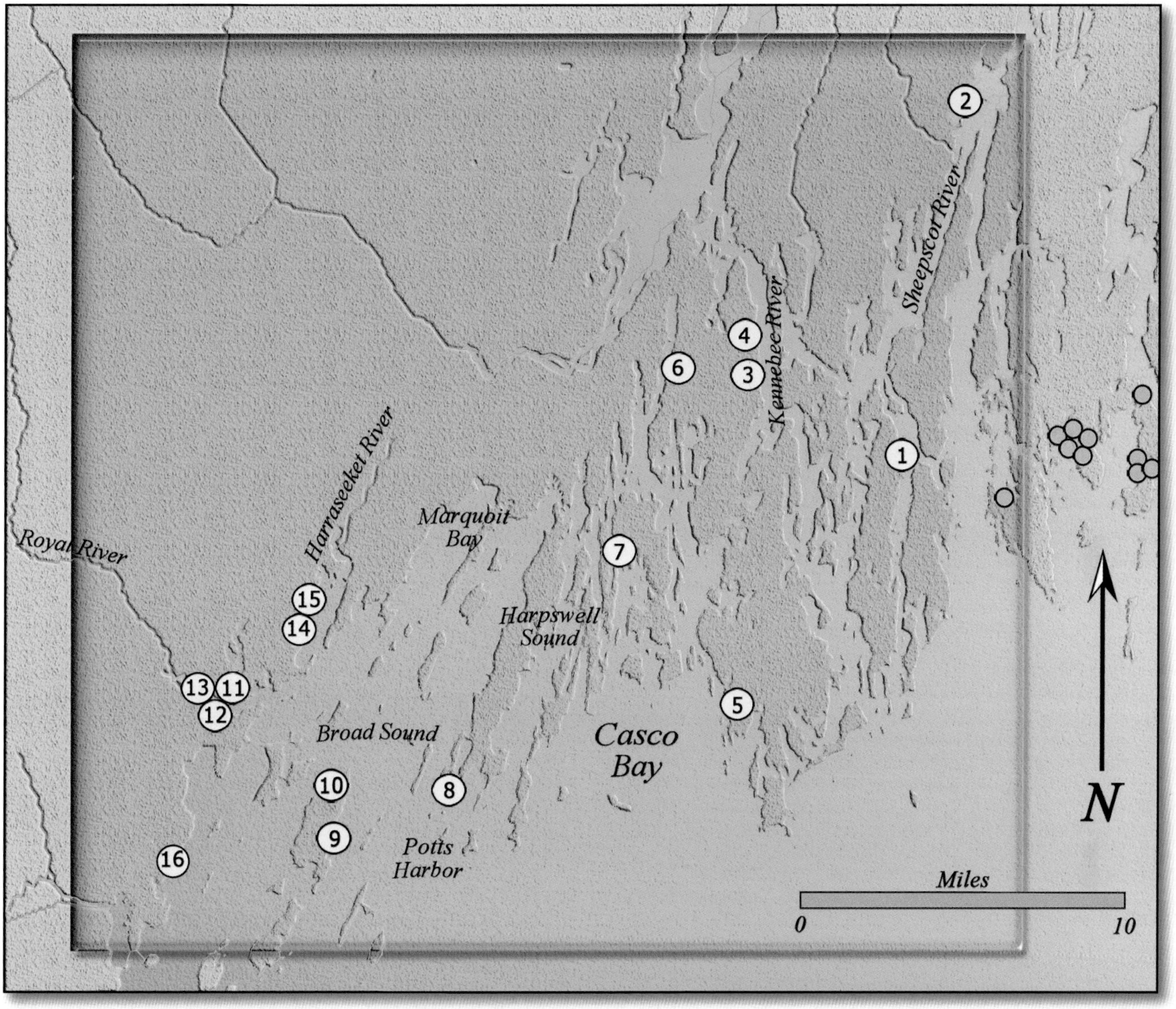

MAP	MARINA	HARBOR	PAGE
1	**Robinhood Marine Center**	*Sheepscot River*	*154*
2	**Wiscasset Town Pier**	*Sheepscot River*	*155*
3	**Maine Maritime Museum**	*Kennebec River*	*156*
4	**Kennebec Tavern & Marina**	*Kennebec River*	*157*
5	**Sebasco Harbor Resort**	*Casco Bay*	*158*
6	**New Meadows Marina**	*New Meadows River*	*159*
7	**Great Island Boat Yard**	*Quahog Bay*	*160*
8	**Dolphin Marina & Restaurant**	*Potts Harbor*	*161*
9	**Chebeague Island Boat Yard**	*Casco Bay*	*162*
10	**Chebeague Island Inn Moorings**	*Broad Sound*	*163*
11	**Royal River Boat Yard**	*Royal River*	*164*
12	**Yankee Marina & Boatyard**	*Royal River*	*165*
13	**Yarmouth Boat Yard**	*Royal River*	*166*
14	**Strouts Point Wharf Company**	*Harraseeket River*	*167*
15	**Brewer South Freeport Marine**	*Harraseeket River*	*168*
16	**Handy Boat Service**	*Falmouth River*	*169*

RATINGS: 1-5 for Marina Facilities & Amenities,  1-2 for Boatyard Services,  1-2 for MegaYacht Facilities,  for Something Special.

SERVICES:  for CCM – Certified Clean Marina,  for Pump-Out, 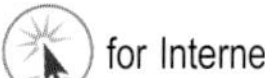 for Internet,  for Fuel, for Restaurant,  for Provisioning nearby,  for Catamaran-friendly,  for SportFish Charter,  for Pool/Beach, and for Golf within a mile. *For an explanation of ACC's Ratings, see page 8.*

Robinhood Marine Center

Robinhood Marine Center

340 Robinhood Road; Georgetown, ME 04548

Tel: (207) 371-2525; (800) 443-3625 **VHF: Monitor** Ch. 9 **Talk** Ch. 71
Fax: (207) 371-2899 **Alternate Tel:** (207) 371-2525
Email: yachts@robinhoodmarinecenter.com **Web:** See Marina Notes*
Nearest Town: Woolwich/Bath *(7 mi.)* **Tourist Info:** (207) 443-9751

Navigational Information

Lat: 43°51.200' **Long:** 069°44.100' **Tide:** 11 ft. **Current:** 2 kt. **Chart:** 13293
Rep. Depths (*MLW*): Entry 70 ft. **Fuel Dock** 10 ft. **Max Slip/Moor** 65 ft./65 ft.
Access: Sheepscot River to Goose Rock Passage

Marina Facilities *(In Season/Off Season)*

Fuel: *unbranded* - Gasoline, Diesel
Slips: 135 Total, 10-20 Transient **Max LOA:** 65 ft. **Max Beam:** n/a
Rate *(per ft.)*: **Day** $4.00/Inq. **Week** $14 **Month** $36
Power: 30 amp Incl., **50 amp** Incl., **100 amp** n/a, **200 amp** n/a
Cable TV: No **Dockside Phone:** No
Dock Type: Floating, Long Fingers, Alongside, Wood
Moorings: 72 Total, 25 Transient **Launch:** None, Dinghy Dock
Rate: Day $35 **Week** $175 **Month** $500
Heads: 2 Toilet(s), 2 Shower(s) *(dressing rooms)*, Book Exchange
Internet: Yes *(Wi-Fi, Free)* **Laundry:** 1 Washer(s), 1 Dryer(s)
Pump-Out: Full Service, 1 Central **Fee:** Free **Closed Heads:** No

Marina Operations

Owner/Manager: Warren Harbison **Dockmaster:** Kelly Rickards
In-Season: n/a, 8am-8pm **Off-Season:** n/a, 8am-3:30pm
After-Hours Arrival: Tie up at fuel dock or pick up vacant mooring
Reservations: Yes, Preferred **Credit Cards:** Visa/MC, Dscvr
Discounts: Boat/US **Dockage:** 10% **Fuel:** n/a **Repair:** n/a
Pets: Welcome, Dog Walk Area **Handicap Access:** Yes, Heads

Marina Services and Boat Supplies

Services - Docking Assistance, Boaters' Lounge, Dock Carts **Communication -** Mail & Package Hold, Fax in/out *(Free)*, FedEx, DHL, UPS, Express Mail **Supplies - OnSite:** Ice *(Block, Cube)*, Ships' Store, CNG *(exchange)* **OnCall:** Bait/Tackle, Propane

Boatyard Services

OnSite: Travelift *(55T - open end)*, Forklift *(35T Con-O-Lift)*, Crane *(18T)*, Hydraulic Trailer *(20T Con-O-Lift)*, Engine mechanic *(gas, diesel)*, Electrical Repairs, Electronic Sales, Electronics Repairs, Hull Repairs, Rigger, Bottom Cleaning, Brightwork, Air Conditioning, Refrigeration, Compound, Wash & Wax, Interior Cleaning, Propeller Repairs, Woodworking, Inflatable Repairs, Metal Fabrication, Painting, Awlgrip, Yacht Building, Yacht Broker *(David Perry)* **OnCall:** Divers, Life Raft Service, Upholstery **Dealer for:** Raymarine, Heart Interface, Cruisaire, Seafrost, Yanmar, Clarion, Westerbeke, Harken. **Member:** ABBRA, ABYC **Yard Rates:** $47-70/hr., Haul & Launch $9/ft. + Lab, Power Wash $2/ft. + Lab **Storage:** In-Water $8/sq.ft./season, On-Land Season - Outside $6.25/sq.ft.; Inside: $11/sq./ft

Restaurants and Accommodations

OnSite: Restaurant *(The Osprey Restaurant 371-2530, L $8-12, D $15-22, Seafood & Pub Fare - 11am-11pm, Kitchen closes 9pm.)*, Lite Fare *(The Tavern at Riggs Cove 371-2530)* **Near:** Restaurant *(Robinhood Meeting House 371-2188, D $24-28, 5:30 - 9pm. Pub night Weds - entrees under $12.)* **Under 1 mi:** Inn/B&B *(Tide's End Farm 371-9050, $100-175, Just across Rigg's Cove)* **3+ mi:** Seafood Shack *(Five Island Lobster 371-2990, 7 mi.)*, Inn/B&B *(Coveside B&B 371-2807, $135-200, 7 mi.)*, *(The Mooring 371-2790, $140-200, 7 mi.)*, *(Gray Havens 371-2616, $160-280, 7 mi.)*

Recreation and Entertainment

OnSite: Picnic Area, Grills, Cultural Attract *(Friday night bands - 4-7pm)*, Galleries *(Old Rigging Shop Studio - a bit of local history)*, Special Events *(Wednesday Lectures 7pm)* **Under 1 mi:** Horseback Riding *(Tides End Farm 371-9050 - dressage, eventing, lessons)* **3+ mi:** Golf Course *(Bath Country Club 442-8411, 12 mi.)*, Park *(Reid State Park - 1.5 mi. of beaches, salt marsh, dunes, tidal pools, bath house, fireplaces, picnic tables, 8 mi.)*, Museum *(Georgetown Historical Society 371-9200 Wed 10am-5pm, Sat 10am-noon, 4.5 mi.)*, Sightseeing *(119 acre Josephine Newman Sanctuary 781-2330 - 2 mi. walking trails & abundant mosquitoes, 6 mi.)*

Provisioning and General Services

OnSite: Farmers' Market *(Dave Berry's Merrymeeting Farm market boat - organic produce & other treats)*, Library *(Books, periodicals, puzzles)* **1-3 mi:** Protestant Church *(Baptist)* **3+ mi:** Market *(Georgetown Store 371-2106, 4.5 mi.)*, Supermarket *(Shaw's 443-9179, 8 mi.)*, Bank/ATM *(Mid-Coast 443-5531, 7 mi.)*, Bookstore *(Bath Books 443-9338, 8 mi.)*, Pharmacy *(Wilsons 442-8786, 8 mi.)*, Hardware Store *(Roger's 443-3542, 8 mi.)*

Transportation

OnSite: Courtesy Car/Van *(2 courtesy cars available all hours)* **OnCall:** Water Taxi *(Mid-Marine 371-2288)*, Rental Car *(Enterprise 882-8393)*, Taxi *(Platinum Plus 443-9166 - from Bath)* **Airport:** Portland Int'l. *(40 mi.)*

Medical Services

911 Service **OnCall:** Ambulance **3+ mi:** Doctor *(Bath Family 443-4471, 8 mi.)*, Dentist *(Bath Family 442-7581, 8 mi.)*, Veterinarian *(Bath Animal 443-9006, 9 mi.)* **Hospital:** Mid-Coast 729-0181 *(15 mi.)*

Setting -- The pitch-perfect, playful village that is Robinhood Marine edges unspoiled Riggs Cove. Arched footbridges protect the dinghy basin while providing easy access to the large network of upscale docks - and mooring field beyond. Winding paths, softened by abundant flowers, link the upland amenities housed in a treasure-trove of restored 18thC buildings - a cozy library, history gallery, General Store (chandlery), screened gazebo, bathhouse and The Osprey restaurant with an al fresco deck all perch along the shore. Attention to detail is evident at every turn.

Marina Notes -- *www.robinhoodmarinecenter.com. Marine parts/supplies (General Store). Magnet for yacht club cruises. Fuel dock open until 8pm summer. Dockage by hour, night or season. Free Wi-Fi on all docks. Library well-stocked with paperbacks to read, take or leave. Dock house open 8am-8pm in summer, till 3 pm in Sept. Full service boatyard 20-person craft & tech team. Builds Robinhood sail & power boats. Spartan Marine, in General Store - high quality marine hardware. Bathhouse: On a small hill. Two large showers & 2 heads. Laundry washer/dryer, chairs, folding table, coffee vending machine.

Notable -- Two courtesy cars are available for shopping and museum visits, and two courtesy boats for fun - a Cape Dory Typhoon Daysailer and spectacular pulling boat. Maritime history buffs may enjoy The Gallery at Riggs Cove's 200 years of articles and photographs of this site when it was Riggsville Wharf. For casual dining (inside or on the small waterside deck), the Osprey Restaurant, now run by the gang from Montsweag Roadhouse, serves seafood and pub food. Nearby, celebrity chef Michael Gagne's Robinhood Free Meetinghouse serves American fusion in a handsomely restored Greek-revival 1855 church.

Navigational Information

Lat: 43°59.980' **Long:** 069°39.870' **Tide:** 6 ft. **Current:** 5 kt. **Chart:** 13293
Rep. Depths (*MLW*): Entry 30 ft. **Fuel Dock** n/a **Max Slip/Moor** 15 ft./22 ft.
Access: Sheepscot R., turn to port at Ft. Edgecomb - docks to port

Marina Facilities *(In Season/Off Season)*

Fuel: No
Slips: 10 Total, 10 Transient **Max LOA:** 50 ft. **Max Beam:** n/a
Rate *(per ft.)*: **Day** $1.00 **Week** n/a **Month** n/a
Power: 30 amp Incl., **50 amp** Incl., **100 amp** n/a, **200 amp** n/a
Cable TV: No **Dockside Phone:** No
Dock Type: Floating, Alongside, Wood
Moorings: 115 Total, 2 Transient **Launch:** No, Dinghy Dock
Rate: Day $15 **Week** n/a **Month** n/a
Heads: 2 Toilet(s)
Internet: No **Laundry:** None
Pump-Out: OnSite, Self Service **Fee:** Free **Closed Heads:** No

Marina Operations

Owner/Manager: William Sutter (Harbormaster) **Dockmaster:** Same
In-Season: Year Round, 9am-5pm **Off-Season:** n/a
After-Hours Arrival: Call in advance
Reservations: No **Credit Cards:** Cash Only
Discounts: None
Pets: Welcome **Handicap Access:** Yes, Heads, Docks

Wiscasset Town Pier

Water Street; Wiscasset, ME 04578

Tel: (207) 882-8200 **VHF: Monitor** n/a **Talk** n/a
Fax: n/a **Alternate Tel:** (207) 380-1922
Email: n/a **Web:** n/a
Nearest Town: Wiscasset **Tourist Info:** (207) 563-8340

Marina Services and Boat Supplies

Communication - FedEx, UPS, Express Mail **Supplies - Near:** Ice *(Cube)* **3+ mi:** Bait/Tackle *(Wiscasset Bait 882-9293, 3.5 mi.)*

Boatyard Services

Nearest Yard: Boothbay Region Boatyard (207) 633-2970

Restaurants and Accommodations

OnSite: Restaurant *(Le Garage 882-5409, L $7-18, D $11-27, spectacular views from renovated 1920 garage)* **Near:** Restaurant *(Sarah's Cafe & Twin Schooner 882-7504, L & D $5-17, Pizzas $6-19, 11am-8pm)*, *(Marketplace Cafe 882-9375, L $6-12)*, Seafood Shack *(Red's Eats 882-6128, L $4-16, take-away)*, *(Sprague's Lobster 882-7814, take away. No lines, picnic tables on the river)*, Pizzeria *(Happy's 882-9275)*, Inn/B&B *(Marston House 882-6010, $100, also an antique shop)*, *(Carew 687-2052, $120, also an antique shop & gallery)*, *(Snow Squall 882-6892, $90-107)* **Under 1 mi:** Restaurant *(Bintliff's Ocean Grill 882-9401)*, Hotel *(Sheepscot Harbour Resort & Cottages 882-6343, $140-450)* **1-3 mi:** Restaurant *(Sea Basket 882-6581, BYO)*, Inn/B&B *(The Squire Tarbox Inn 882-7693, $115-200)*

Recreation and Entertainment

OnSite: Picnic Area **Near:** Jogging Paths, Hike/Bike Trails, Park *(Sunken Garden - Main St.; Waterfront - Water & Fore Sts.)*, Cultural Attract *(Musical Wonder House 882-7163 $10-45/8-10. 1852 sea captain mansion - 2,000 music boxes)*, Galleries *(Maine Art 882-7511; Wiscasset Bay 882-7682; Sheepscot River Pottery 882-9410 - one mi.)*

Under 1 mi: Museum *(Castle Tucker 1807 House 882-7169 $5; Nickels-Sortwell Federal-era mansion 882-6218 $5 Wed-Sun; Old Lincoln County Jail 882-6817 $4/2 - 1.5 mi. south)* **1-3 mi:** Sightseeing *(Fort Edgecomb Memorial Park 882-7777 - 1809 Octagonal Blockhouse with outstanding lookout views)* **3+ mi:** Fitness Center *(Curves 882-8300, 3.5 mi.)*

Provisioning and General Services

Near: Gourmet Shop *(Treats 882-6192)*, Wine/Beer *(Treats)*, Bakery *(Treats)*, Bank/ATM *(Key 882-7274)*, Post Office, Protestant Church, Library *(Wiscasset 882-7161 Internet, copy machine)*, Beauty Salon *(River View 882-7345)*, Retail Shops *(20 + antique shops - pick up a map)* **1-3 mi:** Convenience Store, Market *(Huber's 882-5544 Fire - re-opening late 2011)*, Dry Cleaners *(J&J 319-7519)*, Hardware Store *(Ames 882-7710)*, Clothing Store, Copies Etc. *(Ship4You 319-7519)* **3+ mi:** Supermarket *(Shaw's 882-8424, 4 mi.)*, Pharmacy *(Waltz 563-3128, 7 mi.)*

Transportation

OnCall: Taxi *(Wicked Good 563-6225 - from Damariscotta)*, Airport Limo *(Mid-Coast 800-937-2424)* **Near:** InterCity Bus *(Concord Trailways 800-639-3317)* **Airport:** Wiscasset/Portland Jetport *(5 mi./50 mi.)*

Medical Services

911 Service **OnCall:** Ambulance **Near:** Doctor *(Wiscasset Family 882-6008)*, Dentist *(Grosser 882-6843)*, Chiropractor *(West Family 882-7800)* **Under 1 mi:** Optician *(Sheepscot Eye 882-9566)* **1-3 mi:** Veterinarian *(Coastal 882-9458)* **Hospital:** Miles Mem. 563-1234 *(8.5 mi.)*

Setting -- About 13 miles from the mouth of the Sheepscot River, the Wiscasset Town Pier's three rugged docks and Belgian-block Harbor Master's building lie to port - just south of the Davis Island/Route 1 Bridge. Above the docks, window-walled porches wrap the three-story, hip-roofed Le Garage restaurant - which take full advantage of the spectacular views. Next door, the diminutive but lively Wiscasset Yacht Club tries to accommodate visiting cruisers. Across the road is the 1870 brick Customs House. Wiscasset's main drag - traffic-congested Route 1 - is 0.2 mile north. A destination worthy of a detour.

Marina Notes -- Dockage on northern float - free three-hour tie-up or $1/ft. overnight. Dinghy floats for mooring field. Mimimal services. Harbormaster - 350-0113. Pump-out. Aging wood docks. Gas available at Edgecomb Eddy. Diesel fuel at the North End Coop on Westport Island. Deep, well-protected harbor. Adjacent private Wiscasset Yacht Club (882-4058): limited side-tie dockage, tender floats and moorings. Eddy Marina (882-7776): 10 slips & 10 moorings in The Eddy cove, just east of Ft. Edgecomb. Bathhouse: Belgian block municipal heads. Dimly lit heads with tiled floors. Note; Laundry & showers at W.Y.C.

Notable -- While the Town Pier is less than impressive, Wiscasset - meaning "at the hidden outlet" - is the self-proclaimed "prettiest village in Maine." It boasts mid-19thC. sea captain's clapboard mansions, Federal-style brick commercial buildings, organic cafés, restaurants and authentic fish shacks. Browse boutiques, antique shops and galleries for treasures; stop by the Musical Wonders House for unique music boxes. Follow the lines to Red's Eats touted as purveyors of the best lobster rolls in Maine. Across the river, octagonal Fort Edgecomb was built in 1808 to protect Maine shipping interests from the British.

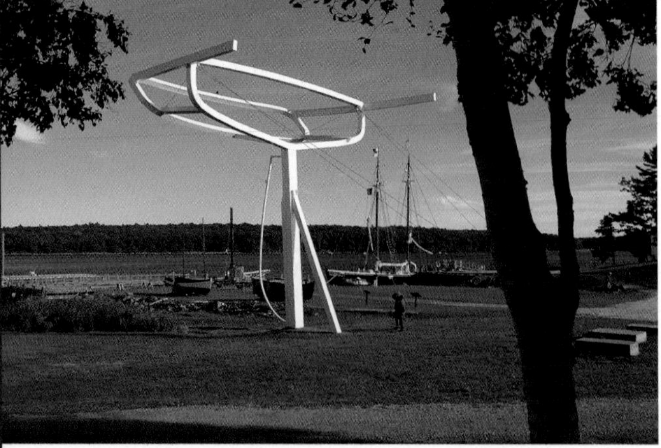

Maine Maritime Museum

243 Washington Street; Bath, ME 04530

Tel: (207) 443-1316 **VHF: Monitor** n/a **Talk** n/a
Fax: (207) 443-1665 **Alternate Tel:** n/a
Email: reservations@maritimeme.org **Web:** mainemartimemuseum.org
Nearest Town: Bath *(1.4 mi.)* **Tourist Info:** (207) 443-9751

Navigational Information

Lat: 43°53.689' **Long:** 069°48.889' **Tide:** 9 ft. **Current:** 4 kt. **Chart:** n/a
Rep. Depths (*MLW*): Entry 20 ft. **Fuel Dock** n/a **Max Slip/Moor** 300 ft./50 ft.
Access: 10 miles up the Kennebec River from Gulf of Maine

Marina Facilities *(In Season/Off Season)*

Fuel: No
Slips: 1 Total, 1 Transient **Max LOA:** 150 ft. **Max Beam:** n/a
Rate *(per ft.)*: **Day** $2.50* **Week** n/a **Month** n/a
Power: 30 amp n/a, **50 amp** n/a, **100 amp** n/a, **200 amp** n/a
Cable TV: No **Dockside Phone:** No
Dock Type: Fixed, Floating, Alongside, Wood
Moorings: 7 Total, 7 Transient **Launch:** No, Dinghy Dock
Rate: Day $30 **Week** n/a **Month** n/a
Heads: 2 Toilet(s), 2 Shower(s) *(dressing rooms)*
Internet: No **Laundry:** Yes
Pump-Out: No **Fee:** n/a **Closed Heads:** Yes

Marina Operations

Owner/Manager: Amy Lent **Dockmaster:** Christine Titcomb
In-Season: May-Oct, 8am-4:30pm **Off-Season:** Closed
After-Hours Arrival: Take an empty mooring, Check-in in morning
Reservations: Yes, Preferred **Credit Cards:** Visa/MC, Dscvr, Amex
Discounts: Member discount 10% **Dockage:** n/a **Fuel:** n/a **Repair:** n/a
Pets: No **Handicap Access:** Yes, Heads, Docks

Marina Services and Boat Supplies

Communication - Fax in/out, FedEx, UPS, Express Mail **Supplies - 1-3 mi:** Ice *(Cube)*, Bait/Tackle *(Kennebec Angler 442-8239)*, Propane *(Seawall 443-8818)*

Boatyard Services

Nearest Yard: New Meadows Marina (207) 443-4254

Restaurants and Accommodations

Under 1 mi: Pizzeria *(The Cabin 443-6224, sands, salads, too)* **1-3 mi:** Restaurant *(Starlight Café 442-3005)*, *(Beale Street BBQ & Grill 442-9514)*, *(Kennebec Tavern 442-9636, L & D $8-26)*, *(Solo Bistro 443-3373, D $12-25, $22 prix fixe)*, *(J.R. Maxwell's 443-2014, L & D $8-19)*, *(Byrne's Irish Pub 443-6776)*, *(Admiral's Steakhouse 443-2555)*, Lite Fare *(Mae's Café & Bakery 442-8577, B $5-13, L $9-14)*, Hotel *(The Inn at Bath 443-4294, $150-190)*, *(Holiday Inn 443-9741, $75-300, pets welcome)*, *(Hampton Inn 386-1310, $125-300)*, Inn/B&B *(Galen C. Moses House 442-8771, $119-259)*, *(Kennebec 443-5324, $110-185)*

Recreation and Entertainment

OnSite: Picnic Area, Playground, Museum *(Maine Maritime $12/9 Daily 9:30am-5pm)* **Near:** Fitness Center *(Universe Gym 442-0180)* **1-3 mi:** Tennis Courts, Golf Course *(Bath G.C. 442-8411)*, Boat Rentals *(H2O Outfitters)*, Fishing Charter *(Obsession 442-8581)*, For Kids *(Bath Skate Park 443-8900)*, Video Rental *(Movie Gallery 443-8954)*, Cultural Attract *(Chocolate Church Arts Center 442-8455; Studio Theater of Bath 443-2418)*, Sightseeing *(Walking tour maps or borrow podcasts from Train Station Info)*, Galleries *(Front St. - antique stores & art galleries)*, Special Events *(Friday night Concerts at Patten Library Park; Art Walk - 3rd Fridays 5-7pm)* **3+ mi:** Horseback Riding *(Sable Oaks 443-4006, 5 mi.)*

Provisioning and General Services

OnSite: Bookstore *(Large maritime books & gift shop)* **1-3 mi:** Supermarket *(Shaw's 443-9179)*, Delicatessen, Bakery *(Mae's 442-8577)*, Farmers' Market *(Waterfront Park Thu & Sat 8:30am-12:30pm)*, Lobster Pound, Bank/ATM, Post Office, Catholic Church, Protestant Church, Library *(Bath 443-5141)*, Beauty Salon *(Bath Harir 443-1786)*, Barber Shop, Dry Cleaners, Laundry, Pharmacy *(CVS 443-9097, Walgreens 443-1786)*, Hardware Store *(Rogers ACE 443-2552)*, Florist, Department Store *(Reny's)*, Copies Etc. *(Bath Printing 443-3411)* **3+ mi:** Liquor Store *(ABC 729-5837, 8 mi.)*

Transportation

OnSite: Local Bus *(Bath Trolley $1/pp, loops museum, the town, and outlying shopping center & supermarket)* **OnCall:** Rental Car *(Enterprise 882-8393)*, Taxi *(Bath 443-4009)*, Airport Limo *(Drew's 443-9166)* **1-3 mi:** Bikes *(Bath Cycle 442-7002 $18/day)*, InterCity Bus *(Concord Trailways)*, Rail *(Eastern Maine RR 866-637-2457- Brunswick, Bath, Wiscasset, Rockland $16-25 1-way)* **Airport:** Portland Int'l. *(38 mi.)*

Medical Services

911 Service **Near:** Dentist *(Bruce Verrill 443-5491)*, Chiropractor *(Bath Family Chiro 443-1244)* **1-3 mi:** Doctor *(Bath Family 443-4471)*, Optician *(Farrar 442-0580)*, Veterinarian *(Bath 443-9006)* **3+ mi:** Holistic Services *(Sweetwater Spa 443-4723, 4 mi.)* **Hospital:** Mid-Coast 729-0181 *(8 mi.)*

Setting -- Ten miles up the Kennebec, just south of Bath Iron Works, the museum complex rises above the western bank. A mooring field, floating docks and 75-foot pier give boating visitors access to this former 19th-century shipyard. The beautiful, black-hulled schooner "Sherman Zwicker" usually docks at the pier. Sprawled across 25-acres of rolling lawn, the main brick ediface and five original buildings host exhibits that interpret Maine's maritime heritage and Bath's early years. Dramatic life-size white bow and stern sculptures outline the ghost footprint of the "Wyoming," the largest wooden sailing ship ever built.

Marina Notes -- *Wharf designed for large vessels 60-300 ft. Museum established 1962. Check in at Admissions Desk. Dockage or mooring fee includes 2 museum passes. Pets only in South parking lot. Picnic area. Attractive Long Reach Hall (capacity 125-200), Donnell House & Percy & Small Shipyard rentable for group functions. Trolley makes all of Bath accessible. Bathhouse: "Visiting Yachtsmen's Building" includes tiled heads, roomy showers, laundry.

Notable -- The MMM, a magnet for maritime-history buffs and families, includes the Percy & Small Shipyard, the only intact wooden shipyard in the U.S. (the "Wyoming" was built here). Permanent and rotating exhibits fill ten acres of galleries with lobstering dioramas, shipbuilding displays, a Victorian-era home, the "Sherman Zwicker," plus children's interactive experiences The contemporary Maritime History building focuses on life at sea and maritime technology. The Boat Shop teaches traditional boat-building techniques. Seasonal tours include the Bath Iron Works and boat cruises - from 50-minute river excursions to four-hour-long adventures. Bath Iron Work, very prominent when cruising the river, builds Navy destroyers and large merchant & commercial vessels.

Navigational Information
Lat: 43°54.825' **Long:** 069°48.748' **Tide:** 6 ft. **Current:** 5 kt. **Chart:** 13293
Rep. Depths (*MLW*): Entry 41 ft. **Fuel Dock** 20 ft. **Max Slip/Moor** 20 ft./40 ft.
Access: 10 miles up the Kennebec River just north of the Route 1 bridge

Marina Facilities *(In Season/Off Season)*
Fuel: *89/93* - Slip-Side Fueling, Gasoline, On Call Delivery
Slips: 60 Total, 10 Transient **Max LOA:** 32 ft. **Max Beam:** 12 ft.
Rate *(per ft.)*: **Day** $1.50 **Week** $150 **Month** n/a
Power: 30 amp n/a, **50 amp** n/a, **100 amp** n/a, **200 amp** n/a
Cable TV: No **Dockside Phone:** No
Dock Type: Floating, Wood
Moorings: 8 Total, 3 Transient **Launch:** None, Dinghy Dock
Rate: Day $30 **Week** $100 **Month** $200
Heads: 2 Toilet(s)
Internet: No **Laundry:** None
Pump-Out: No **Fee:** n/a **Closed Heads:** No

Marina Operations
Owner/Manager: Gene Nygaard **Dockmaster:** Steve Zanco/Jeff Sheires
In-Season: May 15-Oct 15, 8am-8pm **Off-Season:** Oct 15-May 15, 8am-6pm
After-Hours Arrival: Call in advance
Reservations: Yes, Preferred **Credit Cards:** Visa/MC, Dscvr, Din, Amex
Discounts: None
Pets: Welcome **Handicap Access:** Yes, Heads, Docks

Kennebec Tavern & Marina

119 Commercial Street; Bath, ME 04530

Tel: (207) 442-9636 **VHF: Monitor** n/a **Talk** n/a
Fax: (207) 386-0397 **Alternate Tel:** n/a
Email: kennebectavern@suscom-maine.net **Web:** n/a
Nearest Town: Bath *(0.1 mi.)* **Tourist Info:** (207) 443-9751

Marina Services and Boat Supplies
Services - Docking Assistance, Security *(Locked gate)*, Trash Pick-Up **Communication -** Pay Phone, FedEx, UPS, Express Mail **Supplies - OnSite:** Ice *(Block, Cube)* **Near:** Ships' Store, Bait/Tackle *(Kennebec Angler 442-8239, Eels, worms)* **Under 1 mi:** Propane *(Roger's)*

Boatyard Services
Nearest Yard: BEC Marine (207) 443-3022

Restaurants and Accommodations
OnSite: Restaurant *(Kennebec Tavern L $8-20, D $13-28, L & D $8-26 11am-9pm, Sun Brunch $15/10 10am-2pm)* **Near:** Restaurant *(MaryEllenz Caffé 442-0960, D $8-20)*, *(Maxwells 443-2014, L & D $8-19)*, *(Beale St. Grille 442-9514, D $8-14)*, *(Solo Bistro 443-3373, D $12-25)*, Lite Fare *(Mae's Café & Bakery 442-8577, B $5-13, L $9-14)*, *(Darling's Dog House $10 Lobster Roll)*, *(Cafe Creme 443-6454, Wi-Fi)*, Pizzeria *(Mario's 443-4126)*, Inn/B&B *(Kennebec 443-5324, $110-185)*, *(The Inn at Bath 443-4294, $150-190, Pets)*, *(Galen C. Moses 442-8771, $119-259)*, *(Benjamin F. Packard 443-6004, $90-130)* **Under 1 mi:** Pizzeria *(Cabin 443-6224, pastas, subs. Del.)* **1-3 mi:** Hotel *(Holiday Inn 443-9741, $75-300)*

Recreation and Entertainment
OnSite: Fishing Charter *(Obsession 442-8581)* **Near:** Hike/Bike Trails, For Kids *(Bath Indoor Skateboard Park 443-8900)*, Video Rental *(Movie Gallery 443-8954)*, Park *(Waterfront)*, Tours *(Eastern Maine RR - Bath to Rockland $42 RT)*, Cultural Attract *(Chocolate Church Arts 442-8455; Studio Theater 443-1606; Friday night Patten Park Concerts)*, Sightseeing *(3 walking tours - Download podcasts from cityofbath.com or borrow from Train Station Info Center)*, Galleries *(Front St.)* **Under 1 mi:** Playground, Tennis Courts, Fitness Center *(Universe Gym 442-0180)*, Boat Rentals *(H2, Outfitters)* **1-3 mi:** Golf Course *(Bath G.C. 442-8411)*, Museum *(Bath Maritime 443-1316 $12/9)* **3+ mi:** Horseback Riding *(Sable Oak 443-4006, 4 mi.)*

Provisioning and General Services
Near: Provisioning Service, Convenience Store, Market *(Brackett's IGA 443-2012 across street)*, Delicatessen *(Front Street 443-9815)*, Health Food *(Bath Natural 442-8012)*, Bakery *(Mae's 442-8577)*, Farmers' Market *(Waterfront Park Thu & Sat 8:30-12:30)*, Bank/ATM, Post Office, Protestant Church, Library *(443-5141)*, Beauty Salon, Barber Shop, Dry Cleaners, Laundry, Bookstore *(Bath Book Shop 443-9338)*, Pharmacy *(CVS 443-3307)*, Florist **Under 1 mi:** Liquor Store *(New Meadows 443-8818)*, Catholic Church, Hardware Store *(Coastal 443-6089)* **1-3 mi:** Supermarket *(Shaw's 443-9179)*, Fishmonger *(Gilmore's)*, Department Store *(Reny's Discount)*

Transportation
OnSite: Local Bus *(Trolley $1/pp)* **OnCall:** Rental Car *(Enterprise 882-8393)*, Taxi *(Platinum Plus 443-9166)* **Near:** Bikes *(Bath Cycle 442-7002 $18/day)*, Rail *(Eastern Maine RR 866-637-2457- Brunswick, Bath, Wiscasset, Rockland $16-25 1-way)* **Under 1 mi:** InterCity Bus *(Concord Trailways)* **Airport:** Portland Int'l. *(40 mi.)*

Medical Services
911 Service **Near:** Doctor *(Bath Family 443-4471)*, Optician *(Farrar 442-0580)* **Under 1 mi:** Dentist *(Bath Family 442-7581)*, Chiropractor *(Bath Family 443-1244)*, Veterinarian *(Bath 443-9006)* **1-3 mi:** Holistic Services *(Sweetwater Spa 443-4723)* **Hospital:** Mid-Coast 729-0181 *(8 mi.)*

Setting -- On the Kennebec River, just north of the Sagadahoc and Carlton Bridges, The Tavern's two long, side-tie, smaller-boat docks parallel the bulkhead. Bright blue umbrellas and a blue-and-gray striped awning shade the large waterside deck while a small gray dockhouse oversees the boating operation. It's a short walk to the shops, boutiques and cafes of Bath's architecturally and culturally compelling downtown - one steeped in the legacy of 5,000 launched ships.

Marina Notes -- Established 1997. 100 year-old building restored as Kennebec Tavern - a light-filled, casual restaurant with expansive river views. Minimal boater services. Gas dock. Max LOA 35 ft. Sailboats only on moorings due to tides & docking system. New seawall and bigger 400-ft. deck. Attractive, spacious Seguin Hall available for private events. Bathhouse: Inside Tavern's entrance. Varnished wood & tile. Shared with restaurant.

Notable -- Bath has been a shipbuilding center since the 17th century and offers much to today's visiting mariner -- including the well-executed Maine Maritime Museum (1.7 miles downriver) and the Hobby Shoppe (443-4605) which specializes in ships' models. Bath Iron Works, the town's largest employer, builds navy ships and large commercial vessels; it's a secure defense site - witnessed by the white buoys that create a 400 foot security perimeter on the river. One of the museum's trolley tours includes the BIW's yard; christenings are open to the public. To tour Bath's Historic District, borrow or download a podcast of the self-guided walking tours or copy a map from sagadahocpreservation.org. They will certainly enhance more plebian excursions. The Chocolate Church Arts Center sponsors cultural events, from concerts to art exhibits to plays. The hourly trolley loops the marina, museum and Route One shopping center.

PHOTOS ON DVD: 16

  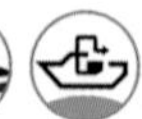    

Sebasco Harbor Resort

PO Box 75; 29 Kenyon Road; Sebasco Estates, ME 0456

Tel: (207) 389-1161; (800) 225-3819 **VHF: Monitor** Ch. 9 **Talk** Ch. 12
Fax: (207) 389-2004 **Alternate Tel:** n/a
Email: mlynch@sebasco.com **Web:** www.sebasco.com
Nearest Town: Bath *(15 mi.)* **Tourist Info:** (207) 443-9751

Navigational Information

Lat: 43°45.580' **Long:** 069°51.550' **Tide:** 9 ft. **Current:** 1 kt. **Chart:** 13290
Rep. Depths (*MLW*): Entry 6 ft. **Fuel Dock** 6 ft. **Max Slip/Moor** -/20 ft.
Access: Eastern shore Casco Bay marker by Cupola at Sebasco Harbor

Marina Facilities *(In Season/Off Season)*

Fuel: Gasoline
Slips: 0 Total, 0 Transient **Max LOA:** 60 ft. **Max Beam:** n/a
Rate *(per ft.)*: **Day** n/a **Week** n/a **Month** n/a
Power: 30 amp n/a, **50 amp** n/a, **100 amp** n/a, **200 amp** n/a
Cable TV: No **Dockside Phone:** No
Dock Type: Floating
Moorings: 25 Total, 23 Transient **Launch:** Yes (Free), Dinghy Dock
Rate: Day $40 **Week** $175 **Month** n/a
Heads: 2 Toilet(s), 2 Shower(s)
Internet: Yes *(Wi-Fi, DT, Jacks, Free)* **Laundry:** 3 Washer(s), 3 Dryer(s)
Pump-Out: Full Service, 1 Central **Fee:** $5 **Closed Heads:** Yes

Marina Operations

Owner/Manager: Michael J Lynch **Dockmaster:** Same
In-Season: Jun-LabDay, 8am-8pm **Off-Season:** n/a
After-Hours Arrival: Pick up mooring ball marked SHR (if available)
Reservations: Yes, Preferred **Credit Cards:** Visa/MC, Dscvr, Amex
Discounts: None
Pets: Welcome, Dog Walk Area **Handicap Access:** No

Marina Services and Boat Supplies

Services - Trash Pick-Up **Communication -** Pay Phone, FedEx, DHL, UPS, Express Mail **Supplies - OnSite:** Ice *(Block, Cube)* **Near:** Bait/Tackle, Live Bait

Boatyard Services

Near: Hydraulic Trailer, Engine mechanic *(gas, diesel)*, Electrical Repairs, Hull Repairs, Divers. **Nearest Yard:** Casco Bay B.W. (207) 389-1300

Restaurants and Accommodations

OnSite: Restaurant *(Pilot House D $14-23, B 7:30-9am, D 5:30-9pm Mon-Sat, Grand Buffet Cornelius Room 6-8:30pm Sun. Spa Menu avail.)*, *(Ledges Pub 1130am-9pm)*, Hotel *(Sebasco Harbor Main Lodge $199-390, EP add $48pp for MAP - 37 rooms in Inn & 10 in Lighthouse)*, *(Harbor Village Suites $209-500)*, *(Fair Winds Spa Suites $259-420)*, Condo/Cottage *(Sebasco Harbor Cottages $250-2300, EP add $48pp for MAP)* **Near:** Inn/B&B *(Rock Gardens Inn 389-1339, $120-185pp, MAP - Note - rates per person. Inn rooms or 2-4 bedroom cottages. S.H.R. amenities avail.)* **Under 1 mi:** Lite Fare *(North Creek Farm 389-1341, L $6.50-7.50, 11am-3:30pm, 11 seats inside or in the gardens, soups, sandwiches, panini, pies, gelato, sorbet)* **1-3 mi:** Seafood Shack *(Anna's Water's Edge 389-1803, L $4-16, D $4-30, 2 mi. by road, less by dinghy - at the town landing. Kids' $7. Shore Dinner $30 - inside or on deck)*

Recreation and Entertainment

OnSite: Pool, Spa, Playground *(Camp Merritt children's program)*, Tennis Courts *(Free, racquet rental)*, Golf Course *(S.H.R. 9-hole course - 9 holes $28, 18 holes $43, 3-hole Lake Course $10/all day - club rentals $15)*, Fitness Center *(Well-equipped, sauna)*, Boat Rentals *(Sea Spray Kayaks & Paddle Boards $15-25/hr, $25-50/day, classes, too; Two 14 ft. aluminum w/ 6 hp motors $25/hr.; two 17 ft. O'Days $20/hr.)*, Bowling *(Quarterdeck Rec Center - Vintage candlepins plus ping pong, pool tables, pinball, foosball, air hockey & a juke box)*, Fishing Charter *(Kayak Striper Fishing)*, Tours *(Sea Spray Kayak Tours 888-349-7772, Half-Day $50/10; Van tours of Historic Phippsburg; Train Excursion Bath to Rockland - van to Bath)*, Sightseeing *("The Ruth" Sebasco's 38 ft. 1935 Handy - offers many nature excursions and adventures - including a lobstering & fishing cruise)* **Near:** Cultural Attract *(Sebasco Art Workshops at Rock Gardens Inn 389-1339)* **3+ mi:** Beach *(Popham Beach, 5 mi.)*

Provisioning and General Services

OnSite: Bank/ATM, Retail Shops *(Gift Shop, Pro-Shop)*, Copies Etc. *(Fax, too)* **Under 1 mi:** Gourmet Shop *(North Creek Farm 389-1341- 9am-6:30pm)*, Wine/Beer *(North Creek Farm)*, Green Grocer *(North Creek)*, Post Office **1-3 mi:** Lobster Pound **3+ mi:** Supermarket *(Shaw's (443-9179), 15 mi.)*, Library *(Totman 389-2309, 4 mi.)*, Pharmacy *(CVS 443-9097, 15 mi.)*

Transportation

OnSite: Bikes **OnCall:** Rental Car *(Enterprise 725-1344)*, Taxi **Airport:** Portland Int'l. *(50 mi.)*

Medical Services

911 Service **OnSite:** Holistic Services *(Fairwinds Spa 371-5100 - full spa services 50 min Massage $90)* **OnCall:** Ambulance **Hospital:** Mid-Coast 729-0181 *(15 mi.)*

Setting -- At the tip of rocky Phippsburg peninsula, 550 acres of pristine woodlands, flourishing gardens, bent grass fairways, a salt water pool, and a plethora of amenities sprawl along a lovely 14,000-foot stretch of Sebasco Harbor. Managed by a small red dockhouse, the mooring field lies In the shadow of a fat, white wedding-cake lighthouse - protected by the ledges at the base of Harbor Island. Forty-plus buildings, from renovated turn-of-the-century to recent reproductions, house lodgings, recreation facilities, water-view restaurants, and a full-service spa - all promising an upscale step back into old Maine.

Marina Notes -- Founded in the 1930s - continually updated. Boaters welcome for day or overnight. Reservations recommended. Moorings only (2-7 ton granite blocks) with complimentary Launch service (8am-8pm, MemDay-LabDay) & dinghy dock. Temporary Dockside tie-up (not after hours). Boating guests same as resort guests. Fitness center, guest rates for golf, tennis and all amenities. Facilities available to anchored boaters $25/day. Book a room, mooring is free. Add'l mooring Casco Bay Boatworks (389-1300). Bathhouse: In fitness center locker room - ceramic-tile heads & showers.

Notable -- Sebasco Harbor Resort offers guests a broad range of options in a buffed-up, low-key, family atmosphere. A stunningly sited, large salt-water pool sits on a rocky peninsula that juts into the harbor. Two water-view restaurants: Pilot House & Ledges Pub plus the Cornelius Room serve three meals complemented by outdoor bakes and breakfasts. 130 rooms, many newly renovated, range from the original Inn to 6-bedroom cottages. A calendar of adult and children's activities augment Camp Merritt and the Quarterdeck Rec Center for kids and the new Fairwinds Spa for adults. Most services are 15 miles away.

PHOTOS ON DVD: 25

Navigational Information
Lat: 43°54.608' **Long:** 069°52.183' **Tide:** n/a **Current:** n/a **Chart:** 13290
Rep. Depths (*MLW*): Entry 5 ft. **Fuel Dock** n/a **Max Slip/Moor** 5 ft./-
Access: Straight up the New Meadows River to navigable head

Marina Facilities *(In Season/Off Season)*
Fuel: Gasoline
Slips: 60 Total, 10 Transient **Max LOA:** 40 ft. **Max Beam:** n/a
Rate *(per ft.)*: **Day** $1.00 **Week** n/a **Month** n/a
Power: 30 amp Incl., **50 amp** n/a, **100 amp** n/a, **200 amp** n/a
Cable TV: No **Dockside Phone:** No
Dock Type: Floating, Long Fingers, Alongside, Wood
Moorings: 0 Total, 0 Transient **Launch:** n/a
Rate: Day n/a **Week** n/a **Month** n/a
Heads: 2 Toilet(s), 2 Shower(s)
Internet: No **Laundry:** None
Pump-Out: OnSite, Self Service **Fee:** $5 **Closed Heads:** Yes

Marina Operations
Owner/Manager: John Fitzpatrick **Dockmaster:** Same
In-Season: Year Round, 8am-5pm **Off-Season:** n/a
After-Hours Arrival: Call in advance
Reservations: Yes, preferred **Credit Cards:** Visa/MC
Discounts: None
Pets: Welcome **Handicap Access:** No

New Meadows Marina

450 Bath Road; Brunswick, ME 04011

Tel: (207) 443-6277 **VHF: Monitor** Ch. 9 **Talk** n/a
Fax: (207) 443-5227 **Alternate Tel:** n/a
Email: marina@gwi.net **Web:** newmeadowsmarina.com
Nearest Town: Brunswick/Bath *(3 mi.)* **Tourist Info:** (207) 725-6658

Marina Services and Boat Supplies
Services - Docking Assistance **Communication -** FedEx, UPS, Express Mail **Supplies - OnSite:** Ice *(Cube)*, Ships' Store **Near:** Bait/Tackle *(Bath Lobster Supply 386-3225)* **1-3 mi:** Propane *(U-Haul 729-8779)*

Boatyard Services
OnSite: Crane, Hydraulic Trailer *(EZ Loader)*, Launching Ramp, Engine mechanic *(gas)*, Electrical Repairs, Electronic Sales, Electronics Repairs, Bottom Cleaning, Brightwork, Compound, Wash & Wax, Interior Cleaning, Propeller Repairs *(H & H Propeller)* **OnCall:** Divers **Dealer for:** Yamaha.

Restaurants and Accommodations
OnCall: Pizzeria *(Dominos 443-4343)* **Near:** Motel *(New Meadows 44-395-91 , $55-85)*, Condo/Cottage *(New Meadows River 442-9299)* **1-3 mi:** Restaurant *(Scarlet Begonia's 721-0403, L & D $5-15)*, *(Golden Chopsticks 729-3388, L & D $7-14)*, *(Applebee's 72-199-20)*, *(Beale St. BBQ 442-9514, L $9-18, D $9-18)*, *(Galley 443-9888, B $2-7, L $6-15, D $6-15)*, *(China Rose 725-8813)*, Snack Bar *(Witch Spring Hill Ice Cream 11-9 Hot dogs, too)*, Fast Food *(McDs, Wendy's, BK, Taco Bell, KFC)*, Pizzeria *(Papa John's 721-9990)*, Motel *(Days Inn 725-8883)*, Inn/B&B *(Inn at Bath 443-4294)* **3+ mi:** Restaurant *(Pedro O'Hara's 373-1300, L $8-$16, D $10-21, 5 mi., Irish-Mexican Cuisine)*, *(Great Impasta 729-5858, L $6-14, D $11-20, 5 mi.)*

Recreation and Entertainment
OnSite: Boat Rentals *(17 ft. Whaler, 20 ft. Pursuit or Mako $150-325/day)* **1-3 mi:** Golf Course *(Bath Country Club)*, Fitness Center *(Curves 725-1800, Planet 725-2944, U.S. Gym)*, Bowling *(Spare Time 729-0154)*, Movie Theater *(Regal Cinema 10 798-4505)* **3+ mi:** For Kids *(Bath Skate Park 443-8900, 3.5 mi.)*, Museum *(Maine Maritime Museum 442-0961; Museum of Art 725-3275, Free & Peary-MacMillan Arctic Museum, Free at Bowdoin, 4 mi.)*, Cultural Attract *(Maine State Theater 725-8769, 5 mi.)*, Sightseeing *(Brunswick Hist. Dist., 5 mi.)*

Provisioning and General Services
Near: Protestant Church, Beauty Salon *(Tranquility 443-2300)* **Under 1 mi:** Bookstore *(Thistle Rare & Antique 443-9031; Hardcover Cafe 725-7033 - 2 mi.; Borders 721-1178 - 3 mi.)* **1-3 mi:** Supermarket *(Shaw's Supermarket 721-9996)*, Delicatessen *(Sam's Italian)*, Health Food *(Bath Natural Market 442-8012)*, Green Grocer *(Swango's Farm Stand)*, Bank/ATM, Post Office, Catholic Church, Synagogue, Laundry *(Wash Tub 443-9885 - next to Bath Shaw's)*, Pharmacy *(Walgreens 443-1786)*, Hardware Store *(Lowe's 373-7016)*, Retail Shops *(Cooks Corner Mall 721-8966)*, Department Store *(Wal-Mart 725-0773 ; Target)*, Copies Etc. *(Staples 725-2741)* **3+ mi:** Library *(Patten 443-5141 , 3.5 mi.)*

Transportation
OnCall: Rental Car *(Enterprise 725-1344)*, Taxi *(Brunswick 729-3688)*, Airport Limo *(Mid-Coast 236-2424)* **Under 1 mi:** InterCity Bus *(Concord Trailways)* **1-3 mi:** Rail *(Eastern Maine RR - Brunswick, Bath, Wiscasset, Rockland $16-27)* **Airport:** Wiscaset/Portland JetPort *(11 mi./36 mi.)*

Medical Services
911 Service **Near:** Doctor *(Katz 442-0350)*, Holistic Services *(Sweet Water Day Spa 443-4723 - 1 hr massage $65)* **1-3 mi:** Dentist *(Jesse Albert 443-9721)*, Chiropractor *(Holland 443-2635)*, Veterinarian *(Bath Brunswick 729-4188)* **Hospital:** Mid Coast 729-0181 *(2.2 mi.)*

Setting -- At the navigable head of the New Meadows River, this small, rustic marina provides a destination for boaters exploring the oft over-looked, peaceful waterway. A few houses and towering pines line the bank, and a flag pole sits at the head of the single, very long dock that slices through the center of the river. Bath Road can be seen just behind the single-story, gray marina store, office and gas station and fuel dock.

Marina Notes -- Family owned, full-service marina. 50 years of boat repair experience. Extremely well-supplied chandlery - anything you might need in stock or they'll have it the next day. Winter storage (with Spring re-commissioning, painting, teak cleaning, oiling, waxing etc). 4-6 ft. of draft all the way to the docks. A combination of slips (closer to the marina) and side-tie dockage (further down river). Water to all, power to most with small lighthouse pedestals. Bathhouse: Cramped, full baths with tiled floors - head, sink & shower. No laundry.

Notable -- Three miles from Bath and five miles from Brunswick downtowns, New Meadows is the closest berth to Brunswick and the culture and summer festivals on the Bowdoin College Campus - five miles away. It's worth a rental car or taxi ride, to visit the Maine State Theater, International Music Festival and the historic Bowdoin College Museum of Art, which re-opened in 2007 after a $21 million addition to the 1894 copper-domed building that doubled the galleries housing its small but important collection. Closer at hand (3 miles), the Cook's Corner Mall complex delivers 30 stores including a Borders, Staples, Shaw's supermarket, Hoyt's 10-screen cinema, T.J. Max, Bookland, Sears, U.S. Gym, WalMart, more plus every known fast food franchise.

Great Island Boat Yard

419 Harpswell Islands Road; Harpswell, ME 04079

Tel: (207) 729-1639 **VHF: Monitor** Ch. 9 **Talk** Ch. 10
Fax: (207) 729-1139 **Alternate Tel:** n/a
Email: info@greatislandboatyard.com **Web:** greatislandboatyard.com
Nearest Town: Brunswick *(7 mi.)* **Tourist Info:** (207) 725-8797

Navigational Information
Lat: 43°49.792' **Long:** 069°54.915' **Tide:** 10 ft. **Current:** 0 kt. **Chart:** 13290
Rep. Depths (*MLW*): Entry 12 ft. **Fuel Dock** 4.5 ft. **Max Slip/Moor** 10 ft./12 ft
Access: Casco Bay to Merriconeag Sound to Quahog Bay

Marina Facilities *(In Season/Off Season)*
Fuel: *ValvTect* - Gasoline, Diesel
Slips: 67 Total, 3 Transient **Max LOA:** 75 ft. **Max Beam:** n/a
Rate *(per ft.)*: **Day** $3.00/Inq. **Week** $15 **Month** $35
Power: 30 amp Incl., **50 amp** Incl., **100 amp** n/a, **200 amp** n/a
Cable TV: No **Dockside Phone:** No
Dock Type: Floating, Long Fingers, Wood
Moorings: 43 Total, 5 Transient **Launch:** No, Dinghy Dock
Rate: Day $35 **Week** $175 **Month** $500
Heads: 2 Toilet(s), 2 Shower(s), Book Exchange
Internet: Yes *(Wi-Fi, Free)* **Laundry:** None
Pump-Out: Full Service, 1 Central **Fee:** Free **Closed Heads:** Yes

Marina Operations
Owner/Manager: Steve & Stephanie Rowe **Dockmaster:** Bob Sharp
In-Season: Year Round, 8am-4:30pm **Off-Season:** n/a
After-Hours Arrival: Call in advance
Reservations: Yes, Required **Credit Cards:** Visa/MC, Dscvr
Discounts: None
Pets: Welcome, Dog Walk Area **Handicap Access:** Yes, Heads, Docks

Marina Services and Boat Supplies
Services - Docking Assistance, Boaters' Lounge, Trash Pick-Up, Dock Carts **Communication -** Pay Phone, FedEx, DHL, UPS, Express Mail **Supplies - OnSite:** Ice *(Block, Cube)*, Ships' Store **3+ mi:** Bait/Tackle *(Naples 693-3638, 7 mi.)*, Propane *(U-Haul 729-8779, 7 mi.)*

Boatyard Services
OnSite: Travelift *(35T)*, Crane, Hydraulic Trailer, Launching Ramp, Engine mechanic *(gas, diesel)*, Electrical Repairs, Electronic Sales, Electronics Repairs, Hull Repairs, Rigger, Divers, Bottom Cleaning, Brightwork, Air Conditioning, Refrigeration, Compound, Wash & Wax, Interior Cleaning, Propeller Repairs, Woodworking, Metal Fabrication, Painting, Awlgrip, Total Refits, Yacht Building, Yacht Broker **OnCall:** Canvas Work, Yacht Interiors **Near:** Sail Loft. **1-3 mi:** Upholstery. **Dealer for:** Yanmar, Engine Parts. **Member:** ABBRA, ABYC - 15 Certified Tech(s), Other Certifications: 4 NMEA **Yard Rates:** $42-70/hr., Haul & Launch $9.50/ft. **Storage:** On-Land Out $6/sq.ft. In $8.50/sq.ft., Heated $12/sq.ft.

Restaurants and Accommodations
1-3 mi: Inn/B&B *(Quahog Bay Inn 725-9995, $110-295)* **3+ mi:** Restaurant *(Block & Tackle 725-5690, 5 mi.)*, Seafood Shack *(Moody's 800-729-5687, 3.3 mi.)*, *(Hawke's Lobster 721-0472, 5 mi.)*, *(Cook's Lobster House 833-2818, L $7-13, D $10-25, 8 mi.)*, Motel *(Days Inn 725-8883, 5.5 mi.)*

Recreation and Entertainment
OnSite: Special Events *(Jazz on the Docks - several times during season)* **Near:** Jogging Paths, Hike/Bike Trails **3+ mi:** Golf Course *(Brunswick Golf Club 725-8224, 7 mi.)*, Bowling *(Yankee Lanes 725-2963, 7 mi.)*, Movie Theater *(Evening Star 729-5486, 7 mi.)*, Museum *(Museum of Art 725-3275, Free & Peary-MacMillan Arctic Museum, Free at Bowdoin, 8 mi.)*, Cultural Attract *(Maine State Theater 725-8769, 8 mi.)*

Provisioning and General Services
1-3 mi: Lobster Pound **3+ mi:** Market *(Watsons' General Store - Cundys Harbor 725-7794, 5 mi.)*, Supermarket *(Shaw's 725-8751, 6 mi.)*, Farmers' Market *(Brunswick Tue & Fri 8am-3pm, 7 mi.)*, Library *(Orrs Island Library 833-7811, 5 mi.)*, Pharmacy *(Shaw's 721-9996, 7 mi.)*, Hardware Store *(Lowe's 373-7016, 7 mi.)*, Copies Etc. *(Staples 725-2741, 7 mi.)*

Transportation
OnSite: Courtesy Car/Van *(staff will provide rides at mutually convenient times)* **OnCall:** Rental Car *(Enterprise 882-8393)*, Taxi *(Brunswick 729-3688)*, Airport Limo *(Platinum Plus Limo 443-9166)* **3+ mi:** InterCity Bus *(Concord Trialways, 6 mi.)* **Airport:** Portland Int'l. *(40 mi.)*

Medical Services
911 Service **OnCall:** Ambulance *(NE Mobile Ambulance 725-1010 - 8 mi.)* **3+ mi:** Veterinarian *(Sunray Animal Clinic 725-6398, 4 mi.)* **Hospital:** Mid Coast 729-0181 *(5.5 mi.)*

Setting -- East of Bailey and Orr's Islands, GIBY lies in protected Orrs Cove off Quahog Bay on Sebascodegan Island. A spectacular contemporary office and chandlery overlooks the floating docks that sprawl along 800 feet of frontage - berthing an array of quality vessels. Maples shade the comfy chairs and picnic tables on the waterside deck. Seven acres of boatyard facilities are discreetly tucked behind a wall of greenery adding to the sense of quiet, rural isolation.

Marina Notes -- CCM. Established in the early 70's. In '05, Steve & Stephanie Rowe took the helm. Up to 70 ft. LOA on docks, 75 ft. on moorings (inspected annually) - manages 130 ft. with notice. Full service boatyard focused on major fiberglass and wood boat refits as well as maintenance. Boaters' Lounge. New 7000-sq ft indoor workspace, full rig shop, trailer, 35 ton travel lift hauls to 65 ft. LOA (up to 130 ft. when reserved in advance). New fuel tanks. 30,000 sq. ft. heated storage. 23 employees, 17 certified marine techs. Direct owner involvementm; open shop policy. Ships store stocks maintenance products & clothing; anything else overnighted. Bathhouse: Inside main building. Well-lit, airy new heads & showers, white tiled walls, gray tile floors.

Notable -- A jazz band plays several times over summer - "Jazz on the Dock." Relax, read, fish, and enjoy the unique Maine quiet. Quahog Bay promises protected, pristine coves for dinghy explorations. Several seafood "shacks" are 3-5 miles, and most services are in Cooks Corner Mall (5.5 mi.). Seven miles away, Brunswick's Bowdoin College features several excellent museums, including the recently expanded, superb art museum, Maine State Music Theater, and a summer music festival. Brunswick's affluent past also spawned an historic district of Federal mansions.

Navigational Information

Lat: 43°44.341' **Long:** 070°02.401' **Tide:** 9 ft. **Current:** 2 kt. **Chart:** 13290
Rep. Depths (*MLW*): Entry 40 ft. **Fuel Dock** 15 ft. **Max Slip/Moor** 15 ft./40 ft.
Access: Past Little Birch Island, after Horse Island and Thumb Cap

Marina Facilities *(In Season/Off Season)*

Fuel: *ValvTect* - Gasoline, Diesel
Slips: 48 Total, 10 Transient **Max LOA:** 250 ft. **Max Beam:** 30 ft.
Rate *(per ft.)*: **Day** $2.75/Inq. **Week** Inq. **Month** Inq.
Power: 30 amp Incl., **50 amp** Incl., **100 amp** Incl., **200 amp** n/a
Cable TV: No **Dockside Phone:** No
Dock Type: Floating, Long Fingers, Wood
Moorings: 80 Total, 15 Transient **Launch:** Yes (Incl.)
Rate: Day $20 **Week** n/a **Month** n/a
Heads: 2 Toilet(s)
Internet: No **Laundry:** None
Pump-Out: OnSite, Self Service **Fee:** Free **Closed Heads:** Yes

Marina Operations

Owner/Manager: Mimi Saxton **Dockmaster:** Chris Saxton
In-Season: May-Oct, 8am-8pm **Off-Season:** Nov-Apr, Closed
After-Hours Arrival: Pick up mooring or slip
Reservations: Yes, Required **Credit Cards:** Visa/MC
Discounts: None
Pets: Welcome, Dog Walk Area **Handicap Access:** Yes, Heads, Docks

Dolphin Marina & Restaurant

515 Basin Point Rd; Harpswell, ME 04079

Tel: (207) 833-5343 **VHF: Monitor** Ch. 9 **Talk** Ch. 14
Fax: n/a **Alternate Tel:** (207) 833-6000
Email: dolphin67@gwi.net **Web:** www.dolphinmarinaandrestaurant.com
Nearest Town: Brunswick *(15 mi.)* **Tourist Info:** (207) 725-8797

Marina Services and Boat Supplies

Services - Docking Assistance, Boaters' Lounge, Security *(7pm - 7am)*, Trash Pick-Up, Dock Carts **Communication -** Mail & Package Hold, Phone Messages, Fax in/out, UPS **Supplies - OnSite:** Ice *(Block, Cube)* **3+ mi:** Propane *(Morse's Market, 5 mi.)*

Boatyard Services

OnSite: Travelift *(35T)*, Launching Ramp, Engine mechanic *(gas, diesel)*, Electrical Repairs, Hull Repairs, Divers, Bottom Cleaning, Brightwork, Compound, Wash & Wax, Propeller Repairs, Woodworking, Metal Fabrication, Total Refits **OnCall:** Air Conditioning, Refrigeration **Member:** ABBRA **Yard Rates:** $52/hr., Haul & Launch $10/ft., Power Wash $1/ft., Bottom Paint $5/ft. **Storage:** On-Land $20/ft.

Restaurants and Accommodations

OnSite: Restaurant *(Dolphin Marina 833-6000, L & D $6-29, 11:30am-9pm - May-Oct. Reportedly the best fish chowder in Midcoast Maine)* **1-3 mi:** Restaurant *(Common Table Themed Dinners 833-5564, D $20-25, Fri & Sat Only, 6-8pm, 2-3-course Prix Fixe, BYOB, Res. Req.)*, Seafood Shack *(Morse's at Estes 833-6340, L & D $3-25, Kids' $4-7 8am-11pm, Outside Grill - steak & BBQ)*, *(Potts Harbor Lobster 833-5190)*, *(Ash Cove Lobster 833-5156)*, Inn/B&B *(Common Table Inn & Event Center 833-5564, $110-125)* **3+ mi:** Inn/B&B *(Harpswell Inn 833-5509, $80-200, 6 mi.)*

Recreation and Entertainment

OnSite: Beach, Picnic Area, Grills, Playground **Near:** Jogging Paths **1-3 mi:** Tennis Courts, Sightseeing *(Bailey Island Cribstone Bridge)*, Galleries *(Local Harpswell Craft Guild members mark their studios - mostly along Route 123 - with a Blue Heron sign.)*

Provisioning and General Services

1-3 mi: Convenience Store *(Bailey Island General Store 833-2400)*, Lobster Pound *(Potts Harbor 833-5190)*, Post Office, Catholic Church, Protestant Church, Synagogue **3+ mi:** Supermarket *(Shaw's or Hannaford 729-1604, 15 mi.)*, Gourmet Shop *(Store On Orrs 833-2301, 4 mi.)*, Library *(Orr's Island 833-7811, 4 mi.)*, Pharmacy *(CVS Brunswick 729-0414, 12 mi.)*

Transportation

OnCall: Rental Car *(Enterprise 725-1344 - from Brunswick)*, Taxi *(Brunswick Taxi 729-3688 - 15 mi. from Brunswick)* **Airport:** Portland Int'l. *(45 mi.)*

Medical Services

911 Service **OnCall:** Ambulance *(6 mi.)* **3+ mi:** Doctor *(Weaver 833-7364, 11 mi.)*, Veterinarian *(D'Onofrio 833-6091, 5 mi.)* **Hospital:** Midcoast 373-3635 *(15 mi.)*

Setting -- At the tip of Harpswell Neck at Basin Point, Dolphin has a 360-degree panoramic view of Potts Harbor including Half Way Rock Lighthouse and neighboring Orr's and Bailey Islands. The highly visible "Dolphin" sign welcomes boaters to the all-new network of floating slips that connect to the parking lot over a new stationary wharf. Perched on a rise, the very popular restaurant features wide windows and a dock with views of the harbor and Basin Point. The small islands that dot the Bay, and the ledges to the south, turn this mile-wide bay into a safe harbor.

Marina Notes -- CCM. Founded 1966. Second generation at the helm. Major marina re-fit underway (not reflected in photos, rates in flux). Completed for 2011: new fuel station, dock system with slips, 30, 50 & 100A power. Designed to accommodate vessels to 250 ft. Dock attended mid-June thru LabDay. Comp. day dockage or mooring for diners. Launch service 8am to 6:30/7pm daily. Bathhouse: New boaters lounge with heads, showers & laundry planned for 2012.

Notable -- Dolphin's food has been revered by the foodie press for years. It's famous for its fish chowder, lobster stew, and blueberry muffins (from the adjacent blueberry field) - and well worth a detour. The atmosphere is down-home comfort and well-used varnished wood -- a favorite of local fishermen and Bowdoin professors. The enlarged dining space and new dining deck are welcome additions. It's open for lunch & dinner daily during the season and also caters Lobster Bakes at the end of the Point (Fleet Captains take note). Basin Cove is a dinghy destination for birdwatching. Common Table Inn and eatery is a 2.3 mile hike and Harpswell Guild artists are scattered along Rte 123 - watch for the Blue Heron Sign. Most provisioning and general services are 15 miles.

Chebeague Island Boat Yard

24 Niblic Circle; Chebeague Island, ME 04017

Tel: (207) 846-4146 **VHF: Monitor** n/a **Talk** n/a
Fax: (207) 846-7832 **Alternate Tel:** n/a
Email: ciby@chebeague.net **Web:** www.chebegueislandboatyard.com
Nearest Town: Yarmouth *(5 mi.)* **Tourist Info:** (207) 772-5800

Navigational Information

Lat: 43°43.774' **Long:** 070°06.621' **Tide:** 9 ft. **Current:** n/a **Chart:** 13290
Rep. Depths (*MLW*): Entry 20 ft. **Fuel Dock** 4 ft. **Max Slip/Moor** -/20 ft.
Access: Luckse Snd to E shore of Great Chebeague

Marina Facilities *(In Season/Off Season)*

Fuel: Gasoline, Diesel
Slips: 0 Total, 0 Transient **Max LOA:** n/a **Max Beam:** n/a
Rate *(per ft.)*: **Day** n/a **Week** n/a **Month** n/a
Power: 30 amp n/a, **50 amp** n/a, **100 amp** n/a, **200 amp** n/a
Cable TV: No **Dockside Phone:** No
Dock Type: Fixed, Floating, Alongside, Concrete
Moorings: 100 Total, 20 Transient **Launch:** No, Dinghy Dock
Rate: Day $25 **Week** n/a **Month** n/a
Heads: 2 Toilet(s), 2 Shower(s) *(dressing rooms)*
Internet: Yes *(Wi-Fi - The Niblic, Free)* **Laundry:** None
Pump-Out: OnCall **Fee:** $10 **Closed Heads:** Yes

Marina Operations

Owner/Manager: Paul Balesca **Dockmaster:** Same
In-Season: Jun-Sep, 7:30am-4:30pm** **Off-Season:** Oct-May, 11:30-4:30
After-Hours Arrival: Casual
Reservations: Yes, Preferred **Credit Cards:** Visa/MC
Discounts: None
Pets: Welcome **Handicap Access:** Yes, Heads, Docks

Marina Services and Boat Supplies

Services - Docking Assistance, Dock Carts **Communication -** UPS, Express Mail **Supplies - OnSite:** Ships' Store *(The Niblic)*

Boatyard Services

OnSite: Railway, Forklift, Crane, Hydraulic Trailer, Launching Ramp, Engine mechanic *(gas, diesel)*, Electronics Repairs, Hull Repairs, Rigger, Brightwork, Compound, Wash & Wax, Woodworking, Painting **OnCall:** Divers, Metal Fabrication **Near:** Sail Loft, Canvas Work. **Member:** ABYC - 1 Master Certified Tech(s), Other Certifications: MMTA

Restaurants and Accommodations

OnSite: Lite Fare *(The Niblic B & L, Soups, sandwiches, baked goods, coffee)* **Under 1 mi:** Seafood Shack *(Calder's Clam Shack 846-5046, L $7-18)* **1-3 mi:** Restaurant *(Chebeague Inn 846-5155, 75 seat, fine-dining - western sunset views)*, Inn/B&B *(Chebeague Inn 846-5155, $145-295, 21 guests room in a restored 1920's Inn. Inn will transport guests and diners from the BY)*

Recreation and Entertainment

Near: Beach *(Indian Point, Chandler Cove, Hamilton Beach, Bennett Cove, Division Point, Rose Point)*, Picnic Area, Jogging Paths, Fishing Charter, Party Boat, Volleyball, Park **1-3 mi:** Pool *(Chebeague Island Recreation Center 846-5068 - Olympic size)*, Playground *(Chebeague Is. School)*, Tennis Courts *(Chebeague Is. Tennis Club 846-7958)*, Golf Course *(Great Chebeague Golf Club 846-9478)*, Fitness Center *(Chebeague Is. Rec.)*, Museum *(Museum of Chebeague History 846-4351, 846-5237 - a restored 1871 schoolhouse open daily)*, Galleries *(Boathouse Gallery at The Niblic; plus further away - Juniper Knee Gallery - original artwork from the 1700's artist Bill Holmbom, Chebeague Library)*

Provisioning and General Services

OnSite: Wine/Beer *(The Niblic 846-1015)*, Bakery *(The Niblic)*, Post Office, Clothing Store *(The Niblic)* **Near:** Market *(Doughty's Island 846-9997)* **1-3 mi:** Delicatessen *(Calder's Clam Shack)*, Fishmonger *(Calder's Clam Shack)*, Catholic Church *(United Methodist - Catholic Mass Sat. 6:15pm)*, Protestant Church *(United Methodist - Sun. 10am)*, Library, Retail Shops *(Island Riches 846-4986)*

Transportation

OnCall: Taxi *(Chebeague Is. 846-8687 - tours too)* **Near:** Bikes *("Bike Man" - Free, call 846-7829)*, Ferry Service *(CTC 846-3700, Casco Bay Lines 774-7871)* **Airport:** Portland Int'l Jetport *(15 mi.)*

Medical Services

911 Service **OnCall:** Ambulance **Under 1 mi:** Doctor *(Chebeague Clinic 846-4988 - Physicians Ass't)* **Hospital:** Maine Medical Center - Ferry to Cousins Island then 10 mi. by road *(13 mi.)*

Setting -- Nestled between the two ferry landings on the largest of Casco Bay's 300-plus islands, Chebeague Island Boat Yard's main float leads to a small dockhouse and the haul-out railway to the modest gray work shed. Further upland, the recent two-story, tan-and-white main building hosts The Niblic shop and, on the second floor, The Boat House event space and gallery annotated with a white railed deck that overlooks the mooring field and nearby Crow Island.

Marina Notes -- **Open Mon-Sat Summer, Offseason Tues-Fri 7:30am-4:30pm, Sat 7:30am-11:30am. Log onto their Webcam to see the weather. Located between the two ferry landings. Newly expanded docking space and water accessibility. The Boat House has a new special event space (weddings, receptions, club cruises) with a deck and gorgeous water & island views. Open year-round. Fuel (gas & diesel), boat storage (Winter and Summer), launching, moorings, mechanical services, boat repair. Winter and Spring maintenance packages available. Bathhouse: New, fresh showers & heads.

Notable -- The Niblic, a nicely merchandised shop, wears many hats: it offers free Wi-Fi, soups and sandwiches, sells drinks, supplies, gifts and clothing, and its gallery showcases local artists and artisans. Borrow a bike from the "Bike Man" to explore the 3½ mile long by 1½ mile wide island, dotted with Greek Revival houses built by the stone sloopers who carried ballast for 19thC. ships. Picnic at one of the many beaches, hit the links at the Chebeague Island Golf Club or enjoy a sunset cocktail on the Chebeague Inn's porch. Chebeague Island Recreation Center offers tennis, a pool and fitness center. Cruise to Eagle Island - once home to North Pole Explorer Admiral E. Peary. Pick up a mooring; and either dinghy in to the float or ask a ranger for a ride - 729-3343 $4.50/1.

Navigational Information

Lat: 43°45.092' **Long:** 070°06.498' **Tide:** 9 ft. **Current:** n/a **Chart:** 13290
Rep. Depths (*MLW*): Entry 5 ft. **Fuel Dock** n/a **Max Slip/Moor** -/8 ft.
Access: Broad Sound ot NW side of Great Chebeague Island

Marina Facilities *(In Season/Off Season)*

Fuel: No
Slips: 0 Total, 0 Transient **Max LOA:** 125 ft. **Max Beam:** n/a
Rate *(per ft.)*: **Day** $0 **Week** n/a **Month** n/a
Power: 30 amp n/a, **50 amp** n/a, **100 amp** n/a, **200 amp** n/a
Cable TV: No **Dockside Phone:** No
Dock Type: n/a
Moorings: 8 Total, 8 Transient **Launch:** Yes (Incl.), Dinghy Dock
Rate: Day $25* **Week** n/a **Month** n/a
Heads: 4 Toilet(s)
Internet: Yes *(Wi-Fi, Free)* **Laundry:** None
Pump-Out: No **Fee:** n/a **Closed Heads:** Yes

Marina Operations

Owner/Manager: Casey Prentice **Dockmaster:** Same
In-Season: May-Oct, 8am-9:30pm **Off-Season:** n/a
After-Hours Arrival: Call in advance
Reservations: Yes* **Credit Cards:** Visa/MC, Dscvr, Amex
Discounts: None
Pets: No **Handicap Access:** No

Chebeague Island Inn

61 South Road; Chebeague Island, ME 04017

Tel: (207) 846-5155 **VHF: Monitor** Ch. 9 **Talk** Ch. 9
Fax: n/a **Alternate Tel:** n/a
Email: info@chebeagueislandinn.com **Web:** www.chebeagueislandinn.com
Nearest Town: Yarmouth *(5 mi.)* **Tourist Info:** (207) 772-5800

Marina Services and Boat Supplies

Supplies - OnSite: Ice *(Cube)* **Near:** Ice *(Block)*

Boatyard Services

Nearest Yard: Chebeague Island Boat Yard (207) 846-4146

Restaurants and Accommodations

OnSite: Restaurant *(Chebeague Island Inn 846-5155, L $11-18, D $16-38, L: 11:30am-2:30pm, D: 5:30-9:30pm, Sun Brunch $10-18, 10:30am-2:30pm)*, Lite Fare *(Sunset Landing Hors' Doeuvres $5-18 2:30-9pm, Tue-Sun - try the lobster corn dog)*, Inn/B&B *(Chebeague Island Inn 846-5155, $190-350, 21 rooms, garden or ocean view)* **Near:** Inn/B&B *(Sunset House 939-7923, Weekly)* **Under 1 mi:** Snack Bar *(Calder's Clam Shack 846-5046, L $7-18, take-out)*, Lite Fare *(Doughty's Island Market 846-9997)* **1-3 mi:** Snack Bar *(The Nublic at CIBY)*

Recreation and Entertainment

OnSite: Picnic Area *(also nearby)*, Tennis Courts *(Chebeague Inn 846-5155)* **Near:** Beach *(Indian Point, Chandler Cover, Hamilton Beach, Bennett Cove, Division Point, Rose Point)*, Grills, Golf Course *(Great Chebeague Golf Course 846-9478 - 9 water-view holes founded in 1920)*, Jogging Paths, Hike/Bike Trails *(Paths cut through forest and edge the sea)*, Volleyball, Museum *(Chebeague Island Historical Society 846-5237 - a restored 1871 schoolhouse open daily)*, Tours *(Eagle Island Schooner voyage - Home of North Pole Explorer Admiral E. Peary. Marie L Tours - Capt. Claire Ross 846-1254 $30/25 at Stone Pier)*, Galleries *(Juniper Knee, The Nublic at)* **Under 1 mi:** Heated Pool *(Chebeague Island Recreation Center - Olympic size)*, Playground *(Chebeague Is. School)*, Fitness Center *(Chebeague Is. Rec Center)*

Provisioning and General Services

Near: Delicatessen *(Calder's Clam Shack)*, Fishmonger *(Calder's Clam Shack)*, Newsstand *(Cobbler Shop)*, Clothing Store *(Cobbler Shop)* **Under 1 mi:** Market *(Doughty's Island 846-9997)*, Green Grocer *(Second Wind Farm)*, Catholic Church *(Chebeague United Methodist - Catholic Mass Sat. 6:15pm)*, Protestant Church *(Chebeague United Methodist)*, Library *(Chebeague 846-4351 Wi-Fi)*

Transportation

OnSite: Bikes *(complimentary for Inn guests)* **Near:** Water Taxi *(Portland Express Water Taxi 415-8493 - from Stone Wharf - 25 min.)* **1-3 mi:** Ferry Service *(From Chandler Cove Wharf - Casco Bay Lines 774-7871 - One hr. 20 min. to Portland at Commercial & Franklin Sts.; Chebeauge Transportation 846-3700 - 15 min. to Cousins Island near Yarmouth)* **Airport:** Portland International Jetport *(10 mi.)*

Medical Services

911 Service **OnCall:** Ambulance **Under 1 mi:** Dentist *(Chebeague Clinic 846-4988 - Physicians Ass't)* **Hospital:** Maine Medical Center - Ferry to Cousins Island then 10 mi. by road *(13 mi.)*

Setting -- On one of Maine's most picturesque islands, the romantic Chebeague Inn's small mooring field lies below the elegantly restored 1880 Greek revival hotel. Perched on a grassy knoll, the three-story, butter-yellow Inn is wrapped by closed and open porches furnished with period wicker that enjoy spectacular sunsets. It's cradled by coastal pines, edged on two sides by a beautiful golf course and sports views of Stone Wharf and the anchorage.

Marina Notes -- *Private moorings for restaurant or inn guests only. Free while dining. $25 fee for diners or inn guests spending the night on the mooring. Complimentary launch service for all. Built in 1925, Major restoration finished 2004. New owner/managers May 2010. Mother & son team Gerri & Casey Prentice at the helm. Transient dock tie-ups at town-owned/operated Stone Wharf $5/hr Mon-Thurs, $7/hr Fri-Sun. Or anchor off Stone Wharf. Skiffs, tenders or punts tie-up for $10/half day, $20/full day. Contact Harbor Master: 846-3184. Bathhouse: Top-drawer ceramic tile heads in the Inn.

Notable -- The elegantly restored inn features a wood-paneled Great Room with a field stone fireplace and comfy chairs - a striking counterpoint to the bright dining room with white linens and modern leather strap chairs. Boaters are making a detour for Chef Justin Rowe's contemporary, locally-sourced American cuisine served on the formal Hillcrest Porch or in the more casual dining room - or cocktails and hors d'oeuvres in the Sunset Landing room. Bikes, fishing poles and equipment for tennis, lawn bowling, badminton and croquet are available to guests. Nicely appointed, airy rooms, punctuated with shots of color, highlight local artists and artisans. Bike this four-mile long island - head to Chandler Cove Wharf, stop at Calder's Clam Shack and head back to the Inn for dinner.

Royal River Boat Yard

307 Bayview Street; Yarmouth, ME 04096

Tel: (207) 846-9577 **VHF: Monitor** n/a **Talk** n/a
Fax: (207) 846-6571 **Alternate Tel:** n/a
Email: forinfo@royalriverboat.com **Web:** n/a
Nearest Town: Yarmouth *(1.6 mi.)* **Tourist Info:** (207) 846-3984

Navigational Information

Lat: 43°47.722' **Long:** 070°10.131' **Tide:** 9 ft. **Current:** 1 kt. **Chart:** 13290
Rep. Depths (*MLW*): Entry 10 ft. **Fuel Dock** 10 ft. **Max Slip/Moor** 10 ft./-
Access: Casco Bay to Royal River, follow markers

Marina Facilities *(In Season/Off Season)*

Fuel: Gasoline, Diesel
Slips: 60 Total, 4 Transient **Max LOA:** 50 ft. **Max Beam:** n/a
Rate *(per ft.)*: **Day** $2.75 **Week** n/a **Month** n/a
Power: 30 amp Incl., **50 amp** Incl., **100 amp** n/a, **200 amp** n/a
Cable TV: No **Dockside Phone:** No
Dock Type: Floating, Alongside, Wood
Moorings: 0 Total, 0 Transient **Launch:** n/a
Rate: Day n/a **Week** n/a **Month** n/a
Heads: 2 Toilet(s), 1 Shower(s)
Internet: Yes *(Wi-Fi, Free)* **Laundry:** 1 Washer(s), 1 Dryer(s)
Pump-Out: OnSite, Self Service **Fee:** Free **Closed Heads:** Yes

Marina Operations

Owner/Manager: Alan J. Dugas **Dockmaster:** n/a
In-Season: May-Oct, 7am-6pm **Off-Season:** Nov-Apr, 7am-5pm
After-Hours Arrival: Call ahead, tie up where instructed
Reservations: Yes **Credit Cards:** Visa/MC, Dscvr, Amex
Discounts: None
Pets: Welcome **Handicap Access:** No

Marina Services and Boat Supplies

Services - Docking Assistance, Trash Pick-Up **Communication -** FedEx, UPS, Express Mail **Supplies - OnSite:** Ice *(Block, Cube)*, Ships' Store **Under 1 mi:** Marine Discount Store *(Landing Boat Supply 846-3777)* **1-3 mi:** Propane *(Downeast Energy 846-5507)*

Boatyard Services

OnSite: Travelift *(2 - 50T)*, Forklift, Launching Ramp, Engine mechanic *(gas, diesel)*, Electrical Repairs, Electronic Sales, Electronics Repairs, Hull Repairs, Rigger, Sail Loft, Canvas Work, Bottom Cleaning, Brightwork, Air Conditioning, Refrigeration, Compound, Wash & Wax, Interior Cleaning, Propeller Repairs, Woodworking, Inflatable Repairs, Painting **OnCall:** Divers, Metal Fabrication **Dealer for:** Mercury. **Member:** ABYC

Restaurants and Accommodations

OnCall: Pizzeria *(Domino's 846-6911)* **Near:** Restaurant *(Deer Run Tavern 846-9555)*, *(Royal River Grillhouse 846-1226, L $9-13, D $18-28, Sun Brunch $10-19 - by dinghy)*, Pizzeria *(De Nuccis 846-8646)* **Under 1 mi:** Lite Fare *(Binga's Wingas 846-8736)* **1-3 mi:** Restaurant *(Seagrass Bistro 846-3885, D $24-25)*, *(Muddy Rudder 846-3082, L $8-14, D $15-22)*, Pizzeria *(Pat's Pizza 846-3701)*, Motel *(Brookside Motel 846-5512, $65-135)*, Hotel *(Freeport Inn 865-3106, $60-120)*

Recreation and Entertainment

Near: Picnic Area *(Lower Falls Landing - by dinghy)* **Under 1 mi:** Video Rental *(Blockbuster 846-0465)* **1-3 mi:** Pool *(Casco Bay "Y")*, Beach, Playground, Fitness Center *("Y")*, Other *(Yarmouth Clam Festival, First Week of July)*, Park *(Royal River)*, Museum *(Yarmouth Historical Society 846-6259)*, Sightseeing *(DeLorme corporate headquarters 846-7000 Eartha, world's largest globe)*, Special Events *(3-day Yarmouth Clam Festival, starts third Friday in July 846-3984)* **3+ mi:** Golf Course *(Freeport C.C. 865-0711, 4 mi.)*

Provisioning and General Services

Under 1 mi: Convenience Store, Market *(Rosemont 846-1234 - bakery, wine, too)*, Supermarket *(Hannaford 846-5941)*, Wine/Beer *(Hannaford)*, Liquor Store *(Hannaford)*, Bakery, Bank/ATM, Post Office, Beauty Salon *(Studio 88 846-1646)*, Pharmacy *(Hannaford)*, Hardware Store *(Ace Coastal 846-6767)* **1-3 mi:** Green Grocer, Fishmonger, Lobster Pound, Catholic Church *(Sacred Heart Parish)*, Protestant Church, Library *(Yarmouth 846-4763)*, Dry Cleaners, Laundry, Newsstand, Florist, Copies Etc.

Transportation

OnCall: Rental Car *(Enterprise 772-0030; Hometown 846-2470 - 2 mi.)*, Taxi *(Yarmouth 846-9336; Freeport 865-9494)* **Airport:** Portland Int'l. *(10 mi.)*

Medical Services

911 Service **Near:** Dentist *(Bayview 846-0979)* **Under 1 mi:** Veterinarian *(Yarmouth Vet Center 846-6515)* **1-3 mi:** Doctor *(Clemetson 415-2700)*, Chiropractor *(Yarmouth 846-1481)* **Hospital:** Maine Medical Center 781-1700 *(8 mi.)*

Setting -- About 2 miles from the mouth of the Royal River, past the marshes on the river's eastern bank, this tidy boat yard lies to starboard. Two large, gray boat sheds perch above the small network of floating docks. The immediate surroundings are relatively unspoiled and home to great blue heron, sandpipers and the occasional cormorant. Just a little further up the river, civilization looms on the opposite bank beginning with the Lower Falls Landing.

Marina Notes -- Family operation now includes 3rd generation. Town dredges channel near docks. Most dockage "alongside." Dependable hurricane hole. 60 slips, 4 reserved for transients. Two large work sheds. 2 50-ton travelifts can haul significant vessels. Service is available 7 days. Extensive dry land storage and commodious inside work and storage areas. Note: At high tide, this tidal channel can be tricky to navigate (the shallows are hidden), but stick to the channel markers and you'll be fine. Bathhouse: two recent, full baths with showers and tiled floors.

Notable -- Across and up the river -- just a short dinghy distance -- is the Royal River Grillhouse Restaurant in the Lower Falls Landing complex (adjacent to Yankee Marina) - the rebuilt Cannery. The annual 3-day Yarmouth Clam Festival, third Friday in July, features river races, craft fairs, a parade, local music, art shows, carnival rides, happy crowds - and clams. The corporate headquarters for the map-makers DeLorme (1.5 mi.) is home to "Eartha." At 42 feet in diameter, it's the world's largest rotating globe.. Yarmouth village (a 10-minute walk) is home to plenty of restaurants, craft shops and provisions. A 3-mile trip up Route 1 leads to the shopping Mecca of Freeport.

  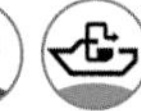

Navigational Information

Lat: 43°47.711' **Long:** 070°10.414' **Tide:** 9 ft. **Current:** 1 kt. **Chart:** 13290
Rep. Depths (*MLW*): Entry 8 ft. **Fuel Dock** n/a **Max Slip/Moor** 9 ft./9 ft.
Access: Casco Bay to the Royal River past R18

Marina Facilities *(In Season/Off Season)*

Fuel: No
Slips: 112 Total, 3 Transient **Max LOA:** 60 ft. **Max Beam:** n/a
Rate *(per ft.)*: **Day** $1.50 **Week** n/a **Month** n/a
Power: 30 amp Incl., **50 amp** Incl., **100 amp** n/a, **200 amp** n/a
Cable TV: No **Dockside Phone:** No
Dock Type: Floating, Wood, Aluminum, Composition
Moorings: 0 Total, 0 Transient **Launch:** n/a
Rate: Day n/a **Week** n/a **Month** n/a
Heads: 2 Toilet(s), 1 Shower(s)
Internet: No **Laundry:** 1 Washer(s), 1 Dryer(s)
Pump-Out: OnSite, Self Service, 1 Central **Fee:** $5 **Closed Heads:** Yes

Marina Operations

Owner/Manager: Deborah A. Delp **Dockmaster:** Ben Stevens
In-Season: May-Oct, 7am-5pm **Off-Season:** Nov-Apr, 7am-4pm
After-Hours Arrival: Call in advance
Reservations: Yes, Required **Credit Cards:** Visa/MC, Dscvr
Discounts: None
Pets: Welcome, Dog Walk Area **Handicap Access:** Yes, Heads, Docks

Yankee Marina & Boatyard

PO Box 548; 142 Lafayette Street; Yarmouth, ME 04096

Tel: (207) 846-4326 **VHF: Monitor** Ch. 9 **Talk** Ch. 9
Fax: (207) 846-3629 **Alternate Tel:** n/a
Email: yankee@yankeemarina.com **Web:** www.yankeemarina.com
Nearest Town: Yarmouth *(0.6 mi.)* **Tourist Info:** (207) 846-3984

Marina Services and Boat Supplies

Services - Docking Assistance, Security, Trash Pick-Up **Communication -** Mail & Package Hold, Fax in/out, FedEx, DHL, UPS, Express Mail **Supplies - OnSite:** Ice *(Block, Cube)* **Near:** Ships' Store *(Landing Boat Supply 846-3777)* **1-3 mi:** Propane *(Freeport Hardware 865-9557)* **3+ mi:** Bait/Tackle *(Maine Fishing Bait & Tackle 829-4606, 4 mi.)*

Boatyard Services

OnSite: Travelift *(15T & 60T)*, Railway *(30T Ramp to 60 ft. LOA)*, Forklift, Launching Ramp, Engine mechanic *(gas, diesel)*, Electrical Repairs, Electronic Sales, Electronics Repairs, Hull Repairs, Rigger, Sail Loft *(Maine Sailing Partners 846-6400)*, Bottom Cleaning, Brightwork, Air Conditioning, Refrigeration, Compound, Wash & Wax, Interior Cleaning, Woodworking, Painting, Awlgrip, Total Refits **OnCall:** Hydraulic Trailer, Divers **Near:** Propeller Repairs, Yacht Broker *(East Coast Yacht Sales)*. **Dealer for:** Westerbeke, Espar, Sea Frost, Awlgrip, Interlux, Marine Air, Grunnert, Yanmar. **Member:** ABBRA, ABYC - 5 Certified Tech(s) **Yard Rates:** Power Wash $2.25/ft. **Storage:** On-Land $4.35-5.35 incl Haul/Launch

Restaurants and Accommodations

OnSite: Restaurant *(Royal River Grillhouse 846-1226, L $8-13, D $18-28, Sun Brunch $10-19, Happy Hr. 2:30-5pm)* **Under 1 mi:** Restaurant *(Grill 233 846-3633, L $10-14, D $10-24)*, *(Down-East Village Restaurant 846-5161, B $3-8, L $6-12, D $10-20)*, *(Muddy Rudder 846-3082, L $8-14, D $9-21)*, *(Seagrass Bistro D $24-25)*, *(China Taste 846-6668)*, Lite Fare *(Clayton's Gourmet 846-1117, B $4-5.50, L $4-9, M-F 7am-7pm, Sat 7-5)*, *(Bruce's Burrito's 846-6330, L $3-8, veg, too)*, Pizzeria *(Romeo's 846-1473)*, *(Pat's 846-3701)*, Motel *(Down East Village 846-5161, $77-130)*

Recreation and Entertainment

Under 1 mi: Picnic Area, Fitness Center *(Fitness Success 332-6248; Sanctuary Health & Yoga 846-1162)*, Hike/Bike Trails *(Royal River Park)*, Video Rental *(Blockbuster 846-0465)*, Park *(Royal River - waterfall cascades just past the bridge)*, Museum *(Yarmouth Historical Soc. 846-6259)*, Cultural Attract *(Wednesday night concerts, R.R. Park)*, Special Events *(3-day Yarmouth Clam Festival, starts 3rd Friday July 846-3984)* **1-3 mi:** Sightseeing *(DeLorme 846-7000 Eartha, world's largest globe)* **3+ mi:** Golf Course *(Freeport C.C. 865-0711, 4 mi.)*

Provisioning and General Services

Near: Beauty Salon *(Celadon 846-3481)* **Under 1 mi:** Market *(Rosemont 846-1234)*, Supermarket *(Hannaford 846-5941)*, Delicatessen *(Clayton's Gourmet 846-1117)*, Wine/Beer *(Rosemont)*, Liquor Store, Bakery *(Rosemont)*, Bank/ATM, Post Office, Catholic Church, Protestant Church, Library *(846-4763)*, Dry Cleaners *(Anthony's 846-9956)*, Laundry, Bookstore *(Royal River 846-8006)*, Pharmacy *(Rite Aid 846-1222)*, Hardware Store *(Goff's 846-5932)*, Florist, Retail Shops, Copies Etc. *(Yarmouth 846-9567)*

Transportation

OnCall: Taxi *(Yarmouth 846-9336)* **1-3 mi:** Rental Car *(Casco Bay Ford 846-5577)* **Airport:** Portland Int'l. *(15 mi.)*

Medical Services

911 Service **Near:** Doctor *(Johnson 846-6200)* **Under 1 mi:** Dentist *(Bayview 846-0979)*, Chiropractor *(Yarmouth 846-1481)*, Holistic Services *(Lucinda's Day Spa 829-3100)*, Optician *(Insight 847-3800)*, Veterinarian *(Yarmouth 846-6515)* **Hospital:** Maine Medical 781-1700 *(6 mi.)*

Setting -- Yankee Marina's six acres roll along the quiet western bank of the Royal River close to its navigable head. Onshore it's strictly boatyard - with a village of gray work sheds and few boater amenities. Adjacent is the attractive, sprawling, natural-sided Royal River Grillhouse and beyond, just upriver, the handsome Lower Falls Landing complex, a restored three-story, gray-shingled former sardine cannery, which houses a few useful marine businesses.

Marina Notes -- CCM. Founded in 1967, family owned & operated for over 3 decades. A serious boatyard first and a marina second. Fully staffed year-round. ABYC, ABBRA, CMET, FCC and manufacturer-certified technicians. Commissioning yard for Grand Banks, J-boats, & Grand Soleil. Northern New England's only service center for Grand Banks & Eastbay. Outside winter storage for up to 200 boats. Seasonal dockage for 100 boats. Specializes in repairs, refits, customizations - heated workspaces with effective dust collection & ventilation systems. Maine Sailing Partners sail loft onsite. Landing Boat Supplies, a very well-supplied chandlery, in Lower Falls. Fuel downriver at Royal River Boat Yard. Bathhouse: One full bath & one half with varnished wood, tiled floors.

Notable -- Popular, waterfront Royal River Grillhouse Restaurant features traditional Maine fare in lovely dining rooms or outside on multiple decks - all with panoramic views of the river and marina. It's part of Lower Falls Landing, also home to Maine Cottage Furniture, East Coast Yacht Sales indoor showroom (Sabre, Jboats, Freedom, Grand Banks), and Landing Boat Supply. The Yarmouth Clam Festival has been held every year since 1965 and draws well over 100,000 visitors on the weekend of the third Friday in July - a parade, food, food, food, carnival rides, crafts, a clam-shucking contest, and foot races.

PHOTOS ON DVD: 14

Yarmouth Boat Yard

PO Box 214; 72 Lafayette Street; Yarmouth, ME 04096

Tel: (207) 846-9050; (888) 401-4581 **VHF: Monitor** n/a **Talk** n/a
Fax: (207) 846-9050 **Alternate Tel:** n/a
Email: steve@ybyboats.com **Web:** www.yarmouthboatyard.com
Nearest Town: Yarmouth *(0.6 mi.)* **Tourist Info:** (207) 846-3984

Navigational Information

Lat: 43°47.861' **Long:** 070°10.597' **Tide:** 10 ft. **Current:** 1 kt. **Chart:** 13290
Rep. Depths (*MLW*): Entry 6 ft. **Fuel Dock** 8 ft. **Max Slip/Moor** 6 ft./6 ft.
Access: Casco Bay, up Royal River to the fixed bridge

Marina Facilities *(In Season/Off Season)*

Fuel: No
Slips: 150 Total, 6 Transient **Max LOA:** 35 ft. **Max Beam:** n/a
Rate *(per ft.)*: **Day** $1.00 **Week** $6 **Month** n/a
Power: 30 amp Incl., **50 amp** n/a, **100 amp** n/a, **200 amp** n/a
Cable TV: No **Dockside Phone:** No
Dock Type: Fixed, Floating
Moorings: 2 Total, 0 Transient **Launch:** n/a
Rate: Day n/a **Week** n/a **Month** n/a
Heads: 1 Toilet(s), 1 Shower(s) *(dressing rooms)*
Internet: No **Laundry:** None
Pump-Out: OnCall, Full Service **Fee:** n/a **Closed Heads:** No

Marina Operations

Owner/Manager: Steve Arnold **Dockmaster:** Shawn Dumas
In-Season: Year-Round, 8am-5pm* **Off-Season:** n/a
After-Hours Arrival: Call ahead
Reservations: Yes, Preferred **Credit Cards:** Visa/MC
Discounts: None
Pets: Welcome **Handicap Access:** No

Marina Services and Boat Supplies

Communication - Phone Messages, Fax in/out, FedEx, DHL, UPS, Express Mail *(Sat Del)* **Supplies - OnSite:** Ships' Store **Near:** Ice *(Block)*, Marine Discount Store *(Landing Boat Supply 846-3777)* **1-3 mi:** Propane *(Freeport Hardware 865-9557)*

Boatyard Services

OnSite: Forklift *(4T)*, Launching Ramp, Engine mechanic *(gas)*, Electrical Repairs, Electronic Sales, Electronics Repairs, Hull Repairs, Rigger *(Bayview Rigging & Sails)*, Sail Loft, Bottom Cleaning, Brightwork, Compound, Wash & Wax, Interior Cleaning **OnCall:** Divers **Near:** Canvas Work, Air Conditioning, Refrigeration. **Dealer for:** Honda, Suzuki, Mercury, Yamaha & Evinrude engines plus Pursuit, Mako, Seacraft and Eastern boats.

Restaurants and Accommodations

OnCall: Pizzeria *(Domino's 846-6911)* **Near:** Restaurant *(Royal River Grillhouse 846-1226, L $8-13, D $18-28, Sun Brunch $10-19)* **Under 1 mi:** Restaurant *(Seagrass Bistro 846-3885, D $24-25)*, *(The Muddy Rudder 846-3082, L $8-14, D $9-21)*, *(Grill House 233 846-3633, L $10-14, D $10-24)*, Lite Fare *(Binga's Wingas 846-8736)*, Pizzeria *(Romeo's 846-1473)*, *(Pat's 846-3701)*, Motel *(Down East Village 846-5161, $77-130)* **1-3 mi:** Fast Food *(McD's)*, Motel *(Brookside 846-5512, $65-135)*

Recreation and Entertainment

Under 1 mi: Picnic Area, Fitness Center *(Fitness Success 332-6248; Sanctuary Health & Yoga 846-1162)*, Hike/Bike Trails *(Royal River Park)*, Video Rental *(Blockbuster 846-0465)*, Park *(Royal River)*, Museum *(Yarmouth Hist. Society 846-6259)*, Special Events *(Outdoor performances - Royal River Park Wed.)* **1-3 mi:** Tennis Courts, Sightseeing *(DeLorme Map Store 846-7100 - Eartha, world's largest globe)* **3+ mi:** Golf Course *(Freeport C.C. 865-0711, 4 mi.)*

Provisioning and General Services

Near: Beauty Salon *(Celadon 846-3481)* **Under 1 mi:** Convenience Store, Market *(Rosemont 846-1234 - bakery, wine, too)*, Supermarket *(Hannaford 846-5941)*, Wine/Beer *(Hannaford)*, Liquor Store *(Hannaford)*, Bakery *(Rosemont)*, Bank/ATM, Post Office, Catholic Church, Protestant Church, Library *(Yarmouth 846-4763)*, Dry Cleaners *(Anthony's 846-9956)*, Laundry, Bookstore *(Royal River 846-8006)*, Pharmacy *(Rite Aid 846-1222)*, Hardware Store *(Ace Coastal 846-6767)*, Florist *(RR Station)*, Clothing Store *(Goff's 846-5932)* **1-3 mi:** Fishmonger, Lobster Pound, Meat Market

Transportation

OnCall: Rental Car *(Casco Bay Ford 846-5577)*, Taxi *(Yarmouth 846-9336; Freeport 865-9494)* **Under 1 mi:** InterCity Bus *(Concord Trailways)*
Airport: Portland Int'l. *(15 mi.)*

Medical Services

911 Service **OnCall:** Ambulance **Under 1 mi:** Dentist *(Bayview 846-0979)*, Chiropractor *(Yarmouth 846-1481)*, Holistic Services *(Lucinda's Day Spa 829-3100)*, Optician *(Insight 847-3800)*, Veterinarian *(Yarmouth 846-6515)* **1-3 mi:** Doctor *(Clemetson 415-2700)* **Hospital:** Maine Medical Center 781-1700 *(6 mi.)*

Setting -- Hard by the Route 295 bridge, just past the commanding three-story Lower Falls Landing complex, three nicely maintained, recent, smaller boat docks poke into the River among the mud flats. Onshore, two large, gray work sheds provide yard services and extensive inside storage. It's an easy walk from this simple facility to the well-reviewed Royal River Grillhouse and a longer trek to the village of Yarmouth.

Marina Notes -- *Sat 9am-4pm, closed Sun. Established in 1948. New docks & pedestals '09 & 30 more slips. Over 200 storage units, two full-service bays. 4-ton forklift haul-out. Some dry stack and dry storage. Painting, detailing, winterization, engine repowers, maintenance. Ships' store with extensive inventory - $1 million of OEM & aftermarket marine parts in stock. Sail loft & chandlery in Lower Falls. Bathouse: 2010 - New full bath with shower open 24/7.

Notable -- Lower Falls Landing, adjacent to the south, includes Landing Boat Supply, East Coast Yacht Sales, Maine Cottage Furniture plus the popular Grillhouse Restaurant - well-known for its traditional Maine fare, pleasant location, and panoramic views of the harbor. The village, (roughly a 0.6 mile walk) is a mix of 18th and 19th-century brick buildings, many now housing shops, churches, Yarmouth Academy and town hall - and home to the Yarmouth Clam Festival, held every year the third weekend in July. Just beyond, Royal River Park's lawns and waterfalls offer an inviting picnic ground and paved walking paths for those looking for a little exercise. Three miles up the road, see the 42-foot rotating globe "Eartha" at DeLorme Map Company's headquarters, as well as their Map Shop, which sells the useful Maine Atlas and Gazatteer (7 days, 9:30am-6pm, 800 642-0970). The Freeport Outlets and L.L. Bean are 4 miles away.

Navigational Information

Lat: 43°49.210' **Long:** 070°06.400' **Tide:** 10ft. **Current:** 3 kt. **Chart:** 13290
Rep. Depths (*MLW*): Entry 20 ft. **Fuel Dock** 18 ft. **Max Slip/Moor** 18 ft./60 ft.
Access: Broad Sound to R6 at Whaleboat Island to G1 to R4

Marina Facilities *(In Season/Off Season)*

Fuel: Gasoline, Diesel
Slips: 120 Total, 2 Transient **Max LOA:** 65 ft. **Max Beam:** 20 ft.
Rate *(per ft.)*: **Day** $2.25 **Week** $10 **Month** $24
Power: 30 amp Incl., **50 amp** Incl., **100 amp** Incl., **200 amp** n/a
Cable TV: No **Dockside Phone:** No
Dock Type: Floating, Long Fingers, Wood
Moorings: 15 Total, 3 Transient **Launch:** Private Launch 252-8876, Ch. 9
Rate: Day $30 **Week** $180 **Month** $720
Heads: 2 Toilet(s), 2 Shower(s)
Internet: No **Laundry:** None
Pump-Out: OnSite, Full Service **Fee:** $5 **Closed Heads:** Yes

Marina Operations

Owner/Manager: Charleen Durgin **Dockmaster:** Eric Bodwell
In-Season: MemDay-LabDay, 8am-7pm **Off-Season:** Sep-May, 8am-4:30pm
After-Hours Arrival: Call ahead for instructions
Reservations: Yes, Preferred **Credit Cards:** Visa/MC
Discounts: None
Pets: Welcome **Handicap Access:** No

Strouts Point Wharf Company

PO Box 95; 5 Wharf Road; South Freeport, ME 04078

Tel: (207) 865-3899 **VHF: Monitor** Ch. 9 **Talk** Ch. 9
Fax: (207) 865-4407 **Alternate Tel:** n/a
Email: dockmaster@stroutspoint.com **Web:** stroutspoint.com
Nearest Town: Freeport *(2 mi.)* **Tourist Info:** (207) 865-1212

Marina Services and Boat Supplies

Services - Docking Assistance, Trash Pick-Up, Dock Carts **Communication -** Mail & Package Hold, Fax in/out, FedEx, UPS, Express Mail **Supplies - OnSite:** Ice *(Block, Cube)*, Ships' Store **1-3 mi:** Bait/Tackle *(L.L. Bean 865-4761)*, Propane *(Freeport Hardware 865-9557)*

Boatyard Services

OnSite: Travelift *(25T)*, Engine mechanic *(gas, diesel)*, Electrical Repairs, Electronics Repairs, Hull Repairs, Rigger, Bottom Cleaning, Brightwork, Refrigeration **Dealer for:** Honda. **Yard Rates:** $30-74/hr., Haul & Launch $0.50-0.75/sq.ft., Power Wash Incl., Bottom Paint $0.70-0.80/sq.ft. **Storage:** On-Land Out $4.60-6.60/sq.ft. In $8.70-10.70/sq.ft.

Restaurants and Accommodations

OnCall: Pizzeria *(Domino's 865-6111)* **Near:** Seafood Shack *(Harraseeket Lunch 865-4888, L & D $5-20 Cash only. 11am-8:45pm. Baskets, Sands, Lobsters, steamers - Town Wharf courtesy dockage)* **1-3 mi:** Restaurant *(Jameson Tavern 865-4196, L $8-25, D $10-27, Kids' $4-6, Tap Room for pub fare)*, *(Gritty McDuff's 865-4321, L & D $8-13 Brew pub)*, *(Corsican 865-9421, L & D $8-16 - Pizza)*, *(Maine Dining Room 865-9377, L $4-13, D $15-26, in the Harraseeket Inn)*, Pizzeria *(Antonia's 865-6863)*, Motel *(Village Inn 865-3236, $85-110)*, *(Freeport Inn 865-3106, $60-150)*, Inn/B&B *(Kendall Tavern B&B 865-1338, $70-175)*, *(Harraseeket Inn 865-9377, $150-205)*

Recreation and Entertainment

Near: Hike/Bike Trails, Park *(Wolfe's Neck Woods S.P. 865-4465)*, Sightseeing *(Atlantic Seal Cruises 865-6112 at town wharf. 40 ft. 28-pass vessel. Seal & Osprey Watch plus trips to Senguin Is. & Robt. E. Peary House at Eagle Is.$55/40-$35/25)* **1-3 mi:** Beach *(Winslow Memorial)*, Playground, Tennis Courts, Golf Course *(Freeport C.C. 865-0711)*, Boat Rentals *(L.L. Bean Kayaking 90 min $20, 4 hrs $60)*, Fishing Charter *(L.L.Bean Fly Casting $20)*, Museum *(Harrington House 865-3170)*, Cultural Attract *(L.L. Bean Summer in the Park - Sat 7:30pm, Free)*

Provisioning and General Services

Near: Convenience Store *(Village Market)*, Lobster Pound *(Harraseeket 865-3535 next door 7am-8:45pm)*, Bank/ATM *(Harraseeket Lunch)*, Post Office, Protestant Church **1-3 mi:** Market *(Bow Street 865-6631)*, Supermarket *(Shaw's 865-0094; Bow Street 865-6631)*, Gourmet Shop, Delicatessen, Health Food *(Royal River 865-0046)*, Wine/Beer *(Old World Gourmet 865-4477)*, Liquor Store, Bakery, Farmers' Market *(Fri- 3-7pm Discovery Park 865-3985)*, Meat Market, Catholic Church, Library *(865-3307)*, Beauty Salon, Dry Cleaners, Bookstore *(Annie's 865-3406, Sherman's 869-9000)*, Pharmacy *(Shaw's-Osco 865-0094)*, Hardware Store *(Freeport 865-9557)*, Florist, Retail Shops *(Freeport Factory Outlets - 150 shops)*

Transportation

OnCall: Rental Car *(Enterprise 725-1344)*, Taxi *(Freeport 865-9494)* **Near:** Local Bus *(L.L. Bean Shuttle, Town Landing)*, Ferry Service *(Bustins Is.)* **1-3 mi:** InterCity Bus *(Trailways)* **Airport:** Portland Int'l. *(18 mi.)*

Medical Services

911 Service **1-3 mi:** Doctor *(Coastal 865-2225)*, Dentist *(Alta 865-1900)*, Chiropractor *(Freeport 865-1183)*, Holistic Services *(Center Studio 865-0086 Massage $75)* **3+ mi:** Veterinarian *(Freeport 865-3673, 4 mi.)* **Hospital:** Mid-Coast 373-6175 *(11 mi.)*

Setting -- A half mile up the Harraseeket, one of Maine's snuggest harbors, a seemingly old-time Maine boatyard veneer hides a modern, well-equipped facility with an expansive, uniquely constructed, year-round dock system at its feet. Strouts Point's craftsmanship is evident in the the noteworthy dock and building designs - a shingled office stands just above the docks backed by two large work sheds. Views are of Wolf's Neck Park, just across the river.

Marina Notes -- Off season open Mon-Fri only. Family-owned for generations. Highly regarded woodworkers & yacht restorers specialize in wooden boats - especially Concordia Yawls. New dock layout accommodates larger boats (100A power). Sturdy, year-round system utilizes unique continuous laminated beam structure, no mechanical joints, tethered with mooring cables. Climate controlled shed, with translucent walls & 12 x 20 ft. skylight, holds up to ten 50 ft. yachts; smaller repair & woodworking shop holds two with a special dust collection ventilation system. Parking $8/day, $12/nt, $30/wk. Launch ME (Ch. 9 or 252-8876) for launch service. Add'l moorings: harbormaster on Ch.9 or Ring's Marine (865-6143). Bathhouse: Sparkling white tile with fiberglass, glass-doored showers.

Notable -- Harraseeket Lunch is a very short walk - if you just want lobster, use the separate window to minimize the wait. A bit further, the Village Store prepares picnic lunches and hot entrées to go. Quiet South Freeport, seemingly far removed from the bustle of Freeport, is just two miles away by taxi or L.L Bean Shuttle. Interspersed among a variety of eateries and lodgings, Freeport's vintage buildings house over 150 outlets. The centerpiece is L.L. Bean's original flagship store (24/7 - 877-755-2326) with an indoor trout pond, plus the Outlet, two specialized satellites and the active adventure Outdoor Discovery

Brewer South Freeport Marine

PO Box 119; 31 Main Street; South Freeport, ME 04078

Tel: (207) 865-3181 **VHF: Monitor** Ch. 9 **Talk** Ch. 10
Fax: (207) 865-3183 **Alternate Tel:** n/a
Email: bsf@byy.com **Web:** www.byy.com/freeport
Nearest Town: Freeport *(2 mi.)* **Tourist Info:** (207) 865-1212

Navigational Information

Lat: 43°49.270' **Long:** 070°06.280' **Tide:** 10 ft. **Current:** 3 kt. **Chart:** 13290
Rep. Depths (*MLW*): Entry 20 ft. **Fuel Dock** 13 ft. **Max Slip/Moor** 16 ft./20 ft.
Access: Broad Sound to R6 at Whaleboat Island to G1 to R4

Marina Facilities *(In Season/Off Season)*

Fuel: *ValvTect* - Slip-Side Fueling, Gasoline, Diesel
Slips: 100 Total, 4 Transient **Max LOA:** 145 ft. **Max Beam:** 20 ft. ft.
Rate *(per ft.)*: **Day** $2.50* **Week** Inq. **Month** Inq.
Power: 30 amp incl, **50 amp** incl, **100 amp** n/a, **200 amp** n/a
Cable TV: No **Dockside Phone:** No
Dock Type: Floating, Long Fingers, Short Fingers, Pilings, Wood, Compositi
Moorings: 15 Total, 0-15 Transient **Launch:** No, Dinghy Dock
Rate: Day $30 **Week** $180 **Month** $720
Heads: 5 Toilet(s), 3 Shower(s) *(dressing rooms)*, lounge, Book Exchange
Internet: Yes *(Wi-Fi, Free)* **Laundry:** 1 Washer(s), 1 Dryer(s)
Pump-Out: OnSite, Full Service, 1 Central **Fee:** $5 **Closed Heads:** Yes

Marina Operations

Owner/Manager: John S. Brewer **Dockmaster:** Kristin Peterson
In-Season: May-Oct, 8am-6pm **Off-Season:** Nov-April, 8am-4:30pm
After-Hours Arrival: Call ahead for instructions
Reservations: Yes, Required **Credit Cards:** Visa/MC, Dscvr, Amex
Discounts: Brewer Club Members **Dockage:** n/a **Fuel:** over 100 gal. **Rep**
Pets: Welcome, Dog Walk Area **Handicap Access:** Yes, Heads

Marina Services and Boat Supplies

Services - Docking Assistance, Boaters' Lounge, Trash Pick-Up, Dock Carts **Communication -** Mail & Package Hold, Fax in/out, FedEx, UPS, Express Mail *(Sat Del)* **Supplies - OnSite:** Ice *(Block, Cube)* **Near:** Ships' Store **1-3 mi:** Bait/Tackle *(L.L. Bean 865-4761)*, Propane *(Freeport Hardware 865-9557)*, CNG *(Landing Boat Supply, Yarmouth 846-3777)*

Boatyard Services

OnSite: Travelift *(35T)*, Forklift, Crane, Hydraulic Trailer, Engine mechanic *(gas, diesel)*, Electrical Repairs, Hull Repairs, Rigger, Sail Loft, Divers, Bottom Cleaning, Brightwork, Interior Cleaning, Woodworking, Painting, Awlgrip, Total Refits, Yacht Broker **OnCall:** Electronics Repairs, Canvas Work, Air Conditioning, Refrigeration **Dealer for:** Mercruiser, Yanmar, Westerbeke, Sealand, Yamaha. **Member:** ABBRA, ABYC - 2 Certified Tech (s) **Yard Rates:** $35-68/hr., Haul & Launch $1/sq.ft. *(blocking incl.)* **Storage:** On-Land Out: $3.30/sq.ft. In: $8.40-12/sq.ft.

Restaurants and Accommodations

OnCall: Pizzeria *(Domino's 846-6911)* **Near:** Seafood Shack *(Harraseeket Lunch & Lobster 865-4888, L & D $5-20 Cash only. 11am-8:45pm. Baskets, Sandwiches)*, Snack Bar *(Village Market 865-4230)* **1-3 mi:** Restaurant *(Jameson Tavern 865-4196, L $8-25, D $10-27, Kids' $4-6)*, *(Broad Arrow Tavern L & D $10-30, Brick Oven pizza too)*, *(Harraseeket Inn Maine Dining Room 865-9377, L $4-13, D $15-26, Sun Brunch $26)*, *(Gritty McDuff's 865-4321, L & D $8-13)*, Fast Food *(McD's)*, Pizzeria *(The Corsican 865-9421)*, *(Siano's 865-9665, Stone Oven)*, Hotel *(Hilton Garden 865-1433, $170-300)*, Inn/B&B *(Freeport 865-3106, $60-170)*, *(Harraseeket 865-9377, $150-285)*, *(181 Main Street 865-9623, $85-110)*

Recreation and Entertainment

OnSite: Picnic Area, Grills **Near:** Sightseeing *(Atlantic Seal Cruises 865-6112, town wharf, $55/40-$35/25)* **Under 1 mi:** Park *(Audubon's Mast Landing Sanctuary - dinghy upstream at high tide)* **1-3 mi:** Beach *(Winslow Mem.)*, Golf Course *(Freeport C.C. 865-0711)*, Museum *(Harrington House 865-3170)*, Cultural Attract *(L.L. Bean concerts - Sat 7:30pm, Free)*

Provisioning and General Services

Near: Convenience Store *(Village Market 865-4230)*, Gourmet Shop, Wine/Beer *(Village)*, Bakery, Lobster Pound *(Harraseeket 865-3535 - 7am-8:45pm)*, Bank/ATM, Post Office, Protestant Church **1-3 mi:** Market *(Bow Street 865-6631)*, Supermarket *(Shaw's 865-0094)*, Health Food *(Royal River 865-0046)*, Liquor Store *(Bow Street)*, Farmers' Market *(Fri- 3-7pm Discovery Park 865-3985)*, Catholic Church, Library, Beauty Salon, Laundry, Bookstore *(Annie's 865-3406, Sherman's 869-9000)*, Pharmacy *(CVS 865-6324)*, Hardware Store *(Freeport 865-9557)*, Florist, Retail Shops *(Freeport Factory Outlets - 150 shops)*

Transportation

OnCall: Water Taxi *(Launch Me Ch. 9, 252-8876, May-Oct)*, Rental Car *(Enterprise 725-1344)*, Taxi *(Freeport 865-9494, Brunswick 729-3688)*, Airport Limo *(Outward Exp 865-0890)* **Near:** Local Bus *(L.L. Bean Shuttle)* **1-3 mi:** InterCity Bus *(Concord Trailways)* **Airport:** Portland Int'l. *(12 mi.)*

Medical Services

911 Service **1-3 mi:** Doctor *(Coastal 865-2225)*, Dentist *(Alta 865-1900)*, Chiropractor *(Freeport 865-1183)*, Holistic Services *(Center Studio 865-0086 Massage $75)* **Hospital:** Mid-Coast 729-0181 *(11 mi.)*

Setting -- Tucked up the protected, deep-water tidal Harraseeket River, this exceptionally well-maintained boatyard and marina is just past Strouts Point, the Town Wharf and red-shingled Harraseeket Lunch & Lobster on the port side. The diminutive gray dockhouse oversees the fuel pumps and welcomes boaters. Perched on the bulkheaded upland, two small gray-shingled buildings with wine awnings and lobster buoys are backed by a massive two-story gray and white work shed and office. Brewers is surrounded by active clam flats and lobster docks - with unspoiled Wolfe's Neck Woods State Park across the water.

Marina Notes -- CCM. *Over 50 ft. $3/ft. 220 feet of floating face dock. Busy full-service boatyard/marina supported by entire Brewers chain. Reservations beginning Jan 1st. Call when 1/4 mile out; dockhands help with lines. Very useful Welcome Packets. All mechanical service, Awlgrip, wood & fiberglass finish, hull repairs, interior joinery. Parking $10/day. $50/wk. Harraseeket Y.C. (865-4949) & Rings (865-6143). Private Launch ME (Ch. 9 or 252-8876) for service. Bathhouse: Full baths in small Customer Lounge - tan quarry tile floors, fiberglass, glass-doored shower stalls, laundry facilities.

Notable -- Right next door, Harraseeket Lunch & Lobster serves baskets, sandwiches, lobsters, steamers, crabs (live and cooked) at picnic tables overlooking the town wharf. The Village Store is a short walk for picnics, entrées to go, ice cream and groceries. L.L. Bean's massive flagship store (24/7) and three satellites anchor Freeport's restored historic buildings that house 150 designer outlets, restaurants, inns - all a 2-mile taxi ride away. Bean's Discovery Schools (888-552-3261) offers 90-minute ($20) Walk-on Adventures - fly-casting, archery, skeet shooting, kayaking - plus full-day and week-long courses.

Navigational Information
Lat: 43°43.700' **Long:** 070°12.580' **Tide:** 9 ft. **Current:** 5 kt. **Chart:** 13290
Rep. Depths (*MLW*): Entry 25 ft. **Fuel Dock** 8 ft. **Max Slip/Moor** -/32 ft.
Access: Casco Bay through Hussey Sound

Marina Facilities *(In Season/Off Season)*
Fuel: Gasoline, Diesel
Slips: 40 Total, 1 Transient **Max LOA:** 65 ft. **Max Beam:** n/a
Rate *(per ft.)*: **Day** $3.00* **Week** n/a **Month** n/a
Power: 30 amp Incl., **50 amp** n/a, **100 amp** n/a, **200 amp** n/a
Cable TV: No **Dockside Phone:** No
Dock Type: Floating, Alongside, Wood
Moorings: 40 Total, 20 Transient **Launch:** Yes (Free), Dinghy Dock
Rate: Day $30 **Week** $210 **Month** $840
Heads: 2 Toilet(s), 2 Shower(s)
Internet: Yes *(WiFi, Free)* **Laundry:** Yes
Pump-Out: OnSite, Full Service, 1 Central **Fee:** $5 **Closed Heads:** No

Marina Operations
Owner/Manager: Jay Hallett **Dockmaster:** Rob Van Os
In-Season: May-Oct, 8am-9pm **Off-Season:** Nov-Apr, Closed
After-Hours Arrival: Call in advance
Reservations: Yes, Preferred **Credit Cards:** Visa/MC, Dscvr
Discounts: None
Pets: Welcome, Dog Walk Area **Handicap Access:** Yes, Heads, Docks

Handy Boat Service

215 Foreside Road; Falmouth, ME 04105

Tel: (207) 781-5110 **VHF: Monitor** Ch. 9 **Talk** Ch. 9
Fax: (207) 781-7534 **Alternate Tel:** n/a
Email: handyboat@maine.rr.com **Web:** www.handyboat.com
Nearest Town: Falmouth *(.5 mi.)* **Tourist Info:** (207) 772-5800

Marina Services and Boat Supplies
Services - Docking Assistance **Communication -** Mail & Package Hold, Phone Messages, Fax in/out *($1.50)*, FedEx, DHL, UPS *(Sat Del)* **Supplies - OnSite:** Ice *(Block, Cube)*, Ships' Store *(The Boathouse - Sailing Gear 781-0939)*, CNG **Under 1 mi:** Propane *(Walmart)* **3+ mi:** West Marine *(761-7600, 6 mi.)*, Marine Discount Store *(Hamilton Marine 774-1772, 6 mi.)*

Boatyard Services
OnSite: Travelift *(35T)*, Engine mechanic *(gas, diesel)*, Electrical Repairs, Electronic Sales, Electronics Repairs, Hull Repairs, Rigger, Sail Loft *(Hallett 781-7070)*, Canvas Work, Divers, Bottom Cleaning, Brightwork, Air Conditioning, Refrigeration, Compound, Wash & Wax, Interior Cleaning, Woodworking, Upholstery, Yacht Interiors, Painting, Awlgrip, Total Refits, Yacht Broker *(New Wave)* **OnCall:** Propeller Repairs, Inflatable Repairs, Life Raft Service, Metal Fabrication **Under 1 mi:** Launching Ramp. **Dealer for:** Westerbeke, Universal, Yanmar engines. **Member:** ABBRA, ABYC, Other Certifications: MMTA **Yard Rates:** $75/hr., Haul & Launch $12-17/ft. *(blocking $16-23/ft.)*, Power Wash $3.50/ft., Bottom Paint $11.25-13.75/ft. **Storage:** On-Land $49-85/ft.

Restaurants and Accommodations
OnSite: Restaurant *(Falmouth Sea Grill 781-5658, L & D $9-21, 7 days 11:30am-close. Sunday brunch.)* **OnCall:** Pizzeria *(Falmouth 781-5251, D $7-16)* **Under 1 mi:** Restaurant *(Lotus Chinese 781-3453)*, Lite Fare *(Foreside Tavern 781-4255, L $7-13, D $7-25)*, Pizzeria *(Ricetta's 781-3100, D $6-18)*, Inn/B&B *(1802 House 967-5632, $146-219)* **1-3 mi:** Fast Food *(Subway, Wendy's, McD's)*, Lite Fare *(Stonyfield Cafe 781-8889, L & D $6-8, Kids $5)*, Motel *(Falmouth Inn 781-2120, $45-100)*

Recreation and Entertainment
Near: Beach, Sightseeing *(Gisland Farm)* **Under 1 mi:** Movie Theater *(Hoyts 781-5616)*, Video Rental, Park **1-3 mi:** Tennis Courts, Golf Course *(Riverside Municipal 797-3524)*, Fitness Center, Hike/Bike Trails *(Gisland Farm 781-2330 Mon-Sat, 9am-5pm; Sun 12-4pm)* **3+ mi:** Museum *(Yarmouth Historical Society 846-6259; Narrow Gauge Railroad & Museum 828-0814, 4 mi.)*

Provisioning and General Services
Under 1 mi: Market *(Town Landing Market 781-2128)*, Lobster Pound *(Town Landing Market)*, Catholic Church, Florist **1-3 mi:** Supermarket *(Shaw's 781-4520)*, Gourmet Shop, Delicatessen, Health Food, Wine/Beer *(Cork & Barrel 781-7955)*, Liquor Store, Bakery, Fishmonger, Meat Market, Bank/ATM, Post Office, Protestant Church, Library *(Falmouth Memorial 781-2351)*, Beauty Salon, Barber Shop, Dry Cleaners, Bookstore, Pharmacy, Newsstand, Hardware Store, Clothing Store, Department Store *(Wal-Mart 781-3879)*, Copies Etc. *(Mail Boxes Etc. 781-4866, Staples)* **3+ mi:** Synagogue *(4 mi.)*, Buying Club *(BJ's, Sams, 5 mi.)*

Transportation
OnCall: Rental Car *(Enterprise 772-0030)*, Taxi *(Mermaid Transport 800-696-2463)* **Airport:** Portland Int'l. *(6 mi.)*

Medical Services
911 Service **OnCall:** Ambulance **1-3 mi:** Chiropractor *(Saulter 781-2003)*, Holistic Services *(Litrocapes Massage 415-7103)*, Veterinarian *(Falmouth 781-4028)* **3+ mi:** Doctor *(Martin's Point Health Care 828-2402, 5 mi.)* **Hospital:** Maine Medical Center 662-0111 *(5 mi.)*

Setting With panoramic views of Casco Bay and many of its islands, Handy Boat's stunning mooring field is served by a pair of floating docks that lead to a small village of weathered shingled buildings and a red-trimmed white shed. Inside are a well-reviewed restaurant, extensive chandlery, and sail loft and surrounded by attractively landscaped grounds and a full-service boatyard. Residential, recreational Falmouth harbor is the largest anchorage in Maine.

Marina Notes -- *Overnight dockage rarely available. Founded in 1934. Hallett family at the helm for more than 40 years. Sold in '08, Jay Hallett still GM. 300 moorings with launch service: 8am-8pm summer, see Dock House for shoulder season schedule. Dry storage for 150. Temporary tie-ups limited to 20 min. Pump-out dock accessible 2 hrs. each side of high tide (pump-out also at Falmouth Town Landing). 5,500 sq. ft. Hallett Canvas & Sail loft for advanced racing sails. The Boathouse marine hardware store - home of Handy Skiff & Handy Cat. plus Handy outboard Bracket. Parking $10/day. Provisioning transport possible. Bathhouse: New heads, showers & laundry in 2011. Note: Adj. Portland Y.C. (Ch.68) - moorings to members of recip. clubs.

Notable -- Dine at the nearly dockside Falmouth Sea Grill and pub (recently voted one of the best in Portland) either inside or on the deck with elegant Casco Bay views and piano music on weekends. Handy also offers Sailing & Coastal Cruising Certificate Courses ($495-550) as well as Basic Intro, Refresher, Basic Navigation, and Sail Trim Lessons ($70-360), or private Lessons ($50/hr.). About 2.5 miles, the Maine Audubon Society protects Gisland Farm's 60 acres with 2½ miles of trails along Presumpscot River's coastal salt marshes (781-2330). Most anything needed is at Falmouth Shopping Center 1.7 miles away.

PHOTOS ON DVD: 19

Sabre Yachts Corporation

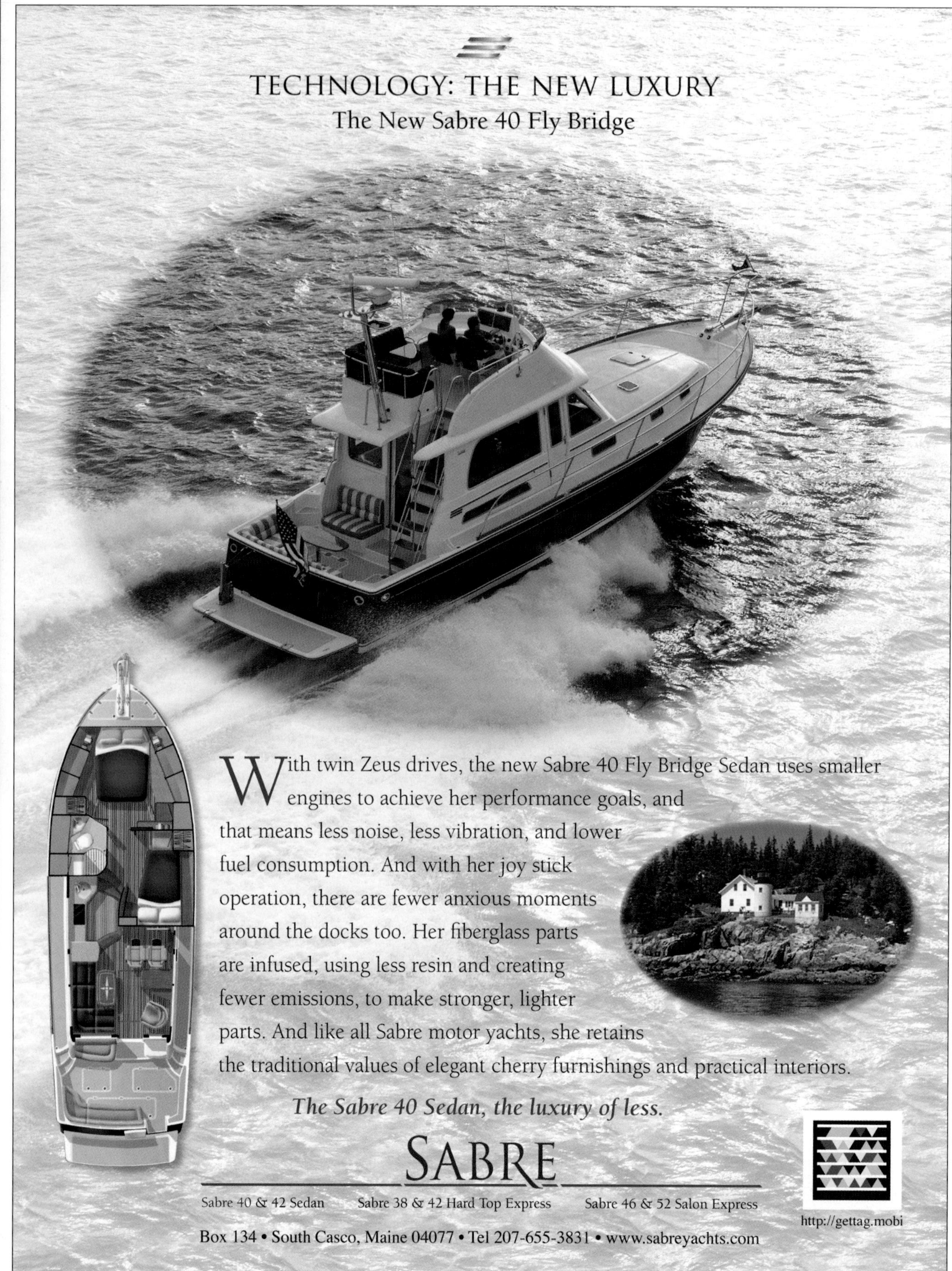

9. ME – Casco Bay, Portland & The Beaches

Atlantic Ocean
N
Portland
Cape Elizabeth
Saco River
Saco Bay
Mousam River
Kennebunkport
Kennebunk River
Cape Neddick
York River
York Harbor
Casco Bay
Back Cove
Portland
Portland River
Peaks Island
South Portland
Miles
0
16

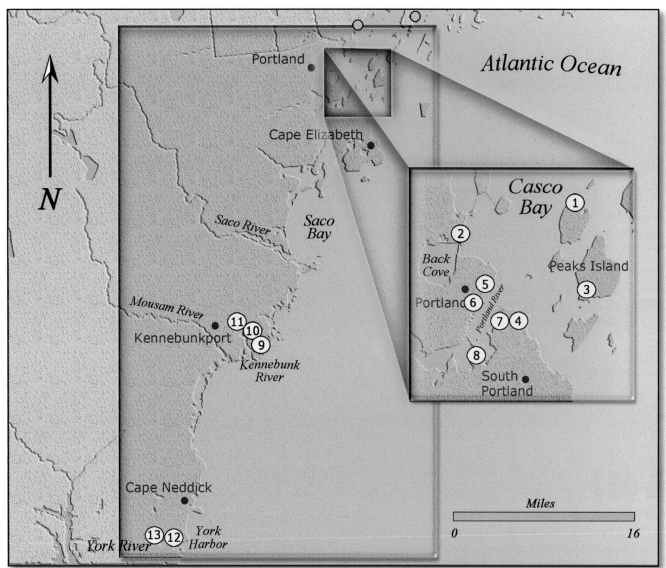

MAP	MARINA	HARBOR	PAGE	MAP	MARINA	HARBOR	PAGE
1	**Diamond's Edge Marina**	*Casco Bay*	172	8	**South Port Marine**	*Portland Harbor*	179
2	**Maine Yacht Center**	*Casco Bay*	173	9	**Chick's Marina**	*Kennebunk River*	180
3	**Peaks Island Marina**	*Casco Bay*	174	10	**Kennebunkport Marina**	*Kennebunk River*	181
4	**Spring Point Marina**	*Casco Bay*	175	11	**Yachtsman Marina**	*Kennebunk River*	182
5	**Portland Yacht Services**	*Portland Harbor*	176	12	**York Town Docks & Moorings**	*York Harbor*	183
6	**DiMillo's Old Port Marina**	*Portland Harbor*	177	13	**Donnell's Dockage**	*York Harbor*	184
7	**Sunset Marina**	*Portland Harbor*	178				

RATINGS: 1-5 for Marina Facilities & Amenities,  1-2 for Boatyard Services,  1-2 for MegaYacht Facilities,  for Something Special.

SERVICES:  for CCM – Certified Clean Marina,  for Pump-Out,  for Internet,  for Fuel,  for Restaurant, for Provisioning nearby,  for Catamaran-friendly,  for SportFish Charter,  for Pool/Beach, and  for Golf within a mile. *For an explanation of ACC's Ratings, see page 8.*

Diamond's Edge Marina

Great Diamond Island; Portland, ME

Tel: (207) 766-5694 **VHF: Monitor** Ch. 9 **Talk** n/a
Fax: (207) 766-5804 **Alternate Tel:** (207) 766-5694
Email: bms@prenticehospitality.com **Web:** www.diamondsedge.com
Nearest Town: Portland *(3 mi.)* **Tourist Info:** (207) 772-5800

Navigational Information

Lat: 43°41.079' **Long:** 070°11.495' **Tide:** 9 ft. **Current:** n/a **Chart:** 13290
Rep. Depths (*MLW*): Entry 20 ft. **Fuel Dock** n/a **Max Slip/Moor** 12 ft./-
Access: Northeast end of Great Diamond Island

Marina Facilities *(In Season/Off Season)*

Fuel: No
Slips: 45 Total, 10 Transient **Max LOA:** 50 ft. **Max Beam:** n/a
Rate *(per ft.)*: **Day** $3.00 **Week** n/a **Month** n/a
Power: 30 amp Incl., **50 amp** Incl., **100 amp** n/a, **200 amp** n/a
Cable TV: No **Dockside Phone:** No
Dock Type: Floating, Long Fingers, Alongside, Wood
Moorings: 0 Total, 0 Transient **Launch:** n/a, Dinghy Dock
Rate: Day n/a **Week** n/a **Month** n/a
Heads: 2 Toilet(s), 2 Shower(s) *(dressing rooms)*
Internet: No **Laundry:** 2 Washer(s), 2 Dryer(s)
Pump-Out: OnSite, Full Service **Fee:** Free **Closed Heads:** Yes

Marina Operations

Owner/Manager: Bryan Smith **Dockmaster:** Same
In-Season: May-Sep, 8am-5pm **Off-Season:** Oct-Apr, Closed
After-Hours Arrival: Call in advance
Reservations: Yes **Credit Cards:** Visa/MC, Amex
Discounts: None
Pets: Welcome **Handicap Access:** No

Marina Services and Boat Supplies

Services - Docking Assistance **Supplies - 3+ mi:** Propane *(Breggy Oil & Propane Service 772-4631, 5 mi.)*

Boatyard Services

Nearest Yard: Handy Boat Service (207) 781-5110

Restaurants and Accommodations

OnSite: Restaurant *(Diamond's Edge Restaurant 766-5850, L $9-18, D $25-35, Also events, weddings, club cruises)*, Lite Fare *(General Store 766-0078, B $2.50-5, L $5-17, D $5-17, Rolls, wraps, sandwiches, fish & chips, live or steamed lobster, beer, wine, ice cream)* **Near:** Condo/Cottage *(Diamond Cove Rentals 766-3005, Historic & Beach cottages - most weekly)* **Under 1 mi:** Inn/B&B *(Chestnut Hill Bed & Breakfast 766-5272, $100-155, on Long Island)* **3+ mi:** Restaurant *(Chebeague Island Inn 846-5155, L $11-18, D $16-38, 3 mi., Sun Brunch $10-18 - by water)*, Inn/B&B *(Hilton Garden Inn Portland Downtown Waterfront 780-0780, $220-289, 4 mi.)*

Recreation and Entertainment

OnSite: Volleyball *(All Lawn games: volleyball, bocce ball, lawn bowling, croquet, & badminton)* **Near:** Hike/Bike Trails *(Miles of scenic trails)*, Museum *(Fort McKinley - artifacts & DVDs of old photos - by app't)*, Tours *(Fort McKinley Tour - rshoemaker@phoenixmanagementcompany.com - Roger Shoemaker)*, Galleries *(Diamonds Edge Gallery - a restored military wagon shed featuring the work of Maine artisans)* **3+ mi:** Golf Course *(Great Chebeague Island Inn 846-5155 - by water, 3 mi.)*, Sightseeing *(Portland Discovery Tours 774-6498, 4 mi.)*

Provisioning and General Services

OnSite: Convenience Store *(General Store 766-0078 Staples, snacks, beer, wine, sandwiches, convenience items)*, Wine/Beer *(or Old Port Wine Merchants 772-9463)*, Lobster Pound, Newsstand **1-3 mi:** Hardware Store *(Peaks Island Hardware Co 766-5300)* **3+ mi:** Supermarket *(Hannaford 799-7359, 7 mi.)*, Pharmacy *(Rite Aid 774-0344, 5 mi.)*

Transportation

OnSite: Ferry Service *(Casco Bay Lines 774-7871 from GDI Pier $8.85/4.40 RT at south end or Diamond Cove Pier $10/5 RT on-site.)* **OnCall:** Water Taxi *(Portland Express - Gene 415-8493; Island 799-1818; Presumpscot 879-2562; Portland Express 415-8493 - to 6 pass. $60 1-way day, $90 night; Chebeague Island Inn - Bryan 846-5155)* **Airport:** Portland Int'l Jetport - 30 min. by ferry, then 8 mi. by land *(8 mi.)*

Medical Services

No 911 Service **Near:** Holistic Services *(Nine Stones Spa 766-0999)* **1-3 mi:** Doctor *(Peaks Island Health Center 766-2929)* **3+ mi:** Veterinarian *(Brackett Street 772-3385, 5 mi.)* **Hospital:** Mercy 879-3000 *(5 mi.)*

PHOTOS ON DVD: 20

Setting -- Tucked into the west side of Diamond Cove on the northeast corner of Great Diamond Island, the marina is surrounded by Fort McKinley's rejuvenated 19thC. brick buildings - now the centerpiece of an upscale development. Slips branch from the main pier, which is topped by a bright blue awning. One hundred fifty yards from the docks, stylishly casual, well-regarded Diamond's Edge Restaurant occupies the restored Quartermaster's storehouse.

Marina Notes -- Complimentary dinner/unch dockage. Wide slips. Dinghy dockage. Year-round ferry to Portland (dogs allowed with a ticket) - 2nd stop on Great Diamond at marina. Seasonal general store sells beer, wine, sandwiches & fresh lobster. Restaurant provides implements for lawn games: volleyball, bocce ball, lawn bowling, croquet, & badminton. Note: pool, tennis courts, fitness center, indoor basketball, duckpins, pinball, billiards available *only* to Diamond Cove residents/tenants. Bathhouse: Well-maintained, spacious full baths with tiled floors.

Notable -- Permeated with history, two-mile long Great Diamond Island was once a creative retreat frequented by artists and writers including Henry Wadsworth Longfellow and Harriet Beecher Stowe. With the advent of the Spanish-American War in 1891, the island was converted to Fort McKinley to protect Casco Bay - remaining a military base until 1945. Today the 19thC. base's brick barracks and gracious Queen Anne-style officer's houses have been elegantly restored as second homes surrounding the National Registered Parade Grounds. They are part of car-free Diamond Cove, an upscale community that covers most of the island's northern end. The restaurant is a special-occasion destination for Portlanders - the lawn's the favored spot; the porch a close second.

Navigational Information
Lat: 43°40.752' **Long:** 070°15.107' **Tide:** 9 ft. **Current:** 5 kt. **Chart:** 329
Rep. Depths (*MLW*): Entry 10 ft. **Fuel Dock** 16 ft. **Max Slip/Moor** 15 ft./-
Access: Portland Harbor Head N to Pomroy Rock then W/NW to RR Bridge

Marina Facilities *(In Season/Off Season)*
Fuel: Gasoline, Diesel, High-Speed Pumps
Slips: 80 Total, 3 Transient **Max LOA:** 150 ft. **Max Beam:** 30 ft.
Rate *(per ft.)*: **Day** $3.00 **Week** n/a **Month** n/a
Power: 30 amp $15, **50 amp** $25, **100 amp** $50, **200 amp** n/a
Cable TV: Yes By arrangement **Dockside Phone:** No
Dock Type: Floating, Long Fingers, Alongside, Concrete, Wood
Moorings: 0 Total, 0 Transient **Launch:** n/a, Dinghy Dock
Rate: Day n/a **Week** n/a **Month** n/a
Heads: 4 Toilet(s), 3 Shower(s) *(dressing rooms)*, Hair Dryers
Internet: Yes *(Wi-Fi, Free)* **Laundry:** 2 Washer(s), 2 Dryer(s)
Pump-Out: Full Service, Self Service **Fee:** $5 **Closed Heads:** Yes

Marina Operations
Owner/Manager: Brian Harris **Dockmaster:** Dana Randlett
In-Season: May16-Oct14, 8am-6pm **Off-Season:** n/a
After-Hours Arrival: Call ahead
Reservations: Yes, Preferred **Credit Cards:** Visa/MC, Dscvr, Amex
Discounts: None
Pets: Welcome, Dog Walk Area **Handicap Access:** Yes, Heads, Docks

Maine Yacht Center

100 Kensington Street; Portland, ME 04101

Tel: (207) 842-9000 **VHF: Monitor** Ch. 9 **Talk** Ch. 71 or 68
Fax: (207) 842-9274 **Alternate Tel:** n/a
Email: karen@maineyacht.com **Web:** www.maineyacht.com
Nearest Town: Portland *(2 mi.)* **Tourist Info:** (207) 772-2811

Marina Services and Boat Supplies
Services - Docking Assistance, Boaters' Lounge, Security *(24)*, Trash Pick-Up, Dock Carts, 3 Phase **Communication -** Mail & Package Hold, Fax in/out, FedEx, DHL, UPS, Express Mail **Supplies - OnSite:** Ice *(Block, Cube)*, Ships' Store, Propane **1-3 mi:** West Marine *(761-7600)*, Marine Discount Store *(Hamilton 774-1772)*, Bait/Tackle *(Tackle 773-3474)*

Boatyard Services
OnSite: Travelift *(80T to 80 ft. LOA, 23 ft. beam)*, Hydraulic Trailer *(40T)*, Electrical Repairs, Electronic Sales, Electronics Repairs, Hull Repairs, Rigger, Brightwork, Woodworking, Yacht Interiors, Painting, Awlgrip, Total Refits **OnCall:** Sail Loft, Canvas Work, Divers, Bottom Cleaning, Air Conditioning, Refrigeration, Inflatable Repairs, Life Raft Service, Metal Fabrication **Member:** ABYC - 3 Certified Tech(s) **Yard Rates:** $55/hr., Haul & Launch $7/ft. *(blocking $10/ft.)*, Power Wash $35 **Storage:** On-Land Outside: $4/sq.ft.; Inside: $12/sq.ft.

Restaurants and Accommodations
Near: Restaurant *(Veranda Thai 874-0045, L $7-11, D $7-15, Delivers)*, *(Veranda Noodle Bar 874-9090, L & D $10-17)*, Lite Fare *(Steve & Renee's Diner 775-2722, Veg. Options)*, *(G Quattrucci's Variety 773-0424)*, Pizzeria *(Pizza Time 774-2222)* **1-3 mi:** Restaurant *(Silly's 772-0360, L & D $6-15 + pizza, Veg options)*, *(Bar Lola 775-5652, D $8-18, Small/large plates, $39 prix fix 5-course)*, *(Blue Spoon 773-1116, L $7-11, D $8-19)*, *(Front Room 773-3366, B $4-9, L $4-9, D $6-19, Brunch every day)*, Seafood Shack *(DiMillo's Floating Restaurant 772-2216, L $7-19, D $19-23)*, Hotel *(Portland Regency 774-4200, $140-359)*, *(Hilton Garden Inn Waterfront 780-0780, $160-350)*, Inn/B&B *(Wild Iris Inn 775-0224, $85-175)*

Recreation and Entertainment
OnSite: Picnic Area, Grills, Special Events *(4th of July barbecue - live band, great view of east promenade fireworks)* **1-3 mi:** Dive Shop, Tennis Courts *(Portland AC 781-2671)*, Movie Theater *(Nickelodeon 772-9751)*, Video Rental *(Movie Gallery 879-2414)*, Museum *(Portland Observatory 774-5561; Inst of Contemp Art 879-5742)*, Cultural Attract *(Portland Stage 774-1043)* **3+ mi:** Golf Course *(Riverside Municipal G.C. 797-3524, 4 mi.)*

Provisioning and General Services
Under 1 mi: Convenience Store *(Cumberland 780-8032)*, Delicatessen *(City Deli 772-9620)*, Liquor Store *(ABC 767-3845)*, Library *(Portland 871-1700)*, Pharmacy *(Martin's Pt. 828-2402)* **1-3 mi:** Supermarket *(Hannaford 761-5967)*, Health Food *(Whole Foods 774-7711)*, Wine/Beer *(Old Port 772-9463)*, Farmers' Market *(Public Market 228-2056)*, Bank/ATM, Post Office, Hardware Store *(Maine Green 780-1500)*

Transportation
OnSite: Courtesy Car/Van **OnCall:** Rental Car *(Enterprise 772-0030)*, Taxi *(ABC 772-8685; American 749-1600)*, Airport Limo *(Airport Cab 899-5335)* **1-3 mi:** Bikes *(Back Bay 773-6906; Cycle Mania 774-2933)*, Ferry Service *(Casc Bay 774-7871 - to the islands)* **3+ mi:** Rail *(Amtrak 780-1000, 3.5 mi.)* **Airport:** Portland Int'l Jetport *(6 mi.)*

Medical Services
911 Service **Under 1 mi:** Doctor *(Martin's Point Health Care 828-2402)*, Dentist *(Community Dental 874-1028)* **1-3 mi:** Chiropractor *(Goulding 775-6782)*, Holistic Services *(Renew Day Spa 899-0109)*, Veterinarian *(Forest Avenue 797-7509)* **Hospital:** Mercy 879-3000 *(3 mi.)*

Setting -- In East Deering, just north of the Portland peninsula paralleling the old railroad bridge, an enormous breakwater protects the Maine Yacht Center's long, concrete U-shaped docks - 80 slips are edged by almost 1,800 feet of side-tie dockage. At the head of the docks, a massive concrete pier hosts the travelift bay and leads to the equally massive, two-story, pale-gray shed and office. The surrounding upland is largely residential.

Marina Notes -- CCM. Established in 2006. Limited transient space. Phone reservation preferred; credit card deposit required. Call on approach for line handling. Single & 3-phase to 100A. Pre-cast, Swedish-built, floating breakwater (990 ft long by 14 ft. wide) extends 4 ft beneath surface, weighs 650 tons - 100% effective system against wind waves. Wonderful window-walled boaters' & crew lounge with leather sofas, comfy arm chairs, tables and chairs, coffee service, Wi-Fi, even a spyglass - airy ambiance and great views. Ships' store with basic boating supplies, snacks, drinks. Well-supplied Parts dept, too. Known for refit work: 80-ton travelift, 8 ft. fairway channel, 31 ft. shed door. 37,000 sq. ft. indoor, heated storage & refit facility. 67 ft. X 21 ft. paint shed. Bathhouse: Attractive heads with beige quarry tile floors, separate handicap-accessible shower room with fiberglass surround, hair dryer. High-capacity washers/dryers.

Notable -- Veteran Manager Brian Harris has brought professional ocean racer refit expertise to Maine - the yard rebuilt Rich Wilson's Open 60 "Great American 3" for the Vendee Globe. The technical knowledge required for these light, powerful racing machines benefits all refits. While the boat is getting a make-over, it's a short cab ride to Old Port for traditional seafood restaurants, serious museums, quirky boutiques, live entertainment and the historic waterfront.

PHOTOS ON DVD: 24

Peaks Island Marina

98 Island Ave; Peaks Island, ME

Tel: (207) 766-5783 **VHF: Monitor** Ch. 9 **Talk** n/a
Fax: (207) 766-2507 **Alternate Tel:** n/a
Email: lplant@maine.rr.com **Web:** n/a
Nearest Town: Peaks Island **Tourist Info:** (207) 772-2811

Navigational Information

Lat: 43°39.317' **Long:** 070°11.967' **Tide:** 9 ft. **Current:** n/a **Chart:** 13292
Rep. Depths (*MLW*): Entry 35 ft. **Fuel Dock** 10 ft. **Max Slip/Moor** 10 ft./35 ft.
Access: Off the main Portland Channel, next to ferry dock

Marina Facilities *(In Season/Off Season)*

Fuel: *Diesel via Jerry Cans* - Gasoline, Diesel
Slips: 4 Total, 4 Transient **Max LOA:** 100 ft. **Max Beam:** n/a
Rate *(per ft.)*: **Day** $2.50* **Week** n/a **Month** n/a
Power: 30 amp n/a, **50 amp** n/a, **100 amp** n/a, **200 amp** n/a
Cable TV: No **Dockside Phone:** No
Dock Type: Floating, Alongside, Wood
Moorings: 10 Total, 5 Transient **Launch:** No, Dinghy Dock
Rate: Day $30 **Week** n/a **Month** n/a
Heads: None
Internet: No **Laundry:** None
Pump-Out: No **Fee:** n/a **Closed Heads:** Yes

Marina Operations

Owner/Manager: Danielle Plant **Dockmaster:** Same
In-Season: May-Oct, 9am-5pm **Off-Season:** Nov-Apr, Closed
After-Hours Arrival: Call in advance.
Reservations: Yes **Credit Cards:** Visa/MC
Discounts: None
Pets: Welcome **Handicap Access:** No

Marina Services and Boat Supplies

Services - Docking Assistance **Supplies - Near:** Ice *(Block, Cube)*, Propane *(Near laundromat)*

Boatyard Services

Nearest Yard: Portland Yacht Services (207) 774-1067

Restaurants and Accommodations

Near: Restaurant *(Peaks Island House 776-4400, L $8-17, D $15-19)*, *(Inn On Peaks Island Pub 766-5100, L $8-18, D $8-20, Owned by Shipyard Brewing)*, *(Peaks Island House 76-644-00 , L $8-15, D $15-19)*, *(Cockeyed Gull 76-628-00 , B $3-10, L $9-18, D $9-39, Deck with view of Fort Gorges-Sunsets! Korean influence)*, Snack Bar *(Downfront 766-5500, ice cream)*, *(Hanigan's Island Market 766-2351, take-out sandwiches & pizza)*, Lite Fare *(Peak's Café 766-2600, B & L $2-20 - Famous cinnamon buns)*, Inn/B&B *(Inn On Peaks Island 766-5100, $175-300)*, *(Peaks Island House 766-4406, $145-265)*, *(Eighth Maine Regiment Memorial 766-5086, $99-139)*

Recreation and Entertainment

Near: Jogging Paths, Boat Rentals *(Casco Bay Kayak Rentals 766-2650)*, Hike/Bike Trails *(4 miles around the island shore)*, Museum *(Fifth Maine Regiment 766-3330, Umbrella Cover Museum 766-4496 $2, Eighth Maine Regiment Memorial 766-5086)*, Tours *(Maine Island Kayaks 766-2373 $65/half day, $110/full day)*, Sightseeing *(Spirit of Peaks Island Tours 766-5514 $15/8, 11am, 1 & 3pm - by golf cart)*, Galleries *(10 - including Gem Gallery 766-5600, Handwoven Baskets, City Point View, K. Newell Crafts, Richard Boyd Pottery)*, Special Events *(Peaks Fest - 3rd wknd Jun, Island Art Walks - 4 Sats, June-Aug - 10 open galleries)* **Under 1 mi:** Park *(Peaks Island Land Preserve)* **1-3 mi:** Picnic Area **3+ mi:** Golf Course *(South Portland Golf Course 775-0005 - by ferry, 7 mi.)*

Provisioning and General Services

Near: Market *(Hannigan's Island Market 766-2351 Remarkably well-supplied)*, Wine/Beer *(Hannigan's)*, Liquor Store *(Hannigan's)*, Farmers' Market *(Wildnut Farm Market 680-9261 Sat 8:30am-12:30pm - organic produce, free-range chickens)*, Fishmonger *(Peaks Island Shellfish 766-2601 - Oysters)*, Lobster Pound *(Forest City Seafood)*, Bank/ATM *(Maine Bank & Trust)*, Protestant Church *(St. Christopher, Brackett United Methodist, Memorial United, P.I. Baptist, Holy Trinity Espicopal at Brackett)*, Library *(Portland 766-5540 - in community building)*, Laundry, Newsstand *(Hannigan's)*, Copies Etc. *(Library)* **1-3 mi:** Pharmacy *(Rite Aid 774-0344 - Portland)* **3+ mi:** Supermarket *(Hannaford 799-7359, 6 mi.)*

Transportation

OnCall: Water Taxi *(Island 799-1818; Presumpscot 879-2562; Portland Express 415-8493 - to 6 pass. $50 1-way day, $80 night)* **Near:** Bikes *(Brady & Wyatts 766.5631)*, Ferry Service *(Casco Bay Line to Portland - 14 RTs a day in summer 6:15am-11:30pm $7.70/3.85 RT)*

Medical Services

911 Service **OnCall:** Ambulance *(Peaks Island CERT Community Emergency Response Team - 21 volunteers 781/962-2662)* **Near:** Doctor *(Peaks Island Health Center 766-2929)*, Veterinarian *(Island Veterinary Service 772-3885 Weekly on boat at Public Landing)* **Hospital:** Mercy 879-3000 - by ferry *(4 mi.)*

PHOTOS ON DVD: 21

Setting -- Across from the 19th-Century Fort Gorges, Peaks Island Marina is on the west side near the massive Forest City ferry wharf and Town Landing lettered "Peak's" in red. A bright yellow "Fuel" sign resting on a green tank and a large dredge mark the marina. A network of docks float just below the village's cluster of quirky shops, inns, gallleries and eateries. Most of the small island community's services and amenities are a short walk.

Marina Notes -- *$2.50/ft. - 20ft minimum for overnight stays with reservations. Limited dock space, call ahead (Ch. 9 monitored irregularly). Gas onsite but diesel at top of hill - take jerry cans. Lunch tie-ups or afternoon visits - under 36ft, $10/hr, over 36ft, $20/hr. Mooring day-rentals based on availability. Few services - fuel, small shop. No power. Bathhouse: None. Note: Add'l dockage at Jones Landing (766-5652) mostly seasonal, but check.

Notable -- About 1,000 year-rounders and 5,000 summer residents make this three-square-mile island a lively place. Coastal views, an artsy vibe, the charming village and the almost hourly ferry service also make it a popular summer day trip - the ferry's been making the 20-minute passage to Portland since 1880. Rent a bike from Brad & Wyatt's sweet little shop to circle the island on the five-mile paved waterfront path - great ocean views from largely undeveloped Backshore or climb up to Battery Steele. Or take an organized golf cart or kayak tour. Stop at the Fifth Maine Regiment Museum, C. 1888, which houses the state's largest Civil War collection, and the Eighth Maine Regiment Memorial. Stroll Island Avenue's shops and peruse the bulletin board at Hannigan's Market for highlights of the latest happenings - including the popular Sunday reggae concerts at Jones Landing and the occasional Saturday Peaks Arts Walks.

   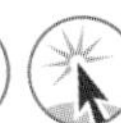 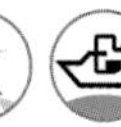  

Navigational Information
Lat: 43°39.005' **Long:** 070°13.883' **Tide:** 9 ft. **Current:** 1 kt. **Chart:** 13292
Rep. Depths (*MLW*): Entry 10 ft. **Fuel Dock** 8 ft. **Max Slip/Moor** 10 ft./-
Access: Casco Bay to Portland Harbor east of breakwater

Marina Facilities *(In Season/Off Season)*
Fuel: Gasoline, Diesel, High-Speed Pumps
Slips: 265 Total, 30 Transient **Max LOA:** 175 ft. **Max Beam:** n/a
Rate *(per ft.)*: **Day** $2.50/Inq.* **Week** $12.50-15 **Month** n/a
Power: 30 amp $8, **50 amp** $8, **100 amp** $15, **200 amp** n/a
Cable TV: Yes, Incl. **Dockside Phone:** No
Dock Type: Floating, Long Fingers, Alongside, Concrete, Wood
Moorings: 0 Total, 0 Transient **Launch:** n/a
Rate: Day n/a **Week** n/a **Month** n/a
Heads: 4 Toilet(s), 4 Shower(s)
Internet: Yes *(Wi-Fi, Free)* **Laundry:** 2 Washer(s), 2 Dryer(s)
Pump-Out: OnSite, OnCall, Full Service **Fee:** $10 **Closed Heads:** No

Marina Operations
Owner/Manager: Mike Soucy **Dockmaster:** Josh Gosselin
In-Season: Apr-Oct 1, 8am-8pm **Off-Season:** Oct 1-Apr 1, 8am-4pm
After-Hours Arrival: Call ahead
Reservations: Yes, Preferred **Credit Cards:** Visa/MC, Dscvr, Amex
Discounts: Volume Discount **Dockage:** n/a **Fuel:** n/a **Repair:** n/a
Pets: Welcome, Dog Walk Area **Handicap Access:** Yes, Heads, Docks

Spring Point Marina

PO Box 2350; 1 Spring Point Drive; South Portland, ME 04106

Tel: (207) 767-3254; (800) 262-8652 **VHF: Monitor** Ch. 9 **Talk** Ch. 69
Fax: (207) 767-5940 **Alternate Tel:** (207) 289-0500
Email: spmarina@portharbormarine.com **Web:** www.portharbormarine.com
Nearest Town: Portland *(3 mi.)* **Tourist Info:** (207) 772-2811

Marina Services and Boat Supplies
Services - Docking Assistance, Room Service to the Boat, Security, Dock Carts **Communication -** Mail & Package Hold, Phone Messages, FedEx, DHL, UPS, Express Mail **Supplies - OnSite:** Ice *(Block, Cube)*, Ships' Store, Marine Discount Store, Bait/Tackle **1-3 mi:** West Marine *(761-7600)*, Propane *(Advantage Gases & Tools 797-0840)*, CNG *(Advantage)*

Boatyard Services
OnSite: Travelift *(35T)*, Forklift *(10T)*, Hydraulic Trailer, Engine mechanic *(gas, diesel)*, Electrical Repairs, Electronic Sales, Electronics Repairs, Hull Repairs, Canvas Work, Bottom Cleaning, Brightwork, Compound, Wash & Wax, Painting, Yacht Broker **OnCall:** Crane, Divers, Air Conditioning, Refrigeration, Interior Cleaning, Propeller Repairs, Inflatable Repairs, Upholstery **Near:** Launching Ramp, Metal Fabrication. **Dealer for:** Sea Ray, Grady White, Boston Whaler, Sailfish, Triumph, Yamaha, Mercury, Mercruiser, Albemarle & Zodiac. **Member:** ABYC **Yard Rates:** $95/hr., Haul & Launch $6.50/ft. **Storage:** In-Water $106/ft., On-Land $50/ft

Restaurants and Accommodations
OnSite: Restaurant *(Joe's Boathouse 741-2780, L $10-16, D $18-28, Sun Brunch $8-16, Lobsters $23/lb.)* **OnCall:** Pizzeria *(Pizza Joint 767-3220)* **Near:** Lite Fare *(158 Pickett St. Cafe 799-8998, renowned bagels)*, Condo/Cottage *(Breakwater 799-1549)* **Under 1 mi:** Restaurant *(David's 388 347-7388, D $14, 6 tables, $8 apps, $14 mains)*, *(Salt Water Grill 799-5400, L $7-10, D $10-23)* **1-3 mi:** Restaurant *(Beale St. BBQ 767-0130, L $7-10, D $12-18)*, Fast Food *(McD's, Wendy's, Dunkin')*, Lite Fare *(Mr. Bagel 767-4756)*, Motel *(Maine Motel 774-8284, $50-100)*, Hotel *(Portland Regency 774-4200, $120-270)*, Inn/B&B *(Inn by the Sea 799-3134, $400-500)*

Recreation and Entertainment
OnSite: Picnic Area, Grills, Boat Rentals, Fishing Charter *(Reel Action 671-2979)* **Near:** Beach, Park **Under 1 mi:** Playground, Tennis Courts, Video Rental *(Blockbuster 741-2713)* **1-3 mi:** Golf Course *(Sable Oaks 775-6257)*, Fitness Center *(Snap 799-0864)*, Movie Theater *(Nickelodeon 772-9751)*, Museum *(Portland Head Light 799-2661, $2/1, 10am-4pm)*

Provisioning and General Services
Under 1 mi: Convenience Store *(Broadway Getty 799-6421)*, Hardware Store *(True Value 799-6191)* **1-3 mi:** Supermarket *(Hannaford 799-7359)*, Delicatessen, Wine/Beer *(Hannaford)*, Liquor Store, Farmers' Market *(Sun 9am-3pm, 15 Ocean St. 221-0404)*, Bank/ATM *(Bank of America)*, Post Office *(871-8451)*, Catholic Church *(772-7489)*, Protestant Church, Library, Beauty Salon *(Peinado 741-2500)*, Barber Shop *(Haircuts 767-7332)*, Dry Cleaners *(799-2960)*, Bookstore *(Nonesuch 799-2659)*, Pharmacy *(Rite Aid 799-2261)*, Copies Etc. *(UPS 767-1826)*

Transportation
OnCall: Water Taxi *(Portland Exp. 451-8493)*, Rental Car *(Enterprise 772-0030)*, Taxi *(American 749-1600)*, Airport Limo *(ABC 772-8685)* **Near:** Local Bus *(774-0351)* **1-3 mi:** Bikes *(Cycle Mania 774-2933)*, Rail *(Boston)*, Ferry Service *(to local islands 774-7871)* **Airport:** Portland Int'l. *(5 mi.)*

Medical Services
911 Service **Under 1 mi:** Doctor *(Sabean 767-2146)*, Dentist, Holistic Services *(Serenity 846-9696)*, Veterinarian *(Cape 799-2188)* **1-3 mi:** Chiropractor *(Healing Arts 799-0972)* **Hospital:** Mercy 879-3000 *(3 mi.)*

Setting -- Nestled between the Spring Point Ledge Light breakwater and a massive tanker unloading terminal, Port Harbor's Spring Point Marina sits just outside the entrance to Portland Harbor. Eight docks berth 250 slips plus a 350-foot face dock. At the head of the pier, dining decks line the contemporary, gray-shingled Joe's Boathouse and Dockhouse - backed by a large gray boat shed. The outer slips look at the Caso Bay's islands and 1866 Fort Gorges.

Marina Notes -- *Up to 40 ft. $2.50/ft. 41 ft + $3/ft. On approach - slips to port, fuel station & side-tie to starboard. Formerly South Portland Shipyard, active in WWII. Buildings converted from a cannery in 1965 - now largest marina in Maine. Full-service BY. Large chandlery. Self-serve fueling 5am-10pm, full-serve dockhouse 8am-5pm Mon-Thu, 8am-8pm Fri-Sun. Hosts 4 fishing tournaments, a poker run & two boat shows. Also manages adjacent Breakwater Marina dockominiums. Special events up to 60 in Joe's Dockhouse $250 plus meals. Bathhouse: Full baths with tiled floors. Laundry - separate building behind Joe's.

Notable -- Dine inside or out at Joe's Boathouse Restaurant with views of the marina and out to the bay; they'll even deliver to the boat. (Mon-Sat 11am-3pm, 5-9:30pm, Sun 9am-3pm, 5-9pm). Kids feed the seals and fish right off the docks. Or, on the site of Fort Preble, lunch at Southern Maine Community College's Culinary Arts Dining Room (Wed-Fri $12) and check out McKernan Hospitality Center's spectacular bay-front spaces for club cruise events. Two miles south, on Cape Elizabeth, the iconic Portland Head Light has famously protected the harbor since 1787. The former Keeps Quarters, now a museum, houses a fresnel lens collection and historic exhibits. Beautiful 90-acre Fort Williams Park surrounds the light with hiking trails, picnic areas, playing fields, tennis courts & beach.

PHOTOS ON DVD: 23

Portland Yacht Services

Portland Yacht Services

58 Fore Street; Portland, ME 04101

Tel: (207) 774-1067 **VHF: Monitor** Ch. 9 **Talk** Ch. 10
Fax: (207) 774-7035 **Alternate Tel:** n/a
Email: service@portlandyacht.com **Web:** www.PortlandYacht.com
Nearest Town: Portland *(0 mi.)* **Tourist Info:** (207) 772-2811

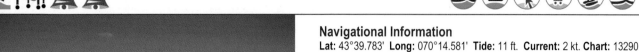

Navigational Information

Lat: 43°39.783' **Long:** 070°14.581' **Tide:** 11 ft. **Current:** 2 kt. **Chart:** 13290
Rep. Depths (*MLW*): Entry 30 ft. **Fuel Dock** n/a **Max Slip/Moor** 20 ft./40 ft.
Access: North side of Portland Harbor

Marina Facilities *(In Season/Off Season)*

Fuel: No
Slips: 128 Total, 10 Transient **Max LOA:** 150 ft. **Max Beam:** n/a
Rate *(per ft.)*: **Day** $1.75/Inq. **Week** Inq. **Month** Inq.
Power: 30 amp Incl., **50 amp** Incl., **100 amp** $3, **200 amp** n/a
Cable TV: No **Dockside Phone:** No
Dock Type: Floating, Long Fingers, Short Fingers, Pilings, Alongside, Wood
Moorings: 24 Total, 18 Transient **Launch:** No, Dinghy Dock
Rate: Day $45 **Week** $250 **Month** n/a
Heads: 5 Toilet(s), 5 Shower(s) *(dressing rooms)*
Internet: Yes *(Wi-Fi, Free)* **Laundry:** 1 Washer(s), 1 Dryer(s)
Pump-Out: Full Service, 1 Central **Fee:** $5 **Closed Heads:** No

Marina Operations

Owner/Manager: Jason Curtis **Dockmaster:** Matthew Ridgway
In-Season: May 15-Oct 15, 8am-7pm **Off-Season:** Oct 16-May 14, 8am-5pm
After-Hours Arrival: Call ahead
Reservations: Yes, Preferred **Credit Cards:** Visa/MC
Discounts: None
Pets: Welcome, Dog Walk Area **Handicap Access:** Yes, Heads, Docks

Marina Services and Boat Supplies

Services - Docking Assistance, Concierge, Boaters' Lounge, Security *(24, Cameras)*, Trash Pick-Up, Dock Carts, European Voltage **Communication -** Mail & Package Hold, Fax in/out, FedEx, DHL, UPS **Supplies - OnSite:** Ice *(Block, Cube)*, Ships' Store **Near:** Marine Discount Store *(Hamilton 774-1772)*, Bait/Tackle *(Tackle Shop 773-3474)* **1-3 mi:** West Marine *(761-7600)*, Propane *(U-Haul)*, CNG *(Portland Welding)*

Boatyard Services

OnSite: Forklift, Crane, Hydraulic Trailer *(35T)*, Launching Ramp, Engine mechanic *(gas, diesel)*, Electrical Repairs, Electronic Sales, Electronics Repairs, Hull Repairs, Rigger, Sail Loft, Canvas Work, Divers, Bottom Cleaning, Brightwork, Air Conditioning, Refrigeration, Compound, Wash & Wax, Woodworking, Metal Fabrication, Painting, Awlgrip, Total Refits **OnCall:** Interior Cleaning, Propeller Repairs, Upholstery **Near:** Inflatable Repairs *(Chase Leavitt)*, Life Raft Service. **Dealer for:** Crusader, Mercruiser, Nanni, OMC, Perkins, Volvo, Westerbeke, Yanmar, Johnson, Evinrude, Mercury, Suzuki, Bombardier, Nanni Diesel, etc. **Member:** ABBRA, ABYC - 20 Certified Tech(s) **Yard Rates:** $80/hr., Haul & Launch $8.50-11.50/ft. *(blocking $25/stand)*, Power Wash $4/ft., Bottom Paint $14-18/ft. **Storage:** On-Land Out: $4/sq.ft. In: $7/sq.ft., Heated: $13/sq.ft.

Restaurants and Accommodations

Near: Restaurant *(Bar Lola 775-5565, D $8-18)*, *(Front Room 773-3366, B $4-9, L $4-9, D $6-19)*, *(Hugo's 774-8538, D $21-24)*, *(Village Café 772-5320, D $18-35)*, *(Gilbert's Chowder 871-5636, L & D $6-20)*, *(Benkay 773-5555, L $7-17, D $11-25, Omakase $35-45)*, Lite Fare *(Duck Fat 774-8080, $6-13 Paninis)*, Hotel *(Hilton Garden 780-0780, $160-350)*, *(Residence Inn 761-1660)* **Under 1 mi:** Restaurant *(Back Bay Grill 772-8833, D $18-33)*, *(Street & Co. 775-0887, D $18-29)*

Recreation and Entertainment

OnSite: Picnic Area, Grills, Boat Rentals *(Small sailboats)*, Hike/Bike Trails *(Eastern Prom)*, Museum *(Maine R.R. 828-0814 $10/6)* **Near:** Beach *(East End)*, Playground, Tennis Courts, Park *(Ft. Allen)*, Sightseeing *(Portland Observatory 774-5661)* **Under 1 mi:** Fitness Center *(Portland Regency Hotel Spa 871-7054)*, Movie Theater *(Nickelodeon 772-9751)*, Video Rental *(Videoport 773-1999)* **3+ mi:** Golf Course *(S. Portland 775-0005, 4 mi.)*

Provisioning and General Services

Near: Convenience Store *(7-11)*, Market *(Micucci's Italian 775-1854)*, Bakery *(2 Fat Cats 347-5144)*, Fishmonger *(3 Sons 761-0825)*, Bank/ATM, Post Office, Catholic Church, Protestant Church, Synagogue, Library *(772-4581)*, Beauty Salon, Dry Cleaners, Pharmacy *(Rite Aid 774-0344)*, Copies Etc. *(Express 775-2444)* **Under 1 mi:** Supermarket *(Whole Foods 774-7711, Del.)*, Wine/Beer *(Downeast 828-2337)*, Liquor Store *(Downeast)*, Farmers' Market *(Wed, Monument Sq.)*

Transportation

OnCall: Water Taxi *(415-8493)*, Rental Car *(Enterprise 772-0030)*, Taxi *(ABC 772-8685)* **Near:** Bikes *(Cycle Mania 774-2933)*, Local Bus *(Explorer 774-9891, Metro 774-0351)* **Airport:** Portland Int'l. *(5 mi.)*

Medical Services

911 Service **Under 1 mi:** Doctor, Dentist, Chiropractor **1-3 mi:** Veterinarian *(Brackett St.)* **Hospital:** Maine Medical 662-0111 *(1 mi.)*

PHOTOS ON DVD: 24

Setting -- At the mouth of the Fore River, between East End Beach and the Casco Bay Ferry Terminal, the Portland Company Complex spans over 10 waterfront acres. PYS's three sets of well-maintained, wooden docks and its "just offshore" mooring field lead to a quasi-industrial, rustic upland. Large, re-purposed brick locomotive factory buildings and antique trains dot the interior - just beyond the Eastern Prominade Trail and narrow guage railroad tracks.

Marina Notes -- CCM. Founded in 1981. 400 ft. transient dockage. 22 ft. mlw plus 9 ft. of tide. 4,000-lb. moorings. 30, 50 & 100A power. Full-service yard with two full-time riggers & many other specialists - wood, fiberglass, composites. 3 hydraulic trailers haul to 40 tons. Ships' store carries odd parts. More than a dozen other services in complex: N.E. Fiberglass (773-3537), Navigator Publishing - "Ocean Navigator" & "Professional Mariner" (772-2466), Maine Learning Center's Coast Guard Licensing Courses. Maine Boatbuilders Show & parking. Bathhouse: Small, old heads. Or use museum's when it's open.

Notable -- For railroad buffs, the onsite Maine Narrow Gauge Railroad Co. & Museum (828-0814) houses a fascinating collection of locomotives and coaches used from 1878-1945. Daily excursions along Casco Bay, using the museum's exhibits, on the hour, 10am-Noon & 2-4pm. The 2.1-mile waterfront Eastern Prom Trail runs right along the marina waterfront heading around the point past Ft. Allen Park and East End Beach. Or walk inland to the red wooden Portland Observatory Maritime Signal Tower at the top of Munjoy Hill - 103 steps up for a birds' eye view. Also near are the well-preserved U.S. Customs House and daily fish auction at Maine State Pier. It's less than a mile to Old Port's entertainment, boutiques, restaurants, micro brews, markets, galleries and museums.

    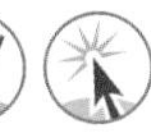 

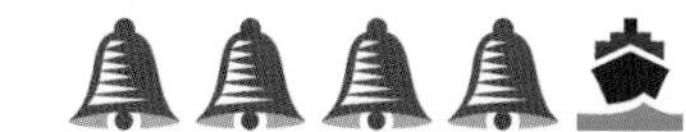

DiMillo's Old Port Marina

Navigational Information

Lat: 43°39.276' **Long:** 070°15.039' **Tide:** 9 ft. **Current:** 1 kt. **Chart:** 13290
Rep. Depths (*MLW*): Entry 30 ft. **Fuel Dock** 30 ft. **Max Slip/Moor** 30 ft./-
Access: Portland Harbor, north side

Marina Facilities *(In Season/Off Season)*

Fuel: Slip-Side Fueling, Gasoline, Diesel
Slips: 120 Total, 15 Transient **Max LOA:** 250 ft. **Max Beam:** n/a
Rate *(per ft.)*: **Day** $3.95/$1.50* **Week** Inq. **Month** $15-22
Power: 30 amp $10, **50 amp** $20, **100 amp** $40, **200 amp** n/a
Cable TV: Yes, Incl. **Dockside Phone:** Yes, Inq.
Dock Type: Floating, Long Fingers, Pilings, Concrete, Wood, Composition
Moorings: 0 Total, 0 Transient **Launch:** n/a
Rate: Day n/a **Week** n/a **Month** n/a
Heads: 2 Toilet(s), 2 Shower(s)
Internet: Yes *(Office)* **Laundry:** 2 Washer(s), 2 Dryer(s)
Pump-Out: OnSite, Full Service, Self Service **Fee:** $5 **Closed Heads:** No

Marina Operations

Owner/Manager: Sarah Foshay **Dockmaster:** Same
In-Season: May-Sept, 7am-9pm **Off-Season:** Oct-Apr, 8am-9pm
After-Hours Arrival: Call ahead for instruction
Reservations: Required **Credit Cards:** Visa/MC, Dscvr, Amex
Discounts: None **Dockage:** n/a **Fuel:** Volume **Repair:** n/a
Pets: Welcome, Dog Walk Area **Handicap Access:** No

DiMillo's Old Port Marina

1 Long Wharf; Portland, ME 04101

Tel: (207) 773-7632 **VHF: Monitor** Ch. 9 **Talk** Ch. 71
Fax: (207) 699-2777 **Alternate Tel:** n/a
Email: sarah@dimillos.com **Web:** www.dimillos.com
Nearest Town: Portland *(0 mi.)* **Tourist Info:** (207) 772-2811

Marina Services and Boat Supplies

Services - Docking Assistance, Security *(Security cameras)*, Dock Carts **Communication -** Pay Phone (2), FedEx, DHL, UPS *(Sat Del)* **Supplies - OnSite:** Ice *(Block, Cube)* **Near:** Ships' Store *(Hamilton Marine 774-1772, Vessel Services 772-5718)*, West Marine *(761-7600)* **Under 1 mi:** Bait/Tackle *(Bait Lady 871-0551)*, Propane

Boatyard Services

OnSite: Yacht Broker **OnCall:** Divers **Near:** Travelift *(150T)*, Railway, Launching Ramp, Engine mechanic *(gas, diesel)*, Electrical Repairs, Electronic Sales, Electronics Repairs, Rigger, Sail Loft, Brightwork, Air Conditioning, Refrigeration, Propeller Repairs, Inflatable Repairs. **Nearest Yard:** Gowen Marine (207) 773-1761

Restaurants and Accommodations

OnSite: Restaurant *(DiMillo's Floating Restaurant 772-2216, L $7-15, D $18-35, Kids' $4-8)* **Near:** Restaurant *(Portland Lobster 775-2112)*, *(Vignola 772-1330, D $11-21, Sun Brunch $11-15)*, *(Street & Co., 775-0887, D $15-25)*, *(Fore Street 775-2717, D $25-30)*, Seafood Shack *(J's Oyster 772-4828, L $8-12, D $10-17)*, Lite Fare *(Black Tie 756-6230, L $8-12)*, *(Market Street Eats 773-3135)*, *(Gritty McDuff 772-2739, $8-13 Brew Pub)*, *(Becky's Diner 773-7070, B $4-8, L $4-12, D $4-20, 4am+)*, Pizzeria *(Bill's 774-6166)*, Hotel *(Portland Harbor 775-9090, $140-330)*, *(Regency 774-4200, $120-270)*

Recreation and Entertainment

OnSite: Fishing Charter **Near:** Dive Shop, Fitness Center, Hike/Bike Trails *(Harbor Walk)*, Party Boat, Movie Theater *(Nickelodeon 772-9751)*, Video Rental *(Videoport 773-1999)*, Tours *(Trolley 774-0808 $18)*, Galleries *(Maine Potters 774-1633)* **Under 1 mi:** Heated Pool *("Y" 874-1111)*, Beach *(East End)*, Picnic Area *(Eastern Prom)*, Playground, Tennis Courts *(Eastern Prom)*, Museum *(Victoria Mansion 772-4841; Longfellow House 774-1822; Children's 828-1234 $9; Portland Museum of Art 775-6148 $10/4)*, Cultural Attract *(Portland Stage 774-0465)* **3+ mi:** Golf Course *(Sable Oaks 775-6257, 4 mi.)*

Provisioning and General Services

OnSite: Lobster Pound, Bank/ATM, Copies Etc. **OnCall:** Dry Cleaners, Laundry *(Same Day)* **Near:** Convenience Store *(Dead River 773-5841)*, Health Food, Wine/Beer *(Old Port 772-9463)*, Bakery, Farmers' Market *(Monument Sq. Wed, 7am-2pm, Deering Oaks Sat 7am-Noon 883-5750)*, Fishmonger *(Harbor 775-0251)*, Post Office, Catholic Church, Protestant Church, Synagogue, Library *(Portland 871-1700)*, Beauty Salon, Barber Shop, Bookstore, Pharmacy *(Rite Aid 774-0344)*, Hardware Store **Under 1 mi:** Supermarket *(Whole Foods 774-7711)*, Liquor Store *(ABC 767-3845)*

Transportation

OnCall: Water Taxi *(Portland Exp.)*, Rental Car *(Hertz 797-7156)*, Taxi *(ASAP 791-ASAP)* **Near:** Bikes *(Cycle-Mania 774-2933)*, Local Bus *(Metro 774-0351)*, InterCity Bus *(Trailways/Greyhound)*, Ferry Service *(Casco Bay Ferry)* **1-3 mi:** Rail *(to Boston)* **Airport:** Portland Int'l. *(5 mi.)*

Medical Services

911 Service **Near:** Doctor *(Scamman 772-6710)*, Dentist *(Young 874-1055)*, Chiropractor *(Old Port 871-0787)*, Holistic Services *(Paradiso 879-7414)* **Under 1 mi:** Veterinarian *(Brackett St. 772-3385)* **Hospital:** Mercy 879-3000 *(1 mi.)*

Setting -- On Long Wharf, in the midst of Portland's vibrant Old Port neighborhood, the marina's docks lie alongside a hard-to-miss, stylishly converted 206-foot, blue-and-white car ferry - DiMillo's Floating Restaurant. It divides the marina into East Side with five docks berthing 100 slips and a long fuel/face dock and West Side with 20 slips. The marina office, shop and bathhouse are on the ferry's landside. Bustling Portland Pier and Chandler Wharf flank the docks.

Marina Notes -- CCM *$2.95 to 39 ft. $3.95 40 ft. up. 30 ft. min. Built in 1978 by Tony DiMillo. DiMillo's on the Waterfront restaurant moved to the ferry in 1982. Reserve in July & August. Helpful Welcome Package - maps, guides, local mags. Service-focused staff, many liveaboards. Volume fuel discounts, 24-hr. credit card pumps. 24-hr. token-operated pump-out. Oil disposal. Piling breakwater slows roll; closer to the shore, quieter the ride. Bathhouse: Nicely renovated brown & white ceramic tiled full baths. Navy ceramic tiled handicap shower. Matching laundry - 2 stacked washers & dryers, soap dispenser, book swap.

Notable -- The 700-ton floating restaurant, with a cruise-ship ambiance and massive 65-foot beam, seats over 600 guests in the First Deck Dining Room, Port Side Lounge, Second Deck Dining Rooms and three Outside Decks - all with marina or harbor views (no reservations but call to be added to wait list half hour before leaving the boat). Banquet service and event spaces ($150-$1000 room fee) make it a good club cruise destination. Portland is the arts and culture center of Maine, and this heart-of-the-action location puts it all within a short walk - 150 shops, 55 restaurants and pubs, 30 galleries, plus concerts, museums, theaters and top-tier hotels. Don't miss First Friday Art walks, the annual Old Port Festival on June's 2nd Sunday, and the Casco Islands' ferry down the street.

PHOTOS ON DVD: 25

Sunset Marina

231 Front Street; South Portland, ME 04106

Tel: (207) 767-4729 **VHF: Monitor** Ch. 9 **Talk** Ch. 12
Fax: (207) 767-4721 **Alternate Tel:** n/a
Email: sunset@maine.rr.com **Web:** www.sunset-marina.com
Nearest Town: Portland *(1 mi.)* **Tourist Info:** (207) 772-2811

Navigational Information

Lat: 43°39.030' **Long:** 070°14.560' **Tide:** 10 ft. **Current:** 1 kt. **Chart:** 13292
Rep. Depths (*MLW*): Entry 20 ft. **Fuel Dock** 10 ft. **Max Slip/Moor** 20 ft./-
Access: Casco Bay to Portland Harbor, first facility on port side

Marina Facilities *(In Season/Off Season)*

Fuel: Slip-Side Fueling, Gasoline, Diesel, High-Speed Pumps
Slips: 150 Total, 20 Transient **Max LOA:** 250 ft. **Max Beam:** 20 ft.
Rate *(per ft.)*: **Day** $2.25/n/a **Week** 10.00 **Month** 28
Power: 30 amp $3, **50 amp** $5, **100 amp** n/a, **200 amp** n/a
Cable TV: No **Dockside Phone:** No
Dock Type: Floating, Long Fingers, Pilings, Alongside, Wood
Moorings: 0 Total, 0 Transient **Launch:** n/a, Dinghy Dock
Rate: Day n/a **Week** n/a **Month** n/a
Heads: 2 Toilet(s), 2 Shower(s) *(dressing rooms)*, Hair Dryers
Internet: Yes *(Wi-Fi, Free)* **Laundry:** 2 Washer(s), 2 Dryer(s)
Pump-Out: OnSite, Self Service, 1 Central **Fee:** $5 **Closed Heads:** Yes

Marina Operations

Owner/Manager: Daniel & Elaine Lilley **Dockmaster:** Same
In-Season: May-Oct, 8am-8pm **Off-Season:** Nov-Apr, Closed
After-Hours Arrival: Call ahead for instructions
Reservations: Yes, Preferred **Credit Cards:** Visa/MC, Dscvr, Amex
Discounts: None
Pets: Welcome **Handicap Access:** No

Marina Services and Boat Supplies

Services - Docking Assistance, Security *(24 Hrs., Closed Circuit TV)*, Trash Pick-Up, Dock Carts **Communication -** Mail & Package Hold, Fax in/out *(Free)*, FedEx, DHL, UPS, Express Mail **Supplies - OnSite:** Ice *(Block, Cube)* **Near:** Ships' Store *(South Port Marine)* **Under 1 mi:** West Marine *(761-7600)* **1-3 mi:** Propane *(Advantage 797-0840)*, CNG *(Advantage)*

Boatyard Services

OnSite: Engine mechanic *(gas, diesel)*, Electrical Repairs, Electronics Repairs, Divers, Bottom Cleaning **OnCall:** Forklift, Crane, Hydraulic Trailer, Compound, Wash & Wax, Propeller Repairs, Inflatable Repairs, Upholstery, Metal Fabrication **Near:** Air Conditioning, Refrigeration. **Yard Rates:** $70/hr., Haul & Launch $8/ft. *(blocking incl.)*, Power Wash Incl. **Storage:** In-Water $2/ft., On-Land $33/ft. incl. H&L

Restaurants and Accommodations

OnSite: Restaurant *(Salt Water Grille 799-5400, L $10-17, D $18-26, Bar menu $10-18)* **OnCall:** Pizzeria *(Pizza Hut 799-0455)* **Under 1 mi:** Restaurant *(Snow Squall 799-0811, B $6-12, L $9-12, D $9-22, Happy hour Wed-Fri, 5-7)*, *(Fresh! 699-2646, L & D)*, *(Joe's Boathouse 741-2780)*, *(David's 388 347-7388, D $14, 6 tables, $8 apps - excellent)*, *(Zeta Cafe 541-9382)*, Fast Food *(Subway)* **1-3 mi:** Hotel *(Portland Harbor 798-9090, $180-340)*, *(Regency 774-4200, $120-270)*, *(Holiday Inn 775-2311, $110-170)*, Inn/B&B *(Pomegranate 772-1006, $95-235)*

Recreation and Entertainment

OnSite: Picnic Area, Grills **Near:** Playground, Jogging Paths *(Green Belt)*, Park *(Bug Light)* **Under 1 mi:** Beach *(Willard)*, Dive Shop *(Aqua 772-4200)*, Fitness Center *(Body of Work 741-5280)* **1-3 mi:** Tennis Courts *(Eastern Prom)*, Golf Course *(So. Portland 775-0005)*, Movie Theater *(Nickelodeon 772-9751)*, Video Rental *(Blockbuster 741-2713)*, Museum *(Museum of Art 775-6148 $10/2; Children's 828-1234 $9; Victoria Mansion 772-4841 $7/3)*, Cultural Attract *(PORTopera 879-7678 at Merrill Aud.)*

Provisioning and General Services

Near: Convenience Store *(Broadway Getty 799-6421)*, Delicatessen *(Anania's 774-8104 - wraps, pizzas, whoopie pies)*, Bank/ATM, Post Office, Catholic Church, Beauty Salon **Under 1 mi:** Supermarket *(Hannaford 799-7359)*, Gourmet Shop *(Browne 775-3118)*, Wine/Beer, Liquor Store *(ABC 767-3845)*, Bakery *(One Fifty Ate 799-8998)*, Farmers' Market *(Sun 9am-3pm, 15 Ocean St. 221-0404)*, Protestant Church, Library *(767-7660)*, Dry Cleaners, Bookstore *(Nonesuch 799-2659)*, Pharmacy *(Rite Aid 774-0344)* **1-3 mi:** Green Grocer *(Portland 761-9232)*, Fishmonger *(Free Range 774-8469)*, Lobster Pound *(Portland 699-2400)*, Synagogue, Hardware Store *(Drillen 799-4133)*, Copies Etc. *(UPS 767-1826)*

Transportation

OnCall: Water Taxi *(Preseumpscot 879-2562)*, Rental Car *(Enterprise 772-0030)*, Taxi *(ABC 772-8685)* **Near:** Local Bus *(774-0351)* **1-3 mi:** Bikes *(Gorham 773-1700)*, Rail *(Boston 780-1000)* **Airport:** Portland Int'l. *(5 mi.)*

Medical Services

911 Service **OnCall:** Ambulance **Near:** Holistic Services *(Serenity Day Spa 767-1946)* **Under 1 mi:** Doctor *(Freedman 799-8596)*, Dentist, Chiropractor *(Healing Arts 799-0972)*, Veterinarian *(Cape Vet Clinic 799-2788)* **Hospital:** Mercy 879-3000 *(2.5 mi.)*

Setting -- On the east shore of the Fore River, just past the magnificent Portland Breakwater (Bug) Lighthouse, Sunset sits directly across Portland Harbor from the historic Old Port district - easily identified by the adjacent green "storage tank farm." 770 feet of face dock form an "L-shaped" enclosure that protects five docks that host 150 slips. The single main pier leads from the dockhouse and fueling station to the marina office and the venerable Saltwater Grille's two-story, gray-shingled contemporary; porches and decks take advantage of the spectacular Portland skyline views and sunsets.

Marina Notes -- Owned/operated by the Lilley family since 1994, formerly Channel Crossing. 20 slips reserved for transients - to 250 ft. LOA. Marina maintains a dinghy dock in the heart of Old Port. Limited groceries and provisions onsite. Free Wi-Fi. Some onsite boatyard services and dry winter storage. Presumpcot Water Taxi $30 across harbor ($60 at night), $50 to islands to 6 pass. Bathhouse: Newly renovated heads, showers and laundry at marina office.

Notable -- At the head of the fairway, Mark Loring's Salt Water Grille serves Maine seafood in a large, airy, glass-walled dining room with amazing views. Get even closer to the view on the screened porch, furnished with contemporary wicker, or on the wide, umbrella-covered front deck. A short walk east, nine-acre Bug Light Park features the famous lighhouse, resembling a 4th-century Greek monument, plus a gift shop, small museum, and the Liberty Ship Memorial. The "Green Belt," a mile-long pedestrian walk along the South Portland waterfront, provides a shortcut to two shopping areas. It's also a quick dinghy or water taxi ride across the harbor to revitalized Old Port district for restuarnats, entertainment, sightseeing - and especially the Congress St. Downtown Arts District.

    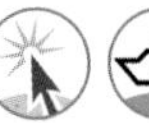 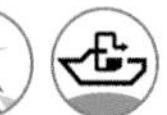

Navigational Information
Lat: 43°38.300' **Long:** 070°15.130' **Tide:** 9 ft. **Current:** 1 kt. **Chart:** 13292
Rep. Depths (*MLW*): **Entry** 8 ft. **Fuel Dock** 8 ft. **Max Slip/Moor** 13 ft./-
Access: Inner harbor by Casco Bay Bridge - 1 NM from Fore River mouth

Marina Facilities *(In Season/Off Season)*
Fuel: *Irving* - Gasoline, Diesel, High-Speed Pumps
Slips: 170 Total, 10 Transient **Max LOA:** 150 ft. **Max Beam:** 50 ft.
Rate *(per ft.)*: **Day** $1.75/Inq.* **Week** n/a/$12 **Month** n/a/$18
Power: 30 amp Incl., **50 amp** Incl., **100 amp** Incl., **200 amp** n/a
Cable TV: Yes, Incl. **Dockside Phone:** No
Dock Type: Floating, Long Fingers, Short Fingers, Pilings, Wood
Moorings: 0 Total, 0 Transient **Launch:** No
Rate: Day n/a **Week** n/a **Month** n/a
Heads: 2 Toilet(s), 2 Shower(s) *(dressing rooms)*
Internet: Yes *(Wi-Fi, Fee)* **Laundry:** 2 Washer(s), 2 Dryer(s)
Pump-Out: Self Service, 170 InSlip **Fee:** $5 **Closed Heads:** Yes

Marina Operations
Owner/Manager: Kip Reynolds **Dockmaster:** Eric Fortier
In-Season: MemDay-LabDay, 8am-6pm** **Off-Season:** Sep-May, 9am-5pm
After-Hours Arrival: Call in advance
Reservations: Yes, Preferred **Credit Cards:** Visa/MC, Dscvr
Discounts: Boat/US **Dockage:** 5% **Fuel:** n/a **Repair:** n/a
Pets: Welcome, Dog Walk Area **Handicap Access:** Yes, Heads, Docks

South Port Marine

14 Ocean Street; South Portland, ME 04106

Tel: (207) 799-8191 **VHF: Monitor** Ch.16 **Talk** Ch. 78
Fax: (207) 767-5937 **Alternate Tel:** n/a
Email: marina@southportmarine.com **Web:** www.southportmarine.com
Nearest Town: Portland *(0.25 mi.)* **Tourist Info:** (207) 772-2811

Marina Services and Boat Supplies
Services - Docking Assistance, Security *(24 hr., Police & TV monitor)*, Dock Carts, 3 Phase **Communication -** Mail & Package Hold, Fax in/out *($1)*, FedEx, DHL, UPS, Express Mail *(Sat Del)* **Supplies - OnSite:** Ice *(Block, Cube)*, Ships' Store, Live Bait **Under 1 mi:** Propane *(Advantage 772-3746)*, CNG *(Advantage)* **1-3 mi:** West Marine *(761-7600)*, Marine Discount Store *(Hamilton Marine)*

Boatyard Services
OnSite: Travelift *(16T)*, Forklift, Crane, Hydraulic Trailer *(35T)*, Launching Ramp, Engine mechanic *(gas, diesel)*, Electrical Repairs, Electronic Sales, Electronics Repairs, Hull Repairs, Rigger, Divers, Brightwork, Air Conditioning, Refrigeration, Compound, Wash & Wax, Interior Cleaning, Woodworking, Metal Fabrication, Painting, Awlgrip, Yacht Broker **OnCall:** Sail Loft, Canvas Work, Propeller Repairs, Inflatable Repairs, Upholstery **Dealer for:** Mercury, Mercruiser, Yamaha, Southport Boatworks, Scout Boats, Yanmar Engines, Echo Rowing Shells. **Member:** ABBRA, ABYC **Yard Rates:** $65-75/hr., Haul & Launch $8.50/ft., Power Wash $2.75/ft., Bottom Paint $11/ft. **Storage:** In-Water $97/ft., On-Land Inq.

Restaurants and Accommodations
OnSite: Restaurant *(Snow Squall 799-0811, L $9-12, D $9-22, Happy hour Wed-Fri, 5-7pm, Sun Brunch $6-12)* **OnCall:** Pizzeria *(Pizza Hut 799-0455)* **Near:** Restaurant *(Fresh! 699-2646, L & D)*, *(Bridgeway 799-5418)*, *(Zeta Cafe 409-5127)*, Pizzeria *(Papa Mios)* **Under 1 mi:** Restaurant *(Salt Water Grille 799-5400, L $7-10, D $18-26, Bar menu $10-18)*, *(Beale Street BBQ 767-0130, L & D $8-24)*, *(Thai Taste 767-4599, L $7-10, D $10-17)*, Hotel *(Holiday Inn 775-2311, $110-170)*, *(Regency 774-4200, $120-270)*

Recreation and Entertainment
OnSite: Picnic Area, Grills **Near:** Playground, Dive Shop, Fitness Center *(Ocean 767-1831)*, Video Rental *(Blockbuster 741-2713)*, Park *(Mill Creek)* **Under 1 mi:** Museum *(Victoria Mansion 772-4841 $15/5, Museum of Art 775-6148, Children's Museum 828-1234 $9, Museum of African Tribal Art 871-7188)*, Cultural Attract *(PORTopera 879-7678 at Merrill Aud.)* **1-3 mi:** Beach, Tennis Courts *(Eastern Promenade)*, Golf Course *(So. Portland 775-0005)*, Movie Theater *(Nickelodeon 772-9751)*

Provisioning and General Services
OnSite: Convenience Store, Wine/Beer, Lobster Pound **Near:** Supermarket *(Hannaford 799-7359)*, Delicatessen, Liquor Store *(ABC 767-3845)*, Bakery, Farmers' Market *(Sun 9am-3pm, 15 Ocean St.)*, Bank/ATM, Post Office, Catholic Church, Library *(767-7660)*, Beauty Salon, Dry Cleaners, Bookstore *(Nonesuch 799-2659)*, Pharmacy *(Rite Aid 799-2261)*, Hardware Store *(True-Value 799-6191)*, Retail Shops *(Waterfront Market/Mill Creek)*, Copies Etc. *(UPS 767-1826)* **Under 1 mi:** Gourmet Shop *(Aurora 871-9060)*, Green Grocer *(Portland 761-9232)*, Protestant Church **1-3 mi:** Synagogue

Transportation
OnCall: Water Taxi *(879-2562)*, Rental Car *(Enterprise 772-0030)*, Taxi *(S. Portland 767-5200)* **Near:** Local Bus **1-3 mi:** InterCity Bus *(Trailways 828-1151)*, Rail *(Boston)*, Ferry Service **Airport:** Portland Int'l. *(4 mi.)*

Medical Services
911 Service **OnCall:** Ambulance **Near:** Doctor *(Freedman 799-8596)*, Dentist, Holistic Services, Veterinarian *(Cape Vet Clinic 799-2788)* **Under 1 mi:** Chiropractor *(Healing Arts 799-0972)* **Hospital:** Mercy 879-3000 *(1 mi.)*

Setting -- Off the southside of Portland Harbor, well-manicured South Port is tucked into a very quiet basin protected by a dry storage peninsula. In the shadow of the nearby Casco Bay Bridge, four sets of docks surround the gray-sided, red-roofed Anchorage Place condominiums. A small dockside picnic area relaxes under a matched set of mature trees, and an arched bridge connects docks "A" and "C." The travelift bay sits at the head of the basin's narrow arm.

Marina Notes -- *under 42 ft. $1.75/ft. & over 43 ft. $2.50/ft. **In-season closes 5pm Sun-Wed, Off-season closes earlier on weekends. Owned by Reynolds Family since 1996. Reserve for July & Aug - up to 1 yr in advance. Token-operated 24-hr. pump-out. Full-service BY on adjacent peninsula with large work shed - 16-ton travelift hauls to 36T, 72 ft. Chandlery with a small convenience store. Bathhouse: Just past garden. Beige tile floor, glass-doored, fiberglass shower enclosure. New airy, bright laundry off to one side of ships' store. 2 washers & 2 stacked dryers, folding table, soap dispenser, book exchange, radio, brochures. Note: Stay in channel then follow private lighted red/green day markers on three pile clusters. 'No Wake Zone' - $100 fines.

Notable -- At the rear of the marina property, the Snow Squall Restaurant re-opened under new management, adding an attractive patio (Wed-Sat,11:30am-Close, Sun 8am-Close - Mon & Tue closed). The nearby Waterfront Market area, including Mill Creek Mall, promises many other eateries, shops, support services, and provisioning resources. 10-acre Mill Creek Park features a pond with fountain, rose garden, a gazebo and special events like summer concert and Art in the Park. A walk/bike ramp climbs from Knight park to the South Portland end of the Casco Bay Bridge's bike lane to Portland's Commercial Street.

PHOTOS ON DVD: 20

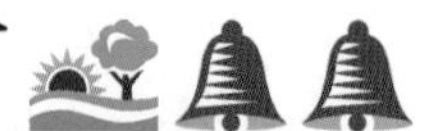

Chick's Marina

PO Box 2758; 75 Ocean Avenue; Kennebunkport, ME 04046

Tel: (207) 967-2782 **VHF: Monitor** Ch. 9 **Talk** Ch. 68
Fax: (207) 967-2034 **Alternate Tel:** n/a
Email: chicksmarina@roadrunner.com **Web:** www.chicksmarina.com
Nearest Town: Kennebunkport *(0.5 mi.)* **Tourist Info:** (207) 967-0857

Navigational Information

Lat: 43°21.180' **Long:** 070°28.440' **Tide:** 9 ft. **Current:** 3 kt. **Chart:** 13286
Rep. Depths (*MLW*): Entry 7 ft. **Fuel Dock** 7 ft. **Max Slip/Moor** 7 ft./-
Access: 0.5 mi. from Kennebunk R. entrance jetty, just off G13 to starboard

Marina Facilities *(In Season/Off Season)*

Fuel: Slip-Side Fueling, Gasoline, Diesel
Slips: 50 Total, 10 Transient **Max LOA:** 150 ft. **Max Beam:** n/a
Rate *(per ft.)*: **Day** $4.00* **Week** n/a **Month** n/a
Power: 30 amp $10, **50 amp** $20, **100 amp** $40, **200 amp** n/a
Cable TV: Yes, Incl. **Dockside Phone:** No
Dock Type: Floating, Short Fingers, Alongside, Wood
Moorings: 0 Total, 0 Transient **Launch:** n/a
Rate: Day n/a **Week** n/a **Month** n/a
Heads: 2 Toilet(s), 2 Shower(s) *(dressing rooms)*, Book Exchange
Internet: Yes *(Wi-Fi, Free)* **Laundry:** 1 Washer(s), 1 Dryer(s)
Pump-Out: OnSite **Fee:** $5 **Closed Heads:** Yes

Marina Operations

Owner/Manager: Lillian Fox **Dockmaster:** Same
In-Season: Jul-Sep, 8am-6pm **Off-Season:** Oct-Jun, 8am-4pm
After-Hours Arrival: Call first
Reservations: Yes, Preferred **Credit Cards:** Visa/MC, Amex
Discounts: None
Pets: Welcome, Dog Walk Area **Handicap Access:** No

Marina Services and Boat Supplies

Services - Docking Assistance, Security, Trash Pick-Up, Dock Carts **Communication -** Fax in/out, FedEx, UPS **Supplies - OnSite:** Ice *(Block, Cube)*, Ships' Store **3+ mi:** Propane *(Downeast 985-3154, 5 mi.)*

Boatyard Services

OnSite: Launching Ramp, Engine mechanic *(gas, diesel)*, Electrical Repairs, Electronic Sales, Brightwork, Compound, Wash & Wax, Interior Cleaning, Woodworking, Inflatable Repairs **OnCall:** Hydraulic Trailer, Sail Loft, Canvas Work, Divers, Air Conditioning, Refrigeration, Propeller Repairs

Restaurants and Accommodations

OnCall: Pizzeria *(Atlantic 967-0333)* **Near:** Restaurant *(95 Ocean at Nonantum 967-4050, D $12-30, Kids' $5-7, Sun Brunch $16, Pre-theater $20), (Striper's at Breakwater 967-5333, L $9-25, D $18-29, Lounge $9-14, Sun Br. $8-23)*, Seafood Shack *(Mabel's Lobster 967-2562, L $8-16, D $14-30)*, Hotel *(Nonantum Resort 967-4050, $130-260)*, Inn/B&B *(Captain Lord 967-3141, $150-500), (Yachtsman Lodge 967-2511, $170-350), (Breakwater Inn 967-3118, $150-475)* **Under 1 mi:** Restaurant *(Bandaloop 967-4994, D $17-29), (Alisson's 967-4841, L $9-15, D $9-23), (One Dock 967-2621, D $17-31, Small Plates $6-13), (Grissini 967-2211, D $18-29)*, Snack Bar *(Clam Shack 967-7321, Detour!)*, Hotel *(The Colony 967-3331, $150-800)* **1-3 mi:** Restaurant *(White Barn 967-2321, D $98, Prix Fixe)*

Recreation and Entertainment

OnSite: Picnic Area, Grills **Near:** Fishing Charter *(Cast-Away 284-1740)* **Under 1 mi:** Beach *(Arundel, Gooch's Beach - Trolley)*, Tennis Courts, Boat Rentals *(Harbor Adventures Kayaks 363-8466)*, Tours *(Nott House Guided Tours 967-2751, Free, Village Walking Tour $7 - 11am Thu., Self-Guided $4/book; Coastal Maine Kayak 967-6065)*, Sightseeing *(First Chance 967-5507 Whale Watch $48/28, Lobster Tour $20/15)* **1-3 mi:** Golf Course *(Cape Arundel 967-3494)*, Horseback Riding *(Rockin' Horse 967-4288)*, Museum *(Kennebunkport History 967-8180; Seashore Trolley 967-2800 $8/4.50 - 4 mi.)* **3+ mi:** Cultural Attract *(Arundel Barn, 4 mi.)*

Provisioning and General Services

OnSite: Newsstand **Near:** Fishmonger *(Port 967-2081)* **Under 1 mi:** Convenience Store *(Port Mobil 967-4255)*, Market *(HB Provisions 967-5762 Country store & deli. Delivers $50+)*, Gourmet Shop, Delicatessen, Wine/Beer *(Down East 967-9171)*, Liquor Store *(HB Provisions)*, Bank/ATM, Post Office, Catholic Church, Protestant Church *(1824 S. Congregational)*, Library *(Graves 967-2778 - 1883 Customs House)*, Beauty Salon, Bookstore *(Kennebooks 967-6136)*, Pharmacy *(Colonial 967-4442)*, Hardware Store *(Port 967-2371)*, Copies Etc. *(Ocean Exp. 967-0500)* **1-3 mi:** Dry Cleaners **3+ mi:** Supermarket *(Hannaford 985-9135, 5 mi.)*, Farmers' Market *(Sat 8am-1pm, Grove St. Village Pharm 985-1755, 4 mi.)*

Transportation

OnCall: Rental Car *(Enterprise 985-7493)*, Taxi *(Coastal 229-0783)*, Airport Limo *(Imperial 282-2386)* **Near:** Local Bus *(InTown Trolley 967-3686 Day $13/6)* **1-3 mi:** Bikes *(Cape-Able 967-4382)* **Airport:** Portland Int'l. *(25 mi.)*

Medical Services

911 Service **Near:** Holistic Services *(Breakwater Inn 967-5333)* **1-3 mi:** Veterinarian *(Homeport 967-2517)* **3+ mi:** Doctor *(Kennebunk Walk-in 985-3726, 4 mi.)* **Hospital:** SMMC 283-7000 *(5 mi.)*

PHOTOS ON DVD: 18

Setting -- A half mile up the Kennebunk River, Chick's 300-foot face dock parallels and protects the inner slips. A contemporary, gray-shingled two-story office and an inviting, sunny patio with comfortable Adirondack-style chairs and picnic tables overlook the river and heavily wooded Franciscan Monastery on the far shore. Ocean Avenue follows the river past beautifully restored Federal-style and Greek-Revival houses and mansions turned resorts.

Marina Notes -- *30 ft. min. to 49 ft. $4/ft., 50-69 ft. $5/ft., 70-99 ft. $6/ft. Over 100 ft. $7/ft. Founded late '60s by boat builder Booth Chick. Current owners at helm since 1990. 300-ft transient face dock space. Reserve with deposit in summer. New fuel dock & power in '08. Radio from river's mouth for dock assist. Marine supplies, drinks, newspapers, logo clothing. Comp. coffee, pastries & afternoon cookies. Concierge services for boats (cleaning, wash-down, in-slip fueling, boat provisioning) & boaters (car, kayak, bicycle rentals, taxi, dinner reservations). Vol Fuel discount. Winter storage: Inside heated $80/ft., Out $50-60/ft. River dredged '07, marina in '09 to 7 ft. Bathhouse: New full baths in '08 - vanities, pale blue walls, wood plank floors, fiberglass shower stalls. Laundry.

Notable -- It's a lovely half-mile inland to lively, posh Dock Square where high-end luxe shops, galleries and restaurants rub shoulders with seafood shacks and quirky stores. Stroll the streets - or take a walking tour - past the 17th & 18thC. homes of sea captains and owners of the shipyards that once lined the Kennebunk - or the remains of the later grand hotels and summer cottages from turn of the last century. It's a half-mile seaward to Arundel beach. In Town Trolley passes the door (10-5) following Cape Arundel's rocky shore - watch for a waterspout near Walker's Point - and then heading back to Dock Square.

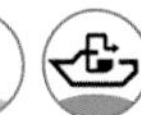

Navigational Information

Lat: 43°21.455' **Long:** 070°28.470' **Tide:** 9 ft. **Current:** 3 kt. **Chart:** 13286
Rep. Depths (*MLW*): Entry 6 ft. **Fuel Dock** n/a **Max Slip/Moor** 8 ft./-
Access: 0.6 miles from the mouth of the Kennebunk River on east side

Marina Facilities *(In Season/Off Season)*

Fuel: No
Slips: 41 Total, 2 Transient **Max LOA:** 65 ft. **Max Beam:** n/a
Rate *(per ft.)*: **Day** $3.50/Inq. **Week** n/a **Month** n/a
Power: 30 amp Incl., **50 amp** Incl., **100 amp** n/a, **200 amp** n/a
Cable TV: No **Dockside Phone:** No
Dock Type: Floating, Long Fingers, Pilings, Alongside, Wood
Moorings: 0 Total, 0 Transient **Launch:** n/a, Dinghy Dock
Rate: Day n/a **Week** n/a **Month** n/a
Heads: 2 Toilet(s), 2 Shower(s)
Internet: No **Laundry:** None
Pump-Out: OnSite, Full Service **Fee:** $5 **Closed Heads:** Yes

Marina Operations

Owner/Manager: Cathy Norton **Dockmaster:** Same
In-Season: May 15-Oct 15, 8am-5pm **Off-Season:** Oct 16-May 14, 8am-4pm
After-Hours Arrival: Call during business hours to arrange
Reservations: Yes, Preferred **Credit Cards:** Visa/MC, Amex
Discounts: None
Pets: Welcome, Dog Walk Area **Handicap Access:** Yes, Heads, Docks

Kennebunkport Marina

PO Box 2734; 67 Ocean Avenue; Kennebunkport, ME 04046

Tel: (207) 967-3411 **VHF: Monitor** Ch. 9 **Talk** Ch. 71
Fax: (207) 967-9808 **Alternate Tel:** n/a
Email: kristynr@roadrunner.com **Web:** www.kennebunkportmarina.com
Nearest Town: Kennebunkport *(0.5 mi.)* **Tourist Info:** (207) 967-8600

Marina Services and Boat Supplies

Services - Docking Assistance, Boaters' Lounge, Trash Pick-Up, Dock Carts **Communication -** Fax in/out, FedEx, DHL, UPS, Express Mail **Supplies - OnSite:** Ice *(Block, Cube)*, Ships' Store, Bait/Tackle

Boatyard Services

OnSite: Hydraulic Trailer, Launching Ramp, Engine mechanic *(gas, diesel)*, Electrical Repairs, Electronic Sales, Divers, Brightwork, Compound, Wash & Wax, Interior Cleaning **OnCall:** Bottom Cleaning, Propeller Repairs, Inflatable Repairs, Upholstery, Metal Fabrication **Dealer for:** Mercury. **Yard Rates:** $85/hr., Power Wash $5/ft. **Storage:** On-Land $44/ft.

Restaurants and Accommodations

OnSite: Condo/Cottage *(Lovely, waterside 1-bedroom cottage - kitchen, w/d, deck)* **OnCall:** Pizzeria *(Atlantic Pizza 967-0033)* **Near:** Restaurant *(Arundel Wharf 967-3444, L $5-12, D $14-30)*, *(Pier 77 967-8500, L $9-18, D $18-28)*, *(Stripers 967-5333, L $9-25, D $8-29)*, *(Hurricane 967-9111, L $10-18, D $19-39)*, Hotel *(Nonantum Resort 967-4050, $130-260)*, Inn/B&B *(Maine Stay Inn & Cottages 967-2117, $170-275)*, *(Yachtsman Lodge 967-2511, $170-350)* **Under 1 mi:** Restaurant *(Alisson's 967-4841, L $8-15, D $9-23)*, *(Bartley's Dockside 967-6244, L $8-26, D $13-26, casual)*, *(Bandaloop 967-4994, D $17-29)*, Snack Bar *(Clam Shack 967-3321)* **1-3 mi:** Restaurant *(White Barn 967-2321, D $98, 4-course prix fixe)*, Inn/B&B *(White Barn 967-2321, $350+)*

Recreation and Entertainment

OnSite: Picnic Area, Grills, Boat Rentals *(Kayaks, Canoes, Skiffs, Power boats)* **Under 1 mi:** Beach *(Arundel, Colony)*, Tours *(Nott House - 1899 School House 967-2751, Village Walking Tour $7 - 11am Thu & Sat, Self-Guided $4/book)*, Sightseeing *(First Chance Whale Watch 967-5507 $48/28)* **1-3 mi:** Tennis Courts *(Edgcomb 967-5791)*, Golf Course *(Cape Arundel 967-3494)*, Museum *(Kennebunkport History Center 967-8180, Tue-Fri 10-4, Sat 10-1; Seashore Trolley 967-2800 $8/4.50 - 4 mi.)*

Provisioning and General Services

Near: Fishmonger *(Port 967-2081)*, Bank/ATM, Pharmacy *(Colonial 967-4442)* **Under 1 mi:** Convenience Store *(Port Mobil 967-4255)*, Health Food *(Market Day 967-5577)*, Wine/Beer *(Down East 967-9171)*, Bakery *(Port 967-2263)*, Post Office, Catholic Church, Protestant Church, Library *(Graves 967-2778)*, Beauty Salon, Bookstore *(Kennebooks 967-6136)*, Hardware Store *(Port 967-2371)*, Florist **3+ mi:** Supermarket *(Hannaford 985-9135, 5 mi.)*, Liquor Store *(Garden St. 985-2081, 5 mi.)*, Farmers' Market *(Sat 8am-1pm, Grove St. 985-1755, 4 mi.)*

Transportation

OnCall: Rental Car *(Enterprise 985-7493, Harbor Village Scooters 590-5151)*, Taxi *(Coastal 229-0783)*, Airport Limo *(Imperial 282-2386)* **Near:** Local Bus *(Trolley - Day $15/5, 8-stops 10-5)* **1-3 mi:** Bikes *(Cape-Able 967-4382)* **3+ mi:** Rail *(Boston-Wells, 8 mi.)* **Airport:** Portland Int'l. *(25 mi.)*

Medical Services

911 Service **Near:** Holistic Services *(Breakwater Spa 967-5333)* **Under 1 mi:** Doctor *(Freeman 967-3726)* **1-3 mi:** Veterinarian *(Homeport 967-2517)* **3+ mi:** Chiropractor *(Kennebunk 985-2900, 5 mi.)* **Hospital:** Southern Maine Medical Center 283-7000 *(5 mi.)*

Setting -- Six-tenths of a mile up the Kennebunk River, Kennebunkport's brand-new, "U-shaped" docks lie between Chick's and Yachtsman's Marinas. A gravel picnic area fronts the pretty gray-shingled, hipped-roof marina building - and leads to the two carefully maintained docks - an adjacent small cottage juts out over the water on pilings. Across the river, a wall of tall pines creates a sense of calm seclusion that belies reality.

Marina Notes -- CCM **Off-season closed Sat & Sun. Closed Dec 20-Jan 2. New owners 2010. All docks replaced 2010 with new electrical and water hook-ups. Reservations preferred. Confirm depths. Boatyard services, Incl. engine mechanics. Over Road hydraulic trailer also available. Well-supplied marine store - with large port-holed doorway - boating & fishing supplies, maps, charts. Boat rentals: Kayaks & Canoes $25/2 hrs., $45 half-day, Double $45/2 hrs., $60/half-day, Skiff $30/hr. Bathhouse: Recent, heads and showers nicely done in pale blue. Note: Possible dockage at Arundel Yacht Club (967-3060).

Notable -- The small, gray, over-water, one-bedroom rental cottage features a kitchen, laundry and private deck with panoramic river views. It's a short walk to Dock Square, the center of the frenzied, small port town. Chic shops, galleries and dozens of eateries - from very pricey fine dining to famous seafood shacks - have taken up residence in historic edifices. Restored early Federal-style former ships' captains' homes and late-19th-century summer houses dot the surrounding historic district. Hike or bike Parson's Way out to Porpoise Point, passing Walker Point (the Bush family home), St. Ann's Church, and trails to the mid-tide natural phenomena: blowing cave and spouting rock. Or take the trolley tour that passes spectacular ocean views and stops at arcs of sandy beach.

PHOTOS ON DVD: 15

Yachtsman Lodge and Marina

Yachtsman Marina

PO Box 560; Ocean Avenue; Kennebunkport, ME 04046

Tel: (207) 967-2511; (800) 992-2487 **VHF: Monitor** n/a **Talk** n/a
Fax: (207) 967-5056 **Alternate Tel:** (207) 967-2321
Email: innkeeper@yachtsmanlodge.com **Web:** www.yachtsmanlodge.com
Nearest Town: Kennebunkport *(0.4 mi)* **Tourist Info:** (207) 967-8600

Navigational Information

Lat: 43°21.550' **Long:** 070°28.586' **Tide:** 9 ft. **Current:** 3 kt. **Chart:** 13286
Rep. Depths (*MLW*): Entry 6 ft. **Fuel Dock** n/a **Max Slip/Moor** 6 ft./-
Access: .6 mi. from Kennebunk River entrance on the east side

Marina Facilities *(In Season/Off Season)*

Fuel: Diesel
Slips: 54 Total, 10 Transient **Max LOA:** 100 ft. **Max Beam:** 20 ft.
Rate *(per ft.)*: **Day** $6.00* **Week** n/a **Month** n/a
Power: 30 amp $25, **50 amp** $25, **100 amp** n/a, **200 amp** n/a
Cable TV: No **Dockside Phone:** No
Dock Type: Floating, Alongside, Wood
Moorings: 0 Total, 0 Transient **Launch:** n/a, Dinghy Dock
Rate: Day n/a **Week** n/a **Month** n/a
Heads: 2 Toilet(s), 2 Shower(s) *(dressing rooms)*, Hair Dryers,
Internet: Yes *(Wi-Fi, Free)* **Laundry:** None
Pump-Out: No **Fee:** n/a **Closed Heads:** Yes

Marina Operations

Owner/Manager: Lucila Peretti **Dockmaster:** Same
In-Season: May 15-Oct 15, 7am-9pm **Off-Season:** Closed
After-Hours Arrival: No after hours arrival
Reservations: Yes, Required **Credit Cards:** Visa/MC, Amex
Discounts: None
Pets: Welcome **Handicap Access:** No

Marina Services and Boat Supplies

Services - Docking Assistance, Concierge, Dock Carts **Communication -** Fax in/out, FedEx, DHL, UPS, Express Mail *(Sat Del)* **Supplies - OnSite:** Ice *(Cube)* **Near:** Ships' Store *(Kennebunkport Marina)*, Bait/Tackle **3+ mi:** Propane *(Downeast Energy 985-3154, 4 mi.)*

Boatyard Services

Nearest Yard: Chick's Marina (207) 967-2782

Restaurants and Accommodations

OnSite: Motel *(Yachtsman Lodge 967-2511, $170-380, Pet Friendly $25/day)* **Near:** Restaurant *(Bandaloop 967-4994, D $17-29)*, *(One Dock 967-2621, D $17-31, Small Plates $6-13)*, *(Stripers at Breakwater 967-5333, L $9-25, D $18-29, Lounge 3pm+ $9-14, Sun Br. $8-23)*, *(95 Ocean at Nonantum 967-4050, D $12-30, Kids' $5-7, Sun Brunch $16, Pre-theater $20)*, Snack Bar *(Clam Shack 967-3321, Detour!)*, Pizzeria *(Atlantic Pizza 967-0033)*, Inn/B&B *(Nonantum Resort 967-4050, $130-260)*, *(Captain Lord 967-3141, $150-500)* **Under 1 mi:** Restaurant *(Grissini Italian 967-2211, D $18-29)*, Seafood Shack *(Mabel's Lobster Claw 967-2562, L $8-16, D $14-30)* **1-3 mi:** Restaurant *(White Barn Inn 967-2321, D $98, 4-course Prix Fixe, 5 diamonds, 5 stars)*, Inn/B&B *(White Barn Inn 967-2321, $330-700)*

Recreation and Entertainment

OnSite: Boat Rentals *(Canoes, complimentary)*, Fishing Charter **Near:** Jogging Paths, Hike/Bike Trails, Tours *(Nott House Guided Tour 967-2751, Free; Village Walking Tour $7 - 11am Thu & Sat., Self-Guided $4/book; Coastal Maine Kayak 967-6065; Schooner Eleanor 967-8809 $40 - 55 ft. gaff-rigged)*, Sightseeing *(First Chance 967-5507 Whale Watch $48/28, Lobster Tour $20/15; Nautilus Whale Watch 967-0707)* **Under 1 mi:** Beach, Park, Museum *(Kennebunkport History Center 967-8180; Seashore Trolley 967-2800 $8/4.50 - 4 mi.)* **1-3 mi:** Tennis Courts *(Edgcomb Club 967-5791)*, Golf Course *(Cape Arundel 967-3494)*, Horseback Riding *(Rockin' Horse Stables 967-4288)* **3+ mi:** Cultural Attract *(Arundel Barn 985-5552, 4 mi.)*

Provisioning and General Services

Near: Bakery, Bank/ATM, Post Office, Beauty Salon *(Fringe 967-8551)*, Pharmacy *(Colonial 967-4442)* **Under 1 mi:** Convenience Store *(Port Mobil 967-4255)*, Market *(HB Provisions 967-5762 Country store Del $50+, B & L too)*, Wine/Beer *(HB)*, Fishmonger *(Port 967-2081)*, Catholic Church, Protestant Church, Library *(Graves 967-2778)*, Bookstore *(Kennebooks 967-6136)*, Hardware Store *(Cape 967-2021)*, Copies Etc. *(Ocean Exposure 967-0500)* **1-3 mi:** Barber Shop, Laundry *(Maytag 967-5066)* **3+ mi:** Supermarket *(Hannaford 985-9135, 5 mi.)*, Liquor Store *(Garden St., 5 mi.)*, Farmers' Market *(Sat 8am-1pm, Grove St. Village Pharm 985-1755, 4 mi.)*

Transportation

OnSite: Bikes *(or Cape-Able 967-4382)* **OnCall:** Rental Car *(Enterprise 985-7493)*, Taxi *(Coastal 229-0783)*, Airport Limo *(Imperial 282-2386)* **Near:** Local Bus *(InTown Trolley 967-3686 Day $13/6)* **3+ mi:** Rail *(Wells, 8 mi.)* **Airport:** Portland Int'l. *(25 mi.)*

Medical Services

911 Service **Near:** Holistic Services *(Breakwater Spa 967-5333 50 min. massage $105)* **Under 1 mi:** Doctor *(Freeman 967-3726)* **1-3 mi:** Veterinarian *(Homeport 967-2517)* **3+ mi:** Chiropractor *(Kennebunk 985-2900, 5 mi.)* **Hospital:** So. Maine Med. 283-7000 *(5 mi.)*

Setting -- Yachtsman's two long side-tie docks sprout lotus-like from a central pier reflecting the two arms of the carefully landscaped single-story boutique inn on the shore. Three sets of slips, berthing a bevy of good looking yachts, fill the center. Colorful flower beds, punctuated by contemporary sculpture, soften the edges of the patios. At the nexus of the inn's two motel-like arms, an umbrella-shaded patio hosts breakfast and afternoon tea.

Marina Notes -- *In Season rates from $4-6/ft. Owned by U.S. Hotels Group. Local sister properties: Beach House, Breakwater & White Barn Inns, Chase Hill Events, Grissini Bistro. Obvious attention to detail throughout. Reservations critical. Complimentary espresso, cappuccino, tea, continental breakfast, afternoon tea - as well as bikes & canoes. Bathhouse: Exceptional full bath rooms with raised tile showers, granite vanities, complimentary towel service.

Notable -- The bones of a standard motel have been transformed into 30 beautifully appointed, cathedral-ceilinged, nautically themed rooms, with glass doors that step out onto private, riverside patios. Mahogany-trimmed bead board walls, generous furnishings and luxe amenities have earned it high praise. About 0.4 mile upriver, the bustling village, centered on Dock Square, boasts chic boutiques, local crafts, upscale galleries and lots of good food - casual cafes, pricey restaurants, seafood shacks, provisioning sources. The neighboring 1853 Greek Revival Nott House museum is emblematic of the surrounding late-18th-century restored homes of shipyard owners & clipper captains. Walking seaward, Nonatum Resort and The Colony are luxurious, grand-style vestiges of the 19th-century glamorous summer colony period. It's four miles to the Seashore Trolley Museum with 200 antique streetcars - the largest collection in the world.

PHOTOS ON DVD: 22

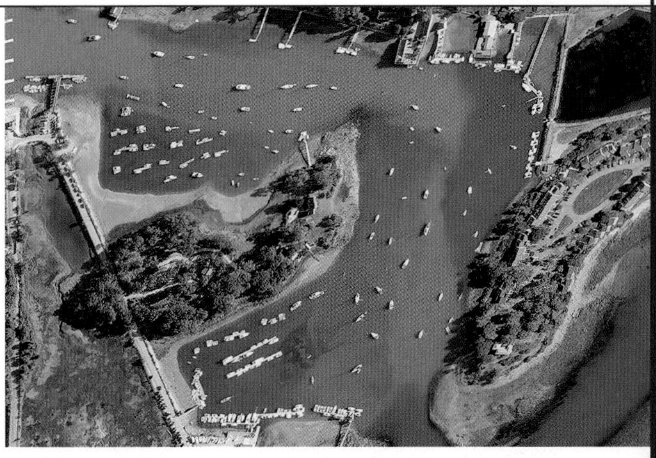

York Town Docks & Moorings

Harris Island Rd & Lilac Lane; York Harbor, ME 03909**

Tel: (207) 363-1000 **VHF: Monitor** Ch. 9 **Talk** Ch. 6
Fax: (207) 363-1019 **Alternate Tel:** (207) 363-0433
Email: d.day@yorkmaine.org **Web:** www.yorkmaine.org
Nearest Town: York *(3 mi.)* **Tourist Info:** (207) 363-4422

Navigational Information

Lat: 43°07.773' **Long:** 070°38.748' **Tide:** 8 ft. **Current:** 4 kt. **Chart:** 13283, '
Rep. Depths (*MLW*): Entry 24 ft. **Fuel Dock** n/a **Max Slip/Moor** 9 ft./9 ft.
Access: York Harbor to York River - past Bragdon Island

Marina Facilities *(In Season/Off Season)*

Fuel: No
Slips: 10 Total, 8 Transient **Max LOA:** 50 ft. **Max Beam:** n/a
Rate *(per ft.)*: **Day** $1.00* **Week** n/a **Month** n/a
Power: 30 amp n/a, **50 amp** n/a, **100 amp** n/a, **200 amp** n/a
Cable TV: No **Dockside Phone:** No
Dock Type: Floating, Alongside, Wood
Moorings: 10 Total, 6 Transient **Launch:** No, Dinghy Dock
Rate: Day $25 **Week** n/a **Month** n/a
Heads: None
Internet: No **Laundry:** None
Pump-Out: OnCall, Full Service **Fee:** Free **Closed Heads:** Yes

Marina Operations

Owner/Manager: Dan Day (Hrbrmstr) **Dockmaster:** Joe Hogan (Ass't)
In-Season: May 15-Sep 15, 8am-5pm **Off-Season:** Oct-Apr, Closed
After-Hours Arrival: Call during Business Hours to arrange
Reservations: No **Credit Cards:** n/a
Discounts: None
Pets: Welcome, Dog Walk Area **Handicap Access:** No

Marina Services and Boat Supplies

Services - Docking Assistance **Communication -** FedEx, UPS, Express Mail **Supplies - Near:** Ice *(Block, Cube)*, Ships' Store *(York Harbor Marine 363-3602)*, Bait/Tackle **Under 1 mi:** Propane *(Downeast 363-4331)*

Boatyard Services

OnCall: Electronics Repairs, Sail Loft, Canvas Work, Air Conditioning, Refrigeration, Woodworking, Inflatable Repairs **Near:** Railway, Launching Ramp, Engine mechanic *(gas, diesel)*, Electrical Repairs, Hull Repairs, Rigger, Divers, Bottom Cleaning, Brightwork, Propeller Repairs, Metal Fabrication. **Nearest Yard:** York Harbor Marine (207) 363-3602

Restaurants and Accommodations

Near: Restaurant *(Dockside 363-2722, L $7-11, D $11-23)*, Seafood Shack *(Foster's Downeast Clambake 363-3255, L $6-24, D $8-24)*, Inn/B&B *(Dockside Guest Qtrs 363-2868, $105-275, 25 rooms)*, *(Chapman Cottage 363-2059, $135-225)* **Under 1 mi:** Restaurant *(1637 at York Harbor Inn 363-5119, D $9-33, Early bird $19, Ship's Cellar Pub $9-33, Late nite $8-17, Sun Brunch $10-29)*, *(Harbor Porches at Stageneck 363-3850, L $12-15, D $20-28, Sun Brunch $12-18)*, Seafood Shack *(Foster's Downeast 363-2643, Events at Pavilion)*, Lite Fare *(Rick's 363-5584, 5am-2pm, Dinner Wed & Thur to 8pm)*, *(Rowen Tree 363-2035)*, *(Bagel Basket 363-1244)*, *(Sandpiper Grill at Stageneck 363-3854, $8-23)*, Pizzeria *(York House of 363-6171)*, Hotel *(Stage Neck Inn 363-3850, $135-325)*, Inn/B&B *(York Harbor 363-5119, $110-350)*, *(Edwards' Harborside 363-3037, $110-320)*

Recreation and Entertainment

OnSite: Fishing Charter *(Shearwater Charters 363-5324; Bigger 'n Better 800-526-8172; 774-200-3020)*, Tours *(Capt. Gile's Lobster Boat Tours 408-1194; Harbor Adventures Kayak & Bike Tours 363-8466 $45-65)* **Near:** Tennis Courts **Under 1 mi:** Beach *(York Harbor)*, Golf Course *(Ledges 351-3000)*, Fitness Center *(Yoga on York 363-9642)*, Video Rental *(Red Box, Hannaford's)*, Museum *(Sayward-Wheeler House 384-2454 $5; Old York Historical Society 363-4974 10am-5pm, Mon-Sat. $6/3 for one bldg, $12/5 for ten bldgs)*, Sightseeing *(Ghostly Tours 363-0000)*

Provisioning and General Services

Under 1 mi: Convenience Store *(Cumberland)*, Market *(Frisbee's 1828 439-0014)*, Supermarket *(Hannaford 363-5357)*, Liquor Store *(ABC 351-1673)*, Bakery *(When Pigs Fly 363-0612)*, Bank/ATM, Post Office, Catholic Church, Protestant Church *(1747 First Parish)*, Library, Barber Shop, Dry Cleaners *(We Care 363-9918)*, Laundry, Pharmacy *(Hannaford 363-5928)*, Retail Shops *(York Village Shopping Center-Rite Aid 363-4312)* **1-3 mi:** Gourmet Shop *(Stonewall 351-2712)*, Delicatessen *(York 351-3012)*, Wine/Beer *(Clown 351-3063)*, Farmers' Market *(Sat. 9-noon 363-4422 - Stonewall)*, Fishmonger *(Finestkind 363-5000)*, Hardware Store *(True Value 363-7090)*

Transportation

OnCall: Rental Car *(Enterprise 351-1790)*, Taxi *(Checker 603-750-7777)* **Under 1 mi:** Bikes *(Berger's 363-4070)* **1-3 mi:** InterCity Bus *(York Trolley Company 363-9600)* **Airport:** Portsmouth/Portland *(13 mi./43 mi.)*

Medical Services

911 Service **Under 1 mi:** Doctor *(York 363-8430)*, Dentist *(Gray 363-2166)*, Chiropractor *(Molda 363-5656)*, Holistic Services *(Stage Neck363-3850)* **1-3 mi:** Veterinarian *(Village 351-1530)* **Hospital:** York 363-4321 *(.8 mi.)*

Setting -- Past Dockside Guest Quarters and York Harbor Marine on Harris Island, the protected York Town mooring field - awash in downeast yachts and working boats - lies to starboard just around the Bragdon Island point. Just beyond, the York Town Dock sits in front of the Route 3, Lilac Lane fixed bridge. The Harbormaster's small, shingled, shed sits at the top of the ramp overlooking the docks and down the river. Old York Village is a half mile across the bridge.

Marina Notes -- *Flat rate $25-35. **Mailing address: 186 York Street. No services at Town dock except Pump-Out boat. Full range of yard services at nearby York Harbor Marine Services (363-3298) - factory-certified technicians,an active drystack storage operation, and well-equipped ships' store, but no transient dockage. Bathhouse: None. But YHMS' heads, showers & laundry available to mooring guests for a fee.

Notable -- The Town Docks are an inauspicious, but convenient, entree to this quiet, fashionable summer colony with expansive greenways and strong ties to its 17th and 18th century roots. Having successfully fought development for over a century, York is now one of the most historically well-preserved and documented towns in New England. Old York Historical Society maintains ten restored buildings - mini-museums scattered about the charming village, including Jefferds Tavern and the 1653 Old Goal (Maine's primary prison until the Civil War). Hike across Lilac Lane bridge to Wiggly Bridge then through the woods to the John Hancock Warehouse & Wharf and George Marshall Store Gallery. York Village is another half mile. At the Lusty family's nearby Dockside Guest Quarters, a 19th-century Maine House, four multi-unit out buildings, a gazebo, a popular water-front restaurant and guest dockage sprawl across 7 acres.

PHOTOS ON DVD: 24

Donnell's Dockage

PO Box 472; 18 Simpsons Lane; York Harbor, ME 03911**

Tel: (207) 363-4308 **VHF: Monitor** n/a **Talk** n/a
Fax: n/a **Alternate Tel:** (207) 363-5324
Email: n/a **Web:** n/a
Nearest Town: Town of York *(0.8 mi.)* **Tourist Info:** (207) 363-4422

Navigational Information

Lat: 43°07.980' **Long:** 070°38.550' **Tide:** 8 ft. **Current:** 4 kt. **Chart:** 13283
Rep. Depths (*MLW*): Entry 10 ft. **Fuel Dock** 10 ft. **Max Slip/Moor** 10 ft./-
Access: Up River beyond Stage Neck on the northeast side

Marina Facilities *(In Season/Off Season)*

Fuel: No
Slips: 6 Total, 6 Transient **Max LOA:** 85 ft. **Max Beam:** n/a
Rate *(per ft.)*: **Day** $2.00/Inq.* **Week** Inq. **Month** Inq.
Power: 30 amp $5, **50 amp** $8, **100 amp** $10, **200 amp** n/a
Cable TV: No **Dockside Phone:** No
Dock Type: Fixed, Floating, Alongside, Wood
Moorings: 0 Total, 0 Transient **Launch:** n/a
Rate: Day n/a **Week** n/a **Month** n/a
Heads: None
Internet: No **Laundry:** None
Pump-Out: No **Fee:** n/a **Closed Heads:** Yes

Marina Operations

Owner/Manager: Mary Coite / Dan Donnell **Dockmaster:** Same
In-Season: May-Oct, 7am-8pm **Off-Season:** Nov-Apr, Closed
After-Hours Arrival: Call ahead
Reservations: Yes **Credit Cards:** Cash/Check only
Discounts: None
Pets: Welcome, Dog Walk Area **Handicap Access:** No

Marina Services and Boat Supplies

Services - Docking Assistance, Trash Pick-Up **Communication -** Phone Messages, FedEx, DHL, UPS, Express Mail **Supplies - Near:** Ice *(Block, Cube)*, Ships' Store *(York Harbor Marine 363-3602)*, Bait/Tackle **Under 1 mi:** Propane *(Downeast Energy 363-4331)*

Boatyard Services

OnSite: Launching Ramp **OnCall:** Divers, Bottom Cleaning, Brightwork **Near:** Engine mechanic *(gas, diesel)*, Electrical Repairs, Electronic Sales, Electronics Repairs, Hull Repairs. **Nearest Yard:** York Harbor Marine Services (207) 363-3602

Restaurants and Accommodations

Near: Restaurant *(Sandpiper Grill at Stageneck L & D $8-23 casual)*, *(Harbor Porches at Stageneck Inn B $8, L $12-15, D $20-28, Fine Dining, Sun Brunch $12-18)*, *(1637 at York Harbor Inn B $8, D $9-33, Early bird $19, Ship's Cellar Pub $9-33, Late nite $8-17, Sun Brunch $10-29)*, Seafood Shack *(Fosters Downeast Clambake 363-3255, L $6-24, D $8-24)*, Hotel *(Stage Neck Inn 363-3850, $135-325)*, Inn/B&B *(Edwards Harborside 363-3037, $110-320, guest dockage)*, *(York Harbor 363-5119, $110-350)* **Under 1 mi:** Restaurant *(Dockside 363-2722, L $7-11, D $11-23)*, Lite Fare *(Rick's 363-5584, 5am-2pm, Dinner Wed & Thur to 8pm)*, *(Bagel Basket 363-1244)*, *(Rowen Tree 363-2035)*, Pizzeria *(York House 363-6171)*

Recreation and Entertainment

OnSite: Picnic Area, Fishing Charter *(Striper Charters 363-5324)* **Near:** Beach, Tennis Courts, Video Rental *(Red Box, Hannaford)*, Park, Special Events *(York Days - Late Jul-Early Aug - 10 days)* **Under 1 mi:** Dive Shop, Fitness Center *(Yoga on York 363-9642)*, Museum *(Old York Historical Society 363-4974 10am-5pm, Mon-Sat. $6/3 one bldg, $12/5 for 10; Sayward-Wheeler House 384-2454)*, Sightseeing *(Ghostly Tours 363-0000; Capt. Gile's Lobster Boat Tours 408-1194; Harbor Adventures Kayak & Bike Tours 363-8466 $45-65)* **1-3 mi:** Golf Course *(Ledges 351-3000)*

Provisioning and General Services

OnSite: Lobster Pound **Near:** Supermarket *(Hannaford 363-5357)*, Post Office, Pharmacy *(Hannaford 363-5928; Rite Aid 363-4312)* **Under 1 mi:** Convenience Store *(Cumberland)*, Liquor Store *(ABC 351-1673)*, Bakery *(When Pigs Fly 363-0612)*, Bank/ATM, Catholic Church, Protestant Church, Library, Barber Shop, Dry Cleaners *(We Care 363-9918)*, Laundry, Hardware Store *(True-Value 363-7090)*, Florist, Retail Shops *(York Village Shopping Center)* **1-3 mi:** Gourmet Shop *(Stonewall Kitchen 351-2712)*, Delicatessen *(York 351-3012)*, Wine/Beer *(The Clown 351-3063)*, Farmers' Market *(Sat. 9am-noon 363-4422 - Stonewall)*

Transportation

OnSite: Courtesy Car/Van *(for grocery shopping)* **OnCall:** Rental Car *(Enterprise 351-1790)*, Taxi *(Sunshine 363-7600)*, Airport Limo *(Coastal 229-0783)* **Near:** Bikes *(Bergers 363-4070)* **1-3 mi:** InterCity Bus *(York Trolley Company 363-9600)* **Airport:** Portsmouth/Portland Int'l. *(13 mi./43 mi.)*

Medical Services

911 Service **Near:** Dentist *(Gray 363-2166)*, Holistic Services *(Stage Neck Inn Spa 363-3850, 60-min Massage $90)* **Under 1 mi:** Doctor *(York Fam 363-8430)*, Chiropractor *(Molda 363-5656)* **1-3 mi:** Veterinarian *(Village 351-1530)* **Hospital:** York 363-4321 *(1 mi.)*

PHOTOS ON DVD: 18

Setting -- The reverse "S" of the York River passes Harris Island's Dockside Guest Quarters and York Harbor Marine to port and expansive Stage Neck Inn Resort to starboard. On the northeast bank, just beyond the Agamenticus Yacht Club, Donnell's first substantial main pier leads to a a long white pavilion backed by a two-story white clapboard house. The second pier leads to a classic, weathered-shingle dockhouse. Historic York Harbor village is an easy walk.

Marina Notes -- *$2/ft. up to 50 ft., $2.75/ft. for 50 ft.+. Estab. in 1947 by Daniel Donnell. Family owned/operated ever since. **Two adjacent docks - one run by second-generation Mary Donnell Coite (363-5324 - 39 Varrell Lane) and the other by her father, Daniel Donnell (363-4308 - 18 Simpsons Lane). New docks in 1998, 100-amp service. Basic amenities but gracious service, good protection & great location. Owners take guests to supermarket & historic sites. Yard services across river at York Harbor Marine Services. Bathhouse: None.

Notable -- It's 1,200 feet seaward to crescent-shaped Harbor Beach; from there a mile-long cliffwalk passes classic "summer cottages" ending at Long Sands Beach. Near the docks are two inns and the impressive Stage Neck Inn Resort with four eateries, indoor and outdoor pools, clay tennis courts and spectacular ocean views. Mile-long Fisherman's Walk begins at Donnell's and runs along the river over the restored 1930's Wiggley steel mini-suspension bridge, which crosses the Barrelle's Millpond outflow through Steedman Woods. At the end are two of the Old York Historical Society's ten restored buildings: 18th. C John Hancock Warehouse & Wharf (dinghy landing for closer access to York Village), and the 1867 George Marshall Store Gallery - featuring contemporary art.

10. ME/NH/MA – Piscataqua to Merrimack Rivers

York Harbor
Kittery
Kittery Point
Piscataqua River
Great Bay
Newmarket
Atlantic Ocean
Exeter
Hampton
Hampton Harbor
Ram Island
Kingston
Amesbury
Merrimack River
Newburyport
N
Miles
0 10

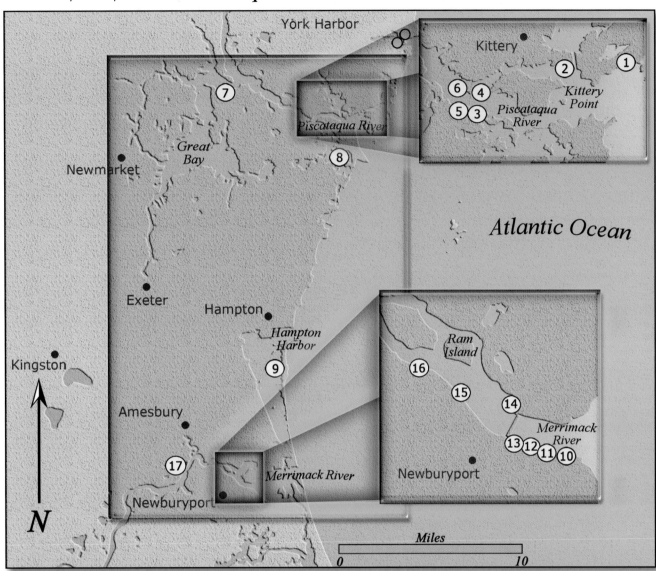

MAP	MARINA	HARBOR	PAGE	MAP	MARINA	HARBOR	PAGE
1	**Kittery Point Town Wharf**	*Pepperrell Cove*	186	10	**Newburyport Harbor Marina**	*Merrimack River*	195
2	**Kittery Point Yacht Yard**	*Piscataqua River*	187	11	**Newburyport Waterfront Park**	*Merrimack River*	196
3	**Prescott Park Municipal Dock**	*Piscataqua River*	188	12	**Hilton's Marina**	*Merrimack River*	197
4	**Badgers Island East**	*Piscataqua River*	189	13	**Windward Yacht Yard**	*Merrimack River*	198
5	**The Marina at Harbour Place**	*Piscataqua River*	190	14	**Cove Marina**	*Merrimack River*	199
6	**Badgers Island Marina**	*Piscataqua River*	191	15	**Newburyport Boat Basin**	*Merrimack River*	200
7	**Great Bay Marine**	*Piscataqua River*	192	16	**Merri-Mar Yacht Basin**	*Merrimack River*	201
8	**Wentworth by the Sea Marina**	*Little Harbor*	193	17	**Marina at Hatter's Point**	*Merrimack River*	202
9	**Hampton River Marina**	*Hampton Harbor*	194				

RATINGS: 1-5 for Marina Facilities & Amenities, 1-2 for Boatyard Services, 1-2 for MegaYacht Facilities, for Something Special.

SERVICES: for CCM – Certified Clean Marina, 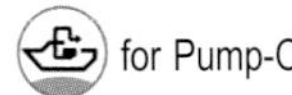 for Pump-Out,  for Internet, 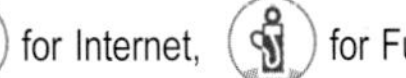 for Fuel,  for Restaurant,  for Provisioning nearby, for Catamaran-friendly,  for SportFish Charter,  for Pool/Beach, and  for Golf within a mile. *For an explanation of ACC's Ratings, see page 8.*

Kittery Point Town Wharf

Bellamy Lane*; Kittery, ME 03904

Tel: (207) 439-0452 **VHF: Monitor** Ch. 9 **Talk** Ch. 68
Fax: n/a **Alternate Tel:** (207) 451-0829
Email: n/a **Web:** www.kittery.org
Nearest Town: Kittery *(3 mi.)* **Tourist Info:** (207) 363-4422

Navigational Information

Lat: 43°04.946' **Long:** 070°42.212' **Tide:** 10 ft. **Current:** 4 kt. **Chart:** 13278
Rep. Depths (*MLW*): Entry 12 ft. **Fuel Dock** 12 ft. **Max Slip/Moor** -/30 ft.
Access: Piscataqua River to Pepperell Cove

Marina Facilities *(In Season/Off Season)*

Fuel: No
Slips: 0 Total, 0 Transient **Max LOA:** 60 ft. **Max Beam:** n/a
Rate *(per ft.)*: **Day** n/a **Week** n/a **Month** n/a
Power: 30 amp n/a, **50 amp** n/a, **100 amp** n/a, **200 amp** n/a
Cable TV: No **Dockside Phone:** No
Dock Type: n/a
Moorings: 20 Total, 5 Transient **Launch:** No, Dinghy Dock
Rate: Day $20 **Week** $140 **Month** Inq.
Heads: 1 Toilet(s)
Internet: No **Laundry:** None
Pump-Out: OnCall **Fee:** $10 **Closed Heads:** Yes

Marina Operations

Owner/Manager: Bion Pike (Hrbmstr) **Dockmaster:** Same
In-Season: May-Oct, 24 hrs. **Off-Season:** Nov-Apr, On Call
After-Hours Arrival: n/a
Reservations: No **Credit Cards:** Cash/Check only
Discounts: None
Pets: Welcome **Handicap Access:** Yes, Heads, Docks

Marina Services and Boat Supplies

Communication - FedEx, UPS, Express Mail **Supplies - OnSite:** Ice *(Cube)* **Under 1 mi:** Ships' Store *(Kittery Point Y.Y. 439-9582)* **3+ mi:** West Marine *(603-436-8300, 5 mi.)*, Propane *(Energy 439-1702, 4 mi.)*

Boatyard Services

OnSite: Divers, Bottom Cleaning **OnCall:** Engine mechanic *(gas, diesel)*, Electronics Repairs, Rigger, Sail Loft, Compound, Wash & Wax, Interior Cleaning **Under 1 mi:** Travelift, Electronic Sales, Hull Repairs. **Nearest Yard:** Kittery Point Yacht Yard (207) 439-9582

Restaurants and Accommodations

OnSite: Restaurant *(Captain & Patty's 439-3655, L $8-25, D $16-35, 11am-9pm. New management Summer '10.)* **Under 1 mi:** Seafood Shack *(Chauncey Creek 439-1030, Market price. Colorful picnic tables, inside/out. Group Lobster Bakes $30-34/pp. BYO - by dink)*, Pizzeria *(Town Pizza 439-1265, Subs, Greek foods, moussaka)* **1-3 mi:** Restaurant *(Anneke Jans 439-0001, D $15-34, Dramatic Scandinavian-chic)*, Seafood Shack *(Warren Lobster House 439-1630, L $7-16, D $15-18, Salad Bar, Kids' $4-6.50)*, Lite Fare *(Loco Cocos Tacos 438-9322, L & D $3.50-11)*, Pizzeria *(AJ's 439-9700, same owners as Anneke Jans - wood-burning grills, flat bread pizza)*, Inn/B&B *(Enchanted Nights B& B 439-1489, $35-250)*, *(Inn at Portsmouth Harbor 439-4040, $155-215)*, Condo/Cottage *(Litson Villa 439-5000, $55-150)* **3+ mi:** Restaurant *(Warren's Lobster House 439-1630, L $5-8, D $15-35, 4 mi.)*, *(Quarterdeck 439-5198, L $5-10, D $10-15, 4 mi.)*

Recreation and Entertainment

OnSite: Tours *(Capt & Patty's 439-8976, 451-8156, 6 tours daily, Tue-Sun)* **Near:** Picnic Area *(Ft. McClary)*, Grills, Playground, Park *(Fort McClary State Park 439-2845 $2)*, Galleries *(Kittery Art Assoc. 451-9384, Fri. Concerts)* **1-3 mi:** Beach *(Ft. Foster, Seapoint)*, Horseback Riding *(Little Brook 439-7708)*, Video Rental *(Movie Gallery 439-2338)*, Museum *(Kittery Historical & Naval Society 439-3080 $3/1.50, Tue-Sat 10am-4pm)* **3+ mi:** Golf Course *(Pease G.C. 603 433-1331, 9 mi.)*

Provisioning and General Services

OnSite: Market *(Enoteca Italiana 439-7216 - necessary groceries, prepared foods, handmade mozzarella & ricotta)*, Wine/Beer *(Enoteca)*, Liquor Store, Bakery *(Enoteca)* **Near:** Post Office **Under 1 mi:** Bank/ATM, Protestant Church **1-3 mi:** Fishmonger *(Seaview 439-1599)*, Catholic Church, Library *(Rice 439-1553)*, Beauty Salon *(Cuts by Courtney 439-2609)*, Dry Cleaners *(We Care 439-4131)*, Pharmacy *(Rite Aid 438-9079)*, Hardware Store *(Ace 439-4150)* **3+ mi:** Supermarket *(Hannaford 603-436-6669, 4.5 mi.)*, Bookstore *(River Run 603-431-2100; Gulliver's Travels 603-431-5556, 4 mi.)*, Retail Shops *(Kittery Outlets 439-7993, 3.5 mi.)*

Transportation

OnCall: Rental Car *(Enterprise 603-433-1177)*, Taxi *(Checker 603-750-7777)* **Airport:** Portsmouth Int'l/Portland Int'l. *(7.5 mi./50 mi.)*

Medical Services

911 Service **OnCall:** Ambulance **1-3 mi:** Doctor *(Kittery Family Practice 439-4430)*, Dentist *(Breslin 439-4400)*, Chiropractor *(Alebro 439-3358)*, Holistic Services *(Portsmouth Harbor Inn & Spa 439-4040 - Massage $95/55-min.)*, Veterinarian *(Piscataqua 439-2661)* **Hospital:** Portsmouth Regional 603-559-4131 *(4 mi.)*

Setting -- Set in classic Maine Pepperell Cove, the Town Wharf's mooring field lies between Fort McClary Park and Moore's Island with spectacular views to the river's mouth and the ocean beyond. The long, stationary pier leads to the small shingled harbormaster's dock house, backed by three-story, gray-shingled Captain and Patty's eatery and upscale Enoteca Italiana Market. The kaleidoscope of dinghies tied to the floats speaks to the harbor's diversity.

Marina Notes -- *Mailing Address: 200 Rogers Road. Two week max Stay. Harbormaster at Town Hall: 207-439-0452 ext. 301, Cell: 207-451-0829. Only 5 transient moorings but superb bottom for anchoring. No services just dinghy dock. Bathhouse: Single public head - tile walls, cement floor - behind harbormasters office (only open during office hours). Note: Try Kittery Point Yacht Club on Goat Island, for transient moorings (Ch. 78 or 603-436-9303).

Notable -- A cruiser's bonanza, Enoteca, an Italian-style grocer, recently opened in the old Frisbee's space. Owned by Chris Souder, a former sommelier, it stocks an impressive wine and beer selection to match the fine hand-made cheeses, pastries and prepared dishes - fresh local produce, too. The original 1680 Frisbee's building (for years Cap'n Simeon's Galley), is now occupied by Captain and Patty's offering down-home Italian with typical Maine decor and spectacular views. Captain & Patty's also offers 80-minute historical Piscataqua River Tours; Capt. Neill Odams spins tales of the area's early days. Stroll Kittery's cobbled lanes lined with charming old homes, including privately owned Lady Pepperell's Mansion - an example of early American Palladian-style architecture. Fort McClary State Park makes a good picnic destination or dinghy/walk a mile up tidal Chauncey Creek to the Lobster Pier for crustaceans in the

Navigational Information
Lat: 43°04.970' **Long:** 070°43.340' **Tide:** 10 ft. **Current:** 4 kt. **Chart:** 13278
Rep. Depths (*MLW*): Entry 24 ft. **Fuel Dock** n/a **Max Slip/Moor** 24 ft./24 ft.
Access: Portsmouth Harbor to Kittery Beach Channel - no Bridge

Marina Facilities *(In Season/Off Season)*
Fuel: No
Slips: 12 Total, 8 Transient **Max LOA:** 95 ft. **Max Beam:** n/a
Rate *(per ft.)*: **Day** $2.00 **Week** Inq. **Month** Inq.
Power: 30 amp $5, **50 amp** $8, **100 amp** n/a, **200 amp** n/a
Cable TV: No **Dockside Phone:** No
Dock Type: Floating, Alongside, Wood
Moorings: 43 Total, 12 Transient **Launch:** No, Dinghy Dock
Rate: Day $40 **Week** $240 **Month** Inq.
Heads: 2 Toilet(s), 2 Shower(s)
Internet: No **Laundry:** None
Pump-Out: No **Fee:** n/a **Closed Heads:** Yes

Marina Operations
Owner/Manager: Tom Allen/John Glessner **Dockmaster:** Same
In-Season: Year-Round, 7:30am-5pm, Sat. 8am-noon **Off-Season:** n/a
After-Hours Arrival: Call on the VHF for instructions
Reservations: Yes, Required **Credit Cards:** Visa/MC, Amex
Discounts: None
Pets: Welcome **Handicap Access:** No

Kittery Point Yacht Yard

PO Box 838; 48 Bowen Road; Kittery, ME 03904

Tel: (207) 439-9582 **VHF: Monitor** Ch. 69 **Talk** Ch. 8
Fax: (207) 439-4298 **Alternate Tel:** n/a
Email: tallen@kpyy.net **Web:** www.kpyy.net
Nearest Town: Kittery *(2 mi.)* **Tourist Info:** (603) 439-1319

Marina Services and Boat Supplies
Services - Docking Assistance, Trash Pick-Up, Dock Carts **Communication -** Pay Phone, FedEx, UPS, Express Mail **Supplies - OnSite:** Ice *(Block, Cube)*, Ships' Store **1-3 mi:** Bait/Tackle *(Kittery Trading 439-2700)* **3+ mi:** West Marine *(603-436-8300, 5 mi.)*

Boatyard Services
OnSite: Travelift *(70T)*, Railway *(100T)*, Hydraulic Trailer *(35T Brownell)*, Engine mechanic *(gas, diesel)*, Electrical Repairs, Electronic Sales, Electronics Repairs, Hull Repairs, Rigger, Bottom Cleaning, Brightwork, Air Conditioning, Refrigeration, Compound, Wash & Wax, Interior Cleaning, Propeller Repairs, Woodworking, Painting, Awlgrip, Total Refits **OnCall:** Canvas Work, Divers, Inflatable Repairs, Upholstery, Metal Fabrication **Dealer for:** Westerbeke, Yanmar, Kohler, CAT. **Member:** ABBRA, ABYC **Yard Rates:** $69/hr., Haul & Launch $8/ft., Power Wash $5/ft.

Restaurants and Accommodations
Under 1 mi: Restaurant *(Captain & Patty's 439-3655, L $8-25, D $16-35, New Mgt, 2010)* **1-3 mi:** Restaurant *(Anneke Jans 439-0001, D $15-34, Fine Dining, Shorter by dinghy)*, Seafood Shack *(Warren's Lobster House 439-1630, L $7-16, D $15-18, Salad Bar, Kids' $4-6.50)*, Lite Fare *(Loco Coco's Tacos 438-9322, L & D $3-11)*, *(Sunrise Grille 439-5748, B & L, 6:30am-2pm, 7 days)*, Pizzeria *(AJ's 439-9700, flat bread pizza)*, *(Town 439-1265, Subs, Greek)*, Motel *(Coachman 439-4434, $60-110)*, Inn/B&B *(Chickadee 439-0672, $119)*, *(Portsmouth Harbor Inn 439-4040, $155-250)*

Recreation and Entertainment
OnCall: Fishing Charter **Near:** Galleries *(Kittery Art Assoc. 451-9384, Fri. Concerts)* **Under 1 mi:** Picnic Area *(Ft. McClary)*, Grills, Playground, Park *(Fort McClary S.P. 439-2845 $2)*, Museum *(Kittery Historical & Naval Society 439-3080 $3/1.50, Tue-Sat 10am-4pm)*, Tours *(Capt & Patty's 439-8976 - History Cruises)* **1-3 mi:** Beach *(Ft. Foster, Seapoint)*, Video Rental *(Movie Gallery 439-2338)* **3+ mi:** Golf Course *(Pease 603-433-1331, 8 mi.)*

Provisioning and General Services
Near: Protestant Church **Under 1 mi:** Market *(Enoteca Italiana 439-7216 - necessary groceries, prepared foods, handmade mozzarella & ricotta)*, Wine/Beer *(Enoteca)*, Liquor Store, Bakery *(Enoteca)*, Bank/ATM, Post Office, Catholic Church, Library *(Rice 439-1553)*, Beauty Salon *(Cuts by Courtney 439-2609)*, Barber Shop, Laundry, Pharmacy *(Rite Aid 438-9079)*, Hardware Store *(Ace 439-4150)*, Florist **1-3 mi:** Health Food *(Rising Tide 439-8898)*, Fishmonger *(Seaview 439-1599)*, Dry Cleaners *(We Care 439-4131)*, Bookstore *(River Run 603-431-2100; Gulliver's Travels 603-431-5556)*, Retail Shops *(Kittery Outlets 439-7993)*, Copies Etc. *(Kittery Biz Ctr. 439-5704)* **3+ mi:** Supermarket *(Hannaford 603-436-6669, 3.5 mi.)*

Transportation
OnCall: Rental Car *(Enterprise 603-433-1177)*, Taxi *(Checker 603-750-7777)* **Airport:** Portsmouth Int'l/Portland Int'l. *(6.5 mi./50 mi.)*

Medical Services
911 Service **Under 1 mi:** Doctor *(Kittery Family 439-4430)*, Dentist *(Breslin 439-4400)*, Chiropractor *(Alebro 439-3358)*, Veterinarian *(Piscataqua 439-2661)* **1-3 mi:** Holistic Services *(Portsmouth Harbor Inn & Spa 439-4040 - Mass. $95/55-min.)* **Hospital:** Portsmouth Regional 603-436-5110 *(3 mi.)*

Setting -- Up the Piscataqua River, past Pepperell Cove, KPYY occupies a protected peninsula bordered by the Back Channel and Spruce Creek. The mooring field and main pier, surrounded by side-tie docks and dinghy floats, look across the channel to Seavey Island's northeast tip. At the top of the ramp, a pretty two story, weathered Dutch Colonial houses the ships' store and office. The adjacent railway leads to the boatyard and dry storage part of the property.

Marina Notes -- CCM. Yard since 1963. Formerly Dion's. Bought by Manchester Marine in 1999. Acquired Patten Y.Y. in '07 (1.5 miles above the Memorial Bridge in Elliot). KPYY's onsite full service yard: Dry storage capacity up to 200 boats. System installs, repowers, rebuilds, custom welding, electrical, electronics, A/C, plumbing, carpenter, fiberglass repair. Employs more than two dozen craftsmen with decades of experience full-time, year-round. Bathhouse: Two full baths. Tile floors, fiberglass shower stall with glass doors. Available during business hours only.

Notable -- On Seavy Island, the Portsmouth Naval Shipyard and its Museum are open by appointment (438-5550). Less than a mile east, past the classic 1729 Congregational Church, Fort McClary's 27-acre historic site (7 days 9am-dusk) is a good picnic destination - at tables or on blankets on the lovely lawn that surrounds the 1846 blockhouse. Continue on to Captain & Patty's eatery and Enoteca Italiana Market at the town wharf. About a mile northwest, tiny Kittery hosts most necessary services; a mile further Kittery Historical and Naval Museum hosts a hodgepodge of fascinating artifacts near the Kittery Trading Post (439-2700) and small circle of local shops. The 120-store Kittery Outlets, a 1.25-mile-long complex of 13 smaller outlets, is another mile northwest on Rte 1.

PHOTOS ON DVD: 16

Prescott Park Municipal Dock

PO Box 1103; Shaw Building, Marcy St.; Portsmouth, NH 03802

Tel: (603) 431-8748 **VHF: Monitor** Ch. 9 **Talk** n/a
Fax: (603) 436-1034 **Alternate Tel:** n/a
Email: prescott@worldpath.net **Web:** www.cityofportmouth.com
Nearest Town: Portsmouth **Tourist Info:** (603) 610-5510

Navigational Information

Lat: 43°04.658' **Long:** 070°45.121' **Tide:** 6 ft. **Current:** 9 kt. **Chart:** 13278
Rep. Depths (*MLW*): Entry 10 ft. **Fuel Dock** n/a **Max Slip/Moor** 10 ft./-
Access: Piscataqua River past Goat Island, just east of the Memorial Bridge

Marina Facilities *(In Season/Off Season)*

Fuel: No
Slips: 22 Total, 16 Transient **Max LOA:** 55 ft. **Max Beam:** 16 ft.
Rate *(per ft.)*: **Day** $1.75* **Week** n/a **Month** n/a
Power: 30 amp Incl., **50 amp** n/a, **100 amp** n/a, **200 amp** n/a
Cable TV: No **Dockside Phone:** No
Dock Type: Floating, Long Fingers, Concrete, Wood
Moorings: 0 Total, 0 Transient **Launch:** n/a
Rate: Day n/a **Week** n/a **Month** n/a
Heads: 7 Toilet(s)
Internet: No **Laundry:** None
Pump-Out: OnCall, Full Service **Fee:** Free **Closed Heads:** Yes

Marina Operations

Owner/Manager: Michael Warhurst **Dockmaster:** Same
In-Season: Apr-Oct, 9am-5pm** **Off-Season:** Nov-Mar, Closed
After-Hours Arrival: Call first
Reservations: Yes, Preferred **Credit Cards:** Cash/Check only
Discounts: None
Pets: Welcome **Handicap Access:** Yes, Heads, Docks

Marina Services and Boat Supplies

Services - Trash Pick-Up **Communication -** Pay Phone, FedEx, UPS
Supplies - Near: Ice *(Block, Cube)* **Under 1 mi:** Ships' Store *(Navtronics 436-2544)*, Propane *(Sea 3 431-5990)* **1-3 mi:** West Marine *(436-8300)*

Boatyard Services

OnCall: Engine mechanic *(gas, diesel)*, Electrical Repairs, Electronics Repairs, Rigger, Sail Loft, Divers, Air Conditioning, Refrigeration **Near:** Launching Ramp. **Nearest Yard:** Kittery Point Yacht Yard (207) 439-9582

Restaurants and Accommodations

OnSite: Lite Fare *(Fresh Local Truck Everything from scratch - CIA chef)*
Near: Restaurant *(Rosa 436-9715, D $12-22)*, *(Café Mediterrano 427-5563, L $8-12, D $14-25)*, *(Library - Steak House 431-5202, L $8-17, D $23-35, Rockingham House)*, *(Press Room 431-5186, L & D $8-13, live music)*, *(Mombo at Strawbery Banke 433-2340, L $12-19, D $19-34)*, *(Common Man 334-6225, D $18-24)*, Lite Fare *(Geno's Chowder & Sandwich 427-2070)*, *(Dos Amigos 373-6001, L $3-8)*, Inn/B&B *(Ale House Inn 431-7660, $130-185)*, *(Governor's House 427-5140, $159-239)*, *(Inn at Strawbery Banke 436-7242, $100-170)*, *(Sise Inn 433-1200, $119-279)*

Recreation and Entertainment

OnSite: Playground, Special Events *(Prescott Park Arts Festival 436-2848)*
Near: Pool, Picnic Area, Grills, Tennis Courts, Fishing Charter *(Sushi Hunter 231-4662)*, Park *(Portsmouth's Maritime Museum - U.S.S. Albacore - a 205-ft. decommissioned '53 submarine)*, Museum *(Strawbery Banke 433-1100, Children's Museum 742-2002 Mon-Sat 10am-5pm, Sun 1-5pm, $4/3 - engagingly illuminates the area's maritime history)*, Cultural Attract *(Seacoast Repertory 433-4472; The Music Hall 436-2400)*, Sightseeing *(Isles of Shoals Steamship Co. 431-5500)* **Under 1 mi:** Bowling *(Bowl O Rama 436-0504)* **1-3 mi:** Golf Course *(Wentworth 433-3050)*, Movie Theater *(Regal Fox Run 431-4200)*

Provisioning and General Services

Near: Gourmet Shop *(Stonewall Kitchen 422-7303)*, Delicatessen, Health Food *(Portsmouth 436-1722)*, Liquor Store, Bakery *(Ceres Street 436-6518)*, Bank/ATM, Post Office, Catholic Church, Protestant Church, Library *(427-1540, Internet)*, Barber Shop, Laundry, Bookstore, Pharmacy *(CVS 431-0231)*, Florist, Copies Etc. *(Jiffy Copy Center 436-8286)* **Under 1 mi:** Supermarket *(Hannaford 436-6669)*, Wine/Beer *(Ceres Street 431-2640)*, Farmers' Market *(Sat 8am-1pm City Hall)*, Fishmonger *(Sanders Fish Market 436-4568)*, Lobster Pound, Synagogue, Dry Cleaners **1-3 mi:** Hardware Store *(Jackson's 439-1133)*

Transportation

OnCall: Taxi *(Blue Star Taxi 436-2774)* **Near:** Local Bus *(Coast Trolley 743-5777)*, InterCity Bus *(C&J Trailways 430-1100, Greyhound 433-3210)* **Under 1 mi:** Bikes *(Papa Wheelies 427-2060)*, Rental Car *(Budget 431-1986)* **Airport:** Pease/Logan Int'l. *(4 mi./55 mi.)*

Medical Services

911 Service **Near:** Doctor *(Brown 373-0664)*, Chiropractor *(Grazier 436-8406)*, Optician *(Eye Look 436-7771)* **Under 1 mi:** Dentist *(Dinnerman 436-0535)*, Holistic Services *(Portsmouthh Spa 433-0059, Mass $70/50 min.)* **1-3 mi:** Veterinarian *(Piscataqua 207- 439-2661)* **Hospital:** Portsmouth Reg 436-5110 *(3.5 mi.)*

PHOTOS ON DVD: 24

Setting -- Two sets of slips sit right on the fast moving Piscataqua with views of the Portsmouth Navy Shipyard and Kittery Landing. A lively crowd of smaller motorboats party hardy on hot summer afternoons while ovenight transients scope out the entertainment events at the top of the ramps on lovely Prescott Park's inviting greensward. Vibrant downtown Portsmouth is an easy walk; dozens of restaurants and shops line charming Bow Street and Market Square.

Marina Notes -- *Flat Rate: 21-30 ft. $50, 31-40 ft $70, 41-50 ft. $85, 51-55 ft. $100. Hourly rate: 21-30 Ft. $8, 31-40 ft. $10, 41-50 ft. $12, over 50 ft. $15. Max LOA 55 ft. (only 2 slips this size). Max stay 72-hours - but dockmaster has discretion. **Varies. Reservation requires payment in advance by check/cash. New 30-amp pedestals on both docks. Fuel at Fish Co-op. Bring extra fenders. No pets in the Park. Must leash dogs & leave/enter dock through north parking lot. Take a local perspective - this is a public park accessible by boat. Bathhouse: Municipal, cinderblock public heads - dawn to dusk, no showers.

Notable -- Gracious, impeccably maintained walkways, gardens, fountains, and more than 500 varieties of annuals provide a backdrop for the Prescott Park Arts Festival, a summer-long celebration of the arts featuring outdoor theatre, music, dance, children's performances, and special events -- Jazz, Folk, Chowder and Chili Festivals. A fitting prelude to the remarkable Strawbery Banke Restoration directly across Marcy Street. The "Museum," a ten-acre restoration of one of Portsmouth's first settlements, includes 45 buildings from 1695-1850's - each restored to its prime period. From April to November, it offers activities, tours and special events (7 days, 10am-5pm, 2 day-pass $15/10, fam $40). The Seacoast Repertory Theatre is a block west, and the Children's Museum is 3 blocks

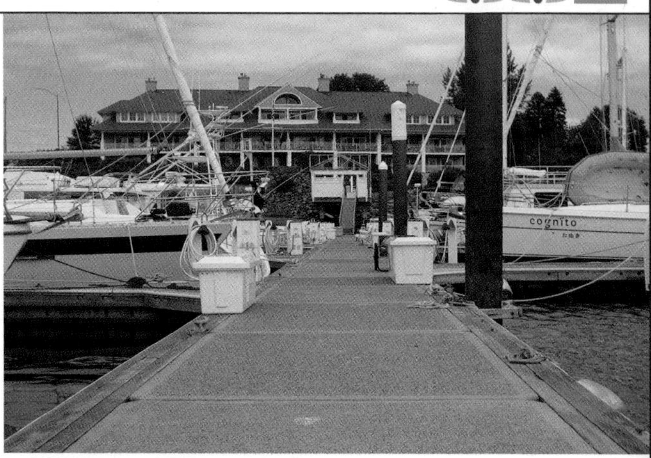

Navigational Information

Lat: 43°04.900' **Long:** 070°45.080' **Tide:** 10 ft. **Current:** 4 kt. **Chart:** 13278
Rep. Depths (*MLW*): Entry 34 ft. **Fuel Dock** n/a **Max Slip/Moor** 12 ft./-
Access: Past Portsmouth Navy Yard, on starboard side - before bridge

Marina Facilities *(In Season/Off Season)*

Fuel: No
Slips: 26 Total, 2 Transient **Max LOA:** 125 ft. **Max Beam:** n/a
Rate *(per ft.)*: **Day** $3.00/Inq.* **Week** Inq. **Month** Inq.
Power: 30 amp $10, **50 amp** $20, **100 amp** $40, **200 amp** n/a
Cable TV: Yes **Dockside Phone:** No
Dock Type: Floating, Long Fingers, Pilings, Concrete, Aluminum
Moorings: 0 Total, 0 Transient **Launch:** n/a
Rate: Day n/a **Week** n/a **Month** n/a
Heads: 2 Toilet(s), 2 Shower(s)
Internet: Yes *(Broadband - Lounge, Free)* **Laundry:** 1 Washer(s), 1 Dryer(s)
Pump-Out: OnCall, Full Service **Fee:** Free **Closed Heads:** No

Marina Operations

Owner/Manager: Island Marine Service **Dockmaster:** Justin Kelcourse
In-Season: May-Oct, 10am-6pm** **Off-Season:** Nov-Apr, Closed
After-Hours Arrival: Take end dock
Reservations: Yes, Preferred **Credit Cards:** Cash or Travelers Checks only
Discounts: None
Pets: Welcome **Handicap Access:** Yes, Heads

Badgers Island East

4 Island Avenue; Kittery, ME 03904

Tel: (207) 439-1661 **VHF: Monitor** Ch. 9 **Talk** Ch. 68
Fax: (207) 438-9715 **Alternate Tel:** n/a
Email: info@badgersislandmarina.com **Web:** badgersislandmarina.com
Nearest Town: Portsmouth, NH *(0.5 mi.)* **Tourist Info:** (603) 610-5510

Marina Services and Boat Supplies

Services - Boaters' Lounge, Trash Pick-Up **Communication -** FedEx, DHL, UPS, Express Mail **Supplies - OnSite:** Ice *(Cube)* **Near:** Boat/US, Live Bait, Propane *(Jackson's)*, CNG **1-3 mi:** Ships' Store *(Jackson's Marine Hardware 439-1133, Kittery Trading Post 439-2700)*, West Marine *(603-436-8300)*, Bait/Tackle *(Kittery Trading Post 439-2700)*

Boatyard Services

OnCall: Engine mechanic *(gas, diesel)*, Electrical Repairs, Electronics Repairs, Canvas Work, Divers, Bottom Cleaning, Brightwork, Air Conditioning, Refrigeration, Compound, Wash & Wax, Interior Cleaning **Near:** Launching Ramp, Propeller Repairs, Woodworking, Metal Fabrication, Painting. **Nearest Yard:** Island Marine Service (207) 439-3810

Restaurants and Accommodations

Near: Restaurant *(Warren's Lobster House 439-1630, L $6-11, D $12-17)*, *(Rosa 603-436-9715, L $4-10, D $7-18)*, Seafood Shack *(Morrison's Lobster 439-2501)*, Pizzeria *(Badgers Island 439-5996)*, Hotel *(Inn at Portsmouth Harbor 439-4040, $95-175)*, Inn/B&B *(Portsmouth Harbor 439-4040)* **Under 1 mi:** Hotel *(Sheraton Harborside 603-431-2300, $135-450)*, Inn/B&B *(Inn at Strawbery Banke 603-436-7242, $85-150)* **1-3 mi:** Seafood Shack *(Bob's Clam Hut 439-4919)*, Inn/B&B *(Coachman Inn 439-4434, $110-135)*

Recreation and Entertainment

Near: Park *(Prescott Park, Portsmouth)*, Museum *(Kittery Historical - Naval Museum)*, Cultural Attract *(Portsmouth Music Hall 603-436-2400; Seacoast Repertory Theater 603- 433-4793 603)*, Sightseeing *(Strawbery Banke, Portsmouth Historical District 603-433-1100)*, Special Events *(Prescott Park Arts Festival 436-2848 - all summer)* **Under 1 mi:** Movie Theater *(Portsmouth)* **1-3 mi:** Bowling *(Bowl USA 603-431-4292)*, Video Rental *(Atlantic Video 603-431-2331)* **3+ mi:** Golf Course *(Pease Golf Course - Great Bay Golf Course 603-433-1331)*

Provisioning and General Services

Near: Fishmonger *(Herbert 703-0431)* **Under 1 mi:** Gourmet Shop *(Terra Cotta Pasta 475-3025)*, Health Food *(Portsmouth 603-436-1722)*, Wine/Beer *(Ceres Street 603-431-2640)*, Liquor Store *(Garys 603-436-5854)*, Bakery *(Beach Pea Baking 439-3555)*, Green Grocer *(Golden Harvest 439-2113)*, Lobster Pound *(Seaview 439-1599)*, Library, Pharmacy *(Rite Aid 439-1966)*, Hardware Store *(Ace 439-4150)*, Copies Etc. *(Johnson Printing 439-2567)* **1-3 mi:** Supermarket *(Hannaford 603-436-6669; Shaw's 603-436-0323)*, Farmers' Market *(Sat 8am-1pm - Portsmouth City Hall)*, Post Office, Protestant Church *(North Church)*, Synagogue, Retail Shops *(Kittery Outlet Stores)*

Transportation

OnCall: Taxi *(Blue Star 603-436-2774)*, Airport Limo *(Regal 800-709-3500; Great Bay 800-820-6117)* **Under 1 mi:** Rental Car *(Budget 603-436-2588; Enterprise 800-736-8222)*, InterCity Bus *(Greyhound 603-436-0163)* **Airport:** Portsmouth Int'l/Portland Int'l. *(5 mi./55 mi.)*

Medical Services

911 Service **Near:** Dentist *(Swallow 439-3390)*, Chiropractor *(Henderson 439-0190)*, Holistic Services *(Portsmouth Harbor Sap 439-4040 - massage $85/55 min.)* **Under 1 mi:** Doctor *(Gear 603-610-0235)*, Veterinarian *(Piscataqua 439-2661)* **Hospital:** Portsmouth Reg. 603-436-5110 *(4 mi.)*

Setting -- Just past the Portsmouth Navy Yard, on the Piscataqua River's Eastern bank, Badger Island East's secure dockage lies right across from Portsmouth's historic Strawbery Banke Museum and Prescott Park - seaward of the Route One Memorial Bridge. The docks are backed by a very attractive, three-story, gray-shingled, contemporary condominium complex that is surrounded by lovely, manicured gardens.

Marina Notes -- *to 40 ft. $3/ft, 41-70 ft. $4/ft., 71-125ft. $5/ft. **staffed Wed-Sun only. Formerly Kittery Landing Marina. Acquired by Darren LaPierre, Island Marine (owner of Badgers Island Marina). Limited transient dockage - call ahead for reservations. Boater's lounge (with internet access, teak chairs, and TV) plus office & bathhouse on first floor of condo. Gate-protected docks. Strong current makes for challenging docking - ask for an assist. Expect some roll. Pump-out available with advance notice. Bathhouse: Inviting full baths, quarry-tile floors, fiberglass shower stalls plus laundry in boaters' lounge.

Notable -- About a half mile north on Rte 1, Kittery's "Gourmet Alley" is an enticing mix of wonderful shops and local eateries. 2 miles further north, the Kittery Outlets sprawl 1.25 miles along Rte 1 with over 120 designer outlet stores, plus the well-known Kittery Trading Post. Down the block from the marina, Warren's Lobster House is a local institution with inside or outside waterfront dining - but locals say take a cab to Bob's Clam Hut for a true Maine experience. Kittery Historical and Naval Museum is about a mile from the docks (10am-4pm, June-Oct, $3/$1.50) as is Lady Pepperell's American-Palladian mansion. Most other services are a ten-minute walk over the bridge in Portsmouth, NH - as is the historic district with Strawbery Banke Museum and Prescott Park.

PHOTOS ON DVD: 15

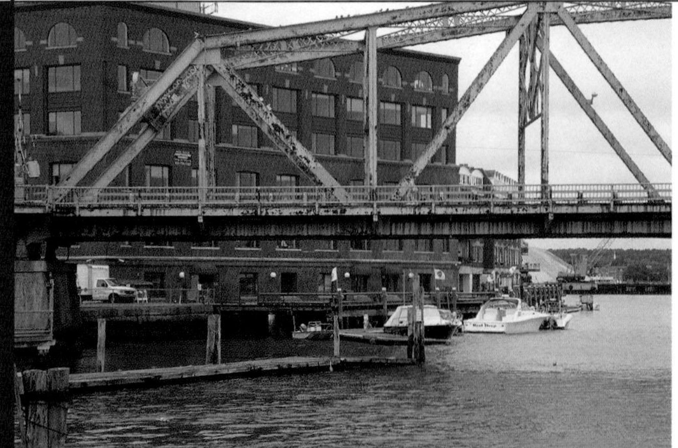

The Marina at Harbour Place

One Harbour Place; Portsmouth, NH 03801

Tel: (603) 436-0915; (978) 430-7104 **VHF: Monitor** n/a **Talk** n/a
Fax: n/a **Alternate Tel:** n/a
Email: marinaharbourplace@yahoo.com **Web:** marinaharbourplace.com
Nearest Town: Portsmouth **Tourist Info:** (603) 610-5510

Navigational Information
Lat: 43°04.736' **Long:** 070°45.210' **Tide:** 6 ft. **Current:** 9 kt. **Chart:** 13278
Rep. Depths (*MLW*): Entry 10 ft. **Fuel Dock** n/a **Max Slip/Moor** 10 ft./-
Access: Past Goat Island, to port immediately after Memorial Bridge

Marina Facilities *(In Season/Off Season)*
Fuel: No
Slips: 12 Total, 5 Transient **Max LOA:** 155 ft. **Max Beam:** 30 ft.
Rate *(per ft.)*: **Day** $2.00* **Week** $14 **Month** n/a
Power: 30 amp $10, **50 amp** $15, **100 amp** n/a, **200 amp** n/a
Cable TV: No **Dockside Phone:** No
Dock Type: Floating, Alongside, Concrete, Wood
Moorings: 0 Total, 0 Transient **Launch:** n/a, Dinghy Dock
Rate: Day n/a **Week** n/a **Month** n/a
Heads: 2 Toilet(s), 2 Shower(s)
Internet: Yes *(Wi-Fi, Free)* **Laundry:** 2 Washer(s), 2 Dryer(s)
Pump-Out: OnCall, Full Service **Fee:** Free **Closed Heads:** Yes

Marina Operations
Owner/Manager: Capt. Steve Root **Dockmaster:** Same
In-Season: Year Round, 9am-5pm **Off-Season:** n/a
After-Hours Arrival: Call (603) 781-4528
Reservations: Yes, Preferred **Credit Cards:** Visa/MC
Discounts: None
Pets: Welcome **Handicap Access:** No

Marina Services and Boat Supplies
Services - Security *(24)* **Supplies - Under 1 mi:** Ice *(Block, Cube, Shaved)* **1-3 mi:** West Marine *(436-8300)*, Bait/Tackle *(Bait Lady 431-3170)* **3+ mi:** Propane *(Davis Oil Service 207-439-1324 , 4 mi.)*

Boatyard Services
Nearest Yard: Kittery Point Yacht Yard (207) 439-9582

Restaurants and Accommodations
Near: Restaurant *(Portsmouth Brewery 431-1115, D $12-18)*, *(Press Room 431-5186, L & D $8-13 Live music, 7 nights & Wed-Sat lunch)*, *(Dolphin Striker 431-5222, D $20-28)*, *(Jumpin' Jay's Fish Cafe 766-3474)*, *(River House 431-2600, D $10-25, Kids' $5-6 - overlooking the tugs)*, *(Wellington Room 431-2989, D $21-34, River view)*, *(Victory 766-0960)*, Lite Fare *(Cava Tapas & Wine Bar 319-1575, L & D $5-16)*, *(Colby's 436-3033, B & L)*, Pizzeria *(Downtown Brickoven 430-8582)*, Hotel *(Sheraton 431-2300, $175-245)*, Inn/B&B *(Bow Street 431-7760, $120-185)*, *(Inn At Strawberry Banke 436-7242, $100-170)*, *(Sise 433-1200, $119-279)*, *(Ale House 431-7760)*

Recreation and Entertainment
Near: Spa, Picnic Area, Playground, Park, Museum *(Strawbery Banke Museum 433-1100 $15; Port of Portsmouth Maritime Museum 436-3680 $5/2)*, Tours *(Isles of Shoals 431-5500 $25 6 miles to 9 island archipelago)*, Cultural Attract *(Seacoast Repertory Theater 433-4472; The Music Hall 436-2400)*, Sightseeing *(Portsmouth Harbor Cruises 800-76-0915; Three walking tours from Market Square tourism Kiosk - Map $2)*, Galleries, Special Events *(Prescott Park Arts Festival - all summer)* **Under 1 mi:** Boat Rentals *(Seafari Charters 207-439-5068)*, Fishing Charter *(Dafari 207-439-5068)* **1-3 mi:** Fitness Center *(Portsmouth Athletic 431-1430)*, Bowling *(Bowl-O-Rama 436-0504)*, Movie Theater *(Hoyts Newington 431-4200)* **3+ mi:** Golf Course *(Pease G.C. 433-1331, 4 mi.)*

Provisioning and General Services
Near: Market *(Richardson's 433-9176)*, Gourmet Shop *(Stonewall Kitchen 422-7303)*, Delicatessen *(Moe's 436-2327)*, Health Food *(Portsmouth Health Food 436-1722)*, Wine/Beer *(Ceres Street 431-2640)*, Fishmonger *(Olde Mill 436-4568)*, Bank/ATM, Post Office, Catholic Church, Protestant Church, Synagogue, Beauty Salon, Barber Shop, Dry Cleaners, Laundry, Bookstore *(Riverrun 431-2100; Gulliver's 431-5556)*, Newsstand **Under 1 mi:** Farmers' Market *(City Hall Sat 8am-1pm)*, Library *(Portsmouth 427-1540)*, Pharmacy *(CVS 431-0234)* **1-3 mi:** Supermarket *(Shaw's 436-0323; Hannaford 436-6669)*, Liquor Store *(NH State 436-4806)*, Hardware Store *(Ricci 436-7480)* **3+ mi:** Department Store *(Fox Run Mall, 3.5 mi.)*

Transportation
OnCall: Taxi *(Anchor 436-1888; Blue Star 436-2774)* **Near:** Local Bus *(Coast Trolley Loop 743-5777 from Market Sq.- Fox Run Mall)*, InterCity Bus *(Concord Coach 430-1100; Greyhound 433-3210)* **Under 1 mi:** Bikes *(Papa Wheelie's 427-2060)* **1-3 mi:** Rental Car *(Budget 431-1986)* **Airport:** Portsmouth Int'l/Portland Jetport *(4.5 mi./47 mi.)*

Medical Services
911 Service **Near:** Doctor *(Gear 610-0235)*, Chiropractor *(Kragen 436-2115)*, Holistic Services *(Portsmouth Spa 433-0059)* **Under 1 mi:** Dentist *(McArdle 430-1010)* **1-3 mi:** Veterinarian *(Piscataqua 439-2661)* **Hospital:** Portsmouth 436-5110 *(2.5 mi.)*

PHOTOS ON DVD: 17

Setting -- Just past the Memorial Bridge, in the shadow of a five-story brick condo and a brick office building - joined by an expansive wood-planked deck - the marina's long side-tie floating docks edge the Piscataqua's southern shore. It's directly across from Badger's Island Marina and sports a front-row view of the bustling river activity.The Seacoast Repertory Theatre is next door and all of historic, revitalized downtown Portsmouth is just steps away.

Marina Notes -- *504 ft. linear floating dockage; dedicated 200+ foot transient float. Manages 100-ton vessels. Day rate $5/2 hrs. Operated by Portsmouth Towing (781-4528 - Towboat-US). Most secure downtown site. Limited marina services. Garage parking seven days. Temp. N.H. boating license available at Wentworth. Open deck area is site of many tented functions - fleet captains take note (569-4786). Bathhouse: modern, tiled group, locker room-style showers (but located in office building's garage - not accessible Sundays). Coin-op Laundry. Note: Bridge opens on demand at hour & half hour, Ch. 13.

Notable -- Location! Location! A cultural magnet with a large number of carefully-preserved Colonial buildings, today's Portsmouth demands a lay-day or two. Within a few blocks of Harbour Place, many cultural, culinary and retail attractions make this an interesting entry to this historic New England town. The Seacoast Rep, one of several venues, has a full schedule of live shows. Visit the USS Albacore Sub at Portsmouth Maritime Museum, the 10-acre Strawbery Banke Restoration, a complex of 40 revolutionary-era buildings or any of the eight historic house museums. A restaurant revival makes the town a gourmet's delight. Market Square is home to upscale shops, cafes and the tourism kiosk which sells the Harbor Trail Walking Tour map and also offers guided tours.

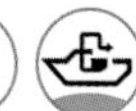

Navigational Information
Lat: 43°04.890' **Long:** 070°45.310' **Tide:** 10 ft. **Current:** 4 kt. **Chart:** 13278
Rep. Depths (*MLW*): Entry 40 ft. **Fuel Dock** n/a **Max Slip/Moor** 40 ft./-
Access: Piscataqua River, past Navy Yard, under bridge - starboard side

Marina Facilities *(In Season/Off Season)*
Fuel: No
Slips: 27 Total, 3 Transient **Max LOA:** 100 ft. **Max Beam:** n/a
Rate *(per ft.)*: **Day** $3.00/Inq.* **Week** n/a **Month** Inq.
Power: 30 amp $10, **50 amp** $20, **100 amp** $40, **200 amp** n/a
Cable TV: No **Dockside Phone:** No
Dock Type: Floating, Long Fingers, Short Fingers, Pilings, Concrete
Moorings: 0 Total, 0 Transient **Launch:** n/a
Rate: Day n/a **Week** n/a **Month** n/a
Heads: 2 Toilet(s), 2 Shower(s)
Internet: No **Laundry:** 1 Washer(s), 1 Dryer(s)
Pump-Out: OnCall, Full Service **Fee:** Free **Closed Heads:** No

Marina Operations
Owner/Manager: Island Marine **Dockmaster:** Vinnie Huneke
In-Season: May-Oct, **8am-4:30pm **Off-Season:** Nov-Apr, Closed
After-Hours Arrival: Take end dock
Reservations: Yes, Preferred **Credit Cards:** Cash/Travelers' Checks only
Discounts: None
Pets: Welcome **Handicap Access:** Yes, Heads

Badgers Island Marina

27 Badgers Island West; Kittery, ME 03904

Tel: (207) 451-8174; (207) 439-3810 **VHF: Monitor** Ch. 9 **Talk** Ch. 68
Fax: (207) 438-9715 **Alternate Tel:** n/a
Email: islandmarineservice@comcast.net **Web:** badgersislandmarina.com
Nearest Town: Portsmouth, NH *(0.5 mi.)* **Tourist Info:** (207) 439-1319

Marina Services and Boat Supplies
Services - Trash Pick-Up **Communication -** FedEx, UPS, Express Mail
Supplies - OnSite: Ice *(Block, Cube)*, Ships' Store **Under 1 mi:** Bait/Tackle *(Kittery Trading 439-2700)* **1-3 mi:** West Marine *(603-436-8300)*

Boatyard Services
OnSite: Railway *(100T)*, Crane, Launching Ramp, Engine mechanic *(gas, diesel)*, Electrical Repairs, Hull Repairs, Bottom Cleaning, Brightwork, Compound, Wash & Wax, Propeller Repairs, Painting **OnCall:** Electronics Repairs, Rigger, Divers, Air Conditioning, Refrigeration, Woodworking, Metal Fabrication **Dealer for:** Mercury, Mercruiser, Honda. **Yard Rates:** $85/hr., Haul & Launch $8.50/ft. each way *(blocking incl.)*, Bottom Paint $18-22/ft.
Storage: On-Land Out: $39/ft.; Inside: $7.50/sq.ft.

Restaurants and Accommodations
Near: Restaurant *(Weathervane 439-0335, L & D $8-25)*, *(Warren's Lobster House 439-1630, L $7-19, D $13-23)*, Seafood Shack *(Morrison's Lobsters 439-2501)*, Pizzeria *(Badger's Island 439-5996)*, Hotel *(Sheraton Harborside 603-431-2300, $175-245)*, Inn/B&B *(Portsmouth Harbor 439-4040, $115-215)* **Under 1 mi:** Restaurant *(Dolphin Striker 603-431-5222, L $7-15, D $15-23)*, *(The Rosa 603-436-9715, D $12-22)*, Inn/B&B *(Bow Tie 603-431-7760, $120-185)*, *(Inn at Strawbery Banke 603-436-7242, $100-170)*, *(Enchanted Garden 439-1489, $60-350)*

Recreation and Entertainment
Near: Jogging Paths, Sightseeing *(Seafari Charters 439-5068; Isles of Shoals Steamship 603-431-5500, $25)* **1-3 mi:** Picnic Area *(Ft. McClary)*, Grills, Bowling *(Bowl O Rama 603-436-0504)*, Museum *(Strawbery Banke, Colonial Dames House 603-430-7968, $15; Port of Portsmouth Maritme Museum 436-3680, $5; Children's Museum of Portsmouth)*, Cultural Attract *(Seacoast Repertory 603-433-4793; The Music Hall 603-436-2400)*
3+ mi: Golf Course *(Pease G.C. 603-436-5001 - 27 holes, 4.5 mi.)*

Provisioning and General Services
Near: Gourmet Shop *(Stonewall 603-422-7303)*, Fishmonger *(Cape Island 439-6407; Herbert 703-0431)* **Under 1 mi:** Market *(Richardson's 603-433-9176)*, Wine/Beer *(Ceres St. 603-431-2640)*, Liquor Store *(Gary's 603-436-5854)*, Library *(Rice 439-1553)*, Beauty Salon, Bookstore *(Gulliver's 603-431-5556)* **1-3 mi:** Supermarket *(Shaw's 603-436-0323; Mobil on the Run 439-6713)*, Farmers' Market *(Sat 8am-1pm, Port. City Hall)*, Bank/ATM, Post Office, Catholic Church, Protestant Church, Synagogue, Pharmacy *(Rite Aid 439-1966)*, Hardware Store *(Kittery Ace 439-4150)*, Retail Shops *(Kittery Outlets)*, Copies Etc. *(Sir Speedy 603-433-4664)*

Transportation
OnCall: Rental Car *(Enterprise 603-433-1177)*, Taxi *(Anchor 603-436-1888, Checker 603-750-7777)*, Airport Limo *(Seacoast 603-431-9880)* **1-3 mi:** InterCity Bus *(Concord 603-430-1100)* **Airport:** Portsmouth Int'l/Portland *(5 mi./55 mi.)*

Medical Services
911 Service **OnCall:** Ambulance **Near:** Dentist *(Swallow 439-3390)*, Chiropractor *(Henderson 439-0190)*, Holistic Services *(Portsmouth Harbor Spa 439-4040 Massage $85/55-min.)* **Under 1 mi:** Doctor *(Gear 603-610-0235)*, Veterinarian *(Piscataqua 439-2661)* **Hospital:** Portsmouth Regional 603-436-5110 *(4 mi.)*

PHOTOS ON DVD: 17

Setting -- Just above the Memorial Bridge, Badgers Island Marina lies on the river's north shore directly across from Marina at Harbour Place and the revitalized Portsmouth waterfront. The imposing three-story, gray-shingled, neo-Victorian Badgers Island West condominium rises above the docks making the marina hard to miss. Wide, redwood-stained, railed boardwalks edge the docks and lead to the upland; inviting picnic tables and comfortable sitting areas offer skyline views, busy harbor scenes plus sublime sunsets. Adjacent is the attractive corporate headquarters of Weathervane Seafood restaurant.

Marina Notes -- *to 40 ft. $3/ft, 41-70 ft. $4/ft., 71-125ft. $5/ft. **Mon-Fri only. Limited transient dockage. Pump-out provided by local EPA Service. Island Marine Service's main office 1.5 mi. inland: 32 Route 236. Full BY services between two facilities including 100 ton railway. Strong current after going under the bridge - Piscataqua means "branching with a strong current." Staff helps with tie-up. Bathhouse: Small, recent facilities, fiberglass shower stalls, tile floor.

Notable -- Warren's Lobster House is a reasonably short walk away as are several other eateries. Provisions are readily available in Portsmouth - a half-mile walk across the bridge (river current recommends against a dinghy ride) or a half mile north along Rte One's "Gourmet Alley." Lovely Prescott Park features a summer-long Arts Festival and adjacent Strawbery Banke outdoor "Museum" is a ten-acre restoration of one of Portsmouth's first settlements with forty-five beautifully restored buildings that date from 1695-1850's.Three blocks farther south is the hands-on Children's Museum of Portsmouth. The Isles of Shoals Steamship Co. takes the angst out of visiting this nine-island archipelago. The famous 120-store, four-mall Kittery Outlet Center is a short three mile cab ride.

Great Bay Marine

61 Beane Lane; Portsmouth, NH 03801

Tel: (603) 436-5299 **VHF: Monitor** Ch. 68 **Talk** Ch. 68
Fax: (603) 436-9834 **Alternate Tel:** n/a
Email: email@greatbaymarine.com **Web:** www.greatbaymarine.com
Nearest Town: Portsmouth *(5 mi.)* **Tourist Info:** (603) 610-5510

Navigational Information

Lat: 43°06.930' **Long:** 070°50.113' **Tide:** 6 ft. **Current:** 4 kt. **Chart:** 13283
Rep. Depths (*MLW*): Entry 30 ft. **Fuel Dock** 6 ft. **Max Slip/Moor** 6 ft./30 ft.
Access: About 6 miles from mouth of the Piscataqua River

Marina Facilities *(In Season/Off Season)*

Fuel: *89 Octane* - Gasoline, Diesel
Slips: 128 Total, 9 Transient **Max LOA:** 60 ft. **Max Beam:** n/a
Rate *(per ft.)*: **Day** $2.00* **Week** Inq. **Month** Inq.
Power: 30 amp Incl., **50 amp** Incl., **100 amp** n/a, **200 amp** n/a
Cable TV: No **Dockside Phone:** No
Dock Type: Fixed, Floating, Long Fingers, Pilings, Alongside, Concrete, Woo
Moorings: 72 Total, 5 Transient **Launch:** n/a, Dinghy Dock (Yes)
Rate: Day $30 **Week** Inq. **Month** Inq.
Heads: 8 Toilet(s), 5 Shower(s) *(dressing rooms)*, Book Exchange
Internet: Yes *(Wi-Fi, Free)* **Laundry:** 2 Washer(s), 2 Dryer(s)
Pump-Out: Self Service, 1 Central **Fee:** Free **Closed Heads:** Yes

Marina Operations

Owner/Manager: Ellen Griffin Saas **Dockmaster:** Ulrich Saas
In-Season: May-Oct, 8am-4:30pm **Off-Season:** Nov-Apr, 8am-4:30pm
After-Hours Arrival: Call ahead
Reservations: Yes, Preferred **Credit Cards:** Visa/MC, Dscvr
Discounts: None
Pets: Welcome **Handicap Access:** Yes, Heads, Docks

Marina Services and Boat Supplies

Services - Docking Assistance, Boaters' Lounge, Security *(24 Hrs., Live onsite)*, Trash Pick-Up, Dock Carts **Communication -** Mail & Package Hold, Phone Messages, FedEx, DHL, UPS, Express Mail *(Sat Del)* **Supplies - OnSite:** Ice *(Block, Cube)*, Ships' Store, Bait/Tackle, CNG **1-3 mi:** Propane *(Sea 3 431-5990)* **3+ mi:** West Marine *(436-8300, 6 mi.)*

Boatyard Services

OnSite: Travelift *(36T)*, Forklift *(15T)*, Crane, Hydraulic Trailer, Launching Ramp, Engine mechanic *(gas, diesel)*, Electronic Sales, Electronics Repairs, Hull Repairs, Rigger, Bottom Cleaning, Brightwork, Compound, Wash & Wax, Interior Cleaning, Propeller Repairs, Woodworking, Inflatable Repairs, Painting, Awlgrip **OnCall:** Electrical Repairs, Sail Loft, Divers, Air Conditioning, Refrigeration, Life Raft Service, Upholstery, Metal Fabrication **Dealer for:** Avon, Honda, Yanmar, Westerbeke, Volvo, Mercruiser, Valu-Flush. **Member:** ABBRA, ABYC - 3 Certified Tech(s), Other Certifications: Honda, Mercruiser, Yanmar **Yard Rates:** $45-80/hr., Haul & Launch $6/ft each way *(blocking incl.)*, Power Wash $4/ft., Bottom Paint $18-22/ft. *(paint incl.)* **Storage:** In-Water $70/ft, On-Land Outside $33/ft. Inside $70/ft.*

Restaurants and Accommodations

OnSite: Lite Fare *(Fresh Local - Bayside 766-4441, Sat & Sun only, 8am-2pm.Seasonal, Cash & Checks)* **1-3 mi:** Restaurant *(New Asia 431-3121, Lunch Buffet)* **3+ mi:** Restaurant *(Bugaboo Creek Steak House 422-0921, 4 mi.)*, *(Redhook Ale Brewery & Cataqua Public House 430-8600, 4 mi.)*, *(Texas Roadhouse 433-7427, 4 mi., L & D $8-20 Kids' $3-8)*, *(Olive Garden 436-8400, 4 mi.)*, *(Chipotle Mexican Grill 433-5981, 4 mi.)*, *(Ixtapa 430-2825, 4 mi.)*, Hotel *(Hampton Inn 431-6111, 4 mi.)*, *(Courtyard 436-2121, 4 mi.)*

Recreation and Entertainment

OnSite: Picnic Area, Grills **1-3 mi:** Beach, Fitness Center *(Planet Fitness 750-0001)*, Movie Theater *(Regal Fox Run 431-4200)* **3+ mi:** Golf Course *(Pease G.C. 433-1331, 5 mi.)*, Cultural Attract *(Seacoast Repertory 433-4472, 5 mi)*

Provisioning and General Services

Near: Catholic Church **Under 1 mi:** Bank/ATM **1-3 mi:** Convenience Store *(Mobil 427-6952)*, Supermarket *(Market Basket 436-0413; Hannaford 436-6669 - 5 mi.)*, Fishmonger *(Los' Seafood & Oriental Market 431-0022)*, Lobster Pound, Post Office, Protestant Church, Synagogue, Pharmacy *(WalMart Pharmacy 433-6129)*, Department Store *(WalMart)* **3+ mi:** Gourmet Shop *(Portsmouth, 5 mi.)*, Wine/Beer *(5 mi.)*, Liquor Store *(NH 436-4806, 5 mi.)*, Library *(427-1540, Internet access, 6 mi.)*, Bookstore *(Barnes & Noble 422-7733, 4 mi.)*, Hardware Store *(Home Depot 422-0856, 4 mi.)*, Retail Shops *(Fox Run Mall, 4 mi.)*, Buying Club *(BJs 427-0400, 4 mi.)*, Copies Etc. *(Staples 334-3423, 4 mi.)*

Transportation

OnCall: Rental Car *(Enterprise 433-1177, National 334-6000 - 3 mi.)*, Taxi *(Rickingham 501-0960)*, Airport Limo *(Great Bay 800-820-6117)* **1-3 mi:** Local Bus *(Coast 743-5777)* **Airport:** Pease/Logan Int'l. *(2mi./55 mi.)*

Medical Services

911 Service **1-3 mi:** Doctor, Dentist *(Atlantic Family 430-9009)*, Holistic Services, Optician *(Harbor 430-0211)* **3+ mi:** Chiropractor *(Port City 433-2447, 5 mi.)*, Veterinarian *(Lafayette 431-0020, 5 mi.)* **Hospital:** Portsmouth Reg 436-5110 *(5.5 mi.)*

PHOTOS ON DVD: 18

Setting -- Six miles up the Piscataqua, a quarter-mile west of the fixed General Sullivan Bridge, quiet, inland Great Bay Marine is surrounded by the fishing boats and birding marshes of Trickys Cove - with views of unspoiled islands, the bridge and distant Durham. A rock and earth berm separates two sets of slips, a long side-tie dock stretches into the mooring field, and a 36-acre upland hosts dry storage, work sheds and the main gray clapboard two-story building.

Marina Notes -- *Rates vary. Established in 1956 by the Griffin Family, current owner/operators. Expansive, immaculate ships store & parts counters. Extensive BY services include dedicated, fully enclosed fiberglass & paint shops. Specializes in engine repowering. **Storage rates include haul, launch & bottom wash. Quiet place to wait out bad weather. Bathhouse: Basic, inviting, painted cinder block heads & showers. Note: Issues temp NH boating license.

Notable -- Onsite CIA Chef Josh Lanahan's "Local Fresh Bayside" serves locavore fare on weekends at tables inside and red picnic tables out - everything is homemade, fresh and noteworthy (find them at Wentworth and their well-known truck at Prescott Park's Art Fest events). Many shops and malls are within a few miles as is the University of New Hampshire - Durham. Dozens of casual chain restaurants surround Newington and Fox Run Malls. Tour Redhook Ale Brewery and stop at their outdoor beer garden or dine in their onsite pub (11:30am-9pm Mon-Sat, noon-6pm Sun). On the eastern shore, the Great Bay National Wildlife Refuge, home to an abundance of wildlife, includes some endangered species such as the American Bald Eagle, Peregrine Falcon and Osprey. Great Bay's warm water makes for very good fishing. 19th-century Newington village's lanes, byways and historic district are good for walks or runs.

Navigational Information
Lat: 43°03.518' **Long:** 070°43.261' **Tide:** 9 ft. **Current:** 2 kt. **Chart:** 13278
Rep. Depths (*MLW*): Entry 10 ft. **Fuel Dock** 12 ft. **Max Slip/Moor** 12 ft./10 ft.
Access: From R "2KR" at Portsmouth Harbor entrance steer 300 degrees

Marina Facilities *(In Season/Off Season)*
Fuel: Gasoline, Diesel, High-Speed Pumps
Slips: 150 Total, 25 Transient **Max LOA:** 250 ft. **Max Beam:** n/a
Rate *(per ft.)*: **Day** $3.85/$3.60* **Week** n/a **Month** Inq.
Power: 30 amp $15, **50 amp** $25, **100 amp** $50, **200 amp** n/a
Cable TV: Yes, Incl **Dockside Phone:** No
Dock Type: Floating, Long Fingers, Alongside, Concrete
Moorings: 2 Total, 0 Transient **Launch:** Yes, Dinghy Dock
Rate: Day n/a **Week** n/a **Month** n/a
Heads: 8 Toilet(s), 8 Shower(s) *(dressing rooms)*, Hair Dryers
Internet: Yes *(Wi-Fi, Free)* **Laundry:** 5 Washer(s), 5 Dryer(s), Iron Board
Pump-Out: OnSite, Self Service, 1 Central **Fee:** Free **Closed Heads:** Yes

Marina Operations
Owner/Manager: Capt. Doug Voss **Dockmaster:** Same
In-Season: Jul-Sep 15, 8am-8pm **Off-Season:** Oct-Jun, 8am-5pm
After-Hours Arrival: Contact Security on Ch. 71
Reservations: Preferred **Credit Cards:** Visa/MC, Amex
Discounts: None **Dockage:** n/a **Fuel:** $.10/500 gals. **Repair:** n/a
Pets: Welcome, Dog Walk Area **Handicap Access:** Yes, Heads, Docks

Wentworth by the Sea Marina

PO Box 2079; 116 Morgans Way; New Castle, NH 03854

Tel: (603) 433-5050 **VHF: Monitor** Ch. 71 **Talk** Ch. 71
Fax: (603) 427-1092 **Alternate Tel:** n/a
Email: concierge@wentworthmarina.com **Web:** wentworthmarina.com
Nearest Town: Portsmouth *(3 mi.)* **Tourist Info:** (603) 610-5510

Marina Services and Boat Supplies
Services - Docking Assistance, Concierge, Room Service to the Boat, Security *(24)*, Trash Pick-Up, Dock Carts, 3 Phase **Communication -** Pay Phone (2), FedEx, UPS **Supplies - OnSite:** Ice *(Block, Cube)*, Ships' Store, Live Bait *(Frozen, too)* **1-3 mi:** West Marine *(436-8300)*, Bait/Tackle *(Kittery Trading Post 207-439-2700)*, Propane *(Sea 3 431-5990)*

Boatyard Services
OnCall: Divers, Bottom Cleaning, Brightwork, Air Conditioning, Refrigeration, Compound, Wash & Wax, Interior Cleaning **Nearest Yard:** Great Bay (603) 436-5299

Restaurants and Accommodations
OnSite: Restaurant *(Latitudes 422-7322, L & D $10-28)*, Lite Fare *(Fresh Local Dockside 559-1006, B $4-12, L $6.50-12.50, Del to boat)* **Near:** Restaurant *(Roosevelt's Lounge 422-7322, D $19-32, Tue-Sun 5-10pm Marriott)*, *(Wentworth Dining Room B $10-17, L $10-25, D $25-38, Marriott)*, Snack Bar *(Ice House $2-9)*, Hotel *(Marriott Wentworth-by-The-Sea just above marina)* **Under 1 mi:** Restaurant *(BG's Boathouse 431-1074, D $13-21, Dinghy Dockage)* **1-3 mi:** Restaurant *(Dolphin Striker 431-5222, L $7-15, D $15-23)*, *(Mombo at Strawbery Banke 433-2340, L $12-19, D $19-34)*, Hotel *(Sheraton 431-2300, $175-245)*, Inn/B&B *(Sise Inn 433-1200, $199)*

Recreation and Entertainment
OnSite: Heated Pool *(Dawn-Dusk, 2 passes)*, Picnic Area, Grills, Tennis Courts *(comp. at Hotel)*, Fitness Center, Video Rental **Near:** Beach *(via dinghy)* **Under 1 mi:** Dive Shop, Boat Rentals *(Portsmouth Kayaks 559-1000 Half $45, Full $65, Tours too $45-75)*, Park *(Ft. Stark 436-1552)* **1-3 mi:** Playground, Museum *(Strawbery Banke 433-1100 10-acre, 40 restorations $15/10; Wentworth Coolidge 436-6607; Children's Museum 436-3853)*, Sightseeing *(Odiorne Point S.P. & Seacoast Science Center 436-8043 $5/2)*, Special Events *(Prescott Park Arts Festival - all summer)* **3+ mi:** Golf Course *(Pease G.C. 433-1331, 7 mi.)*, Cultural Attract *(Portsmouth Seacoast Rep 433-4472; The Music Hall 436-2400, 3.5 mi.)*

Provisioning and General Services
OnSite: Bank/ATM, Newsstand **Under 1 mi:** Convenience Store, Market *(Henry's 430-2008)*, Gourmet Shop *(DK's 319-8140)*, Lobster Pound *(Ricker 436-6421)*, Post Office, Dry Cleaners, Florist **1-3 mi:** Delicatessen *(Bread Box 436-1631)*, Wine/Beer *(Corks & Curds 431-5564)*, Liquor Store *(Gary's 436-5854)*, Bakery *(Red Ginger 373-6791)*, Farmers' Market *(Sat 8am-1pm)*, Catholic Church, Protestant Church, Synagogue, Library *(431-6773)*, Beauty Salon *(Solari 430-0030)*, Barber Shop, Bookstore *(Gulliver's 431-5556)* **3+ mi:** Supermarket *(Hannaford 436-6669, 4 mi.)*, Pharmacy *(CVS 431-0234, 4 mi.)*, Department Store *(WalMart, 5 mi.)*, Buying Club *(BJ's, 5 mi.)*

Transportation
OnSite: Courtesy Car/Van **OnCall:** Rental Car *(Enterprise 433-1177; Hertz 422-6707)*, Taxi *(Checker 750-7777)*, Airport Limo *(Seacoast 431-9880)*
Airport: Pease/Logan Int'l. *(5 mi./55 mi.)*

Medical Services
911 Service **Near:** Holistic Services *(Wentworth Spa 422-7322 Massage $100/50-min.)* **Under 1 mi:** Doctor *(Worrell 436-2260)* **1-3 mi:** Dentist *(Atlantic 430-9009)*, Chiropractor *(Port City 433-2447)* **Hospital:** Portsmouth 436-5110 *(6 mi.)*

Setting -- Safely tucked into Little Harbor, just south of the Piscataqua's mouth, meticulously run Wentworth's five main docks host 150 immaculate slips. The regal edifice of the sprawling, red-roofed Marriott Wentworth-by-the-Sea Grand Hotel and Spa looms above the marina. Quaint, non-commercial New Castle is a world unto itself - but the many pleasures of historic Portsmouth are minutes away by capable dinghy, bike, or courtesy car.

Marina Notes -- *36-50 ft. $3.85/3.60, 51-70 ft. $4.50/4.25, 71-99 ft. $5.15/4.90, 100 ft.+ $5.50/5.25. Dock length or vessel LOA whichever greater. 5 nights+ $3.60/ft. 100A 1-phase $50/day, 100A, 3-phase $55/day. Max dinghy size 11 ft, larger incurs fee. No transient moorings. Two courtesy cars (1.5 hrs., first come). Concierge services, uniformed dock hands, guide boat escorts for incoming vessels. Book exchange. Tent on Boardwalk for large groups. Repair services on-call. Bathhouse: Luxe granite mixes with cinderblock - but still very lovely. 2 sets: at flagpole above "A" dock & above "D" dock with laundry.

Notable -- Seasonal "Snack Shack" eatery makes camp under a tent on the boardwalk (Fri 11am-8pm, Sat 7am-8pm, Sun 7am-3pm) to supplement Chef Daniel Dumont's creative, locavore fare at Latitudes dockside restaurant. Dine near the cozy fireplace, next to the window-wall or out on the teak deck overlooking the docks - adjacent to the heated pool and hot tub. At the separately-managed hotel, the swank Wentworth Dining Room and Roosevelt's Lounge offer higher-end choices. The exquisite hotel invites a night ashore or, at least, a day at the spa. Portsmouth, an oasis for writers, artists, musicians and chefs, delivers diverse cultural offerings, unique shops (no sales tax!), restaurants and historic sites. Pick up a self-guided tour map and just walk.

PHOTOS ON DVD: 25

Hampton River Marina

PO Box 1500; 55 Harbor Road; Hampton, NH 03843

Tel: (603) 929-1422 **VHF: Monitor** Ch. 11 **Talk** Ch. 11
Fax: (603) 926-3054 **Alternate Tel:** n/a
Email: info@hamptonrivermarina.com **Web:** www.hamptonrivermarina.com
Nearest Town: Hampton *(0.2 mi.)* **Tourist Info:** (603) 610-5510

Navigational Information

Lat: 42°54.004' **Long:** 070°49.054' **Tide:** 9 ft. **Current:** 3 kt. **Chart:** 13278
Rep. Depths (*MLW*): Entry 7 ft. **Fuel Dock** 6 ft. **Max Slip/Moor** 10 ft./-
Access: From ocean, follow channel markers to harbor.

Marina Facilities *(In Season/Off Season)*

Fuel: No
Slips: 144 Total, 10 Transient **Max LOA:** 60 ft. **Max Beam:** 18 ft.
Rate *(per ft.)*: **Day** $2.75 **Week** $16.50 **Month** n/a
Power: 30 amp $4, **50 amp** n/a, **100 amp** n/a, **200 amp** n/a
Cable TV: No **Dockside Phone:** No
Dock Type: Floating, Long Fingers, Wood
Moorings: 0 Total, 0 Transient **Launch:** n/a, Dinghy Dock (Free)
Rate: Day n/a **Week** n/a **Month** n/a
Heads: 6 Toilet(s), 4 Shower(s)
Internet: No **Laundry:** 2 Washer(s), 2 Dryer(s)
Pump-Out: OnSite, OnCall **Fee:** n/a **Closed Heads:** Yes

Marina Operations

Owner/Manager: Darla and Charles Noble **Dockmaster:** Kevin Bailey
In-Season: Apr-Oct, 8am-4:30pm **Off-Season:** Nov-Mar, 9am-4pm
After-Hours Arrival: Call ahead for information
Reservations: Yes, Required **Credit Cards:** Visa/MC, Dscvr, Amex
Discounts: Fuel **Dockage:** n/a **Fuel:** $0.10/gal **Repair:** n/a
Pets: Welcome **Handicap Access:** Yes, Docks

Marina Services and Boat Supplies

Services - Docking Assistance, Security *(24 Hrs., On site)*, Trash Pick-Up, Dock Carts **Communication -** FedEx, UPS **Supplies - OnSite:** Ice *(Block, Cube)*, Ships' Store, Bait/Tackle **1-3 mi:** West Marine *(474-7170)*

Boatyard Services

OnSite: Travelift *(25T)*, Engine mechanic *(gas, diesel)*, Electrical Repairs, Hull Repairs, Bottom Cleaning, Compound, Wash & Wax, Propeller Repairs **Under 1 mi:** Upholstery, Yacht Interiors, Metal Fabrication. **1-3 mi:** Electronic Sales, Electronics Repairs. **3+ mi:** Canvas Work, Divers, Brightwork, Air Conditioning, Refrigeration. **Yard Rates:** $65/hr., Haul & Launch $6.25-8.25/ft. *(blocking $2/ft.)*, Power Wash $2.75/ft., Bottom Paint $14/ft. **Storage:** On-Land $0.75/ft./day

Restaurants and Accommodations

Near: Restaurant *(Ocean Wok 926-6633, L & D $8-13 Szechuan, Cantonese, Hong Kong)*, *(Wally's 926-6954, L & D $5-20, pizza too. Kids' $4.25)*, *(Thai Cuisine 929-7272)*, Seafood Shack *(Happy Clam 929-1536)*, Lite Fare *(Coffee Break Cafe)*, Pizzeria *(Cristy's 929-4496)*, Motel *(Hampton Harbor 926-4432, $99)*, Inn/B&B *(Regal Inn 926-7758, $100)* **Under 1 mi:** Restaurant *(Boardwalk Inn 929-7400, D $12-21)*, *(Sea Ketch 926-0324, B $3-10, L $4-10, D $11-25, Kids' $4-7)*, *(Ron's Landing 929-2122)*, *(La Bec Rouge 926-5050, Live entertainment)*, *(Mama's Leone 926-5576)*, *(Purple Urchin 929-0800, L & D $8-26, Kids' $5)*, Pizzeria *(Beach-Nut 926-6688)* **3+ mi:** Lite Fare *(Airfield Cafe 964-1654, B $2-7.50, L $4-10, 5 mi., 7am-2pm)*

Recreation and Entertainment

OnSite: Picnic Area **Near:** Beach, Boat Rentals *(Adventure Charters 926-4648 Jet Skis $75/hr.)*, Fishing Charter *(Al Guaron 926-2469; Yellowbird 929-1995; Smith & Gilmore 926-3503)*, Park *(Hampton Beach)*, Cultural Attract *(Hampton Beach Casino Ballroom 929-4100 - concerts & events)* **Under 1 mi:** Video Arcade *(Laser Storm 929-4077)* **3+ mi:** Tennis Courts *(Smart 926-2276, 4 mi.)*, Golf Course *(Sagamore Hampton G.C. 964-5341, 6 mi.)*, Sightseeing *(Fuller Gardens 964-5414 $7/3, 5 mi.)*

Provisioning and General Services

Near: Convenience Store *(Patriots Corner 926-7087)*, Delicatessen *(Syrian Subs 926-4854)*, Lobster Pound *(State Pier 926-1488)*, Pharmacy *(Rexall 926-2224)* **Under 1 mi:** Wine/Beer *(NH #73)*, Liquor Store *(NH #73 926-3372)*, Fishmonger *(Alan's 929-1162)*, Bank/ATM, Post Office **1-3 mi:** Catholic Church, Protestant Church, Library *(474-2044)*, Beauty Salon *(Shear Illusions 474-9798)*, Dry Cleaners, Laundry *(Centre 926-9681)*, Florist **3+ mi:** Supermarket *(Shaw's 474-2320, 5 mi.)*, Hardware Store *(Hampton Centre 929-7900, 4 mi.)*

Transportation

OnCall: Rental Car *(Avis 926-6363; Enterprise 964-4442)*, Taxi *(Blue Star 964-7710; Abba 926-8294)*, Airport Limo *(Seacoast 531-2377)* **1-3 mi:** Bikes *(Ocean Cycles 926-5757)* **Airport:** Hampton/Manchester/Portsmouth Int'l *(5 mi./19 mi./40 mi.)*

Medical Services

911 Service **1-3 mi:** Doctor *(Ferrell 926-5788)*, Dentist *(Hampton Family 929-3969)*, Chiropractor *(Hampton Family 926-7369)*, Veterinarian *(Health & Wellness 926-5500)* **Hospital:** Anna Jaques 978-463-1000 *(8 mi.)*

PHOTOS ON DVD: 17

Setting -- A quarter mile from the ocean, just beyond the Route 1-A drawbridge, the marina's slips lie along the starboard shore below a 3-story natural-shingled condo and lots of boats on the hard. Cut into the upland, a wide basin hosts five docks while another "U-shaped" dock sits right on the river. The small gray office, on a little patch of lawn sprinkled with picnic tables, looks across the river to unspoiled Commons Island and distant Seabrook nuclear plant.

Marina Notes -- Bulkhead-style wave attenuator breaks up wakes or waves created by the wind/current interaction. Limited amenities onsite but an active upgrade and modernization program. Basic boatyard services - mostly haul, launch and storage. Active dry stack operation. Primarily a powerboat marina; sailboats find river entrance challenging. Bathhouse: Bright blue walls, fiberglass shower stalls - modern and simple.

Notable -- Easy ocean access (no long "wake-free" ride upriver) along with easy walking distance to popular Hampton Beach's old-time boardwalk and lively nightlife are casual HRM's best features. The bustling Hampton Beach boardwalk scene is far enough to not disturb but close enough for the young-at-heart to indulge their cotton candy and arcade game fantasies. Not an upscale resort town; shopping tends toward T-shirts and board shorts (no sales tax) and food to basic franchises. Also nearby is the greyhound race track for those with a gambling spirit. Ocean water is cold but surf can be the best for 500 miles. A five-mile excursion north, the seaside, 19th-century Fuller Gardens, one of the region's last estate gardens, displays over 2,000 roses, a Japanese garden and massive English perennial plantings. Inland, the Hampton Airfield features exciting aerial tours in a bi-plane or helicopter (964-6749) and the Airfield Cafe.

Navigational Information

Lat: 42°48.706' **Long:** 070°51.924' **Tide:** 9 ft. **Current:** 5 kt. **Chart:** 13274
Rep. Depths (*MLW*): Entry 13 ft. **Fuel Dock** 13 ft. **Max Slip/Moor** 13 ft./-
Access: First major facility to port, opp Nun 22

Marina Facilities *(In Season/Off Season)*

Fuel: *ValvTect* - Gasoline, Diesel, High-Speed Pumps
Slips: 70 Total, 10 Transient **Max LOA:** 150 ft. **Max Beam:** 25 ft.
Rate *(per ft.)*: **Day** $3.25* **Week** n/a **Month** n/a
Power: 30 amp $10, **50 amp** $18, **100 amp** $40, **200 amp** n/a
Cable TV: No **Dockside Phone:** No
Dock Type: Floating, Long Fingers, Alongside, Concrete, Wood
Moorings: 0 Total, 0 Transient **Launch:** n/a
Rate: Day n/a **Week** n/a **Month** n/a
Heads: 4 Toilet(s), 4 Shower(s) *(dressing rooms)*
Internet: Yes *(Wi-Fi, Free)* **Laundry:** None
Pump-Out: OnCall *(Boat Fri-Sun 9am-5pm)* **Fee:** Free **Closed Heads:** Yes

Marina Operations

Owner/Manager: Randall Lyons **Dockmaster:** Jay Larcome
In-Season: May-Oct 15, 8am-6pm **Off-Season:** Oct 16-Apr, 9am-5pm
After-Hours Arrival: Hail on 9
Reservations: Yes, Recommended **Credit Cards:** Visa/MC, Dscvr, Amex
Discounts: Store & Rest 15% **Dockage:** n/a **Fuel:** $.20 **Repair:** n/a
Pets: Welcome **Handicap Access:** No

Newburyport Harbor Marina

Rear 51 Water St.; Newburyport, MA 01950

Tel: (978) 462-3990 **VHF: Monitor** Ch. 9 **Talk** n/a
Fax: (978) 462-3991 **Alternate Tel:** (978) 465-9110
Email: info@newburyportmarinas.com **Web:** newburyportmarinas.com
Nearest Town: Newburyport *(0.5 mi.)* **Tourist Info:** (978) 462-6680

Marina Services and Boat Supplies

Services - Docking Assistance, Security *(24)*, Trash Pick-Up
Communication - FedEx, UPS, Express Mail **Supplies - OnSite:** Ice *(Block, Cube)*, Ships' Store, Marine Discount Store, Bait/Tackle, Live Bait
Under 1 mi: CNG **1-3 mi:** Propane *(Germinara 463-9059)*

Boatyard Services

Nearest Yard: Windward Yacht Yard (978) 462-6500

Restaurants and Accommodations

OnSite: Restaurant *(Starboard Galley 462-1326, L $8-17, D $13-26)*, *(River Merrimac Bar & Grille 463-4040, D $15-30, Fine Dining. Tavern $9-16)* **Near:** Restaurant *(10 Center 462-6652, D $18-30)*, *(Not Your Average Joe's 462-3808, L $9-12, D $9-18)*, *(Andaman Thai 499-8424)*, *(Grog 465-8008, L & D $9-20)*, Lite Fare *(Revitalive Cafe 462-0639, Raw, Vegan)*, Inn/B&B *(Compass Rose 465-1568, $169-249)*, *(Essex St. 465-3148, $120-270)* **1-3 mi:** Restaurant *(Plum Island Grille 463-2290, L $12-22, D $15-29, Lunch weekends)*, Seafood Shack *(Bob Lobster 465-7100, also market)*, Hotel *(Blue Inn 465-7171, $195-1095, South Beach in New England)*

Recreation and Entertainment

OnSite: Picnic Area, Grills, Fitness Center *(Natural High 499-0993)*, Fishing Charter *(Atlantis 463-7765; Kelly Ann 618-5893)* **Near:** Dive Shop, Tennis Courts, Jogging Paths *(Bartlett Mall)*, Video Rental *(Express 463-3066)*, Museum *(Custom House Maritime 462-8681 $7/5, 10am-4pm)*, Cultural Attract *(Maudslay Arts Center 499-0050)*, Galleries, Special Events *(music,& arts, fests all summer)* **Under 1 mi:** Pool *("Y" 462-7622)*, Park *(Bartlett Mall, Frog Pond & Old Hill Burying Ground)* **3+ mi:** Beach *(Plum Island's Parker River Natinal Wildlife Refuge $2 - water rarely exceeds 68 degrees, 3 mi.)*, Golf Course *(Ould Newbury 465-9888 non-member M-F, 8 mi)*

Provisioning and General Services

Near: Convenience Store *(Richdale 465-9808)*, Gourmet Shop *(Joppa 462-4662)*, Delicatessen *(Black Duck 462-0323)*, Liquor Store *(Grand Trunk 499-4441)*, Bakery *(Nutcracker 465-8482, Greta's 465-1709)*, Farmers' Market *(Sun 9am-1pm, Tannery Marketplace)*, Bank/ATM, Protestant Church, Library *(465-4428)*, Beauty Salon *(Interlocks 465-3010)*, Barber Shop *(Inn Street 462-9900)*, Bookstore *(Jabberwocky 465-9359; Book Rack 462-8615)*, Pharmacy *(24-hour CVS 462-5339)*, Newsstand *(Fowle's 463-9824)*, Retail Shops *(Tannery Marketplace - shops, food, galleries, concerts)* **Under 1 mi:** Post Office, Catholic Church, Synagogue, Dry Cleaners *(Panda 465-8081)*, Hardware Store *(Kelly's True Value 462-2951)* **1-3 mi:** Supermarket *(Shaw's 462-7121)*, Health Food *(Natural Grocer 463-8713)*

Transportation

OnCall: Rental Car *(Enterprise 499-0021)*, Taxi *(Seacoast 499-9990; London Livery 462-4442; Newburyport Pedicab 465-1496)*, Airport Limo *(Four Star 463-5466)* **1-3 mi:** InterCity Bus, Rail *(Boston train: MBTA 800-392-6100 or www.mbta.com)* **Airport:** Boston Logan *(40 mi.)*

Medical Services

911 Service **OnCall:** Ambulance **Near:** Doctor *(Yerks 499-2200)*, Dentist *(Koglin 465-5041)*, Chiropractor *(McFadden 462-297)*, Holistic Services *(Sacred Tree 462-1890 60-min massage $75)*, Optician *(Newburyport Optique 465-2405)* **Under 1 mi:** Veterinarian *(Animal Wellness 499-9908)*
Hospital: Anna Jaques 463-1000 *(1.5 mi.)*

Setting -- The first marina to port as the Merrimack River narrows, a two-story dark red building built on a sturdy pier oversees three main docks that support 70 nicely maintained floating slips largely populated by sportfishers and other powerboats - the fuel dock is on the most western T-head. A wide deck surrounds the office and small, gated dock houses provide entry to each of the dock ramps. Set on the outskirts of the town center, a quarter mile from Market Square, the ambiance is quieter with more wide-open river views - albeit less protected. The wide Ipe Riverfront Boardwalk begins a few blocks west.

Marina Notes -- *Up to 49 ft. $3.25/ft., 50-99 ft.:$4/ft; 100 ft.+ $4.50/ft. One of four marinas in Newburyport Marina Corporation - also Hilton's, Windward, & Newburyport Boat Basin. 65% seasonal, 35% transient. Primary Newburyport Marina transient dockage unless a "downtown" location is specified. Well supplied small ship's store. Complimentary "valet" docking for those uneasy with river currents. Bathhouse: Simple, serviceable, white, fully tiled full baths.

Notable -- A block southeast, more than fifty local shops, eateries, galleries, mind-body and cultural experiences plus the Sunday Farmers' Market are in the Tannery Historic Marketplace, a two-story restored mill. A block west, the 1835 Custom House Maritime Museum features all manner of maritime exhibits. But the real treasure for many is three miles east: Plum Island's 11 miles of beautiful beach and wild marsh, disturbed by very little commercialism except noteworthy Bob Lobster, Blue Inn and Plum Island Grill. The island's southern end is 4,662 acre Parker River National Wildlife Refuge, a feeding, resting and nesting habitat for over 300 species of resident and migratory birds, For non-bird watchers, there are interpretive trails, surf fishing, shell fishing, and kayaking.

PHOTOS ON DVD: 23

Newburyport Waterfront Park City Marina

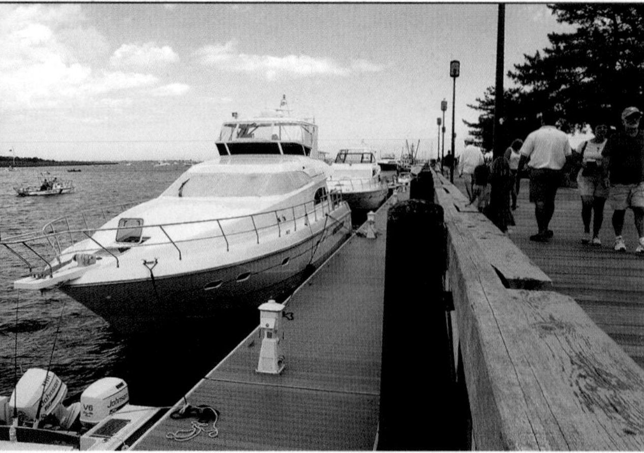

Newburyport Waterfront Park

346R Merrimac Street; Newburyport, MA 01950

Tel: (978) 465-9110 **VHF: Monitor** Ch. 12 **Talk** Ch. 12
Fax: (978) 462-1826 **Alternate Tel:** n/a
Email: info@newburyportmarinas.com **Web:** cityofnewburyport.com
Nearest Town: Newburyport **Tourist Info:** (978) 462-6680

Navigational Information
Lat: 42°48.754' **Long:** 070°52.125' **Tide:** 9 ft. **Current:** n/a **Chart:** 13274
Rep. Depths (*MLW*): Entry 14 ft. **Fuel Dock** 14 ft. **Max Slip/Moor** 14 ft./-
Access: Past Newburyport Harbor, about 3 nm from mouth

Marina Facilities *(In Season/Off Season)*
Fuel: *ValvTect* - Gasoline, Diesel, High-Speed Pumps
Slips: 30 Total, 30 Transient **Max LOA:** 150 ft. **Max Beam:** 30 ft.
Rate *(per ft.)*: **Day** $1.00* **Week** n/a **Month** n/a
Power: 30 amp Incl., **50 amp** Incl., **100 amp** n/a, **200 amp** n/a
Cable TV: Yes **Dockside Phone:** No
Dock Type: Floating, Alongside, Wood
Moorings: 4 Total, 4 Transient **Launch:** No, Dinghy Dock
Rate: Day $25 **Week** n/a **Month** n/a
Heads: 9 Toilet(s), 8 Shower(s)
Internet: No **Laundry:** Yes
Pump-Out: OnCall *(Boat Fri-Sun 9am-5pm)* **Fee:** Free **Closed Heads:** Yes

Marina Operations
Owner/Manager: Paul Hogg (Hrbrmstr) **Dockmaster:** Same
In-Season: MemDay-ColDay, 4am-4pm **Off-Season:** Oct-May, Closed
After-Hours Arrival: Call earlier in the day
Reservations: No **Credit Cards:** Visa/MC, Dscvr, Amex
Discounts: None
Pets: Welcome **Handicap Access:** Yes, Heads

Marina Services and Boat Supplies
Services - Docking Assistance, Security *(City police on site)* **Communication -** Pay Phone, FedEx, UPS **Supplies - Near:** Ice *(Cube)* **1-3 mi:** Propane *(U-Haul 462-3058)*

Boatyard Services
Nearest Yard: Windward Yacht Yard (978) 462-6500

Restaurants and Accommodations
Near: Restaurant *(Ten Center Street 462-6652, L $6-15, D $18-30)*, *(Grog 465-8008, L & D $9-20)*, *(Glenn's 465-3811, D $21-29, Small Plates too)*, *(Rockfish 465-6601, D $14-18, Live Music Fri & Sat. Small Plates too)*, *(Not Your Average Joe's 462-3808, L $9-12, D $9-13)*, *(Black Cow 499-8811, L $10-29, D $10-36, Pub $10-18)*, *(Agave Mexican 499-0428)*, Lite Fare *(Purple Onion 465-9600, $5-11, Kids' $4-7)*, Pizzeria *(Oregano 462-5013)*, Inn/B&B *(Garrison Inn 499-8500, $105-120)*, *(Clark Currier Inn 465-8363, $125-195)*, *(Essex Street Inn 465-3148, $120-270)*

Recreation and Entertainment
OnSite: Park *(Waterfront Park)*, Tours *("Yankee Clipper" 682-2293 Harbor & Eco $16/8-$30/15)*, Sightseeing *(Newburyport Whale Watch 499-0832)*, Special Events *(Yankee Homecoming - late July)* **Near:** Fishing Charter *(Atlantis 463-7765; Kelly Ann 618-5893)*, Video Rental *(Express Video 463-3066)*, Museum *(Custom House Maritime 462-8681$3/2, Cushing House 462-2681 $4/1.50, 21-room Federalist Mansion)*, Cultural Attract *(Firehouse Center for the Arts 462-7336 Films, live theater)*, Galleries *(Maudslay Arts Center 499-0050)* **Under 1 mi:** Playground, Fitness Center *(Natural High 499-0993)*, Jogging Paths *(Bartlett Mall)*, Boat Rentals *(Plum Island Kayaks 462-5510 $60-80/day)*, Hike/Bike Trails *(Skate Park)* **1-3 mi:** Movie Theater *(Screening Room 462-3456)* **3+ mi:** Beach *(Plum Island's Parker River Nat'l Wildlife Refuge $2 - water rarely exceeds 68 deg. but scenery spectacular., 3 mi.)*, Golf Course *(Amesbury G.&C.C. 388-5153, 5 mi.)*

Provisioning and General Services
Near: Bakery *(Praline's 499-8278)*, Post Office, Catholic Church, Protestant Church, Synagogue, Library *(465-4428)*, Beauty Salon *(Interlocks 465-3010)*, Bookstore *(Book Rack 462-8615; Jabberwocky 465-9359 - .6 mi.)* **Under 1 mi:** Convenience Store *(Richdale 465-9808)*, Gourmet Shop *(Joppa 462-4662)*, Delicatessen, Liquor Store *(New England Wine & Spirits 462-2131)*, Farmers' Market *(Sun 9am-1pm, Tannery Marketplace)*, Dry Cleaners, Pharmacy *(Lynch 462-2232)*, Hardware Store *(Lunt True Value 465-6650)*, Retail Shops *(The Tannery Marketplace - shops, food, galleries, concerts)* **1-3 mi:** Health Food *(Natural Grocer 463-8713)* **3+ mi:** Supermarket *(Shaw's 462-7121, 4 mi.)*

Transportation
OnCall: Rental Car *(Enterprise 499-002)*, Taxi *(Seacoast 499-9990; Walkeys 462-7722)* **Near:** Bikes *(Riverside 465-5566)* **Under 1 mi:** InterCity Bus *(Concord)*, Rail *(Boston commuter link)* **Airport:** Pease/Logan Int'l. *(20 mi./55 mi.)*

Medical Services
911 Service **Near:** Doctor *(McAuley 557-880)*, Dentist *(Reczek 462-2530)*, Chiropractor *(Active Life 463-8881)*, Holistic Services *(Spa Paradiso 462-5530 60-min Massage $85)*, Optician *(Newburyport 465-2405)* **Hospital:** Anna Jacques 463-1000 *(1.3 mi.)*

Setting -- The municipal city marina is a centerpiece of this revitalized and picturesque early Federalist town. Top-quality, side-tie floating docks lie along the wide 1100-foot Ipe Riverfront Boardwalk that edges the river and a deep rectangular basin that cuts into the adjacent Waterfront Promenade Park - and hosts the dinghy dock. Just beyond, restaurants and unique, local shops line the bustling brick-paved Market Square Historic District and nearby side streets.

Marina Notes -- *$0.50/ft. overnight dockage rate only for 7pm-7am. Separate fees for daytime, 7am-7pm: Under 21 ft. $2/hr., 21-40 ft. $3/hr., 41-60 ft. $4/hr., over 60 ft. $6/hr. Overnight transients pay the daytime fees plus overnight rate. Maximum 72 hour tie-up. New docks & pedestals 2002. Yellow mooring balls. Free pump-out boat Fri-Sun 9am-5pm. Self-Serve, 24-hr. pump-out at Cashman Park MemDay-MidOct. Bathhouse: Municipal issue group heads.

Notable -- Settled in 1635 as part of "Newberry Plantation," Newburyport's downtown was leveled by a fire in 1811, so the charming, upscale Market Square Historic District, just steps from the dock and boardwalk, is "only" 200 years old. Today the town is a model of preservation that works. Pick-up a walking tour guide at the nearby tourism kiosk; Newburyport boasts the largest stock of American Federalist brick buildings in the state. Stroll State and High Streets lined with the houses built by early sea captains and ship owners. A couple blocks east, the 1835 Custom House Maritime Museum, designed by Robert Mills (Washington Monument & U.S. Treasury), features vaulted ceilings, a cantilevered stairway and six galleries filled with exhibits. Walk a half mile inland to beautiful Bartlett Mall park, Frog Pond and the adjacent Old Hill Burying Grounds. Three miles east, Plum Island offers an 11-mile beach and amazing birding.

PHOTOS ON DVD: 24

Navigational Information
Lat: 42°48.805' **Long:** 070°52.319' **Tide:** 9 ft. **Current:** 5 kt. **Chart:** 13274
Rep. Depths (*MLW*): Entry 12 ft. **Fuel Dock** n/a **Max Slip/Moor** 12 ft./-
Access: Just past Newburyport Waterfront Park

Marina Facilities *(In Season/Off Season)*
Fuel: No
Slips: 65 Total, 3 Transient **Max LOA:** 100 ft. **Max Beam:** 30 ft.
Rate *(per ft.)*: **Day** $3.25* **Week** n/a **Month** n/a
Power: 30 amp $10, **50 amp** $18, **100 amp** n/a, **200 amp** n/a
Cable TV: No **Dockside Phone:** No
Dock Type: Floating, Long Fingers, Wood
Moorings: 0 Total, 0 Transient **Launch:** no
Rate: Day n/a **Week** n/a **Month** n/a
Heads: 2 Toilet(s), 2 Shower(s)
Internet: Yes *(Wi-Fi, Free)* **Laundry:** 1 Washer(s), 1 Dryer(s)
Pump-Out: OnCall *(Boat Fri-Sun 9-5)* **Fee:** Free **Closed Heads:** Yes

Marina Operations
Owner/Manager: Randall Lyons **Dockmaster:** Jay Larcome
In-Season: May-Oct 15, 8am-6pm **Off-Season:** Oct 16-Apr, 9am-5pm
After-Hours Arrival: Call 978-360-1821
Reservations: Yes, Recommended **Credit Cards:** Visa/MC, Dscvr, Amex
Discounts: Restaurants & Retail **Dockage:** n/a **Fuel:** $.20 **Repair:** n/a
Pets: Welcome **Handicap Access:** No

Hilton's Marina

54 Merrimac Street; Newburyport, MA 01950

Tel: (978) 462-3990 **VHF: Monitor** Ch. 9 **Talk** Ch. 11
Fax: (978) 465-1826 **Alternate Tel:** (978) 465-9110
Email: info@newburyportmarinas.com **Web:** hiltonsmarina.com
Nearest Town: Newburyport **Tourist Info:** (978) 462-6680

Marina Services and Boat Supplies
Services - Docking Assistance, Trash Pick-Up **Communication -** FedEx, UPS, Express Mail **Supplies - Near:** Ice *(Block, Cube)*, Bait/Tackle, Live Bait **Under 1 mi:** Ships' Store *(Newburyport Hbr Marina 462-3990)* **1-3 mi:** Propane *(Germinara 463-9059)*

Boatyard Services
OnSite: Travelift *(25T & 85T)*, Crane *(22T)* **OnCall:** Hydraulic Trailer, Engine mechanic *(gas, diesel)*, Electrical Repairs, Electronics Repairs, Hull Repairs, Divers, Bottom Cleaning, Propeller Repairs, Inflatable Repairs

Restaurants and Accommodations
OnSite: Restaurant *(Black Cow 499-8811, L $10-23, D $10-28, Pub $10-23)*, Coffee Shop *(Plum Island 465-1444)* **Near:** Restaurant *(Michael's Harborside 462-7785, L $8-29, D $10-29)*, *(Glenn's Rest & Cool Bar 465-3811, L $9-20, D $21-29, Lunch Thu-Sun, Entertainment Sun night)*, *(Not Your Average Joe's 462-3808, L $9-13, D $9-19)*, *(Ten Center 462-6652, L $9-18, D $15-36)*, *(David's Tavern 462-8077, D $9-34, Garrison Inn)*, Hotel *(Essex Street 465-3148, $85-175, 37 rooms)*, Inn/B&B *(Compass Rose 225-8195, $215-249)*, *(Garrison 499-8500, $170-300)*

Recreation and Entertainment
OnSite: Tours *(Newburyport Whale Watch 499-0832 $45/30)*, Sightseeing *(Plum Island Eco-Tours 273-2060 $30/15)* **Near:** Fishing Charter *(Atlantis 463-7765; Kelly Ann 618-5893)*, Video Rental *(Express 463-3066)*, Park *(Waterfront & Somerby's Landing Sculpture Park)*, Cultural Attract *(Firehouse Center for the Arts 462-7336; Music festivals throughout the summer)*, Galleries **Under 1 mi:** Picnic Area, Playground *(Cashman & Cushing Parks)*, Tennis Courts *(Cashman Park)*, Fitness Center *(Natural High 499-0993)*, Jogging Paths *(Bartlett Mall)*, Hike/Bike Trails *(Skate Park - Low St.)* **1-3 mi:** Beach *(Plum Island)* **3+ mi:** Golf Course *(Ould Newbury 465-9888 non-member Mon-Fri only, 8 mi.)*

Provisioning and General Services
Near: Convenience Store *(Richdale 465-9808)*, Delicatessen *(Joppa's 462-4662)*, Liquor Store *(Grand Trunk 499-4441)*, Bakery *(Greta's 465-1709)*, Bank/ATM, Post Office, Catholic Church, Protestant Church, Synagogue, Library *(465-4428)*, Beauty Salon *(Spa Paradiso 462-5530)*, Barber Shop *(Inn Street 462-9900)*, Dry Cleaners *(Panda 465-8081)*, Laundry, Bookstore *(Book Rack 462-8615; Jabberwocky 465-9359)*, Pharmacy *(CVS 24-hour 462-5339)*, Newsstand *(Fowle's 463-9824)*, Florist **Under 1 mi:** Wine/Beer *(New England Wine & Spirits 462-2131)*, Farmers' Market *(Sun 9am-1pm, Tannery Marketplace)*, Lobster Pound *(Bob Lobster)* **1-3 mi:** Supermarket *(Shaw's 462-7121)*

Transportation
OnCall: Rental Car *(Enterprise 499-0021)*, Taxi *(Seacoast 499-9990; London Livery 462-4442; Newburyport Pedicab 465-1496)*, Airport Limo *(Port City 225-8486)* **Near:** Bikes *(Riverside 465-5566)* **1-3 mi:** Rail *(Boston MBTA 800-392-6100)* **Airport:** Plum Island /Logan Int'l *(3 mi./40 mi.)*

Medical Services
911 Service **Under 1 mi:** Veterinarian *(Animal Wellness 499-9908)* **1-3 mi:** Dentist *(Newburyport 462-9611)*, Chiropractor *(Healthcare Complete 499-9355)*, Holistic Services *(Dr. Dan's Healing Center 462-0023)*, Optician *(Watts 462-2020)* **Hospital:** Anna Jaques 463-1000 *(1.3 mi.)*

Setting -- Just upriver from the town marina, two long docks, hosting 65 slips, stretch into the river. The head of "B" dock is dominated by the Black Cow restaurant's expansive waterfront dining deck, topped by a cathedral pink metal roof. Quieter "A" dock is home to the Plum Island Coffee Roasters' white, two-story, Newburyport Whale Watch and the travelift bay. Walk through rustic parking lots and dry boat storage to Newburyport's Market Square Historic District

Marina Notes -- *Up to 49 ft. $3.25/ft., 50-99 ft.:$4/ft; 100 ft.+ $4.50/ft. One of the four local Newburyport Marinas. Primary contact point - Newburyport Harbor Marina, which assigns Hilton's slips. Upgraded power planned for other facilities. Travelifts shared with Windward. Other BY services accessed through main office (465-9110). For those unaccustomed to tight docking in a fast river current, shared dockmaster (Ch. 9 or 462-3990) will serve as pilot (complimentary service, just ask). Bathhouse: High-end, modern, white-tiled with black trim & laundry shared with Windward. Adjacent is a pleasant porch.

Notable -- With the Black Cow Tap & Grill's lively crowds, Plum Island Coffee and the two wildlife tours, Hilton's is action central. The restaurant's waterfront deck is perfect in fair weather or in a breeze, choose the attractive window-walled dining room. Twice a day in season, Newburyport Whale Watch's 100-foot "Prince of Whales" heads out in search of Humpbacks, Minkes, Finbacks, and even the occasional Great Blue. Except on Mondays when they voyage to the mythical Isles of Shoals accompanied by an Audubon Society naturalist. Plum Island EcoTours leaves from the Black Cow dock and wanders through the Parker River National Wildlife Refuge's Great Marsh. Their 28-passenger "Joppa Flats" cruises three rivers that are home to over 300 species of birds.

PHOTOS ON DVD: 18

Windward Yacht Yard

McKay's Wharf; Newburyport, MA 01950

Tel: (978) 462-6500 **VHF: Monitor** Ch. 9 **Talk** Ch. 11
Fax: (978) 462-3484 **Alternate Tel:** (978) 465-9110
Email: info@newburyportmarinas.com **Web:** www.windwardyachtyard.com
Nearest Town: Newburyport *(0.25 mi.)* **Tourist Info:** (978) 462-6680

Navigational Information

Lat: 42°48.824' **Long:** 070°52.373' **Tide:** 9 ft. **Current:** 3 kt. **Chart:** 13274
Rep. Depths (*MLW*): Entry 10 ft. **Fuel Dock** 12 ft. **Max Slip/Moor** 12 ft./12 ft.
Access: 2nd marina after City Landing; to port just before bascule bridge

Marina Facilities *(In Season/Off Season)*

Fuel: *ValvTect* - Gasoline, Diesel, High-Speed Pumps
Slips: 150 Total, 20 Transient **Max LOA:** 100 ft. **Max Beam:** 30 ft.
Rate *(per ft.)*: **Day** $3.50* **Week** n/a **Month** n/a
Power: 30 amp $10, **50 amp** $18, **100 amp** n/a, **200 amp** n/a
Cable TV: Yes, Inq* **Dockside Phone:** No
Dock Type: Fixed, Wood, Composition
Moorings: 15 Total, 0 Transient **Launch:** No, Dinghy Dock
Rate: Day n/a **Week** n/a **Month** n/a
Heads: 4 Toilet(s), 4 Shower(s) *(dressing rooms)*
Internet: Yes *(Wi-Fi, Free)* **Laundry:** 1 Washer(s), 1 Dryer(s)
Pump-Out: OnCall *(Boat Fri-Sun 9am-5pm)* **Fee:** Free **Closed Heads:** Yes

Marina Operations

Owner/Manager: Randall Lyons **Dockmaster:** Jay Larcome
In-Season: May-Oct 15, 6am-8pm **Off-Season:** Oct 16-Apr, 9am-5pm
After-Hours Arrival: Dockmaster 978-360-1821
Reservations: Yes, Preferred **Credit Cards:** Visa/MC, Dscvr, Amex, Check
Discounts: Food & Retail 15% **Dockage:** n/a **Fuel:** $0.20 **Repair:** n/a
Pets: Welcome, Dog Walk Area **Handicap Access:** Yes, Heads, Docks

Marina Services and Boat Supplies

Services - Docking Assistance, Security, Trash Pick-Up, Dock Carts **Communication -** Fax in/out, FedEx, UPS, Express Mail *(Sat Del)* **Supplies - OnSite:** Ice *(Block, Cube)*, Bait/Tackle, Live Bait **Near:** Ships' Store **Under 1 mi:** Propane *(Lunt & Kellys 465-6650)*

Boatyard Services

OnSite: Travelift *(25/80T)*, Forklift, Crane *(22T)*, Hydraulic Trailer, Engine mechanic *(gas, diesel)*, Electrical Repairs, Electronics Repairs, Hull Repairs, Canvas Work, Divers, Bottom Cleaning, Brightwork, Compound, Wash & Wax, Interior Cleaning, Propeller Repairs, Woodworking, Upholstery, Painting, Awlgrip **OnCall:** Rigger, Sail Loft, Air Conditioning, Refrigeration, Inflatable Repairs **Yard Rates:** $48-90/hr., Haul & Launch $6-15/ft., Bottom Paint $16/ft. **Storage:** On-Land $50/ft.

Restaurants and Accommodations

OnSite: Restaurant *(Michael's Harborside 462-7785, L & D $8-29. Kids' Meal $5.50. Music Upstairs Lounge week-ends)* **Near:** Restaurant *(Black Cow 499-8811, L $10-29, D $10-36, Pub $10-18)*, *(Glenn's Rest & Cool Bar 465-3811, D $21-29, Music)*, *(Ten Center Street 462-6652, L $6-15, D $18-30)*, *(The Purple Onion 465-9600, L & D $6-11)*, *(Mr. India 465-8600, L & D $10-20 Nepali & Himalayan. Kids $5-7. Del.)*, Coffee Shop *(Plum Island 465-1444)*, Pizzeria *(Nicks 465-9853)*, Inn/B&B *(Essex St. 465-3148, $150-270)*, *(Garrison 499-8500, $170-300)*, *(Greenleaf 465-5816, $125-275)*

Recreation and Entertainment

OnSite: Picnic Area **Near:** Hike/Bike Trails *(Clipper City Rail Trail)*, Video Rental *(Blockbuster 463-3741)*, Park *(Somerby's Landing Sculpture)*, Tours *(Plum Island Eco-Tours 273-2060 $30/15 "Joppa Flata")*, Cultural Attract *(Firehouse Center for the Arts 462-7336 $12-22)*, Special Events *(8-day Yankee Homecoming, Fri. night concerts)* **Under 1 mi:** Tennis Courts, Fishing Charter *(Atlantis 463-7765)*, Museum *(Cushing House 462-2681 $4/1; Customs House 462-8681 $3/2)* **1-3 mi:** Beach *(Plum Island)*, Movie Theater *(Screening Room 462-3456)* **3+ mi:** Golf Course *(Amesbury G.& C.C. 388-5153, 5 mi.)*, Bowling *(Leo's 388-2010, 5 mi.)*

Provisioning and General Services

Near: Gourmet Shop *(Grand Trunk 499-4441)*, Delicatessen *(Green Beans 518-7256)*, Health Food, Wine/Beer *(Leary's 462-4451)*, Bank/ATM, Post Office, Catholic Church, Protestant Church, Synagogue, Library *(465-4428)*, Beauty Salon, Barber Shop, Dry Cleaners, Laundry, Bookstore *(Book Rack 462-8615; Jabberwocky 465-9359)*, Pharmacy *(Lynch 462-2232; CVS 462-5164)*, Clothing Store *(Talbot's 463-0699)* **Under 1 mi:** Market *(Byfield 's General 462-1099)*, Liquor Store *(New England 462-2131)*, Bakery *(Praline's 499-8278)*, Farmers' Market *(Sun 9am-1pm, Tannery)*, Hardware Store *(Lunt True Value 462-2951)* **1-3 mi:** Supermarket *(Shaw's 462-7121)*, Lobster Pound *(Bob Lobster 465-7100)*, Department Store *(K-Mart 462-8521)*

Transportation

OnCall: Rental Car *(Enterprise 499-0021)*, Taxi *(Port 465-2333)* **Under 1 mi:** Rail *(MBTA Boston)* **Airport:** Pease/Logan Int'l. *(20 mi./50 mi.)*

Medical Services

911 Service **Near:** Doctor *(Lwr Merrimac 462-2345)*, Dentist *(Newburyport 462-9611)*, Chiropractor *(Healthcare 499-9355)*, Holistic Services *(Interlocks Spa 465-3010)* **Hospital:** Anna Jacques 463-1000 *(1 mi.)*

PHOTOS ON DVD: 19

Setting -- The last in-town marina to port, Windward straddles the rumbling Route One bascule bridge with two long upscale docks seaward off McKay's Wharf and another two large docks on the far side. White-railed boardwalks lead to a nicely furnished deck fronting the attractive gray contemporary office. Michael's Harborside's imposing barn-red home looms above the docks; umbrella-topped tables crowd two decks, and a blue awning protects a third.

Marina Notes -- *Up to 49 ft. $3.25/ft., 50-99 ft. $4/ft; 100 ft.+ $4.50/ft. **Cable TV at some slips. Slips assigned by Newburyport Harbor dockmaster. A & B docks (known as River's Edge) on upriver side of bridge, C & D docks on town side. New docks. Two travel lifts & most boatyard services (shared with Hilton's). Good security. Free "valet" service for docking in swift current. Bathhouse: Shared with Hilton's. Well-done, quality heads, showers & laundry.

Notable -- Three of Newburyport's most popular restaurants - Michael's Harborside, Black Cow and Glenn's - are feet from the boat and all offer weekend entertainment. A few more feet away are Newburyport 's upscale shops, galleries, museums, cultural attractions, myriad festivals - and more eateries. Follow the paved 1.1 mile Clipper City Rail Trail under the bridge along the new pier/walkway then turn left and head inland to the MBTA commuter station to Boston - or go straight along the waterfront boardwalk to Cashman Park, which sports a nautically-themed playground, tennis & basketball courts, ball field, and soccer fields. In 1965, Lyndon Johnson proclaimed Newburyport the birthplace of the Coast Guard; the town vigorously protects its title with a monument behind the Customs House Maritime Museum and with one irrefutable fact: the first Revenue Cutter "Massachusetts" was built right here at MacKay Shipyard in 1791.

Navigational Information

Lat: 42°49.086' **Long:** 070°52.449' **Tide:** 9 ft. **Current:** 3 kt. **Chart:** 13274
Rep. Depths (*MLW*): Entry 17 ft. **Fuel Dock** n/a **Max Slip/Moor** 15 ft./-
Access: Merrimack River, under the bascule bridge, first marina to starboard

Marina Facilities *(In Season/Off Season)*

Fuel: No
Slips: 142 Total, 2 Transient **Max LOA:** 55 ft. **Max Beam:** 18 ft.
Rate *(per ft.)*: **Day** $2.50 **Week** $14 **Month** $37
Power: 30 amp Incl., **50 amp** Incl., **100 amp** n/a, **200 amp** n/a
Cable TV: Yes, Incl. 15 channels **Dockside Phone:** No
Dock Type: Floating, Long Fingers, Alongside, Composition
Moorings: 14 Total, 0 Transient **Launch:** No, Dinghy Dock
Rate: Day n/a **Week** n/a **Month** n/a
Heads: 4 Toilet(s), 2 Shower(s)
Internet: Yes *(Wi-Fi, Free)* **Laundry:** 1 Washer(s), 1 Dryer(s)
Pump-Out: OnCall *(Boat Fri-Sun 9am-5pm)* **Fee:** Free **Closed Heads:** Yes

Marina Operations

Owner/Manager: Brian Mullen **Dockmaster:** Same
In-Season: May 15-Oct 15, 8am-8pm **Off-Season:** Oct 16-May 14, Closed
After-Hours Arrival: Call in advance
Reservations: Yes, Preferred **Credit Cards:** Cash/Check only
Discounts: None
Pets: Welcome, Dog Walk Area **Handicap Access:** Yes, Heads, Docks

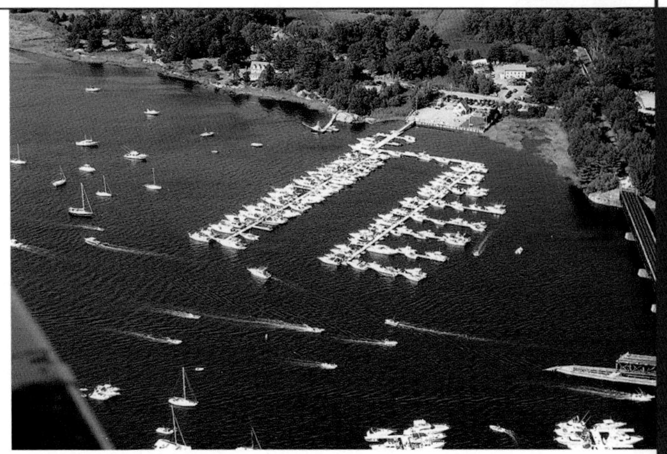

Cove Marina

8 Friedenfels Street; Salisbury, MA 01952

Tel: (978) 462-4998 **VHF: Monitor** Ch. 9 **Talk** Ch. 10
Fax: n/a **Alternate Tel:** n/a
Email: covemarina@verizon.net **Web:** www.covemarina.net
Nearest Town: Newburyport *(0.5 mi.)* **Tourist Info:** (978) 462-6680

Marina Services and Boat Supplies

Services - Docking Assistance, Dock Carts **Communication -** FedEx, UPS **Supplies - OnSite:** Ice *(Block, Cube)* **Near:** Ships' Store *(at Bridge Marina)*, Bait/Tackle *(at Bridge Marina)* **Under 1 mi:** Propane *(Kelly's True Value 462-2951)* **3+ mi:** West Marine *(603-474-7997, 5 mi.)*

Boatyard Services

OnSite: Forklift, Engine mechanic *(gas)*, Electrical Repairs, Woodworking **OnCall:** Divers, Bottom Cleaning, Brightwork, Compound, Wash & Wax, Interior Cleaning, Propeller Repairs, Upholstery, Yacht Interiors **Near:** Travelift, Crane, Hydraulic Trailer, Engine mechanic *(diesel)*, Hull Repairs, Rigger. **Nearest Yard:** Bridge Marina (978) 462-2274

Restaurants and Accommodations

Near: Restaurant *(Stripers Grille 499-0400, L $7-14, D $15-28, at Bridge Marina)*, Lite Fare *(Fishtale Diner 465-1674, B $4-10, L $6-12)*, *(Marsh View Café 465-1199, B $3-8, L $5-10)*, Inn/B&B *(The Inn at Stripers Grille 463-3343, $79, at Bridge Marina)* **Under 1 mi:** Restaurant *(Michael's Harborside 462-7785, L $8-19, D $10-29, easy dinghy access)*, *(Black Cow 499-8811, L $10-23, D $10-28, Pub $8-23, easy dinghy access)*, *(Park Lunch 465-9817, L & D $3-17)*, *(Mapow Sushi-Thai 499-7795, L $7-14, D $10-36, Vegan too)*, Pizzeria *(Angelinas 462-9696)*, Inn/B&B *(Essex Street 465-3148, $85-175)*, *(Newburyport B & B 463-4637, $140-160)*, *(Clark Currier 465-8363, $125-185)*, *(Garrison Inn 499-8500, $170-300)*

Recreation and Entertainment

OnSite: Picnic Area, Grills, Playground **Near:** Hike/Bike Trails *(Old Eastern Marsh)*, Fishing Charter *(Bridge Marina)* **Under 1 mi:** Movie Theater *(Screening Room 462-3456)*, Video Rental *(Express 463-3066)*, Museum *(Custom House Maritime 462-8681$3/2)*, Cultural Attract *(Firehouse Center for the Arts 462-7336)*, Galleries *(Newburyport Art Assoc. 465-8769)* **1-3 mi:** Beach *(Salisbury Beach)*, Dive Shop *(Mac Dougali 388-1234)* **3+ mi:** Golf Course *(Amesbury G & C 388-5153, Evergreen G.C. 463-8600, 4 mi.)*, Bowling *(Lafayette Lanes 388-4338, 5 mi.)*

Provisioning and General Services

Under 1 mi: Gourmet Shop *(Joppa 462-4662)*, Wine/Beer *(Leary's 462-4451)*, Farmers' Market *(Sun 9am-1pm, Tannery Marketplace)*, Fishmonger *(David's 462-2504)*, Bank/ATM, Post Office, Catholic Church, Protestant Church, Synagogue, Library *(465-4428)*, Beauty Salon *(Stylz 465-2111)*, Barber Shop *(Inn St. 462-9900)*, Bookstore *(The Book Rack 462-8615)*, Pharmacy *(Lynch 462-2232)*, Hardware Store *(Kelly's True Value 462-2951)* **1-3 mi:** Supermarket *(Shaw's 462-7121)*, Health Food *(Natural Grocer 463-8713)*, Liquor Store *(R & L 465-5491)*, Dry Cleaners, Laundry, Department Store *(Marshall's, K-Mart)*, Copies Etc. *(UPS Store 388-9144)*

Transportation

OnCall: Rental Car *(Enterprise 499-0021)*, Taxi *(Port Taxi 465-2333)*, Airport Limo *(Cassidy Limo 465-9509)* **3+ mi:** Rail *(MBTA to Boston, 4 mi.)* **Airport:** Pease/Logan Int'l. *(20 mi./50 mi.)*

Medical Services

911 Service **1-3 mi:** Doctor *(Lower Merrimac 462-2345)*, Dentist *(Newburyport 462-9611)*, Holistic Services *(Dr. Dan Eyink's Healing Center 462-0023)*, Optician *(Watts 462-2020)*, Veterinarian *(Carr 462-7101)* **Hospital:** Anna Jacques 463-1000 *(2 mi.)*

Setting -- Just west of the Gillis/Route One Bridge on the river's north bank, Cove's two long main docks stretch far out into the river. On shore, a tidy tan, two-story near "A" frame office is surrounded by neat gravel, edged with lawn and sprinkled with white Adirondack-style chairs, picnic tables and a contemporary play gym. Pretty expanses of marsh lie just beyond creating a quiet oasis that's an easy walk across the bridge to all bustling Newburyport.

Marina Notes -- Family owned & operated. Founded 1989, acquired by Mullens in 1995. Dockhands on duty 8am-8pm, 7 days. Primarily seasonal mid-size power boats. Transient slide-tie & dinghy dockage close to shore or larger vessels on T-head - a long walk to terra firma. Accommodating staff. Good, fiberglass docks. Winter storage to 30 ft. (Haul, store, launch $27/ft.) Mechanic onsite but most BY services & fuel downriver at Bridge Marina (no transients) or across river at several marinas. Port Taxi picks up groceries or takes cruisers to store, train station or airport. Bathhouse: Tiled, well-lighted, fiberglass shower stalls.

Notable -- One of the Merrimack's best "fishing holes" is right off the marina - throw out a line for carp, salmon, bass, catfish, eel or striped bass. For a land-based diversion, hike or bike the new, paved 1.4 mile Old Eastern Marsh Trail. The entrance is adjacent to the marina and runs north through unspoiled sections of the Great Marsh to Salisbury Square where it connects to the Beach Road Bike Lanes and on to Salisbury Beach Center and the State Reservation. Stripers and several casual restaurants are a short walk; more notable ones are just across the bridge or short "power" dinghy ride, as are Newburyport's historic sites and shops. Rowing across is not for the faint of heart - so be sure to have a good motor.

PHOTOS ON DVD: 16

Newburyport Boat Basin

346R Merrimac Street; Newburyport, MA 01950

Tel: (978) 465-9110 **VHF: Monitor** Ch. 71 **Talk** Ch. 71
Fax: (978) 465-1826 **Alternate Tel:** (978) 462-3990
Email: info@newburyportmarinas.com **Web:** newburyportmarinas.com
Nearest Town: Newburyport *(1 mi.)* **Tourist Info:** (978) 462-6680

Navigational Information

Lat: 42°49.248' **Long:** 070°52.779' **Tide:** 7 ft. **Current:** 3 kt. **Chart:** 13274
Rep. Depths (*MLW*): Entry 10 ft. **Fuel Dock** n/a **Max Slip/Moor** 12 ft./-
Access: 2.3 miles upriver, under bridge, to port

Marina Facilities *(In Season/Off Season)*

Fuel: No
Slips: 230 Total, 10 Transient **Max LOA:** 65 ft. **Max Beam:** 20 ft.
Rate *(per ft.)*: **Day** $3.00 **Week** $11 **Month** $23
Power: 30 amp $10, **50 amp** $18, **100 amp** n/a, **200 amp** n/a
Cable TV: No **Dockside Phone:** No
Dock Type: Floating, Long Fingers, Alongside, Wood
Moorings: 0 Total, 0 Transient **Launch:** n/a
Rate: Day n/a **Week** n/a **Month** n/a
Heads: 3 Toilet(s), 3 Shower(s)
Internet: Yes *(Wi-Fi, Free)* **Laundry:** None
Pump-Out: OnCall *(Boat Fri-Sun 9am-5pm)* **Fee:** Free **Closed Heads:** Yes

Marina Operations

Owner/Manager: Randall Lyons **Dockmaster:** Jay Larcome
In-Season: May-Sep 15, 8am-4pm **Off-Season:** Sep 16-Apr, 8am-4pm
After-Hours Arrival: Call in advance
Reservations: Yes, Preferred **Credit Cards:** Visa/MC, Dscvr, Amex
Discounts: Retail 15% off **Dockage:** n/a **Fuel:** n/a **Repair:** n/a
Pets: Welcome, Dog Walk Area **Handicap Access:** No

Marina Services and Boat Supplies

Services - Docking Assistance, Boaters' Lounge, Dock Carts **Communication -** FedEx, UPS, Express Mail **Supplies - OnSite:** Ice *(Block, Cube)* **Near:** Ships' Store *(Newburyport Marinas office)*, Bait/Tackle, Propane *(Lunt & Kelly 465-6650)*, CNG *(Merri Mar)* **1-3 mi:** West Marine *(603-474-7997)*

Boatyard Services

OnSite: Hydraulic Trailer *(35T)*, Launching Ramp, Engine mechanic *(gas)*, Hull Repairs, Bottom Cleaning, Painting **Yard Rates:** $95/hr., Haul & Launch $6/ft.- 1wat *(blocking add'l.)*, Bottom Paint $16/ft.

Restaurants and Accommodations

Near: Lite Fare *(Riverside Cafe 225-6999)*, Inn/B&B *(Newburyport 463-4637, $75-160)* **Under 1 mi:** Restaurant *(Ten Center St. 462-6652, L $9-18, D $15-36, Sun Brunch $11-18)*, *(Finest Kind 462-9131)*, *(Park Lunch 465-9817, L & D $3-21)*, *(Michael's Harborside 462-7785, L & D $8-29)*, *(Black Cow 499-8811, L $10-29, D $10-36, Pub $10-23)*, *(Joseph's 462-1188, D $16-28, piano bar)*, *(Mr. India 465-8600, L & D $10-20 Nepali & Himalayan too. Kids $5-7. Delivers.)*, Lite Fare *(Plum Island 465-1444)*, Pizzeria *(Famous 462-9644)*, Hotel *(Garrison Inn 499-8500, $170-300)*, Inn/B&B *(Essex Street 465-3148, $150-175)*

Recreation and Entertainment

OnSite: Picnic Area, Grills, Fishing Charter *(Rocky Point 360-4346)* **Near:** Park *(Cashman)* **Under 1 mi:** Playground, Tennis Courts *(Cashman Park)*, Fitness Center *(Fitness Factory 465-2546)*, Video Rental *(Blockbuster 463-3741)*, Special Events *(Yankee Homecoming)* **1-3 mi:** Beach *(Plum Island)*, Golf Course *(Amesbury 388-5153)*, Boat Rentals *(P.I. Kayak 462-5510)*, Movie Theater *(Newburyport 462-3456)*, Museum *(Customs House 462-8681)*, Cultural Attract *(Firehouse Center for Arts 462-7336)*

Provisioning and General Services

Near: Health Food *(Natural Grocer 463-8713)* **Under 1 mi:** Convenience Store *(Richdale 465-9808)*, Supermarket *(Shaw's 462-7121)*, Gourmet Shop *(Grand Trunk 499-4441 - wine, too)*, Delicatessen *(Warren St. 465-1288)*, Liquor Store *(New England 462-2131)*, Bakery *(Greta's 465-1709)*, Bank/ATM, Post Office, Catholic Church, Protestant Church, Synagogue, Library *(465-4428)*, Beauty Salon *(Interlocks 465-3010)*, Barber Shop *(Inn Street 462-9900)*, Dry Cleaners *(Panda 465-8081)*, Pharmacy *(CVS 462-5339 - 24 hrs.)*, Hardware Store *(Lunt True Value 462-2951)*, Retail Shops *(Shopping Mall - K-Marts, Marshalls, etc.)* **1-3 mi:** Farmers' Market *(Sun 9am-1pm, Tannery Marketplace)*, Fishmonger *(Bob Lobster 465-7100)*, Bookstore *(Jabberwocky 465-9359)*

Transportation

OnCall: Rental Car *(Enterprise 499-0021)*, Taxi *(Port 465-2333)*, Airport Limo *(Four Star 463-5466)* **Under 1 mi:** Bikes *(Riverside 465-5566)*, InterCity Bus *(Concord)* **1-3 mi:** Rail *(MBTA to Boston 800-392- 6100)*
Airport: Logan Int'l *(50 mi.)*

Medical Services

911 Service **Near:** Veterinarian *(Carr 462-7101)* **Under 1 mi:** Doctor *(Lower Merrimac 462-2345)*, Dentist *(Newburyport 462-9611)*, Chiropractor *(Healthcare 499-9355)*, Holistic Services *(Spa Paradiso 462-5530)*, Optician *(Watts 462-2020)* **Hospital:** Anna Jacques 463-1000 *(0.8 mi.)*

PHOTOS ON DVD: 14

Setting -- Upriver of the Route 1 bascule bridge, past Windward's Rivers Edge and Newburyport Yacht Club, nine new Ipe-decked docks stretch along the southern shore linked to the upland by three walkways. Immediately dockside, pots of flowers grace the small gray ships' store; just inland, an attractive. low-slung shingled office hosts the amenities and the handy boaters' lounge. North and west are soothing views of pristine Ram Island, marsh and shorebirds.

Marina Notes -- Re-built in '07 with Ipe (Brazilian hardwood) docks. Expanded slip sizes and fareways. Part of the 4-site Newburyport Marinas; benefits from shared services. Power $10/nt, $35/wk, $75/mo. Docking assistance available. Small, well-supplied ships store with some clothing, beverages, ice, boat supplies, tackle & good supply of fresh bait (clams, mackerel, herring vac-pacs, flats of herring). Comfortable boater's lounge with fireplace, sofa & TV. Onsite boat yard - outboard mechanic, haul/launch to 40 ft. Winter & summer dry storage for 110 boats. Drawbridge opens on hour and half 6am-10pm; when closed air draft 35 ft. mhw & 42 ft. at mlw. Bathhouse: Renovated '07; commodious tiled full bath, fiberglass shower surround, with curtain.

Notable -- A short walk downriver, waterfront Cashman Park features an enclosed toddler play area, creative playground, tennis and basketball courts and ball and soccer fields. At its eastern end, a raised boardwalk leads to the paved 1.1-mile Clipper City Rail Trail to the train station. Elegant Atkinson Common park is a short half mile walk and it's just a mile to the heart of bustling Newburyport with a remarkable array of restaurants, shops, and artistic activities. Galleries, historic walks, house museums and theatrical productions abound. Or head three miles west to Maudslay Park and the Theater in the Open.

Navigational Information

Lat: 42°49.440' **Long:** 070°53.234' **Tide:** 9 ft. **Current:** 3 kt. **Chart:** 13274
Rep. Depths (*MLW*): Entry 20 ft. **Fuel Dock** n/a **Max Slip/Moor** 12 ft./50 ft.
Access: 3.5 nm on port side, just past buoy #26.

Marina Facilities *(In Season/Off Season)*

Fuel: No
Slips: 50 Total, 5 Transient **Max LOA:** 100 ft. **Max Beam:** 25 ft.
Rate *(per ft.)*: **Day** $1.50 **Week** n/a **Month** n/a
Power: 30 amp Inq., **50 amp** Inq., **100 amp** n/a, **200 amp** n/a
Cable TV: No **Dockside Phone:** No
Dock Type: Floating, Long Fingers, Alongside, Composition
Moorings: 30 Total, 5 Transient **Launch:** Yes (Free), Dinghy Dock
Rate: Day $20 **Week** n/a **Month** n/a
Heads: 2 Toilet(s), 2 Shower(s), Book Exchange
Internet: Yes *(Wi-Fi, Free)* **Laundry:** None
Pump-Out: OnCall *(Boat Fri-Mon 9am-5pm)* **Fee:** Free **Closed Heads:** Yes

Marina Operations

Owner/Manager: W. Jay Lesynski, Jr. **Dockmaster:** Same
In-Season: Year round, 7 am-7pm **Off-Season:** n/a
After-Hours Arrival: Call ahead. Dock attendant will meet you
Reservations: Yes, Preferred **Credit Cards:** Visa/MC, Dscvr
Discounts: None
Pets: Welcome, Dog Walk Area **Handicap Access:** Yes, Heads, Docks

Merri-Mar Yacht Basin

364 Merrimac Street; Newburyport, MA 01950

Tel: (978) 465-3022 **VHF: Monitor** Ch. 16 **Talk** Ch. 10
Fax: (978) 465-1443 **Alternate Tel:** n/a
Email: mmyb@comcast.net **Web:** merrimar.com
Nearest Town: Newburyport *(1.2 mi.)* **Tourist Info:** (978) 462-6680

Marina Services and Boat Supplies

Services - Docking Assistance, Boaters' Lounge, Security, Trash Pick-Up, Dock Carts **Communication -** Fax in/out, FedEx, UPS, Express Mail *(Sat Del)* **Supplies - OnSite:** Ice *(Block, Cube)*, Ships' Store, Propane, CNG

Boatyard Services

OnSite: Travelift *(50T)*, Forklift *(15T)*, Crane *(20T)*, Hydraulic Trailer *(50T)*, Engine mechanic *(gas, diesel)*, Electrical Repairs, Electronic Sales, Electronics Repairs, Hull Repairs, Rigger, Sail Loft, Canvas Work, Divers, Bottom Cleaning, Brightwork, Air Conditioning, Refrigeration, Compound, Wash & Wax, Interior Cleaning, Propeller Repairs, Woodworking, Inflatable Repairs, Metal Fabrication, Painting, Awlgrip, Yacht Broker **OnCall:** Upholstery, Yacht Interiors **Near:** Launching Ramp. **Dealer for:** Yanmar, Mercruiser, Cummins, Kohler, Northern Lights, Crusader, Volvo. **Yard Rates:** $85/hr., Haul & Launch $5/ft. *(blocking $3/ft.)*, Power Wash $3/ft.

Restaurants and Accommodations

Near: Inn/B&B *(Newburyport 463-4637, $139-199)* **Under 1 mi:** Restaurant *(Michael's Harborside 462-7785, L $6-12, D $7-17, dinghy dock)*, *(Black Cow 499-8811, D $17-32, dinghy)*, *(Glenn's Restaurant & Cool Bar 465-3811, D $17-30, live piano music Wed, Fri, & Sun night)*, *(David's Tavern 462-8077, D $8-28)*, *(Finest Kind 462-9131, D $15-25, A local fave)*, *(Mr. India 465-8600, L & D $10-20 Nepali & Himalayan, too. Kids $5-7. Del)*, *(China One 462-6900, Take-Out, Delivers)*, Fast Food *(Wendy's)*, Lite Fare *(D'Angelo's Grilled Sandwiches 465-5408)*, *(Park Lunch 465-9817, L & D $3-21)*, *(Riverside Cafe 225-6999)*, Pizzeria *(Famous Pizza 462-9644)* **1-3 mi:** Motel *(Fairfield Inn 388-3400)*, Inn/B&B *(Garrison Inn 499-8500, $170-300)*

Recreation and Entertainment

OnSite: Picnic Area *(Spacious wood deck)*, Grills **Under 1 mi:** Playground, Tennis Courts, Fitness Center *(Yoga Ctr 463-4354)*, Hike/Bike Trails *(Clipper City Rail Trail)*, Video Rental *(Blockbuster 463-3741)*, Park *(Atkinson Common)* **1-3 mi:** Beach *(Plum Island)*, Golf Course *(Amesbury G.& C.C. 388-5153)*, Movie Theater *(Screening Room 462-3456)*, Museum *(Custom House 462-8681 $3/2)*, Cultural Attract *(Theater in the Open, Maudslay S.P. 465-2572)* **3+ mi:** Bowling *(Lafayette 388-4338, 4 mi.)*

Provisioning and General Services

Near: Health Food *(Natural Grocer 463-8713)*, Beauty Salon *(Mindi's 465-8880)* **Under 1 mi:** Supermarket *(Shaw's 462-7121)*, Delicatessen *(Warren St. 465-1288)*, Bank/ATM, Catholic Church, Protestant Church, Synagogue, Library *(465-4428)*, Dry Cleaners, Pharmacy *(Rite-Aid 462-5084)*, Retail Shops *(Port Plaza - Marshalls, K-Mart, banks, restaurants)* **1-3 mi:** Gourmet Shop *(Joppa 462-4662)*, Liquor Store *(Leahy's 462-4451)*, Farmers' Market *(Sun 9am-1pm, Tannery)*, Post Office, Laundry *(near Customs House)*, Bookstore *(Jabberwocky 465-9359)*, Hardware Store *(Lunt 465-6650)*

Transportation

OnCall: Rental Car *(Enterprise 499-0021)*, Taxi *(Port 465-2333)* **Near:** Local Bus *(to downtown Newburyport)* **Under 1 mi:** Rail *(MBTA to Boston 800-392-6100)* **Airport:** Pease/Logan Int'l. *(20 mi./50 mi.)*

Medical Services

911 Service **Near:** Chiropractor *(HealthCare 499-9355)*, Veterinarian *(Carr Is. 462-7101)* **Under 1 mi:** Doctor *(Lower Merrimac 462-2345)*, Dentist *(Newburyport 462-9611)* **Hospital:** Anna Jacques 463-1000 *(1 mi.)*

Setting -- Upriver, a mile past downtown Newburyport and the bascule bridge, venerable Merri-Mar's spider web of docks sprawls along the quiet south bank. Long stretches of side-tie floats parallel the shore, and slips radiate from the main dock. On the upland, an expansive deck fronts the large yellow clapboard building that houses the ships' store, amenities and leads to the attached work shed. Across the narrowing river, past the marina's mooring field, are views of unspoiled Ram Island and Carr Island Wildlife Management Reserve - an off-season home to a growing population of Bald Eagles.

Marina Notes -- Founded in 1956. Service-oriented family business helmed by three generations. Serious repair work available. Numerous engine and mechanical dealer authorizations. Well-stocked ships' store very handy for supplies or parts. Only closed loop waste water filtration system in area. Requires (and rents) dustless vacuum sanding system. Be aware that pipes replace cleats on the floating docks. Moorings serviced by launch & dinghy dock - rowing is not an option. Good place to leave the boat - especially if work needs to be done. Bathhouse: Basic and not new - in the office. Can be distant from boat.

Notable -- A monument memorializes the famous 1853 Clippership "Dreadnought," built on this site by Currier & Townsend. A half-mile inland, historic Atkinson Common sports elaborate gardens, a lily pond, walking /biking paths, tennis courts, a gazebo and stone tower. 0.8 mile east, Cashman Park has a maritime playground, tennis and basketball courts, and a boardwalk that links to the Clipper City Rail Trail to Newburyport's waterfront or the train depot.Two miles west Maudslay S.P. promises immense stands of laurel, panoramic river views, well-landscaped grounds, Theater in the Open & Boat Camp (463-2233).

PHOTOS ON DVD: 16

Marina at Hatter's Point

PO Box 151; 60 Merrimac St.; Amesbury, MA 01913

Tel: (978) 388-7333 **VHF: Monitor** Ch. 9 **Talk** Ch. 9
Fax: (978) 388-6060 **Alternate Tel:** n/a
Email: paula@marinaathatterspoint.com **Web:** marinaathatterspoint.com
Nearest Town: Amesbury *(1.7 mi.)* **Tourist Info:** (978) 388-3178

Navigational Information

Lat: 42°50.181' **Long:** 070°55.709' **Tide:** 5 ft. **Current:** 4 kt. **Chart:** 13274
Rep. Depths (*MLW*): Entry 6 ft. **Fuel Dock** n/a **Max Slip/Moor** 6 ft./-
Access: About 6 mi. up the Merrimack

Marina Facilities *(In Season/Off Season)*

Fuel: No
Slips: 135 Total, 5 Transient **Max LOA:** 65 ft. **Max Beam:** n/a
Rate *(per ft.)*: **Day** $1.50* **Week** n/a **Month** n/a
Power: 30 amp Incl., **50 amp** Add'l Fee, **100 amp** n/a, **200 amp** n/a
Cable TV: No **Dockside Phone:** No
Dock Type: Floating, Alongside, Wood
Moorings: 0 Total, 0 Transient **Launch:** n/a
Rate: Day n/a **Week** n/a **Month** n/a
Heads: 4 Toilet(s), 2 Shower(s) *(dressing rooms)*
Internet: Yes *(Wi-Fi, Free)* **Laundry:** 1 Washer(s), 1 Dryer(s)
Pump-Out: Onsite *(8am-5pm)*, Self Service **Fee:** Free **Closed Heads:** Yes

Marina Operations

Owner/Manager: Paula McPartland** **Dockmaster:** Andy Knapp
In-Season: May 15-Oct 15, 8am-5pm **Off-Season:** Oct 16-May 14, 9am-4pm
After-Hours Arrival: Call in advance
Reservations: Yes, Recommended **Credit Cards:** Visa/MC
Discounts: None
Pets: Welcome **Handicap Access:** Yes

Marina Services and Boat Supplies

Services - Boaters' Lounge, Security *(24 hrs.)* **Communication -** FedEx, DHL, UPS, Express Mail **Supplies - OnSite:** Ice *(Block, Cube)* **3+ mi:** West Marine *(603-474-7170, 11 mi.)*

Boatyard Services

OnCall: Engine mechanic *(gas, diesel)*, Bottom Cleaning, Air Conditioning, Compound, Wash & Wax, Inflatable Repairs **Nearest Yard:** Merri-Mar Yacht Basin (978) 465-3022

Restaurants and Accommodations

OnCall: Pizzeria *(Domino's 834-0008)* **Under 1 mi:** Lite Fare *(Whistling Tea Kettle 388-5250, B & L)*, *(Irene's Sub & Pizza 388-3060)*, Pizzeria *(Amesbury House 388-9878)* **1-3 mi:** Restaurant *(Barking Dog 388-9537, L $7.50-12, D $10-23, Pub $6.50-11, Kids' $5.50)*, *(Ristorant Molise 388-4844, D $18-26, 4-course Prix Fixe $27, Tue-Sun. Fine dining)*, *(Acapulco's 834-4000, L $8-12, D $10-16)*, *(Weiloon Cafe 388-7521, sushi)*, *(Hollow Cafe 388-5460, B $3-10, L $4-8.50, D $8-17, Kids' $2-6 Mon-Thu 6am-7pm, Fri 6am-8pm, Sat & Sun 6am-1pm - CVS Plaza)*, Fast Food *(McD's)*, Pizzeria *(Sal's 388-5400)*, Hotel *(Marriott Fairfield 388-3400, $114-159)*

Recreation and Entertainment

OnSite: Picnic Area *(Large deck)*, Grills **Under 1 mi:** Playground *(Amesbury Sports Park 388-5788 $20/3hrs. $30/day. OGO & Summer Tubing)*, Museum *(Bartlett 388-4528 - a house museum. Exhibits relate to Amesbury region. Fri & Sun 1-4pm, Sat 10am-4pm)*, Sightseeing *(Lowell's Boat Shop 834-0050 established 1793. National Landmark & Working Museum dedicated to wooden boat building)* **1-3 mi:** Golf Course *(Amesbury Golf 388-5153 - 9 holes $20)*, Bowling *(Leo's 388-2010)*, Movie Theater *(Stage Two Cinema Pub 388-6555 Amesbury; Cinemagic 499-9494 Salisbury)*, Video Rental *(Movie Gallery 388-8541)*, Tours *(John Greenleaf Whittier Home 388-1337; Macy Colby House 388-1500 C.1654)*, Cultural Attract *(Maudslay Theater in the Open 465-2572; Amesbury Playhouse Dinner Theater 388-9444)*, Galleries *(Cedar St.)*

Provisioning and General Services

Under 1 mi: Liquor Store *(Route 110 388-5857)*, Bank/ATM *(Provident)*, Protestant Church, Beauty Salon *(Trendz 834-0468)*, Barber Shop *(Bellavance 388-9125)* **1-3 mi:** Supermarket *(Super Stop & Shop 388-7588)*, Wine/Beer *(Carriagetown 388-0066)*, Post Office *(CVS Plaza)*, Catholic Church, Synagogue, Library *(388-8148)*, Laundry, Bookstore, Pharmacy *(CVS 834-0606; Rite Aid 834-0014)*, Hardware Store *(Eastern Lumber 388-0366)*, Department Store *(K-Mart 462-8521)*

Transportation

OnCall: Rental Car *(Enterprise 499-0021)*, Taxi *(Walkey Livery 388-7755)*, Airport Limo *(Seacoast 465-8820)* **Under 1 mi:** Bikes *(Amesbury Skate & Sport 388-4544)*, Local Bus *(MRTA to Newburyport & Haverhill)* **1-3 mi:** InterCity Bus *(C&J 800-258-7111 to Boston, Portsmouth)* **3+ mi:** Rail *(Newburyport MBTA, 5 mi.)* **Airport:** Logan Int'l *(38 mi.)*

Medical Services

911 Service **OnCall:** Ambulance **Under 1 mi:** Doctor *(Lahey Clinic 388-5050)*, Dentist *(Ditolla 388-4323)*, Veterinarian *(Merrimack Valley 388-3074)* **1-3 mi:** Chiropractor *(Cutting 388-7133)*, Holistic Services *(Raya Med Spa 834-9909)* **Hospital:** Anna Jacques 463-1044 *(3.7 mi.)*

Setting -- Three miles upriver from Newburyport, the 1870s Merrimac Hat Factory, now resurrected as the handsome brick-and-glass Hatters Point luxury condominium, rises on the north bank above the marina. Manicured plantings and a gravel promenade edge the river above a wide expanse of quality, side-tie moorage - three "E" shaped sets of docks parallel the current. Across the river, Maudslay State Park's wall of green provides boaters an unspoiled view.

Marina Notes -- *Discount after 3 days **New local owners '09 Jay McPartland, Jay Knapp & Michael Picard (Knapp's installed docks and built marinas for 30 years). 50A small additional charge. Seasonal $90/ft. Marina office and heads in temporary building. Phase II of the condominium development - on hold as of this writing -- holds prospect of permanent bathouse and other amenities. As of publication, few services available onsite. Protected anchorage in a big blow. Fresh water makes a good place to leave the boat. Bathhouse: Although temporary, modern, pleasant full baths.

Notable -- Primeval stands of white pine, surrounded by thickets of natural Mountain Laurel, hug 450-acre Maudslay State Park's shoreline creating a tall canopy for nesting Bald Eagles. Find the Binoculars. Unfortunately, this glorious park is a look, don't touch, experience since the entrance is 3 miles by road. However, a mile-walk along the river leads to the Lowell's Boat Shop's 1793 barn red buildings. The U.S.'s oldest continuously operating boat builder, it is the preeminent builder of legendary Banks Dories - watch them being constructed or floating at their docks. The closest restaurants and services are about an 0.8 mile walk to Macy Street. More are about 1.3 miles, and the Amesbury and Salisbury Mills Village Historic District and Market Square is 1.7 miles away.

11. MA – North Shore

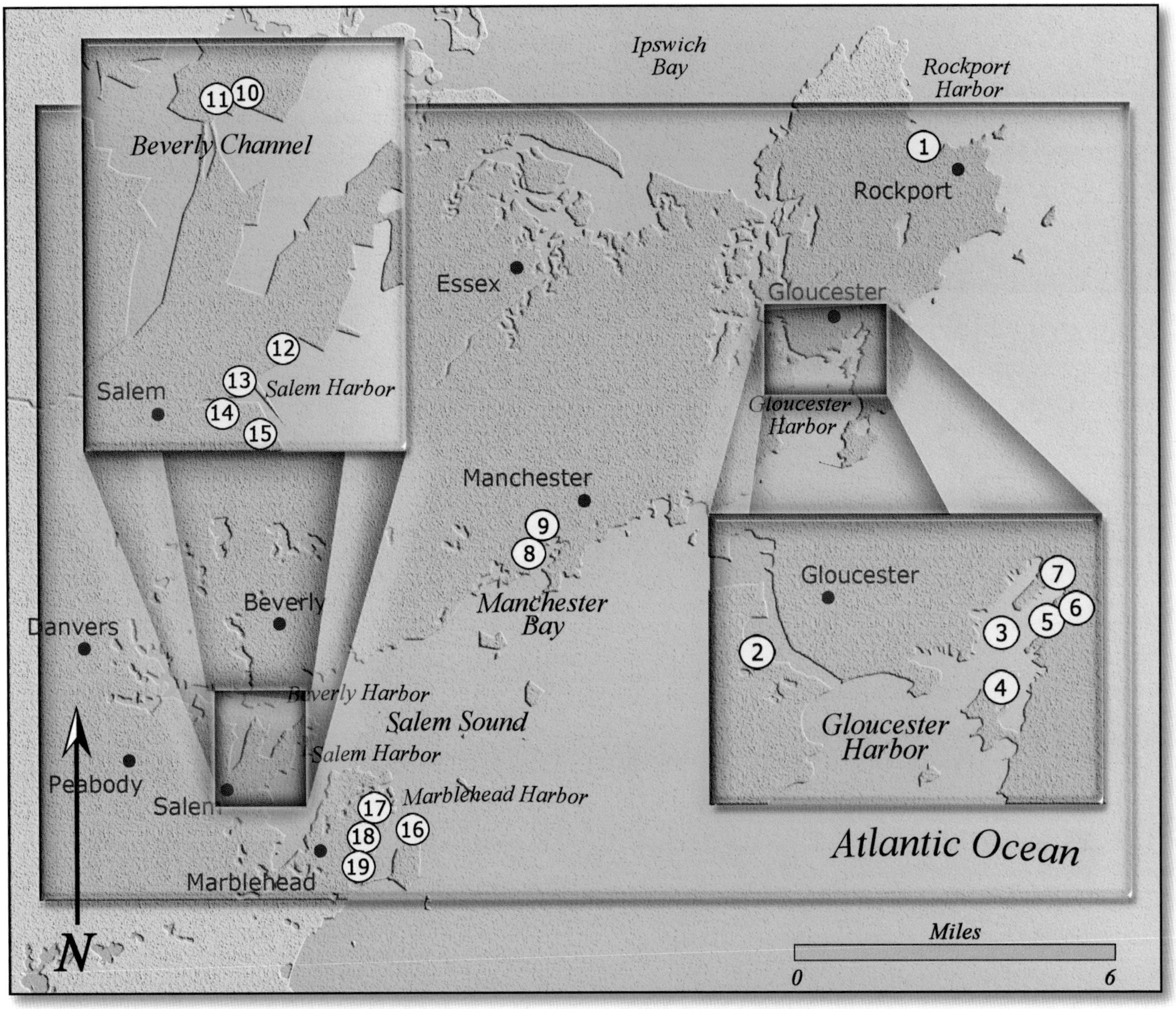

MAP	MARINA	HARBOR	PAGE
1	**Rockport Harbor**	*Rockport Harbor*	204
2	**Cape Ann's Marina Resort**	*Blynman Canal*	205
3	**Gloucester Harbor Moorings**	*Gloucester Harbor*	206
4	**Madfish Grille**	*Smith Cove*	207
5	**East Gloucester Marine**	*Gloucester Harbor*	208
6	**Brown's Yacht Yard**	*Gloucester Harbor*	209
7	**Pier 7/Enos Marine**	*Cripple Cove*	210
8	**Crocker's Boat Yard**	*Manchester Harbor*	211
9	**Manchester Marine**	*Manchester Harbor*	212
10	**Beverly Port Marina**	*Danvers River*	213
11	**Glover Wharf Municipal Marina**	*Danvers River*	214
12	**Brewer Hawthorne Cove Marina**	*Salem Harbor*	215
13	**Pickering Wharf Marina**	*Salem Harbor*	216
14	**Salem Water Taxi**	*Salem Harbor*	217
15	**Fred J. Dion Yacht Yard**	*Salem Harbor*	218
16	**Corinthian Yacht Club**	*Marblehead Harbor*	219
17	**Tucker's Wharf Municipal Docks**	*Marblehead Harbor*	220
18	**Boston Yacht Club**	*Marblehead Harbor*	221
19	**Dolphin Yacht Club**	*Marblehead Harbor*	222

RATINGS: 1-5 for Marina Facilities & Amenities, 1-2 for Boatyard Services,  1-2 for MegaYacht Facilities,  for Something Special.

SERVICES: for CCM – Certified Clean Marina, 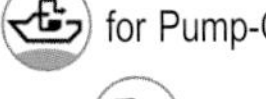 for Pump-Out, 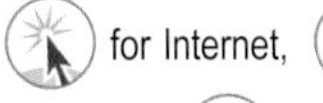 for Internet,  for Fuel,  for Restaurant, for Provisioning nearby, for Catamaran-friendly,  for SportFish Charter,  for Pool/Beach, and  for Golf within a mile. *For an explanation of ACC's Ratings, see page 8.*

Rockport Harbor

Broadway & Mt. Pleasant Street; Rockport, MA 01966

Tel: (978) 546-9589 **VHF: Monitor** Ch. 9 **Talk** Ch. 19
Fax: (978) 546-7297 **Alternate Tel:** n/a
Email: harbormaster@town.rockport.ma.us **Web:** www.town.rockport.ma.us
Nearest Town: Rockport **Tourist Info:** (978) 546-6575

Navigational Information

Lat: 42°66.089' **Long:** 070°61.504' **Tide:** 9 ft. **Current:** n/a **Chart:** 13279
Rep. Depths (*MLW*): Entry 10 ft. **Fuel Dock** n/a **Max Slip/Moor** 6 ft./-
Access: Enter lobster-shaped harbor between two breakwaters

Marina Facilities *(In Season/Off Season)*

Fuel: No
Slips: 8 Total, 8 Transient **Max LOA:** 50 ft. **Max Beam:** n/a
Rate *(per ft.)*: **Day** $1.00* **Week** n/a **Month** n/a
Power: 30 amp Incl., **50 amp** n/a, **100 amp** n/a, **200 amp** n/a
Cable TV: No **Dockside Phone:** No
Dock Type: Fixed, Alongside, Wood
Moorings: 0 Total, 0 Transient **Launch:** n/a, Dinghy Dock (no)
Rate: Day n/a **Week** n/a **Month** n/a
Heads: 2 Toilet(s), 1 Shower(s)
Internet: Yes *(Wi-Fi - Sandy Bay Y.C.)* **Laundry:** None
Pump-Out: OnSite, Full Service **Fee:** Free **Closed Heads:** Yes

Marina Operations

Owner/Manager: Rosemary Lesch, Scott Story (Hrbrmstrs) **Dockmaster:** n/a
In-Season: May-Sep, 7am-3pm **Off-Season:** Oct-Apr, Closed
After-Hours Arrival: Call in advance
Reservations: Yes **Credit Cards:** Cash Only
Discounts: None
Pets: Welcome **Handicap Access:** No

Marina Services and Boat Supplies

Supplies - OnSite: Ice *(Block, Cube)* **Under 1 mi:** Propane *(Smith Ace 546-2229)* **3+ mi:** Ships' Store *(Yankee 290-4415, 4 mi.)*

Boatyard Services

OnCall: Engine mechanic *(gas, diesel)*, Electrical Repairs *(Voyager 768-7143)*, Electronics Repairs *(Voyager)* **Under 1 mi:** Launching Ramp. **Nearest Yard:** Brown's Gloucester (978) 281-3200

Restaurants and Accommodations

Near: Restaurant *(Ellen's Harborside 546-2512, L & D $7-18 - since 1954)*, *(Brackett's Oceanview 546-2797, L $9-18, D $13-22)*, *(My Place 546-9667, L $12-18.50, D $27-38, at the tip of the neck)*, Seafood Shack *(Roy Moore Lobster 546-6696, D $12-25)*, *(Fish Shack 546-6667, L & D $6-18, Kids' $5)*, Snack Bar *(Top Dog 546-0006)*, Coffee Shop *(Bean and Leaf 546-7500, B $4-10, Wi-Fi)*, Lite Fare *(Red Skiff 546-7649)*, *(Red Skiff 546-7647, B & L)*, *(Hula Moon 546-2572, Hawaii)*, Pizzeria *(Rockport 546-6066)*, Motel *(Eagle House 546-6292, $85-130)*, *(Bearskin Neck 546-6677, $109-179)*, Inn/B&B *(Tuck Inn 546-7260, $106-176)*, *(Inn on Cove Hill 546-2701, $130-235)*

Recreation and Entertainment

OnSite: Picnic Area **Near:** Beach, Playground *(Millbrook Meadow)*, Fishing Charter *(Cast Away's 546-3959 21 & 26 ft. Whalers; Northcoast Anglers Fly Fishing 395-5871)*, Museum *(Sandy Bay Historical Soc. 546-9533 $5/Free 1832 Sewall-Scripture House & 1711 Old Castle)*, Tours *(North Shore Kayak Tours 546-5050 $40/25 2hrs; Tall Ship "Formidable" Pirate Cruises 729-2929; Fudge Ripple 527-8994 $25/ 45-min. harbor ride, Fri-Sun)*, Cultural Attract *(Shalin Liu Performance Center 546-7391 Rockport Music - classical, jazz, folk, opera & film)*, Sightseeing *(Motif No. 1 - classic red fishing shack; 1658 Cooperage Shop 546-2958; Thacher Island 546-7697)*, Galleries *(Art Association 546-6604; Bearskin Neck)* **1-3 mi:** Golf Course *(Rockport G.C. 546-3340)*, Park *(Rockport's Sea Rocks & Halibut Point State Park 546-2997 - trail maps at the visitors' center)*

Provisioning and General Services

Near: Gourmet Shop *(Lula's 546-0010)*, Bakery *(Helmut's Strudel 546-2824- Don't miss it!; Rockin' Cupcakes 309-3380; Coffee Shop 546-9443)*, Bank/ATM, Post Office *(546-2694)*, Catholic Church, Protestant Church, Library *(546-6934)*, Beauty Salon, Barber Shop, Dry Cleaners *(Rockport 546-9988)*, Bookstore *(Toad Hall 546-7323)*, Pharmacy *(Rite Aid 546-7521)*, Hardware Store *(Smith Ace 546-2229)*, Florist **Under 1 mi:** Convenience Store *(Cumberland Farms 546-9180)*, Market *(IGA 546-2844)*, Laundry *(Loco-Motion 546-9468)* **1-3 mi:** Supermarket *(Shaw's 281-4844)*

Transportation

OnCall: Rental Car *(Enterprise 281-3288)*, Taxi *(A&K 281-6161)*, Airport Limo *(A-1 281-8121; Atlantic 281 5550)* **Near:** Bikes *(North Shore 546-5050)*, Water Taxi *(Fudge Ripple leaves Town Wharf Fri-Sun, every hour)*, Local Bus *(CATA 283-7278 Gloucester)* **Under 1 mi:** Rail *(MBTA Boston 617-222-3200)* **Airport:** Logan Int'l *(34 mi.)*

Medical Services

911 Service **Near:** Doctor *(Wedmore 546-2535)*, Chiropractor *(Engel 546-1111)* **Under 1 mi:** Dentist *(Sandfield 546-6333)* **1-3 mi:** Veterinarian *(Cape Ann 546-2502)* **3+ mi:** Optician *(Cutler 281-8809, 5 mi)* **Hospital:** Addison Gilbert 283-4000 *(5 mi.)*

Setting -- The quintessential New England fishing village, Rockport Harbor welcomes boaters to slips and tie-ups fitted in here and there among old piers and wharves right in the middle of the action. The Town Wharf, shared with Sandy Bay Yacht Club, divides the harbor into the North Basin for mainly commercial vessels and the South Basin for smaller recreational craft. Rockport is a magnet for daytrippers attracted to the colorful setting and myriad activities.

Marina Notes -- *Daytime tie-up, no charge. Overnight $1/ft. Managed jointly by the harbormasters and Sandy Bay Yacht Club, who try to squeeze everyone in (Ass't Harbormasters Ron Petoff & Story Reed). Not a traditional marina -- a combination of municipal tie-ups and those of the yacht club, which accepts transients on its launch and docks when space is available. Reasonable fee - oriented toward tourism promotion. No transient moorings but good holding for anchoring off the Bearskin Neck beach or in nearby Sandy Bay - dinghy to T-Wharf. Bathhouse: Basic, public & a long walk. Use the yacht club's.

Notable -- Once a fishing village, the original shacks and clapboard houses are now eateries, galleries, bars, shops of every stripe that stretch down Bearneck toward several sandy -- but chilly -- ocean beaches. Don't miss a musical event at the exceptional, glass-walled Shalin Liu Performance Center. Two and a half miles from the harbor, Thacher Island is a fun kayak destination with twin 1789 lighthouses, hiking trails, a museum and National Wildlife Refuge; alternatively take their launch on Wed or Sat morning (reserve 599-2590) or tie the big boat to one of two moorings & dinghy to the ramp. Halibut Point State Park, three miles via Granite Street, features a former quarry surrounded by trails leading to panoramic sea views and a renovated WW II Fire Tower.

PHOTOS ON DVD: 23

Navigational Information
Lat: 42°36.743' **Long:** 070°40.815' **Tide:** 9 ft. **Current:** 5 kt. **Chart:** 13281
Rep. Depths (*MLW*): Entry 10 ft. **Fuel Dock** 7 ft. **Max Slip/Moor** 7 ft./-
Access: Gloucester Harbor to Blynman Canal, far side on port side

Marina Facilities *(In Season/Off Season)*
Fuel: Gasoline, Diesel, High-Speed Pumps
Slips: 275 Total, 10 Transient **Max LOA:** 120 ft. **Max Beam:** n/a
Rate *(per ft.)*: **Day** $3.50/$2.5 **Week** Inq. **Month** Inq.
Power: 30 amp $3, **50 amp** $6, **100 amp** n/a, **200 amp** n/a
Cable TV: No **Dockside Phone:** No
Dock Type: Floating, Long Fingers, Alongside, Wood
Moorings: 3 Total, 3 Transient **Launch:** No, Dinghy Dock
Rate: Day $30 **Week** n/a **Month** n/a
Heads: 4 Toilet(s), 2 Shower(s) *(dressing rooms)*
Internet: Yes *(Wi-Fi, Free)* **Laundry:** 2 Washer(s), 2 Dryer(s)
Pump-Out: Full Service **Fee:** Free **Closed Heads:** Yes

Marina Operations
Owner/Manager: Andrew & Tobin Dominick **Dockmaster:** n/a
In-Season: May-Oct 15, 7am-7pm **Off-Season:** Oct 16-Apr, 8am-4pm
After-Hours Arrival: Call Ch 10, go to lobby
Reservations: Yes, Preferred **Credit Cards:** Visa/MC, Dscvr, Din, Amex
Discounts: None
Pets: Welcome, Dog Walk Area **Handicap Access:** Yes, Docks

Cape Ann's Marina Resort

75 Essex Avenue; Gloucester, MA 01930

Tel: (978) 283-2112 **VHF: Monitor** Ch. 10 **Talk** Ch. 10
Fax: (978) 282-4314 **Alternate Tel:** (978) 283-2116
Email: dockmaster@capeannmarina.com **Web:** www.capeannmarina.com
Nearest Town: Gloucester *(1 mi.)* **Tourist Info:** (978) 281-8865

Marina Services and Boat Supplies
Services - Docking Assistance, Concierge, Boaters' Lounge, Security *(24 hrs.)* **Communication -** Fax in/out, FedEx, UPS, Express Mail **Supplies - OnSite:** Ice *(Block, Cube)*, Ships' Store, Bait/Tackle **Near:** Propane *(Tony's Mobil Mart 283-8998)*

Boatyard Services
OnSite: Travelift *(15, 20 & 70T)*, Forklift, Crane, Hydraulic Trailer, Engine mechanic *(gas, diesel)*, Electrical Repairs, Electronic Sales, Electronics Repairs, Hull Repairs, Bottom Cleaning, Brightwork, Air Conditioning, Refrigeration, Compound, Wash & Wax, Interior Cleaning, Propeller Repairs, Woodworking, Painting **Dealer for:** Suzuki, Interlux, Yamaha, Worldcat, Everglades. **Yard Rates:** $65-90, Haul & Launch $6-7/1-way *(blocking $4-4.50/ft.)*, Power Wash $6.50-7/ft. **Storage:** On-Land $59-61/ft. haul incl.

Restaurants and Accommodations
OnSite: Lite Fare *(Mile Marker One Waterside Tent Bar & Café)*, Motel *(Cape Ann's 283-2112, $75-250)* **Near:** Restaurant *(The Causeway 281-5256, Casual, seafood)*, Inn/B&B *(Manor 283-0614, $61-145)* **Under 1 mi:** Restaurant *(Elliott at the Blackburn 282-1919, L & D $5-13 Music Thu-Sat)*, *(Gloucester House 283-1812, L $11-16, D $16-30)*, *(Pilot House BBQ 283-0131)*, *(Horizon Chinese 283-8815, L $6, D $7-14)*, *(Latitude 43 281-0223, L $8-13, D $17-27, Sushi, Taven $8-12, Music)*, Coffee Shop *(Morning Glory 281-1851)*, Lite Fare *(Cupboard 281-1908, Stage Fort)*, Pizzeria *(Sebastian's 283-4407)*, Inn/B&B *(Babson Court 281-4469, $125-210)*

Recreation and Entertainment
OnSite: Heated Pool, Spa, Picnic Area, Grills, Fishing Charter *(Tuna Hunter, First Light Angler, Kayman Charters)*, Party Boat *(72 ft., 65T Lady Sea 559-1978 $64/54)*, Tours *("Anni" River Tours, Free)* **Near:** Tennis Courts, Movie Theater *(Gloucester 283-9188)* **Under 1 mi:** Beach, Playground, Bowling *(Cape Ann 283-9753)*, Park *(Stage Fort Park)*, Cultural Attract *(West End Theater 281-0680)*, Sightseeing *(Yankee Whale Watch 283-0313 $45/29)* **1-3 mi:** Video Rental *(Red Box 733-2693)*, Museum *(Hammond Castle 283-7673 $10/6; Sargent House 281-2432)*, Galleries **3+ mi:** Golf Course *(Cape Ann 768-7544, 7 mi.)*

Provisioning and General Services
OnSite: Newsstand **Near:** Convenience Store *(Mobil Mart 283-8998)*, Wine/Beer, Liquor Store *(Causeway 283-4313)* **Under 1 mi:** Supermarket *(Shaw's 283-2601)*, Farmers' Market *(Thur, 3-6:30pm, 65 Rogers St.)*, Green Grocer *(Farmer John 283-2575)*, Bank/ATM, Protestant Church, Synagogue, Library *(Sawyer 281-9763)*, Pharmacy *(CVS 283-8489, Walgreens 283-7361)*, Hardware Store **1-3 mi:** Health Food *(Common Crow 283-1665)*, Fishmonger *(Turners 281-8535)*, Post Office, Catholic Church, Beauty Salon, Laundry, Bookstore *(The Bookstore 281-1548)*

Transportation
OnSite: Local Bus *(CATA 283-7278)* **OnCall:** Rental Car *(Enterprise 281-3288)*, Taxi *(Atlantic 281-5550)* **Under 1 mi:** Rail *(MBTA to Boston)*
Airport: Logan Int'l. *(32 mi.)*

Medical Services
911 Service **OnSite:** Chiropractor *(Zubricki 978-283-2116)*, Holistic Services *(Spa 283-2116 Massage 60 min/$75)* **Under 1 mi:** Doctor *(Sagall 625-9608)*, Dentist *(Ahlin 283-4500)* **Hospital:** Addison Gilbert 283-4000 *(1 mi.)*

Setting -- In a sheltered basin on the heavily trafficked Blynman Canal, just south of the busy drawbridge, this full-service marina berths 275 slips on six main docks along a peninsula jam-packed with a three-story, waterfront motel, wellness center, large indoor pool, tented event space, an alfresco waterside eatery, boatyard and several opportunities for anglers. Away from the commercial main harbor, the views are of the docks, canal, and peaceful salt water marshes.

Marina Notes -- Takes 110 ft. yachts on South Basin dock. Books Southeast Harbor moorings for vessels to 150 ft. - includes all amenities & dinghy dockage. Extensive boatyard services. Three travelifts (15, 20 & 70T), 24/7 security & personnel. Indoor heated pool (80 deg.) with jacuzzi (7:30am-9:30pm), game room, laundry (7am-9:30pm), large ships' store & tackle shop, comp. coffee. Mile Marker One Tent Bar and Café fronts an event tent for 20-300 people (fleet captains note). Brick picnic and grill area overlooks docks. "Resort" might be overstatement. No elevator. Bathhouse: Tiled shower stalls with curtains.

Notable -- A bit out of the Gloucester mainstream, Cape Ann offers a great deal to do right onsite in a boaty, down-home environment - and is an easy mile walk or dinghy ride to most everything else. In addition to the pool and day spa, there's a fleet of sport fishing boats and a party (head) boat - which can create a lot of activity early in the early morning. Practically across the street, there's a movie theater, convenience store, casual restaurant and beer/liquor shop - and the local Cape Ann regional bus stops right onsite. Walk to the Fisherman's Monument, Pavilion Beach, Stage Fort Park, concerts, tennis, playground, and an esplanade. Or hop the bus to Beauport where the 1920's austere Hammond Castle brims with medieval relics.

PHOTOS ON DVD: 18

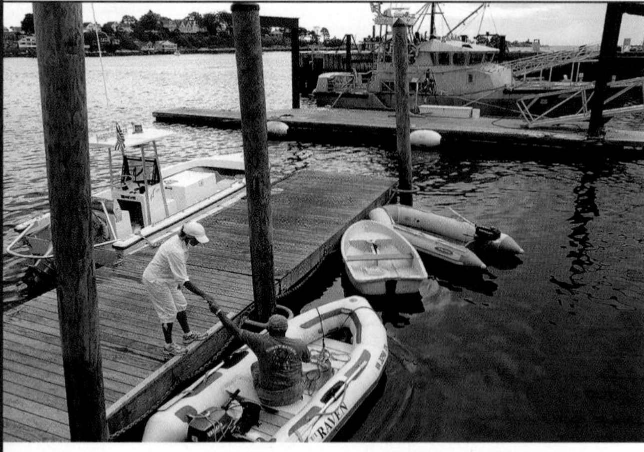

Gloucester Harbor Moorings

19 Harbor Loop; Gloucester, MA 01930

Tel: (978) 282-3012 **VHF: Monitor** Ch. 16 **Talk** Ch. 12, 14
Fax: (978) 281-4188 **Alternate Tel:** n/a
Email: jcaulkett@ci.gloucester.ma.us **Web:** gloucester-ma.gov
Nearest Town: Gloucester *(0.2 mi.)* **Tourist Info:** (978) 281-8865

Navigational Information

Lat: 42°36.000' **Long:** 070°36.000' **Tide:** 9 ft. **Current:** n/a **Chart:** 13281
Rep. Depths (*MLW*): Entry 25 ft. **Fuel Dock** n/a **Max Slip/Moor** -/16 ft.
Access: Gloucester Harbor Channel to Inner Harbor

Marina Facilities *(In Season/Off Season)*

Fuel: No
Slips: 0 Total, 0 Transient **Max LOA:** 100 ft. **Max Beam:** n/a
Rate *(per ft.)*: **Day** n/a **Week** n/a **Month** n/a
Power: 30 amp n/a, **50 amp** n/a, **100 amp** n/a, **200 amp** n/a
Cable TV: No **Dockside Phone:** No
Dock Type: n/a
Moorings: 28 Total, 28 Transient **Launch:** No, Dinghy Dock
Rate: Day $25 **Week** n/a **Month** n/a
Heads: None
Internet: No **Laundry:** None
Pump-Out: OnCall *(Boat)*, Full Service **Fee:** Free **Closed Heads:** Yes

Marina Operations

Owner/Manager: James Caulkett (Hrbrmstr) **Dockmaster:** Same
In-Season: Year Round, 8am-4pm **Off-Season:** n/a
After-Hours Arrival: Pick up any available mooring, check-in next morning
Reservations: Yes, Preferred **Credit Cards:** Cash/Check only
Discounts: None
Pets: Welcome **Handicap Access:** No

Marina Services and Boat Supplies

Communication - FedEx, UPS, Express Mail **Supplies - Near:** Propane *(Building Center 283-3060)* **Under 1 mi:** Ice *(Block, Cube)*, Ships' Store *(Rose's Marine 283-0293)*

Boatyard Services

Nearest Yard: Brown's (978) 281-3200

Restaurants and Accommodations

Near: Restaurant *(Alchemy Tapas & Bistro 281-3997, L $7-12, D $13-20, & Sharing plates. Sun Brunch $6-16, Kids' $5.50)*, *(Savory Skillet 281-4042)*, *(Halibut Point 281-1900, L $4-14, D $11-16, Wi-Fi, 3 HD TVs, Local Fave)*, *(Jalapenos 283-8228, D $11-17)*, *(Cape Ann Gloucester House 283-1812, L $11-16, D $16-30, On Seven Seas Wharf)*, *(Topside Grill 281-1399, L $7-15, D $9-23, Pub $8-10)*, *(Passport 281-3680)*, *(Latitudes 281-0223, L $8-13, D $17-27)*, Seafood Shack *(Capt. Carlo's 283-6342, Fried, waterfront)*, Lite Fare *(Sunny Day Café 281-3997)*, *(Super Magnolias 281-5310, B $4-10, L $6-11)*, Pizzeria *(Leonardo's 281-7882, Del.)* **Under 1 mi:** Motel *(Crows Nest 281-2965, $55-75)*, Inn/B&B *(Babson Court 281-4469, $100-225)*, *(Harbor View 283-2277, $99-180)*, *(Julietta House 281-2300, $125-150)*

Recreation and Entertainment

Near: Heated Pool *("Y" or Cape Ann Resort $12/6)*, Fitness Center *("Y" 283-0470 Showers!)*, Movie Theater *(Cape Ann 309-8448)*, Park *(St. Peter's)*, Museum *(Whale Center of New Eng. 281-6351 Free; Schooner Adventure 281-8079; Gloucester Maritime Heritage 281-0470 $5/2; Cape Ann Historical 283-0455 $8/4)*, Tours *(Lobstering 283-1979 $16/8)*, Sightseeing *(Whale Watch $45/30: Capt. Bill's 283-6995; Cape Ann 283-5110; Seven Seas 283-1776)*, Special Events *(St. Peter's Fiesta - late Jun, Schooner Fest - LabDay)* **Under 1 mi:** Beach *(Pavilion, Niles)*, Picnic Area *(Stage Fort)*, Playground, Tennis Courts *(Stage Fort)*, Fishing Charter *(Cape Ann Marina)*, Party Boat *(Lady Sea 559-1978 $64/54)*, Cultural Attract *(West End Theater 281-0680; Gloucester Stage 281-4099)* **1-3 mi:** Bowling *(Cape Ann 283-9753)* **3+ mi:** Golf Course *(Cape Ann 768-7544, 7 mi.)*

Provisioning and General Services

Near: Health Food *(Common Crow 283-1665)*, Wine/Beer, Liquor Store *(Liquor Locker 283-0630)*, Farmers' Market *(Thu, 3-6:30pm, 65 Rogers St.)*, Lobster Pound, Bank/ATM, Post Office, Protestant Church, Beauty Salon *(Fatima's 281-5583)*, Barber Shop, Laundry *(Home Style 281-4805)*, Bookstore *(The Bookstore 281-1548)*, Pharmacy *(CVS 281-2450)*, Hardware Store *(Building Center 283-3060)* **Under 1 mi:** Supermarket *(Shaw's 283-2601)*, Green Grocer *(Farmer John 283-2575)*, Fishmonger *(Connolly 283-4443)*, Catholic Church, Synagogue, Library *(Sawyer 281-9763 Wi-Fi)*, Dry Cleaners *(DeMarco 283-4464)*

Transportation

OnCall: Rental Car *(Enterprise 281-3288)*, Taxi *(A&K 281-6161)*, Airport Limo *(Atlantic 281-5550)* **Near:** Local Bus *(CATA Trolley 283-7278 circles Cape Ann peninsula plus routes to Shaw's, Rockport, Hammond Castle & Magnolia Sq.)* **Under 1 mi:** Rail *(to Boston)* **Airport:** Logan Int'l. *(32 mi.)*

Medical Services

911 Service **Near:** Doctor *(Sauer 281-0600)*, Dentist *(Mina 283-1692)*, Chiropractor *(Gosselin 281-4977)*, Holistic Services *(West End 283-7100)*
Hospital: Addison Gilbert 283-4000 *(2 mi.)*

Setting -- Sprinkled mainly in Southeast Harbor with a handful in the Inner Harbor and Stage Head, the moorings lie amid colorful long-haul fishing trawlers, scallop draggers and lobster boats. The primary dinghy dockage is Solomon Jacob Landing, near the Coast Guard Station where the Harbormaster's brick-red, two-story home backs the centrally located floats. It's a quick walk to the Maritime Heritage Center, Whale Center of New England and "downtown."

Marina Notes -- Harbomaster's launch checks-in boaters & collects fees. 15 moorings in Southeast Harbor, 9 in Inner Harbor, 4 in Stage Head. Town moorings marked by orange balls. Anchoring is an option. Jacobs Public Landing on back side of float in Harbor Cove off Harbor Loop. Designated by yellow striping. All mid-section distances from this point. Good protection in Easterly or Northeasterly blow. Additional dinghy dockage at Cripple Cove Landing. Fuel at North Shore Fishing (283-6880) which may have dockage. Try Beacon Marine too (283-2380). Bathhouse: none.

Notable -- The oldest fishing port in Massachusetts, Gloucester was founded in 1623. Less gentrified, more authentic than the other North Shore harbors, it is rich in maritime lore. Named one of the top five whale watch destinations in the world by the WWF, the harbor is home to four dedicated boats and the Whale Center of New England. Cape Ann Historical Society curates the largest collection of marine art by Gloucester native Fitz Hugh Lane. More of Gloucester's artistic side can be found in the quirky Rocky Neck Art Colony across the harbor. The "Perfect Storm" map highlights key places from Sebastian Unger's book on the loss of Gloucester trawler Andrea Gail. The Stage Fort Shuttle stops near the Harbormaster's Office, loops though town, and rims the waterfront.

Navigational Information

Lat: 42°36.476' **Long:** 070°39.352' **Tide:** 9 ft. **Current:** n/a **Chart:** 13281
Rep. Depths (*MLW*): Entry 15 ft. **Fuel Dock** n/a **Max Slip/Moor** 11 ft./-
Access: Massachusetts Bay to Gloucester Harbor to Smith Cove

Marina Facilities *(In Season/Off Season)*

Fuel: No
Slips: 8 Total, 8 Transient **Max LOA:** 140 ft. **Max Beam:** n/a
Rate *(per ft.)*: **Day** $5.00 **Week** Inq. **Month** n/a
Power: 30 amp Incl., **50 amp** Incl., **100 amp** Incl., **200 amp** n/a
Cable TV: No **Dockside Phone:** No
Dock Type: Fixed, Alongside, Wood
Moorings: 0 Total, 0 Transient **Launch:** n/a
Rate: Day n/a **Week** n/a **Month** n/a
Heads: 1 Toilet(s)
Internet: No **Laundry:** None
Pump-Out: OnCall, Self Service **Fee:** n/a **Closed Heads:** Yes

Marina Operations

Owner/Manager: Nicole Ahern **Dockmaster:** Same
In-Season: Apr-Oct, 10am-Mid **Off-Season:** n/a
After-Hours Arrival: Call ahead/check in at restaurant
Reservations: Yes, Required **Credit Cards:** Visa/MC, Din, Amex
Discounts: None
Pets: Welcome **Handicap Access:** No

Madfish Grille & The Studio

PO Box 630; 79/51 Rocky Neck Avenue; Gloucester, MA 01930

Tel: (978) 281-4554 **VHF: Monitor** n/a **Talk** n/a
Fax: (978) 281-4557 **Alternate Tel:** (617) 543-2977
Email: n/a **Web:** www.madfishgrille.com
Nearest Town: Gloucester *(2.5 mi.)* **Tourist Info:** (978) 283-1601

Marina Services and Boat Supplies

Services - Docking Assistance, Trash Pick-Up, 3 Phase **Communication -** Mail & Package Hold, FedEx, UPS, Express Mail **Supplies - OnSite:** Ice *(Block, Cube)* **Under 1 mi:** Ships' Store *(Brown's Y.Y.)* **1-3 mi:** Bait/Tackle *(3 Lanterns 281-2080)*, Propane *(Foster's Grills 283-1275)*

Boatyard Services

OnCall: Air Conditioning, Refrigeration **Near:** Travelift *(85T)*, Railway *(2 to 500T)*, Launching Ramp, Engine mechanic *(gas, diesel)*, Electrical Repairs, Electronic Sales, Electronics Repairs, Hull Repairs, Rigger, Divers, Bottom Cleaning, Brightwork, Compound, Wash & Wax, Metal Fabrication, Awlgrip, Total Refits. **Nearest Yard:** Glocester Marine Railway (978) 283-2775

Restaurants and Accommodations

OnSite: Restaurant *(The Studio 283-4123, D $17-21, free dock 'n dine)*, *(Madfish Grille 281-4554, L $7-17, D $15-29, free dock 'n dine)* **Near:** Restaurant *(Rudder 283-7967, L $7-11, D $10-26, Gloucester's oldest, impromptu staff entertainment, free dock 'n dine)*, *(Rockaway House 283-2597)* **Under 1 mi:** Restaurant *(Duckworth's Bistrot 282-4426, D $10-20, The Best! Half Plates, Veg, too.)*, Lite Fare *(Smokin' Jims BBQ 283-1025, Take-out Wed-Sun)*, Pizzeria *(Espresso 283-0600)*, Inn/B&B *(Colonial Inn 281-1953, $70-135)* **1-3 mi:** Motel *(Atlantis Oceanfront 283-0014, $145-230)*, Hotel *(Bass Rocks 283-7600, $199-360)*, *(Ocean View 283-6200)*

Recreation and Entertainment

OnSite: Sightseeing *(Rocky Neck Historic Art Trail - 12 historic sites)* **Near:** Picnic Area, Grills, Playground, Boat Rentals, Hike/Bike Trails, Park **Under 1 mi:** Beach *(Niles Beach)*, Fitness Center, Fishing Charter *(Drama 490-6926)*, Cultural Attract *(Gloucester Stage Co. 281-4099)*, Galleries *(North Shore Arts Assoc. 283-1857)*, Special Events *(St. Peter's Fiesta)* **1-3 mi:** Heated Pool *(Cape Ann Resort $12/6)*, Dive Shop, Tennis Courts, Bowling *(Cape Ann 283-9753)*, Movie Theater, Video Rental *(Blockbuster 283-6210)*, Museum *(Beauport Sleeper-McCann House 283-1857 $10/5, 45-room, 1907 oceanfront mansion)*, Tours *(Yankee Whale Watch 283-0313 $45/29)* **3+ mi:** Golf Course *(Rockport G.C. 546-3340, 6 mi.)*

Provisioning and General Services

Near: Bank/ATM **Under 1 mi:** Convenience Store *(Richdale 283-2179)*, Lobster Pound *(Live 283-2820)*, Protestant Church, Beauty Salon *(Twin Boutique 281-4430)*, Hardware Store *(Cape Ann Hardwood 283-5369)* **1-3 mi:** Supermarket *(Stop & Shop 283-4405)*, Health Food *(Common Crow 283-1665)*, Wine/Beer, Liquor Store *(Liquor Locker 283-0630)*, Bakery *(Virgilio's 283-5295, Pizza)*, Farmers' Market *(Thu, 3-6:30pm)*, Post Office, Catholic Church, Synagogue, Library *(281-9763)*, Laundry *(Home Style)*, Bookstore *(Dogtown 281-5599)*, Pharmacy *(CVS 283-7480)*

Transportation

OnCall: Rental Car *(Enterprise 281-3288)*, Taxi *(A & K 281-6161)*, Airport Limo *(Atlantic 281-5550)* **Near:** Local Bus *(CATA 283-7278 - around harbor)* **1-3 mi:** Bikes *(Harborside 281-7744)*, Rail *(MBTA Commuter)* **Airport:** Logan Int'l. *(35 mi.)*

Medical Services

911 Service **Under 1 mi:** Doctor *(Pearce 282-460)*, Dentist *(Family 281-4022)* **1-3 mi:** Chiropractor *(Atlantic 282-4994)*, Veterinarian *(Seaport 283-8883)* **Hospital:** Addison Gilbert 283-4000 *(3.5 mi.)*

Setting -- The docks of Madfish Grille and The Studio Lounge & Deck overlook Smith Cove on Rocky Neck - the famous artists' colony known for its funky ambiance and non-stop galleries. Tides determine whether the boat's view is the underside of 200-year-old pilings or glorious harbor vistas. Both eateries offer inside and alfresco dining. The Sudio features an expansive, partially covered, dining deck with Cabana bar. Think Key West with a fleece for evening.

Marina Notes -- Two restaurant docks run by the same family with good food and music, music, music. No marine services - just dockage. The Studio (283-4123) max LOA 100 ft.; Madfish 130 ft (but the yacht's superstructure can block diners' views) Two 100A with 3-phase. Free short-term dining dockage. Prefers mid-week overnight transients. Madfish is larger with more varied entertainment - rock to blues with popular dancing to live reggae on Sunday nights. The Studio, once home to Hugh Breckenridge Art School, has a piano bar that runs from romantic to sing-along. Bathhouse: Restaurants' heads only.

Notable -- Perhaps the oldest art colony in America, Rocky Neck was home to important realist painters like Winslow Homer and Edward Hopper. Walk in their footsteps with the 12-stop Rocky Neck Historic Art Trail brochure from the Visitors' Center. Saltbox shacks house galleries (open 10am-10pm) that exhibit traditional and modern art, photography, jewelry, quilts, antiques and clothing (Sigrid Olsen's studio is nearby). The North Shore Arts Association (283-1857, Mon-Sat 10am-5pm, Sun noon-5pm), at the entrance to The Neck, is ground zero for the Colony with 300 artist members. For maritime junkies, the venerable 1859 Gloucester Marine Railway, the oldest continuously operating one in the U.S., is right next door - it hauls lightships, schooners, and fishing trawlers.

PHOTOS ON DVD: 23

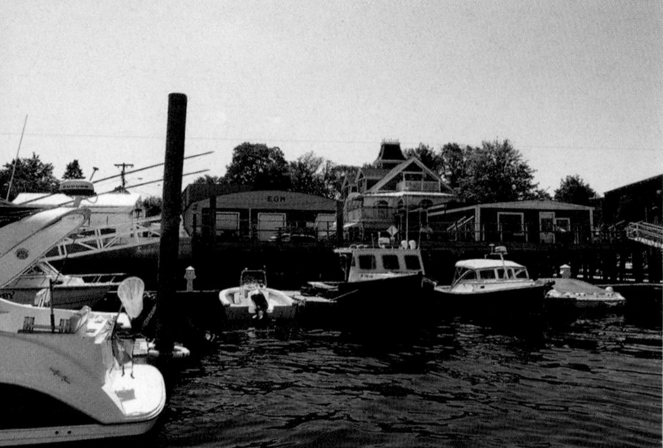

East Gloucester Marine

111 East Main Street; Gloucester, MA 01930

Tel: (978) 281-0982 **VHF: Monitor** Ch. 9 **Talk** n/a
Fax: n/a **Alternate Tel:** (978) 479-8077
Email: n/a **Web:** www.theharborroom.com
Nearest Town: Gloucester *(1 mi.)* **Tourist Info:** (978) 283-1601

Navigational Information

Lat: 42°36.726' **Long:** 070°39.034' **Tide:** 9 ft. **Current:** n/a **Chart:** 13281
Rep. Depths (*MLW*): Entry 12 ft. **Fuel Dock** n/a **Max Slip/Moor** 12 ft./-
Access: Inner Harbor to South Channel

Marina Facilities *(In Season/Off Season)*

Fuel: No
Slips: 60 Total, 5 Transient **Max LOA:** 100 ft. **Max Beam:** n/a
Rate *(per ft.)*: **Day** $3.00 **Week** n/a **Month** n/a
Power: 30 amp Incl., **50 amp** Incl., **100 amp** n/a, **200 amp** n/a
Cable TV: No **Dockside Phone:** No
Dock Type: Floating, Long Fingers, Alongside, Wood
Moorings: 0 Total, 0 Transient **Launch:** n/a
Rate: Day n/a **Week** n/a **Month** n/a
Heads: 2 Toilet(s), 2 Shower(s)
Internet: No **Laundry:** None
Pump-Out: OnCall *(Boat)*, Full Service **Fee:** Free **Closed Heads:** Yes

Marina Operations

Owner/Manager: Manuel Quesada **Dockmaster:** Same
In-Season: May 1-Oct 15, 7am-4pm **Off-Season:** Oct 16-Apr 30, Closed
After-Hours Arrival: Call in advance
Reservations: Yes **Credit Cards:** Visa/MC, Amex
Discounts: None
Pets: Welcome **Handicap Access:** No

Marina Services and Boat Supplies

Services - Docking Assistance, Trash Pick-Up **Communication -** FedEx, UPS, Express Mail **Supplies - OnSite:** Ice *(Block, Cube)* **Near:** Ships' Store *(Brown's 281-3200)*, Bait/Tackle *(Winchester 281-1619)*, Live Bait **1-3 mi:** Propane *(Foster's 283-1131)*

Boatyard Services

OnCall: Engine mechanic *(gas, diesel)*, Electrical Repairs, Electronics Repairs *(Voyager 768-7143)*, Sail Loft *(Doyle 740-5950)*, Divers *(Cape Ann 281-8082)*, Bottom Cleaning, Air Conditioning, Refrigeration, Propeller Repairs **Nearest Yard:** Brown's Yacht Yard (978) 281-3200

Restaurants and Accommodations

OnSite: Lite Fare *(Smokin' Jims BBQ 283-1025, Take-out Wed-Sun)* **Near:** Coffee Shop *(Zeke's Place 283-7817, B & L)* **Under 1 mi:** Restaurant *(Alchemy 281-3997, L $7-14, D $12-10)*, *(Madfish Grille 281-4554, L $7-17, D $15-29, Short dinghy or 1.2 mi. walk)*, *(Rudder 283-7967, L $7-11, D $10-26, Kids' $8, Dinghy dock)*, *(Duckworth's Bistrot 282-4426, D $10-30, The Best! Half Plates, Veg, too.)*, *(Studio 283-4123, Deck Seating, Great Views)*, *(Gloucester House 283-1812, L $11-17, D $11-27, Dinghy)*, Seafood Shack *(Captain Carlo's Fish Market 283-6342, Dinghy)*, Motel *(Vista 281-3410, Good Harbor Beach)*, Hotel *(Bass Rocks Inn 283-7600, $199-360)*, *(Atlantis Oceanfront 283-0014, $145-230)*, Inn/B&B *(Williams 283-4931, $50-75)*

Recreation and Entertainment

OnSite: Picnic Area, Galleries *(StudioVo 282-0269)* **Near:** Playground, Fishing Charter *(Capt. Bill 283-6995)*, Tours *(Yankee Whale Watch 283-0313 $45/29)* **Under 1 mi:** Beach *(Niles or Good Harbor)*, Cultural Attract *(Gloucester Stage Co. 281-4099)*, Sightseeing *(Rocky Neck Art Colony - Painters Path)* **1-3 mi:** Heated Pool *(Cape Ann Resort $12/6; "Y")*, Movie Theater *(Gloucester 283-9188)*, Video Rental *(Blockbuster 283-6210)*, Museum *(Beauport Sleeper-McCann House 283-0800 $10/5; Hammond Castle 283-7673; Sargent House 281-2432)* **3+ mi:** Golf Course *(Rockport Golf 546-3340, 5 mi.)*, Bowling *(Cape Ann Bowl 283-9753, 5 mi.)*

Provisioning and General Services

Near: Convenience Store *(Richdale 283-2179; Last Stop 281-2616 Wi-Fi)*, Protestant Church **Under 1 mi:** Supermarket *(Stop & Shop 283-4405)*, Bank/ATM, Catholic Church, Library *(Sawyer 281-9763)*, Beauty Salon *(Salon Unique 283-5572)*, Laundry *(Home Style 281-4805)*, Hardware Store *(Cape Ann Hardwood 283-5369)*, Retail Shops *(E. Gloucester Shopping Mall)* **1-3 mi:** Health Food *(Common Crow 283-1665)*, Wine/Beer *(Liquor Locker 283-0630)*, Liquor Store, Farmers' Market *(65 Rogers St.; Thu, 3-6:30pm)*, Post Office, Synagogue, Pharmacy *(CVS 283-8489)*

Transportation

OnCall: Rental Car *(Enterprise 281-3288)*, Taxi *(A & K 281-6161)*, Airport Limo *(Atlantic 281-5550)* **Near:** Local Bus *(CATA 283-7278 throughout Cape Ann area)* **Under 1 mi:** Bikes *(Harborside 281-7744)* **1-3 mi:** Rail *(MBTA to Boston)* **Airport:** Boston Logan *(32 mi.)*

Medical Services

911 Service **Near:** Dentist *(Harborside 546-3821)*, Holistic Services *(Divine Spa 282-7730)* **Under 1 mi:** Doctor *(Anscombe 559-0001)*, Chiropractor *(Gloucester 281-0049)*, Veterinarian *(Seaport 283-8883)* **Hospital:** A.G. 283-4000 *(2.5 mi.)*

Setting -- EGM is the first transient-friendly facility on the Inner Harbor's South Channel. The Harbor Room, a pretty, neo-Victorian event space, overlooks the two sets of docks that host a mixture of recreational and working vessels. Dark green picnic tables march across a large, adjacent expanse of waterside deck - occasionally covered by a tent. A three-bay, curved-roof work shed, small office, an art studio and barbecue eatery complete the upland. The East Gloucester cultural scene is closeby, and the more-touristed part of Gloucester is a quick dinghy ride across the harbor to the Solomon Jacobs Public Landing.

Marina Notes -- Management balances their "Harbor Room" function operation upstairs and their marina operation below. Two side-by-side sets of docks I & II berths boats to 100 ft. Adjacent Brown's Yacht Yard, reachable on a continuous floating dock array, offers a well-supplied chandlery and fuel. Bathhouse: Fully tiled, impeccable, nicely decorated heads and showers belie the marina's otherwise utilitarian nature.

Notable -- The Harbor Room (559-0999, 281-0982), which sits above the docks, is a beautifully renovated, turn-of-the-last-century, 1200-square-foot event space that opens onto a large railed deck with panoramic harbor views (fleet captains note - $150-200/hr.). For a take-out feast on the boat, onsite Smokin' Jim's delivers authentic Tennessee-style Bar-B-Q from a half-dozen oil drum smokers surrounded by bloom-filled planters. For an opposite experience, one of Gloucester's best eateries, Duckworth's Bistro, is 0.4 mile up the road. At the top of the docks, a small red-clapboard building hosts Rober Viau's art and design studio - check out the hand-carved "lobster" Adirondack chairs or the gaggle of kids taking a summer class. More art is just up the road at North Shore Arts.

PHOTOS ON DVD: 15

Navigational Information
Lat: 42°36.717' **Long:** 070°38.991' **Tide:** 9 ft. **Current:** n/a **Chart:** 13281
Rep. Depths (*MLW*): Entry 12 ft. **Fuel Dock** 12 ft. **Max Slip/Moor** 12 ft./22 ft.
Access: South Channel of Gloucester Harbor

Marina Facilities *(In Season/Off Season)*
Fuel: *Gulf* - Slip-Side Fueling, Gasoline, Diesel
Slips: 15 Total, 6 Transient **Max LOA:** 70 ft. **Max Beam:** 14 ft.
Rate *(per ft.)*: **Day** $2.50/$1.75 **Week** Inq. **Month** Inq.
Power: 30 amp incl, **50 amp** incl., **100 amp** n/a, **200 amp** n/a
Cable TV: No **Dockside Phone:** No
Dock Type: Floating, Long Fingers, Wood
Moorings: 3 Total, 3 Transient **Launch:** No, Dinghy Dock
Rate: Day $25 **Week** $150 **Month** n/a
Heads: 4 Toilet(s), 3 Shower(s)
Internet: No **Laundry:** None
Pump-Out: OnCall, Full Service **Fee:** Free **Closed Heads:** Yes

Marina Operations
Owner/Manager: Peter Bent **Dockmaster:** Valerie Quinn & Greg Porter
In-Season: May-Oct, 8am-5pm* **Off-Season:** Nov-Apr, Inq.
After-Hours Arrival: Call for info
Reservations: Yes, Preferred **Credit Cards:** Visa/MC, Dscvr, Amex, Gulf
Discounts: None
Pets: Welcome **Handicap Access:** No

Brown's Yacht Yard

Rear 139 East Main Street; Gloucester, MA 01930

Tel: (978) 281-3200 **VHF: Monitor** Ch. 9 **Talk** Ch. 19
Fax: (978) 281-3201 **Alternate Tel:** n/a
Email: info@brownsyy.com **Web:** www.brownsyy.com
Nearest Town: Gloucester *(1.5 mi.)* **Tourist Info:** (978) 283-1601

Marina Services and Boat Supplies
Communication - Fax in/out, FedEx, DHL, UPS, Express Mail **Supplies - OnSite:** Ice *(Block, Cube)*, Ships' Store **Near:** Bait/Tackle *(Winchester 281-1619)* **1-3 mi:** Propane *(Foster's 283-1131)*

Boatyard Services
OnSite: Travelift *(35T)*, Forklift, Engine mechanic *(gas, diesel)*, Hull Repairs, Rigger, Bottom Cleaning, Brightwork, Compound, Wash & Wax, Interior Cleaning, Woodworking, Inflatable Repairs *(Zodiac)* **OnCall:** Electronics Repairs, Canvas Work, Divers, Propeller Repairs **Dealer for:** Zodiac, Dyer, Evinrude, Johnson, Vanguard, Yamaha. **Member:** ABBRA, ABYC **Yard Rates:** $40-60/hr., Haul & Launch $6/ft. *(blocking $4/ft.)*, Power Wash $6/ft. **Storage:** On-Land $50/ft./season

Restaurants and Accommodations
Near: Coffee Shop *(Zeke's Place 283-7817, B & L)*, Lite Fare *(Smokin' Jim's BBQ 283-1055, Take-out, picnic tables - Next Door)* **Under 1 mi:** Restaurant *(Madfish Grille 281-4554, L $7-17, D $15-29, walk or dinghy)*, *(The Rudder 283-7967, L $7-11, D $10-26, Kids' $8. Dinghy Dock)*, *(Studio 283-4123, or short dinghy ride, Deck seating, great views)*, *(Duckworth's Bistrot 282-4426, D $10-30, Highly rated. Half Plates, veg too)*, Motel *(Vista Motel 281-3410, Good Harbor Beach)*, Inn/B&B *(Williams Guest House 283-4931)* **1-3 mi:** Restaurant *(Gloucester House 283-1812, L $6-12, D $9-25)*, Hotel *(Bass Rocks Ocean Inn 283-7600, $239 up)*

Recreation and Entertainment
Near: Tours *(Yankee Whale Watch 283-0313 $45/29)*, Galleries *(North Shore Arts Association 283-1857 - 300 artists)* **Under 1 mi:** Beach *(Niles)*, Playground, Fishing Charter, Cultural Attract *(Gloucester Stage Co. 281-4099)*, Sightseeing *(Rocky Neck Art Colony - long walk or short dinghy ride)* **1-3 mi:** Heated Pool *(Cape Ann Resort $12/6; "Y")*, Tennis Courts, Jogging Paths, Video Rental *(Blockbuster 283-6210)*, Museum *(Beauport Sleeper-McCann House 283-0800 $10/5; Hammond Castle 283-7673, Sargent House 281-2432)*, Special Events *(St. Peters Fiesta - Late June; Schooner Fest - LabDay)* **3+ mi:** Golf Course *(Cape Ann 768-7544, 7 mi.)*, Bowling *(Cape Ann Bowl 283-9753, 3 + mi.)*

Provisioning and General Services
Near: Convenience Store *(Richdale 283-2179; Last Stop Variety 281-2616 Wi-Fi)*, Fishmonger *(International 283-1324)*, Bank/ATM, Protestant Church **Under 1 mi:** Supermarket *(Stop & Shop 283-4405, Shaw's)* **1-3 mi:** Health Food *(Common Crow 283-1665)*, Wine/Beer, Liquor Store *(Liquor Locker 283-0630)*, Bakery, Farmers' Market *(Thu, 3-6:30pm)*, Lobster Pound *(Turner 281-7172; Live Lobster 283-2820)*, Post Office, Catholic Church, Synagogue, Library *(281-9763)*, Beauty Salon, Barber Shop, Dry Cleaners, Laundry *(Home Style 281-4805)*, Bookstore *(281-1548)*, Pharmacy *(CVS 283-8489)*

Transportation
OnCall: Rental Car *(Enterprise 281-3288)*, Taxi *(Atlantic 281-5550)* **Near:** Bikes *(Joes 283-3638)*, Local Bus *(CATA (283-7278) around harbor, Rockport & to beaches)* **1-3 mi:** Rail *(MBTA)* **Airport:** Logan Int'l. *(35 mi.)*

Medical Services
911 Service **Near:** Dentist *(Family 281-4022)* **Under 1 mi:** Doctor *(Pearce 282-4600)*, Chiropractor *(Atlantic 282-4994)*, Veterinarian *(Seaport 283-8883)* **Hospital:** Addison Gilbert 283-4000 *(2.5 mi.)*

Setting -- Just past East Gloucester Marine, on the south side of the South Channel, Brown's big blue sheds, travelift and Gulf fuel sign stand out among the chock-a-block docks. Good slips and side-ties with full-race pedestals attract an upscale mix of pleasure craft. A working boatyard that pretends to be nothing more, its docks are well-protected with views of the active Gloucester working harbor and the state commercial fish pier 300 yards across the Channel.

Marina Notes -- *Open 7 days MemDay-LabDay, then 5.5 days. Excellent, old-timey, very well-equipped ships' store. Historic reputation for service and repairs - 35-ton lift, hull, engine, wood & fiberglass repairs, painting, sailboat rigging plus Zodiac sales & repairs. Evinrude, Johnson & Yamaha outboard service. Gas & Diesel. Bathhouse: Rustic heads & showers. Note: Eastern Point Y.C. (283-3520) may have transient moorings ($25) with launch.

Notable -- Away from the tourism hubbub, this quiet side of the harbor offers good access to the Atlantic beaches, some excellent restaurants, and East Gloucester's cultural scene. The North Shore Arts Association (0.4 mi.) features a stunning gallery space in a refurbished harbor-side building; it exhibits work from its 300 artist members and offers workshops for children and adults. For intimate, professional theater, the Gloucester Stage Company is another 0.3 mile. One of the Visitor Center's Maritime Trails walking tours is the Painters Path, which begins 0.3 mile away and covers the wonderful galleries and restaurants of famous Rocky Neck Art Colony (a total 1 mile walk or dinghy to one of the Neck's restaurant docks). The music scene at Studio and Madfish Grille is definitely worth an evening or two. A little over a mile south, Niles Beach is at the harbor entrance or walk a mile north to gorgeous Good Harbour beach.

PHOTOS ON DVD: 18

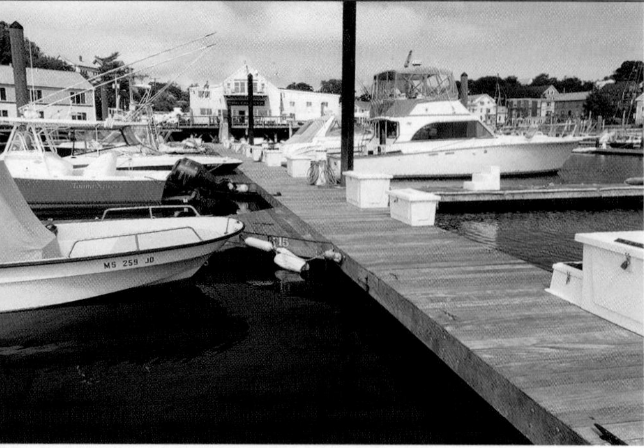

Pier 7/Enos Marine

51 Parker Street; Gloucester, MA 01930

Tel: (978) 281-1935 **VHF: Monitor** n/a **Talk** n/a
Fax: (978) 281-4107 **Alternate Tel:** (978) 479-5455
Email: diane@enosmarine.com **Web:** www.enosmarine.com
Nearest Town: Gloucester *(0.5 mi.)* **Tourist Info:** (978) 283-1601

Navigational Information

Lat: 42°36.886' **Long:** 070°38.942' **Tide:** 9 ft. **Current:** n/a **Chart:** 13281
Rep. Depths (*MLW*): Entry 20 ft. **Fuel Dock** n/a **Max Slip/Moor** 30 ft./-
Access: Main channel to Inner Harbor, then South Channel

Marina Facilities *(In Season/Off Season)*

Fuel: No
Slips: 40 Total, 3 Transient **Max LOA:** 120 ft. **Max Beam:** 18 ft.
Rate *(per ft.)*: **Day** $3.00/Inq. **Week** Inq. **Month** n/a
Power: 30 amp $10, **50 amp** $20, **100 amp** n/a, **200 amp** n/a
Cable TV: Yes **Dockside Phone:** No
Dock Type: Floating, Long Fingers, Wood
Moorings: 10 Total, 1 Transient **Launch:** No
Rate: Day $35 **Week** n/a **Month** n/a
Heads: 2 Toilet(s), 2 Shower(s)
Internet: No **Laundry:** None
Pump-Out: OnCall *(Boat)* **Fee:** Free **Closed Heads:** Yes

Marina Operations

Owner/Manager: Diane Rule-Enos **Dockmaster:** Same
In-Season: May-Aug, 7am-4pm **Off-Season:** Sep-Nov, 8am-4pm*
After-Hours Arrival: Call in advance
Reservations: Yes **Credit Cards:** Cash only
Discounts: None
Pets: Welcome **Handicap Access:** Yes, Docks

Marina Services and Boat Supplies

Services - Boaters' Lounge, Trash Pick-Up **Communication -** FedEx, UPS **Supplies - OnSite:** Ice *(Block, Cube)*, Ships' Store **Near:** Bait/Tackle *(New England Marine 281-2080; 3 Lanterns 281-2080)*, Propane *(Fosters 283-1275)*

Boatyard Services

OnSite: Engine mechanic *(gas)* **Near:** Launching Ramp. **Nearest Yard:** Brown's Yacht Yard (978) 281-3200

Restaurants and Accommodations

Near: Restaurant *(Charlie's Place 281-5002, Dive Diner)*, Coffee Shop *(Zeke's Place 283-7817, B & L)*, *(Lee's 281-3873, B & L)*, Lite Fare *(Smokin' Jim's BBQ 283-1055, Take-out, picnic tables)*, Pizzeria *(La Rosa's 283-0303, Del. Great reviews.)* **Under 1 mi:** Restaurant *(Alchemy 281-3997, L $7-12, D $13-20, Tapas, Half Plates)*, *(Duckworth's Bistrot 282-4426, D $10-30, The Best! Half Plates, Veg, too.)*, *(Halibut Point 281-1900, L $4-14, D $11-16)*, Lite Fare *(Crow's Nest 281-2965, Perfect Storm hang-out)*, Pizzeria *(Leonardo's 281-7882, Del.)*, Motel *(Atlantis Oceanfront 283-0014, $145-230)*, Hotel *(Bass Rocks Ocean 283-7600, $199-360)*, Inn/B&B *(Williams 283-4931, $50-75)*, *(Crow's Nest 281-2965, $55-75)*

Recreation and Entertainment

Near: Picnic Area, Playground *(Cripple Cove)*, Boat Rentals, Hike/Bike Trails, Fishing Charter *(Amanda 281-2080; Coastal 800-877-5110; Drama 490-6926)*, Movie Theater, Park *(Gordon Thomas)*, Sightseeing *(Whale Watch $45/30: Cape Ann 283-5110; Yankee Fleet 283-0313; Capt. Bill's 283-6995; Seven Seas 283-1776)* **Under 1 mi:** Beach *(Good Harbor)*, Fitness Center *(Fitness Zone 281-5761)*, Bowling, Video Rental *(Blockbuster 283-6210; Redbox)*, Museum *(Whale Center of New England 281-6351 Free; Gloucester Maritime Heritage 281-0470 $5/2; Cape Ann Historical 283-0455 $8/4)*, Tours *(Cape Ann Lobstering 283-1979)*, Cultural Attract *(Gloucester Stage Co. 281-4099 $15-30 classic & contemporary works)* **1-3 mi:** Pool *(Cape Ann Resort $12/6)* **3+ mi:** Golf Course *(Rockport 283-0014, 5 mi.)*

Provisioning and General Services

Near: Convenience Store *(White Hen 283-6868)*, Fishmonger *(Connolly)*, Bank/ATM, Post Office, Catholic Church, Protestant Church, Beauty Salon, Bookstore *(281-1548)*, Florist **Under 1 mi:** Supermarket *(Shaw's 281-4844)*, Health Food *(Common Crow 283-1665)*, Wine/Beer, Liquor Store *(Liquor Locker 283-0630)*, Bakery *(Virgilio's 283-5295 - Pizza)*, Farmers' Market *(Thu 3-6pm)*, Library *(281-9763)*, Dry Cleaners *(NE 283-4545)*, Laundry *(Home Style 281-4805)*, Pharmacy *(CVS 283-7480)*, Hardware Store *(Harbor Loop 283-3060)*, Retail Shops *(E. Gloucester Shop Ctr.)*

Transportation

OnCall: Rental Car *(Enterprise 281-3288)*, Taxi *(A & K 281-6161)*, Airport Limo *(Atlantic 281-5550)* **Near:** Local Bus *(CATA Trolley 283-7278 circles harbor plus routes to Shaw's, Rockport, Hammond Castle & Magnolia Sq.)* **Under 1 mi:** Rail *(MBTA to Boston)* **Airport:** Logan Int'l. *(32 mi.)*

Medical Services

911 Service **Near:** Dentist *(Harborside 546-3821)*, Holistic Services *(Divine Spa 282-7730)* **Under 1 mi:** Doctor *(Anscombe 559-0001)*, Chiropractor *(Gloucester 281-0049)*, Veterinarian *(Seaport 283-8883)* **Hospital:** Addison Gilbert 283-4000 *(2 mi.)*

Setting -- At the head of the Inner Harbor's South Channel, past the long, drive-on State Fish Pier and its L-shaped basin, the gray, two-story "Trawler" clubhouse sits at the end of a long, well-maintained dock. Inside old timey fish-house detail, creaky wooden floors, cozy sofas with mismatched chairs and a full kitchen make this an enticing, well-used hangout. On the deck, umbrella-topped tables and chairs take advantage of the long view up the "habbah."

Marina Notes -- *Sat 8-2, Sun Closed. Jan-Mar Tue-Fri 9-3. Family-owned since 1973. Engine mechanic Jay Enos grew up in marine business. BY services $90/hr. Small, well-maintained dock. Dealer for Honda, AB Inflatables & Maritime Skiff. Adjacent Lighthouse Marina may have slips. More extensive services and fuel at Brown's Yacht Yard & Gloucester Marine Railways - 0.2 mi. at the beginning of South Channel. Bathhouse: Fiberglass shower stalls, curtains.

Notable -- This small, efficient Cripple Cove facility has an enviable, well-protected location a bit out of the tourist fray. It's the closest docks to Harbor Beach, a gorgeous, sandy half-mile sprawl with snack bar, showers, life guards (and a $25 parking fee that minimizes the numbers - but it's easily walkable). Some really lovely oceanfront hotels are a mile due east of Enos. For those looking for a spot to throw out a line or are enamored of working vessels, the Gloucester State Fish Pier is worth a stroll. The heart of the four-century-old fishing industry, it is 20 miles from Stellwagen Bank where the ultimate catch is bluefin tuna. Recreational charters are nearby for the big catch - or buy a one-day clam harvest permit from city hall along with maps and schedules. A mile around the harbor, the Maritime Center, Whale Center of New England and Cape Ann Museum all tell different parts of the Gloucester story. Pick up a walking tour map.

PHOTOS ON DVD: 14

Crocker's Boat Yard

PO Box 268; 15 Ashland Ave.; Manchester, MA 01944

Tel: (978) 526-1971; (888) 332-6004 **VHF: Monitor** Ch. 78 **Talk** Ch. 78
Fax: (978) 526-7625 **Alternate Tel:** n/a
Email: skip@crockersboatyard.com **Web:** crockersboatyard.com
Nearest Town: Manchester *(0.3 mi.)* **Tourist Info:** (978) 283-1601

Navigational Information

Lat: 42°34.289' **Long:** 070°46.475' **Tide:** 8.5 ft. **Current:** n/a **Chart:** 13274
Rep. Depths (*MLW*): Entry 8 ft. **Fuel Dock** n/a **Max Slip/Moor** 7 ft./15 ft.
Access: Straight into Manchester Harbor -- on west side

Marina Facilities *(In Season/Off Season)*

Fuel: No
Slips: 16 Total, 2 Transient **Max LOA:** 50 ft. **Max Beam:** 16 ft.
Rate *(per ft.)*: **Day** $2.00 **Week** Inq. **Month** Inq.
Power: 30 amp Incl., **50 amp** n/a, **100 amp** n/a, **200 amp** n/a
Cable TV: No **Dockside Phone:** No
Dock Type: Floating, Wood
Moorings: 10 Total, 4 Transient **Launch:** No
Rate: Day $25 **Week** $125 **Month** n/a
Heads: 2 Toilet(s)
Internet: No **Laundry:** None
Pump-Out: OnCall **Fee:** Free **Closed Heads:** No

Marina Operations

Owner/Manager: Skip Crocker/Chris Walsh **Dockmaster:** Same
In-Season: Apr-Oct, 7am-4:30pm **Off-Season:** Nov- Mar, 7am-3:30pm
After-Hours Arrival: Call Ahead
Reservations: Yes **Credit Cards:** Visa/MC, Cash/Check
Discounts: None
Pets: Welcome **Handicap Access:** No

Marina Services and Boat Supplies

Services - Dock Carts **Communication -** FedEx, DHL, UPS, Express Mail **Supplies - OnSite:** Ships' Store **OnCall:** Propane, CNG **Near:** Ice *(Cube)* **3+ mi:** West Marine *(978-777-5940, 8 mi.)*

Boatyard Services

OnSite: Travelift *(35T)*, Crane *(7T)*, Hydraulic Trailer *(10 & 20T)*, Engine mechanic *(gas, diesel)*, Hull Repairs, Rigger, Divers, Bottom Cleaning, Brightwork, Air Conditioning, Refrigeration, Compound, Wash & Wax, Interior Cleaning, Woodworking, Painting, Awlgrip, Total Refits, Yacht Building **OnCall:** Electrical Repairs, Electronics Repairs, Inflatable Repairs, Life Raft Service, Upholstery, Yacht Interiors, Metal Fabrication **Near:** Yacht Broker. **Under 1 mi:** Launching Ramp, Electronic Sales. **3+ mi:** Sail Loft *(4 mi.)*, Canvas Work *(4 mi.)*. **Dealer for:** Yanmar, Universal, Crusader, Interlux, Petit. **Member:** ABBRA, ABYC - 2 Certified Tech(s), Other Certifications: ABBRA Crane & travelift **Yard Rates:** $65-95/hr., Haul & Launch $8.50/ft., Power Wash $5/ft., Bottom Paint $17/ft. **Storage:** In-Water $6.50/ft., On-Land $6.50/ft.

Restaurants and Accommodations

Near: Inn/B&B *(Old Corner Inn 526-4996, $90-175, weekly rates, too)* **Under 1 mi:** Restaurant *(Landing at 7 Central 526-7494, L $6-17, D $9-25)*, *(Calas 525-3304, L $9-15, D $10-25)*, *(Nicholas Seafood & Grille 704-9253)*, Snack Bar *(Capt. Dusty's Ice Cream 526-1663)*, Coffee Shop *(Christo's 526-4558)*, Lite Fare *(Beach Street Café 526-8049, B & L)*

Recreation and Entertainment

Near: Beach *(Singing Beach)*, Park **Under 1 mi:** Cultural Attract *(Concerts at Masconomo Park - Tues 6-8pm. Free)* **1-3 mi:** Picnic Area *(Misery Islands - $3 fee)*, Fitness Center *(Manchester Athletic Club 526-4610)*, Hike/Bike Trails, Fishing Charter **3+ mi:** Golf Course *(Cape Ann Golf 768-7544, 4 mi.)*, Movie Theater *(Cabot Street Cinema 927-3677, 8 mi.)*

Provisioning and General Services

Near: Convenience Store *(Richdale 526-7294)*, Delicatessen, Bank/ATM, Post Office, Library *(526-7711)*, Pharmacy *(Allens 526-1321)* **Under 1 mi:** Market *(Crosby's 526-4444 - delivers to boat)*, Wine/Beer *(Harrigans 526-8440)*, Liquor Store, Beauty Salon *(Bogart 525-3221)*, Laundry *(Sunshine 526-4921)*, Hardware Store *(Manchester 526-7775)* **1-3 mi:** Gourmet Shop *(Vidalia's 998-4814)*, Fishmonger *(Essex 768-7233)*, Bookstore *(Beverly Farms 927-2122)*, Copies Etc. *(Daily Printing 927-4630)* **3+ mi:** Supermarket *(Super Stop & Shop 232-0021, 8 mi.)*

Transportation

OnCall: Rental Car *(Enterprise 524-9555)*, Taxi *(Cab Express 927-0400)* **Near:** Rail *(MBTA commuter to Boston)* **Under 1 mi:** Bikes *(Seaside Cycle 526-1200)* **Airport:** Logan Int'l. *(25 mi.)*

Medical Services

911 Service **Near:** Dentist *(Bacsik 526-7477)* **Under 1 mi:** Doctor *(Bush 526-7143)*, Holistic Services *(Seaside Spa 526-8400)*, Optician *(Twin Oaks 525-2345)*, Veterinarian *(Manchester 526-9500)* **Hospital:** Gloucester 283-4000 *(5 mi.)*

Setting -- Cruising into protected, picturesque Manchester Harbor, past Manchester Yacht Club, a red-roofed gazebo stands sentinel above the Tucks Point town floats. A third of a mile further, past lovely shoreside "cottages," Crocker's Boat Yard's mooring field and docks are tucked into a placid cove. The pretty, well-maintained down-east yachts contrast with the working yard's grey, corrugated-metal storage and work sheds perched high above the docks and rocks.

Marina Notes -- Established 1946 by Eileen & Sturgis Crocker (son of renowned wooden yacht deisgner Sam Crocker). Third generation at the helm. Max 45 ft. LOA on moorings with dinghy dock. Respected, full-service boatyard. ABYC & ABBRA trained staff. Wood & fiberglass repairs/restorations, systems upgrades, electrical, electronics, rigging. Boat transport to 45 ft. Manchester Y.C. (526-4595) may have moorings. Bathhouse: Snug, older, with varnished knotty pine wainscot. Note: Head of navigation: fixed Boston & Maine railroad bridge, about 1 mile above harbor entrance.

Notable -- Fashionable, sedate, peaceful Manchester-by-the-Sea is characterized by large but harmonious waterfront homes and a charming town center with historic buildings occupied by a dozen and a half low-key shops and top-notch restaurants. Walk or dinghy to the four town docking facilities (1 hr. limit, 45 ft. max LOA). Stroll the leafy lanes starting at the intersection of School, Union and Central Streets, past 19thC. Federal-style and colonial homes. At 12:20pm, listen to the carillon in the Congregational church bell tower. Buy an ice cream at Capt. Dusty's, then walk to spectacular, wide Singing Beach (named for the sound of your feet through the sand), where there are lifeguards, food stands, and restrooms. Or take in a free concert at Masconomo Park (Tuesdays 6-8pm).

PHOTOS ON DVD: 25

Manchester Marine

17 Ashland Ave.; Manchester-by-the-Sea, MA 01944

Tel: (978) 526-7911 **VHF: Monitor** Ch. 9, 72 **Talk** Ch. 72
Fax: (978) 526-8638 **Alternate Tel:** n/a
Email: jprescott@manchestermarine.com **Web:** manchestermarine.com
Nearest Town: Manchester *(0.2 mi.)* **Tourist Info:** (978) 283-1601

Navigational Information

Lat: 42°34.289' **Long:** 070°46.410' **Tide:** 8.5 ft. **Current:** n/a **Chart:** 13274
Rep. Depths (*MLW*): Entry 8 ft. **Fuel Dock** 7 ft. **Max Slip/Moor** 7 ft./10 ft.
Access: Manchester Channel past Norton's Point

Marina Facilities *(In Season/Off Season)*

Fuel: *unbranded* - Gasoline, Diesel
Slips: 40 Total, 1 Transient **Max LOA:** 60 ft. **Max Beam:** 16 ft.
Rate *(per ft.)*: **Day** $2.50* **Week** $12 **Month** Inq.
Power: 30 amp Incl., **50 amp** Incl., **100 amp** n/a, **200 amp** n/a
Cable TV: No **Dockside Phone:** Yes, Switchboard, 5 line(s)
Dock Type: Fixed, Long Fingers, Wood
Moorings: 2 Total, 2 Transient **Launch:** No, Dinghy Dock
Rate: Day $50 **Week** $12/ft. **Month** n/a
Heads: 2 Toilet(s), 2 Shower(s)
Internet: No **Laundry:** None
Pump-Out: Full Service, 1 Central, 1 Port **Fee:** Free **Closed Heads:** No

Marina Operations

Owner/Manager: Mac Donaldson **Dockmaster:** Jonathan Prescott
In-Season: MemDay-LabDay, 8am-4pm** **Off-Season:** Sep, 7am-3pm
After-Hours Arrival: Call ahead
Reservations: Yes, Recommended **Credit Cards:** Visa/MC
Discounts: None
Pets: Welcome **Handicap Access:** No

Marina Services and Boat Supplies

Services - Docking Assistance, Dock Carts **Communication -** Mail & Package Hold, Phone Messages, Fax in/out, FedEx, UPS, Express Mail **Supplies - OnSite:** Ice *(Block, Cube)*, Ships' Store, Propane *(Foster's 283-1131)*, CNG **3+ mi:** West Marine *(978-777-5940, 8 mi.)*

Boatyard Services

OnSite: Travelift *(30T)*, Crane *(22T)*, Hydraulic Trailer *(35T Brownell)*, Engine mechanic *(gas, diesel)*, Electrical Repairs, Electronics Repairs, Hull Repairs, Rigger, Canvas Work, Air Conditioning, Refrigeration, Compound, Wash & Wax, Woodworking, Upholstery, Metal Fabrication, Painting, Total Refits, Yacht Broker *(New Wave Yachts)* **OnCall:** Sail Loft, Propeller Repairs **Dealer for:** Yanmar, Raymarine, Mastervolt, Harken, Leisure Fuel, Sea Frost, Vacuflush. **Member:** ABBRA - 2 Certified Tech(s), ABYC - 6 Certified Tech(s), Other Certifications: NMEA, MMTA. **Yard Rates:** $55-95/hr., Haul & Launch $10/ft. *(blocking incl.)*, Power Wash $5/ft., Bottom Paint $18/ft. **Storage:** On-Land Inside $10.50/sq.ft. Out $5.50/sq.ft.

Restaurants and Accommodations

Near: Inn/B&B *(Old Corner Inn 526-4996, $90-175)* **Under 1 mi:** Restaurant *(The Landing at Central 526-7494, L $6-17, D $9-25)*, *(Cala's 525-3304, L $9-15, D $10-25)*, *(Nicholas Seafood & Grille 704-9253)*, Snack Bar *(Capt. Dusty's Ice Cream)*, Coffee Shop *(Christo's 526-4558)*, Lite Fare *(Beach St.Cafe 526-8049, B $5, L $5-10, B & L)* **1-3 mi:** Pizzeria *(Harry's Pizza & Deli 921-4777)*, Inn/B&B *(Magnolia 525-3642, $80-135)* **3+ mi:** Motel *(Wingaersheek 281-0100, $65-160, 5 mi.)*, Inn/B&B *(Essex River House 768-6800, $109-139, 4 mi.)*

Recreation and Entertainment

OnSite: Grills **Near:** Beach *(Singing Beach)*, Jogging Paths, Park **Under 1 mi:** Video Rental *(Redbox at Shaw's)*, Cultural Attract *(Music in Masconomo Park - Tue, 6-8pm, Jul & Aug)* **1-3 mi:** Picnic Area *(Misery Islands - $3 fee)*, Fitness Center *(Manchester Athletic 526-4610)* **3+ mi:** Golf Course *(Cape Ann 768-7544, 4 mi.)*, Movie Theater *(Cabot St. 927-3677, 8 mi.)*, Museum *(Essex Ship Building Museum 768-7541, 4 mi.)*

Provisioning and General Services

Near: Convenience Store *(Richdale 526-7294)*, Gourmet Shop *(Essen's 526-9995)*, Wine/Beer *(Crosby's 526-4444)*, Liquor Store *(Harrigan's 526-8440)*, Bank/ATM, Post Office, Library *(526-7711 Internet)*, Pharmacy *(Allens 526-1321)* **Under 1 mi:** Market *(Crosby's 526-4444 - delivers)*, Beauty Salon *(Mila's 526-8505)*, Laundry *(Sunshine 526-4921)*, Hardware Store *(Manchester 526-7775)*, Retail Shops **1-3 mi:** Bookstore *(Beverly Farms 927-2122)*, Copies Etc. *(Daily Printing 927-4630)* **3+ mi:** Supermarket *(Shaw's 232-9104, 8 mi.)*, Fishmonger *(Essex 768-7233, 4 mi.)*

Transportation

OnCall: Rental Car *(Enterprise 524-9555)*, Taxi *(City 921-1111)* **Near:** Rail *(MBTA commuter 800-392-6100)* **Under 1 mi:** Bikes *(Seaside Cycle 526-1200)* **Airport:** Logan Int'l. *(25 mi.)*

Medical Services

911 Service **Near:** Dentist *(McDuffee 526-4012)* **Under 1 mi:** Doctor *(Bush 526-7143)*, Holistic Services *(Seaside Spa 526-8400)*, Veterinarian *(Manchester 526-9500)* **Hospital:** Gloucester 283-4000 *(6 mi.)*

Setting -- Just past Crocker's on Cheever's Point, Manchester Marine's immaculate barn-red office and massive sheds rise above quality docks and sheltered, atmospheric Manchester Harbor. The carefully maintained, full-service boatyard attracts gorgeous downeast yachts that congregate here for their beauty treatments. Charming Manchester-by-the-Sea, reeking of New England charm, is about a half-mile walk or dinghy ride past large, gracious homes.

Marina Notes -- *30 ft. min. **MemDay-LabDay Fri-Sun 8am-5pm. Sep Sat & Sun 8-4. In 1899, W.B. Calderwood built yachts here, including 12 Alden designs, then sub chasers for WWII. Post war, Gordon Abbott, Sr. bought & modernized yard, naming it Manchester Marine. Several owners later, in 2004, Steve Brox became majority shareholder & President. Slips, moorings (max.45 ft. in inner-harbor mooring outside for larger vessels) & dinghy dock. 13,000 sq.ft. heated repair bays, 28,000 sq. ft. indoor storage, large rigging loft, 2,500 sq. ft. climate-controlled spray booth. Stores over 200 yachts. Dealer for Sabre, Hanse, Everglades, Robalo. Bathhouse: Modern, tiled, private; close to docks. Note: Recip. privileges at Manchester YC (526-4595).

Notable -- The well-cared-for town, yachts, and Brahmin gentry make Manchester an inviting low-key destination. Singing Beach, a beautiful sweep of fine white sand, is an easy walk. Stroll the town with its impeccably restored 19thC houses, beautiful churches, well-supplied Crosby's Marketplace, a laundry, shops that cater to its well-heeled populace, a selection of restaurants and most other needed services. Find Internet access at the Union Street library. Dinghy to summer concerts at Masconomo Park, which hosts one of the Town's four floats. Or take a longer dinghy excursion to nearby Misery Islands for a picnic.

PHOTOS ON DVD: 22

   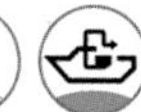

Navigational Information
Lat: 42°32.440' **Long:** 070°53.042' **Tide:** 8 ft. **Current:** 3 kt. **Chart:** 13275
Rep. Depths (*MLW*): Entry 27 ft. **Fuel Dock** 24 ft. **Max Slip/Moor** 24 ft./-
Access: Beverly Harbor Channel past Tuck Point

Marina Facilities *(In Season/Off Season)*
Fuel: *87/89/93* - Gasoline, Diesel, High-Speed Pumps
Slips: 180 Total, 20 Transient **Max LOA:** 200 ft. **Max Beam:** n/a
Rate *(per ft.)*: **Day** $2.75/$1* **Week** Inq. **Month** Inq.
Power: 30 amp Incl., **50 amp** Incl., **100 amp** Incl., **200 amp** n/a
Cable TV: No **Dockside Phone:** No
Dock Type: Floating, Long Fingers, Wood, Composition
Moorings: 0 Total, 0 Transient **Launch:** n/a, Dinghy Dock
Rate: Day n/a **Week** n/a **Month** n/a
Heads: 4 Toilet(s), 4 Shower(s)
Internet: Yes *(Office)* **Laundry:** 2 Washer(s), 2 Dryer(s)
Pump-Out: OnCall, Full Service **Fee:** Free **Closed Heads:** Yes

Marina Operations
Owner/Manager: Frank Kinzie **Dockmaster:** Sue Kinzie
In-Season: May 15-Oct 15, 8am-8pm **Off-Season:** Oct 16-May 14, 8am-6pm
After-Hours Arrival: Call and leave message
Reservations: Yes **Credit Cards:** Visa/MC, Dscvr
Discounts: None
Pets: Welcome **Handicap Access:** No

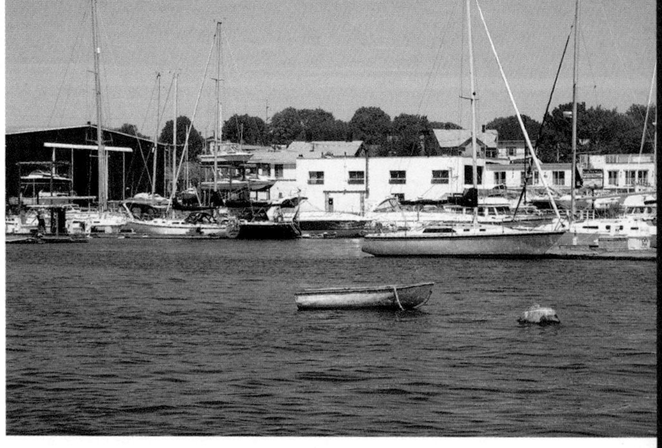

Beverly Port Marina

43 Water Street; Beverly, MA 01915

Tel: (978) 232-3300 **VHF: Monitor** Ch. 79 **Talk** Ch. 79
Fax: (978) 232-3329 **Alternate Tel:** (978) 232-3333
Email: boatbase1@aol.com **Web:** www.beverlyportmarina.com
Nearest Town: Beverly *(0.2 mi.)* **Tourist Info:** (978) 744-0004

Marina Services and Boat Supplies
Services - Docking Assistance, Trash Pick-Up, 3 Phase **Communication -** Mail & Package Hold, Fax in/out *(Free)*, FedEx, DHL, UPS **Supplies - OnSite:** Ice *(Cube)*, Ships' Store **OnCall:** Propane **Under 1 mi:** Bait/Tackle *(Als 927-3312)* **3+ mi:** West Marine *(535-7332, 7 mi.)*

Boatyard Services
OnSite: Travelift *(2-35Ts)*, Forklift, Engine mechanic *(gas, diesel)*, Electrical Repairs, Electronic Sales, Electronics Repairs, Hull Repairs, Rigger, Divers, Bottom Cleaning, Brightwork, Compound, Wash & Wax, Interior Cleaning, Propeller Repairs, Inflatable Repairs, Life Raft Service **OnCall:** Air Conditioning **1-3 mi:** Sail Loft, Canvas Work. **Dealer for:** Donzi, Pro-Line, Honda, Lund, Quintrex, Avon, Volvo, Yamaha, Merc. **Yard Rates:** $115/hr., Haul & Launch $16/ft. *(blocking incl.)*, Power Wash $4.75/ft., Bottom Paint $15-18/ft. *(paint incl.)* **Storage:** In-Water $54/ft/seas., On-Land Inside $120/ft., Outside $54/ft.

Restaurants and Accommodations
Near: Restaurant *(Cafe Salerno Rest & Deli 927-1979, L & D $6-16, Pizza)*, *(Anchor Pub 921-0504)*, *(Goat Hill Grille 927-9263)*, Pizzeria *(Beverly House 922-8400, Delivers)*, *(Luigi's 922-2828, Delivers)* **Under 1 mi:** Restaurant *(Beverly Depot 927-5402)*, *(The Black Lobster at Stromberg Cove 744-1863, L $8-13, D $8-33, Across bridge; Kids' $6, Bar $6-10. Dock. Weekend entertainment)*, *(Chianti Cafe 921-2233, D $13-29)*, *(Casa De Lucca 922-7660, L $6-9, D $9-17, Pizza)*, *(Organic Cafe 922-0004, B $3-8, L $7-17, D $7-17, Kids' Half price)*, *(Chianti Tuscan 921-2233)*, Inn/B&B *(Clipper Ship 745-8022)* **1-3 mi:** Hotel *(Hawthorne 744-4080, $114-315)*, Inn/B&B *(Salem Inn 741-0680, $139-259)*

Near: Picnic Area, Grills, Dive Shop *(Undersea 927-9551)*, Fishing Charter *(Fat Tuna 473-9110)*, Museum *(Beverly Hist. Soc. 922-1186)* **Under 1 mi:** Beach, Playground, Bowling *(Bowl-O-Mat 922-1140)*, Movie Theater *(Cabot St. 927-3677)* **1-3 mi:** Tennis Courts *(Beverly Golf & Tennis 922-9072)*, Golf Course *(Beverly G&T)*, Fitness Center *(Beverly 927-0920)*, Boat Rentals *(Kayak Center 922-5322, $15/1.5 hrs.)*, Video Rental

Provisioning and General Services
OnSite: Newsstand **Near:** Convenience Store, Wine/Beer, Fishmonger *(Rowand 927-1871)*, Lobster Pound *(Lynch 921-8088)*, Beauty Salon *(Cottage Spa 479-8411)* **Under 1 mi:** Market *(One Stop 922-9343)*, Delicatessen *(Gloria 922-3613)*, Health Food *(Organic Rainbow 927-4600)*, Liquor Store *(Cosgroves 744-4000)*, Bank/ATM, Post Office, Catholic Church, Protestant Church, Library *(Beverly 921-6062)*, Dry Cleaners *(Sam's 922-4745)*, Laundry, Pharmacy *(Walgreens 921-0506)*, Hardware Store *(Moynihan 927-0032)* **1-3 mi:** Supermarket *(Stop & Shop 232-0021)*, Synagogue, Bookstore *(Annie's 922-0028)*, Copies Etc. *(Staples 922-3339)*

Transportation
OnSite: Courtesy Car/Van **OnCall:** Rental Car *(Enterprise 524-9555)*, Taxi *(City 921-1111)* **Under 1 mi:** Bikes *(Brown's 922-0376)*, Rail *(MBTA to Boston 800-392-6100)* **Airport:** Logan Int'l. *(15 mi.)*

Medical Services
911 Service **Near:** Chiropractor *(Russell 927-2607)* **Under 1 mi:** Doctor *(Trautman 922-0357)*, Dentist *(Kowalski 373-4600)*, Holistic Services *(Berry LMT 969-2555)*, Veterinarian *(Beverly 927-5453)* **1-3 mi:** Optician *(Scott Clark 922-4732)* **Hospital:** Beverly 921-7077 *(2 mi.)*

Setting -- Past Jubilee Yacht Club and a gray and white condo complex, Beverly Port's enormous red storage shed, two-story white office and ships' store, and busy fuel dock make it easy to spot. The 400 deep-water slips lie seaward of the Beverly-Salem Bridge and opposite Salem Power Plant's distinctive, white-and-blue oil tanks. The landside surroundings tend toward industrial, but Beverly's shopping, fine dining and historic district are an easy walk.

Marina Notes -- *Rates $2.75/ft. to 44 ft. $3.75/ft. 45 ft +. Family-owned & operated, with powerboat focus. Sponsors "Poker Runs." Courtesy car if pre-arranged. Busy hi-speed 80 ft. fuel dock 8am-8pm May-Oct, 9am-5pm Nov-Apr. Four lifts - two 35-ton travelifts and 2 forklifts (boats up to 42 ft). Can manage boats to 200 feet. Mix of composite and wood docks. Recently upgraded power & water. 100A service with 3-phase on C&D docks. Mechanics & service personnel on duty seven days during summer. Only indoor valet rack storage in Boston area - to 42 ft. Cable TV & phone long term only. Bathhouse: Well-maintained, attractive black-and-white tiled; showers with private dressing rooms, laundry. Note: Good protection in northeast blow.

Notable -- Called the Garden City, Beverly has an aging stock of summer homes and gardens built here by wealthy Bostonians. The Historical Society offers guided tours of three historic residences - 1636 Balch House, 18thC John Cabot House, and 1695 John Hale House (Tue-Fri, 10am-4pm, Sat noon-4pm, each $4).The theater-in-the-round North Shore Music Theater, the largest in Massachusetts, reopened in 2010. Cabot St. Cinema (927-3677) a restored 1920s art deco "palace," hosts Le Grand David's Spectacular Magic Company and art house films. Beaches are part of Independence and Lynch Parks.

PHOTOS ON DVD: 20

Glover Wharf Municipal Marina

PO Box 211; 1 Water Street*; Beverly, MA 01915

Tel: (978) 921-6059 **VHF: Monitor** Ch. 16 **Talk** Ch. 12
Fax: (978) 921-8592 **Alternate Tel:** n/a
Email: dmcpherson@beverlyma.gov **Web:** harbormasters.org/beverly
Nearest Town: Beverly *(1.5 mi.)* **Tourist Info:** (978) 232-9559

Navigational Information

Lat: 42°32.417' **Long:** 070°53.181' **Tide:** 8 ft. **Current:** 3 kt. **Chart:** 13275
Rep. Depths (*MLW*): Entry 23 ft. **Fuel Dock** n/a **Max Slip/Moor** 12 ft./24 ft.
Access: Beverly Harbor Channel, last facility before bridge

Marina Facilities *(In Season/Off Season)*

Fuel: No
Slips: 28 Total, 2 Transient **Max LOA:** 50 ft. **Max Beam:** n/a
Rate *(per ft.)*: **Day** $2.00 **Week** Inq. **Month** Inq.
Power: 30 amp Metered, **50 amp** n/a, **100 amp** n/a, **200 amp** n/a
Cable TV: Yes Seasonal only **Dockside Phone:** No
Dock Type: Floating, Wood
Moorings: 12 Total, 12 Transient **Launch:** No, Dinghy Dock
Rate: Day $5 **Week** $35 **Month** $150
Heads: 2 Toilet(s)
Internet: No **Laundry:** None
Pump-Out: OnCall, Full Service, 1 Port **Fee:** Free **Closed Heads:** Yes

Marina Operations

Owner/Manager: Town of Beverly **Dockmaster:** Lou Bochynski
In-Season: May-Sep, 8am-12am **Off-Season:** Oct-Apr, 8am-6pm
After-Hours Arrival: Call in advance
Reservations: Yes **Credit Cards:** Cash/Check only
Discounts: None
Pets: Welcome **Handicap Access:** No

Marina Services and Boat Supplies

Services - Security *(8am-12am)* **Communication -** FedEx, DHL, UPS, Express Mail **Supplies - OnCall:** Propane **Near:** Ice *(Block, Cube)*, Ships' Store *(Beverly Port Marina)* **Under 1 mi:** Bait/Tackle *(Al's 927-3312)* **3+ mi:** West Marine *(535-7332, 7 mi.)*, Boat/US *(777-5940, 4 mi.)*

Boatyard Services

OnCall: Bottom Cleaning, Refrigeration **Under 1 mi:** Launching Ramp. **Nearest Yard:** Beverly Port Marina (978) 232-3300

Restaurants and Accommodations

Near: Restaurant *(Anchor Pub 921-0504)*, *(Cafe Salerno 927-1979, $6-16 & pizza)*, *(Goat Hill Grille 232-9292, D $7.50-22)*, *(Casa DeLucca 922-7660, L $6-11, D $10-17, Kid's menu; take-out.)*, Pizzeria *(Beverly 922-8400, Del.)*, *(Luigi 922-2828)* **Under 1 mi:** Restaurant *(99 740-8999, L $8-18, D $8-18, L&D $8-18 across the bridge)*, *(Black Lobster at Stromberg Cove 744-1863, L $8-13, D $8-33, Over the bridge; Kids' $6, Bar $6-10. Dock. Weekend entertain.)*, *(Beverly Depot 927-5402)*, *(Chianti Cafe 921-2233, D $13-29)*, *(Siam Delight 922-8514, Thai Food)* **1-3 mi:** Motel *(Beverly Garden Suites 922-7535, $79-129)*, Inn/B&B *(Clipper Ship 745-8022)*

Recreation and Entertainment

OnSite: Picnic Area, Park **Near:** Grills, Dive Shop *(Undersea Divers 927-9551)*, Fishing Charter *(Fat Tuna Guides 473-9110)*, Museum *(Beverly Historical Soc. 922-1186)*, Tours *(Guided tours of three historic residences - 1636 Balch House, 18thC John Cabot House & 1695 John Hale House)* **Under 1 mi:** Beach, Playground, Bowling *(Bowl-O-Mat 922-1140)*, Movie Theater *(Cabot Street Cinema 927-3677)*, Video Rental *(Redbox)*, Cultural Attract *(Cabot Street Theatre Magic Show 927-3677)* **1-3 mi:** Tennis Courts *(Beverly Golf & Tennis 922-9072)*, Golf Course *(Beverly G&T)*, Fitness Center *(Beverly Athletic Club 927-0920)*, Boat Rentals *(Kayak Center 922-5322, Lynch Park $15/1.5 hrs.)*

Provisioning and General Services

Near: Convenience Store, Wine/Beer, Fishmonger *(Rowand 927-1871)*, Lobster Pound *(Lynch 921-8088)*, Beauty Salon *(Cottage Spa 479-8411)*, Newsstand, Copies Etc. *(Best Press 921-0456)* **Under 1 mi:** Market *(One Stop 922-9343)*, Delicatessen *(Gloria 922-3613)*, Health Food *(New Leaf 927-5955)*, Liquor Store *(Cosgroves 744-4000)*, Bank/ATM, Post Office, Protestant Church, Library *(Beverly 921-6062)*, Dry Cleaners *(Sam's 922-4745)*, Laundry *(Home Style 927-6460)*, Pharmacy *(Rite Aid 927-5850)*, Hardware Store *(Moynihan 927-0032)* **1-3 mi:** Supermarket *(Stop & Shop 232-0021)*, Catholic Church, Synagogue, Bookstore *(Annie's 922-0028)*

Transportation

OnCall: Rental Car *(Enterprise 524-9555)*, Taxi *(City of Beverly 921-1111)* **Near:** Bikes *(Brown's 922-0376)* **Under 1 mi:** Rail *(MBTA to Boston 800-392-6100)* **1-3 mi:** Ferry Service *(Boston-Salem Ferry 741-0220)* **Airport:** Logan Int'l. *(20 mi.)*

Medical Services

911 Service **OnCall:** Ambulance **Near:** Chiropractor *(Russell Center 927-2607)* **Under 1 mi:** Doctor *(Trautman 922-0357)*, Dentist *(Kowalski 373-4600)*, Holistic Services *(Berry LMT 969-2555; Beverly Holistic Health 524-4888)*, Veterinarian *(Beverly 927-5453)* **1-3 mi:** Optician *(Scott Clark 922-4732)* **Hospital:** Beverly 921-7077 *(2 mi.)*

Setting -- Just past Beverly Port Marina, to starboard on the Danvers River, Glover Wharf lies in the lee of the bustling Salem Bridge. Carpozza Pier, a long public wharf on the site of the historic Old Ferryway Landing, divides the municipal facility into working vessels' docks to the west and recreational boats to the east. A white, two-story cape cod houses the Harbormaster's office. The inner moorings are just off the end of the main pier opposite the seemingly ever-present white-and-blue National Grid tanks on the Salem shore - and the dinghy dock is just below the large, 3-story weathered shingle contemporary.

Marina Notes -- *Mailing Address: 11 Cabot St. Dockage plus 4 moorings in inner harbor just off the Carpozza Pier & 8 moorings off Misery and Little Misery Islands. No launch service; could be a wet dinghy ride from outer mooring field. No dedicated transient slips -- only those vacated by seasonal tenants. Redevelopment of two vacant, rundown buildings await construction crews. Marine services and fuel at the adjacent Beverly Port Marina (large barn red shed). Harbormaster manages the energetic small motorboat traffic on the river. Bathhouse: One full bath plus Port-a-Pottie.

Notable -- Established in the 17thC, the Public Ferryway is one of the oldest "still in use" Common Landing places in the U.S. - and a popular fishing spot. An active port since 1636, Beverly stakes its claim as a birthplace of the American Navy. Take the dinghy or big boat to 83-acre Great Misery Island administered by Trustees of Reservations (926-8687, $5/3). More than two miles of trails pass wild habitats, the ruins of an old resort, and spectacular harbor views. Wade across to 4-acre Little Misery Island to see the wreck of steamship "The City of Rockland." Salem is across the bridge - a good hike or a short cab ride.

PHOTOS ON DVD: 14

  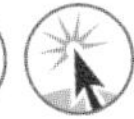 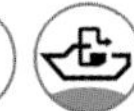

Navigational Information
Lat: 42°31.301' **Long:** 070°52.914' **Tide:** 9 ft. **Current:** n/a **Chart:** 13275
Rep. Depths (*MLW*): **Entry** 10 ft. **Fuel Dock** n/a **Max Slip/Moor** 8 ft./10 ft.
Access: Massachusetts Bay to Salem Channel to Salem Harbor

Marina Facilities *(In Season/Off Season)*
Fuel: Gasoline, Diesel
Slips: 110 Total, 30 Transient **Max LOA:** 65 ft. **Max Beam:** 15 ft.
Rate *(per ft.)*: **Day** $2.50/Inq. **Week** $14 **Month** $45/30
Power: 30 amp $5, **50 amp** $10, **100 amp** n/a, **200 amp** n/a
Cable TV: Yes Seasonal **Dockside Phone:** Yes Seasonal
Dock Type: Floating, Long Fingers, Wood
Moorings: 150 Total, 10 Transient **Launch:** Yes (Free), Dinghy Dock
Rate: Day $45 **Week** $270 **Month** $400
Heads: 4 Toilet(s), 4 Shower(s), Book Exchange
Internet: Yes *(Wi-Fi, Free)* **Laundry:** 2 Washer(s), 2 Dryer(s)
Pump-Out: OnCall, 1 Port **Fee:** Free **Closed Heads:** Yes

Marina Operations
Owner/Manager: Noah Flaherty **Dockmaster:** Ben Kopp
In-Season: May-Oct, 8am-8pm **Off-Season:** Nov-Apr, 8am-5pm
After-Hours Arrival: Call in advance
Reservations: Yes, Preferred **Credit Cards:** Visa/MC, Dscvr
Discounts: None
Pets: Welcome, Dog Walk Area **Handicap Access:** Yes

Brewer Hawthorne Cove Marina

10 White Street; Salem, MA 01970

Tel: (978) 740-9890 **VHF: Monitor** Ch. 8 **Talk** Ch. 8
Fax: (978) 740-9994 **Alternate Tel:** n/a
Email: hcm@byy.com **Web:** www.byy.com/salem
Nearest Town: Salem *(0.4 mi.)* **Tourist Info:** (978) 744-0004

Marina Services and Boat Supplies
Services - Docking Assistance, Concierge, Boaters' Lounge, Security *(24 Hrs.)*, Trash Pick-Up, Dock Carts **Communication -** Fax in/out, FedEx, UPS **Supplies - OnSite:** Ice *(Block, Cube)*, Ships' Store **Under 1 mi:** Bait/Tackle *(Jerry's 744-1547)*, Propane *(U-Haul 744-6030)*

Boatyard Services
OnSite: Travelift *(35T)*, Engine mechanic *(gas, diesel)*, Hull Repairs, Rigger, Divers, Bottom Cleaning, Woodworking **Near:** Electrical Repairs, Electronic Sales, Electronics Repairs *(Mass Marine)*, Propeller Repairs *(H&H 744-3806)*. **Dealer for:** Awlgrip, Fischer Panda, Furlex, Max-prop, Yanmar, Westerbeke, Mercury, Sea-Land, Side-Power. **Member:** ABBRA, ABYC **Yard Rates:** $55/hr., Haul & Launch $8/ft., Power Wash $3.25, Bottom Paint $13/ft. *(paint incl.)* **Storage:** On-Land $10/ft./mo.

Restaurants and Accommodations
OnCall: Pizzeria *(Upper Crust 741-2787)* **Near:** Restaurant *(In a Pig's Eye 741-4436, L $3-8, D $6-13, Sun Brunch)*, *(Grapevine 745-9335, D $10-27)*, *(Witch's Brew 745-8717)*, Hotel *(Hawthorne 744-4080, $114-315, 3 historic buildings)* **Under 1 mi:** Restaurant *(Sixty2 on Wharf 744-0062, D $10-26)*, *(Rockafella's 745-2411, L $7-11, D $13-24, Sun Brunch $9-13)*, Fast Food *(Boston Hot Dog, Wendy's)*, Inn/B&B *(Daniels House 744-5709)*, *(Morning Glory 741-1703, $125-220)*, *(Stepping Stone 741-8900, $95-150)*

Recreation and Entertainment
OnSite: Picnic Area, Grills **Near:** Boat Rentals, Park, Cultural Attract *(Salem NPS Maritime Historic Site 740-1660 $5/3)*, Sightseeing *(House of The 7 Gables 744-0991 $12.50/7.50)* **Under 1 mi:** Pool, Beach *(Winter Island 745-9430)*, Playground, Movie Theater *(Museum Place 744-3700; AMC Loews 750-9785, 3.5 mi)*, Video Rental *(West Coast 745-4005)*, Museum *(Peabody Essex 745-9500 $15/3; Pirate 741-2800 $8/6; Witch Museum 744-1692 $8/6)*, Tours *(Salem Harbor Tours - Salem Water Taxi 745-6050)*, Galleries *(Marine Arts 745-5000)* **1-3 mi:** Dive Shop *(Undersea 927-9551)*, Tennis Courts *(Beverly Golf & Tennis 922-9072)*, Golf Course *(Olde Salem Green 744-2149)*, Fitness Center *(Healthworks 745-7390)*, Bowling *(Bowl-O-Mat 922-1140)*, Fishing Charter *(Fat Tuna 473-9110)*

Provisioning and General Services
Near: Convenience Store, Delicatessen, Liquor Store *(Bung Hole 744-2251)*, Catholic Church, Florist **Under 1 mi:** Supermarket *(Shaw's 741-8660)*, Farmers' Market *(Derby Sq. Thu 3-7pm)*, Green Grocer *(Milk & Honey 744-6639)*, Bank/ATM, Post Office, Protestant Church, Library *(Athenaeum 744-2540)*, Beauty Salon, Barber Shop, Dry Cleaners, Laundry, Bookstore *(Pyramid 745-7171)*, Pharmacy *(CVS 744-2224)*, Hardware Store *(Winer Bros 744-0780)*, Copies Etc. *(Mail Boxes 745-9191)* **1-3 mi:** Synagogue

Transportation
OnCall: Water Taxi *($5 1-way)*, Rental Car *(Enterprise 741-2780)*, Taxi *(Witch City 508/507-8294)*, Airport Limo *(George 777-3377)* **Near:** Local Bus *(Trolley)*, Ferry Service *(to Boston 741-0220)* **Under 1 mi:** Bikes *(Salem Cycle 741-2222)*, Rail *(to Boston)* **Airport:** Logan Int'l. *(15 mi.)*

Medical Services
911 Service **Under 1 mi:** Doctor *(North Shore 825-7100)*, Dentist *(Fisher 744-1209)* **1-3 mi:** Chiropractor *(Kantorosinski 741-3477)*, Veterinarian *(All Creatures 740-0290)* **Hospital:** North Shore 741-1200 *(1.4 mi)*

Setting -- The first marina to starboard after entering historic and well-protected Salem Harbor, three long docks host 110 slips. Onshore, a welcoming deck overlooks the marina and the wide, attractive, boat-laden harbor; a two-story, gray-shingled building houses the office and amenities, and the remainder of the site is filled with an active boatyard and on-the-hard storage. Located on the edge of the busy historic area, the marina is flanked on the north by the Salem-Boston Blaney Street ferry dock and to the south by the House of the Seven Gables Historic Site. The heart of Salem is a 0.4 mile walk.

Marina Notes -- *Acquired by Brewer Yacht Yard Group in Oct. 2010. Complete facility renovation in '08. Large tented patio, two grilling stations. Full-service yard with 35 ton lift, Winter storage for 150 boats. Airy, wicker-furnished seating area outside laundry. Sea Tow onsite. Bathhouse: Inviting group heads. Beadboard wainscot, tile floors, tile and fiberglass shower stalls. Large laundry area. Note: Brewer owns Salem Water Taxi as well, but to date they are totally separate operations, but this may change and some more services may be shared. Inquire.

Notable -- Nathaniel Hawthorne's muse, the 1668 House of the Seven Gables, with its steeply pitched roofs and secret staircase, is the oldest wooden mansion in New England. Several other structures, including Hawthorne's birthplace and two cololonial revival gardens, complete the complex. The Salem Maritime National Historic Site and 1819 Federal-style brick Custom House are 0.3 miles. The remainder of Salem's treasure trove of historic and not-so-historic delights are a short walk further. Dramatic Peabody Essex Museum houses over a million objects, many brought from the Orient by Salem ships' captains.

PHOTOS ON DVD: 20

Pickering Wharf Marina

23 Congress Street; Salem, MA 01970

Tel: (978) 744-2727 **VHF: Monitor** Ch. 9 **Talk** Ch. 8
Fax: (978) 740-6728 **Alternate Tel:** n/a
Email: pwmarina@rockettrealty.com **Web:** www.pickeringwharf.com
Nearest Town: Salem **Tourist Info:** (978) 744-0004

Navigational Information

Lat: 42°31.165' **Long:** 070°53.279' **Tide:** 9 ft. **Current:** n/a **Chart:** 13275
Rep. Depths (*MLW*): Entry 10 ft. **Fuel Dock** n/a **Max Slip/Moor** 7 ft./-
Access: Salem Harbor to white/black lighthouse

Marina Facilities *(In Season/Off Season)*

Fuel: No
Slips: 100 Total, 3 Transient **Max LOA:** 120 ft. **Max Beam:** n/a
Rate *(per ft.)*: **Day** $2.75/Inq. **Week** $10 **Month** Inq.
Power: 30 amp $3, **50 amp** $5, **100 amp** n/a, **200 amp** n/a
Cable TV: Yes, incl **Dockside Phone:** No
Dock Type: Floating, Alongside, Wood
Moorings: 0 Total, 0 Transient **Launch:** n/a, Dinghy Dock
Rate: Day n/a **Week** n/a **Month** n/a
Heads: 2 Toilet(s), 2 Shower(s), Book Exchange
Internet: Yes *(Wi-Fi, Free)* **Laundry:** 1 Washer(s), 1 Dryer(s)
Pump-Out: OnCall, Full Service **Fee:** Free **Closed Heads:** Yes

Marina Operations

Owner/Manager: Richard Rockett **Dockmaster:** Tom Moran
In-Season: May-Oct, 7:30am-10pm **Off-Season:** Nov-Apr, 8am-4pm
After-Hours Arrival: Call in advance
Reservations: Yes **Credit Cards:** Visa/MC, Amex
Discounts: None
Pets: Welcome, Dog Walk Area **Handicap Access:** Yes

Marina Services and Boat Supplies

Services - Docking Assistance, Security *(24)*, Trash Pick-Up, Dock Carts **Communication -** Mail & Package Hold, Phone Messages, Fax in/out, FedEx, DHL, UPS, Express Mail **Supplies - OnSite:** Ice *(Cube)* **1-3 mi:** Bait/Tackle *(Petes 744-2262)*, Propane *(U-Haul 744-6030)*

Boatyard Services

OnCall: Engine mechanic *(gas, diesel)*, Divers, Bottom Cleaning, Compound, Wash & Wax, Interior Cleaning, Woodworking, Inflatable Repairs, Upholstery **Nearest Yard:** Dion's (978) 744-0844

Restaurants and Accommodations

OnSite: Restaurant *(Finz Seafood 744-8485, L $9-17, D $16-26, waterside)*, *(Capt's 741-0555, L $8-46, D $10-46, waterside)*, *(Victoria Station 745-3400, L $8-27, D $9-29, waterside, gluten-free menu)*, *(Sixty2 on Wharf 744-0062, D $10-26)*, *(Regatta Pub 740-8788, B $8-16, L $8-21, D $8-21, Patio dining, Kids' menu)*, Hotel *(Salem Waterfront 740-8788, $135-269)* **Near:** Restaurant *(The Grapevine 745-9335, D $10-27)*, *(Nathaniel's 825-4311, B $6-15, D $11-28, Piano Thu-Sat, Tavern Menu $8-19, Sun Jazz Brunch $16)*, Hotel *(Hawthorne 744-4080, $114-315)* **Under 1 mi:** Inn/B&B *(Salem Inn 741-0680, $119-259)*, *(Amelia Payson 744-8304, $135-175)*

Recreation and Entertainment

OnSite: Heated Pool, Fitness Center, Tours *("Fame" 729-7600 $30.15, Privateer schooner, 3 sailings/day; Salem Heritage Trail - red-line; Salem Trolley 744-5469 $12)*, Cultural Attract **Near:** Movie Theater *(Museum Place 744-3700)*, Park, Museum *(Peabody Essex 745-9500 $15/3; Pirate 741-2800 $8/6; Witch Museum 744-1692 $8/6; House of The Seven Gables 744-0991 $12.50/7.50)*, Sightseeing *(Salem NPS Maritime Historic Site 740-1660 $5/3)* **Under 1 mi:** Beach, Picnic Area, Grills, Playground, Video Rental *(Redbox)* **1-3 mi:** Dive Shop *(Undersea 927-9551)*, Golf Course *(Olde Salem Greens 744-2149)*, Bowling *(Bowl-O-Mat 922-1140)*

Provisioning and General Services

OnSite: Beauty Salon *(Fringe 745-5500)*, Retail Shops **Near:** Convenience Store, Delicatessen *(Red's 745-3527)*, Liquor Store *(Bung Hole 744-2251)*, Bakery *(A&J King 744-4881)*, Bank/ATM, Post Office, Catholic Church, Protestant Church, Barber Shop, Dry Cleaners, Laundry, Bookstore *(Pyramid 745-7171)*, Pharmacy *(CVS 744-2224)*, Hardware Store *(Winer Bros 744-0780)*, Florist **Under 1 mi:** Market *(Crosby's)*, Supermarket *(Shaw's 741-8660)*, Farmers' Market *(Derby Sq. Thu 3-7pm)*, Green Grocer *(Milk & Honey 744-6639)*, Synagogue, Library *(Athenaeum 744-2540)*, Copies Etc. *(Mail Boxes 745-9191)* **1-3 mi:** Health Food *(Organic Rainbow 927-4600)* **3+ mi:** Buying Club *(Costco, BJ's, 6 mi.)*

Transportation

OnCall: Water Taxi *(Salem $10 1-Way)*, Taxi *(Adventure 774-2112)*, Airport Limo *(George 777-3377)* **Near:** InterCity Bus *(MBTA 800-392-6100)* **Under 1 mi:** Bikes *(Salem Cycle 741-2222)*, Rental Car *(Hertz 745-5275; Enterprise 741-2780)*, Local Bus *(Salem Trolley)*, Rail *(Commuter to Boston)*, Ferry Service *(Salem-Boston 741-0220)* **Airport:** Logan Int'l. *(14 mi.)*

Medical Services

911 Service **Near:** Doctor *(North Shore 825-7100)*, Dentist *(Fisher 744-1209)* **Under 1 mi:** Chiropractor *(Kantorosinski 741-3477)*, Veterinarian *(All Creatures 740-0290)* **Hospital:** North Shore - Salem 741-1215 *(1.5 mi.)*

Setting -- Tucked into Salem Harbor, between the National Park Service's Salem Maritime Historic Site on Derby Wharf and a jarringly modern white five-story office building, the upscale docks surround Pickering Wharf, a six-acre, tastefully-designed, commercial and residential low-rise village and recent, luxury full-service hotel. Immediately beyond are the rich historic remnants of a busy 18th- and 19th-century port and reminders of its macabre 17th-century past.

Marina Notes -- Professional dock staff. Wi-Fi throughout property. Indoor heated pool and well-equipped fitness center in onsite Salem Waterfront Hotel. Complimentary Fax, Print & Copy services. Preponderance of motorboats; tight maneuvering. Dock 'n Dine $0.25/foot for two hours. Pump-Out Boat Ch 9 Sat, Sun, Wed & Hols. Salem Water Taxi stops at bridge. Bathhouse: Modern, convenient; tiled floor, fiberglass shower stalls, wall paper. Casual laundry.

Notable -- Five restaurants are onsite - Finz, Capt's, Regatta Pub, Victoria Station, Sixty2 on Wharf - plus a coffee house, boutiques, galleries, crafts and gift shops, a salon, pet groomer, hotel and the schooner "Fame." And all of Salem's many attractions are within easy walking distance. Start at the Visitor Center at 10 Liberty St. The nine-acre federal Salem Maritime Site has a dozen restored buildings, including the Custom House, "Friendship" cargo vessel and Pedrick Store House on Derby Wharf, all open daily 9am-5pm (740-1660). Do not miss Moshe Safdie's soaring Peabody Essex Museum, the oldest private museum in the U.S. Founded by Salem ships' captains, it boasts 30 galleries housing vast Asian artifacts and the world's largest maritime art collection. Salem is steeped in Witch kitsch: Witch Museum, Witch Dungeon, and Witch House just scratch the surface. Haunted Happenings is a month-long Halloween.

11. MA: NORTH SHORE

PHOTOS ON DVD: 23

Navigational Information
Lat: 42°31.137' **Long:** 070°53.362' **Tide:** 9 ft. **Current:** n/a **Chart:** 13275
Rep. Depths (*MLW*): Entry 15 ft. **Fuel Dock** n/a **Max Slip/Moor** 10 ft./15 ft.
Access: Salem Channel to Salem Harbor mooring field

Marina Facilities *(In Season/Off Season)*
Fuel: No
Slips: 0 Total, 0 Transient **Max LOA:** 60 ft. **Max Beam:** 20 ft.
Rate *(per ft.)*: **Day** n/a **Week** n/a **Month** n/a
Power: 30 amp n/a, **50 amp** n/a, **100 amp** n/a, **200 amp** n/a
Cable TV: No **Dockside Phone:** No
Dock Type: n/a
Moorings: 120 Total, 10 Transient **Launch:** Yes (Free), Dinghy Dock
Rate: Day $45 **Week** $270 **Month** $400**
Heads: 4 Toilet(s), 4 Shower(s) *(dressing rooms)*, Book Exchange
Internet: No **Laundry:** 2 Washer(s), 2 Dryer(s)
Pump-Out: OnCall, Full Service, 1 Central **Fee:** n/a **Closed Heads:** Yes

Marina Operations
Owner/Manager: Noah Flaherty **Dockmaster:** Ben Kopp
In-Season: May-Oct, 8 am-10 pm **Off-Season:** Nov-Apr, Closed
After-Hours Arrival: Call in advance for assignment
Reservations: Yes **Credit Cards:** Visa/MC, Dscvr
Discounts: None
Pets: Welcome **Handicap Access:** No

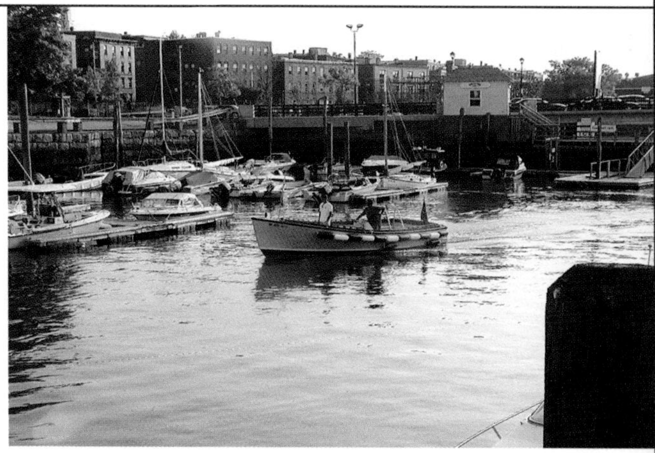

Salem Water Taxi

10 White Street*; Salem, MA 01970

Tel: (978) 745-6070 **VHF: Monitor** Ch. 68 **Talk** Ch. 68
Fax: (978) 740-9994 **Alternate Tel:** n/a
Email: info@salemwatertaxi.com **Web:** www.salemwatertaxi.com
Nearest Town: Salem **Tourist Info:** (978) 744-0004

Marina Services and Boat Supplies
Supplies - OnSite: Ice *(Block, Cube)* **Under 1 mi:** Ships' Store *(Hawthorne Cove)*, Propane *(U-Haul 744-6030)* **1-3 mi:** Bait/Tackle *(Petes 927-3312)*

Boatyard Services
Nearest Yard: Brewer Hawthorne Cove Marina (978) 740-9890

Restaurants and Accommodations
Near: Restaurant *(Regatta Pub 740-8788, B $8-16$8-16, D $8-21)*, *(Nathaniel's 744-4080, B $6-15, D $11-28, Live piano Thu-Sat, Tavern $8-19, Sun Jazz Brunch $17)*, *(Salem Beer Works 745-2337, L & D $9-23)*, *(Cilantro 745-9436, D $16-26, Mexican)*, *(Sixty2 on Wharf 744-0062, D $10-26)*, *(Victoria Station 745-3400, L $8-27, D $9-27, Also gluten-free menu)*, *(The Grapevine 745-9335, D $10-27)*, *(Finz 744-8485, L $9-17, D $16-26)*, *(The Old Spot 745-5656, L $6.50-9, D $8-17)*, Hotel *(Hawthorne 744-4080, $114-315)*, *(Salem Waterfront 740-8788, $135-269)*, Inn/B&B *(Stepping Stone 741-8900, $95-150)*, *(Suzannah Flint House 744-5281, $150-400)*

Recreation and Entertainment
OnSite: Tours *(Salem Harbor Tours $5, 20-30 min.)* **Near:** Boat Rentals, Movie Theater *(Cinema Salem 744-1400)*, Video Rental *(West Coast 745-4005)*, Park, Museum *(Peabody Essex 745-9500 $15/3 - 16-room Yin Yu Tang Qing dynasty house +$4; Pirate 741-2800 $8/6; Witch Museum 744-1692 $8/6; House of the Seven Gables 744-0991 $12.50/7.50)*, Sightseeing *(Salem Maritime National Historic Site 740-1650 Free; "Fame" 729-7600 $30.15, Privateer schooner, 3 sailings/day; Salem Heritage Trail - red-line; Salem Trolley 744-5469 $12)*, Galleries *(Marine Arts 745-5000)* **Under 1 mi:** Pool *(Forest River Park)*, Beach, Playground *(Palmer Cove Park)*, Fitness Center *(Extra Effort 476-4120)*, Cultural Attract *(Pioneer Village)* **1-3 mi:** Dive Shop *(Undersea 927-9551)*, Golf Course *(Olde Salem Green 744-2149)*, Bowling *(Bowl-O-Mat 922-1140)*

Provisioning and General Services
Near: Convenience Store *(Bany 744-3331)*, Gourmet Shop *(Pamplemousse 745-2900)*, Delicatessen *(Derby 741-2442; Salem Bros. 741-4648)*, Liquor Store *(Bung Hole 744-2251)*, Bank/ATM, Post Office, Catholic Church, Protestant Church, Beauty Salon *(Fringe 745-5500)*, Barber Shop, Dry Cleaners *(Salem 744-8333)*, Laundry, Bookstore *(Pyramid 745-7171)*, Pharmacy *(CVS 744-2224)*, Hardware Store *(Winer Bros 744-0780)*, Florist, Retail Shops *(Essex Street Pedestrian Mall)* **Under 1 mi:** Market *(Crosby's Marketplace 745-3571)*, Supermarket *(Shaw's 741-8660)*, Health Food *(Organic Rainbow 927-4600)*, Wine/Beer *(Salem 741-9463)*, Farmers' Market *(Derby Sq. Thu 3-7pm)*, Green Grocer *(Milk & Honey 219-4125)*, Meat Market, Synagogue, Library *(Salem 744-0860)*, Copies Etc. *(Mail Boxes Etc 745-9191)* **1-3 mi:** Department Store *(Target 224-4000)*

Transportation
OnSite: Water Taxi **OnCall:** Rental Car *(Enterprise 741-2780)*, Taxi *(Tri-City 744-4772)*, Airport Limo *(George 777-3377)* **Near:** Bikes *(Urbane 594-5174)* **Under 1 mi:** Rail *(to Boston)*, Ferry Service *(to Boston 741-0220)*
Airport: Logan *(14 mi.)*

Medical Services
911 Service **Near:** Doctor *(North Shore 825-7100)*, Dentist *(Fisher 744-1209)*, Chiropractor *(Du Pilka 745-6224)* **Under 1 mi:** Veterinarian *(All Creatures 740-0290)* **Hospital:** North Shore - Salem 741-1200 *(1.5 mi.)*

Setting -- Snugged up at the head of the channel behind Pickering Wharf, Salem Water Taxi's little, crayon-yellow house perches on the Congress Street Bridge above the Public Landing. From this "in-town" base, a short walk to the Historic district, it manages a large mooring field in the center of Salem Harbor. The bright-yellow "Water Taxi" launches are easy to spot as they buzz about the harbor.

Marina Notes -- *Under same management/ownership as Brewer Hawthorne Cove Marina (which shares the above mailing address). All "middle section" distances are from the Congress Street Landing. **Season Pass $270: 2 days per week incl. launch. Moorings 3500-pound blocks with 3/4" or 1" pennants. Unlimited launch service 8am-10pm. Complimentary dinghy if needed. All marine services at Hawthorne Cove plus comp. washdown dock, showers, and laundry, as of publication, included in the mooring fee (but call to confirm, as this may change). Bathhouse: At Brewer Hawthorne Cove. Inviting group heads. Beadboard wainscot, tile floors, tile and fiberglass shower stalls. Large laundry area.

Notable -- Salem Taxi's Congress Street location at the Public Landing is very handy to all Salem sites. Just beyond Pickering Wharf's restaurants and shops, the National Park Service's Maritime National Historic Site hosts the replica schooner "Friendship" and several restored buildings including Custom House. The "painted red line" Heritage Trail starts here at the Visitors Center. Stroll the McIntire District - especially Chestnut Street lined with magnificent sea captains' houses built by the largesse of privateers and, later, the East Indies and China trade. World-class Peabody Essex Museum features much of the loot.

PHOTOS ON DVD: 17

Fred J. Dion Yacht Yard

Fred J. Dion Yacht Yard

23 Glendale Street; Salem, MA 01970

Tel: (978) 744-0844 **VHF: Monitor** Ch. 9 **Talk** n/a
Fax: (978) 745-7258 **Alternate Tel:** n/a
Email: fjdions@msn.com **Web:** n/a
Nearest Town: Salem *(1.2 mi.)* **Tourist Info:** (978) 744-0004

Navigational Information

Lat: 42°31.366' **Long:** 070°52.986' **Tide:** 9 ft. **Current:** 1 kt. **Chart:** 13275
Rep. Depths (*MLW*): Entry 8 ft. **Fuel Dock** 7 ft. **Max Slip/Moor** 8 ft./8 ft.
Access: Salem Harbor main Channel to G3 then private Channel

Marina Facilities *(In Season/Off Season)*

Fuel: Diesel, On Call Delivery
Slips: 18 Total, 10 Transient **Max LOA:** 100 ft. **Max Beam:** n/a
Rate *(per ft.)*: **Day** $3.50 **Week** Inq. **Month** Inq.
Power: 30 amp Incl., **50 amp** Incl., **100 amp** n/a, **200 amp** n/a
Cable TV: No **Dockside Phone:** No
Dock Type: Floating, Alongside, Wood
Moorings: 13 Total, 6 Transient **Launch:** Yes (Free)
Rate: Day $35 **Week** Inq. **Month** Inq.
Heads: 1 Toilet(s), 1 Shower(s)
Internet: No **Laundry:** None
Pump-Out: OnCall, Full Service, 1 Port **Fee:** Free **Closed Heads:** Yes

Marina Operations

Owner/Manager: Fred Atkins **Dockmaster:** Todd Mentuck
In-Season: May-Oct, 7am-4pm **Off-Season:** Nov-April, 8am-4pm
After-Hours Arrival: Prior arrangement.
Reservations: Yes, Required **Credit Cards:** Visa/MC, Amex
Discounts: None
Pets: Welcome **Handicap Access:** No

Marina Services and Boat Supplies

Communication - Phone Messages, Fax in/out, FedEx, UPS, Express Mail **Supplies - OnSite:** CNG **Near:** Ice *(Block, Cube)* **Under 1 mi:** Ships' Store *(Boston 631-1800)*, Propane *(U-Haul 744-6030)* **1-3 mi:** West Marine *(781-639-6451)*, Bait/Tackle *(Al's 927-3312)*

Boatyard Services

OnSite: Travelift *(50T)*, Railway, Forklift, Crane, Hydraulic Trailer, Engine mechanic *(gas, diesel)*, Electrical Repairs, Hull Repairs, Rigger, Sail Loft, Canvas Work, Bottom Cleaning, Brightwork, Air Conditioning, Refrigeration, Interior Cleaning, Woodworking, Metal Fabrication, Painting **Dealer for:** Westerbeke, Cummins, Universal, Edson. **Yard Rates:** $70-80/hr., Haul & Launch $6-7.5/ft., Power Wash $2.50 **Storage:** On-Land $65-90/ft.

Restaurants and Accommodations

Near: Restaurant *(Jade House 744-3360)*, *(River Merrimack 463-4040)*, *(Okea Grill & Sushi 607-0060)*, Pizzeria *(Christina's 744-0700)*, Inn/B&B *(Coach House 744-4092, $130-299)* **Under 1 mi:** Restaurant *(The Grapevine 745-9335, D $10-27)*, *(Salem Jade 744-3360)*, *(Bertini's 744-1436, L & D $5-15)*, Fast Food *(Subway, McDs, BK)*, Lite Fare *(Sidelines Sports Bar 745-5870, college bar)*, Pizzeria *(Engine House 745-1744, L & D $5-15 Calzones, Subs, Pizza, etc.)*, Hotel *(Hawthorne Hotel 744-4080, $114-315)*, Inn/B&B *(Salem Inn 741-0680, $119-259)*

Recreation and Entertainment

Near: Pool *(Forest River Park)*, Picnic Area, Playground *(Palmer Cove)*, Cultural Attract *(Pioneer Village 867-4767 $6/Free)*, Sightseeing *(Salem Trolley 744-5469 $15/5 all-day)* **Under 1 mi:** Tennis Courts *(River Forest Park, Salem State)*, Movie Theater *(Cinema Salem 744-1400)*, Video Rental *(West Coast 745-4005)*, Museum *(Peabody Essex 745-9500)*, Tours *(Haunted Footsteps 745-0666)* **1-3 mi:** Beach *(Winter Island/Waikiki)*, Dive Shop *(Undersea 927-9551)*, Golf Course *(Olde Salem 744-2149)*, Fitness Center *(Healthworks 745-7390)*, Bowling *(Metro Bowl 531-0500)*

Provisioning and General Services

Near: Wine/Beer, Liquor Store *(Salem 744-2335)*, Bank/ATM, Protestant Church, Synagogue, Beauty Salon *(Andrew Michaels 741-4900)* **Under 1 mi:** Convenience Store *(Sunny Corner 741-0079)*, Supermarket *(Crosby's 745-3571)*, Gourmet Shop *(Pamplemousse 745-2900)*, Bakery *(Bagel World 741-5225)*, Farmers' Market *(Derby Sq. Thu 3-7pm)*, Post Office, Catholic Church, Library *(Athenaeum 744-2540)*, Barber Shop *(Pringle's 744-2216)*, Dry Cleaners *(Royal 741-3337)*, Laundry *(Salem 745-4892)*, Pharmacy *(CVS 744-2224)*, Hardware Store *(Winer Bros 744-0780)*, Florist *(Darlene 745-6967)*, Copies Etc. *(Mail Boxes 745-9191)* **1-3 mi:** Health Food *(Whole Foods 592-2200)*, Retail Shops *(Hawthorne Sq. Mall, Target)*

Transportation

OnCall: Rental Car *(Enterprise 741-2780)*, Taxi *(Liberty 744-7440)*, Airport Limo *(Adventure 774-2112)* **Near:** Local Bus *(Salem Trolley)* **Under 1 mi:** Bikes *(Urbane 594-5174)* **1-3 mi:** Water Taxi *(Salem 745-6070)*, Rail *(MBTA)*, Ferry Service *(to Boston)* **Airport:** Logan Int'l *(15 mi.)*

Medical Services

911 Service **Under 1 mi:** Doctor *(No. Shore 825-7100)*, Dentist *(Fisher 744-1209)*, Chiropractor *(Kantorosinski 741-3477)*, Optician *(Salem 607-0086)*, Veterinarian *(Hawthorne 741-2300)* **Hospital:** Salem 741-1200 *(2 mi.)*

Setting -- The centerpiece of a small protected cove near the head of Salem Harbor, bounded on the north by Palmer Cove and on the south by River Forest Park, this historic boatyard sports two long docks that accommodate larger vessels "alongside." A launch services a mooring field just offshore. The ambiance is pure old-time working yard and doesn't pretend to be anything more. Look for the F.J. Dion and North Sails sign on the big gray shed.

Marina Notes -- Family-owned and operated since 1914. Year-round, full-time professional staff. Launch service to mooring field. Repair, restoration and storage of sail and power boats. Refinishing, mechanical services, rigging. Hauling to 75 ft. and overland transport up to 45 ft. Indoor & outdoor storage for boats to 60 ft. LOA. The antique buildings could use a restorative hand. Bathhouse: Office hours only but useable and tidy.

Notable -- About 0.3 mile south, the extensive Forest River Park features picnic areas, a playground, two beaches, salt-water pool, baseball diamond and the Pioneer Village - a three-acre living history museum bult in the 1930's that includes a range of 17thC. Colonial-era buildings from wigwams to Governor's Faire House as well as medicinal and culinary gardens (noon to 4pm). The original site of the 1626 Massachusetts Bay Colony. Salem's puritanical legacy - the witch trials fueled by Boston's Rev. Cotten Mather - have been the financial engine that has kept it prosperous long after the decline of its maritime prowess. A bit over a mile to the edge of the historic area, attractions range from hokey to well-done witchery to the truly superb Maritime National Historic Site (Orientation Center offers a free overview film (740-1660) and Peabody Essex Museum, which displays roughly one million artifacts from around the world in 30 galleries.

PHOTOS ON DVD: 12

Navigational Information

Lat: 42°30.202' **Long:** 070°50.209' **Tide:** 10 ft. **Current:** .5 kt. **Chart:** 13275
Rep. Depths (*MLW*): Entry 30 ft. **Fuel Dock** n/a **Max Slip/Moor** -/30 ft.
Access: Just inside the harbor, beyond Marblehead Light, directly to port

Marina Facilities *(In Season/Off Season)*

Fuel: No
Slips: 0 Total, 0 Transient **Max LOA:** 90 ft. **Max Beam:** n/a
Rate *(per ft.)*: **Day** n/a **Week** n/a **Month** n/a
Power: 30 amp n/a, **50 amp** n/a, **100 amp** n/a, **200 amp** n/a
Cable TV: No **Dockside Phone:** No
Dock Type: n/a
Moorings: 350 Total, 4-10 Transient **Launch:** Yes (Incl.), Dinghy Dock
Rate: Day $45 **Week** n/a **Month** n/a
Heads: 6 Toilet(s), 6 Shower(s)
Internet: Yes *(Wi-Fi, Free)* **Laundry:** 1 Washer(s), 1 Dryer(s)
Pump-Out: OnCall, Full Service **Fee:** n/a **Closed Heads:** Yes

Marina Operations

Owner/Manager: Robert Hastings, Jr. **Dockmaster:** Staff
In-Season: June-Aug, 8am-11pm **Off-Season:** May & Sep-Oct, 9am-6pm
After-Hours Arrival: Call in advance
Reservations: Yes **Credit Cards:** Visa/MC
Discounts: None
Pets: Welcome **Handicap Access:** No

Corinthian Yacht Club

PO Box 401; 1 Nahant Street; Marblehead, MA 01945

Tel: (781) 631-0005 **VHF: Monitor** Ch. 9 **Talk** Ch. 9
Fax: (781) 631-4968 **Alternate Tel:** n/a
Email: rhastings@corinthianyc.org **Web:** www.corinthianyc.org
Nearest Town: Marblehead *(2 mi.)* **Tourist Info:** (781) 631-2868

Marina Services and Boat Supplies

Services - Docking Assistance, Security, Dock Carts **Communication -** Pay Phone, DHL, UPS, Express Mail **Supplies - OnSite:** Ice *(Block, Cube)* **1-3 mi:** Ships' Store *(Lynn Marine 631-1305)*, West Marine *(639-6451)*, Bait/Tackle *(Boat Shop 631-5348)*

Boatyard Services

OnSite: Launching Ramp **Under 1 mi:** Travelift, Electrical Repairs *(Boatworks 631-7565)*, Electronic Sales *(Boatworks)*, Electronics Repairs, Sail Loft *(Doyle)*. **Nearest Yard:** Marblehead Trading Co. (781) 639-0029

Restaurants and Accommodations

OnSite: Restaurant *(Corinthian Y.C. Dining Room D $15-30, Casual Fare $9-18)*, Snack Bar *(Cont. breakfast, sandwiches, burgers)*, Lite Fare *(Corinthian Grille L $9-18, Pub food, sandwiches to light entrées)* **Near:** Inn/B&B *(Seagull 631-1893, $140-250)*, *(Lady Winnette Cottage 631-8579, $125-150)* **Under 1 mi:** Restaurant *(Barnacle 631-4236, L & D $12.50-22 Kid's menu)*, *(Maddie's Sail Loft 631-9824)*, Inn/B&B *(Harborside House 631-1032)*, *(Harbor Light 631-2186, $145-365)* **1-3 mi:** Restaurant *(Landing 639-1266, L $9-20, D $11-32)*, *(Pellino's 631-3344, D $13-35, Highly rated)*

Recreation and Entertainment

OnSite: Heated Pool, Beach, Tennis Courts, Jogging Paths **Near:** Picnic Area, Fishing Charter *(Sigler Guide 639-7763)*, Park *(Chandler Hovey Lighthouse Point; Castle Rock)*, Sightseeing *(Marblehead Neck - 3-mile loop on Ocean & Harbor Aves.)* **Under 1 mi:** Video Rental *(Chet's 631-9550)*, Museum *(Marblehead 631-1768)*, Cultural Attract *(Marblehead Little Theatre 631-9697)*, Galleries *(Acorn 631-6030)* **1-3 mi:** Playground, Fitness Center *(Gravity Fitness 631-6533)* **3+ mi:** Golf Course *(Olde Salem 978-744-2149, 3.5 mi)*, Movie Theater *(Salem 978-744-1400, 3.5 mi)*

Provisioning and General Services

Under 1 mi: Convenience Store *(7-Eleven 631-9351)*, Supermarket *(Crosby's 631-1741)*, Gourmet Shop *(Shubie's 631-0149)*, Delicatessen *(Muffin Shop 631-8223)*, Liquor Store *(Haley's 631-0169)*, Bakery *(Muffin Shop)*, Lobster Pound *(Marblehead 631-0787)*, Bank/ATM, Protestant Church, Beauty Salon, Barber Shop, Dry Cleaners *(Marblehead 631-0526)*, Laundry *(Marblehead 631-0526)*, Bookstore *(The Spirit of '76 631-7199)*, Pharmacy *(CVS 639-1412)*, Newsstand *(Howard's 639-0546)*, Florist *(Flores Mantilla 631-9483)* **1-3 mi:** Wine/Beer, Post Office, Catholic Church, Synagogue, Library *(Marblehead 631-1480)*, Hardware Store *(Green's ACE 639-2257)* **3+ mi:** Department Store *(Target 978-224-4000, 4.5 mi)*

Transportation

OnCall: Rental Car *(Enterprise 978/741-2780)*, Taxi *(VanGo 978/729-5998)*, Airport Limo *(476-5720)* **1-3 mi:** Bikes *(Marblehead 631-1570)*, Rail *(MBTA to Boston 800-392-6100)*, Ferry Service *(Salem Ferry 978/741-0220)* **Airport:** Logan Int'l. *(15 mi.)*

Medical Services

911 Service **OnCall:** Ambulance **Under 1 mi:** Dentist *(Rice 631-3162)*, Holistic Services *(SeaStone Massage 631-4449)*, Optician *(Marblehead 631-6600)*, Veterinarian *(Marblehead Animal Hospital 639-1300)* **1-3 mi:** Doctor *(North Shore 631-5454)*, Chiropractor *(Marblehead 639-0808)* **Hospital:** North Shore - Salem 978-741-1200 *(4 mi.)*

Setting -- Just past Marblehead Light, on the harbor's eastern shore, the gracious,19th-century turreted-and-gabled clubhouse perches high on a rocky ledge. The lovely verandas, porches, dining and living rooms sport 180-degree panoramic vistas across the yacht-filled harbor, out to the South Channel and along a shore lined with elegant shingle-style homes. The extensive facilities include a pool, tennis, club launch, big-boat and dinghy docks and one-design hoist.

Marina Notes -- Founded in 1885. A private club that welcomes visitors without reciprocity. Splendid setting and spectacular value. Luxurious surroundings, first-rate hospitality, facilities and services. Observe dress code: Dining Room & Porch - collared shirt & slacks for men; comparable attire for women. Dining Room - Jackets & ties Sat. after 6pm. Function facilities (accommodating 60-180) available to other YCs. Above distances *around* harbor. Quicker "nearby" access to Tucker's Wharf town landing by dinghy or CYC launch. Bathhouses: Simply lovely. Beadboard cabinets, soft striped wallpaper, corian & artwork.

Notable -- Exclusive, picture-perfect, residential Marblehead Neck is home to turn-of-the-century "cottages," spectacular mansions, noteworthy gardens. and even a private stone castle that gives its name to Castle Rock Park. Just north of CYC, Lighthouse Lane leads to windswept 3.7-acre Chandler Hovey Park, home of the Marblehead LIght Tower, with picnic tables, pavilions, swimming - and spectacular views. About a mile south, Audubon's Marblehead Neck Wildlife Sanctuary occupies the center of the Neck - a fall and spring haven for migratory birds like warblers, it's a magnet for birders. Despite it's private enclave ambiance, the Neck has ten right-of-ways to both the ocean and harbor waterfront - some to small sandy beaches, others step down to rocky coves.

PHOTOS ON DVD: 23

Tucker's Wharf Municipal Docks

9 Ferry Lane at Tucker's Wharf; Marblehead, MA 01945

Tel: (781) 631-2386 **VHF: Monitor** Ch. 16 **Talk** Ch. 14
Fax: (781) 631-7888 **Alternate Tel:** n/a
Email: cdalferro@marblehead.org **Web:** www.marblehead.org
Nearest Town: Marblehead **Tourist Info:** (781) 639-8469

Navigational Information

Lat: 42°30.248' **Long:** 070°50.833' **Tide:** 10 ft. **Current:** 1 kt. **Chart:** 13275
Rep. Depths (*MLW*): Entry 20 ft. **Fuel Dock** n/a **Max Slip/Moor** 20 ft./20 ft.
Access: Marblehead Harbor, follow fairway along western shore

Marina Facilities *(In Season/Off Season)*

Fuel: *Marblehead Trading* - Gasoline, Diesel
Slips: 6 Total, 6* Transient **Max LOA:** 100 ft. **Max Beam:** n/a
Rate *(per ft.)*: **Day** $3.50/n/a **Week** n/a **Month** n/a
Power: 30 amp incl, **50 amp** incl, **100 amp** n/a, **200 amp** n/a
Cable TV: No **Dockside Phone:** No
Dock Type: Floating, Alongside, Wood
Moorings: 0 Total, 0 Transient **Launch:** n/a, Dinghy Dock
Rate: Day n/a **Week** n/a **Month** n/a
Heads: 2 Toilet(s)
Internet: No **Laundry:** 1 Washer(s), 1 Dryer(s)
Pump-Out: Self Service, 1 Central **Fee:** Free **Closed Heads:** Yes

Marina Operations

Owner/Manager: Charles Dalferro (Harbormaster) **Dockmaster:** same
In-Season: May 16-Oct, 7:30am-11pm **Off-Season:** Nov-May 15, 7:30-3pm
After-Hours Arrival: Take any open slip, check in in the morning
Reservations: Yes **Credit Cards:** Visa/MC
Discounts: None
Pets: Welcome **Handicap Access:** No

Marina Services and Boat Supplies

Communication - Pay Phone, FedEx, DHL, UPS, Express Mail **Supplies - Near:** Ice *(Block, Cube)*, Ships' Store *(Lynn Marine 631-1305)* **Under 1 mi:** Bait/Tackle *(Boat Shop 631-5348)* **1-3 mi:** West Marine *(639-6451)*

Boatyard Services

Near: Travelift, Railway, Crane, Engine mechanic *(gas, diesel)*, Electrical Repairs, Electronics Repairs, Hull Repairs, Rigger, Sail Loft, Canvas Work, Bottom Cleaning, Brightwork, Air Conditioning, Refrigeration, Propeller Repairs, Painting. **Nearest Yard:** Marblehead Trading (781) 639-0029

Restaurants and Accommodations

OnSite: Restaurant *(The Landing 639-1266, L $9-20, D $11-32, overlooking docks & harbor)* **Near:** Restaurant *(The Barnacle 631-4236, L & D $13.23 Kids' $5-9)*, *(Maddie's Sail Loft 631-9824)*, *(Jack Tar 631-2323, D $9-23)*, Lite Fare *(Driftwood 631-1145, B & L)*, *(Muffin Shop 631-8223, B $4-7.25, L $5-18)*, Inn/B&B *(Harbor Light 631-2186, $145-365)*, *(Brimblecomb Hill 631-3172, $95-125)*, *(Herreshoff Castle 631-1950, $200, A real stone castle. Two-night min. No children)* **Under 1 mi:** Pizzeria *(Marblehead 631-4898)*, Inn/B&B *(Marblehead 631-1430, $99-250)*

Recreation and Entertainment

Near: Video Rental *(Chet's 631-9550)*, Park *(Crocker)*, Museum *(Marblehead Hist. Soc. 631-1768; 1768 Jeremiah Lee Mansion 631-1069; King Hooper Mansion 631-2608)*, Cultural Attract *(Summer Jazz 631-1528 Unitarian Church)*, Sightseeing *(Historic District)* **Under 1 mi:** Beach *(Fort Beach at Sewall)*, Picnic Area *(West to Crocker Park or East to Fort Sewall)*, Playground, Fitness Center *(Gravity Fitness 631-6533)*, Fishing Charter *(Sigler Guide 639-7763)* **1-3 mi:** Pool *(One Salem St Pool 586-1668)*, Boat Rentals *(Kayaks at Devereaux Beach)*, Movie Theater *(Salem 978-744-1400)* **3+ mi:** Golf Course *(Olde Salem 744-2149, 3 mi.)*

Provisioning and General Services

Near: Supermarket *(Crosby's 631-1741)*, Gourmet Shop *(Foodies Feast 639-1104)*, Delicatessen *(Muffin Shop 631-8223)*, Liquor Store *(Haley's 631-0169)*, Bakery *(Muffin Shop 631-8223)*, Bank/ATM, Protestant Church, Florist *(Flores Mantilla 631-9483)* **Under 1 mi:** Convenience Store *(7-Eleven)*, Wine/Beer *(Village 631-0570)*, Farmers' Market *(Sat 9am-noon Village St. 631-2868)*, Lobster Pound *(Marblehead Lobster 631-0787)*, Post Office, Catholic Church, Library *(Marblehead 631-1480)*, Beauty Salon, Dry Cleaners *(Marblehead 631-0526)*, Laundry *(Marblehead 631-0526)*, Bookstore *(Spirit of '76 631-7199)*, Pharmacy *(CVS 639-1412)*, Hardware Store *(Green's Ace 639-2257)* **1-3 mi:** Synagogue **3+ mi:** Department Store *(Target 978-224-4000, 3.5 mi.)*

Transportation

OnCall: Rental Car *(Enterprise 978-741-2780)*, Taxi *(VanGo 978-729-5998)*, Airport Limo *(Dependable 639-1020)* **Near:** Rail *("T" to Boston)* **Under 1 mi:** Bikes *(Marblehead 631-1570)* **Airport:** Logan Int'l. *(15 mi.)*

Medical Services

911 Service **Near:** Dentist *(Bolen 631-3799)*, Holistic Services *(Hand in Hand 639-4380)* **Under 1 mi:** Doctor *(Cohn 631-7594)*, Chiropractor *(Marblehead 639-0808)*, Optician *(Marblehead 631-6600)*, Veterinarian *(Marblehead 639-1300)* **Hospital:** North Shore 978-741-1200 *(3 mi.)*

Setting -- In the center of Marblehead's marine whirlwind, Tucker's Wharf is on the harbor's starboard side. Waterside views are of the picturesque harbor, one of the busiest on the North Shore, awash in beautiful boats - mostly sail. Landside is little Phillip T. Clark Public Landing Park, Marblehead Trading's yacht yard and The Landings Restaurant -- all surrounded by the historic district. Spot the weathered-shingle building with the very long gangway.

Marina Notes -- *218 ft. of alongside transient dockage. Maintained by the town & managed by Harbormaster. Sandy Carney in harbormaster's office can help with most questions. Recently rebuilt office with heads. Harbormaster oversees over 2000 moorings permitted to individuals and managed by five yacht clubs. Call individual clubs for mooring assignments. Larger vessel moorings at harbor's mouth also booked through the Y.C.'s. Adjacent Marblehead Trading's three yards offer most marine services. Busy in summer, but pandemonium reigns before biennial Marblehead-to-Halifax Ocean Race (early July) and Race Week (late July). Bathhouses: brand-new & handicap-accessible. Laundry. Additional public heads in Phillip T. Clark Park.

Notable -- Centrally located Tucker's Wharf makes a perfect starting point for a self-guided walking tour of Marblehead's charming historic district; more than 200 impeccably preserved private, colonial-era houses and commercial buildings line a labyrinth of narrow, winding lanes (pick up a map or download an audio tour at visitmarblehead.com). Don't miss the Jeremiah Lee and King Hooper Mansions (home to the Arts Association) and Abbott Hall on Washington Square (now the town offices) where Willard's "Spirit of '76" painting hangs. Head north to Fort Sewell, established in 1644 on Gale's Head, for spectacular views.

11. MA: NORTH SHORE

PHOTOS ON DVD: 19

    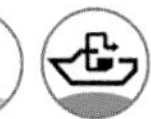

Navigational Information

Lat: 42°30.126' **Long:** 070°51.002' **Tide:** 10 ft. **Current:** .5 kt. **Chart:** 13275
Rep. Depths (*MLW*): Entry 20 ft. **Fuel Dock** 6 ft. **Max Slip/Moor** -/20 ft.
Access: Marblehead Harbor about half way, 3rd facility on Western shore

Marina Facilities *(In Season/Off Season)*

Fuel: *Private* - Gasoline, Diesel
Slips: 0 Total, 0 Transient **Max LOA:** 50 ft. **Max Beam:** n/a
Rate *(per ft.)*: **Day** n/a **Week** n/a **Month** n/a
Power: 30 amp n/a, **50 amp** n/a, **100 amp** n/a, **200 amp** n/a
Cable TV: No **Dockside Phone:** No
Dock Type: n/a
Moorings: 200 Total, 5 Transient **Launch:** Yes (Free), Dinghy Dock
Rate: Day $35 **Week** n/a **Month** n/a
Heads: 4 Toilet(s), 4 Shower(s)
Internet: Yes *(Wi-Fi, Free)* **Laundry:** None
Pump-Out: OnCall, Full Service, 1 Port **Fee:** Free **Closed Heads:** Yes

Marina Operations

Owner/Manager: Bob Pescatore **Dockmaster:** Ken Breen
In-Season: May-Oct, 8am-10pm **Off-Season:** Nov-April, 9am-3pm
After-Hours Arrival: Call same day
Reservations: No **Credit Cards:** Visa/MC, Amex
Discounts: None
Pets: Welcome **Handicap Access:** Yes, Heads, Docks

Boston Yacht Club

One Front Street; Marblehead, MA 01945

Tel: (781) 631-3100 **VHF: Monitor** Ch. 68 **Talk** Ch. 68
Fax: (781) 631-9059 **Alternate Tel:** n/a
Email: dockmaster@bostonyachtclub.net **Web:** www.bostonyachtclub.net
Nearest Town: Marblehead *(0.2 mi.)* **Tourist Info:** (781) 631-2868

Marina Services and Boat Supplies

Services - Boaters' Lounge **Communication -** Pay Phone (1), FedEx, DHL, UPS, Express Mail *(Sat Del)* **Supplies - Near:** Ships' Store *(Lynn Marine 631-1305 7 days)*, CNG *(Forepeak 781-631-7184)* **1-3 mi:** West Marine *(639-6451)*, Propane *(U-Haul 978-744-6030)*

Boatyard Services

OnCall: Engine mechanic *(gas, diesel)*, Divers **Nearest Yard:** Marblehead Trading (781) 639-0029

Restaurants and Accommodations

OnSite: Restaurant *(Boston Y.C. Dining Room, Gazebo & Lounge - Recip. Y.C. Members only*)*, Inn/B&B *(Boston Yacht Club - Ships' Cabins 631-3100, Recip. Y.C. Members only)* **Near:** Restaurant *(The Landing 639-1266, L $9-20, D $11-32, lunch menu in pub at night)*, *(Pellino's Italian 631-3344, D $13-35)*, *(Ataraxis Tavern 639-2100, was Flynnies)*, *(Jack Tar 631-2323, D $9-23, kid's menu)*, *(Sweeney's 631-6469, L & D $7-17)*, Snack Bar *(Coffey Ice Cream 639-1545)*, Coffee Shop *(Driftwood 631-1145)*, Lite Fare *(The Muffin Shop 631-8223, B $4-7.25, L $5-18)*, Pizzeria *(House of Pizza 631-4898)*, Inn/B&B *(Harborside 631-1032)*, *(Marblehead 631-1430, $138-325)*, *(Harbor Light 631-2186, $145-365)*, *(Herreshoff Castle 631-1950, $145-365)*

Recreation and Entertainment

Near: Video Rental *(Chet's 631-9550)*, Park *(Crocker - adjacent)*, Museum *(Jeremiah Lee Mansion 631-1768)*, Cultural Attract *(Marblehead Little Theatre 631-9697)*, Sightseeing *(Historic District)*, Galleries *(Marblehead Arts Assoc in King Hooper Mansion)*, Special Events *(Race Week, late July; Halifax Race July 4)* **Under 1 mi:** Tennis Courts *(Seaside Park - lighted)*, Fitness Center *(Gravity 631-6533)*, Fishing Charter *(Sigler 639-7763)* **1-3 mi:** Beach *(Devereaux)*, Golf Course *(Olde Salem Green 978-744-2149)*, Boat Rentals *(Kayaks at Devereaux Beach)*, Movie Theater *(Salem 978-744-1400)*, Video Arcade *(Salem Willows 978-745-0251)*

Provisioning and General Services

Near: Convenience Store *(7-Eleven)*, Market *(Shubie's 631-0149)*, Supermarket *(Crosby's 631-1741)*, Delicatessen *(Muffin Shop 631-8223)*, Liquor Store *(Haley's Package 631-0169)*, Bakery *(Muffin Shop 631-8223)*, Bank/ATM, Protestant Church, Beauty Salon, Pharmacy *(Walgreens 631-0800)*, Florist *(Flores Mantilla 631-9483)* **Under 1 mi:** Wine/Beer *(Village 631-0570)*, Farmers' Market *(Sat 9am-noon Village Street)*, Lobster Pound *(Marblehead 631-0787)*, Post Office, Catholic Church, Library *(Marblehead 631-1480)*, Barber Shop, Dry Cleaners *(Marblehead 631-0526)*, Laundry *(Marblehead 631-0526)*, Bookstore *(Spirit of '76 631-7199)*, Hardware Store *(Green's 639-2257)*, Copies Etc. *(UPS Store 631-1669)* **1-3 mi:** Synagogue **3+ mi:** Health Food *(Whole Foods 592-2200, 3.3 mi.)*

Transportation

OnCall: Rental Car *(Enterprise 978-741-2780)*, Taxi *(Tri-City 639-2488)*, Airport Limo *(Dependable 639-1020)* **Near:** Rail *(MBTA to Boston)* **Under 1 mi:** Bikes *(Marblehead 631-1570)* **Airport:** Logan Int'l. *(15 mi.)*

Medical Services

911 Service **Near:** Holistic Services *(Hand In Hand 639-4380)*, Veterinarian *(Marblehead 639-1300)* **Under 1 mi:** Chiropractor *(Marblehead 639-0808)*, Optician *(Marblehead 631-6600)* **1-3 mi:** Doctor *(North Shore 631-5454)*, Dentist *(Bolen 631-3799)* **Hospital:** North Shore 978-741-1200 *(3 mi.)*

Setting -- South of the town landing, BYC's large, beautifully maintained three-story, white-trimmed, gray-clapboard clubhouse rises above a set of upscale, floating docks hosting dinghies, launches, fuel tanks and big boat temporary tie-ups. White rockers march along wonderful open porches that overhang the water. Inside lovely living areas, dining spaces and hotel rooms occupy expansive and impeccable quarters. Marblehead's Historic District is a stone's throw.

Marina Notes -- Founded in 1866. Third-oldest yacht club in the country & oldest in New England. Fuel dock (8am-6pm credit cards), Ice, washdown, dinghy docks. Mooring fee includes use of launch, heads & showers only. Summer launch hours 8am-11pm, Check shoulder season sked. *Members of reciprocating yacht clubs (who can charge to their club accounts) have access to: Main Dining Room, Commodore's Lounge Bar, Waterfront Gazebo & 14 hotel rooms (private'shared baths). Smart casual attire. Bathhouses: Main Clubhouse & Yardarm Building Luxurious, wainscot, granite counters, fiberglass stalls.

Notable -- B.Y.C., the only club in historic "Old Town," has played a leading role in America's Cup races and the U.S. Power Squadron founding in 1912. It held the first world women's sailing championship in 1924 and, in 1939, formalized the biennial Marblehead-to-Halifax Ocean Race and hosted the first N.A. World Disabled Sailing Championship. To really appreciate all of Marblehead's history, pick up a self-guided tour map and wander its narrow streets past lovingly preserved small clapboard houses, ship captains' mansions and carefully tended gardens - some that date back to 1629. Interspersed are many eateries, nautically themed shops, galleries, small provisioners and delightful B&Bs. More services are a mile away on Atlantic and Pleasant Streets.

PHOTOS ON DVD: 19

Dolphin Yacht Club

PO Box 905; 17 Allerton Place; Marblehead, MA 01945

Tel: (781) 631-8000 **VHF: Monitor** Ch. 16 **Talk** Ch. 68
Fax: n/a **Alternate Tel:** (781) 639-6399
Email: joeydddd@verizon.net **Web:** www.dolphinyachtclub.com
Nearest Town: Marblehead *(0 mi.)* **Tourist Info:** (781) 639-8469

Navigational Information

Lat: 42°29.912' **Long:** 070°51.061' **Tide:** 10 ft. **Current:** 1 kt. **Chart:** 13275
Rep. Depths (*MLW*): Entry 22 ft. **Fuel Dock** n/a **Max Slip/Moor** -/15 ft.
Access: Marblehead Harbor almost to head, 4th facility to starboard

Marina Facilities *(In Season/Off Season)*

Fuel: No
Slips: 0 Total, 0 Transient **Max LOA:** n/a **Max Beam:** n/a
Rate *(per ft.)*: **Day** n/a **Week** n/a **Month** n/a
Power: 30 amp n/a, **50 amp** n/a, **100 amp** n/a, **200 amp** n/a
Cable TV: No **Dockside Phone:** No
Dock Type: n/a
Moorings: 200 Total, 5 Transient **Launch:** Yes (Free), Dinghy Dock
Rate: Day $25 **Week** Inq. **Month** Inq.
Heads: 2 Toilet(s), 1 Shower(s)
Internet: No **Laundry:** None
Pump-Out: OnCall, Full Service, 1 Port **Fee:** Free **Closed Heads:** Yes

Marina Operations

Owner/Manager: Vin Conte (Commodore) **Dockmaster:** Joe Downes
In-Season: MemDay-LabDay, 8am-8pm **Off-Season:** Sep-Nov, Apr-May*
After-Hours Arrival: Call in advance
Reservations: Yes **Credit Cards:** Visa/MC, Cash, Check
Discounts: None
Pets: Welcome **Handicap Access:** No

Marina Services and Boat Supplies

Services - Trash Pick-Up, Dock Carts **Communication -** Mail & Package Hold, FedEx, DHL, UPS, Express Mail **Supplies - OnSite:** Ice *(Block, Cube)* **Near:** Ships' Store *(Lynn Marine 631-1305, Woods Nautical 631-0221)* **1-3 mi:** West Marine *(639-6451)*, Propane *(U-Haul 978-744-6030)*

Boatyard Services

OnCall: Engine mechanic *(gas, diesel)*, Electronic Sales *(Boatworks 639-7565)*, Divers **Nearest Yard:** Marblehead Trading (781) 639-0029

Restaurants and Accommodations

OnSite: Restaurant *("The View" - Dolphin Y.C. Dining Room 639-6399, Reserve! Outside deck, kids' menu)* **Near:** Restaurant *(Ataraxis Tavern 639-2100), (Mino's Roast Beef 631-7228), (Fen Yang 639-8386), (Pellino's 631-3344, D $13-35, pastas), (Sweeny's 631-6469, L & D $7-17)*, Inn/B&B *(Harborside House 631-1032), (Pheasant Hill 639-4799, $100-180), (Compass Rose 631-7599)* **Under 1 mi:** Restaurant *(Landing 639-1266, L $9-20, D $11-32, dinghy ride), (Barnacle 531-4236, D $12.50-22, kids' menu)*, Lite Fare *(Lime Rickeys 631-6700)*, Inn/B&B *(Notorious Annie's 631-0558, $195-295)*

Recreation and Entertainment

OnSite: Boat Rentals *(Kayaks - loaners)* **Near:** Picnic Area *(Crocker Park)*, Tennis Courts *(Seaside Park - lighted)*, Fitness Center *(Curves 631-2826)*, Video Rental *(Chet's 631-9550)*, Park *(Seaside Park)*, Museum *(Jeremiah Lee Mansion 631-1768 $5/Free)*, Sightseeing *(Marblehead Old Town Historic District Walking Tour)*, Special Events *(Race Week - late July; Halifax Race July 4)* **Under 1 mi:** Beach *(Devereaux Beach 631-3551)*, Fishing Charter *(Sigler 639-7763)*, Cultural Attract *(King Hooper Mansion, Marblehead Streets Assoc. 631-2608 Free)* **1-3 mi:** Pool, Playground, Golf Course *(Olde Salem Green 978-744-2149)*, Movie Theater *(Cinema 978-744-1400)*, Video Arcade *(Salem Willows 978-745-0251)*

Provisioning and General Services

Near: Convenience Store *(7-Eleven)*, Market *(Shubie's 631-0149)*, Farmers' Market *(Village St. Sat am 631-2868)*, Bank/ATM, Catholic Church, Protestant Church, Beauty Salon, Bookstore *(Spirit of '76 631-7199)*, Pharmacy *(CVS 639-1412)*, Hardware Store *(Green's Ace 639-2257)*, Florist *(Flores Mantilla 631-9483)*, Clothing Store, Retail Shops **Under 1 mi:** Supermarket *(Crosby's 631-1741)*, Delicatessen *(Muffin Shop 631-8223)*, Wine/Beer *(Village 631-0570)*, Liquor Store *(Haley's 631-0169)*, Bakery *(Muffin Shop 631-8223)*, Lobster Pound *(Marblehead 631-0787)*, Post Office, Library *(Marblehead 631-1480)*, Barber Shop, Dry Cleaners *(Marblehead 631-0526)*, Laundry **1-3 mi:** Health Food *(Whole Foods 592-2200)*, Synagogue, Copies Etc. *(Staples 978-741-4244)*

Transportation

OnCall: Rental Car *(Enterprise 978-741-2780)*, Taxi *(VanGo 978-729-5998)*, Airport Limo *(Dependable 639-1020)* **Under 1 mi:** Bikes *(Marblehead 631-1570)* **3+ mi:** Rail *(MBTA to Boston, 4.5 mi.)* **Airport:** Logan Int'l. *(15 mi.)*

Medical Services

911 Service **Near:** Optician *(Marblehead 631-6600)*, Veterinarian *(Marblehead 639-1300)* **Under 1 mi:** Doctor *(North Shore 631-5454)*, Dentist *(Bolen 631-3799)*, Chiropractor *(Milone 639-0808)*, Holistic Services *(Hand In Hand 639-4380)* **Hospital:** North Shore 978-741-1200 *(3 mi.)*

Setting -- Almost to the head of Marblehead Harbor, Dolphin's small, brown-shingled clubhouse perches high above its long, tidy launch and dinghy dock. Its white-trimmed decks deliver one of the best panoramas of the tightly packed and beautiful mooring field - well worth climbing the steeply pitched gangway at low tide. Landside, an entirely residential neighborhood translates into quiet evenings.

Marina Notes -- *Reduced hours Spring and Fall. Established 1951. Small and hospitable. A mooring guest is a guest of the Club. Services include launch (Summer 8am-9pm, 10pm Fri & Sat), ice, bathhouse, two decks plus a friendly bar and "The View" dining room (lunch and dinner service Mon-Sat Noon-10pm, Sun to 8pm) in recently remodeled window-walled dining room or on the deck - overlooking the harbor). Dining room available for private functions. Ongoing facility upgrade. Lots of kayakers (a membership category) - wonderful way to explore the nearby coves. No rentals, loaners may be possible. Bathhouse: Neat, small, sweet with wallpaper borders - wicker furnished ante-room.

Notable -- Dolphin is just outside the historic district and an easy walk to 34-acre Seaside Park. Established in 1895, it has lighted tennis courts, a baseball diamond, basketball, and exercise trails. The beaches are also nearby - Riverhead and famous 5.5-acre Devereux on the causeway to "The Neck" with pavilions, benches, picnic tables, restroom facilities, and Lime Ricky's beach shack. D.Y.C. is also closer to the more commercial downtown area that runs along Atlantic and Pleasant Streets. Consider renting a bike to navigate the skinny, one-way streets or dinghy down harbor to the Town Landing.

PHOTOS ON DVD: 17

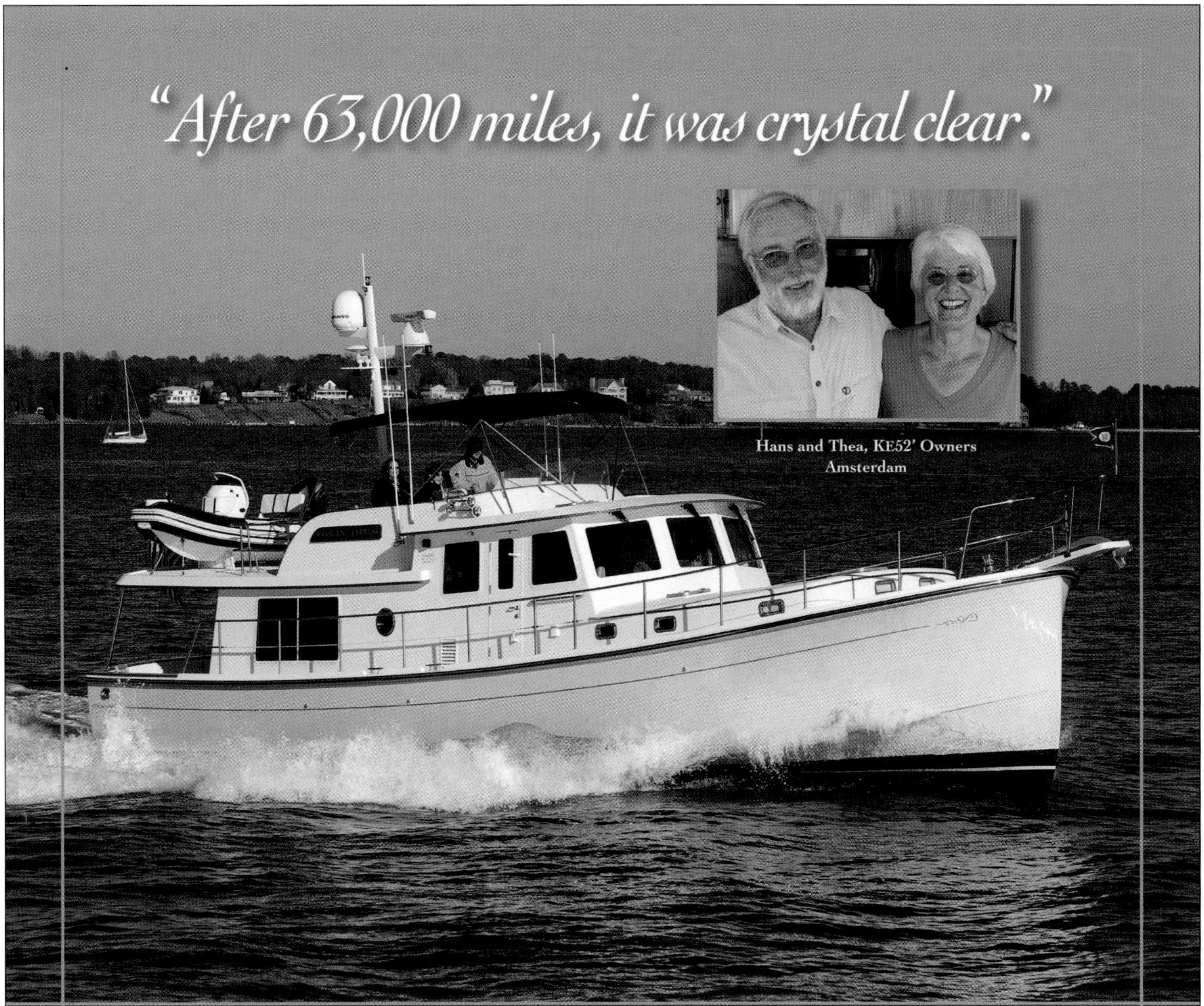
"After 63,000 miles, it was crystal clear."
Hans and Thea, KE52' Owners
Amsterdam

Cruising is our Passion

We know it's yours, too. Enjoy more of your time on the water with the confidence that Maptech products deliver. New England boaters trust the experience, accuracy and local knowledge of the ***Embassy Cruising Guide,*** the legendary ***ChartKit***® and the tough, tear-resistant ***Waterproof Chartbook.*** With these onboard you'll be… Cruising with Confidence.

New England Companion Series

- **Embassy Cruising Guide – New England Coast**
  The most comprehensive and accurate guide available. Local knowledge, navigation advice, photos, and marina information.
- **ChartKit®– Region 2: Block Island, RI to the Canadian Border**
  Full-color reproductions of NOAA charts bundled together in large cruising regions.
- **Compact ChartKit® Narragansett Bay to Nantucket**
  A waterproof version of a smaller geographic area of the ChartKit®.
- **Waterproof Chartbooks – Covering Cape Cod to Mount Desert Island**
  Conveniently sized charts on waterproof pages.

Purchase at your local marine dealer or bookstore.

1-888-839-5551 | www.maptech.com

MAPTECH®

Navigate with Confidence.

12. MA – Boston Harbor Region

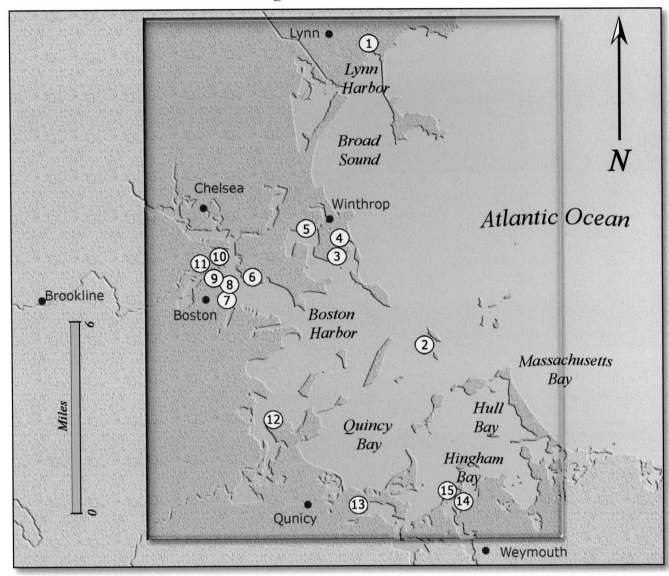

MAP	MARINA	HARBOR	PAGE
1	**Seaport Landing Marina**	*Lynn Harbor*	*226*
2	**Boston Harbor Islands**	*Boston Outer Harbor*	*227*
3	**Winthrop Town Pier**	*President Roads*	*228*
4	**Crystal Cove Marina**	*President Roads*	*229*
5	**Atlantis Marina**	*President Roads*	*230*
6	**Boston Harbor Shipyard & Marina**	*Boston Harbor*	*231*
7	**The Marina at Rowes Wharf**	*Boston Harbor*	*232*
8	**Boston Waterboat Marina**	*Boston Harbor*	*233*
9	**Boston Yacht Haven**	*Boston Harbor*	*234*
10	**Shipyard Quarters Marina**	*Boston Harbor*	*235*
11	**Constitution Marina**	*Boston Harbor*	*236*
12	**Marina Bay**	*Dorchester Bay*	*237*
13	**Captain's Cove Marina**	*Weymouth Fore River*	*238*
14	**Hingham Shipyard Marinas**	*Weymouth Back River*	*239*
15	**Tern Harbor Marina**	*Weymouth Back River*	*240*

RATINGS: 1-5 for Marina Facilities & Amenities, 1-2 for Boatyard Services,  1-2 for MegaYacht Facilities,  for Something Special.

SERVICES: for CCM – Certified Clean Marina,  for Pump-Out, for Internet,  for Fuel, for Restaurant,  for Provisioning nearby, for Catamaran-friendly,  for SportFish Charter, for Pool/Beach, and for Golf within a mile. *For an explanation of ACC's Ratings, see page 8.*

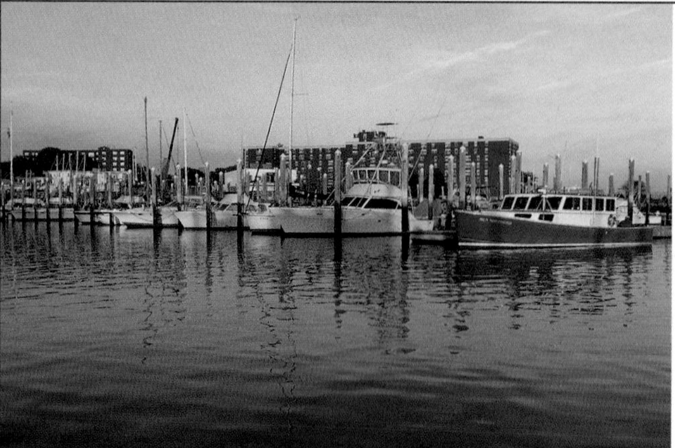

Seaport Landing Marina

154 Lynnway; Lynn, MA 01902

Tel: (781) 592-5821 **VHF: Monitor** Ch. 16 **Talk** Ch. 9
Fax: n/a **Alternate Tel:** n/a
Email: Seaportmarina@verizon.net **Web:** See marina notes
Nearest Town: Lynn *(0.25 mi.)* **Tourist Info:** (781) 592-2900

Navigational Information

Lat: 42°27.496' **Long:** 070°56.631' **Tide:** 9 ft. **Current:** 2 kt. **Chart:** 13275
Rep. Depths (*MLW*): Entry 20 ft. **Fuel Dock** 20 ft. **Max Slip/Moor** 20 ft./15 ft.
Access: Massachusetts Bay to Flip Rock Buoy to Lynn Channel R2

Marina Facilities *(In Season/Off Season)*

Fuel: *Private* - Gasoline, Diesel
Slips: 165 Total, 20 Transient **Max LOA:** 200 ft. **Max Beam:** 50 ft.
Rate *(per ft.)*: **Day** $2.00/$1.00 **Week** n/a **Month** n/a
Power: 30 amp Incl., **50 amp** Incl., **100 amp** n/a, **200 amp** n/a
Cable TV: No **Dockside Phone:** No
Dock Type: Floating, Long Fingers, Pilings, Concrete
Moorings: 400 Total, 0 Transient **Launch:** n/a
Rate: Day n/a **Week** n/a **Month** n/a
Heads: 2 Toilet(s), 2 Shower(s)
Internet: No **Laundry:** 1 Washer(s), 1 Dryer(s)
Pump-Out: OnSite, Self Service **Fee:** Free **Closed Heads:** Yes

Marina Operations

Owner/Manager: James Perry (Hrbrmstr) **Dockmaster:** Derek Locke
In-Season: Apr 15-Oct, 7am-7pm **Off-Season:** Nov-Apr 14, 9am-5pm
After-Hours Arrival: Call ahead on channels 9 or 16
Reservations: Yes **Credit Cards:** Visa/MC, Amex
Discounts: None
Pets: Welcome **Handicap Access:** No

Marina Services and Boat Supplies

Services - Docking Assistance, Concierge, Security *(Security guard)*, Dock Carts **Communication -** Pay Phone (2), FedEx, DHL, UPS, Express Mail *(Sat Del)* **Supplies - OnSite:** Ice *(Block, Cube)*, Ships' Store *(Will order anything for overnight delivery)* **Under 1 mi:** Bait/Tackle *(10 min by boat)*, Propane **3+ mi:** West Marine *(978-639-6451, 6 mi.)*

Boatyard Services

OnCall: Engine mechanic *(gas, diesel)*, Electrical Repairs, Electronics Repairs, Canvas Work **Near:** Travelift, Rigger, Divers, Compound, Wash & Wax, Interior Cleaning, Propeller Repairs. **Under 1 mi:** Launching Ramp. **Nearest Yard:** Lynn Yacht Club (781) 595-9825

Restaurants and Accommodations

OnSite: Restaurant *(The Porthole 595-7733, L $5-18, D $5-24, L 11:30am-4pm, D 4-9:30pm; Live entertainment weekends)* **Near:** Seafood Shack *(Christie's 598-1122, Self-service takeout)*, Coffee Shop *(Capitol Diner 595-9314)* **Under 1 mi:** Restaurant *(Blue Ox 780-5722)*, Fast Food *(Dunkin Donuts, Wendy's, McDs, KFC)*, Inn/B&B *(Diamond District 595-4770, $165-295)* **1-3 mi:** Restaurant *(Green Tea 595-2100, L $5-8, D $9-18, Asian)*, Inn/B&B *(Oceanview 598-6388)*, *(Capt. Jack's 595-7910, $100-350)*

Recreation and Entertainment

OnSite: Special Events *(Bluefish Tournament - Aug, Lynn Harbor Monster Day - Childrens' Fest - 2nd Sat in Aug)* **OnCall:** Boat Rentals *(Vista 258-7344)*, Fishing Charter *(Sheawater 599-1143)* **Near:** Beach *(Lynn & Nahant Beaches - 3-mile sand crescent, favorite of boardsailers)*, Picnic Area, Playground, Jogging Paths, Hike/Bike Trails, Park *(Lynn Heritage State Park - elegantly renovated shoe factory is visitors' center which includes an early 1800s shoe shop plus a 4-acre oceanfront promenade)*, Sightseeing *(Walking tour of original shoe factories - brochure at Lynn Historical Society)* **Under 1 mi:** Tennis Courts *(Gas Wharf Rd. off Lynnway)*, Party Boat *(Walsh's Deep Sea Fishing 592-9505)*, Museum *(City of Lynn Historical Society 592-2465 $4 - restored 1836 house shelters a diverse collection and an extensive research library)* **1-3 mi:** Golf Course *(Kelley Greens 581-0840; Gannon Municipal 592-8238)*

Provisioning and General Services

OnSite: Beauty Salon *(Seaport 593-5410)* **Near:** Convenience Store *(Johnny's 592-4311)*, Liquor Store *(Santo Domingo 598-3272)*, Bank/ATM, Post Office, Catholic Church **Under 1 mi:** Supermarket *(Shaw's 599-8473)*, Gourmet Shop, Delicatessen *(Junction Deli 595-9827)*, Wine/Beer, Farmers' Market *(Thurs. 11am-3pm. Corner Union & Exchange Streets)*, Fishmonger *(Seafood America 581-5180)*, Library, Dry Cleaners, Laundry, Pharmacy *(Walgreens 593-1230)*, Hardware Store *(Beden 592-6260)*, Florist, Retail Shops *(Lynn Marketplace)*, Department Store *(WalMart)*, Copies Etc.

Transportation

OnCall: Rental Car *(Enterprise 581-5000)*, Taxi *(Tom's 595-0049)*, Airport Limo *(All-City 595-0688)* **Near:** Local Bus **Under 1 mi:** Rail *("T" to Boston; Boston Amtrak 8 mi.)* **Airport:** Logan Int'l. *(6 mi.)*

Medical Services

911 Service **OnSite:** Holistic Services *(Seaport Day Spa 593-5410)* **Near:** Dentist *(Seaport 581-2797)*, Chiropractor *(Ryan 595-6560)* **1-3 mi:** Doctor *(Nalesnik 595-9581)* **Hospital:** Union Hospital 581-9200 *(4 mi.)*

Setting -- Seaward of a modest six-story brick residential and professional offices complex and surrounded by a boardwalk, Lynn's large municipal facility is hard to miss after entering the long channel. The expansive network of floating concrete docks shares the harbor with the Lynn and Volunteer Yacht Clubs. Along the boardwalk, an impressive nine-panel mosaic mural depicts the history of Lynn, highlighting its role in the shoe industry. Adjacent is the Lynn Heritage Waterfront Park - the Boston skyline is magnificent at dawn and dusk

Marina Notes -- Web: ci.lynn.ma.us/attractions_waterfront. Slips accommodate boats to 65 ft. LOA, larger vessels on T-heads. Operated by Lynn City; 24-hour security. Ongoing maintenance, but age is showing. Mechanical and other marine services at adjacent yacht clubs. Accommodating staff. Free afternoon tie-up for those taking Horizon's Edge casino boat (800-582-5932). Onsite Porthole seafood restaurant sports views over its parking lot to marina docks. Bathhouse: A bit beyond utilitarian municipal - fully tiled with glass shower stalls. Laundry with coffee pot & microwave.

Notable -- A once gritty manufacturing city, Lynn's fascinating attractions trace its history as an early center of "invisibly stitched" women's shoes. A protective tarriff imposed in the early 19thC. made Lynn the ladies shoe center of the world. Founded in 1897, the Historical Society, a 0.4 mile walk, tells the city's story with diverse collections -- including more shoe stories. A shore-front mile walk leads to Lynn's Diamond Historical District, an enclave of architecturally important 19thC mansions -- many built by shoe manufacturers. For necessities, Lynn Marketplace Mall is about 0.4 mile - beyond Lynn Heritage State Park.

12. MA - BOSTON HARBOR REGION

PHOTOS ON DVD: 19

Navigational Information

Lat: 42°19.268' **Long:** 070°55.864' **Tide:** 10 ft. **Current:** 2 kt. **Chart:** 13272
Rep. Depths (*MLW*): Entry 10 ft. **Fuel Dock** n/a **Max Slip/Moor** 15 ft./20 ft.
Access: Outer Harbor to Gallops, George's, Long Island, Rainford, Peddocks

Marina Facilities *(In Season/Off Season)*

Fuel: No
Slips: 40 Total, 40 Transient **Max LOA:** 80 ft. **Max Beam:** 20 ft.
Rate *(per ft.)*: **Day** $2.00* **Week** n/a **Month** n/a
Power: 30 amp n/a, **50 amp** n/a, **100 amp** n/a, **200 amp** n/a
Cable TV: No **Dockside Phone:** No
Dock Type: Floating, Pilings, Alongside, Concrete
Moorings: 30 Total, 30 Transient **Launch:** No
Rate: Day $30* **Week** n/a **Month** n/a
Heads: 6 Toilet(s), 4 Shower(s)
Internet: No **Laundry:** None
Pump-Out: OnCall, Full Service **Fee:** Free **Closed Heads:** Yes

Marina Operations

Owner/Manager: Tom Cox **Dockmaster:** Cathy Collins
In-Season: May-Oct **Off-Season:** Nov-Apr, Closed
After-Hours Arrival: Call in advance
Reservations: Yes **Credit Cards:** Visa/MC, Dscvr, Amex
Discounts: None
Pets: Welcome **Handicap Access:** No

Boston Harbor Islands

408 Atlantic Avenue, Suite 228; Boston, MA 02210

Tel: (781) 749-5900 **VHF: Monitor** Ch. 69 **Talk** Ch. 69
Fax: (617) 242-3013 **Alternate Tel:** (617) 223-8666
Email: boha_information@nps.gov **Web:** bostonharborislands.org
Nearest Town: Boston *(3 mi.)* **Tourist Info:** (223) 866-6617

Marina Services and Boat Supplies

Services - Trash Pick-Up **Supplies - OnSite:** Ice *(Block, Cube)*, Bait/Tackle *(Capt. Flye's - Fishing Rod rentals, bait)*

Boatyard Services

Nearest Yard: Boston Harbor Shipyard (617) 561-1400

Restaurants and Accommodations

OnSite: Lite Fare *(Jasper White's Summer Shack Lunch & Thurs' night clam bake on Spectacle Island), (George's Island Snack Bar B $3-5, L $5-12, D $5-28, Saturday night clambake on George's Island - Catered Outdoor grill with picnic tables 9:30am-7pm)*

Recreation and Entertainment

OnSite: Beach *(Spectacle - Life-guarded, Umbrellas & Adirondack Chairs; Lovells - un-supervised swimming beach with dunes;)*, Hike/Bike Trails *(Spectacle - 5 miles of trails leading to 157 ft. hill for panoramic views)*, Park, Museum *(Explore National Historic Landmark 1833 Fort Warren & its Visitor Center on George's Island - also picnic grounds, open fields, paved walkways, parade ground)*, Tours *(Sea Kayak Tours - 5 kayaks with leader. Jul & Aug. 1st come. 14 yrs +. 90-min Grape Island tour - Wed, Thu, Sat, Sun. 30-min Intro at Spectacle Mon, Wed, Thurs)* **OnCall:** Dive Shop *(Boston Harbor Diving 617-846-5151)*

Near: Picnic Area *(On George's and most other islands. Plus berry picking for raspberries, blackberries and wild rose hips on Grape)*, Grills *(Beach fires below the high-tide line only)*, Jogging Paths *(Deer Island, a peninsula attached to Winthrop, has 4.5 mi. of trails around perimeter of Treatment Plant and 2 mi. of interior hill trails in 60 acre park 617-788-1170; Peddock's has trails around Ft. Andrews)*, Cultural Attract *(157-acre Thompson, home to an Outward Bound program, marsh tour - Sun with Ranger)*, Sightseeing *(Little Brewster Island's last "manned" lighthouse - Fri, Sat, Sun 10 & 1:30pm 617-223-8666; take a nature walk on Peddocks, see wildflowers on Bumpkin or roses on Great Brewster)*, Special Events *(Over 50 Free events, i.e. Sun. afternoon Jazz at Spectacle; "Wild edibles" tour of Grape Island; old-fashioned baseball; Berklee Rock Concerts at George's Island 617 223 8666)*

Transportation

OnSite: Water Taxi *(From George's Island to Bumpkin, Lovells, Peddocks, & Spectacles 9am-Sundown)*, Ferry Service *(George's & Spectacle Islands to Boston/Long Wharf-North several times daily 223-8666. Plus to Hingham/Hingham Shipyard, Hewetts Cove, Hull at Pemberton Point $14/RT)* **Airport:** Logan Int'l. *(5 mi.)*

Medical Services

911 Service **Hospital:** Mass. General 617-726-2000 *(7 mi.)*

PHOTOS ON DVD: 23

Setting -- Just seven miles from downtown Boston, the 34 Harbor Islands offer quiet, protected, remote anchorages, mooring fields, and overnight slips. Twelve are open for exploration with 30 moorings spread across five of the islands. Start at Spectacle Island's high, 300-foot long pier that protects a small marina. The wind-swept, hilly island features 360-degree harbor and ocean vistas, inviting beaches and a solar-powered, expansive visitors' center.

Marina Notes -- *Spectacle Island: Day $20 to 30 ft., $30 30 ft. plus. Overnight: Thu-Sun $2/ft., $50 min. Moorings $20/day, $30/overnight. 30 moorings located off Long, Peddocks, Gallops, Georges & Rainsford Islands.1200 lb. numbered mushrooms (Pay at marina). Anchoring in coves permitted. Managed by Island Alliance & Hingham Harbor Marina. No electricity. Limited fresh water. Generators off by 11pm. Pets confined to boat to protect native wildlife. Dock at George's Island on first-come basis during daylight hours. Docks at Grape, Bumpkin, Lovells & Peddocks for drop-off only (anchor/moor offshore, then dinghy in). Permit camping on Grape, Bumpkin, Peddocks & Lovells (compost toilets). Bathhouse: On Spectacle. Like new, tile floors, heads, outdoor showers.

Notable -- In sight of downtown Boston, the archipelago promises skyline and ocean views, spectacular sunsets, hiking trails, historic sights, inter-island water shuttles, campsites, and beaches made usable by the Boston Harbor cleanup. The undeveloped islands are quiet except when daytrippers arrive by ferry - but at sundown boaters and campers rule. Virtual Island Caching provides a fun tour. Check out a GPS unit and Site Sheets at the Spectacle Island Visitor Center or use your own GPS and download the sheets (bostonharborislands.org/islandcache-program) and your dink or the inter-island ferries.

Winthrop Town Pier

Winthrop Town Pier

707 Shirley Street; Winthrop, MA 02152

Tel: (617) 839-4000 **VHF: Monitor** Ch. 9 **Talk** Ch. 6
Fax: n/a **Alternate Tel:** (617) 846-3474
Email: cfamolare@aol.com **Web:** www.town.winthrop.ma.us
Nearest Town: Winthrop **Tourist Info:** (617) 846-9898

Navigational Information

Lat: 42°22.016' **Long:** 070°58.411' **Tide:** 10 ft. **Current:** 1 kt. **Chart:** 13270
Rep. Depths (*MLW*): Entry 15 ft. **Fuel Dock** n/a **Max Slip/Moor** 10 ft./-
Access: President Roads to G3

Marina Facilities *(In Season/Off Season)*

Fuel: No
Slips: 30 Total, 5 Transient **Max LOA:** 100 ft. **Max Beam:** n/a
Rate *(per ft.)*: **Day** $2.00 **Week** n/a **Month** n/a
Power: 30 amp Incl., **50 amp** Incl., **100 amp** n/a, **200 amp** n/a
Cable TV: No **Dockside Phone:** No
Dock Type: Floating, Long Fingers, Pilings, Alongside, Wood
Moorings: 0 Total, 0 Transient **Launch:** n/a, Dinghy Dock
Rate: Day n/a **Week** n/a **Month** n/a
Heads: 2 Toilet(s), 2 Shower(s)
Internet: Yes *(Wi-Fi, Free)* **Laundry:** None
Pump-Out: OnSite, Full Service **Fee:** Free **Closed Heads:** Yes

Marina Operations

Owner/Manager: Chuck Famolare (Hrbmstr) **Dockmaster:** Joe Montalto
In-Season: May-Oct 15, 8am-5pm **Off-Season:** Oct 16-Apr, closed
After-Hours Arrival: Call ahead
Reservations: Yes **Credit Cards:** Visa/MC, Amex
Discounts: None
Pets: Welcome **Handicap Access:** Yes, Heads, Docks

Marina Services and Boat Supplies

Services - Docking Assistance, Security **Communication -** FedEx, UPS, Express Mail **Supplies - OnSite:** Ice *(Block, Cube)* **Under 1 mi:** Marine Discount Store *(Ward 846-1421)* **1-3 mi:** Bait/Tackle *(Bob's 846-5896, Fresh & Frozen bait)* **3+ mi:** Propane *(American 387-5065, 5 mi.)*

Boatyard Services

OnCall: Engine mechanic *(gas, diesel)* **Nearest Yard:** Crystal Cove (617) 846-7245

Restaurants and Accommodations

Near: Restaurant *(Winthrop YC 846-9774, D $9-20, open to public)*, *(Trattoria di Parma 846-5867, D $8-14, BYOB)*, *(Alia Ristorante 539-1600)*, *(Gary's 539-0020)*, Snack Bar *(Twist and Shake 846-8500, Ice cream and frozen yogurt)*, Lite Fare *(Panini 846-3839, L & D $6-13)* **Under 1 mi:** Restaurant *(La Siesta 846-2300, L $4-11, D $8-20, Mexican)*, *(Lucky Garden 846-8560, Asian)*, Coffee Shop *(Moonstruck 846-8866, B $5-11)*, *(Jac's Cafe 846-7496, Open 6am-3pm, breakfast and lunch, coffee and bagels)*, Lite Fare *(Cafe Delight 539-1535, L $6-10, dinghy)*, Pizzeria *(Nick's Place 846-9800, Delivers)*, Motel *(Suburban 539-9466, $99)*, Hotel *(Winthrop Arms 846-4000, $93)*, Inn/B&B *(Inn at Crystal Cove 846-9217, $89)*

Recreation and Entertainment

OnSite: Picnic Area, Boat Rentals *(Belle Isle Kayak Adventures 719-2036)*, Fishing Charter *(CJ Victoria 283-5801)* **Near:** Beach *(Winthrop & Yirrell)*, Playground *(Massa)*, Jogging Paths, Party Boat, Park *(Coughlin Park at Point Shirley)*, Museum *(1637 Deane Winthrop House - by appt. 846-8606)* **Under 1 mi:** Golf Course *(Winthrop 846-9775)* **1-3 mi:** Tennis Courts *(Ingleside Park)*, Hike/Bike Trails *(Deer Island)*, Bowling *(Central Park 567-7073)*, Video Rental *(RedBox 733-2693)*, Tours, Cultural Attract *(Suffolk Downs Thoroughbred racing. Recently restored 1935 art deco Clubhouse)*, Sightseeing *(Belle Isle Reservation - 152 acres of salt marsh incl. 28 acres of landscaped park, hiking trails, birding)*, Special Events *(Winthrop Playmakers 539-1175)*

Provisioning and General Services

Near: Convenience Store, Bank/ATM, Post Office, Barber Shop *(Gio's 539-1900)*, Dry Cleaners *(Surf 846-9762)*, Laundry, Pharmacy *(CVS 539-1751)* **Under 1 mi:** Market *(Winthrop Market Place 846-6880)*, Bakery *(Crusty Crumpet 846-0429)*, Meat Market *(The Meat Market 846-6303)*, Protestant Church *(St John's Episcopal Church 846-2363)*, Beauty Salon *(Mally's 846-5444)*, Bookstore *(Winthrop Book Depot 846-3099)*, Florist *(Christopher's 846-7161)*, Clothing Store *(Luna Boutique 846-4644)* **1-3 mi:** Supermarket *(Shaw's 781-286-3750)*

Transportation

OnSite: Ferry Service *(MV Anna to Rowes Wharf 227-4321 $6/3 - Weekdays)* **OnCall:** Rental Car *(Enterprise 561-4488)*, Taxi *(Viking 846-6000)* **Near:** Local Bus *("T" 222-5000 - 712 & 713)* **Under 1 mi:** Rail *(MBTA 222-3200)* **Airport:** Logan Int'l *(6 mi.)*

Medical Services

911 Service **Near:** Doctor *(Desai 846-1318)* **Under 1 mi:** Dentist *(Brooks 846-1811)*, Chiropractor *(Corcoran 846-3502)*, Holistic Services *(Winthrop 539-5744)*, Optician *(Designer 539-3937)* **1-3 mi:** Veterinarian *(E. Boston 567-0101)* **Hospital:** Mass Gen - Revere 781-485-6000 *(3 mi.)*

Setting -- After passing the enormous Deer Island Treatment plant, the Irving H. Streeter Memorial Pier is about a mile to starboard - beyond Snake Island. The sturdy 90-by-24 foot, green-railed ferry wharf and massive steel float and gangways make it easy to spot. Teed off from the wharf are floats hosting 30 stern-to tie-ups for commercial, municipal and recreational vessels plus large yacht T-heads. The upland facilities, part of the ongoing Winthrop Harbor Walk project, share the views of the Boston skyline and Logan airport across the water. The brown-shingled, three-story Winthrop Yacht Club is just north.

Marina Notes -- Owned by town of Winthrop. Redevelopment process started in 2009. All facilities very new. Marina services & fuel at Crystal Cove Marina, less than a quarter mile. Action Mobile Marine comes to dock. Second-generation entrepreneurial harbormaster very proud of this operation. All handicap-accessible. Dining available at adjacent Winthrop YC. No moorings or anchoring - but 6 moorings at Deer Island. Keep a wide berth from Logan airport's security zone. Bathhouse: Municipal but new. Note: Well-protected in a Northerly or Northeasterly blow.

Notable -- Winthrop is bounded on its east side by two long stretches of Atlantic beach just a few blocks walk: Winthrop Shore Drive and Shirley Street. For plane watching, the Town Pier's a great spot (or Point Shirley in Coughlin Park). Deer Island, a 210-acre peninsula attached to Winthrop (one of the Harbor Islands), hosts a $3.8 billion sewage treatment plant that is saving Boston Harbor. Five miles of trails skirt the perimeter past the egg-shaped "digesters" and through the 60-acre park (dogs permitted). Ten overlooks deliver spectacular views. Boston is within view and accessible via ferry, "T" or taxi.

Navigational Information

Lat: 42°22.262' **Long:** 070°58.275' **Tide:** 10 ft. **Current:** 1 kt. **Chart:** 13270
Rep. Depths (*MLW*): Entry 15 ft. **Fuel Dock** n/a **Max Slip/Moor** 7 ft./-
Access: President Roads to G3, follow channel past Winthrop YC

Marina Facilities *(In Season/Off Season)*

Fuel: Gasoline, Diesel, High-Speed Pumps
Slips: 120 Total, 5 Transient **Max LOA:** 75 ft. **Max Beam:** n/a
Rate *(per ft.)*: **Day** $3.00/Inq. **Week** $9 **Month** $31
Power: 30 amp Incl., **50 amp** Incl., **100 amp** n/a, **200 amp** n/a
Cable TV: No **Dockside Phone:** No
Dock Type: Floating, Short Fingers, Wood
Moorings: 0 Total, 0 Transient **Launch:** n/a, Dinghy Dock
Rate: Day n/a **Week** n/a **Month** n/a
Heads: 4 Toilet(s), 4 Shower(s)
Internet: No **Laundry:** 12 Washer(s), 12 Dryer(s)
Pump-Out: OnCall, Full Service, 1 Port **Fee:** Free **Closed Heads:** Yes

Marina Operations

Owner/Manager: Dan Curtin **Dockmaster:** Lloyd Thompson
In-Season: Mar-Dec, 8am-5pm **Off-Season:** Jan-Feb, 8am-4pm
After-Hours Arrival: Call to Pre-arrange
Reservations: Yes, Required **Credit Cards:** Visa/MC, Dscvr, Din
Discounts: None
Pets: Welcome **Handicap Access:** Yes, Heads

Crystal Cove Marina

529 Shirley Street; Winthrop, MA 02152

Tel: (617) 846-7245 **VHF: Monitor** Ch. 10 **Talk** Ch. 10
Fax: (617) 846-4301 **Alternate Tel:** n/a
Email: crystalcovemarina@gmail.com **Web:** crystalcovemarina.com
Nearest Town: Winthrop *(1 mi.)* **Tourist Info:** (617) 846-9898

Marina Services and Boat Supplies

Services - Security *(Video)*, Trash Pick-Up **Communication -** FedEx, DHL, UPS, Express Mail **Supplies - OnSite:** Ice *(Cube)* **Near:** Ice *(Block)* **Under 1 mi:** Ships' Store *(Vista Ward 846-1421)*, Bait/Tackle *(Bob's 846-5896 - live & frozen bait)* **3+ mi:** Propane *(American 387-5065, 5 mi.)*

Boatyard Services

OnSite: Forklift *(20T)*, Crane, Launching Ramp, Engine mechanic *(gas, diesel)*, Electrical Repairs, Electronic Sales, Hull Repairs, Rigger, Bottom Cleaning, Brightwork, Compound, Wash & Wax, Interior Cleaning, Woodworking, Painting **OnCall:** Electronics Repairs, Divers, Air Conditioning, Refrigeration **Yard Rates:** $75/hr., Haul & Launch $16/ft., Power Wash $4/ft. **Storage:** In-Water $30/ft., On-Land $60/ft.

Restaurants and Accommodations

Near: Restaurant *(Trattoria di Parma 846-5867)*, *(Gary's 539-0020, D $9-18, Seafood)*, *(Lucky Garden 846-8560, L $6-12, D $8-16, Szechuan, Hong Kong & Thai food - across the street)*, *(Winthrop Y.C. 846-9774, D $9-20, open to public)*, *(Alia Ristorante 539-1600)*, Snack Bar *(Quick Food)*, *(Twist and Shake 846-8500, Ice cream and frozen yogurt)*, Coffee Shop *(Moonstruck 846-4644, B $4-9, L $5-11)*, Pizzeria *(Domino's 539-3344, next door)*, Inn/B&B *(Inn at Crystal Cove 846-9217, $80-110, Boston Harbor view, Wi-Fi)*, *(Longwood Inn 566-8615, $84-164, Victorian manse, Wi-Fi)* **Under 1 mi:** Restaurant *(La Siesta 846-2300, L $5-12, D $8-20, Mexican)*, *(Winthrop Arms L $6-13, D $12-23, Kids' $7-8, Sun Brunch $8-15)*, Pizzeria *(Nick's Place 846-9800, Del.)*, Hotel *(Winthrop Arms 846-4000, $105, C. 1916, Restored)* **1-3 mi:** Motel *(Suburban Extended Stay 539-9466, $99, part of Choice chain)*

Recreation and Entertainment

Near: Beach *(Winthrop & Yirrell)*, Picnic Area, Playground *(Massa)*, Boat Rentals *(Belle Isle Kayak 719-2036)*, Fishing Charter, Park *(Coughlin or Point Shirley)*, Museum *(1637 Deane Winthrop House - Call 846-8606)* **Under 1 mi:** Tennis Courts *(Ingleside Park)*, Golf Course *(Winthrop G.C. 846-9775)*, Hike/Bike Trails *(Deer Island 788-1170)*

Provisioning and General Services

OnSite: Convenience Store, Laundry *(Commercial Laundry)* **Near:** Wine/Beer, Liquor Store *(Murph's 846-3030 - across street)*, Bakery *(Crusty Crumpet 846-0429)*, Hardware Store *(Shirley 846 2050)* **Under 1 mi:** Market *(Winthrop 846-6880)*, Delicatessen *(Letterie's Italian 846-0351)*, Meat Market *(846-6303)*, Bank/ATM, Post Office, Protestant Church, Library, Beauty Salon *(Mally's 846-5444)*, Barber Shop *(Gio's 539-1900)*, Dry Cleaners *(Surf 846-9762)*, Pharmacy *(CVS 846-9155)* **1-3 mi:** Supermarket *(Shaw's 781-286-3750)*, Catholic Church, Synagogue, Bookstore *(Winthrop 846-3099)*, Copies Etc. *(Staples 781-289-8950)*

Transportation

OnSite: Local Bus *(222-5000 - 712 & 713)* **OnCall:** Rental Car *(Enterprise 781-289-4002)*, Taxi *(Viking 846-6000)* **Near:** Ferry Service *(MV Anna to Rowes Wharf 227-4321 $6/3 - Weekdays)* **Airport:** Logan Int'l. *(6 mi.)*

Medical Services

911 Service **Near:** Doctor *(Desai 846-1318)*, Holistic Services *(Epidermis 212-0938)* **Under 1 mi:** Dentist *(Brooks 846-1811)*, Chiropractor *(Corcoran 846-3502)*, Optician *(Designer 539-3937)* **1-3 mi:** Veterinarian *(East Boston 567-0101)* **Hospital:** Mass Gen - Revere 781-485-6000 *(3 mi.)*

Setting -- Past the Town Pier and Winthrop Yacht Club, C.C.M.'s two main docks, largely populated by smaller boats, are snugged into a well-protected dead-end basin - created by a long, curved man-made jetty. Seaside views are of the town mooring field backed by Logan Airport and the Boston skyline beyond. Landside is a single-story masonry office surrounded by a rustic boatyard. Across the street are a liquor store, pet groomer, Domino's and Thai take-out.

Marina Notes -- Proximity to Boston's Logan Airport and relatively reasonable long-stay rates offers an interesting choice to "leave the boat." Gray-painted docks showing some age. Owners have serious renovation plans, already realized at their nearby Atlantis Marina. Numerous 30A pedestals, more limited 50A service - specify if important. Winthrop town pump-out boat -- hail on Ch. l9. Onsite mechanical services managed by Action Mobile Marine (539-1425), Houghton Marine (631-9338). Commercial laundromat onsite - number of washers/dryers reflects that. Fuel dock. Bathhouse: Institutional, pretty basic.

Notable -- Kids will love the 30 take-offs and landings per hour at nearby Logan airport, adults maybe less so. But it may be a small price for the positives in this small seaside town with big-city access. The Winthrop peninsula, flanked by the Atlantic and Boston Harbor, is slowly garnering the prosperity that its waterfront warrants - grand vistas of the Boston skyline, wide, sandy life-guarded beaches, welcoming merchants with reasonable prices, quick access to open water and parks, preserves and green space with gorgeous views. Fishing has improved thanks to the Boston Harbor clean-up. Touring by boat is a village pastime - visit the Harbor Islands, cruise the inner harbor, watch the July 4 fireworks. And the new ferry makes Boston easily accessible.

Atlantis Marina

550 Pleasant Street; Winthrop, MA 02152

Tel: (617) 846-5262 **VHF: Monitor** Ch. 10 **Talk** n/a
Fax: (617) 846-4301 **Alternate Tel:** n/a
Email: info@atlantismarinadocks.com **Web:** atlantismarinadocks.com
Nearest Town: Winthrop *(1 mi.)* **Tourist Info:** (617) 846-9898

Navigational Information

Lat: 42°22.827' **Long:** 070°59.536' **Tide:** 10 ft. **Current:** 1 kt. **Chart:** 13270
Rep. Depths (*MLW*): Entry 20 ft. **Fuel Dock** n/a **Max Slip/Moor** 30 ft./-
Access: Winthrop Channel; bear left at Winthrop Light

Marina Facilities *(In Season/Off Season)*

Fuel: No
Slips: 100 Total, 70 Transient **Max LOA:** 120 ft. **Max Beam:** n/a
Rate *(per ft.)*: **Day** $3.00 **Week** $9 **Month** $30
Power: 30 amp Incl., **50 amp** incl, **100 amp** n/a, **200 amp** n/a
Cable TV: Yes **Dockside Phone:** Yes
Dock Type: Floating, Long Fingers, Short Fingers, Wood
Moorings: 0 Total, 0 Transient **Launch:** n/a, Dinghy Dock
Rate: Day n/a **Week** n/a **Month** n/a
Heads: 2 Toilet(s), 2 Shower(s) *(dressing rooms)*
Internet: No **Laundry:** None
Pump-Out: OnCall, 1 Port **Fee:** Free **Closed Heads:** Yes

Marina Operations

Owner/Manager: Curtin Associates **Dockmaster:** Lloyd Thompson
In-Season: Year Round **Off-Season:** none
After-Hours Arrival: n/a
Reservations: Yes, Preferred **Credit Cards:** Visa/MC, Dscvr
Discounts: None
Pets: Welcome, Dog Walk Area **Handicap Access:** Yes, Heads, Docks

Marina Services and Boat Supplies

Services - Security *(24 Hrs., Live on-site)*, Dock Carts **Communication -** Mail & Package Hold, Express Mail *(Sat Del)* **Supplies - OnSite:** Ice *(Cube)* **Near:** Bait/Tackle *(Bob's Bait Shack 846-5896)* **1-3 mi:** Ships' Store *(Ward Marine 846-1421)*

Boatyard Services

OnCall: Engine mechanic *(gas, diesel)*, Electrical Repairs, Hull Repairs, Rigger, Canvas Work, Divers, Bottom Cleaning, Brightwork, Air Conditioning, Refrigeration, Compound, Wash & Wax, Interior Cleaning, Propeller Repairs, Woodworking, Inflatable Repairs, Life Raft Service, Upholstery, Yacht Interiors, Metal Fabrication, Painting, Awlgrip, Total Refits, Yacht Design, Yacht Building, Yacht Broker **Near:** Travelift *(30T at Crystal Cove)*, Launching Ramp. **Nearest Yard:** Crystal Cove Marina (617) 846-7245

Restaurants and Accommodations

Near: Restaurant *(Odyssey Grill 846-7200, D $8-15, subs, gyros, delivers)*, Lite Fare *(Papa's Deli 846-1991, Pizza, sandwiches, entrees)*, Pizzeria *(Dominos 567-5551, Dels.)* **Under 1 mi:** Restaurant *(Gary's 539-0020, D $9-19, seafood)*, *(Center Bistro 539-4484)*, *(Paesans 539-1676, L & D $6-16 Italian, BBQ, Pizza)*, *(Kasbah 539-4484, D $15-23, Moroccan. Tapas $5/plate 4/$17)*, Seafood Shack *(Belle Isle 567-1619)*, Pizzeria *(Nick's Place 846-9800, Delivers, Pizza, Subs, Seafood, Calzones 8am-10pm)* **1-3 mi:** Motel *(Suburban 539-9466, $99)*, Hotel *(Winthrop Arms 846-4000, $105)*, Inn/B&B *(Inn At Crystal Cove 846-9217, $90-130)*

Recreation and Entertainment

OnSite: Picnic Area **Near:** Playground *(Ingleside)*, Tennis Courts *(Ingleside Park)*, Jogging Paths, Park *(Ingleside)* **Under 1 mi:** Beach *(Winthrop - life guards)*, Golf Course *(Winthrop G.C. 846-9775)*, Fitness Center *(Kathy's Place 846-6868)*, Boat Rentals *(Belle Isle Kayaks 719-2036 delivers)*, Video Rental *(Blockbuster 561-6053)*, Museum *(1637 Deane Winthrop House - Call 846-8606)*, Sightseeing *(Belle Isle Marsh Preserve)*, Special Events *(Winthrop Playmakers 539-1175 ; 4th of July)* **1-3 mi:** Bowling *(Central Park 567-7073)*, Cultural Attract *(Suffolk Downs Race Track 567-3900)*

Provisioning and General Services

Near: Convenience Store, Delicatessen *(Lunch Box 846-3755; Milanos 567-6718)*, Wine/Beer, Liquor Store *(Swetts 846-0005)*, Bakery, Bank/ATM, Post Office, Barber Shop, Laundry, Pharmacy *(Rite Aid 561-0610)*, Hardware Store *(Ace Woodside 846-2141)*, Florist **Under 1 mi:** Market *(Winthrop 846-6880)*, Fishmonger *(Belle Isle 567-1619)*, Library *(Orient Heights 567-2516)*, Beauty Salon *(Shear Delight 846-9799)*, Bookstore *(Winthrop 846-3099)* **1-3 mi:** Supermarket *(Shaws 781-286-3750)*, Catholic Church, Protestant Church, Synagogue, Dry Cleaners, Copies Etc. *(Staples 289-8950)*

Transportation

OnCall: Rental Car *(Enterprise 561-4488)*, Taxi *(Viking 846-6000)* **Near:** Local Bus **Under 1 mi:** Ferry Service *(MV Anna to Rowes Wharf 227-4321 $6/3 Weekdays)* **Airport:** Logan Int'l. *(4 mi.)*

Medical Services

911 Service **OnCall:** Ambulance **Near:** Dentist *(Carnicelli 846-1280)* **Under 1 mi:** Doctor *(Pransky 846-8622)*, Chiropractor *(Corcoran 846-3502)*, Optician *(Designer Optical)*, Veterinarian *(East Boston 567-0101)* **Hospital:** Mass General-Revere 781-485-6000 *(3 mi.)*

Setting -- Follow the half-circle channel between Logan's main runways to port and the Winthrop peninsula to starboard, then head straight north. On the eastern shore, find four state-of-the-art docks backed by the gray, five-story "Residences at Atlantis Marina" condominium with bowed verandas overlooking the warterway, Logan Airport and the spectacular Boston skyline. The newly rebuilt marina features security, green grass, and a water side promenade.

Marina Notes -- 91 new slips for LOAs to 60 ft. Alongside tie-ups and T-heads for boats up to 120 feet; limited maneuvering room. Newly rebuilt with high quality everything. Only services electricity, heads and water. Very well-protected and secure. Fuel and full mechanical services at Crystal Cove or on-call through Action Mobile Marine. Hail town pump-out boat on Ch. 9. For the quality, security, included electricity and Logan proximity - a good place to leave the boat. Dinghy ride to downtown Winthrop or a mile walk. Bathhouse: Luxurious tile but no showers.

Notable -- Old-fashioned, small-town Winthrop is a 1.6 square mile peninsula with seven miles of shoreline and a lot of green space - including the nearby golf course and Belle Isle Marsh Preserve with kayak access just under the bridge from the docks. Rick Buss at Belle Isle Kayak Adventures provides a unique adventure within the 152-acre Preserve or out in the Harbor (or he'll deliver to the docks - rent from $10/hr to $70/day for fully rigged fishing kayak or take a birding, harbor or fishing tour). Many Winthrop residents are third-generation. The reasonably priced Victorian and Queen Anne housing stock is beginning to gentrify. Winthrop is a good jumping-off point for visiting the Harbor Islands or touring Boston Harbor. Alternatively, Boston is 15 minutes by ferry or car.

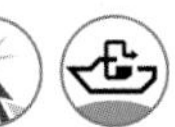

Navigational Information
Lat: 42°21.837' **Long:** 071°02.027' **Tide:** 10 ft. **Current:** 2 kt. **Chart:** 13272
Rep. Depths *(MLW)*: **Entry** 30 ft. **Fuel Dock** 30 ft. **Max Slip/Moor** 30 ft./-
Access: Boston Harbor main channel, past Logan, first facility to starboard

Marina Facilities *(In Season/Off Season)*
Fuel: *ValvTect* - Gasoline, Diesel
Slips: 180 Total, 20 Transient **Max LOA:** 250 ft. **Max Beam:** n/a
Rate *(per ft.)*: **Day** $2.00/$1.50* **Week** $10 **Month** $30
Power: 30 amp $5, **50 amp** $10, **100 amp** Metered, **200 amp** n/a
Cable TV: Yes Monthly **Dockside Phone:** Yes Monthly
Dock Type: Floating, Long Fingers, Wood
Moorings: 0 Total, 0 Transient **Launch:** n/a, Dinghy Dock
Rate: Day n/a **Week** n/a **Month** n/a
Heads: 2 Toilet(s), 2 Shower(s) *(dressing rooms)*, Book Exchange
Internet: Yes *(Wi-Fi, Free)* **Laundry:** 2 Washer(s), 2 Dryer(s)
Pump-Out: OnSite, Full Service, 1 Central **Fee:** Free **Closed Heads:** Yes

Marina Operations
Owner/Manager: Pat Gately **Dockmaster:** Jason Boudrow
In-Season: May 1-Oct 31, 7am-8pm **Off-Season:** Nov 1-Apr 30, 8am-4pm
After-Hours Arrival: Call in advance
Reservations: Yes, Required **Credit Cards:** Visa/MC, Dscvr, Amex
Discounts: Boat/US; Sea Tow **Dockage:** n/a **Fuel:** $0.10 **Repair:** n/a
Pets: Welcome, Dog Walk Area **Handicap Access:** Yes, Heads

Boston Harbor Shipyard

256 Marginal Street; East Boston, MA 02128

Tel: (617) 561-1400 **VHF: Monitor** Ch. 9 **Talk** Ch. 8
Fax: (617) 561-9539 **Alternate Tel:** n/a
Email: pgately@bhsmarina.com **Web:** www.bhsmarina.com
Nearest Town: Boston *(1 mi. by water)* **Tourist Info:** (617) 227-4500

Marina Services and Boat Supplies
Services - Docking Assistance, Room Service to the Boat, Boaters' Lounge, Security *(24 Hrs., Guard)*, Trash Pick-Up, Dock Carts **Communication -** Mail & Package Hold, Phone Messages, Fax in/out, FedEx, DHL, UPS, Express Mail *(Sat Del)* **Supplies - OnSite:** Ice *(Block, Cube, Shaved)*, Bait/Tackle *(Eric's Bait and Tackle)* **Under 1 mi:** Ships' Store **3+ mi:** Marine Discount Store *(CG Edwards 268-4111, 3 mi.)*

Boatyard Services
OnSite: Travelift *(50T)*, Railway *(Graving Dock to 16,500 long tons)*, Forklift, Crane, Engine mechanic *(gas, diesel)*, Electrical Repairs, Hull Repairs, Rigger, Divers, Bottom Cleaning, Brightwork, Compound, Wash & Wax, Interior Cleaning, Propeller Repairs, Woodworking, Metal Fabrication, Awlgrip, Total Refits, Yacht Design, Yacht Building **OnCall:** Electronics Repairs, Canvas Work **Near:** Inflatable Repairs, Life Raft Service. **Member:** ABBRA, ABYC - 2 Certified Tech(s), Other Certifications: Mercruiser **Yard Rates:** Haul & Launch $3.50/ft *(blocking incl.)*

Restaurants and Accommodations
OnSite: Restaurant *(Scups in the Harbor 569-7287, Wed-Fri: Lunch sandwiches, empanadas, soup, Supper - same plus entrees Sat & Sun Brunch 10-3)* **Near:** Restaurant *(Mehak 568-1900, Authentic Pakistani)*, *(Beetcookin' 460-2966)*, Lite Fare *(Pupuseria Mama Blanca 567-5511, Fab El Salvadoran stuffed masa tortillas)*, Pizzeria *(Italian Exp 561-0038)* **Under 1 mi:** Restaurant *(Legal Seafood at Logan 241-2000)*, *(Side St. Café 569-7000)*, *(303 Cafe 569-3001, B $6-10, L $7-12, D $11-15, Wknd Brunch)*, Pizzeria *(Santarpio's 567-9871, best pizza in Boston)*, Hotel *(Embassy Suites 567-5000, $140-200)*, *(Hyatt Harborside 568-1234, $100-250)*

Recreation and Entertainment
OnSite: Picnic Area, Grills, Dive Shop *(Boston 418-5555)*, Fitness Center *(Get Fit Club, 2nd floor, 8am-11pm)*, Fishing Charter *(Dropaline 781-831-3753, also whale watch & harbor island cruises)*, Tours *(Boston Scuba 418-5555, Harbor Island tours)* **Near:** Playground *(Piers Park - special)*, Boat Rentals *(Piers Park Sailing Center)*, Park *(Piers - with 18 tree species)*, Sightseeing *(East Boston Harborwalk - download map)* **Under 1 mi:** Video Rental *(Blockbuster 561-6053)* **1-3 mi:** Beach *(Revere & Constitution)*

Provisioning and General Services
Near: Convenience Store *(White Hen 569-7069)*, Market *(Gloria 567-6373)*, Delicatessen, Bakery *(A & L 569-7597)*, Bank/ATM, Post Office, Beauty Salon, Dry Cleaners, Newsstand, Retail Shops *(Maverick Square)* **Under 1 mi:** Supermarket *(Shaw's 567-4116)*, Liquor Store *(Kappy's 567-9500)*, Library *(569-0271)*, Bookstore *(Brattle 542-0210)*, Pharmacy *(Rite Aid 561-0610)* **1-3 mi:** Hardware Store *(Salem St. 523-4759)*, Department Store *(Target, Revere)*, Buying Club *(Costco)*

Transportation
OnSite: Courtesy Car/Van *(Airport & local mkts)*, Water Taxi *(City 422-0392 $10/Free 1-way)* **OnCall:** Rental Car *(Enterprise)*, Taxi *(E. Boston 567-2700)*, Airport Limo *(Central Sq. 567-3400)* **Near:** Local Bus *("T")* **1-3 mi:** Rail *(South Station)* **Airport:** Logan - Eastie back door *(1 mi.)*

Medical Services
911 Service **Near:** Doctor *(Concentra Urgent Care)* **Under 1 mi:** Dentist *(E. Boston 569-7300)* **1-3 mi:** Chiropractor *(Backworks 451-2225)*, Veterinarian *(So. Boston 269-0610)* **Hospital:** Mass. General *(5 mi.)*

Setting -- Past Logan Airport and Hyatt Hotel, BHSM's long wharf, hosting 5 slip docks and "L-shaped" alongside tie-ups, lies between the shipyard and award-winning six-acre Piers Park. The East Boston marina offers a boatyard ambiance balanced by spectacular, panoramic views of the Boston skyline - a water taxi away - and the park's greensward, pavilions, 600-foot waterside promenade, playground, amphitheater, fitness trail system and sailing center.

Marina Notes -- Established 1989 on site of the historic Bethlehem Steel Shipyard. Only true shipyard in the harbor. 120 ft. Fuel Dock. 258 ft. by 44 ft. graving dock & 50 ton travelift; handles vessels to 16,500 long tons. Unique complimentary breakfast cart on summer weekends & catering service. State-of-the-art fitness center with flat-panel TV. Boater's lounge w/TV, stereo, coffee, sofa and chairs - and upper deck. Good security, guard at main gate and locked gates to each dock. Bait & tackle, Dive Service, Seatow, fishing charters on site. Outer steel floats can handle most megayachts. Comp shuttle to Logan airport & markets. Water taxi accesses all of Boston Harbor. Bathhouse: Nicely tiled but a hike from big boat slips. Attractive, fully tiled laundry

Notable -- In the 19th-century, Donald McKay's fast clipper ships were built in East Boston - laying the groundwork for today's maritime industry. Soon thereafter this became the first stop for the newest wave of immigrants. Today it's a stronghold of Latino culture and home to artists, professionals, born and raised Easties - and some wonderful food and cultural adventures. In the middle of the shipyard, homey Scup's serves an original menu in a painted cinderblock dining room or outside at picnic tables. More eateries are nearby and even more, along with services, are a three-quarter mile walk at Maverick Square.

PHOTOS ON DVD: 20

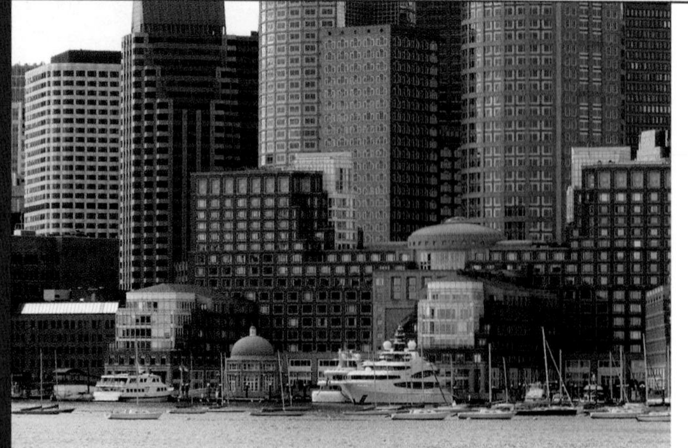

The Marina at Rowes Wharf

30 Rowes Wharf; Boston, MA 02110

Tel: (617) 748-5013 **VHF: Monitor** Ch. 9 **Talk** Ch. 67
Fax: (617) 748-5012 **Alternate Tel:** (617) 425-7500
Email: *See marina notes **Web:** themarinaatroweswharf.com
Nearest Town: Boston **Tourist Info:** (617) 227-4500

Navigational Information

Lat: 42°21.419' **Long:** 071°02.952' **Tide:** 10 ft. **Current:** 2 kt. **Chart:** 13272
Rep. Depths (*MLW*): Entry 30 ft. **Fuel Dock** n/a **Max Slip/Moor** 30 ft./-
Access: Cape Cod Bay to Boston Harbor, first facility on port side

Marina Facilities *(In Season/Off Season)*

Fuel: No
Slips: 38 Total, 18 Transient **Max LOA:** 280 ft. **Max Beam:** n/a
Rate *(per ft.)*: **Day** $6.50/.* **Week** n/a **Month** n/a
Power: 30 amp $30, **50 amp** $40, **100 amp** $75, **200 amp** n/a
Cable TV: Yes **Dockside Phone:** Yes Local
Dock Type: Floating, Concrete, Wood
Moorings: 0 Total, 0 Transient **Launch:** n/a
Rate: Day n/a **Week** n/a **Month** n/a
Heads: 2 Toilet(s), 2 Shower(s)
Internet: Yes *(Biz Center)* **Laundry:** 1 Washer(s), 1 Dryer(s)
Pump-Out: OnSite, OnCall, Self Service **Fee:** Free **Closed Heads:** Yes

Marina Operations

Owner/Manager: Kristan McLaughlin **Dockmaster:** Same
In-Season: May-Oct, 9am-9pm **Off-Season:** Nov-Apr, 9am-5pm
After-Hours Arrival: Call in advance
Reservations: Yes **Credit Cards:** Visa/MC, Amex
Discounts: None
Pets: Welcome **Handicap Access:** No

Marina Services and Boat Supplies

Services - Docking Assistance, Concierge, Room Service to the Boat, Security *(24 hrs.)*, Trash Pick-Up, Dock Carts, 3 Phase, European Voltage **Communication -** Mail & Package Hold, Phone Messages, Fax in/out, FedEx, DHL, UPS, Express Mail **Supplies - OnSite:** Ice *(Cube)* **Under 1 mi:** Bait/Tackle *(Firefly 423-3474, Orvis 742-0288)* **1-3 mi:** Ships' Store *(Edwards 268-4111)*, Propane *(U-Haul 442-5600)*

Boatyard Services

OnCall: Engine mechanic *(gas, diesel)*, Rigger, Canvas Work, Bottom Cleaning, Interior Cleaning **Nearest Yard:** BHSM (617) 561-1400

Restaurants and Accommodations

OnSite: Restaurant *(Intrigue Café 856-7744)*, *(Meritage 439-3995, D $16-32, Small Plates $16, Large $32, Bar Bites 3/$10)*, *(Sea Grille 406-8584, L $15-23, D $19-35, Afternoon tea)*, Hotel *(Boston Harbor 439-7000, $225-2000)* **Near:** Restaurant *(Sel de la Terre 720-1300, D $15-39)*, *(Legal Seafood 227-3115, D $13-35)*, Lite Fare *(Panera Bread 951-1330)*, Hotel *(Hilton 556-0006, $240-380)*, *(InterContinental 747-1000, $210-600)*

Recreation and Entertainment

OnSite: Heated Pool, Fitness Center *(Rowes Wharf Health Club 439-3914 $35/day Fri-Sun, $25/day Mon-Thu)*, Hike/Bike Trails *(HarborWalk)* **Near:** Playground, Fishing Charter *(C.J. Victoria 283-5801)*, Movie Theater *(Simons IMAX 973-5206)*, Video Rental *(Blockbuster Exp)*, Park *(Columbus)*, Museum *(Old State House 720-1713; Children's 426-8855; N.E. Aquarium 973-5200 $22/14)*, Tours *(Boston City Walks 904-2819 $15-25; Discover Boston 742-1440 Trollley & Duck Tours Pkgs $36/18-61/31)*, Sightseeing *(Mass Bay Whale Watching 542-8000; Freedom Trail 357-8300)*, Galleries *(Lannen ship Models 451-2650)* **Under 1 mi:** Cultural Attract *(Improv 263-6887; Boston Opera 259-3400; Lyric 542-4912)* **1-3 mi:** Tennis Courts *(Boston A.C, 269-4300 Free 1-day pass)*, Bowling *(Kings 266-2695)*

Provisioning and General Services

OnSite: Delicatessen, Bank/ATM, Beauty Salon, Dry Cleaners, Laundry, Newsstand, Florist, Copies Etc. *(Business Center)* **Near:** Convenience Store *(7-Eleven)*, Bakery, Fishmonger *(James Hook 423-5500)*, Post Office, Catholic Church, Protestant Church, Synagogue, Pharmacy *(CVS 426-8964)* **Under 1 mi:** Market *(Haymarket 918-9988)*, Gourmet Shop *(Polcari's 227-0786)*, Wine/Beer *(Boston Wine 422-0100)*, Liquor Store *(Federal 367-8605)*, Green Grocer *(Haymarket)*, Library *(BLC 262-0380)*, Bookstore *(Commonwealth 338-6328)*, Hardware Store *(Seaport 426-9988)*, Department Store *(Macy's, Filene's)* **1-3 mi:** Supermarket *(Whole Foods 723-0004)*, Farmers' Market *(Sun 10-4 SOWA 460 Harrison)*

Transportation

OnSite: Ferry Service *(Hingham, Logan)* **OnCall:** Water Taxi *(Rowes Wharf to Logan 406-8584 $10/1-way, $17/RT; City 422-0392)*, Taxi *(Airport 850-0500)* **Near:** Rental Car *(Budget 497-3733)*, Local Bus *("T")* **Under 1 mi:** Rail *(Boston South Station)* **Airport:** Logan Int'l. *(3 mi.)*

Medical Services

911 Service **OnSite:** Holistic Services *(Day Spa)* **OnCall:** Veterinarian *(At Home 753-9300)* **Near:** Doctor *(Harvard Vanguard 654-7000)*, Dentist *(Fanueil Hall 523-4444)* **Under 1 mi:** Chiropractor *(Backworks 728-7246)* **Hospital:** Mass. General 248-1926 *(1 mi.)*

Setting -- Set in the tall, gleaming $193 million Rowes Wharf complex, the "E-shaped" docks are to port after entering the inner harbor - head for the teal domes. At the foot of Boston Harbor Hotel, the marina benefits from its top amenities and panoramic views across the harbor, which attract the megayacht set. Smaller yachts dock bow-in for privacy. Landside views include the impeccable hotel, flower-bedecked outdoor cafe, town houses and commercial vessels.

Marina Notes -- *up to 100ft. $6.50/ft. 100 ft. plus $6.50. Pick-Up/Drop-off $20/hr. **Email: kristan_mclaughlin@equityoffice.com.120 & 208 volts/3 phase. Fuel BHSM & Mystic (293-6247). Pump-out. Ice $4/bag. Hotel guest hospitality from one of Boston's finest - 24-hour room service to boats (856-7728), florist, ATM, car rental, several top eateries and handsome health club, spa & fitness center with pool (Fee). Southern docks for commercial vessels; quieter northern docks for rec boats. Views become pilings at low tide. Bathhouses: Surprisingly simple, modern, tiled, with glass shower doors; close to docks.

Notable -- Chef Daniel Bruce's spectacular, contemporary Meritage and Sea Grille reflect his two decades at the stove. Rowes Wharf Bar serves pub food from 4pm and the Intrigue Bistro Café's wonderful terrace overlooks the docks where there are free concerts or movies weekday evenings in summer (consider when choosing slip). Onsite ferries go to the South Shore and Logan Airport. Many of Boston's attractions, including the financial district, Quincy Market/Faneuil Hall, Aquarium and Freedom Trail, are within an easy walk. Vibrant mile-long, 15-acre Rose Kennedy Greenway winds through five parks (from Chinatown to North End Parks) with festivals, art, performances, food trucks and free Wi-Fi. Boston Harbor Sailing Club runs one-design keelboat races in front of the marina.

    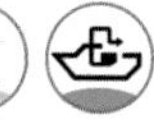

Navigational Information

Lat: 42°21.670' **Long:** 071°02.922' **Tide:** 10 ft. **Current:** 2 kt. **Chart:** 13272
Rep. Depths (*MLW*): Entry 15 ft. **Fuel Dock** n/a **Max Slip/Moor** 30 ft./35 ft.
Access: Follow Harbor channel to Inner Harbor, 3rd facility on port side

Marina Facilities *(In Season/Off Season)*

Fuel: No
Slips: 36 Total, 20 Transient **Max LOA:** 200 ft. **Max Beam:** 26 ft.
Rate *(per ft.)*: **Day** $4.50* **Week** $27 **Month** n/a
Power: 30 amp $15, **50 amp** $30, **100 amp** $55, **200 amp** n/a
Cable TV: No **Dockside Phone:** No
Dock Type: Floating, Long Fingers, Alongside, Wood
Moorings: 12 Total, 5 Transient **Launch:** No, Dinghy Dock
Rate: Day $45 **Week** n/a **Month** n/a
Heads: 2 Toilet(s), 2 Shower(s)
Internet: Yes *(Wi-Fi, Free)* **Laundry:** 1 Washer(s), 1 Dryer(s)
Pump-Out: OnSite, 1 Central, 1 Port **Fee:** Free **Closed Heads:** Yes

Marina Operations

Owner/Manager: Capt Lawrence Cannon **Dockmaster:** Capt. Paul Bramsen
In-Season: May-Oct, 8am-6pm **Off-Season:** Nov-Apr, 8am-2pm
After-Hours Arrival: Call during office hours
Reservations: Yes **Credit Cards:** Visa/MC, Amex
Discounts: None
Pets: Welcome, Dog Walk Area **Handicap Access:** No

Boston Waterboat Marina

66 Long Wharf; Boston, MA 02110

Tel: (617) 523-1027 **VHF: Monitor** Ch. 9 **Talk** Ch. 8
Fax: (617) 523-1215 **Alternate Tel:** n/a
Email: ccannon@bostonwaterboatmarina.com **Web:** See Marina Notes
Nearest Town: Boston **Tourist Info:** (617) 227-4500

Marina Services and Boat Supplies

Services - Docking Assistance, Security *(24 Hrs.)*, Dock Carts, 3 Phase **Communication -** Mail & Package Hold, Fax in/out, FedEx, UPS, Express Mail **Supplies - OnSite:** Ice *(Block, Cube)*, Ships' Store *(Boston Marine & Birch Marine 723-4900)* **Under 1 mi:** Bait/Tackle *(Orvis 742-0288)* **1-3 mi:** Propane *(U-Haul 625-2789)*

Boatyard Services

OnSite: Engine mechanic *(gas, diesel)*, Bottom Cleaning, Brightwork, Air Conditioning, Refrigeration **Nearest Yard:** BHSM (617) 561-1400

Restaurants and Accommodations

OnSite: Restaurant *(Chart House 227-1576, L $11-23, D $24-47)*, *(Oceana 227-0800, D $17-35, L & D $11-23, Sun Brunch)*, Lite Fare *(Harbor Terrace 227-0800, Bar Menu $10-16)*, *(Rudi's 330-7656, L & D $9-16)*, Hotel *(Marriott Long Wharf 227-0800, $349)* **Near:** Restaurant *(Legal Seafoods 227-3115, L $10-18, D $18-28, Plus Gluten-Free, Kids' $5-17)*, *(Joe's 367-8700, L & D $9-24 Wknd Brunch $10-18)*, *(Sel de Terre 720-1300, L $9-16, D $24-38, Wknd Brunch $6-24, Kids $7-9)*, *(Black Rose 742-2286, L & D $8-22 Irish Connection)*, Lite Fare *(Intrigue Café 856-7744, L & D $9-16)*, Hotel *(Boston Harbor 439-7000, $400-2000)*, *(Harborside Inn 723-7500, $199-310)*

Recreation and Entertainment

OnSite: Sightseeing *(Liberty Tall Ships noon-2pm, 3-5pm, 6-8pm)* **Near:** Pool *(Rowes Wharf)*, Playground *(Columbus)*, Fitness Center *(Beacon Hill A.C. 742-0055)*, Hike/Bike Trails *(HarborWalk; Rose Kennedy Greenway)*, Fishing Charter *(C.J. Victoria 283-5801)*, Movie Theater *(Simons IMAX 973-5206)*, Park *(Columbus)*, Tours *(Boston CityWalks 904-2819 $15-25; Discover Boston 742-1440 Trolley & Duck Tours Pkgs $36/18-61/31)* **Under 1 mi:** Video Rental *(Blockbuster Exp)*, Museum *(Paul Revere House 523-1676; Children's 426-8855; Old State House 720-1713; N.E. Aquarium 973-5200 $22/14; Boston Tea Party Ship 269-7150)*, Cultural Attract *(Improv 263-6887; Boston Opera 259-3400; Lyric 542-4912)*

Provisioning and General Services

Near: Convenience Store *(7-Eleven 227-9534)*, Delicatessen *(Salumeria 523-8743)*, Wine/Beer *(Boston Wine 422-0100)*, Farmers' Market *(City Hall Plaza Mon & Wed 11am-6pm)*, Fishmonger *(James Hook 423-5500)*, Bank/ATM, Post Office, Catholic Church, Library *(BLC 262-0380)*, Beauty Salon, Dry Cleaners, Bookstore *(Commonwealth 338-6328)*, Pharmacy *(CVS 951-0312)* **Under 1 mi:** Supermarket *(Stop & Shop 742-6094)*, Gourmet Shop *(Gypsy Kitchen 227-9649)*, Liquor Store *(Cirace 227-3193; Federal 367-8605)*, Hardware Store *(True Value 23-4759)*, Department Store *(Filene's, Macy's)*

Transportation

OnSite: Water Taxi *(City 422-0392)*, Ferry Service *(to Harbor Islands, Provincetown, Logan water shuttle at Rowes Wharf)* **OnCall:** Rental Car *(Enterprise 723-8077)*, Taxi, Airport Limo *(Boston 933-9077)* **Near:** Bikes *(Urban Adven 670-0637)* **Under 1 mi:** Rail **Airport:** Logan Int'l. *(3 mi.)*

Medical Services

911 Service **Near:** Doctor *(Harvard Vanguard 654-7000)*, Holistic Services *(Jacquelyn's Spa 367-138)* **Under 1 mi:** Dentist *(Fanueil Hall 523-4444)*, Chiropractor *(Backworks 728-7246)*, Veterinarian *(Tufts 839-5395)* **Hospital:** Mass. General 638-8000 *(1 mi.)*

Setting -- This low-key, ideally situated facility is the center of the Wharf District's three transient-friendly marinas. Look for the large, red-brick, renovated warehouse, the prow of the Marriott Long Wharf, and the tall ships. At the end of Long Wharf, the three sets of well-protected slips and side-tie dockage have views of the adjacent esplanade and across to East Boston and Logan. The wharf buildings house nautical enterprises, tour kiosks, restaurants with al fresco decks and the Marriott Long Wharf Hotel. Just north, a glorious wisteria-covered pergola in Columbus Park's Rose Kennedy Garden opens to the water.

Marina Notes -- *$4/ft to 45 ft. $4.50/ft. over 45 ft. 30 ft. min. 100A 3-phase $60/day. Web: bostonwaterboatmarina.com. Family-owned for 3 generations. Most private of inner-harbor marinas. Slips oriented to harbor chop to reduce roll. Onsite boat maintenance & repair by Capt. Chris Birch, Birch Marine (723-4900). Outer steel float handles the largest yachts. Small mooring field. Card Access security gate. Fuel at Mystic Marine, Charlestown or at BHSM. For location & saltiness, Boston's "best pick." Bathhouse: Modern, fire-red walls, glass shower doors - handy to slips. Laundry room.

Notable -- Just a block to the New England Aquarium and short 0.4-mile walk west to famous Quincy Market (great for grazing), Faneuil Hall and City Hall Plaza, this delightful home-grown city marina was the departure point for Joshua Slocum's three-year cicumnavigation on "Spray." The onsite 1760's four-story brick Gardiner Building was originally John Hancock's counting house. The Marriott and its multiple bars and restaurants plus the Chart House are steps away along the Harborwalk, which edges the Boston waterfront - with exhibits, decks for lounging, food trucks. A couple blocks inland, walk the Freedom Trail.

12. MA - BOSTON HARBOR REGION

PHOTOS ON DVD: 25

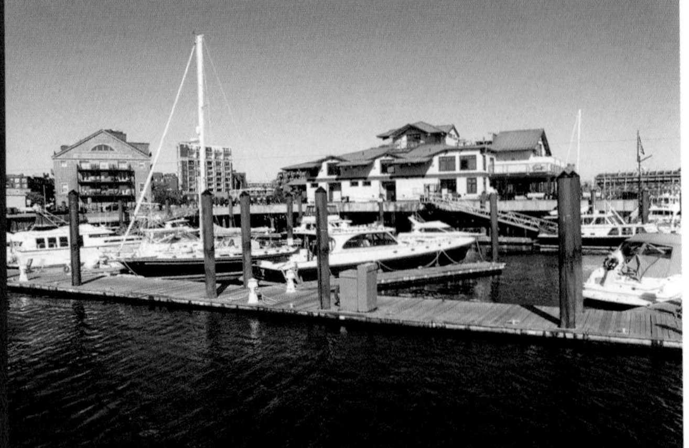

Boston Yacht Haven

87 Commercial Wharf; Boston, MA 02110

Tel: (617) 367-5050 **VHF: Monitor** Ch. 9 **Talk** Ch. 8
Fax: (617) 523-2270 **Alternate Tel:** (617) 523-7352
Email: garyc@byhonline.com **Web:** byhonline.com
Nearest Town: Boston *(0 mi.)* **Tourist Info:** (617) 227-4500

Navigational Information

Lat: 42°21.703' **Long:** 071°02.923' **Tide:** 10 ft. **Current:** 2 kt. **Chart:** 13272
Rep. Depths (*MLW*): Entry 35 ft. **Fuel Dock** n/a **Max Slip/Moor** 35 ft./-
Access: Cape Cod Bay to Boston Inner Harbor, 4th facility on port side

Marina Facilities *(In Season/Off Season)*

Fuel: Slip-Side Fueling, Diesel, High-Speed Pumps, On Call Delivery
Slips: 70 Total, 15 Transient **Max LOA:** 300 ft. **Max Beam:** 40 ft.
Rate *(per ft.)*: **Day** $4.00/Inq.* **Week** $10 **Month** $35
Power: 30 amp $30/day, **50 amp** $40/day, **100 amp** $75/day, **200 amp** Inq
Cable TV: Yes Satellite **Dockside Phone:** No
Dock Type: Floating, Wood, Aluminum
Moorings: 0 Total, 0 Transient **Launch:** n/a
Rate: Day n/a **Week** n/a **Month** n/a
Heads: 6 Toilet(s), 4 Shower(s)
Internet: Yes *(Wi-Fi, Free)* **Laundry:** 2 Washer(s), 2 Dryer(s)
Pump-Out: OnSite, Full Service **Fee:** Free **Closed Heads:** Yes

Marina Operations

Owner/Manager: Gary Coe **Dockmaster:** Frank Goodwin
In-Season: May-Oct 31, 8am-Mid **Off-Season:** Nov 1-Apr 30, 9am-4pm
After-Hours Arrival: Call in advance
Reservations: Yes **Credit Cards:** Visa/MC, Dscvr, Din, Amex
Discounts: None
Pets: Welcome **Handicap Access:** Yes, Heads, Docks

Marina Services and Boat Supplies

Services - Docking Assistance, Boaters' Lounge, Security *(24 Hrs., guard at gate, CCTV/cards)*, Dock Carts, 3 Phase **Communication -** Mail & Package Hold, Phone Messages, Fax in/out, FedEx, UPS, Express Mail *(Sat Del)* **Supplies - OnSite:** Ice *(Cube)* **Near:** Ice *(Block)* **Under 1 mi:** Ships' Store, Bait/Tackle *(Orvis 742-0288)* **1-3 mi:** Propane *(U-Haul 442-5600)*

Boatyard Services

OnCall: Engine mechanic *(gas, diesel)*, Bottom Cleaning **Under 1 mi:** Launching Ramp. **Nearest Yard:** BHSM (617) 561-1400

Restaurants and Accommodations

OnSite: Hotel *(Boston Yacht Haven 523-7352, $175-450, 10 waterfront rooms)* **Near:** Restaurant *(Joe's American 367-8700, L & D $9-24, Wknd Brunch $10-18)*, *(Sel de la Terre 720-1300, L $9-16, D $24-38, Truly special, Wknd Brunch $6-24, Kids $7-9)*, *(Union Oyster House 227-2750, L $7-16, D $15-25, An institution, Oldest in Boston)*, *(Durgin Park 227-2038, L $5-17, D $6-17)*, *(Boston Sail Loft 227-7280)*, *(Legal Seafoods 227-3115, L $10-18, D $18-28)*, *(Oceana 227-0800, L & D $11-23)*, Hotel *(Marriott Long Wharf 227-0800, $349)*, *(Boston Harbor Hotel 439-7000, $400-2000)*

Recreation and Entertainment

Near: Playground *(Columbus Park)*, Fitness Center *(Beacon Hill Athletic Club 742-0055)*, Jogging Paths *(HarborWalk)*, Hike/Bike Trails, Fishing Charter *(C.J. Victoria 283-5801)*, Park *(Columbus)*, Sightseeing *(17th C. Blackstone Block, city's oldest commercial district; The North End & the Freedom Trail)*, Special Events *(Columbus Park Concerts - Aug, Tues eves)* **Under 1 mi:** Movie Theater *(Orpheum 679-0810)*, Video Rental *(North End 367-3533)*, Museum *(N.E. Aquarium 973-5200 $22/14; Paul Revere & Pierce/Hichborn Houses 523-2338 $3.50/1; Old North Church; Old State House 720-1713)*, Tours *(Boston City Walks 904-2819 $15-25)*, Cultural Attract *(Boston Opera 259-3400; Lyric Opera 542-4912)*

Provisioning and General Services

Near: Convenience Store *(7-Eleven 227-9534)*, Gourmet Shop *(Golden Goose 367-3198)*, Delicatessen *(Salumeria 523-8743)*, Green Grocer *(Faneuil Hall Market)*, Fishmonger *(James Hook 423-5500)*, Bank/ATM, Post Office, Catholic Church, Protestant Church, Library *(BLC 262-0380)*, Beauty Salon, Dry Cleaners, Pharmacy *(CVS 227-3728)*, Newsstand, Florist **Under 1 mi:** Market *(Haymarket Int'l 918-9988)*, Wine/Beer *(Wine Bottega 227-6607)*, Liquor Store *(Cirace 227-3193)*, Farmers' Market *(City Hall Plaza Mon & Wed 11am-6pm)*, Synagogue, Laundry, Bookstore *(Commonwealth 338-6328)*, Hardware Store *(Salem St. 523-4759)*, Department Store *(Macy's, Filene's)* **1-3 mi:** Supermarket *(Whole Foods 723-0004)*

Transportation

OnCall: Rental Car *(Enterprise 723-8077)*, Taxi, Airport Limo *(Boston 933-9077)* **Near:** Bikes *(Urban Adven 670-0637)*, Water Taxi *(422-0392)*, Ferry Service *(Salem, Provincetown, Harbor Islands, Hingham)* **Under 1 mi:** Local Bus *("T")*, Rail *(South Station)* **Airport:** Logan Int'l. *(3 mi.)*

Medical Services

911 Service **OnCall:** Veterinarian *(At Home 753-9300)* **Near:** Doctor *(Harvard Vanguard 654-7000)*, Chiropractor *(Backworks 728-7246)*, Holistic Services *(Henia's Day Spa 523-8800)* **Under 1 mi:** Dentist *(Fanueil Hall 523-4444)* **Hospital:** Mass. General 638-8000 *(1 mi.)*

Setting -- Backed by the restored 1830 four-story, stone "Commercial Wharf," a set of three breakwater face docks encloses spacious slips and an elegant two-story contemporary take on a Maine boathouse - topped by an eccentric metal roof. The service-oriented marina operations and thoughtful guest amenities are on the first floor, and a luxurious B&B on the second and third. Views across the harbor and back toward the nearby Boston skyline are breathtaking.

Marina Notes -- *Daily to 35 ft $4/ft., 35.1-80 ft. $4.25/ft., 80.1 and over $5.50/ft. Weekly to 35 ft $22.75/ft., 35.1-80 ft. $26.25/ft., 80.1 and over $33.75/ft; Med-moor $3/ft. Managed by Island Global Yachting (IGY). Excellent security & concierge services. Side-tie megayacht dockage on 123 ton, 300-ft breakwater & on 150 and 100-ft. breakwaters. Yacht club ambiance in like-new condition. Multi-phase, megayacht power: 480 volt (200 & 100A), 240 volt single-phase, 208 volt 3-phase 100A; 240 volt 50A, 120 volt 30A. Radisson wave attenuator. Hi-speed, in-slip fueling. Attractive boaters' lounge and handsome meeting room. Complimentary breakfast. Docks very private and protected. Bathhouse: Ultra modern, granite & ceramic tile. Airy laundry room.

Notable -- The luxe B&B boasts well-appointed guest rooms and suites with private decks, elevator, dedicated parking and attractive public rooms - some shared with boaters. Once home to clipper ships, Commercial Wharf now berths condominiums and, at its head, Joe's American. Immediately adjacent lies very green Columbus Park, part of the exquisite, mile-long Rose Kennedy Greenway. Head west to provision at The Haymarket - a vibrant maze of stalls and pushcarts hawking their wares. Or go north to the North End's Little Italy for more provisioning (think bakeries) or the dozens of eateries along Hanover Street.

12. MA - BOSTON HARBOR REGION

PHOTOS ON DVD: 25

   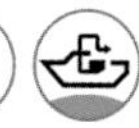 

Navigational Information
Lat: 42°22.404' **Long:** 071°03.021' **Tide:** 10 ft. **Current:** 2 kt. **Chart:** 13272
Rep. Depths (*MLW*): Entry 30 ft. **Fuel Dock** n/a **Max Slip/Moor** 45 ft./-
Access: Inner Harbor, past Coast Guard, straight to Pier 6 & 8 in Navy Yard

Marina Facilities *(In Season/Off Season)*
Fuel: No
Slips: 300 Total, 100 Transient **Max LOA:** 300 ft. **Max Beam:** n/a
Rate *(per ft.)*: **Day** $3.00/$1.00* **Week** $17.50 **Month** $25 per foot
Power: 30 amp $10, **50 amp** $20, **100 amp** $35, **200 amp** n/a
Cable TV: Yes **Dockside Phone:** Yes
Dock Type: Floating, Long Fingers, Pilings, Wood
Moorings: 0 Total, 0 Transient **Launch:** n/a
Rate: Day n/a **Week** n/a **Month** n/a
Heads: 10 Toilet(s), 8 Shower(s), Hair Dryers
Internet: Yes *(Wi-Fi, Free)* **Laundry:** 6 Washer(s), 8 Dryer(s)
Pump-Out: OnSite, Full Service, 1 Central **Fee:** Free **Closed Heads:** Yes

Marina Operations
Owner/Manager: Not disclosed **Dockmaster:** Capt. Jim Pike
In-Season: May-Oct, 8am-8pm **Off-Season:** Nov-Apr, 9am-5pm
After-Hours Arrival: Call in advance
Reservations: Yes **Credit Cards:** Visa/MC, Dscvr
Discounts: Groups 5+ boats **Dockage:** n/a **Fuel:** n/a **Repair:** n/a
Pets: Welcome, Dog Walk Area **Handicap Access:** No

Shipyard Quarters Marina

1 Pier Eight; Charlestown, MA 02129

Tel: (617) 242-2020 **VHF: Monitor** Ch. 16 **Talk** Ch. 71
Fax: (617) 242-5296 **Alternate Tel:** n/a
Email: **See Marina Notes **Web:** shipyardquartersmarina.com
Nearest Town: Boston *(0.25 mi.)* **Tourist Info:** (617) 227-4500

Marina Services and Boat Supplies
Services - Docking Assistance, Concierge, Boaters' Lounge, Trash Pick-Up, Dock Carts, 3 Phase **Communication -** Pay Phone, FedEx, DHL, UPS, Express Mail *(Sat Del)* **Supplies - OnSite:** Ice *(Cube)* **1-3 mi:** Ships' Store *(McLellan Bros 389-5508)*, Bait/Tackle, Propane *(U-Haul 625-2789)*

Boatyard Services
OnCall: Engine mechanic *(gas, diesel)*, Electrical Repairs, Electronics Repairs, Hull Repairs, Rigger, Canvas Work, Divers, Bottom Cleaning, Brightwork, Refrigeration **Nearest Yard:** BHSM (617) 561-1400

Restaurants and Accommodations
OnSite: Restaurant *(Tavern on the Water 242-8040, L & D $9-18, Sun brunch $6-19, Kids' $7)*, Inn/B&B *(Green Turtle 337-0202, $215-260, floating)* **Near:** Restaurant *(Navy Yard Bistro 242-0036, D $16-27)*, *(Tangierino 242-6009, D $12-26)*, *(Copia 242-6742)*, *(Outback 306-6130)*, Lite Fare *(Style Cafe 241-7300)*, *(Sorelle Bakery Cafe 242-5980)*, *(American Bakers Cafe 241-7999)*, Pizzeria *(Kipos 242-4141)*, Hotel *(Marriott's Residence Inn 242-9000, $130-400)*, Inn/B&B *(Constitution 241-8400)* **Under 1 mi:** Restaurant *(Todd English's Olives 242-1999, D $19-35)*

Recreation and Entertainment
OnSite: Picnic Area, Grills, Jogging Paths, Park *(Charlestown Naval Shipyard; 8th Street Circle, 9th St. Circle)*, Sightseeing *(Freedom Trail)* **OnCall:** Fishing Charter *(Hatunamatata 781-910-1039)* **Near:** Pool, Playground, Dive Shop, Museum *(USS Constitution 242-5670 $4/2; Bunker Hill Monument 242-5641; Boston Marine Society 242-0522 - sea captains)* **Under 1 mi:** Fitness Center *(Union 482-1122)*, Video Rental *(Blockbuster 242-9893)* **1-3 mi:** Tennis Courts *(Badminton & Tennis Club 247-8748)*, Bowling *(Central Park 567-7073)*, Movie Theater *(Orpheum 679-0810)*, Cultural Attract *(TD Garden - Celtics, Bruins, events & Sports Museum)* **3+ mi:** Golf Course *(Fresh Pond 349-6282, 6 mi.)*

Provisioning and General Services
OnSite: Bakery, Dry Cleaners **Near:** Delicatessen *(Adam's 241-7110)*, Wine/Beer, Liquor Store *(McCarthy Bros 242-4877)*, Bank/ATM, Laundry *(Mary Ann's 242-9386)*, Newsstand **Under 1 mi:** Convenience Store *(7-Eleven 723-7599)*, Market *(Johnnie's Foodmaster 660-1372)*, Supermarket *(Shaw's 625-4070)*, Farmers' Market *(Thompson Square 241-8866 Wed 2-7pm)*, Post Office, Protestant Church, Library *(242-1248)*, Beauty Salon *(Element 242-3200)*, Bookstore *(Borders 679-0887)*, Pharmacy *(High 242-0415)*, Hardware Store *(Salem St. 523-4759)*, Copies Etc. *(Copy Cop 367-3370)* **1-3 mi:** Gourmet Shop *(Gypsy Kitchen 227 9649)*, Health Food *(Springwell 723-9828)*, Catholic Church, Synagogue

Transportation
OnSite: Local Bus, Ferry Service *(Longwharf $1.70/Free, Also Logan $12)* **OnCall:** Water Taxi *(422-0392 $20/Free 422-0392)*, Rental Car *(Enterprise 723-8077)*, Taxi *(After Hours 242-2666)* **Near:** Bikes **1-3 mi:** InterCity Bus *(Coach 887-2200)*, Rail *(MBTA 222-3200)* **Airport:** Logan Int'l. *(5 mi.)*

Medical Services
911 Service **Near:** Doctor *(Mass Gen 726-2000)* **Under 1 mi:** Dentist *(Goldman 242-0663)*, Chiropractor *(Broadway 685-7775)* **1-3 mi:** Holistic Services *(Chi Wellness 625-1211)*, Veterinarian *(Amster 227-8270)* **Hospital:** Mass. General 726-2000 *(0.1 mi.)*

Setting -- Within the retired, historic 63-acre Charlestown Navy Yard, this large, two-pier marina complex sports 350 slips, mega-yacht side-ties, retail shops, a boardwalk and spectacular Boston skyline views. Abutting a modernistic, 4-story gray condo and 11-story brick contemporary apartment building, Pier Six berths the two-story Tavern on the Water Restaurant. Pier Eight, guarded by an 800-foot floating breakwater, hosts the nerve center - a low-country style contemporary clapboard clubhouse with a pale green roof. Harborwalk edges the water, and parks are interspersed among the wharfs.

Marina Notes -- *to 55 ft. $3/ft. 55 ft.-99 ft. $3.50/ft., Wkly $21/ft. Over 99 ft. $4/ft., Wkly $24.50/ft. July 4th Wknd, add $1/ft. 100A Single-Phase $35, 3-phase $40. Day rate Max 2.5 hrs $20/30/50. **Email:dockmaster@ShipyardQuartersMarina.com. 24 hr. security (CCTV/Card Access). Four way tie-ups. Houseboats & other liveaboards. Pier 6 - more action at onsite Tavern on the Water (11:30am-9pm, 'til 10 wknds - 200-seat patio), better high-tide vistas of Boston & Zakim bridge, limited heads. Pier 8 - quieter, more privacy, access to main heads. Bathhouse: Surprisingly basic.

Notable -- 30-acres of the Charlestown Navy Yard, are now part of the Boston National Historical Park, which includes greenspace, jogging paths, the Harborwalk, the USS Constitution (Old Ironsides) and Museum, USS Cassin Young, Visitors Center and Bunker Hill Monument. Boston's 2.5-mile red-brick historic Freedom Trail passes the marina as well as 16 significant American treasures - including Paul Revere's House, Copps Hill, Old North Church and Kings Chapel. A water taxi and transit authority's water shuttle zip around the harbor - from Charlestown Navy Yard to Long Wharf downtown every 15 minutes.

12. MA - BOSTON HARBOR REGION

PHOTOS ON DVD: 22

Constitution Marina

28 Constitution Road; Boston, MA 02129

Tel: (617) 241-9640 **VHF: Monitor** Ch. 9 **Talk** Ch. 69
Fax: (617) 242-3013 **Alternate Tel:** n/a
Email: sebastian@bosport.com **Web:** www.constitutionmarina.com
Nearest Town: Boston *(0.25 mi.)* **Tourist Info:** (617) 227-4500

Navigational Information

Lat: 42°22.213' **Long:** 071°03.506' **Tide:** 10 ft. **Current:** 2 kt. **Chart:** 13272
Rep. Depths (*MLW*): Entry 30 ft. **Fuel Dock** n/a **Max Slip/Moor** 40 ft./40 ft.
Access: Charles River, turn to port at Coast Guard, on starboard

Marina Facilities *(In Season/Off Season)*

Fuel: No
Slips: 265 Total, 60 Transient **Max LOA:** 150 ft. **Max Beam:** 30 ft.
Rate *(per ft.)*: **Day** $3.00* **Week** $17.50 **Month** $60/30
Power: 30 amp Incl., **50 amp** $15, **100 amp** $45, **200 amp** n/a
Cable TV: Yes **Dockside Phone:** Yes
Dock Type: Floating, Long Fingers, Alongside, Wood, Composition
Moorings: 0 Total, 0 Transient **Launch:** No, Dinghy Dock (Free)
Rate: Day n/a **Week** n/a **Month** n/a
Heads: 5 Toilet(s), 7 Shower(s) *(dressing rooms)*, Book Exchange
Internet: Yes *(Office)* **Laundry:** 3 Washer(s), 4 Dryer(s)
Pump-Out: Full Service, 1 Central, 1 Port **Fee:** Free **Closed Heads:** Yes

Marina Operations

Owner/Manager: Tom Cox **Dockmaster:** Sebastian Da Silva
In-Season: Mar-Nov, 8am-8pm **Off-Season:** Dec-Apr, 9am-5pm
After-Hours Arrival: Call ahead.
Reservations: Yes, Preferred **Credit Cards:** Visa/MC, Dscvr, Amex
Discounts: None
Pets: Welcome, Dog Walk Area **Handicap Access:** Yes, Heads

Marina Services and Boat Supplies

Services - Docking Assistance, Concierge, Boaters' Lounge, Security, Dock Carts **Communication -** Pay Phone (3), FedEx, DHL, UPS, Express Mail *(Sat Del)* **Supplies - OnSite:** Ice *(Block, Cube)* **1-3 mi:** Ships' Store *(CG Edwards 268-4111)*, Marine Discount Store *(CG Edwards 268-4111)*, Bait/Tackle *(Firefly 423-3474)*, Propane *(U Haul 625-2789)*

Boatyard Services

OnSite: Forklift, Crane, Engine mechanic *(gas, diesel)*, Electrical Repairs, Electronics Repairs, Refrigeration **OnCall:** Propeller Repairs

Restaurants and Accommodations

Near: Restaurant *(Olives 242-1999, D $9.25-32.50)*, *(Ironside Grille 242-1384, L & D $7-22)*, *(Figs 242-2229, D $11-19)*, *(Warren Tavern 241-8142, L $8-16, D $10-16, historic)*, *(Max & Dillan's 242-7400, D $6.50-18, Brunch $7-19)*, Lite Fare *(Sorrelle Bakery 242-5980, B $3-5, L $3.50-7)*, Hotel *(Residence Inn 242-9000, $129-$399)* **Under 1 mi:** Hotel *(Boston Garden 720-5544, $100-149)*, *(Bullfinch 624-0202, $100-149)*

Recreation and Entertainment

OnSite: Heated Pool, Picnic Area, Grills, Fitness Center *(Union Gym 482-1122)*, Boat Rentals *(Night Rider 317-6668)*, Hike/Bike Trails **Near:** Fishing Charter *(Ondular 710-5098)*, Volleyball, Park *(City Square, Paul Revere)*, Museum *(USS Constitution, 426-1812 Free; Boston Science 723-2500 $20/17; Old State House 426-1812, $5/1 - 1 mi.)*, Tours *(Greenway Zoomahs 202-9735; North End Market 523-6032)* **Under 1 mi:** Playground, Golf Course *(Newton Commonwealth 630-1971)*, Sightseeing *(Boston by Foot 367-2345)* **1-3 mi:** Bowling *(Central Park 567-7073)*, Movie Theater *(Orpheum 679-0810)*, Cultural Attract *(New England Aquarium 973-5200 $22/14; Citi Performing Arts 482-9393, free)*

Provisioning and General Services

Near: Liquor Store *(Charlestown 242-3600)*, Bakery *(Sorelle 242-5980)*, Farmers' Market *(Thompson Sq. at Main & Austin Sts.)*, Beauty Salon *(Salon 44 242-9745)*, Dry Cleaners *(Town Hill 241-9845)*, Newsstand **Under 1 mi:** Market *(Foodmaster 660-1372)*, Delicatessen *(Tutto Italiano 557-4002)*, Wine/Beer *(Wine Cave 227-7311)*, Green Grocer *(Costa 241-8410)*, Fishmonger *(Mercato del Mare 362-7477)*, Bank/ATM, Post Office *(241-5322)*, Catholic Church, Protestant Church, Library *(Charlestown 242-1248)*, Laundry *(Lavanderia 523-9601)*, Bookstore *(Borders 679-0887)*, Pharmacy *(High 242-0415)*, Hardware Store *(Salem Street True Value 523-4759)*, Florist *(A Wild Floer 242-4214)* **1-3 mi:** Supermarket *(Stop & Shop 666-1024)*, Gourmet Shop *(Gypsy Kitchen 227-9649)*, Health Food *(Topshelf 723-9828)*, Synagogue, Department Store *(Macy's 357-3000)*

Transportation

OnSite: Courtesy Car/Van, Local Bus *(MBTA)*, Ferry Service *(Longwharf $1.70/Free, Also Logan $12)* **OnCall:** Water Taxi *(City 422-0392)*, Rental Car *(Enterprise 723-8077)*, Taxi **Under 1 mi:** Bikes *(Urban AdvenTours 670-0637)* **1-3 mi:** Rail *(MBTA 222-3200)* **Airport:** Logan *(3.5 mi)*

Medical Services

911 Service **Near:** Dentist *(Chally 241-7959)*, Chiropractor *(Charlestown 242-4476)* **Under 1 mi:** Optician *(Vision North 227-2010)* **1-3 mi:** Doctor *(Mass Gen 724-6006)*, Holistic Services *(Chi Wellness 625-1211)*, Veterinarian *(At Home 753-9300)* **Hospital:** Mass. Gen. 726 2000 *(1.3 mi.)*

Setting -- Past the Coast Guard station, the marina lies seaward of the Charles River locks - just east of Old Ironsides. Five docks are tucked into a quiet, protected basin, and another fronts a low-slung brick office building. The three-story, gray clapboard office and clubhouse overlooks the dockside pool. Views are of Boston skyline, the dramatically illuminated Zakim suspension bridge, the Charlestown Navy Yard and a Residence Inn with waterside deck.

Marina Notes -- *To 55 ft. $3/ft. Over 55 ft $4/ft./nt, $24.50.ft/wk. July 4th, add $1/ft., Holidays 2-day min. Day dockage 4 hr. max - to 55 ft. $25, Over 55 ft. $50. 1st 30A free, 2nd $10, 1st 50A $15, 2nd $25, 100A $45. Some basic yard services at this well-managed facility. Inviting, lively pool and sun deck (Only marina pool in Boston). Pleasant boaters' lounge. Attracts sailboats and large yachts. Welcomes flotillas. Perfect perch for July 4th fireworks. Liveaboards & long-term transients. "Bed and Breakfast Afloat" - lodgings on five diverse vessels. Bathhouse: Tiled, commodious full baths off laundry room.

Notable -- Along the Freedom Trail that edges the marina, the venerable USS Constitution, the world's oldest commissioned war ship, and its museum are adjacent to the east. The Trail's Visitor's Center is next door to the west (for maps and brochures). From there, the 2.5-mile trail winds through early American history, stopping at 16 important sites including the Bunker Hill Monument. Harborwalk also traces the waterfront connecting vistas and parks - Tudor Wharf where ice blocks were traded and expansive, green Paul Revere Park. Boston Garden is 0.4 mile away for sporting events or concerts, as is North Station and the North End for Italian dining and provisioning. Best bet is the Museum of Science with its planetarium, 3-D digital and Imax theatre.

PHOTOS ON DVD: 22

Navigational Information
Lat: 42°17.970' **Long:** 071°01.700' **Tide:** 9 ft. **Current:** n/a **Chart:** 13270
Rep. Depths (*MLW*): Entry 13 ft. **Fuel Dock** 13 ft. **Max Slip/Moor** 13 ft./-
Access: Dorchester Bay; Rainbow tank to starboard, to Squantum Channel

Marina Facilities *(In Season/Off Season)*
Fuel: *ValvTect* - Gasoline, Diesel, High-Speed Pumps
Slips: 685 Total, 60 Transient **Max LOA:** 300 ft. **Max Beam:** n/a
Rate *(per ft.)*: **Day** $3.50/$1.25 **Week** $13.50 ($12 over 60') **Month** $33.75*
Power: 30 amp $6.50, **50 amp** $12.50, **100 amp** $40, **200 amp** n/a
Cable TV: No **Dockside Phone:** No
Dock Type: Floating, Pilings, Alongside, Concrete, Wood
Moorings: 0 Total, 0 Transient **Launch:** n/a, Dinghy Dock
Rate: Day n/a **Week** n/a **Month** n/a
Heads: 4 Toilet(s), 7 Shower(s)
Internet: Yes *(Wi-Fii, Free)* **Laundry:** 3 Washer(s), 3 Dryer(s)
Pump-Out: OnSite, Self Service, 2 Central **Fee:** Free **Closed Heads:** Yes

Marina Operations
Owner/Manager: Dave Jensen **Dockmaster:** Paul Jensen
In-Season: Apr 15-Oct, 7am-Dusk **Off-Season:** Nov-Apr 14, 7:30am-5pm
After-Hours Arrival: Call security on Ch. 10
Reservations: Yes **Credit Cards:** Visa/MC, Amex
Discounts: None
Pets: Welcome, Dog Walk Area **Handicap Access:** No

Marina Bay

333 Victory Road; Quincy, MA 02171

Tel: (617) 847-1800; (888) 285-0441 **VHF: Monitor** Ch. 9 **Talk** n/a
Fax: (617) 847-1840 **Alternate Tel:** (617) 479-0277
Email: marinabay@flagshipmarinas.com **Web:** marinabayboston.com
Nearest Town: Quincy *(1 mi.)* **Tourist Info:** (617) 657-0527

Marina Services and Boat Supplies
Services - Docking Assistance, Concierge, Security, Trash Pick-Up, Dock Carts, 3 Phase **Communication -** Pay Phone (4), FedEx, UPS, Express Mail **Supplies - OnSite:** Ice *(Cube)*, Ships' Store **Under 1 mi:** Propane *(Neponset Circle 288-1581)* **1-3 mi:** Bait/Tackle *(P & J 288-7917)*

Boatyard Services
OnSite: Travelift *(35T)*, Forklift, Crane, Engine mechanic *(gas, diesel)*, Electrical Repairs, Electronics Repairs, Hull Repairs, Rigger, Canvas Work, Divers, Bottom Cleaning, Brightwork, Refrigeration, Compound, Wash & Wax, Woodworking, Upholstery, Painting **OnCall:** Propeller Repairs **Dealer for:** Northern Lights, Kohler, Yanmar, Kellog, Manset. **Yard Rates:** $80/hr. **Storage:** In-Water $35/ft., On-Land $35/ft.

Restaurants and Accommodations
OnSite: Restaurant *(Port 305 302-4447)*, *(Siro's 472-4500, L $12-18, D $12-30, Fine Dining. Grilled Pizza, too 11:30am-4pm, 5-10pm, Fri & Sat to 11pm)*, *(Captain Fishbones 471-3511, B $10, L & D $10-24, Kids' $5 Delivers)*, Coffee Shop *(Coffee Break Cafe 773-9420)*, Lite Fare *(Water Club 328-6500, L & D $7-17 Dancing. Function menu)*, *(Bites at the Ocean Club 689-0600, outdoor nightclub)*, *(Chantey 770-4121, D $9-16)*, Pizzeria *(Nonna's Kitchen 471-9101)*, Condo/Cottage *(Marina Bay)* **1-3 mi:** Pizzeria *(Riddick's 436-7848, take-out, salads, too)*, Motel *(Comfort Inn 287-9200)*

Recreation and Entertainment
OnSite: Picnic Area, Grills, Boat Rentals *(Charters Unlimited 328-9224)*, Fishing Charter *(Lurker 460-0501; Boston 833-2759)* **Under 1 mi:** Playground, Park *(Squantum Point)* **1-3 mi:** Golf Course *(Presidents 328-3444)*, Fitness Center *(Planet Fitness 287-8885)*, Bowling *(First Boston Tenpin 825-3800)*, Video Rental *(Redbox)*, Museum *(Josiah Quincy House 227-3956 $5/2.50; Pierce House 288-6041)*, Galleries *(Proart 282-2810)* **3+ mi:** Cultural Attract *(JFK Library 288-6041 $12/9, 5 mi.)*

Provisioning and General Services
OnSite: Convenience Store, Wine/Beer *(Red Bull 479-9398)*, Bank/ATM, Beauty Salon *(Aria 472-1344)*, Dry Cleaners *(Marina Bay 773-7970)*, Laundry *(Full-serv)*, Copies Etc. *(or Staples 2 mi.)* **Under 1 mi:** Library *(376-1320)* **1-3 mi:** Supermarket *(Stop & Shop)*, Delicatessen *(Old Heidelberg 463-3880)*, Liquor Store *(T & T 471-6700)*, Bakery *(Panera 328-5473; Greenhills 825-8187)*, Green Grocer *(Lambert's 436-2997)*, Fishmonger *(Burke's 479-1540)*, Post Office, Catholic Church, Protestant Church, Barber Shop *(Clippers 328-9719)*, Bookstore *(Brattle 542-0210)*, Pharmacy *(CVS 471-0041)*, Hardware Store *(Home Depot 442-6110)*, Florist *(Lopez 265-8801)*, Retail Shops *(South Bay Center 369-6613)*

Transportation
OnSite: Courtesy Car/Van *(Transfer throughout complex and to Quincy)* **OnCall:** Rental Car *(Enterprise 376-4769)*, Taxi *(Pringle 567-1000; Quincy 472-4111)* **Near:** Water Taxi *(MBTA Shuttle)*, Local Bus **1-3 mi:** Bikes **3+ mi:** Rail *(Boston 268-9000, 4 mi.)* **Airport:** Logan Int'l. *(11 mi.)*

Medical Services
911 Service **OnSite:** Dentist *(Marnia Bay 479-8080)*, Holistic Services *(Aria Salon & Spa 472-1344)* **OnCall:** Ambulance **Under 1 mi:** Doctor *(Pitt 847-6995)*, Chiropractor *(Spine Care 282-6400)* **1-3 mi:** Veterinarian *(Hancock 773-0008)* **Hospital:** Carney 296-3114 *(3.5 mi.)*

Setting -- On the Squantum Peninsula at the head of Dorchester Bay, 686 slips, protected by an L-shaped rock breakwater, form the centerpiece of a retail and entertainment complex backed by mid-rise condos. Along the boardwalk, restaurants, bars, nightclubs and useful services occupy Nantucket-style gray-shingled buildings - punctuated by a clocktower. Seaward views are the University of Massachusetts, Harbor Islands and Boston's skyline.

Marina Notes -- *Monthly rate: 30 days can be used over length of the season. Dockmaster 2nd floor tower oversees operation. 25 dedicated transient slips. Concierge service for parts, food, beer, wine & liquor delivery. Courtesy shuttle internally and to Quincy. Multiple pump-outs. Wi-Fi at some slips (inquire!). For quiet & privacy request outer slip. Onsite convenience store. Key-carded dock access. 24/7 Security. Megayacht facilities 100A, 1-phase $40, 3-phase $50. Marine services - re-powers, commissioning-decommissioning, diagnostics, detailing, indoor/outdoor storage, haul/launch with 35-ton travelift. Many marina-sponsored events. Primarily powerboats. Bathhouse: Key carded. 24 hrs. Short walk. Large, well-tended, fully-tiled but not resort-quality. Laundry.

Notable -- Marina Bay's waterside eateries, nightlife, and general party ambiance attract many seasonals as well as Boston week-enders - the wrap-around boardwalk makes boaters part of the scene. In addition to three full-service restaurants with alfresco dining options, there are eight indoor-outdoor bars with light menus, two nightclubs, and three event spaces (Summer House, Gazebos I & II) plus the open-air 62,000 sq. foot Ocean Club with a capacity of 1600 and an open kitchen eatery, four bars, LED fountains, local & national bands, DJs, seaside cabanas, pro volleyball court, ping pong tables and a basketball court.

PHOTOS ON DVD: 22

Captain's Cove Marina

PO Box 6903; 100 Cove Way; Quincy, MA 02169

Tel: (617) 328-3331 **VHF: Monitor** n/a **Talk** n/a
Fax: (617) 773-3840 **Alternate Tel:** (617) 479-2440
Email: steve@captainscovemarina.com **Web:** captainscovemarina.com
Nearest Town: Quincy **Tourist Info:** (617) 479-1111

Navigational Information

Lat: 42°15.206' **Long:** 070°58.939' **Tide:** 9 ft. **Current:** n/a **Chart:** 13270
Rep. Depths (*MLW*): Entry n/a **Fuel Dock** n/a **Max Slip/Moor** 9 ft./-
Access: Weymouth Fore River to Hole Point reach entrance channel

Marina Facilities *(In Season/Off Season)*

Fuel: No
Slips: 222 Total, 17 Transient **Max LOA:** 65 ft. **Max Beam:** 20 ft.
Rate *(per ft.)*: **Day** $2.00/$1.00 **Week** $12 **Month** $35
Power: 30 amp Incl., **50 amp** inq, **100 amp** n/a, **200 amp** n/a
Cable TV: No **Dockside Phone:** No
Dock Type: Floating, Aluminum
Moorings: 0 Total, 0 Transient **Launch:** n/a, Dinghy Dock
Rate: Day n/a **Week** n/a **Month** n/a
Heads: 2 Toilet(s), 2 Shower(s)
Internet: No **Laundry:** None
Pump-Out: OnSite, Self Service **Fee:** Free **Closed Heads:** No

Marina Operations

Owner/Manager: Capt. Steve Rodri **Dockmaster:** Same
In-Season: Apr-Nov, 9am-5pm **Off-Season:** Dec-Mar, 9am-5pm
After-Hours Arrival: Proceed to assigned slip. Prior registration required
Reservations: Yes **Credit Cards:** Visa/MC
Discounts: None
Pets: Welcome, Dog Walk Area **Handicap Access:** Yes, Heads, Docks

Marina Services and Boat Supplies

Services - Security *(Video surveillance)*, Dock Carts **Supplies - OnSite:** Ice *(Block, Cube)* **Under 1 mi:** Bait/Tackle *(Sportsman's Den 770-3884)* **1-3 mi:** Ships' Store *(Anchor Express 376-9999)*, Propane *(U-Haul 781-331-4050)* **3+ mi:** West Marine *(781-356-2100, 4 mi.)*

Boatyard Services

OnCall: Divers, Bottom Cleaning, Brightwork, Interior Cleaning **Nearest Yard:** Hingham Shipyard Marinas (781) 749-6647

Restaurants and Accommodations

Near: Restaurant *(Punjab Café 472-4860, reportedly wonderful Indian food)* **Under 1 mi:** Restaurant *(Mandarin King 786-8889, L $5-7, D $8-16, delivers)*, *(Coop's Bar & Grill 472-2667)*, *(Quincy's Kitchen 786-9992)*, *(Nick's Pizza Roast Beef-Seafood 774-1212)*, *(Inn at Bay Pointe 472-3200, D $16-25)*, Fast Food *(McDs, BK, DQ 479-6488)*, Pizzeria *(Jimmy's 984-0333)*, Inn/B&B *(Brookside House 471-0112, 2-night min)* **1-3 mi:** Motel *(Arbor Inn Motor Lodge 781-337-8070)*, Hotel *(Marriott 472-1000)*

Recreation and Entertainment

OnSite: Picnic Area, Grills **Under 1 mi:** Beach *(Mound Street)*, Fitness Center *("Y" 479-8500)*, Fishing Charter *(Ave Maria 909-2125)*, Video Rental *(Blockbuster 471-5055; Redbox in Stop & Shop)*, Video Arcade, Park *(Mound Saint Beach)*, Museum *(U.S. Naval Ship Building Museum 479-7900 $8/6)*, Galleries *(Maritime Art Prints 479-9107; Quincy Art Association 770-2482)* **1-3 mi:** Pool *(South Shore CC 781-331-1144)*, Dive Shop *(South Shore CC)*, Tennis Courts *(South Shore CC)*, Bowling *(Quincy Ave. 472-3597)*, Tours *(Discover Quincy 657-0527)*, Sightseeing *(Adams Nat'l Historical Park Visitor Ctr 770-1175)* **3+ mi:** Golf Course *(Granite Links 689-1900, 4 mi.)*, Movie Theater *(AMC Braintree 888-62-4386, 4.5 mi)*

Provisioning and General Services

Near: Convenience Store *(Tedeschi 479-1935)*, Laundry *(Friendly 471-1916)*, Pharmacy *(Baxter 773-7733)*, Florist *(Quint's 773-7620)* **Under 1 mi:** Supermarket *(Stop & Shop 773-4510)*, Delicatessen *(Cucina Mia 479-1945)*, Bakery *(Fratelli's 328-7855)*, Bank/ATM, Synagogue, Library *(Thomas Crane 376-1301)*, Beauty Salon *(Shear Stylers 471-6908)*, Dry Cleaners *(Quincy 472-8287)* **1-3 mi:** Health Food *(Good Health 773-4925)*, Wine/Beer *(Gypsy 847-1846)*, Liquor Store *(National 479-3131)*, Green Grocer *(Sunshine Fruit 328-5940)*, Fishmonger *(Carter's 817-2142)*, Post Office, Catholic Church, Protestant Church, Hardware Store *(Curry Ace 843-1616)*, Department Store *(WalMart 745-4390; T.J. Maxx 328-1763)*, Buying Club *(BJ's 857-403-2002)*, Copies Etc. *(Staples 781-331-4282)*

Transportation

OnCall: Rental Car *(Enterprise 376-0429)*, Taxi *(Braintree Cab 781-848-5050)*, Airport Limo *(Brewster Coach 769-9800)* **Under 1 mi:** Bikes *(Anderson 769-9669)*, Ferry Service *(Harbor Express)* **1-3 mi:** Local Bus *(T-line)*, Rail *(Quincy Center)* **Airport:** Logan Int'l. 634-0006 *(12 mi.)*

Medical Services

911 Service **OnCall:** Ambulance **Near:** Dentist *(Parsons 781-545-0039)*, Chiropractor *(Tardanico 479-7231)*, Holistic Services *(Acupuncture @ Balance Matters 429-9176)* **Under 1 mi:** Optician *(Pearle Vision 773-7424)* **1-3 mi:** Doctor *(Harbor Medical 781-545-7243)*, Veterinarian *(VCA 773-8247)* **Hospital:** Quincy Medical Center 773-6100 *(1.9 mi.)*

Setting -- Tucked up the Hole Point Reach channel in Town River Bay, off Weymouth Fore River, the marina lies beneath a 10-story apartment complex - adjacent to Town River Yacht Club. Landward is the expansive green lawn of the apartment complex, and seaward are marshlands and Sprague's large green storage tanks to the north. While not the most scenic, this 200-slip marina is very protected in a big blow and near many historic attractions.

Marina Notes -- *Office address: 218 Willard Street, Quincy, MA 02169 (617) 479-2440. Very few marine services available onsite. Quiet location. Pool not available to marina guests. Primarily smaller powerboats; Very few sailboats. Small group of helpful liveaboards. Good security but only adequate maintenance. Bridge-free access despite its distance from open water. Good parking. Lively group of seasonal slipholders. Manager lives onsite. Bathhouse: Cinderblock building - part of pool entrance. Adequate and relatively close to the slips.

Notable -- Routine commercial services are quite convenient; the Southern Artery, aka Route 3A, one of the main drags of hardscrabble Quincy, is a short walk. A mile away the U.S. Naval & Shipbuilding Museum, home to the USS Salem, the world's only preserved Heavy Cruiser, is located on the site of abandoned Fore River Shipyard. But Quincy is especially noteworthy for the National Park Service "Adams" site. A mecca for history buffs or David McCullough fans, the sprawling complex's visitors' center is a 2-mile cab ride. Tours are required (last one 3:15pm - all internal transportation provided). As part of this excursion, see John Adams' Birthplace (773-1177), Josiah Quincy House (471-4508), and, a bit further, Abigail Smith Adams' Birthplace (335-4205).

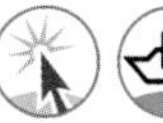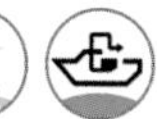

Hingham Shipyard Marinas

24 Shipyard Drive; Hingham, MA 02043

Tel: (781) 749-6647 **VHF: Monitor** Ch. 9 **Talk** Ch. 9
Fax: (781) 740-0700 **Alternate Tel:** n/a
Email: info@hinghamshipyardmarinas.com **Web:** See Marina Notes
Nearest Town: Hingham *(2 mi.)* **Tourist Info:** (617) 479-1111

Navigational Information
Lat: 42°15.210' **Long:** 070°55.290' **Tide:** 10 ft. **Current:** 5 kt. **Chart:** 13270
Rep. Depths (*MLW*): Entry 15 ft. **Fuel Dock** 19 ft. **Max Slip/Moor** 12 ft./-
Access: Hingham Bay to Weymouth Back River, south side

Marina Facilities *(In Season/Off Season)*
Fuel: Gasoline, Diesel
Slips: 500 Total, 20 Transient **Max LOA:** 300 ft. **Max Beam:** n/a
Rate *(per ft.)*: **Day** $3.00 **Week** n/a **Month** Inq.
Power: 30 amp $5, **50 amp** $10, **100 amp** Inq., **200 amp** Inq
Cable TV: No **Dockside Phone:** Yes
Dock Type: Floating, Alongside, Concrete, Wood
Moorings: 100 Total, 10 Transient **Launch:** Yes (Incl.), Dinghy Dock
Rate: Day $1.75/ft. **Week** Inq. **Month** Inq.
Heads: 8 Toilet(s), 8 Shower(s)
Internet: Yes *(Wi-Fi, Free)* **Laundry:** 1 Washer(s), 1 Dryer(s)
Pump-Out: OnSite, Full Service, 1 Central **Fee:** Free **Closed Heads:** Yes

Marina Operations
Owner/Manager: Cherie Rudzinsky **Dockmaster:** Vincent DiTullio
In-Season: May-Oct, 8am-10pm **Off-Season:** Nov-Apr, 9am-5pm*
After-Hours Arrival: See Security
Reservations: Yes **Credit Cards:** Visa/MC
Discounts: None
Pets: Welcome, Dog Walk Area **Handicap Access:** Yes, Heads, Docks

Marina Services and Boat Supplies
Services - Docking Assistance, Room Service to the Boat, Security *(24 Hrs.)*, Dock Carts **Communication -** Pay Phone, FedEx, UPS, Express Mail **Supplies - OnSite:** Ice *(Block, Cube)*, Ships' Store **Near:** Ice *(Shaved)* **Under 1 mi:** Propane *(U-Haul 331-4050)* **1-3 mi:** Bait/Tackle *(Fore River 617-770-1397)* **3+ mi:** West Marine *(356-2100, 7.5 mi.)*

Boatyard Services
OnSite: Travelift *(35T)*, Forklift, Crane, Engine mechanic *(gas, diesel)*, Electrical Repairs, Electronics Repairs, Hull Repairs, Rigger, Canvas Work, Bottom Cleaning, Brightwork, Air Conditioning, Refrigeration, Compound, Wash & Wax, Interior Cleaning, Propeller Repairs, Woodworking, Inflatable Repairs, Upholstery, Yacht Interiors, Metal Fabrication, Painting, Awlgrip, Yacht Broker **OnCall:** Sail Loft, Divers **Yard Rates:** $98/hr. **Storage:** In-Water $37/ft., On-Land $50-55/ft.

Restaurants and Accommodations
Near: Restaurant *(Hingham Beer Works 749-9774, L $8-13, D $9-23, Kids $4)*, *(Typhoon Asian 749-8484, L $9-18, D $14-48)*, *(Alma Nove 749-3353, L $10-18, D $18-29, waterfront patio with firepit)*, Snack Bar *(Red Mango Frozen yogurt, smoothies)*, Lite Fare *(Panera Bread 925-1370, Wi-Fi)*, Pizzeria *(Pizzapalooza 741-8400)* **Under 1 mi:** Restaurant *(Ninety Nine 740-8599, L & D $10-18)*, Fast Food *(McDs, BK)*

Recreation and Entertainment
OnSite: Picnic Area, Grills **Near:** Fitness Center *(Body Scape 749-0600)*, Movie Theater *(Patriot Cinemas 749-8780)*, Galleries *(South Shore Art 749-2100)* **Under 1 mi:** Park *(Stoddard's Neck)* **1-3 mi:** Pool *(South Shore C.C. 749-8479)*, Beach, Playground, Tennis Courts *(South Shore C.C.)*, Golf Course *(South Shore C..C)*, Bowling *(South Shore C.C.)*, Museum *(Bare Cove Fire 749-0028, USS Salem 617-479-7900, $8/Free; Hingham Historical Society's Old Ordinary 17thC tavern 749-7721 $3/1)*

Provisioning and General Services
Near: Market *(Fresh Market 740-2066)*, Delicatessen *(The Launch 741-8900)*, Wine/Beer *(Fresh Market)*, Liquor Store, Bakery *(Panera Bread 749-3643)*, Beauty Salon *(Supercuts 740-4414)*, Retail Shops *(Shipyard Village - Bed, Bath & Beyond, Old Navy, Talbots Outlet, Eastern Mountain Sports, Petco)* **Under 1 mi:** Supermarket *(Stop & Shop 749-1143)*, Bank/ATM, Dry Cleaners *(Twin City 749-2626)*, Laundry **1-3 mi:** Convenience Store *(7-Eleven)*, Farmers' Market *(Bathing Beach Sat 10am-2pm)*, Green Grocer *(Fruit Ctr 749-7332)*, Fishmonger *(Hingham Lobster 749-1984)*, Post Office, Catholic Church, Protestant Church, Library *(340-5036)*, Bookstore *(Benefics 337-8676)*, Pharmacy *(Rite Aid 749-0487)*, Hardware Store *(Lowe's 340-5964)*, Copies Etc. *(Staples 331-4282)*

Transportation
OnCall: Rental Car *(Enterprise 682-6166)*, Taxi *(Avalon 337-1562)*, Airport Limo **Near:** Ferry Service *(Rowes Wharf $6; Harbor Islands)* **1-3 mi:** Rail *(West Hingham)* **Airport:** Logan Int'l. *(15.5 mi.)*

Medical Services
911 Service **Near:** Dentist *(Brennan 361-3000)* **Under 1 mi:** Doctor *(Hingham-Weymouth 337-4105)*, Chiropractor *(Rees 741-5300)* **1-3 mi:** Holistic Services *(Saisons 749-2227)*, Optician *(337-8088)* **3+ mi:** Veterinarian *(Hingham 749-1243, 4 mi.)* **Hospital:** S. S. 624-8000 *(7 mi.)*

Setting -- Three miles from open water, head for the three massive gray condo buildings opposite the docks - and the large ferry wharf. A tan, two-story hipped-roof main building with widow's walk oversees the large, well-protected river marina with full-service boatyard, mooring field, easy ferry access to Boston, a boardwalk with views of Boston Harbor and America's oldest light station, and a new, sprawling mall with shops, eateries and services.

Marina Notes -- Web: hinghamshipyardmarinas.com. *Closed Sat & Sun off-season. Formerly Hewitt's Cove & Landfall Marinas. Now under new, service-focused, management. Most amenities upgraded. 30, 50, 100 & 200A service. 500+slips & 100 moorings (field to east of ferry landing). Launch service 7am - 10pm. Gated, quality, concrete-decked docks plus larger, single loaded slips. Wave attenuator minimizes roll from wakes. Internet cafe. Yard services provided by Black Diamond Marine (749-2222). Bathhouse: Recent, inviting, blue & beige-tiled, double-shower curtain dressing rooms.

Notable -- The adjacent Shipyard Village, part of the Launch at Hingham Shipyard, is an open-air mix of well-known shops as well as local boutiques, galleries, Fresh Market (European market-style stalls), a multi-screen movie theater, a half-dozen eateries, an outdoor amphitheater, and a 2-mile-long P.J.'s Way waterfront boardwalk - surrounded by The Moorings, a large in-development luxury residential and office complex. The original Hingham Shipyard employed more than 24,000 during WWII, building six ships per month and more than 275 in all. It's memorialized by a walking tour with descriptive panels (brochure). Charming, upscale Hingham sports several historic sites - the Old Ordinary, a 17thC coach stop, and the Old Ship Meeting House, a 17thC church.

PHOTOS ON DVD: 19

Tern Harbor Marina

275 River Street; North Weymouth, MA 02191

Tel: (781) 337-1964 **VHF: Monitor** Ch. 9 **Talk** n/a
Fax: (781) 337-3718 **Alternate Tel:** n/a
Email: info@ternharbormarina.com **Web:** www.ternharbormarina.com
Nearest Town: Quincy *(3 mi.)* **Tourist Info:** (617) 657-0527

Navigational Information

Lat: 42°15.322' **Long:** 070°55.530' **Tide:** 9 ft. **Current:** n/a **Chart:** 13270
Rep. Depths (*MLW*): Entry 14 ft. **Fuel Dock** n/a **Max Slip/Moor** 15 ft./18 ft.
Access: Hingham Bay to Weymouth Back River, north side

Marina Facilities *(In Season/Off Season)*

Fuel: No
Slips: 146 Total, 10 Transient **Max LOA:** 110 ft. **Max Beam:** n/a
Rate *(per ft.)*: **Day** $2.00* **Week** Inq. **Month** Inq.
Power: 30 amp $5, **50 amp** $10, **100 amp** n/a, **200 amp** n/a
Cable TV: No **Dockside Phone:** No
Dock Type: Floating, Long Fingers, Alongside, Concrete, Wood
Moorings: 15 Total, 2 Transient **Launch:** Yes ($5/trip), Dinghy Dock
Rate: Day $2/ft. **Week** $14/ft. **Month** Inq.
Heads: 6 Toilet(s), 6 Shower(s)
Internet: Yes *(Wi-Fi, Free)* **Laundry:** None
Pump-Out: OnSite, Self Service, 1 Central **Fee:** Free **Closed Heads:** Yes

Marina Operations

Owner/Manager: Paul Trendowicz & Joe Sugar **Dockmaster:** Same
In-Season: Year-Round, 8am-5pm **Off-Season:** n/a
After-Hours Arrival: Call ahead
Reservations: Yes **Credit Cards:** Visa/MC, Dscvr, Amex
Discounts: Restrictions **Dockage:** n/a **Fuel:** n/a **Repair:** n/a
Pets: Welcome **Handicap Access:** Yes, Heads

Marina Services and Boat Supplies

Services - Docking Assistance, Security *(Cameras)*, Trash Pick-Up, Dock Carts **Communication -** Mail & Package Hold, Fax in/out, FedEx, UPS, Express Mail **Supplies - OnSite:** Ice *(Block, Cube)*, Ships' Store **1-3 mi:** Bait/Tackle *(Fore River 770-1397)*, Propane *(U-Haul 331-4050)*

Boatyard Services

OnSite: Travelift *(35T)*, Forklift, Hydraulic Trailer, Engine mechanic *(gas, diesel)*, Electronics Repairs, Hull Repairs *(Custom 337-0055)*, Bottom Cleaning, Air Conditioning, Refrigeration, Compound, Wash & Wax, Propeller Repairs **OnCall:** Rigger, Brightwork **Under 1 mi:** Launching Ramp. **Dealer for:** Wellcraft. **Yard Rates:** Haul & Launch $9/ft., Power Wash $2.50/ft. **Storage:** On-Land $1/ft./day

Restaurants and Accommodations

OnCall: Pizzeria *(Domino's 740-4131)* **1-3 mi:** Restaurant *(The 99 340-9000, D $9-18, L & D $9-18)*, *(Margaritas Mexican 331-0303)*, *(Typhoon Asian 749-8484, L $9-18, D $14-48)*, Snack Bar *(Red Mango)*, Fast Food *(Alma Nove 749-3353, L $9-18, D $18-29)*, *(McDonald's 331-0966)*, Pizzeria *(Pizzapalooza 741-8400)*, *(Rose & Vicki 340-0111)*, Motel *(Arbor Inn 337-8070)* **3+ mi:** Inn/B&B *(Brookside House 617-471-0112, 4.5 mi)*

Recreation and Entertainment

OnSite: Party Boat *(Tern Marine 337-1964)* **Near:** Beach, Picnic Area *(Webb Mem. Park)*, Park *(Webb)* **Under 1 mi:** Grills, Video Rental *(Redbox)* **1-3 mi:** Fitness Center *(BodyScapes 749-0600)*, Boat Rentals *(ABC 331-6700)*, Fishing Charter *(Ave Maria 909-2125)*, Movie Theater *(Patriot Cinemas 749-8780)*, Museum *(Bare Cove Fire 749-0028)*, Sightseeing *(USS Salem 479-7900)*, Galleries *(B. G. 749-2411)* **3+ mi:** Pool *(South Shore C.C. 331-1144, 3.5 mi.)*, Tennis Courts *(So. Shore, 3.5 mi.)*, Golf Course *(So. Shore, 3.5 mi.)*, Bowling *(So. Shore 749-8400, 3.5 mi)*

Provisioning and General Services

Under 1 mi: Supermarket *(Super Stop & Shop 749-1143)*, Florist *(Stop & Shop)* **1-3 mi:** Convenience Store *(7-Eleven 331-0942)*, Market *(The Fresh Market 740-2824)*, Delicatessen *(Michele's 331-2988)*, Wine/Beer *(Hingham 740-9393)*, Liquor Store *(Ellis 335-9463)*, Bakery *(Panera 749-3643)*, Farmers' Market, Bank/ATM, Post Office, Catholic Church, Protestant Church, Library *(Weymouth 340-5036)*, Beauty Salon *(Supercuts 740-4414)*, Barber Shop, Dry Cleaners *(Dependable 335-7477)*, Laundry *(Wash 'n Dry 749-9814)*, Pharmacy *(CVS 335-3331)*, Hardware Store *(Lowe's 340-5964)*, Retail Shops *(The Launch at Hingham Shipyard)*, Copies Etc. *(Staples)* **3+ mi:** Synagogue *(4 mi.)*, Department Store *(WalMart 617-745-4390, 4 mi.)*, Buying Club *(BJs 335-8500, 5 mi.)*

Transportation

OnCall: Rental Car *(682-6166)*, Taxi *(Boston's Best 337-2277)*, Airport Limo *(Avalon 617-479-4399)* **1-3 mi:** InterCity Bus *(P & B 508-746-0378 to Boston)*, Ferry Service *(to Rowes Wharf, Boston)* **3+ mi:** Rail *(West Hingham 617-222-3200, 3.5 mi.)* **Airport:** Logan Int'l. *(16.5 mi.)*

Medical Services

911 Service **1-3 mi:** Doctor *(Krista 740-0333)*, Dentist *(Smile 836-5230)*, Chiropractor *(So. Shore 335-7671)*, Holistic Services *(Meridians Centre 331-0400)*, Optician *(My-Optics 337-8088)* **3+ mi:** Veterinarian *(Weymouth 337-0400, 4.2 mi.)* **Hospital:** Quincy 617-773-6100 *(5.3 mi.)*

Setting -- Cruise up Weymouth Back River, past Hingham Shipyard Marinas to port, Tern Harbor is to starboard in the shadow of a stark three-building apartment complex. A multi-level, three-story contemporary, backed by a large storage and work shed, overlooks the four sets of quality docks. Commercial and recreational traffic, as well as the commuter ferry to Boston, ply the river. The largely residential neighborhood offers inviting recreational options.

Marina Notes -- *Rates: $2.25/ft. weekends, $2/ft. weekdays, $3/ft. holidays. **8am-5pm Mon-Fri, Sat 9am-4pm, Sun 10am-2pm. Slips to 65 ft. Face dock to 150 ft. with 14 ft. MLW. Full-service boatyard with virtually all mechanical services available onsite. Recently renovated. Mostly powerboats. Bathhouse: Lovely painted cinderblock & ceramic tile with fiberglass stall showers. No laundry.

Notable -- It's a short walk to Wessagussett Beach - a long sweep of sand with views of the Boston skyline. A bit further is the entrance to William K. Webb Park, three connected drumlins that are now part of the Harbor Islands National Recreation Area. Twelve of the other 34 delightful Boston Harbor Islands are open to visitors - a good day trip (day moorings $10, overnight $25). A dinghy ride across Back River (listed above as 1-3 mi. by land) nets the recently completed Hingham Shipyard Village - a sprawling, upscale, open-air mall of markets, restaurants, shops and a movie theater (tie-up at the Shipyard). Or take the fast ferry to Rowes Wharf in Boston's downtown (Faneuil Hall/Quincy Market). Hingham's impressive, municipally owned South Shore Country Club offers a day pass with access to a swimming pool, 10-lane candlepin bowling alley, three tennis courts, and a Stiles 18-hole, par-72 golf course - originally built in 1922.

13. MA – South Shore & The Outer Cape

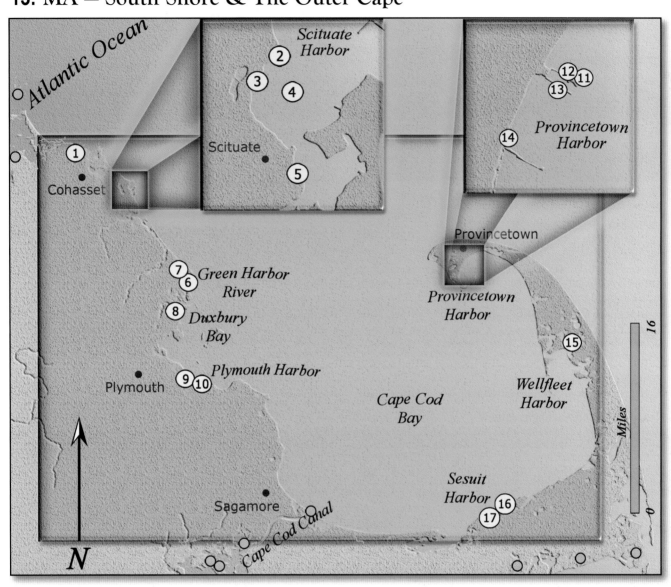

MAP	MARINA	HARBOR	PAGE	MAP	MARINA	HARBOR	PAGE
1	**Cohasset Harbor Marina**	*Cohasset Cove*	242	10	**Plymouth Yacht Club**	*Plymouth Harbor*	251
2	**Scituate Harbor Yacht Club**	*Scituate Harbor*	243	11	**Provincetown Public Pier**	*Provincetown Harbor*	252
3	**Scituate Harbor Marina**	*Scituate Harbor*	244	12	**Provincetown Harbor Marina**	*Provincetown Harbor*	253
4	**Waterline Moorings**	*Scituate Harbor*	245	13	**Provincetown Marina**	*Provincetown Harbor*	254
5	**Cole Parkway Municipal Marina**	*Scituate Harbor*	246	14	**Flyer's Boatyard Moorings**	*Provincetown Harbor*	255
6	**Taylor Marine**	*Green Harbor River*	247	15	**Town of Wellfleet Marina**	*Wellfleet Harbor*	256
7	**Green Harbor Marina**	*Green Harbor River*	248	16	**Northside Marina**	*Sesuit Harbor*	257
8	**Duxbury Town Pier**	*Duxbury Bay*	249	17	**Town of Dennis Marina**	*Sesuit Harbor*	258
9	**Brewer Plymouth Marine**	*Plymouth Harbor*	250				

RATINGS: 1-5 for Marina Facilities & Amenities,  1-2 for Boatyard Services,  1-2 for MegaYacht Facilities,  for Something Special.

SERVICES:  for CCM – Certified Clean Marina,  for Pump-Out,  for Internet,  for Fuel,  for Restaurant,  for Provisioning nearby, for Catamaran-friendly,  for SportFish Charter,  for Pool/Beach, and  for Golf within a mile. *For an explanation of ACC's Ratings, see page 8.*

Cohasset Harbor Marina

Cohasset Harbor Marina

33 Parker Avenue; Cohasset, MA 02025

Tel: (781) 337-1964 **VHF: Monitor** n/a **Talk** n/a
Fax: (781) 337-3718 **Alternate Tel:** n/a
Email: info@cohassetharbormarina.com **Web:** cohassetharbormarina.com
Nearest Town: Boston *(16 mi.)* **Tourist Info:** (781) 383-1010

Navigational Information

Lat: 42°14.337' **Long:** 070°49.145' **Tide:** 10 ft. **Current:** n/a **Chart:** 13269
Rep. Depths (*MLW*): Entry 5 ft. **Fuel Dock** n/a **Max Slip/Moor** 6 ft./-
Access: Minot's Lt to "Gangway" to Cohasset Hbr into Cohasset Cve SE side

Marina Facilities *(In Season/Off Season)*

Fuel: No
Slips: 75 Total, 3 Transient **Max LOA:** 42 ft. **Max Beam:** 14 ft.
Rate *(per ft.)*: **Day** $3.00 **Week** n/a **Month** n/a
Power: 30 amp $5*, **50 amp** $10, **100 amp** n/a, **200 amp** n/a
Cable TV: No **Dockside Phone:** No
Dock Type: Floating, Wood
Moorings: 0 Total, 0 Transient **Launch:** n/a
Rate: Day n/a **Week** n/a **Month** n/a
Heads: 2 Toilet(s)
Internet: No **Laundry:** None
Pump-Out: OnCall, 1 Port **Fee:** Free **Closed Heads:** Yes

Marina Operations

Owner/Manager: Joe Sugar **Dockmaster:** Bill Jackson
In-Season: May15-Oct15, 7:30am-5pm** **Off-Season:** Oct16-May14, Closed
After-Hours Arrival: Call in advance
Reservations: Yes, Required **Credit Cards:** Cash only
Discounts: None
Pets: Welcome **Handicap Access:** No

Marina Services and Boat Supplies

Services - Trash Pick-Up **Communication -** FedEx, UPS, Express Mail **Supplies - Under 1 mi:** Ice *(Cube)* **3+ mi:** Ships' Store *(North River 545-7811, 7 mi.)*, Bait/Tackle *(Belsan 781-545-9400, 4.5 mi.)*

Boatyard Services

Near: Launching Ramp. **Nearest Yard:** Mill River Marine (781) 383-1207

Restaurants and Accommodations

Under 1 mi: Restaurant *(Olde Salt House 383-2203, D $12-25)*, *(Bia Bistro 383-0464, D $18-32)*, *(Atlantica 383-0900, D $19-38, Bar Menu $10-16, Kids' $5-8, Sun Brunch 10-2)*, *(Zapps at Red Lion Inn 383-1704)*, *(Golden Rooster 545-4404)*, Snack Bar *(Seaport Ice Cream Town Wharf)*, Lite Fare *(5 South Main 383-3555, L & D)*, Inn/B&B *(Cohasset Harbor Inn 383-6550, $119-279)*, *(Red Lion 383-1704)* **1-3 mi:** Fast Food *(Wendy's)*, Pizzeria *(Cosmo's 383-0020)* **3+ mi:** Hotel *(Oceanside Inn 544-0002, $109-249, 4.4 mi.)*

Recreation and Entertainment

Under 1 mi: Beach *(Bassing's Beach)*, Fitness Center *(Body Studio 383-2999)*, Park *(Cohasset Common)* **1-3 mi:** Pool *(Cohasset 383-7463)*, Playground *(Hatherly)*, Tennis Courts *(Hatherly Country Club 545-9891)*, Golf Course *(Hatherly CC)*, Horseback Riding *(Longmeadow 544-3097)*, Video Rental *(Redbox, Blockbuster Express)*, Museum *(Cohasset Historical Society's Maritime Museum 383-1434 - explains Minot's Light - three buildings, each worth a stop 383-1434)*, Tours *(Walker 383-3129)*, Cultural Attract *(South Shore Music Circus 383-9850)*, Galleries *(South Shore Art Center 383-2787; Dalton Fine Arts 544-3200; Blue Heron 383-3210)*, Special Events *(St. Stephen's Church Carillon Concerts Sun 6pm 383-1083 features 57-bell carillon; Cohasset Arts Festival on the Common)* **3+ mi:** Boat Rentals *(Fairwind 383-2090, 4.4 mi.)*, Bowling *(Satuit Bowlaway 545-9726, 5.3 mi.)*, Fishing Charter *(Mass Bay Guides 545-6516, 4.4 mi.)*, Movie Theater *(Patriot 544-3130, 5 mi.)*, Sightseeing *(Wompatuck S.P., 4 mi.)*

Provisioning and General Services

Under 1 mi: Market *(Tedeschi 383-9470)*, Delicatessen *(Village 383-8181)*, Liquor Store *(Village Wine and Spirits 383-8886)*, Bakery *(French Memories 383-2216)*, Farmers' Market *(Thu 2:30-6:30pm Cohasset Common 781-383-2284)*, Bank/ATM, Post Office *(383-0320)*, Catholic Church, Dry Cleaners *(Dependable 383-9629)*, Newsstand **1-3 mi:** Convenience Store *(Egypt 544-3013)*, Supermarket *(Shaw's 383-2315)*, Health Food *(All the Best 383-3005)*, Wine/Beer *(Canandaigua 545-7656)*, Green Grocer *(Holy Hill 383-1455)*, Fishmonger *(Mullaney's 383-1181)*, Protestant Church, Library *(Paul Pratt Mem. 383-1348)*, Beauty Salon, Bookstore *(Buttonwood 383-2665)*, Pharmacy *(Walgreens 383-1773)*, Hardware Store *(Aubuchon 383-0053)*, Florist *(Stop & Shop 383-2101)*, Retail Shops *(Cushing Plaza)*

Transportation

OnCall: Rental Car *(Enterprise 383-2966)*, Taxi *(Scituate 383-8294)* **1-3 mi:** Bikes *(Cohasset Cycle 383-0707)*, Rail *(North Scituate MBTA to Boston 800-392-6100)* **Airport:** Logan Int'l. *(24 mi.)*

Medical Services

911 Service **Near:** Optician *(Baldry 383-8555)* **Under 1 mi:** Doctor *(Goldenson 545-6226)*, Dentist *(Thompson 383-1450)* **1-3 mi:** Holistic Services *(Adamo 383-3011)* **3+ mi:** Chiropractor *(Scituate Harbor 781-545-7388, 4.5 mi.)* **Hospital:** South Shore 340-8000 *(13 mi.)*

Setting -- Thread your way a half mile into the cove, past the Cohasset Yacht Club - and then make a sharp turn to port. A single, well-protected dock sprawls along the marsh, connected to the upland by a boardwalk and sturdy steel ramp. On shore, a white, one-story modular bungalow houses the office and amenities. The slips sport views of the quiet marsh, sand beach and of the Cohasset Sailing Club next door - notable for its replica of the top of Minot's Light.

Marina Notes -- *Power 20A & 50A. **Hours: Mon-Thu 7:30am-5pm, Fri-Sat 8am-7pm, Sun 8am-5pm. Pump-out boat; radio harbourmaster (Ch. 16, 383-0863). No boatyard services onsite. Mechanical service by McAnn's Marine 630-2011. Local lore has it that the Minot Light's 1-4-3 flash means "I Love You." Very shallow harbor. Bathhouse: Separate building. Aging, rustic full baths with small tub. Note: Also Mill River Marine for slip or mooring (383-1207).

Notable -- Quiet, unassuming Cohasset Harbor Marina offers entry to the charming seaside village of Cohasset - less than a mile walk; two blocks are lined with small restaurants, galleries, gift shops, and a convenience store. A half-mile from the marina, pretty Cohasset Harbor Inn has a fine dining restaurant, Atlantica, with window walls filled with harbor views, and the more casual waterside eatery Old Salt House. A bit further, the Red Lion Inn, founded in 1704, features a spectacular barn-like function room and a more casual brasserie. Some of the best national acts perform seasonally in the South Shore Music Circus tent, a mile plus from the marina. The town landing permits 30-minute tie-ups and is closer to the village. Leave time for a long walk along Atlantic Avenue and Jerusalem Road past beautiful old homes and estates. Boston is 16 NM by water, 30 miles by land or 20 minutes via the new Greenbush train.

Navigational Information

Lat: 42°12.129' **Long:** 070°43.416' **Tide:** 9 ft. **Current:** n/a **Chart:** 13269
Rep. Depths (*MLW*): Entry 10 ft. **Fuel Dock** n/a **Max Slip/Moor** -/8 ft.
Access: Cape Cod Bay to Scituate Harbor RW "SA," 1st facility to starboard

Marina Facilities *(In Season/Off Season)*

Fuel: No
Slips: 90 Total, 0 Transient **Max LOA:** 50 ft. **Max Beam:** n/a
Rate *(per ft.)*: **Day** $3.00 **Week** n/a **Month** n/a
Power: 30 amp n/a, **50 amp** n/a, **100 amp** n/a, **200 amp** n/a
Cable TV: No **Dockside Phone:** No
Dock Type: Floating, Long Fingers, Short Fingers, Alongside, Wood
Moorings: 40 Total, 15 Transient **Launch:** Yes (Free)
Rate: Day $35 **Week** n/a **Month** n/a
Heads: 2 Toilet(s), 3 Shower(s) *(dressing rooms)*, Book Exchange
Internet: No **Laundry:** None
Pump-Out: OnCall, 1 Port **Fee:** Free **Closed Heads:** Yes

Marina Operations

Owner/Manager: Nancy Anderson **Dockmaster:** Same
In-Season: LateMay-MidOct, 8a-11p* **Off-Season:** MidOct-MidMay, Closed
After-Hours Arrival: Call first and pick up mooring.
Reservations: No **Credit Cards:** Visa/MC, Cash or check
Discounts: None
Pets: Welcome, Dog Walk Area **Handicap Access:** No

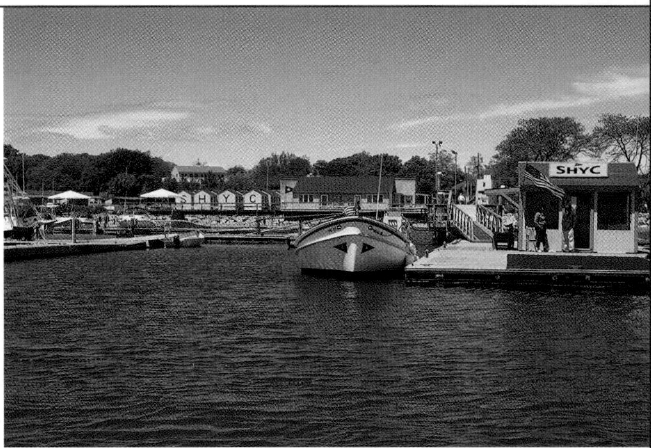

Scituate Harbor Yacht Club

PO Box 275; 84 Jericho Road; Scituate, MA 02066

Tel: (781) 545-0372 **VHF: Monitor** Ch. 9 **Talk** Ch. 9
Fax: (781) 545-2612 **Alternate Tel:** n/a
Email: shyc_manager@shyc.net **Web:** www.shyc.net
Nearest Town: Scituate *(0.5 mi.)* **Tourist Info:** (781) 545-4000

Marina Services and Boat Supplies

Services - Concierge, Security *(6pm-12am)*, Dock Carts **Communication -** Mail & Package Hold, Phone Messages, FedEx, UPS, Express Mail **Supplies - OnSite:** Ice *(Block, Cube)* **1-3 mi:** Ships' Store *(North River 545-7811)*, Bait/Tackle *(Belsan 545-9400)*

Boatyard Services

OnCall: Engine mechanic *(gas, diesel)*, Electrical Repairs, Electronics Repairs, Rigger, Canvas Work, Divers, Bottom Cleaning, Brightwork **Nearest Yard:** Scituate Boat Works (781) 545-0487

Restaurants and Accommodations

OnSite: Restaurant *(SHYC 545-7926, D $17-22)* **Near:** Restaurant *(Barker Tavern 545-6533)*, Lite Fare *(Satuit Tavern L & D $4-19 Kids' $5-7)*, Inn/B&B *(Inn at Scituate Harbor 545-5550, $119-175)* **Under 1 mi:** Restaurant *(Riva 545-5881, B $6-10, D $6-18)*, *(TK O'Malley Sports Café 545-4012, L $5-13, D $9-14)*, *(Mill Wharf & Chesters 545-3999, L $7-20, D $12-20, Pub $8-20 Kids' $7)*, *(Phin's 545-1110, B, L & D)*, *(Oro 378-2465, D $6-28)*, Coffee Shop *(Dunkin' Donuts 545-5345)*, Pizzeria *(Harbor House 545-5407)*

Recreation and Entertainment

Near: Beach *(Museum)*, Park **Under 1 mi:** Dive Shop *(Waterline 545-4154)*, Bowling *(Satuit Bowlaway 545-9726)*, Fishing Charter *(Enoch 264-5151; Elizabeth Marie 864-7154)*, Movie Theater *(Patriot 545-3130)*, Video Rental *(Hennessy News 545-6940)*, Galleries *(Scituate Art Assoc 545-6150; Little House of Arts 545-6100)* **1-3 mi:** Playground *(Hatherly)*, Golf Course *(Widows Walk 544-7777)*, Fitness Center *(Bay State A.C. 545-2249)*, Museum *(Scituate Hist. Soc 545-1083 - 9 sites incl. Maritime Museum 545-5565)*, Sightseeing *(Scituate Lighthouse)* **3+ mi:** Tennis Courts *(Scituate Racket 545-1184, 4 mi.)*, Tours *(No. River Wildlife Sanctuary, 4 mi.)*, Cultural Attract *(So. Shore Music Circus 383-9850, 6 mi.)*

Provisioning and General Services

Near: Barber Shop, Newsstand, Clothing Store **Under 1 mi:** Market *(Village 545-4896)*, Wine/Beer *(Front Street 545-4050)*, Liquor Store *(Harborside 545-0059)*, Fishmonger *(Mullaney's 545-5000)*, Bank/ATM *(Scituate Federal)*, Catholic Church, Protestant Church, Beauty Salon *(KA Ricco 545-7772)*, Dry Cleaners *(Cleaning Corner 545-0066)*, Laundry *(Superwash 545-9673)*, Bookstore *(Front Street 545-5011)*, Pharmacy *(CVS 545-0240)*, Hardware Store *(Satuit 545-8370)*, Florist *(Flowers & Festivities 545-0929)* **1-3 mi:** Convenience Store *(Dad's 545-7030)*, Bakery *(Morning Glories 545-3400)*, Farmers' Market *(Wed, 3-7 pm Country Way & Gannett Rd.)*, Green Grocer *(Tree Berry 545-7750)*, Post Office, Library *(Scituate 545-8727)* **3+ mi:** Supermarket *(Stop & Shop 383-9281, 5 mi.)*, Retail Shops *(Cushing Plaza, 5 mi.)*

Transportation

OnCall: Water Taxi *(545-4154, Ch. 9 $10)*, Rental Car *(Enterprise 383-2966)*, Taxi *(Cohasset 383-8294)* **Under 1 mi:** Airport Limo *(Abbey Road 749-9727)* **1-3 mi:** InterCity Bus *(P&B 508-746-0378)*, Rail *(to Boston 617-222-3200)* **Airport:** Logan Int'l. *(28 mi.)*

Medical Services

911 Service **Near:** Dentist *(Bradford 545-0039)* **Under 1 mi:** Chiropractor *(Scituate 545-7388)* **1-3 mi:** Doctor *(Pozatek 545-6565)*, Veterinarian *(Driftway 545-0952)* **Hospital:** So. Shore 624-8000 *(12 mi.)*

Setting -- The first facility to starboard, this attractively landscaped and impeccably maintained private club sits on a low bluff overlooking the outer harbor. Look for a rock bulkhead lined with a gray-shingled low-rise trimmed in blue, a row of small individual bathhouses, colorful umbrellas and the glass-fronted modified "A" frame dining room. Its docks radiate from a boardwalk-like pier - surrounded by a large mooring field.

Marina Notes -- **Shorter hours Mon-Thurs. Open to all cruisers. Mooring fee includes launch service (7 days during Jul & Aug), club heads and showers, use of the club dining room (Dinner Wed-Sun, $15-25 -- jackets and ties required), and bright, nicely furnished expansive lounge and veranda. Two private water taxi services if you miss the last launch. Note: Club pool and tennis courts not available to transients. Pump-out boat calls at moorings. Occasional slip available but watch depths! Bathhouse: Modern, tiled, private club quality. Note: Additional moorings may be available from the Satuit Boat Club next door.

Notable -- An alternative to the lovely club dining room, a week's worth of interesting restaurants, along with extensive services, are an easy walk (or shorter dinghy ride) in the classic New England beach town of Scituate. Walk the opposite direction for the beach and the Scituate Lighthouse, which dates to the early 19th century when it played a key role in the War of 1812 (545-1083, by appointment). One of the Scituate Historical Society's nine sites, The Maritime and Irish Mossing Museum, The Driftway, has artifacts from the wreck of the steamship "Pinthis" along with three centuries of South Shore seafaring life. Heritage Days in early August are a big draw. The town band shell hosts weeknight concerts.

PHOTOS ON DVD: 25

Scituate Harbor Marina

PO Box 295; 9 Seamore Road; Scituate, MA 02066

Tel: (781) 545-2165 **VHF: Monitor** Ch. 9 **Talk** Ch. 12
Fax: (781) 545-6754 **Alternate Tel:** n/a
Email: info@scituateharbormarina.com **Web:** scituateharbormarina.com
Nearest Town: Scituate *(0.4 mi.)* **Tourist Info:** (781) 545-4000

Navigational Information

Lat: 42°12.070' **Long:** 070°43.540' **Tide:** 9 ft. **Current:** n/a **Chart:** 13269
Rep. Depths (*MLW*): Entry 12 ft. **Fuel Dock** 12 ft. **Max Slip/Moor** 12 ft./-
Access: Cape Cod Bay to Scituate Harbor RW "SA," 3rd facility to starboard

Marina Facilities *(In Season/Off Season)*

Fuel: *Gulf* - Gasoline, Diesel
Slips: 90 Total, 5 Transient **Max LOA:** 75 ft. **Max Beam:** 16 ft.
Rate *(per ft.)*: **Day** $2.50 **Week** Inq. **Month** n/a
Power: 30 amp Incl., **50 amp** Incl., **100 amp** n/a, **200 amp** n/a
Cable TV: No **Dockside Phone:** No
Dock Type: Floating, Long Fingers
Moorings: 0 Total, 0 Transient **Launch:** n/a
Rate: Day n/a **Week** n/a **Month** n/a
Heads: 1 Toilet(s), 1 Shower(s)
Internet: No **Laundry:** None
Pump-Out: OnCall, Full Service **Fee:** Free **Closed Heads:** Yes

Marina Operations

Owner/Manager: Dobber Reynolds **Dockmaster:** Jim Breen
In-Season: Jun-Oct 10, 8am-7pm* **Off-Season:** Oct 11-May, 9am-6pm
After-Hours Arrival: Tie up at fuel dock.
Reservations: Yes** **Credit Cards:** Visa/MC, Dscvr, Din, Amex
Discounts: None
Pets: Welcome, Dog Walk Area **Handicap Access:** No

Marina Services and Boat Supplies

Services - Docking Assistance, Security *(24 Hrs., Gate/cameras)*, Trash Pick-Up, Dock Carts **Communication -** Pay Phone, FedEx, UPS, Express Mail **Supplies - OnSite:** Ice *(Block, Cube)* **1-3 mi:** Ships' Store *(No. River 545-7883; Erickson 829-0433, 5 mi.)*, Bait/Tackle *(Belsan 545-9400)*

Boatyard Services

OnSite: Launching Ramp, Electrical Repairs **OnCall:** Electronics Repairs, Hull Repairs, Rigger, Canvas Work, Divers, Bottom Cleaning, Brightwork **Near:** Refrigeration. **Nearest Yard:** Scituate Boat Works (781) 545-0487

Restaurants and Accommodations

Near: Restaurant *(Barker Tavern 545-6533, D $18-42, Prix Fixe $30, Kids $5-7, Sun Dinner $19, Eli's Pub $10-15)*, Lite Fare *(Satuit Tavern 545-2500, L & D $5-19 Lunch Fri-Sun. Kids')*, Inn/B&B *(Inn at Scituate Harbor 545-5550, $119-175)* **Under 1 mi:** Restaurant *(Riva 545-5881, B $6-18, D $6-18)*, *(Phin's 545-1110, B, L D)*, *(Mill Wharf & Chesters 545-3999, L $7-14, D $14-25)*, *(Oro 378-2465, D $6-28)*, Coffee Shop *(Atlantic Bagel 545-1331)*, Pizzeria *(Harbor House 545-5407)*

Recreation and Entertainment

Near: Beach *(Museum, Pegotty, Sand Hills)*, Park, Sightseeing *(Scituate Lighthouse)*, Special Events *(Heritage Days - early August)* **Under 1 mi:** Dive Shop *(Waterline 545-4154)*, Bowling *(Satuit 545-9726)*, Fishing Charter *(Elizabeth Marie 864-7154)*, Movie Theater *(Patriot 545-3130)*, Video Rental *(Hennessy News 545-6940)*, Galleries *(Scituate Art Assn 545-6150; Little House of Arts 545-6100)* **1-3 mi:** Playground *(Hatherly)*, Tennis Courts *(Hatherly CC 545-9891)*, Golf Course *(Widows Walk G.C. 544-7777)*, Fitness Center *(Bay State A.C. 545-2249)*, Museum *(Maritime 545-5565)* **3+ mi:** Pool *(Cohasset 383-9463, 6.2 mi)*, Tours *(No. River Wildlife Sanctuary 837-9400, 4 mi.)*, Cultural Attract *(So. Shore Music Circus 383-9850, 6 mi.)*

Provisioning and General Services

Near: Gourmet Shop *(Front Street 545-4050)*, Bank/ATM *(Bankers Capital)* **Under 1 mi:** Market *(Village 545-4896)*, Wine/Beer *(Front Street Gourmet 545-4050)*, Liquor Store *(Harborside 545-0059)*, Fishmonger *(Mullaney's 545-5000)*, Catholic Church, Protestant Church, Library *(Scituate 545-8727)*, Beauty Salon *(Zuki's 545-5605)*, Dry Cleaners *(Kenny's 545-7670)*, Laundry *(Superwash 545-9673)*, Bookstore *(Front Street 545-5011)*, Pharmacy *(CVS 545-0240)*, Hardware Store *(Satuit 545-8370)*, Florist *(Flowers & Festivities 545-0929)* **1-3 mi:** Convenience Store *(Dad's 545-7030)*, Bakery *(Morning Glories 545-3400)*, Farmers' Market *(Wed, 3-7pm)*, Green Grocer *(Tree Berry Farm 545-7750)*, Post Office *(545-4829)* **3+ mi:** Supermarket *(Stop & Shop 383-9281, 4.5 mi.)*, Retail Shops *(Cushing Plaza, 5 mi.)*

Transportation

OnCall: Water Taxi *(545-4154 or Ch. 9)*, Rental Car *(Verc 383-9339; Enterprise 383-2966)*, Taxi *(Cohasset 383-8294)*, Airport Limo *(Abbey Rd. 749-9727)* **1-3 mi:** InterCity Bus *(P&B 746-0378 to Boston)*, Rail *(Boston 800-392-6100)* **Airport:** Logan Int'l. *(27 mi.)*

Medical Services

911 Service **OnCall:** Ambulance **Near:** Dentist *(Bradford 545-0039)* **Under 1 mi:** Chiropractor *(Scituate Harbor Chiropractic 545-7388)*, Holistic Services *(Spascape 545-1200)* **1-3 mi:** Doctor *(Harbor Medical 545-7243)*, Veterinarian *(Driftway 545-0952)* **Hospital:** South Shore 624-8000 *(14 mi.)*

Setting -- The next major facility past the yacht club and Satuit Boat Club, SHM is identified by by the bright red floating dockhouse and busy fuel dock. A neat tree of well-maintained docks leads to a 125-foot fixed pier. On the upland, there's a parking lot and a large, shuttered, gray, clapboard restaurant. The gray and burgundy Barker Tavern complex perches above the slips. Views are of the outer harbor mooring field and the western shore dotted with eateries.

Marina Notes -- *Office closed weekdays Sep 1-Oct 10. Seasonal operation. **Reservations up to 7 days in advance. Founded in the 1960's (originally as O'Neil's or The Lobster House). Current owner, Dobber Reynolds, worked here from age 12. First managed, then leased and finally purchased the facility in 1993. Caters to sport fishers heading to the renowned fishing grounds twenty miles out. Cable TV seasonal only. No grilling on docks. Bathhouse: Useable shower in dock building and a Porta-Pottie at the edge of the parking lot. (Alternatively, walk/dinghy to town docks for comp. bathhouse).

Notable -- Just up the hill, overlooking the marina, atmospheric Barker Tavern, a restored C. 1634 dwelling & garrison (one of the country's oldest English houses), offers elegant fine dining in a charming, beamed room and lighter fare in Eli's Pub - Tuesday-Saturday evenings and Sunday dinner. They'll also arrange take-out. Nearby is the low-key, immaculate Satuit Tavern and within half a mile are a wide variety of reasonably priced eateries, commercial businesses and historic structures in the sweet village. Visit Kustis's Carving shop for a peek into real craftsmanship (210-2219). Take the dinghy (or Cedar Point/Waterline launch) to Museum Beach or walk east 0.3 miles and then another 0.7 miles to the Old Scituate Light.

Navigational Information

Lat: 42°12.020' **Long:** 070°43.390' **Tide:** 9 ft. **Current:** n/a **Chart:** 13269
Rep. Depths (*MLW*): Entry 10 ft. **Fuel Dock** n/a **Max Slip/Moor** 10 ft./12 ft.
Access: Cape Cod Bay to Scituate Harbor RW "SA" to mooring field

Marina Facilities *(In Season/Off Season)*

Fuel: No
Slips: 0 Total, 0 Transient **Max LOA:** 50 ft. **Max Beam:** 15 ft.
Rate *(per ft.)*: **Day** n/a **Week** n/a **Month** n/a
Power: 30 amp n/a, **50 amp** n/a, **100 amp** n/a, **200 amp** n/a
Cable TV: No **Dockside Phone:** No
Dock Type: n/a
Moorings: 100 Total, 25 Transient **Launch:** Yes (Free), Dinghy Dock (Free)
Rate: Day $35 **Week** Inq. **Month** Inq.
Heads: 8 Toilet(s), 4 Shower(s)
Internet: No **Laundry:** None
Pump-Out: OnCall, Full Service **Fee:** Free **Closed Heads:** Yes

Marina Operations

Owner/Manager: Fran McMillen **Dockmaster:** none
In-Season: May-Oct, 8am-10pm **Off-Season:** Nov- Apr, Closed
After-Hours Arrival: cell: 781-858-3128
Reservations: Yes **Credit Cards:** n/a
Discounts: None
Pets: Welcome, Dog Walk Area **Handicap Access:** No

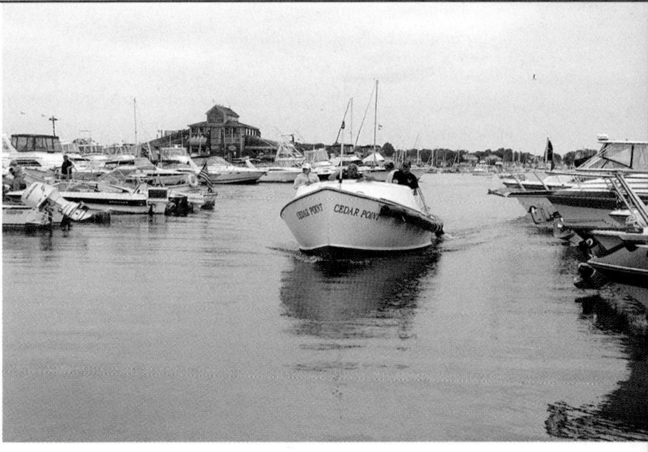

Waterline Moorings

PO Box 35; 79 Cole Parkway; Scituate, MA 02066

Tel: (781) 545-4154; (781) 545-2130 **VHF: Monitor** Ch. 9 **Talk** Ch. 9
Fax: (781) 545-5215 **Alternate Tel:** (781) 545-2130
Email: n/a **Web:** n/a
Nearest Town: Scituate *(0 mi.)* **Tourist Info:** (781) 545-4000

Marina Services and Boat Supplies

Services - Concierge, Room Service to the Boat, Security *(24 Hrs.)*, Trash Pick-Up, Dock Carts **Communication -** Pay Phone (3), FedEx, UPS, Express Mail **Supplies - OnCall:** Ice *(Block, Cube)* **1-3 mi:** Ships' Store *(N. River 545-7811)*, Bait/Tackle *(Belsan 545-9400)*

Boatyard Services

OnCall: Engine mechanic *(gas, diesel)*, Electrical Repairs, Electronics Repairs, Hull Repairs, Rigger *(Foster's 545-7003)*, Sail Loft, Divers, Bottom Cleaning, Brightwork, Air Conditioning, Refrigeration, Compound, Wash & Wax, Interior Cleaning, Propeller Repairs, Woodworking, Inflatable Repairs, Metal Fabrication **Nearest Yard:** Scituate Boat Works (781) 545-0487

Restaurants and Accommodations

Near: Restaurant *(Riva L & D $6-18)*, *(Mill Wharf & Chesters 545-3999, L $7-20, D $12-20, Lite fare up at Mill Wharf, Dinner down at Chesters)*, *(TK O'Malley's Sports Café 545-4012, L $5-13, D $9-14)*, *(Phin's 544-1110)*, *(Oro 378-2465, D $6-28)*, Pizzeria *(Harbor House 545-5407)*, Inn/B&B *(Allen House 545-8221)* **Under 1 mi:** Inn/B&B *(The Inn at Scituate Harbor 545-5550, $119-175)* **1-3 mi:** Restaurant *(Pub at Widows Walk 248-5138)*

Recreation and Entertainment

OnSite: Dive Shop *(Waterline 545-4154)* **Near:** Jogging Paths, Boat Rentals *(Labrador 498-4716)*, Bowling *(Bowlaway 545-9726)*, Fishing Charter *(Enoch 264-5151)*, Movie Theater *(Patriot 545-3130)*, Video Rental *(Hennessy News 545-6940)*, Galleries *(Scituate Art 545-6150; Silverstorm 545-1251)* **Under 1 mi:** Beach *(Peggotty)*, Park **1-3 mi:** Playground, Tennis Courts *(Hatherly 545-9891)*, Golf Course *(Widows Walk G.C. 544-7777)*, Fitness Center *(Bay State 545-2249)*, Museum *(Maritime 545-5565, Scituate Historical Society 545-1083)* **3+ mi:** Horseback Riding *(Longmeadow 544-3097, 3.2 mi.)*, Tours *(No. River Wildlife Sanctuary 837-9400, 4 mi.)*, Cultural Attract *(So. Shore Music Circus 383-9850, 7 mi.)*

Provisioning and General Services

Near: Market *(Village 545-4896)*, Wine/Beer *(Front Street 545-4050)*, Liquor Store *(Harborside Wine and Spirits 545-0059)*, Fishmonger *(Summer Shack 740-9555)*, Lobster Pound *(Mullaney's 545-5000)*, Bank/ATM, Catholic Church, Library *(Scituate 545-8727)*, Beauty Salon *(Zuki's 545-5605)*, Dry Cleaners *(Cleaning Corner 545-0066)*, Laundry *(Super Wash 545-9673)*, Bookstore *(Front Street 545-5011)*, Pharmacy *(CVS 545-0240)*, Newsstand, Hardware Store *(Satuit 545-8370)*, Florist *(Flowers & Festivities 545-0929)*, Retail Shops *(Front Street)* **Under 1 mi:** Protestant Church **1-3 mi:** Convenience Store *(Dad's 545-7030)*, Bakery *(Morning Glories 545-3400)*, Green Grocer *(Tree Berry Farm 545-7750)*, Post Office *(545-4829)* **3+ mi:** Supermarket *(Stop & Shop 383-9281, 5 mi.)*, Farmers' Market *(Wed 3-7pm, Country Way & Gannett Rd., 4 mi.)*

Transportation

OnCall: Rental Car *(Enterprise 383-2966; Verc 383-9339)*, Taxi *(Coastal 383-0120)* **1-3 mi:** InterCity Bus *(P&B 508-746-0378)*, Rail *(Boston)*
Airport: Logan Int'l. *(27 mi.)*

Medical Services

911 Service **Near:** Dentist *(Bradford 545-0039)*, Chiropractor *(Scituate Harbor 545-7388)* **1-3 mi:** Doctor *(Pozatek 545-6565)*, Holistic Services *(Spascape 545-1200)* **Hospital:** Pembroke 829-7000 *(9 mi.)*

Setting -- Waterline's moorings are sprinkled throughout Scituate's outer and inner harbors intermingled with those of the yacht club, private owners and other suppliers - and are serviced by Scituate Launch "Cedar Point." Waterline makes the centrally located Cole Parkway Town Pier, in the inner harbor, its home port; those facilites are available to Waterline customers. Lovely, historic Scituate's Front Street is feet away.

Marina Notes -- Inaugurated in 1995 to provide "island class" service in Scituate Harbor. Waterline sells, services & inspects mooring systems - primary provider in harbor. Dive services. Choose Inner Harbor for quick access to town or Outer Harbor for a quieter spot. Harbor max 12 feet mlw. Service-oriented management and staff - just ask. Free Sunday morning coffee, donuts and newspapers for mooring customers. "Dinner on board" restaurant service. Takes trash. Discount for repeat customers or extended stay. Runs pump-out boat. No anchoring permitted in harbor. Bathhouse: Modern ceramic-tile baths in harbormaster building. Note: Satuit Boat Club (545-9752) & Bay Rider may have moorings (508-221-8405, Ch. 9)

Notable -- The launch stop at Cole Parkway is in the middle of charming, real, untouristed Scituate - surrounded by restaurants, services and supplies. All summer, there are Friday night concerts - Bach to Rock - in Band Shell. During Heritage Days (early August), shops move into the streets, and music performances continue through the weekend. The new Scituate Marine Park houses Scituate Boatworks for full yard services. For ocean swimming, pebbly Peggoty Beach is a 0.6 mile walk. Municipally-owned Widow Walk Golf Course, voted the South Shore's #1 course, is a 1.5-mile hike.

PHOTOS ON DVD: 18

Cole Parkway Municipal Marina

100 Cole Parkway; Scituate, MA 02066

Tel: (781) 545-2130 **VHF: Monitor** Ch. 9 **Talk** Ch. 14
Fax: (781) 545-5215 **Alternate Tel:** (781) 545-2139
Email: See marina notes **Web:** www.town.scituate.ma.us/harbormaster
Nearest Town: Scituate **Tourist Info:** (781) 545-4000

Navigational Information

Lat: 42°11.697' **Long:** 070°43.392' **Tide:** 9 ft. **Current:** n/a **Chart:** 13267
Rep. Depths (*MLW*): Entry 12 ft. **Fuel Dock** n/a **Max Slip/Moor** 10 ft./12 ft.
Access: Cape Cod Bay to Scituate Inner Harbor

Marina Facilities *(In Season/Off Season)*

Fuel: No
Slips: 300 Total, 6-10 Transient **Max LOA:** 50 ft. **Max Beam:** 15 ft.
Rate *(per ft.)*: **Day** $3.00 **Week** n/a **Month** n/a
Power: 30 amp $5, **50 amp** $10, **100 amp** n/a, **200 amp** n/a
Cable TV: No **Dockside Phone:** No
Dock Type: Floating, Long Fingers, Wood
Moorings: 0 Total, 0 Transient **Launch:** n/a, Dinghy Dock (Free)
Rate: Day n/a **Week** n/a **Month** n/a
Heads: 8 Toilet(s), 4 Shower(s)
Internet: Yes **Laundry:** None
Pump-Out: OnCall, Full Service **Fee:** Free **Closed Heads:** Yes

Marina Operations

Owner/Manager: Mark Patterson (Hrbmstr) **Dockmaster:** Ed Gibbons (Ass't)
In-Season: May 15-Oct 15, 8am-4pm* **Off-Season:** Oct 16-May 14, 8-4**
After-Hours Arrival: Call Harbormaster's cell: 781-858-3128
Reservations: Yes **Credit Cards:** Visa/MC, Cash or check
Discounts: None
Pets: Welcome, Dog Walk Area **Handicap Access:** Yes, Heads

Marina Services and Boat Supplies

Services - Docking Assistance, Security *(7 days, Guard and patrol boat)*, Trash Pick-Up, Dock Carts **Communication -** Pay Phone **Supplies - OnSite:** Ice *(Block, Cube)* **Near:** Bait/Tackle *(Belsan 545-9400; Mass Bay 545-6516)* **1-3 mi:** Marine Discount Store *(N. River Marina)*

Boatyard Services

OnSite: Travelift *(35T)*, Hydraulic Trailer, Launching Ramp, Engine mechanic *(gas, diesel)*, Electronic Sales, Electronics Repairs, Hull Repairs, Rigger, Canvas Work, Divers, Bottom Cleaning, Air Conditioning, Refrigeration, Compound, Wash & Wax, Painting **OnCall:** Propeller Repairs **Yard Rates:** $00/hr., Haul & Launch $00/ft. *(blocking incl.)*, Power Wash $0/ft., Bottom Paint $00/ft. **Storage:** On-Land $00/ft.

Restaurants and Accommodations

Near: Restaurant *(Phin's 545-1110, L $4-13, D $12-17)*, *(Chester's & Mill Wharf 545-3999, L $4-14, D $14-20, Casual upstairs, Formal down)*, *(TK O'Malley's 545-4012, L $5-13, D $5-14, sports bar)*, *(Riva 545-5881, L & D $6-18 Italian gourmet)*, *(Oro 378-2465)*, Coffee Shop *(Morada Cafe 544-3144, $3-10)*, Pizzeria *(Marias 545-2323, & subs)*, *(Harbor House 545-5407)*, Inn/B&B *(The Inn at Scituate Harbor 545-5500, $120-175)* **Under 1 mi:** Restaurant *(Barker Tavern 545-6533, D $18-42, $30 Prix Fixe)*

Recreation and Entertainment

OnSite: Dive Shop *(Waterline)*, Cultural Attract *(Fri night Band concerts; Scituate Maritime Center - maritime history exhibits, courses, programs)*, Special Events *(Heritage Days 1st weekend in Aug)* **Near:** Beach *(Peggotty)*, Bowling *(Satuit Bowlaway 545-9726)*, Fishing Charter *(Labrador 498-4716)*, Movie Theater *(Patriot 545-3130)*, Video Rental *(Hennessy News)*, Galleries *(Scituate Arts 545-6150)* **Under 1 mi:** Park *(Kent St.)* **1-3 mi:** Tennis Courts *(Scituate Racket 545-1184)*, Golf Course *(Widows Walk 544-7777)*, Fitness Center *(Bay State 545-2249)*, Museum *(Scituate Hist 545-1047 - 9 sites incl. Lawson Tower 545-1083, built by copper magnate in 15thC Roman-style to camouflage water tower, now houses carillon bells)*

Provisioning and General Services

Near: Market *(Village 545-4896)*, Gourmet Shop *(Front St. 545-4050)*, Wine/Beer *(Front St.)*, Liquor Store *(Harborside 545-0059)*, Bakery, Fishmonger *(Coastal 545-7650)*, Lobster Pound *(Mullaney's 545-5000)*, Bank/ATM, Catholic Church, Protestant Church, Beauty Salon *(Zuki's 545-5605)*, Barber Shop, Dry Cleaners, Laundry *(Super Wash 545-7445)*, Bookstore *(Front Street 545-5011)*, Pharmacy *(CVS 545-1531)*, Hardware Store *(Satuit 545-8370)*, Florist, Retail Shops *(Front St.)* **Under 1 mi:** Post Office **1-3 mi:** Library *(545-8727)* **3+ mi:** Supermarket *(Stop & Shop, 5 mi.)*, Farmers' Market *(Wed 3-7pm, Country Way & Gannett Rd., 4 mi.)*

Transportation

OnCall: Rental Car *(Enterprise 383-2966; Verc 383-9339)*, Taxi *(Coastal 383-0120; Cohasset Limo 545-6600)* **1-3 mi:** Bikes *(Seacoast Cycle & Sports 545-7000)*, Rail *(Greenbush)* **Airport:** Logan Int'l. *(27 mi.)*

Medical Services

911 Service **Near:** Dentist *(Parsons 545-0039)*, Chiropractor *(Scituate Harbor 545-7388)*, Holistic Services *(S. Shore Acupuncture 545-1345)* **1-3 mi:** Doctor *(Harbor Medical 545-5225; Pozatek 545-6565)* **Hospital:** South Shore 340-8000 *(15 mi.)*

Setting -- Tucked behind the breakwater, Cole Parkway and the new Scituate Maritime Center offer the only transient dockage in the protected, convenient Inner Harbor. Spread out along the town park, the slips share the basin with a modest mooring field, a flock of sportfishers hard by the Mill Wharf, and Chester's - two of the town's principal watering holes. Low-slung, blue-gray shingled buildings, flanked by elegant three-story neo-Victorian condos, house the offices and amenities. At the southeast corner, the Maritime Center sports another dock array backed by the new historical and event space and boatyard.

Marina Notes -- *May-Oct, 7 days 8am-4pm, Security 4pm-Midnight. **Off-season 8am-4pm, Mon-Fri only. Email: harbormaster@town.scituate.ma.us. New Scituate Maritime Center, with 100 more slips, event & history center and full-service Scituate Boat Works boatyard with a 35-ton lift. Accommodating, helpful staff. Two mooring launch services operate from marina: Waterline (545-4154) & Bay Rider (508-221-8405), both Ch. 9. Bathhouse: Recent, inviting ceramic tile, shower curtains in harbormaster building; another new set in Maritime Center.

Notable -- Delightful, unfussy "downtown" Scituate, with small-town commerce of every stripe, is barely a one-block walk through the parking lot. In 2010, the town opened the impressive 1200-square foot Scituate Maritime Center with a wonderful 2500 sq. ft. harborfront deck. Built on the site of 3-acre Young's Boatyard, it includes exhibits on the town's maritime history, heads and a harborfront meeting room that holds 50-90 (Fleet captains note, $300 fee). Friday night concerts are held at the band shell overlooking the Cole Parkway docks. For ocean swimming, Pegotty beach is across the road from the Maritime Center.

Navigational Information
Lat: 42°04.916' **Long:** 070°38.724' **Tide:** 9.5 ft. **Current:** 2 kt. **Chart:** 13252
Rep. Depths (*MLW*): Entry 7 ft. **Fuel Dock** 6 ft. **Max Slip/Moor** 6 ft./-
Access: First facility to starboard

Marina Facilities *(In Season/Off Season)*
Fuel: *Unbranded* - Gasoline, Diesel
Slips: 135 Total, 3 Transient **Max LOA:** 50 ft. **Max Beam:** 15 ft.
Rate *(per ft.)*: **Day** $2.00/$1 **Week** $10 **Month** n/a
Power: 30 amp Incl., **50 amp** n/a, **100 amp** n/a, **200 amp** n/a
Cable TV: No **Dockside Phone:** No
Dock Type: Floating, Long Fingers, Short Fingers, Wood
Moorings: 0 Total, 0 Transient **Launch:** n/a
Rate: Day n/a **Week** n/a **Month** n/a
Heads: 2 Toilet(s), 2 Shower(s) *(dressing rooms)*
Internet: No **Laundry:** None
Pump-Out: Full Service, 1 Central **Fee:** $5 **Closed Heads:** Yes

Marina Operations
Owner/Manager: John Taylor **Dockmaster:** Same
In-Season: Apr-Nov, 9am-6pm **Off-Season:** n/a
After-Hours Arrival: Call ahead
Reservations: Yes **Credit Cards:** Visa/MC, Dscvr, Amex
Discounts: None
Pets: Welcome, Dog Walk Area **Handicap Access:** Yes

Taylor Marine

PO Box 697; 95 Central Ave.; Ocean Bluff-Brant Rock, MA 02020

Tel: (781) 837-9617 **VHF: Monitor** n/a **Talk** n/a
Fax: (781) 834-6344 **Alternate Tel:** (781) 837-9617
Email: taylormarinecorp@aol.com **Web:** n/a
Nearest Town: Brant Rock *(0.5 mi.)* **Tourist Info:** (508) 872-1620

Marina Services and Boat Supplies
Services - Docking Assistance, Trash Pick-Up, Dock Carts
Communication - Mail & Package Hold, FedEx, UPS, Express Mail
Supplies - OnSite: Ice *(Block, Cube)* **Near:** Ships' Store *(New England Marine 888-834-9301)* **Under 1 mi:** Bait/Tackle *(Green Harbor 834-3474)*

Boatyard Services
OnSite: Crane *(2T)*, Hydraulic Trailer *(Two)*, Engine mechanic *(gas, diesel)*, Electrical Repairs **OnCall:** Hull Repairs, Propeller Repairs, Woodworking **Near:** Launching Ramp, Divers, Bottom Cleaning. **Yard Rates:** Haul & Launch $6.50/ft., Power Wash $4/ft. **Storage:** On-Land $4/ft./mo.

Restaurants and Accommodations
Under 1 mi: Restaurant *(Fairview 834-9144, L $9-15, D $10-26)*, *(Venus II 837-6368, L & D $5-17, Kids $5, Greek Pizza, Grinders too)*, *(Haddad's Ocean Café 837-2722)*, Fast Food *(DQ)*, Lite Fare *(Arthur & Pat's 834-9755, B $4-12, L $4-15)*, Hotel *(Fairview 834-9144, $175-250)* **1-3 mi:** Restaurant *(Mandarin & Tokyo 837-4440)*, Pizzeria *(Santoros 837-9001)*, *(Papa Gino's 834-6661, Delivery)*

Recreation and Entertainment
Near: Beach *(Sunrise Beach)*, Playground, Tennis Courts, Jogging Paths, Fishing Charter *(Black Rose 508-269-1882)*, Park *(Brant Rock Marsh)* **Under 1 mi:** Sightseeing *(Massachusetts Audubon Society's wildlife sanctuaries 575-1552)*, Special Events *(Marshfield Fair - Aug 834-6629)* **1-3 mi:** Video Rental *(Blockbuster Express)*, Museum *(Winslow Mansion, Daniel Webster's Study 837-5753 $3/1; Marshfield Historical Society 834-0100 Nathaniel Winsor, King Ceasar & Gershom Bradford Houses)*
3+ mi: Dive Shop *(N. Atlantic 834-4087 , 4.5 mi.)*, Golf Course *(Green Harbor G.C. 834-7303, 4.5 mi.)*, Galleries *(Porcello 837-7776, 4.5 mi.)*

Provisioning and General Services
Under 1 mi: Market *(Brant Rock 834-8839)*, Fishmonger *(Brant Rock Fish 834-6231)*, Bank/ATM *(Brant Rock Market)*, Post Office, Protestant Church, Laundry *(Brant Rock 834-6682)*, Newsstand **1-3 mi:** Convenience Store *(Rexhame 837-3374)*, Liquor Store *(Ocean Bluff 834-6000)*, Bakery *(Leo's 837-3300)*, Farmers' Market, Catholic Church, Beauty Salon *(Salon 1160 837-6699)*, Barber Shop, Dry Cleaners *(Marshfields 834-1911)* **3+ mi:** Supermarket *(Stop & Shop 924-5050, 8.5 mi.)*, Wine/Beer *(Vintages 934-0300, 4.5 mi.)*, Green Grocer *(Haymarket South 837-0949, 4.5 mi.)*, Library *(Ventress 834-5535, 4.5 mi.)*, Pharmacy *(CVS 837-5381, 4.5 mi.)*, Florist *(Artistic 837-6251, 3.5 mi.)*, Department Store *(Marshall's 837-1171 , 4 mi.)*

Transportation
OnCall: Rental Car *(Enterprise 585-4218)*, Taxi *(Green Harbor 837-1234; Travler 834-1900)*, Airport Limo *(Aerobus 837-1234)* **Near:** InterCity Bus *(Cape Cod to Boston)* **3+ mi:** Bikes *(Bikeway 837-2453, 5 mi.)*, Rail *(Greenbush/Plymouth, 12 mi.)* **Airport:** Logan *(30 mi.)*

Medical Services
911 Service **OnCall:** Ambulance **1-3 mi:** Dentist *(Glynn 834-7575)* **3+ mi:** Doctor *(Ikeda 934-6390, 6.5 mi.)*, Chiropractor *(Duxbury Sports 934-0020, 5 mi.)*, Holistic Services *(Stone Acupuncture 223-0130; Colligan LMT 834-4347, 5 mi.)*, Veterinarian *(VCA 837-1141, 3.5 mi.)* **Hospital:** Jordan 746-2000/South Shore 749-1691 *(16 mi./18 mi.)*

Setting -- Enter Green Harbor River's tight channel and find Taylor immediately to starboard. Three main docks, tucked into a rectangular basin, parallel the waterway. Onshore, a weathered, shingled two-story office oversees 135 slips filled with sport fish boats. Views are of unspoiled marsh and the three other facilities further upriver: the busy town pier, where commercial fishermen load and unload, Green Harbor Yacht Club and Green Harbor Marina at its head.

Marina Notes -- Few frills, but the sportfishermen like it that way. Only diesel pump in town (staffed 14 hours a day in season). Does not monitor the VHF -- stop by the gas dock or call John Taylor on cell - he's been on premises for 40 years. Army Corps of Engineers regularly manages shoaling problem at the river's mouth. Active commercial fishermen at adjacent town pier; otherwise buy your fish up the street at Brant Rock Fish market. Dinghy up to the tackle shop at Green Harbor Marine. Bathhouse: Fully tiled, but basic at best; bit of a hike from outer docks.

Notable -- Well-protected Green Harbor River provides easy access to and from Stellwagen Bank for sport fishing and whale watching -- and offers a safe port in a storm. The old-fashioned, low-key beach community of Brant Rock Beach is a bit over a half-mile walk. There are restaurants and basic commercial needs - nothing fancy, just invitingly down home. The main attraction is the Atlantic, rather cool but very clean these days - a wide sweep of beach is nearby. For history buffs, taxi to the 1699 Winslow Mansion, built by Plymouth Colony Governor Edward Winslow. Also on the grounds are Daniel Webster's law office and a coach museum, Wed-Sun 11am-3pm (837-5753, $3/1).

PHOTOS ON DVD: 18

Green Harbor Marina

PO Box 338; 239 Dyke Road; Green Harbor, MA 02041

Tel: (781) 837-1181 **VHF: Monitor** Ch. 9 **Talk** Ch. 65
Fax: (781) 834-0163 **Alternate Tel:** (781) 837-4415
Email: ghm@greenharbormarina.net **Web:** greenharbormarina.com
Nearest Town: Green Harbor *(0.5 mi.)* **Tourist Info:** (508) 872-1620

Navigational Information

Lat: 42°05.100' **Long:** 070°39.000' **Tide:** 9 ft. **Current:** 5 kt. **Chart:** 13253
Rep. Depths (*MLW*): Entry 9 ft. **Fuel Dock** 7 ft. **Max Slip/Moor** 8 ft./-
Access: Green Harbor River, second facility to port

Marina Facilities *(In Season/Off Season)*

Fuel: Gasoline
Slips: 185 Total, 2 Transient **Max LOA:** 60 ft. **Max Beam:** n/a
Rate *(per ft.)*: **Day** $2.50/Inq. **Week** Inq. **Month** n/a
Power: 30 amp Incl., **50 amp** Incl., **100 amp** n/a, **200 amp** n/a
Cable TV: No **Dockside Phone:** No
Dock Type: Floating, Short Fingers, Pilings, Wood
Moorings: 0 Total, 0 Transient **Launch:** n/a
Rate: Day n/a **Week** n/a **Month** n/a
Heads: 4 Toilet(s), 4 Shower(s)
Internet: Yes *(Wi-Fi, Free)* **Laundry:** None
Pump-Out: OnSite, 1 Central **Fee:** Free **Closed Heads:** Yes

Marina Operations

Owner/Manager: Ray Stauff **Dockmaster:** Same
In-Season: Year Round, 8am-5pm* **Off-Season:** n/a
After-Hours Arrival: Call VHF 65 - will direct you to slip
Reservations: Yes **Credit Cards:** Visa/MC
Discounts: None
Pets: Welcome **Handicap Access:** No

Marina Services and Boat Supplies

Services - Docking Assistance, Dock Carts **Communication -** Mail & Package Hold, Phone Messages, Fax in/out, FedEx, UPS, Express Mail *(Sat Del)* **Supplies - OnSite:** Ice *(Cube)*, Ships' Store, Bait/Tackle *(Green Harbor 834-3473)*, Live Bait **3+ mi:** Propane *(Kingston 585-6511, 7 mi.)*

Boatyard Services

OnSite: Hydraulic Trailer *(to 55 ft.)*, Launching Ramp, Engine mechanic *(gas, diesel)*, Electrical Repairs, Electronic Sales, Electronics Repairs, Hull Repairs, Bottom Cleaning, Brightwork, Compound, Wash & Wax, Interior Cleaning, Propeller Repairs **OnCall:** Canvas Work, Air Conditioning, Refrigeration, Woodworking, Upholstery, Metal Fabrication **Dealer for:** Mercruiser, Yanmar, Westerbeke. **Member:** ABBRA **Yard Rates:** $85/hr., Haul & Launch $8/ft. *(blocking $2/ft.)*, Power Wash $3.50/ft., Bottom Paint $15/ft. **Storage:** On-Land Out $47/ft.; In $76/ft.**

Restaurants and Accommodations

OnSite: Restaurant *(Ocean Deck 339-793-2899, 3pm-1am)* **Near:** Snack Bar *(The Coffee Shack 5am-6pm, smoothies, pastries, newspapers)* **Under 1 mi:** Restaurant *(Haddad's Ocean Café 837-2722)*, *(Fairview 834-9144, L $9-15, D $10-26)*, *(Venus II 837-6368, L & D $5-17, Kids $5, Greek Pizza, Grinders too)*, Snack Bar *(Brant Rock Variety)*, Lite Fare *(Arthur & Pat's 834-9755, B $4-12, L $4-15, famous breakfasts)*, Inn/B&B *(Fairview 834-9144, $175-300)* **1-3 mi:** Pizzeria *(Santoro's 837-9001)*, *(Dimitri's 934-0941)*

Recreation and Entertainment

OnSite: Picnic Area, Fishing Charter *("Lease II" 344-3836, "Cathyann" 878-6798, "Ocean Runner" 508-697-7947, "Big Fish" 834-7504, "Easter Viking" 582-9761, "Reel Time" 508-747-6720, "Big Mac" 837-0308, "Relentless" 871-2113, "Seabarone" 223-2501, "Ridla" 233-1298)* **Near:** Playground, Tennis Courts **Under 1 mi:** Beach *(Brant Rock)*, Park *(Wharf Creek)*, Special Events *(Marshfield Fair - Aug)* **1-3 mi:** Fitness Center *(Duxbury 934-2798)*, Video Rental *(Blockbuster Express)*, Museum *(Marshfield Hist. Society 834-0100, $5; Winslow Mansion, Daniel Webster's Study 837-5753 $3/1)* **3+ mi:** Golf Course *(Green Harbor 834-7303, 3 mi.)*

Provisioning and General Services

Near: Gourmet Shop, Bank/ATM, Post Office, Laundry *(834-6682)*, Newsstand **Under 1 mi:** Market *(Brant Rock 837-8839)*, Liquor Store *(Ocean Bluff 834-6000)*, Fishmonger *(Brant Rock 834-6231)*, Catholic Church, Protestant Church, Barber Shop **1-3 mi:** Wine/Beer *(Vintages 934-0300)*, Bakery *(Leo's 837-3300)*, Library, Beauty Salon *(Newbury St. 837-0468)*, Dry Cleaners *(Marshfield 834-1911)*, Florist *(Artistic 837-6251)* **3+ mi:** Supermarket *(Star Osco 837-5100, 3.5 mi.)*, Pharmacy *(CVS 837-5381, 4 mi.)*, Hardware Store *(John Foster 837-2821, 3.5 mi.)*

Transportation

OnCall: Rental Car *(Enterprise 585-4218)*, Taxi *(Green Harbor 834-3300; Traveler 834-1900)*, Airport Limo *(Aerobus 837-1234; Marshfield 837-2289)* **Near:** Local Bus **Airport:** Marshfield/Logan Int'l. *(3 mi./30 mi.)*

Medical Services

911 Service **1-3 mi:** Dentist *(Glynn 834-7575)*, Holistic Services *(Alexandra's Day Spa 934-7075)* **3+ mi:** Doctor *(Ikeda 934-6390, 5 mi.)*, Chiropractor *(Duxbury 934-0020, 4 mi.)*, Veterinarian *(So. River 837-5611, 3.5 mi.)* **Hospital:** Jordan 746-2000/So. Shore 749-1691 *(14.5 mi./18 mi.)*

Setting -- A quarter mile from the ocean, just past the yacht club, this large, comprehensive facility is home port to sport fish charters and recreational vessels that troll the Stellwagen Bank. A small, monogrammed lighthouse announces the entrance to the set of six docks that fan out along the western shore. On the upland, next to the full-service boatyard. A pair of two-story gray clapboard buildings house the ships' store, tackle shop and, some seasons, a restaurant.

Marina Notes -- *Closed Sat offseason. **Storage rate includes Haul & Launch, bottom wash. Hydraulic trailer & full array of reasonable mechanical and other BY services. Large, well-stocked marine store, ten sport-fish charters onsite. Well-stocked Green Harbor Bait & Tackle shop plus a tuna dealer/processor for immediate ice-down, transfers and sales. Only Luhrs dealer in New England. Gas only (go to Taylor for diesel). River is tight, and moored boats don't always swing in unison. Bathhouse: Carefully tended ceramic tile heads. Note: Army Corps dredging channel to 100 ft wide, 8 ft. deep. Marina being dredged, too.

Notable -- Loaded to the gills with Cabo, Luhrs, and other battlewagons, there's no mistaking the fishing focus of this marina. Its easy access to Race Point, and Stellwaggon Bank lures anglers looking for Bluefin Tuna, Cod, Haddock, Stripers, Blues, and Flounder. The venerable Green Harbor Tuna Club sponsors a multi-species, season-long tournament, as well as Cod, Bluefish, and two Bluefin Tournaments - one reserved for lady anglers. The handicap-accessible, second floor Ocean Deck restaurant serves light fare and dinner seven days inside and on the new deck with views across the boatyard to the marina and river beyond. It's a half mile to the edge of the quirky Green Harbor/Brant Rock village, which has a few services, supplies, a variety of eateries and a nice beach.

Navigational Information
Lat: 42°02.312' **Long:** 070°40.178' **Tide:** 9 ft. **Current:** n/a **Chart:** 13253
Rep. Depths (*MLW*): Entry 9 ft. **Fuel Dock** n/a **Max Slip/Moor** -/8 ft.
Access: Duxbury Bay, turn to port at G11, follow channel to end

Marina Facilities *(In Season/Off Season)*
Fuel: No
Slips: 0 Total, 0 Transient **Max LOA:** 45 ft. **Max Beam:** n/a
Rate *(per ft.)*: **Day** n/a **Week** n/a **Month** n/a
Power: 30 amp n/a, **50 amp** n/a, **100 amp** n/a, **200 amp** n/a
Cable TV: No **Dockside Phone:** No
Dock Type: n/a
Moorings: 150 Total, 5 Transient **Launch:** Yes ($10-15)
Rate: Day $30 **Week** n/a **Month** n/a
Heads: 2 Toilet(s)
Internet: No **Laundry:** None
Pump-Out: Full Service, 1 Central, 1 Port **Fee:** Free **Closed Heads:** Yes

Marina Operations
Owner/Manager: Donald C. Beers (HM) **Dockmaster:** Jake Emerson
In-Season: May-Oct, 8am-8pm **Off-Season:** Nov-Apr, 9am-5pm
After-Hours Arrival: Call in advance
Reservations: No **Credit Cards:** n/a
Discounts: None
Pets: Welcome **Handicap Access:** No

Duxbury Town Pier

Mattakeesett Court*; Duxbury, MA 02332

Tel: (781) 934-2866 **VHF: Monitor** Ch. 16 **Talk** Ch. 12
Fax: (781) 934-9011 **Alternate Tel:** n/a
Email: See Marina Notes **Web:** www.duxburyharbormaster.org
Nearest Town: Duxbury *(0.1 mi.)* **Tourist Info:** (508) 830-1620

Marina Services and Boat Supplies
Services - Security **Communication -** Pay Phone, FedEx, UPS **Supplies - Near:** Ice *(Cube)*, Ships' Store *(Bayside 934-0561)*, Bait/Tackle *(Duxbury 934-0242)* **3+ mi:** Propane *(Kingston 585-6511, 4 mi.)*

Boatyard Services
Near: Travelift *(35T)*, Engine mechanic *(gas, diesel)*, Electrical Repairs, Electronics Repairs, Hull Repairs, Rigger, Sail Loft, Bottom Cleaning, Propeller Repairs, Painting. **Nearest Yard:** Long Point (781) 934-5302

Restaurants and Accommodations
Near: Restaurant *(Winsor House 934-0991)*, Inn/B&B *(Winsor House Inn 934-0991, $140-210)* **Under 1 mi:** Inn/B&B *(Powder Point 934-7727, $165-350)* **1-3 mi:** Restaurant *(Wildflower Café 934-7814, B $4, L $6, D $10-22, Sun Brunch, Early bird break $4 before 9am, Dinner Thu-Sat 4-6pm $11, Box lunch to-go $6)*, *(Tsang's Café 934-8222)*, *(Blakeman's 837-3112, D $4-15, Thu-Sun 5-8pm, Lobsters Mkt Price)*, *(Milepost Tavern 934-6801, L $6-16, D $16-25)*, Snack Bar *(Lunch Room)*, Fast Food *(Dunkin Donuts 934-5225)*, Lite Fare *(Depot St. Market 934-2863, $12-18 Take & Bake for 3)*, Pizzeria *(Duxbury 934-6568)*, *(Dimitri's 934-0941, & Subs)*

Recreation and Entertainment
OnSite: Picnic Area **Near:** Jogging Paths, Boat Rentals *(Winsor House 934-0991)*, Fishing Charter *(High Hook 291-1304; Swamp Yankee 508-465-0414)*, Museum *(Duxbury Rural & Hist. Soc. 934-6106; Alden House 934-9092 $5/3 & Maj. Judah Alden House 934-2886 1.4 mi.)* **Under 1 mi:** Pool *(Percy Walker 934-2464)*, Playground **1-3 mi:** Beach *(Duxbury)*, Golf Course *(North Hill G.C. 934-3249)*, Fitness Center *(Gymnastics 934-5145; Duxbury 934-2798)*, Park *(Back River Marsh; Isabelle Freeman Sanctuary; Myles Stadish SP)*, Galleries *(Art Complex Museum 934-6634 Wed-Sun, 1-4pm; John Young 934-8464)* **3+ mi:** Horseback Riding *(Timberhill 582-2276, 5 mi.)*, Bowling *(Kingston 585-5151; Alley Cat 585-2191, 4.5 mi.)*

Provisioning and General Services
Near: Market *(Sweetsers 934-6000)*, Wine/Beer *(La Maison Du Vin 934-6393)*, Bakery *(French Memories 934-9020)*, Fishmonger *(Snug Harbor 934-8167 fresh & take-out)*, Post Office, Protestant Church, Florist *(Tangent 934-5855)* **1-3 mi:** Convenience Store *(Hall's 934-0985; Millbrook 934-2921)*, Delicatessen *(The Deli 934-2875)*, Liquor Store *(Duxbury 934-2431)*, Bank/ATM, Catholic Church, Library *(934-2721)*, Beauty Salon *(London 934-5181)*, Dry Cleaners *(Cleanist 934-2210)*, Bookstore *(Once Upon A Time 934-9788; Wickham 934-6955)*, Pharmacy *(Rite Aid 934-6556)* **3+ mi:** Supermarket *(Stop & Shop 582-3700, 4.5 mi.)*, Green Grocer *(Cretinon's 585-5531, 4.5 mi.)*, Hardware Store *(Aubuchon 934-6556, 4 mi.)*

Transportation
OnCall: Taxi *(Traveler 834-1900)*, Airport Limo *(Aerobus 837-1234)* **Near:** Rental Car *(Verc 934-5608; Enterprise 747-1212 oncall)* **Under 1 mi:** InterCity Bus *(P&B 746-0378 Ptown to Boston)* **3+ mi:** Rail *(Plymouth, 6.5 mi.)* **Airport:** Plymouth/Logan Int'l. *(5 mi./35 mi.)*

Medical Services
911 Service **Near:** Doctor *(Ikeda 934-6390)* **1-3 mi:** Dentist *(Pellegrini 934-2311)*, Chiropractor *(Krowski 934-5114; Duxbury Sports 934-0020)*, Holistic Services *(Alexandra's Day Spa 934-7075)*, Veterinarian *(Duxbury 934-5300)* **Hospital:** Jordan 746-2000 *(12 mi.)*

Setting -- Protected by skinny, seven-mile Duxbury Beach, the crowded mooring field fills broad, shallow Snug Harbor. The diminutive gray-shingled Harbormaster's office overlooks Duxbury Town Pier - flanked by Duxbury Bay Maritime School's impressive new two-story ediface and Duxbury Y.C.'s burgundy-trimmed Tudorish structures. Picturesque, upscale land views are interrupted by Bayside Marine's drystacks and Long Pointe Marine's yard.

Marina Notes -- *Mailing Address: 878 Tremont Street. Email: jakeemerson@duxburyharbormaster.org. Harbormaster controls all transient moorings (avail. when owner away). Tender float at Town Pier. Fuel at adjacent Bayside Marine. Rafting allowed. Inner basin moorings up to 45 ft.; 1 mile out, 2-Rock moorings up to 80 ft. Two launches: Bay Rider (Ch.10, 225-5934) & Bayside Marine (Ch.9). Free loaner dinks at town float (oars only). If anchoring, someone must stay with boat. Free pump-out on pier (max 30 min tie-up), plus pump-out boat. Bathhouse: Separate small building back of property. Basic heads; no showers or laundry. Duxbury Y.C. (Ch.11, 934-2122, 934-5815) accommodates reciprocal YC members - launch, pool, tennis & golf.

Notable -- Adjacent to the town pier, Duxbury Bay Maritime School offers an extraordinary number of sailing, rowing, kayaking, windsurfing, ecology and boating workshops for children and adults - a compelling reason to lay-over. Spectacular Duxbury Beach at Powder Point makes a perfect day-trip - board sailing, bathhouse, snack bar and "must-do" supper at Blakeman's on the rustic screened porch of an old beach house. Founded in 1628 by Myles Standish & John Alden as a Plymouth outpost, Duxbury's lanes are dotted with restored period homes. Kayaks aboard? Explore Back River's serene, pretty tidal marshes.

13. MA - SOUTH SHORE & THE OUTER CAPE
PHOTOS ON DVD: 20

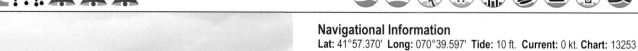

Brewer Plymouth Marine

14 Union Street; Plymouth, MA 02360

Tel: (508) 746-4500 **VHF: Monitor** Ch. 9 **Talk** Ch. 72
Fax: (508) 746-2883 **Alternate Tel:** n/a
Email: bpm@byy.com **Web:** www.byy.com/Plymouth
Nearest Town: Plymouth *(0.2 mi.)* **Tourist Info:** (508) 747-7525

Navigational Information

Lat: 41°57.370' **Long:** 070°39.597' **Tide:** 10 ft. **Current:** 0 kt. **Chart:** 13253
Rep. Depths (*MLW*): Entry 9 ft. **Fuel Dock** 12 ft. **Max Slip/Moor** 12 ft./-
Access: Duxbury Pier Light, Plymouth Harbor Channel, to port at G 9

Marina Facilities *(In Season/Off Season)*

Fuel: *Texaco* - Gasoline, Diesel, On Call Delivery
Slips: 110 Total, 40 Transient **Max LOA:** 150 ft. **Max Beam:** n/a
Rate *(per ft.)*: **Day** $3.50* **Week** Inq. **Month** n/a
Power: 30 amp Incl., **50 amp** Incl., **100 amp** n/a, **200 amp** n/a
Cable TV: Yes **Dockside Phone:** No
Dock Type: Floating, Long Fingers, Alongside, Concrete
Moorings: 0 Total, 0 Transient **Launch:** n/a
Rate: Day n/a **Week** n/a **Month** n/a
Heads: 6 Toilet(s), 6 Shower(s)
Internet: Yes *(Wi-Fi, Free)* **Laundry:** 2 Washer(s), 3 Dryer(s)
Pump-Out: OnSite, Full Service **Fee:** Free **Closed Heads:** Yes

Marina Operations

Owner/Manager: Tim Moll **Dockmaster:** Chris Smith
In-Season: Summer, 8am-6pm **Off-Season:** Fall-Win-Sprg, 8am-4:30pm
After-Hours Arrival: Check in the next morning
Reservations: Yes **Credit Cards:** Visa/MC, Dscvr, Amex
Discounts: None
Pets: Welcome **Handicap Access:** Yes

Marina Services and Boat Supplies

Services - Docking Assistance, Security, Dock Carts **Communication -** Mail & Package Hold, Phone Messages, Fax in/out, FedEx, UPS **Supplies - OnSite:** Ice *(Block, Cube)*, Bait/Tackle *(Fishermans Outfitter 747-7440)* **1-3 mi:** West Marine *(830-3150)*, Propane *(Dunlap's 746-2627)*

Boatyard Services

OnSite: Travelift *(2 60T)*, Forklift *(20,000 lb.)*, Crane *(spars to 70 ft.)*, Engine mechanic *(gas, diesel)*, Electrical Repairs, Electronics Repairs, Hull Repairs, Rigger, Canvas Work, Bottom Cleaning, Brightwork, Refrigeration, Awlgrip, Total Refits **OnCall:** Divers, Propeller Repairs **Dealer for:** Cummins, Caterpillar, Mercruiser, Cat, Westerbeke, Yanmar. **Member:** ABBRA, ABYC - 6 Certified Tech(s) **Yard Rates:** $65-95/hr., Haul & Launch $8-12/ft., Bottom Paint $12/ft. **Storage:** On-Land $28/ft.

Restaurants and Accommodations

OnSite: Restaurant *(14 Union 747-4503, L $10-15, D $16-25, Jazz Brunch $8-18)* **Near:** Restaurant *(Water St. Cafe 746-2050, B $4-11, L $5-7)*, *(San Diego's 747-0048, L $7-9, D $8-14)*, *(Hearth 'n Kettle 747-7405, B $6-9, L & D $8-20)*, *(Persey's 732-9876, L & D $3-11)*, Pizzeria *(Bella 747-1870)*, *(Stevie's 746-3395)*, Inn/B&B *(Gov. Bradford 746-6200, $100-150)*, *(John Carver 746-7100, $150-190)* **Under 1 mi:** Restaurant *(Lobster Hut 746-2270, L $4-11, D $6-19)*, *(Isaac's 830-0001, L $8-15, D $12-23)*, *(Wood's Seafood 746-0261, L & D $7-18+)*, Hotel *(Best West. 746-2222, $99-199)*

Recreation and Entertainment

OnSite: Grills, Fishing Charter *(Reel Time 774-437-1882)* **Near:** Beach *(Stephen Fields)*, Park *(Brewster Gardens; Pilgrim Memorial)*, Museum *(Pilgrim Hall 746-1620 $8/5; 1749 Court House 830-4075)*, Tours *(Jenny Grist Mill $6/4, Plymouth Hist. $10/8 747-4544; Plymouth Belle 747-3434)*, Cultural Attract *(Plymouth Phil. 746-8008)*, Sightseeing *(Mayflower II 746-1622 $10/7)* **Under 1 mi:** Fitness Center *(Shakin-n-Groovin 747-2077)*, Boat Rentals *(Plymouth 245-3996 PWCs, kayaks)*, Party Boat *(Capt. John 746-2643)* **3+ mi:** Golf Course *(Squirrel Run 746-5001, 4 mi.)*

Provisioning and General Services

Near: Convenience Store *(Tedeschi 746-9304)*, Health Food *(Common Sense 732-0427)*, Wine/Beer *(Wine Barrel 830-9511)*, Bank/ATM, Post Office, Protestant Church, Synagogue, Beauty Salon *(Tuscany 747-7211)*, Dry Cleaners, Laundry **Under 1 mi:** Liquor Store *(Richards 747-3311)*, Bakery *(Blue Binds 747-0462)*, Farmers' Market *(Courthouse Sat am)*, Fishmonger *(Reliable 746-1970)*, Catholic Church, Library *(830-4250)*, Pharmacy *(Rite Aid 746-2227)*, Hardware Store *(Benny's 746-7949)* **1-3 mi:** Supermarket *(Shaw's 747-2325)*, Retail Shops *(Standish Mall)*

Transportation

OnCall: Rental Car *(Enterprise 747-1212)*, Taxi *(Traveler 732-8294)* **Near:** Local Bus *(Trolley)*, InterCity Bus *(P & B 746-0378 - Boston/P-Town)* **Under 1 mi:** Ferry Service *(P-Town 747-2400)* **1-3 mi:** Bikes *(Martha's 746-2109)*, Rail *(617-268-9000 Boston)* **Airport:** Logan/Plymouth *(42 mi./1.6 mi.)*

Medical Services

911 Service **Near:** Doctor *(PMG 224-2224)*, Dentist *(Aveni 746-1918)*, Chiropractor *(Whitefield 747-2722)*, Holistic Services *(Beach Plum Spa 746-7100)*, Optician *(Eyewear 747-0096)* **Under 1 mi:** Veterinarian *(Court St. 747-0774)* **Hospital:** Jordan 746-2000 *(1.5 mi.)*

Setting -- Located in historic Plymouth Harbor, the marina's two-story, hip-roofed building, housing Union 14 restaurant, the office and ships store, sports a wrap-around veranda that overlooks the expansive network of quality docks. Two large, gray work sheds anchor the extensive boat yard operation. The slips and the restaurant's blue-tented deck and upper-level dining room all enjoy panoramic views of the harbor, Mayflower II, Plymouth Rock Memorial and, beyond, to Plymouth Beach - a narrow barrier peninsula dotted with old summer homes. Brewer also benefits from an L-shaped jetty that protects the inner harbor.

Marina Notes -- *slips plus 325 ft side-tie dockage. CCM. Founded in 1947 as Plymouth Marine railways. Present facility built in 1981, purchased & rebuilt by Brewer in 1992. Well-managed, very clean, good security. Dredged to 12 ft. mlw at face dock, 8-10 ft. throughout basin. Winter storage for 200 vessels, rack storage for 40. State-of-the-art, 10,000 sq.ft. service building with 33-ft high doors & 20,000-sq. ft. shed houses 42 yachts indoors. Good service techs with strong mechanical background. Bathhouse: Modern, well-tended, full-tiled, glass shower doors - flowers & dressing rooms. Also used by restaurant clients.

Notable -- Plymouth is a destination harbor deserving a layday or three. Most of the sites are within easy walking distance. Find a copy of the 20-sites "Pilgrim Path" tour at the Visitors Center (120 Water St.) or download one and a free audio tour from pilgrimpathtours.com. Also notable are First House, 1627 House, the Pilgrim Hall Museum - the nation's oldest public museum, and Plimoth Plantation (746-1622 $24/14) a living history museum that recreates a 1627 English Village and the Wampanoag Homesite (2.5 miles near Pilgrim Sands Beach). The Plymouth Trolley (Day -$15/7.50) circles all the historic sites.

Navigational Information
Lat: 41°57.332' **Long:** 070°39.476' **Tide:** 10 ft. **Current:** 0 kt. **Chart:** 13253
Rep. Depths (*MLW*): Entry 10 ft. **Fuel Dock** n/a **Max Slip/Moor** -/50 ft.
Access: Duxbury Pier Light, to port at G9, to Plymouth Harbor Channel

Marina Facilities *(In Season/Off Season)*
Fuel: No
Slips: 0 Total, 0 Transient **Max LOA:** 50 ft. **Max Beam:** n/a
Rate *(per ft.)*: **Day** n/a **Week** n/a **Month** n/a
Power: 30 amp n/a, **50 amp** n/a, **100 amp** n/a, **200 amp** n/a
Cable TV: No **Dockside Phone:** No
Dock Type: n/a
Moorings: 300 Total, 10 Transient **Launch:** Yes (Free), Dinghy Dock
Rate: Day $45* **Week** n/a **Month** n/a
Heads: Toilet(s), Shower(s)
Internet: No **Laundry:** 1 Washer(s), 1 Dryer(s)
Pump-Out: OnCall *(MemDay-LabDay)* **Fee:** Free **Closed Heads:** Yes

Marina Operations
Owner/Manager: Rebecca Darsch **Dockmaster:** Robert Webb
In-Season: May-Oct, 7am-10pm **Off-Season:** Nov-Apr, 8am-8pm
After-Hours Arrival: Call in advance
Reservations: Yes **Credit Cards:** Visa/MC
Discounts: None
Pets: Welcome **Handicap Access:** No

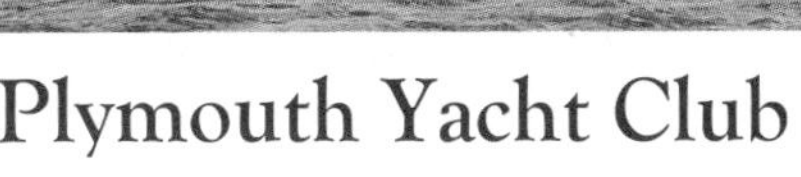

Plymouth Yacht Club

34 Union Street; Plymouth, MA 02360

Tel: (508) 747-0473 **VHF: Monitor** Ch. 8 **Talk** Ch. 8
Fax: (508) 747-2015 **Alternate Tel:** n/a
Email: pyclub@comcast.net **Web:** plymouthyachtclub.org
Nearest Town: Plymouth *(0.2 mi.)* **Tourist Info:** (508) 747-7525

Marina Services and Boat Supplies
Services - Docking Assistance, Boaters' Lounge, Dock Carts
Communication - FedEx, UPS, Express Mail **Supplies - OnSite:** Ice *(Block, Cube)* **Near:** Bait/Tackle *(Fishermans Outfitter 747-7440)* **1-3 mi:** West Marine *(830-3150)*, Propane *(Dunlap's 746-2627)*

Boatyard Services
Nearest Yard: Brewer Plymouth Marine (508) 746-4500

Restaurants and Accommodations
Near: Restaurant *(Water Street Cafe 746-2050, B $4-11, L $5-8)*, *(14 Union 747-4503, L $10-15, D $16-25, Sun Jazz Brunch $8-18)*, *(Cafe Strega 732-9996, L $11-17, D $18-24)*, *(San Diego Mexican 747-0048, L $7-9, D $8-20)*, *(Shangri-La Indian 747-2353, L & D $14-21)*, Pizzeria *(Bella 747-1870)*, *(Stevie's 746-3395)*, Motel *(Blue Anchor 746-9551)*, Inn/B&B *(Gov Bradford 746-6200, $100-150)* **Under 1 mi:** Restaurant *(Hearth & Kettle 747-4705, B $7-11, L & D $12-20)*, *(Issac's 830-0001, L $8-15, D $12-23)*, *(Wood's Seafood 746-0261, L & D $7-18+)*, *(Lobster Hut 746-2270, L $4-11, D $6-19)*, Inn/B&B *(John Carver 746-7100, $150-190)*

Recreation and Entertainment
Near: Beach *(Stephens Field)*, Playground, Tennis Courts *(Stephens Field)*, Fishing Charter *(Reel Time 774 437-1882)*, Park *(Brewster Gardens; Pilgrim Memorial)*, Museum *(Pilgrim Hall 746-1620 $8/5; 1749 Court House 830-4075; Mayflower Society $4/1)*, Tours *(Jenny Grist Mill $6/4, Plymouth Hist. $10/8 747-4544; Ghost Tours 813-2244)*, Cultural Attract *(Plymouth Philharmonic 746-8008)*, Sightseeing *(Mayflower II 746-1622 $10/7; Pilgrim Path 10 sites)*, Galleries *(Kusmin 746-9215; Wilson & Heywood 732-0170)*
Under 1 mi: Boat Rentals *(Plymouth 245-3996 PWCs, kayaks)*, Party Boat *(Capt. John 746-2643)* **3+ mi:** Golf Course *(Squirrel Run 746-5001, 5 mi.)*

Provisioning and General Services
Near: Convenience Store *(Tedeschi 746-9304)*, Health Food *(Common Sense 732-0427)*, Wine/Beer *(Wine Barrel 830-9511)*, Farmers' Market *(Thur 2:30-6:30pm, Stephen's Field)*, Bank/ATM, Post Office, Protestant Church, Synagogue, Beauty Salon *(Verona 746-7979)*, Dry Cleaners *(Reliable 746-0520)*, Laundry *(746-3688)*, Newsstand, Copies Etc. *(Shiretown 747-2809)* **Under 1 mi:** Market *(Sabor 747-7690)*, Delicatessen *(Court St. 747-4299)*, Liquor Store *(Richards 747-3311)*, Bakery *(Blue Blinds 747-0462)*, Fishmonger *(Reliable 746-1970)*, Catholic Church, Library *(830-4250 Web)*, Pharmacy *(Medicine Shoppe 747-1247)*, Florist *(Petal Pusher 746-0035)* **1-3 mi:** Supermarket *(Shaw's 747-2325)*, Hardware Store *(Home Depot 830-6702)*, Retail Shops *(Standish Mall)*, Department Store *(Marshall's; Kohls)*, Buying Club *(BJs 591-1009)*

Transportation
OnCall: Rental Car *(Enterprise 747-1212)*, Taxi *(SeaBreeze 888-0774)* **Near:** Local Bus *(Trolley)*, InterCity Bus *(P & B 746-0378 P-town/Boston)* **Under 1 mi:** Ferry Service *(P-town 747-2400)* **1-3 mi:** Bikes *(Martha's 746-2109)*, Rail *(617-268-9000 MBTA)* **Airport:** Logan/Plymouth *(42 mi./1.6 mi.)*

Medical Services
911 Service **Near:** Doctor *(PMG 224-2224)*, Dentist *(Aveni 746-1918)*, Optician *(Eyewear 747-0096)* **Under 1 mi:** Chiropractor *(Whitfield 747-2722)*, Holistic Services *(Acupuncture Healing 309-2362)*, Veterinarian *(Pilgrim 746-5003)* **Hospital:** Jordan 746-2000 *(1.5 mi.)*

Setting -- Right next to Brewer's, small, engaging Plymouth Yacht Club offers a convenient location with spectacular views of Plymouth, the Mayflower II, and the harbor -- from its mooring field, its front lawn, and from its second and third-floor decks, which are attractively furnished with comfortable tables and chairs.

Marina Notes -- *Mooring technically free, the fee is for use of the Club's launch and its other facilities: Top Side Bar, decks, heads, shower, & laundry. Founded 1890. Reservations require payment in advance, cancellation 4-6 days, forfeit 50%, 1-3 days, forfeit 100%. Launch hours: Jul & Aug 7:30am-10pm Sun-Thu, 7:30am-11pm Fri, Sat; shoulder season 8am-10pm. Pump-out boat MemDay-LabDay 7 days, Ch.9. Topside Bar open 4-10pm Tue-Thu & Sat & Sun 4-11pm Fri, 2-10pm. several special dining events each week. Lovely main floor Event Room overlooking harbor accommodates 150. Call Harbormaster Timothy Routhier (830-4182) in advance for vessels over 40 ft. LOA. Bathhouse: Pretty shower curtains, vanity skirts. Simple but inviting. Laundry.

Notable -- Everything in this historic 1620 town is within easy reach. Walk the Pilgrim Path through Brewster Garden past more than 20 sites (maps at 130 Water St. Visitors Center). It's 0.3 mi. to Plymouth Rock, the Park & Mayflower II. For a more sedentary excursion, Plymouth Rock Trolley passes 40 sites, including the yacht club ($15/7.50). Contemporary action can be found at the main commercial wharf (0.7 mi.) where the fishing trawlers unload. At the living history museum, Plimoth Plantation, costumed villagers go about early 17thC lives living in thatched-roof cottages and tending authentic plants and livestock. There's also an adjacent Wampanoag Homesite (746-1622 $24/14, with Mayflower II $28/18). The Plymouth-Provincetown Ferry leaves from the State Pier.

Provincetown Public Pier

260 Commercial St.; Provincetown, MA 02657

Tel: (508) 487-7030 **VHF: Monitor** Ch. 9 **Talk** Ch. 8
Fax: (508) 487-7005 **Alternate Tel:** n/a
Email: see Marina Notes **Web:** provincetownpublicpiercorporation.com
Nearest Town: Provincetown *(0 mi.)* **Tourist Info:** (508) 487-3424

Navigational Information

Lat: 42°02.970' **Long:** 070°10.921' **Tide:** 12 ft. **Current:** 1 kt. **Chart:** 13249
Rep. Depths (*MLW*): Entry 13 ft. **Fuel Dock** 5 ft. **Max Slip/Moor** 14 ft./30 ft.
Access: Cape Cod Bay to Long Point; inside breakwater to west docks

Marina Facilities *(In Season/Off Season)*

Fuel: Gasoline, Diesel, On Call Delivery
Slips: 30 Total, 30 Transient **Max LOA:** 150 ft. **Max Beam:** 20 ft.
Rate *(per ft.)*: **Day** $3.00* **Week** Inq. **Month** Inq.
Power: 30 amp Incl., **50 amp** Incl., **100 amp** n/a, **200 amp** n/a
Cable TV: No **Dockside Phone:** No
Dock Type: Long Fingers, Concrete
Moorings: 0 Total, 0 Transient **Launch:** n/a, Dinghy Dock
Rate: Day n/a **Week** n/a **Month** week
Heads: 6 Toilet(s)
Internet: No **Laundry:** None
Pump-Out: OnCall, Full Service, 1 Port **Fee:** Free **Closed Heads:** Yes

Marina Operations

Owner/Manager: Rex McKinsey (HM) **Dockmaster:** John Davidson
In-Season: May-Oct, 24 hrs.** **Off-Season:** Closed
After-Hours Arrival: Call in advance
Reservations: Yes **Credit Cards:** Visa/MC
Discounts: None
Pets: Welcome **Handicap Access:** Yes, Heads, Docks

Marina Services and Boat Supplies

Services - Docking Assistance, Security *(24 Hrs., Night watch)* **Communication -** Pay Phone, FedEx, UPS **Supplies - OnSite:** Ice *(Cube)* **Near:** Ships' Store *(Lands End 487-0784)* **Under 1 mi:** Bait/Tackle *(Nelsons 487-0034)*, Propane *(F A Days 487-0041)*

Boatyard Services

OnSite: Divers **OnCall:** Engine mechanic *(gas, diesel)*, Air Conditioning, Refrigeration **Nearest Yard:** Flyer's Boatyard (508) 487-0898

Restaurants and Accommodations

Near: Restaurant *(Patio American 487-4003, B $8-10, L $14--27, D $14-46), (Squealing Pig 487-5804, B $11-14, L, & D $11-18), (Napis 487-1145, L $15-20, D $18-34), (Mayflower 487-0121), (Lobster Pot 487-0842, L & D $18-30, Kids' $5-8)*, Pizzeria *(George's 487-3744), (Red Shack 487-7422)*, Inn/B&B *(Moffett 487-6615, $60-174), (Secret Garden 487-9027, $60-175)* **Under 1 mi:** Restaurant *(Front Street 487-9715, L & D $17-25), (Mews 487-1500, D $18-32, Cafe $9-17)*, Hotel *(Anchor Inn 487-0432, $260-400)*

Recreation and Entertainment

OnSite: Fishing Charter *(Ginny G 487-3191; Beth Ann 487-0034)*, Party Boat *(Cee Jay 487-4330)*, Museum *(Whydah Pirate 487-8899;)*, Tours *(Dolphin Whalewatching 800-826-9300 $41/33; Pirate Adventures 487-1010)*, Galleries *(Blueberry Lane Pottery 487-2810; Unique Images 487-0561)* **Near:** Beach *(right & left of pier)*, Movie Theater *(Whaler's Wharf 487-4269)*, Sightseeing *(Art's Dune Tours 487-1950 $25/17; Alpha Whale Watch 221-5920)*, Special Events *(Portuguese Fest, late June; Carnival Mid-Aug)* **Under 1 mi:** Fitness Center *(Ptown 487-2776)*, Video Rental *(City 487-4493; Redbox)*, Cultural Attract *(Ptown Playhouse 487-0955; Ptown Theater 487-7487)* **3+ mi:** Golf Course *(Highland 487-9207, 8 mi.)*

Provisioning and General Services

Near: Gourmet Shop *(Cape Cod 487-2273)*, Farmers' Market *(Sat 11am-4pm, Town Hall)*, Fishmonger *(Townsend 487-5161)*, Bank/ATM, Hardware Store *(Lands End 487-0784)*, Copies Etc. *(Copy Caps 349-1300)* **Under 1 mi:** Market *(Far Land 487-0045; Ptown Gen 487-0300; Tedeschi 487-6810)*, Supermarket *(Stop & Shop 487-3738)*, Health Food *(Bradford 487-9784)*, Wine/Beer *(Perry's 487-0140)*, Liquor Store *(Yardarm 487-0700)*, Bakery *(Connie's 487-2167)*, Green Grocer *(J&E 487-3627)*, Post Office *(487-0368)*, Catholic Church, Protestant Church, Library *(487-7094)*, Beauty Salon *(Good Scents 487-3393)*, Dry Cleaners *(Prestige 487-9835)*, Laundry *(Ptown 487-3030)*, Bookstore *(Voyager 487-0848)*, Pharmacy *(S&S 487-0069)*

Transportation

OnSite: Water Taxi *(Flyers to Long Point 487-0898 $15/RT)* **OnCall:** Rental Car *(Enterprise 487-0009)*, Taxi *(Mercedes 487-8294)*, Local Bus *(The Shuttle)* **Near:** Bikes *(Arnold's 487-0844)*, InterCity Bus *(P & B 746-0378)*, Ferry Service *(Boston Harbor 617-227-4321; Boston Bay 877-783-3779 May-Oct)* **Under 1 mi:** Airport Limo *(Black & White 487-7800)*, Rail *(Ptown)* **Airport:** Ptown *(3 mi.)*

Medical Services

911 Service **Near:** Holistic Services *(Blu Day Spa 487-5506)* **Under 1 mi:** Doctor *(Ptown Med Group 487-3505)*, Dentist *(Graves 487-9395)*, Chiropractor *(Heitzman 487-3799)*, Veterinarian *(Ptown 487-2191)*
Hospital: Cape Cod 771-1800 *(48 mi.)*

Setting -- Protected by a long stone wave attenuator, two large piers flanked by mooring fields reach out into Provincetown Harbor. Provincetown Public Pier lies along the first and most easterly of the two - MacMillan Wharf. The harbormaster's low-slung gray-shingled office oversees the mix of pleasure craft and commercial fishing fleet with views of "downtown" and the tall Pilgrim Monument. Ferries and whale-watch tour boats make it easy to spot.

Marina Notes -- *$195 min. Limits dockage to vessels 65 LOA or more. **Onsite Staffed 8am-4pm, Mon-Fri. Email: mckinsey@provincetown-ma.gov. Managed by the Provincetown Public Pier Corporation. Wheelchair-accessible float for 15-minute tie-ups and a dingy dock. Book July 4 and mid-August Carnival in January. U.S. Coast Guard port. Truck delivery of diesel fuel - Marcey Oil 487-0219 & Cape Cod Oil 487-0205. Ice available but "not for human consumption." Good power pedestals. Pump-out boat 10am-4pm daily (487-7030 orCh 12). Self-service pump-out on courtesy float between MacMillan & Fishermen's Wharfs. Bathhouse: Next to Harbormaster's Office - open to public. Newly built, tiled. Note: Moorings - Provincetown Yacht Club 538-9010.

Notable -- In 1620, the Mayflower sailed into Provincetown Harbor paving the way for today's non-stop tourist season. A whalewatching fleet capitalizes on the proximity to the Stellwagen Bank National Marine Sanctuary and Fast Ferries connect the Wharf to Boston and Plymouth. All of delightful, exuberant, fun P-town is within easy walking distance for great shopping, gallery-hopping and a sophisticated restaurant scene. Hike, boat, shuttle, or taxi to Race Point (487-1256) and the National Seashore's ocean beach and hiking trails. Or bike the 8 miles of paths through 4,000 diverse acres. Better yet, party 'til dawn.

  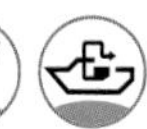   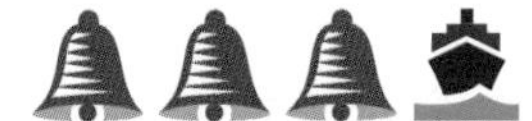

Navigational Information

Lat: 42°02.975' **Long:** 070°10.935' **Tide:** 12 ft. **Current:** 1 kt. **Chart:** 13249
Rep. Depths (*MLW*): Entry 20 ft. **Fuel Dock** n/a **Max Slip/Moor** 15 ft./-
Access: Cape Cod Bay to Long Point; inside breakwater to east docks

Marina Facilities *(In Season/Off Season)*

Fuel: Diesel, On Call Delivery
Slips: 14 Total, 6 Transient **Max LOA:** 140 ft. **Max Beam:** 35 ft.
Rate *(per ft.)*: **Day** $5.00/Inq.* **Week** n/a **Month** n/a
Power: 30 amp $35, **50 amp** $35, **100 amp** $35, **200 amp** n/a
Cable TV: No **Dockside Phone:** No
Dock Type: Floating, Long Fingers, Concrete
Moorings: 0 Total, 0 Transient **Launch:** n/a
Rate: Day n/a **Week** n/a **Month** n/a
Heads: 1 Toilet(s)
Internet: No **Laundry:** None
Pump-Out: OnCall, Full Service, 1 Port **Fee:** Free **Closed Heads:** Yes

Marina Operations

Owner/Manager: Ken Kinkor **Dockmaster:** Barry Clifford
In-Season: May 15-Oct **Off-Season:** Nov-May 14
After-Hours Arrival: Call in advance
Reservations: Yes, Required **Credit Cards:** Visa/MC, Dscvr, Amex
Discounts: None
Pets: Welcome **Handicap Access:** Yes, Heads, Docks

Provincetown Harbor Marina

PO Box 493; 16 MacMillan Wharf; Provincetown, MA 02657

Tel: (508) 487-8899 **VHF: Monitor** Ch. 9 **Talk** Ch. 12
Fax: (508) 487-8899 **Alternate Tel:** (508) 247-7451
Email: whydahmuseum@yahoo.com **Web:** marinaprovincetown.com
Nearest Town: Provincetown **Tourist Info:** (508) 487-3424

Marina Services and Boat Supplies

Services - Docking Assistance, Security *(24/7)* **Communication -** FedEx, UPS, Express Mail *(Sat Del)* **Supplies - OnSite:** Ice *(Block, Cube)* **Near:** Ships' Store *(Lands End 487-0784)* **Under 1 mi:** Bait/Tackle *(Nelsons 487-0034)*, Propane *(FA Days 487-0041)*

Boatyard Services

OnSite: Divers **OnCall:** Engine mechanic *(gas, diesel)*, Electrical Repairs, Electronic Sales, Electronics Repairs, Bottom Cleaning, Brightwork, Propeller Repairs **Nearest Yard:** Flyer's (508) 487-0898

Restaurants and Accommodations

Near: Restaurant *(Napis 487-1145, L $15-20, D $18-34)*, *(The Lobster Pot 487-0842, L $18-28, D $18-28, Kids' $5-8)*, *(Old Colony Tap 487-2361)*, *(Crown & Anchor 487-1430, L $11-18, D $12-26, 6 bars)*, Fast Food *(John's Footlong 487-7434)*, Lite Fare *(Karoo 487-6630, So. African)*, Pizzeria *(George's 487-3744)*, Inn/B&B *(Moffett 487-6615, $55-174)*, *(Secret Garden 487-9027, $60-175)*, *(Lotus 487-4644, $140-260)*, *(Crown & Anchor $95-295)* **Under 1 mi:** Restaurant *(Ross' Grill 487-8878, L $10-20, D $22-40)*, *(Mojo's 487-3140, $8-15)*, *(Pepe's Wharf 487-8717, L $13-29, D $13-29)*, *(Devon's 487-4773, B $5.50-$11.50, D $20-30)*, *(Bistro at Crowne Pt 487-6767)*, *(Ciro & Sal's 487-6444)*, Inn/B&B *(Christopher's 487-9263, $70-285)*

Recreation and Entertainment

OnSite: Fishing Charter *(Ginny G 487-3191)*, Party Boat *(CeeJay 487-4330)*, Museum *(Whydah Pirate 487-8889)* **Near:** Beach, Tours *(Pirate Adventures 487-1010; Viking Harbor Cruises 487-7323)*, Sightseeing *(Alpha Whale Watch 221-5920; Art's Dune 487-1950)* **Under 1 mi:** Fitness Center *(Ptown Gym 487-2776)*, Movie Theater *(Whalers Wharf 487-4269; New Art 487-9222)*, Video Rental *(City 487-4493; Redbox)*, Cultural Attract *(P-town Playhouse 487-0955)* **3+ mi:** Golf Course *(Highland 487-9201, 7.5 mi)*

Provisioning and General Services

Near: Farmers' Market *(Sat 11am-4pm, Town Hall)*, Fishmonger *(Townsend 487-5161)*, Bank/ATM, Hardware Store *(Lands End 487-0784)* **Under 1 mi:** Convenience Store *(Tedeschi's 487-6810)*, Market *(Far Land 487-0045)*, Supermarket *(Stop & Shop 487-3738)*, Health Food *(Bradford 487-9784)*, Wine/Beer *(Perry's 487-0140)*, Liquor Store *(Yardarm 487-0700)*, Bakery *(Connie's 487-2167)*, Green Grocer *(J&E 487-3627)*, Post Office, Catholic Church, Protestant Church, Library *(Provincetown 487-7094)*, Beauty Salon *(Good Scents 487-3393)*, Barber Shop, Dry Cleaners *(Prestige 487-9835)*, Laundry, Bookstore *(Voyager 487-0848)*, Pharmacy *(Stop & Shop 487-3738)*, Florist *(P-town 487-2047)*

Transportation

OnSite: Local Bus *(The Shuttle)*, InterCity Bus *(P&B to Boston 888-751-8800)*, Ferry Service *(to Boston: Bay State 487-9284; Boston Harbor Cruises 617-227-4321 $30-40 RT; Capt John to Plymouth $27 RT)* **OnCall:** Rental Car *(Enterprise 487-0009)*, Taxi *(Mercedes 487-8294; Cape 487-2222)* **Near:** Bikes *(Arnold's 487-0844)* **Under 1 mi:** Airport Limo *(Black & White 487-7800)*, Rail *(P-town)* **Airport:** P-town *(3 mi.)*

Medical Services

911 Service **Near:** Chiropractor *(Andrulot 487-0704)* **Under 1 mi:** Doctor *(Outer Cape 487-9395)*, Dentist *(Graves 487-9395)*, Veterinarian *(P-town 487-2191)* **Hospital:** Cape Cod 771-1800 *(48 mi.)*

Setting -- At the end of McMillan Wharf's western side, Provincetown Harbor's small complement of sturdy, sheltered dockage surrounds the large, brown-shingled building housing the Expedition Whydah Pirate Museum and Provincetown Harbor Marina offices. The rest of the wharf is occupied by the Provincetown Public Pier. This protected location affords spectacular views of the town, harbor and setting sun - while still being in the heart of Ptown.

Marina Notes -- *30-89 ft. $5/ft., 90-140 ft. $6/ft. Prepaid reservations only. Min. 35 ft. charge. Two-night min. Fri-Sun July & Aug. Formerly Provincetown Yacht Marina. Most mechanical services on call. Great views. Adjoins the Public Pier and shares some facilities. Stone wave attenuator protects piers. Dockside diesel delivery from Marcey Oil 487-0219 & Cape Cod Oil 487-0205. Pump-out boat (10am-4pm daily 487-7030, Ch 12). Self-service pump-out on courtesy float between MacMillan & Fishermen's Wharfs. Bathhouse: Simple, tile & steel, or use heads at Provincetown Public Pier.

Notable -- In 1717, the pirate flagship Whydah Galley, containing treasure looted from fifty ships, went down off Marconi Beach. In 1984, it was discovered. Today, a National Geographic "Special Event" archeological mission based at the Expedition Whydah Sea Lab & Learning Center displays the world's only pirate shipwreck treasure (10am-8pm, $10/8). The Ptown Shuttle bases at the foot of MacMillan Wharf stops at gorgeous, uncrowded Race Point Beach (487-1256), the spectacular National Seashore and much of the "Outer Cape." Commercial Street, the heart of Ptown, is just steps from the wharf: lively nightlife, a diverse selection of restaurants, special events, attractions, shops, galleries, and a fun, vivid street life.

PHOTOS ON DVD: 18

Provincetown Marina

PO Box 1042; Ryder St. Extension; Provincetown, MA 02657

Tel: (508) 487-0571 **VHF: Monitor** Ch. 9 **Talk** n/a
Fax: (508) 487-0571 **Alternate Tel:** n/a
Email: n/a **Web:** n/a
Nearest Town: Provincetown **Tourist Info:** (508) 487-3424

Navigational Information

Lat: 42°02.950' **Long:** 070°11.003' **Tide:** 12 **Current:** 1 kt **Chart:** 13249
Rep. Depths (*MLW*): Entry 13 ft. **Fuel Dock** n/a **Max Slip/Moor** 12 ft./15 ft.
Access: Cape Cod Bay to Long Point

Marina Facilities *(In Season/Off Season)*

Fuel: Gasoline
Slips: 36 Total, 30 Transient **Max LOA:** 65 ft. **Max Beam:** 15 ft.
Rate *(per ft.)*: **Day** $2.50* **Week** n/a **Month** n/a
Power: 30 amp Incl., **50 amp** Incl, **100 amp** n/a, **200 amp** n/a
Cable TV: No **Dockside Phone:** No
Dock Type: Fixed, Short Fingers, Pilings, Wood
Moorings: 100 Total, 50 Transient **Launch:** Yes (Free), Dinghy Dock
Rate: Day $45 **Week** $270 **Month** n/a
Heads: 4 Toilet(s), 4 Shower(s)
Internet: Yes *(Wi-Fi, $5)* **Laundry:** None
Pump-Out: OnSite **Fee:** n/a **Closed Heads:** Yes

Marina Operations

Owner/Manager: Not disclosed **Dockmaster:** Beth Townsend
In-Season: May-Oct **Off-Season:** Nov-April
After-Hours Arrival: n/a
Reservations: yes **Credit Cards:** Visa/MC, Amex
Discounts: None
Pets: Welcome **Handicap Access:** No

Marina Services and Boat Supplies

Services - Docking Assistance, Dock Carts **Communication -** FedEx, UPS **Supplies - OnSite:** Ice *(Block, Cube)* **Near:** Ships' Store *(Lands End 487-0784)* **Under 1 mi:** Bait/Tackle *(Nelson's 487-0034)*, Propane *(Days 487-0041)*

Boatyard Services

Nearest Yard: Flyer's Boatyard (508) 487-0898

Restaurants and Accommodations

Near: Restaurant *(Lobster Pot 487-0842, L & D $18-28, Kids' $5-8)*, *(Napi's 487-1145, L $15-20, D $18-34)*, *(Old Colony Tap 487-2361)*, *(Pepe's Wharf 487-8717, L & D $13-29)*, Lite Fare *(Karoo 487-6630)*, Pizzeria *(George's 487-3744)*, *(Twisted Sister 487-6973)*, Inn/B&B *(Moffett House 487-6615, $55-174)*, *(Secret Garden 487-9027, $60-175)* **Under 1 mi:** Restaurant *(The Mews 487-1500, D $18-32, Cafe $9-17)*, *(Vorelli's 487-2778, D $16-30)*, *(Ross' 487-8878, L $10-20, D $22-40)*, Inn/B&B *(Somerset House 487-0383, $80-145)*, *(Gabriel's at Ashbrooke 487-3232, $125-380)*

Recreation and Entertainment

Near: Beach, Fishing Charter *(Lighthouse 224-4616)*, Party Boat *(Cee Jay 487-4330)*, Museum *(Whydah Pirate 487-8899; Provincetown 487-1310; Provincetown Art 487-1750)*, Tours *(Pirate Adventures 487-1010; Art's Dune Tours 487-1950; Portuguese Princess 487-2651- naturalist-led)*, Sightseeing *(Alpha 221-5920 & Dolphin Whale Watch tours 800-826-9300)*, Galleries *(Blueberry Lane Pottery 487-2810; Unique Images 487-0561; Tao Water Art 487-8880; Bowersock 487-4994)* **Under 1 mi:** Fitness Center *(Ptown Gym 487-2776)*, Boat Rentals *(Flyer's 487-0898)*, Video Rental *(City Video 487-4493; Redbox)*, Cultural Attract *(P-town Playhouse 487-0955; P-town Theater 487-7487)* **3+ mi:** Golf Course *(Highland G.C. 487-9201, 7.5 mi)*

Provisioning and General Services

Near: Fishmonger *(Townsend's 487-5161)*, Bank/ATM, Hardware Store *(Lands End 487-0784)* **Under 1 mi:** Convenience Store *(Tedeschi 487-6810)*, Market *(Far Land 487-0045)*, Supermarket *(Stop & Shop 487-3738)*, Health Food *(Bradford 487-9784)*, Wine/Beer *(Perry's 487-0140)*, Liquor Store *(Yardarm 487-0700)*, Bakery *(Connie's 487-2167)*, Farmers' Market *(Sat 11am-4pm, Town Hall)*, Green Grocer *(J&E Fruit 487-3627)*, Post Office, Catholic Church, Protestant Church, Library *(487-7094)*, Beauty Salon *(Good Scents 487-3393)*, Dry Cleaners *(Prestige 487-9835)*, Laundry *(P-town 487-3030)*, Bookstore *(Voyager 487-0848)*, Pharmacy *(S&S 487-0069)*, Florist *(P-town 487-2047)*, Copies Etc. *(P-town 487-2679)*

Transportation

OnCall: Rental Car *(Enterprise 487-0009)*, Taxi *(Mercedes 487-8294)* **Near:** Bikes *(Arnold's 487-0844)*, Local Bus *(Shuttle & Flex)*, InterCity Bus *(P & B 746-0378; Peter Pan 800-343-9999)*, Ferry Service *(Bay State $79/58; Boston Harbor)* **Under 1 mi:** Airport Limo *(B & W 487-7800)*, Rail *(Ptown)* **Airport:** Ptown *(3 mi.)*

Medical Services

911 Service **Near:** Holistic Services *(Blue Day Spa 487-5506)* **Under 1 mi:** Doctor *(Outer Cape 487-9395)*, Dentist *(Graves 487-9395)*, Chiropractor *(Conscious Choice 487-3799)*, Veterinarian *(Provincetown 487-2191)* **Hospital:** Cape Cod 771-1800 *(48 mi.)*

Setting -- A massive, weathered-shingled building with two chimneys and a small Citgo sign sit on the end of the more western pier where Provincetown's largest, most complete and quietest facility stretches along Fisherman's Wharf. A launch-serviced mooring field sprawls further to the west. From the docks and the moorings, there are spectacular vistas of this timeless village and beautiful harbor -- especially at sunset. Ptown village is just steps away.

Marina Notes -- *$100 min. Launch Service: 8am-11pm weekdays; 8am-midnight weekends.Mix of older and newer pedestals. Websites often confuse this private facility with the town marina. Needs some updating. Casual fuel dock on west side - only one in area. Club-quality launch. Harbor's stone wave attenuator helps the slosh, but in a slip, athwartships to the wave action, may be some roll. Proximity to Stellwagen Bank attracts many sport fishers. Reserve in Jan for Portuguese Fest (late June), July 4 & mid-Aug Carnival.). Pump-out boat (10am-4pm, 7 days 487-7030 & Ch. 12); Self-serve pump on float between marina & MacMillan Wharf. Bathhouse: Rustic, tiled, in need of updating; token-operated showers - $1 for 3.5 min. Note: Muni. Dinghy dock 7 hrs. free.

Notable -- "They Also Faced the Sea" on the side of the main wharf building are pictures of women relatives of Provincetown fishermen (learn more at the Harbormaster's Office). A popular fish market is at the pier's base next to the local beach. For a more extravagant sweep of sand, take Flyer's water shuttle to Long Point or bike to spectacular Race Point. Most of the action is along Commercial Street, but Ptown is so much more: a smorgasboard of cultural, musical, artistic, gastronomic, natural diversions: Whale-watching, naturalist-conducted excursions, Province Lands - 8 miles of bike paths through 4,000 acres.

Flyer's Boatyard & Moorings

PO Box 561; 131A Commercial Street; Provincetown, MA 02657

Tel: (508) 487-0898; (800) 750-0898 **VHF: Monitor** Ch. 9 **Talk** Ch. 11
Fax: (508) 487-3875 **Alternate Tel:** (508) 487-0898
Email: noahsantos@flyersboats.com **Web:** www.flyersboats.com
Nearest Town: Provincetown *(0.25 mi.)* **Tourist Info:** (508) 487-3424

Navigational Information
Lat: 42°02.734' **Long:** 070°11.460' **Tide:** 10 ft. **Current:** 1 kt. **Chart:** 13249
Rep. Depths (*MLW*): Entry 18 ft. **Fuel Dock** n/a **Max Slip/Moor** -/15 ft.
Access: Long Point, cross harbor bearing WNW, 1.4 miles to inner harbor

Marina Facilities *(In Season/Off Season)*
Fuel: No
Slips: 0 Total, 0 Transient **Max LOA:** 100 ft. **Max Beam:** n/a
Rate *(per ft.)*: **Day** n/a **Week** n/a **Month** n/a
Power: 30 amp n/a, **50 amp** n/a, **100 amp** n/a, **200 amp** n/a
Cable TV: No **Dockside Phone:** No
Dock Type: n/a
Moorings: 50 Total, 18 Transient **Launch:** Yes (Free**), Dinghy Dock
Rate: Day $45 **Week** $200 **Month** Inq.
Heads: 3 Toilet(s), 2 Shower(s) *(dressing rooms)*
Internet: Yes *(Office)* **Laundry:** 1 Washer(s), 1 Dryer(s)
Pump-Out: OnCall *(487-7030 or Ch. 12)* **Fee:** Free **Closed Heads:** Yes

Marina Operations
Owner/Manager: Noah Santos **Dockmaster:** Malcolm Hunter
In-Season: May 15-Oct 15, 8am-6pm **Off-Season:** Oct 16-May 14, 9a-4p
After-Hours Arrival: Pick-up mooring by Coast Guard piers - look for sign
Reservations: Yes **Credit Cards:** Debit Cards/Cash only
Discounts: None
Pets: Welcome **Handicap Access:** Yes, Heads

Marina Services and Boat Supplies
Services - Docking Assistance **Communication -** Pay Phone (1), FedEx, UPS, Express Mail *(Sat Del)* **Supplies - OnSite:** Ice *(Block)*, Ships' Store **Near:** Bait/Tackle *(Nelson's 487-0034)*, Propane *(Days 487-0041)*

Boatyard Services
OnSite: Railway, Forklift, Engine mechanic *(gas, diesel)*, Electrical Repairs, Electronic Sales, Electronics Repairs, Hull Repairs, Rigger, Divers, Bottom Cleaning, Brightwork, Compound, Wash & Wax, Interior Cleaning, Propeller Repairs, Woodworking, Inflatable Repairs, Painting, Awlgrip, Total Refits **Near:** Launching Ramp. **Dealer for:** Evinrude, Johnson.

Restaurants and Accommodations
Near: Restaurant *(Lorraine's 487-6074, D $15-26)*, *(Sal's Place 487-1279, D $16-23)*, *(Martin House 487-6555)*, *(Monkey Bar 487-2879)*, *(Enzo 487-7555, B $6-9, D $14-30, Brunch $8-10)*, *(Jimmy's Hideaway 487-1011, D $19-33, Tavern $11-18)*, Lite Fare *(Karoo 487-6630, D $12-20, Veg, too.)*, Motel *(Masthead 487-0523, $99-489, plus moorings and launch)*, *(Boatslip Resort 487-1669, $150-190)*, Inn/B&B *(Prince Albert 487-1850, $125-350)*, *(Carriage House 487-3387)*, *(Crown Pt. Historic 487-6767)*

Recreation and Entertainment
OnSite: Beach, Boat Rentals *(Kayaks $50-70/day, Sunfish $80, Rhodes 19 $130, Powerboats $180-400)* **Near:** Fitness Center *(Mussel Beach 487-0001)*, Horseback Riding *(Bayberry Hollow 487-6584)* **Under 1 mi:** Tennis Courts *(Herring Cove 487-9512)*, Fishing Charter *(Capt Jim's 237-7701)*, Party Boat *(Cee Jay 487-4330)*, Movie Theater *(Whaler's Wharf 487-4269)*, Video Rental *(City 487-4493)*, Museum *(Pilgrim Monument & Provincetown 487-1310; Whydah 487-8899)*, Cultural Attract *(Ptown Art 487-1750; Ptown Playhouse 487-0955; Ptown Theater 487-7487)*, Sightseeing *(Alpha Whalewatch 221-5920)*, Galleries **1-3 mi:** Tours *(Nat'l Seashore self-guided nature trails 487-1256)* **3+ mi:** Golf Course *(Highland 487-9201, 8 mi.)*

Provisioning and General Services
Near: Convenience Store *(Ptown General 487-0300)*, Gourmet Shop *(Cheese Market 487-3032)*, Wine/Beer *(Perrys 487-0140)*, Newsstand, Florist *(Wildflower 487-6732)* **Under 1 mi:** Supermarket *(Stop & Shop)*, Liquor Store *(Big Vin's 487-0635)*, Farmers' Market *(Sat 11am-4pm, Town Hall)*, Fishmonger *(Townsend's 487-5161)*, Bank/ATM, Post Office, Catholic Church, Protestant Church, Library *(Ptown 487-7094)*, Beauty Salon *("Salon 54" 487-4247)*, Dry Cleaners *(Prestige 487-9835)*, Laundry, Bookstore *(Ptown 487-0964)*, Pharmacy *(Adams 487-0069)*, Hardware Store *(Conwell 487-0150)*, Copies Etc. *(Mail Spot 487-6650)*

Transportation
OnSite: Water Taxi *(Long Pt 487-0898 $15 RT, Sunset $30)* **OnCall:** Rental Car *(Enterprise 487-0009, Thrifty 487-9418)*, Taxi *(Ptown 487-8294; Cape Cab 487-2222; Mercedes 487-3333)* **Near:** Bikes *(Gale Force 487-4849)*, Local Bus *(The Shuttle)* **Under 1 mi:** InterCity Bus *(P&B 746-0378)*, Rail *(Ptown)*, Ferry Service *(Boston-Plymouth)* **Airport:** Ptown *(3.5 mi.)*

Medical Services
911 Service **Near:** Holistic Services *(West End Spa 487-1872)* **Under 1 mi:** Doctor *(Ptown Med 487-3505)*, Dentist *(Ptown 487-2800)*, Chiropractor *(Andrulot 487-0704)*, Optician *(Shiffman 487-4333)*, Veterinarian *(Herring Cove 487-6449)* **Hospital:** Cape Cod 771-1800 *(48 mi.)*

Setting -- Just before the long, fixed Coast Guard pier, pick out Flyers on the western edge of Provincetown's dense shoreline. Look for floating wood docks lined with small rental craft, a bright orange-railed gangway, and a marine railway. On shore is a two-story, weathered-shingled main building edged with verandas and a concrete patio populated by green tables and chairs. The mooring field offers great views of Provincetown and Long Point - and sunsets.

Marina Notes *over 50 ft: $1/ft supplement. **Unlimited free launch service 8am to 8pm - to Flyers dock or MacMillan Wharf in the heart of the village. After hours launch fee $2/each way. Radio for mooring assignment - only go to float in the dink. For big boat loading/unloading, tie up at the town dock. Pump-out boat 10am-4pm, daily. Unique, service-oriented moorings/launch operation since 1945. Small service yard handles fiberglass dinghies to 80 ft. wood fishing draggers. Largest small craft boat rental operation on the Cape: kayaks, skiffs, sailboats, power boats (by the hour, half-day or day). Dry storage for boats to 28 ft. Sailing School - Beginner to Bare Boat. Waterfront, weekly 3-4 bedroom apartment 487-3064. Bathhouse: Small, white cinderblock heads & showers.

Notable -- Take Flyer's ten-minute party shuttle trip to Long Point - the hook of the Cape. The pontoon boats land right on the beach in the shadow of Long Point Lighthouse for a delightful beach walk or picnic excursion to this three-mile stretch of uncivilized beach - great way to meet people. All of Provincetown's delights are an easy walk, including Pilgrim Monument and Herring Cove Beach - or the Ptown Shuttle stops a block away. Bike the Province Land's trails through dunes, bogs, and to the beaches. The July 4 and mid-August Carnival are great fun and very, very crowded - you'll know you're not in Kansas anymore.

PHOTOS ON DVD: 17

Town of Wellfleet Marina

Town of Wellfleet Marina

255 Commercial Street; Wellfleet, MA 02667

Tel: (508) 349-0320 **VHF: Monitor** Ch. 9 **Talk** Ch. 16
Fax: (508) 349-0320 **Alternate Tel:** n/a
Email: wfmarina@townofwellfleet.org **Web:** wellfleetma.org
Nearest Town: Wellfleet *(0.25 mi.)* **Tourist Info:** (508) 349-2510

Navigational Information

Lat: 41°55.789' **Long:** 070°01.697' **Tide:** 10 ft. **Current:** 1 kt. **Chart:** 13250
Rep. Depths (*MLW*): Entry 6 ft. **Fuel Dock** 6 ft. **Max Slip/Moor** 6 ft./6 ft.
Access: Cape Cod Bay to G1, follow channel into Wellfleet Harbor

Marina Facilities *(In Season/Off Season)*

Fuel: Gasoline, Diesel
Slips: 185 Total, 5 Transient **Max LOA:** 55 ft. **Max Beam:** 16 ft.
Rate *(per ft.)*: **Day** $2.00* **Week** $14/124 **Month** n/a
Power: 30 amp $2, **50 amp** n/a, **100 amp** n/a, **200 amp** n/a
Cable TV: No **Dockside Phone:** No
Dock Type: Floating, Alongside, Concrete, Wood
Moorings: 15 Total, 15 Transient **Launch:** Yes, Dinghy Dock
Rate: Day $36/5 **Week** $252/31 **Month** n/a
Heads: 2 Toilet(s), 1 Shower(s)
Internet: No **Laundry:** None
Pump-Out: Full Service, 1 Port **Fee:** Free **Closed Heads:** Yes

Marina Operations

Owner/Manager: Michael Flanagan (Hbrmstr) **Dockmaster:** Mike May
In-Season: May 15-Oct 15, 24 hrs. **Off-Season:** Oct 16-May 14, 8am-5pm**
After-Hours Arrival: Call in advance
Reservations: Yes **Credit Cards:** Cash/Check only
Discounts: None
Pets: Welcome **Handicap Access:** Yes, Heads, Docks

Marina Services and Boat Supplies

Services - Security *(24 Hrs., night watchman)*, Trash Pick-Up **Communication -** FedEx, UPS **Supplies - OnSite:** Ice *(Block, Cube)* **Near:** Bait/Tackle *(Wellfleet Marine 349-6417)* **Under 1 mi:** Ships' Store *(Bay Sails 349-3840)* **3+ mi:** Propane *(Snow's, 13 mi.)*

Boatyard Services

OnSite: Launching Ramp, Engine mechanic *(gas, diesel)* **Nearest Yard:** Flyers Provincetown (508) 487-0518

Restaurants and Accommodations

OnSite: Seafood Shack *(Mac's 349-9611, L & D $5-30 Kid's $6-7.50)* **Near:** Restaurant *(Book Store & Restaurant 349-3154, B $4-13, L $5-20, D $14-23)*, *(Pearl 349-2999, L $9-19, D $16-30)*, Seafood Shack *(Mac's Shack 349-6333, D $10-30, kids' $6-9)*, Inn/B&B *(Stone Lion 349-9565, $140-220)* **Under 1 mi:** Restaurant *(Wicked Oyster 349-3455)*, *(Winslow's Tavern 349-6450)*, *(PJ's Family 349-2126, L&D 5:50-29; kid's $2.50-$10)*, Pizzeria *(Wellfleet Town 349-6400)*, *(Juice 349-0535)*, Motel *(Duck Creeke 349-9333, $90-135)*, Inn/B&B *(Aunt Sukie's 349-0525, $215-295)* **1-3 mi:** Restaurant *(Moby Dick's Seafood 349-9795, L&D $11-24)*, Inn/B&B *(Chez Sven 349-6823, $150-200)*, *(Oyster Cove 349-2994, $225-495)*

Recreation and Entertainment

OnSite: Boat Rentals *(Wellfleet Marine 349-2233 Small sail & powerboats $50-80/hr.)*, Fishing Charter *(Cape Mariner 349-6003; Capt Coakley 349-0951; Jac's Mate 255-2978; Snooper 237-4600)* **Near:** Beach *(Mayo)*, Tennis Courts *(Wellfleet 349-0330)*, Galleries *(dozens - Frying Pan 349-0011; Left Bank 349-7939)* **Under 1 mi:** Hike/Bike Trails *(25 mi. Rail Trail 896-3491 to So. Dennis)*, Museum *(Wellfleet Historical 349-9157)* **1-3 mi:** Golf Course *(Chequessett 349-3704)*, Park *(Pilgrim Spring)*, Cultural Attract *(Wellfleet Harbor Actors Theater 349-6835)* **3+ mi:** Movie Theater *(Wellfleet Drive-In & Cinema 349-7176, 6 mi.)*, Tours *(Outer Cape Jeep Tours 487-8802, 6 mi.)*, Sightseeing *(Wellfleet Bay Wildlife 349-2615, 6 mi.)*

Provisioning and General Services

OnSite: Fishmonger *(Macs 349-0404; The Boathouse)* **Under 1 mi:** Market *(Wellfleet 349-3156)*, Delicatessen *(The Box Lunch 349-3509)*, Liquor Store *(Wellfleet Spirits 349-3731)*, Bakery *(Sweet Baking 349-1094)*, Green Grocer *(Hatch's Produce)*, Bank/ATM *(Wellfleet Marketplace)*, Post Office *(349-6117)*, Protestant Church, Library *(Wellfleet 349-0310)*, Bookstore *(Herridge 349-1323)*, Hardware Store *(Mid-Cape Home Centers 349-3734)*, Florist *(Kelley's Flowers 349-9861)* **1-3 mi:** Wine/Beer *(Wellfleet Wine 349-6880)*, Catholic Church, Beauty Salon *(Local Color 349-6974)* **3+ mi:** Supermarket *(Stop & Shop 255-5288, 12 mi.)*, Pharmacy *(CVS 240-2759, 13 mi.)*

Transportation

OnCall: Rental Car *(Enterprise 255-2997)*, Taxi *(Wellfleet 349-8294)* **Under 1 mi:** InterCity Bus *(P&B 746-0378 Provincetown to Boston)* **1-3 mi:** Bikes *(Idle Times 349-9161/255-8281)* **3+ mi:** Rail *(Truro, 6 mi.)* **Airport:** Provincetown *(17 mi.)*

Medical Services

911 Service **Under 1 mi:** Holistic Services *(Laughing Hearts Acupuncture 349-7700)*, Veterinarian *(Duck Creek 349-7870)* **1-3 mi:** Doctor *(Outer Cape 349-3131)*, Dentist *(Coulter 349-6471)* **Hospital:** Cape Cod - Hyannis 771-1800 *(34 mi.)*

Setting -- Tucked into picturesque Wellfleet Harbor, behind Shirttail Point, one of the most accessible and protected marinas on the Outer Cape, this municipal facility is blissfully uncommercial with views of boats, marsh and sky. The harbormaster's two-story, weathered brown shingle building, perched above a massive rock escarpment, overlooks a comfortable, unpretentious mix of pleasure craft and working boats - and still hosts an active fishing industry.

Marina Notes -- *Dockage Flat Rate $52/nt. for first 30 feet plus $2/ft. over that. Power $5/nt, $10/wk. Floats & Rafts dockage $36/nt. Mooring Rate $36/nt. for first 30 feet plus $2/ft. over that. Offseason Dockage $21/nt., $124/wk. Offseason Moorings $5/nt., $21/wk. **Offseason Hours - closed Sat & Sun. Recent major renovation and dredging. Stern-to, no finger piers. Launch service 7 days 8am-7pm operated by Wellfleet Marine (Ch. 9 or 349-2233) included in fee - loaner rowing dinghies provided at other times. Pump-out Boat 349-0320. Bathhouse: Rustic, cinder-block building; utilitarian at best - showers $1 token.

Notable -- Practically dockside, Mac's Seafood offers more than the expected - take-out to picnic tables overlooking Mayo Beach. A week's worth of fine dining is within walking distance, including spiffy, two-story Pearl with decks that look across to the docks. Stroll to small, quiet Wellfleet for necessities, some low-key chic, the impressive Wellfleet Harbor Actor's Theatre, and a map of the art zone. If Mayo Beach isn't enough, then the Cape Cod Nat'l Seashore is 2.5 miles - with sundowners at the Beachcomber. In the 19thC, Wellfleet dominated the oyster business; today it has re-emerged with the advent of aquaculture. Join the fun with a permit from Town Hall. Cloudy? Visit Marconi Station (site of the first transatlantic broadcast) or the drive-in theater's flea market.

Northside Marina

PO Box 1415; 357 Sesuit Neck Road; South Dennis, MA 02660

Tel: (508) 385-3936 **VHF: Monitor** Ch. 7/9 **Talk** Ch. 7
Fax: (508) 385-3938 **Alternate Tel:** n/a
Email: dan@northsidemarina.com **Web:** www.northsidemarina.com
Nearest Town: Brewster *(2 mi.)* **Tourist Info:** (508) 398-3568

Navigational Information

Lat: 41°45.241' **Long:** 070°09.141' **Tide:** 10 ft. **Current:** 1 kt. **Chart:** 13246
Rep. Depths (*MLW*): Entry 6 ft. **Fuel Dock** 4 ft. **Max Slip/Moor** 6 ft./-
Access: Cape Cod Bay due south of the G "1S" buoy

Marina Facilities *(In Season/Off Season)*

Fuel: Gasoline, Diesel, High-Speed Pumps
Slips: 120 Total, 5 Transient **Max LOA:** 70 ft. **Max Beam:** 20 ft.
Rate *(per ft.)*: **Day** $2.00/$1 **Week** n/a **Month** Inq.
Power: 30 amp Incl., **50 amp** Incl., **100 amp** n/a, **200 amp** n/a
Cable TV: Yes, Call Comp. **Dockside Phone:** Yes, Call Comp.
Dock Type: Floating, Wood
Moorings: 0 Total, 0 Transient **Launch:** n/a
Rate: Day n/a **Week** n/a **Month** n/a
Heads: 2 Toilet(s), 1 Shower(s) *(dressing rooms)*
Internet: No **Laundry:** None
Pump-Out: OnSite, Self Service, 1 Central **Fee:** free **Closed Heads:** Yes

Marina Operations

Owner/Manager: Dan Schadt **Dockmaster:** none
In-Season: May 15-Oct 15, 8am-5pm **Off-Season:** Oct 15-May 14, Mon-Fri*
After-Hours Arrival: Call the day before
Reservations: Yes, Preferred **Credit Cards:** Visa/MC, Amex
Discounts: None
Pets: Welcome, Dog Walk Area **Handicap Access:** Yes, Heads, Docks

Marina Services and Boat Supplies

Services - Docking Assistance, Boaters' Lounge, Dock Carts **Communication -** Mail & Package Hold, Fax in/out *(Free)*, FedEx, DHL, UPS, Express Mail **Supplies - OnSite:** Ice *(Cube)*, Ships' Store **Near:** Bait/Tackle **3+ mi:** Propane *(Eastern 760-2778, 5 mi.)*

Boatyard Services

OnSite: Travelift *(35T)*, Forklift, Launching Ramp, Engine mechanic *(gas, diesel)*, Electrical Repairs, Electronic Sales, Electronics Repairs, Hull Repairs, Rigger, Canvas Work, Divers, Bottom Cleaning, Brightwork, Air Conditioning, Refrigeration, Compound, Wash & Wax, Interior Cleaning, Propeller Repairs, Woodworking, Inflatable Repairs, Upholstery, Painting, Awlgrip, Total Refits **Yard Rates:** $65/hr., Power Wash $4, Bottom Paint $10/ft. *(paint incl.)* **Storage:** In-Water $35/ft., On-Land $25/ft.

Restaurants and Accommodations

OnSite: Restaurant *(Sesuit Harbor Café 385-6134, B $3-7, L & D $5-17)* **Under 1 mi:** Restaurant *(Marshside 385-4010, L $5-20, D $14-25, Kids' $4-8)* **1-3 mi:** Restaurant *(Red Pheasant 385-2133, B $10-16, L $10-16, D $20-33)*, *(Scargo Café 385-8200, L $10-24, D $17-31)*, *(Lost Dog Pub 385-6177, L $4-11, D $7-14, Kids' $5-7)*, *(Gracie's Table 385-5600, Spanish tapas, Top reviews)*, *(Blue Moon Bistro 385-7100, D $12-32)*, Pizzeria *(Evan Dennis 258-3228)*, Motel *(Briarcliffe 385-3464, $79-209)*, *(Sesuit Harbor 385-3326, $90-150)*, Inn/B&B *(Scargo Manor 595-0034, $130-275)*

Recreation and Entertainment

OnSite: Fishing Charter *(Sportfish charters 23-34 ft. 385-8991)* **Near:** Beach, Park *(Sesuit Harbor West)*, Tours *(Lobster Roll Cruises 385-1686 $27-42)* **1-3 mi:** Tennis Courts *(Sesuit 385-2200)*, Golf Course *(Dennis Pines 385-8347)*, Fitness Center *(Cape Cod Health 385-2166)*, Party Boat *(Albatross 385-3244)*, Movie Theater *(Cape Cinema 385-2503)*, Video Rental *(Blockbuster Express)*, Museum *(Fine Arts 385-4477 $8/Free; Natural History 896-3867, 3.5 mi, $8/7)*, Cultural Attract *(Cape Playhouse 877-385-3911)*

Provisioning and General Services

1-3 mi: Convenience Store *(Tedeschi's 385-4858)*, Market *(Dennis 385-3215)*, Delicatessen *(Mercantile 385-3877)*, Wine/Beer *(Harvest Gallery 385-2444)*, Liquor Store *(Swan River 394-1740)*, Bakery *(Underground 385-4700)*, Bank/ATM *(Cape Cod Coop 385-9212)*, Post Office, Catholic Church, Protestant Church, Library *(385-2255)*, Beauty Salon *(Hair Studio 385-5558)*, Dry Cleaners *(Prestige 385-2589)*, Hardware Store *(True Value 385-3999)*, Florist *(Blossoms 385-0093)*, Copies Etc. *(Fratus 896-1878)* **3+ mi:** Supermarket *(Stop & Shop 394-4535, 5 mi.)*, Pharmacy *(Rite Aid 362-2114, 4 mi.)*, Department Store *(Marshalls 760-3722, 4 mi.)*

Transportation

OnCall: Rental Car *(Enterprise 398-4555; Thrifty 430-1171)*, Taxi *(Ocelot 423-4213)*, Airport Limo *(Town Car 896-6129)* **1-3 mi:** InterCity Bus *(P&B 746-0378 Players Plaza)* **3+ mi:** Bikes *(Barbara's 760-4723, 5 mi.)*, Rail *(South Dennis, 6 mi.)* **Airport:** Chatham *(13 mi.)*

Medical Services

911 Service **1-3 mi:** Doctor *(Bickford 367-8372)*, Dentist *(Fortenberry 385-3004)*, Chiropractor *(Singleton 385-9999)*, Holistic Services *(Hands-On 385-8882)*, Veterinarian *(Dennis 385-8323)* **Hospital:** C.C. 771-1800 *(12 mi.)*

Setting -- Enter the sandy, narrow channel flanked by rock jetties and pretty beaches. Northside is the first facility to starboard. Perched above the network of 120 slips, umbrella-topped redwood picnic tables front the long, low, gray-shingled home of the Sesuit Harbor Cafe. The marina's large gray work sheds, housing the office and ships store, rise behind. Walk to the edge of the incoming channel for spectacular views of the marsh, the jetties and Cape Cod Bay.

Marina Notes -- *Off season hours: Mon-Fri 9am-4pm, Closed Sat & Sun. Mostly powerboats and sport fishers due to shallow channel and cold water. Full-service boatyard with 35-ton travelift and busy dry stack operation for 150 boats to 26 ft. Only fuel dock in area - very busy also serves adjacent town piers. A welcome harbor of refuge - the only choice for miles. Bathhouse: Just the basics. Attractive, speckle-painted cinder-block steps up the ambiance.

Notable -- Onsite Sesuit Harbor Cafe can be busy with day-trippers and occasional functions with tents and bridesmaids - but conveniently serves three meals a day. Beaches are a specialty of this stretch of the Cape - there are peaceful marsh views and a glorious, unspoiled town beach just across the channel - a 30-second dinghy ride - or walk to lovely Harborview Beach on the marina side that serves the quiet, surrounding residential neighborhood. This is the Cape Cod of solitude and cool water, not the tourist-filled shopping scene several miles South. An 0.8 mile walk inland nets a small strip mall with an upscale family restaurant, Marshside, and Tedeschi's convenience & liquor store. If bikes are aboard, Cape Cod Art Museum is 2.5 miles away and famous Captain Frosty's Fish & Chips shack (385-8548) is about three miles (clam rolls!). This part of the Cape abounds in antique shops, old family homes, and cozy B&Bs.

PHOTOS ON DVD: 20

Town of Dennis Marina

PO Box 2060; 351 Sesuit Neck Road; South Dennis, MA 02660

Tel: (508) 385-5555 **VHF: Monitor** Ch. 16, 18, 21, 66 **Talk** Ch. 66
Fax: (508) 394-8309 **Alternate Tel:** (508) 760-6159
Email: tclen@town.dennis.ma.us **Web:** www.town.dennis.ma.us
Nearest Town: Dennis *(2 mi.)* **Tourist Info:** (508) 896-3500

Navigational Information

Lat: 41°45.131' **Long:** 070°09.239' **Tide:** 12 ft. **Current:** 3 kt. **Chart:** 13246
Rep. Depths (*MLW*): Entry 6.5 ft. **Fuel Dock** n/a **Max Slip/Moor** 10 ft./-
Access: Cape Cod Bay S1 buoy south to 1A lighted buoy follow chamber

Marina Facilities *(In Season/Off Season)*

Fuel: No
Slips: 260 Total, 5 Transient **Max LOA:** 45 ft. **Max Beam:** n/a
Rate *(per ft.)*: **Day** $2.00/$1-1.50* **Week** Inq. **Month** n/a
Power: 30 amp $10, **50 amp** $10, **100 amp** n/a, **200 amp** n/a
Cable TV: No **Dockside Phone:** No
Dock Type: Floating, Long Fingers, Pilings, Wood
Moorings: 1 Total, 1 Transient **Launch:** n/a, Dinghy Dock
Rate: Day $1.50/ft. **Week** $1/ft. **Month** n/a
Heads: 2 Toilet(s), 2 Shower(s)
Internet: Yes *(Inc)* **Laundry:** None
Pump-Out: OnSite, Self Service **Fee:** Free **Closed Heads:** Yes

Marina Operations

Owner/Manager: Terry Clen (HbrMstr) **Dockmaster:** Rick Lemont
In-Season: MemDay-LabDay, 8am-12am **Off-Season:** Winter, 8am-4pm**
After-Hours Arrival: Call ahead
Reservations: Yes **Credit Cards:** Check/Cash only
Discounts: None
Pets: Welcome **Handicap Access:** Yes, Heads, Docks

Marina Services and Boat Supplies

Services - Trash Pick-Up, Dock Carts **Communication -** FedEx, UPS **Supplies - Near:** Ice *(Block, Cube, Shaved)*, Ships' Store *(Northside)*, Live Bait **3+ mi:** Propane *(Eastern 760-2778, 5 mi.)*

Boatyard Services

OnSite: Launching Ramp **Nearest Yard:** Northside (508) 385-3936

Restaurants and Accommodations

Near: Restaurant *(Sesuit Harbor Café 385-6134, B $3-7, L & D $5-17 - Cold & hot sandwiches, salads, Kids' $4-8)* **Under 1 mi:** Restaurant *(Marshside 385-4010, L $9-20, D $19-27, Overlooks Sesuit Creek, Kid's $4-8)*, Snack Bar *(Lost Dog Public 385-6177, L $4-14, Kids' $5-7)*, Pizzeria *(Evan Dennis 258-3228)* **1-3 mi:** Restaurant *(Red Pheasant 385-2133, B $10-16, L $10-16, D $20-33)*, *(Grumpys 385-2911, B $3-10, L $5-9)*, *(Kate's Seafood 896-9517)*, Motel *(Sesuit Harbor Motel 385-3326, $90-150)*, Inn/B&B *(Brewster By the Sea 896-3910, $165-350)* **3+ mi:** Hotel *(Kingfisher Lodging 385-5883, $110, 3.5 mi.)*, Inn/B&B *(Isaiah Clark House 896-2223, $179, 4 mi.)*

Recreation and Entertainment

OnSite: Party Boat *(Albatross 385-3244, $35/30, 4 hrs)*, Tours *(Lobster Roll Cruise 385-1686 $27-42)* **Near:** Beach *(Harborview Beach)*, Fishing Charter *(Northside Marina)*, Park *(Sesuit Harbor West; Wm. P. Stone Conservation Area)* **Under 1 mi:** Video Rental *(Blockbuster Express)* **1-3 mi:** Tennis Courts *(Sesuit 385-2200)*, Golf Course *(Dennis Pines 385-8347)*, Fitness Center *(Cape Cod 385-2166)*, Movie Theater *(Cape Cinema 385-2503)*, Museum *(Cape Fine Arts 385-4477; Cape Cod Natural History, 3.4 mi., 896-3867; New England Fire & History, 4.5 mi. 896-5711)*, Cultural Attract *(Cape Playhouse 877-385-3911)*, Galleries *(Barry's Barn 385-6632; Worden Hall 385-9289)* **3+ mi:** Horseback Riding *(Emerald Hollow 685-6811, 4.5 mi.)*

Provisioning and General Services

Under 1 mi: Convenience Store *(Tedeschi's 385-4858)*, Liquor Store *(Swan River 394-1740)*, Bank/ATM *(Cape Cod Coop)*, Post Office *(Postal Express & More 217-8235)* **1-3 mi:** Market *(Dennis 385-3215)*, Delicatessen *(Mercantile 385-3877)*, Wine/Beer *(Harvest Gallery 385-2444)*, Bakery *(Underground 385-4700)*, Farmers' Market *(Mon Jul-Oct 2-6pm, Dennisport)*, Catholic Church, Protestant Church, Library *(Jacob Sears Memorial 385-8151)*, Beauty Salon *(Hair Studio 385-5558)*, Dry Cleaners *(Prestige 385-2589)*, Bookstore *(Kings Way 896-3639)*, Hardware Store *(True Value 385-3999)*, Florist *(Blossoms 385-0093)*, Copies Etc. *(Fratus 896-1878)* **3+ mi:** Supermarket *(Super Stop & Shop 394-4535, 4.5 mi.)*, Pharmacy *(Rite Aid 362-2114, 4 mi.)*, Department Store *(Marshalls 760-3722, 3.5 mi.)*

Transportation

OnCall: Rental Car *(Thrifty 430-1171)*, Taxi *(Ocelot 432-4213)*, Airport Limo *(Town Car 896-6129)* **Under 1 mi:** InterCity Bus *(P&B 746-0378 Provincetown to Boston at Players Plaza)* **3+ mi:** Bikes *(Barbara's 760-4723, 4.5 mi.)*, Rail *(South Dennis, 5.7 mi.)* **Airport:** Barnstable *(11 mi.)*

Medical Services

911 Service **1-3 mi:** Doctor *(Bickford 367-8372)*, Dentist *(Fortenberry 385-3004)*, Chiropractor *(Singleton 385-9999)*, Holistic Services *(Hands-On 385-8882)*, Veterinarian *(Dennis 385-8323)* **3+ mi:** Optician *(Mid Cape 398-8822, 4.5 mi.)* **Hospital:** Cape Cod 771-1800 *(11.5 mi.)*

Setting -- Past the breakwater and Northside Marina, boatyard and fuel dock, the narrow, scenic channel widens into quiet, protected Sesuit Harbor. A tiny shingled harbormaster's shack oversees this large municipal facility that fills the basin with 250 slips. On the west side, six large main docks accommodate seasonals, transients, sport fish charters and the easy-to-spot, red-and-white Lobster Roll cruise boat at the end of a T-head.

Marina Notes -- *Summer $2/ft., Spring/Fall $1.50/ft. Late Fall. Early Spring, Winter $1/ft. **7 days a week June 25 - Sept 6, 8am-Midnight; Shoulder & winter season Mon-Fri 8am-4pm. 250 slips divided between the east and west sides. Responds to Sesuit or Dennis on VHF. Sportfish oriented; few sailboats due to shallow entry: 6.5 ft. mlw in center of channel, 5 ft. at sides (lighted entrance). Helpful Harbormaster's staff; need anything? Just ask. Need fish? Walk the docks and ask again. Pump-out on Commercial Pier. Bathhouse: Small, functional, wood, Cape cutesy - very nice and private.

Notable -- The beaches on both sides of the channel are a delight: totally uncommercial and untouristed with views of dunes and marsh. For an alternate experience, Dennis Parasail (385-UFLY) offers five different parasail rides and four-stroke jet skis. The marina basin narrows to Sesuit Creek - an inviting dinghy ride that winds south through beautiful, unspoiled marsh. It affords easier access to Marshside restaurant and Tedeschi convenience & liquor store from the small dock at the creek's head. Call a cab to get to the many fine restaurants, quaint antique shops, and other attractions like Cape Cinema, a fine arts film house in a 1930's movie theater that premiered The Wizard of Oz. A full-equity theatre, Cape Playhouse offers daily shows and a children's program.

The Multihull Company

The World's Leader in Multihull Sales and Service

WWW.MULTIHULLCOMPANY.COM

Our Brokers

Phillip Berman, President
215-508-2704
Phil@multihullcompany.com

Alexis de Boucaud, Florida
484-744-2740
Alexis@multihullcompany.com

As the world's largest international catamaran and trimaran brokerage,we can assist you with the purchase or sale of a multihull anywhere in the world.

The Multihull Company offers several distinct differences, from its pioneering buyer/broker program, developed by President and founder Phillip Berman, himself a world champion catamaran racer and author, to its international print advertisements that reach just the right buyers and sellers of catamarans, to its monthly newsletters that actually help readers understand the current market, the latest trends in sailing, and even tackling the most recent conversations on electrical systems, helm station placement, daggerboards versus keels, etc, to our powerful online presence and social-media know how and U.S. and European Boat Show participation.

Visit us at www.multihullcompany.com to see why The Multihull Company is truly the choice of sailors around the world. We offer even the casual browser the means to understand the current market with expert videos, articles and an extensive selection of catamarans and trimarans listed for sale.

Matthew Dunning, West Coast
206-297-1151
Matthew@multihullcompany.com

Derek Escher, Rhode Island
617-803-8976
Derek@multihullcompany.com

Darrel McDaniel, Florida
954-309-6101
Darrel@multihullcompany.com

Gordon Forbes, Caribbean
868-678-8051
Gordon@multihullcompany.com

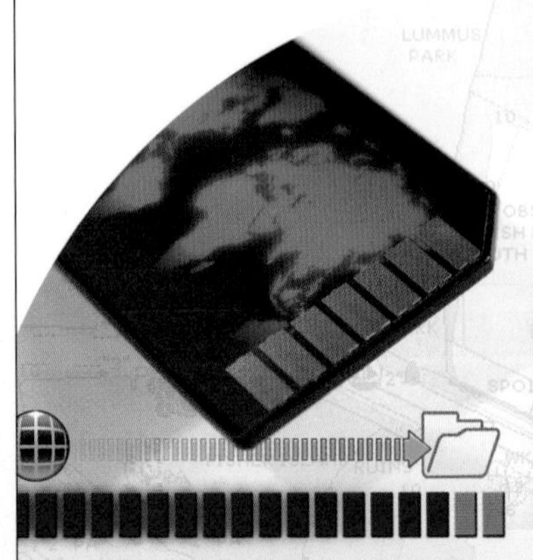

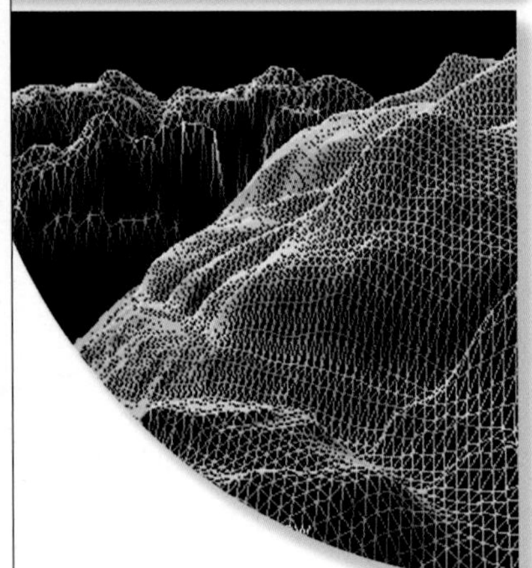

More than a bookstore...

...the world's leading marine navigational resource.

Worldwide Nautical Chart Agent

As a U.S. chart agent for all the major hydrographic offices around the world, we offer the best selection of up-to-date paper charts for wherever your adventure takes you, from Fiji to Greece & back again.

PC Software & Electronic Charts

The 21st century has changed the way we sail with the rise of electronic charts. However, some are better than others for different parts of the world. We pride ourselves on being experts on the latest nautical software and electronic charts for wherever you cruise.

Chart Plotter Cartridges Made Here...

...while you wait we can burn the latest chart cartridges for your C-Map, Navionics & Garmin chart plotters, in the store...in just a few minutes. Why buy off-the-shelf chips never knowing the age of the data? Bluewater will burn the most up-to-date information available while you browse our new store.

...and of course books!

We have nearly 35,000 titles available with the latest cruising guides, travel guides, novels, government publications, log books and more for you to explore. Can't make it to a store? Browse online at ***www.BluewaterWeb.com.***

Call: 954-763-6533 or go online:
www.BluewaterWeb.com

1811 Cordova Road
Fort Lauderdale, FL 33316

Bluewater Books & Charts
Serving the nautical community with the best selection of nautical books and charts for over 20 years

We are more than that. We also provide the latest technologies in electronic navigation software, chart updates, chart cartridges and more! Our chart coverage extends around the world. As an official chart agent for many Hydrographic Offices, we offer only the latest charts for anywhere you want to cruise.

14. MA – Buzzards Bay

North Lakeville
Wareham
Cape Cod Canal
Buzzards Bay
Onset Bay
Forestdale
Sippican Harbor
Red Brook Harbor
Smith Mills
Fairhaven
Mattapoisett Harbor
Fiddlers Cove
Falmouth
New Bedford Harbor
South Westport
Apponagansett Harbor
Quissett Harbor
Westport Harbor
N
Miles
0
10

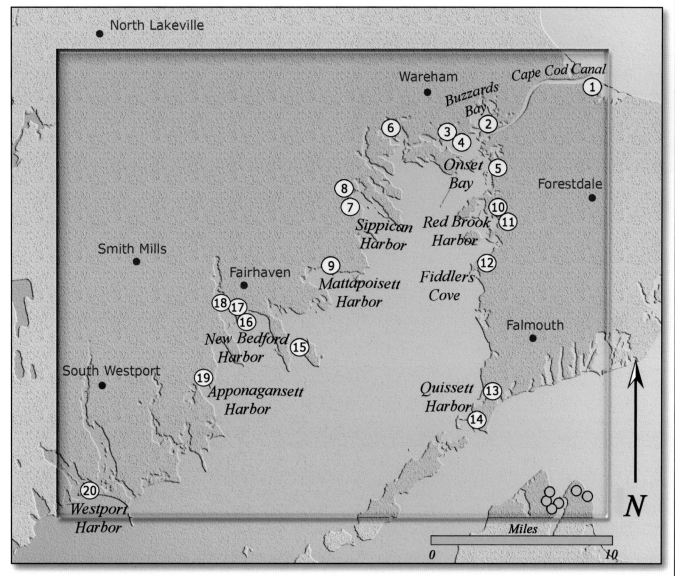

MAP	MARINA	HARBOR	PAGE	MAP	MARINA	HARBOR	PAGE
1	**Sandwich Marina**	*Cape Cod Canal*	262	11	**Parker's Boat Yard**	*Red Brook Harbor*	272
2	**Taylor's Point Marina**	*Cohasset Narrows*	263	12	**Brewer Fiddler's Cove Marina**	*Megansett Harbor*	273
3	**Point Independence Yacht Club**	*Onset Bay*	264	13	**Quissett Harbor Boatyard**	*Quissett Harbor*	274
4	**Onset Bay Marina**	*Onset Bay*	265	14	**Woods Hole Marine**	*Eel Pond*	275
5	**Monument Beach Marina**	*Phinney's Harbor*	266	15	**Earl's Marina**	*Nasketucket Bay*	276
6	**Zecco Marina**	*Wareham River*	267	16	**Fairhaven Shipyard & Marina**	*New Bedford Harbor*	277
7	**Barden's Boat Yard**	*Sippican Harbor*	268	17	**Acushnet River Safe Boating Marina**	*New Bedford Harbor*	278
8	**Burr Bros. Boats**	*Sippican Harbor*	269	18	**Pope's Island Marina**	*New Bedford Harbor*	279
9	**Mattapoisett Boatyard**	*Mattapoisett Harbor*	270	19	**New Bedford Yacht Club**	*Apponagansett Harbor*	280
10	**Kingman Yacht Center**	*Red Brook Harbor*	271	20	**F. L. Tripp & Sons, Inc.**	*Westport Harbor*	281

RATINGS: 1-5 for Marina Facilities & Amenities,  1-2 for Boatyard Services,  1-2 for MegaYacht Facilities,  for Something Special.

SERVICES:  for CCM – Certified Clean Marina,  for Pump-Out,  for Internet,  for Fuel,  for Restaurant,  for Provisioning nearby, for Catamaran-friendly,  for SportFish Charter,  for Pool/Beach, and  for Golf within a mile. *For an explanation of ACC's Ratings, see page 8.*

Sandwich Marina

PO Box 1393; 25 Ed Moffitt Drive; Sandwich, MA 02563

Tel: (508) 833-0808 **VHF: Monitor** Ch. 9/16 **Talk** Ch. 8
Fax: (508) 833-8026 **Alternate Tel:** n/a
Email: ebbasin@townofsandwich.net **Web:** sandwichmarina.com
Nearest Town: Sandwich *(1 mi.)* **Tourist Info:** (508) 833-9755

Navigational Information

Lat: 41°46.295' **Long:** 070°30.104' **Tide:** 11 ft. **Current:** n/a **Chart:** 13246
Rep. Depths (*MLW*): Entry 11 ft. **Fuel Dock** 11 ft. **Max Slip/Moor** 11 ft./-
Access: Buzzard's Bay/Cape Cod Bay to Cape Cod Canal

Marina Facilities *(In Season/Off Season)*

Fuel: Gasoline, Diesel, High-Speed Pumps
Slips: 200 Total, 24 Transient **Max LOA:** 110 ft. **Max Beam:** 25 ft.
Rate *(per ft.)*: **Day** $2.25/1.50 **Week** n/a **Month** n/a
Power: 30 amp $12, **50 amp** $18, **100 amp** $30, **200 amp** n/a
Cable TV: No **Dockside Phone:** No
Dock Type: Floating, Long Fingers, Concrete, Wood
Moorings: 0 Total, 0 Transient **Launch:** n/a
Rate: Day n/a **Week** n/a **Month** n/a
Heads: 4 Toilet(s), 2 Shower(s)
Internet: Yes *(Office)* **Laundry:** None
Pump-Out: OnCall, Full Service, 1 Central **Fee:** $5 **Closed Heads:** Yes

Marina Operations

Owner/Manager: Gregory E. Fayne (Hrbmstr) **Dockmaster:** Same
In-Season: MemDay-LabDay, 24 hrs. **Off-Season:** Sep-May, 7am-3pm*
After-Hours Arrival: Call in advance Ch. 9 or 16
Reservations: Yes, Preferred **Credit Cards:** Visa/MC, Dscvr, Amex
Discounts: None
Pets: Welcome **Handicap Access:** No

Marina Services and Boat Supplies

Services - Docking Assistance, Security *(24 Hrs.)* **Communication -** Pay Phone, FedEx, UPS **Supplies - OnSite:** Ice *(Block, Cube)* **Near:** Ships' Store *(Sandwich Ship 888-0200)* **1-3 mi:** Bait/Tackle *(Canal 833-2996)*

Boatyard Services

OnSite: Divers **OnCall:** Engine mechanic *(gas, diesel)*, Air Conditioning, Refrigeration **Nearest Yard:** Brewer Plymouth (508) 746-4500

Restaurants and Accommodations

OnSite: Restaurant *(Aqua Grille 888-8889, L & D $7-25, Sun Brch $7-14, Prix Fixe $18 M-F)* **Near:** Restaurant *(Seafood Sam's 888-4629, L & D $5-19)*, *(Capt. Scott's 888-1675)* **Under 1 mi:** Restaurant *(Bobby Byrne's 888-6088, L & D $8-19)*, *(Marshland 888-9824, B $4-10, L $6-10, D $6-18)*, *(Hemisphere 888-6166, L & D $9-22)*, *(Belfry's Bistro 888-8550, L $10-18, D $12-39, Sun Br $10-22)*, *(Belfry's Painted Lady L $9-15, D $9-33)*, Lite Fare *(Cafe Chew 888-7717, B $2-4, L $6-10)*, Pizzeria *(Lelli's 833-7322)*, Inn/B&B *(Sandwich Lodge 888-2275, $69-250)*, *(Inn at Sandwich 888-6958, $139-189)*, *(Belfry Inne $145-295)*, *(Annabelle 833-1419, $160-245)*

Recreation and Entertainment

OnSite: Picnic Area, Playground, Hike/Bike Trails *(14-mi. loop alongside canal)* **Near:** Dive Shop *(Aqua Center 888-3444)*, Fishing Charter *(Laura-Jay 888-4033; One Shot 833-3500; The Hookie 617-888-2222)*, Tours *(USACE's Visitors Center - history & films on Canal. A must!)* **Under 1 mi:** Beach *(Town Neck - at canal's eastern entrance)*, Video Rental *(Redbox)*, Park *(Scusset Beach Reservation)*, Museum *(Sandwich Glass 888-0251, $5/1.25; Thornton Burgess 888-4668, Don.)*, Sightseeing *(Sandwich Boardwalk; Green Briar Nature Ctr; Michael Magyar's Glass Studio 888-6681, 4 mi.)* **1-3 mi:** Cultural Attract *(Heritage Museums & Gardens $15/7 888-3300)* **3+ mi:** Golf Course *(Sandwich Hollows G.C. 888-3384, 5 mi.)*, Movie Theater *(Heritage 833-7777, 4 mi.)*

Provisioning and General Services

Near: Delicatessen *(Global 888-0210)*, Fishmonger *(Joe's Lobster 888-2971 Voted the best, prepared foods, packs for travel)*, Beauty Salon *(Great Lengths 888-5165)* **Under 1 mi:** Convenience Store *(Tedeschi 833-1657)*, Supermarket *(Stop & Shop 833-1302 - 0.6 mi.)*, Gourmet Shop *(Brown Jug 888-4669)*, Wine/Beer *(Paradise 888-8810)*, Liquor Store *(Merchant Sq. 888-8242)*, Bakery *(Marshlands)*, Farmers' Market *(9am-1pm Tues, Village Green)*, Bank/ATM, Post Office *(833-0951)*, Protestant Church, Dry Cleaners *(Capeway 888-6865)*, Bookstore *(Retlok's 564-4859)*, Pharmacy *(CVS 888-4333)*, Newsstand, Hardware Store *(Aubuchon 888-5035)*, Florist *(Village 888-6080)*, Copies Etc. *(Cape Biz Solutions 833-2100)* **1-3 mi:** Library *(888-0625)* **3+ mi:** Catholic Church *(4 mi)*

Transportation

OnCall: Rental Car *(Thrifty 888-8333)*, Taxi *(Passport 563-2688)*, Airport Limo *(Limos to Logan 546-6786)* **Under 1 mi:** Bikes *(Cape Cod 888-8030)* **1-3 mi:** InterCity Bus *(P&B 746-0378)* **Airport:** Cape Cod *(8 mi.)*

Medical Services

911 Service **Near:** Chiropractor *(Back In Motion 833-0433)*, Optician *(See Breeze 888-3821)* **Under 1 mi:** Doctor *(Espinosa 833-1569)*, Dentist *(Dinn 888-1515)*, Veterinarian *(Shawme 833-0883)* **1-3 mi:** Holistic Services *(Beach Plum Spa 888-3622)* **Hospital:** Cape Cod 771-1800 *(15 mi.)*

PHOTOS ON DVD: 24

Setting -- Strategically located at the east end of the Cape Cod Canal, just north of the power station, it's hard to miss the large sheltered basin cut into the low-lying vegetation. The shingled harbormaster's shack is the nerve center, but first up are the red roofs of the Coast Guard station, the glittering steel lifeboats - and the nearby Corps of Engineer's Cape Cod Canal Visitors' Center. Over 200 slips berth a commercial fishing fleet, pleasure craft and sportfishers.

Marina Notes -- *Fuel Dock 7am-8pm, 7 days. Offseason 8:30am-2:30pm. Pump-out 8am-4pm (closed offseason). Built by Sandwich, MA in 1989 on the site of a former Harbor of Refuge & managed by the town. 24 dedicated transient slips, 42 commercial & remainder seasonal. Reservations accepted starting April 1. Busy commercial and recreational sport fish scene & Coast Guard station. Launch Ramp $10. For group events, Aqua Grille - 250 for cocktails, 200 for sit-down. Winter dry storage $20/ft., incl pressure washing. Bathhouses: Basic steel, cinderblock with cement floor, minimal privacy.

Notable -- Established in 1639, Sandwich is the oldest town on the Cape - a quintessential, richly historical New England village a mile walk from the docks. For 100 years, it was home to one of the country's largest glass factories; visit the Sandwich Glass Museum for the whole story. Kids aboard? On the far side of town, the Thornton Burgess Museum is a paen to the well-known naturalist and children's author ("Peter Cottontail"); a bit further, Green Briar Nature Center features Jam Kitchen. Two miles away, the 76-acre Heritage Plantation hosts several museums: auto, history, folk art, a 1912 carousel and kids' discovery center. Closer to home, walk or bike the paths along the seven-mile canal. Adjacent Aqua Grille's windowed dining room and deck overlook the basin.

Taylor's Point Marina

1 Academy Drive; Buzzards Bay, MA 02532

Tel: (508) 759-2512 **VHF: Monitor** Ch. 9 **Talk** Ch. 9
Fax: (508) 759-0725 **Alternate Tel:** (508) 759-0621
Email: rdawley@townofbourne.com **Web:** www.townofbourne.com
Nearest Town: Buzzards Bay *(0.1 mi.)* **Tourist Info:** (508) 759-6000

Navigational Information

Lat: 41°44.700' **Long:** 070°37.200' **Tide:** 4 ft. **Current:** 4 kt. **Chart:** 13230
Rep. Depths (*MLW*): Entry 6 ft. **Fuel Dock** 8 ft. **Max Slip/Moor** 8 ft./-
Access: Turn NW into Channel at G25 of Cape Cod Canal

Marina Facilities *(In Season/Off Season)*

Fuel: Gasoline, Diesel, High-Speed Pumps
Slips: 148 Total, 2 Transient **Max LOA:** 50 ft. **Max Beam:** 15 ft.
Rate *(per ft.)*: **Day** $2.50/$2 **Week** $15 **Month** n/a
Power: 30 amp Incl., **50 amp** Incl., **100 amp** n/a, **200 amp** n/a
Cable TV: Yes **Dockside Phone:** Yes
Dock Type: Floating, Long Fingers, Pilings, Alongside, Wood, Aluminum
Moorings: 0 Total, 0 Transient **Launch:** n/a
Rate: Day n/a **Week** n/a **Month** n/a
Heads: 11 Toilet(s), 7 Shower(s) *(dressing rooms)*
Internet: No **Laundry:** 1 Washer(s), 1 Dryer(s)
Pump-Out: OnSite, 1 Central, 1 Port **Fee:** Free **Closed Heads:** Yes

Marina Operations

Owner/Manager: Bob Dawley **Dockmaster:** Same
In-Season: Mem-LabDay, 7am-6pm **Off-Season:** Sep-May, 7am-6pm
After-Hours Arrival: Call ahead
Reservations: No **Credit Cards:** Visa/MC, Dscvr, Amex
Discounts: Frequent Fueler **Dockage:** n/a **Fuel:** n/a **Repair:** n/a
Pets: Welcome, Dog Walk Area **Handicap Access:** Yes, Heads, Docks

Marina Services and Boat Supplies

Services - Docking Assistance, Boaters' Lounge, Security *(Biz Hrs.)*, Dock Carts **Communication -** Mail & Package Hold, FedEx, UPS, Express Mail **Supplies - OnSite:** Ice *(Block, Cube)*, Ships' Store **1-3 mi:** Bait/Tackle *(Cape Cod Charlie's 759-2611)* **3+ mi:** West Marine *(10 mi.)*

Boatyard Services

OnSite: Launching Ramp **OnCall:** Canvas Work, Divers, Bottom Cleaning **Nearest Yard:** Onset Bay Marina (508) 273-0357

Restaurants and Accommodations

Near: Restaurant *(Krua Thai 759-9662)*, Seafood Shack *(East Wind Lobster 759-1857, L & D $4-17 Kids' $6-9)*, Pizzeria *(Effie's 759-2224)* **Under 1 mi:** Restaurant *(Lobster Pot 759-3876, L & D $4-18, Kids' $7-9)*, *(Buzzards Bay Tavern 743-5493)*, *(Captain Al's Tiki Bar 759-0811, Dinghy, too)*, *(Ella's Wood Burning Oven 759-3600, D $15-17, Pizzas $7-19)*, Lite Fare *(Leo's Breakfast 759-7557)*, Motel *(Buttermilk Bay 743-0800, $95-190)* **1-3 mi:** Restaurant *(Lindsey's Family 759-5544, L $5-10, L & D $6-27, Gluten-Free)*, Motel *(Rosewood 291-0442)*, Hotel *(Quality Inn 759-0800, $89-139)*

Recreation and Entertainment

OnSite: Picnic Area, Grills **Near:** Sightseeing *(National Marine Life Ctr. 743-9888)*, Galleries *(Artisans 743-7555)*, Special Events *(Scallop Fest -Sep; Jul 4 Parade, Weekly concerts)* **Under 1 mi:** Bowling *(Ryan Family 759-9892)* **1-3 mi:** Beach *(Scusset Beach State Reserv.)*, Dive Shop *(Buzzards Bay 291-7282)*, Golf Course *(Bay Pointe 759-8802)*, Fitness Center *(Old Iron 291-7479)*, Boat Rentals *(Cape Cod Canal 295-3883)*, Video Rental *(Entertainment & More 291-4200)*, Park *(Bourne 759-7873)*, Museum *(Aptucxet Trading Post 759-9487 $4/2, $10 per family; Bourne Historical Society, 759-8167; Bourne Society Historic House 759-6120)* **3+ mi:** Horseback Riding *(Wunda Farm 743-9926, 4 mi.)*

Provisioning and General Services

Near: Convenience Store *(Cumberland Farms 743-9974)*, Farmers' Market *(Fri 10am-2pm, CofC)*, Fishmonger *(Eastwind 759-1857)*, Beauty Salon *(Village 743-9956)*, Florist *(Lilly-Belles 759-8021)* **Under 1 mi:** Liquor Store *(Liberty 759-5120)*, Bank/ATM, Post Office *(759-4160)*, Catholic Church, Protestant Church, Library *(Hurley 830-5034)*, Dry Cleaners *(Capeway 759-3548)* **1-3 mi:** Supermarket *(Stop & Shop 295-3377)*, Bakery *(Cakes by Lil 759-9366; Honey Dew Donuts)*, Green Grocer *(Mazzilli's 759-5901)*, Synagogue, Laundry *(Laundry Center 759-4966)*, Bookstore *(Artisana)*, Pharmacy *(CVS 759-1097)*, Hardware Store *(Sears Hometown 291-7733)*

Transportation

OnCall: Rental Car *(Enterprise 759-2299)*, Taxi *(Road Runner 759-2337)*, Airport Limo *(Limos to Logan 546-6786)* **Near:** Bikes *(Sailworld 759-6559)*, Local Bus, InterCity Bus *(P&B 771-6191; Bonanza, 888-751-8800 Wareham to Boston, TF Green, Hyannis)*, Rail *(Buzzards Bay)* **Airport:** Cape Cod/Logan Int'l *(21 mi./62 mi.)*

Medical Services

911 Service **Near:** Holistic Services *(Balance Massage Spa 759-6409)*, Optician *(See Breeze 759-0011)*, Veterinarian *(Buzzards Bay 759-2521)* **Under 1 mi:** Dentist *(Canal Side 759-272)*, Chiropractor *(Buzzards Bay 759-8852)* **1-3 mi:** Doctor *(Bourne Walk-In 743-0322)* **Hospital:** Falmouth 548-5300 *(16 mi.)*

Setting -- Tucked into a tight basin at Cohasset Narrows,around Taylors Point from the western end of the Cape Cod Canal, the municipal marina's modern, single-story office perches high on artificial rockpile. With a long view of the dock-filled basin, it is also well-protected from any storm surge. On the south side of the marina, the Massachusetts Maritime Academy occupies the entire Point. On the north side, across the tracks, is little Buzzards Bay's Main Street.

Marina Notes -- Formerly Bourne Marina operated by Maritime Academy for hands-on training. Now one of three marinas owned by Town of Bourne (Town Hall: 759-0600) & operated by Dept. of Natural Resources. Clean and orderly municipal facility - fuel and a good location. Friendly, mostly powerboat, seasonals welcome transients to lounge/ships' store combo and picnic tent with grills. Bathhouse: Well-tended municipal cinderblock and stainless steel.

Notable -- A short walk from the docks, the slightly scruffy commercial part of Buzzards Bay, one of seven Bourne villages, sports some antique, thrift, gift and collectible shops, along with a few eateries and useful provisioners. Stop by the Cape Cod Canal Chamber of Commerce in the historic red railroad station for a little background on the 1914 canal - now managed by the U.S. Army Corps of Engineers. Nearby National Marine Life Center, a non-profit, rehabilitation & release hospital that treats stranded sea turtles and seals, welcomes visitors to its Discovery Center (10am-5pm). A short walk across the point, near the iconic vertical-lift railroad bridge, the seven-mile Cape Cod Canal Park lines the waterway with paved bike paths. Or head three miles across the Bourne Bridge to the Aptucxet Trading Post, a reproduction of the 1627 original that sports an herb garden, saltworks, and a RR depot built for Grover Cleveland.

PHOTOS ON DVD: 20

Point Independence Yacht Club

Point Independence Yacht Club

PO Box 367; 15-17 Independence Lane; Onset, MA 02558

Tel: (508) 295-3972 **VHF: Monitor** Ch. 9 **Talk** Ch. 10
Fax: n/a **Alternate Tel:** n/a
Email: prenticesteven@yahoo.com **Web:** none
Nearest Town: Onset *(0.6 mi.)* **Tourist Info:** (508) 295-7072

Navigational Information

Lat: 41°44.440' **Long:** 070°38.937' **Tide:** 4 ft. **Current:** n/a **Chart:** 13236
Rep. Depths (*MLW*): Entry 14 ft. **Fuel Dock** 6 ft. **Max Slip/Moor** 6 ft./7 ft.
Access: West end of Cape Cod Canal; turn NW into Channel at G21

Marina Facilities *(In Season/Off Season)*

Fuel: Gasoline, Diesel
Slips: 100 Total, 8 Transient **Max LOA:** 50 ft. **Max Beam:** n/a
Rate *(per ft.)*: **Day** $3.00/Inq.* **Week** Inq. **Month** Inq.
Power: 30 amp $10, **50 amp** $20, **100 amp** n/a, **200 amp** n/a
Cable TV: Yes Incl **Dockside Phone:** No
Dock Type: Fixed, Floating, Short Fingers, Pilings, Wood
Moorings: 45 Total, 30 Transient **Launch:** No, Dinghy Dock
Rate: Day $30 **Week** $180 **Month** $700
Heads: 6 Toilet(s), 4 Shower(s), Book Exchange
Internet: No **Laundry:** 2 Washer(s), 3 Dryer(s)
Pump-Out: OnSite, OnCall, 1 Central, 1 Port **Fee:** Free **Closed Heads:** Yes

Marina Operations

Owner/Manager: Steve Prentice **Dockmaster:** same
In-Season: May-Oct, 9am-9pm **Off-Season:** closed
After-Hours Arrival: Make prior arrangements
Reservations: Yes, Preferred **Credit Cards:** Visa/MC, Dscvr
Discounts: None
Pets: Welcome, Dog Walk Area **Handicap Access:** Yes, Heads, Docks

Marina Services and Boat Supplies

Services - Docking Assistance, Dock Carts **Communication -** Pay Phone (1), FedEx, DHL, UPS, Express Mail **Supplies - OnSite:** Ice *(Block, Cube)* **Under 1 mi:** Bait/Tackle *(Macos 759-9836)* **1-3 mi:** Ships' Store *(Fastech 732-9779)* **3+ mi:** Propane *(Roby's 295-3737, 8 mi.)*

Boatyard Services

OnSite: Launching Ramp **Nearest Yard:** Onset Bay (508) 295-0338

Restaurants and Accommodations

OnSite: Seafood Shack *(Pt. Independence Friday Fish Fry)* **Near:** Restaurant *(Stonebridge Bistro 291-2229, D $13-20, Pizzas $9-11.50)*, Inn/B&B *(Pt. Independence 273-0466, $219-279)*, *(Harbor Watch 295-4600, $150-275)*, *(Harborview Inn 295-4123)* **Under 1 mi:** Snack Bar *(Kenny's Taffy 295-8828)*, Lite Fare *(Pier View 295-5968, B 6am-noon, Stephen's Lounge 11am-1am, DJ wknds)*, Pizzeria *(Marc Anthony's 295-5956)* **1-3 mi:** Restaurant *(Ella's Wood Burn 759-3600, D $4-17, Pizza, $7-19)*, *(Lindsey's 759-5544, L & D $5-27 Kids' $6-9)*, *(Barnacle Bills 759-1822)*, *(Bailey's Surf N Turf 295-1700, L $5-13, D $11-24)*, *(Beachmoor 759-7522)*, *(Charlie's Place 295-6656, L & D $6-18, Kids' $4-5)*, *(Rice Bowl Asian 291-1206)*, Seafood Shack *(Lobster Pot 759-3876, L & D $4-17, Kids' $7-9)*

Recreation and Entertainment

OnSite: Beach, Picnic Area, Grills **Near:** Boat Rentals *(Stone Bridge Marina 295-8003 - small power boats)* **Under 1 mi:** Playground, Dive Shop *(Buzzards Bay 291-7282)*, Golf Course *(759-8802)*, Fishing Charter *(Neat Lady 295-9402 at Town Pier)*, Movie Theater *(Weekly at town pavilion; Flagship 291-4100 - 9 mi.)*, Video Rental *(Blockbuster 295-9151)*, Park *(Prospect)*, Museum *(Porter Thermometer 295-5504 - by app't)*, Sightseeing *(Cape Cod Canal Cruises 295-3883 - Town Pier)*, Special Events *(Prospect Park Band Concerts Fri. 7pm,; Cape Verdean Fest & Blues Fest - Aug)* **1-3 mi:** Fitness Center *(Old Iron Gym 291-7479)*, Bowling *(Ryan 759-9892)*

Provisioning and General Services

Near: Synagogue **Under 1 mi:** Market *(Onset Village 291-1440)*, Supermarket *(Stop & Shop 295-337)*, Bank/ATM *(Village Market)*, Post Office, Protestant Church, Beauty Salon *(Total Image 295-2535)*, Bookstore *(Artisana 291-2726)* **1-3 mi:** Convenience Store *(7-Eleven 295-0500)*, Delicatessen *(Subway 295-1148)*, Liquor Store *(Mayflower 759-5358)*, Bakery *(Cakes by Lil 759-9366)*, Green Grocer *(Mazilli's 759-5901)*, Fishmonger *(Eastwind 759-1857)*, Catholic Church, Library, Dry Cleaners *(Capeway 759-3548)*, Pharmacy *(CVS 295-3880)*, Hardware Store *(Onset 295-0020)*, Florist *(Lily-Belles 759-8021)*, Department Store *(WalMart 295-8890)* **3+ mi:** Retail Shops *(Wareham Crossing via OWL, 6 mi.)*

Transportation

OnCall: Rental Car *(Thrifty 291-3200, Enterprise 759-2299)*, Taxi *(Wareham 295-5459)*, Airport Limo *(Limos to Logan 800-546-6786)* **Under 1 mi:** Local Bus *(OWL to Wareham - no Sun service)* **1-3 mi:** Bikes *(Sailworld 759-6559)* **Airport:** Logan Int'l/Barnstable *(60 mi./25 mi.)*

Medical Services

911 Service **Near:** Dentist *(Prime 322-7144)*, Holistic Services *(Tarra Dean Spa 295-2535)* **1-3 mi:** Doctor *(Thomas 759-9428))*, Chiropractor *(Watterson 273-0002)*, Optician *(Sea Breeze 759-0011)*, Veterinarian *(Animal Hse 759-4522)* **Hospital:** Southcoast 295-3848 *(4 mi.)*

PHOTOS ON DVD: 20

Setting -- Just beyond Onset Bay Marina. PIYC's attractive, two-story gray clubhouse, topped by a pyramidal roof, sits at the head of a long pier - two sets of docks fan out on either side. A low-slung pavilion anchors the landward end of the pier, and a prominent fuel dock houses the Bay end. On the far side are a lovely crescent-shaped strand of beach and a dinghy dock. Surrounded by a residential community, the landscape and seascape are low-key and quiet.

Marina Notes -- *Mon-Thu, $2.75/ft. Fri-Sun. Founded 1903 by Bostonians summering in Onset, a popular 19thC. resort served by trains & steamers. Now a small, equity-ownership yacht club open to all (no reciprocity issues). Primarily power boats, many sport fishers. Clubhouse with great bar & second-story deck open to visitors - as is Friday night Seafood Fry. Good security, friendly atmosphere. No launch, dinghy dock. Bathhouse: Well-kept, tiled heads, separate showers. Laundry. Note: Add'l moorings & dockage at Onset Town Pier (295-8160) when marina's full - also short-term tie-up for dinks & yachts for shopping.

Notable -- Step back in time to the gradually gentrifying Victorian village; it's 0.6-mile walk. Stroll the crooked leafy lanes lined with some well-maintained historic homes and then hit the town pier for saltwater taffy and fudge. Kids can cavort on the sandy beach and warm water. "Downtown" Onset is basically one street - Onset Avenue - which runs along the hill above the Town Pier. There are a few eateries, a highly rated hardware store, gift, antique and clothing shops, and a well-supplied market. Alternatively, spend a family day at Wareham's Water Wizz, a small water park (295-3255 - $30/15, after 4pm $20/10). For serious supplies, take the OWL to Wareham Crossing. Anglers can transit the canal to the Stellwagen bank in two hours, or cruise south to "the Hole" in less than one.

Onset Bay Marina

PO Box 780; 3 Green Street; Onset, MA 02558

Tel: (508) 295-0338 **VHF: Monitor** Ch. 9 **Talk** n/a
Fax: (508) 295-8873 **Alternate Tel:** n/a
Email: info@onsetbay.com **Web:** www.onsetbay.com
Nearest Town: Village of Onset *(1 mi.)* **Tourist Info:** (508) 295-7072

Navigational Information

Lat: 41°44.313' **Long:** 070°38.818' **Tide:** 4 ft. **Current:** n/a **Chart:** 13236
Rep. Depths (*MLW*): Entry 6 ft. **Fuel Dock** 10 ft. **Max Slip/Moor** 10 ft./9 ft.
Access: West end of Cape Cod Canal; turn NW into Channel at G21

Marina Facilities *(In Season/Off Season)*

Fuel: *Citgo* - Gasoline, Diesel
Slips: 120 Total, 8 Transient **Max LOA:** 120 ft. **Max Beam:** n/a
Rate *(per ft.)*: **Day** $3.00/$1.50* **Week** Inq. **Month** Inq.
Power: 30 amp Incl., **50 amp** Incl., **100 amp** n/a, **200 amp** n/a
Cable TV: Yes Incl. **Dockside Phone:** No
Dock Type: Floating, Long Fingers, Wood
Moorings: 34 Total, 10 Transient **Launch:** No, Dinghy Dock (no)
Rate: Day $30 **Week** n/a **Month** n/a
Heads: 2 Toilet(s), 2 Shower(s)
Internet: Yes *(wireless available)* **Laundry:** 1 Washer(s), 1 Dryer(s)
Pump-Out: OnSite, Full Service, 1 Central **Fee:** Free **Closed Heads:** Yes

Marina Operations

Owner/Manager: Joanne Hamilton **Dockmaster:** Greg Glavin
In-Season: May-Oct, 7am-6pm **Off-Season:** Nov-Apr, 8am-4:30pm
After-Hours Arrival: Call in advance
Reservations: Yes, Preferred **Credit Cards:** Visa/MC, Amex
Discounts: None
Pets: Welcome **Handicap Access:** No

Marina Services and Boat Supplies

Services - Docking Assistance, Security, Dock Carts **Communication -** Pay Phone, FedEx, DHL, UPS, Express Mail **Supplies - OnSite:** Ice *(Block, Cube, Shaved)* **1-3 mi:** Ships' Store *(Fastech 732-9779)*, Bait/Tackle *(Macos 759-9836)* **3+ mi:** West Marine *(748-3833, 8.5 mi.)*

Boatyard Services

OnSite: Forklift, Launching Ramp, Engine mechanic *(gas, diesel)*, Electrical Repairs, Electronic Sales, Electronics Repairs, Hull Repairs, Canvas Work, Bottom Cleaning, Brightwork, Air Conditioning, Interior Cleaning, Propeller Repairs, Woodworking, Metal Fabrication, Painting, Awlgrip **Yard Rates:** $65/hr., Haul & Launch $10/ft. *(blocking $3 ft.)*, Power Wash $3.50/ft. **Storage:** In-Water $40/ft., On-Land $67/ft.

Restaurants and Accommodations

Near: Motel *(Holly Hurst 291-2200, $95-250)*, Inn/B&B *(Pt. Independence 273-0466, $135-239)*, *(Lazy Bean 295-4949, $175-200)* **Under 1 mi:** Restaurant *(Stonebridge Bistro 291-2229, D $13-20, Pizzas $9-11.50. Full liquor; easy dinghy ride)*, Lite Fare *(Pier View 295-5968, B only 6am-noon, Stephen's Lounge 11am-1am, DJ wknds)*, *(Victorian Cafe 678-0477)*, Pizzeria *(Marc Anthony's 295-5956)* **1-3 mi:** Restaurant *(Lindsey's Family Restaurant 759-5544, L & D $5-27 Kids' $6-9)*, *(Ella's Wood Burning Oven 759-3600, D $4-17, Pizza, $7-19)*, *(Breakfast Nook 759-5950)*, *(Beachmoor 759-7522)*, *(Charlie's Place 295-6656, L & D $6-18, Kids' $4-5)*, Seafood Shack *(Lobster Pot 759-3876, L & D $4-17, Kids' $7-9)*

Recreation and Entertainment

OnSite: Picnic Area, Grills **Under 1 mi:** Beach, Playground, Dive Shop *(Buzzards Bay 291-7282)*, Golf Course *(Bay Pointe 759-8802)*, Boat Rentals *(Stone Bridge Marina 295-8003)*, Movie Theater *(Weekly at town pavilion)*, Park *(Onset Beach)*, Sightseeing *(Cape Cod Canal Cruises 295-3883)* **1-3 mi:** Fitness Center *(Old Iron 291-7479)*, Bowling *(Ryan 759-9892)*, Video Rental *(Redbox)*, Museum *(Porter Thermometer 295-5504 - by app't)*

Provisioning and General Services

Under 1 mi: Market *(Onset Village 291-1440)*, Fishmonger *(East Wind 759-1857)*, Bank/ATM, Post Office *(295-8672)*, Protestant Church, Synagogue, Library, Beauty Salon *(Mr. Carter's 295-8733)*, Bookstore *(Artisana 291-2726)*, Hardware Store *(Onset 295-0020)* **1-3 mi:** Convenience Store *(7-Eleven 295-0500)*, Supermarket *(Stop & Shop)*, Liquor Store *(Mayflower 759-5358)*, Bakery *(Cakes by Lil 759-9366)*, Green Grocer *(Mazzilli's 759-5901)*, Catholic Church, Dry Cleaners *(Capeway 759-3548)*, Pharmacy *(WalMart 295-8890)*, Florist *(Lily-Belles 759-8021)*, Retail Shops *(Wareham Crossing)*, Department Store *(WalMart)*

Transportation

OnCall: Rental Car *(Enerprise 759-2299)*, Taxi *(Wareham 295-5459)*, Airport Limo *(Limos to Logan 800-546-6786)* **Under 1 mi:** Local Bus *(OWL to Wareham)* **1-3 mi:** Bikes *(Sailworld 759-6559)*, InterCity Bus *(P & B Bus Wareham & Boston 746-0378)* **Airport:** Logan/Cape Cod *(60 mi./18 mi.)*

Medical Services

911 Service **Near:** Dentist *(Prime 322-7144)*, Holistic Services *(Pt Independence Inn)* **1-3 mi:** Doctor *(Thomas 759-9428)*, Chiropractor *(Watterson 273-0002)*, Optician *(Sea Breeze 759-0011)*, Veterinarian *(Animal Hse 759-4522)* **Hospital:** Southcoast 295-3848 *(4 mi.)*

Setting -- This protected full-service facility provides a welcome, quiet respite before or after a trip through the canal. Find the big pale-grey sheds nestled in the trees, with the serious sportfishermen docked out front. The large dock array uses a lot of the scarce deep water while the small boats inhabit the 30-story rack structures. Sporting a big red "Citgo" sign, a gray-sided dockhouse oversees the fueling station and manages the slips.

Marina Notes -- *$36 min. Professional, well-regarded operation. Hauling and storage for boats to 70 ft. Full-service yard with high octane fuel. Amenities include lounging decks, grills, and snacks in dockhouse. Caters to sport fishers. Take a mooring for better breeze or quieter setting. Active dry stack storage business. Bathhouse: Simple, cinderblock set away from docks in nicely landscaped area. Note: Onset Town Pier (295-8160) accommodates transient yachts at docks and moorings when marina's full -- offers temporary tie-up for dinks and yachts.

Notable -- A 20-minute walk or quick dinghy ride from the docks, Onset is a delightful, quirky Victorian village - though its crinolines are just a bit tattered. It boasts calm, pleasant beaches, an ice cream/saltwater taffy/fudge wonderland, an eclectic mix of inviting shops, galleries, eateries, and watering holes and an impressive stock of gingerbread houses - some restored as B&Bs. Pick up a walking tour brochure from the Onset Bay Association (4 Union Avenue) - and end the stroll at Onset Bluffs for sunset. Dick Porter's Thermometer Museum displays a portion of his astounding 5000-plus collection that has put him in Guinness and Ripley's. Wareham Crossing (Target, LL Bean outlet, Borders, Staples, Best Buy, JCPenney and 3 restaurants - 6 miles) is on the OWL bus route.

PHOTOS ON DVD: 22

Monument Beach Marina

24 Emmons Road; Monument Beach, MA 02553

Tel: (508) 759-3105 **VHF: Monitor** Ch. 9 **Talk** Ch. 11
Fax: (508) 759-8026 **Alternate Tel:** n/a
Email: rdawley@townofbourne.com **Web:** www.townofbourne.com
Nearest Town: Bourne *(3 mi.)* **Tourist Info:** (508) 759-6000

Navigational Information
Lat: 41°42.862' **Long:** 070°36.938' **Tide:** 4 ft. **Current:** 3 kt. **Chart:** 13236
Rep. Depths (*MLW*): Entry 40 ft. **Fuel Dock** 6 ft. **Max Slip/Moor** 8 ft./30 ft.
Access: West of Wings Neck to Phinney's Harbor

Marina Facilities *(In Season/Off Season)*
Fuel: *93* - Gasoline, High-Speed Pumps
Slips: 61 Total, 3 Transient **Max LOA:** 50 ft. **Max Beam:** 13 ft.
Rate *(per ft.)*: **Day** $1.50/Inq. **Week** Inq. **Month** n/a
Power: 30 amp Incl., **50 amp** n/a, **100 amp** n/a, **200 amp** n/a
Cable TV: No **Dockside Phone:** No
Dock Type: Floating, Wood, Vinyl
Moorings: 35 Total, 1 Transient **Launch:** No, Dinghy Dock
Rate: Day $25 **Week** n/a **Month** n/a
Heads: 2 Toilet(s)
Internet: No **Laundry:** None
Pump-Out: OnCall, Full Service, 1 Port **Fee:** Free **Closed Heads:** Yes

Marina Operations
Owner/Manager: Bob Dawley **Dockmaster:** Jim Ryan
In-Season: May-Oct, 9am-5pm **Off-Season:** Nov-Apr, Closed
After-Hours Arrival: Tie up and see attendant at 9 am the next day
Reservations: Yes **Credit Cards:** Visa/MC, Dscvr, Amex
Discounts: None
Pets: Welcome **Handicap Access:** Yes, Heads, Docks

Marina Services and Boat Supplies
Services - Docking Assistance, Dock Carts **Communication -** Pay Phone (1), FedEx, UPS, Express Mail **Supplies - Near:** Ice *(Block, Cube)* **1-3 mi:** West Marine, Bait/Tackle *(Eastman's 548-6900)*, Live Bait *(Harbor Bait 759-6555)* **3+ mi:** CNG *(Parker's Boat Yard, 4 mi.)*

Boatyard Services
OnSite: Launching Ramp **Nearest Yard:** Parker's B.Y. (508) 563-9366

Restaurants and Accommodations
OnSite: Snack Bar *(Breakfast entrees & expected variety of sandwiches to take-out)* **Under 1 mi:** Restaurant *(Lobster Trap 759-3992, $7-20, Kids' $5-7, BYO)*, Lite Fare *(Deb's Veggie Depot 743-5057, 10am-6pm, take-out too)* **1-3 mi:** Restaurant *(Hollyberrys 759-8955)*, *(Sunset Grille at Brookside CC L $9-12, D $9-24, Sun Br $7-12)*, Pizzeria *(Evan 759-9111)*, Motel *(Quality Inn 759-0800)*, Inn/B&B *(Cape Cod Country 564-5857, $110-160)*, *(Holly House by Canal 759-2864)*, *(Wood Duck 564-6404, $99-149)* **3+ mi:** Restaurant *(Stir Crazy 564-6464, 3.2 mi., Cambodian, Kids' menu)*

Recreation and Entertainment
OnSite: Beach, Picnic Area, Fishing Charter *(Lincoln Bros, 808-6476)* **Under 1 mi:** Park *(Shore Road Ballfied)*, Galleries *(A2z Modern 743-7557 furniture, glass)* **1-3 mi:** Tennis Courts, Golf Course *(Brookside Club 743-0705)*, Fitness Center *(B-Strong 759-7111)*, Video Rental *(Blockbuster Exp.)*, Museum *(Aptucxet Trading Post 759-9487 $4/2, $10 per family Mon-Sat 10am-5pm Sun 2-5pm; Bourne Historical Center 759-6928)*, Cultural Attract **3+ mi:** Horseback Riding *(Haland Stables 540-2552, 5 mi.)*

Provisioning and General Services
Under 1 mi: Convenience Store *(Cumberland 743-9314)*, Post Office *(759-5347)*, Beauty Salon *(Madd Cutter 759-2994)* **1-3 mi:** Market *(Pocasset Country 564-4258)*, Delicatessen *(Pocasset 563-7017)*, Wine/Beer *(Monument 759-1951)*, Liquor Store *(Portside 563-3012)*, Bakery *(Wicked Sweets 392-9588)*, Bank/ATM, Catholic Church, Protestant Church, Library *(Bourne 759-0644)*, Laundry *(Laundry Ctr 759-4966)*, Pharmacy *(Denmarks 990-2207)*, Hardware Store *(Pocasset 563-6042)*, Copies Etc. *(Accurate 759-2129)* **3+ mi:** Supermarket *(Stop & Shop 833-1302, 8 mi.)*, Synagogue *(6 mi.)*, Florist *(Bourne 759-421, 3.5 mi.)*

Transportation
OnCall: Rental Car *(Enterprise 759-2299)*, Taxi *(Road Runner 759-2337)*, Airport Limo *(Green Shuttle 563-6476)* **Under 1 mi:** Bikes **1-3 mi:** InterCity Bus *(P&B 771-6191; Bonanza 888-751-8800 to Boston, TF Green, Hyannis)* **Airport:** Cape Cod/Logan Int'l *(18 mi./64 mi.)*

Medical Services
911 Service **1-3 mi:** Doctor *(Bourne Fam 743-0899)*, Dentist *(Murphy 564-6663)*, Optician *(Eye Health of Bourne 743-9044)*, Veterinarian *(All Pets 367-6076)* **3+ mi:** Chiropractor *(Upper Cape Chiro 548-9999, 5 mi.)* **Hospital:** Falmouth 548-5300 *(11 mi.)*

PHOTOS ON DVD: 18

Setting -- Embraced by the wide arms of Phinney's Harbor, on the eastern side of Mashnee Dike, one of Bourne's three municipal marinas promises a long, well-built, "U"-shaped wooden pier with floating slips, a cinderblock snack bar and bathhouse - sporting a vibrant mural - and a beautiful, wide, real sand beach. The gas shack, labeled "Monument Beach" in big blue letters, is easy to spot. Views are across the busy, yet quiet, harbor to exclusive Mashnee Island.

Marina Notes -- 42 ft. max at docks & 50 ft. on moorings. Owned by Town of Bourne & operated by the Department of Natural Resources. Marina Manager, Bob Dawley operates out of Taylor's Point Marina. Pier rebuilt in 2005. No marina services. High-octane gas (no diesel). Watch your draft! Primarily smaller and gasoline-powered boats in part due to limited water. Helpful seasonal staff, and lifeguards at beach. Few transient berths & moorings, but anchoring allowed. Nice refuge from Buzzards Bay's square waves to/from the Cape Cod Canal. Pump-out boat Ch. 9, 7 days, 10am-4pm in season - stationed here. Bathhouse: Public & Private. Municipal-grade, painted cinderblock, gang showers for the boys & outdoor one, too.

Notable -- The first town in Cape Cod on the way from Boston, it remains surprsingly quiet, inexpensive, and overwhelmingly residential - an excellent place for the kids to let off steam. There are few commercial or culinary attractions, but the Lobster Trap restaurant and Village Market are within three quarters of a mile. A bit further afield are Aptucxet Trading Post Museum - a replica of a 1627 trading post with Native American, Pilgrim and early Phoenician relics - plus saltworks and Grover Cleveland's RR station. Quahogs (large clams) are a big draw - alas Bourne does not sell temp, non-resident licenses.

Navigational Information
Lat: 41°45.143' **Long:** 070°42.558' **Tide:** 4 ft. **Current:** 3 kt. **Chart:** 13236
Rep. Depths (*MLW*): Entry 6 ft. **Fuel Dock** 6 ft. **Max Slip/Moor** 6 ft./7 ft.
Access: Buzzards Bay to Wareham River

Marina Facilities *(In Season/Off Season)*
Fuel: *Texaco* - Gasoline, Diesel, High-Speed Pumps
Slips: 120 Total, 10 Transient **Max LOA:** 50 ft. **Max Beam:** 17 ft.
Rate *(per ft.)*: **Day** $3.00 **Week** $12 **Month** $40
Power: 30 amp Incl., **50 amp** n/a, **100 amp** n/a, **200 amp** n/a
Cable TV: No **Dockside Phone:** No
Dock Type: Fixed, Long Fingers, Short Fingers, Pilings, Wood
Moorings: 60 Total, 2 Transient **Launch:** No, Dinghy Dock
Rate: Day $20/day **Week** n/a **Month** n/a
Heads: 4 Toilet(s), 2 Shower(s) *(dressing rooms)*
Internet: No **Laundry:** None
Pump-Out: Full Service, 1 Central, 1 Port **Fee:** Free **Closed Heads:** Yes

Marina Operations
Owner/Manager: Tony Zecco **Dockmaster:** same
In-Season: Year-Round, 8am-4:30pm **Off-Season:** none
After-Hours Arrival: Call fuel dock
Reservations: Yes **Credit Cards:** Visa/MC, Dscvr, Din, Amex
Discounts: None
Pets: Welcome, Dog Walk Area **Handicap Access:** Yes, Heads, Docks

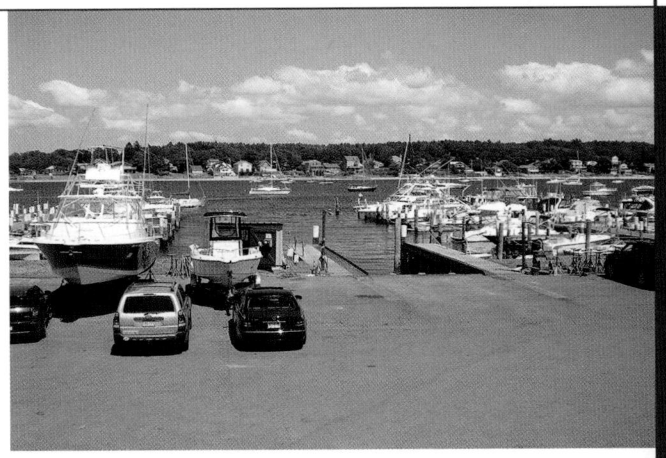

Zecco Marina

2 Warr Avenue; Wareham, MA 02571

Tel: (508) 295-0022 **VHF: Monitor** Ch. 9 **Talk** Ch. 9
Fax: (508) 295-5361 **Alternate Tel:** n/a
Email: greg_dorn@zeccomarine.com **Web:** www.zeccomarine.com
Nearest Town: Wareham *(0.3 mi.)* **Tourist Info:** (508) 759-6000

Marina Services and Boat Supplies
Services - Docking Assistance, Security *(12 Hrs.)*, Trash Pick-Up, Dock Carts **Communication -** Pay Phone, FedEx, UPS, Express Mail **Supplies - OnSite:** Ice *(Block, Cube)*, Ships' Store **Near:** Bait/Tackle *(M & D 291-0820)* **3+ mi:** West Marine *(748-3833, 5 mi.)*

Boatyard Services
OnSite: Travelift *(35T)*, Railway, Forklift, Crane, Launching Ramp, Engine mechanic *(gas, diesel)*, Electrical Repairs, Electronics Repairs, Hull Repairs, Canvas Work, Bottom Cleaning, Brightwork, Air Conditioning, Refrigeration, Compound, Wash & Wax, Propeller Repairs, Woodworking, Metal Fabrication, Painting, Awlgrip **Dealer for:** Proline, OMC, Mercruiser, Volvo Penta. **Member:** ABBRA, ABYC - 4 Certified Tech(s), Other Certifications: Puffin, Evinrude & Johnson, Mercruiser, OMC Cobra, Volvo Penta **Yard Rates:** $69/hr., Haul & Launch $8/ft. *(blocking incl.)*, Power Wash $3.50/ft.

Restaurants and Accommodations
Near: Restaurant *(Country Kitchen 967-9173, B, L & D, Kids')* **Under 1 mi:** Restaurant *(Narrows Crossing 295-9345)*, *(Woh Lun 295-3122)*, *(Piperbeaus 295-3356)*, Snack Bar *(Frakenstein Dogs)*, Pizzeria *(Fat Paulies 295-6100)*, Inn/B&B *(Cranberry Garden 295-9475)* **1-3 mi:** Restaurant *(China Garden 295-7792)*, Lite Fare *(Tihonet 295-5437, L $5-7, Del, min $10)*, Motel *(Briarwood Beach 295-2766, $90-150)*, Inn/B&B *(Ginn Inn 295-1313)* **3+ mi:** Inn/B&B *(Point Independence 273-0466, $219-279, 4 mi.)*

Recreation and Entertainment
OnSite: Picnic Area, Grills **Under 1 mi:** Museum *(Capt. John Kendrick Maritime 291-2274; Fearing Tavern)* **1-3 mi:** Pool *("Y" 295-9622 $10/4)*, Beach *(Swifts via OWL)*, Playground *(Water Wizz Water Park 295-3255)*, Fitness Center *("Y")*, Boat Rentals *(Atlantic 295-8005)*, Video Rental *(Redbox)*, Tours *(A.D. Makepeace 322-4028 Cranberry bogs, small groups)* **3+ mi:** Golf Course *(Bay Pointe C.C. 759-8802, 5 mi.)*

Provisioning and General Services
Near: Wine/Beer *(Trio 291-7110)*, Bank/ATM, Catholic Church **Under 1 mi:** Supermarket *(Shaw's 295-7813)*, Gourmet Shop *(Gourmet & Gourmand 295-1915)*, Liquor Store *(Jug Shop 295-7449)*, Bakery *(Merchant's Way 295-3264)*, Post Office *(295-0968)*, Protestant Church, Library *(295-2343)*, Beauty Salon *(Looks Unlim. 295-4204)*, Dry Cleaners *(Town & Country 295-0053)*, Laundry *(Wareham 295-9833)*, Pharmacy *(CVS 291-6289)* **1-3 mi:** Convenience Store *(Swifty 295-6278)*, Market *(Tihonet Village 295-5437)*, Delicatessen *(Melina's 273-0130)*, Green Grocer *(Nesralla Farm 295-0105)*, Fishmonger *(Seahorse 748-6714)*, Hardware Store *(Home Depot 291-7051)*, Florist *(Wareham 295-5855)*, Retail Shops *(Wareham Crossing)*

Transportation
OnCall: Rental Car *(Enterprise 759-2299)*, Taxi *(Wareham 295-5459)*, Airport Limo *(Green Shuttle 563-6476)* **Near:** Local Bus *(OWL 800-433-5995 to Onset, Boune, Cranberry Plaza - no Sun)*, InterCity Bus *(Bonanza 295-3665 at Deca's)* **Airport:** Cape Cod/Logan Int'l *(23 mi./60 mi.)*

Medical Services
911 Service **Near:** Dentist *(Foote 295-6002)*, Ambulance **Under 1 mi:** Doctor *(Fitzpatrick 291-4359)*, Chiropractor *(Dacunha & Costa 291-6119)*, Optician *(Mass. 295-2193)* **3+ mi:** Veterinarian *(Marion 748-1203, 4.5 mi.)*
Hospital: Southcoast 295-3848 *(0.4 mi.)*

Setting -- Up the sheltered Wareham River, four main docks march along the port shore dominated by large green-trimmed, gray-metal work and storage sheds on the 15-acre upland. Paved parking lots edge the docks; picnic tables on a long stretch of grass and lounge chairs on a small raised deck are nods to creature comfort. Views are of marsh mixed with beach, and further upriver of red brick mill buildings - now British Landing condos.

Marina Notes -- Founded 1939. Formerly Warr's Marina. A long-established family run facility. Marina and its affiliate Dick's Marine Service (759-3753) provide full yard services - 4 ABYC certified techs. Good choice for a haul-out if leaving the boat for a while. Bathhouse: Low gray building behind parking lot. Inside, well-maintained cinder block and beadboard, with private areas. Note: Additional dockage and moorings at Wareham Town Pier 295-8160, Ch.9.

Notable -- The long ride in from Buzzards Bay (it's the "innermost" point) puts Zecco close to Wareham's amenities - in a well-protected area. The historic village, one of the cranberry capitals of the world, starts at the railroad bridge about a half mile north. Settled in 1687, it has an interesting cache of a dozen 17th- to 19th-century buildings; heading north start with Kendrick House, then the Captain John Kendrick Maritime Museum to the 1690 Fearing's Tavern Museum and the 1819 Tremont Nail Co. In between are Tobey Homestead, a Nantucket Lighthouse, Schoolhouse, Union Chapel, and Old Meeting House - call the Historical Society (295-6839). The Wareham Gatemen, a semi-pro baseball team (295-3956), and the Minot Forest Nature Walk (295-7070) are compelling local attractions. Cape Cod Shipbuilding, a classic small sailboat builder, is also in town and a big mall, Wareham Crossing, is 2.5 miles (via the OWL bus).

Barden's Boat Yard

PO Box 577; 2 Island Wharf; Marion, MA 02738

Tel: (508) 748-0250; (800) 548-0250 **VHF: Monitor** Ch. 68 **Talk** n/a
Fax: (508) 748-2478 **Alternate Tel:** n/a
Email: bardensboatyard@comcast.net **Web:** www.bardensboatyard.com
Nearest Town: Marion **Tourist Info:** (508) 759-6000

Navigational Information

Lat: 41°42.285' **Long:** 070°45.668' **Tide:** 4 ft. **Current:** 0 kt. **Chart:** 13236
Rep. Depths (*MLW*): Entry 14 ft. **Fuel Dock** 6 ft. **Max Slip/Moor** -/13 ft.
Access: Sippican Harbor, past Ram Island, first boatyard to port

Marina Facilities *(In Season/Off Season)*

Fuel: Gasoline, Diesel
Slips: 16 Total, 0 Transient **Max LOA:** 60 ft. **Max Beam:** 16 ft.
Rate *(per ft.)*: **Day** n/a **Week** n/a **Month** n/a
Power: 30 amp incl, **50 amp** n/a, **100 amp** n/a, **200 amp** n/a
Cable TV: No **Dockside Phone:** No
Dock Type: Floating, Short Fingers, Wood
Moorings: 85 Total, 10 Transient **Launch:** Yes (Free)
Rate: Day $40 **Week** $200 **Month** n/a
Heads: 2 Toilet(s), 2 Shower(s)
Internet: Yes *(Wi-Fi - entire harbor)* **Laundry:** None
Pump-Out: OnCall, Full Service, 1 Port **Fee:** Free **Closed Heads:** Yes

Marina Operations

Owner/Manager: Fred Coulson **Dockmaster:** Same
In-Season: Year Round, 8am-5pm* **Off-Season:** n/a, 7:30am-4pm
After-Hours Arrival: Call ahead for instructions
Reservations: No **Credit Cards:** Visa/MC
Discounts: None
Pets: Welcome **Handicap Access:** No

Marina Services and Boat Supplies

Services - Dock Carts **Communication -** FedEx, UPS, Express Mail
Supplies - OnSite: Ice *(Block, Cube)* **Under 1 mi:** Ships' Store *(Burr)* **3+ mi:** Propane *(Sea Gas 758-4338, 5 mi.)*

Boatyard Services

OnSite: Travelift *(35T to 60 ft.)*, Forklift, Crane, Hydraulic Trailer, Engine mechanic *(gas, diesel)*, Hull Repairs, Rigger, Bottom Cleaning, Compound, Wash & Wax, Woodworking, Painting **OnCall:** Electrical Repairs, Electronics Repairs, Sail Loft, Canvas Work, Divers, Air Conditioning, Refrigeration, Propeller Repairs, Inflatable Repairs, Metal Fabrication
Dealer for: Yanmar, Johnson. Other Certifications: Yanmar, Westerbeke, Evinrude, MMTA **Yard Rates:** $60-85, Haul & Launch $9/ft 1-way, Bottom Paint $12/ft. *(paint incl.)* **Storage:** On-Land In; $7/sq.ft. Out: $2-6.50 sq.ft.

Restaurants and Accommodations

Near: Inn/B&B *(Village Landing 748-0350, $130-135)* **Under 1 mi:** Restaurant *(Wave 748-2986, L & D $6-17 kids' $4-8, Pizza, Wknd Break., Entertain.)*, *(Sippican Cafe 748-0176, B $3-8, L $3-8, D $7-22, Kids' $4-6, Local fave, good reviews)*, *(House of Thai 500-2020)*, Pizzeria *(Santoro's 748-9599)*, *(Rose & Vicki 748-1333, Plus Subs, wraps, salads, pies, cookies, cakes - Del.)*, Inn/B&B *(Pineywood Farm 748-3925, $165)*

Recreation and Entertainment

Near: Picnic Area, Playground, Museum *(Marion Natural History 748-2098 Wed noon-4pm, Fri noon-2pm, Sat 10am-1pm, Summer kids' programs; 1834 Sippican Historical Society)*, Cultural Attract *(Marion Art Center 748-1266 - Concerts, lectures, plays, musicals, classes, summer art camp; Marion Music Hall 748-9556)*, Galleries *(Marion Art Center - 2 galleries & theater walls Tue-Fri 1-5pm, Sat 10am-2pm, Free)* **Under 1 mi:** Beach *(Silvershell - walk, pkg permit req.)*, Tennis Courts *(Marion Indoor 748-2889)*, Boat Rentals *(Burr Bros. 748-0541)* **1-3 mi:** Fishing Charter *(Bounty Hunter 748-3474)*, Park *(Washburn Memorial)* **3+ mi:** Golf Course *(Marion GC 748-0199, 3.5 mi.)*, Bowling *(Bowlmor 758-6783, 5 mi.)*

Provisioning and General Services

Near: Market *(Marion General 748-0340)*, Liquor Store *(Spirits 748-0004)*, Post Office *(748-3847)*, Catholic Church, Protestant Church, Library *(748-1252)*, Bookstore *(Bookstall 748-1041)*, Retail Shops *(Front Street)* **Under 1 mi:** Convenience Store *(Cumberland Farms)*, Fishmonger *(Tasty 748-3127)*, Bank/ATM *(Bank of America)*, Beauty Salon *(Karma 748-1540)*, Barber Shop, Dry Cleaners *(Mayhews 748-2353)*, Florist *(Always 748-1777)* **1-3 mi:** Wine/Beer *(Leo's 500-4884)* **3+ mi:** Supermarket *(Shaw's 295-7813, 4.5 mi.)*, Green Grocer *(How on Earth 758-1341 Local, seasonal, 3.5 mi.)*, Pharmacy *(Rite Aid 295-5772, 4.5 mi.)*

Transportation

OnCall: Rental Car *(Enterprise 759-2299)*, Taxi *(Wareham 295-5459)*, Airport Limo *(Churchill 295-8343)* **1-3 mi:** InterCity Bus *(Bonanza 800-751-8800)* **Airport:** New Bedford/TF Green/Logan Int'l *(15 mi./48 mi./60 mi.)*

Medical Services

911 Service **Near:** Dentist *(McSweeny 748-1380)* **Under 1 mi:** Chiropractor *(Coastal 748-3224)* **1-3 mi:** Doctor *(Wallace 748-9749)*, Veterinarian *(Marion 748-1203)* **Hospital:** Southcoast 295-3848 *(5.5 mi.)*

Setting -- Beautiful, three-sided Sippican Harbor weaves in and around coves, islands and unspoiled salt marsh. 750 moorings dot this primarily sailboat haven and Barden's manages 90 of them. Tucked between the Beverly Yacht Club and Municipal Wharf, its park-like sprawling shoreside facility includes two main docks, stone-bulkheaded grass earth berms, two two-story shingled buildings that house the offices and amenities plus the yard's looming gray sheds.

Marina Notes -- *Yard hours 7:30am-4pm Mon-Fri. Family business since 1927. Boatyard with helix moorings; no transient slips. Seasonal launch on 21 ft. Crosby - MemDay-LabDay 8am-6pm Mon-Thu, 8am-9:30pm weekends. Shoulder season, hours vary. 35-ton travelift & full yard services here & at 2nd inland facility - 10,000 sq. ft. of inside storage. Valet service for fueling $25. Dry stack in/out service for boats to 32 ft. Pump-out & water on adjacent town dock (Ch.9. 748-3535). Bathhouse: Skip the basic boatyard facilities; walk next door to the town pier's fresh checkerboard-tile heads & showers.

Notable -- Marion is worth a detour as much for its village as for its harbor; Barden is within its historic heart. Lovely vintage homes and 18th and 19th C. architectural gems, housing commercial ventures and cultural attractions, line stopped-in-time leafy lanes. For a delightful hour or two, take the Marion Art Center' s walking tour (marionartcenter.org/Town_Tour.htm). On and around Front Street are the Marion Music Hall, General Store, Library, Post Office, Marion Natural History Musuem, Sippican Historical Society - many gifts from Marion's fairy godmother Elizabeth Tabor.Dinghy up-harbor to the northern Town Pier for West Marine, some popular restaurants and the commercial Rte 6 strip. Or dinghy to the sandspit in the harbor's Southeast corner for a kick-back afternoon.

Navigational Information

Lat: 41°42.790' **Long:** 070°45.926' **Tide:** 4 ft. **Current:** 0 kt. **Chart:** 13236
Rep. Depths (*MLW*): Entry 6 ft. **Fuel Dock** 6 ft. **Max Slip/Moor** 6 ft./12 ft.
Access: Buzzards Bay to the head of Sippican Harbor

Marina Facilities *(In Season/Off Season)*

Fuel: *Texaco* - Gasoline, Diesel
Slips: 30 Total, 2 Transient **Max LOA:** 70 ft. **Max Beam:** 18 ft.
Rate *(per ft.)*: **Day** $3.00/Inq. **Week** $16.50 **Month** Inq.
Power: 30 amp Incl., **50 amp** Incl., **100 amp** Incl., **200 amp** n/a
Cable TV: No **Dockside Phone:** No
Dock Type: Floating, Concrete
Moorings: 100 Total, 10 Transient **Launch:** Yes (Free), Dinghy Dock
Rate: Day $40 **Week** $225 **Month** n/a
Heads: 2 Toilet(s), 2 Shower(s)
Internet: Yes *(Wi-Fi - entire harbor, Free)* **Laundry:** None
Pump-Out: OnCall, Full Service **Fee:** Free **Closed Heads:** Yes

Marina Operations

Owner/Manager: Dennis Joaquin **Dockmaster:** Carl Arruda
In-Season: MemDay-LabDay, 8am-8pm* **Off-Season:** Sep-May, 8am-4:30pm
After-Hours Arrival: Must arrive during office hours
Reservations: No **Credit Cards:** Visa/MC, Amex
Discounts: None
Pets: Welcome **Handicap Access:** No

Burr Bros. Boats

309 Front Street; Marion, MA 02738

Tel: (508) 748-0541 **VHF: Monitor** Ch. 68 **Talk** n/a
Fax: (508) 748-0963 **Alternate Tel:** n/a
Email: burrbros@burrbros.com **Web:** www.burrbros.com
Nearest Town: Marion **Tourist Info:** (508) 759-6000

Marina Services and Boat Supplies

Services - Docking Assistance, Security, Trash Pick-Up, Dock Carts **Communication -** Pay Phone (1), FedEx, UPS, Express Mail **Supplies - OnSite:** Ice *(Block, Cube)*, Ships' Store, CNG **Near:** West Marine *(748-3833)* **3+ mi:** Propane *(Sea Gas 758-4338, 6 mi.)*

Boatyard Services

OnSite: Travelift *(55T)*, Forklift, Crane, Hydraulic Trailer, Launching Ramp, Engine mechanic *(gas, diesel)*, Electrical Repairs, Electronic Sales, Electronics Repairs, Hull Repairs, Rigger, Divers, Bottom Cleaning, Brightwork, Air Conditioning, Refrigeration, Compound, Wash & Wax, Interior Cleaning, Propeller Repairs, Woodworking, Inflatable Repairs, Metal Fabrication, Painting, Awlgrip, Total Refits **OnCall:** Sail Loft, Canvas Work, Upholstery **Dealer for:** Yanmar, Mercury, Yamaha, OMC, Laser, Sunfish, Honda, Vacuflush. **Member:** ABBRA, ABYC **Yard Rates:** $29-129/hr., Haul & Launch $7.50 + lab, Power Wash $1.50/ft + lab **Storage:** On-Land Heat $8.25/sq.ft; In $6/sq.ft.; Out $5/sq.ft

Restaurants and Accommodations

Near: Restaurant *(Sippican Café 748-0176, B $3-8, L $3-8, D $7-22, Popular with locals)*, *(House of Thai 500-2020)*, *(The Wave 748-2986, L & D $6-17, kids' $4-8, Pizza, Wknd Break., Entertain.)*, Snack Bar *(Uncle Jon's Coffee 748-0063, Lots of prepared food)*, Pizzeria *(Santoro's 748-9599)* **Under 1 mi:** Restaurant *(Tasty Seafoods 748-3127)*, Pizzeria *(Rose & Vicki 748-1333, Plus Subs, wraps, salads, pies, cookies, cakes - Del.)*, Inn/B&B *(Village Landing 748-0350, $130-135)* **1-3 mi:** Restaurant *(Frigate Steak House 748-0970)*, *(Gateway Tavern 291-6040, L & D $8-27, Veg Menu, too)*, Motel *(Briarwood 295-2766)*, Inn/B&B *(Pineywood Farm 748-3925, $165)*

Recreation and Entertainment

Near: Picnic Area, Playground **Under 1 mi:** Tennis Courts *(Marion 748-2889)*, Park *(Washburn Mem)*, Museum *(Marion Natural History 748-2098)*, Cultural Attract *(Marion Art Center 748-1266)*, Galleries *(Front Street 748-1078)* **1-3 mi:** Beach *(Silvershell)*, Golf Course *(Marion G.C. 748-0199)*

Provisioning and General Services

Near: Convenience Store *(Cumberland Farms 748-0417)*, Farmers' Market, Bank/ATM, Beauty Salon *(Uppercut 748-1641)*, Dry Cleaners *(Mayhews 748-2353)*, Laundry *(Mattapoisett 758-6711 - picks up)*, Florist *(Always 748-1777)* **Under 1 mi:** Market *(Marion General 748-0340)*, Wine/Beer *(Leo's 500-4884)*, Liquor Store *(Marion 748-2319)*, Bakery *(Flour Girls 241-2553)*, Fishmonger *(Seahorse 748-6714)*, Post Office *(748-3847)*, Catholic Church, Protestant Church, Library *(Taber 748-1252)*, Bookstore *(Bookstall 748-1041)* **3+ mi:** Supermarket *(Shaws 295-7813, 4 mi.)*, Green Grocer *(How On Earth 758-1341, 4 mi.)*, Pharmacy *(Rite Aid 295-5772, 4 mi.)*, Hardware Store *(Aubuchon 295-2123, 4 mi.)*

Transportation

OnCall: Rental Car *(Hertz 295-2314)*, Taxi *(Wareham 295-5459)*, Airport Limo *(Just in Time 961-2434; Business Rider 007-0010)* **1-3 mi:** Bikes *(South Coast 758-6666)* **Airport:** New Bedford/TF Green/Logan Int'l *(15 mi./48 mi./60 mi.)*

Medical Services

911 Service **Under 1 mi:** Dentist *(McSweeney 748-1380)*, Chiropractor *(Coastal 748-3224)*, Veterinarian *(Marion 748-1203)* **1-3 mi:** Doctor *(Wallace 748-9749)* **Hospital:** Southcoast 295-3848 *(5 mi.)*

Setting -- At the head of beautiful Sippican Harbor, just beyond the northern municipal pier, this seemingly plain-Jane facility dominates the shoreline. A half-dozen large, gray work sheds sporting an antique Texaco sign and signature brick-red doors, house the full-service marina and top-notch boatyard operation. Well-tended Hinckleys and custom yachts berth at its network of concrete docks and in its mooring field. Beyond is one of the loveliest villages on the bay.

Marina Notes -- *Open until 9pm Fri & Sun. LabDay-MemDay Mon-Thu 8am-4:30pm, Fri Sun 8am 6pm. Estab. 1946; Family run. "Club-quality" launch service: Jul 20-LabDay Mon-Thu & Sat 8am-8pm, Fri & Sun 8am-9pm. Shoulder season shorter hrs. Helix mooring anchors. 55-ton travelift. Dedicated Awlgrip facility, custom woodworking, inside storage. Three new add'l large sheds (2 at inland site). Renovated, well-stocked ships' store. Casual Lounge. Pump-out & water at town docks (Harbormaster 748-3535). Bathhouse: Very basic, gray-tiled, pine wainscot. Separate shower rooms. 2nd floor of street-side building.

Notable -- Burr's mooring field is closer to the village than the yard (dinghy to southern town dock), but the boatyard is very close to the businesses and eateries on commercial Route 6 (0.1 mile). Stroll the quintessential New England village; all of the organizations and services are housed in restored 18th and 19thC. buildings. See Town Hall, the Library, Museum, General Store, Music Hall, Marion Art Center (amateur theatrical events, two art galleries, Art Camp, concerts, more), well-known Tabor Academy and a plethora of charming homes. Events abound - July 4th parade & fireworks, Monday night Town Dock concerts, Art in the Park, and, hosted by Beverly Yacht Club, the Marion to Bermuda Race in odd-number years and Buzzards Bay Regatta in even ones.

PHOTOS ON DVD: 20

Mattapoisett Boatyard

PO Box 1030; 32 Ned's Point Road; Mattapoisett, MA 02739

Tel: (508) 758-3812 **VHF: Monitor** Ch. 68 **Talk** Ch. 68
Fax: (508) 758-2527 **Alternate Tel:** n/a
Email: dave@mattapoisettboatyard.com **Web:** mattapoisettboatyard.com
Nearest Town: Mattapoisett *(1 mi.)* **Tourist Info:** (508) 999-5231

Navigational Information
Lat: 41°39.150' **Long:** 070°47.900' **Tide:** 5 ft. **Current:** n/a **Chart:** 13230
Rep. Depths (*MLW*): Entry 12 ft. **Fuel Dock** 6 ft. **Max Slip/Moor** 12 ft./19 ft.
Access: Buzzard's Bay, past Ned's Point Light, first facility to starboard

Marina Facilities *(In Season/Off Season)*
Fuel: *Shell* - Gasoline, Diesel
Slips: 6 Total, 2 Transient **Max LOA:** 50 ft. **Max Beam:** n/a
Rate *(per ft.)*: **Day** $2.00/Inq. **Week** Inq. **Month** Inq.
Power: 30 amp Incl., **50 amp** n/a, **100 amp** n/a, **200 amp** n/a
Cable TV: No **Dockside Phone:** No
Dock Type: Fixed, Wood
Moorings: 200 Total, 15 Transient **Launch:** Yes (Free)
Rate: Day $35 **Week** $225 **Month** n/a
Heads: 2 Toilet(s), 1 Shower(s)
Internet: No **Laundry:** None
Pump-Out: OnSite, Full Service, 1 Central **Fee:** Free **Closed Heads:** Yes

Marina Operations
Owner/Manager: David Kaiser **Dockmaster:** Same
In-Season: Year-Round, 8am-8pm **Off-Season:** n/a, 8am-5pm
After-Hours Arrival: Call ahead
Reservations: Yes **Credit Cards:** Visa/MC, Din, Amex, Tex
Discounts: None
Pets: Welcome **Handicap Access:** No

Marina Services and Boat Supplies
Services - Docking Assistance, Trash Pick-Up, Dock Carts **Communication -** Pay Phone, FedEx, DHL, UPS, Express Mail *(Sat Del)* **Supplies - OnSite:** Ice *(Block, Cube)*, Ships' Store **1-3 mi:** Propane *(Sea 758-4338)* **3+ mi:** West Marine *(748-3833, 5 mi.)*

Boatyard Services
OnSite: Travelift *(35T)*, Engine mechanic *(gas, diesel)*, Electrical Repairs, Electronics Repairs, Hull Repairs, Rigger, Canvas Work, Bottom Cleaning, Brightwork, Refrigeration, Compound, Wash & Wax, Interior Cleaning, Woodworking, Painting **OnCall:** Propeller Repairs, Inflatable Repairs **Near:** Sail Loft. **Yard Rates:** $65, Haul & Launch $10/ft

Restaurants and Accommodations
OnCall: Pizzeria *(Nick's 758-2277)* **Under 1 mi:** Restaurant *(The Pub at Kinsale Inn 758-4922, L $6-10, D $8-25, 7 days, 11am-10pm, Sun Br $18/9)*, *(Leeward 758-3148)*, Lite Fare *(Oxford Creamery 758-3847)*, *(On the Go 758-9922, L $5-9, $4-9, soups, salads, wraps)*, Inn/B&B *(Kinsale Inn 758-4922, $90-110, 3 rooms, live entertainment)*, *(Mattapoisett Inn 758-9733, $115-295, 3 rooms & apt.)* **1-3 mi:** Restaurant *(Mattapoisett Chowder House 758-2333, L&D $6-18)*, *(Turks Seafood 758-3117, L&D $3-13; Kids' $4-7)* **3+ mi:** Hotel *(Hampton Inn 990-8500, $100-149, 5.5 mi)*

Recreation and Entertainment
Near: Volleyball *(Town Beach)*, Park *(Shipyard)* **Under 1 mi:** Hike/Bike Trails, Video Rental *(Blockbuster Exp)*, Special Events *(Harbor Days 3rd week July)* **1-3 mi:** Golf Course *(Reservation G. C. 758-3792)*, Bowling *(Bowlmor 758-6783)*, Museum *(Mattapoisett Hist. Soc. 758-2844 - carriages & other 19th century artifacts)* **3+ mi:** Fishing Charter *(Bounty Hunter 748-3474, 4 mi.)*, Cultural Attract *(Marion Art Center 748-1266, 4.5 mi)*

Provisioning and General Services
Under 1 mi: Convenience Store *(Tedeschi's 758-9301)*, Wine/Beer *(Seahorse 758-3821)*, Bakery *(Shipyard Galley 758-9408)*, Protestant Church, Library *(758-4171)*, Beauty Salon *(Sisters 758-3722)*, Barber Shop *(Mattapoisett Clipper 758-9212)*, Laundry *(Mattapoisett 758-6711)*, Florist *(Mattapoisset 758-4025)*, Copies Etc. *(Mailbox 758-9700)* **1-3 mi:** Delicatessen *(Gail's Goodies 758-3900)*, Liquor Store *(Village 758-4334)*, Green Grocer *(How on Earth 758-1341)*, Bank/ATM *(Bank of America)*, Post Office, Dry Cleaners *(Mayhew's 758-4272)*, Hardware Store *(Mahoney True Value 758-6921)* **3+ mi:** Market *(Marion General 748-0340, 4.5 mi.)*, Supermarket *(Shaw's 993-9996, 6 mi.)*, Farmers' Market *(Sun 1-4pm, Fairhaven, 5.5 mi.)*, Catholic Church *(4.5 mi)*, Pharmacy *(Walgreens 993-7498, 5 mi)*, Department Store *(WalMart 993-8100, 6 mi)*

Transportation
OnCall: Rental Car *(Enterprise 759-2299; Rent-A-Wreck of New Bedford 984-7300 - 8 mi.)*, Taxi *(Checker 999-9994)*, Airport Limo *(Just in Time 961-2434)* **Under 1 mi:** Local Bus *(SERTA to Fairhaven Mall)* **Airport:** New Bedford 979-1410 *(11 mi)*

Medical Services
911 Service **OnCall:** Ambulance **Under 1 mi:** Dentist *(Tavares 758-2571)*, Holistic Services *(Spascape Day 758-2008)*, Veterinarian *(Mattapoisett 758-6400)* **1-3 mi:** Doctor *(Southcoast 758-3781)* **3+ mi:** Chiropractor *(Barley 997-9100, 4.5 mi.)* **Hospital:** Southcoast 997-1515 *(9.6 mi.)*

PHOTOS ON DVD: 15

Setting -- On the Easterly, leeward shore of unspoiled Mattapoisett Harbor, the docks and work sheds of Mattapoisett Boatyard are striking against the uncluttered shoreline. Three large, gray and weathered-shingle sheds are surrounded by a casual, bustling working yard crammed with boats on the hard. A mile up the harbor - by land, boatyard launch or dink - is the pretty, low-key historic village.

Marina Notes -- Founded in 1962 by Arthur W. McLean; family still operates the yard. Well-stocked parts department. Launch serves both boatyard's own dock & Long Wharf town dock during daylight hours. Approx 800 moorings spread throughout the harbor and outlying beach areas; 200 belong to Mattapoisett Boatyard. Second 2.5-acre inland yard - Cap't Dave's Consignment Shop downstairs for gear. Dinghy docks: boatyard, Long Wharf, and town beach. Mattapoisett Yacht Club berths here. Bathhouse: Rustic, painted walls, practically outdoor shower.

Notable -- Veterans Park at Ned's Point, a short walk seaward, sports a wide open greensward with spectacular views of Buzzards Bay, a popular windsurfing destination, it's also home to the 160-year-old-landmark Ned's Point Light. At the head of the harbor, Long Wharf, Mattapoisett's town dock - built on the original granite piers designed for tall ships - is surrounded by Shipyard Park. The flagpole is the mizzen mast of the last of 400 whalers built here - 1878 "Wanderer." Across Water Street, charming 1799 Kinsale Inn, Pub & Wine Bar serves seven days. Stroll the quiet streets where restored 18th and 19thC. houses speak to Mattapoisett's heyday as a ship-building center. Commercial Route 6 follows the harbor contours about 4 blocks from the water.

  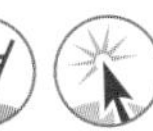 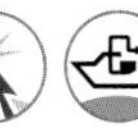  

Navigational Information

Lat: 41°40.547' **Long:** 070°36.971' **Tide:** 4 ft. **Current:** 0 kt. **Chart:** 13236
Rep. Depths (*MLW*): Entry 6 ft. **Fuel Dock** 10 ft. **Max Slip/Moor** 10 ft./12 ft.
Access: Buzzards Bay - East End to Pocasset Harbor to Red Brook

Marina Facilities *(In Season/Off Season)*

Fuel: Gasoline, Diesel
Slips: 235 Total, 30 Transient **Max LOA:** 100 ft. **Max Beam:** n/a
Rate *(per ft.)*: **Day** $3.50* **Week** n/a **Month** n/a
Power: 30 amp Incl., **50 amp** Incl., **100 amp** n/a, **200 amp** n/a
Cable TV: No **Dockside Phone:** No
Dock Type: Floating, Long Fingers, Short Fingers, Pilings, Alongside, Wood
Moorings: 130 Total, 15 Transient **Launch:** Yes (Free), Dinghy Dock
Rate: Day $50 **Week** $315 **Month** n/a
Heads: 12 Toilet(s), 12 Shower(s), Book Exchange
Internet: Yes *(Wi-Fi, Inq.)* **Laundry:** 3 Washer(s), 3 Dryer(s)
Pump-Out: OnSite, Self Service, 1 Central **Fee:** Free **Closed Heads:** Yes

Marina Operations

Owner/Manager: John Burman **Dockmaster:** Tara Plugge
In-Season: June-Sep, 8am-8pm **Off-Season:** Oct-May, 8am-5pm
After-Hours Arrival: Call in advance and check-in in the morning
Reservations: Yes, Preferred **Credit Cards:** Visa/MC, Dscvr, Amex
Discounts: None
Pets: Welcome, Dog Walk Area **Handicap Access:** No

Kingman Yacht Center

PO Box 408; 1 Shipyard Lane; Cataumet, MA 02534

Tel: (508) 563-7136 **VHF: Monitor** Ch. 9 **Talk** Ch. 71
Fax: (508) 563-6493 **Alternate Tel:** n/a
Email: harbormaster@kingmanyachtcenter.com **Web:** See marina notes
Nearest Town: Pocasset *(1 mi.)* **Tourist Info:** (508) 759-3122

Marina Services and Boat Supplies

Services - Docking Assistance, Dock Carts **Communication -** Mail & Package Hold, Phone Messages, Fax in/out *($1)*, FedEx, DHL, UPS, Express Mail *(Sat Del)* **Supplies - OnSite:** Ice *(Block, Cube)*, Ships' Store *(Boater's Essentials)*, Bait/Tackle *(Latitude 41)*

Boatyard Services

OnSite: Travelift *(60T)*, Crane, Hydraulic Trailer, Engine mechanic *(gas, diesel)*, Electrical Repairs, Electronics Repairs, Hull Repairs, Rigger, Upholstery, Yacht Interiors, Metal Fabrication, Painting, Awlgrip, Total Refits, Yacht Broker **OnCall:** Air Conditioning, Refrigeration, Propeller Repairs **Dealer for:** Yanmar, Cummins, Caterpillar, Westerbeke, Kohler, Volvo-Penta, Flexiteek. **Member:** ABBRA, ABYC **Yard Rates:** $99/hr., Haul & Launch $11/ft. *(blocking incl.)*, Power Wash $3.50/ft., Bottom Paint $8-10/ft. **Storage:** In-Water $36/ft., On-Land from $5.30/sq.ft.

Restaurants and Accommodations

OnSite: Restaurant *(The Chart Room & Piano Bar 563-5350, L $3-16, D $10-22, 11:30am-3pm, 5:30-10pm, Light fare 11:30am-10:00pm)* **1-3 mi:** Restaurant *(Corner Café 563-6944)*, *(Silver Lounge 563-2410, D $8-16)*, *(Courtyard 563-1818, D $9-20)*, *(Parrot Grill 563-2117, D $10-15)*, *(Beach House 564-5029, L $8-11, D $8-17)*, *(Golden Place 563-2828, L&D $8-10)*, Pizzeria *(Prime Time 563-1900)*, *(N. Falmouth 563-6966)*, Inn/B&B *(No. 9 563-9199, $125-144)* **3+ mi:** Hotel *(Sea Crest 540-9400, $130-385, 5 mi.)*

Recreation and Entertainment

OnSite: Picnic Area, Grills, Galleries *(Watershed - area artists)* **Near:** Beach *(Bassett's Island - mile long beach)*, Hike/Bike Trails *(Nivling-Alexander Reserve)*, Fishing Charter *(Diablo 733-4357)* **Under 1 mi:** Sightseeing *(Dinghy to Barlow's landing)* **1-3 mi:** Tennis Courts *(Cape & Island 759-5636)*, Fitness Center *(Balanced 563-1100)*, Movie Theater *(Regal Cinemas 563-7554)* **3+ mi:** Golf Course *(Ballymeade 540-4005, 4 mi.)*, Horseback Riding *(Highlander Farm 563-6866, 5 mi.)*, Museum *(Aptucxet Trading Post 759-9487, 5 mi.)*

Provisioning and General Services

OnSite: Convenience Store *(Latitude 41 - 6:30am-8:30pm Essential provisions)*, Retail Shops *(Latitude 41 - Fresh Produce, Vera Bradley, gifts, etc; Periwinkles Gifts - souvenirs)* **Under 1 mi:** Protestant Church **1-3 mi:** Market *(Pocasset Country 564-4258)*, Bakery *(Beach Plum 563-3434)*, Green Grocer *(Jack in the Beanstalk 564-4305)*, Fishmonger *(Cataumet 564-5956)*, Bank/ATM, Post Office, Catholic Church, Library *(563-2922)*, Beauty Salon *(Villager 563-6732)*, Dry Cleaners, Hardware Store *(Pocasset 563-6042)* **3+ mi:** Supermarket *(Stop & Shop 743-9563 - Pharmacy, 5 mi.)*, Liquor Store *(Monument 759-1951, 4 mi.)*

Transportation

OnSite: Courtesy Car/Van **OnCall:** Rental Car *(Enterprise 759-2299)*, Taxi *(A A 563-9944; No. Falmouth 548-2900)*, Airport Limo *(Passport 563-2688)* **1-3 mi:** Bikes *(Bike Zone 563-2333)* **3+ mi:** InterCity Bus *(Bonanza to TF Green & Boston, 5 mi.)* **Airport:** Barnstable/TF Green *(21 mi./70 mi.)*

Medical Services

911 Service **Under 1 mi:** Doctor *(Baxley 563-5507)* **1-3 mi:** Dentist *(Dembro 563-9596)*, Chiropractor *(Up. Cape 563-9996)* **3+ mi:** Veterinarian *(Falmouth 563-7147, 3.5 mi.)* **Hospital:** Falmouth 548-5300 *(9.5 mi.)*

Setting -- The largest marina on the Cape, bustling Kingman dominates pristine Red Brook Harbor alongside quieter Parker's. Entry is through the serpentine North (deeper) or South channels skirting Bassett's Island and its gorgeous beach. Head for the massive white steel sheds with Kingman emblazoned in 4-foot letters. The land facilities sit on a peninsula surrounded by docks. An enclosed basin "behind" the marina holds mostly seasonals; the harborside docks berth the transients and dock & diners. Lounge chairs perch on the small point overlooking the harbor, in front of The Chart Room, lending a festive ambiance.

Marina Notes -- Website: KingmanYachtCenter.com. *50-65 ft. $4.50/ft; over 65 ft. $5.50/ft. $50 minimum. Founded 1932. Full payment required with reservation, refund 7 days in advance less $20. Fuel & Pump-out dock 8am-7:30pm in season (or Bourne Pump-out Boat Ch.9). Moorings (most 8,000 lbs) include launch & courtesy loading dock. Dock & Launch crew 8am-9pm, Ch.71. Comprehensive, high-volume service & repair facility. Tire floating wave attenuator minimizes wash. Dockside phone & cable for longer stays. Ships' store open 7 days plus KYC parts store. Emergency towing. Affiliated Kingman Yacht Club offers reciprocal slips & moorings to other YCs. Bathhouse: Two sets of heads, one with laundry. Modern, tile, formica with full baths.

Notable -- Kingman's Island includes a gift shop, ships' store, convenience store, gallery and destination restaurant: The Chart Room, a permanently beached New Jersey Railroad barge with indoor or covered porch seating plus cocktails on the point. KYC's impressive green initiatives include: Largest commercial photo voltaic solar system on the Cape generates 25% of electrical needs, biofuel, recycled pressure water and rain gardens to filter storm water.

PHOTOS ON DVD: 24

Parker's Boat Yard

PO Box 38; 68 Red Brook Harbor Road; Cataumet, MA 02534

Tel: (508) 563-9366 **VHF: Monitor** Ch. 69 **Talk** n/a
Fax: (508) 563-3899 **Alternate Tel:** n/a
Email: pby@verizon.net **Web:** www.parkersboatyard.com
Nearest Town: Falmouth *(10 mi.)* **Tourist Info:** (508) 759-6000

Navigational Information

Lat: 41°40.469' **Long:** 070°36.850' **Tide:** 2 ft. **Current:** n/a **Chart:** 13236
Rep. Depths (*MLW*): Entry 6 ft. **Fuel Dock** 7 ft. **Max Slip/Moor** 7 ft./8 ft.
Access: East of Wings Neck traffic light near entrance to Cape Cod Canal

Marina Facilities *(In Season/Off Season)*

Fuel: Gasoline, Diesel
Slips: 9 Total, 1 Transient **Max LOA:** 45 ft. **Max Beam:** n/a
Rate *(per ft.)*: **Day** $3.00/$2 **Week** n/a **Month** n/a
Power: 30 amp Incl., **50 amp** n/a, **100 amp** n/a, **200 amp** n/a
Cable TV: No **Dockside Phone:** No
Dock Type: Long Fingers, Wood
Moorings: 130 Total, 6+ Transient **Launch:** Yes (Free), Dinghy Dock
Rate: Day $46 **Week** Inq. **Month** Inq.
Heads: 2 Toilet(s), 2 Shower(s), Book Exchange
Internet: Yes *(Office)* **Laundry:** None
Pump-Out: OnSite, Full Service, 1 Central **Fee:** Free **Closed Heads:** Yes

Marina Operations

Owner/Manager: Bruce & Patti Parker **Dockmaster:** Same
In-Season: Jun-Aug, 8am-8pm **Off-Season:** Sep-May, 8am-5pm
After-Hours Arrival: n/a
Reservations: Yes **Credit Cards:** Visa/MC
Discounts: None
Pets: Welcome, Dog Walk Area **Handicap Access:** No

Marina Services and Boat Supplies

Services - Docking Assistance, Boaters' Lounge, Trash Pick-Up, Dock Carts **Communication -** Mail & Package Hold, Phone Messages, FedEx, DHL, UPS, Express Mail **Supplies - OnSite:** Ice *(Block, Cube)*, Ships' Store, CNG **1-3 mi:** Bait/Tackle *(Bad Fish 563-3474)*

Boatyard Services

OnSite: Travelift *(35T)*, Crane, Engine mechanic *(gas, diesel)*, Electrical Repairs, Electronic Sales, Hull Repairs, Rigger, Bottom Cleaning, Brightwork, Compound, Wash & Wax, Interior Cleaning, Woodworking, Metal Fabrication, Painting, Awlgrip, Yacht Broker **OnCall:** Electronics Repairs, Divers, Air Conditioning, Refrigeration, Propeller Repairs, Inflatable Repairs **Under 1 mi:** Launching Ramp. **Member:** ABBRA, ABYC - 4 Certified Tech (s), Other Certifications: CCMT, MMT, YBAA **Yard Rates:** $90/hr, Haul & Launch $9 1-way, $14/ft. Short, Power Wash $3.75/ft, Bottom Paint $12.50/ft **Storage:** On-Land Out $60/ft., In $115/ft

Restaurants and Accommodations

Near: Restaurant *(Chart Room 563-5350, L $3-16, D $10-22, by dinghy)* **Under 1 mi:** Inn/B&B *(Wood Duck Inn 564-6404, $99-149, 3 rooms)*, *(No. 9 563-9199, $125-144)* **1-3 mi:** Restaurant *(Silver Lounge 563-2410)*, *(Courtyard 563-1818, D $9-20)*, *(Parrot Bar & Grill 563-2117, D $10-15)*, *(My Tin Man 617-529-2251, Dinner)*, *(Beach House 392-9679, L&D $9-17)*, *(Patriot Diner 392-9679)*, *(Golden Place 563-2828, L&D $8-10)*, *(Stir Crazy 564-6464, L&D Cambodian)*, Lite Fare *(Beach Plum 563-3434)*, *(Daily Brew 564-4755)*, Pizzeria *(Prime Time 563-1900)*, *(Dean's 563-5971)*

Recreation and Entertainment

OnSite: Picnic Area, Grills, Fitness Center **Near:** Beach *(Bassett's Island - dinghy)*, Hike/Bike Trails *(Nivling-Alexander Reserve)* **Under 1 mi:** Fishing Charter *(Diablo 733-4357)*, Park *(Clifton Boyer Conservation)* **1-3 mi:** Boat Rentals *(Cape Cod Kayak 563-9377 & Tours)*, Movie Theater *(Regal 563-7554)*, Galleries *(333; Day Hill)* **3+ mi:** Golf Course *(Ballymeade 540-4005, 3.5 mi.)*, Horseback Riding *(Highlander 563-6866, 4 mi.)*

Provisioning and General Services

Near: Protestant Church **Under 1 mi:** Post Office **1-3 mi:** Convenience Store *(Tedeschi 563-3713)*, Market *(Pocasset Country 564-4258)*, Gourmet Shop *(West Falmouth 548-1139)*, Liquor Store *(Portside 563-3012)*, Bakery *(Beach Plum)*, Green Grocer *(Jack in the Beanstalk 564-4305)*, Fishmonger *(Cataumet 564-5956)*, Bank/ATM, Catholic Church, Library *(563-2922)*, Beauty Salon *(Villager 563-6732)*, Dry Cleaners *(Capeway 563-9899)*, Hardware Store *(Pocasset 563-6042)* **3+ mi:** Supermarket *(Stop & Shop 743-9563 Pharmacy, 5 mi.)*

Transportation

OnSite: Courtesy Car/Van **OnCall:** Rental Car *(Enterprise, 759-2299)*, Taxi *(Roadrunner 759-2337; Bourne 759-4004)* **1-3 mi:** Bikes *(Arts 563-7379)* **3+ mi:** InterCity Bus *(Bonanza 759-7715, 5.5 mi.)* **Airport:** Barnstable/TF Green *(22 mi./70 mi.)*

Medical Services

911 Service **Under 1 mi:** Doctor *(Baxley 563-5507)* **1-3 mi:** Dentist *(Braund 564-4317)*, Chiropractor *(Upper Cape 563-9996)*, Veterinarian *(Falmouth 563-7147)* **Hospital:** Falmouth 548-5300 *(9 mi.)*

PHOTOS ON DVD: 23

Setting -- Parker's charming weathered-shingled sheds, festooned with clever woodworking, look out over quiet, protected, mooring-filled Red Hook Harbor to Bassetts Island. From the club-quality launches to the immaculately raked yards, PBY has certainly scaled up the classic boatyard ambiance - clearly an artist is in residence adding another dimension. The harbor is almost exclusively pleasure craft, and the surrounding community rural and residential.

Marina Notes -- Family owned since 1948. Knowledgeable, professional, ship-shape full-service yard focusing on sailboats. Well-stocked marine store. Mechanics, machine shop, fiberglass, carpentry, Awlgrip refinishing, rigging, winter storage. Dealer for Volvo, Yanmar, Universal, Westerbeke. Good onsite chandlery. Loaner car for supermarket or restaurant runs. Bourne Pump-out Boat VHF Ch.9. Well-equipped exercise room, ping pong, foosball, and even basketball. Bathhouse: Lovely. fresh full baths. Beadboard trim with nautical murals, charming accents, privacy.

Notable -- Near the Buzzards Bay end of the Cape Cod Canal, Red Brook Harbor is an ideal transit point. Several beaches, including the beautiful stretch of sand along Bassetts Island, adjacent harbors Megansett and Squeteague and small coves invite a dinghy lay-day. For iffy days, Parker's has a fitness room, ping pong, foosball, basketball and, most important, a courtesy car. Nearby, 40-acre Nivling-Alexander Reserve offers wooded land trails overlooking cranberry bogs and Red Brook Pond. If there are bikes aboard, it's 2.5 miles to the new head of the Shining Sea Bikeway that runs 10.7 miles to Woods Hole with 16 "points of interest" along the way. The Bonanza Bus stop is 5.5 miles away with service to Boston and Providence.

Navigational Information
Lat: 41°38.808' **Long:** 070°38.160' **Tide:** 3 ft. **Current:** n/a **Chart:** 13236
Rep. Depths (*MLW*): Entry 7 ft. **Fuel Dock** 7 ft. **Max Slip/Moor** 7 ft./-
Access: Megansett Harbor to R6 to Fiddler's Cove

Marina Facilities *(In Season/Off Season)*
Fuel: *ValvTect* - Gasoline, Diesel
Slips: 105 Total, 3 Transient **Max LOA:** 65 ft. **Max Beam:** n/a
Rate *(per ft.)*: **Day** $3.00 **Week** Inq. **Month** Inq.
Power: 30 amp $20, **50 amp** n/a, **100 amp** n/a, **200 amp** n/a
Cable TV: Yes **Dockside Phone:** No
Dock Type: Floating, Long Fingers, Composition
Moorings: 0 Total, 0 Transient **Launch:** n/a
Rate: Day n/a **Week** n/a **Month** n/a
Heads: 9 Toilet(s), 9 Shower(s) *(dressing rooms)*
Internet: Yes *(Wi-Fi - Beacon, Sub.)* **Laundry:** 1 Washer(s), 1 Dryer(s)
Pump-Out: Full Service **Fee:** Free **Closed Heads:** Yes

Marina Operations
Owner/Manager: Amy Griffin-Ofc Mgr **Dockmaster:** Fred Sorrento
In-Season: Apr-Nov, 8am-6pm **Off-Season:** Dec-Mar, 8am-5pm
After-Hours Arrival: Call in advance
Reservations: Yes **Credit Cards:** Visa/MC, Dscvr, Amex
Discounts: None
Pets: Welcome **Handicap Access:** Yes, Heads, Docks

Brewer Fiddler's Cove Marina

42 Fiddlers Cove Road; North Falmouth, MA 02556

Tel: (508) 564-6327 **VHF: Monitor** Ch. 9 **Talk** Ch. 8
Fax: (508) 564-6724 **Alternate Tel:** n/a
Email: fcm@byy.com **Web:** www.byy.com
Nearest Town: Falmouth *(5 mi.)* **Tourist Info:** (508) 548-8500

Marina Services and Boat Supplies
Services - Docking Assistance, Boaters' Lounge, Trash Pick-Up, Dock Carts **Communication -** FedEx, UPS, Express Mail **Supplies - OnSite:** Ice *(Block, Cube)*, Ships' Store **1-3 mi:** Bait/Tackle *(Bad Fish 563-3474)*

Boatyard Services
OnSite: Travelift *(35T)*, Forklift, Crane, Engine mechanic *(gas, diesel)*, Hull Repairs, Rigger, Bottom Cleaning, Compound, Wash & Wax, Interior Cleaning, Woodworking, Inflatable Repairs, Painting **OnCall:** Electronic Sales, Electronics Repairs, Canvas Work, Divers, Air Conditioning, Refrigeration, Propeller Repairs, Upholstery, Yacht Interiors **Member:** ABBRA, ABYC **Yard Rates:** $78-98/hr.

Restaurants and Accommodations
Under 1 mi: Restaurant *(Wild Harbor Market 563-2011)* **1-3 mi:** Restaurant *(Courtyard Rest & Pub 563-1818, D $9-20)*, *(Beach House 564-5029, D $8-17, Early bird 4-6)*, *(Silver Lounge 563-2410)*, *(My Tin Man 617-529-2251, Dinner)*, *(Parrot Bar & Grill 563-2117, L&D $10-15)*, *(Food For Thought 548-4498)*, Lite Fare *(Baccari's Diner 563-3041, B&L $4-10; Kids' $3, Supper Fri. 5-8pm)*, Pizzeria *(North Falmouth 563-6966)*, *(Prime Time 563-3190)*, Hotel *(Sea Crest Resort 540-9400, $130-385)*, *(Upton Jean 548-5524)*, Inn/B&B *(No. 9 563-9199, $125-144)*

Recreation and Entertainment
OnSite: Picnic Area, Playground **Near:** Jogging Paths **1-3 mi:** Pool *(Ballymeade 540-4005)*, Beach *(Old Silver Beach)*, Golf Course *(Ballymeade Country Club 540-4005)*, Fitness Center *(Balanced 563-1100)*, Boat Rentals *(Cape Cod Kayak 563-9377)*, Fishing Charter *(Diablo 733-4357)*, Park *(Nye Park)*, Galleries *(Gallery 333 564-4467; Day Hill 564-4657)* **3+ mi:** Horseback Riding *(Haland Stables 540-2552, 3.5 mi)*, Hike/Bike Trails *(Shining Trail Bike Path, 4 mi.)*

Provisioning and General Services
Near: Bookstore *(Retlok's 564-4859)*, Newsstand **Under 1 mi:** Bank/ATM **1-3 mi:** Convenience Store *(Tedeschi 563-3713)*, Market *(JP's 548-2759)*, Liquor Store *(No. Falmouth 563-3331)*, Bakery *(Beach Plum 563-3434)*, Green Grocer *(Jack in the Beanstalk 564-4305)*, Fishmonger *(Cataumet 564-5956)*, Post Office *(563-7388)*, Catholic Church, Protestant Church, Library *(North Falmouth 563-2922)*, Beauty Salon *(Darolyn 563-7400)*, Barber Shop, Dry Cleaners *(Cataumet 563-6052)*, Pharmacy *(No. Falmouth 564-4459)*, Hardware Store *(No. Falmouth 564-6160)*, Copies Etc. *(Mira 563-5704)* **3+ mi:** Supermarket *(Shaw's 617-298-0969, 8 mi.)*, Synagogue *(5.5 mi.)*

Transportation
OnCall: Rental Car *(Enterprise 540-7784)*, Taxi *(A A 563-9944)*, Airport Limo *(Any Occasion 477-7300)* **1-3 mi:** Bikes *(Bike Zone 563-2333)*, InterCity Bus *(Bonanza 888-751-8800)* **3+ mi:** Ferry Service *(Edgartown & Oak Bluffs, 7 mi.)* **Airport:** Barnstable/TF Green *(20 mi./75 mi.)*

Medical Services
911 Service **Under 1 mi:** Dentist *(Adams 563-5052)* **1-3 mi:** Doctor *(Wrede 564-6262)*, Chiropractor *(Upper Cape 563-9996)*, Holistic Services *(Healing Arts 563-9130)*, Veterinarian *(Falmouth 563-7147)* **Hospital:** Falmouth 548-5300 *(7.5 mi.)*

Setting -- Just off Megansett Harbor, tucked away in a well-protected, man-made cove, this attractively landscaped, carefully maintained facility hits a home run with a beautiful "cape cod contemporary" turreted, decked, and gray-shingled clubhouse. Eel grass, bayberry and rosa rugosa soften the four main dock areas. Mechanical services base in the large shed - one side faced with a pleasant, gray-shingled colonial office building. Views from the slips are across the cove entrance to the harbor beyond and of the large homes - many contemporary - lining the shore.

Marina Notes -- Full-service boatyard with excellent creature comforts. Accommodates 250 boats on the hard: heated indoor storage during work or outdoors, Window-walled clubhouse - a galley, reading room with fireplace, card tables, pool table, TV area, laundry and bathhouse. Service building & 35-ton travelift sited & landscaped to enhance views from slips. Special treatment for Brewer Customers. Dredged entrance channel marked with private buoys. Bathhouse: 8 private rooms in Clubhouse. Ceramic tile, beautifully appointed. Laundry. Note: Moorings possible from Megansett Yacht Club (563-9812).

Notable -- A true oasis, this part of the Cape is primarily residential with few attractions and remains very quiet and untouristed. Explore by bike, dinghy or on foot to see lovely seaside gardens. Take the dinghy into Squeteague (best at high tide), a harbor at the east end of Megansett Harbor near the yacht club. A little over two miles by land or around Nyes Neck by dinghy, daytrip to popular Old Silver Beach - a lovely, stretch of sand with no surf, warm tidal pools, bathhouse, snack bars and life guards. Bonanza Bus line runs along Route 28 - south to Woods Hole and north to Plymouth, Logan, TF Green.

PHOTOS ON DVD: 22

Quissett Harbor Boatyard

Quissett Harbor Boatyard

PO Box 46; 36 Quissett Harbor Road; Falmouth, MA 02541

Tel: (508) 548-0506 **VHF: Monitor** Ch. 9 **Talk** n/a
Fax: (508) 540-8991 **Alternate Tel:** n/a
Email: quissett@cape.com **Web:** n/a
Nearest Town: Woods Hole *(1.25 mi.)* **Tourist Info:** (508) 548-5500

Navigational Information

Lat: 41°32.655' **Long:** 070°39.113' **Tide:** 5 ft. **Current:** .5 kt. **Chart:** 13229
Rep. Depths (*MLW*): Entry 9 ft. **Fuel Dock** 16 ft. **Max Slip/Moor** -/25 ft.
Access: 1 mi. NE of Woods Hole Passage; look for entrance flasher R2

Marina Facilities *(In Season/Off Season)*

Fuel: No
Slips: 0 Total, 0 Transient **Max LOA:** 75 ft. **Max Beam:** n/a
Rate *(per ft.)*: **Day** n/a **Week** n/a **Month** n/a
Power: 30 amp n/a, **50 amp** n/a, **100 amp** n/a, **200 amp** n/a
Cable TV: No **Dockside Phone:** No
Dock Type: Fixed, Floating
Moorings: 25 Total, 12 Transient **Launch:** No, Dinghy Dock (Free)
Rate: Day $40* **Week** $175 **Month** Inq.
Heads: 1 Toilet(s)
Internet: No **Laundry:** None
Pump-Out: OnCall *(Boat)*, Full Service **Fee:** Free **Closed Heads:** Yes

Marina Operations

Owner/Manager: Weatherly Barnard Dorris **Dockmaster:** Richard Dorris
In-Season: Jun-Sep, 8am-6pm **Off-Season:** Oct-May, 9am-4:30pm
After-Hours Arrival: Pick up a mooring marked "QBY" in the outer harbor
Reservations: No **Credit Cards:** Cash/Check only
Discounts: None
Pets: Welcome **Handicap Access:** No

Marina Services and Boat Supplies

Services - Trash Pick-Up **Communication -** FedEx, UPS, Express Mail **Supplies - OnSite:** Ice *(Block, Cube)* **1-3 mi:** West Marine *(457-6500)*, Bait/Tackle *(Eastman's Sport 548-6900)*

Boatyard Services

OnSite: Railway *(10T)*, Engine mechanic *(gas, diesel)*, Divers, Brightwork, Propeller Repairs, Woodworking, Yacht Broker **Dealer for:** Dyer dinghy. **Yard Rates:** Power Wash $50 **Storage:** On-Land $6/ft./mo.

Restaurants and Accommodations

Under 1 mi: Inn/B&B *(Woods Hole Passage 495-0248, $99-325)* **1-3 mi:** Restaurant *(Landfall 548-1758, L $5-16, D $9-38, Kids' $4-8)*, *(Capt Kidd 548-8563, L $9-21, D $10-35, Kids' $7)*, *(Fishmonger 540-5376)*, *(Shuckers 548-3850, L $6-9, D $10-20)*, *(Phusion 457-3100)*, *(Quick's Hole 495-0792, D $5-15)*, *(Osteria La Civetta 540-1616, L $12-15, D $15-28)*, Lite Fare *(Pie in the Sky 540-5475)*, Pizzeria *(Steve's 457-9454)*, Motel *(Nautilus 548-1525, $118-225)*, *(Sleepy Hollow 548-1986, $108-274)*

Recreation and Entertainment

Near: Beach, Hike/Bike Trails *(Shining Seas Path)* **Under 1 mi:** Park *(Peterson Farm)*, Special Events *(Falmouth Road Race, Aug; Wood Hole Film Fest, July)* **1-3 mi:** Tennis Courts *(Falmouth Sports Center 548-7384)*, Fitness Center *(Anytime 548-0230)*, Video Rental *(Redbox)*, Museum *(Woods Hole Historical 548-7270, Free)*, Tours *(Falmouth Historical Society Walking Tour 548-4857; Woods Hole Oceanographic Institute Exhibit WHOI 289-2252 Free; Marine Biological Laboratory 289-7423 Free)*, Cultural Attract *(Falmouth Theatre Guild 548-0400; College Light Opera 548-0668-Reserve; Woods Hole Theater 540-6525)*, Sightseeing *(Nat'l Marine Fisheries Aquarium 495-2267 Don)* **3+ mi:** Golf Course *(Falmouth C.C. 548-3211, 8 mi)*, Movie Theater *(Falmouth 495-0505, 3.5 mi)*

Provisioning and General Services

1-3 mi: Convenience Store *(Tedeschi 457-1191)*, Market *(Windfall 548-0099)*, Gourmet Shop *(Windfall Market 548-0099)*, Health Food *(Amber Waves 540-3538)*, Wine/Beer *(Falmouth 548-4824)*, Liquor Store *(Old Barn 548-4855)*, Bakery *(Pie in the Sky 540-5475)*, Farmers' Market *(Thur Noon-6pm, Peg Noonan Park)*, Bank/ATM, Post Office, Catholic Church, Protestant Church, Library *(Woods Hole 548-8961)*, Beauty Salon *(A Cut Above 548-5508)*, Laundry *(Falmouth 548-3911)*, Bookstore *(Eight Cousins 548-5548)*, Pharmacy *(Rite Aid 495-2991)*, Hardware Store *(Eastman's 548-0407)* **3+ mi:** Supermarket *(Shaw's 617-298-0969, 3.5 mi.)*, Retail Shops *(Falmouth Mall via WOOSH, 3.5 mi)*

Transportation

OnCall: Rental Car *(Enterprise 540-7784)*, Taxi *(Falmouth 548-3100)*, Airport Limo *(All Town 548-7166)* **Near:** Local Bus *(WHOOSH 800-352-7155 $1/Free - to Woods Hole or Falmouth)* **1-3 mi:** Bikes *(Corner 540-4195)*, InterCity Bus *(Bonanza)*, Ferry Service *(to Martha's Vineyard)* **Airport:** Cape Cod/T.F.Green *(18 mi./80 mi.)*

Medical Services

911 Service **1-3 mi:** Doctor *(Haam 540-7423)*, Dentist *(Woods Hole 548-6655)*, Chiropractor *(Upper Cape 548-9999)*, Holistic Services *(Bellezza 299-8300)*, Optician *(Sia 774-763-0366)* **3+ mi:** Veterinarian *(Deer Run 548-3406, 4 mi)* **Hospital:** Falmouth 548-5300 *(2.7 mi.)*

Setting -- On the eastern shore of the inner harbor, WHB's weatherbeaten, brown sheds, docks dotted with pots of flowers and small railway are the only signs of commercialism in this lovely, protected, deep harbor. Its packed dinghy dock services a crowded mooring field mostly populated by sailboats, including a fleet of Herreshoff cats and many classic downeast yachts. The shoreline is edged by beautifully wooded old summer estates and conservation lands.

Marina Notes -- *Outer harbor moorings: $30. Established in 1960's. Old-style, family owned and operated boatyard. Wood is the preferred material, and old money pays for it. Some mechanical services. Railway hauls to 40 ft. 1 short-term slip for work or water. Good refuge from beating into the prevailing southwesterly. Water, ice & a busy dinghy dock. A stop on many yacht club cruises. Pump-out boat serves the harbor. Brewer or Kingman to the North are other options for fuel and/or repairs. Bathhouse: One porta-john. Note: Quissett Yacht Club 457-1055 - on the west side of inner harbor - few amenities.

Notable -- Walk out to "The Knob" in the Cornelia L. Carey Bird Sanctuary (on the northwest end of the harbor) - a little over a mile round-trip nets views of the Elizabeth Islands, a small hike-in beach and spectacular seaside sunsets. More trails wind through 13 acres of protected lands. Many attractions, culinary and biological, await you in Woods Hole, where you'll find numerous one-of-a-kind restaurants and the famed Oceanographic Institution along with several other marine research facilities. Falmouth is equally as accessible. The WHOOSH trolley is a 0.2 mile walk away, and runs twice an hour to Woods Hole and Falmouth. The Shining Sea Bikeway is a couple of miles. This paved ten-mile rail trail weaves across an ancient coastal plane ending in Woods Hole.

PHOTOS ON DVD: 22

  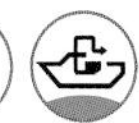 

Woods Hole Marine

PO Box 746; 91A Water Street; Woods Hole, MA 02543

Tel: (508) 540-2402 **VHF: Monitor** Ch. 9 **Talk** Ch. 72
Fax: (508) 540-7927 **Alternate Tel:** n/a
Email: info@woodsholemarine.com **Web:** www.woodsholemarine.com
Nearest Town: Falmouth *(4 mi.)* **Tourist Info:** (508) 548-8500

Navigational Information
Lat: 41°31.478' **Long:** 070°40.232' **Tide:** 1.5 ft. **Current:** n/a **Chart:** 13235
Rep. Depths (*MLW*): Entry 10 ft. **Fuel Dock** n/a **Max Slip/Moor** 7 ft./20 ft.
Access: Woods Hole Passage to Great Harbor, through bridge into Eel Pond

Marina Facilities *(In Season/Off Season)*
Fuel: No
Slips: 22 Total, 1 Transient **Max LOA:** 55 ft. **Max Beam:** 18 ft.
Rate *(per ft.)*: **Day** $2.00/Inq. **Week** Inq. **Month** Inq.
Power: 30 amp Incl., **50 amp** n/a, **100 amp** n/a, **200 amp** n/a
Cable TV: No **Dockside Phone:** No
Dock Type: Fixed, Short Fingers, Pilings, Wood
Moorings: 37 Total, 1 Transient **Launch:** No, Dinghy Dock
Rate: Day $65 **Week** Inq. **Month** Inq.
Heads: 3 Toilet(s), 1 Shower(s)
Internet: Yes *(Wi-Fi, Free)* **Laundry:** None
Pump-Out: OnCall, Full Service **Fee:** Free **Closed Heads:** Yes

Marina Operations
Owner/Manager: Buzz Harvey **Dockmaster:** Karen Kraus
In-Season: Jun-LabDay, 8am-7pm **Off-Season:** LabDay-May, 10am-2pm
After-Hours Arrival: Call in advance
Reservations: Yes, Preferred **Credit Cards:** Visa/MC, Amex
Discounts: None
Pets: No **Handicap Access:** Yes, Heads, Docks

Marina Services and Boat Supplies
Services - Trash Pick-Up **Communication -** FedEx, UPS, Express Mail
Supplies - Near: Ice *(Cube)* **3+ mi:** West Marine *(457-6500, 5 mi.)*

Boatyard Services
OnSite: Divers **Nearest Yard:** Falmouth Marine (508) 548-4600

Restaurants and Accommodations
OnSite: Restaurant *(Shuckers 540-3850, L $9-18, D $16-21)* **Near:** Restaurant *(Fishmonger's 540-5376, B $5-16, L $7-18, D $7-18)*, *(Lee-Side 548-9744)*, *(Naked Lobster 540-4848)*, *(Captain Kidd 548-8563, L $9-21, D $10-26, Kids' $7)*, *(Landfall 548-1758, L $5-16, D $9-38, Kids $4-8)*, *(Phusion Grille 457-3100, B, L & D)*, Lite Fare *(Quick's Hole 495-0792, $5-20)*, *(Pie in the Sky 540-5475, B & L $3-8, Internet)*, Inn/B&B *(Woods Hole Inn 495-0248, $99-325)* **Under 1 mi:** Restaurant *(Dome 548-0800)*, Motel *(Nautilus Motor Inn 548-1525, $58-158)*, *(Sleepy Hollow 548-1986, $108-274)*, *(Sands of Time 548-6300, $95-165)*

Recreation and Entertainment
Near: Hike/Bike Trails *(Shining Path to Falmouth)*, Museum *(Woods Hole Historical 548-7270, Free - Walking Tour)*, Tours *(WHOI - Woods Hole Oceanographic Institute Exhibit Center 289-2252 Free, Reserv. Req. - 1 hr. walking tour wkdays; Marine Biological Laboratory 289-7423 Free. 1 hr. tours by reservation)*, Cultural Attract *(Woods Hole Theater 540-6525, Community Hall)*, Sightseeing *(National Marine Fisheries Aquarium 495-2267 Donation, Visit gray seals LuSeal & Bumper)*, Galleries *(Local Colors 548-2549)*, Special Events *(Woods Hole Film Fest - late July)* **Under 1 mi:** Fishing Charter *(Get the Net 804-347-2353)*, Park *(Woods Hole; Nobska Light)* **1-3 mi:** Beach *(Surf Drive 548-8623)* **3+ mi:** Movie Theater *(Falmouth Cinema Pub 495-0505, 5 mi.)*

Provisioning and General Services
Near: Bakery *(Pie in the Sky 540-5475)*, Bank/ATM, Post Office *(548-0604)*, Library *(Woods Hole Oceanographic Institute 289-7423, tours)*, Newsstand **3+ mi:** Convenience Store *(Tedeschi 457-1191, 4 mi.)*, Supermarket *(Shaw's 617-298-0969, 5 mi.)*, Liquor Store *(Kappy's 548-2600, 5 mi.)*, Farmers' Market *(Tues & Sat Noon-3pm, Peg Noonan Park, 4 mi.)*, Catholic Church *(4 mi.)*, Protestant Church *(4 mi.)*, Beauty Salon *(Cut Above 548-5508, 3.5 mi.)*, Dry Cleaners *(Capeway 548-3222, 4 mi.)*, Bookstore *(Eight Cousins 548-5548, 4 mi.)*, Pharmacy *(Rite Aid 495-2991, 4.5 mi.)*, Hardware Store *(Eastman's Ace 548-0407, 4 mi.)*

Transportation
OnCall: Rental Car *(Enterprise 540-7784)*, Taxi *(Falmouth 548-3100)*, Airport Limo *(Leslee's 548-1888)* **Near:** Local Bus *(WOOSH Trolley to Falmouth & mall $2 every 30 min, 9:30am-10pm)*, InterCity Bus *(Bonanza to Boston, Providence, NY & airports 888-751-8800)*, Ferry Service *(Steamship Authority to Martha's Vineyard $8/4.25)* **3+ mi:** Bikes *(Corner 540-4195, 4 mi.)* **Airport:** Cape Cod/T.F. Green *(20 mi./82 mi.)*

Medical Services
911 Service **OnCall:** Ambulance **Near:** Dentist *(Woods Hole 548-6655)* **3+ mi:** Doctor *(Zartarian 548-0232, 4.5 mi.)*, Chiropractor *(Upper Cape 548-9999, 4.5 mi.)*, Holistic Services *(Bellezza 299-8300, 4 mi.)*, Optician *(Sia 774-763-0366, 4 mi.)*, Veterinarian *(Deer Run 548-3406, 6 mi.)* **Hospital:** Falmouth 548-5300 *(4.5 mi.)*

Setting -- The new drawbridge is the velvet rope into placid, protected Eel Pond and WHM's two long docks and mooring field. At the head of the docks, Shucker's occupies the first floor of a weathered-shingle townhouse; the marina office the upstairs. The slips and moorings have wonderful views of fishermen's shacks and the brick buildings of the Oceanographic Institution - WHOI. Just steps up a cobblestone path is the heart of tiny, bustling Woods Hole.

Marina Notes -- Owned by Buzz Harvey since 1980. Bridge Tender on Ch. 13. Pets not allowed. Manages boat hauling and delivery with Here to There 495-HAUL. Wet & dry Storage. Diver on staff. Carries Interstate batteries & chargers. Dockage plus Eel Pond and Great Harbor moorings. Protected from wild currents of "The Hole." No launch. Limited space so book early! Bathhouse: Shared with restaurant. Lovely tiled, modern, private. Shower in marina office.

Notable -- Schizophrenic Woods Hole is home port to the Martha's Vineyard car ferries and four international oceanographic research institutes, making summers a mashup of thousands of tourists, scientists and students. Cruisers interested in the oceans and their flora and fauna will be enthralled at the attractions open to the public. The Marine Biological Labs (MBL), established in 1888, offers tours (Mon-Sat, 10am-4pm). See some of the research vessels with a tour of Woods Hole Oceanographic Institutes' Exhibit Center - WHOI - the largest private marine research center in the world (Mon-Sat 10am-4:30pm, Sun 12-4:30pm). The National Marine Fisheries' Aquarium (Mon-Fri 11am-4pm), the first in the U.S., is fraying around the edges but still impressive with 16 tanks and a new seal pool. Bike the four-mile Shining Sea bike path to Falmouth - with a stop at Nobska Light, or take the WHOOSH to Falmouth Center.

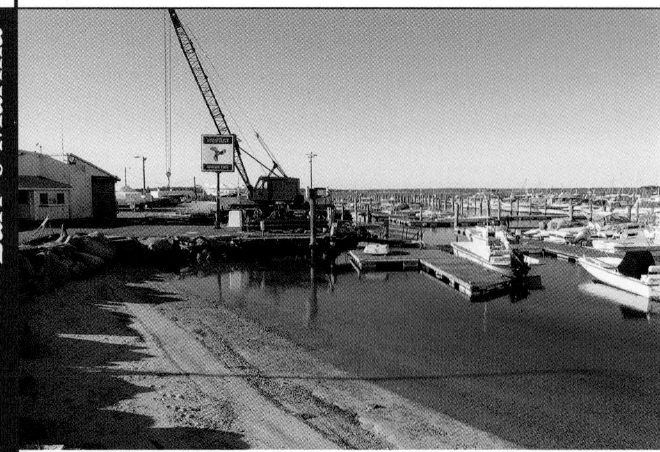

Earl's Marina

56 Goulart Memorial Drive; Fairhaven, MA 02719

Tel: (508) 993-8600 **VHF: Monitor** Ch. 18 **Talk** n/a
Fax: n/a **Alternate Tel:** n/a
Email: James@earlsmarina.com **Web:** www.earlsmarina.com
Nearest Town: Fairhaven *(6 mi.)* **Tourist Info:** (508) 999-5231

Navigational Information

Lat: 41°35.801' **Long:** 070°50.591' **Tide:** 3 ft. **Current:** n/a **Chart:** 13230
Rep. Depths (*MLW*): Entry 8 ft. **Fuel Dock** 6 ft. **Max Slip/Moor** 10 ft./10 ft.
Access: North and west of West Island

Marina Facilities *(In Season/Off Season)*

Fuel: Gasoline, Diesel
Slips: 115 Total, 8 Transient **Max LOA:** 50 ft. **Max Beam:** n/a
Rate *(per ft.)*: **Day** $1.50* **Week** n/a **Month** n/a
Power: 30 amp Incl., **50 amp** n/a, **100 amp** n/a, **200 amp** n/a
Cable TV: No **Dockside Phone:** No
Dock Type: Floating, Long Fingers, Alongside, Wood
Moorings: 70 Total, 10 Transient **Launch:** No, Dinghy Dock
Rate: Day 1.50/ft **Week** n/a **Month** n/a
Heads: 4 Toilet(s), 4 Shower(s)
Internet: No **Laundry:** None
Pump-Out: OnSite, Self Service **Fee:** Free **Closed Heads:** Yes

Marina Operations

Owner/Manager: Dave Herbert **Dockmaster:** Same
In-Season: Apr-Oct, 8am-5pm **Off-Season:** Nov-Mar, Closed
After-Hours Arrival: Call to inquire
Reservations: No **Credit Cards:** Visa/MC, Amex
Discounts: None
Pets: Welcome **Handicap Access:** No

Marina Services and Boat Supplies

Services - Security **Communication -** FedEx, UPS, Express Mail
Supplies - OnSite: Ice *(Block, Cube)*

Boatyard Services

OnSite: Crane, Hydraulic Trailer, Launching Ramp, Engine mechanic *(gas, diesel)*, Electrical Repairs, Electronics Repairs, Hull Repairs, Brightwork
Yard Rates: $85, Haul & Launch $8-10/ft. **Storage:** On-Land $21/ft.

Restaurants and Accommodations

OnSite: Snack Bar *(Down the Hatch 993-3434, cash only)* **OnCall:** Pizzeria *(Yiayia's 990-1919)* **3+ mi:** Restaurant *(Riccardi's 996-4100, 4 mi., L&D $4-14, Kids' $3-5)*, *(Sivalai Thai 999-2527, 3.5 mi., L&D)*, *(Peking Palace 990-8660, L $8-9, D $11-12, 4.5 mi., Kids' $1)*, *(99 992-9951, 4 mi., Brunch & D$8-14, Kids' $4-6)*, *(Pasta House 993-9913, L $7-14, D $8-26, 5 mi.)*, Motel *(Hampton Inn 990-8500, $100-149, 4.5 mi.)*, Hotel *(Holiday Inn Express 997-1281, $89-139, 6 mi.)*, Inn/B&B *(Polish Manor 774-206-6143, $85, 5.5 mi.)*

Recreation and Entertainment

OnSite: Picnic Area, Grills **Near:** Park *(Hoppy's Landing)* **1-3 mi:** Beach *(West Island)*, Galleries *(Arthur Moniz 992-6050)* **3+ mi:** Golf Course *(Reservation G.C. 758-3792, 7.5 mi.)*, Party Boat *(Capt Leroy 992-8907, 6 mi)*, Museum *(New Bedford Whaling 997-0046 $10/6; NB Art 961-3072 $3/5, 7.5 mi.)*, Cultural Attract *(Zeiterion Theatre 997-5664, 7.5 mi)*

Provisioning and General Services

3+ mi: Convenience Store *(Fairhaven 997-6777, 3.5 mi.)*, Supermarket *(Shaw's 993-9996, 4.5 mi.)*, Wine/Beer *(Cardoza's 992-4477, 4 mi.)*, Liquor Store *(Little Bay 997-2967, 4 mi.)*, Farmers' Market *(Sun 1-4pm, Fairhaven High School, 4 mi.)*, Bank/ATM *(Webster, 4.5 mi)*, Catholic Church *(5.5 mi)*, Protestant Church *(5 mi)*, Beauty Salon *(Jan's 996-2551, 3.5 mi)*, Pharmacy *(Walgreens 993-7498, 4.5 mi)*, Hardware Store *(Fairhaven Lumber 993-2611, 5 mi.)*

Transportation

OnCall: Rental Car *(Enterprise 999-9400)*, Taxi *(Checker 999-9994)*, Airport Limo *(Just in Time 961-2434)* **Airport:** New Bedford 979-1410 *(10 mi.)*

Medical Services

911 Service **OnCall:** Veterinarian *(Kindred Spirits Mobile 264-1238)*, Ambulance **1-3 mi:** Holistic Services *(Accupointe 991-5911; Bayshore Massage 979-5587)* **3+ mi:** Doctor *(Marvell 992-5546, 4.5 mi.)*, Dentist *(Camacho 994-2255, 5 mi.)*, Chiropractor *(Gateway 999-4400, 4.5 mi.)*
Hospital: St. Luke's 997-1515 *(8.5 mi.)*

PHOTOS ON DVD: 18

Setting -- On Long Island tucked into Nasketucket Bay, two long docks berthing 115 boats look across to the northwest shore of West Island. The docks are protected by homemade wave attenuators - tires stacked on pilings. The popular Down the Hatch casual outdoor beach bar along with older sheds give the place a Carribbean look and feel. A causeway connects the island to West Island and the State Reservation and to the Sconicut Neck mainland.

Marina Notes -- *Slips $30 min., Moorings $25 min. Family owned & operated since 1958 - 3rd generation at the helm. Marina has the necessities (fuel, mechanics, crane - along with most key yard services), hydraulic trailer for haul-out, committed staff, a very protected location but little else. No provisions or stores are nearby. 70 moorings, no launch. Thin water and remote - but fun. Bathhouse: Quite nice, prefabricated, mounted on a construction trailer - glass shower doors. Note: Need to motor around West Island to reach the marina. Anchoring permitted; use town float - walk twenty feet across the causeway.

Notable -- Down the Hatch features light deli food and music all the time - with live entertainment on the week-ends. Once the weekend live music stops, the isolated location promises quiet at night. West Island is a major sailboarding spot, with stiff wind and flat water. The 338-acre West Island State Reservation is an Audobon "A" rated bird habitat, home to more than 35 rare and common species (and to deer ticks, too, beware!). Marked hiking trails criss-cross the "backside" of the island passing salt marshes, ponds, mud flats, rocky headlands, hardwood forests, sandy beaches - and several active weather stations streaming video. Hoppy's Landing, south of the causeway, is home to a new state pier, gangway, float and boat ramp.

Navigational Information
Lat: 41°37.782' **Long:** 070°54.229' **Tide:** 4 ft. **Current:** n/a **Chart:** 13230
Rep. Depths (*MLW*): **Entry** 23 ft. **Fuel Dock** 17 ft. **Max Slip/Moor** 15 ft./-
Access: Buzzards Bay to Acushnet River, through hurricane barrier

Marina Facilities *(In Season/Off Season)*
Fuel: *ValvTect* - Gasoline, Diesel, High-Speed Pumps
Slips: 165 Total, 20 Transient **Max LOA:** 150 ft. **Max Beam:** n/a
Rate *(per ft.)*: **Day** $3.25/$2.75 **Week** $21 **Month** $82.50
Power: 30 amp $10.50, **50 amp** $18.40, **100 amp** $52.50, **200 amp** n/a
Cable TV: No **Dockside Phone:** No
Dock Type: Fixed, Floating, Long Fingers, Alongside, Concrete, Wood
Moorings: 0 Total, 0 Transient **Launch:** n/a, Dinghy Dock
Rate: Day n/a **Week** n/a **Month** n/a
Heads: 4 Toilet(s), 4 Shower(s), Book Exchange
Internet: Yes *(Wi-Fi, Free)* **Laundry:** 1 Washer(s), 1 Dryer(s)
Pump-Out: OnCall, Full Service, 1 Port **Fee:** Free **Closed Heads:** Yes

Marina Operations
Owner/Manager: Kevin McLauqhlin **Dockmaster:** Fred Stenquist
In-Season: May-Oct, 7:30am-7pm **Off-Season:** Nov-Apr, 7:30am-4pm
After-Hours Arrival: Pull alongside Valvtect fuel dock
Reservations: Yes, Preferred **Credit Cards:** Visa/MC, Dscvr
Discounts: None
Pets: Welcome, Dog Walk Area **Handicap Access:** Yes, Heads, Docks

Fairhaven Shipyard & Marina

50 Fort Street; Fairhaven, MA 02719

Tel: (508) 999-1600 **VHF: Monitor** Ch. 9 **Talk** Ch. 10
Fax: (508) 999-1650 **Alternate Tel:** n/a
Email: fred@fairhavenshipyard.com **Web:** www.fairhavenshipyard.com
Nearest Town: New Bedford *(3 mi.)* **Tourist Info:** (508) 970-4085

14. MA - BUZZARDS BAY

Fairhaven Shipyard & Marina

Marina Services and Boat Supplies
Services - Docking Assistance, Boaters' Lounge, Security *(24 Hrs., Watchmen)*, Trash Pick-Up, Dock Carts, 3 Phase **Communication -** Pay Phone, FedEx, UPS **Supplies - OnSite:** Ice *(Block, Cube)*, Ships' Store **Under 1 mi:** Bait/Tackle *(Fairhaven Bait 996-8682)* **1-3 mi:** West Marine *(994-1122)*, Propane *(Sea Fuels 992-2323)*

Boatyard Services
OnSite: Travelift *(330T, 120T & 35T)*, Railway *(4 to 1000T)*, Forklift, Crane, Engine mechanic *(gas, diesel)*, Electrical Repairs, Electronic Sales, Hull Repairs, Rigger, Sail Loft, Bottom Cleaning, Brightwork, Air Conditioning, Compound, Wash & Wax, Propeller Repairs, Woodworking, Metal Fabrication, Painting, Awlgrip, Total Refits **Member:** ABBRA, ABYC **Yard Rates:** $85-$87.50/hr., Haul & Launch $9-17/ft., Power Wash $70/hr. **Storage:** On-Land Inside $8.50/sq.ft., Outside $45/ft.

Restaurants and Accommodations
Under 1 mi: Restaurant *(Margarets 992-9942, B $3-5, L $6-10, D $14-20, BYO)*, *(Elizabeth's 993-1712, L $8-14, D $12-25)*, *(Pumpernickel's 990-2026, D $9-21)*, *(Hot Rod Grille 858-5503, B&L)*, Pizzeria *(Minerva 997-5120)*, Hotel *(Seaport Inn & Marina 997-1281, $89-139, docks)*, Inn/B&B *(Polish Manor 206-6143, $85)*, *(Delano Homestead 992-5552, $100-110)* **1-3 mi:** Restaurant *(Waterfront Grill 997-7010, D $14-19, Kids' $6, Sun Br. $8-17)*, *(99 Restaurant L $7, D $11-20)*, *(Riccardis 996-4100, L&D $4-14)*

Recreation and Entertainment
OnSite: Picnic Area, Grills **Near:** Fishing Charter *(Bayside 525-5071)* **Under 1 mi:** Beach *(Ft Phoenix)*, Park *(Cushman; Fort Phoenix; Dike)*, Sightseeing *(Visitors' Center Historic Walking Tours 979-4085)* **1-3 mi:** Dive Shop *(Bob's 992-2662)*, Fitness Center *(Lite Weights 858-5878)*, Party Boat *(Capt Leroy 992-8907)*, Museum *(Whaling Museum 997-0046 $10/6; New Bedford Art 961-3072)*, Tours *(NB Harbor 984-4979)*, Cultural Attract *(Zeiterion 997-5664 & Festival Theaters 991-5212)* **3+ mi:** Golf Course *(New Bedford 996-9393, 5 mi.)*, Movie Theater *(Flagship 985-3000, 4.5 mi)*

Provisioning and General Services
Under 1 mi: Liquor Store *(Moriarty 984-0490)*, Bank/ATM, Post Office, Catholic Church, Protestant Church, Library *(992-5342)*, Beauty Salon *(Julie's 993-4485)* **1-3 mi:** Supermarket *(Shaw's 993-9996)*, Wine/Beer *(Cardoza's 992-4477)*, Farmers' Market *(Thu 2-7pm, Wings Court; Sat 9am-1pm, Clasky Common)*, Synagogue, Dry Cleaners, Laundry, Pharmacy *(Fairhaven 997-0006)*, Hardware Store *(Rite Aid 999-2920)*, Department Store *(Fairhaven Mall, WalMart)*

Transportation
OnSite: Bikes **OnCall:** Water Taxi *(Whaling City 984-4979)*, Rental Car *(Enterprise 999-9400)*, Taxi *(Yellow 999-5213)* **Under 1 mi:** Local Bus *(SRTA - New Bedford or Fairhaven Mall)* **1-3 mi:** InterCity Bus *(American Eagle to Boston; Bonanza, to Providence, NYC)*, Ferry Service *(Cuttyhunk & Martha's Vineyard)* **Airport:** TF Green/New Bedford *(30 mi./7.5 mi.)*

Medical Services
911 Service **Under 1 mi:** Dentist *(Sistare 999-4683)*, Chiropractor *(Baron 997-4302)*, Holistic Services *(Blue Lotus 287-0864 massage)* **1-3 mi:** Doctor *(Landry 992-5546)*, Veterinarian *(New England 996-6700)* **Hospital:** St. Luke's 997-1515 *(3.5 mi.)*

Setting -- Inside New Bedford's Hurricane Barrier, large steel fishing vessels rub shoulders with pleasure yachts at the first marine complex to starboard. A marina and serious shipyard blend into an attractive facility where a 440-ton travelift looms over carefully tended patches of grass and abundant pots of flowers. The massive sheds to the north, formerly D.N. Kelley, expand the operation to a total 16 acres. Views are across to New Bedford's commercial waterfront.

Marina Notes -- Estab. 1879. Family operation. Fixed pier dockage to 200 ft. LOA, concrete floats to 120 ft., 18 ft. depth. Includes DN Kelley - now "North Yard." Gated access. Superyacht focus & accommodation. Yachtsman's Haven lounge with snacks & covered deck. Largest travelift in U.S. at 440 tons, plus 300-ton, 100-ton & 35-ton for smaller jobs & 4 railways to 1000 tons. 100amp power, 1 & 3-phase ($105). Fuel dock 7:30am-7pm. 24-hr. emergency haul-out & repair. Sandblasting, spray painting, authorized Awlgrip applicator. Crane Service, spars to 150 ft. Bathhouse: Modern, tiled & cinderblock showers.

Notable -- Many boaters will find a close-up view of this massive shipyard operation quite fascinating. Outside the gates lies an historic town with magnificent European-style public buildings. From 1885-1906, Standard Oil tycoon Henry Huttleson Rogers gifted many public buildings to Fairhaven - most considered true architectural gems. Join a free walking tour (Tue & Thu 10am) or pick up a map of either the historic district or the 3.5-mile Phoenix bike trail at the Visitors Center (43 Center St.). Flat topography makes for an easy walk or bike ride. About a half-mile away are several good restaurants, an ice cream shack, and Fort Phoenix State Beach & Historical Park. The first naval battle of the American revolution was fought in Fairhaven; the fort was erected shortly thereafter.

PHOTOS ON DVD: 23

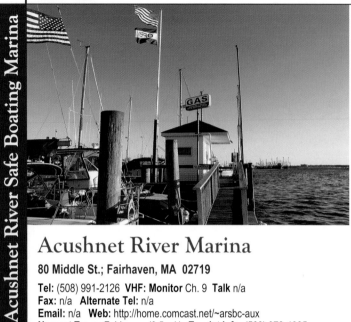

Acushnet River Marina

80 Middle St.; Fairhaven, MA 02719

Tel: (508) 991-2126 **VHF: Monitor** Ch. 9 **Talk** n/a
Fax: n/a **Alternate Tel:** n/a
Email: n/a **Web:** http://home.comcast.net/~arsbc-aux
Nearest Town: Fairhaven *(0.5 mi.)* **Tourist Info:** (508) 979-4085

Navigational Information
Lat: 41°38.366' **Long:** 070°54.547' **Tide:** 3 ft. **Current:** 1 kt **Chart:** 13230
Rep. Depths (*MLW*): Entry 23 ft. **Fuel Dock** 15 ft. **Max Slip/Moor** 16 ft./-
Access: Buzzards Bay to Acushnet River, through hurricane barrier

Marina Facilities *(In Season/Off Season)*
Fuel: Gasoline
Slips: 150 Total, 5 Transient **Max LOA:** 60 ft. **Max Beam:** 15 ft.
Rate *(per ft.)*: **Day** $1.00 **Week** n/a **Month** n/a
Power: 30 amp Inc., **50 amp** n/a, **100 amp** n/a, **200 amp** n/a
Cable TV: No **Dockside Phone:** No
Dock Type: Floating, Long Fingers, Wood
Moorings: 0 Total, 0 Transient **Launch:** No
Rate: Day n/a **Week** n/a **Month** n/a
Heads: 4 Toilet(s), 4 Shower(s)
Internet: No **Laundry:** None
Pump-Out: OnSite, Self Service **Fee:** Free **Closed Heads:** Yes

Marina Operations
Owner/Manager: Lee J. Baumgartner **Dockmaster:** Joe Alcobia
In-Season: May-Oct, 7am-4pm **Off-Season:** Nov-Apr, Closed
After-Hours Arrival: Call ahead
Reservations: No **Credit Cards:** Visa/MC, Dscvr
Discounts: None
Pets: Welcome **Handicap Access:** No

Marina Services and Boat Supplies
Services - Docking Assistance, Boaters' Lounge **Communication -** FedEx, UPS **Supplies - OnSite:** Ice *(Block, Cube)* **Near:** Ice *(Shaved)*, West Marine *(992-8484)*, Bait/Tackle *(Fairhaven Bait 996-8682)* **1-3 mi:** Propane *(SeaFuels 992-2323)*

Boatyard Services
OnCall: Engine mechanic *(gas, diesel)*, Electrical Repairs **Nearest Yard:** Fairhaven Shipyard (508) 999-1600

Restaurants and Accommodations
Near: Restaurant *(Wah May 992-8668)*, *(Skipper's Bar & Grille 999-1112)*, Pizzeria *(Minerva 997-5120)*, Hotel *(Seaport Inn & Marina 997-1281, $89-139, Docks)* **Under 1 mi:** Restaurant *(Elizabeth's 993-1712, L $8-14, D $10-24)*, *(Margaret's 992-9942, B $3-5, L $6-10, D $10-24, BYO, Local Fave)*, *(Waterfront Grill 997-7010, D $14-19, Kids')*, *(Freestone's 993-7477, D 10-24)*, *(Pumpernickel's 990-2026, D $9-21)*, Lite Fare *(Hot Rod Grille 858-5503, B & L)*, Pizzeria *(Palace 984-1500)*, Motel *(Huttleston 997-7655)*, Inn/B&B *(Delano Homestead 992-5552, $100-150)*, *(Polish Manor 774-206-6143, $85)* **1-3 mi:** Restaurant *(Candleworks 997-1294, L $5-15, D $12-26)*, *(Ninety-Nine 992-9951, D $9-14, Kids' $4-6)*, *(Riccardi's 996-4100, L&D $4-14)*, Fast Food *(BK, McD's, Wendys)*

Recreation and Entertainment
Near: Tennis Courts *(Cushman)*, Park *(Cushman)*, Sightseeing *(Fairhaven Historic District; Old Stone Schoolhouse)* **Under 1 mi:** Beach *(Ft. Phoenix - 1.2 mi.)*, Dive Shop *(Bob's 992-2662)*, Fishing Charter *(Bayside 525-5071)*, Party Boat *(Capt. Leroy's 992-8907 $65)*, Video Rental *(Redbox)*, Cultural Attract *(Zeiterion 994-2900 & N.B Fest Theaters 991-5212)* **1-3 mi:** Fitness Center *(Lite Weights 858-5878)*, Bowling *(Wonder 993-1746)*, Museum *(N.B. Whaling Museum 997-0046; N.B. Art 961-3072)* **3+ mi:** Golf Course *(New Bedford 993-9393, 4 mi.)*, Movie Theater *(Flagship 985-3000, 3.5 mi.)*

Provisioning and General Services
Near: Convenience Store *(Cumberland Farms 990-9779)*, Liquor Store *(Moriarty 984-0490)* **Under 1 mi:** Wine/Beer *(Douglas 997-0311)*, Bakery *(Homlyke 996-2336)*, Fishmonger *(Kyler's 984-5150)*, Bank/ATM, Post Office, Catholic Church, Protestant Church, Library *(Millicent 992-5342)*, Beauty Salon *(Carol's 997-1412)*, Dry Cleaners *(Delken 996-9277)*, Laundry, Pharmacy *(CVS 999-0790)*, Hardware Store *(Fairhaven 997-3307)*, Florist *(Darling's 993-4020)*, Retail Shops *(Fairhaven Mall, WalMart)* **1-3 mi:** Supermarket *(Shaw's 993-9996)*, Gourmet Shop *(Wainer 800 423-8383)*, Synagogue

Transportation
OnCall: Water Taxi *(Whaling City 984-4979)*, Rental Car *(Enterprise 994-8289)*, Taxi *(Yellow 993-5213)*, Airport Limo *(Just In Time 961-2434)* **Near:** Local Bus *(SRTA - New Bedford or Fairhaven Mall)* **1-3 mi:** InterCity Bus *(American Eagle to Boston; Bonanza to Providence & NY)*, Ferry Service *(Cuttyhunk & M.V.)* **Airport:** TF Green/New Bedford *(30 mi./7 mi.)*

Medical Services
911 Service **Under 1 mi:** Dentist *(Sistare 999-4683)*, Chiropractor *(Fairhaven 997-3600)*, Holistic Services *(Blue Lotus Massage 287-0864)*, Veterinarian *(New England 996-6700)* **1-3 mi:** Doctor *(Metromedic Walk-In 997-2900)* **Hospital:** St. Luke's 997-1515 *(2.5 mi.)*

PHOTOS ON DVD: 20

Setting -- Upriver to starboard, past the two large Fairhaven Shipyard facilities, this Coast Guard Auxiliary marina is marked by a big "Gas" sign above a small white dockhouse and a tree of stern-to slips branching off from a single main pier. Views are of the Route 6 bridge and New Bedford commercial shore.

Marina Notes -- Home to USCG Auxillary Flotilla 1N65, managed independently by ARSBC, Inc. No mechanical services or parts -- just stern-to docks (no finger piers!), good gas prices, and friendly, helpful, boating savvy seasonals - just ask. Camaraderie translates into good security. Dry storage in winter. Rafting allowed where practical. Diesel at N.B. fishermen's coop or at Fairhaven Shipyard. Bathhouse: Basic, formica in C.G. Aux headquarters. Note: Launch service & moorings available from Whaling City, Capt. Jeff Pontiff 984-4979. Dockage also next door at Seaport Inn & Marina (former Holiday Inn) for boats to 70 ft.

Notable -- Flotilla 1N65 of the Coast Guard Auxillary maintains the marina and clubhouse for its members and guests - and to educate the public about boating; fellow Coast Guard Auxiliary members will be greeted warmly. Their onsite bar is open on weekends. Visible from the docks, the architecturally significant public buildings poke above the Fairhaven skyline. Native Henry Huttleston Rogers made millions with Standard Oil and the Virginia Railway and gave back to his hometown by erecting magnificent public buildings (1890-1908) influenced by European architecture. Among his gifts were a luxurious high school, Town Hall, Taber Masonic lodge, Unitarian Church, Tabitha Inn, Millicent Library, and a "modern" water-and-sewer system - all in use today. Take the free Visitor's Center tour (979-4085) or walk the area with brochure in hand. Busy, commercial Huttleston Avenue (aka Route 6) is conveniently just two blocks.

Navigational Information

Lat: 41°38.379' **Long:** 070°54.792' **Tide:** 3 ft. **Current:** 1.5 kt. **Chart:** 13230
Rep. Depths (*MLW*): Entry 9 ft. **Fuel Dock** n/a **Max Slip/Moor** 11 ft./-
Access: Buzzards Bay to New Bedford Harbor to Pope's Island

Marina Facilities *(In Season/Off Season)*

Fuel: No
Slips: 198 Total, 6 Transient **Max LOA:** 150 ft. **Max Beam:** 40 ft.
Rate *(per ft.)*: **Day** $3.25/Inq. **Week** n/a **Month** n/a
Power: 30 amp Incl., **50 amp** Incl., **100 amp** n/a, **200 amp** n/a
Cable TV: No **Dockside Phone:** No
Dock Type: Fixed, Floating, Long Fingers, Alongside, Concrete, Wood
Moorings: 0 Total, 0 Transient **Launch:** No
Rate: Day n/a **Week** n/a **Month** n/a
Heads: 8 Toilet(s), 8 Shower(s), Book Exchange
Internet: No **Laundry:** 4 Washer(s), 4 Dryer(s)
Pump-Out: OnSite, Full Service, 1 Central **Fee:** Free **Closed Heads:** Yes

Marina Operations

Owner/Manager: Martin Manley **Dockmaster:** 3 seasonal
In-Season: Apr-Oct, 8am-7pm **Off-Season:** Nov-Mar, Closed
After-Hours Arrival: VHF Channel 74 or 9
Reservations: Yes, Required **Credit Cards:** Visa/MC, Dscvr, Amex
Discounts: None
Pets: Welcome, Dog Walk Area **Handicap Access:** Yes, Heads, Docks

Pope's Island Marina

102 Pope's Island; New Bedford, MA 02740

Tel: (508) 979-1456 **VHF: Monitor** Ch. 9 **Talk** Ch. 74
Fax: (508) 979-1469 **Alternate Tel:** (508) 979-1469
Email: dyuille@newbedford-ma.gov **Web:** see marina notes
Nearest Town: Fairhaven *(0.1 mi.)* **Tourist Info:** (508) 997-1250

Marina Services and Boat Supplies

Services - Docking Assistance, Security *(24 Hrs., Gated)*, Trash Pick-Up, Dock Carts **Communication -** Pay Phone, FedEx, UPS **Supplies - OnSite:** Ice *(Block, Cube)* **Near:** West Marine *(994-1122)* **1-3 mi:** Bait/Tackle *(Fairhaven 996-8682)*, Propane *(Sea Fuels 992-2323)*

Boatyard Services

OnCall: Engine mechanic *(gas, diesel)*, Divers, Bottom Cleaning, Compound, Wash & Wax, Interior Cleaning, Upholstery **Nearest Yard:** Fairhaven Shipyard (508) 999-1600

Restaurants and Accommodations

Near: Fast Food *(Dunkin' Donuts)*, Lite Fare *(Skippers Lounge 999-1112)*, Hotel *(Seaport Inn & Marina 997-1281, $89-139)* **Under 1 mi:** Restaurant *(Candleworks 997-1294, L $5-15, D $12-26)*, *(Elizabeth's 993-1712, L $8-14, D $10-24)*, *(Pumpernickels 990-2026, L&D $9-12)*, *(Freestone's City 993-7477, L & D $8-23)*, *(Margaret's 992-9942, B $3-8, L $6-10, D $12-25, BYO)*, *(Spicy Lime 992-3330, L&D $7-16)*, Pizzeria *(Minerva's 997-5120)*, *(Sarducci's 990-7827)*, Inn/B&B *(Delano 992-5552, $100-150)*, *(Polish Manor 774-206-6143, $85)* **1-3 mi:** Restaurant *(Catwalk 994-3355, L&D $9-16)*

Recreation and Entertainment

OnSite: Picnic Area, Playground **Near:** Dive Shop *(Bob's 992-2662)*, Hike/Bike Trails *(Phoenix)*, Party Boat *(Capt. LeRoy 992-8907)* **Under 1 mi:** Pool *(N.B. "Y" 997-0734 $10/6)*, Tennis Courts *(Cushman Park)*, Fitness Center *("Y")*, Park *(N.B. Whaling Nat'l Historical, Free)*, Museum *(N.B. Whaling 997-0046 $10/6; Seamen's Bethel; N.B. Art 961-3072 $5/Free)*, Cultural Attract *(Zeiterion Theaters 994-2900)*, Sightseeing *(Oceanarium 994-5400 $7.50/5.50)* **1-3 mi:** Beach *(Ft Phoenix)*, Bowling *(Wonder 993-1746)*, Fishing Charter *(Bayside 525-5071)* **3+ mi:** Golf Course *(Whaling City 996-9393, 3.5 mi.)*, Movie Theater *(Flagship 985-3000, 3.5 mi.)*

Provisioning and General Services

Near: Beauty Salon *(Wash House 992-7155)*, Newsstand *(NewsBreak)*, Hardware Store *(Fairhaven 997-3307)*, Florist *(Darling's 993-4020)* **Under 1 mi:** Convenience Store *(Fish Is. 991-3474)*, Liquor Store *(Moriarty 984-0490)*, Bakery *(Homlyke 996-2336)*, Farmers' Market *(Thu 2-7pm, Wings Court; Sat 9am-1pm, Clasky Common)*, Fishmonger *(Blue Waters 997-9651)*, Bank/ATM, Post Office, Catholic Church, Protestant Church, Library *(992-5342)*, Dry Cleaners *(Bush 992-7622)*, Laundry *(Super 999-4770)*, Pharmacy *(Walgreens 984-4434)* **1-3 mi:** Supermarket *(Shaw's 993-9996)*, Gourmet Shop *(Wainer 999-6408)*, Health Food *(Down to Earth)*, Wine/Beer *(Douglas 997-0311)*, Synagogue, Retail Shops *(Fairhaven Mall)*

Transportation

OnCall: Rental Car *(Avis 999-6900, Enterprise 994-8289)*, Taxi *(Checker 999-4545; Yellow 999-5213)* **Near:** Water Taxi *(Whaling City 984-4979)*, Local Bus *(SRTA to Fairhaven Mall)* **Under 1 mi:** InterCity Bus *(Bonanza 990-3366, American Eagle 993-5040)* **1-3 mi:** Ferry Service *(Marthas Vineyard, Cuttyhunk)* **Airport:** New Bedford/TF Green *(4 mi./28mi.)*

Medical Services

911 Service **Under 1 mi:** Doctor *(Greater New Bedford Med 992-6553)*, Dentist *(Dehni 996-3131)*, Chiropractor *(Fairhaven 997-3600)*, Holistic Services *(Blue Lotus 287-0864)*, Veterinarian *(New England 996-6700)*
Hospital: St. Luke's 979-1515 *(2 mi.)*

Setting -- Motor dead ahead upriver to the large network of docks, smack in the middle of the river, on Pope Island. Flanked by two bridges, three sets of parallel docks - including 350 ft. alongside - are tied to the island by a long boardwalk that leads right through the two-story shingled harbormaster's office. Expanses of lawn with views of the busy harbor and hurricane barrier host picnic tables and benches; commercial Route 6 is out the back door.

Marina Notes -- URL: www.ci.new-bedford.ma.us/portofnewbedford/gettingaround/popesisland.html. Opened 1993. Operated by New Bedford's Harbor Development Comm. Good security includes a 24-hr. electronic gate & single entrance that requires passing the dockmaster's office. Conference Room. Onsite pump-out plus pump-out boat. West Marine & True Value Hardware across Rte. 6. Bathhouse: Fully tiled, spacious group heads with fresh shower curtains. Laundry. Note: Moorings from N.B. Whaling City water taxi, Capt. Jeff Pontiff 984-4979. More dockage at Seaport Inn & Marina.

Notable -- It's less than a mile walk to the 34-acre New Bedford Whaling Nat'l. Historical Park (or take the free shuttle from Rte 6th & 10 just over the bridge). The Park's Visitors' Center (33 William St. 9am-5pm) has maps and brochures of the 70 whaling-related structures within the 13-block area. The Whaling Museum is a half block - climb aboard the half-scale, fully-rigged 89 ft. whaling bark "Lagoda." The adjacent 1832 Seamen's Bethel is immortalized in Herman Melville's Moby Dick as the "Whaleman's Chapel." For fans, there's also a Moby Dick Trail. Stop at the N.B. Visitors Center on the harbor front, the Oceanarium in the former power plant, and the free Summer Nights Concerts in Whaling Park. It's also a hard-working fishing town with the occasional raucous crowd.

PHOTOS ON DVD: 17

New Bedford Yacht Club

P.O. Box P4; 208 Elm Street; South Dartmouth, MA 02748

Tel: (508) 997-0762 **VHF: Monitor** Ch. 68 **Talk** n/a
Fax: (508) 992-1299 **Alternate Tel:** n/a
Email: info@nbyc.com **Web:** www.nbyc.com
Nearest Town: Dartmouth *(0.1 mi.)* **Tourist Info:** (508) 999-5231

Navigational Information
Lat: 41°35.098' **Long:** 070°56.622' **Tide:** 3.5 ft. **Current:** 1 kt. **Chart:** 13229
Rep. Depths (*MLW*): Entry 18 ft. **Fuel Dock** 9 ft. **Max Slip/Moor** 9 ft./18 ft.
Access: North of Dumpling Rocks to Apponagansett Bay to R12

Marina Facilities *(In Season/Off Season)*
Fuel: *Texaco* - Gasoline, Diesel
Slips: 100 Total, 3 Transient **Max LOA:** 60 ft. **Max Beam:** n/a
Rate *(per ft.)*: **Day** $3.25 **Week** n/a **Month** n/a
Power: 30 amp Incl, **50 amp** n/a, **100 amp** n/a, **200 amp** n/a
Cable TV: No **Dockside Phone:** No
Dock Type: Fixed, Floating, Long Fingers, Alongside, Wood
Moorings: 100 Total, 10 Transient **Launch:** Yes (Inc.), Dinghy Dock
Rate: Day $50 **Week** n/a **Month** n/a
Heads: 6 Toilet(s), 4 Shower(s) *(dressing rooms)*, Hair Dryers
Internet: Yes *(Wi-Fi, Free)* **Laundry:** None
Pump-Out: OnCall *(Ch.9, 999-0759)*, Full Service **Fee:** Free **Closed Heads:**

Marina Operations
Owner/Manager: Marilyn P. Sams **Dockmaster:** Joe Cosme
In-Season: Jun 15-LabDay, 8am-10pm **Off-Season:** LabDay-Sep, 8am-7pm
After-Hours Arrival: Mid Jun-LabDay open 'til 10pm
Reservations: No **Credit Cards:** Visa/MC
Discounts: None
Pets: Welcome, Dog Walk Area **Handicap Access:** Yes

Marina Services and Boat Supplies
Services - Docking Assistance, Boaters' Lounge, Security *(Overnight)*, Trash Pick-Up, Dock Carts **Communication -** Mail & Package Hold, Fax in/out *($1)*, FedEx, UPS **Supplies - OnSite:** Ice *(Block, Cube)* **Near:** Ships' Store **1-3 mi:** Bait/Tackle *(Uncle Ken's 991-3022)*, Propane *(Boc 997-9457)* **3+ mi:** West Marine *(994-1122, 5 mi.)*

Boatyard Services
OnSite: Launching Ramp **Near:** Travelift, Crane, Hydraulic Trailer, Engine mechanic *(gas, diesel)*, Electrical Repairs, Electronics Repairs, Sail Loft *(Doyle)*. **Nearest Yard:** Cape Yachts (adjacent) (508) 994-4444

Restaurants and Accommodations
OnSite: Restaurant *(The Galley - NBYC Dining Room 997-0762, D $8-22, Wed-Sun)*, Snack Bar *(NBYC Snack Bar L Mon-Fri 11:30am-2pm midJun-midAug)*, Lite Fare *(Earle's Place Lounge)* **Near:** Restaurant *(Black Bass Grille 999-6975, L $6-13, D $12-27, brick oven pizza, too. Inside or out, local fave)*, Snack Bar *(Dockside Ice Cream 996-8799)*, Lite Fare *(Cecily's Café 994-1162, B $6, L $9, D $10-27)* **Under 1 mi:** Restaurant *(Ying's Dynasty 993-3380)*, Lite Fare *(Karen's Cafe 993-5263)*, Pizzeria *(Papa Gino's 997-3334)* **1-3 mi:** Restaurant *(Ma Raffa's 992-8467, L&D $4-12)*, Pizzeria *(Friendly 996-5511)*, Inn/B&B *(Orchard Beach 984-3475, $125-250)* **3+ mi:** Hotel *(Fairfield Inn 774-634-2000, 4 mi.)*, Inn/B&B *(Captain Haskell's 999-3933, $117+, 3.5 mi.)*

Recreation and Entertainment
Near: Playground, Tours *(Natural Resources Trust Walking Tours 991-2289)* **Under 1 mi:** Beach *(Knowles)*, Park *(Apponagansett Point)* **1-3 mi:** Tennis Courts, Golf Course *(Whale City G.C. 996-9393)*, Fitness Center *(Planet Fitness 991-2920)*, Bowling *(Wonder Bowl 993-1746)* **3+ mi:** Horseback Riding *(Old Dartmouth 993-8438, 3.5 mi.)*, Museum *(N.B. Whaling 997-0046 $10/6; Rotch-Jones-Duff House 997-1401 $5/2, 4 mi.)*, Cultural Attract *(Zeiterion Theater 997-5664, 3.5 mi.)*, Sightseeing *(N.B. Whaling Nat'l Historical, Free, 4 mi.)*

Provisioning and General Services
Near: Protestant Church, Laundry *(Cape Yachts next door)*, Florist *(Flora 996-2332)*, Clothing Store *(The Packet 994-0759)* **Under 1 mi:** Convenience Store *(CV Variety 999-4900 - pizza, too; Cumberland Farms 990-9729)*, Bank/ATM, Library *(999-0726)*, Beauty Salon *(Hair Center 997-1414)*, Dry Cleaners *(Delken)* **1-3 mi:** Supermarket *(Stop & Shop 993-1791)*, Delicatessen *(Dartmouth Market 997-0225)*, Wine/Beer *(Douglas 992-3387)*, Liquor Store *(Freitas 997-9602)*, Bakery *(Sunrise 984-7706)*, Fishmonger *(Cape 995-6724 996-6724)*, Post Office, Catholic Church, Pharmacy *(Rite Aid 990-3875)*, Hardware Store *(Benny's 992-8406)*

Transportation
OnCall: Rental Car *(Enterprise 999-9400)*, Taxi *(Checker 999-9994)*, Airport Limo *(EZ Rider 992-3785)* **3+ mi:** Ferry Service *(MV & Cuttyhunk, 4.5 mi.)*
Airport: New Bedford/TF Green *(37 mi./35 mi.)*

Medical Services
911 Service **Near:** Holistic Services *(Kane & Co. Massage 999-9996)* **1-3 mi:** Doctor *(Gravel 961-5184)*, Dentist *(Mercier 994-5278)*, Chiropractor *(Dartmouth 997-5636)* **3+ mi:** Veterinarian *(Buttonwood 996-3159, 3.5 mi.)*
Hospital: St. Luke's 979-1515 *(3 mi.)*

PHOTOS ON DVD: 25

Setting -- Up the Apponagansett River (and not in New Bedford), NBYC's extensive network of docks and large mooring field are to starboard, bounded by marsh. This private, hospitable club boasts a a century-old gracious clubhouse with spectacular views of Padanaram Harbor from its dining room and deck. A large white dockside tent hosts cruise and club events. The charming little village of So. Dartmouth/Padanaram is a couple of blocks' walk.

Marina Notes -- Private club founded in 1877. Welcomes all boaters to docks, moorings, snack bar, lounge and dining room. Launch: 8am-10pm daily mid-June to LabDay, shoulder season shorter hours. Fuel shack for ice - 20-min. tie-up limit enforced. Pump-out: - Dartmouth Harbormaster, Ch.9, 999-0759. 3-day max. stay. Anchoring & limited rafting allowed. In season: Earle's Place cocktail lounge, Tue-Sun 4:30-10pm. Snack Bar Mon-Fri 11:30am- 2pm. The Galley Wed-Sun 5:30-9pm (Reservations req). Bathhouse: Inviting tiled, painted concrete block and teak showers & heads on the south side of the clubhouse. Open 24 hours. Note: No transient facilities at Davis & Tripp. Concordia revitalized as Cape Yachts/South Wharf (with laundry).

Notable -- A very active sailboat cruising and racing club, NBYC hosts the Buzzards Bay Regatta in odd-numbered years. Kids will love exploring in the dink, especially to the ice cream and seafood shack in the park on the opposite shore above the drawbridge. In the village are a couple of restaurants, some unique shops and the Dartmouth Natural Resources Trust, which offers a book of 40 miles of walking trails through its 1,530 acres in 52 Reserves. The 55-acre Lloyd Center for Environmental Studies (990-0505), about 4 miles away, features five walking trails with views out to Buzzards Bay, Mishaum Pt, and the islands.

Navigational Information

Lat: 41°30.801' **Long:** 071°04.618' **Tide:** 3 ft. **Current:** 3 kt. **Chart:** 13218
Rep. Depths (*MLW*): Entry 10 ft. **Fuel Dock** 15 ft. **Max Slip/Moor** 12 ft./10 ft.
Access: Westport Harbor, 1st docks to starboard

Marina Facilities *(In Season/Off Season)*

Fuel: *Texaco* - Gasoline, Diesel
Slips: 178 Total, 5 Transient **Max LOA:** 65 ft. **Max Beam:** 15 ft.
Rate *(per ft.)*: **Day** $4.00/1 **Week** $21/3/50 **Month** $65/10
Power: 30 amp Incl., **50 amp** Incl., **100 amp** n/a, **200 amp** n/a
Cable TV: No **Dockside Phone:** No
Dock Type: Fixed, Short Fingers, Pilings, Wood
Moorings: 218 Total, 20 Transient **Launch:** Yes ($1/pp-1way), Dinghy Dock
Rate: Day $42.50** **Week** $215 **Month** $745
Heads: 5 Toilet(s), 5 Shower(s) *(dressing rooms)*, outside shower
Internet: Yes *(Boaters' Lounge)* **Laundry:** 2 Washer(s), 2 Dryer(s)
Pump-Out: OnSite, OnCall, 1 Central, 1 Port **Fee:** Free **Closed Heads:** Yes

Marina Operations

Owner/Manager: Richard Picard **Dockmaster:** Scott Gifford
In-Season: Jun-LabDay, 7am-5pm* **Off-Season:** LabDay-May, 8am-4pm
After-Hours Arrival: Call ahead
Reservations: Yes, Preferred **Credit Cards:** Visa/MC, Dscvr, Amex, Tex
Discounts: None
Pets: Welcome, Dog Walk Area **Handicap Access:** Yes, Heads, Docks

F. L. Tripp & Sons

PO Box 23; 211 Cherry & Webb Rd.; Westport Point, MA 02791
Tel: (508) 636-4058 **VHF: Monitor** Ch. 9 **Talk** Ch. 8
Fax: (508) 636-4178 **Alternate Tel:** (508) 636-4058
Email: rpicard@fltripp.com **Web:** www.fltripp.com
Nearest Town: Westport *(6 mi.)* **Tourist Info:** (508) 999-5231

Marina Services and Boat Supplies

Services - Docking Assistance, Boaters' Lounge, Security *(8 hrs., Night watch)*, Dock Carts **Communication -** Pay Phone (1), FedEx, UPS, Express Mail **Supplies - OnSite:** Ice *(Block, Cube)*, Ships' Store **Under 1 mi:** Bait/Tackle *(Westport Marine 636-8100 - by dink)* **3+ mi:** Propane *(Southeast 636-2632, 10 mi.)*

Boatyard Services

OnSite: Travelift, Crane *(18T)*, Engine mechanic *(gas, diesel)*, Electrical Repairs, Electronic Sales, Electronics Repairs, Hull Repairs, Rigger, Divers, Bottom Cleaning, Brightwork, Air Conditioning, Refrigeration, Compound, Wash & Wax, Interior Cleaning, Propeller Repairs, Woodworking, Metal Fabrication, Painting, Yacht Broker *(Tripp's Marine Brokerage)* **Near:** Launching Ramp. **Yard Rates:** $85/hr., Haul & Launch $19.60-23/ft. *(blocking incl.)*, Power Wash $4/ft., Bottom Paint $9.75-11.60/ft. **Storage:** In-Water $27/ft., On-Land inside $57.50/ft., Outside $40/ft.

Restaurants and Accommodations

OnSite: Restaurant *(Westport Y.C. Friday Dinner 636-8885, D $8-18)* **Near:** Restaurant *(Back Eddy 636-6500, L $7-15, D $7-26, Mon-Wed 5-10pm, Thu-Sun Noon-10pm)*, Inn/B&B *(Paquachuck 636-4398, $175, 8 rooms, dock, ice, waterside deck)* **3+ mi:** Restaurant *(Bayside Seafood 636-5882, 3.5 mi., B,L&D $10-15)*, *(Marguerite's 636-3040, 6 mi., B,L&D)*

Recreation and Entertainment

OnSite: Beach *(or across to West or Horseneck)*, Picnic Area, Grills *(propane)*, Fishing Charter *(Marsha England)*, Tours *(Westport River Eco Tours 636-3016, Thu & Fri 10am & 1pm $35)* **Near:** Jogging Paths, Hike/Bike Trails, Museum *(Historic Westport Point)*, Sightseeing *(Cherry & Webb Conservation Area's well-marked trails - Westport Watershed Alliance wrwa.com)* **1-3 mi:** Park *(Horseneck Beach Reservation 636-8816)*, Galleries *(Westport Art 636-2114)*, Special Events *(River Day Celebrations Late June)* **3+ mi:** Golf Course *(Acoaxet 636-4730, 9 mi.)*, Horseback Riding *(Driftway Meadows 636-8864, 7 mi.)*

Provisioning and General Services

OnSite: Copies Etc. *(at Tripp's Office)* **Under 1 mi:** Post Office **1-3 mi:** Bakery *(Kamgans Cake-alicious 525-9069; Perry's Bakery 636-8858 - 5 mi.)* **3+ mi:** Convenience Store *(Partners Village Store 636-2572 books, gifts, and deli, 5 mi.)*, Supermarket *(Lee's Supermarket 636-3348, 6 mi.)*, Health Food *(Gooseberry Natural Foods 636-2241, 5 mi.)*, Wine/Beer *(Westport Vineyard 636-3423 Mon-Sat 11am-5pm Tastings $7, Tours Sat 1 & 3pm, 6 mi.)*, Liquor Store *(Old Westport Beer & Wine 636-3892; Just Beer Brewery 636-2288, 5 mi.)*, Green Grocer *(Hilltop Farm 617-851-6319, 5.5 mi.)*, Fishmonger *(Westport Lobster 636-8500, 5 mi.)*, Bank/ATM *(6 mi.)*, Pharmacy *(Westport Apothecary 636-5957, 6 mi.)*, Hardware Store *(Westport Ace 636-8853, 8 mi.)*

Transportation

OnCall: Rental Car *(Enterprise 999-9400)*, Taxi *(Westport 636-6910)*
Airport: New Bedford/TF Green *(18 mi./43 mi.)*

Medical Services

911 Service **3+ mi:** Doctor *(Westport Fam 636-5101, 5 mi.)*, Dentist *(Jusseaume 636-5111, 5 mi.)*, Veterinarian *(Acoaxet 636-8382, 10 mi.)*
Hospital: St. Lukes 979-1515 *(15 mi.)*

Setting -- Directly to starboard, after entering the fast-flowing, tidal Westport River, Tripp's large-shingled sheds back a network of docks that sprawl along the bulkhead. Two picnic areas are dockside, and a lovely boaters' lounge, ships' store and bathhouse occupy a waterfront building. Seaward views are of the mooring field and unspoiled Westport Harbor. Landward are windblown dunes and the three-mile stretch of Horseneck State Beach.

Marina Notes -- *Office 8am-4pm, Boatyard Mon-Fri, 7am-3:30pm Launch MemDay-LabDay Sun-Thurs 8am- 8pm, Fri- Sat 8am-10pm, LabDay-ColDay Mon-Thu 7am 3:30pm, Fr-Sun 8am- 6pm, **Mooring fees - under 33 ft. LOA $190/wk, $530/mo. Most yard services and a well-inventoried ship's store. Boats to 65 ft. LOA dockside, 55 ft. LOA on a mooring - transients mostly at West end, look for small yellow float. Launch $1/pp - also drops off at Back Eddy and village. Boater's lounge with internet & book exchange - next to laundry. Tripp Anglers Boats built here. Pump-out onsite or Westport Harbormaster boat (Ch. 9). Bathhouse: Modern, half-tiled showers. Note: Moorings from Westport Harbormaster 363-1105 or adjacent Westport Yacht Club 636-8885 (recip only).

Notable -- Pretty, flower-bedecked Westport Yacht Club hosts Seafood Fridays open to all, and nearby Back Eddy offers fine dining and a casual raw bar. Walk across the road to spectacular West Beach or further to 2-mile-long Horseneck. Dinghy or launch to the tiny village of Westport Point - anchored by 170-year-old Paquachuck Inn. Explore Westport River, a productive estuarine habitat - the East (Noquochoke) branch's four islands and West (Acoaxet) branch's eight. Westport Watershed Alliance offers weekly kids' programs at Cherry & Webb Beach. Five miles north, on Main Road, find a small gaggle of useful shops.

PHOTOS ON CVD: 25

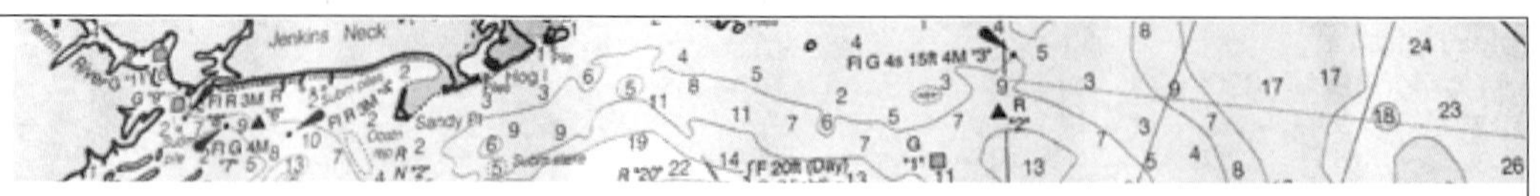

Your Daily Online Boating Magazine

Mad Mariner is a daily boating magazine that offers definitive coverage of topics ranging from diesel mechanics to cooking. But it is also a resource, a searchable archive—thousands of stories—that allows boaters to read and research on demand.

Mad Mariner is the modern equivalent of a dockside chat, where readers can share stories, nurture dreams and get high-quality information—and this dock extends around the globe.

Mad Mariner's staff works hard to present information in lively and engaging new formats, with resources that are not available in the print world.

Boat reviews have real-time pricing. How-to stories have animated graphics. And important topics like marine medicine and electronic charting are given proper treatment—long, in-depth series that give you a full understanding of the subject.

From our weekly video and podcast offerings to daily news updates, we try to do things differently. Check it out for free with a 30-day, no obligation trial.

See more at www.madmariner.com

15. MA – Cape Cod South Shore

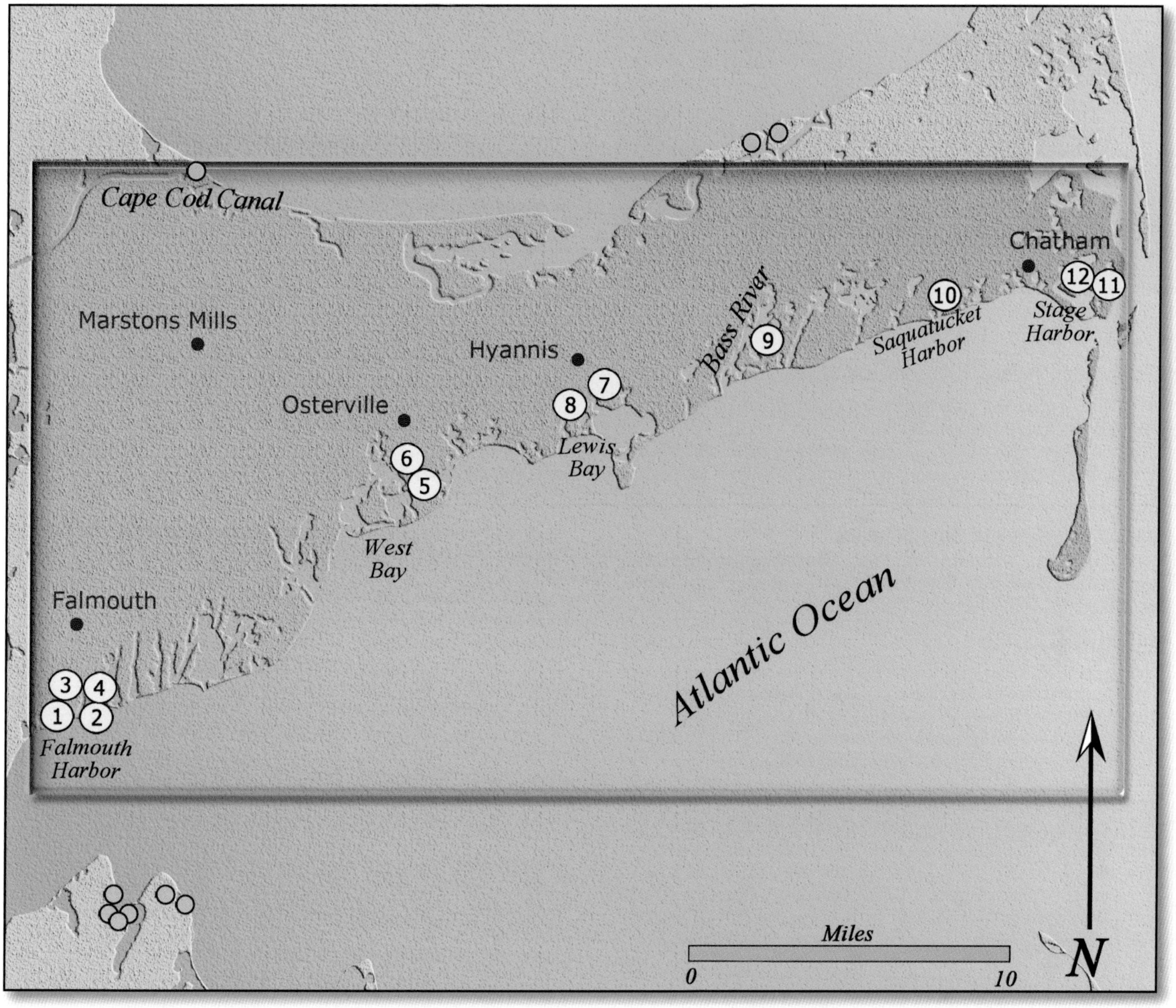

MAP	MARINA	HARBOR	PAGE
1	**Falmouth Marine Yachting Center**	*Falmouth Harbor*	284
2	**MacDougalls' Cape Cod Marine**	*Falmouth Harbor*	285
3	**Falmouth Harbor Town Marina**	*Falmouth Harbor*	286
4	**East Marine**	*Falmouth Harbor*	287
5	**Oyster Harbors Yacht Basin**	*Osterville Crosby Basin*	288
6	**Crosby Yacht Yard**	*Osterville Crosby Basin*	289
7	**Hyannis Marina**	*Hyannis Harbor*	290
8	**Bismore Park Bulkhead**	*Hyannis Harbor*	291
9	**Bass River Marina**	*Bass River*	292
10	**Saquatucket Harbor Marina**	*Saquatucket Harbor*	293
11	**Chatham Harbormaster Moorings**	*Stage Harbor*	294
12	**Stage Harbor Marine**	*Stage Harbor*	295

RATINGS: 1-5 for Marina Facilities & Amenities,  1-2 for Boatyard Services,  1-2 for MegaYacht Facilities,  for Something Special.

SERVICES: for CCM – Certified Clean Marina,  for Pump-Out, for Internet,  for Fuel, for Restaurant,  for Provisioning nearby, for Catamaran-friendly,  for SportFish Charter,  for Pool/Beach, and  for Golf within a mile. *For an explanation of ACC's Ratings, see page 8.*

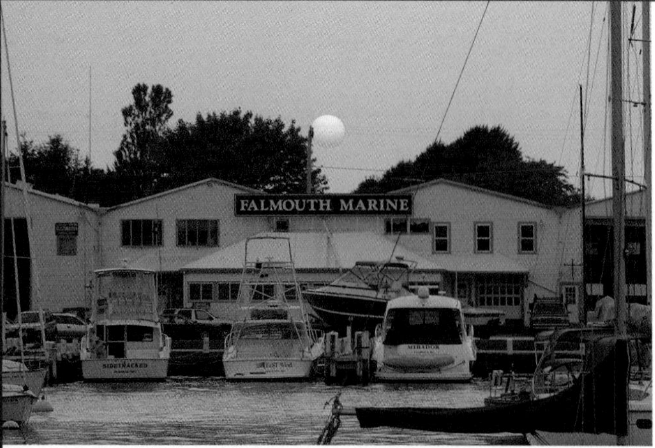

Falmouth Yachting Center

278 Scranton Avenue; Falmouth, MA 02540

Tel: (508) 548-4600 **VHF: Monitor** Ch. 9 **Talk** Ch. 68
Fax: (508) 540-0297 **Alternate Tel:** n/a
Email: dockmaster@falmouthmarine.com **Web:** www.falmouthmarine.com
Nearest Town: Falmouth *(0.5 mi.)* **Tourist Info:** (800) 526-8532

Navigational Information

Lat: 41°32.777' **Long:** 070°36.304' **Tide:** 2 ft. **Current:** 2 kt. **Chart:** 13229
Rep. Depths (*MLW*): Entry 9 ft. **Fuel Dock** 8 ft. **Max Slip/Moor** 8 ft./10 ft.
Access: Vineyard Sound to Falmouth Harbor to Inner Harbor, port side

Marina Facilities *(In Season/Off Season)*

Fuel: *Mobil* - Slip-Side Fueling, Gasoline, Diesel
Slips: 15 Total, 15 Transient **Max LOA:** 70 ft. **Max Beam:** 22 ft.
Rate *(per ft.)*: **Day** $3.00/Inq. **Week** Inq. **Month** Inq.
Power: 30 amp $12.50, **50 amp** $25, **100 amp** n/a, **200 amp** n/a
Cable TV: Yes **Dockside Phone:** No
Dock Type: Fixed, Floating, Long Fingers, Pilings, Alongside, Wood
Moorings: 15 Total, 15 Transient **Launch:** No, Dinghy Dock
Rate: Day $50 **Week** n/a **Month** n/a
Heads: 2 Toilet(s), 2 Shower(s) *(dressing rooms)*
Internet: No **Laundry:** None
Pump-Out: Full Service **Fee:** Free **Closed Heads:** Yes

Marina Operations

Owner/Manager: Jack Erikson **Dockmaster:** Deborah Selleck
In-Season: May 15-Oct 15, 7:30am-7:30pm **Off-Season:** Oct 16-May 14*
After-Hours Arrival: Call ahead
Reservations: No **Credit Cards:** Visa/MC, Mobil, Exxon
Discounts: None
Pets: Welcome, Dog Walk Area **Handicap Access:** No

Marina Services and Boat Supplies

Services - Docking Assistance, Dock Carts **Communication -** Fax in/out, FedEx, UPS, Express Mail **Supplies - OnSite:** Ice *(Block, Cube)* **Under 1 mi:** West Marine *(457-6500)*

Boatyard Services

OnSite: Travelift *(70T)*, Crane, Engine mechanic *(gas, diesel)*, Hull Repairs, Rigger, Bottom Cleaning, Brightwork, Compound, Wash & Wax, Interior Cleaning, Propeller Repairs, Woodworking, Painting, Awlgrip **Near:** Electrical Repairs. **Yard Rates:** $95/hr., Haul & Launch $3.50/ft. *(blocking $6.50/ft.)*, Power Wash $2.50, Bottom Paint $25-55/ft.

Restaurants and Accommodations

OnSite: Restaurant *(Flying Bridge 548-2700, L&D $10-26, Kids' $3-10)* **Near:** Seafood Shack *(Clam Shack 540-7758)* **Under 1 mi:** Restaurant *(Boathouse at Pier 37 388-7573)*, *(Betsy's Diner 540-0060, B $4-9, L $4-9, D $4-14, Kid's $6)*, *(Peking Palace 540-8204, L&D $5-32)*, Pizzeria *(Paul's 548-5838)*, Motel *(Falmouth 548-3623, $159+)*, *(Mariner 548-1331, $115-245)*, *(Falmouth 540-2500, $85-150)*, Inn/B&B *(Red Horse 548-0053, $90-265)*

Recreation and Entertainment

Near: Beach *(Surf Drive - sail board rentals)*, Fishing Charter *(Sea Dog 540-1421)*, Party Boat *(Patriot 648-2626 Vineyard Snd $60/35 all day, Sportfish $70/40)* **Under 1 mi:** Fitness Center *(Anytime 548-0230)*, Video Rental *(Redbox)*, Park *(Falmouth Marine)* **1-3 mi:** Tennis Courts *(Falmouth Sports 548-7384)*, Hike/Bike Trails *(Shining Sea to Woods Hole)*, Bowling *(Trade Center 548-7000)*, Movie Theater *(Falmouth 495-0505)*, Museum *(On the Green 548-4857)*, Cultural Attract *(Highfield Hall 495-1878)* **3+ mi:** Golf Course *(Cape Cod C.C. 563-9842, 5.5 mi.)*

Provisioning and General Services

Near: Market *(Windfall 548-0099 Prepared food, too)* **Under 1 mi:** Convenience Store *(7-Eleven 540-7878)*, Health Food *(Amber Waves 540-3538)*, Liquor Store *(Kappy's 548-2600)*, Bakery *(Mary Ellen's 540-9696)*, Bank/ATM, Post Office, Protestant Church, Library *(Falmouth 457-2555)*, Beauty Salon *(Rumors 548-9100)*, Laundry *(Town 548-5030)*, Bookstore *(Booksmith 540-6064)*, Pharmacy *(Rite Aid 495-2991)*, Hardware Store *(Eastman's 548-0407)*, Florist *(Allen's 540-9798)*, Copies Etc. *(Staples 495-0800)* **1-3 mi:** Supermarket *(Shaw's 617-298-0969)*, Wine/Beer *(Falmouth 548-4824)*, Fishmonger *(Falmouth 540-0045)*, Catholic Church, Retail Shops *(Falmouth Mall 540-8329)*, Department Store *(WalMart; TJ Maxx)*

Transportation

OnSite: Ferry Service *(Pied Piper to MV 548-4800 $10)* **OnCall:** Courtesy Car/Van, Rental Car *(Enterprise 540-7783)*, Taxi *(Independent 444-8700)* **Near:** Bikes *(Holiday 540-3549)*, Water Taxi *(Patriot 548-2626 $10 to Oak Bluffs)* **Under 1 mi:** Airport Limo *(Robin's 548-0561)*, Local Bus *(Sea-Line Woods Hole & Mashpee, WOOSH to Woods Hole 352-7155)* **1-3 mi:** InterCity Bus *(Bonanza 548-7588)* **Airport:** Cape Cod/Logan *(16 mi./75 mi.)*

Medical Services

911 Service **Under 1 mi:** Doctor *(Braconier 548-0111)*, Dentist *(Mitchell 548-2432)*, Chiropractor *(Mulcahy 457-0440)*, Holistic Services *(Comfort Zone 540-8889)*, Optician *(Sajban 444-8691)* **1-3 mi:** Veterinarian *(Deer Run 548-3406)* **Hospital:** Falmouth 548-5300 *(2 mi.)*

PHOTOS ON DVD: 22

Setting -- Through the jetties, past the red-and-blue Patriot Party Boats, FMYC's slips and side-tie dockage line the bulkhead to port. A white picket fence separates the slips from the long row of peaked-roof, white-and-gray sheds and the expansive boatyard operation. The "Pied Piper" ferry to Edgartown anchors one end, and massive Flying Bridge restaurant stretches along the waterfront at the other. Views are across the mooring field to the harbor entrance.

Marina Notes -- *Oct 16-May 14 7:30am-4:30pm, closed weekends. Founded 1939 to handle the "magnificent yachts that cruised the coast." More boatyard than marina - but flower pots step up the ambiance. Skilled yacht care specialists, FMYC invariably gets it right. 70-ton travelift. Side-tie dockage option. Most slips lie perpendicular to the harbor wash, to minimize roll. Busy weekends but quiet weekdays. Fuel also available at MacDougalls' and at Patriot at harbor entrance. Use the dink to cross over to MacDougalls' or up-harbor to the Boathouse. Bathhouse: Not fancy but modern and somewhat private.

Notable -- The venerable, classic Clam Shack overlooks the harbor entrance next to the red white and blue Patriot Fishing and Sightseeing Cruises and a good beach is just beyond. Flying Bridge's multiple dining rooms, bars and live music weekends, straddles FMYC and the town dock - take refuge on the deck. The marina is on the "Village" (West) side of the harbor, putting some of the best shopping on the Cape and more watering holes all within easy walking distance through the historic district ending at the Village Green and the Museums on the Green. On the way, there's a market, liquor store, laundry and tackle shop. The hassle-free "Pied Piper" Edgartown ferry leaves from here, and the nearby free Patriots Shopping Shuttle goes to Falmouth Mall and Falmouth Plaza.

 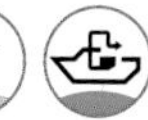 

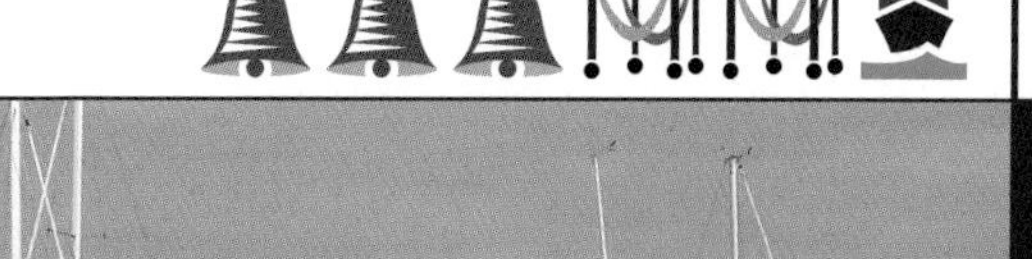

Navigational Information
Lat: 41°32.815' **Long:** 070°36.126' **Tide:** 2 ft. **Current:** 2 kt. **Chart:** 13229
Rep. Depths (*MLW*): Entry 10 ft. **Fuel Dock** 10 ft. **Max Slip/Moor** 12 ft./-
Access: Falmouth Harbor R16 to G1 light into Falmouth Inner Harbor

Marina Facilities *(In Season/Off Season)*
Fuel: Gasoline, Diesel, High-Speed Pumps
Slips: 100 Total, 25 Transient **Max LOA:** 150 ft. **Max Beam:** n/a
Rate *(per ft.)*: **Day** $4.25/Inq.* **Week** Inq. **Month** Inq.
Power: 30 amp $20, **50 amp** $40, **100 amp** $90, **200 amp** n/a
Cable TV: Yes, Incl. **Dockside Phone:** No
Dock Type: Fixed, Floating, Short Fingers, Alongside, Wood, Aluminum
Moorings: 0 Total, 0 Transient **Launch:** No, Dinghy Dock
Rate: Day n/a **Week** n/a **Month** n/a
Heads: 4 Toilet(s), 4 Shower(s) *(dressing rooms)*
Internet: Yes *(Wi-Fi, Free)* **Laundry:** 3 Washer(s), 3 Dryer(s)
Pump-Out: Full Service, 1 Central **Fee:** Free **Closed Heads:** Yes

Marina Operations
Owner/Manager: Tom Stainton **Dockmaster:** Chris Aubut
In-Season: May-Sept, 7am-7pm **Off-Season:** Oct-April, 7:30am-5pm
After-Hours Arrival: Call in advance
Reservations: Yes **Credit Cards:** Visa/MC, Amex, Debit Cards
Discounts: None
Pets: Welcome **Handicap Access:** Yes, Heads, Docks

MacDougalls' Cape Cod Marine

15. MA - CAPE COD SOUTH SHORE

MacDougalls' Cape Cod Marine

145 Falmouth Heights; Falmouth, MA 02540

Tel: (508) 548-3146 **VHF: Monitor** Ch. 16, 9 **Talk** Ch. 71
Fax: (508) 548-7262 **Alternate Tel:** (774) 836-2481
Email: info@macdougalls.com **Web:** www.macdougalls.com
Nearest Town: Falmouth *(0.8 mi.)* **Tourist Info:** (800) 526-8532

Marina Services and Boat Supplies
Services - Docking Assistance, Boaters' Lounge, Crew Lounge, Dock Carts **Communication -** Pay Phone (2), FedEx, UPS, Express Mail **Supplies - OnSite:** Ice *(Block, Cube)*, Ships' Store, CNG **Under 1 mi:** West Marine *(457-6500)*, Bait/Tackle *(Eastman's 548-6900)*

Boatyard Services
OnSite: Travelift *(150 T)*, Forklift, Crane, Engine mechanic *(gas, diesel)*, Electrical Repairs, Electronics Repairs, Hull Repairs, Rigger, Canvas Work, Bottom Cleaning, Air Conditioning, Refrigeration, Compound, Wash & Wax, Interior Cleaning, Propeller Repairs, Woodworking, Painting, Awlgrip, Total Refits **Dealer for:** North Sails, EZ2CY, Hatteras, Sabre, Back Cove, Nordhavn, Grand Banks, Caterpillar, Cummins Marine, Detroit Diesel, Westerbeke, Yanmar. **Yard Rates:** $95/hr.

Restaurants and Accommodations
Near: Restaurant *(British Beer 540-9600, L $7-11, D $13-18)*, *(The Avenue 388-7594, Seafood & Pizza)*, *(Casino Wharf fx 540-6160, $18-40 on beach)*, Motel *(Falmouth Heights 548-3623, $159+)*, *(Mariner's Point 457-0300, $115-245)*, *(Seaside Inn 540-4120, $59-325)*, *(Hiltz's 540-2499)* **Under 1 mi:** Restaurant *(The Boathouse at Pier 37 388-7573, Live Bands)*, *(Roo Bar 548-8600, D $11-25)*, *(Flying Bridge 548-2700, L&D $10-26, Kids' $3-10)*, *(Falmouth Raw Bar 548-7729, $17-45 take out)*, *(Betsy's Diner 540-0060, B & L $4-9. D $4-14, Kids' $6)*, Pizzeria *(Paul's 548-5838)*

Recreation and Entertainment
OnSite: Picnic Area, Grills **Near:** Beach *(Falmouth Heights)* **Under 1 mi:** Hike/Bike Trails *(Shining Sea Bike Path)* **1-3 mi:** Tennis Courts *(Falmouth 457-2567)*, Fitness Center *(Anytime 548-0230)*, Party Boat *(Patriot 548-2626)*, Movie Theater *(Falmouth 495-0505)*, Museum *(On the Green 548-4857)*, Cultural Attract *(College Light Opera 548-0668; Cape Cod Theatre 457-4242)* **3+ mi:** Golf Course *(Falmouth CC 548-3211, 5.5 mi.)*

Provisioning and General Services
OnSite: Copies Etc. **Under 1 mi:** Convenience Store *(7-Eleven 540-7878)*, Market *(Windfall 548-0099)*, Gourmet Shop *(Bean & Cod 548-8840)*, Health Food *(Amber Waves 540-3538)*, Wine/Beer *(Kappy's 548-2600)*, Liquor Store *(John's 548-2287)*, Bakery *(Mary Ellen's 540-9696)*, Farmers' Market *(Thur Noon-6pm - Noonan Park)*, Bank/ATM, Beauty Salon *(Artisan 540-9432)*, Dry Cleaners *(Park 548-0907)*, Laundry *(Falmouth 548-3911)*, Bookstore *(Booksmith 540-6064)*, Pharmacy *(Rite Aid 495-2931)*, Florist *(Allen's 540-9798)* **1-3 mi:** Supermarket *(Shaw's 617-298-0969)*, Post Office, Catholic Church, Protestant Church, Library, Hardware Store *(Eastman's 548-0407)*, Retail Shops *(Falmouth Mall; Falmouth Plaza)*

Transportation
OnCall: Rental Car *(Enterprise 540-7784)*, Taxi *(Independent 444-8700)*, Airport Limo *(All Town 548-7166)* **Near:** Bikes *(Holiday 540-3549)*, Local Bus *(Sea-Line; WOOSH Woods Hole 800-352-7155)*, Ferry Service *(Edgartown & Oak Bluffs)* **Airport:** Cape Cod/Logan *(16 mi./75 mi.)*

Medical Services
911 Service **Under 1 mi:** Doctor *(Von Haam 540-7423)*, Dentist *(Mitchell 548-2432)*, Chiropractor *(Mulcahy 457-0440)*, Holistic Services *(Comfort Zone 540-8889)*, Optician *(Cambridge 495-0332)* **1-3 mi:** Veterinarian *(Deer Run 548-3406)* **Hospital:** Falmouth 548-5300 *(2.5 mi.)*

Setting -- Past Falmouth Yacht Club, to starboard, MacDougalls' is easily visible from the Harbor's mouth. A large network of docks, usually with a few megayachts on the T-heads, is backed by striking red-and-gray work sheds topped by silver roofs and vent stacks. Spread across five tightly packed and very ship-shape acres, luxe boater amenities rub shoulders with newly renovated, top-shelf yard facilities. Historic Falmouth Heights is out the "back door".

Marina Notes -- *Under 30 ft. $3.75/ft. In business since 1938, on site of Phinney catboat yard. Fuel dock 7am-7pm, Jun 15-Sep 14, Shoulder 8:30am-5pm. Ships Store May-ColDay M-F 7;30-5, Sat 7:30-12pm. Shoulder M-F 7:30-4. Closed Nov-Apr. Posh dockside gray shingled "The Landing" - airy customer lounge with comfortable rattan furniture,TV, galley and separate computer area. Newish docks and pedestals. To 100A with single phase. Full-service, first-line boatyard - most complete in harbor. Renovated, green facilities (2008) managed by professional project management system, include state-of-the-art laminar flow paint spray booth. Weekly rates avail. Bathhouse: Club quality. Mexican and ceramic tile, molded sinks, dressing areas.

Notable -- Beyond the marina, upscale Falmouth Heights, a picturesque stretch of large Victorian summer "cottages," sits on a bluff overlooking the water - some gazing down on the hamlet's narrow Vineyard Sound beach that lies along Grand Avenue as do two popular beachside eateries. Falmouth Center is just under a mile; dinghy to the town dock at the harbor head for more restaurants and mile walk along Main Street to the village center where the museums, eateries, shops, and provisioning rival larger towns. Or take the WHOOSH bus along Main Street or to the two shopping malls or to Woods Hole.

PHOTOS ON DVD: 22

Falmouth Harbor Town Marina

Falmouth Harbor Town Marina

180 Scranton Avenue; Falmouth, MA 02540

Tel: (508) 457-2550 **VHF: Monitor** Ch. 9, 16 **Talk** Ch. 12
Fax: (508) 457-2525 **Alternate Tel:** n/a
Email: falhmast@falmouthmass.us **Web:** www.falmouthmass.us
Nearest Town: Falmouth *(0.3 mi.)* **Tourist Info:** (508) 548-8500

Navigational Information

Lat: 41°32.947' **Long:** 070°36.207' **Tide:** 2 ft. **Current:** 2 kt. **Chart:** 13229
Rep. Depths (*MLW*): Entry 9 ft. **Fuel Dock** 6 ft. **Max Slip/Moor** 9 ft./-
Access: Falmouth Harbor R16 to G1 light to Falmouth Inner Harbor

Marina Facilities *(In Season/Off Season)*

Fuel: No
Slips: 60 Total, 10 Transient **Max LOA:** 250 ft. **Max Beam:** 21 ft.
Rate *(per ft.)*: **Day** $2.75/1.50* **Week** n/a **Month** n/a
Power: 30 amp $20, **50 amp** $30, **100 amp** n/a, **200 amp** n/a
Cable TV: Yes **Dockside Phone:** No
Dock Type: Fixed, Long Fingers, Alongside, Wood
Moorings: 0 Total, 0 Transient **Launch:** n/a, Dinghy Dock (Free)
Rate: Day n/a **Week** n/a **Month** n/a
Heads: Toilet(s), Shower(s)
Internet: No **Laundry:** None
Pump-Out: OnCall, Full Service, 1 Port **Fee:** free **Closed Heads:** Yes

Marina Operations

Owner/Manager: Gregg Fraser (Hbrmstr) **Dockmaster:** Eileen Sprague
In-Season: Apr-Oct, 8am-6pm **Off-Season:** Nov-Mar, Closed
After-Hours Arrival: Call in advance
Reservations: Yes **Credit Cards:** Visa/MC, Check/Cash
Discounts: None
Pets: Welcome **Handicap Access:** Yes, Docks

Marina Services and Boat Supplies

Services - Docking Assistance **Communication -** FedEx, UPS, Express Mail **Supplies - OnCall:** Ships' Store *(Stem To Stern Mobile 563-6553)* **Near:** Ice *(Block, Cube)*, West Marine *(457-6500)* **Under 1 mi:** Bait/Tackle *(Eastman's 548-6900)*

Boatyard Services

Nearest Yard: Falmouth Marine (508) 548-4600

Restaurants and Accommodations

Near: Restaurant *(Flying Bridge 548-2700, L & D $10-26. Kids' $3-10)*, *(The Boathouse 388-7573)*, *(Falmouth Raw Bar 548-7729, L & D $10-25)*, Lite Fare *(D'Angelo's 548-8980)*, Motel *(Inn Season 548-4300, $70-109)*, *(Mariner 548-1331, $115-245)*, *(Motel 7 Seas 548-1110)* **Under 1 mi:** Restaurant *(Betsy's Diner 540-0060, B $4-9, D $4-14)*, *(Clam Shack 540-7758, $5-$25 'til 8pm)*, *(Bangkok Thai 495-3760, L $10-16, D $10-37)*, *(Quarterdeck 548-9900, L $7-12, D $12-22)*, *(Nimrod 540-4132)*, *(Hearth & Kettle 548-6111, B $6-12, L $7-19, D $7-19)*, *(Liam Maguire's 548-0285, L $7-15)*, *(La Cucina Sul Mare 548-5600)*, Pizzeria *(Paul's 548-5838)*

Recreation and Entertainment

OnSite: Fishing Charter *(Bluefin 457-9194; Sea Dog 540-1421)* **Near:** Picnic Area, Video Rental *(Redbox)* **Under 1 mi:** Beach *(Surf Drive)*, Fitness Center *(Anytime 548-0230)*, Bowling *(Trade Center 548-7000)*, Party Boat *(Patriot 648-2626)*, Galleries *(Falmouth Artists Guild 540-3304)* **1-3 mi:** Tennis Courts *(Falmouth 548-7384)*, Hike/Bike Trails *(Shining Sea to Woods Hole)*, Movie Theater *(Falmouth 495-0505)*, Museum *(Museums on the Green 548-4857)*, Cultural Attract *(College Light Opera 548-2211; Falmouth Theatre 548-0400; Cape Cod Theatre 457-4242)* **3+ mi:** Golf Course *(Falmouth 548-3211, 5 mi.)*

Provisioning and General Services

Near: Convenience Store *(7-Eleven 540-7878)*, Market *(Windfall 548-0099)*, Bank/ATM, Dry Cleaners *(Park 548-0907)*, Laundry *(Town 548-5030)* **Under 1 mi:** Supermarket *(Shaw's 617-298-0969)*, Gourmet Shop *(Bean & Cod 548-8840)*, Health Food *(Amber Waves 540-3538)*, Wine/Beer *(Murphy's 540-7724)*, Liquor Store *(John's 548-2287)*, Bakery *(Mary Ellen's 540-9696)*, Farmers' Market *(Thur Noon-6pm, Peg Noonan Park)*, Post Office *(457-0158)*, Catholic Church, Protestant Church, Library *(457-2555 Wi-Fi)*, Beauty Salon *(Hair Reflections 548-3344)*, Bookstore *(Booksmith 540-6064)*, Pharmacy *(Rite Aid 495-2991)*, Hardware Store *(Eastmans 548-0407)*, Florist *(Allen's 540-9798)*, Copies Etc. *(Falmouth 457-4985)* **1-3 mi:** Retail Shops *(Falmouth Mall, Falmouth Plaza, WalMart, TJ Maxx)*

Transportation

OnCall: Rental Car *(Enterprise 540-7784)*, Taxi *(Independent 444-8700)*, Airport Limo *(All Town 548-7166)* **Near:** Local Bus *(Sea-Line Woods Hole & Mashpee, WOOSH to Woods Hole 352-7155)*, Ferry Service *(to Edgartown 548-4800)* **Under 1 mi:** Bikes *(Holiday 540-3549)* **1-3 mi:** InterCity Bus *(Bonanza 548-7588)* **Airport:** Cape Cod/Logan *(16 mi./75 mi.)*

Medical Services

911 Service **Under 1 mi:** Doctor *(Von Haam 540-7423)*, Dentist *(Mitchell 548-2432)*, Chiropractor *(Mulcahy 457-0440)*, Holistic Services *(Comfort Zone 540-8889)*, Optician *(Cambridge 495-0332)* **1-3 mi:** Veterinarian *(Deer Run 548-3406)* **Hospital:** Falmouth 548-5300 *(2 mi.)*

Setting -- Past Falmouth Marine Yachting Center and Flying Bridge Restaurant, the municipal marina's stern-to docks are strung along the portside bulkhead. The Harbormaster's office in the long, low-slung, shingled land base, is the centerpiece of Bigelow Marine Park - a hefty, refreshing stretch of greensward with a promenade, benches, a music pavilion and docks for pleasure craft, working boats and sportfish charters.

Marina Notes -- *$2.75/ft. Jul-Aug, 30 ft. min, $1.50/ft Jun 16-30, $1/ft. Apr 15-Jun 15 & Sep 1-Nov 15. Rates double after 14 days; triple after 23. Max stay 30 days. Most docks perpendicular to the harbor axis; inquire about a planned expansion which could alter that. In high summer, some transients may be alongside at Robbins Road (to 50 ft.), Davis Marine Park Bulkhead side-tie (to 80 ft.) or Tides Bulkhead side-tie (to 250 ft.) at harbor entrance (9 ft.mlw). Reserve early (10% deposit). Pump-out boat base. No grilling on docks. Bathhouse: Clearly municipal. Stainless steel but very modern with some privacy.

Notable -- The Falmouth Town Band performs every Thurs 7-8:30pm at the Oscar Wolf Bandshell - also home to other large events. Just up the street are the Windfall Market, for gourmet/deli items, groceries, and ready-to-ea food, plus a laundromat, tackle shop, and liquor store. A little further, picturesque "downtown" Falmouth Village's main street is lined with shops, restaurants, galleries, services - and ends at the Village Green with the Historical Society's Museums and restored 18thC sea captains' houses. On a lay-day, rent bikes to travel the 4-mile Shining Sea bike path, from Ice Arena to Woods Hole Steamship Authority - starts a mile away. Close by are ferries to both Edgartown and Oak Bluffs on Martha's Vineyard - and the popular Surf Drive beach.

PHOTOS ON DVD: 25

Navigational Information

Lat: 41°32.949' **Long:** 070°36.064' **Tide:** 2 ft. **Current:** 2 kt. **Chart:** 13229
Rep. Depths (*MLW*): Entry 10 ft. **Fuel Dock** 10 ft. **Max Slip/Moor** 8 ft./-
Access: Falmouth Harbor R16 to G1 light to Falmouth Inner Harbor

Marina Facilities *(In Season/Off Season)*

Fuel: *ValvTect* - Gasoline, Diesel, High-Speed Pumps
Slips: 15 Total, 2 Transient **Max LOA:** 50 ft. **Max Beam:** n/a
Rate *(per ft.)*: **Day** $3.00/Inq. **Week** Inq. **Month** Inq.
Power: 30 amp $10, **50 amp** $12, **100 amp** n/a, **200 amp** n/a
Cable TV: Yes **Dockside Phone:** No
Dock Type: Fixed, Long Fingers, Pilings, Alongside, Wood
Moorings: 0 Total, 0 Transient **Launch:** n/a
Rate: Day n/a **Week** n/a **Month** n/a
Heads: 2 Toilet(s)
Internet: No **Laundry:** None
Pump-Out: Full Service **Fee:** free **Closed Heads:** Yes

Marina Operations

Owner/Manager: Susann Koelsch **Dockmaster:** Jesse White
In-Season: April-Oct, 7:30am-4:30pm **Off-Season:** Nov-Mar, 8am-4pm
After-Hours Arrival: Call in advance
Reservations: Yes **Credit Cards:** Visa/MC, Dscvr, Amex
Discounts: None
Pets: Welcome **Handicap Access:** No

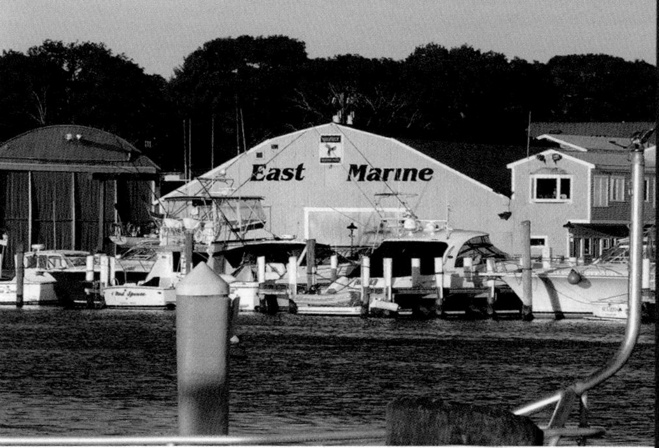

East Marine

PO Box 610; 89 Falmouth Heights Road; Falmouth, MA 02540

Tel: (508) 540-3611 **VHF: Monitor** Ch.16 **Talk** n/a
Fax: (508) 540-2385 **Alternate Tel:** n/a
Email: gm@eastmarine.com **Web:** www.eastmarine.com
Nearest Town: Falmouth *(1 mi.)* **Tourist Info:** (508) 548-8500

Marina Services and Boat Supplies

Services - Docking Assistance, Security **Communication -** FedEx, UPS, Express Mail **Supplies - OnSite:** Ice *(Block, Cube)* **Under 1 mi:** West Marine *(457-6500)*, Bait/Tackle *(Eastman's 548-6900)* **1-3 mi:** Ships' Store *(Green Pond 540-0877)*

Boatyard Services

OnSite: Travelift *(35T)*, Crane, Hydraulic Trailer, Engine mechanic *(gas, diesel)*, Electrical Repairs, Electronics Repairs, Hull Repairs, Compound, Wash & Wax, Painting **OnCall:** Divers **Dealer for:** Yanmar, Mercury/Mercruiser, Yamaha. **Member:** ABBRA, ABYC **Yard Rates:** Haul & Launch $10-20/ft. **Storage:** In-Water $28/ft.

Restaurants and Accommodations

Near: Restaurant *(The Boathouse 388-7573, L $12-18, D $18-26, Live Bands)*, *(Falmouth Raw Bar 548-7729, L & D $10-25)*, *(Flying Bridge 548-2700, L $6-26, D $14-26, Dinghy)*, Pizzeria *(Paul's 548-5838)*, Motel *(Hiltz's 540-2499)*, *(Falmouth Heights 548-3623, $159+)*, *(Red Horse Inn 548-0053, $9-265)* **Under 1 mi:** Restaurant *(Roo Bar 548-4600, D $11-28)*, Seafood Shack *(Clam Shack 540-7758, Dinghy)*, Lite Fare *(Molly's 457-1666)*

Recreation and Entertainment

Near: Picnic Area, Grills, Playground, Dive Shop, Jogging Paths **Under 1 mi:** Beach *(Falmouth Heights)*, Fitness Center *(Anytime 548-0230)*, Hike/Bike Trails *(Shining Sea to Woods Hole)*, Bowling *(Trade Center 548-7000)*, Fishing Charter *(Bluefin 548-9498)*, Party Boat *(Patriot 648-2626)*, Movie Theater *(Falmouth Mall 540-2169)*, Video Rental *(Redbox)*, Galleries *(Falmouth Artists Guild 540-3304)* **1-3 mi:** Tennis Courts *(Falmouth 548-7384)*, Museum *("On the Green" 548-4857)*, Cultural Attract *(College Light Opera 548-2211; Falmouth Theatre 548-0400; Cape Cod Theatre 457-4242)* **3+ mi:** Golf Course *(Galmouth C.C. 548-3211, 5 mi.)*

Provisioning and General Services

Near: Bank/ATM, Protestant Church **Under 1 mi:** Convenience Store *(7-Eleven 540-7878)*, Market *(Windfall 548-0099)*, Supermarket *(Shaw's 617-298-0969)*, Gourmet Shop *(Bean & Cod 548-8840)*, Health Food *(Amber Waves 540-3538)*, Wine/Beer *(Kappy's 548-2600)*, Liquor Store *(John's 548-2287)*, Bakery *(Mary Ellen's 540-9696)*, Farmers' Market *(Thur Noon-6pm - Noonan Park)*, Fishmonger *(Falmouth 540-0045)*, Lobster Pound, Post Office *(548-5361)*, Catholic Church, Library *(Falmouth 457-2555)*, Beauty Salon *(Hair Reflections 548-3344)*, Dry Cleaners *(Park 548-0907)*, Laundry *(Town 548-5030)*, Bookstore *(Booksmith 540-6064)*, Pharmacy *(Rite Aid 495-2991)*, Hardware Store *(Eastman's 548-0407)*, Florist *(Allen's 540-9798)*, Retail Shops *(Falmouth Mall; Walmart)*, Copies Etc. *(Staples 495-0800)*

Transportation

OnCall: Rental Car *(Enterprise 540-7784)*, Taxi *(Independent 444-8700)* **Near:** Bikes *(Holiday 540-3549)*, Local Bus *(Sea-Line 800-352-7155, WHOOSH to Woods Hole 352-7155)*, Ferry Service *(MV - Edgartown or Oak Bluffs)* **Airport:** Cape Cod/Logan *(16 mi./75 mi.)*

Medical Services

911 Service **Near:** Dentist *(Mitchell 548-2432)* **Under 1 mi:** Doctor *(Von Haarn 540-7423)*, Chiropractor *(Mulcahy 457-0440)*, Holistic Services *(Comfort Zone 540-8889)*, Optician *(Cambridge 495-0332)* **1-3 mi:** Veterinarian *(Deer Run 548-3406)* **Hospital:** Falmouth 548-5300 *(2 mi.)*

Setting -- Deep into the harbor on the starboard side, past the big, red MacDougalls' shed, East Marine is distinguished by smaller off-white sheds with their signature curved roofs. A quintessential old-time New England yard, it's not fancy, just solid and professional. The town marina is across the harbor, and East Marine's sibling North Marine is almost to the harbor head. A mile north are the newer malls. A mile west along Main Street is Falmouth Center.

Marina Notes -- Valvtect fuel and mechanical services in a good, protected location. Do-it-yourself permitted. Many mechanical services provided by nearby North Marine. Fuel dock shares the "ditch" with the travelift. Extensive winter boat storage. Limited transient space. Once on the shore of Deacons Pond, Army Corps dredged it into Falmouth Harbor in early 1900's. Bathhouse: Useable, simple painted full bathroom with fiberglass shower stall.

Notable -- The ferry to Oak Bluffs, MV is almost onsite for a day trip. Conveniently at the head of the harbor are Falmouth Raw Bar and The Boathouse. For services, more eateries and good supplies, stroll the mile and a half along Main Street to the Village Green (or take the WOOSH) - stop at Molly's Tea Room. A cluster of museums depict colonial Cape Cod - 1790 Julia Wood House, a barn and 1730 Conant House are surrounded by formal gardens. The Falmouth Commodores baseball team plays at Guv Fuller Field - less than a half-mile walk from the docks. A similar walk in the other direction yields Falmouth Heights Beach. Home to the Cape's first summer colony, many of the Height's original Shingle-style mansions overlook the narrow strip of sand. Take the WHOOSH to Woods Hole. Or, with bikes in tow, head to the 10-mile Shining Sea trail; bike 4 miles along the water to Woods Hole, stopping at Nobska Light -- then bus back.

PHOTOS ON DVD: 20

Oyster Harbors Yacht Basin

122 Bridge Street; Osterville, MA 02655

Tel: (508) 428-2017; (866) 482-6115 **VHF: Monitor** n/a **Talk** n/a
Fax: (508) 420-5398 **Alternate Tel:** n/a
Email: mattc@oysterharborsmarine.com **Web:** oysterharborsmarine.com
Nearest Town: Osterville *(0.5 mi.)* **Tourist Info:** (508) 790-3077

Navigational Information

Lat: 41°37.430' **Long:** 070°23.691' **Tide:** 3 ft. **Current:** 1 kt. **Chart:** 13229
Rep. Depths (*MLW*): Entry 6.5 ft. **Fuel Dock** 7 ft. **Max Slip/Moor** 7 ft./6 ft.
Access: Nantucket Sound, West Bay to North Bay Channel

Marina Facilities *(In Season/Off Season)*

Fuel: Gasoline, Diesel
Slips: 110 Total, 5 Transient **Max LOA:** 105 ft. **Max Beam:** n/a
Rate *(per ft.)*: **Day** $4.00 **Week** n/a **Month** n/a
Power: 30 amp Incl., **50 amp** Incl., **100 amp** n/a, **200 amp** n/a
Cable TV: No **Dockside Phone:** No
Dock Type: Fixed, Floating, Long Fingers, Wood
Moorings: 25 Total, 5 Transient **Launch:** No, Dinghy Dock
Rate: Day $35 **Week** n/a **Month** n/a
Heads: 2 Toilet(s), 2 Shower(s)
Internet: No **Laundry:** None
Pump-Out: OnCall, Full Service **Fee:** Free **Closed Heads:** Yes

Marina Operations

Owner/Manager: Peter Maryott **Dockmaster:** Matt Carstensen
In-Season: Year-Round, 8am-4pm **Off-Season:** n/a
After-Hours Arrival: Call ahead
Reservations: Yes, preferred **Credit Cards:** Visa/MC, Dscvr, Amex
Discounts: None
Pets: Welcome **Handicap Access:** Yes, Heads, Docks

Marina Services and Boat Supplies

Services - Docking Assistance, Concierge, Trash Pick-Up, Dock Carts **Communication -** Mail & Package Hold, FedEx, UPS **Supplies - OnSite:** Ice *(Block, Cube)*, Ships' Store *(also Seaworthy 477-9911)* **1-3 mi:** Bait/Tackle *(Sportsport 775-3096)* **3+ mi:** Propane *(Corp 775-5001, 7 mi.)*

Boatyard Services

OnSite: Travelift *(75T)*, Forklift, Hydraulic Trailer, Engine mechanic *(gas, diesel)*, Electrical Repairs, Electronic Sales, Electronics Repairs, Hull Repairs, Rigger, Sail Loft, Canvas Work, Bottom Cleaning, Brightwork, Air Conditioning, Refrigeration, Compound, Wash & Wax, Interior Cleaning, Propeller Repairs **Dealer for:** Sportfish yachts: Cabo, Tiara, Viking.

Restaurants and Accommodations

Near: Restaurant *(Islander 428-6719, D $13-27)* **Under 1 mi:** Restaurant *(Five Bays Bistro 420-5559, D $20-35)*, *(Osterville Village 428-1005)*, Seafood Shack *(Wimpy's 428-6300, L $7-21, D $8-26)*, Lite Fare *(Noah's Wrap 420-8777)*, *(Earthly Delights 420-2206, to go)*, Pizzeria *(Sweet Tomatoes 420-1717)* **1-3 mi:** Restaurant *(Tugboats 428-2600, D $14-27, Kids' $5-10)*, Motel *(Centerville Corners 246-7881, $75-195)* **3+ mi:** Restaurant *(Regatta 428-5715, D $24-36, 5 mi., Tap Room $12-25 Do not miss!)*, Motel *(Ocean View 775-1962, $89-269, 4 mi.)*, Inn/B&B *(Green Mountain 778-4278, $115-130, 4 mi.)*

Recreation and Entertainment

Near: Picnic Area **Under 1 mi:** Park *(Armstrong-Kelley)*, Museum *(Osterville Historical Soc 428-5861 - farmers' market, too)*, Galleries *(Bridge on the Cape 428-4969; Schulz 428-8770)*, Special Events *(Village Day - July - 3rd weekend)* **1-3 mi:** Beach *(Dowses)*, Tennis Courts *(Osterville Bay School)*, Golf Course *(New Seabury 477-9400)*, Fitness Center *(Osterville 428-3775)* **3+ mi:** Horseback Riding *(Holly Hill 428-2621, 3.5 mi.)*, Movie Theater *(Regal Cinemas 771-7872, 6 mi.)*, Cultural Attract *(Cape Cod Melody 775-5630, 5 mi.)*

Provisioning and General Services

Under 1 mi: Convenience Store *(Cumberland 420-8168)*, Market *(Fancy's 428-6954)*, Delicatessen *(Cheese & Sandwich Shop 428-9085)*, Liquor Store *(Osterville 428-6327)*, Farmers' Market *(Fri, 9am-2pm Osterville Historical Museum)*, Bank/ATM, Post Office *(428-6680)*, Catholic Church, Protestant Church, Library *(428-5757)*, Beauty Salon *(Leona 420-7812)*, Dry Cleaners *(Centerville 420-6118)*, Bookstore *(By the Sea 420-9400)*, Hardware Store *(House & Garden 428-6911)* **1-3 mi:** Wine/Beer *(Craigville 420-0321)*, Fishmonger *(Osterville 420-0500)*, Synagogue, Florist *(Flowersticks 420-7966)* **3+ mi:** Supermarket *(Stop and Shop 428-1278, 3.5 mi.)*, Pharmacy *(Rite Aid 428-3525, 3.5 mi.)*

Transportation

OnCall: Rental Car *(Enterprise 778-8293)*, Taxi *(Checker 771-8294)*, Airport Limo *(Cape Cod Airport Shuttle 771-8294)* **Near:** Local Bus *(CCRTA Woods Hole, Orleans, Hyannis)* **Airport:** Barnstable/Logan *(8 mi./73 mi.)*

Medical Services

911 Service **Under 1 mi:** Holistic Services *(Peace of Mind 45-7399)*, Optician *(Simply 420-4231)* **1-3 mi:** Doctor *(Osterville 428-2620)*, Dentist *(Osterville 428-2443)*, Chiropractor *(Bober 420-0495)* **3+ mi:** Veterinarian *(Mid Cape 428-2989, 4 mi.)* **Hospital:** Cape Cod 771-1800 *(8.5 mi.)*

PHOTOS ON DVD:

Setting -- Cruse form West Bay, past Wianno Yacht Club, through the bascule bridge into North Bay. Immediately to starboard are the recently renovated, immaculate OHYB facilities. Across the tight fairway, on Little Island, Oyster Harbors' two additional long shingled sheds, topped by cupolas, back many more docks. This narrow stretch, chock-a-block with docks, opens up into almost circular North Bay edged by quiet salt marsh and large summer homes.

Marina Notes -- An active dealership for high-end sportfish lines - masters of high-touch customer care. Routinely manages stem-to-stern winterizing, commissioning, and everything in between for demanding clientele. Otherwise, a typical upscale Cape Cod boatyard, with few frills and amenities. Large solar project on roof of new building. Few attractions, other than fine summer living, minimizes the transient business. Anchoring allowed in North Bay. Bathhouse: Recent, wood paneling above white tile, checkboard trim. Note: No transient facilities at Wianno YC. Many unoccupied moorings in N.Bay for storm use.

Notable -- It's less than a mile stroll through the affluent, gracious, low-key village on the east side of the bascule bridge. Browse the fine galleries, unique local shops and easily three-days worth of eateries. Little Island is a pleasant walk but expect to be turned away from "Oyster Harbors" on Great Island. Water-based explorations are best in the dink - along the shore, the bays can be shallow; the houses (actually mansions) are worth the trip. Include a visit to Cotuit in western West Bay, which has a dinghy dock. It's about two miles to wide, uncrowded Dowses Beach at the entrance to East Bay - with both bay and ocean frontage (bikes are good, but a car sans Parking Permit is not). Village Day is the third weekend in July and Fall Fest's at the end of September.

   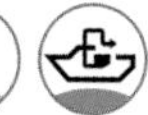

Navigational Information
Lat: 41°35.433' **Long:** 070°23.389' **Tide:** 3 ft. **Current:** 1 kt. **Chart:** 13229
Rep. Depths (*MLW*): Entry 6 ft. **Fuel Dock** 10 ft. **Max Slip/Moor** 10 ft./9 ft.
Access: Nantucket Sound, through West Bay, through bascule bridge

Marina Facilities *(In Season/Off Season)*
Fuel: *ValvTect* - Gasoline, Diesel, High-Speed Pumps
Slips: 125 Total, 15 Transient **Max LOA:** 60 ft. **Max Beam:** n/a
Rate *(per ft.)*: **Day** $4.50 **Week** n/a **Month** n/a
Power: 30 amp $15, **50 amp** $30, **100 amp** n/a, **200 amp** n/a
Cable TV: No **Dockside Phone:** No
Dock Type: Fixed, Long Fingers, Wood
Moorings: 80 Total, 10 Transient **Launch:** No
Rate: Day $60* **Week** $350 **Month** $950
Heads: 4 Toilet(s)
Internet: Yes *(Wi-Fi, Free)* **Laundry:** None
Pump-Out: OnCall *(Reserve)*, Full Service **Fee:** Free** **Closed Heads:** Yes

Marina Operations
Owner/Manager: Greg Egan (VP) **Dockmaster:** Tom Meara
In-Season: Year-Round, 9am-5pm **Off-Season:** n/a
After-Hours Arrival: Call in advance
Reservations: Yes **Credit Cards:** Visa/MC, Dscvr, Amex
Discounts: None
Pets: Welcome **Handicap Access:** Yes, Heads

Crosby Yacht Yard

72 Crosby Circle; Osterville, MA 02655

Tel: (508) 428-6900; (877) 491-9759 **VHF: Monitor** Ch. 9 **Talk** Ch. 68
Fax: (508) 428-0323 **Alternate Tel:** n/a
Email: contact@crosbyyacht.com **Web:** www.crosbyyacht.com
Nearest Town: Osterville *(0.7 mi.)* **Tourist Info:** (508) 790-3077

Marina Services and Boat Supplies
Services - Docking Assistance, Dock Carts **Communication -** Phone Messages, FedEx, UPS, Express Mail **Supplies - OnSite:** Ice *(Block, Cube)* **3+ mi:** West Marine *(862-2700, 6 mi.)*, Bait/Tackle *(Sports Port 775-3096, 5 mi.)*, Propane *(Aubuchon Hardware 428-7100, 7 mi.)*

Boatyard Services
OnSite: Travelift *(70T)*, Railway, Forklift *(2)*, Engine mechanic *(gas, diesel)*, Electrical Repairs, Electronic Sales, Electronics Repairs, Hull Repairs, Rigger, Bottom Cleaning, Brightwork, Compound, Wash & Wax, Propeller Repairs, Woodworking, Inflatable Repairs, Painting, Awlgrip, Total Refits, Yacht Building **Dealer for:** Scout Boats.. **Member:** ABBRA, Other Certifications: MMTA, CCMTA, YBAA, MRAA, CPYB **Yard Rates:** $112/hr., Haul & Launch $15/RT **Storage:** On-Land 26-35 ft. $7.55/sq.ft.; 35+ ft. $8.20/sq.ft.

Restaurants and Accommodations
OnSite: Restaurant *(The Islander at Crosby Boat Yard 428-6719, L $8-15, D $14-29, Seasonal, Lunch & Dinner 7 days summer, Dinner Wed-Sun, Lunch wknds shoulder season)* **Under 1 mi:** Restaurant *(Wimpy's 428-6300, L $7-21, D $8-26, Kids' $6-7; Brunch $7-15)*, *(Five Bays Bistro 420-5559, D $20-35)*, *(Osterville Village 428-1005)*, Lite Fare *(Earthly Delights 420-2206, To Go)* **1-3 mi:** Motel *(Centerville Corners 246-7881, $75-195)*, Inn/B&B *(Long Dell 775-2750)* **3+ mi:** Restaurant *(Regatta of Cotuit 428-5715, D $25-36, 5 mi., Tap Room $12-25)*

Recreation and Entertainment
Under 1 mi: Picnic Area, Tennis Courts *(Osterville Bay School)*, Park *(Armstrong-Kelley)*, Museum *(Osterville Historical Soc 428-5861)* **1-3 mi:** Beach *(Dowses)*, Golf Course *(New Seabury 477-9400)*, Fitness Center *(Osterville 428-3775)*, Hike/Bike Trails **3+ mi:** Horseback Riding *(Holly Hill 428-2621, 3.5 mi.)*

Provisioning and General Services
Under 1 mi: Convenience Store *(Cumberland 420-8168)*, Market *(Fancy's 428-6954)*, Gourmet Shop *(Osterville Cheese 428-9085)*, Delicatessen *(Earthly Delights)*, Liquor Store *(Osterville 428-6327)*, Farmers' Market *(Fri, 9-2 Osterville Museum)*, Fishmonger *(Premier 420-1115)*, Bank/ATM *(Citizens Bank; TD Bank 428-5700)*, Catholic Church, Protestant Church, Library *(Osterville 428-5757)*, Beauty Salon *(Jamila 420-1912)*, Dry Cleaners *(Centerville 420-6118)*, Hardware Store *(House & Garden 428-6911)*, Florist *(Flowersticks 420-7966)* **1-3 mi:** Wine/Beer *(Craigville 420-0321)*, Synagogue **3+ mi:** Supermarket *(Stop & Shop 428-1278, 4 mi.)*, Pharmacy *(CVS 428-9638, 3.5 mi.)*

Transportation
OnCall: Rental Car *(Enterprise 778-8293)*, Taxi *(Checker 771-8294)*, Airport Limo *(Cape Cod 771-8294)* **Near:** InterCity Bus *(CCRTA Woods Hole, Orleans, Hyannis)* **Airport:** Barnstable/Logan *(8 mi./73 mi.)*

Medical Services
911 Service **OnCall:** Ambulance **Under 1 mi:** Dentist *(Osterville Family 428-2443)*, Chiropractor *(Bober 420-0495)*, Holistic Services *(Osterville Massage 428-5436)*, Optician *(Simply Eyewear 420-4231)* **3+ mi:** Doctor *(Midcape Medical Ctr 771-4092, 6 mi.)*, Veterinarian *(Mid Cape 428-2989, 3.5 mi.)* **Hospital:** Cape Cod 771-1800 *(8.5 mi.)*

Setting -- A bottle-neck of docks, the narrow entrance to West Bay is home to Oyster Harbors, Nauticus Marine and venerable Crosby's, the last to starboard. A large, new, white shed and several weathered-shingled classic yard buildings -- one housing a top shelf restaurant - overlook three long docks stretching out into the fairway. Sylvan views up the bay where it widens into a large circular basin surrounded by luxurious waterfront homes - many dating to the 19thC.

Marina Notes -- *Moorings: To 21ft. $50; 22-31 ft. $55; 32ft. & Up $60. Week 22-31ft. $325; 32 ft & Up -$350. Month 22-31 ft. $850; 32 ft. +$950. **Call for pump out reservation. Boatyard established here in 1850 -- this the oldest continuously operating yard in the US. Builds famous Crosby Catboat, as well as Wianno Senior, Crosby Striper, Canyon, Hawk, and a line of Tugs. Plus full resorations. Moorings: further up Cotuit Bay, out of sight of yard and across West Bay near Cotuit Pier dinghy dock. Fuel dock 7 days May-Sep, off -season call. West Bay Bridge (790-6330) for schedule. Bathhouse: Utilitarian at best.

Notable -- Osterville's favorite eatery, Islander (sibling to Hyannis' Island Merchant) delivers Carribbean-meets-Cape-Cod cuisine in the middle of the boatyard. The charming, low-key village is a delightful respite from the summer throngs. A half-dozen eateries, trendy boutiques, elegant home goods, galleries, provisioners, the post office and library line a quarter-mile stretch of Wianno Avenue and Main Street. Take a stroll through the pretty community and walk across the bridge to Little Island. Great Island, the "Oyster Harbors" community, is off-limits by road but not to a dinghy out for an afternoon sightseeing tour. Just 0.4 mile from the docks, Osterville Historical Museum showcases various sailing vessels in an 1824 sea captain's house and 18thC. Cammet House.

PHOTOS ON DVD: 9

Hyannis Marina

1 Willow Street; Hyannis, MA 02601

Tel: (508) 790-4000 **VHF: Monitor** Ch. 9, 72 **Talk** Ch. 72
Fax: (508) 775-0851 **Alternate Tel:** n/a
Email: carla@hyannismarina.com **Web:** www.hyannismarina.com
Nearest Town: Hyannis *(0.5 mi.)* **Tourist Info:** (508) 362-5230

Navigational Information

Lat: 41°38.992' **Long:** 070°16.438' **Tide:** 3 ft. **Current:** 1 kt. **Chart:** 13229
Rep. Depths (*MLW*): Entry 16 ft. **Fuel Dock** 14 ft. **Max Slip/Moor** 14 ft./-
Access: Lewis Bay to Hyannis Inner Harbor

Marina Facilities *(In Season/Off Season)*

Fuel: *Texaco* - Slip-Side Fueling, Gasoline, Diesel, High-Speed Pumps
Slips: 180 Total, 25 Transient **Max LOA:** 200 ft. **Max Beam:** 40 ft.
Rate *(per ft.)*: **Day** $4.00* **Week** Inq. **Month** Inq.
Power: 30 amp $15, **50 amp** $38, **100 amp** Metered, **200 amp** n/a
Cable TV: Yes, Incl. **Dockside Phone:** Yes, Incl., Switchboard Incl., Availab
Dock Type: Fixed, Floating, Long Fingers, Alongside, Concrete, Wood
Moorings: 0 Total, 0 Transient **Launch:** n/a
Rate: Day n/a **Week** n/a **Month** n/a
Heads: 12 Toilet(s), 12 Shower(s) *(dressing rooms)*
Internet: Yes *(Wi-Fi, Free)* **Laundry:** 6 Washer(s), 6 Dryer(s)
Pump-Out: OnSite, Full Service, 3 Port **Fee:** Free **Closed Heads:** Yes

Marina Operations

Owner/Manager: Carla A Sullivan **Dockmaster:** same
In-Season: May-Oct, 8am-8pm **Off-Season:** Nov-Apr, 8am-5pm
After-Hours Arrival: See security guard, onsite 24 hrs.
Reservations: Yes **Credit Cards:** Visa/MC, Dscvr, Tex
Discounts: None
Pets: Welcome, Dog Walk Area **Handicap Access:** Yes, Heads, Docks

Marina Services and Boat Supplies

Services - Docking Assistance, Concierge, Boaters' Lounge, Security *(24 Hrs., Gate, Guard)*, Dock Carts, 3 Phase **Communication -** Pay Phone, FedEx, UPS **Supplies - OnSite:** Ice *(Block, Cube)*, Ships' Store **Under 1 mi:** Propane *(Amerigas 775-0686)* **1-3 mi:** West Marine *(862-2700)*

Boatyard Services

OnSite: Travelift *(50T)*, Forklift, Launching Ramp, Engine mechanic *(gas, diesel)*, Electrical Repairs, Electronics Repairs, Hull Repairs, Rigger, Bottom Cleaning, Brightwork, Air Conditioning, Refrigeration, Woodworking, Painting, Awlgrip, Yacht Broker **OnCall:** Propeller Repairs **Yard Rates:** $59 & $112/hr., Haul & Launch $12 & 16/ft. *(blocking $85)*, Power Wash $3/ft., Bottom Paint $19/ft. *(paint incl.)* **Storage:** On-Land $48-50/ft.

Restaurants and Accommodations

OnSite: Restaurant *(Tugboats 775-6433, L&D $12-29, Kids' $3-10)*, *(Trader Ed's 790-8686, L&D $6-17, Kids' $5-6)* **Near:** Restaurant *(Dockside 470-1383, B $6-10, L&D $9-27, Kids' $6-8)*, Motel *(Anchor 775-0357, $69-429)* **Under 1 mi:** Restaurant *(Spanky's 771-2770, D $10-15)*, *(Black Cat 778-1233, L $8-19, D $10-35, Dink)*, *(Baxter's Boat House 775-7040, L&D $8-34, Dink)*, *(Island Merchant 771-1337, D $12-27)*, *(Colombo's 790-5700, L $10-20, D $15-22, Late $8-14; Kids' $6-8)*, *(Embargo 771-9700, D $11-28, Tapas $5-13)*, Lite Fare *(Box Lunch 790-5855, Del.)*, Pizzeria *(Palio 771-7004)*

Recreation and Entertainment

OnSite: Pool, Picnic Area, Grills, Playground **Under 1 mi:** Bowling *(Ryan 775-3411)*, Park *(Aselton)*, Museum *(C.C. Maritime 775-1273, $5/4; J.F.K. 790-3077; $12/9)*, Tours *(Hyannis Harbor 790-0696, $16-32/8-24; Hyannis Pirate Adv. 394-9100; C.C R.R. 771-3800, $21/17; C.C. Duckmobiles 790-2111, $17/5)*, Cultural Attract *(Melody Tent 775-5630)*, Sightseeing *(Olde C.C. Trolley 771-8687)* **1-3 mi:** Beach *(Veteran's; Kalmus; Sea St.)*, Dive Shop *(Sea Sports 790-1217)*, Golf Course *(Twin Brook 862-6980)*, Fitness Center *(Fitness 500 815-4520)*, Movie Theater *(Regal 771-7872)*

Provisioning and General Services

Under 1 mi: Market *(Christy's 771-0900)*, Supermarket *(Shaw's 775-7611)*, Delicatessen *(La Petite France 775-1067)*, Wine/Beer *(Grain & Vine 775-0660)*, Farmers' Market *(Wed 3-6pm Hyannis Comm. Ctr.)*, Green Grocer *(Fresh 771-1770)*, Bank/ATM, Post Office, Catholic Church, Protestant Church, Library *(775-2280)*, Beauty Salon *(Maria Bonita 815-4540)*, Dry Cleaners *(Spartan 775-8119)*, Laundry *(Clothesline 778-1976)*, Hardware Store *(Ace 775-0620)*, Florist *(Shaw's)* **1-3 mi:** Health Food *(Trader Joe's 790-3008)*, Liquor Store *(Hyannis 775-1205)*, Bakery *(Pain D'Avignon 778-8588)*, Fishmonger *(Cote 771-6218)*, Synagogue, Bookstore *(B&N 862-6310)*, Pharmacy *(CVS 775-8462)*, Retail Shops *(Cape Cod Mall)*

Transportation

OnSite: Courtesy Car/Van, Local Bus *(HAT 385-8326)* **OnCall:** Taxi *(Exec. 776-3379)*, Airport Limo *(C.C. 771-2640)* **Near:** InterCity Bus *(P & B 746-0378)*, Ferry Service *(Nantucket, MV 778-2600)* **Under 1 mi:** Bikes *(Sea Sports 790-1217)*, Rental Car *(Trek 771-2459)* **Airport:** Barn. *(1.5 mi.)*

Medical Services

911 Service **Near:** Doctor *(Papavasilliou 771-0006)*, Dentist *(Falla 775-8416)* **Under 1 mi:** Chiropractor *(Harborside 775-1935)* **1-3 mi:** Veterinarian *(Barnstable 778-6555)* **Hospital:** Cape Cod 771-1800 *(0.1 mi.)*

Setting -- Enter Lewis Bay and follow the well-marked channel into the busy inner harbor - the deepest on the Cape. Past the Hyannis Yacht Club, the large, first-class marina is to starboard, distinguished by the original brown, shingled Quonset hut - now the office and marine store. This historic structure has been overshadowed by a four-acre compound of enormous state-of-the-art work white sheds and well-designed, water-side amenities buildings that includes an inviting pool and two restaurants. The bustling tourist haven lies on the opposite shore beyond the Bismore Park Bulkhead Dock on Ocean Street .

Marina Notes -- *to 35 ft. $3.50/ft, 36-79 ft. $4/ft, 80 ft.+$5/ft. Family owned/operated for over 40 yrs. Professional operation. Focuses on unique needs of a wide range of vessels & delivers. High-speed fuel, tall pilings, two eateries, harborside pool, ship's store, 3 courtesy cars, playground, Wi-Fi on all docks, Internet "cafe" in laundry room. Extensive megayacht services & facilities - 100A 1 & 3-phase. Turns over charters in hours. Sportfish services. Dealer for Sea Ray, Contender, Mercury, Intrepid, Key West, Jupiter. Bathhouse: Sparkling white-tiled group heads with stainless partitions & pretty sea motif.

Notable -- Trader Ed's poolside eatery and raw bar is the fun center of marina life (head of A & B docks). Centrally-located, upscale Tugboats looks across the main dock and harbor from two dining areas with awning-topped decks. All of Hyannis' services and attractions are an easy walk - including a transportation hub that extends far beyond the Cape. On the way to the shopping district (Main & South Streets) and J.F.K. Memorial Library, stop at the fascinating Cape Cod Maritime Museum (with interactive kids' area). Or daytrip to Nantucket or Martha's Vineyard on nearby ferries. Memorial Day's Figawi Race bases here.

PHOTOS ON DVD: 25

Navigational Information

Lat: 41°38.966' **Long:** 070°16.767' **Tide:** 4 ft. **Current:** 1 kt **Chart:** 13229
Rep. Depths (*MLW*): Entry 16 ft. **Fuel Dock** 13 ft. **Max Slip/Moor** 10 ft./-
Access: Follow channel into harbor, then west

Marina Facilities *(In Season/Off Season)*

Fuel: No
Slips: 26 Total, 8 Transient **Max LOA:** 100 ft. **Max Beam:** n/a
Rate *(per ft.)*: **Day** $2.75* **Week** n/a **Month** n/a
Power: 30 amp $7.25, **50 amp** $7.25, **100 amp** n/a, **200 amp** n/a
Cable TV: No **Dockside Phone:** No
Dock Type: Fixed, Short Fingers, Wood
Moorings: 0 Total, 0 Transient **Launch:** No
Rate: Day n/a **Week** n/a **Month** n/a
Heads: 2 Toilet(s)
Internet: No **Laundry:** None
Pump-Out: OnSite, OnCall, 1 Central **Fee:** Free **Closed Heads:** Yes

Marina Operations

Owner/Manager: Dan Horn **Dockmaster:** Joe Gibbs
In-Season: Year-round, 24 hrs. **Off-Season:** n/a
After-Hours Arrival: Call ahead
Reservations: Yes **Credit Cards:** Visa/MC, Amex
Discounts: None
Pets: Welcome **Handicap Access:** Yes, Heads

Bismore Park Marina

180 Ocean St.; Hyannis, MA 02601

Tel: (508) 790-6327 **VHF: Monitor** Ch. 9 **Talk** n/a
Fax: (508) 790-6275 **Alternate Tel:** n/a
Email: harbormaster@town.barnstable.ma.us **Web:** town.barnstable.ma.us
Nearest Town: Hyannis **Tourist Info:** (508) 362-5230

Marina Services and Boat Supplies

Services - Docking Assistance **Supplies - Near:** Ice *(Block, Cube, Shaved)*, Ships' Store *(Hyannis 790-4000)*, Live Bait *(Hy-Line B&T)* **Under 1 mi:** Bait/Tackle *(Powder Horn 775-8975)*, Propane *(C.C. 771-4807)* **1-3 mi:** West Marine *(862-2700)*

Boatyard Services

Nearest Yard: Hyannis Marina (508) 790-4000

Restaurants and Accommodations

Near: Restaurant *(Black Cat 778-1233, L $8-19, D $10-35)*, *(Trader Ed's 367-2162, dink)*, *(Raw Bar 775-8800, music)*, *(Spanky's Seafood 771-2770, L & D $8-32, Kids' $5-8)*, *(Tugboats 775-6433, L & D $12-29)*, Motel *(Hyannis Holiday 775-1639, $83-217)*, *(Harbor House 771-1880, $124-540)*, Hotel *(Seacoast 775-3828, $78-158)* **Under 1 mi:** Restaurant *(Alberto's 778-1770)*, *(Fazio's 775-9400, D $13-22)*, *(Baxter's Seafood 775-7040, L&D $8-34, dink)*, *(Island Merchant 771-1337, D $13-22)*, *(British Beer 771-1776, L $7-10, D $9-18)*, *(Alberto's 778-1770, L $13-17, D $15-35)*, Fast Food *(McD, BK)*, Pizzeria *(Palio 771-7004)*, *(Scottie's 790-9500)*, Hotel *(Cape Cod 775-3000, $69-199)*

Recreation and Entertainment

OnSite: Picnic Area, Party Boat *(Hy-Line "Sea Queen" 775-7185)*, Park, Galleries *(HyArts Shanties)* **Near:** Museum *(C.C. Maritime 775-1723 $5/4; J.F. Kennedy 790-3077 $12/9)*, Tours *(Hyannis Harbor 790-0696, $16-32/ $8)* **Under 1 mi:** Beach *(Veterans)*, Dive Shop *(Sea Sports 790-1217)*, Golf Course *(Twin Brooks 775-7775)*, Fitness Center *(Fitness 500 815-4520)*, Bowling *(Ryan Fam 775-3411)*, Cultural Attract *(Comedy Lounge 771-1700; C.C. Melody Tent 775-5630; C.C. baseball 862-5352)*, Sightseeing *(C.C. Duckmobiles 790-2111, $17/5)* **1-3 mi:** Horseback Riding *(Paradise 398-5679)*, Movie Theater *(Regal 771-7872)*, Video Rental *(Blockbuster 790-3430)*

Provisioning and General Services

Near: Market *(Christy's 470-1551)*, Delicatessen *(La Petite 775-1067)*, Protestant Church **Under 1 mi:** Supermarket *(Shaw's 775-7611)*, Wine/Beer *(Woods Hole 775-3380)*, Liquor Store *(Hyannis 775-1205)*, Bakery *(Great Cape 534-9368)*, Farmers' Market *(Wed 3-6pm Comm. Ctr.)*, Green Grocer *(Fresh 771-1770)*, Bank/ATM, Post Office *(775-2603)*, Catholic Church, Synagogue, Library *(Hyannis 775-2280)*, Beauty Salon *(By Design 775-4455)*, Dry Cleaners *(Centerville 771-5500)*, Laundry *(Clothesline 778-1976)*, Pharmacy *(Rite Aid 771-6511)*, Hardware Store *(Bradford's 775-0620)*, Florist *(Magnolia 790-0452)*, Copies Etc. *(Fed Ex 778-9454)* **1-3 mi:** Health Food *(Trader Joe's)*, Fishmonger *(Cote 771-6218)*, Bookstore *(B&N 862-6310)*, Retail Shops *(Cape Cod Mall)*, Buying Club *(BJ's 568-4035)*

Transportation

OnSite: Ferry Service *(Hy-Line 778-2688)* **OnCall:** Taxi *(Exec. 776-3379)*, Airport Limo *(C.C. 771-2640)* **Near:** Rental Car *(Thrifty 771-2057)*, Local Bus *(CCRT 775-8504; HAT 385-8326)* **Airport:** C.C./Logan *(2 mi./80 mi.)*

Medical Services

911 Service **Under 1 mi:** Doctor *(Mid-Upper Cape 778-0300)*, Dentist *(Mid Cape 775-1955)*, Chiropractor *(Hands On 790-8787)*, Holistic Services *(Revitalife 836-0920)*, Optician *(Snyder 775-0881)* **1-3 mi:** Veterinarian *(Barnstable 778-6555)* **Hospital:** Cape Cod 771-1800 *(0.5 mi.)*

Setting -- Follow the channel into the inner harbor; then head 150 yards to port where the docks stretch along the Bismore Park bulkhead - which berths ferries, fishing boats and pleasure craft. The harbormaster and a tourism kiosk are in the white, revitalized, cupola-topped Mitchell Building. The brick Walkway to the Sea, lined with pole-mounted lobster buoys, winds past the HyArts shanties to Aselton Park - ending at the Village Green and Main Street retail area.

Marina Notes -- *Commercial $1.50/ft. Recently renovated harbormaster's office, very busy operation. One of 4 Barnstable town marinas. Harbor berths 500 comm. & rec. vessels, plus whale-watch vessel, tour & fishing boats & two ferry operations. Bathhouse: Recent, high-quality concrete & steel, but no showers or laundry. Note: Anchoring in Lewis Bay permitted, good access to beach or Hyannis YC - but long dinghy ride to town.

Notable -- Hyannis plans to extend the delightful wave-patterned "Walkway" all the way around the harbor. The onsite Hy-Line Landing homes the Coffee Table Cafe and the Raw Bar. Free musical and theatrical performances are held summer evenings in nearby Aselton Park at the head of the harbor - the Cape Cod Maritime Museum is on the northeast edge. Walk two blocks through the lovely Village Green (with Iyannough statue) to Main and North Streets for more dining and the bustling shopping district. The John F. Kennedy Museum is in the middle of town in Old Town Hall (which includes the baseball league exhibits in The Dugout). 0.6 mile south, the JFK Memorial is next to the Veterans Park beach. Hyannis is the Cape's transportation hub - a shuttle circles the shopping & historic district, the ferries go to Nantucket and the Vineyard, a local bus heads out to the malls, buses go to Boston and beyond, and the airport is two miles.

PHOTOS ON DVD: 25

Bass River Marina

PO Box 355; 140 Main Street; West Dennis, MA 02670

Tel: (508) 394-8341 **VHF: Monitor** Ch. 71 **Talk** Ch. 71
Fax: (508) 394-1660 **Alternate Tel:** n/a
Email: manager@bassrivermarina.com **Web:** www.bassrivermarina.com
Nearest Town: Dennis *(3 mi.)* **Tourist Info:** (508) 790-2921

Navigational Information

Lat: 41°39.960' **Long:** 070°10.610' **Tide:** n/a **Current:** n/a **Chart:** 13229
Rep. Depths (*MLW*): Entry 4 ft. **Fuel Dock** n/a **Max Slip/Moor** 4 ft./-
Access: Vineyard Snd, river ent. marked by R2 Bell. Under bridge, to starboar

Marina Facilities *(In Season/Off Season)*

Fuel: Gasoline
Slips: 158 Total, 7 Transient **Max LOA:** 40 ft. **Max Beam:** 14 ft.
Rate *(per ft.)*: **Day** $3.50* **Week** $16 **Month** $49
Power: 30 amp Incl., **50 amp** n/a, **100 amp** n/a, **200 amp** n/a
Cable TV: Yes **Dockside Phone:** No
Dock Type: Floating, Wood
Moorings: 0 Total, 0 Transient **Launch:** n/a
Rate: Day n/a **Week** n/a **Month** n/a
Heads: 2 Toilet(s), 2 Shower(s) *(dressing rooms)*, Book Exchange
Internet: Yes *(Wi-Fi, Free)* **Laundry:** None
Pump-Out: Full Service, 1 Central **Fee:** Free **Closed Heads:** Yes

Marina Operations

Owner/Manager: Robert Bratton **Dockmaster:** Same
In-Season: May-Nov, 8am-5pm Mon-Fri** **Off-Season:** Dec-April, Closed
After-Hours Arrival: n/a
Reservations: Yes, Required **Credit Cards:** Visa/MC, Dscvr, Amex
Discounts: Boat/US **Dockage:** 25% **Fuel:** n/a **Repair:** n/a
Pets: Welcome **Handicap Access:** Yes

Marina Services and Boat Supplies

Services - Docking Assistance, Dock Carts **Communication -** FedEx, UPS, Express Mail **Supplies - OnSite:** Ice *(Block, Cube)*, Ships' Store **Under 1 mi:** Bait/Tackle *(Sportsman's 398-4125)*, Live Bait *(Riverview 394-1036)* **3+ mi:** Propane *(Eastern 760-2778, 3.5 mi)*

Boatyard Services

OnSite: Travelift, Forklift, Engine mechanic *(gas, diesel)*, Electrical Repairs, Electronic Sales, Electronics Repairs, Hull Repairs, Canvas Work, Bottom Cleaning, Air Conditioning, Refrigeration, Compound, Wash & Wax, Interior Cleaning, Propeller Repairs, Painting **Dealer for:** Volvo Penta, Larson, Zodiac, Yamaha. **Yard Rates:** $100/hr., Haul & Launch $18/ft., Power Wash $7/ft., Bottom Paint $18/ft. **Storage:** On-Land $30/ft.

Restaurants and Accommodations

OnSite: Restaurant *(Summer Shanty 394-0400, L&D $6-27, Live music Thur-Sun)* **Near:** Restaurant *(Marathon 394-3379, L&D $4-23)*, *(Sundancers 394-1600, L&D $7.50-13, Kids' $6-7)*, *(Crow's Nest 760-3335)*, Motel *(Barnacle 394-8472, $45-200)* **Under 1 mi:** Restaurant *(Riverway Lobster 398-2172, D $10-26)*, *(O'Shea's 398-8887)*, *(Olympia Seafood 394-2612)*, *(Doyle's 760-1000)*, *(Jerk Cafe 394-1944)*, Pizzeria *(Paradise 398-9177)*, Motel *(Beach'n Towne 398-2311)*, *(Capt. Johnathan 398-1832)*, Inn/B&B *(Ambassador 394-4000)* **1-3 mi:** Restaurant *(Kreme 'n Kone 394-0808, L&D $4-19, Seafood for 50 yrs! Inside/deck)*, *(Ocean House 394-0700, D $16-26, pizza, late night)*

Recreation and Entertainment

OnSite: Picnic Area, Boat Rentals **Near:** Park *(Horsefoot Cove)* **Under 1 mi:** Galleries *(Sullivan 394-3555; O'Neil 398-0233, 1 mi.)* **1-3 mi:** Beach *(West Dennis)*, Tennis Courts *(Mid-Cape 394-3511)*, Golf Course *(Blue Rock 398-9295)*, Fitness Center *(Mid-Cape 394-3511)*, Bowling *(Ryan Fam 394-5644)*, Movie Theater *(Entertainment 394-4700)*, Video Rental *(Redbox; Blockbuster Exp)*, Museum *(C.C. Cultural Center 394-7100)*, Cultural Attract *(Harwich Jr. Theatre 432-2002; Cape Symphony 362-1111)*

Provisioning and General Services

Near: Liquor Store *(Finley's 398-8391)*, Library *(West Dennis 398-2050)*, Beauty Salon *(Andreas 760-0666)* **Under 1 mi:** Market *(West Dennis 394-5500)*, Delicatessen *(Jelly Belly 394-9090)*, Green Grocer *(International 258-3232)*, Post Office *(398-4292)*, Catholic Church, Protestant Church, Dry Cleaners *(Princess 398-5516)*, Hardware Store *(Anchor 398-3691)*, Florist *(Kevin's 800-962-6290)* **1-3 mi:** Convenience Store *(7-Eleven 398-7487)*, Supermarket *(Shaws 394-0995)*, Health Food *(Dennisport 760-3043)*, Wine/Beer *(Yarmouth 760-2006)*, Bakery *(Great Island 760-0007)*, Fishmonger *(Chatham 394-1181)*, Bank/ATM, Pharmacy *(CVS 398-8800)*

Transportation

OnCall: Rental Car *(Enterprise 778-8293)*, Taxi *(Cape 790-0222)* **1-3 mi:** Bikes *(Barbara's 760-4723)* **Airport:** Barnstable 775-2020 *(7 mi.)*

Medical Services

911 Service **OnCall:** Ambulance **Under 1 mi:** Dentist *(Amorosi 394-2066)* **1-3 mi:** Doctor *(C.C. Medical 394-7113)*, Chiropractor *(Network 394-9355)*, Holistic Services *(C.C. Body & Soul 760-5667)*, Optician *(Sheinkopf 398-6333)* **Hospital:** Cape Cod 771-1800 *(6.2 mi.)*

Setting -- Upriver, under the 15-foot fixed Main Street bridge, the marina is immediately to starboard in Horsefoot Cove. Four very long floating docks fan out from the ship-shape jam-packed upland. An attractive, two-story white clapboard office is backed by massive storage and work sheds. The Compass Rose Summer Shanty waterfront bar and restaurant adds a lively note to the ambiance. The eatery and slips enjoy beautiful, wide-open marsh views.

Marina Notes -- *Weekdays $3/ft. Holidays $4.50/ft. **Sat-Sun 8am-5pm. Estab 1958. Powerboats only - air draft 15 ft. Good ships store. Extensive mechanical services. Permanent slipholders have a lively social scene and speak well of the marina operation. Most commercial services are along the roadway and within walking distance. Gasoline only--no diesel. Bathhouse: Modern, nicely decorated with private dressing rooms.Far from the outer docks.

Notable -- Summer Shanty's boaters' menu of fried, broiled and grilled seafood comes with entertainment from 4-11pm, Thursday through Sunday - and they even deliver to the boat. Hard by Route 28, aka Main Street, Bass River offers easy access to many West Dennis supplies and services. Gift shops, jewelry shops, small unique stores, and more restaurants stretch along Main Street. Housed in historic structures, the Cultural Center of Cape Cod offers workshops, exhibits and entertainment. South Yarmouth is just west across the bridge. Beside more eateries, markets and Ryan Amusements (bowling and video games), a stretch along Pleasant Street, right on the river, is lined with the Greek Revival and Federal-style homes of the area's 19th C. elite. The H2O Hyannis-Orleans bus runs along Route 28 and connects in Hyannis with the SeaLine, the Barnstable Villager, and Bonanza/B.P. service to Boston and Providence.

    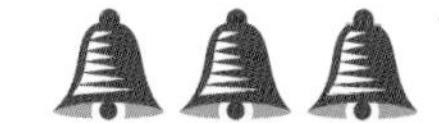

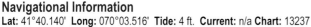

Navigational Information
Lat: 41°40.140' **Long:** 070°03.516' **Tide:** 4 ft. **Current:** n/a **Chart:** 13237
Rep. Depths (*MLW*): Entry 6 ft. **Fuel Dock** n/a **Max Slip/Moor** 14 ft./6 ft.
Access: Nantucket Sound, follow channel straight ahead through breakwater

Marina Facilities *(In Season/Off Season)*
Fuel: No
Slips: 195 Total, 10 Transient **Max LOA:** 65 ft. **Max Beam:** 16 ft.
Rate *(per ft.)*: **Day** $2.50/1.25* **Week** Inq. **Month** Inq.
Power: 30 amp $11, **50 amp** n/a, **100 amp** n/a, **200 amp** n/a
Cable TV: No **Dockside Phone:** No
Dock Type: Floating, Long Fingers, Pilings, Wood
Moorings: 0 Total, 0 Transient **Launch:** n/a, Dinghy Dock
Rate: Day n/a **Week** n/a **Month** n/a
Heads: 8 Toilet(s), 4 Shower(s)
Internet: No **Laundry:** None
Pump-Out: OnSite, Full Service, 1 Central **Fee:** Inc **Closed Heads:** Yes

Marina Operations
Owner/Manager: Thomas Leach **Dockmaster:** Michelle Morris
In-Season: Jun-Sep 15, 24 hrs. **Off-Season:** Sep 16-May, closed
After-Hours Arrival: Call Tom's cell 508-237-9291
Reservations: Yes **Credit Cards:** Visa/MC, Cash/Checks only
Discounts: None
Pets: Welcome, Dog Walk Area **Handicap Access:** Yes, Heads, Docks

Saquatucket Harbor Marina

PO Box 207; 715 Main Street; Harwich, MA 02645

Tel: (508) 430-7532 **VHF: Monitor** Ch. 16 **Talk** Ch. 68, 66
Fax: (753) 430-7535 **Alternate Tel:** (508) 237-1860
Email: harbor@town.harwich.ma.us **Web:** www.threeharbors.com
Nearest Town: Harwich Port *(.5 mi.)* **Tourist Info:** (508) 430-1165

Marina Services and Boat Supplies
Services - Docking Assistance, Security, Trash Pick-Up, Dock Carts **Communication -** Mail & Package Hold, Fax in/out *($1)*, FedEx, UPS, Express Mail **Supplies - OnSite:** Ice *(Block)* **1-3 mi:** Ships' Store *(Allen Harbor Marine 432-0353)*, Bait/Tackle *(Sunrise 430-4117)*

Boatyard Services
OnSite: Launching Ramp **OnCall:** Engine mechanic *(gas, diesel)* **Nearest Yard:** Allen Harbor Marine (508) 432-0353

Restaurants and Accommodations
OnSite: Restaurant *(Brax Landing 432-5515, L&D $7-22 Kids' $6-11 Sun Br. $17/9)* **Near:** Snack Bar *(Schoolhouse Ice Cream)*, Motel *(Coachman 432-0707, $95-230)* **Under 1 mi:** Restaurant *(Cape Sea Grill 432-4745, D $23-36)*, *(L'Alouette 430-0405, D $18-30)*, *(Port 430-5410, D $19-28)*, *(Hot Stove 432-9911, L&D $7-15)*, Lite Fare *(Dino's 432-0700, B $3-9, L $3-4)*, *(Lighthouse Cafe 432-5399, B $7-12, L $7-15)*, Pizzeria *(George's 432-3144)*, *(Ember 430-0407)*, Inn/B&B *(Seadar by the Sea 432-0264, $90-400)*, *(Captain's Quarters 432-1991, $119-139)*

Recreation and Entertainment
OnSite: Picnic Area, Fishing Charter *(Magellan 277-8090; Capt'n & Tonnaire 246-6691; Striper 432-4025; Fishtales 432-3783; Sue-Z 432-3294)*, Party Boat *(Yankee 432-2520, 60 passengers, Half day $28, 8am or 12:30pm; Capn' Kid 430-0066, 2 hr family fishing trips $25, 45 pass.)*, Tours *(Monomoy Island Excursions 430-7772 $35/30 refuge & seals)* **Under 1 mi:** Beach *(Merkel)*, Golf Course *(Harwich Port 432-0250)*, Park *(Thompson Field; Yasuna)*, Galleries *(820 Main St 430-7622; Kreeger Pottery 432-6398)* **1-3 mi:** Video Rental *(Redbox; Video Store 430-5211)*, Museum *(Brooks Academy at Harwich Historical Soc. 432-8089)*, Cultural Attract *(Harwich Junior Theatre 432-2002)*, Special Events *(Harwich Mariners at Whitehouse Field 432-2000; Cranberry Fest - Sep)* **3+ mi:** Horseback Riding *(Saltwater Farm 246-3609, 3.5 mi.)*, Movie Theater *(Regal 430-1162, 4 mi.)*

Provisioning and General Services
Under 1 mi: Convenience Store *(Cumberland)*, Delicatessen *(Mason Jar 432-1803)*, Liquor Store *(Harwich 430-0000)*, Bakery *(Bonatt's 432-7199)*, Fishmonger *(Maguro 432-8812)*, Bank/ATM, Protestant Church, Beauty Salon *(Heather's 430-1617)*, Hardware Store *(True Value 432-1113)*, Florist *(White 432-5540)*, Copies Etc. *(Red River 432-3000)* **1-3 mi:** Market *(Star 432-3433)*, Supermarket *(Stop & Shop 432-1803)*, Farmers' Market *(3-6pm Thur, Harwich Hist. Soc.)*, Post Office, Catholic Church, Library *(Harwich 430-7562)*, Laundry *(Harwich 432-0552)*, Pharmacy *(CVS 430-0660)*, Retail Shops *(333 Main Street)*

Transportation
OnSite: Ferry Service *(Freedom to Nantucket 432-8999 $39/29 1-way)* **OnCall:** Rental Car *(Enterprise)*, Taxi *(Eldredge 945-0068)*, Airport Limo *(Carriage House 432-6696)* **Under 1 mi:** Local Bus *(H2O 385-8326 & Flex - Star Market to Provincetown)* **Airport:** Barnstable *(20 mi.)*

Medical Services
911 Service **Under 1 mi:** Doctor *(Macy 432-0887)* **1-3 mi:** Dentist *(Dowgiallo 432-3118)*, Chiropractor *(Wright 432-7002)*, Holistic Services *(Sol Spa 432-8772)*, Optician *(Cape Cod 432-0020)* **3+ mi:** Veterinarian *(Pleasant Bay 432-5500, 3.5 mi.)* **Hospital:** Cape Cod 771-1800 *(12 mi.)*

Setting -- The buoyed entrance channel (aka Andrews Creek) just east of Wychmere Harbor, leads through quiet marsh opening into the rectangular Saquatucket basin - literally filled with docks berthing a mix of pleasure craft, working vessels, and charter boats. In the northwest corner, the pyramid-roofed Brax Landing restaurant perches on a hill. In the center of the upland is the single-story, shingled office and amenities building with black shutters.

Marina Notes -- *$1.75/ft. under 35 ft.in season, $1.50 off-season. Summer reservations - 3 night min, stay, 2 week max. Off-season first come, first served. Open May 1-Nov 15 for recreational boaters. Municipal marina, one of three Harwich harbors. Carved out of the marsh and Andrews River in 1969. Tom Leach Harbormaster since 1973. Fuel removed in '07, now Freedom ferry to Nantucket dock. Army Corps dredges channel to 6 ft. mlw. Larger boats put on the outside for more elbow room. Fuel available at Wychmere Harbor & Allen Harbor. Mechanics on call. Everything orderly and well-maintained. Bathhouse: Stark steel & formica public heads on outside of building. Boaters-only heads & showers through office. More commodious, but still institutional. Laundry.

Notable -- The long channel puts the marina just off Route 28 giving convenient access to Harwich Port's stretch of restaurants and services. Venerable Brax Landing, operated since 1976 by the Brackett Family, offers all-glass dining rooms, a harborside patio with blue umbrella-topped tables and a second-floor deck - with long marina views. Cranberry farming got its start here; learn more at Brooks Academy. The H2O Hyannis-Orleans bus runs along Route 28 connecting in Hyannis with Bonanza/B.P. to Boston and Providence. The Freedom ferry to Nantucket leaves at 8am, 11:30am, and 5:45pm for the 80-minute crossing.

Chatham Harbormaster Moorings

613 Stage Harbor Rd.*; Chatham, MA 02633

Tel: (508) 945-5185 **VHF: Monitor** Ch. 16 **Talk** Ch. 66
Fax: (508) 545-5121 **Alternate Tel:** (508) 545-5186
Email: srocanello@chatham-ma.gov **Web:** www.town.chatham.ma.us
Nearest Town: Chatham *(1.3 mi.)* **Tourist Info:** (508) 945-5199

Navigational Information

Lat: 41°39.987' **Long:** 069°57.984' **Tide:** 4 ft **Current:** 2 kt **Chart:** 13229
Rep. Depths (*MLW*): Entry 8 ft. **Fuel Dock** n/a **Max Slip/Moor** -/8 ft.
Access: Nantucket Sound to Chatham Roads

Marina Facilities *(In Season/Off Season)*

Fuel: Gasoline, Diesel
Slips: 0 Total, 0 Transient **Max LOA:** n/a **Max Beam:** n/a
Rate *(per ft.)*: **Day** n/a **Week** n/a **Month** n/a
Power: 30 amp n/a, **50 amp** n/a, **100 amp** n/a, **200 amp** n/a
Cable TV: No **Dockside Phone:** No
Dock Type: n/a
Moorings: 30 Total, 20 Transient **Launch:** No
Rate: Day $25** **Week** n/a **Month** n/a
Heads: 2 Toilet(s), 1 Shower(s)
Internet: No **Laundry:** None
Pump-Out: OnSite, Self Service **Fee:** Free **Closed Heads:** Yes

Marina Operations

Owner/Manager: Stuart F.X. Smith (Harbormaster) **Dockmaster:** Same
In-Season: April-Oct, 8am-4pm **Off-Season:** Nov-March, 8am-4pm
After-Hours Arrival: Call in advance
Reservations: Yes **Credit Cards:** Cash/Check only
Discounts: None
Pets: Welcome **Handicap Access:** No

Marina Services and Boat Supplies

Services - Trash Pick-Up **Supplies - Near:** Ice *(Block, Cube)*, Ships' Store *(Stage Harbor Marina; Seafever)* **1-3 mi:** Bait/Tackle *(Cape 945-3501)*

Boatyard Services

OnSite: Launching Ramp **OnCall:** Engine mechanic *(gas, diesel)* **Nearest Yard:** Stage Harbor (508) 945-1860

Restaurants and Accommodations

OnCall: Pizzeria *(Nick's 945-4680)* **Under 1 mi:** Motel *(Bradford 945-1030, $115-475)* **1-3 mi:** Restaurant *(Vining Bistro 945-5033, D $20.50-29), (Chatham Bars 945-0096, B $9-26, L $14-27, D $18-33, Tavern L $12-27, D $12-31. Beach $14-22 The Gold Standard), (Pate's 945-9777), (Chatham Squire 945-0945, L $7-19, D $10-22), (Wildgoose Tavern 945-5590, B $6-9.50, L $7-14, D $9-28), (Red Nun 348-0469, D $10-21), (Blue Coral 348-0485), (Captain's Table 945-1961, D $5-18), (Roobar 945-9988, D $12-29)*, Hotel *(Chatham Bars 945-0096, $500)*, Inn/B&B *(Old Harbor 945-4434, $129-329), (Chatham Wayside 945-5550, $120-495), (Queen Anne 945-0394, $120-415)*

Recreation and Entertainment

Under 1 mi: Beach *(Chatham Lighthouse)*, Tennis Courts *(Chatham)*, Fitness Center *(7:30am Yoga on South Beach 945-7643; Chatham Health 945-3555)*, Hike/Bike Trails *(8-mile circuit - map at CofC)*, Fishing Charter *(Chatham 945-7806)*, Park *(Chase Park - lawn bowling & 18thC.Old Grist Mill)*, Museum *(Atwood House 945-2493 - 1752 house tells Chatham's story, incl. a frozen 1947 fishing camp; Mayo House 945-6098)*, Sightseeing *(1876 Chatham Lighthouse)*, Galleries *(C.C. Photography 367-2180; Artful Hand 945-5681)*, Special Events *(Fri night band concerts - Main St; Chatham Athletics at Veterans Field)* **1-3 mi:** Playground *(A fab Leathers' design across from Railroad museum)*, Golf Course *(Chatham Seaside 945-4774)*, Boat Rentals *(Pleasant Bay 945-7245)*, Tours *(Cape Arial Tours 945-2563)*, Cultural Attract *(Monomoy Theatre 945-1589)* **3+ mi:** Horseback Riding *(Saltwater 246-3609, 5 mi.)*, Movie Theater *(Regal 430-1162, 5.5 mi.)*

Provisioning and General Services

Under 1 mi: Protestant Church **1-3 mi:** Market *(Chatham Village 945-9783)*, Health Food *(Chatham Natural 945-4139)*, Wine/Beer *(Chatham 945-0639)*, Liquor Store *(Liquor Locker 945-0501)*, Bakery *(Chatham 945-3229)*, Bank/ATM *(Bank of America; Cape Cod Five Cents)*, Post Office *(945-6054)*, Catholic Church, Library *(Town of Chatham 945-5170)*, Beauty Salon *(Salon Fabulous 945-7860)*, Dry Cleaners *(Princess 945-2584)*, Bookstore *(Yellow Umbrella 945-0144)*, Hardware Store *(Chatham 945-0107)*, Florist *(Manson 945-0080)* **3+ mi:** Supermarket *(Stop & Shop 432-5000, 5 mi.)*

Transportation

OnCall: Rental Car *(Enterprise 555-2997)*, Taxi *(Eldredge 945-0068)*, Airport Limo *(Kon 945-2941)* **1-3 mi:** Bikes *(Chatham Cycle 945-8981)*, Local Bus *(H2O 385-8326 from Chatham Rotary)* **Airport:** Cape Cod *(26 mi.)*

Medical Services

911 Service **Under 1 mi:** Holistic Services *(Le Petite Day Spa 237-8783)* **1-3 mi:** Doctor *(Mees 945-0187)*, Dentist *(Montbach 945-9595)*, Chiropractor *(McClennen 945-7755)*, Optician *(Bass River 945-1127)*, Veterinarian *(Stoney Hill 945-0151)* **Hospital:** Cape Cod 771-1800 *(19 mi.)*

PHOTOS ON DVD: 19

Setting -- At Cape Cod's elbow, the Stage Harbor mooring field is sheltered by Morris Island. It is delightfully calm with vistas of windswept dunes, weathered cottages and salt marsh. The harbormaster inhabits a typical Cape, wood-shingled lair with a second-story veranda and bouquet of antennas - a dinghy dock at its foot. Stage Harbor Yacht Club is just to the southeast. It's a mile to the spectacular Chatham light and beach; a bit further or a dinghy ride to the village.

Marina Notes -- *Mailing Address: Town Hall 549 Main St. **2 Week Max. Rental & "courtesy" moorings in outer harbor, denoted by letters "V" through "Z" on blue balls. Town uses elastic Hazelet rodes. No launch service. Use dinghy to get to harbormaster shack. Tends toward thin water. Marine services and small ship's store at Stage Harbor Marine, 0.3 mi. near Mill Pond Bridge. Bathhouse: Newly built, basic gray & white municipal. Outdoor shower lovers - nicely done, shingled one. Note: Anchoring allowed on south side of entrance channel, West of Stage Harbor buoy "8."

Notable -- Two worlds happily collide; low-key, artsy, old-moneyed summer Chatham and the hard-working year-round fishing fleet. Both appreciate their sweet, picturesque village, flower-bedecked summer cottages and charming commercial strip. Dinghy up the harbor, under the Mill Pond bridge, to the landing at the head of Little Mill Pond - the heart of town is one block away. Or, take a longer dinghy ride up Oyster Pond River to the grocery store. On foot? Walk a half mile north to the Atwood House Museum or a bit further to the Grist Mill. From the harbormaster's dinghy dock, it's a mile across the bridge to spectacular Chatham Light and its gorgeous sweep of beach.The fishing fleet and pier are in Chatham Harbor, a channel to the East (risky for non-locals).

  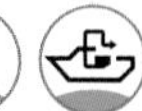

Navigational Information

Lat: 41°39.994' **Long:** 069°58.011' **Tide:** 4 ft. **Current:** n/a **Chart:** 13229
Rep. Depths (*MLW*): Entry 10 ft. **Fuel Dock** 6 ft. **Max Slip/Moor** 8 ft./12 ft.
Access: Chatham Roads to G1/R2, follow the Stage Harbor Channel

Marina Facilities *(In Season/Off Season)*

Fuel: Gasoline, Diesel
Slips: 30 Total, 3 Transient **Max LOA:** 115 ft. **Max Beam:** n/a
Rate *(per ft.)*: **Day** $2.00/$1.50 **Week** Inq. **Month** Inq.
Power: 30 amp Incl., **50 amp** n/a, **100 amp** n/a, **200 amp** n/a
Cable TV: No **Dockside Phone:** No
Dock Type: Floating, Short Fingers, Pilings, Alongside, Wood
Moorings: 44 Total, 10 Transient **Launch:** Yes (Incl.), Dinghy Dock
Rate: Day $35/25 **Week** $190/150 **Month** n/a
Heads: 2 Toilet(s)
Internet: No **Laundry:** None
Pump-Out: OnCall *(Boat)* **Fee:** Free **Closed Heads:** Yes

Marina Operations

Owner/Manager: Andrew Meincke **Dockmaster:** Same
In-Season: Year-Round, 8am-5pm **Off-Season:** n/a
After-Hours Arrival: Call in advance
Reservations: Yes** **Credit Cards:** Visa/MC, Amex
Discounts: None
Pets: Welcome **Handicap Access:** No

Stage Harbor Marine

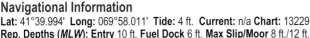

PO Box 646; 80 Bridge Street; Chatham, MA 02633

Tel: (508) 945-1860 **VHF: Monitor** Ch. 9 **Talk** Ch. 8
Fax: (508) 945-2522 **Alternate Tel:** n/a
Email: andy@stageharbormarine.com **Web:** www.stageharbormarine.com
Nearest Town: Chatham *(1 mi.)* **Tourist Info:** (508) 945-5199

Marina Services and Boat Supplies

Services - Docking Assistance, Trash Pick-Up, Dock Carts **Communication -** Pay Phone, FedEx, UPS, Express Mail **Supplies - OnSite:** Ice *(Block, Cube)*, Ships' Store **1-3 mi:** Bait/Tackle *(Cape 945-3501)* **3+ mi:** Propane *(Snow's 255-1090, 10 mi.)*

Boatyard Services

OnSite: Launching Ramp, Engine mechanic *(gas)*, Electronic Sales, Hull Repairs, Rigger, Bottom Cleaning, Brightwork, Compound, Wash & Wax, Woodworking, Painting **OnCall:** Engine mechanic *(diesel)*, Electrical Repairs, Canvas Work, Propeller Repairs, Inflatable Repairs **Dealer for:** Stamas Yachts, Cobra, Beacon Boats, Edgewater, Mercury. **Yard Rates:** $60/hr., Haul & Launch $5/ft., Power Wash $4, Bottom Paint $12/ft. *(paint incl.)* **Storage:** On-Land $19/ft.

Restaurants and Accommodations

OnCall: Pizzeria *(Nick's 945-4680)* **Under 1 mi:** Hotel *(Surfside 945-9757)*, Inn/B&B *(Bradford Inn 945-1030, $115-475)* **1-3 mi:** Restaurant *(Vining 945-5033, D $20.50-29)*, *(Chatham Squire 945-0942, L $7-19, D $10-22)*, *(Impudent Oyster 945-3545, L&D)*, *(Blue Coral 348-0485, L&D)*, *(Wildgoose 945-5590, B $6-9.50, L $7-14, D $9-28)*, *(Red Nun 348-0469, D $10-21)*, *(Captain's Table 945-1961, D $5-18)*, *(Camparis 945-9123)*, Motel *(Wayside 945-5550, $120-495)*, Hotel *(Cranberry 945-9232, $120-315)*

Recreation and Entertainment

Under 1 mi: Beach *(Chatham Light; Oyster Pond)*, Picnic Area, Grills, Tennis Courts *(Chatham 945-0464)*, Park *(Chase)*, Museum *(Atwood House 945-2493, $5/3)*, Sightseeing *(Chatham Lighthouse; Monomoy National Wildlife Refuge 945-0594, 1.8 mi.)* **1-3 mi:** Pool *(Chatham 945-3555)*, Playground *(Across from RR Museum)*, Golf Course *(Seaside Links 945-4774)*, Fitness Center *(Chatham Health 945-3555)*, Boat Rentals *(Pleasant Bay 945-7245)*, Hike/Bike Trails, Tours *(Cape Ariel Tours 945-2363)*, Cultural Attract *(Monomoy Theater 945-1589)*

Provisioning and General Services

Under 1 mi: Farmers' Market *(Veterans Park Thur 945-1555 8am-noon)*, Bank/ATM, Protestant Church, Newsstand **1-3 mi:** Market *(Chatham Village 945-9783)*, Health Food *(Natural Foods 945-4139)*, Wine/Beer *(Chatham 945-0639)*, Liquor Store *(Liquor Locker 945-0501)*, Bakery *(Chatham 945-3229)*, Fishmonger *(Nickersons 945-0145)*, Post Office *(945-6054)*, Catholic Church, Library *(Chatham 945-5170)*, Beauty Salon *(Salon Fabulous 945-7860)*, Dry Cleaners *(Princess 945-2584)*, Bookstore *(Cabbages & Kings 945-1603)*, Pharmacy *(CVS 945-4340)*, Hardware Store *(Chatham 945-0107)*, Florist *(Manson 945-0088)* **3+ mi:** Supermarket *(Stop & Shop 432-5000, 5 mi.)*, Copies Etc. *(UPS Store 945-2716, 5 mi.)*

Transportation

OnCall: Rental Car *(Enterprise 555-2997)*, Taxi *(Eldredge 945-0068)*, Airport Limo *(Kon 945-2941)* **Under 1 mi:** Local Bus, InterCity Bus **1-3 mi:** Bikes *(Chatham 945-8981)* **Airport:** Cape Cod *(23 mi)*

Medical Services

911 Service **Under 1 mi:** Holistic Services *(Le Petite Spa 237-8783)* **1-3 mi:** Doctor *(Mees 945-0187)*, Dentist *(Chatham Dental 945-0207)*, Chiropractor *(Chatham 945-3131)*, Optician *(Bass River 945-1127)*, Veterinarian *(Stoney Hill 945-0151)* **Hospital:** Cape Cod 771-1800 *(19 mi.)*

Setting -- In protected Stage Harbor, a third of a mile east of the Stage Harbor Yacht Club and the Harbormaster shack, this buttoned-up, primarily power boat marina and boatyard is easily identified by the 1-1/2 story weathered-shingle structure with barn-red doors and blue-and-white sign - the only commercial venture in this quiet harbor. Hard by the picturesque bridge that marks the beginning of the Mill Pond, the docks have long views of the pristine mooring field.

Marina Notes -- Fuel and a well-stocked ships' store onsite. Handles boats to about 45 ft. Most mechanical services and trades, some on call. Launch serves much of the harbor; will also stop at the landing near town - a mile upriver. Dinghy up the western side (Oyster Pond River) to access the west end of town, including the supermarket. Internet access at Eldridge Library. Useful base for offshore fishing or runs up the outside. Harbormaster: 945-5185. Bathhouse: very basic, but private, no shower. Note: Anchoring allowed west of buoy 8 on the south side of the channel. Free town "courtesy" moorings, too.

Notable -- Stage Harbor is unspoiled, rustic and marshy with quaint summer homes along the shore. In contrast, upscale Main Street and the surrounding lanes are lined with chic shops, many with a maritime flair, elegant restaurants, luxurious inns, cottages and stately houses with flower-filled gardens - ask about the bow-shaped roofs. It's a magnet for summer visitors who don't flinch at the price tag. Visit the fish pier in Chatham Harbor -- but go overland as the Harbor is somewhat difficult to navigate and a bit thin. Many great beaches are nearby - especially at Chatham light. Nine-mile long Monomoy Island, part of the 7600-acre Monomoy National Wildlife Refuge, can be accessed by tours or private boat for bird and seal watching. Check in with the Visitors Center on Morris Island.

PHOTOS ON DVD: 25

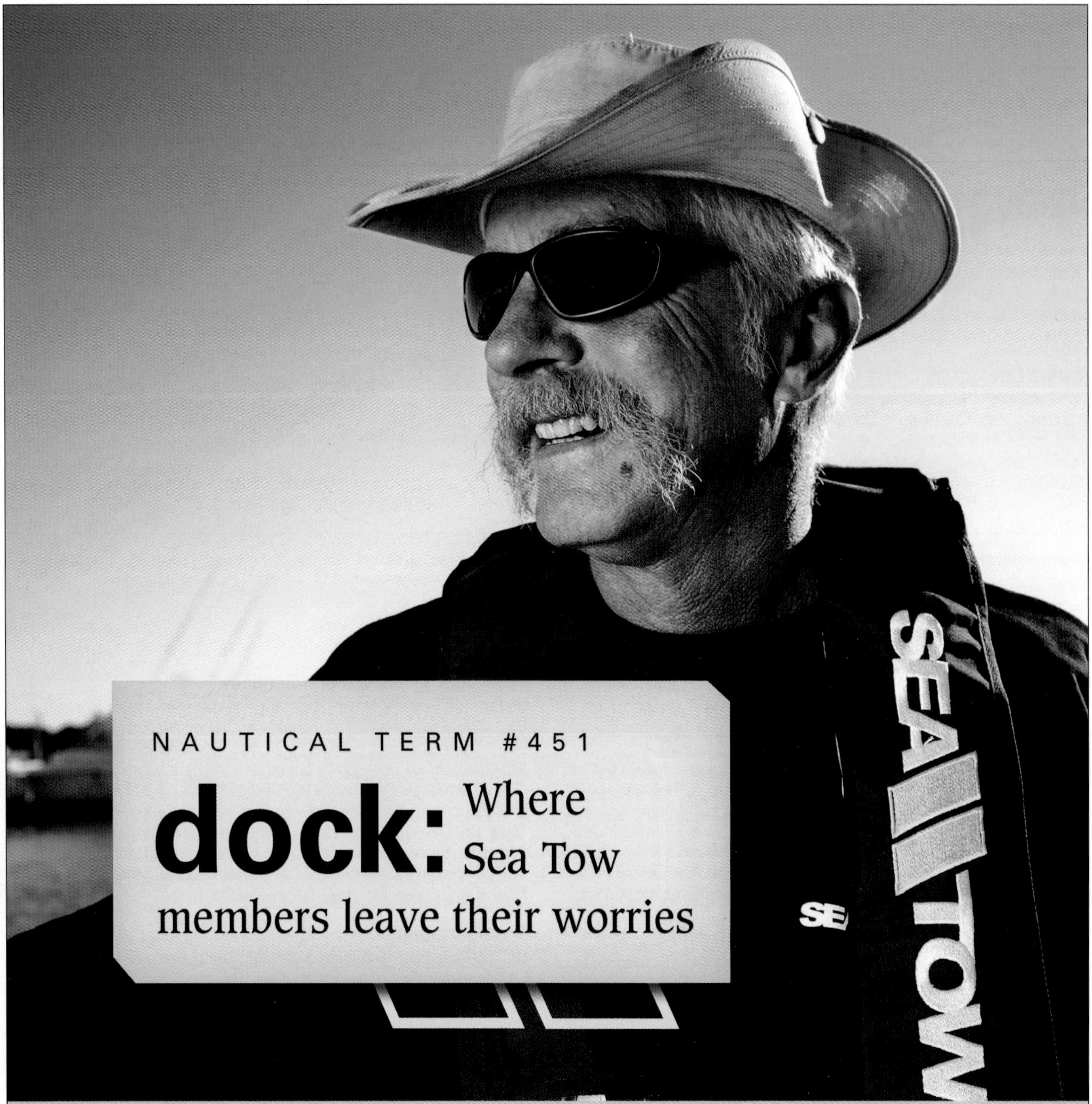

Sea Tow Services International, Inc.

WWW.SEATOW.COM

16. MA – The Islands

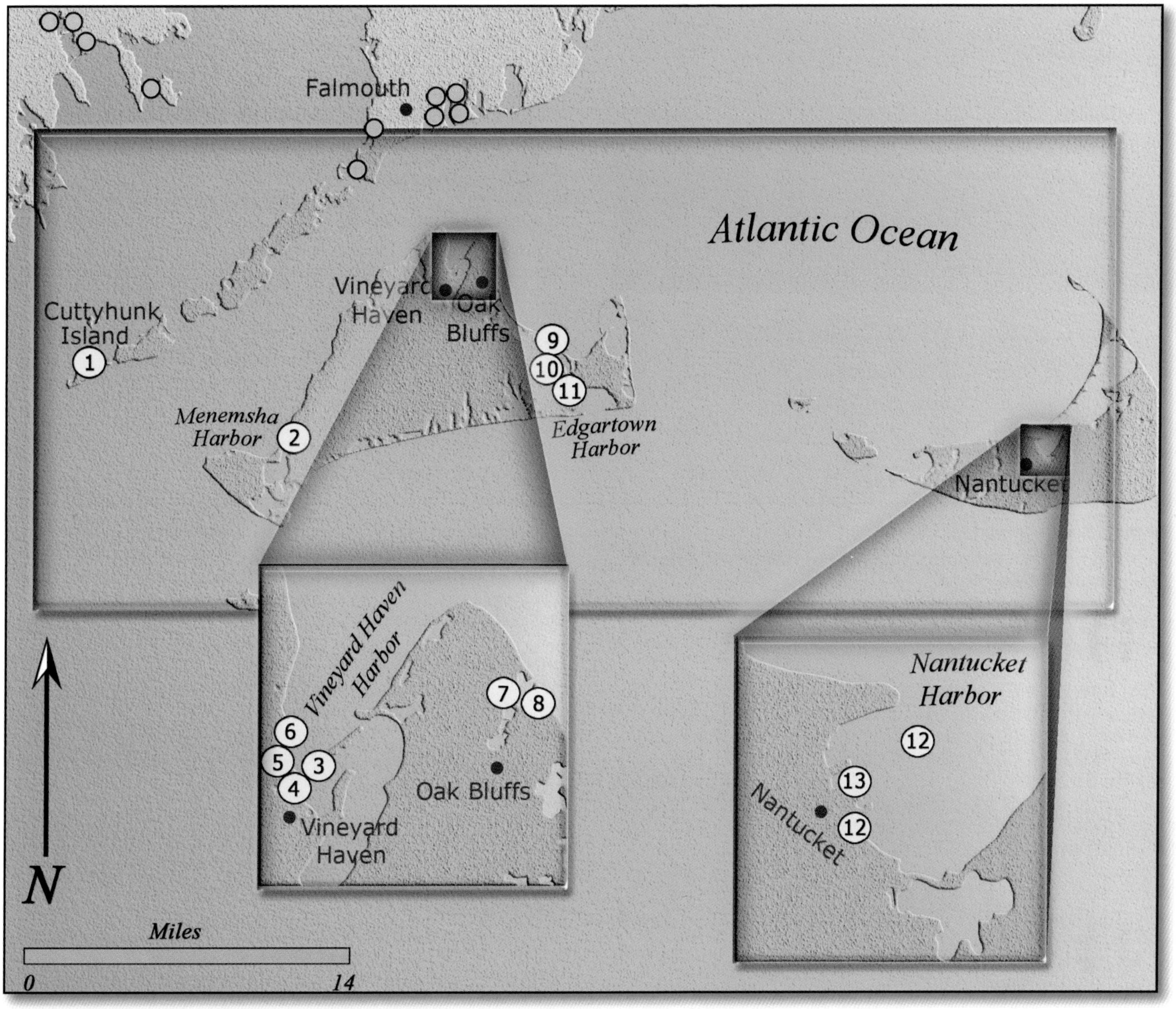

MAP	MARINA	HARBOR	PAGE
1	**Cuttyhunk Town Marina**	*Cuttyhunk Pond*	298
2	**Menemsha Harbor**	*Menemsha Harbor*	299
3	**Tisbury Wharf**	*Vineyard Haven Harbor*	300
4	**Vineyard Haven Marina**	*Vineyard Haven Harbor*	301
5	**Black Dog Wharf**	*Vineyard Haven Harbor*	302
6	**Owen Park Town Dock**	*Vineyard Haven Harbor*	303
7	**Oak Bluffs Marina**	*Oak Bluffs Harbor*	304
8	**Dockside Market Place & Marina**	*Oak Bluffs Harbor*	305
9	**North Wharf Moorings**	*Edgartown Harbor*	306
10	**Mad Max Marina**	*Edgartown Harbor*	307
11	**Harborside Inn**	*Edgartown Harbor*	308
12	**Nantucket Moorings**	*Nantucket Harbor*	309
13	**Nantucket Boat Basin**	*Nantucket Harbor*	310

RATINGS:  1-5 for Marina Facilities & Amenities,  1-2 for Boatyard Services,  1-2 for MegaYacht Facilities,  for Something Special.

SERVICES: for CCM – Certified Clean Marina,  for Pump-Out, for Internet,  for Fuel, for Restaurant,  for Provisioning nearby, for Catamaran-friendly,  for SportFish Charter,  for Pool/Beach, and  for Golf within a mile. *For an explanation of ACC's Ratings, see page 8.*

Cuttyhunk Town Marina

PO Box 28; 28 Tower Hill Road; Cuttyhunk, MA 02713

Tel: (508) 990-7578 **VHF: Monitor** Ch. 9 **Talk** Ch. 10
Fax: n/a **Alternate Tel:** n/a
Email: none **Web:** none
Nearest Town: New Bedford *(14 mi.)* **Tourist Info:** (508) 999-5231

Navigational Information

Lat: 41°25.453' **Long:** 070°55.685' **Tide:** 3 ft. **Current:** n/a **Chart:** 13229
Rep. Depths (*MLW*): Entry 12 ft. **Fuel Dock** 12 ft. **Max Slip/Moor** 6 ft./6 ft.
Access: Buzzard's Bay or Vineyard Sound. Follow channel!

Marina Facilities *(In Season/Off Season)*

Fuel: *At Ferry Dock* - Slip-Side Fueling, Gasoline, Diesel
Slips: 99 Total, 50 Transient **Max LOA:** 100 ft. **Max Beam:** n/a
Rate *(per ft.)*: **Day** $3.00/Inq.* **Week** Inq. **Month** Inq.
Power: 30 amp $20, **50 amp** $30, **100 amp** n/a, **200 amp** n/a
Cable TV: No **Dockside Phone:** No
Dock Type: Fixed, Floating, Wood
Moorings: 46 Total, 46 Transient **Launch:** No, Dinghy Dock
Rate: Day $40 **Week** n/a **Month** n/a
Heads: 4 Toilet(s)
Internet: Yes *(Wi-Fi, $12)* **Laundry:** None
Pump-Out: Onsite *(Wed & Sun AM only)*, Full Service **Fee:** Free **Closed He**

Marina Operations

Owner/Manager: George Isabel (Hrbrmstr) **Dockmaster:** Same
In-Season: Jul-Sep 10, 8am-6pm **Off-Season:** Sep 11-Oct 15, 8am-3pm
After-Hours Arrival: Call VHF Ch. 9 or 508 993-6490
Reservations: Yes, for slips only **Credit Cards:** Cash only
Discounts: None
Pets: Welcome **Handicap Access:** No

Marina Services and Boat Supplies

Services - Docking Assistance **Communication -** Pay Phone **Supplies - Near:** Ice *(Block, Cube, Shaved)*

Boatyard Services

Nearest Yard: Fairhaven Shipyard (508) 999-1600

Restaurants and Accommodations

OnSite: Seafood Shack *(The Fish Market boiled lobster to go - order in afternoon, pick-up at 6pm sharp)*, Snack Bar *(Ice Cream Stall)*, *(Island Dogs)* **OnCall:** Raw Bar *(Harbor Shellfish & Raw Bar Ch.72. 11:30-1 & 3-6:30pm dockside, 5:15-7:30pm in harbor - Doz: clams $16, oysters $20, shrimp $18)* **Near:** Snack Bar *(Ferry Depot)*, Lite Fare *(Bart's Cart B & L $5-12, On Broadway, Fri-Tues Fried clams, shrimp, chicken, fish & lobster roll)*, Pizzeria *(Soprano's 992-7530, Ch. 72, pizza oven in garage, 4 picnic tables)*, Inn/B&B *(Avalon Club, The Inn at Cuttyhunk 997-8388, $150, 11 guest rooms)* **Under 1 mi:** Lite Fare *(Cuttyhunk Fishing Club 992-5585, B $5-8, 8-11am)*, Inn/B&B *(Cuttyhunk Fishing Club B&B 992-5585, $165-185, 8 guest rooms, break not incl.)*

Recreation and Entertainment

OnSite: Fishing Charter *(Linesider 991-7352; Seahawk 997-6387; Revenge 994-8913; Old Squaw & Wahini 999-1263; Dorsal 992-8181; Lisa G. 965-7362; Rudy J 993-7427; Island time 542-4266; Lehner 992-5131)* **Near:** Beach *(Barges, Church's & Channel)*, Picnic Area, Jogging Paths, Boat Rentals *(303-929-2475 Kayaks $40/2hrs)*, Hike/Bike Trails *(Cliff Walk - from the Avalon to the Ponds)*, Movie Theater *(Town Hall - DVDs on big screen TV + popcorn)*, Museum *(Historical Society Museum 984-4611 - Open July-LabDay, Wed 2-4pm, Thur-Sat. 10:30-12:30 & 2-4pm, Sun 10am-4pm)*, Sightseeing *(Bird and Wildlife Sanctuary; Cuttyhunk Cemetery; Naval Artillery batteries from WW II; Naval Look-out at top of hill)*, Galleries *(Pea in Your Pants 603-321-6326; Ironworks Studio 748-6744)*, Special Events *(Jul 4th Parade, Clam Bakes)*

Provisioning and General Services

OnSite: Fishmonger *(Capt. Borges Old Squaw on Dock - lobsters & fish 2-6pm)* **OnCall:** Liquor Store *(Cordoza's in New Bedford 992-4477)* **Near:** Convenience Store *(Cuttyhunk Market & General Store 993-6490)*, Bank/ATM *(at Corner Store)*, Post Office *(9am-3pm, Sat 9-noon)*, Catholic Church, Protestant Church *(Cuttyhunk Union Methodist - Summer Sundays: Episcopal 8am, Roman Catholic 9am, Sunday School 10am, Methodist 11am, Hymn Sing 7:45pm, Evening Vespers 8pm)*, Library *(Mon & Thur 9-11:30am, Tues & Fri 2:30-5pm)*, Retail Shops *(Cuttyhunk Corner Store 984-7167; Seagirl Gifts 990-9820)*

Transportation

OnCall: Water Taxi *(Cuttyhunk Seahorse 789-3250 $35/$20)* **Near:** Bikes *(303-929-2475 $15/hr.)*, Rental Car *(Golf Carts 496-1538)*, Ferry Service *(992-0200 to New Bedford 992-1432 $25/20 1-way, Same day RT $40/30, Summer Mon-Thu 4pm, Fri 4 & 8pm, Sat 11am & 4pm, Sun 12 & 5pm)* **Airport:** New Bedford - via ferry *(25 mi.)*

Medical Services

911 Service **Near:** Doctor *(MDs at Avalon House 8:30-9:30am & First Aid at Fish Dock 9am-4pm)* **Hospital:** St. Luke's 979-1515 by ferry *(25 mi.)*

Setting -- Six and a half nautical miles south of New Bedford and eight miles west of Menemsha, Martha's Vineyard, 580-acre Cuttyhunk is quiet, unspoiled and delightfully backward. Past the de-commissioned Coast Guard Station, the protected inner harbor moorings lie in Cuttyhunk Pond. A network of slips hug a shoreline edged with a neat row of fishing shacks. Views from the harbor are of the hills, packed with haphazardly perched houses.

Marina Notes -- *Mon-Thu $2/ft. 1 -4 hour tie-up: $25. **Cannot reserve moorings. No mechanical services, limited provisions (BYO). Town dinghy dock available to all. 2-boat rafts permitted in good weather. Gosnold Fuel at ferry dock. 40 Outer Harbor moorings avail. from: Frog Pond to left of entrance channel $35/day, orange balls, Ch. 72, 992-7530 (or 443-480-0046) and Jenkins Ch. 9, northeast of harbor, blue stripe. No reservations. Pick up empty mooring; boat will be by to collect fee. Sealed heads required; pump-out Wed & Sun am only. Trash collection $5/ bag. SeaTow 877-266-6955. Internet Wi-Fi at T-1 speed (888-658-1688 or Duane & Lexi Lynch 997-6387) $12/day, $25/wk. Bathhouse: basic cinderblock and concrete.

Notable -- The largest of the 16 Elizabeth Islands, Cuttyhunk feels like a throwback to the fifties. The library, museum, church, town hall, one-room school, and post office are a short hike, halfway up the hill. Continue to the look-out at the top - on a clear day, there are 360-degree views to The Vineyard and Rhode Island. Around the other side, the lovely 1864 Cuttyhunk Fishing Club B&B serves breakfast overlooking Vineyard Sound - a perfect early morning destination. Almost all of Cuttyhunk is privately owned except the wharf area, where a plethora of charter operations signal the seriousness of the fishing.

PHOTOS ON DVD: 24

Navigational Information
Lat: 41°21.215' **Long:** 070°45.960' **Tide:** 4 ft. **Current:** 5 kt. **Chart:** 13218
Rep. Depths (*MLW*): Entry 7 ft. **Fuel Dock** 7 ft. **Max Slip/Moor** 7 ft./7 ft.
Access: 100 yards past entrance, turn left into basin

Marina Facilities *(In Season/Off Season)*
Fuel: *Texaco* - Slip-Side Fueling, Gasoline, Diesel
Slips: 100 Total, 17+ Transient **Max LOA:** 55 ft. **Max Beam:** n/a
Rate *(per ft.)*: **Day** $2.50/Inq.* **Week** n/a **Month** n/a
Power: 30 amp $5, **50 amp** $10, **100 amp** n/a, **200 amp** n/a
Cable TV: No **Dockside Phone:** No
Dock Type: Fixed, Floating, Long Fingers, Alongside, Wood
Moorings: 10 Total, 10 Transient **Launch:** No, Dinghy Dock (Free)
Rate: Day $30** **Week** n/a **Month** Inq.
Heads: 2 Toilet(s), 2 Shower(s) *(dressing rooms)*
Internet: Yes *(Squid Row Wi-Fi, Free)* **Laundry:** None
Pump-Out: OnCall, Full Service **Fee:** Free **Closed Heads:** Yes

Marina Operations
Owner/Manager: Dennis Jason **Dockmaster:** Same
In-Season: Jun-Oct 15, 7am-8pm **Off-Season:** Oct 16-May, 7am-4pm
After-Hours Arrival: Call on VHF Ch 9
Reservations: No, but inquire same day after 7am **Credit Cards:** Visa/MC
Discounts: None
Pets: Welcome **Handicap Access:** No

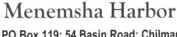

Menemsha Harbor

PO Box 119; 54 Basin Road; Chilmark, MA 02535

Tel: (508) 645-2846 **VHF: Monitor** Ch. 9 **Talk** Ch. 8
Fax: (508) 645-2110 **Alternate Tel:** (508) 645-2100
Email: harbor@chilmarkma.gov **Web:** wwww.chilmarkma.gov
Nearest Town: Chilmark *(2 mi.)* **Tourist Info:** (508) 693-0085

Marina Services and Boat Supplies
Services - Docking Assistance **Communication -** FedEx, UPS, Express Mail **Supplies - OnSite:** Ice *(Cube)*, Ships' Store *(Chilmark Chandlery 645-9562)*, Live Bait **3+ mi:** West Marine *(693-2906, 12 mi.)*, Propane *(Island 696-6122; AmeriGas 693-0441, 11 mi.)*

Boatyard Services
Nearest Yard: Martha's Vineyard Shipyard (508) 693-0400

Restaurants and Accommodations
Near: Restaurant *(Homeport 645-2679, D $35-70, 3-course prix fixe; Brunch $11-29; Kids' $7-9; Back-Door Take-Out & Raw Bar $12-26, Del.)*, *(Menemsha Cafe 645-9902)*, Seafood Shack *(Larsen's 645-2680)*, *(The Bite 645-9239, D $8-28, Famous Fried Clams & more - picnic tables)*, Lite Fare *(Menemsha Galley 645-9819, 11am-9pm, best lobster roll!)* **Under 1 mi:** Restaurant *(Beach Plum 645-9454)*, Hotel *(Beach Plum Inn & Restaurant 645-9454, $225-750)*, Inn/B&B *(Menemsha Inn & Cottages 645-2521, $270-700)*, *(Captain R. Flanders 645-3123, $140-300)* **1-3 mi:** Pizzeria *(Chilmark Store 645-3739)* **3+ mi:** Restaurant *(Chilmark Tavern 645-9400, D $16-45, 4 mi., Brunch $14-22; Bar Menu $14-18)*

Recreation and Entertainment
OnSite: Beach, Picnic Area **Near:** Fishing Charter *(Red Tail Offshore 645-6131; Lauren C. 645-2993, Menemsha Blues 645-3778)* **Under 1 mi:** Hike/Bike Trails *(Gay Head to Chilmark)* **1-3 mi:** Playground *(Chilmark School)*, Tennis Courts, Park *(Menemsha Hills; Fulling Mill Brook Conserv. Area)* **3+ mi:** Golf Course *(Farm Neck 693-3057, 15 mi.)*, Horseback Riding *(Arrowhead 693-8831, 7.5 mi.)*, Movie Theater *(MV Film Fest 645-9599, 4 mi.)*, Museum *(Aquinna Cultural 645-7900, 7 mi.)*, Sightseeing *(Gay Head Lighthouse 645-2211, 7 mi.)*, Galleries *(Gossamer 645-7978, 6 mi.)*, Special Events *(West Tisbury Agricultural Fair - late Aug, 6 mi.)*

Provisioning and General Services
OnSite: Lobster Pound *(Menemsha Fish 645-2282 - local bay scallops)* **Near:** Convenience Store *(Menemsha Market & Post Office)*, Fishmonger *(Larsen's Fish 645-2680)*, Post Office *(645-3501)* **1-3 mi:** Market *(Chilmark 645-3739)*, Bank/ATM *(Sovereign 645-2608)*, Protestant Church, Library *(Aquinnah 645-2314, Chilmark 645-3360)*, Beauty Salon *(Barn 645-2145)* **3+ mi:** Supermarket *(Cronig's 693-2234, 6 mi.)*, Bakery *(Fella's 693-6924, 6.5 mi.)*, Farmers' Market *(Wed & Sat 9-Noon, West Tisbury, 6 mi.)*, Catholic Church *(8 mi.)*, Synagogue *(8 mi.)*, Pharmacy *(Conroy's 693-7070, 11 mi.)*, Hardware Store *(Up Island 693-9977, 6.5 mi.)*

Transportation
OnCall: Bikes *(Martha's 693-6593 - 12 mi.)*, Taxi *(Mario's 693-8399)*, Airport Limo *(Vineyard 693-3996)* **Near:** Local Bus *(MVTA 693-9440 accesses the entire island)*, Ferry Service *(Hugh Taylor's Menemsha Bike Ferry 645-5154 across Menemsha Creek $7RT 8am-6pm)* **3+ mi:** Rental Car *(Budget 693-1911, 10 mi.)* **Airport:** Martha's Vineyard *(10.5 mi.)*

Medical Services
911 Service **3+ mi:** Doctor *(Vineyard Walk-in Clinic 693-4400, 11 mi.)*, Dentist *(D'Ambrosio 693-8285, 7 mi.)*, Chiropractor *(Vineyard 693-3800, 6.5 mi.)*, Holistic Services *(Body Balance 645-2333, 5 mi.)*, Optician *(Finkelstein 693-3517, 12 mi.)*, Veterinarian *(My Pet's 693-4040, 11 mi.)* **Hospital:** Martha's Vineyard 693-0410 *(13 mi.)*

Setting -- At the western end of Martha's Vineyard, rolling hills drop down to marsh and shoreline. Just inside the narrow entrance to Menemsha Harbor is an authentic, small-scale working fishing village, with wind-blown, buoy-bedecked buildings that house casual shops, justly popular seafood shacks and several fishing charters - a low-key, laid-back alternative to the bustle of the eastern harbors. Frequent dramatic sunsets include an occasional green flash.

Marina Notes -- *$10/4hrs. Max Stay 2 weeks. **Moorings 2 Inside basin $30/nt/per boat, rafting allowed. 8 Outside Basin $20/nt, no rafting. Med moor & side-tie docks. No reserv. Morning of arrival call for space avail. Mailing Add: 401 Middle Road. Off-season: 645-2100 x 2846. Commercial groundfish draggers, lobster trappers & recreational anglers. Coast Guard Station. Wi-Fi - Menemsha Texaco. Bathhouse: Modern, municip. concrete, coin op showers (quarters).

Notable -- Menemsha Harbor is a gateway to Chilmark with its rolling hills, stone fences, and breathtaking coastline as well as dramatic Aquinnah (formerly Gay Head) with mile-long, 150-foot colorful clay bluffs and native American crafts - a center of Wampanoag culture. Nearby Menemsha Beach has food kiosks, heads and a view of the returning fleet. Closeby are luxury country inns that attract bold-faced names from around the globe; the draws are off-radar, spectacular scenery and fish. Known for its lobster and swordfish, Larsen's and on-site Menemsha fish markets also offer prepared dishes to eat al fresco. Beetlebung Corner (1.7 mi.) houses the library, school, tennis courts, community center and Community Church flea market (Wed & Sat). In West Tisbury, the Artisan's Fair is held every Sunday (10am-2pm). MVTA's bus system puts the rest of the island within easy reach - inexpensively. Chilmark is "dry," so BYOB.

  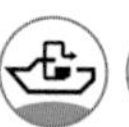   

Tisbury Wharf

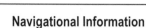

PO Box 1317; 144 Beach Road; Vineyard Haven, MA 02568

Tel: (508) 693-9300 **VHF: Monitor** Ch. 9 **Talk** Ch. 9
Fax: (508) 696-8436 **Alternate Tel:** n/a
Email: info@tisburywharf.com **Web:** www.tisburywharf.com
Nearest Town: Vineyard Haven **Tourist Info:** (508) 693-4486

Navigational Information
Lat: 41°27.202' **Long:** 070°35.762' **Tide:** 4 ft. **Current:** 1 kt. **Chart:** 13238
Rep. Depths (*MLW*): Entry 20 ft. **Fuel Dock** 12 ft. **Max Slip/Moor** 14 ft./-
Access: Past breakwater to southeast corner of harbor

Marina Facilities *(In Season/Off Season)*
Fuel: *Shell* - Gasoline, Diesel, High-Speed Pumps
Slips: 20 Total, 20 Transient **Max LOA:** 300 ft. **Max Beam:** n/a
Rate *(per ft.)*: **Day** $4.25/2.50* **Week** n/a **Month** n/a
Power: 30 amp $5, **50 amp** $10, **100 amp** $20, **200 amp** n/a
Cable TV: No **Dockside Phone:** No
Dock Type: Fixed, Wood
Moorings: 0 Total, 0 Transient **Launch:** n/a
Rate: Day n/a **Week** n/a **Month** n/a
Heads: 4 Toilet(s), 4 Shower(s)
Internet: Yes *(Wi-Fi, Free)* **Laundry:** None
Pump-Out: OnSite, Full Service **Fee:** Free **Closed Heads:** Yes

Marina Operations
Owner/Manager: Noreen Baker **Dockmaster:** Same
In-Season: May 15-Oct 5, 8am-6pm **Off-Season:** Oct 6-May 14, 10am-4pm
After-Hours Arrival: Call in advance
Reservations: Yes **Credit Cards:** Visa/MC, Din, Amex
Discounts: None
Pets: Welcome **Handicap Access:** Yes, Heads, Docks

Marina Services and Boat Supplies
Services - Docking Assistance, Concierge, Trash Pick-Up **Communication -** Phone Messages, Fax in/out, FedEx, UPS **Supplies - OnSite:** Ice *(Block, Cube)* **Near:** Ships' Store *(MV Shipyard 693-0400)*, West Marine *(693-2906)* **1-3 mi:** Bait/Tackle *(Dick's 693-7669)*, Propane *(Island 696-6122)*

Boatyard Services
Nearest Yard: Martha's Vineyard Shipyard (508) 693-0400

Restaurants and Accommodations
Near: Restaurant *(Blue Canoe 693-3332, L&D $14-35)*, *(Saltwater 338-4666, D $22-40)*, Seafood Shack *(Net Result 693-6071, Take Out $3.50-34)*, Lite Fare *(Artcliff 693-1224, B $5-11, L $10-15)*, Pizzeria *(Rocco's Island 693-1125)*, Motel *(Vineyard Harbor 693-3334, $99-250)* **Under 1 mi:** Restaurant *(Le Grenier 693-4906, D $28-39, French cuisine)*, *(Zephrus 693-3416, D $18-30, L&D $6-20)*, *(Golden Dragon 693-4417, Chinese)*, Lite Fare *(Waterside Market 693-8899, B $5-9, L $7-13)*, Hotel *(Mansion House 693-2200, $99-299)*, *(Captain Dexter House 693-6564)*, Inn/B&B *(1720 House 693-6407, $85-250)*, *(Harbor Landing 693-2600, $70-215)*, *(Crocker House 693-1151, $125-225)*

Recreation and Entertainment
OnSite: Beach *(or Eastville)* **Near:** Playground, Boat Rentals *(Wind's Up 693-4252 Kayaks $16-21/hr.)*, Tours *(MV Sightseeing 627-8687 $29/10; Vineyard Haven History 627-2529 $12/Free)*, Galleries *(Seaworthy 693-0153; Gould Photog 693-7373)* **Under 1 mi:** Pool *(Mansion House 693-2200 $16/11)*, Tennis Courts *(East Chop)*, Fitness Center *(Mansion House $16/11 Day)*, Park *(Veterans Mem.)*, Cultural Attract *(Vineyard Playhouse 693-6450; Katherine Cornell Theater)* **1-3 mi:** Dive Shop *(Vineyard 693-0288)*, Golf Course *(Farm Neck 693-3057)*, Sightseeing *(East Chop Light)*

Provisioning and General Services
OnSite: Farmers' Market *(Tues 9am-1pm)* **Near:** Convenience Store *(Cumberland Farms)*, Supermarket *(Stop & Shop 696-8339)*, Delicatessen *(M B 693-6200)*, Bakery *(Black Dog 693-4786)*, Fishmonger *(Net Result 693-6071)*, Post Office *(693-2818)*, Beauty Salon *(Maggie's)*, Bookstore *(Riley's Reads 696-7957)*, Pharmacy *(Vineyard Scripts 693-7979)*, Hardware Store *(Hinckley Ace 693-0075)*, Florist *(Nochi 693-9074)* **Under 1 mi:** Health Food *(Vineyard Grocer 696-8914)*, Bank/ATM *(MV Savings; Bank of MV)*, Catholic Church, Protestant Church, Synagogue, Library *(Vineyard Haven 696-4211)*, Copies Etc. *(Educomp 693-0803)* **1-3 mi:** Gourmet Shop *(Martha's Vineyard 693-3688)*, Wine/Beer *(Vineyard Wine & Cheese 693-0943)*, Liquor Store *(Jim's 693-0236)*, Dry Cleaners *(Men at Work 982-9675)*, Laundry *(Vineyard 693-7389)*

Transportation
OnCall: Taxi *(Island 693-3705; Vineyard 693-3996)* **Near:** Bikes *(Martha's 693-6593)*, Rental Car *(Budget 693-1911; Adventure 693-1959)*, InterCity Bus *(MVTA 693-9440)*, Ferry Service *(Woods Hole, New Bedford-Steamship Authority)* **Airport:** Martha's Vineyard 693-7022 *(6.5 mi.)*

Medical Services
911 Service **Near:** Doctor *(Pagan 693-7730)*, Dentist *(Mills 693-7300)*, Chiropractor *(Berger 693-4668)* **Under 1 mi:** Holistic Services *(Polished Day Spa 939-0800)*, Optician *(Finkelstein 693-3517)* **1-3 mi:** Veterinarian *(My Pet's 693-4040)* **Hospital:** Martha's Vineyard 693-0410 *(1 mi.)*

Setting -- Set slightly away from the hubbub of Vineyard Haven, this austere facility consists of three main wharfs spread along the eastern shore - framed by other marine-related businesses, including the famed Martha's Vineyard Shipyard. The first, "North" dock sports a Shell fueling station manned by an attractive yellow dock house. On the shore, welcoming porches front a two-story, brown-shingled Cape Cod office building. The long docks reach far enough into the harbor to provide a pleasant view of the array of classic wooden sailing vessels that moor here - and to benefit from the prevailing southwest breeze.

Marina Notes -- *Day dockage - vessels under 40 ft. $12/hr, 1-3 hrs. 41+ ft., call; Call also for weekly, monthly rates. A steady effort to upgrade. Focus on larger, self-sufficient yachts. Winslow, the house dog, and his master keep a close eye on things. Well-maintained fixed docks with power/water, comfortable sofa area in office. Mechanical & other BY services next door at MV Shipyard. Bathhouse: Tiled, modern, private with glass-door shower stalls.

Notable -- Down Island Farmers & Artisans Market sets up on the marina grounds every Tuesday. A quarter-mile walk, Vineyard Haven's small, tree-shaded village, a pleasing mix of shingled Cape Codders and sea captain's mansions, is the Vineyard's commercial center and transportation hub. It offers fine and casual restaurants, good shopping, provisioning sources, a year-round ferry and buses to everywhere. For an overview of the entire island, consider MV Sightseeing's 2.5-hour bus tour of six towns. To get to know the local village, take Vineyard History's 75-minute "Ghosts, Gossip & Scandal" walking tour. Eastville Pt. and Lagoon Bridge Park beaches are walking distance; Sound beach is a two-mile bike or bus ride to East Chop. (V.H. is no longer a dry town.)

Navigational Information
Lat: 41°27.215' **Long:** 070°35.934' **Tide:** 2 ft. **Current:** 1 kt. **Chart:** 13238
Rep. Depths (*MLW*): Entry 20 ft. **Fuel Dock** 10 ft. **Max Slip/Moor** 12 ft./35 ft.
Access: Past the breakwater to 2nd set of docks east of of Ferry Terminal

Marina Facilities *(In Season/Off Season)*
Fuel: Slip-Side Fueling, Gasoline, Diesel, High-Speed Pumps
Slips: 40 Total, 40 Transient **Max LOA:** 200 ft. **Max Beam:** 40 ft.
Rate *(per ft.)*: **Day** $4.25* **Week** Inq. **Month** n/a
Power: 30 amp $15, **50 amp** $35, **100 amp** $70, **200 amp** n/a
Cable TV: Yes, free **Dockside Phone:** Yes
Dock Type: Fixed, Long Fingers, Pilings, Alongside, Wood
Moorings: 25 Total, 25 Transient **Launch:** Yes (3), Dinghy Dock
Rate: Day $45/25** **Week** Inq. **Month** Inq.
Heads: 6 Toilet(s), 4 Shower(s) *(dressing rooms)*, Hair Dryers
Internet: Yes *(Wi-Fi & Slipside, Free)* **Laundry:** 1 Washer(s), 2 Dryer(s)
Pump-Out: OnCall, Full Service, 1 Central **Fee:** Free **Closed Heads:** Yes

Marina Operations
Owner/Manager: Liz Wild **Dockmaster:** Jo Wild
In-Season: May-Oct, 7am-Midnight **Off-Season:** Nov-Apr, Closed
After-Hours Arrival: Call in advance
Reservations: Yes **Credit Cards:** Visa/MC, Amex
Discounts: None
Pets: Welcome **Handicap Access:** Yes, Heads, Docks

Vineyard Haven Marina

PO Box 4203; 52 Beach Road; Vineyard Haven, MA 02568

Tel: (508) 693-0720; (508) 693-7377 **VHF: Monitor** Ch. 9 **Talk** Ch. 10
Fax: (508) 696-9341 **Alternate Tel:** (978) 771-7133
Email: vineyardhavenmarina@vineyard.net **Web:** www.mvhm.com
Nearest Town: Vineyard Haven *(1 block)* **Tourist Info:** (508) 693-0085

Marina Services and Boat Supplies
Services - Docking Assistance, Concierge, Boaters' Lounge, Crew Lounge, Security *(24 Hrs.)*, Trash Pick-Up, Dock Carts **Communication -** Mail & Package Hold, Phone Messages, Fax in/out, FedEx, UPS, Express Mail **Supplies - OnSite:** Ice *(Block, Cube)*, West Marine *(693-2906)* **Near:** Ships' Store *(MV Shipyard 693-0400)*, Propane *(Vineyard 693-4232)*

Boatyard Services
OnCall: Divers **Nearest Yard:** Gannon & Benjamin (508) 693-4658

Restaurants and Accommodations
OnSite: Restaurant *(Blue Canoe 693-3332, L & D $14-35)* **Near:** Restaurant *(Black Dog 693-9223, B $5-9, L $6-13, D $12-26)*, *(Zephrus 693-3416, L $6-15, D $18-30)*, *(Lola's 693-6093, D $20-40)*, *(Golden Dragon Chinese 693-4417)*, Seafood Shack *(Net Result 693-6071)*, Lite Fare *(Waterside Market 693-8899, B $5-9, L $7-13)*, *(Artcliffe Diner 693-1224, B $5-11, L $10-15)*, Pizzeria *(Rocco's 693-1125)*, Motel *(Vineyard Harbor 693-4300, $99-250)*, Inn/B&B *(Mansion House 693-2200, $99-319+)*, *(Harbor Landing 693-2600, $70-215)*

Recreation and Entertainment
OnSite: Beach, Picnic Area, Grills, Special Events *(Shark tournament - end-July)* **Near:** Heated Pool *(Mansion House 693-2200 $16/11)*, Playground, Fitness Center *(Mansion House Day Pass $16/11)*, Boat Rentals *(Winds Up 693-4252 Kayaks $16-21/hr.)*, Tours *(MV Eco Adventures 696-7842)*, Sightseeing *(MV Sightseeing 627-8687 $29/10; Vineyard Haven History 627-2529 $12/Free)*, Galleries *(Seaworthy 693-0153; Jaba's 696-7772)* **Under 1 mi:** Movie Theater *(Capawock 696-9200)*, Park *(Veterans)*, Cultural Attract *(Vineyard Playhouse 693-6450; Katharine Cornell 693-6450)* **1-3 mi:** Dive Shop *(Vineyard 693-0288)*, Golf Course *(Farm Neck 693-3057)*, Fishing Charter *(MV Sporfishing 693-5142)*, Party Boat *(The Skipper 693-1238)*

Provisioning and General Services
Near: Convenience Store *(Cumberland Farms 693-8729)*, Supermarket *(Stop & Shop 696-6047)*, Gourmet Shop *(Vineyard 693-5181)*, Delicatessen *(MB 693-6200)*, Bakery *(Tropical 696-4999)*, Farmers' Market *(Tues 9am-1pm, Tisbury Wharf)*, Fishmonger *(Net Result 693-6071)*, Lobster Pound, Bank/ATM, Post Office *(228-4477)*, Protestant Church, Library *(696-4211)*, Beauty Salon *(Maggie's 693-2875)*, Bookstore *(Riley's Reads 696-7957; Bunch of Grapes 693-2291)*, Pharmacy *(Vineyard Scripts 693-7979)*, Hardware Store *(Hinckley Ace 693-0075)*, Florist *(Nochi 693-9074)*, Copies Etc. *(EduComp 693-0803)* **Under 1 mi:** Health Food *(Vineyard Grocer 696-8914)*, Catholic Church, Synagogue, Dry Cleaners *(Vineyard 693-7389)* **1-3 mi:** Wine/Beer, Liquor Store *(Jim's 693-0236)*

Transportation
OnCall: Taxi *(Atlantic 693-7110)* **Near:** Bikes *(Martha's 693-6593)*, Rental Car *(Adventure 693-1959)*, InterCity Bus *(MVTA 693-9440)*, Ferry Service *(Woods Hole, New Bedford)* **Airport:** Martha's Vineyard *(6 mi.)*

Medical Services
911 Service **Near:** Doctor *(Pagan 693-7730)*, Dentist *(Lagoon 693-5068)*, Chiropractor *(Berger 693-4668)*, Holistic Services *(Holistic Spa 338-4744; Vineyard Acupuncture 693-3060)*, Optician *(Finkelstein 693-3517)* **Under 1 mi:** Veterinarian *(My Pet's 693-4040)* **Hospital:** Martha's Vineyard 693-0410 *(1.3 mi.)*

Setting -- Deep in the harbor, east of Gannon & Benjamin Marine, this petite, nicely landscaped boutique marina caters to its guests as if a small hotel. At the head of the long, fixed wharf manned from an old tugboat cabin, a two-story, gray-shingled building houses the amenities. On the first floor, an attractively appointed lounge opens onto a well-furnished porch overlooking a small beach. A large, second-floor dining deck fronts the self-service bar and crew lounge.

Marina Notes -- *50-99 ft.- $4.65/ft, over 100' $5/ft **Moorings $25/night in shoulder season. 100A service. Dockside phone & cable. Vessels to 200 ft. dockside or on deep water moorings. Concierge services, privacy, numerous amenities, liquor delivery service, rental cars, jeeps, scooters. Second floor Pilot House deck with capacious teak tables & chairs, propane grills plus inside bar where crews & boaters hang out & mingle. Bathhouse: Modern, private, fully-tiled including shower stalls. Laundry, Irons, Ironing boards. Note: Add'l moorings from Vineyard Haven Launch Ch.72, 693-7030. Note: V.H. no longer dry.

Notable -- Just to the west of the dock, dine at the Blue Canoe Waterfront Grille (formerly Mediterranean) in the airy window-walled enclosed porch, the cozy second floor ship-like dining room or on the waterfront upper deck - overlooking the boat and harbor. Vineyard Haven's burgeoning shipwright and preservationist industry has populated the anchorage with spectacular wooden sailing vessels, many built by neighboring Gannon & Benjamin - including the 65-foot "Charlotte" - the subject of a 2011 documentary. A West Marine is onsite, an Ace hardware store's across the street and - within a few blocks - several restaurants, B&Bs, shops and wonderful provisioning including a supermarket. Nearby Che's Lounge sports live music on Saturday and open-mike Wednesday.

PHOTOS ON DVD: 24

Black Dog Wharf

Black Dog Wharf

PO Box 429; 1 Beach Street Ext.; Vineyard Haven, MA 02568

Tel: (508) 693-3854 **VHF: Monitor** Ch. 72 **Talk** Ch. 72
Fax: (508) 693-1881 **Alternate Tel:** n/a
Email: office@theblackdogtallships.com **Web:** www.theblackdogwharf.com
Nearest Town: Vineyard Haven *(0.1 mi.)* **Tourist Info:** (508) 693-0085

Navigational Information

Lat: 41°27.263' **Long:** 070°35.988' **Tide:** 2 ft. **Current:** 1 kt. **Chart:** 13238
Rep. Depths (*MLW*): Entry 20 ft. **Fuel Dock** n/a **Max Slip/Moor** 10 ft./17 ft.
Access: Past breakwater to east side of the Ferry Terminal

Marina Facilities *(In Season/Off Season)*

Fuel: No
Slips: 18 Total, 18 Transient **Max LOA:** 120 ft. **Max Beam:** 16 ft.
Rate *(per ft.)*: **Day** $4.00/2.50* **Week** n/a **Month** n/a
Power: 30 amp $17.50, **50 amp** $40, **100 amp** n/a, **200 amp** n/a
Cable TV: No **Dockside Phone:** No
Dock Type: Fixed, Pilings, Alongside, Wood
Moorings: 22 Total, 2 Transient **Launch:** Yes ($4)
Rate: Day $40 **Week** n/a **Month** n/a
Heads: 2 Toilet(s), 2 Shower(s)
Internet: Yes *(Wi-Fi, Free)* **Laundry:** 2 Washer(s), 2 Dryer(s)
Pump-Out: OnSite, Full Service, 1 Central **Fee:** Free **Closed Heads:** Yes

Marina Operations

Owner/Manager: Morgan Douglas **Dockmaster:** Shawn Ahearn
In-Season: Jun 15-LabDay, 9am-5pm **Off-Season:** Sep-June 14, closed
After-Hours Arrival: Call for instructions
Reservations: Yes **Credit Cards:** Visa/MC, Amex
Discounts: None
Pets: Welcome, Dog Walk Area **Handicap Access:** No

Marina Services and Boat Supplies

Services - Docking Assistance, Trash Pick-Up **Communication -** Pay Phone, FedEx, UPS, Express Mail **Supplies - OnSite:** Ice *(Block, Cube)* **Near:** West Marine *(693-2906)*, Propane *(Vineyard 693-4232)* **Under 1 mi:** Ships' Store *(MV Shipyard 693-0400)* **1-3 mi:** Marine Discount Store *(Island Marine 696-7502)*

Boatyard Services

Nearest Yard: Martha's Vineyard Shipyard (508) 693-0400

Restaurants and Accommodations

OnSite: Restaurant *(Black Dog Tavern 693-9223, B $7-10, L $8-20, D $15-34, No Res., Beer & wine! Sun Brunch $7-15)*, Lite Fare *(Black Dog Bakery 693-4786, 5:30am-8pm)* **Near:** Restaurant *(Blue Canoe 693-3332, L&D $14-35)*, *(Le Grenier 693-4906, D $28-39)*, *(Zephrus 693-3416, L&D $6-20)*, *(Golden Dragon 693-4417)*, Lite Fare *(Artcliff Diner 693-1224, B $5-11, L $10-15)*, Pizzeria *(Bob's 693-8266)*, Motel *(Vineyard Harbor 693-3334, $99-250)*, Hotel *(Mansion House 693-2200, $99-299, Health Club)*, *(Harbor Landing 693-2600, $70-215)*, Inn/B&B *(Captain Dexter's 693-6564, $100-275)* **Under 1 mi:** Restaurant *(Lola's 693-6093, D $20-40)*, Lite Fare *(Black Dog Cafe 696-8190, B $3-5, L $7-12, D $7-12, 7am-8pm)*

Recreation and Entertainment

OnSite: Picnic Area, Boat Rentals *(Black Dog Tall Ships)*, Special Events *(Shark Tourn - July)* **Near:** Heated Pool *(Mansion House 693-2200 $16/11)*, Beach *(Owen Park)*, Fitness Center *(Mansion House $16/11)*, Park *(Veterans)*, Tours *(MV Sightseeing 627-8687 $29/10; Vineyard Haven History 627-2529 $12/Free)*, Cultural Attract *(Vineyard Playhouse 693-6450; Katharine Cornell 693-6450)* **Under 1 mi:** Fishing Charter *(MV Sporfishing 693-5142)*, Movie Theater *(Capawock 696-9200)* **1-3 mi:** Golf Course *(Farm Neck 693-3057)*, Sightseeing *(East Chop Light)*

Provisioning and General Services

OnSite: Bakery *(Black Dog 693-4786)*, Retail Shops *(Black Dog Gen Store)* **Near:** Convenience Store *(Cumberland Farms 693-8729)*, Supermarket *(Stop & Shop 696-6047)*, Delicatessen *(M B 693-6200)*, Fishmonger *(Net Result 693-6071)*, Bank/ATM, Post Office *(693-2818)*, Protestant Church, Beauty Salon *(Maggie's 693-2875)*, Bookstore *(Bunch of Grapes 693-2291)*, Pharmacy *(Vineyard Scripts 693-7979)*, Florist *(Nochi 693-9074)* **Under 1 mi:** Gourmet Shop *(MV Coffee 693-2223)*, Health Food *(Vineyard 696-8914)*, Wine/Beer *(Vineyard 693-6385)*, Farmers' Market *(Tues 9-1 693-9300)*, Catholic Church, Synagogue, Library *(Vineyard Haven 696-4211)*, Laundry *(Vineyard 693-7389)*, Hardware Store *(Hinckley Ace 693-0075)* **1-3 mi:** Liquor Store *(Jim's Package 693-0236)*

Transportation

OnCall: Taxi *(Island 693-3705)*, Airport Limo *(Vineyard 693-3996)* **Near:** Bikes *(Martha's 693-6593)*, Rental Car *(AA 696-5300; Adventure 693-1959)*, Local Bus *(Tisbury's Shuttle)*, InterCity Bus *(MVTA 693-9440)*, Ferry Service *(Woods Hole, New Bedford)* **Airport:** Martha's Vineyard 693-7022 *(6 mi.)*

Medical Services

911 Service **Near:** Doctor *(Pagan 693-7730)*, Dentist *(Lagoon 693-5068)*, Chiropractor *(Berger 693-4668)*, Holistic Services *(Holistic Spa 338-4744)*, Optician *(Finkelstein 693-3517)* **Under 1 mi:** Veterinarian *(My Pet's 693-4040)* **Hospital:** Martha's Vineyard 693-0410 *(1.4 mi)*

Setting -- 200 feet southeast of the Steamship Authority Ferry Dock, the Black Dog Wharf with its eponymous Tavern, Bakery, General Store and Tall Ships are right in the center of Vineyard Haven. Look for the cluster of weathered, brown-shingled buildings flying the big flag adorned with a "Martha's Vineyard Whitefoot" Labrador and the stunning schooners moored just offshore. A half-roofed salt-box dock house sits in the middle of the single long wharf.

Marina Notes -- *$4/ft. to 49 ft., 50-99 ft. $4.75/ft; over 100 ft, $5.00/ft. 35 ft. min. Add $1/ft for shark tourney. Lunch/Dinner Day dockage $15/hr. Cancellation beyond 72 hrs, 1 night dockage forfeited; within 72 hrs, no refund. Formerly Vineyard Haven Maritime. AKA Coastwise Wharf Co. 2-night weekend min. Alongside & "stern-to" med-moor dockage. Rafting often required. Comp. Black Dog coffee/doughnuts around 8am. V.H. Launch Ch. 72 or 693-7030 berths here. Bathhouse: Modern, warm, wood with private dressing rooms, Laundry w/ 2 washers, 2 commercial dryers.

Notable -- Coastwise (aka Black Dog) created the wooden boat industry in Vineyard Haven; Black Dog Tall Ships hosts a kids' summer camp and offers three-hour day sails as well on its three schooners ($60/40-$70/50). The flagship, 108-foot square topsail "Shenandoah," was designed by Coastwise owner Capt. Robert S. Douglas and built by Gamage Shipyard in 1964. Literally the only schooner without auxiliary power, she carries 36 passengers. The 1926 90-foot, ex-pilot schooner "Alabama" hosts 49 passengers and "Chantey" six passengers. Black Dog Tavern opened in 1971; famous for its Black-out Cake, its Lab logo is now recognized the world over. Out the backdoor, the vortex of "Five Corners," the village's commercial hub, is wild on weekends when the ferry arrives.

PHOTOS ON DVD: 20

Navigational Information

Lat: 41°27.439' **Long:** 070°35.940' **Tide:** 2 ft. **Current:** 1 kt. **Chart:** 13238
Rep. Depths (*MLW*): Entry 12 ft. **Fuel Dock** n/a **Max Slip/Moor** 6 ft./12 ft.
Access: Vineyard Harbor past breakwater, starboard into mooring field

Marina Facilities *(In Season/Off Season)*

Fuel: No
Slips: 10 Total, 10 Transient **Max LOA:** 55 ft. **Max Beam:** 16 ft.
Rate *(per ft.)*: **Day** $1.00/Inq.* **Week** Inq. **Month** Inq.
Power: 30 amp n/a, **50 amp** n/a, **100 amp** n/a, **200 amp** n/a
Cable TV: No **Dockside Phone:** No
Dock Type: Fixed, Wood
Moorings: 30 Total, 30 Transient **Launch:** Yes ($2), Dinghy Dock
Rate: Day $50 **Week** n/a **Month** n/a
Heads: 2 Toilet(s), 2 Shower(s)
Internet: No **Laundry:** None
Pump-Out: OnCall *(Boat Ch.71, 9am-4pm)* **Fee:** Free **Closed Heads:** Yes

Marina Operations

Owner/Manager: Jay Wilbur (Hrbrmstr) **Dockmaster:** John Crocker
In-Season: Jun 15-Sep 15, 7:30am-7:30pm **Off-Season:** Sep 16-Jun 14, Inq.
After-Hours Arrival: VHF or pick up empty mooring/alongside dock
Reservations: No **Credit Cards:** Cash/Check only
Discounts: None
Pets: Welcome, Dog Walk Area **Handicap Access:** No

Owen Park Town Dock

PO Box 1239; Owen Park Way; Vineyard Haven, MA 02568**

Tel: (508) 696-4249 **VHF: Monitor** Ch. 9 **Talk** Ch. 69
Fax: (508) 693-5876 **Alternate Tel:** n/a
Email: n/a **Web:** n/a
Nearest Town: Vineyard Haven **Tourist Info:** (508) 693-0085

Marina Services and Boat Supplies

Services - Docking Assistance, Trash Pick-Up, Dock Carts **Communication -** Pay Phone, FedEx, UPS, Express Mail **Supplies - OnCall:** Ice *(Block)* **Near:** Propane *(Vineyard 693-4232)* **Under 1 mi:** Ships' Store *(MV Shipyard 693-0400)*, Bait/Tackle *(Roberts 696-8925)*

Boatyard Services

Nearest Yard: Martha's Vineyard Shipyard (508) 693-0400

Restaurants and Accommodations

Near: Restaurant *(Le Grenier 693-4906, D $28-39, French)*, *(Zephrus 693-3416, $6-20)*, *(Golden Dragon 693-4417, Chinese)*, Lite Fare *(Waterside Market 693-8899, B $5-9, L $7-13)*, Pizzeria *(Bob's 693-8266)*, Motel *(Vineyard Harbor 693-3334, $99-250)*, Inn/B&B *(Mansion House 693-2200, $99-299)*, *(1720 House 693-6407, $85-250)*, *(Captain Dexter House 693-6564)* **Under 1 mi:** Restaurant *(Blue Canoe Waterfront Cafe 693-3332, L&D $14-35)*, *(Lola's 693-6093, D $20-40)*, Lite Fare *(Artcliff Diner 693-1224, B $5-11, L $10-15)*

Recreation and Entertainment

OnSite: Beach *(Owen Park)*, Picnic Area, Playground, Park, Cultural Attract *(Concerts in the Park, Sun 8pm; Vineyard Playhouse 693-6450)* **Near:** Heated Pool *(Mansion House 693-2200)*, Fitness Center *(Mansion House $16/11 Day Pass)*, Movie Theater *(Capawock 696-9200)*, Tours *(MV Sightseeing 627-8687 $29/10; Vineyard Haven History 627-2529 $12/Free)*, Galleries *(Jaba's 696-7772; Gould Photography 693-7373; Seaworthy 693-0153)* **Under 1 mi:** Boat Rentals *(Wind's Up 693-1699 Kayaks $16-21/hr.; Island Water Sports 693-7767 Power boats, Skiffs, Inflatables)* **1-3 mi:** Golf Course *(Farm Neck 693-3057)*, Party Boat *(The Skipper 693-1238)*, Sightseeing *(East Chop Light)*

Provisioning and General Services

Near: Convenience Store *(Cumberland Farm 693-8729)*, Supermarket *(Stop & Shop 696-6047)*, Delicatessen *(Blues Cafe 693-6200)*, Lobster Pound, Bank/ATM, Protestant Church, Library *(Vineyard Haven 696-4211)*, Bookstore *(Bunch of Grapes 693-2291)*, Pharmacy *(Leslie's 693-0008)*, Newsstand, Florist *(Nochi 693-9074)*, Retail Shops **Under 1 mi:** Health Food *(Vineyard Grocer 696-8914)*, Bakery *(Black Dog 693-4786)*, Farmers' Market *(Tues 9am-1pm, Tisbury Wharf)*, Fishmonger *(Net Result 693-6071)*, Post Office *(693-2818)*, Synagogue, Beauty Salon *(Maggie's 693-2875)*, Laundry *(Vineyard Cleaners 693-7389)*, Hardware Store *(Hinckley & Sons Ace 693-0075)*, Copies Etc. *(Tisbury 693-4222)* **1-3 mi:** Wine/Beer *(Vineyard 693-6385)*, Liquor Store *(Jim's 693-0236)*, Catholic Church, Dry Cleaners *(Men at Work 982-9675)*

Transportation

OnCall: Taxi *(Island 693-3705; Atlantic 693-7110)*, Airport Limo *(Vineyard 693-3996)* **Near:** Bikes *(Martha's 693-6593)*, Rental Car *(Hertz 693-4196)*, InterCity Bus *(MVTA 693-9440)*, Ferry Service *(Woods Hole; New Bedford 997-1688)* **Airport:** Martha's Vineyard 693-7022 *(6.5 mi.)*

Medical Services

911 Service **OnSite:** Ambulance **Near:** Chiropractor *(Berger 693-4668)*, Holistic Services *(Holistic Spa 338-4744)*, Optician *(Finkelstein 693-3517)* **Under 1 mi:** Doctor *(Pagan 693-7730)*, Dentist *(Lagoon 693-5068)* **1-3 mi:** Veterinarian *(My Pet's 693-4040)* **Hospital:** MV 693-0410 *(1.7 mi.)*

Setting -- Tucked behind the breakwater in the western side of Vineyard Haven Harbor, this municipal mooring field is bound on the east by the active ferry channel. On the shore, a single dock leads to a small, gray-shingled salt-box surrounded by a lovely, beachy garden that houses the Harbormaster's Office and bathhouse. Owen Park features a wide swath of sandy beach with a lifeguard stand backed by an oasis of lawn - on the fringe of the bustling, pretty village.

Marina Notes -- *4pm-10am $1/ft. dockage - only after all private marinas are full. 10am-4pm temporary T-head tie-ups : to 25 ft. LOA $5/hr.; over 25 ft. $10/hr. **Mailing address: 51 Spring Street. Moorings run parallel to breakwater. Over 40 ft. LOA - Rows A-E. Uunder 40 ft .- rows F & higher. Pale blue & black balls with 2-ton blocks on heavy chain. Rafting up to 3 boats permitted. No power on docks; generators not allowed. Engines & generators on moorings 9am-9pm only. Dinghy docks on north side of both Town Dock & Steamship Dock or land on beach. Launch Ch.72. Dumpster at Owen Park - not ferry dock. Bathhouse: All tile, basic municipal. Note: Anchorage north of breakwater & Lagoon Pond. Add'l moorings - Gannon & Banjamin, Marciel & MV Shipyard.

Notable -- Stroll the William Street Historic District where some grand, old captains' houses survived the 1883 fire that devastated 60 buildings. Stop by the 1844 "Association Hall" - an architectural gem that houses the town offices and Katherine Cornell Theater. The year-round ferry dock is the transportation hub of the island - bike and car rentals, cabs, and an extensive bus system make all six towns easily accessible. Most services, supplies and eateries are closeby - including a supermarket across from the ferry dock. The luxe Mansion House welcomes boaters to its indoor pool, fitness center and showers. VH is not dry.

Oak Bluffs Marina

PO Box 1327; 310 Circuit Ave. Extension; Oak Bluffs, MA 02557

Tel: (508) 693-4355 **VHF: Monitor** Ch. 71/9 **Talk** Ch. 71
Fax: (508) 693-7402 **Alternate Tel:** n/a
Email: obmarina@comcast.net **Web:** oakbluffsmarina.com
Nearest Town: Oak Bluffs **Tourist Info:** (508) 693-0085

Navigational Information

Lat: 41°27.522' **Long:** 070°33.653' **Tide:** 3 ft. **Current:** n/a **Chart:** 13238
Rep. Depths (*MLW*): Entry 7 ft. **Fuel Dock** 12 ft. **Max Slip/Moor** 12 ft./12 ft.
Access: Nantucket Sound to Oak Bluffs Harbor

Marina Facilities *(In Season/Off Season)*

Fuel: *Church's* - Gasoline, Diesel
Slips: 80 Total, 75 Transient **Max LOA:** 105 ft. **Max Beam:** n/a
Rate *(per ft.)*: **Day** $3.50/$3* **Week** Inq. **Month** Inq.
Power: 30 amp $15, **50 amp** $20, **100 amp** n/a, **200 amp** n/a
Cable TV: No **Dockside Phone:** No
Dock Type: Fixed, Long Fingers, Short Fingers, Pilings, Alongside
Moorings: 45 Total, 45 Transient **Launch:** Yes ($4 RT)
Rate: Day $40/30 **Week** Inq. **Month** Inq.
Heads: 6 Toilet(s), 6 Shower(s)
Internet: Yes *(Wi-Fi, Free)* **Laundry:** None
Pump-Out: Onsite *(Ch. 71)*, Self Service **Fee:** Free **Closed Heads:** Yes

Marina Operations

Owner/Manager: Todd Alexander **Dockmaster:** Same
In-Season: Jun 15-LabDay, 8am-8pm **Off-Season:** Sep-Jun**, 9am-5pm
After-Hours Arrival: Recommend arrival before 6pm
Reservations: Yes **Credit Cards:** Visa/MC
Discounts: None
Pets: Welcome, Dog Walk Area **Handicap Access:** Yes

Marina Services and Boat Supplies

Services - Docking Assistance, Trash Pick-Up **Communication -** Pay Phone, FedEx, UPS, Express Mail **Supplies - Near:** Ice *(Cube)* **Under 1 mi:** Bait/Tackle *(Sharks Land 696-8272)* **1-3 mi:** Ships' Store *(MV Ship 693-0400)*, West Marine *(693-2906)*, Propane *(AmeriGas 693-0441)*

Boatyard Services

Nearest Yard: MV Shipyard (508) 693-0400

Restaurants and Accommodations

Near: Restaurant *(Giordano's 693-0184, L $8-16, D $13-22, Pizza, too)*, *(Fishbones Grille 696-8227, Waterfront cafe, L&D $9-24, Kids' $5-7)*, *(Zapotec Southwestern 693-6800, L&D $15-20, Kids' $8)*, *(Sweet Life Café 696-0200, D $32-42, Fine Dining)*, *(O-Sun Hibachi 696-0220)*, *(Nancy's 693-0006, Upstairs dining, Snack Bar Mid-East veg options)*, *(Coop de Ville 693-3420, L&D $6-25 open air clam shack)*, *(Offshore Ale 693-2626, BrewPub)*, *(Sharky's Cantina 693-7501, L&D $14-39)*, *(Sidecar 693-6261)*, *(Park Corner Bistro 696-9922, D $15-29)*, Lite Fare *(Linda Jean's 693-4093, B $4-6, L $6-18, D $6-18)*, *(Biscuits 693-2033, B&L)*, *(Skinny's Fat Sandwiches 693-5281)*, Pizzeria *(Paesan's 693-9990)*, Motel *(Nashua 693-0043, $69-219)*, *(MV Surfside 693-2500, $100-250)*, Hotel *(Wesley 693-6611, $230-320)*, Inn/B&B *(Dockside 693-2966, $180-450)*, *(Oak Bluffs 693-7171, $250-345)*

Recreation and Entertainment

OnSite: Beach *(OB Town)* **Near:** Picnic Area, Hike/Bike Trails *(to Edgartown)*, Party Boat *(The Skipper 693-1238 Half Day $60/40)*, Movie Theater *(Strand 696-8300)*, Video Arcade, Park *(Trinity)*, Museum *(Cottage at MV Camp Meeting 693-0525 $2)*, Tours *(MV Sightseeing 693-4681)*, Sightseeing *(1876 Flying Horse Carousel $1.50; MV Camp Meeting & 1879 Trinity Park Tabernacle)*, Galleries *(Arts District - Dukes Cty Ave.)*, Special Events *(Illumination mid-Aug; Shark Tourny - mid-July)* **Under 1 mi:** Dive Shop *(Vineyard 693-0288)* **1-3 mi:** Golf Course *(Farm Neck 693-3057)*

Provisioning and General Services

Near: Market *(Reliable 693-1102; Our Market 693-3000)*, Delicatessen *(Slice of Life 693-3838, Cafe, too)*, Wine/Beer *(Vineyard 693-0943)*, Liquor Store *(Jim's 693-0236)*, Bakery *(MV's Cafe/Bakery 693-3688)*, Bank/ATM, Post Office, Catholic Church, Protestant Church, Beauty Salon *(Guys N' Dolls 693-1602)*, Dry Cleaners *(Men at Work 982-9675)*, Laundry *(Wash Ashore 696-6999)*, Bookstore *(Sun Porch 693-3880)*, Pharmacy *(Conroy's 696-0700)*, Copies Etc. *(Da Rosa's 693-0110)* **Under 1 mi:** Fishmonger *(Moby Dick's 693-0748)*, Library *(Oak Bluffs 693-9433)* **1-3 mi:** Supermarket *(Stop & Shop 696-6047)*, Farmers' Market *(Tues 9am-1pm, Tisbury Wharf, VH)*, Synagogue, Hardware Store *(Hinckley 693-0075)*

Transportation

OnCall: Taxi *(Tisbury 693-7475)*, Airport Limo *(Coach & Concierge 693-3006)* **Near:** Bikes *(Ride On 693-2076)*, Rental Car *(Sun 'n Fun 693-5457; AA Island 696-5211)*, Local Bus *(MVTA 693-9440)*, Ferry Service *(to Falmouth 548-4800 & Hyannis 778-2600)* **Airport:** MV 693-7022 *(7.5 mi.)*

Medical Services

911 Service **Near:** Holistic Services *(Guys N' Dolls Spa 693-1602)* **Under 1 mi:** Doctor *(Vineyard Family Med. 693-0019)* **1-3 mi:** Dentist *(Pedro 693-6872)*, Chiropractor *(La Coste 696-3060)* **3+ mi:** Veterinarian *(My Pet's 693-4040, 3.5 mi.)* **Hospital:** MV 693-0410 *(1.5 mi.)*

Setting -- Right in the heart of quaint, funky, high-energy Oak Bluffs, 60 moorings sit in the midst of this placid, well-protected "lake." Eighty transient berths rim the eastern and southern shores - most are stern-to with cement combining and ladders at each berth. The largest facility in the Vineyard's most crowded harbor, it offers easy access to a plethora of eateries, nightlife, attractions and transportation that ring the shore.

Marina Notes -- *Slips: 30-40 ft. $3/2.25; 41-69 ft. $3.50/3; 70-99 ft. $4.50/4; over 100 ft. $5.50/5. 2-night min. weekends, 30 ft. min. **Shoulder seasons: Mid-May to mid-June (except MemDay) & LabDay to ColDay. Closed Oct-Feb. Reservations for slips only (call or online in Feb.) 2-night deposit. 80% refund only if cancelled 10+ days. Power: 30A $15/10, 2x30A $30/20, 50A $20/15. Ext. cords often needed. Moorings; first come first served, rafting expected (but can decline). Launch Ch. 71, Late Jun-LabDay, 8am-10pm; weekends in shoulder season $4pp/RT. Some finger piers. Most slips stern-to, med-moor. Self-Serve Pump-out dock for LOAs to 40 ft. Pump-out boat for larger vessels (Ch. 71). Special services for groups. Generators off by 10pm. Fuel at Church's (889-4834). Bathhouse: Brightly painted cinderblock & steel decor, tucked away at southwest corner near Our Market. New heads & showers planned.

Notable -- Oak Bluff's famously lively social scene includes most of the Vineyard's clubs. Expect a bit of a circus atomosphere at the height of the season - especially if a cruise ship is in port. The 1876 Flying Horses Carousel in center of town is arguably the oldest in the country. Wesleyan Grove's rows of over 300 brightly colored 19thC. gingerbread cottages circle the 1879 open-air Trinity Park Tabernacle - site of weekly concerts. Start the tour at Cottage Museum.

Navigational Information

Lat: 41°27.527' **Long:** 070°33.505' **Tide:** 3 ft. **Current:** 1 kt. **Chart:** 13238
Rep. Depths (*MLW*): Entry n/a **Fuel Dock** 12 ft. **Max Slip/Moor** 8 ft./-
Access: Nantucket Sound to port side of Oak Bluffs Harbor

Marina Facilities *(In Season/Off Season)*

Fuel: *Church's* - Gasoline, Diesel
Slips: 10 Total, 8 Transient **Max LOA:** 60 ft. **Max Beam:** 16 ft.
Rate *(per ft.)*: **Day** $3.50/$2.50 **Week** n/a **Month** n/a
Power: 30 amp $10, **50 amp** $15, **100 amp** n/a, **200 amp** n/a
Cable TV: Yes Incl. **Dockside Phone:** No
Dock Type: Fixed, Long Fingers, Alongside, Wood
Moorings: 0 Total, 0 Transient **Launch:** Yes, Dinghy Dock
Rate: Day n/a **Week** n/a **Month** n/a
Heads: 6 Toilet(s), 6 Shower(s)
Internet: No **Laundry:** None
Pump-Out: OnCall *(Ch. 71)*, Full Service **Fee:** Free **Closed Heads:** Yes

Marina Operations

Owner/Manager: Terry McCarthy **Dockmaster:** same
In-Season: MidJun-LabDay, 7-8 **Off-Season:** May-MidJun & Sep-Oct, 9-5
After-Hours Arrival: Call ahead
Reservations: Yes **Credit Cards:** Visa/MC
Discounts: None
Pets: Welcome **Handicap Access:** Yes, Heads, Docks

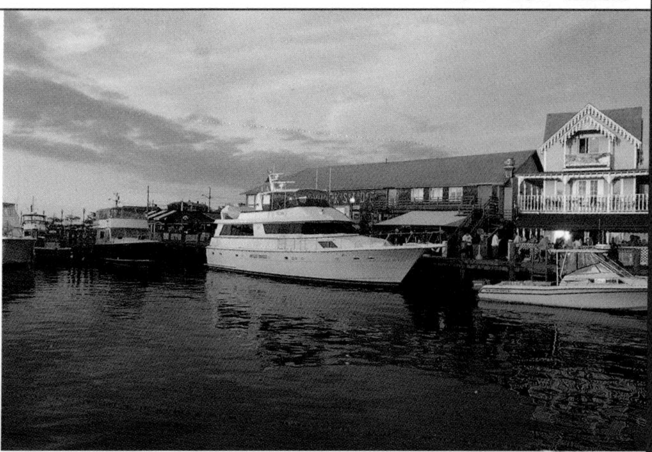

Dockside Market Place & Marina

PO Box 1386; 12 Circuit Avenue Ext; Oak Bluffs, MA 02557

Tel: (508) 693-3392 **VHF: Monitor** Ch. 9 **Talk** n/a
Fax: (508) 696-7624 **Alternate Tel:** n/a
Email: mvdockside@gmail.com **Web:** none
Nearest Town: Oak Bluffs **Tourist Info:** (508) 693-0085

Marina Services and Boat Supplies

Services - Docking Assistance, Security *(16 Hrs., On duty dock)*, Trash Pick-Up **Communication -** Pay Phone (2), FedEx, UPS, Express Mail **Supplies - Near:** Ice *(Cube)* **Under 1 mi:** Bait/Tackle *(Sharks Landing 696-8272)* **1-3 mi:** Ships' Store *(MV 693-0400)*, West Marine *(693-2906)*, Propane *(Vineyard 693-4232)*

Boatyard Services

OnSite: Divers **Nearest Yard:** M.V. Shipyard (508) 693-0400

Restaurants and Accommodations

OnSite: Restaurant *(Coop De Ville 693-3420, L $6-17, D $15-37, open air clam shack)* **Near:** Restaurant *(Giordano's 693-0184, L $8-16, D $13-22, Pizza, too)*, *(Fishbones 696-8227, L&D $10-24; Kids' $5-7)*, *(Nancy's 693-0006, Upstairs dining, Snack Bar)*, *(Sweet Life 696-0200, D $24-37)*, *(Sidecar Cafe 693-6261)*, *(Zapotec 693-6800, L&D $15-20; Kids' $8)*, *(Offshore Ale 693-2626, BrewPub)*, *(Sharky's Cantina 693-7501, L&D $14-39)*, *(O-Sun Hibachi 696-0220, L $8-11, D $12-18)*, *(Park Corner 696-9922, D $15-29)*, Lite Fare *(Biscuits 693-2033, B&L)*, *(Sand Bar 693-7111)*, Pizzeria *(Paesan's 693-9990)*, Motel *(MV Surfside 693-2500, $100-255)*, Inn/B&B *(Dockside 693-2966, $200-250)*, *(Madison 693-2760, $89-319)*

Recreation and Entertainment

OnSite: Boat Rentals *(MV Watersports 693-8476 parasailing, jet skis, water ski)* **Near:** Beach *(Town Beach)*, Hike/Bike Trails *(to Edgartown)*, Fishing Charter *(Banjo 693-3154)*, Party Boat *(Skipper 693-1238)*, Movie Theater *(Strand 696-8300)*, Video Arcade, Park *(Trinity)*, Museum *(Cottage at MV Camp Meeting 693-0525 $2)*, Tours *(MV Sightseeing 693-4681)*, Sightseeing *(Flying Horse Carousel 693-9481 $1.50; MV Camp Meeting & 1879 Trinity Park Tabernacle)* **1-3 mi:** Golf Course *(Farm Neck 693-3560)*

Provisioning and General Services

OnSite: Retail Shops *(Black Dog, Handworks, Dockside Jewelers)* **Near:** Convenience Store *(Jim's 693-0236)*, Market *(Reliable 693-1102; Our Market 693-3000)*, Gourmet Shop *(MV Gourmet 693-3688)*, Delicatessen *(Slice of Life 693-3838, Cafe, too)*, Wine/Beer *(Vineyard Wine & Cheese 693-0943)*, Liquor Store *(Jim's Package 693-0236)*, Bakery *(MV Gourmet 693-3688)*, Meat Market, Bank/ATM, Post Office *(693-7737)*, Catholic Church, Beauty Salon *(Guys N' Dolls 693-1602)*, Dry Cleaners *(Men at Work 982-9675)*, Laundry *(Wash Ashore 696-6999)*, Bookstore *(Sun Porch 693-3880)*, Pharmacy *(Conroy's 696-0700)*, Newsstand, Copies Etc. *(Da Rosa's 693-0110)* **Under 1 mi:** Fishmonger *(Moby Dick's 693-0748)*, Protestant Church, Library *(Oak Bluffs 693-9433)* **1-3 mi:** Supermarket *(Stop & Shop 696-6047)*, Farmers' Market *(Tues 9am-1pm, Tisbury Wharf, VH)*, Synagogue, Hardware Store *(Hinckley 693-0075)*, Florist *(Nochi 693-9074)*

Transportation

OnSite: Ferry Service *(HiLine & Island Queen)* **OnCall:** Taxi *(Tisbury 693-7475)*, Airport Limo *(Coach & Concierge 693-3006)* **Near:** Bikes *(MV 696-6255; Anderson 693-9346)*, Rental Car *(Budget 497-1820)*, Local Bus *(MVTA 693-9440)* **Airport:** Martha's Vineyard 693-7022 *(7.5 mi.)*

Medical Services

911 Service **Near:** Holistic Services *(Guys N' Dolls Spa 693-1602)* **Under 1 mi:** Doctor *(Vineyard Family 693-0019)* **1-3 mi:** Dentist *(Casey 693-6872)*, Chiropractor *(La Coste 696-3060)* **Hospital:** MV 693-0410 *(1.5 mi.)*

Setting -- On the east side of calm, sheltered, but hyper-busy, boat-filled Oak Bluffs Harbor, the marina's two piers book-end a long face dock - which lies alongside the concrete Boardwalk, known as The Strip. Dockside Market Place's 15 shops and restaurants share the upland with more eateries, ferry docks, verandas, beachy bars, live music and point-n-shoot tourists in a festive party atmosphere. Large Victorian-era houses overlook the south shore.

Marina Notes -- Fuel at adjacent Church's. Additional electric service planned. Repeat visitors reserve in January; newcomers reserve March 1. Very helpful dockhands, particularly useful in this tight lay-out. No rafting. Outdoor bars & cafes literally steps from the docks. Late-July shark tournament busiest weekend. Pump-out Boat. Bathhouse: Painted cinderblock public heads & showers in harbor's southwest corner - shared with municipal marina. Laundry across street.

Notable -- For two months, Oak Bluffs is the brash, fun, effervescent adolescent of the three harbor towns. In September it quietly returns to its roots. Seek refuge in the 34-acre Wesleyan Grove (aka M.V. Camp Meeting Assoc.), where Methodist Summer Camp meetings have taken place since 1835. Accessed through the Circuit Avenue Arcade, over 300 brightly painted, small Carpenter Gothic Victorian ginger-bread cottages ring the open-air 1879 Trinity Park Tabernacle - the site of summer evening concerts. The Flying Horses Carousel has been operating since 1876. Bicycle rentals abound; about 15 bus routes intersect with bike paths making the whole island accessible. Oak Bluffs is also served by five ferry companies: Hy-Line to Hyannis/Nantucket, Island Queen to Falmouth, New England to New Bedford, Steamship Authority to Woods Hole, Vineyard Fast Ferry to Quonset Point, RI - very convenient for crew changes.

PHOTOS ON DVD: 23

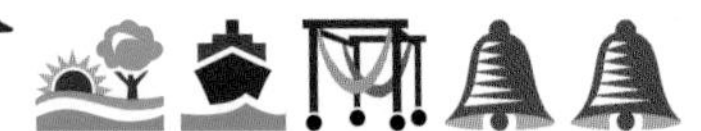     

North Wharf & Moorings

PO Box 739; 1 Morse Street; Edgartown, MA 02539

Tel: (508) 627-4746 **VHF: Monitor** Ch. 9/16 **Talk** Ch. 74
Fax: (508) 627-6123 **Alternate Tel:** n/a
Email: edgharbor@gmail.com **Web:** www.edgartownharbor.com
Nearest Town: Edgartown **Tourist Info:** (508) 693-0085

Navigational Information
Lat: 41°23.065' **Long:** 070°30.463' **Tide:** 2 ft. **Current:** 3 kt. **Chart:** 13238
Rep. Depths (*MLW*): Entry 19 ft. **Fuel Dock** 20 ft. **Max Slip/Moor** 20 ft./20 ft.
Access: First commercial dock on starboard side

Marina Facilities *(In Season/Off Season)*
Fuel: *Shell* - Gasoline, Diesel, On Call Delivery
Slips: 33 Total, 4 Transient **Max LOA:** 130 ft. **Max Beam:** 27 ft.
Rate *(per ft.)*: **Day** $4.00/$2* **Week** n/a **Month** n/a
Power: 30 amp Incl., **50 amp** Incl., **100 amp** n/a, **200 amp** n/a
Cable TV: No **Dockside Phone:** No
Dock Type: Fixed, Floating, Long Fingers, Alongside, Wood
Moorings: 100 Total, 75 Transient **Launch:** Yes, Dinghy Dock
Rate: Day $40 **Week** n/a **Month** n/a
Heads: 2 Toilet(s), 3 Shower(s)
Internet: No **Laundry:** None
Pump-Out: OnSite, OnCall, Full Service **Fee:** Free **Closed Heads:** Yes

Marina Operations
Owner/Manager: Charles Blair (Hbrmstr) **Dockmaster:** Same
In-Season: May-Nov, 7am-9pm **Off-Season:** Dec-Apr, Closed
After-Hours Arrival: Call VHF 74
Reservations: Yes, Preferred **Credit Cards:** Visa/MC, Dscvr, Amex
Discounts: None
Pets: Welcome **Handicap Access:** Yes, Heads, Docks

Marina Services and Boat Supplies
Services - Docking Assistance, Security *(20 Hrs., Patrol)*, Trash Pick-Up **Communication -** FedEx, UPS, Express Mail **Supplies - OnSite:** Ice *(Block, Cube)*, Ships' Store *(Edgartown Marine 627-6500)* **Near:** Bait/Tackle *(Capt. Porky's 627-7117)* **3+ mi:** West Marine *(693-2906, 8 mi)*, Propane *(Vineyard 693-5080, 5.5 mi)*

Boatyard Services
OnSite: Travelift *(35T - Edgartown Marine)*, Engine mechanic *(gas, diesel)*, Electronic Sales, Hull Repairs, Brightwork, Painting **OnCall:** Divers, Bottom Cleaning, Compound, Wash & Wax, Interior Cleaning, Propeller Repairs

Restaurants and Accommodations
Near: Restaurant *(Newes 627-4397, L&D $7-17)*, *(L'Etoile Restaurant 627-5187, D $14-47)*, *(Seafood Shanty 627-8622, L $11-16, D $18-33)*, *(Chesca's 627-1234, D $26-36)*, *(David Ryan's 627-4100, L $8-30, D $8-38)*, *(Quarterdeck Seafood 627-5346)*, *(Atlantic Fish & Chophouse 627-7001)*, *(Among the Flowers 627-3233)*, *(Detente 627-8810, D $28-30)*, Lite Fare *(Humphrey's 627-7029)*, Pizzeria *(Lattanzi's 627-9084)*, Hotel *(Harbor View 627-7000, $350-1250)*, Inn/B&B *(Kelley House 627-7000, $135-1600)*, *(Colonial 627-4711, $135-895)*, *(Edgartown 627-4794, $75-300)*

Recreation and Entertainment
Near: Beach *(Lighthouse & Fuller St.)*, Hike/Bike Trails *(to Oak Bluffs)*, Fishing Charter *(Larry's 627-5088; Capt. Porky's 627-7117)*, Movie Theater *(Edgartown 627-8008)*, Tours *(Cape Poge Light 627-3599 $25/12; Edgartown Light Thu-Mon, 11-5, $5)*, Cultural Attract *(Performing Arts Ctr. 627-4442 - Old Whaling Church)*, Sightseeing *(Ferry to Chappy; Historic District; Biplane rides 627-7677 2 mi.)*, Galleries *(Eisenhauer 627-7003; MV 627-4881; Belushi 939-9322)* **Under 1 mi:** Playground, Video Rental *(Redbox)*, Park *(Cannonball)*, Museum *(MV 627-4441, $7/4; Vincent House 627-8017)* **1-3 mi:** Golf Course *(Farm Neck 693-3057)*

Provisioning and General Services
Near: Gourmet Shop *(Soigne 627-8489; Katama General Store 627-5071)*, Delicatessen *(Skinny's 627-6990)*, Bank/ATM, Post Office, Catholic Church, Protestant Church, Library *(Edgartown 627-4221)*, Beauty Salon *(Pure Touch 939-3123)*, Bookstore *(Edgartown 627-8463)*, Hardware Store *(Edgartown 627-4338)*, Florist *(Cottage Garden 627-3528)* **Under 1 mi:** Market *(Depot 627-1299)*, Supermarket *(Stop & Shop 627-9522)*, Liquor Store *(Al's 627-4347)*, Bakery *(Tropical 627-3773)*, Fishmonger *(Edgartown 627-3791)*, Copies Etc. *(Mailroom 627-7704)* **1-3 mi:** Green Grocer *(Morning Glory Farm 627-9674)*, Pharmacy *(Stop & Shop 627-5107)*

Transportation
OnCall: Water Taxi *(Old Port Ch. 68)*, Taxi *(Jon's 627-4677)* **Near:** Bikes *(Cutler 627-4052)*, InterCity Bus *(MVTA to all towns)*, Ferry Service *(to Falmouth 548-9400; to Chappaquiddick 627-9794 - 7am-Mid $12/car, $4/pp)* **Under 1 mi:** Rental Car *(AA Is. 627-6800)* **Airport:** MV *(5.5 mi.)*

Medical Services
911 Service **OnCall:** Ambulance **Near:** Doctor *(Hoak 627-1044)*, Holistic Services *(Higher Knead 627-5308)* **Under 1 mi:** Dentist *(Orazem 627-8090)* **1-3 mi:** Optician *(Visual As Specs 627-1342)*, Veterinarian *(Vineyard 627-5292)* **3+ mi:** Chiropractor *(La Coste 696-3060, 6.5 mi.)* **Hospital:** Martha's Vineyard 693-0410 *(8 mi.)*

Setting -- After rounding Starbuck Neck under the gaze of squat, cast iron Edgartown Light, the mooring field sprawls along the narrow harbor. Filled with perfectly turned-out yachts, the field boasts views of the Greek Revival Whaling Church's 92-foot Steeple rising above elegant 19th Century homes set on the hill. The North Wharf land base and big-yacht dock is the first commercial facility along the harborfront and houses Edgartown Marine yacht yard.

Marina Notes -- *50 ft. min. fee. Town-owned. Face docks to 130 ft. Slips to 90 ft. Fuel Dock. Blue-ball mooring field for LOAs under 40 ft., first come. Yellow-ball field for LOAs 40-60 ft. by reservation (2-week max.). Rafting $20. Refunds 10 days prior to arrival less 15%. Dinghy dock onsite & dinghy float at Atlantic Restaurant (west of EYC). Oldport launch (Ch.68) docks at North Wharf & next to Mad Max (& Lure Grill 627-3663 at South Beach). Water at Memorial Wharf, North Wharf (while fueling) & Water Barge opposite green can #9. Pump-out: Boat or Memorial Wharf (9am-4pm). Dog walk beach - Chappy Ferry slip south to first dock. Not at North Wharf. Edgartown Marine (627-4388): chandlery, haul-out, yard services & storage. Bathhouse: Basic fiberglass & formica.

Notable -- Once a prosperous whaling center, Edgartown's narrow streets and brick sidewalks are lined with stately black-shuttered, white neo-classical houses built by ships' captains, fleet owners and China-trade merchants. About a hundred years ago, it reinvented itself as a passionate, patrician yachting center - claiming the title sailing capital of the world. The calm Lighthouse and Fuller Street Beaches are an easy walk north, and surf-pounded South Beach is a 3-mile bike or Rte 8 bus ride. Chappaquiddick is a naturalist's delight - the exquisite Mytoi Japanese garden a surprising counterpoint to the wild preserves.

PHOTOS ON DVD: 24

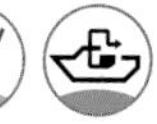

Navigational Information

Lat: 41°23.330' **Long:** 070°30.671' **Tide:** 2 ft. **Current:** 3 kt. **Chart:** 13238
Rep. Depths (*MLW*): Entry 15 ft. **Fuel Dock** n/a **Max Slip/Moor** 15 ft./-
Access: Head South from R2 bell located in Nantucket Sound

Marina Facilities *(In Season/Off Season)*

Fuel: No
Slips: 9 Total, 9 Transient **Max LOA:** 150 ft. **Max Beam:** 30 ft.
Rate *(per ft.)*: **Day** $8.75/Inq.* **Week** Inq. **Month** Inq.
Power: 30 amp $25, **50 amp** $50, **100 amp** n/a, **200 amp** n/a
Cable TV: No **Dockside Phone:** No
Dock Type: Fixed, Short Fingers, Pilings, Alongside, Wood
Moorings: 0 Total, 0 Transient **Launch:** n/a
Rate: Day n/a **Week** n/a **Month** n/a
Heads: None
Internet: No **Laundry:** None
Pump-Out: OnCall, Full Service, 2 Port **Fee:** Free **Closed Heads:** Yes

Marina Operations

Owner/Manager: Robert Colacray **Dockmaster:** Seasonal
In-Season: May 25-Oct 10, 9am-6pm **Off-Season:** Oct 11-May 24, Closed
After-Hours Arrival: Call (508) 627-7400 for instructions
Reservations: Yes, for 2 night min. **Credit Cards:** Visa/MC
Discounts: None
Pets: Welcome **Handicap Access:** No

Mad Max Marina

PO Box 2821; 25 Dock Street; Edgartown, MA 02539

Tel: (508) 627-7400 **VHF: Monitor** Ch. 9 **Talk** Ch. 71
Fax: (508) 627-7245 **Alternate Tel:** n/a
Email: none **Web:** www.madmaxmarina.com
Nearest Town: Edgartown **Tourist Info:** (508) 693-4486

Marina Services and Boat Supplies

Services - Docking Assistance, Trash Pick-Up **Communication -** FedEx, UPS, Express Mail **Supplies - OnSite:** Ice *(Block, Cube)* **Near:** Ships' Store *(MV Shipyard 627-6000)* **Under 1 mi:** Bait/Tackle *(Coop's 627-3909)* **3+ mi:** Propane *(Vineyard 693-5080, 5.5 mi)*

Boatyard Services

Nearest Yard: North Wharf - Edgartown Marine (508) 627-4388

Restaurants and Accommodations

OnSite: Restaurant *(Seafood Shanty 627-8622, L $11-19, D $20-33, Waterfront view)*, *(Quarterdeck 627-5346)* **Near:** Restaurant *(David Ryans 627-4100, L $8-30, D $7-38)*, *(Chesca's 627-1234, D $26-36)*, *(L'Etoile Restaurant 627-5187, D $14-47)*, *(Atlantic Fish & Chophouse 627-7001)*, *(Among the Flowers 627-3233)*, Lite Fare *(Humphrey's 627-7029)*, Pizzeria *(Lattanzi's 627-9084)*, Hotel *(Harbor View 627-7000, $385-1200)*, Inn/B&B *(Kelley House 627-7000, $135-1600)*, *(Daggett House 627-4600)*, *(Edgartown 627-4794, $75-300)*, *(Colonial Inn 627-4711, $135-895)*

Recreation and Entertainment

OnSite: Boat Rentals *(2 hr. Sail on "Mad Max" $60/55 2 & 6pm)* **Near:** Playground, Fishing Charter *(Larry's 627-5088; Capt. Porky's 627-7117)*, Movie Theater *(Edgartown 627-8008)*, Museum *(MV 627-4441, $7/4; Vincent House 627-8017; Old Whaling Church; Fisher House)*, Cultural Attract *(Performing Arts Ctr. 627-4442 at Old Whaling Church)*, Sightseeing *(Trustees of Reservation Cape Poge Nat. Hist $40/18 & Wasque Surf-Casting Tours $60/25 693-5005; Biplane Rides 627-7677 2 mi.)* **Under 1 mi:** Beach *(Ferry to East Beach or Bus Rte 8 to South Beach)*, Hike/Bike Trails *(to Oak Bluffs)*, Video Rental *(Redbox)*, Park *(Cannonball)* **1-3 mi:** Golf Course *(Farm Neck 693-3057)*, Fitness Center *(Vineyard 627-3393)*

Provisioning and General Services

Near: Delicatessen *(Skinny's 627-6990)*, Wine/Beer, Bakery *(MV 627-5880)*, Fishmonger *(Edgartown 627-3791)*, Bank/ATM, Post Office *(627-1100)*, Catholic Church, Protestant Church, Library *(Edgartown PL 627-4221)*, Beauty Salon *(Boucle 627-3853)*, Barber Shop, Bookstore *(Edgartown 627-8463)*, Newsstand, Hardware Store *(Edgartown 627-4338)*, Florist *(Cottage Garden 627-3528)* **Under 1 mi:** Market *(Depot 627-1299)*, Supermarket *(Super Stop & Shop 627-9522)*, Gourmet Shop *(Soigne 627-8489; Katama General Store 627-5071)*, Liquor Store *(Al's 627-4347)*, Pharmacy *(Stop & Shop 627-5107)* **1-3 mi:** Green Grocer *(Katama Farm 627-5071)*, Copies Etc. *(Allanbrook 627-3035)* **3+ mi:** Laundry *(Airport 693-5005, 6 mi.)*

Transportation

OnCall: Water Taxi *(Oldport Launch Ch. 68, $3)*, Taxi *(John's 627-4677)*, Airport Limo *(Coach & Concierge 693-3006)* **Near:** Bikes *(Cutler Bike 627-4052)*, Local Bus *(MVTA 693-9440 15 major routes cover the island)*, Ferry Service *("On Time" to Chappaquidick Island 627-9794 7am-Mid every 5 min. - RT $12/car, $4/pp; to Falmouth 548-9400 1-way $25/15)* **Under 1 mi:** Rental Car *(Island Auto Rental 627-6800)* **Airport:** MV 693-7022 *(5.5 mi.)*

Medical Services

911 Service **OnCall:** Ambulance **Near:** Doctor *(Hoak 627-1044)*, Holistic Services *(Higher Knead 627-5308)* **Under 1 mi:** Dentist *(Orazem 627-8090)* **1-3 mi:** Optician *(Visual As Specs 627-1342)*, Veterinarian *(Vineyard 627-5292)* **Hospital:** Martha's Vineyard 693-0410 *(8 mi.)*

Setting -- Occupying a prime, central location in this beautiful harbor, Mad Max lies just past the Memorial Town Dock in front of the Seafood Shanty restaurant - seaward of Edgartown Yacht Club. The big, bright-red catamaran with the Mad Max logo lying along the T-head makes it hard to miss. Smaller boats berth in a pretty, brick-rimmed basin backed by an attractive three-story, natural-shingled office; larger vessels side-tie on the deeper, outer docks.

Marina Notes -- *Flat Rate: Max beam 14 ft & draft 7 ft - to 39 ft. $275, 40-45 ft., $350 (basin slips). Unlimited beam & 14 ft. draft (face docks) - 50-59 ft. $600, 60-69 ft. $675, 70-79 ft. $750, 80-85 ft. $850, 86-160ft Call. 2-3 boats traveling in company rafted on outer dock $375 each. Weekends - Fri & Sat booking required. Holiday weekends - 3 night min. Water available here or from Water Barge opposite Green Can #9. Fuel at North Wharf or delivered by Island Fuel 627-9955. Docks shared with daytrippers embarking on Mad Max. Bathhouse: None. Showers at Edgartown Visitors' Center (Church St.). No laundry.

Notable -- The eponymous "Mad Max," a 60-foot catamaran, sails twice daily from the marina. With a 70-foot mast and 25-foot beam, she's a stand-out in the staid, affluent harbor where hulls sporting a downeast sheer are de rigeur. Edgartown, a compact jewel, is made for walking. Pick up a map and start on North Water Street lined with exquisite 19thC. Greek Revival and Federal style houses built by whaling ship captains and fleet owners. Many house one-of-a-kind shops, boutiques, art galleries, museums. Rising above the skyline, the 1843 Old Whaling Church's 92-foot steeple is a navigation aid. Rent a bike; take the ferry to Chappy. Visit Wasque Reservation and Cape Pogue Wildlife Refuge on a guided tour or simply enjoy East Beach and the Mytoi Japanese garden.

PHOTOS ON DVD: 20

Harborside Inn

Harborside Inn

PO Box 67; 3 South Water Street; Edgartown, MA 02539

Tel: (508) 627-4321 **VHF: Monitor** Ch. 10 **Talk** Ch. 10
Fax: (508) 627-7566 **Alternate Tel:** n/a
Email: info@TheHarborsideInn.com **Web:** www.TheHarborsideInn.com
Nearest Town: Edgartown *(0.1 mi.)* **Tourist Info:** (508) 693-0085

Navigational Information

Lat: 41°23.322' **Long:** 070°30.761' **Tide:** 2 ft. **Current:** 3 kt. **Chart:** 13238
Rep. Depths (*MLW*): Entry 21 ft. **Fuel Dock** n/a **Max Slip/Moor** 6 ft./-
Access: Past Chappaquiddick Point, the last set of docks to starboard

Marina Facilities *(In Season/Off Season)*

Fuel: No
Slips: 15 Total, 15 Transient **Max LOA:** 125 ft. **Max Beam:** n/a
Rate *(per ft.)*: **Day** $6.50* **Week** n/a **Month** n/a
Power: 30 amp n/a, **50 amp** n/a, **100 amp** n/a, **200 amp** n/a
Cable TV: No **Dockside Phone:** No
Dock Type: Fixed, Alongside, Wood
Moorings: 0 Total, 0 Transient **Launch:** n/a, Dinghy Dock
Rate: Day n/a **Week** n/a **Month** n/a
Heads: Toilet(s)
Internet: Yes *(free)* **Laundry:** None
Pump-Out: OnCall *(Boat Ch.74)* **Fee:** Free **Closed Heads:** Yes

Marina Operations

Owner/Manager: Joseph Badot **Dockmaster:** Same
In-Season: MidApr-MidNov, 7am-10pm **Off-Season:** midNov-MidApr, Closed
After-Hours Arrival: Please call ahead
Reservations: Yes **Credit Cards:** Visa/MC, Amex
Discounts: None
Pets: No **Handicap Access:** No

Marina Services and Boat Supplies

Services - Docking Assistance, Trash Pick-Up **Communication -** Fax in/out, FedEx, UPS, Express Mail **Supplies - Near:** Ice *(Block, Cube)*, Ships' Store *(MV Ship 627-6000)*, Bait/Tackle *(Capt. Porky's 627-7117)* **3+ mi:** West Marine *(693-2906, 8 mi)*, Propane *(Vineyard 693-5080, 5 mi)*

Boatyard Services

Nearest Yard: North Wharf--Edgartown Marine (508) 627-4388

Restaurants and Accommodations

OnSite: Hotel *(Harborside Inn 627-4321, $225+, 2-night min.)* **Near:** Restaurant *(L'Etoile 627-5187, D $14-47)*, *(Chesca's 627-1234, D $26-36)*, *(Alchemy 627-9999, D $28-38, Bar menu: $14-18)*, *(Atria 627-5850, D $16-36)*, *(Seafood Shanty 627-8622, L $15-19, D $20-29)*, *(Quarterdeck 627-5346)*, *(Atlantic Fish & Chophouse 627-7001, L $11-23, D $11-40, Adjacent, Dock)*, *(Newes from America 627-4397, L&D: $7-17)*, *(Among the Flowers 627-3233)*, *(David Ryan's 627-4100, D $8-30)*, *(The Wharf 627-9966, D $7-24, Across Street, Kids' $5-8. Music, Pub 12 beers on tap)*, Lite Fare *(Humphrey's 627-7029)*, Pizzeria *(Lattanzi's 627-9084)*, Hotel *(Kelley House 627-7000, $135-1600)*, Inn/B&B *(Colonial 627-4711, $135-425)*, *(Edgartown 627-4794, $75-300)*, *(Charlotte 627-4751, $350-950)*

Recreation and Entertainment

OnSite: Pool, Spa **Near:** Beach *(ferry to East Beach)*, Hike/Bike Trails *(to Oak Bluffs)*, Movie Theater *(Edgartown 627-8008)*, Museum *(MV 627-4441, $7/4; Vincent House 627-8017; Old Whaling Church; Fisher House)*, Tours *(Cape Poge Nat. Hist 627-3599 $40/18)*, Cultural Attract *(Performing Arts Ctr. 627-4442 at Old Whaling Church)*, Sightseeing *(Walking Tour: Roam Water, Main, School, Summer & Winter Sts.)*, Galleries *(North Water 627-6002; Willoughby 627-3369; Edgartown Scrimshaw 627-9439; Carin Eliot 627-3073)* **Under 1 mi:** Fishing Charter *(Larry's 627-5088)*, Park *(Cannonball)* **1-3 mi:** Golf Course *(Farm Neck 693-3057)*

Provisioning and General Services

OnSite: Beauty Salon *(Pure Touch 939-3123)*, Florist *(Cottage Garden 627-3528)*, Retail Shops *(Lazy Frog)* **Near:** Delicatessen *(Skinny's 627-6990)*, Liquor Store *(Great Harbour 627-4390)*, Bakery *(MV 627-5880)*, Bank/ATM, Catholic Church, Protestant Church, Library *(Edgartown 627-4221)*, Bookstore *(Edgartown 627-8463)*, Hardware Store *(Edgartown 627-4338)* **Under 1 mi:** Market *(Depot 627-1299; Katama General 627-5071)*, Supermarket *(Stop & Shop 627-9522)*, Gourmet Shop *(Soigne 627-8489)*, Fishmonger *(Edgartown 627-3791)*, Post Office, Pharmacy *(Stop & Shop 627-5107)* **1-3 mi:** Green Grocer *(Morning Glory Farm 627-9003)*

Transportation

OnCall: Water Taxi *(Oldport Launch Ch.68, $3-4/pp)*, Taxi *(Jon's 627-4677)*, Airport Limo *(Coach & Concierge 693-3006)* **Near:** Bikes *(Wheel Happy 627-5928)*, Local Bus *(MVTA - 15 rtes.)*, Ferry Service *(to Chappy 627-9794 7am-Mid - RT $12/car, $4/pp; to Falmouth 548-9400 1-way $25/15)* **Under 1 mi:** Rental Car *(Island 627-6800)* **Airport:** MV 693-7022 *(5.5 mi.)*

Medical Services

911 Service **OnSite:** Holistic Services *(288-5251)* **Under 1 mi:** Doctor *(Hoak 627-1044)*, Dentist *(Orazem 627-8090)*, Veterinarian *(Vineyard 627-5292)* **1-3 mi:** Optician *(Visual As Specs 627-1342)* **3+ mi:** Chiropractor *(La Coste 696-3060, 5 mi.)* **Hospital:** Martha's Vineyard 693-0410 *(8 mi.)*

Setting -- Tucked into a basin just past the Edgartown Yacht Club, Harborside's three long, fixed docks march along the impeccably manicured waterfront. Verandas front white, multi-story buildings that surround the lush greensward. A kidney-shaped pool overlooks the docks, rose beds line brick walks, and 19th C. houses host the amenities. Views across the busy, narrow harbor are of Chappaquiddick Island. The village's Main Street is a block away.

Marina Notes -- *Flat Rate: to 50 ft. $310; 51-60 ft. $375; 61-70 ft. $435; over 80 ft. $500. 2 night min. stay, 3 nights holidays. Originally 7 small houses; it has grown over time. Secure & private. No electricity on docks, only water. Transient vessels need marine head & generator or inverter. Reserve far in advance. 90-room interval-ownership resort operates like a luxury inn - rooms rented when owners not in residence. Pool & whirlpool avail to boaters. Grills & laundry are not. Children welcome. No pets. Pump-out boat Ch.74 or at Memorial Wharf facility (9am-4pm). Bathhouse: none. Note: No reciprocity at Edgartown YC.

Notable -- Several popular restaurants are within a block of Harborside, as are the shops in neo-classical buildings along Main Street. The Martha's Vineyard Historical Society's also a short walk. A glowing Gay Head Light fresnel lens welcomes visitors to the complex of historic buildings that tell the island's rich 350-year story; particularly interesting exhibits include the Francis Foster Maritime Gallery's ships' logs, mariner's souvenir memorabilia, scrimshaw, early portraits and a depiction of the conversion of whale blubber to lamp oil. Stop at the Farm Institute on the way south to famous surf-pounded South Beach State Park (Bus Rte 8). Three blocks north, the Chappaquiddick "On Time" ferry is the gateway to the My Toi garden, East Beach, Cape Poge and Wasque Reservations.

PHOTOS ON DVD: 23

    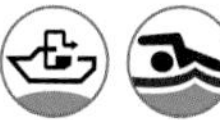 

Navigational Information
Lat: 41°17.164' **Long:** 070°05.339' **Tide:** 3 ft. **Current:** n/a **Chart:** 13242
Rep. Depths (*MLW*): Entry 20 ft. **Fuel Dock** n/a **Max Slip/Moor** -/100 ft.
Access: Nantucket Sound to Nantucket Harbor

Marina Facilities *(In Season/Off Season)*
Fuel: *Gray Lady Marine* - Diesel
Slips: 0 Total, 0 Transient **Max LOA:** 100 ft. **Max Beam:** n/a
Rate *(per ft.)*: **Day** n/a **Week** n/a **Month** n/a
Power: 30 amp n/a, **50 amp** n/a, **100 amp** n/a, **200 amp** n/a
Cable TV: No **Dockside Phone:** No
Dock Type: n/a
Moorings: 125 Total, 125 Transient **Launch:** Yes (Ch. 68, $4/pp/1-way,)
Rate: Day $65* **Week** n/a **Month** n/a
Heads: 2 Toilet(s), 2 Shower(s)
Internet: Yes *(Wiblast 325-7606)* **Laundry:** Yes
Pump-Out: OnCall *(Boat)*, Full Service **Fee:** Free **Closed Heads:** Yes

Marina Operations
Owner/Manager: Dennis & Wendy Metcalfe **Dockmaster:** Same
In-Season: May-Oct, 7am-7pm **Off-Season:** Nov-April, Closed
After-Hours Arrival: Call before 5pm Ch. 68 or by phone
Reservations: Yes **Credit Cards:** Visa/MC, Amex
Discounts: May/Sep - Inq. **Dockage:** n/a **Fuel:** n/a **Repair:** n/a
Pets: Welcome, Dog Walk Area **Handicap Access:** No

Nantucket Moorings

85 Batlett Road; Nantucket, MA 02554**

Tel: (508) 228-4472 **VHF: Monitor** Ch. 68 **Talk** Ch. 68
Fax: (508) 228-7441 **Alternate Tel:** n/a
Email: nantucket.moorings@gmail **Web:** www.nantucketmoorings.com
Nearest Town: Nantucket *(0.1 mi.)* **Tourist Info:** (508) 228-1700

Marina Services and Boat Supplies
Communication - Pay Phone, FedEx, DHL, UPS, Express Mail **Supplies - OnCall:** Ice *(Block, Cube)* **Near:** Ships' Store *(Brant Point 228-6244; Nantucket 228-2300)*, Bait/Tackle *(Cross Rip 228-4900)* **1-3 mi:** Propane *(Nantucket 228-6240)*

Boatyard Services
Nearest Yard: Grey Lady Marine (508) 228-6525

Restaurants and Accommodations
Near: Restaurant *(Lobster Trap 228-4200, L&D $12-30)*, *(Arno's 228-7001, B $8-20, L $9-20, D $15-28, Kids' Menus)*, *(Straight Wharf 228-4499, L $10-16, D $28-39, Bar $8-20, 3 courses $25, Brunch: $11-19)*, *(Boarding House 228-9622, D $28-34)*, *(Rope Walk 228-8886, D $22-34, Kids' $12)*, *(Fifty Six Union 228-6135, D $16-36)*, *(Slip 14 228-2033, L&D)*, *(Black-Eyed Susans 325-0308, D $12-25, BYOB, Break, too)*, Lite Fare *(Company of the Cauldron 228-4016, D $58-64, 4 course prix fixe)*, Inn/B&B *(Union Street 888-517-0707, $160-550)*, *(Cottages at the Boat Basin 325-1499, $159-499)* **Under 1 mi:** Pizzeria *(Steamboat Wharf 228-1131)*, Hotel *(Jared Coffin 228-2400, $155-470)*, *(White Elephant 228-2500, $350-1300)*

Recreation and Entertainment
Near: Beach *(Brant Point; Children's, Francis St., Jetties)*, Playground *(Children's Beach)*, Dive Shop *(Sunken Ship 228-9226)*, Fitness Center *(Studio 901-5211)*, Boat Rentals *(Sea Nantucket - Kayaks 228-7499 $15/hr.)*, Hike/Bike Trails *(5 paths - 25 mi.)*, Fishing Charter *(Topspin Fishing 228-7724)*, Movie Theater *(Dreamland 228-5356, Starlight 228-4479)*, Video Rental *(Blockbuster; Redbox)*, Museum *(Nantucket Whaling 228-1894, $15/8; Nantucket Historical 228-1894; Mitchell Nat. Science 228-0898)*, Tours *(Nant. Adventures 228-6365 -Tuckernuck & Muskeget $100; Nantucket Is. 228-0334; Gail's 228-6557 $20-25; Coskata-Coatue Wildlife 228-6799 $40/15)* **Under 1 mi:** Tennis Courts *(Jetties 325-5334)* **1-3 mi:** Pool *(Nantucket Comm. 228-7262 $8)*, Golf Course *(Miacomet 325-0333)*

Provisioning and General Services
Near: Convenience Store *(Cumberland Farms)*, Market *(Fresh 825-2100)*, Supermarket *(Grand Union 228-9756)*, Gourmet Shop *(Nantucket 228-6447)*, Delicatessen *(Walter's 228-0010)*, Health Food *(Nantucket Nat 228-3947)*, Wine/Beer *(Fresh)*, Liquor Store *(Murray's 228-0071)*, Bakery *(Nantucket 228-2797)*, Farmers' Market *(Sat 9am-1pm, St. Mary's)*, Fishmonger *(Sayle's 228-4599)*, Bank/ATM, Post Office *(228-4477)*, Catholic Church, Protestant Church, Synagogue, Library *(228-1110)*, Beauty Salon *(Island Flair 325-7100)*, Laundry *(Nantucket 228-4597)*, Bookstore *(Mitchell's 228-1080; Nantucket 228-4000)*, Pharmacy *(Nantucket 228-0180)*, Florist *(Trillium 228-4450)* **Under 1 mi:** Hardware Store *(Marine 228-0900)*

Transportation
OnCall: Water Taxi *(325-1350, Ch.68)*, Taxi *(Val's 228-9410; Cranberry 825-9793)* **Near:** Bikes *(Young's 228-1151)*, Rental Car *(Nantucket 228-7474)*, Local Bus *(NRTA 228-7025, 7am-11:30pm)*, Ferry Service *(Hyline & Steamship Auth. to Cape Cod)* **Airport:** Nantucket *(2.5 mi.)*

Medical Services
911 Service **Under 1 mi:** Doctor *(Ouellette 228-0035)*, Dentist *(Roberts 228-5508)*, Chiropractor *(Nantucket 325-4777)* **1-3 mi:** Veterinarian *(Angell 228-1491)* **Hospital:** Nantucket 825-8100 *(0.6 mi.)*

Setting -- Past the small lighthouse and red-roofed Coast Guard station, the sprawling mooring field sits in the center of this stunning harbor - directly across the channel from Nantucket Boat Basin. Unparalleled views of historic Nantucket Town, the Congregational Church steeple rising above the skyline, are magic at sunset. Nantucket Town Pier, 100 yards south of Main Street, serves as the dinghy landing and service center for the 125 moorings and the anchorage.

Marina Notes *Up to 40 ft. $65, 41-59 ft. $70, 60-79 ft. $80, 80-100 Ft. $105 **All distances from Town Pier Dinghy Dock, 34 Washington Street. Reservations: Non-refundable pre-pay for 2 nights; 3 on holiday wknds. Cancellation; under 7 nights, forfeit 2 nts, etc. Date changes permitted. Raft up to 3 settled weather (disc.). Escort to mooring. "69 Delivers" - Ch. 69 for ice, etc. Boat Basin Launch to foot of Main St. (Ch. 68, 325-1350). At Nantucket Town Pier (12 ft. depths, 2-story brown building at foot of long pier): Eight dinghy docks, water, ice, pump-out, recycling, trash disposal (clear bags req.), & 10 trans. slips, under 30 ft. LOA, $5/hr. $25/nt. flat rate. Cannot sleep aboard! (Contact Harbormaster 228-7261). Bathhouse: Group - Simple, tile & fiberglass.

Notable -- Once the whaling capital of the world, this beautiful island morphed into a premier pleasure craft port of call. "Town" is a short walk from the launch drop and Town Pier Dinghy Dock. Flanking cobblestone lanes, carefully preserved antique buildings house elegant inns, superb restaurants, chic shops, top galleries. The impressive Whaling Museum, in a former spermaceti candle factory, is one of the Historical Association's 20 buildings. Bike or shuttle to 'Sconset, Madaket, or the 20 beaches that dot 110 miles of shoreline. Dinghy to Children's (playground, Sunday concerts) or Jetties Beaches (changing rooms, guards).

PHOTOS ON DVD: 25

Nantucket Boat Basin

PO Box 2580; Swain's Wharf; Nantucket, MA 02554

Tel: (508) 325-1350; (800) 626-2628 **VHF: Monitor** Ch. 9 **Talk** Ch. 11
Fax: (508) 228-8941 **Alternate Tel:** n/a
Email: gbassett@niresorts.com **Web:** www. nantucketboatbasin.com
Nearest Town: Nantucket **Tourist Info:** (508) 228-0925

Navigational Information
Lat: 41°17.036' **Long:** 070°05.639' **Tide:** 3 ft. **Current:** n/a **Chart:** 13242
Rep. Depths (*MLW*): Entry 12 ft. **Fuel Dock** 12 ft. **Max Slip/Moor** 15 ft./-
Access: Nantucket Sound to Nantucket Harbor

Marina Facilities *(In Season/Off Season)*
Fuel: *Mobil* - Gasoline, Diesel, High-Speed Pumps
Slips: 242 Total, 150 Transient **Max LOA:** 400 ft. **Max Beam:** n/a
Rate *(per ft.)*: **Day** $5.50/$4* **Week** Inq. **Month** Inq.
Power: 30 amp $20, **50 amp** $55, **100 amp** $75, **200 amp** n/a
Cable TV: Yes, $10 **Dockside Phone:** Yes, $8, Switchboard, up to 8 line(s)
Dock Type: Fixed, Long Fingers, Pilings, Alongside, Wood
Moorings: 0 Total, 0 Transient **Launch:** n/a, Dinghy Dock
Rate: Day n/a **Week** n/a **Month** n/a
Heads: 18 Toilet(s), 18 Shower(s)
Internet: Yes *(Wi-Fi, Free)* **Laundry:** 9 Washer(s), 9 Dryer(s)
Pump-Out: OnSite, OnCall, Full Service **Fee:** Free **Closed Heads:** Yes

Marina Operations
Owner/Manager: Geo. H Bassett, Jr CMM **Dockmaster:** Christina Martin
In-Season: Mid-Jun-LabDay, 7am-7pm **Off-Season:** LabDay-Jun, 8am-5pm
After-Hours Arrival: Call ahead
Reservations: Yes **Credit Cards:** Visa/MC, Dscvr, Din, Amex, Mobil
Discounts: Pre/Post Season **Dockage:** Inq. **Fuel:** n/a **Repair:** n/a
Pets: Welcome, Dog Walk Area **Handicap Access:** No

Marina Services and Boat Supplies
Services - Docking Assistance, Concierge, Security *(7pm-8am)*, Trash Pick-Up, Dock Carts, 3 Phase **Communication -** Pay Phone (3), FedEx, DHL, UPS, Express Mail **Supplies - OnSite:** Ice *(Block, Cube)* **Near:** Ships' Store *(Nantucket 228-2300)*, Bait/Tackle *(Cross Rip 228-4900)*

Boatyard Services
Nearest Yard: Grey Lady Marine (508) 228-6525

Restaurants and Accommodations
OnSite: Restaurant *(Ropewalk 228-8886, D $22-34, Kids' $12)*, *(Straight Wharf 228-4499, L $10-16, D $28-39, Bar $8-20, Br: $11-19)*, *(Slip 14 228-2033, L&D)*, Lite Fare *(Provisions 228-3258)*, Condo/Cottage *(Cottages at Boat Basin 325-1499, $159-499, 29 studio-2 bed)* **OnCall:** Restaurant *(Toppers 228-0145, L $20-25, D $34-52)*, Hotel *(Wauwinet 228-0145, $600-1000, Free launch)* **Near:** Restaurant *(Lobster Trap 228-4200, L&D $12-30)*, *(Boarding House 228-9622, D $10-34)*, *(Fifty Six Union 228-6135, D $13-36)*, *(Company of the Cauldron 228-4016, D $58-64, 4-course)*, *(Black-Eyed Susan's 325-0308, D $12-26, BYOB, B)*, *(Club Car 228-1101, D $24-45, L & piano bar)*, Pizzeria *(Steamboat Wharf 228-1131)*, Inn/B&B *(Jared Coffin 228-2400, $85-395)* **Under 1 mi:** Restaurant *(Brant Point Grill 325-1320, D $25-39, Bar menu)*, Hotel *(White Elephant 228-2500, $350-1300)*

Recreation and Entertainment
OnSite: Fishing Charter *(Herbert T 228-6655)* **Near:** Beach *(Children's, playground)*, Fitness Center *(Studio 901-5211)*, Boat Rentals *(Sea Nantucket Kayaks 228-7499 $15/hr.)*, Hike/Bike Trails *(to Madaket or Surfside)*, Movie Theater *(Starlight 228-4479; Dreamland 228-5356)*, Museum *(Nantucket Whaling 228-1894, $15/8; Maria Mitchell Aquarium 228-5387, Loines & Vestal Observatories 228-9273 & Natural Science 228-0898)*, Tours *(Nantucket Adventures 228-6365; Shearwater Whale Watch $155/138 & Seal Cruises $95/75 228-7037)* **Under 1 mi:** Tennis Courts *(Jetties)*, Park *(Lily Pond)* **1-3 mi:** Golf Course *(Miacomet 325-0333)* **3+ mi:** Sightseeing *(792-acre Coskata-Coatue Refuge 228-6799 $40/15 at Wauwinet, 6 mi.)*

Provisioning and General Services
Near: Convenience Store *(Cumberland Farm)*, Market *(Fresh 825-2100)*, Supermarket *(Grand Union 228-9756)*, Gourmet Shop *(Nantucket 228-6447)*, Delicatessen *(Walter's 228-0010)*, Health Food *(Nantucket Nat. 228-3947)*, Wine/Beer *(Fresh)*, Liquor Store *(Murray's 228-0071)*, Farmers' Market *(Sat 9am-1pm, St. Mary's)*, Fishmonger *(Sayle's 228-4599)*, Bank/ATM, Post Office *(228-4477)*, Catholic Church, Protestant Church, Synagogue, Library *(228-1110)*, Beauty Salon *(Darya 228-0550)*, Laundry *(Nantucket 228-4597)*, Bookstore *(Mitchell's 228-1080; Bookworks 228-4000)*, Pharmacy *(Nantucket 228-0180)* **Under 1 mi:** Hardware Store *(Marine 228-0900)*

Transportation
OnCall: Water Taxi, Taxi *(Val's 228-9410; Toppy's 228-7874)*, Airport Limo *(Cranberry 825-9793)* **Near:** Bikes *(Young's 228-1151)*, Rental Car *(Nantucket 228-1999)*, Local Bus *(NRTA)*, Ferry Service *(Hyline & Steamship Authority to Cape)* **Airport:** Nantucket *(2.8 mi.)*

Medical Services
911 Service **Under 1 mi:** Doctor *(LePore 228-4846)*, Dentist *(Roberts 228-5508)* **1-3 mi:** Chiropractor *(Nantucket 325-4777)*, Veterinarian *(Angell 228-1491)* **Hospital:** Nantucket 825-8100 *(0.7 mi.)*

PHOTOS ON DVD: 25

Setting -- In the heart of historic Nantucket Town, this world-class marina's 242 slips are woven gracefully along three wharfs: Straight (north), Old South (center), and Swain's (south). Inner slips berth smaller yachts while the megayachts side-tie to the outer piers. Above the fuel dock, the dockmaster's two-story operations center looks out across the charming, cozy, flower-bedecked rental cottages and weathered-shingle galleries and eateries that edge the docks.

Marina Notes -- *Rates: Slips: 35-59 ft. $5.50/ft., 60-99 ft. $6.50/ft., Side-tie: 100-124 ft. $7/ft. ($6.75 med-moor); 125 ft. up: $7.75/ft. (Over 100 ft, less $5/ft for med-moor). Reservations recommended. 2-night min.& 2 nt. deposit to reserve, 3 nt. deposit for longer stays (1st 2 nts. & last nt.). Cancel 30 days out $50 fee, within 30 days half deposit. Inquire about 1-night. Clear trash bags req. (avail. at Chandlery), recycling, non-toxic boat soap, etc. Dockside pumpout. Supply own power, telephone, TV cords. Concierge "desk" on each wharf (325-1360). Bathhouse: Luxe, granite, tile & beadboard group heads. Open to all boaters.

Notable -- Just steps away, "town" is a registered historic district . The surrounding 54-square mile island is a National Historic Landmark and an international megayacht magnet. Fine dining, along with high-end shopping and golf, compete with the beaches and other natural attractions. Wander the brick and cobblestone streets, self-guided tour map in hand, to enjoy the exquisitely restored 18th- and19th-C. homes and buildings that whaling built. Especially noteworthy, the Whaling Museum illustrates the island's first glory days - along with the Historical Association's 20 other properties. NRTA shuttles and 25 miles of bicycle paths criss-cross the island to the moors and beaches. See the wild northeast end; Wauiwinet Resort's complimentary launch picks up here.

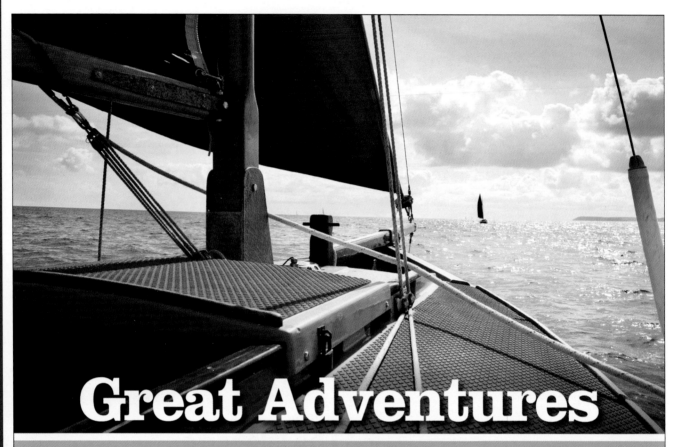

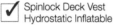

17. RI – Sakonnet River & Newport Harbor

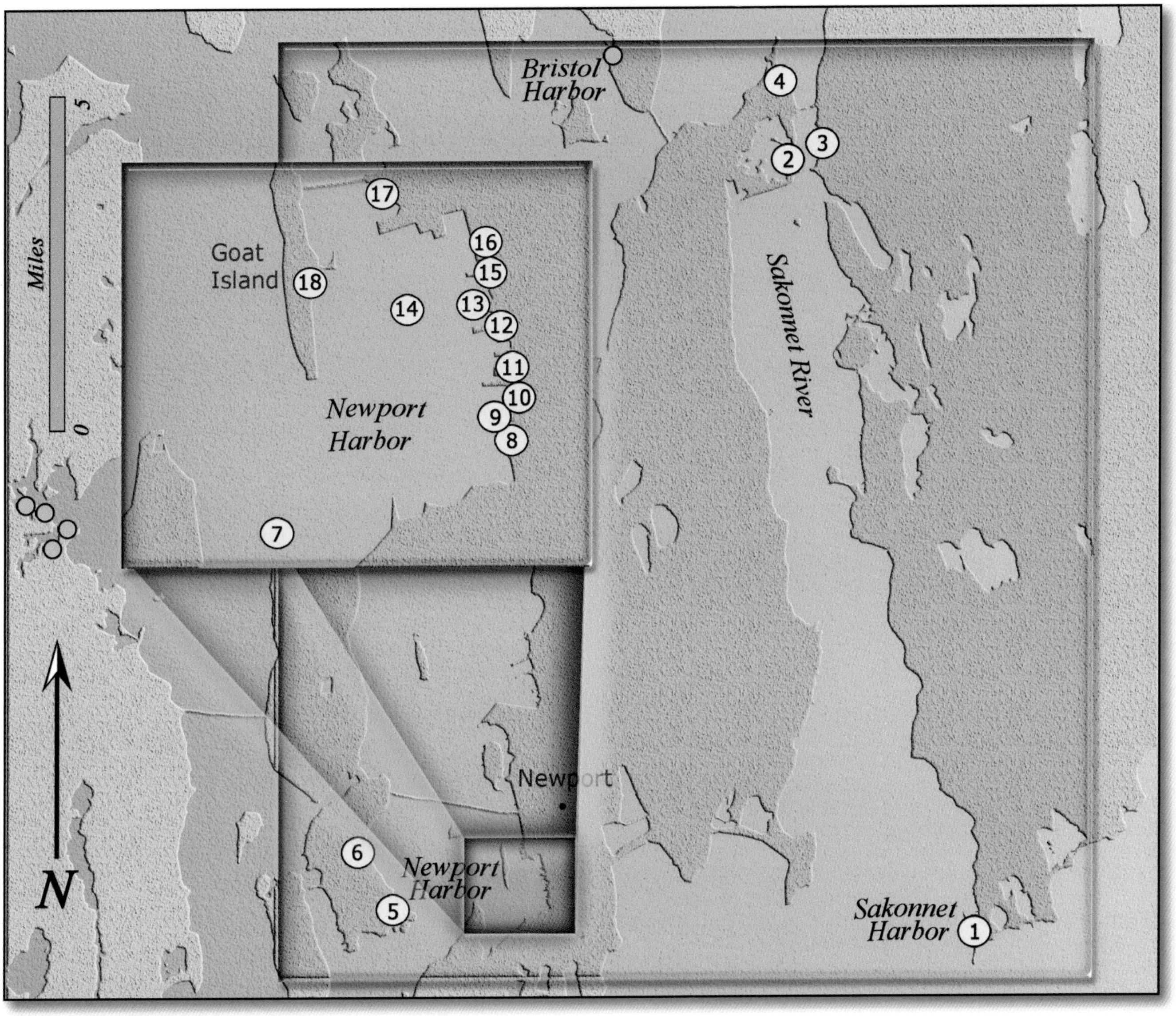

RATINGS: 1-5 for Marina Facilities & Amenities,  1-2 for Boatyard Services,  1-2 for MegaYacht Facilities,  for Something Special.

SERVICES:  for CCM – Certified Clean Marina,  for Pump-Out,  for Internet,  for Fuel, for Restaurant,  for Provisioning nearby,  for Catamaran-friendly,  for SportFish Charter,  for Pool/Beach, and  for Golf within a mile. *For an explanation of ACC's Ratings, see page 8.*

Sakonnet Point Marina

5 Bluff Head Avenue; Little Compton, RI 02837

Tel: (401) 635-4753 **VHF: Monitor** Ch. 9 **Talk** Ch. 6
Fax: (401) 331-7418 **Alternate Tel:** (401) 635-6352
Email: J.Peter.Sullivan@hotmail.com **Web:** n/a
Nearest Town: Compton *(4.7 mi.)* **Tourist Info:** (800) 976-5122

Navigational Information

Lat: 41°27.539' **Long:** 071°11.434' **Tide:** 3 ft. **Current:** 2 kt **Chart:** 13221
Rep. Depths (*MLW*): Entry 25 ft. **Fuel Dock** n/a **Max Slip/Moor** 18 ft./-
Access: Mouth of Sakonnet River. Breakwater into harbor

Marina Facilities *(In Season/Off Season)*

Fuel: Gasoline, Diesel, On Call Delivery
Slips: 31 Total, 4 Transient **Max LOA:** 80 ft. **Max Beam:** 15 ft.
Rate *(per ft.)*: **Day** $3.00 **Week** n/a **Month** n/a
Power: 30 amp Incl., **50 amp** Incl., **100 amp** n/a, **200 amp** n/a
Cable TV: No **Dockside Phone:** No
Dock Type: Floating, Wood
Moorings: 0 Total, 0 Transient **Launch:** n/a, Dinghy Dock
Rate: Day n/a **Week** n/a **Month** n/a
Heads: 4 Toilet(s), 4 Shower(s) *(dressing rooms)*
Internet: No **Laundry:** 2 Washer(s), 2 Dryer(s)
Pump-Out: No **Fee:** n/a **Closed Heads:** Yes

Marina Operations

Owner/Manager: Peter Sullivan **Dockmaster:** Same
In-Season: May 15-Oct 15, 7am-7pm **Off-Season:** Oct 16-May 14, Closed
After-Hours Arrival: Call ahead
Reservations: Yes **Credit Cards:** Cash/Check only
Discounts: None
Pets: Welcome **Handicap Access:** Yes, Heads, Docks

Marina Services and Boat Supplies

Services - Docking Assistance, Trash Pick-Up, Dock Carts **Communication -** FedEx, UPS, Express Mail **Supplies - OnSite:** Ice *(Cube)*, Live Bait

Boatyard Services

OnSite: Launching Ramp **Nearest Yard:** F. L. Tripp (508) 636-4058

Restaurants and Accommodations

OnSite: Restaurant *(Sakonnet Point Club* 635-2582, L $8.50-14, D $9-32, Casual fine dining - Sunday Brunch $8-16, Bar Menu, Kids' Menu - Recip. Only)*, Snack Bar *(Pool House* 635-2582, Recip Only)* **Under 1 mi:** Restaurant *(Pietra at The Stone House 1854 635-2222, L $12-19, D $21-42, Inside or on the deck)*, *(Tap Room at Stone House 635-2222, D $11-28, Former speakeasy cellar)*, *(Sakonnet Golf Club 635-4821, B $5-10, L $5-15, D $10-30)*, Inn/B&B *(Stone House 1854 635-2222, $295+, Italianate 1854 Mansion)* **3+ mi:** Restaurant *(Crowthers 635-4388, 6 mi., seafood)*, Lite Fare *(The Commons Lunch 635-4388, B $5-10, L $5-10, D $6-23, 4.5 mi., Casual all day. Great for breakfast or lunch - Johnny cakes & fish sandwiches)*, *(Coop Cafe at Sakonnet Vineyards 800-919-4637, L $4-9, 6 mi., Seasonal Fri-Sun)*, Pizzeria *(A-1 635-8353, 4.5 mi.)*, Inn/B&B *(Edith Pearl 592-0053, $175-350, 5 mi.)*

Recreation and Entertainment

OnSite: Pool *(Recip only*)*, Picnic Area, Grills, Fitness Center *(Recip Only)*, Boat Rentals *(Sakonnet Charters 474-2405 Hinckley 59 ft. fully crewed "Eclipse" - days, weekends, weeks)* **Near:** Beach, Jogging Paths **Under 1 mi:** Tennis Courts *(Sakonnet Golf Club)*, Golf Course *(Sakonnet Golf Club 635-4821- private, call)*, Hike/Bike Trails **1-3 mi:** Park *(Wilbor Woods)*, Museum *(Little Compton Historical Society 635-4035 $5/1. Wilbor House C. 1690 & 19thC. Friends Meeting House Tue-Fri 9am-3pm, Wilbor House Tours Thu-Sun 1-5pm)*, Sightseeing *(Wilbor Woods or Sauchest Wildlife Refuge - across the river)*, Special Events *(Mid-Sep - Little Compton Historic House Tour of 11 properties $25)*

Provisioning and General Services

OnSite: Bank/ATM **Near:** Lobster Pound *(Sakonnet Lobster 635-4371)* **1-3 mi:** Farmers' Market *(Rt 77)* **3+ mi:** Market *(Wilbur's General Store 635-2356, 4.7 mi.)*, Wine/Beer *(Sakonnet Vineyards 635-8486 - Tastings, tours. Founded 1975, 50-acres with Vinifera Varietals, 30,000 cases annually, 6 mi.)*, Green Grocer *(Wishing Stone Farm 635-4274, 4.5 mi.)*, Library *(635-8562 Brownell, 4.7 mi.)*, Pharmacy *(Westport Apothecary 636-5957, 13 mi.)*

Transportation

OnCall: Rental Car *(Enterprise 849-3939)* **3+ mi:** InterCity Bus *(Peter Pan, 24 mi.)*, Rail *(Amtrak, 64 mi.)* **Airport:** New Bedford Regional/T.F. Green *(27 mi./45 mi.)*

Medical Services

911 Service **Under 1 mi:** Holistic Services *(Stone House Spa 592-0523 $120 60 min. massage)* **1-3 mi:** Doctor *(Good Samaritan Medical Center 674-5600)* **3+ mi:** Dentist *(Jusseaume 636-5111, 12 mi.)*, Veterinarian *(East Bay Vet 635-2700, 5 mi.)* **Hospital:** Newport 846-6400 *(28 mi.)*

Setting -- There are more cows than people on this elite, gentrified country peninsula where ancient stone fences divide estates and rolling farm lands. The Sakonnet Point Marina and Yacht club is tucked behind the tip of the peninsula surrounded by Little Compton's superb fishing grounds. The highest building on the point, the stylish, shingled, two-storied, craftsman-style clubhouse, perches on pilings; its walk-around deck overlooks the pool and harbor. A favorite spot for recreational anglers, the high-rock jetty protects well-groomed docks and the small commercial fishing fleet.

Marina Notes -- *Sakonnet Point Club facilities (restaurants, pool, fitness center) only available to members of reciprocating yacht clubs or by permission. Sakonnet Point Marina & Sakonnet Point Club share property but are separate entities. Docks managed by marina. Power & water on Ensign pedestals. Vinyl-edged wood floating docks. Fuel trucked in (Gas Mon & Thu; Diesel Fri). Storage on hard for boats to 24 ft. on trailers. No boatyard services. Bathhouse: Upscale, club-quality heads, showers, dressing rooms & laundry. Note: only protected harbor for miles; excellent gunk hole from sudden storms.

Notable -- Sakonnet Point's well-reviewed club dining room serves lunch and dinner with lighter fare at the Bar or poolside (Also event space - Fleet Captains take note). Or walk up the road to the trendy, luxe 1854 Stone House where acclaimed Chef Paul Jonathan Wade helms the stove at Pietra Restaurant. Sakonnet Point Road, rich in seasonal farm stands, leads to the tiny village. Little Compton is the only coastal harbor between Buzzards Bay and Newport and the only one on the Sakonnet before reaching Fogland Beach. It is quite isolated from most amenities other than those provided by the marina - and the village.

Navigational Information

Lat: 41°37.707' **Long:** 071°13.111' **Tide:** 3 ft. **Current:** 2 kt. **Chart:** 13226
Rep. Depths (*MLW*): Entry 8 ft. **Fuel Dock** 10 ft. **Max Slip/Moor** 18 ft./65 ft.
Access: 10 mi. north of Sakonnet River mouth; 2 mi. south of Mt. Hope Bay

Marina Facilities *(In Season/Off Season)*

Fuel: Gasoline, Diesel
Slips: 82 Total, 20 Transient **Max LOA:** 80 ft. **Max Beam:** 22 ft.
Rate *(per ft.)*: **Day** $2.50/2* **Week** $17 **Month** $40
Power: 30 amp $10, **50 amp** $20, **100 amp** n/a, **200 amp** n/a
Cable TV: No **Dockside Phone:** No
Dock Type: Fixed, Floating, Alongside, Wood
Moorings: 45 Total, 20 Transient **Launch:** No, Dinghy Dock
Rate: Day $30 **Week** $175 **Month** $600
Heads: 2 Toilet(s), 4 Shower(s) *(dressing rooms)*
Internet: Yes *(Wi-Fi - Beacon Comm., Sub.)* **Laundry:** None
Pump-Out: OnSite, Full Service, 1 Central **Fee:** $6 **Closed Heads:** Yes

Marina Operations

Owner/Manager: Brandon Kidd **Dockmaster:** Dave Holden (Service Mgr)
In-Season: Year-Round, 8am-5pm **Off-Season:** n/a
After-Hours Arrival: Call prior to arrival
Reservations: Yes, Preferred **Credit Cards:** Visa/MC, Dscvr
Discounts: None
Pets: Welcome, Dog Walk Area **Handicap Access:** Yes, Heads

Pirate Cove Marina

109 Point Road; Portsmouth, RI 02871

Tel: (401) 683-3030 **VHF: Monitor** Ch. 9 **Talk** Ch. 10
Fax: (401) 683-6914 **Alternate Tel:** (401) 683-3030
Email: info@piratecovemarina.net **Web:** www.piratecovemarina.net
Nearest Town: Newport/Fall River *(8 mi.)* **Tourist Info:** (401) 847-1600

Marina Services and Boat Supplies

Services - Docking Assistance, Security *(Local Police Patrol)*, Trash Pick-Up, Dock Carts **Communication -** Mail & Package Hold, Phone Messages, FedEx, DHL, UPS, Express Mail **Supplies - OnSite:** Ice *(Block, Cube)*, Ships' Store **Under 1 mi:** Bait/Tackle *(Riverside Marine 625-5181)*, Propane *(Humphrey's 624-8800)* **3+ mi:** West Marine *(841-9880, 10 mi.)*

Boatyard Services

OnSite: Travelift *(60T Acme)*, Crane *(35T Terex)*, Engine mechanic *(gas, diesel)*, Hull Repairs, Rigger, Bottom Cleaning, Brightwork, Compound, Wash & Wax, Propeller Repairs, Woodworking, Painting, Awlgrip **Near:** Launching Ramp. **1-3 mi:** Canvas Work. **Yard Rates:** $40-105/hr., Haul & Launch $7-12/ft., Power Wash $4-5.50/ft., Bottom Paint $7-10/ft. **Storage:** In-Water $31/ft., On-Land $40-55/ft. Outdoor; $10/sq.ft. Indoor

Restaurants and Accommodations

Near: Restaurant *(15 Point Road 683-3138, D $16-26, Riverfront Tue-Sat 5-10, Sun 2-10)* **Under 1 mi:** Restaurant *(Scampi 293-5844, L & D $10-25)*, *(El Parque 682-2171, L & D $10-15)*, *(Graziano's 683-0750, B, L & D)*, Inn/B&B *(Bonita's 683-4418)* **1-3 mi:** Pizzeria *(North End 683-6633, Del - grinders, pastas, salads, panini)*, *(Chase Deli 683-5800, Del)*, *(Carmella's 683-0880, Del.)*, Hotel *(Best West Bay Point 683-3600)*

Recreation and Entertainment

OnSite: Picnic Area, Grills **OnCall:** Fishing Charter *(Tiverton Charters 714-6632)* **Near:** Beach *(Teddy's Beach)* **Under 1 mi:** Playground *(Island Park - end of Ormerod Ave.)* **1-3 mi:** Golf Course *(Montaup C.C. 683-0955; Pocasset C.C. 683-7300)*, Fitness Center *(Positive Works 683-2013 Pilates, Gyrotonic)*, Video Rental *(Briggs Video 683-5440)*, Park *(Bertha K Russel Preserve; Black Regiment Memorial)* **3+ mi:** Museum *(Blithewold Mansion & Gardens 253-2707 $10/2, 4.5 mi.)*, Sightseeing *(Green Animals Topiary Gardens 683-1267, 5 mi.)*

Provisioning and General Services

Near: Fishmonger *(Stonebridge Shellfish 683-3805)*, Lobster Pound **Under 1 mi:** Wine/Beer *(Moriarty's 683-4441)*, Liquor Store *(Moriarty's)*, Green Grocer **1-3 mi:** Convenience Store *(Cumberland Farms 682-1733)*, Delicatessen *(Little Corner 683-4318; Chase 683-5800)*, Bank/ATM, Post Office *(683-6803)*, Catholic Church, Protestant Church, Library *(683-9457, Internet access)*, Beauty Salon *(Hair by Donna 683-1133)*, Pharmacy *(Rite Aid 683-1270)*, Hardware Store *(Handren's 293-5290)* **3+ mi:** Market *(Clements 683-0180 - clementsmarket.com - Delivers Sun, Wed & Fri $9 for $50+ orders, 3.5 mi.)*, Supermarket *(Shaw's 508-674-8445; Stop & Shop 675-0391, 5 mi.)*, Department Store *(WalMart 730-2677, 5 mi.)*, Copies Etc. *(Staples 679-4500, 5 mi.)*

Transportation

OnCall: Rental Car *(Enterprise 253-9160)*, Taxi *(Yellow 508-673-2960)*, Airport Limo *(Liesure 683-2683)* **3+ mi:** Rail *(Amtrak 727-7276, 25 mi.)*
Airport: Newport State/TF Green *(10 mi./33 mi.)*

Medical Services

911 Service **Under 1 mi:** Chiropractor *(D C Assoc. 293-0029)* **1-3 mi:** Doctor *(Johnson 683-3300)*, Dentist *(Vanregenmrter 624-9177)*, Holistic Services *(Positive Works 683-2013)*, Veterinarian *(Mt. Hope 683-3743)*
Hospital: Saint Annes 508-235-5000 *(7.5 mi.)*

Setting -- Pirate Cove Marina is located at the head of the Sakonnet River just beyond the remains of an old stone bridge, the remnants of which serve as a jetty and passport to calmer waters. The casually landscaped, well-maintained marina is to port in a protected basin - the single loaded slips are hugged by a wrap-around earth-and-rock breakwater. The dominant land feature is a neat two-story, gray-and-blue building housing the office, heads and ships store adjacent to the fuel dock. Totally protected, salt-water Blue Bell Cove is just across a two-lane road.

Marina Notes -- *up to 4 hrs. $1/ft. Family owned/operated by the Kidd family since 1967. Third generation now at the helm. Year-round 7-day attention. Some residents have been in the marina since its beginning. Fuel dock (7am-6pm, 7 days) - also ice & sundries. Pump out same hours. Heated indoor storage for 35 boats. Full-service boatyard with DIY allowed. Docking assistance. Circular channel for easy access. Most protected marina in the Sakonnet. Underwater pipelines prevent anchoring, but many moorings. Bathhouse: Tiled walls & floors with simple homestyle fixtures & privacy curtains.

Notable -- Several islands with pretty sand beaches make large Blue Bell Cove (also known as The Cove or Old Orchard Cove) perfect for dinghy or kayak explorations and adventures. Clamming and fishing - especially trolling for Blues - is reportedly excellent. West from the marina, the Mount Hope bridge sets the backdrop for stunning sunset photography. Just down the road, Teddy's Beach, a wide arc of sand that has built up against the old Stone Bridge, fronts the river. Park Avenue, the main access road, is lined with a variety of stores and restaurants, and two golf courses are close by.

PHOTOS ON DVD: 19

Standish Boat Yard

Standish Boat Yard

1697 Main Road; Tiverton, RI 02878

Tel: (401) 624-4075 **VHF: Monitor** Ch. 16 **Talk** Ch. 69
Fax: (401) 624-3438 **Alternate Tel:** n/a
Email: standishboat@verizon.net **Web:** standishboatyard.com
Nearest Town: Tiverton *(3 mi.)* **Tourist Info:** (401) 466-2892

Navigational Information

Lat: 41°37.768' **Long:** 071°12.720' **Tide:** 4 ft. **Current:** 2 kt. **Chart:** 13226
Rep. Depths (*MLW*): Entry 35 ft. **Fuel Dock** 10 ft. **Max Slip/Moor** 20 ft./65 ft.
Access: 10 mi. north of Sakonnet River mouth; 2 mi. south of Mt. Hope Bay

Marina Facilities *(In Season/Off Season)*

Fuel: Gasoline, Diesel
Slips: 25 Total, 2 Transient **Max LOA:** 65 ft. **Max Beam:** 16 ft.
Rate *(per ft.)*: **Day** $2.50/Inq. **Week** $25 **Month** $45
Power: 30 amp inc., **50 amp** n/a, **100 amp** n/a, **200 amp** n/a
Cable TV: No **Dockside Phone:** No
Dock Type: Fixed, Floating, Alongside, Wood
Moorings: 65 Total, 15 Transient **Launch:** No, Dinghy Dock
Rate: Day $25 **Week** Inq. **Month** Inq.
Heads: 2 Toilet(s)
Internet: No **Laundry:** None
Pump-Out: Full Service, 1 Central, 1 Port **Fee:** $5 **Closed Heads:** Yes

Marina Operations

Owner/Manager: Ken Hilton **Dockmaster:** Same
In-Season: Year-Round, 8am-5pm **Off-Season:** Closed Sun
After-Hours Arrival: Gas dock or white mooring ball
Reservations: Preferred **Credit Cards:** Visa/MC
Discounts: Safe/Sea **Dockage:** 25% **Fuel:** n/a **Repair:** n/a
Pets: Welcome **Handicap Access:** No

Marina Services and Boat Supplies

Services - Docking Assistance, Dock Carts **Communication -** Phone Messages, Fax in/out, FedEx, DHL, UPS, Express Mail *(Sat Del)* **Supplies - OnSite:** Ice *(Block, Cube)*, Ships' Store, CNG **Under 1 mi:** Bait/Tackle *(Riverside Marine 625-5181)* **1-3 mi:** Propane *(Ferrellgas 624-8013)*

Boatyard Services

OnSite: Crane *(18T)*, Engine mechanic *(gas, diesel)*, Electrical Repairs, Electronic Sales, Hull Repairs, Rigger, Divers, Bottom Cleaning, Brightwork, Air Conditioning, Refrigeration, Compound, Wash & Wax, Interior Cleaning, Woodworking, Painting, Awlgrip, Yacht Broker **Near:** Launching Ramp. **Dealer for:** Albin 27'-45', Mercruiser, Cummings, Yanmar. **Yard Rates:** $75/hr., Haul & Launch $8/ft. *(blocking $2/ft.)*, Power Wash $60-$115., Bottom Paint T&M **Storage:** In-Water $26/ft., On-Land $34/ft

Restaurants and Accommodations

Near: Restaurant *(Stone Bridge 625-5780, L $10-12, D $13-29, Riverfront - inside or deck dining)*, Coffee Shop *(Coastal Roasters 624-2343)* **Under 1 mi:** Restaurant *(Moulin Rouge 624-4320, French, Local Fave)*, Lite Fare *(Black Goose Cafe 816-0882, 6am-9pm Breakfast all day plus sands, salads)*, Pizzeria *(Famous 624-8900)* **1-3 mi:** Restaurant *(Boat House Waterfront 624-6300, L & D $11-26, elegant inside or deck dining - 1.3 mi.)*, Seafood Shack *(Evelyn's Nanaquaket Drive-In 624-3100, L & D $4-20 Dockage. Kids' $5, Beer/wine. 11:30am-8pm)*, Hotel *(Best Western Bay Point 683-3600, $80-120)*, Inn/B&B *(Bonita's 683-4418)*

Recreation and Entertainment

OnSite: Picnic Area, Grills, Boat Rentals *(Cape Dory 33 Charter)* **Near:** Beach *(Grinnel)*, Playground, Park *(Grinnel)*, Museum *(Fort Barton 625-6700 sunrise-sunset)* **1-3 mi:** Tennis Courts *(Tiverton Municipal)*, Golf Course *(Montaup Country Club 683-0955)*, Jogging Paths, Horseback Riding *(Tiverton Equestrian Center 816-0320)*, Video Rental *(Briggs 683-5440)* **3+ mi:** Fitness Center *(Tiverton Health & Fitness 624-3440, 4 mi.)*, Sightseeing *(Tiverton Four Corners Historic District - 13 historic bldgs including Chase-Cory House 624-4013 Sun 2-4:40; Blithewold 253-2707, 5 mi.)*

Provisioning and General Services

Near: Convenience Store *(Cumberland Farms 624-7175)*, Bank/ATM, Catholic Church, Beauty Salon *(Divine 624-6844)*, Newsstand, Florist *(Paul's 624-3310)* **Under 1 mi:** Protestant Church, Barber Shop **1-3 mi:** Market *(Grand Central 624-9914)*, Wine/Beer, Liquor Store *(Tiverton 625-5091)*, Bakery, Post Office, Library *(Tiverton 625-6796)*, Dry Cleaners, Laundry, Pharmacy *(Rite-Aid 624-8411)*, Hardware Store *(Humphrey's 624-8800)* **3+ mi:** Supermarket *(Shaw's 508-674-8445, Stop & Shop 508-675-0391, 5 mi.)*, Retail Shops *(Tiverton Four Corners - antique, crafts, decorative arts, 5 mi.)*

Transportation

OnCall: Rental Car *(Enterprise 508-672-1988)*, Taxi *(B&E Taxi 624-7100)*, Airport Limo *(Fantasy Limo 508-683-6677)* **3+ mi:** InterCity Bus *(Fall River, 10 mi.)*, Rail *(Providence, 25 mi.)* **Airport:** TF Green 737-8222 *(20 mi.)*

Medical Services

911 Service **OnCall:** Ambulance **Near:** Doctor *(Family Physicians 624-1400)*, Dentist *(Jenkins 624-2375)*, Holistic Services *(Divine Spa 624-6844)* **1-3 mi:** Chiropractor *(Chiro Center of Tiverton 624-4111)*, Veterinarian *(Sakonnet 624-6624)* **Hospital:** Saint Annes 508-235-5000 *(6 mi.)*

Setting -- About a quarter-mile north of the remains of the Old Stone Bridge, on the the Tiverton Basin's east bank, Standish's gas dock, lettered roof and miniature lighthouse make it easy to spot. The white, two-story building seems built into the side of the steep river bank; the second-floor deck, sprinkled with tables and chairs, delivers panoramic views. The atmosphere is strictly boatyard with landscaping courtesy of the natural surroundings.

Marina Notes -- Originally built in 1933. Current owners took over in 1969 with second generation now involved. One of the oldest marinas on the Sakonnet or Narragansett Bay. Down-home friendliness in a working-class ambiance. Spacious, convenient fuel dock with pump-out and ice. Boatyard services available with an active Albin dealership on site. Well-stocked ships' store. 65 moorings with additional available from either the town of Tiverton or the Tiverton Yacht Club. No launch service. All docks have power and water, but some are in need of the ongoing maintenance. Bathhouse: Inviting. Tiled floors, faux-painted walls, vanities, fiberglass shower stall with bright curtains. Note: Heady current through the cut, but otherwise calm waters.

Notable -- Grinnel Beach is a short walk south with good fishing, swimming (lifeguard on duty) and a playground. Fort Barton, an original 1778 redoubt built during the American Revolution, was the staging area for the invasion of Aquidneck Island (and the Battle of Rhode Island). A quarter-mile away, it boasts three miles of hiking trails and a 30 ft. observation tower. Evelyn's Drive-In on Nanaquaket Pond is a favorite destination by boat or foot (1.3 mi.). Five miles south, 300-year-old Tiverton Four Corners, a national historic district, is worth a cab - shops occupy restored buildings featuring antiques, textiles, pottery, fine art.

Navigational Information
Lat: 41°38.754' **Long:** 071°13.105' **Tide:** 4 ft. **Current:** 2 kt. **Chart:** 13226
Rep. Depths (*MLW*): Entry 10 ft. **Fuel Dock** 8 ft. **Max Slip/Moor** 10 ft./-
Access: Sakonnet River or Mt. Hope Bay to top of Aquidneck Island

Marina Facilities *(In Season/Off Season)*
Fuel: *ValvTect* - Gasoline, Diesel
Slips: 320 Total, 10 Transient **Max LOA:** 60 ft. **Max Beam:** 15 ft.
Rate *(per ft.)*: **Day** $2.00 **Week** Inq. **Month** Inq.
Power: 30 amp Inc, **50 amp** Inq., **100 amp** n/a, **200 amp** n/a
Cable TV: No **Dockside Phone:** No
Dock Type: Floating, Long Fingers, Pilings, Wood, Vinyl, Composition
Moorings: 0 Total, 0 Transient **Launch:** n/a
Rate: Day n/a **Week** n/a **Month** n/a
Heads: 7 Toilet(s), 5 Shower(s), Book Exchange
Internet: Yes *(Wi-Fi, Free)* **Laundry:** 2 Washer(s), 2 Dryer(s)
Pump-Out: OnSite, Full Service, 1 Central **Fee:** $5 **Closed Heads:** Yes

Marina Operations
Owner/Manager: Jay Burns **Dockmaster:** Same
In-Season: Summer, 8am-8pm **Off-Season:** Fall-Spring, 7:30am-5pm
After-Hours Arrival: Call ahead for instructions
Reservations: Yes, Recommended **Credit Cards:** Visa/MC, Dscvr, Amex
Discounts: None
Pets: Welcome, Dog Walk Area **Handicap Access:** No

Brewer Sakonnet Marina

222 Narragansett Boulevard; Portsmouth, RI 02871

Tel: (401) 683-3551 **VHF: Monitor** Ch. 9 **Talk** Ch. 72
Fax: (401) 683-9188 **Alternate Tel:** n/a
Email: jburns@byy.com **Web:** www.byy.com/portsmouth
Nearest Town: Newport *(18 mi.)* **Tourist Info:** (401) 466-2982

Marina Services and Boat Supplies
Services - Docking Assistance, Security *(Nights)*, Dock Carts
Communication - Pay Phone (4), FedEx, DHL, UPS, Express Mail
Supplies - OnSite: Ice *(Block, Cube)*, Ships' Store **Under 1 mi:** Bait/Tackle *(625-5181 Riverside)* **1-3 mi:** Propane *(624-6395 Phil's Propane)*, CNG *(624-8013 Ferrel Gas)* **3+ mi:** West Marine *(841-9880, 10 mi.)*

Boatyard Services
OnSite: Travelift *(35T)*, Forklift *(6T)*, Crane *(15T)*, Hydraulic Trailer *(20T)*, Launching Ramp, Engine mechanic *(gas, diesel)*, Electrical Repairs, Electronics Repairs, Hull Repairs, Rigger, Canvas Work, Bottom Cleaning, Brightwork, Air Conditioning, Refrigeration, Compound, Wash & Wax, Propeller Repairs, Woodworking, Painting, Awlgrip, Yacht Broker **Dealer for:** Awlgrip, Interlux, Pettit, Furlex, Max-Prop, Espar, SeaLand, Yanmar, Koehler, Westerbeke, Mercruiser, Teak Decking Systems. **Member:** ABBRA - 4 Certified Tech(s), ABYC - 4 Certified Tech(s) **Yard Rates:** $45-$90/hr., Haul & Launch Incl. w/ Storage, Bottom Paint $13.50/ft. **Storage:** In-Water $29/ft., On-Land Out $38-43/ft., Inside $10/sq.ft.

Restaurants and Accommodations
Near: Restaurant *(Boat House 624-6300, L & D $11-26 By dinghy. Courtesy docking. Elegant inside or deck dining)* **Under 1 mi:** Inn/B&B *(Bonita's 683-4418, $179)* **1-3 mi:** Restaurant *(15 Point Road 683-3138, D $16-26, Riverview. 5-9pm, Fri-Sat 'til 10pm, Sun 4-9pm, picks up)*, *(Moulin Rouge 624-4320)*, *(Stone Bridge 625-5780, L $10-12, D $13-29)*, *(El Parque 682-2171, L & D $10-15)*, *(Scampi 693-5844, L & D $10-25)*, Pizzeria *(Chase 683-5800, Delivers)*, *(North End 683-6633, Delivers. Plus grinders, pastas, salads, panini)*, Motel *(Best Western Bay Point 683-3800, $80-120)*

Recreation and Entertainment
OnSite: Pool, Picnic Area, Grills, Playground, Jogging Paths, Volleyball
Near: Park **Under 1 mi:** Golf Course *(Montaup Country Club 683-0955)* **1-3 mi:** Fitness Center *(Peak's 683-6033)*, Horseback Riding *(Upson Downs 683-0453)*, Video Rental *(Briggs 683-5440)* **3+ mi:** Museum *(Blithewold Mansions & Gardens 253-2707 $10/2, 4 mi.)*, Sightseeing *(Battleship Cove 508-678-1100 $15/9 - by water. www.battleshipcove.org, 5 mi.)*

Provisioning and General Services
Near: Bank/ATM **1-3 mi:** Wine/Beer, Liquor Store *(Moriarty's 683-4441)*, Green Grocer *(Grand Central 624-9914)*, Fishmonger *(Stonebridge 683-3805)*, Post Office, Catholic Church, Protestant Church, Library *(683-9457, Internet access)*, Pharmacy *(Rite Aid 683-1270)*, Hardware Store *(624-8800 Humphrey's)* **3+ mi:** Market *(Clements 683-0180 - clementsmarket.com - Delivers Sun, Wed & Fri $9 for $50+ orders $6 for $100+, 5 mi.)*, Supermarket *(Shaw's 508-674-8445; Stop & Shop 675-0391, 5.5 mi.)*, Department Store *(WalMart 508-730-2677, 5 mi)*

Transportation
OnSite: Bikes **OnCall:** Rental Car *(Enterprise 672-1988)*, Taxi *(Rainbow 849-1333)*, Airport Limo *(Fantasy 683-6677)* **3+ mi:** Rail *(Providence Amtrak, 30 mi.)* **Airport:** TF Green 732-3621 *(33 mi.)*

Medical Services
911 Service **1-3 mi:** Doctor *(Miesner/Cummings 625-1001)*, Dentist *(Van Regenmorter/Marks 624-9177)*, Holistic Services *(Positive Works 683-2013)*, Veterinarian *(Sakonnet Vet. Hosp 624-6624)* **Hospital:** Saint Annes 508-235-5000 *(6 mi.)*

Setting -- Located directly before a large fetch of bay, Brewer Sakonnet Marina is now a combination of the original, Sakonnet North, tucked within protected Cedar Island Pond and recently acquired Sakonnet South, which is a bit roomier but directly on the river and more open to the elements. Dockage is a mix of older floating wood and newer composite with updated power and water. Well-executed landscaping and screened picnic areas make for a peaceful retreat. A mix of pool, play areas, games, dog walks, expansive lawn area and sheltered kayaking means there truly is something for the whole family.

Marina Notes -- A Brewer property since 1978. A total of 320 slips between north and south - maintained in Brewer style. South docks added wave protection. North dockage enclosed and very well-protected. Full-service yard with 10,000 sq ft of shop space. Rack & indoor storage plus 6 acres of outdoor service and storage. Master Mercury tech on staff. Member of RIMTA. Brewer Customer Club Card offers free dockage & discounts. Bathhouse: Several heads and showers placed throughout both properties. Decorated with a home-like touch. Tiled floors & fiberglass shower stalls with curtains.

Notable -- Onsite facilities include a pool with Jacuzzi, playground, basketball and volleyball courts, gas grills and screened picnic gazebos with expansive views. Two golf clubs are close by. The Cove is an interesting dinghy-ride destination with small islands, and good fishing and clamming. A five-mile "big boat" cruise north, Battleship Cove is the world's largest naval ship museum - home to five National Historic Landmarks including USS Massachusetts, Destroyer J.P. Kennedy (from "13 Days in October"), National PT Boat and National Destroyermen's Museums, plus a Carousel (slips $12/hr. Moorings $35/night, $5/hr.)

Jamestown Boat Yard

PO Box 347; 60 Racquet Road; Jamestown, RI 02835

Tel: (401) 423-0600 **VHF: Monitor** Ch. 72 **Talk** Ch. 72
Fax: (401) 423-0060 **Alternate Tel:** n/a
Email: brian@jby.com **Web:** www.jby.com
Nearest Town: Jamestown *(1 mi.)* **Tourist Info:** (401) 423-3650

Navigational Information

Lat: 41°28.927' **Long:** 071°21.610' **Tide:** 4 ft. **Current:** 1 kt. **Chart:** 13223
Rep. Depths (*MLW*): Entry 12 ft. **Fuel Dock** n/a **Max Slip/Moor** -/50 ft.
Access: Narragansett Bay, East Passage, left after G11 (The Dumplings)

Marina Facilities *(In Season/Off Season)*

Fuel: No
Slips: 4 Total, 1 Transient **Max LOA:** 75 ft. **Max Beam:** 18 ft.
Rate *(per ft.)*: **Day** $2.50* **Week** n/a **Month** n/a
Power: 30 amp Incl., **50 amp** Incl., **100 amp** n/a, **200 amp** n/a
Cable TV: No **Dockside Phone:** No
Dock Type: Fixed, Floating, Wood
Moorings: 57 Total, 2 Transient **Launch:** n/a, Dinghy Dock
Rate: Day $65* **Week** $410 **Month** n/a
Heads: 2 Toilet(s), 3 Shower(s)
Internet: No **Laundry:** None
Pump-Out: OnCall **Fee:** $6 **Closed Heads:** Yes

Marina Operations

Owner/Manager: Clement Napolitano **Dockmaster:** Brian Thomas
In-Season: May-Oct, 8:30am-4pm **Off-Season:** Oct-May, 7:50am-3:30pm
After-Hours Arrival: Call in Advance
Reservations: Yes **Credit Cards:** Visa/MC, Dscvr, Amex
Discounts: None
Pets: Welcome **Handicap Access:** No

Marina Services and Boat Supplies

Services - Docking Assistance, Dock Carts **Communication -** Mail & Package Hold, Phone Messages, Fax in/out, FedEx, UPS **Supplies - OnSite:** Ice *(Block, Cube)* **Under 1 mi:** Ships' Store *(Conanicut 423-1556)* **1-3 mi:** Bait/Tackle *(Zeeks Creek 423-1170)* **3+ mi:** Marine Discount Store *(Newport Nautical 847-3933, 4 mi.)*, Propane *(Spicer, 6 mi)*

Boatyard Services

OnSite: Railway *(150T)*, Engine mechanic *(gas, diesel)*, Electrical Repairs, Electronic Sales *(Jamestown 423-2253)*, Electronics Repairs, Hull Repairs, Rigger, Divers, Bottom Cleaning, Brightwork, Air Conditioning, Refrigeration, Compound, Wash & Wax, Interior Cleaning, Woodworking, Life Raft Service, Yacht Interiors, Painting, Awlgrip, Total Refits **Dealer for:** Perkins, Volvo Penta, Westerbeke, Universal Marine Air, Grunert-Cruisair, Sea Frost, Espar, Raytheon, Max Prop, Nanni, Yanmar. **Yard Rates:** $80/hr., Haul & Launch $17.50-28/ft *(blocking $1.50-2.50/ft.)*, Power Wash $3/ft, Bottom Paint T&M **Storage:** On-Land Inside $12/sq.ft. Outside $40-55/ft

Restaurants and Accommodations

Under 1 mi: Restaurant *(Tricia's Tropi-Grille 423-1490, L&D $10-20, Kids' $4-6)*, *(Oyster Bar & Grille 423-3380)*, *(Trattoria Simpatico 423-3731, L $9-22, D $13-37, Small plates 3:30+)*, *(Chopmist Charlie's 423-1020, L $7-14, D $10-20, Seafood)*, *(Narragansett Cafe 423-2150, Best Blues - Sundays)*, *(Peking Garden 423-0680)*, Lite Fare *(Slice of Heaven 423-9866, B $6-11, L $8-13, bakery)*, *(East Ferry Market 423-1592)*, Pizzeria *(House of Pizza 423-3060)*, Inn/B&B *(Jamestown 423-1338)* **1-3 mi:** Hotel *(Wyndham Newport Overlook 866-323-3087, $136+)*, Inn/B&B *(Wyndham Bay 866-323-3087, $85+)*, *(East Bay 423-0330, $99-185)*

Recreation and Entertainment

OnSite: Beach, Picnic Area, Grills **Under 1 mi:** Park *(Fort Wetherill SP 423-1771; Jamestown)* **1-3 mi:** Golf Course *(Jamestown G.C. 423-9930)*, Fitness Center *(Jamestown 423-9930)*, Museum *(Jamestown 423-0784 - 19thC. schoolhouse; Jamestown Fire Dept. 423-0062 - antique firefighting equip)*, Sightseeing *(Fort Getty)*, Galleries *(Jamestown 423-3383)*, Special Events *(Newport Jazz Fest - Aug)*

Provisioning and General Services

Under 1 mi: Convenience Store *(Mobil 423-3070)* **1-3 mi:** Market *(McQuade 423-0873)*, Delicatessen *(East Ferry Market & Deli 423-1592)*, Wine/Beer *(Grapes & Gourmet 423-0070)*, Liquor Store *(Bridge 848-9200)*, Bakery *(Village Hearth 423-9282)*, Bank/ATM, Post Office, Catholic Church, Protestant Church, Library *(Jamestown 423-7280)*, Beauty Salon *(Anita 423-2423)*, Dry Cleaners *(Bill Del Nero 423-1142)*, Hardware Store *(Jamestown 423-2722)*, Florist *(Secret Garden 423-0500)* **3+ mi:** Supermarket *(Stop & Shop 848-7200, 7 mi.)*, Pharmacy *(CVS 846-7800, 7 mi.)*

Transportation

OnSite: Courtesy Car/Van **OnCall:** Rental Car *(Enterprise)*, Taxi *(Cozy 846-2500)*, Airport Limo *(A-Airline Exp 295-1100)* **Under 1 mi:** Ferry Service *(to Newport & Ft. Adams)* **3+ mi:** InterCity Bus *(Peter Pan 846-1820, 5 mi.)*, Rail *(Kingstown Amtrak, 17 mi.)* **Airport:** TF Green *(25 mi.)*

Medical Services

911 Service **1-3 mi:** Doctor *(NHCC Med. 423-2616)*, Dentist *(Bush 423-2110)*, Holistic Services *(Ocean Essence 423-9830)*, Veterinarian *(Jamestown 423-2288)* **Hospital:** Newport 846-6400 *(6.5 mi.)*

Setting -- On the eastern shore of Conanicut Island, a two-story weathered-shingle office building manages this top-tier boatyard. A tiny dockhouse overlooks several fixed docks and a dinghy float that services the mooring field. Pockets of flowers try to soften the working ambiance while a jumble of large work sheds crowd the edge of a small, private, sandy beach. All vessels enjoy the panoramic views of famous "House on the Rock" and Claiborne Pell Newport Bridge.

Marina Notes -- *Dockage Flat Rate $100. Moorings to 40 ft. $65nt., $410/wk. 40 ft. & over $85/nt., $535/wk. Formerly Lovering Wharton's supply base. For 3 decades has specialized in elite Nautor's Swan Yachts - largest parts inventory in northeast. Launch runs 7am-9pm MemDay-LabDay, 7am-7pm May & Oct. 9000 sq. ft. inside storage plus outside to 75 ft. Small boaters' lounge with phones and data ports. Courtesy pick-up from Kingston Amtrak station, Newport Transportation Hub (Visitors' Center), New London Ferry & T.F. Green Airport. Crew pick-up from NYC area $150 - 3 days notice. Bathhouse: Two outdoor showers behind main office with swinging privacy doors. One indoor full bath, tiled floors/walls with vanity sink & dressing bench.

Notable -- When Lovering Wharton's estate was confiscated to expand Fort Wetherill in 1904, he built the now-famous three-story, 23-room Clingstone Mansion on a rocky island in the harbor - and the yard was the mainland base. Today, 61-acre Fort Wetherill State Park, a Coast Artillery base from 1899-1946, boasts 100-foot high granite cliffs, a small cove for swimming, picnicking spots - and the mine wharf and tramway system that maintained the 300 mines that protected the harbor during WW II. Directly across from Ft. Adams, it is a prime viewing spot for Tall Ship events & yacht races - and a scuba dive destination.

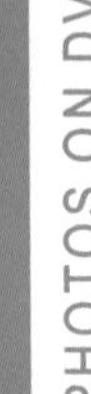
PHOTOS ON DVD: 16

  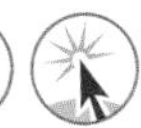 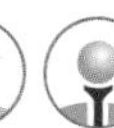 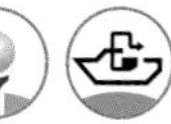

Navigational Information
Lat: 41°29.782' **Long:** 071°21.970' **Tide:** 4 ft. **Current:** 1 kt. **Chart:** 13221
Rep. Depths (*MLW*): Entry 35 ft. **Fuel Dock** 15 ft. **Max Slip/Moor** 22 ft./60 ft.
Access: Narragansett Bay, East Passage, left at G11

Marina Facilities *(In Season/Off Season)*
Fuel: *Texaco* - Gasoline, Diesel, High-Speed Pumps
Slips: 100 Total, 10 Transient **Max LOA:** 175 ft. **Max Beam:** 50 ft.
Rate *(per ft.)*: **Day** $4.75/$2.75* **Week** $31.50/12.25 **Month** n/a
Power: 30 amp $10, **50 amp** $20, **100 amp** $62**, **200 amp** n/a
Cable TV: No **Dockside Phone:** No
Dock Type: Fixed, Floating, Long Fingers, Alongside, Wood
Moorings: 156 Total, 20 Transient **Launch:** 8am-9pm (Free), Dinghy Dock
Rate: Day $54/39-42 **Week** $350/252 **Month** $1410/960-1050
Heads: 6 Toilet(s), 4 Shower(s), Hair Dryers
Internet: Yes *(Wi-Fi, Free)* **Laundry:** None
Pump-Out: OnSite, OnCall, 2 Port, 6 InSlip **Fee:** Free **Closed Heads:** Yes

Marina Operations
Owner/Manager: David Blydenburgh **Dockmaster:** Same
In-Season: Jun-ColDay, 8am-9pm **Off-Season:** Octr-May 30, 8am-5pm
After-Hours Arrival: Contact fuel dock on Ch. 71 or 401-423-7157
Reservations: Required. Phone or Internet. **Credit Cards:** Visa/MC
Discounts: Extended stays **Dockage:** n/a **Fuel:** Volum **Repair:** n/a
Pets: Welcome, Dog Walk Area **Handicap Access:** Yes, Heads

Conanicut Marina

One Ferry Wharf; Jamestown, RI 02835

Tel: (401) 423-1556 **VHF: Monitor** Ch. 71 **Talk** Ch. 71
Fax: (401) 423-7152 **Alternate Tel:** (401) 423-7158
Email: may@conanicutmarina.com **Web:** www.conanicutmarina.com
Nearest Town: Jamestown *(.5 mi.)* **Tourist Info:** (401) 423-3650

Marina Services and Boat Supplies
Services - Docking Assistance, Security *(10 hrs.)*, Dock Carts, 3 Phase **Communication -** Pay Phone, FedEx, UPS, Express Mail **Supplies - OnSite:** Ice *(Block, Cube)* **Near:** Ships' Store *(Conanicut Chandlery 423-1556)* **Under 1 mi:** Bait/Tackle *(Zeeks Creek 423-1170)*

Boatyard Services
OnSite: Crane *(Manitex 35T, 165 ft. high)*, Hydraulic Trailer *(10T, 30T to 60 ft., 60T to 70 ft.)*, Launching Ramp, Engine mechanic *(gas, diesel)*, Electrical Repairs, Electronic Sales, Electronics Repairs, Hull Repairs, Rigger, Divers, Bottom Cleaning, Brightwork, Compound, Wash & Wax, Interior Cleaning, Propeller Repairs, Woodworking, Inflatable Repairs, Metal Fabrication, Painting, Awlgrip, Total Refits **Dealer for:** Honda, Westerbeke, Yanmar, Johnson, Avon, Evinrude, Universal, Yamaha, Nanni Diesel. **Member:** ABBRA, ABYC - 4 Certified Tech(s), Other Certifications: OMC, Honda, IMI, Volvo, Yamaha **Yard Rates:** $85-95/hr., Haul & Launch $10-17/ft., Bottom Paint $19.50/ft. **Storage:** On-Land $7/ft./mo.

Restaurants and Accommodations
OnSite: Lite Fare *(Spinnaker's Café 423-3077, B $2-4, L $2-8, Ice Cream, too)*, *(East Ferry Deli 423-1592, B&L $2-8)* **Near:** Restaurant *(Trattoria Simpatico 423-3731, L $9-22, D $13-37, L Fri-Sun)*, *(Jamestown Oyster Bar 423-3380, L&D $6-18)*, *(Narragansett Cafe 423-2150, Best Blues - Sun)*, *(Chopmist Charlie's 423-1020)*, *(Peking Garden 423-0680)*, Lite Fare *(Slice of Heaven 423-9866, B $6-11, L $8-13, Kids' $4; bakery)*, Pizzeria *(House of Pizza 423-3060)*, Inn/B&B *(East Bay 423-0330, $99-185)* **Under 1 mi:** Hotel *(Wyndham Bay Voyage 866-323-3087, $85+)*, Inn/B&B *(Rose Island 847-4242, $100-195, Become a real lighthouse keeper for a night or a week)*

Recreation and Entertainment
OnSite: Picnic Area, Grills **Near:** Museum *(Jamestown Fire Dept. 423-0062; Jamestown 423-0784; Wright 423-7280 - Indian & Colonial artifacts)* **Under 1 mi:** Playground, Golf Course *(Jamestown G.C. 423-9930)*, Fitness Center *(Jamestown 560-0300)*, Video Rental *(Redbox)*, Park *(Artillery)*, Tours *(Rose Is. Light 847-4242)* **1-3 mi:** Sightseeing *(Jamestown Windmill 423-1798, Beavertail Light 423-9941)*

Provisioning and General Services
OnSite: Delicatessen *(East Ferry 423-1592)*, Wine/Beer *(Grapes & Gourmet 423-0070)*, Lobster Pound **Near:** Convenience Store *(Xtra 423-3070)*, Bank/ATM, Catholic Church, Beauty Salon *(C. Jamieson 423-0905)*, Dry Cleaners *(Del Nero 423-1142)*, Laundry, Pharmacy *(Baker's 423-2800)*, Hardware Store *(Jamestown 423-2722; Conanicut 423-1856)* **Under 1 mi:** Market *(McQuade 423-0873)*, Liquor Store *(Jamestown 423-0100)*, Fishmonger *(Zekes Creek)*, Post Office *(423-0420)*, Protestant Church, Library *(423-7280)*, Florist *(Secret Garden 423-0050)* **3+ mi:** Supermarket *(Stop & Shop 845-2220, 5 mi.)*

Transportation
OnSite: Courtesy Car/Van *(Van 423-7157)*, Local Bus *(RIPTA)*, Ferry Service *(Jamestown & Newport 423-9900 $18/8 RT)* **OnCall:** Rental Car *(Enterprise 849-3939)*, Taxi *(Cozy 846-2500)* **Airport:** TF Green *(22 mi.)*

Medical Services
911 Service **OnCall:** Ambulance **Near:** Dentist *(Bush 423-2110)*, Holistic Services *(Halsosam 423-0103)*, Veterinarian *(Jamestown 423-2288)* **Under 1 mi:** Doctor *(England 423-2616)* **Hospital:** Newport 846-6400 *(5 mi.)*

Setting -- Set on the quiet side of East Passage, two large mooring fields and a wave attenuator buffer Conanicut's extensive network of nicely maintained docks and water taxi landing. On shore, the office and bathhouse join a small strip of shops and casual eateries creating a compact village atmosphere surrounded by a well-groomed city park. Views of Newport, the cruise ships, Rose Island & the bridges add to the appeal.

Marina Notes -- *Dockage Rates to 70 ft. LOA: Hi-Season - MidJun-LabDay, Shoulder - Apr-MidJun & LabDay-Nov, LOW - Dec-Mar ($1.50/ft.). Med-moor $3.75/ft. Over 70 ft. add $0.25-$1/ft. Moorings: to 50 ft. LOA. (Dec-Mar Low $37). Over 50 ft. add $10/nt. **100A 3-phase $100. Founded by Mungers in 1974. Reserve: 2 nt. deposit July/Aug wknds. Cancel: 14-day out full refund. Less, forfeit 1 night + 15%. 1/2 hr Touch/Go & hourly dock/mooring rates. Launch: July-Aug Sun-Thur: 8am-10pm, Fri & Sat 8am-11pm, Shoulder season shorter hrs. Fuel dock 8am-6pm. Self-serve pump-out plus boat (Mon-Fri). Service yard at inland Taylor Point (10 acres inside/outside storage). Boat transport to 70 tons. chandlery 7,000 sq. ft. on Narragansett Ave. Courtesy van to laundry, parking lot & yard (next to McQuade's market, pizzeria, liquor/hardware store & laundrimat). Bathhouse: Comfortable, simply decorated. Tiled floors & walls. No laundry.

Notable -- Ferry to Newport (Waites Wharf, Bowen's Wharf, & Perrotti Park), Ft. Adams, or Rose Island every 90 minutes. Or take a very short walk to Narragansett Avenue lined with a dozen eateries from coffee shops to high-end restaurants and other useful services. Take the ferry to tour 18-acre Rose Island ($5/4, 10am-4pm) with the only working lighthouse maintained by vacationers; visit the Keeper's House museum, picnic area and wildlife refuge.

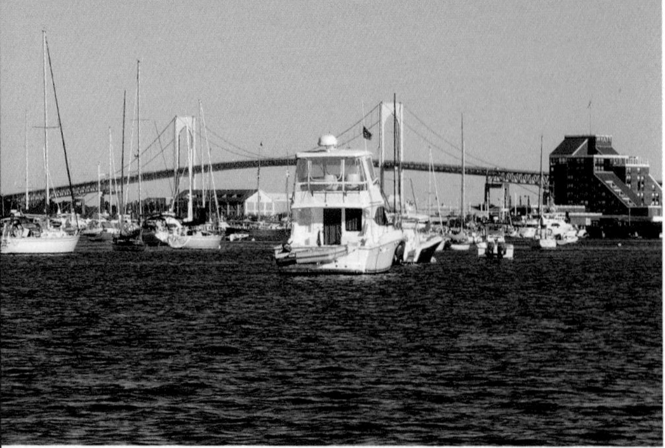

Newport Moorings

Newport, RI 02840

Tel: (401) 846-7535 **VHF: Monitor** Ch. 9 **Talk** Ch. 12
Fax: n/a **Alternate Tel:** (401) 849-2210
Email: n/a **Web:** n/a
Nearest Town: Newport *(0 mi.)* **Tourist Info:** (401) 845-9123

Navigational Information

Lat: 41°28.583' **Long:** 071°19.821' **Tide:** 4 ft. **Current:** n/a **Chart:** 13223
Rep. Depths (*MLW*): Entry 30 ft. **Fuel Dock** n/a **Max Slip/Moor** -/25 ft.
Access: Newport Harbor; Main, Spindle or Brenton Cove Mooring Fields

Marina Facilities *(In Season/Off Season)*

Fuel: No
Slips: 0 Total, 0 Transient **Max LOA:** 70 ft. **Max Beam:** n/a
Rate *(per ft.)*: **Day** n/a **Week** n/a **Month** n/a
Power: 30 amp n/a, **50 amp** n/a, **100 amp** n/a, **200 amp** n/a
Cable TV: No **Dockside Phone:** No
Dock Type: n/a
Moorings: 60 Total, 22 Transient **Launch:** Ch.9 ($2/1-way), Dinghy Dock
Rate: Day CCall **Week** Call **Month** Call
Heads: None
Internet: Yes *(Seamen's Institute, Free)* **Laundry:** None
Pump-Out: OnCall *(Ch. 9 & 73)*, Full Service **Fee:** $15+ **Closed Heads:** Yes

Marina Operations

Owner/Manager: Carl Bolender, Neil Gray, Bill Thoad **Dockmaster:** n/a
In-Season: May 15-Oct 15, 8am-10pm **Off-Season:** Oct 16-May 14, Closed
After-Hours Arrival: Always call first
Reservations: Yes **Credit Cards:** Check/Cash only
Discounts: None
Pets: Welcome **Handicap Access:** No

Marina Services and Boat Supplies

Supplies - Near: Ice *(Block, Cube)*, CNG *(Oldport 847-9109)* **1-3 mi:** Ships' Store *(Bowen's Wharf 849-4999)*, Live Bait, Propane *(Spicer 596-6531)* **3+ mi:** West Marine *(841-9880 , 5 mi)*

Boatyard Services

Nearest Yard: Newport Shipyard (401) 846-6000

Restaurants and Accommodations

OnSite: Fast Food *(Concession Stands)* **1-3 mi:** Restaurant *(Pier 847-3645, L $8-26, D $16-32), (Bouchard 846-0123, D $18-39), (Thai 841-8822, L&D $11-17; Kids' $6), (Red Parrot 847-3800, L&D $13-29; Kids' $2-6), (Sambar 619-2505, D $12-23), (Scales & Shells 846-3474), (Cafe Zelda 849-4002, L $8-19, D $10-35)*, Lite Fare *(Handy 847-9480)*, Pizzeria *(Firehouse 846-1199, Near King Pier)*, Hotel *(Wyndham Newport 866-323-3087, $305+)*, Inn/B&B *(Francis Malbone 846-0392, $165-525), (Admiral Fitzroy 848-8000, $95-355), (Spring Street 847-4767, $119-299)*

Recreation and Entertainment

OnSite: Beach *(Life Guard)*, Picnic Area, Grills, Boat Rentals *(Bareboat 800-661-4013 salboats 42-54 ft.)*, Sightseeing *(Fort Adams SP 847-2400 Guided Tour $10/5, hourly 10am-4pm)*, Special Events *(Folk Fest - late July, JVC Jazz Fest - early Aug)* **1-3 mi:** Playground *(King Park)*, Dive Shop *(Newport 847-9293)*, Tennis Courts *(Nat'l. Tennis Club 849-6672)*, Bowling, Fishing Charter *(Adventure Sports, Long Wharf 849-4820)*, Video Rental *(Redbox)*, Museum *(Rose Island, 847-4242, $5/4; Whitehorne 847-2448, $12/Free; Int'l. Tennis Hall of Fame 849-3990 $9/7)*, Galleries *(Art on the Wharf 845-6858; Newport Potters 619-4880; van der Wal 849-5556)* **3+ mi:** Golf Course *(Newport Nat'l 848-9690, 9 mi.)*, Movie Theater *(Pickens 846-5252, 3.5 mi)*

Provisioning and General Services

1-3 mi: Market *(Max's 849-8088)*, Supermarket *(Stop & Shop 848-7200)*, Delicatessen *(Sig's 847-9668)*, Health Food *(Harvest Nat. 846-8137)*, Wine/Beer *(Bellevue 846-7993)*, Liquor Store *(Fifth Ward 847-4545)*, Bakery *(Katrina's 847-8210)*, Farmers' Market *(Aquidneck 848-0099, 2-6, Wed Memorial Blvd & Chapel St.)*, Fishmonger *(Aquidneck 846-0106)*, Bank/ATM, Post Office *(847-9835)*, Catholic Church, Protestant Church, Library *(847-8720)*, Beauty Salon *(Natural Creations 841-0798)*, Dry Cleaners *(O'Donnell's 846-9635)*, Laundry *(Micki's 847-5972)*, Pharmacy *(Rite Aid 846-1631)*, Hardware Store *(Newport Ace 849-9442)*, Florist *(Bellevue 847-0145)*, Copies Etc. *(UPS 848-7600)* **3+ mi:** Synagogue *(3.5 mi)*, Retail Shops *(Long Wharf Mall, 3.5 mi.)*

Transportation

OnCall: Water Taxi *(Jamestown & Newport 423-9900 $18/8 RT)*, Rental Car *(Enterprise 849-3939)*, Taxi *(Orange 841-0030)*, Airport Limo *(Posh 842-0005)* **Near:** Local Bus *(RIPTA 781-9400)* **1-3 mi:** InterCity Bus *(Bonanza, Peter Pan)*, Ferry Service *(Jamestown, B.I.)* **3+ mi:** Rail *(Kingston Amtrak 800-872-7245, 22 mi.)* **Airport:** TF Green *(30 mi.)*

Medical Services

911 Service **1-3 mi:** Doctor *(Connell 841-8613)*, Dentist *(Newport Dental 847-7662)*, Holistic Services *(Franklin Spa 847-3540)*, Veterinarian *(Newport 849-3401)* **3+ mi:** Chiropractor *(Newport 847-4224, 4 mi)*, Optician *(Brown 846-0101, 3.5 mi)* **Hospital:** Newport 846-6400 *(4 mi)*

Setting -- Sprinkled throughout Newport's mooring fields are sets of privately managed moorings with no proprietary landside facilities. Most are in the middle of Brenton Cove or The Spindle at the southern end of the harbor near Little Ida Lewis Rock. There are a few front-row center in the main mooring field across from Bannister's Wharf and off the historic Point neighborhood just north of Goat Island Causeway. Most locations offer excellent storm protection.

Marina Notes -- *From $40 (under 39 ft.) to $55 (over 60 ft.). Above distances by land from Sail America dinghy float. From other launch/dinghy docks, refer to nearest marina's Report. Independent vendors: Newport Mooring Service - Niel Gray Ch.9, 846-7535 (over 30 years) mushroom anchors to 70 ft. Brenton Cove - Carl Bolender 849-2210, helix anchors, to 60 ft.. & White Cloud - Bill Thoad 527-2754. Other Dinghy Landings: Elm Street Pier, north side Shipyard breakwater, Inn on Long Wharf, Bowens Wharf, Ann Street Pier, West Extension St., King Park. Pump-Out boat (474-0543, Ch.9). Harbormaster Tim Mills (848-6492, Ch.16 &14). Bathhouse: Sail America in Mule Barn - coin-op showers. And Seaman's Institute (7:30-5:30) with heads, showers ($2), Mariners' Lounge (Free Wi-Fi), Maritime Library, Aloha Cafe (7:30-2:30), mail hold, washer/dryer ($1.50), overnight stays, garden, chapel - seamensnewport.org.

Notable -- Hourly tours visit Ft. Adams, the largest coastal fortification in the U.S. Today it also hosts summer concerts and festivals, picnic grounds, Sail America and the Museum of Yachting - 10,000 square feet of boats and exhibits, including two-time America's Cup winner "Courageous." The Elms is an easy walk from King Park dinghy dock. Walk or trolley to the other mansions or the south end of Cliff Walk, a spectacular three-mile trail that passes the "cottages."

    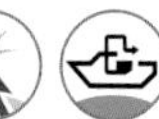 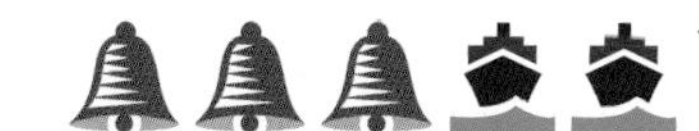

Navigational Information

Lat: 41°28.797' **Long:** 071°19.013' **Tide:** 4 ft. **Current:** n/a **Chart:** 13223
Rep. Depths (*MLW*): Entry 18 ft. **Fuel Dock** n/a **Max Slip/Moor** 13 ft./-
Access: Narragansett Bay, past Ft. Adams, past Little Rock, Ida Lewis

Marina Facilities *(In Season/Off Season)*

Fuel: Slip-Side Fueling, Diesel, On Call Delivery
Slips: 60 Total, 50 Transient **Max LOA:** 200 ft. **Max Beam:** n/a
Rate *(per ft.)*: **Day** $5.00/Inq.* **Week** Inq. **Month** Inq.
Power: 30 amp $12, **50 amp** $30, **100 amp** $65, **200 amp** n/a
Cable TV: No **Dockside Phone:** No
Dock Type: Fixed, Floating, Long Fingers, Alongside, Wood
Moorings: 0 Total, 0 Transient **Launch:** n/a
Rate: Day n/a **Week** n/a **Month** n/a
Heads: 4 Toilet(s), 4 Shower(s) *(dressing rooms)*
Internet: Yes *(Wi-Fi, Free)* **Laundry:** 2 Washer(s), 2 Dryer(s)
Pump-Out: OnCall, Full Service, 2 Port **Fee:** $15+ **Closed Heads:** Yes

Marina Operations

Owner/Manager: Tami Abrunese **Dockmaster:** Cathie Thurston
In-Season: Apr-Nov, 8am-8pm **Off-Season:** Closed
After-Hours Arrival: Call in advance
Reservations: Yes, preferred **Credit Cards:** Visa/MC, Amex, Check
Discounts: None
Pets: Welcome **Handicap Access:** Yes, Heads, Docks

West Wind Marina

Waite's Wharf; Newport, RI 02840

Tel: (401) 849-4300 **VHF: Monitor** Ch. 9 **Talk** n/a
Fax: (401) 847-0862 **Alternate Tel:** n/a
Email: westwindri@aol.com **Web:** www.westwindmarina.com
Nearest Town: Newport *(0 mi.)* **Tourist Info:** (401) 849-8048

Marina Services and Boat Supplies

Services - Docking Assistance, Concierge, Room Service to the Boat, Security, Trash Pick-Up, Dock Carts, 3 Phase **Communication -** Pay Phone, FedEx, DHL, UPS **Supplies - OnSite:** Ice *(Block)* **Under 1 mi:** Ships' Store *(Bowen's Wharf 849-4999)*, Propane *(Spicer 596-6531)*, CNG *(Oldport 847-9109)* **1-3 mi:** West Marine *(841-9880)*

Boatyard Services

OnSite: Engine mechanic *(gas)*, Compound, Wash & Wax, Interior Cleaning **Nearest Yard:** The Newport Shipyard (401) 846-6000

Restaurants and Accommodations

OnSite: Restaurant *(@The Deck Inside 847-3610, D $24-39, open kitchen & fine dining, Veg Option)*, Lite Fare *(@The Deck Outside D $5-$18)*, *(Dockside & Outdoor Riptide Bar Live music 6-9pm)* **OnCall:** Pizzeria *(Firehouse 846-1199)* **Near:** Restaurant *(Bouchard 846-0123, D $18-39, French)*, *(Pier 847-3645, L $8-26, D $18-32, Brunch $8-14)*, *(Thai Cuisine 841-8822, L&D 11-17, Kids' $6)*, *(Sambar 619-2505, D $12-23)*, *(Scales & Shells 846-3474)*, *(Cafe Zelda 849-4002, L $8-19, D $10-35)*, Hotel *(Wellington 849-1770, $112-399)*, Inn/B&B *(Adm. Fitzroy 848-8000, $95-355)*, *(Francis Malbone 846-0392, $165-525)*, *(Spring Street 847-4767, $119-299)* **1-3 mi:** Fast Food *(BK, Taco Bell, McD's 848-0959)*

Recreation and Entertainment

Near: Playground *(Aquidneck Park)*, Dive Shop *(Newport 847-9293)*, Tennis Courts *(Aquidneck)* **Under 1 mi:** Fitness Center *(Pulse 595-8549)*, Fishing Charter *(Sara Star 623-1121)*, Movie Theater *(Jane Pickens 846-5252)*, Video Rental *(Redbox)*, Park *(King; Aquidneck)*, Museum *(Tennis HOF 846-1203, $9/7; Newport Art 848-8200; $10/8)*, Tours *(Classic Cruises 847-0298 historic yachts)*, Cultural Attract *(Firehouse Theater 849-3473)*, Sightseeing *(The Mansions - The Elms 847-1000)* **1-3 mi:** Beach *(Easton's)* **3+ mi:** Golf Course *(Newport Nat'l 848-9690, 5.5 mi.)*

Provisioning and General Services

Near: Market *(Max's 849-8088)*, Bank/ATM, Beauty Salon *(Nat. Creations 841-0798)*, Retail Shops *(Bellevue Mall)* **Under 1 mi:** Supermarket *(Stop & Shop 848-7200)*, Health Food *(Harvest Nat 846-8137)*, Wine/Beer *(Bellevue 846-7993)*, Liquor Store *(Vickers' 847-0123)*, Bakery *(Katrina's 847-8210)*, Fishmonger *(Aquidneck 846-0106)*, Post Office, Catholic Church, Protestant Church, Synagogue, Library *(847-8720)*, Dry Cleaners *(O'Donnell's 846-9635)*, Laundry *(Micki's 847-5972)*, Pharmacy *(CVS 846-7800)*, Hardware Store *(Newport Ace 849-9442)*, Florist *(Broadway 849-4000)*, Copies Etc. *(UPS 848-7600)* **1-3 mi:** Farmers' Market *(Aquidneck 2-6, Wed, Memorial & Chapel)*

Transportation

OnCall: Water Taxi, Rental Car *(Enterprise 849-3939)*, Taxi *(Orange 841-0030)*, Airport Limo *(Posh 842-0005)* **Near:** Bikes *(Segway 619-4010)*, Local Bus *(Trolley)* **Under 1 mi:** InterCity Bus, Ferry Service *(Jamestown, B.I.)* **3+ mi:** Rail *(Amtrak, 20 mi.)* **Airport:** T.F. Green *(27 mi.)*

Medical Services

911 Service **Near:** Veterinarian *(Newport 849-3401)* **Under 1 mi:** Doctor *(Connell 841-8613)*, Dentist *(Newport 847-7662)*, Holistic Services *(Wave Lengths 849-4427)*, Optician *(Brown 846-0101)* **1-3 mi:** Chiropractor *(Newport 847-2248)* **Hospital:** Newport 846-6400 *(1.5 mi.)*

Setting -- The most southern of Newport's transient marinas, West Wind sits on the quieter edge of downtown - out of the hubbub but with easy access to key attractions. Hard to miss, the outer docks extend 350 feet into the harbor and are usually obscured by a cluster of megayachts. The more protected interior berths smaller yachts in slips and med-style dockage. An attractive, shingled, single-story building houses the restaurants, clubs, bathhouse and VIP lounge.

Marina Notes -- *Rates $4-5/ft. Family owned & operated since the mid 90s. Caters to transients, encourages large megayachts to 250 ft. 100A, 3-phase. Public dinghy dock. 24-hr. security with gated access. Concierge service - transport, sightseeing, reservations, etc. Dock hands always available. "On the Docks" waterside VIP Lounge $250 membership. Certified Volvo mechanic. Dealer for Cranchi Yachts of Italy. Boardwalk fronting marina part of Newport Harbor Walk. Gazebos offer shelter while harbor watching. Free parking for guests. Bathhouse: Pleasantly decorated heads & showers. Laundromat.

Notable -- A lot is happening on the entertainment front here. Well-reviewed @The Deck (inside) offers fine dining with an option of sitting kitchen-side to watch the new chef's show. @The Deck's alfresco patio serves more casual fare. Dockside night club, inside, delivers live rock and dancing with a harbor view; @Riptide features live music outside on the dock (6-9pm) every night in season. The closest marina to the Mansions, The Elms is just 0.4 mile. Adjacent municipal dock has a dinghy float and is a water taxi and harbor tour stop. To hike the 3.5-mile Cliff Walk that runs in front of many of the "cottages," take the trolley to either end - down Bellevue to the Ledges or to Easton's Beach (1.5 mi.). A short walk, the NECB baseball league plays at King Park.

PHOTOS ON DVD: 20

Casey's Marina

PO Box 187; Spring Wharf; Newport, RI 02840

Tel: (401) 849-0821 **VHF: Monitor** Ch. 9 **Talk** Ch. 68
Fax: (401) 849-3550 **Alternate Tel:** (401) 640-4458
Email: n/a **Web:** n/a
Nearest Town: Newport **Tourist Info:** (401) 849-8048

Navigational Information

Lat: 41°28.831' **Long:** 071°19.010' **Tide:** 4 ft. **Current:** n/a **Chart:** 13223
Rep. Depths (*MLW*): Entry 22 ft. **Fuel Dock** n/a **Max Slip/Moor** 14 ft./-
Access: Fort Adams to starboard, then straight ahead

Marina Facilities *(In Season/Off Season)*

Fuel: No
Slips: 30 Total, 20 Transient **Max LOA:** 185 ft. **Max Beam:** n/a
Rate *(per ft.)*: **Day** $5.50/$3 **Week** Inq. **Month** Inq.
Power: 30 amp n/a, **50 amp** Incl.*, **100 amp** Incl., **200 amp** n/a
Cable TV: No **Dockside Phone:** No
Dock Type: Fixed, Floating, Long Fingers, Alongside, Wood
Moorings: 0 Total, 0 Transient **Launch:** n/a
Rate: Day n/a **Week** n/a **Month** n/a
Heads: 2 Toilet(s), 2 Shower(s)
Internet: Yes *(Wi-Fi, Free)* **Laundry:** None
Pump-Out: OnCall *(1st 30 gals)*, 2 Port **Fee:** $15 **Closed Heads:** Yes

Marina Operations

Owner/Manager: Bill Casey **Dockmaster:** Same
In-Season: May-Oct, 8am-8pm **Off-Season:** Nov-Apr, Closed
After-Hours Arrival: Call Ahead
Reservations: Yes **Credit Cards:** Visa/MC, Cash or Checks
Discounts: None
Pets: Welcome **Handicap Access:** No

Marina Services and Boat Supplies

Services - Docking Assistance, Concierge, Trash Pick-Up, 3 Phase, European Voltage **Communication -** Fax in/out, FedEx, DHL, UPS, Express Mail **Supplies - OnSite:** Ice *(Block, Cube)* **Near:** CNG *(Oldport 847-9109)* **Under 1 mi:** Ships' Store *(Bowen's Wharf 849-4999)* **1-3 mi:** West Marine *(841-9880)*, Propane *(Spicer 596-6531)*

Boatyard Services

OnSite: Crane *(30T)*, Hydraulic Trailer, Engine mechanic *(gas, diesel)*, Electrical Repairs, Electronics Repairs, Hull Repairs, Rigger, Canvas Work **Member:** ABYC - & ABBRA 3 Certified Tech(s) **Yard Rates:** $95

Restaurants and Accommodations

Near: Restaurant *(Scales & Shells 846-3474)*, *(Café Zelda 849-4002, L $8-19, D $10-35)*, *(@The Deck - inside 847-3610, D $24-39, @The Deck outside $5-18)*, *(Bouchard's 846-0123, D $18-39)*, *(Pier 847-3645, L $8-26, D $16-32)*, *(Handy Lunch 847-9480, B&L)*, *(Thai 841-8822, L&D $11-17, Kids')*, *(Red Parrot 847-3800, D $13-29)*, *(Sambar 619-2505, D $12-23)*, Pizzeria *(Via Via 846-4074)*, Hotel *(Newport Bay 849-8600, $79-379)*, Inn/B&B *(Adm Fitzroy 848-8000, $95-355)*, *(Spring St. 847-4767, $119-299)*

Recreation and Entertainment

Near: Playground *(Aquidneck Park)*, Dive Shop *(Newport 847-9293)*, Tennis Courts *(Aquidneck)*, Video Arcade *(Ryan 46-5774)* **Under 1 mi:** Fitness Center *(Pulse 595-8549)*, Fishing Charter *(Sara Star 623-1121)*, Movie Theater *(Jane Pickens 846-5252)*, Video Rental *(Redbox)*, Park *(King; Touro; Aquidneck)*, Museum *(Whitehorn 847-2448, $12/6; Tennis HOF 846-1203, $9/7)*, Tours *(Classic Cruises 847-0298 historic yachts)*, Sightseeing *(Mansions: The Elms - nearest; Rosecliff 847-1000; Belcourt Castle 846-0669)* **1-3 mi:** Beach *(Easton's)*, Cultural Attract *(Firehouse Theater 849-3473)* **3+ mi:** Golf Course *(Newport Nat'l 848-9690, 5.5 mi.)*

Provisioning and General Services

Near: Market *(Max's 849-8088)*, Fishmonger *(Aquidneck 846-0106)*, Bank/ATM, Post Office *(847-9835)*, Library *(847-8720)*, Beauty Salon *(Natural Creations 841-0798)*, Barber Shop, Newsstand, Clothing Store, Retail Shops *(Bellevue Mall)* **Under 1 mi:** Supermarket *(Stop & Shop 848-7200)*, Delicatessen *(Sig's 847-9668)*, Health Food *(Harvest Natural 846-8137)*, Wine/Beer *(Bellevue 846-7993)*, Liquor Store *(Vickers' 847-0123)*, Bakery *(Katrina's 847-8210)*, Farmers' Market *(Aquidneck 848-0099; 2-6, Wed, Chapel & Memorial)*, Catholic Church, Protestant Church, Synagogue, Dry Cleaners *(O'Donnell's 846-9635)*, Laundry *(Micki's 847-5972)*, Pharmacy *(CVS 849-7800)*, Hardware Store *(Newport Ace 847-9442)*, Copies Etc. *(PDQ 619-2188)*

Transportation

OnCall: Taxi *(Orange 841-0030)*, Airport Limo *(Posh 842-0005)* **Near:** Bikes *(Scooter World 619-1349)*, Local Bus *(Trolley)* **Under 1 mi:** Rental Car *(Hertz 846-1645)*, InterCity Bus, Ferry Service *(to Jamestown, BI)* **3+ mi:** Rail *(Amtrak, Kingston, 20 mi.)* **Airport:** TF Green *(27 mi.)*

Medical Services

911 Service **Near:** Veterinarian *(Newport 849-3401)* **Under 1 mi:** Doctor *(Rocco 849-1113)*, Dentist *(Newport 847-7662)*, Holistic Services *(Flow Acupunc. 835-7770)*, Optician *(Brown 846-0101)* **1-3 mi:** Chiropractor *(Newport 847-4224)* **Hospital:** Newport 846-6400 *(1.5 mi.)*

Setting -- Casey's Marina is a well-established temporary home to some of the largest megayachts visiting Newport. From the outermost docks, the views are of the harbor, chock-a-block with a wide variety of vessels. Landside there is very little to see. There is a neat, one-room shack housing the dock office, a green single-story working building with signage announcing Casey's Marina and the parking lot. Sparse landscaping but all very clean and tidy.

Marina Notes -- *Power: 50A, 100A 3-phase & single-phase, 208 3-phase, 480 100A. Designed & built for transient megayachts. Most dockage is "alongside." 30 ft. interior slips - seasonal only $6,000/yr. Since most large yachts are self-contained worlds, Casey's limits physical facilities but offers some concierge-type services. A storeroom holds advance mail & packages. Takes phone messages. Focuses on needs of yacht crews. Lounge with Internet & free phone. 7 phone lines. Free parking for owners & guests. Overland truck transport to anywhere. Haul up to 50 ft. Broker for Trinity Yachts. Fish & bait store in main building planned. Boat Storage & Fuel 640-4458. Pump-Out Boat ($15 1st 30 gals, $5 Bathhouse: Two full baths.

Notable -- This end of Newport is a bit quieter and quite convenient to a couple of the mansions; the others are accessible via the Yellow #67 Trolley. Take a walking tour of Newport or hike either the Harbor Walk or the 3.5 mile Cliff Walk that fronts many of the "cottages." The "action" part of town is a few blocks north. Nearby West Wind has two eateries, and well-reviewed, pricey Bouchard is three blocks away. Watch shipwrights restore classic sail and power vessels at the International Yacht Restoration School next door (848-5777). Or take a trolley or tender out to Fort Adams to tour the Museum of Yachting (847-1018).

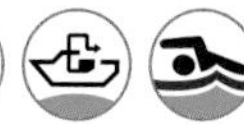

Navigational Information
Lat: 41°28.889' **Long:** 071°18.955' **Tide:** 4 ft. **Current:** n/a **Chart:** 13223
Rep. Depths (*MLW*): Entry 18 ft. **Fuel Dock** n/a **Max Slip/Moor** 10 ft./-
Access: Fourth set of docks in Newport Harbor, east shore

Marina Facilities *(In Season/Off Season)*
Fuel: No
Slips: 45 Total, 8 Transient **Max LOA:** 140 ft. **Max Beam:** 35 ft.
Rate *(per ft.)*: **Day** $5.00* **Week** n/a **Month** n/a
Power: 30 amp $20, **50 amp** $22, **100 amp** $50, **200 amp** n/a
Cable TV: Yes **Dockside Phone:** No
Dock Type: Fixed, Floating, Pilings, Alongside, Wood
Moorings: 0 Total, 0 Transient **Launch:** n/a, Dinghy Dock
Rate: Day n/a **Week** n/a **Month** n/a
Heads: 4 Toilet(s), 4 Shower(s) *(dressing rooms)*
Internet: Yes *(Wi-Fi, Free)* **Laundry:** 1 Washer(s), 1 Dryer(s)
Pump-Out: OnCall *(1st 30 gals)*, 2 Port **Fee:** $15 **Closed Heads:** Yes

Marina Operations
Owner/Manager: Steven M Sullivan **Dockmaster:** Same
In-Season: May 6-Oct 23, 8am-8pm **Off-Season:** Oct 24-May 5, Closed
After-Hours Arrival: Call ahead
Reservations: Yes **Credit Cards:** Visa/MC, Dscvr, Amex
Discounts: None
Pets: Welcome, Dog Walk Area **Handicap Access:** Yes

Newport Marina

Lee's Wharf; Newport, RI 02840

Tel: (401) 849-2293 **VHF: Monitor** Ch. 9 **Talk** Ch. 9
Fax: (401) 849-9503 **Alternate Tel:** (401) 225-1337
Email: info@newportmarina.com **Web:** www.newportmarina.com
Nearest Town: Newport **Tourist Info:** (800) 975-5122

Marina Services and Boat Supplies
Services - Docking Assistance, Boaters' Lounge, Security *(24 hr. video)*, Trash Pick-Up, Dock Carts, 3 Phase **Communication -** FedEx, UPS **Supplies - OnSite:** Ice *(Block, Cube)* **Near:** Ships' Store *(Bowen's 849-4999)*, CNG *(Oldport 847-9109)* **Under 1 mi:** Propane *(Spicer 596-6531)* **1-3 mi:** West Marine *(841-9880)*, Bait/Tackle *(Saltwater 842-0062)*

Boatyard Services
OnCall: Rigger, Divers, Air Conditioning, Refrigeration, Compound, Wash & Wax, Interior Cleaning **Nearest Yard:** Newport Ship (401) 846-6000

Restaurants and Accommodations
Near: Restaurant *(Christie's 847-5400, L $9-19, D $11-23, Sun Br. $8-19)*, *(Scales & Shells 846-3474, Upscales upstairs)*, *(Red Parrot 847-3800, L&D $13-29; Kids' $2-6)*, *(Sambar 619-2505, D $12-23)*, *(Cafe Zelda 849-4002, L $8-18, D $10-35)*, *(The Pier 847-3645, L $8-26, D $16-32, Live music Wed-Sun 6-10pm; New mgmt)*, *(Bouchard 846-0123, D $18-39)*, *(Handy Lunch 847-9480, B&L)*, *(Thai Cuisine 841-8822, L&D $11-17; Kids' $6)*, Pizzeria *(Via Via 846-4074)*, Inn/B&B *(Spring St. 847-4767, $119-299)*, *(Francis Malbone 846-0392, $165-525)*, *(Admiral Fitzroy 848-8000, $95-355)*, *(Forty 1 North 846-8018, $239-1900)*

Recreation and Entertainment
OnSite: Heated Pool, Picnic Area, Grills *(gas)* **Near:** Playground *(Aquidneck)*, Tennis Courts *(Aquidneck Park; Nat'l Tennis Club 849-6672)*, Jogging Paths, Boat Rentals *(Oldport Marine 847-9109 Classic power)*, Tours *(Ghosts 847-8600; Secret Gardens 847-0514)* **Under 1 mi:** Dive Shop *(Newport 847-9293)*, Fitness Center *(Pulse 595-8549)*, Fishing Charter *(Quest 339-8035)*, Movie Theater *(Jane Pickens 846-5252)*, Video Rental *(Redbox)*, Park *(Aquidneck; Touro)*, Museum *(Tennis HOF 846-1203, $9/7; Newport History 846-0813; Newport Art 848-8200, $10/8)*, Cultural Attract *(Firehouse 849-3473)* **1-3 mi:** Beach *(Easton's 1st 849-8430; Gooseberry 847-3958)*, Sightseeing *(The Mansions: Rosecliff & The Elms 847-1000; Belcourt Castle 846-0669; Breakers)* **3+ mi:** Golf Course *(Newport Nat'l 848-9690, 5.5 mi.)*

Provisioning and General Services
Near: Market *(Max's 849-8088)*, Bank/ATM, Post Office, Catholic Church, Protestant Church, Library *(847-8720)*, Beauty Salon *(Visage 847-1606)* **Under 1 mi:** Convenience Store *(7-Eleven)*, Supermarket *(Stop & Shop 848-7200)*, Delicatessen *(Peaceable 846-0036)*, Health Food *(Harvest 846-8137)*, Wine/Beer *(Bellevue 846-7993)*, Liquor Store *(Vickers' 847-0123)*, Bakery *(Katrina's 847-8210)*, Farmers' Market *(Wed 2-6pm Aquidneck)*, Fishmonger *(Aquidneck 846-0106)*, Synagogue, Dry Cleaners *(O'Donnell's 846-9635)*, Laundry *(Micki's 847-5972)*, Pharmacy *(CVS 846-7800)*, Hardware Store *(Newport Ace 849-9442)*, Florist *(Broadway 849-4000)*

Transportation
OnCall: Rental Car *(Enterprise 849-3939)*, Taxi *(Orange 841-0030)*, Airport Limo *(Posh 842-0005)* **Near:** Bikes *(Segway 619-4010)*, Water Taxi *(Harbor)*, Local Bus *(RIPTA)*, Ferry Service **Airport:** TF Green *(27 mi)*

Medical Services
911 Service **Near:** Veterinarian *(Newport 849-3401)* **Under 1 mi:** Doctor *(Rocco 849-1113)*, Dentist *(Newport 847-7662)*, Chiropractor *(Newport 847-4224)*, Optician *(Brown 846-0101)* **Hospital:** Newport 846-6400 *(1.4 mi.)*

Setting -- In the center of the "Newport Yachting Village," an inviting pool overlooks three impeccable, well-maintained, long floating docks - enlivened by the occasional flower pot. An adjacent pier hosts a deck populated with umbrellaed tables and lounge area. At the back of the property, quality propane grills and picnic tables tuck under a white tent. On the north side, four-story, contemporary, Victorian gray town houses wall the basin.

Marina Notes -- *Over 70 ft. LOA & holiday weekends $5.50/ft. Disc. May, Sept, Oct. Add'l Power: 2/30A $22/day, 2/50A $44/day, 100A $50/cord/day + 3-phase. $3 million renovation in '09. Floating 10 ft. wide, composite decked docks, 2 ft. freeboard - internal steel pilings. Reservations cancellable 72 hrs in advance. Heated dockside pool, gas grill area. Pet/child friendly. Lounge area. Pump-out boats, 7 days, 8am-7pm, 474 3011, Ch. 9, ($15 first 30 gals, $5 add'l 30 gals). Free paking, guest parking $10/day. Diesel trucked/barged in. Bathhouse: Bright, airy showers & dressing rooms, home-like ambiance. Laundry.

Notable -- The Pier waterfront restaurant abuts the property. Well-insulated from the hubbub of touristed Newport, all the attractions are still just a short walk out the "back door." A block south, the International Yacht Restoration School (848-5777) rejuvenated many classic yachts, including the 133 ft. Gilded Age "Coronet." Coordinate a visit here with the Museum of Yachting (847-1018) - the Harbor Shuttle stops at both. Stroll Thames Street to America's Cup Avenue - the nexus of the action. Walk to the nearest "cottage," The Elms or take the yellow Trolley line to the more distant mansions - the Astor's Beechwood (846-3772), the Vanderbilt's Belcourt Castle (846-0669, 10am-4pm $10/8) or The Breakers (10am-5pm $15/4 847-1000). Combo tickets available.

PHOTOS ON DVD: 18

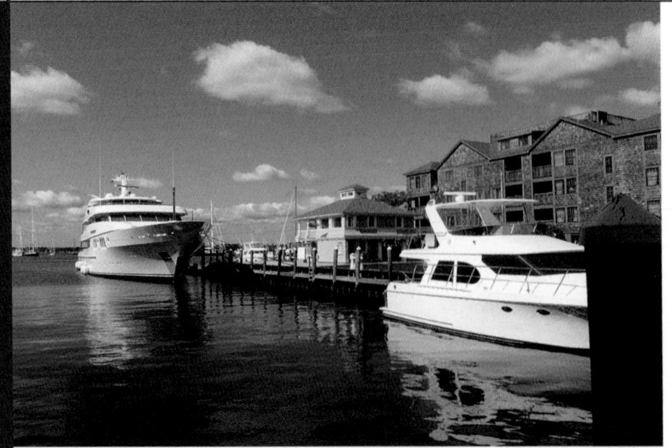

Brown & Howard Wharf Marina

19 Brown & Howard Wharf, 411 Thames St.; Newport, RI 02840

Tel: (401) 846-5100 **VHF: Monitor** Ch. 9 **Talk** Ch. 68
Fax: (401) 751-7088 **Alternate Tel:** (401) 274-6611
Email: kdonovan@brownandhoward.com **Web:** www.paolinoproperties.com
Nearest Town: Newport **Tourist Info:** (401) 521-5000

Navigational Information

Lat: 41°28.844' **Long:** 071°18.969' **Tide:** 4 ft. **Current:** n/a **Chart:** 13223
Rep. Depths (*MLW*): Entry 22 ft. **Fuel Dock** 20 ft. **Max Slip/Moor** 20 ft./-
Access: Ft. Adams to starboard, straight ahead to 3rd set of docks heading N

Marina Facilities *(In Season/Off Season)*

Fuel: No
Slips: 20 Total, 20 Transient **Max LOA:** 250 ft. **Max Beam:** n/a
Rate *(per ft.)*: **Day** $5.50 **Week** n/a **Month** n/a
Power: 30 amp $20, **50 amp** $35, **100 amp** $70, **200 amp** n/a
Cable TV: Yes, Incl. **Dockside Phone:** Yes, Incl.
Dock Type: Fixed, Alongside
Moorings: 0 Total, 0 Transient **Launch:** n/a
Rate: Day n/a **Week** n/a **Month** n/a
Heads: None
Internet: Yes *(Dockside, Free)* **Laundry:** None
Pump-Out: OnCall, Full Service, 2 Port **Fee:** Free **Closed Heads:** Yes

Marina Operations

Owner/Manager: Joseph R. Paolino, Jr. **Dockmaster:** Michael Egar
In-Season: May-Oct 31, 8am-8pm **Off-Season:** Nov 1-Apr 30, Closed
After-Hours Arrival: Call in advance
Reservations: Yes, Preferred **Credit Cards:** Visa/MC, Dscvr, Cash or Check
Discounts: None
Pets: Welcome **Handicap Access:** Yes, Docks

Marina Services and Boat Supplies

Services - Docking Assistance, Trash Pick-Up, 3 Phase **Communication -** Pay Phone, FedEx, DHL, UPS, Express Mail **Supplies - OnSite:** Ice *(Block, Cube)* **Near:** CNG *(Oldport 847-9109)* **Under 1 mi:** Ships' Store *(Bowen's 849-4999)*, Propane *(Spicer 596-6531)* **1-3 mi:** West Marine *(841-9880)* **3+ mi:** Bait/Tackle *(Saltwater Edge 842-0062, 3.3 mi.)*

Boatyard Services

Nearest Yard: Newport Shipyard (401) 846-6000

Restaurants and Accommodations

OnCall: Pizzeria *(Via Via 846-4074)* **Near:** Restaurant *(Red Parrot 847-3800, L $5-15, D $10-24, L&D $13-29; Kids' $2-6)*, *(The Pier 847-3645, L $8-26, D $18-32, Brunch: $8-14 Live Music Wed-Sun 6-10pm.)*, *(Bouchard 846-0123, D $18-39)*, *(Handy Lunch 847-9480, B&L)*, *(Thai Cuisine 841-8822, L&D $11-17; Kids' $6)*, *(Sambar 619-2505, D $12-23)*, *(Scales & Shells 846-3474)*, Inn/B&B *(Admiral Fitzroy 848-8000, $95-355)*, *(Francis Malbone 846-0392, $165-525)*, *(Spring St. 847-4767, $119-299)*

Recreation and Entertainment

Near: Playground, Dive Shop *(Newport 847-9293)*, Tennis Courts *(Aquidneck Park; Nat'l Tennis Club 849-6672)*, Museum *(S. Whithorne 847-2448, $6/12; Tennis HOF 846-1203, $9/7)*, Special Events *(Jazz & Folk Festivals)* **Under 1 mi:** Beach *(Easton's 1st)*, Fitness Center *(Pulse 595-8549)*, Fishing Charter *(Quest 339-8035)*, Movie Theater *(Jane Pickens)*, Video Rental *(Redbox)*, Park *(King, Touro)*, Tours *(Ghost Tours 847-8600; Secret Garden Tour 847-0514)*, Sightseeing *(Cliff Walk)*, Galleries *(Newport Potters 619-4880; Art on the Wharf 845-6858; van der Wal 849-5556)* **1-3 mi:** Cultural Attract *(Firehouse Theater 849-3473)* **3+ mi:** Golf Course *(Newport Nat'l 848-9690, 5.5 mi.)*

Provisioning and General Services

Near: Market *(Max's 849-8088)*, Delicatessen *(Eastside Market/Catering 831-7771)*, Health Food *(Harvest Natural 846-8137)*, Wine/Beer *(Bellevue 846-7993)*, Fishmonger *(Aquidneck 846-0106)*, Bank/ATM, Post Office *(847-9835)*, Library *(847-8720)*, Beauty Salon *(Natural Creations 841-0798)*, Pharmacy *(CVS 846-7800)*, Retail Shops *(Bellevue Mall)* **Under 1 mi:** Supermarket *(Stop & Shop 848-7200)*, Liquor Store *(Vickers' 847-0123)*, Bakery *(Katrina's 847-8210)*, Farmers' Market *(Wed 2-6pm, Aquidneck Memorial & Chapel)*, Catholic Church, Protestant Church, Synagogue, Dry Cleaners *(O'Donnell's 846-9635)*, Laundry *(Micki's 847-5972)*, Hardware Store *(Newport Ace 847-9442)*, Copies Etc. *(UPS 848-7600)* **1-3 mi:** Department Store *(TJ Maxx 841-5910)*, Buying Club *(BJs 848-9242)*

Transportation

OnCall: Rental Car *(Enterprise 849-3939)*, Taxi *(Orange 841-0030)*, Airport Limo *(Posh 842-0005)* **Near:** Bikes *(Segway 619-4010)*, Water Taxi *(Harbor Shuttle $10/6/day)*, Local Bus *(Trolley)*, InterCity Bus *(Bonanza, Peter Pan)*, Ferry Service *(Jamestown)* **3+ mi:** Rail *(Kingston, 20 mi.)* **Airport:** TF Green *(27 mi.)*

Medical Services

911 Service **Near:** Holistic Services *(Flow Acupunc. 835-7770)*, Veterinarian *(Newport 849-3401)* **Under 1 mi:** Doctor *(Connell 841-8613)*, Dentist *(Newport 847-7662)*, Optician *(Brown 846-0101)* **1-3 mi:** Chiropractor *(Newport 847-4224)* **Hospital:** Newport 846-6400 *(1.5 mi.)*

Setting -- Even though it's in the heart of downtown Newport, the 1,400 feet of linear dock wall flanked by 16 elegant, three-story Neo-Victorian residences, provides a buffer from the usual rush and bustle. A very pretty, two-story Shingle-style office building perched on pillars houses the office and future amenities. Landscaping is limited to a uniquely large parking lot (for owners, crew and guests) that helps make it among the most-private large yacht accommodations.

Marina Notes -- Caters to 50- to 250-ft yachts with up to 40 ft. beam. Power: 100 AMP/3 phase, 20V. Plus telephone, cable, water and ice. Minimal landside facilities. Dockmaster's direct line 640-4458. Nov-Apr Management address: 76 Dorrance Street, Providence, RI 02903 Tel: 401-274-6611, Fax: 401-751-7088. Large parking lot, rare in Newport. Neat, clean and maintained. Bathhouse: None. Planned expansion to add lounge, heads & showers; Inquire.

Notable -- Lower Thames Street, one of Newport's main thoroughfares, is at the head of the wharf. Several historic inns along with Federal-style Samuel Whitehorne house are a block away. Walk east across Aquidneck Park, past the impressive library, tennis courts and Edward King House to Bellevue Shopping Center. The Casino Historic District and Tennis Hall of Fame are just beyond as is the weekly Growers' Market. And a bit over a mile, Easton's beach, a lovely sweep of sand, sports gentle waves, a carousel, playground, aquarium, food concessions and Atlantic Beach Club's patio restaurant and bar with live music. Shuttles run to the famous mansions - about half a mile. The Elms is the closest. Get tickets and brochures at the Preservation Society then take the shuttle down Bellevue Ave. to any of the others. The Cliff Walk hike, 3.5 miles from start to finish, fronts many of the "cottages" and can be done in short segments.

Navigational Information
Lat: 41°29.039' **Long:** 071°18.985' **Tide:** 4 ft. **Current:** n/a **Chart:** 13223
Rep. Depths (*MLW*): Entry 14 ft. **Fuel Dock** n/a **Max Slip/Moor** 14 ft./-
Access: Straight into Newport Harbor

Marina Facilities *(In Season/Off Season)*
Fuel: Slip-Side Fueling, Gasoline, Diesel, High-Speed Pumps
Slips: 25 Total, 25 Transient **Max LOA:** 250 ft. **Max Beam:** 42 ft.
Rate *(per ft.)*: **Day** $4.50/Inq.* **Week** n/a **Month** $175
Power: 30 amp $20, **50 amp** $30, **100 amp** $60**, **200 amp** n/a
Cable TV: Yes, Incl. **Dockside Phone:** No
Dock Type: Floating, Long Fingers, Pilings, Alongside, Wood
Moorings: 0 Total, 0 Transient **Launch:** n/a, Dinghy Dock
Rate: Day n/a **Week** n/a **Month** n/a
Heads: 13 Toilet(s), 3 Shower(s)
Internet: Yes *(Wi-Fi, Free)* **Laundry:** None
Pump-Out: 25 InSlip **Fee:** $0.32/gal, $20 min **Closed Heads:** Yes

Marina Operations
Owner/Manager: Mark DelGiudice **Dockmaster:** Casey Civatts
In-Season: May-Oct, 8am-10pm **Off-Season:** Oct-May, Closed
After-Hours Arrival: Call in advance
Reservations: Yes **Credit Cards:** Visa/MC, Dscvr, Din, Amex
Discounts: None
Pets: Welcome **Handicap Access:** No

Marina at Forty 1 Degrees North

351 Thames Street; Newport, RI 02840

Tel: (401) 846-8018 **VHF: Monitor** Ch. 9 **Talk** Ch. 9
Fax: (866) 702-3135 **Alternate Tel:** (401) 662-2620
Email: mdel@41north.com **Web:** www.41north.com
Nearest Town: Newport **Tourist Info:** (401) 845-9123

Marina Services and Boat Supplies
Services - Docking Assistance, Concierge, Room Service to the Boat, Security *(24 hour, Yes)*, Dock Carts, 3 Phase **Communication -** Pay Phone, FedEx, DHL, UPS, Express Mail **Supplies - OnSite:** Ice *(Cube)* **Near:** Ships' Store *(Bowen's 849-4999)*, CNG *(Oldport 847-9109)* **Under 1 mi:** Propane *(Spicer 596-6531)* **1-3 mi:** West Marine *(841-9880)*, Bait/Tackle *(Saltwater Edge 842-0062)*

Boatyard Services
OnSite: Compound, Wash & Wax, Interior Cleaning **Nearest Yard:** Newport Shipyard (401) 846-6000

Restaurants and Accommodations
OnSite: Restaurant *(Christie's 847-5400, L $8-19, D $9-23, Wknd Br. $8-15)*, *(The Grill 846-8018, B $9-19, L $13-36, D $25-50, Wknd Br $13-36)*, Hotel *(Forty 1 North 846-8018, $250-600)* **Near:** Restaurant *(Rhino Bar & Grill 846-0707, D $7-18, Mamba club)*, *(Mooring 846-2260, D $9-44)*, *(22 Bowen's 841-8884, L $10-24, D $23-53)*, *(Black Pearl 846-5264, L $8-26.50, D $7.50-29.50)*, *(Red Parrot 847-3800, D $13-29, Kids' $2-6)*, *(Clarke Cooke 849-2900, L $10-37, D $19-39)*, *(Gas Lamp 845-9300)*, Pizzeria *(Via Via 846-4074, del.)*, Hotel *(Harborside Inn 846-6600, $159-385)*, *(Bannister's Wharf 846-4500, $125-340)*, *(Newport Bay 849-8600, $199-379)*

Recreation and Entertainment
Near: Playground, Tennis Courts *(Aquidneck)*, Boat Rentals *(Oldport Marine)*, Park *(Aquidneck)*, Tours *(Rum Runner II 847-0299; Wayfarer 849-5087; Ghost 841-8600;)* **Under 1 mi:** Beach *(Easton's)*, Dive Shop *(Bubbles 847-4985)*, Fitness Center *(Pulse 595-8549)*, Movie Theater *(Jane Pickens 846-5252)*, Museum *(Newport History 846-0813, $4/2; Tennis HOF 846-1203, $11-15)*, Cultural Attract *(Firehouse 849-3473)*, Sightseeing *(The Mansions: Rosecliff & The Elms 847-1000; Belcourt Castle 846-0669; Breakers)* **3+ mi:** Golf Course *(Jamestown G.C. 423-9930, 5.5 mi.)*

Provisioning and General Services
OnSite: Bank/ATM, Laundry, Newsstand **Near:** Market *(Max's 849-8088)*, Fishmonger *(Aquidneck 846-0106)*, Post Office, Catholic Church, Library *(847-8720)*, Beauty Salon *(Visage 847-1606)* **Under 1 mi:** Supermarket *(Stop & Shop 848-7200)*, Delicatessen *(Pick Pockets 619-1973)*, Health Food *(Harvest Nat 846-8137)*, Wine/Beer *(Bellevue 846-7993)*, Liquor Store *(Spring St. 846-0959)*, Bakery *(Queenie's 619-5968)*, Farmers' Market *(Wed 2-6pm, Chapel & Memorial 848-0099)*, Protestant Church, Synagogue, Dry Cleaners *(Perfect Touch 300-0030)*, Pharmacy *(CVS 846-7800)*, Hardware Store *(Ace 849-9442)*, Florist *(Broadway 849-4000)*, Retail Shops *(Long Wharf Mall)*, Copies Etc. *(UPS 848-7600)* **1-3 mi:** Buying Club *(BJ's 848-9242)*

Transportation
Near: Bikes *(Scooter World 619-1349)*, Water Taxi, Rental Car *(Hertz 846-1645)*, Taxi *(Cozy 846-2500)*, Airport Limo *(Orange 841-0030)*, Local Bus *(RIPTA)*, InterCity Bus, Ferry Service **Airport:** T.F. Green *(27 mi)*

Medical Services
911 Service **Near:** Holistic Services *(Flow Acupuncture 835-7770)* **Under 1 mi:** Doctor *(Gonzalez 848-2160)*, Dentist *(Rosenberg 849-2080)*, Chiropractor *(Newport 847-4224)*, Optician *(Brown 846-0101)*, Veterinarian *(Newport 849-3401)* **Hospital:** Newport 846-6400 *(1.5 mi.)*

Setting -- This elegant, eco-conscious marina resort packs a lot lof high-end luxe into a compact space right on the harbor front. The top-flight Ipe-decked slips and megayacht side-tie docks flow right into the restaurants and hotel public rooms. Dockside cocktail decks and outdoor living areas, sheltered by large market umbrellas, rub shoulders with an airy dining room wide open to the seabreeze. Beautifully appointed guestrooms look across the harbor.

Marina Notes -- *$4.50 7.50/ft **Single-phase, 240-volt, 3-phase $220, 100A & 200A $95, 480-volt service $440. Established 1945, Christie's is Newport's oldest waterfront restaurant. Totally re-built with state-of-the-art docking, yacht services, eateries & hotel. Inner slips accommodate up to 50 ft. LOA; outer docks up to 5 megayachts to 250 ft. each. In-slip pump-out. Live music year 'round, 7 nights 6pm-1am. Dinner/room service available to yachts. Leeds-certified. Parking $25. Flow-through traffic limits privacy. Bathhouse: Three dedicated, lavishly appointed full baths with bordered tile, contemporary fixtures.

Notable -- The white Queen Anne, Shingle-style exterior echos Newport's historic old hotels while the interior is chic, modern, and infused with a touch of Asian. Old world service marries hip amenities (like integrated media systems, I-Pads and low-flow waterfall showers). Two unique restaurants - The Grill on the harbor's edge is more upscale, locovore and Christie's more playful and casual with stylish Latin/Asian cuisine, swing seating and a communal table. 24 guest rooms/suites and four cottage/lofts feature fireplaces, oversized French doors opening onto waterview balconies. A magic switch turns party mode into high gear. Cobblestone Christie's Landing, lined with shops and more eateries, winds its way from the docks to bustling Thames Street.

PHOTOS ON DVD: 25

Newport Yachting Center

Newport Yachting Center

PO Box 550; Commercial Wharf; Newport, RI 02840

Tel: (401) 846-1600 **VHF: Monitor** Ch. 9 **Talk** Ch. 9
Fax: (401) 847-9262 **Alternate Tel:** (401) 846-1600
Email: info@newportyachtingcenter.com **Web:** newportyachtingcenter.com
Nearest Town: Newport **Tourist Info:** (401) 845-9123

Navigational Information

Lat: 41°29.108' **Long:** 071°19.059' **Tide:** 4 ft. **Current:** n/a **Chart:** 13223
Rep. Depths (*MLW*): Entry 22 ft. **Fuel Dock** 17 ft. **Max Slip/Moor** 17 ft./-
Access: Narragansett Bay to Newport Harbor; look for large white tents

Marina Facilities *(In Season/Off Season)*

Fuel: *ValvTect* - Gasoline, Diesel, High-Speed Pumps
Slips: 100 Total, 60 Transient **Max LOA:** 180 ft. **Max Beam:** n/a
Rate *(per ft.)*: **Day** $5.00/2.75-3* **Week** Inq. **Month** Inq.
Power: 30 amp $10, **50 amp** $20, **100 amp** $60, **200 amp** n/a
Cable TV: No **Dockside Phone:** No
Dock Type: Floating, Long Fingers, Alongside, Wood
Moorings: 0 Total, 0 Transient **Launch:** n/a
Rate: Day n/a **Week** n/a **Month** n/a
Heads: 8 Toilet(s), 8 Shower(s) *(dressing rooms)*
Internet: Yes *(Wi-Fi, Free)* **Laundry:** None
Pump-Out: OnSite, Full Service, 1 Central **Fee:** $5/25 gals. **Closed Heads:**

Marina Operations

Owner/Manager: Chuck Moffitt **Dockmaster:** Ray LeBlanc
In-Season: MidMay-MidOct, 8am-8pm **Off-Season:** LateOct-May, 9am-5pm
After-Hours Arrival: Call in advance
Reservations: Yes **Credit Cards:** Visa/MC, Dscvr, Amex
Discounts: Boat/US **Dockage:** 10% **Fuel:** $.10g **Repair:** n/a
Pets: Welcome **Handicap Access:** Yes, Heads, Docks

Marina Services and Boat Supplies

Services - Docking Assistance, Concierge, Security *(24 hr.)*, Trash Pick-Up, Dock Carts, 3 Phase **Communication -** Pay Phone, FedEx, DHL, UPS, Express Mail **Supplies - OnSite:** Ice *(Block, Cube)* **Near:** Ships' Store *(Bowen's 849-4999)*, CNG *(Oldport 847-9109)* **Under 1 mi:** Propane *(Spicer 596-6531)* **1-3 mi:** West Marine *(841-9880)*

Boatyard Services

Nearest Yard: Newport Shipyard (401) 846-6000

Restaurants and Accommodations

OnSite: Restaurant *(The Mooring Seafood 846-2260, L $9-24, D $9-34, Prix Fixe $20 Sun-Wed)*, *(Smokehouse Café 848-9800, L&D $8-24)* **Near:** Restaurant *(22 Bowen's 841-8884, L $10-24, D $19-44)*, *(Black Pearl 846-5264, L $8-27, D $7-29)*, *(Red Parrot 847-3800, D $13-29)*, *(Christie's 847-5400, L $8-19, D $9-23)*, *(Clarke 849-2900, L $10-37, D $19-39)*, *(Fluke 849-7778, D $23-46)*, *(Landing 847-4514, L $9-26, D $17-36)*, Pizzeria *(Via Via 846-4074)*, Hotel *(Newport Bay 849-8600, $199-379)*, *(Harborside Inn 846-6600, $159-385)* **Under 1 mi:** Hotel *(Marriott 849-1000, $275-500)*

Recreation and Entertainment

OnSite: Picnic Area, Cultural Attract *(Events & Concerts all Summer)* **Near:** Pool *(Marriott - Comp.)*, Playground, Tennis Courts *(Aquidneck Park)*, Fitness Center *(Marriott - Comp.)* **Under 1 mi:** Beach *(Easton/1st)*, Dive Shop *(Bubbles 847-4985)*, Hike/Bike Trails *(Cliff Walk)*, Movie Theater *(Jane Pickens 846-5252)*, Video Rental *(Redbox)*, Park *(Aquidneck; Touro)*, Museum *(Touro Synagogue 847-4794; Newport History 846-0813; Newport Art 848-8200; $10/8)*, Tours *(Viking bus 847-6921$24; Native Newporter Walk 662-1407)* **1-3 mi:** Sightseeing *(The Mansions: Rosecliff & The Elms 847-1000; Belcourt Castle 846-0669; Breakers - RIPTA shuttle at gate)* **3+ mi:** Golf Course *(Jamestown G.C. 423-9930, 5.5 mi.)*

Provisioning and General Services

Near: Convenience Store *(JD 842-0545)*, Delicatessen *(Pick Pockets 619-1973)*, Bakery *(Queenie's 619-5968)*, Fishmonger *(Aquidneck 846-0106)*, Bank/ATM, Post Office, Catholic Church, Protestant Church, Library *(847-8720)*, Beauty Salon *(Visage 847-1606)* **Under 1 mi:** Supermarket *(Stop & Shop 848-7200)*, Gourmet Shop *(Le Petit 619-3882)*, Health Food *(A Market Nat 846-8137)*, Wine/Beer *(Bellevue 846-7993)*, Liquor Store *(Vicker's 847-0123)*, Farmers' Market *(Wed 2-6, Chapel & Memorial)*, Synagogue *(Oldest in U.S.)*, Dry Cleaners *(Perfect Touch 300-0030)*, Laundry *(Del Nero 847-6800)*, Pharmacy *(CVS 846-7800)*, Hardware Store *(Newport Ace 849-9442)*, Retail Shops *(Long Wharf; Bellevue)*, Copies Etc. *(UPS)* **1-3 mi:** Buying Club *(BJ's 848-9242)*

Transportation

OnCall: Water Taxi, Rental Car *(Enterprise 849-3939)*, Taxi *(Cozy 846-2500)*, Airport Limo *(Cozy; RIPTA 781-9400)* **Near:** Bikes *(Scooter World 619-1349)*, Local Bus *(RIPTA to Mansions, Cliff Walk)* **Under 1 mi:** InterCity Bus *(Bonanza, Peter Pan)*, Ferry Service *(Jamestown, B.I.)* **3+ mi:** Rail *(Kingston Amtrak, 20 mi.)* **Airport:** TF Green *(27 mi.)*

Medical Services

911 Service **Under 1 mi:** Doctor *(Gonzalez 848-2160)*, Dentist *(Violet 847-3497)*, Chiropractor *(Newport 847-4224)*, Holistic Services *(Marriott 848-6983)*, Veterinarian *(Nwprt 849-3401)* **Hospital:** Newport 846-6400 *(1.2 mi.)*

Setting -- NYC's wharf peninsula is flanked by rows of long side-tie docks interspersed with short double-loaded slips; across the harbor-front end, the marina office backs an easy-access fuel dock. Its unassuming water-side appearance belies the first-class amenities offered by Newport's largest downtown marina. The expansive, carefully maintained complex extends almost to America's Cup Avenue with three permanent event tents that are near extensive parking, two restaurants, a bathhouse, and more offices - all surrounding the long, four-story brick Harborview Condominium.

Marina Notes -- *Mid-Jun-Lab Day $5/ft. July 4th, $5.50, 2 nt min; MemDay wknd $3/ft., Apr-Jun 10 & LabDay-Oct $2.75/ft. Touch/Go $1/ft. 2500 ft. linear dockage, accommodate yachts to 180 ft. Boats rarely rafted these days. Reserve with deposit. Cancel 7 days before arrival, full refund. Part of Newport Harbor Corporation. Comp. access to Marriott pool & fitness center avail. to marina guests (0.4 mi.). Concierge service & event planning - especially club cruises & rendezvous. Parking: guests $10/day, public $20. Bathhouse: One-story shingle-sided structure. Floors & walls fully tiled. Inviting décor, well-maintained.

Notable -- NYC offers an impressive series of summer events and concerts practically dockside - including the Great Chowder Cook-Off, Newport Summer Comedy Series with headliners like Steven Wright and Bob Saget, Nantucket Nectars Sunset Music Series with top talent (Indigo Girls, Doobie Bros.) plus Reggae, Irish, Arts and October Fests. Check the website. September brings Newport's Boat Show when added docks stretch into the harbor. Upscale Moorings restaurant features a waterfront deck under a tan striped awning (a favorite for over 25 years), or follow your nose to down-home Smokehouse Cafe.

Navigational Information
Lat: 41°29.117' **Long:** 071°19.283' **Tide:** 6 ft. **Current:** n/a **Chart:** 13223
Rep. Depths (*MLW*): Entry 25 ft. **Fuel Dock** n/a **Max Slip/Moor** -/25 ft.
Access: Narragansett Bay; head east at Fort Adams to Central Mooring field

Marina Facilities *(In Season/Off Season)*
Fuel: No
Slips: 0 Total, 0 Transient **Max LOA:** n/a **Max Beam:** n/a
Rate *(per ft.)*: **Day** n/a **Week** n/a **Month** n/a
Power: 30 amp n/a, **50 amp** n/a, **100 amp** n/a, **200 amp** n/a
Cable TV: No **Dockside Phone:** No
Dock Type: n/a
Moorings: 115 Total, 17 Transient **Launch:** Yes ($3/pp 1-way), Dinghy Dock
Rate: Day $45-60/30-40* **Week** n/a **Month** $1350-1800
Heads: None
Internet: No **Laundry:** None
Pump-Out: OnCall *(474-0543, Ch.9)* **Fee:** $15/25 gals. **Closed Heads:** Yes

Marina Operations
Owner/Manager: Matt Gineo **Dockmaster:** same
In-Season: MemDay-LabDay, 7am-Mid **Off-Season:** **May, Jun, Sep, Oct
After-Hours Arrival: Pick up cone-shaped buoy marked "Rental"
Reservations: No **Credit Cards:** Visa/MC
Discounts: None
Pets: Welcome **Handicap Access:** No

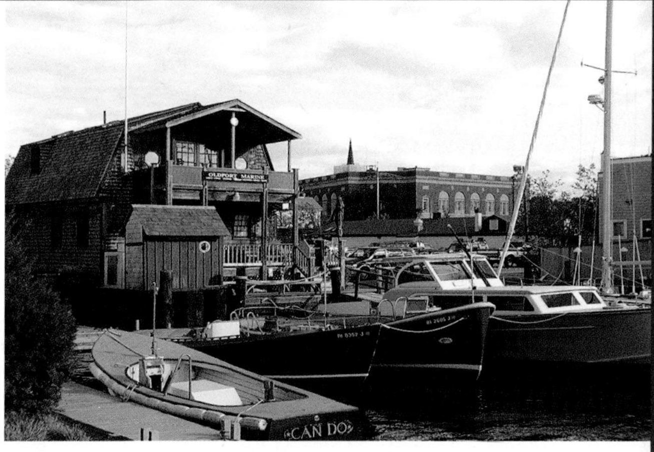

Oldport Moorings

PO Box 141; Sayers Wharf; Newport, RI 02840

Tel: (401) 847-9109 **VHF: Monitor** Ch. 68 **Talk** Ch. 68
Fax: (401) 846-5599 **Alternate Tel:** n/a
Email: matt@oldportmarine.com **Web:** www.Oldportmarine.com
Nearest Town: Newport **Tourist Info:** (401) 845-9123

Marina Services and Boat Supplies
Communication - Fax in/out, FedEx, UPS **Supplies - OnSite:** Ice *(Block, Cube)*, CNG *($18/20)* **Near:** Ships' Store *(Bowen 849-4999)* **Under 1 mi:** Propane *(Spicer 596-6531)* **1-3 mi:** West Marine *(841-9880)*

Boatyard Services
OnSite: Engine mechanic *(gas, diesel)*, Electrical Repairs, Hull Repairs, Divers, Compound, Wash & Wax **Dealer for:** Yanmar, Oldport Launches. **Member:** ABBRA - 2 Certified Tech(s), ABYC - 2 Certified Tech(s)

Restaurants and Accommodations
Near: Restaurant *(Smokehouse Cafe 848-9800, L&D $8-24)*, *(The Mooring 846-2260, L $9-24, D $9-34, Adjacent, waterfront, casual fine dining)*, *(22 Bowen's 841-8884, L $10-24, D $23-53)*, *(Black Pearl 846-5264, L $8-26.50, D $7-30)*, *(Red Parrot 847-3800, D $13-29, Kids' $2-6)*, *(Christie's 847-5400, L $8-19, D $9-23)*, *(Clarke Cooke 849-2900, L $10-37, D $19-39)*, *(Landing 847-4514, L $9-26, D $17-36)*, Pizzeria *(Via Via 846-4074)*, Hotel *(The Newport 847-9000, $242+)*, *(Bannister's Wharf 846-4500, $125-340)*, *(Newport Bay 849-8600, $199-379)*, *(Wyndham 866-323-3087, $140+)*

Recreation and Entertainment
OnSite: Tours *(MV Amazing Grace 847-9109 Harbor tours $15/5; Rum Runner II 847-0299)* **Near:** Tennis Courts *(Aquidneck)*, Video Arcade, Park *(Pergotti)* **Under 1 mi:** Beach *(Easton's 1st)*, Dive Shop *(Bubbles 847-4985)*, Fitness Center *(Pilates 619-4660)*, Hike/Bike Trails *(Cliff Walk north entrance)*, Fishing Charter *(Quest 339-8035)*, Movie Theater *(Jane Pickens 846-5252)*, Video Rental *(Redbox)*, Museum *(S. Whitehorne 847-2448, $6/free; Newport History 846-0813, Free; Tennis HOF 846-1203, $11/free)*, Cultural Attract *(Firehouse 849-3473)*, Sightseeing *(Exploration Aquarium 849-8430; Mansions: Rosecliff & The Elms 847-1000; Belcourt Castle 846-0669; Breakers - RIPTA shuttle at gate)* **3+ mi:** Golf Course *(Newport Nat'l 848-9690, 5.5 mi.)*, Horseback Riding *(Newport Stable 848-5440, 4.5 mi.)*

Provisioning and General Services
Near: Convenience Store *(JD 842-0545)*, Delicatessen *(Pick Pockets 619-1973)*, Liquor Store *(Spring Street 846-0959)*, Bakery *(Queenie's 619-5968)*, Fishmonger *(Aquidneck 846-0106)*, Bank/ATM, Post Office, Catholic Church, Protestant Church, Library *(847-8720)*, Beauty Salon *(Visage 847-1606)* **Under 1 mi:** Supermarket *(Stop & Shop 848-7200)*, Health Food *(A Market Nat 846-8137)*, Wine/Beer *(Bellevue 846-7993 Del.)*, Farmers' Market *(Wed 2-6pm, Memorial & Chapel)*, Synagogue *(Touro, oldest in US)*, Dry Cleaners *(Perfect Touch 300-0030)*, Laundry *(847-5972 Miki's PU/Del)*, Pharmacy *(CVS 846-7800)*, Hardware Store *(Ace 849-9442)*, Florist *(Broadway 849-4000)*, Retail Shops *(Long Wharf & Bellevue Malls)*, Copies Etc. *(UPS 848-7600)*

Transportation
OnSite: Water Taxi *($3)* **OnCall:** Taxi *(Cozy Cab 846-2500)*, Airport Limo *(Posh 842-0005)* **Near:** Bikes *(Scooter World 619-1349)*, Local Bus *(RIPTA Trolley)* **Under 1 mi:** Rental Car *(Budget 846-6116)*, InterCity Bus *(Peter Pan)* **3+ mi:** Rail *(Kingston Amtrak, 19 mi.)* **Airport:** TF Green *(27 mi.)*

Medical Services
911 Service **Under 1 mi:** Doctor *(Gonzalez 846-2160)*, Dentist *(Sunderland 846-4404)*, Chiropractor *(Newport C. 847-4224)*, Optician *(Brown 846-0101)*, Veterinarian *(Newport 849-3401)* **Hospital:** Newport 846-6400 *(1.2 mi.)*

Setting -- For a front row seat on Newport's boat ballet, call Oldport; they own the majority of transient moorings in Central Harbor. Squeezed between Newport Yachting and Bannister's Wharf, a bustling single dock with a covered waiting area is awhirl with tours, taxis and launches. A gambrel-roof tops the attractive, two-story green-and-natural-shingled office. Oldport's distinctive, comfortable launches service all the mooring fields and anchorages.

Marina Notes -- *Up to 49 ft. $45/nt. $1350/mo, 50-65 ft $60/nt, $1800/mo. (over 65 ft. call harbormaster 848-6492, Ch.16 &14). Rafting $30 add'l boat. Shoulder Season: Up to 49 ft. $30/nt. $$1200/mo, 50 65 ft. $40/nt, $1400/mo, After ColDay $700/mo. **Launch: Jul & Aug Sat & Sun to 1am, Shoulder Season - hours get shorter & runs more infrequent, see website. Founded 1972. Office: 8am-5pm Mon-Fri, 10am-4pm Wknds. Water float in harbor. Add'l water plus trash receptacles on Oldport's dock. Repairs/sells diesel engines (largest Yanmar dealer on East Coast), transmissions, generators, engine parts, fuel/oil filters, batteries, alternators, propellers. Builds Oldport Launches. Dinghy landings: Elm St. Pier, north side Shipyard breakwater, Inn on Long Wharf, Bowen's Wharf, Ann Street Pier, West Extension St., King Park. Bathhouse: None. Seaman's Institute (847-4260, 7:30-5:30): Heads, Showers ($2), Mariners' Lounge (Free Wi-Fi), Maritime Library, Aloha Café (7:30-2:30), mail hold, washer/dryer, overnight stays, garden & Chapel. Add'l heads at Perrotti Park - dogs welcome.

Notable -- Just off America's Cup Avenue, Oldport's as centrally located on land as in the harbor. For shopping, galleries and restaurants, Bowen's Wharf is a block. Cliff Walk's north end and Easton's beach are a mile hike, or take RIPTA #67, which runs past the museums, mansions and Cliff Walk North and South.

PHOTOS ON DVD: 18

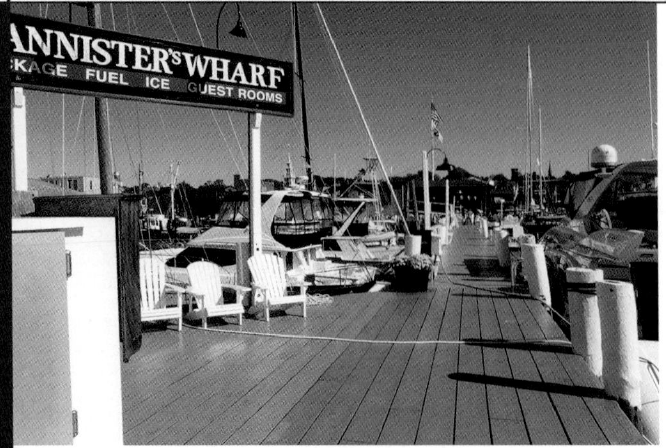

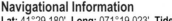

Bannister's Wharf

Bannister's Wharf; Newport, RI 02840

Tel: (401) 846-4556 **VHF: Monitor** Ch. 9 **Talk** Ch. 11
Fax: (401) 846-7732 **Alternate Tel:** (401) 846-4500
Email: bwdocks@aol.com **Web:** www.bannisterswharf.net
Nearest Town: Newport **Tourist Info:** (401) 845-9123

Navigational Information

Lat: 41°29.180' **Long:** 071°19.023' **Tide:** 5 ft. **Current:** n/a **Chart:** 13223
Rep. Depths (*MLW*): Entry 16 ft. **Fuel Dock** 16 ft. **Max Slip/Moor** 16 ft./-
Access: Narragansett Bay to Newport, look for Bannister's Wharf sign

Marina Facilities *(In Season/Off Season)*

Fuel: *Various* - Slip-Side Fueling, Gasoline, Diesel, High-Speed Pumps
Slips: 30 Total, 30 Transient **Max LOA:** 280 ft. **Max Beam:** 34 ft.
Rate *(per ft.)*: **Day** $5.00/Inq.* **Week** Inq. **Month** Inq.
Power: 30 amp $12, **50 amp** $25, **100 amp** $60, **200 amp** n/a
Cable TV: No **Dockside Phone:** Yes
Dock Type: Fixed, Floating, Long Fingers, Short Fingers, Alongside, Wood
Moorings: 0 Total, 0 Transient **Launch:** n/a
Rate: Day n/a **Week** n/a **Month** n/a
Heads: 3 Toilet(s), 3 Shower(s) *(dressing rooms)*, Hair Dryers
Internet: Yes *(Wi-Fi, Free)* **Laundry:** None
Pump-Out: OnCall **Fee:** $15/30gals **Closed Heads:** Yes

Marina Operations

Owner/Manager: Jim McCarthy **Dockmaster:** Same
In-Season: June-Oct, 8am-8pm **Off-Season:** Nov-May, 9am-5pm
After-Hours Arrival: Find a berth and see office in the morning
Reservations: Yes, Required **Credit Cards:** Visa/MC, Dscvr, Amex
Discounts: None
Pets: Welcome **Handicap Access:** No

Marina Services and Boat Supplies

Services - Docking Assistance, Room Service to the Boat, Security *(10pm-5am)*, Trash Pick-Up, Dock Carts, European Voltage **Communication -** Pay Phone, FedEx, DHL, UPS, Express Mail **Supplies - OnSite:** Ice *(Block, Cube)* **Near:** Ships' Store *(Bowen's 849-4999)*, CNG *(Oldport)* **Under 1 mi:** Propane *(Spicer 596-6531)* **1-3 mi:** West Marine *(841-9880)*

Boatyard Services

Nearest Yard: Newport Shipyard (401) 846-6000

Restaurants and Accommodations

OnSite: Restaurant *(The Candy Store & Bistro 849-7778, L $9-34, D $14-44, Brunch $13 or $20)*, *(Black Pearl Patio)*, *(Black Pearl Tavern 846-5264, L $9-20, D $17-30, Commodore Room L&D $22-40)*, *(Clarke Cooke House Porch 849-2900, D $36-59)*, Inn/B&B *(Bannister's Wharf Guest Rooms 846-4500, $75-340, Pets Welcome)* **Near:** Restaurant *(22 Bowen's 841-8884, L $10-24, D $23-53)*, *(Mooring 846-2260, L $9-24, D $9-34)*, *(Red Parrot 847-3800, D $13-29, Kids' $2-6)*, *(Christie's 847-5400, L $8-19, D $9-23)*, *(Fluke 849-7778, D $8-38)*, *(Landing 847-4514, L $9-26, D $17-36)*, Pizzeria *(Via Via)*, Hotel *(Newport 847-9000, $242+)*, Inn/B&B *(Almondy 848-7202, $155-380)*

Recreation and Entertainment

OnSite: Tours *(Classic Yachts: Rum Runner II, Arabella, Madeleine 847-0299 $18-25; Flyer cat 484-2100 $30-35)* **Near:** Playground, Tennis Courts *(Aquidneck Park)*, Video Arcade, Park *(Perotti, Touro)*, Museum *(Newport History 846-0813, free; Sam Whitehorne 847-2448, $6/free; Tennis HOF 846-1203, $11/free)* **Under 1 mi:** Beach *(Easton's)*, Fitness Center *(Pulse 595-8549)*, Hike/Bike Trails *(Cliff Walk 3-5 mi. long)*, Movie Theater *(Jane Pickens 846-5252)*, Video Rental *(Redbox)*, Sightseeing *(Newport Island Train 841-8700 $15/6, Lunch/Dinner Train $37-69; Viking Trolley 847-6921)* **3+ mi:** Golf Course *(Jamestown C.C. 423-9930, 5 mi.)*

Provisioning and General Services

Near: Convenience Store *(JD 842-0545)*, Delicatessen *(Pick Pockets 619-1973)*, Liquor Store *(Spring Street 846-0959)*, Bakery *(Cookie Jar 846-5078)*, Fishmonger *(Aquidneck 846-0106)*, Bank/ATM, Post Office, Protestant Church, Beauty Salon *(Visage 847-1606)* **Under 1 mi:** Market *(Max's 849-8088)*, Supermarket *(Stop & Shop 848-7200)*, Health Food *(A Market 846-8137)*, Wine/Beer *(Bellevue 846-7993)*, Farmers' Market *(Chapel & Memorial 2-6, Wed)*, Catholic Church, Synagogue, Library *(847-8720)*, Dry Cleaners *(Perfect Touch 300-0030)*, Laundry *(Micki's 847-5972 - P/U & Del)*, Pharmacy *(CVS 846-7800)*, Hardware Store *(Ace 849-9442)*, Florist *(Broadway 849-4000)*, Retail Shops *(Long Wharf & Bellevue Malls)*, Copies Etc. *(UPS 848-7600)*

Transportation

OnCall: Water Taxi, Rental Car *(Enterprise)*, Taxi *(Cozy 846-2500)*, Airport Limo *(Rockstar 619-3000)* **Near:** Bikes *(Scooter World 619-1349)*, Local Bus *(Trolley)*, Ferry Service *(Jamestown, B.I.)* **Under 1 mi:** InterCity Bus *(Bonanza, Peter Pan)* **Airport:** TF Green *(27 mi.)*

Medical Services

911 Service **Near:** Optician *(Brown 846-0101)* **Under 1 mi:** Doctor *(Gonzalez 848-2160)*, Dentist *(Sunderland 846-4404)*, Chiropractor *(Newport 847-4224)*, Holistic Services *(Wave Lengths 849-4427)*, Veterinarian *(Newport 849-3401)* **Hospital:** Newport 846-6400 *(1.3 mi)*

Setting -- Historic Bannister's Wharf, a hub of waterfront activity since the 18th century, today offers pleasure craft 30 floating slips and 280 feet of fixed dockage at the end of the ship-shape wharf. A two-story, weathered-shingle building with dark green veranda overlooks the marina - guest rooms above the office and coffee house. Flower boxes adorn a sweet little dockhouse, surrounded by Adirondack-style chairs, that manages the easy-access fuel dock.

Marina Notes -- *Plus 280 ft. fixed pier. 10 of 30 slips 50 ft. Founded 1742 by John Bannister. Quantity discounts on fuel. Most yard services on-call. 100A single-phase. Once home port to Endeavour, Shamrock V, Ticonderoga, & Stars and Stripes. Now Classic yacht tours base here. Boat Show sponsor. Service focused. Docks beautifully maintained. 4 guest rooms & 1 suite on 2nd floor share veranda. Bathhouse: Three recently renovated full baths.

Notable -- One of many wharfs built to support trade between Europe, the Colonies and the West Indies, Bannister's Wharf was always intended as a tie between the upscale commercial and social lives of Newport. The archway that separates marina from wharf is a time machine. Since the late 1800s, this has been a busy marina on an historic street lined with upscale shops, galleries and eclectic eateries - much as it is today. The charming Clarke Cooke House offers several dining options: The Boom Boom Room dance club raises cain below decks; wharf-level Candy Store, a long-time yachtie hangout, opens to the water; the main floor's cozy 18thC.-tavern-like Bistro counterpoints the exquisite, pricey, top-floor trellised Porch (several private rooms available). Next door, Bowen's Wharf berths another 20 retail shops, five galleries, seven restaurants, Aquidneck Lobster & transient yacht services with 490 ft. of dockage (324-4108).

Navigational Information
Lat: 41°29.259' **Long:** 071°19.009' **Tide:** 4 ft. **Current:** n/a **Chart:** 13223
Rep. Depths (*MLW*): Entry 17 ft. **Fuel Dock** n/a **Max Slip/Moor** 8 ft./-
Access: NE Corner of Newport Harbor off Narragansett Bay

Marina Facilities *(In Season/Off Season)*
Fuel: No
Slips: 65 Total, 65 Transient **Max LOA:** 150 ft. **Max Beam:** n/a
Rate *(per ft.)*: **Day** $5.00* **Week** $25 **Month** $600
Power: 30 amp $9, **50 amp** $18, **100 amp** $45, **200 amp** n/a
Cable TV: Yes, Incl. **Dockside Phone:** Yes
Dock Type: Fixed, Floating, Long Fingers, Alongside, Wood
Moorings: 0 Total, 0 Transient **Launch:** n/a
Rate: Day n/a **Week** n/a **Month** n/a
Heads: 8 Toilet(s), 8 Shower(s) *(dressing rooms)*
Internet: Yes *(Wi-Fi, Free)* **Laundry:** 6 Washer(s), 6 Dryer(s)
Pump-Out: OnCall *(474-0543, Ch.9)* **Fee:** $15/25 gals **Closed Heads:** Yes

Marina Operations
Owner/Manager: Ted R Schroeder, CHA **Dockmaster:** Mark Holden
In-Season: Year-Round, 7am-7pm **Off-Season:** n/a
After-Hours Arrival: Call in advance for instructions
Reservations: Yes **Credit Cards:** Visa/MC, Dscvr, Din, Amex
Discounts: None
Pets: Welcome, Dog Walk Area **Handicap Access:** Yes, Heads

Newport Harbor Hotel & Marina

49 America's Cup Avenue; Newport, RI 02840

Tel: (401) 848-3310; (800) 955-2558 **VHF: Monitor** Ch. 9 **Talk** Ch. 9
Fax: (401) 849-6380 **Alternate Tel:** (401) 847-9000
Email: Dockmaster@shanercorp.com **Web:** www.newporthotel.com
Nearest Town: Newport **Tourist Info:** (401) 845-9123

Marina Services and Boat Supplies
Services - Docking Assistance, Concierge, Room Service to the Boat, Boaters' Lounge, Trash Pick-Up, Dock Carts **Communication -** Pay Phone, FedEx, DHL, UPS, Express Mail **Supplies - OnSite:** Ice *(Cube)* **Near:** Ships' Store *(Bowen's Wharf 849-4999)*, CNG *(Oldport 847-9109)* **Under 1 mi:** Propane *(Spicer 596-6531)* **1-3 mi:** West Marine *(841-9880)*

Boatyard Services
Nearest Yard: The Newport Shipyard (401) 846-6000

Restaurants and Accommodations
OnSite: Restaurant *(Pier 49 Seafood 847-9000)*, Hotel *(Newport Harbor 847-9000, $242+)* **Near:** Restaurant *(22 Bowen's 841-8884, L $10-24, D $23-53)*, *(Mooring House 846-2260, D $9-44)*, *(Black Pearl 846-5264, L $8-26.50, D $7.50-29.50)*, *(Barking Crab 846-2722)*, *(Christie's 847-5400, L $8-19, D $9-23)*, *(Fluke 849-7778, D $8-38)*, *(Landing 847-4514, L $9-26, D $17-36)*, Pizzeria *(Lucia 847-6355)*, Hotel *(Bannister's Wharf 846-4500, $125-340)*, *(Newport Bay 849-8600, $199-379)*

Recreation and Entertainment
OnSite: Heated Pool *(Indoor year round)*, Picnic Area, Grills, Fitness Center, Boat Rentals *(Charter America's Cup Yachts 846-9886 - ticketed sails also avail.)* **Near:** Hike/Bike Trails, Fishing Charter *(Double Trouble 508-735-4565)*, Party Boat *(Arabella 849-3033)*, Volleyball, Park *(Perotti)*, Museum *(Newport History 846-0813, Free; Artillery Company 846-8488, Free; Turo Synagogue 847-4794 Guided tours; Newport Art 848-8200)*, Tours *(Classic Cruises 849-5868 incl. Rum Runner, Brandaris, Madeleine; Viking Trolley 847-6921 $24;)* **Under 1 mi:** Tennis Courts *(Nat'l Tennis Club 849-6672)*, Movie Theater *(Jane Pickens 846-5252)*, Video Rental *(Redbox)*, Sightseeing *(Newport Dinner Train 841-8700; Hunter House 847-7516; Exploration Center Aquarium 849-8430)* **1-3 mi:** Beach *(Easton's)*, Cultural Attract *(Newport Playhouse 848-7529)* **3+ mi:** Golf Course *(Newport Nat'l 848-9690, 6.5 mi.)*, Horseback Riding *(Newport Eq. 848-5440, 4 mi.)*

Provisioning and General Services
OnSite: Laundry *(Hotel)* **Near:** Convenience Store *(JD 842-0545)*, Delicatessen *(Pick Pockets 619-1973)*, Liquor Store *(Spring Street 846-0959)*, Bakery *(Cookie Jar 846-5078)*, Fishmonger *(Aquidneck 846-0106)*, Bank/ATM, Post Office, Protestant Church, Beauty Salon *(Martin's 846-7500)* **Under 1 mi:** Market *(Max's 849-8088)*, Supermarket *(Stop & Shop 848-7200)*, Health Food *(A Market 846-8137)*, Wine/Beer *(Newport Cellar 619-3966)*, Farmers' Market *(Wed 2-6pm, Chapel & Memorial)*, Catholic Church, Synagogue, Library *(847-8720)*, Pharmacy *(CVS 846-7800)*, Hardware Store *(Newport Ace 849-9442)*, Florist *(Little Flower 835-5514)*, Retail Shops *(Long Wharf & Bellevue Malls)*

Transportation
OnCall: Rental Car *(Enterprise 849-3939)*, Taxi *(Cozy 846-2500)*, Airport Limo *(Rockstar 619-3000)* **Near:** Bikes *(Scooter World 619-1349)*, Local Bus *(RIPTA Trolley)*, InterCity Bus *(Bonanza, Peter Pan)*, Ferry Service *(Jamestown)* **3+ mi:** Rail *(Kingston, 19 mi.)* **Airport:** TF Green *(27 mi.)*

Medical Services
911 Service **Under 1 mi:** Doctor *(Gonzalez 848-2160)*, Dentist *(Sunderland 846-4404)*, Chiropractor *(Newport 847-4224)*, Optician *(Brown 846-0101)*, Veterinarian *(Newport 849-3401)* **Hospital:** Newport 846-6400 *(1.1 mi.)*

Setting -- NHHM's three dockage areas flow from the expansive front lawn of the 133-room, four-story hotel. Historic yachts, 12-meter racers, and just well-loved pretty boats are eye candy for the hotel guests - fun by day but really impressive when they glow at night. The expected white Adirondack-style lawn chairs line the boardwalk that runs the width of the marina. At the edge of the downtown district, shopping and attractions are right across or down the street.

Marina Notes -- *Holidays, Tall Ships, Jazz/Folk Fests: $5.50/ft. Owned/operated by Shaner Hotel Group. Built 1971, acquired in 1996. Deposit required with reservation. Newly renovated docks with Sullivan Flotation Systems and well-placed pedestals. Phones/data ports on some pedestals (inquire if important). Marina guests have full resort privileges, indoor pool, sauna, heads & showers adjacent to the pool. Onsite gated parking for marina guests - $14/night. Open all year with full services. Bathhouse: Heads & showers are richly decorated with homestyle fixtures. Tiled with wallpapered walls.

Notable -- Home to the legendary America's Cup Yachts; these six 12-meter yachts are available for charter and, occasionally for ticketed sails. For a quieter ride, a small fleet of historic power and sail yachts tour the harbor from NHHM and adjacent Bowen's Wharf. Onsite Pier 49 Restaurant offers fine dining indoors or outside overlooking the docks under bright-blue umbrellas. A ferry to Jamestown via Ft. Adams and Rose Island Light leaves from Bowen's Wharf - with two-dozen shops and restaurants. Past Trinity Church, walk the Historic Hill neighborhood starting at the Newport History Museum in Brick Market Place (or take a tour 841-8770 $12/5). Just beyond Perotti Park, a lean, green stretch that berths the Harbormaster's office is the tourism and transportation center.

PHOTOS ON DVD: 22

Newport Shipyard

Newport Shipyard

1 Washington Street; Newport, RI 02840

Tel: (401) 846-6002 **VHF: Monitor** Ch. 9 **Talk** Ch. 8
Fax: (401) 846-6003 **Alternate Tel:** (401) 846-6000
Email: dockoffice@newportshipyard.com **Web:** www.newportshipyard.com
Nearest Town: Newport **Tourist Info:** (401) 845-9123

Navigational Information

Lat: 41°29.420' **Long:** 071°19.365' **Tide:** 4 ft. **Current:** n/a **Chart:** 13223
Rep. Depths (*MLW*): Entry 21 ft. **Fuel Dock** n/a **Max Slip/Moor** 21 ft./-
Access: Narragansett Bay, turn right before bridge in Newport Harbor

Marina Facilities *(In Season/Off Season)*

Fuel: *Casey's Truck/Barge* - Slip-Side Fueling, Gasoline, Diesel, High-Speed I
Slips: 55 Total, 55 Transient **Max LOA:** 300 ft. **Max Beam:** n/a
Rate *(per ft.)*: **Day** $5.00/$2* **Week** n/a **Month** $135/60.
Power: 30 amp $20**, **50 amp** $30, **100 amp** $60, **200 amp** n/a
Cable TV: Yes, Free **Dockside Phone:** Yes, $10
Dock Type: Floating, Long Fingers, Alongside, Wood
Moorings: 0 Total, 0 Transient **Launch:** n/a
Rate: Day n/a **Week** n/a **Month** n/a
Heads: 8 Toilet(s), 5 Shower(s)
Internet: Yes *(WiFi & Lounge, Free)* **Laundry:** 2 Washer(s), 2 Dryer(s)
Pump-Out: OnCall *(Ch. 9, 474-0543)* **Fee:** $15/25 gals **Closed Heads:** Yes

Marina Operations

Owner/Manager: Eli L. Dana **Dockmaster:** Same
In-Season: May-Oct, 7am-8pm **Off-Season:** Oct-May, 9am-5pm
After-Hours Arrival: Call security on Ch.9
Reservations: Yes, Preferred **Credit Cards:** Visa/MC, Dscvr, Amex
Discounts: None
Pets: Welcome, Dog Walk Area **Handicap Access:** Yes, Heads, Docks

Marina Services and Boat Supplies

Services - Docking Assistance, Concierge, Crew Lounge, Security *(24 Hrs., Gated entrance)*, Dock Carts, 3 Phase, European Voltage **Communication -** Mail & Package Hold, Fax in/out *(Free)*, FedEx, DHL, UPS, Express Mail **Supplies - OnSite:** Ice *(Block, Cube)*, Ships' Store *(8am-5pm)* **Under 1 mi:** Propane *(Newport 847-6878; U-Haul 847-3219)*, CNG *(Oldport)* **1-3 mi:** West Marine *(841-9880)*, Bait/Tackle *(Saltwater Edge 842-0062)*

Boatyard Services

OnSite: Travelift *(330T, 100T, 70T)*, Forklift, Crane *(50T)*, Engine mechanic *(gas, diesel)*, Electrical Repairs, Electronic Sales, Electronics Repairs, Hull Repairs, Rigger, Sail Loft, Canvas Work, Divers, Bottom Cleaning, Brightwork, Air Conditioning, Refrigeration, Propeller Repairs, Woodworking, Inflatable Repairs, Yacht Interiors, Metal Fabrication, Painting, Awlgrip, Total Refits **Dealer for:** Hinckley, Bertram, Brackshoff. **Yard Rates:** $85/hr., Haul & Launch $20-45/ft. *(blocking $5-7/ft.)*, Power Wash $5/ft. **Storage:** On-Land Out $70-85/ft; In $195/ft.

Restaurants and Accommodations

OnSite: Lite Fare *(Belle's B $3.50-8, L $3.50-18)* **Near:** Restaurant *(Barking Crab 846-2722), (Rhumbline 849-3999)*, Lite Fare *(Panera Bread 324-6800), (Mudville Pub 619-1100), (Sushi Go 849-5155, $7-14.50)*, Pizzeria *(Lucia 847-6355)*, Hotel *(Marriott 849-1000, $150-600), (Newport Harbor 849-9000, $140-650), (Capt. Simeon Potter 848-0443)*, Inn/B&B *(Sarah Kendall House 846-3979, $175-350)* **Under 1 mi:** Restaurant *(Brick Alley Pub 849-6334, L $12-22, D $18-28), (22 Bowen's 841-8884, L $10-24, D $23-53), (Black Pearl 846-5264, L $8-26, D $8-30), (Clarke Cooke 849-2900, L $10-37, D $19-39), (Fluke 849-7778, D $8-38)*

Recreation and Entertainment

OnSite: Picnic Area, Grills, Fitness Center **Near:** Boat Rentals *(Adventure Sports 849-4820)*, Park *(Storer, Pergotti, Ballfield)*, Museum *(Newport History 846-0813, Free)*, Tours *(Historic 855-1942; Secret Garden 847-0514; Viking 847-6921)*, Sightseeing *(Newport Dinner Train 841-8700; Hunter House 847-7516)* **Under 1 mi:** Dive Shop *(Bubbles 847-4985)*, Tennis Courts *(Nat'l Tennis 849-6672 Grass Courts)* **3+ mi:** Golf Course *(Newport Nat'l 846-1489, 5 mi)*

Provisioning and General Services

OnSite: Bank/ATM, Copies Etc. **Near:** Bakery *(Panera 324-6800)*, Protestant Church **Under 1 mi:** Convenience Store *(JD 842-0545)*, Supermarket *(Stop & Shop 848-7200)*, Delicatessen *(Pick Pockets 619-1973)*, Health Food *(A Market 846-8137)*, Wine/Beer *(Mitchell's 848-5770)*, Liquor Store *(Bucci's 847-0035)*, Farmers' Market *(Wed 2-6pm, Chapel & Memorial)*, Post Office, Catholic Church, Synagogue, Library, Dry Cleaners *(Perfect 300-0030)*, Laundry *(DN 847-6800)*, Pharmacy *(CVS 846-7800)*, Hardware Store *(Ace 849-9442)*

Transportation

OnCall: Water Taxi *(Oldport)*, Rental Car *(Enterprise)*, Taxi *(Cozy 846-2500)*, Airport Limo *(Posh 842-0005)* **Near:** Local Bus *(Trolley)*, InterCity Bus, Ferry Service **Airport:** TF Green *(27 mi.)*

Medical Services

911 Service **Near:** Dentist *(Sunderland 846-4404)* **Under 1 mi:** Doctor *(Gonzalez 848-2160)*, Chiropractor *(Newport 847-4224)*, Veterinarian *(Newport 849-3401)* **Hospital:** Newport 846-6400 *(1 mi)*

Setting -- Tucked up at the harbor head across from Goat Island, south of the bridge, one of the East Coast's most serious, state-of-the-art megayacht yards also manages a first-class, all-transient marina. Thoughtful planning separates the working yard from the recreational floating docks - both carefully maintained. Fronting the large, main building, white tents and market umbrellas top picnic tables that sit on a plus-size checkerboard that runs along the tarmac.

Marina Notes -- *May 15-Sep $5/ft./nt., $135/ft./mo. Apri 15-May 14 & Oct $3.50/ft./nt, $100/ft./mo. Jan 4-Apr 14 & Nov-Dec $2/ft./nt., $60/ft./mo. Touch 'n Go $2.50/ft (max 4 hrs). **20A $12/nt., 30A $20, 50A $30, 100A $60, 100A, 3-phase $105. Hardwires up to 480 volts 3 phase. Generators for Euro power. Fuel delivery - 100-500 gals by truck, 500+ gals by barge. 20 X 40 ft. Storage Container rentals. Yard hours: 7:30am-4pm. Established 1850s, completely rebuilt 2002. Yard concentrates on yachts 80-300 ft. Marina-wide Wi-Fi, 2 computers/data ports, comp domestic faxes, printing, conf. room in lounge. Inviting, nicely equipped gym with Wii Fit. 18 yacht-service companies onsite. Well-supplied & merchandised Ships Store. Belle's Cafe for breakfast & lunch, inside, al fresco & to go. Fabulous 25-page guide to yacht services & all of Newport. Bathhouse: Sleekly simple group heads, fiberglass shower stalls, glass doors.

Notable -- Walk two blocks north to Hunter House, centerpiece of the architecturally significant Point District, where colonial and Victorian homes line narrow streets. Past the nearby Wyndham Resort and Marriott (with a Day Spa), the information/ transportation hub's intercity buses and trolleys take you anywhere - board 67 to the mansions or either end of Cliff Walk. From Perotti Park, the ferry goes to Rose Light, Ft. Adams and The Museum of Yachting (847-1018).

PHOTOS ON DVD: 25

Navigational Information
Lat: 41°29.226' **Long:** 071°19.592' **Tide:** 4 ft. **Current:** .3 kt. **Chart:** 13223
Rep. Depths (*MLW*): Entry 19 ft. **Fuel Dock** 17 ft. **Max Slip/Moor** 17 ft./-
Access: Narragansett Bay; E Shore of Goat Island in Newport Harbor

Marina Facilities *(In Season/Off Season)*
Fuel: Gasoline, Diesel, High-Speed Pumps
Slips: 175 Total, 20 Transient **Max LOA:** 250 ft. **Max Beam:** 25 ft.
Rate *(per ft.)*: **Day** $4.50* **Week** n/a **Month** $105
Power: 30 amp $15, **50 amp** $30, **100 amp** $50, **200 amp** n/a
Cable TV: Yes, $9 **Dockside Phone:** No
Dock Type: Fixed, Floating, Long Fingers, Pilings, Alongside, Wood
Moorings: 0 Total, 0 Transient **Launch:** n/a, Dinghy Dock
Rate: Day n/a **Week** n/a **Month** n/a
Heads: 6 Toilet(s), 6 Shower(s)
Internet: Yes *(Wi-Fi, Free)* **Laundry:** 3 Washer(s), 3 Dryer(s)
Pump-Out: Self Service **Fee:** $5 **Closed Heads:** Yes

Marina Operations
Owner/Manager: Mike Sweeney **Dockmaster:** Same
In-Season: May 15-Oct, 8am-Dusk **Off-Season:** Nov-May15, 8am-4pm**
After-Hours Arrival: Call ahead
Reservations: Yes **Credit Cards:** Visa/MC, Amex
Discounts: Safe/Sea **Dockage:** 25% **Fuel:** n/a **Repair:** n/a
Pets: Welcome, Dog Walk Area **Handicap Access:** No

Goat Island Marina

5 Marina Plaza; Goat Island, RI 02840

Tel: (401) 849-5655 **VHF: Monitor** Ch. 9 **Talk** Ch. 11
Fax: (401) 848-7144 **Alternate Tel:** (401) 849-1212
Email: boat@newportexperience.com **Web:** www.newportexperience.com
Nearest Town: Newport *(0.5 mi.)* **Tourist Info:** (401) 845-9123

Marina Services and Boat Supplies
Services - Docking Assistance, Concierge, Boaters' Lounge, Security *(24 Hrs., Gated Entrance)*, Trash Pick-Up, Dock Carts, 3 Phase **Communication -** Pay Phone, FedEx, DHL, UPS, Express Mail **Supplies - OnSite:** Ice *(Block, Cube)*, Ships' Store **Under 1 mi:** Propane *(Spicer 596-6531)*, CNG *(Oldport 847-9109)* **1-3 mi:** West Marine *(841-9880)*

Boatyard Services
Nearest Yard: Newport Shipyard 0.25 mi. (401) 846-6000

Restaurants and Accommodations
OnSite: Restaurant *(Marina Cafe & Pub 849-0003, L $8-18, D $8-28, 11:30am-10pm)*, *(Schooner Aurora 849-6683, Lobster Boil & 1.5-hr. sail $37/20, Wed, Thur, Sun)* **Near:** Restaurant *(Pineapples on the Bay 851-1234, L&D $10-21, Kids $7-8, Seasonal, Al Fresco. Raw Bar, Entertainment Fri-Mon)*, *(Windward 851-3325, B $5-15, L $10-22, D $15-35)*, Lite Fare *(Five33 Lounge & The Galley Coffee Bar Hyatt)*, Hotel *(Hyatt Regency 851-1234, $200-480, on Goat Island)* **Under 1 mi:** Restaurant *(Brick Alley 849-6334, L $12-22, D $11-28)*, *(22 Bowen's 841-8884, L $10-24, D $23-53)*, *(Rhumbline 849-3999)*, Pizzeria *(Ronzio 846-9300, Del.)*

Recreation and Entertainment
OnSite: Picnic Area, Playground, Fishing Charter *(Quest 339-8035)* **Near:** Heated Pool *(at Hyatt)*, Beach, Tennis Courts *(Hyatt)*, Golf Course *(Jamestown GC 423-9930)*, Fitness Center *(Hyatt StayFit, pool side)* **Under 1 mi:** Boat Rentals *(Adventure Sports 849-4820)*, Park *(Storer; Pergotti)*, Museum *(Newport History & Historic Hill 846-0813, Free; Artillery Co. 846-8488; Tennis HOF 846-1203, $11/free 2 mi.)*, Tours *(Historic 855-1942; Secret Garden 847-0514; Viking 847-6921)*, Sightseeing *(Dinner Train 841-8700; Hunter House 847-7516)* **1-3 mi:** Movie Theater *(Jane Pickens 846-5252)*, Cultural Attract *(Firehouse 849-3473; The Mansions 847-1000)*

Provisioning and General Services
OnSite: Wine/Beer, Liquor Store **Near:** Beauty Salon *(Hyatt Stillwater)*, Newsstand **Under 1 mi:** Convenience Store *(7-Eleven 846-4501)*, Bakery *(Panera 324-6800)*, Fishmonger *(Aquidneck 846-0106)*, Bank/ATM, Protestant Church, Synagogue, Barber Shop, Dry Cleaners *(Perfect Touch 300-0030)* **1-3 mi:** Supermarket *(Stop & Shop 848-7200)*, Delicatessen *(Portabella 847-8200)*, Health Food *(Harvest Nat 846-8137)*, Farmers' Market *(Memorial & Chapel 2-6, Wed, 848-0099)*, Post Office, Catholic Church, Library *(847-8720)*, Laundry *(Micki's 847-5972 - P/U)*, Pharmacy *(CVS 846-7800)*, Hardware Store *(Newport Ace 849-9442)*, Florist *(Little Flower 835-5514)*, Retail Shops *(Long Wharf Mall)*, Buying Club *(BJ's 848-9242)*, Copies Etc. *(PDQ 619-2188)*

Transportation
OnSite: Bikes, Water Taxi *(Bowen's Wharf)*, Ferry Service *(Jamestown, Ft. Adams 423-9900)* **OnCall:** Rental Car *(Enterprise 849-3939)*, Taxi *(Cozy 846-2500)* **Under 1 mi:** Local Bus, InterCity Bus *(Peter Pan, Bonanza)* **3+ mi:** Rail *(Amtrak, 20 mi.)* **Airport:** TF Green *(27 mi.)*

Medical Services
911 Service **Near:** Holistic Services *(Hyatt Stillwater Spa 851-3225)* **Under 1 mi:** Dentist *(Sunderland 846-4404)*, Optician *(Brown 846-0101)* **1-3 mi:** Doctor *(Gonzalez 848-2160)*, Chiropractor *(Newport 847-4224)*, Veterinarian *(Newport 849-3401)* **Hospital:** Newport 846-6400 *(1.7 mi.)*

Setting -- Isolated on the harbor's west side, away from Newport's summer hubbub, upscale, gated docks deliver spectacular skyline views. Very long, fixed piers extend at an angle to accommodate larger side-tie yachts while floating slips work for smaller boats. On the upland, white tables and chairs dot the bulkhead in front of the two-story "L-shaped" concrete office, punctuated with blue-and-white striped awnings. Adjacent weathered-shingled Marina Cafe features an outside fireplace circle. Across the narrow island, the dramatic Belle Mer event venue looks out over the bay. The Hyatt is a few minutes walk.

Marina Notes -- *Under 80 ft $4.50/ft., over 80 ft. $5.50/ft. Holiday rates $0.50/ft. higher (Jun 30-Jul 8, Sep 1-3, Sep 14-16). 30 ft. min. **Closed week-ends off-season. Optional $9/nt. amenity package - satellite TV, Wi-Fi & 10% restaurant disc. Reserve: 50% deposit & two nt. stay, three on hols. req. (Cancel 7+ days out, refund 85% of deposit or $50.) Striped tent May-Oct (weddings, events, rendezvous). Parking. 10-minute water shuttle to Newport's Bowen's Wharf every half hour. Newport Sailing School (848-2266). Hyatt's Stillwater Spa health club & indoor/outdoor pools ($20/day). Bathhouse: Three full bathrooms.

Notable -- Marina Grille has both a cozy, tableclothed dining room and canopied patio overlooking the Harbor. Longwood's Belle Mer offers six exquisite function spaces totalling 14,000 square feet on six acres at the edge of the bay (Cruise committees take note). Goat Island's diverse history belies the tranquility of its current incarnation. In 1702, Fort Anne was the first of five that protected Newport Harbor. Later pirates were captured, hanged and 26 buried here. In the 1900s, all torpedos for both World Wars were manufactured on G.I.. Still active, Goat Island Light, first built on the site of the Hyatt in 1837, welcomes visitors.

PHOTOS ON DVD: 20

18. RI – Narragansett Bay – East Passage

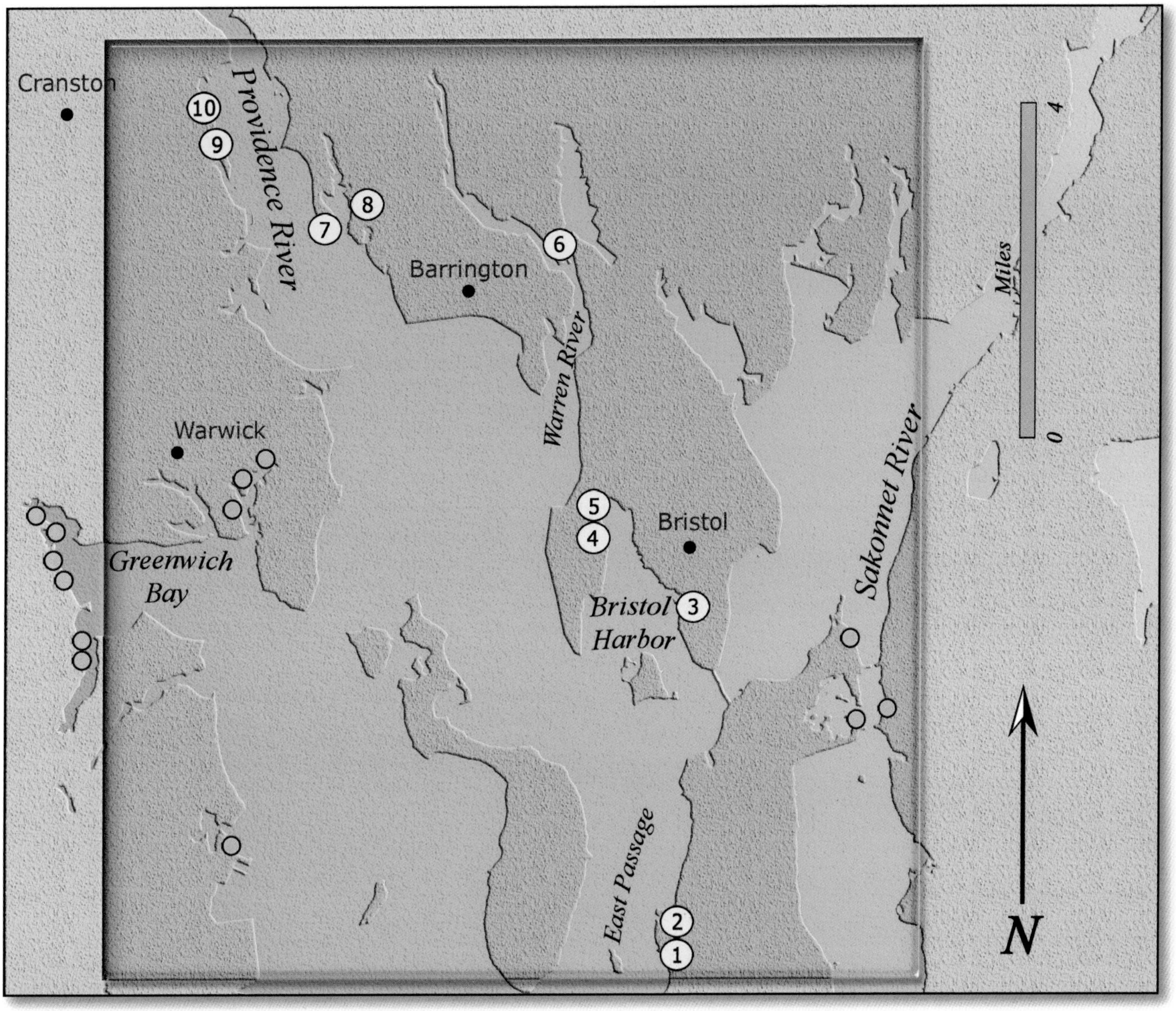

MAP	MARINA	HARBOR	PAGE
1	**Hinckley Yacht Services**	*East Passage*	334
2	**New England Boatworks**	*East Passage*	335
3	**Herreshoff South Wharf**	*Bristol Harbor*	336
4	**Bristol Yacht Club**	*Bristol Harbor*	337
5	**Bristol Marine Co.**	*Bristol Harbor*	338
6	**Barrington Yacht Club**	*Warren River*	339
7	**Bullock Cove Marine**	*Bullock Cove*	340
8	**Brewer Cove Haven Marina**	*Bullock Cove*	341
9	**Rhode Island Yacht Club**	*Providence River*	342
10	**Port Edgewood Marina**	*Providence River*	343

RATINGS: 1-5 for Marina Facilities & Amenities,  1-2 for Boatyard Services,  1-2 for MegaYacht Facilities,  for Something Special.

SERVICES:  for CCM – Certified Clean Marina,  for Pump-Out,  for Internet, 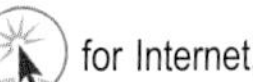  for Fuel, for Restaurant,  for Provisioning nearby,  for Catamaran-friendly,  for SportFish Charter,  for Pool/Beach, and  for Golf within a mile. *For an explanation of ACC's Ratings, see page 8.*

Hinckley Yacht Services

One Little Harbor Landing; Portsmouth, RI 02871

Tel: (401) 683-7100 **VHF: Monitor** Ch. 9 **Talk** n/a
Fax: (401) 683-7118 **Alternate Tel:** n/a
Email: jkerr@hinckleyyachts.com **Web:** www.hinckleyyachtservices.com
Nearest Town: Portsmouth *(1 mi.)* **Tourist Info:** (401) 683-0888

Navigational Information

Lat: 41°35.090' **Long:** 071°17.225' **Tide:** 4 ft. **Current:** n/a **Chart:** 13221
Rep. Depths (*MLW*): Entry 20 ft. **Fuel Dock** 15 ft. **Max Slip/Moor** 35 ft./-
Access: East Passage, 6 miles north of Newport Bridge in Melville

Marina Facilities *(In Season/Off Season)*

Fuel: Gasoline, Diesel, High-Speed Pumps, On Call Delivery
Slips: 100 Total, 50 Transient **Max LOA:** 140 ft. **Max Beam:** 30 ft.
Rate *(per ft.)*: **Day** $1.25* **Week** $30 **Month** $65
Power: 30 amp Incl., **50 amp** Incl., **100 amp** Mtr., **200 amp** n/a
Cable TV: No **Dockside Phone:** No
Dock Type: Floating, Long Fingers, Pilings, Alongside, Concrete, Wood
Moorings: 0 Total, 0 Transient **Launch:** Yes (Incl.), Dinghy Dock
Rate: Day n/a **Week** n/a **Month** n/a
Heads: 2 Toilet(s), 2 Shower(s)
Internet: Yes *(Wi-Fi, Free)* **Laundry:** 2 Washer(s), 2 Dryer(s)
Pump-Out: OnSite, Full Service **Fee:** $5 **Closed Heads:** Yes

Marina Operations

Owner/Manager: James Kerr **Dockmaster:** Same
In-Season: Year-Round, 8am-5pm **Off-Season:** n/a
After-Hours Arrival: Call for security clearance
Reservations: Yes, Preferred **Credit Cards:** Visa/MC, Amex
Discounts: None
Pets: Welcome, Dog Walk Area **Handicap Access:** Yes, Heads

Marina Services and Boat Supplies

Services - Docking Assistance, Concierge, Crew Lounge, Security, Trash Pick-Up, Dock Carts, 3 Phase **Communication -** Pay Phone, FedEx, DHL, UPS, Express Mail *(Sat Del)* **Supplies - OnSite:** Ice *(Block, Cube)*, Ships' Store, Propane **3+ mi:** West Marine *(841-9880, 6 mi.)*

Boatyard Services

OnSite: Travelift *(35 & 160T, 17 ft. draft)*, Forklift, Crane *(18T)*, Hydraulic Trailer *(35T)*, Engine mechanic *(diesel)*, Electrical Repairs, Electronic Sales, Electronics Repairs, Hull Repairs, Rigger, Sail Loft, Canvas Work, Divers, Bottom Cleaning, Brightwork, Air Conditioning, Refrigeration, Compound, Wash & Wax, Interior Cleaning, Propeller Repairs, Woodworking, Upholstery, Yacht Interiors, Metal Fabrication, Painting, Awlgrip, Total Refits **Dealer for:** Hinckley Yachts. **Member:** ABBRA - 4 Certified Tech(s), ABYC - 4 Certified Tech(s) **Yard Rates:** $58-110/hr., Haul & Launch $11-$21/ft. *(blocking incl.)*, Power Wash $2.50-4.50/ft., Bottom Paint $75/hr. **Storage:** On-Land Outside $55/ft. Inside $150/ft. Heated $185/ft.

Restaurants and Accommodations

Near: Restaurant *(Melville Grille 683-4400, L $5-19, D $10-$30, at N.E. Boatworks, 11:30-3pm, Mon-Wed, 'til 8pm Wed-Sat)* **Under 1 mi:** Lite Fare *(Cindy's Cafe 683-5134, B $4-8, L $4-8, 7am-3pm, Yacht Deliveries by 8:30am, 7 days)*, Pizzeria *(West Main 683-1492, Del.)* **1-3 mi:** Restaurant *(Valley Inn 847-9871)*, *(Chris's Diner 683-9814)*, Lite Fare *(Subway)*, *(Custom Coffee House 682-2600, 8am-6pm)* **3+ mi:** Restaurant *(Rocco's 682-1777, 3.2 mi., $9-15)*, Lite Fare *(Food Works 683-4664, 3.2 mi., B&L)*, Motel *(Founders Brook 683-1244, 5 mi.)*, Hotel *(Courtyard 849-8000, $100-140, 5 mi.)*, Inn/B&B *(Shamrock Farm 841-1240, $150-225, 3.5 mi.)*

Recreation and Entertainment

1-3 mi: Fitness Center *(Peak 683-6033)*, Horseback Riding *(Stonegate Farm 683-2776)*, Park *(Heritage)*, Sightseeing *(Green Animals Topiary Gardens 863-1267, $9)* **3+ mi:** Golf Course *(Green Valley 847-9543, 4 mi.)*, Movie Theater *(SSC Holiday 847-3001, 6 mi.)*, Museum *(Prescott Farm 847-6230; Newport Restoration 324-6158, 3.2 mi.)*

Provisioning and General Services

OnCall: Dry Cleaners *(Fernanda's 683-0107, Del.)*, Laundry *(West Main 847-7410, Del.)* **Under 1 mi:** Bakery *(Dunkin Donuts)* **1-3 mi:** Liquor Store *(Ferreira's 683-9598)*, Green Grocer *(De Castro 683-4688)*, Catholic Church, Protestant Church, Beauty Salon *(All About You 683-4443)*, Bookstore *(Journal 683-1955)* **3+ mi:** Supermarket *(Super Stop & Shop 849-5510, 4.5 mi.)*, Farmers' Market *(Aquidneck Middletown, Sat 9am-1pm, 848-0099, 5.5 mi.)*, Post Office *(683-6803, 5 mi.)*, Library *(683-9457, 3.5 mi.)*, Pharmacy *(CVS 682-2098, 3.5 mi.)*, Hardware Store *(Handren's 293-5290, 4 mi.)*

Transportation

OnSite: Courtesy Car/Van *(provisioning/airport)* **OnCall:** Rental Car *(Enterprise 849-3939)*, Taxi *(Orange 841-0030)*, Airport Limo *(Leisure 682-2683)* **Under 1 mi:** Local Bus *(RIPTA #60)* **Airport:** TF Greene *(36 mi.)*

Medical Services

911 Service **1-3 mi:** Dentist *(Aquidneck 683-5990)*, Chiropractor *(Marsh 683-1941)*, Optician *(SpaVana 293-0920)* **3+ mi:** Doctor *(Linden Tree 683-4817, 3.2 mi.)* **Hospital:** Newport 846-6400 *(7 mi.)*

PHOTOS ON DVD: 23

Setting -- Neatly guarded by a large and effective wave attenuator, the marina's 100 slips and 600 feet of side-tie dockage berth some of the world's most beautiful vessels. On the upland, multi-story worksheds and out buildings dominate a minimally landscaped 14-acre yard - it's all about the boat.

Marina Notes -- *Plus 600 ft. pier with 35 ft. draft. Hinckley marinas and service yards extend from Maine to Florida. Little Harbor Marine acquired by The Hinckley Co. in 2001. Docks - mix of older, well-maintained plywood with non-skid surface and newer vinyl docks with long fingers. First-class, full-service boatyard. Lighthouse pedestals. 100A single & 3-phase. Complete array of onsite marina suppliers and services, including yacht designers, brokers, sailing school and yacht charters. Specializes in complete re-fits. Reciprocity agreement with reduced rates for seasonal members of other Hinckley marinas. 600 ft. with 35' draft. 113,000 sq ft shop space. State-of-the-art paint facility for up to150 ft. 113,000 sq ft indoor storage, 5-acres outside. Year-round operation with dockhands/staff on duty 7 days. Bathhouse: Located in main office complex, minimal decor with simple tile floors - but very clean and comfortable.

Notable -- Originally designed by Ted Hood to "accommodate and improve the lives of cruising boaters," the complex has been a key stop for some famous yachts. Mellville Grille (11:30-3pm, Mon-Wed, 'til 8pm Wed-Sat) is a 7-minute walk at E.P.Y.C. Green Animals, a topiary garden with over 80 sculpted trees, a Victoriana collection, plant shop and a picnic grove, is within three miles. A mile away, Cindy's Cafe serves breakfast and lunch plus caters prepared food to yachts - offerings include Soup $30-40/gal, Sandwiches $6/pp, Roast Chicken $12, Dinners $5-10, 10-person min. (after hours 848-7849, Cell 683-8444).

Navigational Information
Lat: 41°35.400' **Long:** 071°17.010' **Tide:** 4 ft. **Current:** n/a **Chart:** 13223
Rep. Depths (*MLW*): Entry 15 ft. **Fuel Dock** 15 ft. **Max Slip/Moor** 15 ft./-
Access: 6 mi. north of Newport Bridge; Between Coggeshall Point & Hinckley

Marina Facilities *(In Season/Off Season)*
Fuel: *ValvTect* - Gasoline, Diesel
Slips: 360 Total, 30 Transient **Max LOA:** 150 ft. **Max Beam:** 22 ft.
Rate *(per ft.)*: **Day** $3.75/$1.90* **Week** $19 **Month** $55
Power: 30 amp Incl., **50 amp** Incl., **100 amp** Incl., **200 amp** n/a
Cable TV: No **Dockside Phone:** No
Dock Type: Floating, Long Fingers, Pilings, Alongside, Wood
Moorings: 0 Total, 0 Transient **Launch:** n/a
Rate: Day n/a **Week** n/a **Month** n/a
Heads: 8 Toilet(s), 8 Shower(s) *(dressing rooms)*, Book Exchange
Internet: Yes *(WiFi, Sub)* **Laundry:** 3 Washer(s), 3 Dryer(s)
Pump-Out: OnSite, Full Service, 1 Central **Fee:** $5 **Closed Heads:** Yes

Marina Operations
Owner/Manager: Stan Piszcz III **Dockmaster:** Same
In-Season: MemDay-LabDay, 7:30-6:30 **Off-Season:** Sep-May, 8:30-3:30
After-Hours Arrival: Call ahead for instructions
Reservations: Yes, Recommended **Credit Cards:** Visa/MC, Amex
Discounts: None
Pets: Welcome, Dog Walk Area **Handicap Access:** Yes, Heads, Docks

New England Boatworks

1 Lagoon Road; Portsmouth, RI 02871

Tel: (401) 683-4000 **VHF: Monitor** Ch. 9 **Talk** n/a
Fax: (401) 683-6774 **Alternate Tel:** n/a
Email: information@neboatworks.com **Web:** www.neboatworks.com
Nearest Town: Portsmouth *(1 mi.)* **Tourist Info:** (401) 683-0888

Marina Services and Boat Supplies
Services - Docking Assistance, Security *(24 Hrs., Gated/Guards)*, Trash Pick-Up, Dock Carts **Communication -** Pay Phone, FedEx, UPS **Supplies - OnSite:** Ice *(Block, Cube)*, Ships' Store *(683-0457)*, Propane, CNG **3+ mi:** West Marine *(841-9880, 6 mi.)*

Boatyard Services
OnSite: Travelift *(88T/50T)*, Forklift, Crane, Hydraulic Trailer, Engine mechanic *(gas, diesel)*, Electrical Repairs, Electronic Sales, Electronics Repairs, Hull Repairs, Rigger, Canvas Work, Bottom Cleaning, Brightwork, Air Conditioning, Refrigeration, Compound, Wash & Wax, Propeller Repairs, Woodworking, Inflatable Repairs, Life Raft Service, Metal Fabrication, Painting, Awlgrip, Total Refits, Yacht Building **Member:** ABBRA - 3 Certified Tech(s), ABYC - 3 Certified Tech(s) **Yard Rates:** $77/hr., Haul & Launch $14/ft. *(blocking incl.)*, Power Wash Incl., Bottom Paint T/M **Storage:** In-Water $31/ft., On-Land $42/ft.

Restaurants and Accommodations
OnSite: Restaurant *(Melville Grille 683-4400, L $5-9, D $10-30, 11:30-3pm, Mon-Wed, 'til 8pm Wed-Sat)* **Under 1 mi:** Lite Fare *(Cindy's Cafe 683-5134, B&L $4-8, 7-3, 7 days. After 3, call catering)*, *(Cindy's Catering 848-7849, Cell 683-8444. Delivers quantity Soups, Sandwiches $6/pp, Dinner entrees $5-10/pp to yachts.)*, Pizzeria *(West Main 683-1492, Del.)* **1-3 mi:** Restaurant *(Valley Inn 847-9871)*, *(Chris's 683-9814)*, Lite Fare *(Subway)*, *(Custom Coffee 682-2600, 8-6)* **3+ mi:** Restaurant *(Rocco's 682-1777, 3.5 mi., L&D $9-15)*, Lite Fare *(Foodworks 683-4664, 3 mi., B&L)*, Motel *(Founders Brook 683-1244, $69-159, 5 mi.)*, Hotel *(Courtyard 849-8000, $100-140, 5 mi.)*, Inn/B&B *(Shamrock Farm 851-1240, $150-225, 4 mi.)*

Recreation and Entertainment
OnSite: Heated Pool, Picnic Area, Grills, Playground, Volleyball **1-3 mi:** Fitness Center *(Peak 683-6033)*, Horseback Riding *(Stonegate Farm 683-2776)*, Video Rental *(Blockbuster Express)*, Park *(Heritage)* **3+ mi:** Golf Course *(Green Valley 847-9543, 4 mi.)*, Movie Theater *(SSC Holiday 847-3001, 6 mi.)*, Museum *(Newport Restoration's Prescott Farm 489-7300, 3.2 mi.)*, Sightseeing *(Green Animals Topiary Gardens 683-1267, 3.3 mi.)*

Provisioning and General Services
OnCall: Dry Cleaners *(Fernanda's 683-0107)*, Laundry *(West Main 847-7410)* **1-3 mi:** Liquor Store *(Ferreira's 683-9598)*, Green Grocer *(De Castro 683-4688)*, Bank/ATM, Catholic Church, Protestant Church, Beauty Salon *(All About You 683-4443)*, Bookstore *(Journal 683-1955)* **3+ mi:** Supermarket *(Stop & Shop 849-5510, 4.5 mi.)*, Farmers' Market *(Middletown 848-0099 Sat 9am-1pm, 5.5 mi.)*, Post Office *(5.5 mi.)*, Library *(Portsmouth 683-9457, 4 mi.)*, Pharmacy *(Rite Aid 683-3062, 3.5 mi.)*, Hardware Store *(Handren's 293-5290, 4.5 mi.)*, Retail Shops *(Eastgate Mall, 3.5 mi.)*

Transportation
OnCall: Rental Car *(Enterprise 324-6834)*, Taxi *(Orange 841-0030)*, Airport Limo *(Leisure 683-2683)* **Near:** Local Bus *(RIPTA #60)* **3+ mi:** Rail *(Amtrak, 25 mi.)* **Airport:** TF Green *(33 mi.)*

Medical Services
911 Service **1-3 mi:** Dentist *(Aquidneck 683-5990)*, Chiropractor *(Marsh 683-1941)*, Holistic Services *(SpaVana 293-0920)* **3+ mi:** Doctor *(Linden Tree 683-4817, 3.4 mi.)*, Veterinarian *(Portsmouth VC 683-0803, 3.5 mi.)*
Hospital: Newport 846-6400 *(7.5 mi.)*

Setting -- Nearly enclosed by a grassy, earth berm built by the Navy during World War II, the extensive network of well-maintained, floating wood docks - the largest in New England - literally fills the basin. 380 slips and side-ties line nine parallel piers that open onto a spacious, exceptionally well-maintained, full-service yard and recreation area with an inviting pool, a volleyball court, picnic pavilion and restaurant - softened by floral displays and greenery.

Marina Notes -- *Includes 1 power cord. Docks resurfaced & pedestals replaced in '08. Pioneer in advanced composite technology. 48,000 sq ft of work sheds & indoor storage, 14 acres outdoor. Hauls to 88 tons, 20 ft. beam. 100A single phase. 4 megayacht slips plus side-tie dockage (for multihulls, too). Large, well-inventoried chandlery. Two new, climate-controlled work sheds replaced WWII Quonset huts left from days when PT boats & torpedoes were manufactured here. Bathhouse: Spacious, comfortable, attractively tiled throughout in rustic beiges, molded corian sinks, tilt mirrors, glass-doors shower stalls.

Notable -- From Dennis Conner's 1983 Americas Cup contender to 2011 entries in the Transatlantic Race & Volvo Ocean Open 70, building strong, fast boats is a NEB tradition. For service or maintenance, this is a very comfortable place for short or extended layovers. A covered picnic area with propane grills sits near the pool overlooking the docks. Mellville's, an off-the-beaten-track local favorite, offers in- and outdoor casual dining. Three miles north, more than 80 century-old trees have been scissored into a wildly whimsical display at Green Animals Topiary Gardens (an antique toy collection, too). Three miles south, 40-acre Prescott Farm, Doris Duke's gift to preserve Aquidneck's history, features an 1812 windmill, six 18thC. builidngs, and exquisite kitchen & herb gardens.

PHOTOS ON DVD: 25

Herreshoff Marine Museum

PO Box 450; 1 Burnside Street; Bristol, RI 02809

Tel: (401) 253-5000 **VHF: Monitor** Ch. 68 **Talk** Ch. 68
Fax: (401) 253-6222 **Alternate Tel:** (401) 253-5000
Email: info@herreshoff.org **Web:** www.herreshoff.org
Nearest Town: Bristol *(0.6 mi.)* **Tourist Info:** (401) 253-7000

Navigational Information

Lat: 41°39.410' **Long:** 071°16.150' **Tide:** 4 ft. **Current:** 3 kt. **Chart:** 13221
Rep. Depths (*MLW*): Entry 12 ft. **Fuel Dock** n/a **Max Slip/Moor** 12 ft./12 ft.
Access: East Side of Harbor - under 107 ft. white flagpole

Marina Facilities *(In Season/Off Season)*

Fuel: No
Slips: 10 Total, 10 Transient **Max LOA:** 180 ft. **Max Beam:** 25 ft.
Rate *(per ft.)*: **Day** $4.00* **Week** $28 **Month** n/a
Power: 30 amp Incl., **50 amp** Incl., **100 amp** n/a, **200 amp** n/a
Cable TV: No **Dockside Phone:** No
Dock Type: Fixed, Floating, Pilings, Alongside, Wood
Moorings: 14 Total, 14 Transient **Launch:** No, Dinghy Dock
Rate: Day $45 **Week** n/a **Month** n/a
Heads: 2 Toilet(s), 2 Shower(s)
Internet: No **Laundry:** None
Pump-Out: OnCall *(Tue & Thur 253-1700)* **Fee:** $5 **Closed Heads:** Yes

Marina Operations

Owner/Manager: Dyer Jones, CEO **Dockmaster:** John Cobb
In-Season: May-Oct, 8am-5pm **Off-Season:** Nov-Apr, Closed
After-Hours Arrival: Pick up mooring and check in next morning
Reservations: Yes, Preferred **Credit Cards:** Visa/MC, Dscvr, Amex
Discounts: Museum Membership **Dockage:** n/a **Fuel:** n/a **Repair:** n/a
Pets: Welcome **Handicap Access:** Yes, Heads, Docks

Marina Services and Boat Supplies

Services - Docking Assistance, Dock Carts **Communication -** FedEx, UPS, Express Mail **Supplies - OnSite:** Ice *(Cube)* **1-3 mi:** Ships' Store *(PK Marine 254-8990)*, Bait/Tackle *(Ocean State 396 5554)* **3+ mi:** West Marine *(245-7405, 4.5 mi.)*, Propane *(Bristol 245-4862, 5 mi.)*

Boatyard Services

OnSite: Forklift, Rigger, Sail Loft, Canvas Work, Bottom Cleaning, Woodworking **Nearest Yard:** Bristol Marine (401) 253-2200

Restaurants and Accommodations

Near: Restaurant *(Lobster Pot 253-9100, L $5-14, D $8-25, L&D $19-30)*, Inn/B&B *(William's Grant Inn 253-4222, $109-199)* **Under 1 mi:** Restaurant *(Roberto's 254-9732, D $14-28)*, *(S.S. Dion 253-2884)*, *(Leo's 253-9300, L&D $6-16; Kids' $7)*, *(Persimmon 254-7474, D $20-31)*, *(LeCentral 396-9965, L $6-17, D $7-38, Brunch $7-13)*, *(Redlefsen's 254-1188, L $5-16, D $6-32)*, *(Tweet's Balzanos 253-9811, L&D $6-14)*, *(Thames Waterside 253-4523)*, *(Hourglass Brasserie 396-9811, L $10-14, D $18-28, fine dining)*, Pizzeria *(Wood St. 254-0852)*, *(Bristol 253-2550)*, Hotel *(Bristol Harbor Inn 254-1444, $95-249)*, Inn/B&B *(Bradford-Dimond-Norris 253-6338)*, *(Rockwell House 253-4222, $100-175)*, *(Sailor's Loft 369-9560, $90-175)*

Recreation and Entertainment

OnSite: Beach, Picnic Area, Museum *(Herreshoff Marine; Bristol Hist Society & Train of Artillery 253-2928, .6 mi)* **Near:** Hike/Bike Trails *(East Bay Bike path)*, Park *(Walley Beach)* **Under 1 mi:** Playground *(Rockwell)*, Tennis Courts *(Town Common)*, Tours *(Blithewold Mansion & Arboretum 253-2707 $10/2)* **1-3 mi:** Fitness Center *(Ultimate 253-3539)*, Fishing Charter *(Can't Imagine 253-2924)*, Video Rental *(Redbox; Blockbuster Express)* **3+ mi:** Golf Course *(Bristol G.C. 254-1282, 3.5 mi.)*, Bowling *(Dudek 245-9471, 5.4 mi.)*, Cultural Attract *(2nd Story Theatre 247-4200, 5 mi.)*, Sightseeing *(Audubon Society's RI Ed. Ctr 245-7500, 3.5 mi.)*

Provisioning and General Services

Near: Beauty Salon *(Caboret 253-6349)* **Under 1 mi:** Convenience Store *(Bristol 253-6864)*, Market *(Goglia 253-9876)*, Delicatessen *(Panini 847-7784)*, Bakery *(Bristol Bagels 254-1390)*, Fishmonger *(Andrade's 253-4529)*, Bank/ATM, Post Office, Catholic Church, Protestant Church, Synagogue, Library *(Bristol 253-6948)*, Dry Cleaners *(Sam's 253-2239)*, Laundry *(State St. 253-9809)*, Bookstore *(Novel Idea 396-9360)*, Pharmacy *(Compagna's 253-8808)*, Hardware Store *(Hope 253-9777)* **1-3 mi:** Supermarket *(Stop & Shop 254-2525)*, Liquor Store *(1776 253-2222)*, Farmers' Market *(Fri 9am-1pm, Colt State Park 222-2781)*

Transportation

OnCall: Water Taxi *(Bristol Marine "Olivia")*, Rental Car *(Enterprise 253-9160)*, Taxi *(Top Shelf 363-2063)*, Airport Limo *(Special Moments 253-9566)* **Near:** Local Bus *(RIPTA #60 Providence/Newport)* **Under 1 mi:** Ferry Service *(Prudence & Hog Is. 253-9808)* **1-3 mi:** InterCity Bus *(N.E. Coach 253-9566)* **3+ mi:** Rail *(Amtrak, 18 mi.)* **Airport:** TF Green *(23 mi.)*

Medical Services

911 Service **Under 1 mi:** Doctor *(Family 254-2121)*, Dentist *(Allen 253-9636)*, Chiropractor *(Bristol 253-1130)*, Holistic Services *(Time ot Unwind 253-1511)* **1-3 mi:** Optician *(Twenty-Twenty 253-2020)*, Veterinarian *(Mt. Hope 683-3743)* **Hospital:** St. Anne's 508-674-5600 *(11 mi.)*

PHOTOS ON DVD: 23

Setting -- Flying flags signal your arrival at the Holy Grail of classic yachting. At the mouth of Bristol Harbor, side-tie floats flank the single, brick-paved wharf and wooden pier - managed by a dockhouse at its head - and surrounded by a large mooring field. Onshore, enthusiasts will appreciate the museum's impressive collection of sailing craft designed by the "Wizard of Bristol" Nathanael Herreshoff - and a smaller exhibit of his power boats.

Marina Notes -- *Museum Members $3/ft., Moorings $35. (Viglilant-level membership $100). Few services other than dockage or moorings. Well-merchandised gift shop. Special rates for owners of classic yachts. Dockage fees include museum entrance (May-Oct, 10am-5pm, 7 day)s. Favorite stop for club cruises & rendezvous; a tent is generally erected on the waterfront. Plans for full-service marina. Dockage at Rockwell Park in town - free for two hours. Bathhouse: Industrial-style heads, enclosed showers with plastic curtains. Open during museum hours.

Notable -- Across the road from the docks, the well-executed Herreshoff Marine Museum complex and open air exhibits berth the America's Cup Hall of Fame (8 winners were Herreshoff's) along with more than 50 sailing and power vessels (and their models) designed and built by the Herreshoff brothers from 1859-1914. Highlights are beautiful Sprite (1859) and Aria (1914). The main building's overhead walkway permits "top-down" viewing of most yachts. Half a mile along richly treed Hope Street, lined with 18th-century homes, Victorian mansions, shops and eateries, Bristol is Americana perfected with the country's oldest July Fourth parade. Lush, spectacular 33-acre Blithwold is an 0.8 mi. walk south. Tour the 45-room English manor house and 200-species arboretum.

  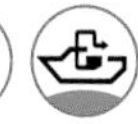 

Navigational Information

Lat: 41°40.560' **Long:** 071°17.334' **Tide:** 4 ft. **Current:** 3 kt. **Chart:** 13224
Rep. Depths (*MLW*): Entry 9 ft. **Fuel Dock** n/a **Max Slip/Moor** -/8 ft.
Access: Bristol Harbor Western Shore - East side of Poppasquash Point

Marina Facilities *(In Season/Off Season)*

Fuel: No
Slips: 0 Total, 0 Transient **Max LOA:** n/a **Max Beam:** n/a
Rate *(per ft.)*: **Day** n/a **Week** n/a **Month** n/a
Power: 30 amp n/a, **50 amp** n/a, **100 amp** n/a, **200 amp** n/a
Cable TV: No **Dockside Phone:** No
Dock Type: Floating, Pilings, Alongside, Wood
Moorings: 50 Total, 20 Transient **Launch:** Yes (Free), Dinghy Dock
Rate: Day $40* **Week** n/a **Month** n/a
Heads: 4 Toilet(s), 4 Shower(s)
Internet: No **Laundry:** None
Pump-Out: OnCall *(Tue & Thur 253-1700)* **Fee:** $5 **Closed Heads:** Yes

Marina Operations

Owner/Manager: Christopher Healey **Dockmaster:** Pete Turenne
In-Season: May 6-Oct 15, 8am-9pm** **Off-Season:** Oct 16-May5, Closed
After-Hours Arrival: Tie up at Courtesy dock.
Reservations: Yes, Preferred **Credit Cards:** Visa/MC, Dscvr, Amex
Discounts: None
Pets: Welcome **Handicap Access:** No

Bristol Yacht Club

PO Box 180; 101 Poppasquash Road; Bristol, RI 02809

Tel: (401) 253-2922 **VHF: Monitor** Ch. 68 **Talk** Ch. 68
Fax: (401) 253-3283 **Alternate Tel:** n/a
Email: steward@bristolyc.com **Web:** www.bristolyc.com
Nearest Town: Bristol *(1.5 mi.)* **Tourist Info:** (401) 245-0750

Marina Services and Boat Supplies

Services - Docking Assistance, Boaters' Lounge, Security *(Two Bristol town police boats patrol harbor)*, Dock Carts **Communication -** Pay Phone, FedEx, UPS, Express Mail **Supplies - OnSite:** Ice *(Block, Cube)* **Near:** Ships' Store *(Bristol Marine)* **1-3 mi:** Bait/Tackle *(Ocean State 254-6066)* **3+ mi:** West Marine *(245-7405, 4 mi.)*, Propane *(Bristol 245-4862, 4 mi.)*

Boatyard Services

OnSite: Crane *(1T)* **Nearest Yard:** Bristol Marine (401) 253-2200

Restaurants and Accommodations

OnSite: Restaurant *(BYC - Friday Night Dinner)* **Under 1 mi:** Restaurant *(Topside 253-9110, L $8-13, D $13-18, Kids' $4-5.50)*, *(Sandbar 253-5485, Famous chowder)*, Hotel *(Point Pleasant Inn 253-0627, $375-625, Resort)* **1-3 mi:** Restaurant *(Quito's 253-4500, L&D $8-28)*, *(Lobster Pot 253-9100, L $5-14, D $8-25, Moorings & dinghy dock)*, *(Redlefsen's Rotisserie 254-1188, L $8-16, D $10-32)*, *(SS Dion 253-2884, D $17-25, Kids' $5-9)*, *(Persimmon 254-7474, D $20-31)*, *(Hourglass Brasserie 396-9811, L $10-14, D $18-28)*, *(Thames Waterside 253-4523)*, Lite Fare *(Hope Diner 253-1759)*, Pizzeria *(Bristol House 253-2550, Del.)*, Motel *(Bristol Motor 253-7600, $137)*, Hotel *(Bristol Harbor Inn 254-1444, $95-249)*, *(Sailor's Loft 396-9560, $90-175)*

Recreation and Entertainment

OnSite: Beach *(or Bristol Town)*, Picnic Area, Grills, Playground **Near:** Hike/Bike Trails *(connect to East Bay Bike Path to Providence)* **Under 1 mi:** Park *(Colt State Park)*, Cultural Attract *(Coggeshall Farm 243-9062, $5/3 - Tue-Sun 10-4)* **1-3 mi:** Tennis Courts *(Town Common)*, Fitness Center *(Ultimate 253-3539)*, Fishing Charter *(Can't Imagine 253-2924)*, Video Rental *(Redbox; Blockbuster Express)*, Museum *(Linden Place 253-0390 $5; Bristol Historic Soc. & Train of Artillery 253-0015; Herreshoff Marine, 253-5000)*, Sightseeing *(Blithewold Mansion & Arboretum 253-2707 $10/2)*, Galleries *(Uncommon Art 396-5757; Brigidi Fine Art 253-2351)* **3+ mi:** Golf Course *(Bristol GC 254-1282, 3.2 mi.)*, Bowling *(Dudek 245-9471, 5 mi.)*

Provisioning and General Services

1-3 mi: Convenience Store *(JD 842-0545)*, Market *(Goglia 253-9876)*, Supermarket *(Stop & Shop 254-2525)*, Gourmet Shop *(Bristol Harbor 396-9033)*, Delicatessen *(Panini 847-7784)*, Liquor Store *(1776 Liquors 253-2222)*, Bakery *(Cake Gallery 254-1911)*, Green Grocer *(Mello's Fruitland 253-6858)*, Fishmonger *(Quito's 253-9042)*, Bank/ATM, Post Office, Catholic Church, Protestant Church, Synagogue, Library *(253-6948)*, Beauty Salon *(New Leaf 254-9333)*, Dry Cleaners *(Independence 253-1939)*, Laundry *(East Bay 253-1613)*, Bookstore *(Novel Idea 396-9360)*, Pharmacy *(CVS 253-2050)*, Hardware Store *(Hope 253-9777)*, Florist *(Bellevue 847-0145)*

Transportation

OnCall: Water Taxi, Rental Car *(Enterprise 253-9160)*, Taxi *(Top Shelf 363-2063)* **Under 1 mi:** Local Bus *(RIPTA #60 Providence/Newport)* **1-3 mi:** Ferry Service *(Prudence & Hog Islands 253-9808)* **3+ mi:** Bikes *(Your Bike 245-9755, 4 mi.)*, Rail *(Amtrak, 18 mi.)* **Airport:** T.F. Green *(25 mi.)*

Medical Services

911 Service **1-3 mi:** Doctor *(Jaffe 438-3300)*, Dentist *(Lukasiewicz 253-9613)*, Chiropractor *(Bristol Group 253-1130)*, Holistic Services *(Alayne Spa 254-1772)*, Optician *(Twenty-Twenty 253-2020)* **3+ mi:** Veterinarian *(Warren 245-8313, 4.4 mi.)* **Hospital:** Newport 846-6400 *(14 mi.)*

Setting -- Lovely BYC, on the western shore of Bristol Harbor, is surrounded by residential Poppasquash Point. The single fixed pier extends out past neat rows of dinghy and launch docks with a small-signed dockhouse perched near the end. The attractive, mansard-roofed, two-story, gray-shingled clubhouse - sporting an inviting front porch, topped by a blue awning - enjoys panoramic harbor views. Add a picnic area, children's play gym and extensive dry storage.

Marina Notes -- *$40 fee for use of facilities, mooring complimentary. **Shoulder hrs, shorter. Founded 1877 as The Zephyr Boat Club by Brown U. students; name changed in 1899. No guest slips. 20 transient moorings with excellent launch service. MemDay-LabDay 8am-9pm Sun-Thu, 'til 10pm Fri-Sat. (Shoulder season shorter hrs). Hail on Ch 68. Also ferries guests to restaurants, parks & attractions across harbor. Clubhouse recently renovated. Welcomes all yachtspeople to all facilities: temp tie-up for loading/unloading & water plus bar, lounge, porch, Friday night dinner, picnic area, beach & play gym. Ice: Blocks 25 lb. $5 & 50 lb. $10, Cubes $2/5 lbs. Bathhouse: Small cinderblock building close to parking lot. Stark white painted walls, tiled floors, curtained showers.

Notable -- It's a short dinghy or launch ride across the harbor to Bristol for fine or casual dining, shopping and sightseeing. Dinghy landings in town at Independence and Rockwell Parks, Bristol Harbor Inn, Herreshoff Museum and Union Street - a good place to watch the famous July 4th parade. Occupying half of Poppasquash Point, 460-acre Colt State Park offers a beach, picnicking, fishing and hiking. A 0.4 mile stroll, 48-acre Coggeshall Farm living history Museum, on Mill Gut Inlet, recreates East Bay agrarian life circa 1799 with vintage tools, farmhouse, outbuildings, heirloom plants, livestock - and workshops.

PHOTOS ON DVD: 22

Bristol Marine

99 Poppasquash Road; Bristol, RI 02809

Tel: (401) 253-2200 **VHF: Monitor** Ch. 69 **Talk** Ch. 69
Fax: (401) 253-0007 **Alternate Tel:** n/a
Email: andy@bristolmarine.com **Web:** www.bristolmarine.com
Nearest Town: Bristol *(1.6 mi.)* **Tourist Info:** (401) 253-7000

Navigational Information

Lat: 41°40.609' **Long:** 071°17.311' **Tide:** 4 ft. **Current:** 3 kt. **Chart:** 13223
Rep. Depths (*MLW*): Entry 12 ft. **Fuel Dock** n/a **Max Slip/Moor** 7 ft./8 ft.
Access: NW corner of Bristol Harbor. East side of Poppasquash Point

Marina Facilities *(In Season/Off Season)*

Fuel: No
Slips: 140 Total, 5 Transient **Max LOA:** 70 ft. **Max Beam:** n/a
Rate *(per ft.)*: **Day** $2.50/$2 **Week** $10.50 **Month** n/a
Power: 30 amp Incl., **50 amp** Incl., **100 amp** n/a, **200 amp** n/a
Cable TV: No **Dockside Phone:** No
Dock Type: Floating, Long Fingers, Alongside, Wood
Moorings: 70 Total, 5 Transient **Launch:** Yes ($3), Dinghy Dock
Rate: Day $35 **Week** $147 **Month** $480
Heads: 1 Toilet(s), 1 Shower(s) *(dressing rooms)*, Book Exchange
Internet: No **Laundry:** None
Pump-Out: OnSite, Full Service, 1 Central **Fee:** $5 **Closed Heads:** Yes

Marina Operations

Owner/Manager: Andy Tysca **Dockmaster:** n/a
In-Season: Year-Round, 6am-5pm* **Off-Season:** n/a
After-Hours Arrival: Call ahead
Reservations: Yes, Recommended **Credit Cards:** Visa/MC, Dscvr, Amex
Discounts: Boat/US **Dockage:** 25% **Fuel:** n/a **Repair:** n/a
Pets: Welcome, Dog Walk Area **Handicap Access:** No

Marina Services and Boat Supplies

Services - Docking Assistance, Dock Carts **Communication -** FedEx, DHL, UPS **Supplies - OnSite:** Ice *(Block, Cube)*, Ships' Store **1-3 mi:** Bait/Tackle *(Ocean State 254-6066)* **3+ mi:** West Marine *(245-7405, 4 mi)*

Boatyard Services

OnSite: Travelift *(50T)*, Forklift *(10T)*, Crane *(7T)*, Engine mechanic *(gas, diesel)*, Electrical Repairs, Electronic Sales *(Raytheon)*, Hull Repairs, Rigger, Canvas Work, Divers, Bottom Cleaning, Brightwork, Compound, Wash & Wax, Propeller Repairs, Woodworking, Upholstery, Yacht Interiors, Painting, Awlgrip, Total Refits, Yacht Design, Yacht Building **Dealer for:** Yanmar; Raytheon. **Member:** ABBRA - 3 Certified Tech(s), ABYC - 3 Certified Tech (s), Other Certifications: International Yacht Restoration; Ocean Circuit
Yard Rates: $70, Haul & Launch $8-10/ft. *(blocking $25)*, Power Wash $2/ft., Bottom Paint Time/Material **Storage:** On-Land $70-85/ft.

Restaurants and Accommodations

Under 1 mi: Restaurant *(Topside 253-9110)*, *(Sandbar 253-5485)*, Inn/B&B *(Pt. Pleasant 253-0627, $375-625)* **1-3 mi:** Restaurant *(Lobster Pot 253-9100, L $5-14, D $8-25, moorings/dinghy dock)*, *(Redlefsens Rotisserie 254-1188, L $8-16, D $10-32)*, *(Quito's 253-4500, L $7-22, D $10-22, L&D $8-28)*, *(SS Dion 253-2884)*, *(Persimmon 254-7474, D $20-31)*, *(Hourglass 396-9811, L&D $19-28)*, Pizzeria *(Bristol 253-2550, Del.)*, Hotel *(Bristol Harbor Inn 254-1444, $95-249)*, Inn/B&B *(Gov Bradford 253-9300)*

Recreation and Entertainment

OnSite: Picnic Area, Grills **Under 1 mi:** Beach *(Bristol Town)*, Tennis Courts, Fitness Center *(Colt S.P.)*, Hike/Bike Trails *(East Bay - Providence)*, Park *(Bristol Town)*, Cultural Attract *(Coggeshall Farm 243-9062, $5/3)* **1-3 mi:** Golf Course *(Bristol GC 254-1282)*, Video Rental *(Redbox; Blockbuster Express)*, Museum *(Linden Place 253-0390 $5 - a "Fair House;" Bristol Historic Society 253-0015; Herreshoff Marine, 253-5000)*, Tours *(Audubon McIntosh Wildlife Refuge 245-7500)*, Sightseeing *(Blithewold Mansion & Arboretum 253-2707 $10/2)*, Galleries *(Bristol Art - Linden Place 253-2095)*

Provisioning and General Services

Under 1 mi: Farmers' Market *(Colt State Park 222-2781 Fri 9-1)* **1-3 mi:** Convenience Store *(JD 842-0545)*, Supermarket *(Stop & Shop 254-2525)*, Delicatessen *(Panini Grill 847-7784)*, Liquor Store *(1776 253-2222)*, Bakery *(Cake Gallery 254-1911)*, Green Grocer *(Mello's 253-6858)*, Fishmonger *(Quito's 253-9042)*, Bank/ATM, Post Office, Catholic Church, Protestant Church, Synagogue, Library *(Bristol 253-6948)*, Beauty Salon *(New Leaf 254-9333)*, Dry Cleaners *(Independence 253-1939)*, Laundry *(East Bay 253-1613)*, Bookstore *(A Novel Idea 396-9360)*, Pharmacy *(Campagna's 253-8808)*, Hardware Store *(Ace 253-8180)*, Florist *(Bellevue 847-0145)*

Transportation

OnSite: Bikes **OnCall:** Water Taxi *($3)*, Rental Car *(Enterprise 253-9160)*, Taxi *(Top Shelf 363-2063)* **Under 1 mi:** Local Bus *(RIPTA #60)* **1-3 mi:** Ferry Service *(Prudence Is. 253-9808)* **Airport:** T.F. Green *(24 mi.)*

Medical Services

911 Service **1-3 mi:** Doctor *(O'Dowd 253-3710)*, Dentist *(Allen 253-9636)*, Chiropractor *(East Bay 253-7475)*, Holistic Services *(Time to Unwind 253-1511)*, Optician *(Twenty Twenty 253-2020)* **3+ mi:** Veterinarian *(Warren 245-8313, 4 mi.)* **Hospital:** Newport 846-6400 *(14 mi.)*

PHOTOS ON DVD: 22

Setting -- Bristol Marine shares quiet, residential Poppasquash Point with adjacent Bristol Yacht Club and 460-acre Colt State Park. A paved pier extends to the single-wood dock flanked by slips and side-tie docks capped by a long, large-yacht-capable T-head. The shingled two-story office complex hosts a half-dozen marine vendors. At the back of the property, three buildings provide indoor storage and work space - and it is all surrounded by dry storage.

Marina Notes -- *Closed Sat & Sun. Club-quality launch & water taxi service - one-trip or ten trip (starting at $3 pp, 1-way, $20 10-trip). In 1998, Clint Pearson's Bristol Yachts found new ownership: dockage was reduced, moorings expanded, a new travelift and many more improvements followed - including new power/water pedestals. Still home to many Bristol yachts; yard manages service and refits (parts no longer avail.) & commissions other brands. 16,000 sq. ft of indoor heated storage. Bathhouse: Single, quite nice full bath. Tiled floor & walls, fiberglass shower stall with curtains, dressing bench.

Notable -- On the "quiet" side of the harbor, the launch service delivers guests to Bristol Marine's docks or across the harbor to the Herreshoff Museum, or "downtown" Bristol where fine restaurants, parks, museums, and sightseeing stretch along lovely Hope Street with colonial and Victorian houses. Bristol Harbor Inn -- in the center of Thames Street Landing - integrates nine historic buildings into a boardwalk-style complex of retail shops and pedestrian walkways. Colt State Park is a mile walk with fitness trails, exercise stations, Chapel-by-the-Sea, and Coggeshall Farm Museum. Under a mile, Bristol Town Beach and Park offers tennis, playgrounds and extensive playing fields, and the 14-mile East Bay paved bike path starts at Independence Parks and runs to Providence.

Navigational Information

Lat: 41°44.104' **Long:** 071°17.655' **Tide:** 4 ft. **Current:** 4 kt. **Chart:** 13221
Rep. Depths (*MLW*): Entry 10 ft. **Fuel Dock** n/a **Max Slip/Moor** 6 ft./10 ft.
Access: Warren River channel to G3, left into Barrington River

Marina Facilities *(In Season/Off Season)*

Fuel: Gasoline, Diesel
Slips: 100 Total, 2 Transient **Max LOA:** 45 ft. **Max Beam:** 14 ft.
Rate *(per ft.)*: **Day** $2.00* **Week** n/a **Month** n/a
Power: 30 amp Incl., **50 amp** n/a, **100 amp** n/a, **200 amp** n/a
Cable TV: No **Dockside Phone:** No
Dock Type: Floating, Long Fingers, Wood
Moorings: 4 Total, 1 Transient **Launch:** Yes (Incl.)
Rate: Day $30 **Week** n/a **Month** n/a
Heads: 6 Toilet(s), 4 Shower(s)
Internet: Yes *(Wi-Fi, Free)* **Laundry:** None
Pump-Out: Full Service, 1 Central **Fee:** Free **Closed Heads:** Yes

Marina Operations

Owner/Manager: Scott L. Nichols **Dockmaster:** Phil Holmes
In-Season: May-Oct, 8am-Sunset **Off-Season:** Nov-Apr, 8am 4:30pm
After-Hours Arrival: Gas Dock
Reservations: Yes **Credit Cards:** Visa/MC, Dscvr
Discounts: None
Pets: Welcome, Dog Walk Area **Handicap Access:** Yes, Heads

Barrington Yacht Club

25 Barton Avenue; Barrington, RI 02806

Tel: (401) 245-1181 **VHF: Monitor** Ch. 68 **Talk** Ch. 68
Fax: (401) 245-0275 **Alternate Tel:** n/a
Email: scott@barringtonyc.com **Web:** www.barringtonyc.com
Nearest Town: Barrington *(1.4 mi.)* **Tourist Info:** (401) 253-7000

Marina Services and Boat Supplies

Services - Docking Assistance, Trash Pick-Up, Dock Carts **Communication -** FedEx, UPS, Express Mail **Supplies - OnSite:** Ice *(Block, Cube)* **Under 1 mi:** Propane *(Bristol 245-4862)* **1-3 mi:** West Marine *(245-7405)*, Bait/Tackle *(Lucky 247-2223)*

Boatyard Services

Nearest Yard: Stanley's Boat Yard (401) 245-5090

Restaurants and Accommodations

OnSite: Snack Bar *(11am-5:30pm, Bar 5:30-8:30pm, Sat & Sun 4-8:30pm)* **Near:** Restaurant *(Tyler Point Grille 247-0017, D $16-33, Burger $10, Prixe Fixe Menu, Kids' $7, Take-Out)* **Under 1 mi:** Restaurant *(Wharf Tavern 245-5043)*, *(Stella Blues 289-0349, L&D $8-27)*, *(Tong D 289-2998, L&D $11-16)*, *(Blount Clam Shack 245-3210)*, Lite Fare *(Sunny Side 247-1200, B $4-13, L $10-14, Brunch $4-14; Kids' $3)*, *(BeBop Burrito 289-9274, $4-6.50, Del.)*, Pizzeria *(Chicago 247-2202, Del.)*, *(Samantha 289-2993, Del.)* **1-3 mi:** Inn/B&B *(Candlewick Inn 247-2425)* **3+ mi:** Hotel *(Holiday Inn Exp 508-672-6857, $86-175, 5 mi.)*, *(Best Western 508-336-4927, 5 mi.)*

Recreation and Entertainment

OnSite: Picnic Area, Grills **Near:** Hike/Bike Trails *(14 mi. paved East Path - Providence/Bristol)*, Sightseeing *(Tyler Point Cemetery - Revolutionary War; Nyatt Point)* **Under 1 mi:** Beach *(Barrington)*, Playground *(Peck Center)*, Dive Shop *(East Bay 247-2420)*, Video Rental *(Redbox)*, Park *(Pema; Belcher Cove)*, Museum *(Warren's Fire 245-3790)*, Cultural Attract *(2nd Story Theater 247-4200 - 1st rate regional theater)*, Galleries *(Imago 245-3348; River Art 289-0820)* **1-3 mi:** Golf Course *(Windmill GC 245-1463)*, Bowling *(Dudek 245-9471)*, Fishing Charter *(Can't Imagine 253-2924)*

Provisioning and General Services

Near: Beauty Salon *(Renaissance 245-7609)* **Under 1 mi:** Convenience Store *(Cumberland Farms 245-5989)*, Supermarket *(Shaw's 245-5882)*, Delicatessen *(Nancy's 289-2930)*, Liquor Store *(Patriot 245-1776)*, Bank/ATM, Post Office *(245-0601)*, Catholic Church, Protestant Church, Library *(Barrington 247-1920 - Internet)*, Dry Cleaners *(Grampa's 245-9288)*, Laundry *(Launder 'n Luxury 245-8060)*, Bookstore *(Barrington 245-7925)*, Pharmacy *(CVS 245-0512; Rite Aid 245-8855)*, Hardware Store *(Mercier's 245-8964)*, Florist *(Greenery 247-7100)*, Copies Etc. *(Petite 595-5781)* **1-3 mi:** Green Grocer *(Johnson's Roadside 508-379-0349)*, Fishmonger *(Blount 245-1800)*, Retail Shops *(Ocean State Plaza)* **3+ mi:** Farmers' Market *(Fri 9am-1pm Colt State Park 222-2781, 5.5 mi.)*, Synagogue *(5 mi.)*, Department Store *(WalMart 508-336-0290; Target 508-336-1117, 5 mi.)*, Buying Club *(Sam's Club 508-336-8262, 5 mi.)*

Transportation

OnCall: Rental Car *(Enterprise 253-9160)*, Taxi *(TAG 450-9861)*, Airport Limo *(GSC 247-1665)* **Near:** Local Bus *(RIPTA 781-9400 #60 on Rte 114 Providence-Newport)* **Under 1 mi:** Bikes *(East Providence 434-3838)* **3+ mi:** Rail *(Amtrak 800-872-7245, 13 mi.)* **Airport:** TF Green *(20 mi.)*

Medical Services

911 Service **Under 1 mi:** Dentist *(Asaro 245-4619)*, Chiropractor *(Barrington 245-7010)*, Veterinarian *(Barrington 245-9226)* **1-3 mi:** Doctor *(Warren Fam. 247-1000)*, Holistic Services *(Naturopathic 742-4531)*, Optician *(Barrington 247-7393)* **Hospital:** Rhode Island 444-4000 *(11 mi.)*

Setting -- This low-key, gracious, family yacht club sits on Tyler Point, between the Warren and Barrington Rivers. Rocking chairs line the broad, 450-foot deck that fronts the stylish, contemporary clubhouse. Bright blue awnings protect the deck and picnic areas at each end of the building. Expansive views across the river are particulary spectacular at sunset. A short way upriver, a fixed bridge ends big boat navigation, creating the sense of a basin.

Marina Notes -- Established 1908. All visiting yachtspeople welcomed to moorings, launch and *members of reciprocating yacht clubs to the transient docks (30A power). Two moored floating docks accommodate side-tie both sides. Launch 8am-8pm. Pool for members only. Large fleets of Optimists and 420s. Pump-out station open 8am-sunset. Large mooring field managed by the town - contact harbormaster Ray Sousa on Ch 16. Bathhouse: Warm and inviting with rich wood trim, tiled floors and homelike touches throughout. Spacious showers with dressing area. Note: Beware ledge near main dock.

Notable -- Recently renovated by the new chef-owner, virtually onsite Tyler Point Grille specializes in seafood and Italian favorites (Sun-Thu 4:30-10pm, Fri & Sat 4:30-11pm). Historic Barrington village, first settled in 1632, is now a lovely, prosperous Providence suburb with deep roots and beautiful old homes - a walk along Rumstick & Mathewson Roads will yield some of the best. It's a 0.7-mile dinghy ride (or mile walk) to the funky Warren waterfront with several restaurants (Wharf & TaVino are "dock & dine"), Firemen's Museum, lots of antique shops, useful services and 2nd Story, one of RI's top regional theaters. On the town common, the 1844 Methodist Church's 160-foot steeple is the visual center of Warren's historic district. Stroll Main and Child Streets.

PHOTOS ON DVD: 20

Bullock Cove Marine

254 Riverside Drive; Riverside, RI 02915

Tel: (401) 433-3010 **VHF: Monitor** n/a **Talk** n/a
Fax: (401) 433-3128 **Alternate Tel:** n/a
Email: kggregory@bullockcovemarine.com **Web:** www.bullockcove.com
Nearest Town: Barrington *(2 mi.)* **Tourist Info:** (401) 438-1212

Navigational Information

Lat: 41°44.794' **Long:** 071°21.354' **Tide:** 4 ft. **Current:** 2 kt. **Chart:** 13221
Rep. Depths (*MLW*): Entry 7 ft. **Fuel Dock** n/a **Max Slip/Moor** 8 ft./-
Access: W. Narragansett Bay-Providence R, 4 mi. Bullock Cove on Starboard

Marina Facilities *(In Season/Off Season)*

Fuel: No
Slips: 49 Total, 2 Transient **Max LOA:** 45 ft. **Max Beam:** 14 ft.
Rate *(per ft.)*: **Day** $2.00 **Week** $14 **Month** $60
Power: 30 amp Incl., **50 amp** n/a, **100 amp** n/a, **200 amp** n/a
Cable TV: No **Dockside Phone:** No
Dock Type: Floating, Pilings, Wood
Moorings: 0 Total, 0 Transient **Launch:** n/a, Dinghy Dock
Rate: Day n/a **Week** n/a **Month** n/a
Heads: 2 Toilet(s), 2 Shower(s)
Internet: No **Laundry:** None
Pump-Out: No **Fee:** n/a **Closed Heads:** Yes

Marina Operations

Owner/Manager: Kennard G. Gregory **Dockmaster:** Same
In-Season: Year Round, 8am-4:30pm **Off-Season:** n/a
After-Hours Arrival: Call in advance
Reservations: Yes, Required **Credit Cards:** Cash only
Discounts: None
Pets: Welcome **Handicap Access:** No

Marina Services and Boat Supplies

Services - Dock Carts **Communication -** FedEx, UPS, Express Mail **Supplies - OnSite:** Ships' Store **1-3 mi:** Bait/Tackle *(Archie's 437-2630)* **3+ mi:** West Marine *(508-336-5004, 5 mi.)*, Propane *(Bristol 245-4862, 6 mi.)*

Boatyard Services

OnSite: Travelift *(35T)*, Crane *(40T)*, Launching Ramp, Electrical Repairs, Hull Repairs, Rigger, Bottom Cleaning, Brightwork, Compound, Wash & Wax, Interior Cleaning, Woodworking, Painting, Awlgrip **Member:** ABYC **Yard Rates:** $70, Haul & Launch $5/ft., Power Wash $2/ft., Bottom Paint $10/ft. **Storage:** In-Water $38/ft., On-Land $35/ft.

Restaurants and Accommodations

Under 1 mi: Restaurant *(New China 433-2288, L&D $8-13)*, Lite Fare *(Rooster's Grill 433-0023)* **1-3 mi:** Restaurant *(Siam Square 433-0123, L&D $11-16)*, Pizzeria *(Town Pizza & Family Restaurant 433-0300, L&D $7-14)*, *(Riverside 490-0005, Del.)*, *(Domino's 433-0200, Del.)* **3+ mi:** Restaurant *(Chiazza Trattoria 247-0303, L $7-15, D $8-25, 4 mi., Kids' $5-7)*, *(TGI Friday's 508-336-2258, 5 mi., L&D $7-16, Kids' menu)*, Hotel *(Best Western 508-336-4927, $80+, 5 mi.)*, *(Comfort Inn 508-336-7900, $85-120, 5 mi.)*

Recreation and Entertainment

Under 1 mi: Picnic Area *(Bullock Point Park)*, Grills, Fitness Center *(Curves 437-4200)*, Video Arcade, Park *(Larisa)*, Sightseeing *(Crescent Park Looff Carousel)* **1-3 mi:** Golf Course *(Silver Springs 434-9697)*, Video Rental *(Redbox; Blockbuster Express)*, Galleries *(Right Angle 433-0051)* **3+ mi:** Movie Theater *(Showcase 800-315-4000, 6.5 mi.)*, Cultural Attract *(Rhode Island Philharmonic 248-7070; 2nd Story Theatre 247-4200, 5 mi.)*

Provisioning and General Services

Under 1 mi: Market *(Crescent 223-7177)*, Bakery *(Honey Dew 433-3219)*, Beauty Salon *(Carousel 433-5466)* **1-3 mi:** Convenience Store *(Chelsey's 433-1300)*, Supermarket *(Shaw's 433-3180)*, Gourmet Shop *(Eastside 831-7771)*, Delicatessen *(Left of Center 228-3008)*, Wine/Beer *(McGreen's 433-0900)*, Liquor Store, Farmers' Market *(Haines Park, East Providence, 222-2781, Wed 2-6)*, Bank/ATM *(Citizens)*, Post Office *(433-2619)*, Catholic Church, Protestant Church *(St Marks Episcopal)*, Library *(433-4877 Internet)*, Dry Cleaners *(Riverside 433-2800)*, Laundry *(ABS 433-2830)*, Pharmacy *(Rite Aid 433-5710)*, Hardware Store *(Barrington 246-0550)*, Florist *(Pretty Pickins 433-6818)*, Retail Shops *(Lakeside Shopping Ctr)* **3+ mi:** Bookstore *(Barrrington 245-7925, 4.5 mi.)*, Buying Club *(Sam's 508-336-8262, 5 mi.)*

Transportation

OnCall: Rental Car *(Enterprise 780-9935)*, Taxi *(E. Providence 434-2000)*, Airport Limo *(TAG 450-9861)* **1-3 mi:** Bikes *(East Providence 437-2453)*, Local Bus *(RIPTA 33 to Providence 781-9400)* **3+ mi:** Rail *(South Attleboro, 11 mi.)* **Airport:** TF Green *(16 mi.)*

Medical Services

911 Service **OnCall:** Ambulance **Under 1 mi:** Holistic Services *(Stage Hands 369-2239)* **1-3 mi:** Doctor *(Steiner 383-9260)*, Chiropractor *(Riverside 433-5559)*, Veterinarian *(Riverside 433-2070)* **3+ mi:** Dentist *(Applebaum 433-2400, 3.5 mi.)* **Hospital:** Rhode Island 444-4000 *(8 mi.)*

PHOTOS ON DVD: 16

Setting -- To port, at the entrance to Bullock Cove, the boatyard sits at the tip of Bullock Neck behind a natural sand barrier in a residential area known as Narragansett Terrace. The floating wood docks run perpendicular to the land - some with slips, others requiring med-mooring. They are floating wood with vinyl edging, lighting, water and older electric connections. On the upland, two red-shingled buildings housing the office and chandlery are surrounded by large stick-built and quonset-style work sheds dominated by a travelift. There is no landscaping; this is pure boatyard and pretends to be nothing more.

Marina Notes -- Originally two boatyards, built prior to WW II, that were combined in 1988. Primarily a small, local boatyard; welcomes transients on a space-is-available basis. Do-it-yourself or full-service. Finish varnishing, fiberglass repair, Awlgrip, carpentry, painting, plus inboard/outboard gas & diesel engine installation and repair. Old-fashioned ships' store with an amazing inventory for a small shop. Bathhouse: Located in main office building with separate entrances. Full private bathrooms, tiled floors/walls, one-piece fiberglass shower stalls with plastic curtains.

Notable -- Barrington experienced a bit of the Gilded Age, and those grand summer "cottages" can be seen from the boat at the mouth of the river along Nayatt Point. BCM's isolated location offers little "nearby." But a 0.7-mile walk yields the Nat'l Historic Landmarked Crescent Park Looff Carousel - an 1895 hippodrome topped by an onion cupola. Sixty-one hand-carved horses, a camel and four coaches ride on a 50-foot platform; of 50 built by Charles I. D. Looff, it's one of the few still operating. Listen for the Neck's rogue colony of 12-inch tall, lime-green-and-gray Monk (aka Quaker) Parakeets; here since the '70s.

Navigational Information

Lat: 41°45.057' **Long:** 071°21.064' **Tide:** 5 ft. **Current:** 2 kt. **Chart:** 13221
Rep. Depths (*MLW*): Entry 10 ft. **Fuel Dock** 8 ft. **Max Slip/Moor** 12 ft./-
Access: Conimicut Point. Follow markers to R18. The cove begins at "G1"

Marina Facilities *(In Season/Off Season)*

Fuel: *ValvTect* - Gasoline, Diesel, On Call Delivery
Slips: 348 Total, 5 Transient **Max LOA:** 150 ft. **Max Beam:** 20 ft.
Rate *(per ft.)*: **Day** $3.00 **Week** $15 **Month** $150
Power: 30 amp $10, **50 amp** $15, **100 amp** n/a, **200 amp** n/a
Cable TV: No **Dockside Phone:** No
Dock Type: Floating, Long Fingers, Pilings
Moorings: 25 Total, 5 Transient **Launch:** yes, Dinghy Dock
Rate: Day $1.50 **Week** $7.50 **Month** $22.50
Heads: 6 Toilet(s), 8 Shower(s)
Internet: Yes *(Wi-Fi, Free)* **Laundry:** None
Pump-Out: OnSite, Self Service, 2 Central **Fee:** n/a **Closed Heads:** Yes

Marina Operations

Owner/Manager: Ray Snow **Dockmaster:** Same
In-Season: Year-Round, M-F 7:30am-4:30pm, S 8am-12 **Off-Season:** n/a
After-Hours Arrival: Call ahead
Reservations: Yes **Credit Cards:** Visa/MC, Dscvr, Amex
Discounts: Reciprocates with Brewer Members **Dockage:** n/a **Fuel:** n/a **R**
Pets: Welcome **Handicap Access:** Yes, Heads

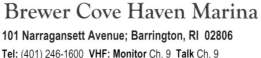

Brewer Cove Haven Marina

101 Narragansett Avenue; Barrington, RI 02806

Tel: (401) 246-1600 **VHF: Monitor** Ch. 9 **Talk** Ch. 9
Fax: (401) 246-0731 **Alternate Tel:** n/a
Email: rsnow@byy.com **Web:** www.byy.com/barrington
Nearest Town: Barrington *(0 mi.)* **Tourist Info:** (401) 275-0750

Marina Services and Boat Supplies

Services - Docking Assistance, Dock Carts **Communication -** Fax in/out *($3)*, FedEx, UPS, Express Mail **Supplies - OnSite:** Ice *(Block, Cube)*, Ships' Store **Under 1 mi:** Bait/Tackle *(Archies 437-2630)* **3+ mi:** West Marine *(508-336-5004, 4.5 mi.)*, Propane *(Bristol 245-4862, 4 mi.)*

Boatyard Services

OnSite: Travelift *(150T)*, Forklift *(15T)*, Crane *(15T)*, Engine mechanic *(gas, diesel)*, Electrical Repairs, Electronics Repairs, Hull Repairs, Rigger, Canvas Work, Bottom Cleaning, Brightwork, Refrigeration, Compound, Wash & Wax, Woodworking, Inflatable Repairs, Upholstery, Metal Fabrication, Painting, Awlgrip, Yacht Broker **Dealer for:** Yanmar, Westerbeke, Kohler, Edson, Spectra Watermakers, Spurs, Sealand, Marine Air, Cruisair, Webasto, Universal, Ocean Marine, Heart Interface-Xantrex, Village Watermakers, Sea Recovery, Sea Frost, Wacco Adler/Barbour, Hatteras. **Member:** ABBRA - 4 Certified Tech(s), ABYC - 4 Certified Tech(s) **Yard Rates:** $89/hr., Haul & Launch $7.50/ft *(blocking $2-3/ft.)*, Power Wash $2-3/ft., Bottom Paint $14.50/ft. **Storage:** In-Water $110/ft., On-Land Out $5/sq.ft. In $9/sq.ft.

Restaurants and Accommodations

Under 1 mi: Restaurant *(Siam Square 433-0123, L&D $9.50-16)*, *(New China 433-2288, $8-13)*, Lite Fare *(Rooster's Grill 433-0023)*, Pizzeria *(Town Family 433-0300, L&D $7-14)*, *(Domino's 433-0200, Del.)* **3+ mi:** Hotel *(Comfort Inn 508-336-7900, $85-120, 4.5 mi.)*

Recreation and Entertainment

OnSite: Pool, Picnic Area, Grills **Near:** Hike/Bike Trails *(East Bay Trail)*, Park *(Haines S.P.)* **Under 1 mi:** Tennis Courts *(Barrington Mid School)* **1-3 mi:** Golf Course *(Silver Spring 434-9697)*, Fitness Center *(360 Total 247-1360)*, Video Rental *(Blockbuster Exp)*, Sightseeing *(Crescent Carousel)* **3+ mi:** Beach *(Barrington 245-9377, 4 mi.)*, Bowling *(Dudek 345-9471, 5 mi.)*, Movie Theater *(Showcase 800-315-4000, 6 mi.)*, Cultural Attract *(2nd Story Theater 247-4200; RI Philharmonic 248-7070, 5 mi.)*

Provisioning and General Services

Near: Farmers' Market *(Wed 2-6pm, Haines SP 222-2781)*, Beauty Salon *(Tufarolo's 246-0922)* **Under 1 mi:** Convenience Store *(Willett Ave 433-1586)*, Supermarket *(Shaw's 433-3180)*, Delicatessen *(Left of Center 228-3008)*, Wine/Beer *(Fest of Vine 521-9463)*, Liquor Store *(McGreen's 433-0900)*, Bank/ATM, Catholic Church, Protestant Church, Dry Cleaners *(Riverside 433-2800)*, Laundry *(Launder + 437-9274)*, Pharmacy *(Rite Aid 433-5710)*, Hardware Store *(Barrington 246-0550)* **1-3 mi:** Bakery *(Honey Dew 433-3219)*, Fishmonger *(Wallis 245-6666)*, Post Office, Library *(433-4877)*, Bookstore *(Barrington 245-7925)*, Retail Shops *(Lakeside Mall)* **3+ mi:** Department Store *(Kohl's, 4.5 mi.)*, Buying Club *(Sam's, 4.5 mi.)*

Transportation

OnSite: Courtesy Car/Van **OnCall:** Rental Car *(Enterprise 438-8550)*, Taxi *(E. Providence 434-2000)*, Airport Limo *(TAG 450-9861)* **Near:** Local Bus *(RIPTA # 33 - Providence, TF Green)* **Under 1 mi:** Bikes *(E. Providence 437-2453)* **3+ mi:** Rail *(S. Attleboro, 11 mi.)* **Airport:** T.F. Green *(17 mi.)*

Medical Services

911 Service **Near:** Doctor *(Jones 289-0992)* **Under 1 mi:** Veterinarian *(Riverside 433-2070)* **1-3 mi:** Dentist *(Moakler 245-2377)*, Chiropractor *(Riverside 433-5559)* **Hospital:** Rhode Island 444-4000 *(8 mi.)*

Setting -- Tucked about halfway up Bullock Cove, expansive BCHM sprawls along the starboard shore. Five long docks host 348 quality slips plus extensive alongside dockage. A small dockhouse mans the on-shore fuel dock and two large travelifts front a massive, gray-blue workshed; several smaller shingled outbuildings house the office and amenities. A private pool sits at the rear of the property completely away from the yard operation, and inviting sand-floored picnic areas overlook A and D docks. The yard-maintained America's Cup yachts provide dock jewelry. Haines State Park borders the marina.

Marina Notes -- 8am-noon on Sat. Over $1 million dollars in improvements since Brewer acquisition. Courtesy Car. Short-term dockage/mooring rate. Sullivan flotation system, vinyl-trimmed wood docks. Ensign pedestals - 30/50 Amp, telephone & cable. Full-service boatyard known 12-Meters, J-Boats, & other high-performance racing machines. Largest travelifts in area. Brewer's Preferred Customer Program. Bathhouse: Beautifully done. Decorated with rich, warm diagonal wood paneling, tiled floors, vanities with large mirror above. Colorful, tiled shower stalls with private dressing rooms.

Notable -- Adjacent 102-acre Haines Memorial State Park offers 33 picnic areas with fireplaces, two ball fields, Paws Path dog walk, jogging trails, Wednesday Farmers' Market - and it's intersected by the East Bay Bike Path, a 14.5-mile 10-foot-wide paved trail between Bristol and Providence with spectacular bay views. Silver Springs Golf course, 2.5 miles north, once the private course for Mobil executives, is now a no-frills 9-hole public course. For a closer look at the Nayatt Point summer "cottages," take Washington Road south about two miles to Nayatt Road. The RIPTA bus to Providence stops nearby.

PHOTOS ON DVD: 23

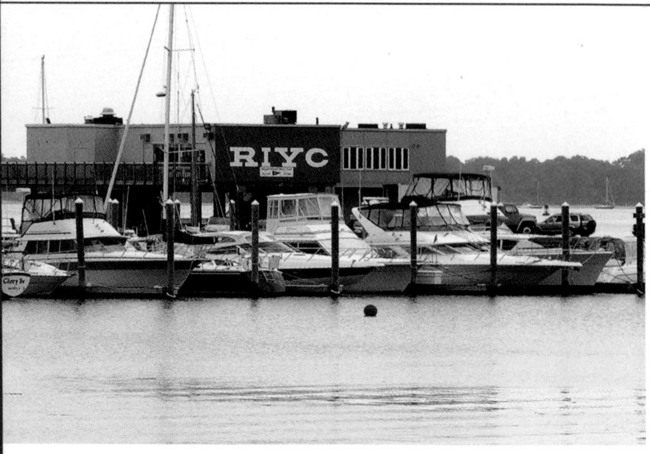

Rhode Island Yacht Club

PO Box; 1 Ocean Ave; Cranston, RI 02905

Tel: (401) 941-0220 **VHF: Monitor** Ch. 78 **Talk** Ch. 78
Fax: n/a **Alternate Tel:** n/a
Email: RIYC1@aol.com **Web:** www.riyc.org
Nearest Town: Pawtuxet Village *(.1 mi.)* **Tourist Info:** n/a

Navigational Information

Lat: 41°46.083' **Long:** 071°23.126' **Tide:** 4 ft. **Current:** 1 kt **Chart:** 13224
Rep. Depths (*MLW*): Entry 8 ft. **Fuel Dock** n/a **Max Slip/Moor** 8 ft./8 ft.
Access: Providence River past Conimicut Point to Stillhouse Cove

Marina Facilities *(In Season/Off Season)*

Fuel: No
Slips: 88 Total, 10 Transient **Max LOA:** 50 ft. **Max Beam:** 14 ft.
Rate *(per ft.)*: **Day** $1.50/$1* **Week** n/a **Month** $70
Power: 30 amp $5, **50 amp** $10, **100 amp** n/a, **200 amp** n/a
Cable TV: No **Dockside Phone:** No
Dock Type: Floating, Long Fingers, Wood
Moorings: 50 Total, 20 Transient **Launch:** No, Dinghy Dock
Rate: Day $20/10 **Week** n/a **Month** n/a
Heads: 2 Toilet(s), 2 Shower(s)
Internet: Yes *(Wi-Fi, Free)* **Laundry:** None
Pump-Out: OnSite, Self Service, 1 Central **Fee:** Free **Closed Heads:** Yes

Marina Operations

Owner/Manager: Ron Diehl **Dockmaster:** Same
In-Season: Apr 15-Nov 15, 9am-5pm **Off-Season:** n/a
After-Hours Arrival: 401-941-3335 & tie up at Courtesy Dock
Reservations: Yes, Recommended **Credit Cards:** Visa/MC
Discounts: None
Pets: Welcome **Handicap Access:** Yes, Heads

Marina Services and Boat Supplies

Services - Boaters' Lounge, Dock Carts **Communication -** Phone Messages, FedEx, UPS, Express Mail **Supplies - OnSite:** Ice *(Block, Cube)* **Near:** Bait/Tackle *(Reel Man 941-6853)* **1-3 mi:** Ships' Store *(Johnson 255-1246)*, Propane *(Stovepipe 941-9333)*

Boatyard Services

Nearest Yard: Frank Pettis (401) 781-2340

Restaurants and Accommodations

OnSite: Restaurant *(RIYC Friday Night 941-0220)* **Under 1 mi:** Restaurant *(Arunothai Cuisine 383-9545, L $8-11, D $9-19)*, *(Basta Italian 461-0330)*, *(Rim Nahm 467-7897, L&D $9-15)*, *(L'Attitude 780-8700, L&D $9-18.50)*, *(Wai Wai House 941-3360, Chinese, Del.)*, Lite Fare *(Mr. Peabody's 941-2258, B $5-$8, 8am-4pm)*, *(Little Fall's 781-8010, Pizza, bakery)*, Pizzeria *(Vivaldi's 461-7511)*, *(Steve's 467-4973)*, Inn/B&B *(Edgewood Manor 781-0099, $89-299, 1905 Greek Revival Mansion)* **1-3 mi:** Hotel *(Independence Place 275-0221)* **3+ mi:** Motel *(Motel 6 467-9800, $50-66, 4 mi)*, Hotel *(Courtyard 467-6900, $114-189, 4 mi)*, *(La Quinta 941-6600, $75, 4 mi)*

Recreation and Entertainment

OnSite: Picnic Area, Grills **Near:** Hike/Bike Trails *(City wide 4.5 miles)* **Under 1 mi:** Tennis Courts, Fitness Center *(Pawtuxet 941-9784)*, Fishing Charter *(Sakonnet 474-2405)*, Park *(Stillhouse Cove; Pawtuxet SP)*, Galleries *(Art & Soul 461-4511; Edgewood 461-7555)* **1-3 mi:** Playground *(Sprague; Park View; Columbia)*, Bowling *(Legion Bowl and Billiards 781-8888)*, Video Rental *(Redbox)*, Museum *(Culinary Arts 598-2805; $7/4; Natural History 785-9457, $2/1 museum; $3/2 planetarium)*, Cultural Attract *(Park Theatre 467-7275; Trinity Repertory 751-5500 - 4 mi)*, Sightseeing *(Carousel Village 785-3510; Roger Williams Park: Zoo 785-3510 & Botanical Center 785-9450)* **3+ mi:** Golf Course *(Button Hole 421-1664, 7 mi)*, Movie Theater *(Cable Car 272-3970, 4.3 mi)*

Provisioning and General Services

Near: Florist *(River's Edge 941-9972)* **Under 1 mi:** Convenience Store *(All Mall 461-6938)*, Market *(Lindsay's 781-6940)*, Wine/Beer *(Edgewood 785-2286)*, Bakery *(Little Fall 781-8010)*, Farmers' Market *(Pawtuxet Village, Sat 9-12, 751-6038)*, Bank/ATM, Protestant Church, Library *(Cranston 781-2450)*, Beauty Salon *(Bucarr's 461-6300)*, Dry Cleaners *(Village 467-8548)*, Laundry *(Edgewood 781-7875)*, Pharmacy *(Cameron 781-1919)*, Hardware Store *(Rocky's 941-8561)* **1-3 mi:** Supermarket *(Shaw's 941-4553)*, Gourmet Shop *(Ocean Pride 943-6690)*, Delicatessen *(Anthony's 461-9100)*, Liquor Store *(IM Gan 467-5558)*, Green Grocer *(Donabedians 941-7617)*, Fishmonger *(Gardner's Wharf)*, Post Office, Catholic Church, Synagogue, Department Store *(WalMart 781-2233)*

Transportation

OnCall: Rental Car *(Enterprise 780-9935)*, Taxi *(Yellow Cab 941-1122)*, Airport Limo *(Whatcheer 486-0840)* **Near:** Local Bus **3+ mi:** Rail *(Amtrak 800-872-7245, 5 mi.)* **Airport:** TF Green *(5 mi.)*

Medical Services

911 Service **Near:** Holistic Services *(Whispering Waters 785-2144)* **Under 1 mi:** Dentist *(Tramonti 785-2707)*, Chiropractor *(Mastronardi 941-2944)* **1-3 mi:** Doctor *(Swen 784-6963)*, Optician *(Double Vision 463-7100)*, Veterinarian *(4 Paws 785-1000)* **Hospital:** Rhode Island 444-4000 *(4 mi)*

Setting -- On the western shore of the Providence River in Stillhouse Cove, an extended breakwater protects the marina and mooring field - and serves as a recreation area with shuffleboard and walking path. A concrete slab on hurricane-proof pilings supports the 1956 starkly modern club house. Tucked beneath is a shaded picnic and storage area. A large observation deck faces the harbor and the one fixed pier that hosts the dockhouse and feeds the floating docks.

Marina Notes -- *Discounted rates for YCA reciprocating members. Founded 1875. Current, storm-proof edifice, built after hurricanes devastated the two previous club houses. Dining room opens Fridays (5-9pm) to the public with DJ or live music. Food & bar open to guests 363 days a year. Commodore Room available for functions at reasonable rates Power Port pedestals. Bathhouse: Located in the club house. Cinderblock walls, cement floors, industrial fixtures, plastic shower curtains. Note: Charts show shallow entrance, but club-funded dredging maintains an 8-foot depth in channel.

Notable -- RIYC sits on the edge of a mature upscale residential neighborhood; it's a short walk from there to the Pawtuxet Village Historic District - the most interesting houses are along Narragansett Avenue. First settled by Roger Williams in the early 18thC, two industries captured the power of the river - mills and ship builders. Then in the 19thC, those mills were converted to textile manufacturing and later the village became a summer resort. Gaspee Days (May-June) celebrates the attack by local patriots on the grounded British revenue schooner "Gaspee" - a precursor to the Revolutionary War. It's two blocks to restaurants, churches, markets and RIPTA buses to Roger Williams Park and Zoo, Providence and T.F. Green Int'l Airport.

Navigational Information
Lat: 41°46.590' **Long:** 071°23.230' **Tide:** 4 ft. **Current:** 3 kt. **Chart:** 13224
Rep. Depths (*MLW*): Entry 9 ft. **Fuel Dock** 9 ft. **Max Slip/Moor** 9 ft./-
Access: Providence river to end of Bullock Point reach (G29) follow channel

Marina Facilities *(In Season/Off Season)*
Fuel: *ValvTect/ Bio-Diesel* - Gasoline, Diesel
Slips: 125 Total, 10 Transient **Max LOA:** 80 ft. **Max Beam:** 20 ft.
Rate *(per ft.)*: **Day** $2.00 **Week** n/a **Month** n/a
Power: 30 amp Incl., **50 amp** n/a, **100 amp** n/a, **200 amp** n/a
Cable TV: No **Dockside Phone:** No
Dock Type: Floating, Long Fingers, Pilings, Alongside, Wood, Vinyl
Moorings: 0 Total, 0 Transient **Launch:** n/a, Dinghy Dock
Rate: Day n/a **Week** n/a **Month** n/a
Heads: 2 Toilet(s), 2 Shower(s)
Internet: Yes *(Wi-Fi, Free)* **Laundry:** 1 Washer(s), 1 Dryer(s)
Pump-Out: OnSite, Self Service, 1 Central **Fee:** Free **Closed Heads:** Yes

Marina Operations
Owner/Manager: Ray Mooney **Dockmaster:** Paul Gorton
In-Season: May-Sep, 8am-5pm* **Off-Season:** Oct-Apr, 9am-4pm
After-Hours Arrival: Tie up at Fuel Dock
Reservations: Yes, Required **Credit Cards:** Visa/MC, Dscvr, Amex
Discounts: None
Pets: Welcome **Handicap Access:** No

Port Edgewood Marina

1129 Narragansett Blvd; Providence, RI 02905

Tel: (401) 941-2000; (877) 325-7060 **VHF: Monitor** n/a **Talk** n/a
Fax: (401) 941-2202 **Alternate Tel:** n/a
Email: portedgewood@aol.com **Web:** www.portedgewood.com
Nearest Town: Cranston *(0.2 mi.)* **Tourist Info:** (401) 785-3780

Marina Services and Boat Supplies
Services - Docking Assistance, Security *(24 hrs., Security cameras)*, Dock Carts **Communication -** Fax in/out, FedEx, UPS, Express Mail **Supplies - OnSite:** Ice *(Block, Cube)*, Ships' Store, CNG **1-3 mi:** Bait/Tackle *(Reel Man 941-6853)* **3+ mi:** Propane *(Warren Petro 821-8021, 3.5 mi.)*

Boatyard Services
OnSite: Travelift *(25T)*, Crane, Launching Ramp, Engine mechanic *(gas, diesel)*, Electrical Repairs, Electronic Sales, Hull Repairs, Canvas Work, Bottom Cleaning, Compound, Wash & Wax, Propeller Repairs, Woodworking, Inflatable Repairs, Life Raft Service **Dealer for:** Mercury; Quicksilver; Banana Boats, MercCruiser Certified. **Member:** ABBRA - 3 Certified Tech(s), ABYC - 3 Certified Tech(s) **Yard Rates:** $65, Haul & Launch $10/ft *(blocking $5/ft)*, Power Wash $2/ft **Storage:** On-Land $85/ft

Restaurants and Accommodations
Under 1 mi: Restaurant *(Yun Nan 351-9311, D $10-25, Del.)*, *(La Mocana 941-4438)*, *(Fire & Ice 781-3050)*, *(El Pez Dorado 781-3050)*, Pizzeria *(Blvd Pizza 781-2730, Del.)*, Inn/B&B *(Albert House 461-0906, Cash only)*, *(Edgewood Manor 781-0099, $89-299, 1905 Historic Reg.)* **1-3 mi:** Restaurant *(El Principe 383-9743)*, *(Rim Nahm 467-7897, L&D $9-15)*, *(L'Attitude 780-8700, L&D $9-18.50)*, Hotel *(Radisson 272-5577)*

Recreation and Entertainment
Near: Museum *(Culinary Arts 598-2805, $7/6; Natural History/Planetarium 785-9457, $2-3/1-2 - 2 mi.)* **Under 1 mi:** Playground *(Columbia Park)*, Tennis Courts *(RWP)*, Fishing Charter *(Sakonnet 474-2405)*, Park *(Stillhouse Cove)*, Galleries *(Edgewood 461-7555; Art & Soul 461-5511)*
1-3 mi: Bowling *(Legion 781-8888)*, Movie Theater *(Cable Car 272-3970)*, Video Rental *(Redbox 467-7631)*, Tours *(Trolley 421-3825)*, Cultural Attract *(Park Theatre, 467-7275; Opera Providence 331-6060, 5 mi.)*, Sightseeing *(Roger Williams Zoo 785-3510 $12/6 & Botanical Ctr 785-9450; Carousel Village 785-3510)* **3+ mi:** Golf Course *(Button Hole 421-1664, 6 mi.)*

Provisioning and General Services
Near: Dry Cleaners *(Perfection 228-7011)* **Under 1 mi:** Convenience Store *(Speedy 461-0324)*, Market *(Correntes 437-6044)*, Health Food *(Vidsana 467-8489)*, Wine/Beer *(Edgewood 785-2286)*, Bakery *(Dan's 272-9773)*, Fishmonger *(Dias 461-4860)*, Bank/ATM, Post Office, Catholic Church, Protestant Church, Library *(Hall 781-2450)*, Beauty Salon *(Rosley's 781-6114)*, Laundry *(Laundromax 780-0727)*, Pharmacy *(Rite Aid 461-6438)*, Hardware Store *(Rocky's Ace 941-8561)*, Florist *(Blooming Mad 941-1140)* **1-3 mi:** Supermarket *(Shaws 941-4553)*, Gourmet Shop *(Gourmet 632-4100)*, Delicatessen *(Anthony's 461-9100)*, Liquor Store *(IM Gan 467-5558)*, Farmers' Market *(Pawtuxet Village, Sat 9-12, 751-6038)*, Green Grocer *(Donabedians 941-7617)*, Synagogue, Department Store *(WalMart 781-2233)*, Copies Etc. *(NE Copy 781-3039)*, Mosque

Transportation
OnCall: Rental Car *(Enterprise 946-3888)*, Taxi *(Yellow 941-1122)*, Airport Limo *(University 228-8588)* **Near:** Local Bus **Airport:** T.F. Green *(6 mi.)*

Medical Services
911 Service **Under 1 mi:** Doctor *(Fallon & Horan 467-3350)*, Dentist *(Comfort 781-5151)*, Chiropractor *(Lighthouse 751-6568)*, Veterinarian *(Hoffman 941-7345)* **Hospital:** Rhode Island 444-4000 *(3 mi.)*

Setting -- In a natural basin on the river's west bank, an extended, low-stone breakwater protects the network of floating wood docks. A huge, gray, arched-roof work/storage shed dominates the north end of the basin, and a smaller two-story office and ships' store, sporting a large water tower on the upper deck, anchors the west side. Recent white vinyl docks edge the basin hosting smaller boat slips and the shore-side fuel station. The ambiance is pure boatyard.

Marina Notes -- *Spring/Fall hours Mon-Fri 9am-5pm; Sat-Sun 9am-3pm. Nov -Closed Sun. Founded 1946. Christopher Migliaccio bought Thorsten's Boat Yard; renamed it Port Edgewood. In 1980, current owners expanded facility to manufacture Don Aronow-designed Banana Boats. Custom work on Carolina Skiffs. Bio-Diesel & gasoline. Mix of older wooden docks with older pedestals & bright-white vinyl. Single picnic table at end of "A" dock. Well-stocked chandlery. Add'l dockage at sister marina in Pawtuxet Cove. Bathhouse: Basic full baths with tile floors & raised fiberglass shower stalls. Laundry with folding table.

Notable -- In the historic Edgewood section, boasting blocks of 19thC. architecture, some of Providence's attractions are a stone's throw. The Culinary Arts Musuem, the world's largest cookery archive, features many fascinating exhibits on the Johnson & Wales Harborside Campus (0.3 mile). It's a mile to the Roger Williams Botanical Garden, then 0.8 mile strolling the 430-acre park's serpentine paths past the Natural History Museum & Planetarium to the Zoo - ranked in the nation's top ten. Less than three miles (nearby #3 bus), exciting "Downcity" is chock-a-block with creative restaurants, extensive art scene, WaterPlace Park and Riverwalk. Just beyond the hurricane gate, Waterfire Providence's 100 bonfires burn along the River accompanied by music and theater.

PHOTOS ON DVD: 22

19. RI – Narragansett Bay – West Passage

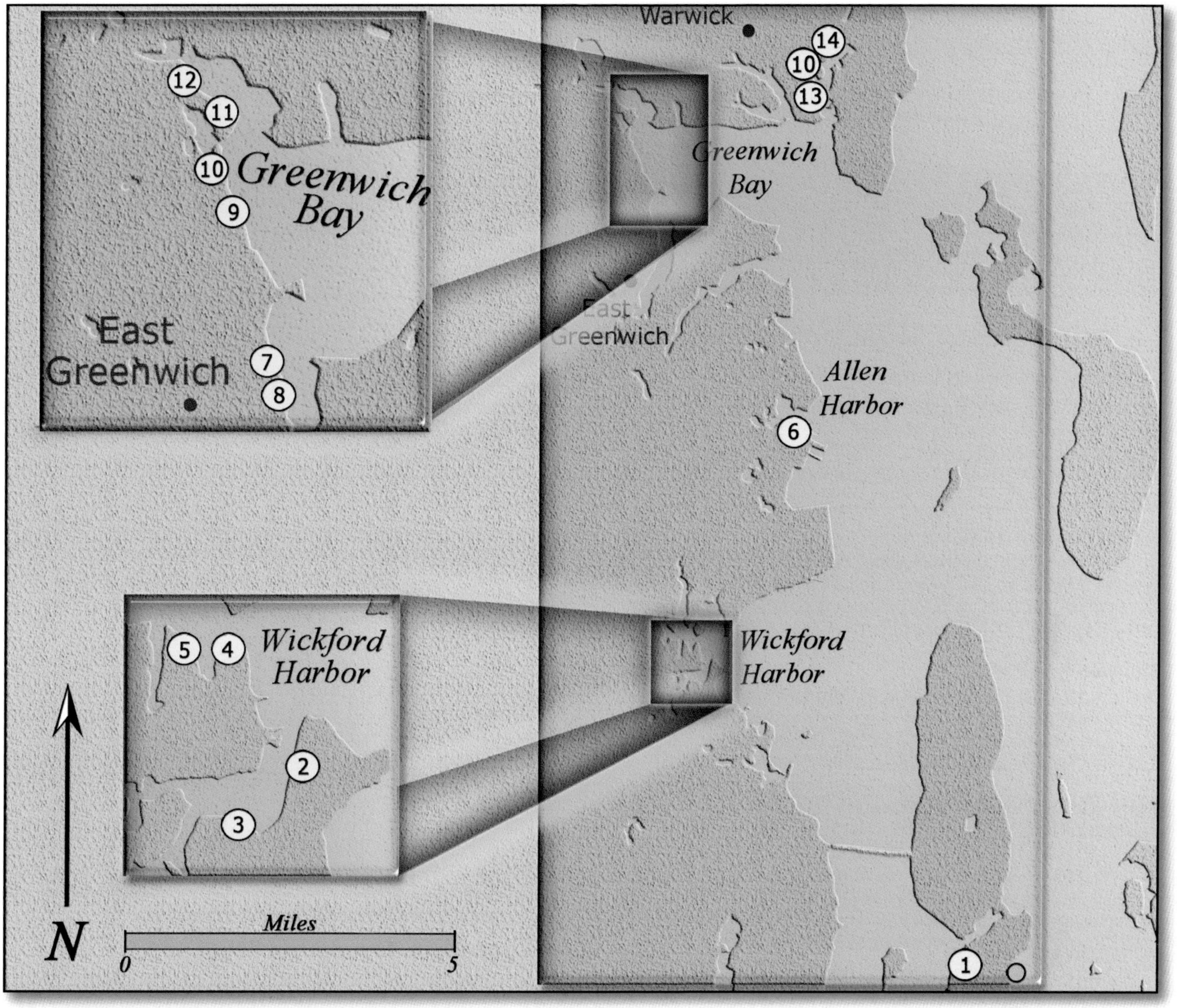

MAP	MARINA	HARBOR	PAGE
1	**Dutch Harbor Boatyard**	*Dutch Island Harbor*	346
2	**Wickford Shipyard**	*Wickford Harbor*	347
3	**Brewer Wickford Cove Marina**	*Wickford Harbor*	348
4	**Pleasant Street Wharf**	*Wickford Harbor*	349
5	**Wickford Marina**	*Wickford Harbor*	350
6	**Allen Harbor Marina**	*Allen Harbor*	351
7	**Norton's Shipyard & Marina**	*Greenwich Cove*	352
8	**Milt's Marina**	*Greenwich Cove*	353
9	**Brewer Yacht Yard Cowesett**	*Greenwich Bay*	354
10	**Brewer Greenwich Bay Marinas**	*Greenwich Bay*	355
11	**Apponaug Harbor Marina**	*Apponaug Cove*	356
12	**Ponaug Marina**	*Apponaug River*	357
13	**Warwick Cove Marina**	*Warwick Cove*	358
14	**Bay Marina**	*Warwick Cove*	359

RATINGS: 1-5 for Marina Facilities & Amenities,  1-2 for Boatyard Services,  1-2 for MegaYacht Facilities,  for Something Special.

SERVICES: for CCM – Certified Clean Marina,  for Pump-Out,  for Internet, for Fuel,  for Restaurant,  for Provisioning nearby,  for Catamaran-friendly,  for SportFish Charter,  for Pool/Beach, and  for Golf within a mile. *For an explanation of ACC's Ratings, see page 8.*

Dutch Harbor Boatyard

252 Narragansett Avenue; Jamestown, RI 02835

Tel: (401) 423-0630 **VHF: Monitor** Ch. 69 **Talk** n/a
Fax: (401) 423-3834 **Alternate Tel:** n/a
Email: info@dutchharborboatyard.com **Web:** dutchharborboatyard.com
Nearest Town: Jamestown *(0.7 mi.)* **Tourist Info:** (401) 423-3650

Navigational Information

Lat: 41°50.000' **Long:** 071°38.433' **Tide:** 4 ft. **Current:** n/a **Chart:** 13221
Rep. Depths (*MLW*): Entry 15 ft. **Fuel Dock** n/a **Max Slip/Moor** -/55 ft.
Access: West Passage to Dutch Island Harbor past steel pier

Marina Facilities *(In Season/Off Season)*

Fuel: No
Slips: 0 Total, 0 Transient **Max LOA:** 60 ft. **Max Beam:** 18 ft.
Rate *(per ft.)*: **Day** n/a **Week** n/a **Month** n/a
Power: 30 amp n/a, **50 amp** n/a, **100 amp** n/a, **200 amp** n/a
Cable TV: No **Dockside Phone:** No
Dock Type: Floating
Moorings: 100 Total, 12 Transient **Launch:** Yes (Free), Dinghy Dock
Rate: Day $50* **Week** n/a **Month** n/a
Heads: 2 Toilet(s), 4 Shower(s)
Internet: No **Laundry:** None
Pump-Out: OnSite, 1 Central **Fee:** Free **Closed Heads:** Yes

Marina Operations

Owner/Manager: Larry & Alison Eichler **Dockmaster:** Same
In-Season: May-MidOct, 8am-9pm** **Off-Season:** MidOct-Apr, 8am-4pm
After-Hours Arrival: Call in advance
Reservations: Yes, Online or phone **Credit Cards:** Visa/MC
Discounts: None
Pets: Welcome **Handicap Access:** No

Marina Services and Boat Supplies

Services - Dock Carts **Communication -** FedEx, DHL, UPS, Express Mail **Supplies - OnSite:** Ice *(Block, Cube)* **Under 1 mi:** Ships' Store *(Conanicut 423-1556)* **1-3 mi:** Bait/Tackle *(Zeeks Creek 423-1170)* **3+ mi:** West Marine *(841-9880, 7 mi.)*, Propane *(Spicer 596-6531, 5.5 mi.)*

Boatyard Services

OnSite: Railway *(30T New)*, Engine mechanic *(gas, diesel)*, Electrical Repairs, Hull Repairs, Rigger, Bottom Cleaning, Brightwork, Compound, Wash & Wax, Interior Cleaning, Woodworking, Painting, Awlgrip **OnCall:** Upholstery, Metal Fabrication **Member:** ABBRA **Yard Rates:** $75/hr.

Restaurants and Accommodations

OnSite: Lite Fare *(The Shack B $2-5, L $4-10, 8am-6pm, picnic tables, Lobster rolls)* **Near:** Restaurant *(PAC Pub 423-9909, L&D $7-14)* **Under 1 mi:** Restaurant *(Chopmist Charlies 423-1020, L $7-10, D $7-19, Casual fine)*, *(Trattoria Simpatico 423-3731, L $9-22, D $13-37, L Fri-Sun)*, *(Tricia's Tropi-grille 423-1490, L&D $12-19; Kids' $4-6)*, *(Narragansett Cafe 423-2150)*, *(Peking Garden 423-0680)*, Seafood Shack *(Jamestown Oyster Bar 423-3380, L&D $6-18)*, Lite Fare *(Slice of Heaven 423-9866, B $6-11, L $8-13, Kids' $4.25)*, Pizzeria *(House of Pizza 423-3060, Del.)*, *(Ace's 423-3282)*, Inn/B&B *(East Bay 423-0330, $99-185)*, *(Lionel Chaplin 423-7469, $120-175, Apt $260)* **1-3 mi:** Restaurant *(Bay Voyage 423-2100, D $22-34, jackets)*

Recreation and Entertainment

OnSite: Fishing Charter *(Sea Ya! 568-4766)* **Near:** Beach *(Mackerel Cove)*, Picnic Area *(Ft. Getty Recreation Area)* **Under 1 mi:** Tennis Courts *(Jamestown G.C.)*, Fitness Center *(Jamestown 560-0300)*, Video Rental *(Redbox; Video Showcase 423-2194)*, Park *(Artillery)*, Galleries *(Jamestown 423-3383)*, Special Events *(Fools' Rules Regatta - Aug)* **1-3 mi:** Golf Course *(Jamestown G.C. 423-9930)*, Museum *(Sydney L. Wright Museum 423-7280; Jamestown Fire Dept. Mem. 423-0062)*, Sightseeing *(Watson Farm 423-0005; Windmill Hill Historic District; Beavertail Lighthouse 423-9941 4 mi.)* **3+ mi:** Movie Theater *(Jane Pickens 846-5252, 6 mi.)*

Provisioning and General Services

Under 1 mi: Convenience Store *(Cumberland 423-2507)*, Market *(McQuade's 423-0879)*, Delicatessen *(East Ferry Mkt & Deli 423-1592)*, Wine/Beer *(Grapes 423-0070)*, Liquor Store *(Jamestown 423-0100)*, Bakery *(Village Hearth 423-9282)*, Fishmonger *(Zeeks Creek 423-1170)*, Bank/ATM *(Bank Newport; Bank of America)*, Post Office *(423-0420)*, Catholic Church, Protestant Church, Library *(Jamestown 423-7280)*, Beauty Salon *(Balayage 560-0642)*, Dry Cleaners *(Del Nero 423-1142)*, Laundry *(Del Nero)*, Pharmacy *(Bakers 423-2800; McQuade's)*, Hardware Store *(Jamestown 423-2722)*, Florist *(Secret Garden 423-0050)*, Clothing Store **3+ mi:** Supermarket *(Stop & Shop 845-2220, 6 mi.)*, Synagogue *(6 mi.)*

Transportation

OnCall: Rental Car *(Enterprise 849-3938)*, Taxi *(Cozy Cabs 846-2500)*, Airport Limo *(Posh 842-0005)* **Under 1 mi:** Ferry Service *(to Newport)* **3+ mi:** InterCity Bus *(5 mi.)*, Rail *(Kingston, 16 mi.)* **Airport:** TF Green *(22 mi.)*

Medical Services

911 Service **Under 1 mi:** Doctor *(NHCC Med. Ass. 423-2616)*, Dentist *(Bush 423-2110)*, Holistic Services *(Ocean Essence 423-9830)*, Veterinarian *(Jamestown 423-2288)* **Hospital:** Newport 846-6400 *(6 mi.)*

Setting -- Located on the western side of Conanicut Island, Dutch Harbor has the best of both worlds -- Jamestown's services, supplies and eateries within three-quarters of a mile coupled with the comparatively unspoiled ambiance of West Passage and one of the last pristine harbors on the bay. Dutch Island, part of the State of Rhode Island Park System, protects the expansive mooring field. Onshore, one fixed pier feeds new floating docks backed by a large, tan work shed and three small-shingled outbuildings - one housing "The Shack." West Ferry is a quiet neighborhood surrounded by farms and conservancy land.

Marina Notes -- *$50 to 45 ft., $60 45+. **In season open 'til 10pm Fri & Sat. Built on the site of Conanicut Ferry Landing - traversed West Passage to Saunderstown. New owners '09; completely renovated. New marine railway, floating docks & mooring launches. Mid-Jun-LabDay 8am-9pm, (to 10pm S&S), shoulder season shorter hours May to ColDay (Hail "Comet" Ch. 69). Snack bar with picnic tables - breakfast, lunch, ice cream; caters cruise events. Self-Serve pump-out. Bathhouse: Recently updated - full baths, tiled floors, attractively decorated - two add'l outdoor showers with spa-style heads.

Notable -- Just south of DHBY, Sheffield Cove, noted for its oysters, is adjacent to 31-acre Ft. Getty Park - with picnic areas, beaches, fishing pier and heads. Straight up and over, the Narragansett Avenue area delivers some notable eateries, neat shops, and most everything cruisers need - including a top local market with prepared food. A four-mile bike ride to the island's south end, Jamestown's top attraction, 155-acre Beavertail State Park, promises gorgeous views, a vehicle loop with four overlooks, hiking trails, ranger-led walks and a picturesque Lighthouse with museum, two keeper houses and small aquarium.

Navigational Information

Lat: 41°34.233' **Long:** 071°26.679' **Tide:** 3 ft. **Current:** .5 kt. **Chart:** 13223
Rep. Depths (*MLW*): Entry 9 ft. **Fuel Dock** 9 ft. **Max Slip/Moor** 7 ft./-
Access: Wickford Harbor, left at G7, first facility to port

Marina Facilities *(In Season/Off Season)*

Fuel: *Shell* - Gasoline, Diesel
Slips: 210 Total, 10 Transient **Max LOA:** 80 ft. **Max Beam:** 26 ft.
Rate *(per ft.)*: **Day** $1.50 **Week** n/a **Month** n/a
Power: 30 amp Incl., **50 amp** Incl., **100 amp** Incl., **200 amp** n/a
Cable TV: No **Dockside Phone:** No
Dock Type: Floating, Long Fingers, Wood
Moorings: 0 Total, 0 Transient **Launch:** n/a
Rate: Day n/a **Week** n/a **Month** n/a
Heads: 2 Toilet(s), 2 Shower(s)
Internet: No **Laundry:** 3 Washer(s), 4 Dryer(s)
Pump-Out: Self Service **Fee:** $10* **Closed Heads:** Yes

Marina Operations

Owner/Manager: Don Fraser **Dockmaster:** Same
In-Season: Year-Round, 8am-4:30pm **Off-Season:** n/a
After-Hours Arrival: Tie up at gas dock
Reservations: Yes **Credit Cards:** Visa/MC, Shell
Discounts: None
Pets: Welcome **Handicap Access:** No

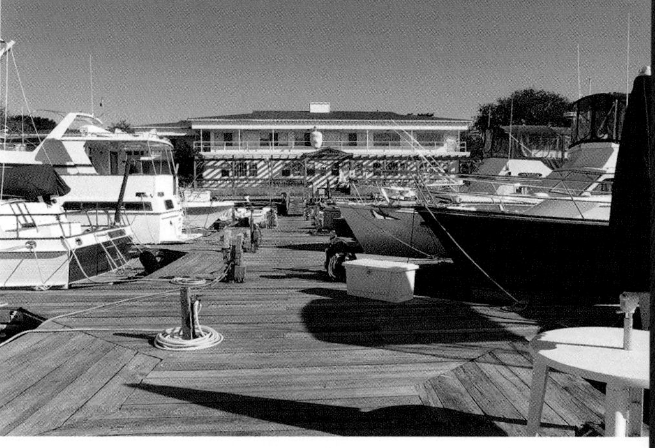

Wickford Shipyard

125 Steamboat Avenue; North Kingstown, RI 02852

Tel: (401) 884-1725 **VHF: Monitor** n/a **Talk** n/a
Fax: (401) 294-7736 **Alternate Tel:** n/a
Email: n/a **Web:** n/a
Nearest Town: Wickford *(0.5 mi.)* **Tourist Info:** (401) 295-5566

Marina Services and Boat Supplies

Services - Docking Assistance **Communication -** Mail & Package Hold, Phone Messages, Fax in/out *($1)*, FedEx, DHL, UPS, Express Mail **Supplies - OnSite:** Ice *(Block, Cube)*, Ships' Store **1-3 mi:** Bait/Tackle *(Quaker Lane 294-9642)*, Propane *(Arrow 294-9547)* **3+ mi:** West Marine *(884-0900, 9 mi)*

Boatyard Services

OnSite: Forklift, Crane, Launching Ramp, Engine mechanic *(gas)*, Hull Repairs, Bottom Cleaning, Brightwork, Compound, Wash & Wax, Metal Fabrication, Total Refits **OnCall:** Divers, Air Conditioning, Refrigeration, Interior Cleaning, Propeller Repairs, Inflatable Repairs, Life Raft Service **Near:** Sail Loft, Canvas Work. **Yard Rates:** $75/hr., Haul & Launch $13/ft. *(blocking incl.)*, Power Wash Incl.

Restaurants and Accommodations

OnCall: Pizzeria *(Chicago 295-1550)* **Under 1 mi:** Restaurant *(Quahog Company 294-2727)*, *(Tavern By The Sea 294-5771, L $7-13, D $17-23)*, *(Wickford Diner 295-5477, B, L, D $3-20)*, Lite Fare *(Bagelz 294-6366)*, *(Beach Rose Cafe 295-2800, $4-10 7am-3/4pm)*, Pizzeria *(Place 294-0800)*, Inn/B&B *(Haddie Pierce 294-7674, $140-160)* **1-3 mi:** Restaurant *(El Tapatio 295-2280, Mexican)*, *(Oak Hill Tavern & BBQ 294-3282, L&D $7-16)*, *(Tucker Seafood 885-2020)*, Motel *(Wickford Motor 294-4852, $65)*, Hotel *(Hamilton Village 295-0700, $99-139)*

Recreation and Entertainment

OnSite: Pool **Near:** Beach, Picnic Area, Grills, Playground, Tennis Courts **Under 1 mi:** Boat Rentals *(Kayak Centre 295-4400)*, Park *(Wilson)*, Sightseeing *(Wickford Historic District, Old Narragansett Church)*, Galleries *(Wickford Art Assoc. 294-6840; Voilà 667-5911; Eveline Luppi 294-9111)* **1-3 mi:** Fitness Center *(West Bay "Y" 295-6501)*, Horseback Riding *(Paramount 662-0520)*, Bowling *(Wickford Lanes 294-9886)*, Museum *(Smith's Castle 294-3521 $6/2;)* **3+ mi:** Golf Course *(No. Kingstown G.C. 294-0684, 6 mi.)*

Provisioning and General Services

Near: Newsstand **Under 1 mi:** Market *(Ryan's 294-9571)*, Gourmet Shop *(Wickford 295-8190)*, Bakery *(Pastry Gourmet 295-8400)*, Bank/ATM, Protestant Church, Library *(294-3306)*, Beauty Salon *(Bambole 294-2260)*, Bookstore *(Book Garden 294-3285)*, Pharmacy *(Rite Aid 294-3662)* **1-3 mi:** Supermarket *(Dave's 268-3991)*, Wine/Beer, Liquor Store *(Colonial 294-4623)*, Green Grocer *(Tower Hill 294-6633)*, Fishmonger *(Gardner's Wharf 295-4600)*, Post Office, Catholic Church, Dry Cleaners *(Rhode Island 294-6930)*, Hardware Store *(Wickford 295-8866)*, Florist *(Wickford 295-5900)*, Retail Shops *(Wickford Junction 294-0020)* **3+ mi:** Department Store *(WalMart 294-0025, 3.5 mi.)*, Copies Etc. *(Staples 295-5505, 3.5 mi)*

Transportation

OnCall: Rental Car *(Enterprise 885-7558)*, Taxi *(M&D 398-1100)*, Airport Limo *(A Airline 295-1100)* **Under 1 mi:** InterCity Bus *(RIPTA Providence)* **1-3 mi:** Rail *(Wickford Junction)* **Airport:** TF Green *(13 mi.)*

Medical Services

911 Service **Under 1 mi:** Chiropractor *(Village 667-7700)*, Holistic Services *(Earth & Ocean 294-2335)*, Optician *(South County 294-4506)* **1-3 mi:** Doctor *(Wickford 295-3120)*, Dentist *(Brunelle 295-2527)*, Veterinarian *(Wickford 295-9739)* **Hospital:** South County 782-8000 *(12 mi)*

Setting -- Starting at the mouth of narrow Wickford Cove, the Shipyard's seven sets of T-shaped docks march along the eastern shore. Beyond the fuel dock, backed by dry storage and large, antique work sheds, a white, two-story, hip-roofed, vaguely colonial building with a barren-wood pergola overlooks the marina. Behind a chain-link fence softened by evergreens and flower-filled planters is a pool. More steel work sheds and smaller out buildings fill the upland.

Marina Notes -- *Free pump-out with Fuel Purchase. Fuel dock at the cove entrance. Attendant usually only marina assistance. Nicely constructed, single-loaded slips with corner pieces. 30A power at some slips. Aging pool only open part-time. Small, sparsely stocked chandlery; boaters lounge next door. Many white or unpainted steel work buildings; maintenance could use a boost. Other commercial entities onsite. Bathhouse: Locked basic, linoleum floors, painted walls. Laundry. Note: For early arrivals, the town has five free 24-hour town moorings to port of harbor entrance (bright orange balls with blue "NK").

Notable -- A half-mile walk, downtown Wickford is truly a fantasy New England harborside village. The model for John Updike's "The Witches of Eastwick," summer is filled with festivals and juried fine arts and crafts shows. It's also a short dinghy ride across the Cove to the town dock - free for a two-hour visit (up to a 40-ft. LOA). From the Shipyard, a mile-long hike circles the Cove: walk along Steamboat Ave, a right on Beach St., another onto Boston Neck Rd - window shop over to the water. Then back onto Boston Neck, across the bridge onto Rte 1A and then to Washington St. Most of the tour focuses on the charming, 1.5-square mile Historic District with dozens of lovingly cared-for 18th & 19thC houses and Old St. Paul's Narragansett Church (1707). It's another mile back.

Brewer Wickford Cove Marina

65 Reynolds Street; North Kingstown, RI 02852

Tel: (401) 884-7014 **VHF: Monitor** Ch. 9 **Talk** Ch. 10
Fax: (401) 294-1541 **Alternate Tel:** n/a
Email: lcolantuono@byy.com **Web:** www.byy.com/wickford
Nearest Town: Wickford *(0.3 mi.)* **Tourist Info:** (401) 295-5566

Navigational Information

Lat: 41°34.091' **Long:** 071°26.873' **Tide:** 4 ft. **Current:** 1 kt. **Chart:** 13221
Rep. Depths (*MLW*): Entry 10 ft. **Fuel Dock** 10 ft. **Max Slip/Moor** 10 ft./-
Access: Wickford Harbor, then 2nd facility to port in Wickford Cove

Marina Facilities *(In Season/Off Season)*

Fuel: *ValvTect* - Gasoline, Diesel
Slips: 155 Total, 10 Transient **Max LOA:** 120 ft. **Max Beam:** 30 ft.
Rate *(per ft.)*: **Day** $3.00 **Week** $15 **Month** $45
Power: 30 amp $10/day, **50 amp** $16.67, **100 amp** n/a, **200 amp** n/a
Cable TV: No **Dockside Phone:** No
Dock Type: Floating, Long Fingers, Pilings, Alongside, Vinyl
Moorings: 44 Total, 6 Transient **Launch:** No, Dinghy Dock
Rate: Day $1.50/ft. **Week** $7.50/ft **Month** $22.50/ft
Heads: 4 Toilet(s), 4 Shower(s) *(dressing rooms)*, Book Exchange
Internet: Yes *(Wi-Fi, Free)* **Laundry:** 1 Washer(s), 1 Dryer(s)
Pump-Out: Self Service, 1 Central, 2 Port **Fee:** $5 **Closed Heads:** Yes

Marina Operations

Owner/Manager: Larry Colantuono **Dockmaster:** Same
In-Season: May-Oct, 7:30am-6pm **Off-Season:** Nov-Apr, 7:30am-5pm
After-Hours Arrival: Call ahead
Reservations: Yes, Required **Credit Cards:** Visa/MC, Dscvr, Amex
Discounts: Brewer Customer Club **Dockage:** n/a **Fuel:** n/a **Repair:** n/a
Pets: Welcome, Dog Walk Area **Handicap Access:** Yes, Heads

Marina Services and Boat Supplies

Services - Docking Assistance, Dock Carts **Communication -** Mail & Package Hold, Phone Messages, Fax in/out *($3)*, FedEx, DHL, UPS, Express Mail **Supplies - OnSite:** Ice *(Block, Cube)*, Ships' Store **Under 1 mi:** Bait/Tackle *(Wickford Rods 667-7363)* **1-3 mi:** Propane *(Arrow 294-9547; Taylor 884-1730)*

Boatyard Services

OnSite: Travelift *(70T)*, Forklift *(4T)*, Crane *(15T)*, Engine mechanic *(gas, diesel)*, Electrical Repairs, Electronics Repairs, Hull Repairs, Rigger, Sail Loft *(Canvasback)*, Canvas Work, Bottom Cleaning, Brightwork, Refrigeration, Compound, Wash & Wax, Interior Cleaning, Woodworking, Inflatable Repairs, Yacht Interiors, Metal Fabrication, Painting, Awlgrip, Total Refits, Yacht Broker **Member:** ABBRA, ABYC **Yard Rates:** $85/hr., Haul & Launch $10-12/ft. hwb *(blocking $3/ft)*, Power Wash $3/ft., Bottom Paint $11/ft. **Storage:** In-Water $40/ft., On-Land $4/sq ft.

Restaurants and Accommodations

Under 1 mi: Restaurant *(Beach Rose 295-2800, $4-10 7am-3/4pm)*, *(Tavern by the Sea 294-5771, L $7-13, D $17-20, Waterfront)*, *(The Place 294-0800)*, Lite Fare *(Wickford Diner 295-5477, B $3-6, L $3-15, Kids' $2-4)*, Hotel *(Hamilton Village 295-0700, $79-139)*, Inn/B&B *(Haddie Pierce House 294-7674, $140-160)* **1-3 mi:** Restaurant *(El Tapatio 295-2280)*, *(Oak Hill Tavern BBQ 294-3282, L&D $7-16)*, Pizzeria *(Kingston 294-1223)*

Recreation and Entertainment

OnSite: Picnic Area, Grills, Fishing Charter **Near:** Beach *(Town Beach)*, Playground, Boat Rentals *(Kayaks 295-4400)* **Under 1 mi:** Tennis Courts *(Wilson Park)*, Park *(Town Dock)*, Sightseeing *(Historic District)*, Galleries *(Wickford Art Assoc 294-6840)* **1-3 mi:** Fitness Center *(West Bay Y 295-6501)*, Horseback Riding *(Jey & Moon 219-2263)*, Bowling *(Wickford 294-9886)*, Video Rental *(Hunt 295-5550)*, Museum *(Smith's Castle 294-3521 $6/2)* **3+ mi:** Golf Course *(No. Kingstown 294-4051, 5.5 mi.)*

Provisioning and General Services

Near: Wine/Beer *(Colonial 294-4623)* **Under 1 mi:** Market *(Dave's 268-3991)*, Gourmet Shop *(Wickford Marketplace)*, Liquor Store *(Wickford 294-4681)*, Bakery *(Pastry Gourmet 295-8400)*, Green Grocer *(Tower Hill 294-6633)*, Fishmonger *(Gardner's 295-4600; Tucker 885-2020)*, Bank/ATM, Post Office, Catholic Church, Protestant Church, Library *(294-3306)*, Beauty Salon *(Bambole 294-2260)*, Bookstore *(Book Garden 294-3285)*, Pharmacy *(Rite Aid 294-3662)*, Florist *(Wickford 295-5900)*, Retail Shops *(Wickford Villlage)* **1-3 mi:** Convenience Store *(Mini-Mart 295-2080)*, Dry Cleaners *(Nguyen 295-1755)*, Hardware Store *(Wickford 295-8866)*, Department Store *(WalMart)* **3+ mi:** Supermarket *(Stop & Shop 268-3808, 4 mi.)*

Transportation

OnCall: Rental Car *(Enterprise 885-7558)*, Taxi *(M&D 398-1100)*, Airport Limo *(A Airline Express 295-1100)* **Under 1 mi:** InterCity Bus *(RIPTA Providence)* **1-3 mi:** Rail *(Wickford Junction)* **Airport:** TF Green *(13 mi.)*

Medical Services

911 Service **Near:** Dentist *(Updike 295-1992)*, Chiropractor *(Village 667-7700)*, Optician *(So.County 294-4506)* **Under 1 mi:** Holistic Services *(Earth & Ocean 294-2335)* **1-3 mi:** Doctor *(Sathya 295-4503)*, Veterinarian *(Wickford 295-9739)* **Hospital:** Newport 846-6400 *(12 mi.)*

PHOTOS ON DVD: 23

Setting -- Edging the nine-foot-wide entrance channel, Brewer's fore-and-aft moorings lead boaters to the matrix of neat, composite docks dominated by a large, soft-green work shed. Wooden boardwalks and wide decks with park benches and picnic areas front attractive, gray-shingled, single-story buildings - all with panoramic views of the marina and Cove. Abundant landscaping steps up the ambiance and helps hide the isolated "working" end of the marina.

Marina Notes -- Recent upgrades - gas grills, fencing, docks, dredging (10 ft.). Tie-fore-and-aft mooring system for boats to 80 feet plus 5 moorings in outer harbor - serviced by a "club-quality" launch. Ensign pedestals. Fuel dock finger piers converted to side-tie to accommodate larger yachts. 100A, single-phase $33, 3-phase $50. Fish-cleaning table with tap. Dinghy dock $10/day, $45/wk, $135/mo. Bathhouse: Separate building. Spacious, exceptional full baths - tiled floors and wainscot with varnished, diagonal tongue & groove wood above. Fiberglass shower stalls with glass doors, dressing bench. Also roll-in shower.

Notable -- It's a half mile to West Main and Brown - the heart of Wickford Village's shopping district with forty unique, locally owned boutiques, galleries, and shops in two 19thC business sectors - the redbrick Avis Block and the brick/stone Gregory Block. Incorporated in 1674, over 95% of the original colonial village is still intact. Stroll the 1.5 square mile historic homes district, which includes the 1707 Narragansett Episcopal Church - the largest collection of colonial houses in the US. Over 300 artists show their work at the Wickford Artists Gallery, south of the marina on the way to the town beach. The Wickford Arts Fair is usually the second weekend in July. A short drive or bike ride away are historic treasures such as Gilbert Stuart's birthplace and Smith's Castle.

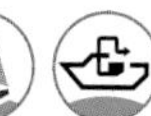

Navigational Information

Lat: 41°34.628' **Long:** 071°26.887' **Tide:** 4 ft. **Current:** .2 kt. **Chart:** 13221
Rep. Depths (*MLW*): Entry 13 ft. **Fuel Dock** 13 ft. **Max Slip/Moor** 13 ft./10 ft.
Access: Wickford Harbor, starboard to R10 & entrance to Mill Cove

Marina Facilities *(In Season/Off Season)*

Fuel: Gasoline, Diesel
Slips: 50 Total, 2 Transient **Max LOA:** 40 ft. **Max Beam:** 13 ft.
Rate *(per ft.)*: **Day** $1.50/$1.50 **Week** $10.50 **Month** $45
Power: 30 amp $0, **50 amp** n/a, **100 amp** n/a, **200 amp** n/a
Cable TV: No **Dockside Phone:** No
Dock Type: Floating, Long Fingers, Alongside, Wood
Moorings: 10 Total, 1 Transient **Launch:** Yes, Dinghy Dock
Rate: Day $35 **Week** n/a **Month** n/a
Heads: 3 Toilet(s), 2 Shower(s), Book Exchange
Internet: No **Laundry:** None
Pump-Out: OnSite, Self Service, 1 Central **Fee:** n/a **Closed Heads:** Yes

Marina Operations

Owner/Manager: Eric Collins **Dockmaster:** Rob Collins
In-Season: Mem-LabDay, 8am-8pm **Off-Season:** Sep-May, 8am-2pm
After-Hours Arrival: Call in advance
Reservations: No **Credit Cards:** Visa/MC
Discounts: None
Pets: Welcome **Handicap Access:** No

Pleasant Street Wharf

160 Pleasant Street; North Kingstown, RI 02852

Tel: (401) 294-2791 **VHF: Monitor** n/a **Talk** n/a
Fax: (401) 295-8032 **Alternate Tel:** n/a
Email: pswinc@verizon.net **Web:** www.pswri.com
Nearest Town: Wickford Village *(0.25 mi.)* **Tourist Info:** (877) 295-7200

Marina Services and Boat Supplies

Communication - FedEx, DHL, UPS **Supplies - OnSite:** Ice *(Block, Cube)* **1-3 mi:** Ships' Store *(Marine Consignment 295-9709)*, Bait/Tackle *(Quaker Lane 294-9642)*, Propane *(Arrow 294-9547)*

Boatyard Services

OnSite: Travelift *(15T)*, Crane, Hydraulic Trailer *(Boat Transport)*, Engine mechanic *(gas, diesel)*, Hull Repairs, Bottom Cleaning, Propeller Repairs, Painting **Yard Rates:** $80/hr., Haul & Launch $10/ft., Power Wash $4/ft., Bottom Paint $18/ft. *(paint incl.)*

Restaurants and Accommodations

Under 1 mi: Restaurant *(Beach Rose Cafe 295-2800, $4-10 7am-3/4pm)*, *(Tavern by the Sea 294-5771, L $7-13, D $17-20)*, *(Wickford Diner 295-5477)*, Pizzeria *(The Place 294-0800)*, Inn/B&B *(Haddie Pierce House 294-7674, $140-160)* **1-3 mi:** Restaurant *(El Tapatio 295-2280, Mexican)*, *(Oak Hill 294-3282, Tavern & BBQ, L&D $7-16)*, *(Tucker Seafood 885-2020)*, *(Gillian's Ale House 667-0900)*, *(Duffy's Tavern 295-0073)*, Pizzeria *(Kingston 294-1223, Del.)*, Motel *(Wickford 294-4852)*, *(Budget Inn 294-4888, $55+)*, Hotel *(Hamilton Village Inn 295-0700, $99-139)*

Recreation and Entertainment

OnSite: Picnic Area, Grills, Fishing Charter *(Reel Dog 935-6734)* **Near:** Hike/Bike Trails, Sightseeing *(Wickford Historic District; Hamilton Mill Village Historic District - 2 mi.)* **Under 1 mi:** Playground, Tennis Courts *(Wilson Park)*, Boat Rentals *(Kayak Centre 295-4400)*, Park *(Wilson)*, Galleries *(Mystic Scrimshanders 294-2262; Voila 667-5911; Five Main 294-6280; Benjamin Thomas 295-7555)* **1-3 mi:** Pool *("Y" 295-6501)*, Beach *(Town Beach)*, Dive Shop *(Oceanus 850-0502)*, Fitness Center *(Fabulous 667-7877)*, Horseback Riding *(Paramount 662-0520)*, Bowling *(Wickford Lanes 294-9886)*, Video Rental *(Hunt 295-5550)*, Museum *(Smith's Castle 294-3521 $6/2)* **3+ mi:** Golf Course *(No. Kingstown Mun. 294-4051, 5 mi.)*

Provisioning and General Services

Near: Fishmonger *(Gardner's Wharf 295-4600)*, Bank/ATM, Beauty Salon *(Magic Mirror 295-2530)* **Under 1 mi:** Market *(Ryan's 294-9571)*, Gourmet Shop *(Wickford Marketplace 667-5940)*, Wine/Beer *(Colonial 294-4623)*, Liquor Store *(Wickford 294-4681)*, Bakery *(Pastry 295-8400)*, Post Office, Protestant Church, Library *(North Kingstown 294-3306 Internet)*, Dry Cleaners *(Security 294-2566)*, Bookstore *(Book Garden 294-3285)*, Pharmacy *(Rite Aid 294-3662)*, Florist *(Wickford 295-5900)*, Retail Shops *(Wickford Village)* **1-3 mi:** Convenience Store *(Mini Mart 295-2080)*, Supermarket *(Dave's 268-3991)*, Delicatessen *(King 295-1243)*, Green Grocer *(Tower Hill 294-6633)*, Catholic Church, Hardware Store *(Wickford Lumber 295-8866)* **3+ mi:** Department Store *(WalMart 294-0025, 3.5 mi.)*

Transportation

OnCall: Rental Car *(Enterprise 885-7558)*, Taxi *(Bay 461-0780)*, Airport Limo *(Air Exp 295-1100)* **Under 1 mi:** InterCity Bus *(RIPTA Providence)* **3+ mi:** Rail *(Wickford Junction, 3.5 mi.)* **Airport:** TF Green *(13 mi.)*

Medical Services

911 Service **Under 1 mi:** Dentist *(Updike 295-1992)*, Chiropractor *(Village 667-7700)*, Holistic Services *(Earth & Ocean 294-2335)*, Optician *(So. County Eye 294-4506)* **1-3 mi:** Doctor *(Sathya 295-1992)*, Veterinarian *(Wickford Vet 295-9739)* **Hospital:** Newport 846-6400 *(12 mi.)*

Setting -- At the entrance to Mill Cove, this delightful, appropriately named, no-frills marina offers a mix of alongside dockage, slips and moorings in a casual, convivial old-time boatyard atmosphere. The dockside picnic area with grills, tables and fish cleaning station fronts the weathered-shingle main building.The Wickford Yacht Club is next door and both are in the middle of the historic district - a third-of-a-mile walk to the main crossroads of Wickford Village.

Marina Notes -- Family owned/operated since 1970. Owners live onsite. Simple electric boxes and water connections along the vinyl-edged, somewhat aging docks. Specializes in boat transport to 40-ft. Fish-cleaning table. Occasional stocked lobster pound (call first). Bathhouse: Quite nice full bathrooms with upscale tiled walls and floor; fiberglass shower stalls with curtains. Note: Add'l moorings from WYC & Harbormaster (294-3311, Ch.12).

Notable -- The 1.5-square-mile Wickford Village Historic District boasts the largest population of 17th- and 18th-century houses in the country. The centerpiece, St. Paul's Narragansett, built in 1701, is the oldest Episcopal church in America. A block off Pleasant and Main Streets, the Town Wharf berths the local fishing fleet and Gardner's Wharf seafood. Supported by the 40 locally-owned shops, galleries and eateries, the Wickford Village Association sponsors a string of events including the Arts Festival in July and Quahog Fest in August. Two miles north, Smith's Castle, a restored 18th-century mansion with historic gardens, started out as a 17th-century trading post that grew into a large plantation. Also well worth a visit, the Gilbert Stuart Museum (4.5 miles south, 294-3001, $7/4) replicates 1750s home with an herb garden, grist mill and docents. The RIPTA #14 bus along Rte 1A saves about half the walking distance.

PHOTOS ON DVD: 24

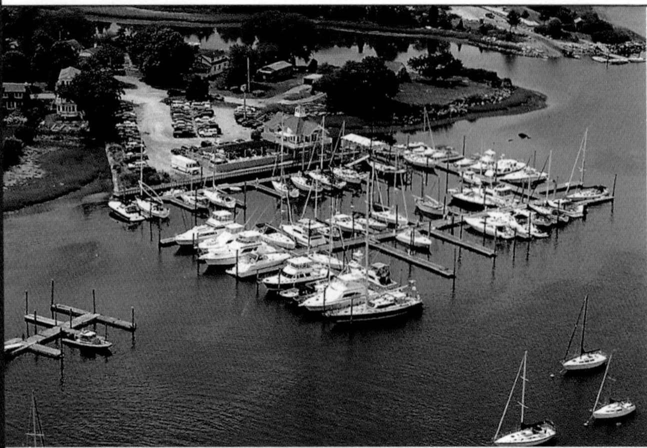

Wickford Marina

PO Box 1402; 67 Esmond Avenue; North Kingstown, RI 02852

Tel: (401) 294-8160 **VHF: Monitor** Ch. 10 **Talk** Ch. 10
Fax: (401) 294-6063 **Alternate Tel:** (401) 294-6063
Email: wickford.marina@verizon.net **Web:** www.wickfordmarina.com
Nearest Town: Wickford *(0.4 mi.)* **Tourist Info:** (401) 295-5566

Navigational Information
Lat: 41°34.600' **Long:** 071°26.960' **Tide:** 4 ft. **Current:** .2 kt. **Chart:** 13221
Rep. Depths (*MLW*): Entry 12 ft. **Fuel Dock** n/a **Max Slip/Moor** 10 ft./-
Access: Wickford Brkwtr to R8. Starboard channell to last marina on port.

Marina Facilities *(In Season/Off Season)*
Fuel: No
Slips: 70 Total, 6 Transient **Max LOA:** 100 ft. **Max Beam:** 16 ft.
Rate *(per ft.)*: **Day** $2.60/$1.75* **Week** $18.20 **Month** n/a
Power: 30 amp $8, **50 amp** $12, **100 amp** n/a, **200 amp** n/a
Cable TV: No **Dockside Phone:** No
Dock Type: Floating, Long Fingers, Wood
Moorings: 0 Total, 0 Transient **Launch:** n/a
Rate: Day n/a **Week** n/a **Month** n/a
Heads: 2 Toilet(s), 2 Shower(s) *(dressing rooms)*
Internet: Yes *(Wi-Fi, Inq.)* **Laundry:** 1 Washer(s), 1 Dryer(s)
Pump-Out: OnSite, Self Service, 1 Central **Fee:** $5 **Closed Heads:** Yes

Marina Operations
Owner/Manager: Paul Galego **Dockmaster:** Same
In-Season: Jun-Oct 15, 8am-5pm **Off-Season:** Oct 15-May, 8am-12pm**
After-Hours Arrival: Tie up to the pump-out station
Reservations: Yes, Required **Credit Cards:** Visa/MC
Discounts: None
Pets: Welcome **Handicap Access:** Yes, Heads, Docks

Marina Services and Boat Supplies
Services - Docking Assistance, Dock Carts **Communication -** Fax in/out *($2)*, FedEx, DHL, UPS, Express Mail **Supplies - OnSite:** Ice *(Block, Cube)* **Under 1 mi:** Ships' Store *(Brewer)* **1-3 mi:** Bait/Tackle *(Wickford Rods 667-7363; Quaker Lane 294-9642)*, Propane *(Taylor 295-0016)*

Boatyard Services
Nearest Yard: Pleasant Street Wharf (401) 294-2791

Restaurants and Accommodations
OnCall: Pizzeria *(The Place 294-0800)*, *(Chicago 295-1550)* **Under 1 mi:** Restaurant *(Tavern by the Sea 294-5771, L $7-13, D $17-20)*, *(Beach Rose Cafe 295-2800, $4-10 7am-3/4pm, waterfront)*, *(Wickford Diner 295-5477)*, *(El Tapatio 295-2280, Mexican)*, *(Oak Hill 294-3282, Tavern & BBQ, L&D $7-16)*, Inn/B&B *(Haddie Pierce 294-7674, $140-160)* **1-3 mi:** Restaurant *(Duffy's Tavern 294-3733, L $4-14, D $6-33, seafood, raw bar, lobsters)*, *(Tucker Seafood 885-2020)*, *(Gillian's Ale House 667-0900)*, Motel *(Hamilton Village 295-0700, $99-139)*, *(Wickford Motor 294-4852)*

Recreation and Entertainment
OnSite: Spa, Picnic Area, Grills, Boat Rentals *(Kayaks, Complimentary)* **Near:** Beach, Jogging Paths *(Wilson Park)*, Hike/Bike Trails *(Wilson Park)* **Under 1 mi:** Tours, Sightseeing *(Wickford Historic District)*, Galleries *(Five Main 294-6280; Mystic Scrimshanders 294-2262; Voila 667-5911; Benjamin Thomas 295-7555)*, Special Events *(Arts Fest - Mid July; Quahog Fest - Late Aug)* **1-3 mi:** Playground *(Wilson Park)*, Dive Shop *(Oceanus 850-0502)*, Tennis Courts *(Wilson Park)*, Fitness Center *(Fabulous 667-7877)*, Horseback Riding *(Paramount 662-0520)*, Bowling *(Wickford Lanes 294-9886)*, Video Rental *(Hunt 295-5550)*, Park *(Wilson)*, Museum *(Smith's Castle 294-3521, $6/2; Seabee 294-7233; Gilbert Stuart 294-3001 - 4.5 mi; Quonset Air 294-9540 - 5.6 mi.)* **3+ mi:** Golf Course *(North Kingstown Muni 294-4051, 5 mi)*, Movie Theater *(Showcase 885-4793, 9 mi)*

Provisioning and General Services
Near: Beauty Salon *(Magic Mirror 295-2530)* **Under 1 mi:** Wine/Beer *(Colonial 294-4623)*, Liquor Store *(Wickford 294-4681)*, Bakery *(Pastry 295-8400)*, Fishmonger *(Gardner's Wharf 295-4600)*, Bank/ATM, Post Office, Protestant Church, Library *(N. Kingstown 294-3306)*, Dry Cleaners *(Security 294-2566)*, Bookstore *(Book Garden 294-3285)*, Pharmacy *(Rite Aid 694-3662)*, Florist *(Wickford 295-5900)*, Retail Shops *(Wickford Village)* **1-3 mi:** Convenience Store *(Mini Mart 295-2080)*, Supermarket *(Dave's 268-3991; Stop & Shop 268-3808 - 4 mi.)*, Green Grocer *(Tower Hill Fruit 294-6633)*, Catholic Church, Hardware Store *(Wickford Lumber 295-8866)* **3+ mi:** Department Store *(WalMart 294-0025, 3.5 mi.)*, Copies Etc. *(Staples 295-5505, 3.5 mi.)*

Transportation
OnSite: Courtesy Car/Van **OnCall:** Rental Car *(Enterprise 885-7558)*, Taxi *(Bay 461-0780)*, Airport Limo *(Airl Exp 295-1100)* **Under 1 mi:** InterCity Bus *(RIPTA #14)* **1-3 mi:** Rail *(Wickford Junc.)* **Airport:** TF Green *(13 mi.)*

Medical Services
911 Service **Under 1 mi:** Dentist *(Updike 295-1992)*, Chiropractor *(Village 667-7700)*, Holistic Services *(Earth & Ocean294-2335)*, Optician *(So. County Eye 294-4506)* **1-3 mi:** Doctor *(Sathya 295-4503)*, Veterinarian *(Wickford 295-9739)* **Hospital:** So. County 471-6777 *(12 mi.)*

PHOTOS ON DVD: 23

Setting -- The cupola atop the two-story, gray-shingled contemporary colonial identifies this thoughtfully designed destination marina in placid Mill Cove. Vinyl-edged, floating wood docks, laid out in a "U"-shape with a single T-head, lead to a dockside yellow-and-white-striped, tented pavilion. Umbrella-topped tables, an elevated hot tub and a pergola above a massive bed of hydrangeas sit on the delightful 3,000-square-foot patio deck overlooking the docks.

Marina Notes -- *32 ft. min. **Tue-Sat. Built in 1997 by current owners on site of century-old Wickford Shellfish Co. 100-foot wide channel from Wickford Cove to docks. Patio equipped with impressive, unique galley with built-in grill, convection oven, pots, utensils, and stocked with condiments - just add food. Hosts groups to 20 boats. Bathhouse: In main building. Nicely done, fully tiled separate rooms - heads with sinks & shower stalls with dressing area & bench.

Notable -- Everything is beautifully maintained - from the flower-filled planters to the pavilion with roll-down screens, comfortable Adirondack-style chairs and a surround-sound system to the terrace, designed with an alfresco "restaurant feel" and large hot tub with panoramic cove views. Borrow kayaks to explore Mill Cove bounded by a 60-acre wildlife sanctuary including Conanicus/Cornelius and Rabbit Islands with sandy beaches. It's a short dinghy ride to Wickford Village docks - or a pleasant half-mile walk through the one-and-a-half square mile historic district densely packed with lovingly restored 18th & 19thC houses. Stop at perfectly preserved "Old" St. Paul's Narragansett Church, built in 1701 (open weekends). Sunday services are held at "New" 1847 St. Paul's Episcopal and at the 1816 Baptist Church. Nearly forty locally owned shops meet most needs. It's a mile to Wilson Park for tennis, playgounds and fields.

Navigational Information
Lat: 41°37.225' **Long:** 071°24.752' **Tide:** 5 ft. **Current:** 1 kt. **Chart:** 13223
Rep. Depths (*MLW*): Entry 8 ft. **Fuel Dock** n/a **Max Slip/Moor** 8 ft./8 ft.
Access: Narragansett Bay to Quanset Point follow channel markers

Marina Facilities *(In Season/Off Season)*
Fuel: No
Slips: 125 Total, 5 Transient **Max LOA:** 35 ft. **Max Beam:** 12 ft.
Rate *(per ft.)*: **Day** $1.50* **Week** $10.50 **Month** $86
Power: 30 amp n/a, **50 amp** n/a, **100 amp** n/a, **200 amp** n/a
Cable TV: No **Dockside Phone:** No
Dock Type: Floating, Long Fingers, Wood
Moorings: 80 Total, 10 Transient **Launch:** Yes ($10), Dinghy Dock ( )
Rate: Day $25 **Week** $175 **Month** $250
Heads: 2 Toilet(s)
Internet: No **Laundry:** None
Pump-Out: OnCall *(Ch 73)*, Full Service **Fee:** Free **Closed Heads:** Yes

Marina Operations
Owner/Manager: William Slater **Dockmaster:** Same
In-Season: Apr-Dec, 8am-4pm **Off-Season:** Jan-Mar, Closed
After-Hours Arrival: Courtesy Dock
Reservations: None **Credit Cards:** Visa/MC, Dscvr
Discounts: None
Pets: Welcome **Handicap Access:** Yes, Heads

Allen Harbor Marina

PO Box 352; 24 Bruce Boyer Road; North Kingstown, RI 02852

Tel: (401) 294-1212 **VHF: Monitor** Ch. 73 **Talk** Ch. 73
Fax: n/a **Alternate Tel:** n/a
Email: n/a **Web:** www.wickfordyc.org
Nearest Town: Wickford Village *(5 mi)* **Tourist Info:** (401) 295-5566

Marina Services and Boat Supplies
Services - Security *(Police Patrol)*, Dock Carts **Communication -** FedEx, UPS, Express Mail **Supplies - OnSite:** Ice *(Cube)* **1-3 mi:** Ships' Store *(Consolidated 398-8849)*, Marine Discount Store *(Consignment 295-9709)*, Bait/Tackle *(Beavertail 215-5062)*, Propane *(Inergy 294-9547)*

Boatyard Services
Nearest Yard: Johnson's

Restaurants and Accommodations
OnCall: Pizzeria *(Pier 886-9899)* **1-3 mi:** Restaurant *(Seven Moons 885-8383, L $5-14, D $11-40, Asian; Kids' $8)*, *(Pagoda 294-2200, $9-29)*, *(Sonoma Grille 295-0800, L $7-10, D $8-17)*, Fast Food *(BK, KFC)* **3+ mi:** Restaurant *(Meritage 884-1255, 5 mi., L&D $10-24)*, *(Walt's Roast Beef 884-9719, 3.5 mi.)*, Lite Fare *(Breakfast Nook 884-6108, 3.5 mi.)*, Motel *(Kingstown 884-1160, $55-89, 4 mi.)*, *(Wickford Motor Inn 294-4852, $55+, 4 mi.)*, Hotel *(Budget Inn 294-4888, $55+, 4 mi.)*, Inn/B&B *(Mrs. B's 885-1712, 4 mi.)*

Recreation and Entertainment
OnSite: Beach, Picnic Area, Grills, Playground, Park *(24 Bruce Boyer St)* **Near:** Special Events *(Quonset Air Show July 4th weekend)* **1-3 mi:** Dive Shop *(Subsalve 884-8801)*, Tennis Courts *(Wilson Park)*, Golf Course *(North Kingstown 294-4051)*, Video Rental *(Amazing Superstores)*, Museum *(Seabee Memorial 294-7233; Quonset Air 294-9540 $7/3 - 3.5 mi.)* **3+ mi:** Bowling *(Kingstown 884-4450, 4.5 mi.)*, Movie Theater *(Showcase 885-4793, 8.5 mi.)*, Sightseeing *(Smith's Castle 294-3521, $6/2; Wickford Historic District, 5.5 mi, 4.5 mi.)*

Provisioning and General Services
1-3 mi: Market *(Dave's 295-0019)*, Beauty Salon *(Supercuts 267-0006)*, Hardware Store *(BB &S Lumber 295-3200)*, Retail Shops *(Yorktown Shopping Center)*, Department Store *(Kohl's 295-7955)* **3+ mi:** Supermarket *(Super Stop & Shop 884-9400, 7 mi.)*, Wine/Beer *(Colonial 294-4623, 4 mi.)*, Liquor Store *(Thorpe's 885-4485, 5 mi.)*, Bank/ATM *(3.5 mi.)*, Post Office *(294-5842, 4 mi.)*, Catholic Church *(4 mi.)*, Protestant Church *(3.5 mi.)*, Library *(Davisville 884-5524, 4.5 mi.)*, Pharmacy *(CVS 885-4920, 4 mi.)*

Transportation
OnCall: Rental Car *(Enterprise 885-7558)*, Taxi *(M&D 398-1100)*, Airport Limo *(Ocean State 826-4300)* **1-3 mi:** Local Bus *(RIPTA)* **3+ mi:** Rail *(Kingston Amtrak, 16 mi.)* **Airport:** TF Green *(12 mi.)*

Medical Services
911 Service **1-3 mi:** Doctor *(Bayside Family HC 295-9706)*, Chiropractor *(Back & Neck 295-8606)* **3+ mi:** Dentist *(Bridgetown Dental 885-2260, 3.5 mi.)*, Holistic Services *(Optimal Health 884-1757, 5 mi.)*, Veterinarian *(Wickford Clinic 295-9739, 3.5 mi.)* **Hospital:** Kent 737-7000 *(11 mi.)*

Setting -- Inside well-protected Allen Harbor, a "summer camp" feeling permeates this small, neat municipal marina. The facility consists of three floating wood docks with finger piers, a separate fixed dock with alongside floating docks for pump-out and a small-boat mooring field. Colorful pots of flowers dot the landscape and brighten the small, single-story, garage-like office building. A horseshoe pit adds to the "camp" ambiance, and covered pavilion with BBQ pit and tables offers the best view of the serene harbor.

Marina Notes -- Originally part of the Davisville Navy facility & Navy Sea Bee's training center, deeded to North Kingstown as a municipal marina. Difficult channel leading into cove - almost impossible for vessels larger than 40 ft. due to sharp turns. Water only; no electricity on docks. 3 marked courtesy docks for short-term visits. Pump-out Ch 73. Large upgraded pavilion rentable for big gatherings. Special rates for N. Kingstown residents. Bathhouse: Separate well-maintained plain white cinderblock building with industrial fixtures. No showers.

Notable -- For a safe port in a sudden storm, this marina is extremely well-protected and offers a quiet place away from it all. Even though it is isolated from walkable resources by the Davis Navy base which surrounds it, there is a shopping center 2.3 miles away anchored by a Kohl's and Dave's Marketplace (an upscale supermarket). Next door to the mall is the in-development Seabees Museum, built and run by Seabees and their families, and the Quonset Air Museum, 3.5 miles from the docks, at the south end of the airport, exhibits 28 aircraft, (C. 1944-1983) plus parts and other artifacts. Wickford Village is 5 miles.

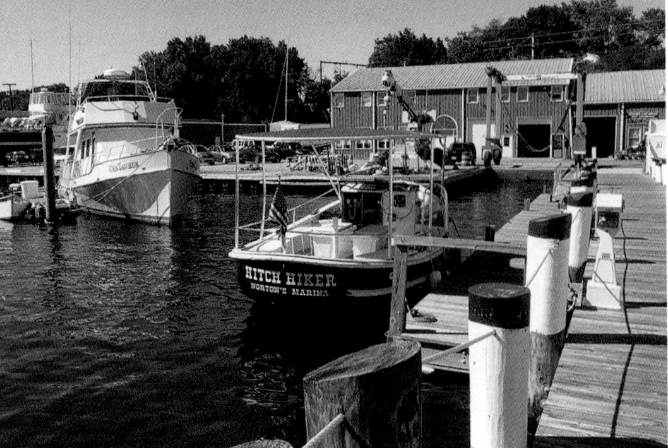

Norton's Shipyard & Marina

PO Box 106; Foot of Division Street; East Greenwich, RI 02818

Tel: (401) 884-8828 **VHF: Monitor** Ch. 9 **Talk** n/a
Fax: (401) 884-3163 **Alternate Tel:** n/a
Email: info@nortonsmarina.com **Web:** nortonsmarina.com
Nearest Town: East Greenwich *(0.5 mi.)* **Tourist Info:** (401) 885-0020

Navigational Information

Lat: 41°39.995' **Long:** 071°26.767' **Tide:** 3 ft. **Current:** 1 kt. **Chart:** 13224
Rep. Depths (*MLW*): Entry 10 ft. **Fuel Dock** n/a **Max Slip/Moor** 15 ft./15 ft.
Access: West Passage to Greenwich Bay to G7 at Greenwich Cove

Marina Facilities *(In Season/Off Season)*

Fuel: No
Slips: 185 Total, 20 Transient **Max LOA:** 300 ft. **Max Beam:** 20 ft.
Rate *(per ft.)*: **Day** $1.50 **Week** $21 **Month** n/a
Power: 30 amp Metered, **50 amp** Metered, **100 amp** Metered, **200 amp** n/a
Cable TV: No **Dockside Phone:** No
Dock Type: Fixed, Floating, Long Fingers, Wood
Moorings: 100 Total, 10 Transient **Launch:** Yes (Incl.), Dinghy Dock
Rate: Day $1.50/ft.** **Week** n/a **Month** n/a
Heads: 3 Toilet(s), 3 Shower(s)
Internet: Yes *(Wi-Fi - Beacon, Free)* **Laundry:** None
Pump-Out: OnCall *(Ch. 9)* **Fee:** $5/30 gal **Closed Heads:** Yes

Marina Operations

Owner/Manager: Patricia Norton **Dockmaster:** Same
In-Season: Apr-Oct, 8am-5pm* **Off-Season:** Nov-Mar, 8am-5pm
After-Hours Arrival: Call ahead
Reservations: Yes, Preferred **Credit Cards:** Visa/MC, Dscvr
Discounts: Safe/Sea **Dockage:** 10% **Fuel:** n/a **Repair:** n/a
Pets: Welcome, Dog Walk Area **Handicap Access:** No

Marina Services and Boat Supplies

Services - Docking Assistance, Dock Carts **Communication -** Mail & Package Hold, Fax in/out *($1/pg)*, FedEx, DHL, UPS, Express Mail **Supplies - OnSite:** Ice *(Block, Cube)*, Ships' Store **1-3 mi:** West Marine *(884-0900)*, Bait/Tackle *(Ray's 738-7878)*, Propane *(Linde 884-0486)*

Boatyard Services

OnSite: Travelift *(35T)*, Crane, Engine mechanic *(gas, diesel)*, Electrical Repairs, Electronic Sales, Electronics Repairs, Hull Repairs, Rigger, Canvas Work, Divers, Brightwork, Compound, Wash & Wax, Interior Cleaning, Woodworking, Painting, Awlgrip **OnCall:** Air Conditioning, Refrigeration, Propeller Repairs, Inflatable Repairs **Dealer for:** Yanmar, Volvo, Mercruiser. **Member:** ABBRA **Yard Rates:** $75/hr., Haul & Launch $5.50-12/ft. *(blocking $2/ft.)*, Power Wash $2/ft., Bottom Paint $14/ft. **Storage:** In-Water $32/ft., On-Land $43/ft. Winter

Restaurants and Accommodations

OnSite: Restaurant *(McKinley's Waterfront 886-1111, L&D $7-15)* **Near:** Restaurant *(Harborside/Lobstermania 884-6363, D $15-27)*, *(Warehouse Tavern at 20 Water St. 885-3700, L&D $6-21)*, *(Pal's 884-9701, L $6-14, D $8-22)*, Pizzeria *(Steve's 885-5652, Del)*, *(Giuseppe's 886-4429, Del)*, Inn/B&B *(Equinox 885-1822)* **Under 1 mi:** Restaurant *(Grille On Main 885-2200, L $7-12, D $13-23)* **1-3 mi:** Fast Food *(Wendy's, McDs, BK)*, Hotel *(Extended Stay 885-3161)*

Recreation and Entertainment

OnSite: Picnic Area, Grills **Near:** Beach *(Goddard SP 884-2010 via dinghy)*, Galleries *(Stephen 884-8979; YJ 885-4329)* **Under 1 mi:** Fitness Center *(Flex Appeal 886-7411)*, Museum *(Varnum House 884-1776; Clouds Hill Victorian 884-4550, 1.5 mi)*, Sightseeing *(Historic E. Greenwich)* **1-3 mi:** Dive Shop *(Anderson's 884-1310)*, Bowling *(Kingstown 884-4450)*, Movie Theater *(Showcase 885-4793)*, Video Rental *(Blockbuster 885-6670)* **3+ mi:** Golf Course *(Goddard SP 884-9834, 3.5 mi.)*

Provisioning and General Services

Near: Farmers' Market *(Goddard SP Fri 9-1)*, Florist *(Stoneblossom 884-3220)* **Under 1 mi:** Convenience Store *(E. Greenwich 886-4811)*, Gourmet Shop *(Greenwich 541-9190)*, Delicatessen *(Simon Says 884-1965)*, Health Food *(Back to Basics 885-2679)*, Liquor Store *(Thorpe's 885-4485)*, Bakery *(Sweet Temptations 884-2404)*, Fishmonger *(Kendall 886-1151)*, Bank/ATM, Catholic Church, Protestant Church, Library, Beauty Salon *(Vogue 886-4064)*, Dry Cleaners *(E. Winds 884-4866)*, Laundry *(Waterford 884-9722)*, Bookstore *(Symposium 886-1600)*, Pharmacy *(CVS 884-7044)*, Copies Etc. *(Allegra 884-9280)* **1-3 mi:** Supermarket *(Dave's 541-7255)*, Wine/Beer *(Savory 886-9463)*, Post Office, Hardware Store *(Benny's 884-9844)*

Transportation

OnCall: Rental Car *(Enterprise 828-5577)*, Taxi *(Bay 461-0780)*, Airport Limo *(Ocean State 826-4300)* **Near:** Local Bus *(RIPTA)* **1-3 mi:** Bikes *(Casters 739-0393)* **Airport:** T.F. Green *(5 mi.)*

Medical Services

911 Service **Under 1 mi:** Dentist *(E. Greenwich 884-6262)*, Chiropractor *(Frye Family 886-4255)*, Holistic Services *(Optimal Health 884-1757)*, Veterinarian *(E. Greenwich 885-2221)* **1-3 mi:** Doctor *(Fallon & Horan 884-2476)*, Optician *(Miller 884-6066)* **Hospital:** Kent 737-7000 *(4 mi.)*

PHOTOS ON DVD: 16

Setting -- At the mouth of Greenwich Cove, the channel passes Norton's north mooring field with a sharp turn to port to the marina. This advantageous location provides both protection and panoramic views of Goddard State Park, Long Point, and Greenwich Bay. Three long docks lie parallel to the shore, the outermost a face dock for side-tie to 300 feet, and, further up the cove, four more lie perpendicular. The well-maintained upland reflects a boatyard focus.

Marina Notes -- *9am-3pm Sat, 10am-2pm Sun. **Morrings - up to 30 ft. LOA only. Family owned/operated since 1945. Two sets of docks (7 total) berth 180 slips separated by a travelift bay. Docking assistance responds quickly when hailed. 100 moorings in 2 fields. Onsite complex of smaller, marine vendors include boat service, riggers and equipment rental plus a discount marine store. Recently replaced 90% of docks, renovated grounds & added a pump-out boat (Ch 9 Mon, Tue, Thu, Sat). West Bay Yacht Club onsite. Bathhouse: Small, separate building. Keycoded full baths showing age, but well-maintained.

Notable -- Just beyond West Bay Yacht Club, McKinley's Waterfront - "The Irish Pub with Italian Grub" - serves lunch and great barfood specials - and stands in as a boaters' lounge. On land, Norton's is close to historic East Greenwich with many specialty shops, liquor, drug and convenience stores. By water, it's a short dinghy ride to 400-acre Goddard Memorial Park for a roped-off, life-guarded beach, horseback riding, swimming, hiking, and picnicking (or take the big boat, and anchor off any of the beaches). Once a sand dune, the park was privately planted by Henry Russell starting in the 1870's, continued by William Goddard, and given to RI in 1927. The Cove's mouth is a popular spot for Tuesday night racing & sailing school maneuvers - Norton's is a good vantage point.

Milt's Marina

PO Box 760; 20 Water Street; East Greenwich, RI 02818

Tel: (401) 885-3700 **VHF: Monitor** n/a **Talk** n/a
Fax: (401) 885-2501 **Alternate Tel:** n/a
Email: n/a **Web:** n/a
Nearest Town: East Greenwich *(0.5 mi.)* **Tourist Info:** (401) 885-0020

Navigational Information

Lat: 41°39.820' **Long:** 071°26.700' **Tide:** 3 ft. **Current:** 1 kt. **Chart:** 13221
Rep. Depths (*MLW*): Entry 10 ft. **Fuel Dock** n/a **Max Slip/Moor** 8 ft./-
Access: West Passage to Greenwich Bay to C7 at Greenwich Cove

Marina Facilities *(In Season/Off Season)*

Fuel: No
Slips: 30 Total, 6 Transient **Max LOA:** 75 ft. **Max Beam:** n/a
Rate *(per ft.)*: **Day** $3.00 **Week** n/a **Month** n/a
Power: 30 amp Incl., **50 amp** Incl., **100 amp** n/a, **200 amp** n/a
Cable TV: No **Dockside Phone:** No
Dock Type: Floating, Long Fingers, Wood
Moorings: 0 Total, 0 Transient **Launch:** n/a
Rate: Day n/a **Week** n/a **Month** n/a
Heads: 2 Toilet(s)
Internet: No **Laundry:** None
Pump-Out: No **Fee:** n/a **Closed Heads:** Yes

Marina Operations

Owner/Manager: Milt Tanner **Dockmaster:** Kristin McCabe
In-Season: Year-Round, 9am-8pm **Off-Season:** n/a
After-Hours Arrival: Call ahead and inquire
Reservations: No **Credit Cards:** Visa/MC, Dscvr, Amex
Discounts: None
Pets: Welcome **Handicap Access:** No

Marina Services and Boat Supplies

Services - Dock Carts **Communication -** Pay Phone **Supplies - Near:** Ice *(Block, Cube)*, Ships' Store *(Norton's)* **1-3 mi:** West Marine *(884-0900)*, Bait/Tackle *(Rays 738-7878)*, Propane *(Linde 884-0486)*

Boatyard Services

Nearest Yard: Norton's Shipyard (401) 854-8828

Restaurants and Accommodations

OnSite: Restaurant *(20 Water Street 885-3700, D $15-24, Mon-Sat 6pm-?, Sun 4pm-?, Deck opens noon weekends, $7-16. Take-Out Menu, too)*, *(Warehouse Tavern 885-3700, L&D $6-21)* **OnCall:** Pizzeria *(Giuseppe's 886-4429)* **Near:** Restaurant *(Pal's 884-9701, D $6-22)*, *(The Grille 885-2200, L&D $7-23)*, *(Harborside-Lobstermania 884-6363, D $15-27)*, *(Hemenway's 336-3920)*, *(Table Twenty-Eight 885-1170, L&D $9-45)*, *(McKinley's 886-1111, L&D $7-15)*, Lite Fare *(Jiggers Diner 884-5388, B $2-4, L $5-7)*, Inn/B&B *(Equinox 885-1822)* **1-3 mi:** Fast Food *(Wendy's, McDs, BK)*, Motel *(Extended Stay 885-3161)* **3+ mi:** Hotel *(Crowne Plaza 732-6000, $153-219, 4 mi.)*, *(Springhill Suites 822-1244, $109-303, 4 mi.)*

Recreation and Entertainment

Near: Beach *(Goddard State Park by dink)*, Picnic Area, Grills, Park *(Crompton Rd; Chepiwanoxet Point; Major Potter Hills; Hemlock Dr)*, Museum *(Varnum House 884-1776; Varnum Memorial Armory 884-4110; Clouds Hill Victorian 884-4550 1.4 mi.)*, Sightseeing *(E. Greenwich Historic District)*, Galleries *(Stephen 884-8979; Pop 884-2973; Thorpe & Verdi 886-7740)* **Under 1 mi:** Fitness Center *(Flex Appeal 886-7411)*, Video Rental *(Blockbuster 885-6670)* **1-3 mi:** Dive Shop *(Anderson's 884-1310)*, Golf Course *(Goddard Park G.C.884-2010; Potowomut G.C. 884-9773)*, Horseback Riding *(C&L 886-5246)*, Bowling *(Kingstown Bowl 884-4450)*, Movie Theater *(Showcase 885-4793)* **3+ mi:** Cultural Attract *(Something Fish Aquarium 732-9970, 4 mi.)*

Provisioning and General Services

Near: Gourmet Shop *(Greenwich Bay 541-9190)*, Delicatessen *(Simon Says 884-1965)*, Bank/ATM, Catholic Church, Protestant Church, Beauty Salon *(Hair Plus 884-2771)*, Bookstore *(Symposium 886-1600)*, Florist *(Stone Blossom 884-3220)* **Under 1 mi:** Convenience Store *(E. Greenwich Farm 886-4811)*, Health Food *(Back to Basics 885-2679)*, Liquor Store *(Thorpe's 885-4485)*, Bakery *(Sweet Temptations 884-2404)*, Fishmonger *(Kendall 886-1151)*, Library *(884-9510)*, Barber Shop *(Ronalds 884-4022)*, Dry Cleaners *(East Winds 884-4866)*, Laundry *(Waterford 884-9772)*, Pharmacy *(CVS 884-7044)*, Copies Etc. *(Allegra 884-9280)* **1-3 mi:** Supermarket *(Dave's 541-7255)*, Wine/Beer *(Savory Grape 886-9463)*, Post Office, Hardware Store *(Salk's 885-2700)*, Department Store *(Marshalls 884-7850)*

Transportation

OnCall: Rental Car *(Enterprise 828-5577)*, Taxi *(M&D 398-1100)*, Airport Limo *(Ocean 826-4300)* **Near:** Local Bus *(RIPTA)* **1-3 mi:** Bikes *(Caster's 739-0393)* **3+ mi:** Rail *(Wickford, 8 mi.)* **Airport:** TF Green *(5 mi.)*

Medical Services

911 Service **OnCall:** Ambulance **Under 1 mi:** Doctor *(Pancholi 885-0063)*, Dentist *(E. Greenwich 884-6262)*, Chiropractor *(Frye 886-4255)*, Holistic Services *(Optimal Health 884-1757)*, Veterinarian *(E. Greenwich 885-2221)* **1-3 mi:** Optician *(Miller 884-6066)* **Hospital:** Kent 737-7000 *(4 mi.)*

Setting -- Just past East Greenwich Yacht Club, on the starboard side of busy Greenwich Cove, Milt's is a small upscale marina at the foot of the Twenty Water Street Restaurant complex. Housed in a renovated 19thC. warehouse, the sleek, three-level eatery features creatively divided spaces, an outdoor bar, patios and decks with magnificent views of the cove and Goddard Memorial State Park - which occupies all of the opposite shore.

Marina Notes -- Established in 1982. Family owned. No marina services, no reservations. Very limited transient dockage, mostly T-heads and bulkheads. Impeccable docks edged in vinyl with relatively recent full-service pedestals. Rating reflects the lack of cruiser amenities. Bathhouse: None. No showers, heads shared with the restaurant - artfully decorated in rich tones with quality materials. Note: Private East Greenwich Yacht Club (884-7700) on north side may have transient slips for reciprocal YC members (attractively landscaped, great clubhouse with rocking-chair porch, full-baths but no reservations either).

Notable -- Twenty Water Street and The Tavern restaurants offer casual, white-tablecloth dining in cozy inside spaces or on the water-side dining decks - with live entertainment Thursday through Sunday evenings. The views from the large, glass-walled second floor Sky Room event space are spectacular. It's easy walking distance to several other restaurants and the village of East Greenwich, an intriguing architectural mash-up of Colonial, Greek Revival, Neo-Gothic, Mid-Victorian and Late-Victorian/Italinate buildings. It is another candidate vying for the title "birthplace of the U.S. Navy - June 12, 1775." Across the cove, 400-acre Goddard Memorial Park has a sandy swimming beach, a 9-hole golf course, bridle paths, walking trails, concerts and picnic areas.

PHOTOS ON DVD: 17

Brewer Yacht Yard Cowesett

100 Folly Landing; Warwick, RI 02886

Tel: (401) 884-0544 **VHF: Monitor** Ch. 9 **Talk** Ch. 72
Fax: (401) 885-5620 **Alternate Tel:** n/a
Email: cruhling@byy.com **Web:** www.byy.com/Warwick
Nearest Town: East Greenwich *(1.5 mi.)* **Tourist Info:** (401) 732-1100

Navigational Information

Lat: 41°40.910' **Long:** 071°26.930' **Tide:** 4 ft. **Current:** n/a **Chart:** 13221
Rep. Depths (*MLW*): Entry 8 ft. **Fuel Dock** n/a **Max Slip/Moor** 10 ft./10 ft.
Access: Western part of Narragansett Bay to Greenwich Cove

Marina Facilities *(In Season/Off Season)*

Fuel: No
Slips: 265 Total, 15 Transient **Max LOA:** 70 ft. **Max Beam:** 18 ft.
Rate *(per ft.)*: **Day** $3.00 **Week** $14 **Month** $60
Power: 30 amp Incl., **50 amp** Incl., **100 amp** n/a, **200 amp** n/a
Cable TV: Yes **Dockside Phone:** No
Dock Type: Floating, Long Fingers, Pilings, Concrete
Moorings: 18 Total, 0 Transient **Launch:** No, Dinghy Dock
Rate: Day n/a **Week** n/a **Month** n/a
Heads: 6 Toilet(s), 6 Shower(s) *(dressing rooms)*, Book Exchange
Internet: Yes *(Wi-Fi, Free)* **Laundry:** None
Pump-Out: OnSite, Self Service, 1 Central **Fee:** Free **Closed Heads:** Yes

Marina Operations

Owner/Manager: Chris Ruhling **Dockmaster:** Matt St. Angleo
In-Season: May-Oct, 8am-5pm* **Off-Season:** Nov-Apr, 8am-5pm Mon-Fri*
After-Hours Arrival: Call in advance and pre-arrange
Reservations: Yes **Credit Cards:** Visa/MC, Dscvr, Amex
Discounts: None **Dockage:** 25% **Fuel:** n/a **Repair:** n/a
Pets: Welcome, Dog Walk Area **Handicap Access:** Yes, Heads

Marina Services and Boat Supplies

Services - Docking Assistance, Concierge, Security *(24 hr. video)*, Dock Carts **Communication -** Mail & Package Hold, Phone Messages, Fax in/out, FedEx, DHL, UPS, Express Mail *(Sat Del)* **Supplies - OnSite:** Ice *(Block, Cube)*, Ships' Store **1-3 mi:** Bait/Tackle *(Ray's 738-7878)* **3+ mi:** West Marine *(884-0900, 4 mi.)*, Propane *(Linde 884-0486, 4 mi.)*

Boatyard Services

OnSite: Travelift *(40T)*, Forklift *(3T)*, Crane *(7T)*, Hydraulic Trailer, Engine mechanic *(gas, diesel)*, Electrical Repairs, Electronic Sales, Electronics Repairs, Hull Repairs, Rigger, Divers, Bottom Cleaning, Brightwork, Compound, Wash & Wax, Interior Cleaning, Propeller Repairs, Woodworking, Inflatable Repairs, Upholstery, Yacht Interiors, Metal Fabrication, Painting, Awlgrip **OnCall:** Sail Loft, Canvas Work, Air Conditioning, Refrigeration **Dealer for:** Kohler, Westerbeke, Yanmar, Mercury. **Member:** ABBRA, ABYC - 3 Certified Tech(s) **Yard Rates:** $68/hr., Haul & Launch $10/ft. *(blocking $2/ft.)*, Power Wash $2, Bottom Paint $14/ft. **Storage:** In-Water $22/ft., On-Land $40/ft.

Restaurants and Accommodations

OnCall: Pizzeria *(Piezoni's 921-2323)* **Near:** Restaurant *(Chelo's Waterfront 884-3000, L $4-9, D $6-13, L&D $7-20; Del.)*, *(Ward's Publick House 884-7008, D $7-16, Draft beer, Irish music Thu & Sun)*, *(Masthead Grill & Creamery 884-1424)* **Under 1 mi:** Fast Food *(BK, Subway)* **1-3 mi:** Restaurant *(Crows Nest 732-6575, L&D $3-21; Del.)*, *(Remington House Inn 736-8388, D $15-19)*, *(Buttonwood Fish & Chips 738-7571)*, *(McKinley's Pub 886-1111, L $7-10, D $10-15)*, *(Post Office 885-4444, Italian)*, *(Grille on Main 885-2200)*, Hotel *(Crowne Plaza 732-6000, $136+)*, *(Greenwich 884-4200)*

Recreation and Entertainment

OnSite: Pool, Spa, Beach, Picnic Area, Grills **Under 1 mi:** Golf Course *(Goddard 884-9834 - dink)* **1-3 mi:** Fitness Center *(Flex Appeal 886-7411)*, Video Rental *(Redbox)*, Park *(Chepiwanoxet Pt.)*, Museum *(Warwick Art 737-0010; Varnum House 884-1776)*, Sightseeing *(Warwick CC Historic District)* **3+ mi:** Movie Theater *(Showcase 885-4793, 4 mi.)*

Provisioning and General Services

Near: Bank/ATM, Beauty Salon *(Marjon 885-0056)*, Dry Cleaners *(Majestic 886-8585)* **Under 1 mi:** Farmers' Market *(Goddard S.P. Fri 9-1)*, Pharmacy *(Knapp 439-8794)*, Retail Shops *(E. Greenwich Ctr)* **1-3 mi:** Convenience Store *(Dan's 738-6190)*, Market *(McKeever's IGA 736-0383)*, Delicatessen *(Simon Says 884-1965)*, Health Food *(Back to Basics 885-2679)*, Wine/Beer *(Thorpe's 885-4485)*, Liquor Store *(Peoples 737-0900)*, Green Grocer *(Pasquale 828-1053)*, Fishmonger *(Captain's 738-6762)*, Post Office, Catholic Church, Protestant Church, Library *(884-9510)*, Hardware Store *(Eagle 737-0400)* **3+ mi:** Supermarket *(Shaw's 823-1820, 3.5 mi.)*

Transportation

OnSite: Courtesy Car/Van **OnCall:** Rental Car *(Enterprise 828-5577)*, Taxi *(Bay 461-0780)*, Airport Limo *(Excel 273-6464)* **Near:** Local Bus *(RIPTA)* **Under 1 mi:** Bikes *(Caster's 739-0393)* **Airport:** T.F. Green *(4 mi.)*

Medical Services

911 Service **Under 1 mi:** Veterinarian *(Cowesett 732-4050)* **1-3 mi:** Doctor *(Petteruti 921-5934)*, Dentist *(E. Greenwich 884-6262)*, Chiropractor *(Frye 886-4255)*, Holistic Services *(Sundance 398-0786)*, Optician *(Apponaug 738-6277)* **Hospital:** Kent County 737-7000 *(2.3 mi.)*

PHOTOS ON DVD: 16

Setting -- Centered on Greenwich Bay's western shore, Cowesett's five main docks are protected by a rip-rapped jetty and wave fence. Two large work sheds and an attractive two-story office and ships' store, with a second-floor deck edged with plantings, are surrounded by parking and boat storage. On the south end, at the water's edge, flower-filled planters set off the lovely brick-paved picnic area and inviting pool with hot tub. Wide-open bay views benefit all.

Marina Notes -- *Office closes at 5pm, ships store at 4:30. Off-season 8am-5pm Mon-Fri, 'til 4pm Sat & Sun. Originally Providence Coal Company, Brewer's purchased in 1981. Ongoing upgrades. Floating, notably clean concrete docks, current pedestals. Breakwater dramatically minimizes wash from wakes but also cuts breeze. Full-service yard. Discounts for Brewer's members. Pool attendant/activities director. Laundry & fuel available at nearby Brewer Greenwich Bay Marina. Bathhouse: Recent, well-maintained heads & showers with dressing rooms.

Notable -- A modest beach is directly adjacent to the marina, ,and a 300-yard dinghy ride takes you to Goddard Memorial State Park with roller-blading, bike paths, a long sweep of life-guarded sand beach, large picnic areas with over 350 picnic tables, hiking paths, a concession stand, weekly farmers' market, a nine-hole golf course, carousel, event building, and C&L Stables with 18 miles of bridal trails. Stroll the streets around the marina, lined with nicely restored houses. Or bike the Post Road on a designated bike lane. About four miles via the local RIPTA #14 bus, Warwick Mall makes a great rainy day destination - with JCPenney's, Target, Macy's, Sports Authority, food court and ten-screen theater. T.F. Green International Airport is nearby - on the same RIPTA bus line.

   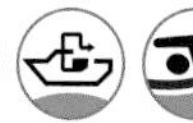 

Navigational Information

Lat: 41°41.126' **Long:** 071°26.972' **Tide:** 5 ft. **Current:** 1 kt. **Chart:** 13221
Rep. Depths (*MLW*): Entry 9 ft. **Fuel Dock** 5 ft. **Max Slip/Moor** 12 ft./-
Access: Narragansett Bay to Greenwich Bay

Marina Facilities *(In Season/Off Season)*

Fuel: Gasoline, Diesel
Slips: 500 Total, 40 Transient **Max LOA:** 150 ft. **Max Beam:** 19 ft.
Rate *(per ft.)*: **Day** $3.00/3 **Week** $19.25 **Month** n/a
Power: 30 amp $10, **50 amp** $20, **100 amp** $50*, **200 amp** n/a
Cable TV: No **Dockside Phone:** No
Dock Type: Fixed, Concrete, Wood
Moorings: 0 Total, 0 Transient **Launch:** n/a, Dinghy Dock
Rate: Day n/a **Week** n/a **Month** n/a
Heads: 6 Toilet(s), 6 Shower(s) *(dressing rooms)*
Internet: Yes *(Wi-Fi, Free)* **Laundry:** 4 Washer(s), 4 Dryer(s)
Pump-Out: OnSite, 1 Central, 1 Port **Fee:** Free **Closed Heads:** Yes

Marina Operations

Owner/Manager: Chris Ruhling **Dockmaster:** Same
In-Season: Year-Round, 8am-5pm **Off-Season:** n/a
After-Hours Arrival: Call pager (401-439-5100 & tie to fuel dock
Reservations: Yes, Preferred **Credit Cards:** Visa/MC, Dscvr, Amex
Discounts: None
Pets: Welcome **Handicap Access:** Yes, Heads

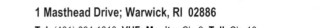

Brewer Greenwich Bay Marinas

1 Masthead Drive; Warwick, RI 02886

Tel: (401) 884-1810 **VHF: Monitor** Ch. 9 **Talk** Ch. 10
Fax: (401) 884-4751 **Alternate Tel:** (401) 478-0368
Email: bgc@byy.com **Web:** www.byy.com
Nearest Town: E. Greenwich *(2 mi.)* **Tourist Info:** (401) 732-1100

Marina Services and Boat Supplies

Services - Docking Assistance, Concierge, Dock Carts, 3 Phase **Communication -** Mail & Package Hold, Phone Messages, FedEx, DHL, UPS **Supplies - OnSite:** Ice *(Block, Cube)*, Ships' Store **Under 1 mi:** Bait/Tackle *(Ray's 738-7878)* **3+ mi:** West Marine *(884-0900, 4 mi)*

Boatyard Services

OnSite: Travelift *(50T, 35T, 25T)*, Forklift, Crane, Engine mechanic *(gas, diesel)*, Electrical Repairs, Electronics Repairs, Hull Repairs, Rigger, Sail Loft, Canvas Work, Divers, Bottom Cleaning, Brightwork, Compound, Wash & Wax, Propeller Repairs, Woodworking, Inflatable Repairs, Upholstery, Yacht Interiors, Painting, Awlgrip **OnCall:** Air Conditioning, Refrigeration **Member:** ABBRA, ABYC **Yard Rates:** $67.50/hr., Haul & Launch $13/ft. *(blocking $2/ft.)*, Power Wash $3/ft., Bottom Paint $9/ft.

Restaurants and Accommodations

OnSite: Restaurant *(Chelo's 884-3000, L&D $7-20 Del.)* **Near:** Restaurant *(Ward's Publick 884-7008, D $7-16, Irish music)*, *(Masthead Grill 884-1424)* **Under 1 mi:** Restaurant *(Crow's Nest 732-6575, L&D $3-21)*, *(Remington House Inn 736-8388, D $15-19)*, Pizzeria *(Piezoni's 921-2323, Del.)* **1-3 mi:** Restaurant *(Eastern Star 738-6162, L&D $5-15, Kids' $5)*, *(Buttonwood Fish & Chips 738-7571)*, *(Greenwood Inn 738-3334, L&D $8-20,Kids' $5-6, Lite $6-7)*, *(China Inn 738-8885, L&D $7-14)*, Fast Food *(BK)*, Hotel *(Crowne Plaza 732-6000, $136+)*, *(Holiday Inn Exp 736-5000, $99+)*

Recreation and Entertainment

OnSite: Pool, Picnic Area, Grills, Playground, Boat Rentals *(Bassett 885-0959)* **Under 1 mi:** Beach *(Chepiwanoxet Pt, Goddard - by dinghy)*, Park *(Chepiwanoxet Pt)*, Museum *(Varnum House 884-1776, $5; Warwick Art 37-0010; Greenwood Vol. Fire 736-8412)* **1-3 mi:** Tennis Courts *(Tennis R.I. 828-4450)*, Fitness Center *("Y" 828-0130)*, Video Rental *(Redbox)*, Sightseeing *(Warwick CC Historic District)* **3+ mi:** Golf Course *(East Greenwich 884-5656, 5 mi.)*, Movie Theater *(Showcase 885-4793, 4 mi.)*

Provisioning and General Services

OnSite: Bank/ATM **Near:** Beauty Salon *(Marjon 885-0056)*, Dry Cleaners *(Majestic 886-8585)* **Under 1 mi:** Convenience Store *(Cumberland Farms 738-7896)*, Farmers' Market *(Goddard Park)*, Catholic Church, Laundry *(Apponaug 738-1868)*, Pharmacy *(Walgreens 737-1952)*, Hardware Store *(National Bldg. 921-0400)*, Retail Shops *(E. Greenwich Shopping Ctr.)* **1-3 mi:** Market *(Dan's 738-6190)*, Supermarket *(Stop & Shop 828-9360; Shaw's)*, Delicatessen *(Simon Says 884-1965)*, Wine/Beer *(Thorpe's 885-4485)*, Liquor Store *(Peoples 737-0900)*, Bakery *(Sweet Temptations 884-2404)*, Green Grocer *(Pasquale 828-1053)*, Fishmonger *(Captain's 738-6762)*, Post Office, Protestant Church, Library *(884-9510)*, Bookstore *(Symposium 886-1600)*, Department Store *(Target 244-1973)*

Transportation

OnCall: Rental Car *(Enterprise 828-5577)*, Taxi *(Apponaug 737-6400)*, Airport Limo *(Excel 273-6464)* **Near:** Local Bus *(RIPTA)* **Under 1 mi:** Bikes *(Caster's 739-0393)* **Airport:** TF Green *(4 mi.)*

Medical Services

911 Service **Near:** Doctor *(Malik 885-3616)* **Under 1 mi:** Veterinarian *(E. G. 885-2221)* **1-3 mi:** Dentist *(McManus 884-2190)*, Chiropractor *(Frye 886-4255)*, Optician *(Apponaug 738-6277)* **Hospital:** Kent 737-7000 *(2.3 mi.)*

Setting -- Massive Greenwich Bay Marina combines three yards. The original 30-acre South yard, situated on the west end of Greenwich Bay south of Arnold Neck, sports 500-slips and a 2,000-foot face dock, mature, manicured landscaping, an inviting pool and Chelo's Waterfront Restaurant - it's easy to spot both day and night. The North and East yards lie along Warwick Cove in the Northeast corner of the Bay. All three are well-tended, reflecting an attention to detail.

Marina Notes -- *100A, 3-Phase $75. Transients mostly at Brewer Greenwich Bay South Yard right on Greenwich Bay. Longer term dockage or shallower draft vessels at BGB North Yard (formerly C-Lark) and adjacent BGB East Yard (formerly Carlson's). All listed on map as #10. Guests have full use of all facilities (including Cowessett). Gas at South Yard (8am-7pm), Gas & Diesel at North Yard. 24 hr. cancellation notice required - otherwise forfeit 1 night deposit. Shuttle golf cart available as dock cart for getting around & loading/unloading. Lovely boaters lounge and pool. Mostly a dockominium but some seasonal. Bathhouse: Behind restaurant but for the exclusive use of marina guests/residents. First-class and well-maintained.

Notable -- At the main south yard, brightly painted, two-story Chelo's restaurant is the popular, engaging upland focus - the first-floor eating areas spill out onto an expansive lawn dotted with umbrella-topped tables while the second floor is wrapped with dining decks. Fire pits, four bars and a bandstand at the water's edge, often occupied by local groups, encourage a lively, party atmosphere. Chelo's delivers to boats docked at the South Yard and neighboring Cowessett. It's open only during the season (closed Nov -Apr) and free Wi-Fi, too! Chelo's and the South Yard docks have long views of Greenwich Bay.

PHOTOS ON DVD: 25

Apponaug Harbor Marina

Apponaug Harbor Marina

Rear 17 Arnolds Neck Drive; Warwick, RI 02886

Tel: (401) 739-5005 **VHF: Monitor** n/a **Talk** n/a
Fax: (401) 738-4459 **Alternate Tel:** n/a
Email: capjak46@cox.net **Web:** www.apponaugmarina.com
Nearest Town: Apponaug *(1 mi.)* **Tourist Info:** (401) 732-1100

Navigational Information

Lat: 41°41.422' **Long:** 071°26.805' **Tide:** 5 ft. **Current:** 2 kt. **Chart:** 13221
Rep. Depths (*MLW*): Entry 6 ft. **Fuel Dock** n/a **Max Slip/Moor** 7 ft./6 ft.
Access: Narragansett Bay to Greenwich Bay to Apponaug Cove

Marina Facilities *(In Season/Off Season)*

Fuel: No
Slips: 348 Total, 10 Transient **Max LOA:** 45 ft. **Max Beam:** 15 ft.
Rate *(per ft.)*: **Day** $1.25 **Week** n/a **Month** n/a
Power: 30 amp Incl., **50 amp** n/a, **100 amp** n/a, **200 amp** n/a
Cable TV: No **Dockside Phone:** No
Dock Type: Floating, Long Fingers, Concrete, Wood, Composition
Moorings: 30 Total, 10 Transient **Launch:** No, Dinghy Dock
Rate: Day $25 **Week** n/a **Month** n/a
Heads: 6 Toilet(s), 6 Shower(s)
Internet: Yes *(Wi-Fi, Free)* **Laundry:** None
Pump-Out: OnSite, Self Service, 1 Central **Fee:** Free **Closed Heads:** Yes

Marina Operations

Owner/Manager: John Dickerson **Dockmaster:** Same
In-Season: Year Round, 8:30am-5pm **Off-Season:** n/a
After-Hours Arrival: Anchor in mooring field
Reservations: Yes, Required **Credit Cards:** Visa/MC, Dscvr
Discounts: Boat/US; Safe/Sea **Dockage:** 25% **Fuel:** n/a **Repair:** n/a
Pets: Welcome **Handicap Access:** Yes, Heads

Marina Services and Boat Supplies

Services - Docking Assistance, Trash Pick-Up, Dock Carts **Communication -** FedEx, DHL, UPS, Express Mail **Supplies - OnSite:** Ice *(Block, Cube)* **Under 1 mi:** Bait/Tackle *(Ray's 738-7878)* **1-3 mi:** Ships' Store *(Bassett 886-7899)*, Propane *(U-Haul 737-8536)* **3+ mi:** West Marine *(884-0900, 5 mi)*

Boatyard Services

OnSite: Travelift *(35T)*, Crane *(25T)* **OnCall:** Engine mechanic *(gas, diesel)*, Electronics Repairs, Rigger *(NE 884-1112)*, Canvas Work, Divers, Bottom Cleaning, Propeller Repairs **Near:** Launching Ramp, Hull Repairs. **Under 1 mi:** Sail Loft *(Doyle 884-4227)*. **Dealer for:** Universal. **Member:** ABBRA **Yard Rates:** $75/hr., Haul & Launch $40/ft.** *(blocking incl.)*, Power Wash $1.50/ft. **Storage:** In-Water $35/ft., On-Land $10/ft./mo.

Restaurants and Accommodations

Under 1 mi: Restaurant *(Remington 736-8388, D $15-19)*, *(Chelo's Waterfront 884-3000, L&D $7-20 Dinghy)*, *(Crow's Nest 732-6575, L&D $6-21 Del)*, *(Ward's Publick House 884-7008)*, *(Masthead Grill 884-1424)*, *(Eastern Star 738-6162, $5-15, Kids' $5)*, Fast Food *(Subway)*, Pizzeria *(Piezoni's 921-2323, Del.)* **1-3 mi:** Restaurant *(Buttonwood Fish & Chips 738-7571)*, *(Greenwood Inn 738-3334, L&D $8-15; Kids' $5-6; Lite $6-7)*, *(China Inn 738-8885, L&D $7-14)*, Hotel *(Crowne Plaza 732-6000, $136+)*, *(Holiday Inn Exp 736-5000, $99+)*, *(Homestead 732-6667, $75+)*

Recreation and Entertainment

OnSite: Beach **Under 1 mi:** Park, Museum *(Warwick Art 737-0010)*, Sightseeing *(Apponaug & Warwick Historic Dist)* **1-3 mi:** Pool *("Y" 828-0130)*, Fitness Center *(Flex Appeal 886-7411)*, Video Rental *(Redbox)* **3+ mi:** Golf Course *(Midville 828-9215, 5 mi.)*, Bowling *(Meadowbrook 737-5402, 5 mi)*, Movie Theater *(Showcase 885-4793, 5 mi.)*

Provisioning and General Services

Under 1 mi: Convenience Store *(Cumberland Farms 738-7896)*, Liquor Store *(Peoples 737-0900)*, Fishmonger *(Twin's 737-1575; Captain's 738-6762)*, Bank/ATM, Library *(739-6411)*, Beauty Salon *(Wave 739-9283)*, Barber Shop *(David's 738-7790)*, Dry Cleaners *(Zoots 885-5513)*, Laundry *(Apponaug 738-1868)*, Pharmacy *(Walgreens 737-1952)* **1-3 mi:** Market *(Trader Joe's 821-5368)*, Supermarket *(Super Stop & Shop 828-9360)*, Health Food *(Back to Basics 885-2679)*, Green Grocer *(Pasquale 828-1053)*, Catholic Church, Protestant Church, Bookstore *(Symposium 886-1600)*, Hardware Store *(Eagle Lumber 737-0400)*, Florist *(Stoneblossom 884-3220)* **3+ mi:** Post Office *(3.5 mi.)*, Retail Shops *(Warwick Mall, 3.7 mi.)*, Department Store *(WalMart 821-1766, 3.8 mi.)*, Buying Club *(Sam's 823-7070, 3.3 mi.)*

Transportation

OnCall: Taxi *(Apponaug 737-6400)*, Airport Limo *(Excel 273-6464)* **Under 1 mi:** Bikes *(Caster's 739-0393)*, Local Bus *(RIPTA 781-9400)* **1-3 mi:** Rental Car *(Thrifty 738-5800; Hertz 737-2189)* **Airport:** TF Green *(4 mi.)*

Medical Services

911 Service **Under 1 mi:** Doctor *(Malik 885-3616)*, Veterinarian *(Cowesett 732-4050)* **1-3 mi:** Dentist *(W. Shore 739-1399)*, Chiropractor *(Toll Gate 738-8154)*, Holistic Services *(Pearl Spa 921-4390)*, Optician *(Apponaug 738-6277)* **Hospital:** Kent County 737-7000 *(2 mi.)*

PHOTOS ON DVD: 16

Setting -- Off the northwest corner of Greenwich Bay in Apponaug Cove, this large, smaller-boat marina offers an expansive network of protected dockage a bit out of the fray - in a quiet, residential environment. The rustic upland hosts a single-story gray-sided office, work shed and small bathhouse. The outer docks and mooring field benefit from wide-open views of the Bay and a cool southwest breeze most of the summer. Kayakers can launch from the secluded beach.

Marina Notes -- **Haul & Launch rate includes storage. AKA Dickerson's Marina. Old family owned marina; two generations currently active. Fixed docks, floating concrete, easily accessed pump-out dock. Docks A -G recently replaced with composite. Do-it-yourself yard provides only launch, haul & storage at reasonable rates. Prior to the sale of Universal Engine to Westerbeke, Apponaug was the East Coast distributor & warehouse. Large remaining inventory of parts for Atomic 4 (gas) and Universal Diesel. Bathouse: Small, cinderblock with cement floor, well-maintained.

Notable -- Apponaug Yacht Club, based here, holds regular social events and Tuesday evening sail races on an ideal course for both novice and experienced crews. Excellent winds and smooth water are the norm.The proximity to excellent transportation could make this a good place to leave the boat for awhile. Newly expanded T.F. Green International Airport is within ten minutes. Nearby RIPTA Park and Ride offers state-wide bus service and the high-speed Acela train services the Northeast corridor. For antique shops and sightseeing, stroll historic Apponaug village, stretched along Post Road between Greenwich Ave. and West Shore. For practical needs, two large malls are within 3 miles with RIPTA shuttle service between them.

Navigational Information
Lat: 41°41.738' **Long:** 071°27.128' **Tide:** 5 ft. **Current:** 2 kt. **Chart:** 13221
Rep. Depths (*MLW*): Entry 4.5 ft. **Fuel Dock** n/a **Max Slip/Moor** 4 ft./4 ft.
Access: Narragansett Bay to NE corner of Greenwich Bay to Apponaug Cove

Marina Facilities *(In Season/Off Season)*
Fuel: Gasoline
Slips: 100 Total, 2 Transient **Max LOA:** 40 ft. **Max Beam:** 12 ft.
Rate *(per ft.)*: **Day** $1.50 **Week** n/a **Month** n/a
Power: 30 amp Incl., **50 amp** Incl., **100 amp** n/a, **200 amp** n/a
Cable TV: No **Dockside Phone:** No
Dock Type: Floating, Long Fingers, Wood
Moorings: 0 Total, 0 Transient **Launch:** n/a
Rate: Day n/a **Week** n/a **Month** n/a
Heads: 6 Toilet(s), 2 Shower(s) *(dressing rooms)*
Internet: No **Laundry:** None
Pump-Out: OnSite, Self Service, 1 Central **Fee:** Free **Closed Heads:** Yes

Marina Operations
Owner/Manager: Raymond Chace **Dockmaster:** Ann Chace
In-Season: Apr 15 - Nov 15, Dawn-Dusk **Off-Season:** n/a
After-Hours Arrival: Call in Advance
Reservations: Yes, Recommended **Credit Cards:** Visa/MC
Discounts: None
Pets: Welcome **Handicap Access:** Yes, Heads

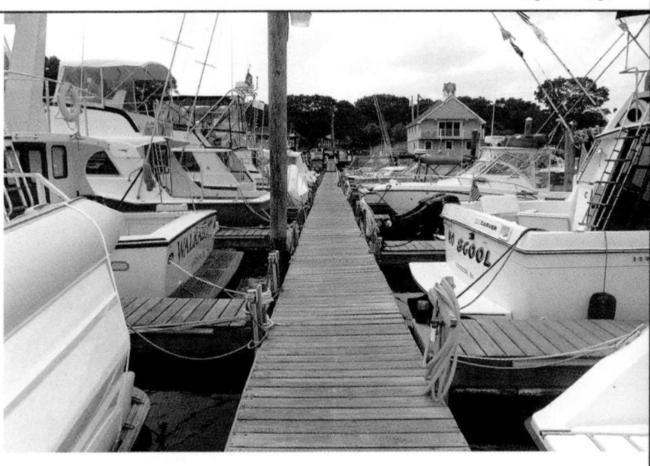

Ponaug Marina

285 Arnold Neck Drive; Warwick, RI 02886

Tel: (401) 884-1976 **VHF: Monitor** n/a **Talk** n/a
Fax: (401) 736-0324 **Alternate Tel:** n/a
Email: ponaug@cox.net **Web:** n/a
Nearest Town: Apponaug *(0.4 mi.)* **Tourist Info:** n/a

Marina Services and Boat Supplies
Communication - FedEx, DHL, UPS, Express Mail **Supplies - OnSite:** Ice *(Block, Cube)*, Bait/Tackle, Live Bait **Under 1 mi:** Ships' Store *(KSP 398-8668)* **1-3 mi:** Boater's World *(823-5952)*, Boat/US *(886-6790)* **3+ mi:** West Marine *(884-0900, 5 mi)*, Propane *(Linde 884-0486, 4 mi)*

Boatyard Services
OnSite: Launching Ramp **OnCall:** Divers *(Underwater Services 1-886-901-3483)* **Near:** Compound, Wash & Wax. **Under 1 mi:** Air Conditioning.
Nearest Yard: Brewer Greenwich Bay (401) 884-1810

Restaurants and Accommodations
Near: Restaurant *(Crow's Nest 732-6575, Delivers; $3-21)*, *(Remington 736-8388, D $15-19)* **Under 1 mi:** Restaurant *(Chelo's Waterfront 884-3000, L&D $7-20)*, *(Ward's Publick House 884-7008)*, *(Masthead Grill & Creamery 884-1424)*, *(Eastern Star 738-6162, L&D $4.50-15.25; Kids' $5.25)*, Fast Food *(BK, Subway, Dunkin, Jersey Mike's)*, Lite Fare *(Hummingbird Cafe)*, Pizzeria *(Piezoni's 921-2323)* **1-3 mi:** Restaurant *(Buttonwood Fish & Chips 738-7571)*, *(Greenwood Inn 738-3334, L&D $8-20; Kids' $4.50-6.25; Lite $6-7)*, *(China Inn 738-8885, L&D $8.15-14)*, Hotel *(Crown Plaza 732-6000, $136+)*, *(Homestead Studio Suites 732-6667, $75+)*, *(Holiday Inn Express 736-5000, $99+)*, *(Radisson 793-3000)*

Recreation and Entertainment
Near: Picnic Area, Playground *(Harris)*, Park *(Or Chepiwanoxet Point; Little Gorton Pond Wetland)* **Under 1 mi:** Boat Rentals *(Bassett 885-0959)*, Museum *(Warwick Art 737-0010)*, Sightseeing *(Warwick C.C. Hist. Dist)* **1-3 mi:** Pool *("Y" 828-0130)*, Beach *(Chepiwanoxet Point)*, Tennis Courts *(Tennis R.I. 828-4450)*, Fitness Center *(Work Out World 739-9002)*, Movie Theater *(Showcase 885-4793)*, Video Rental *(Redbox)* **3+ mi:** Golf Course *(Midville 828-9215, 4 mi.)*, Bowling *(Meadowbrook 737-5402, 4 mi.)*

Provisioning and General Services
Near: Fishmonger *(Twin's 737-1575)*, Library *(Apponaug)* **Under 1 mi:** Convenience Store *(Cumberland Farms 738-7896)*, Liquor Store *(People's 737-0900)*, Bank/ATM, Catholic Church, Protestant Church, Beauty Salon *(Wave 739-9283)*, Dry Cleaners *(Warwick 737-8899)*, Laundry *(Apponaug 738-1868)*, Pharmacy *(Walgreen's 737-1952)*, Hardware Store *(Eagle Lumber 737-0400)*, Retail Shops *(Post Road)* **1-3 mi:** Market *(McKeever's IGA 736-0382)*, Supermarket *(Stop and Shop 828-9360)*, Delicatessen *(Simon Says 884-1965)*, Bakery *(My Bread 738-7956)*, Post Office *(468-1010)*, Barber Shop *(David's 738-7790)*, Florist *(Stoneblossom 884-3220)*, Department Store *(WalMart 821-1766)*, Buying Club *(Sam's 823-7070)* **3+ mi:** Wine/Beer *(Savory Grape 886-9463, 4 mi.)*, Synagogue *(4 mi.)*

Transportation
OnCall: Taxi *(Apponaug 737-6400)*, Airport Limo *(Excel 273-6464)* **Near:** InterCity Bus *(RIPTA)* **Under 1 mi:** Bikes *(Caster's 739-0393)* **1-3 mi:** Rental Car *(Dollar 739-8450; Hertz 737-2189)* **Airport:** T.F. Green *(3 mi.)*

Medical Services
911 Service **OnCall:** Ambulance **Under 1 mi:** Doctor *(DiMarco 738-6565)*, Chiropractor *(Toll Gate 738-8154)*, Veterinarian *(Cowesett 732-4050)* **1-3 mi:** Dentist *(West Shore 739-1399)*, Holistic Services *(Pearl 921-4390)*, Optician *(Apponaug 738-6277)* **Hospital:** Kent 737-7000 *(1.7 mi.)*

Setting -- Tucked deep into Apponaug Cove, just east of the railroad bridge, Ponaug's sprawling docks are exceedingly well-protected. Out of sight of Greenwich Bay, the setting, nevertheless, feels bucolic with open mooring areas, a tidal basin, and a plethora of migratory birds - crossing geese often hold up traffic - that offer photo opportunities at sunrise and sunset. A recent, attractive two-story gray clapboard contemporary berths the offices and bathhouse.

Marina Notes -- Mature family owned marina. Main office is new within the past five years. Docks in good condition with 30-amp electric and water. Rates for long-term and transient dockage currently the lowest in the upper bay region. DIY marina with professional services available nearby. A road separates the grassy grounds from the boat storage. Bathhouse: On the first floor of the main building, like-new heads with concrete floors and fiberglass shower stalls.

Notable -- Ponaug benefits from a convenient location. The property borders the Apponaug Waterfront Park and playground. Ray's Bait and Tackle sits at the marina's edge. Across the road, the Crow's Nest restaurant is a local favorite. Next door are The Changing Tide gift shop, Twin's Shellfish, and Custom Boat Repair. It's a short walk through the tidy, rural, middle-class neighborhood, a mix of summer and year-round homes to busy Four Corners - the city's heart and once the Pequot Trail. Pick up a copy of a walking tour of Apponaug Village, founded in 1735. It highlights 30 buildings that today house many useful services (Call 1-800-4-WARWICK). The RIPTA bus also stops here for exploring more of the area, heading to the two malls, or to the newly expanded T.F. Green International airport. If there's a kayak aboard, it's possible, depending on tide, to paddle all the way to the Post Road.

Warwick Cove Marina

2 Seminole St; Warwick, RI 02889

Tel: (401) 737-2446 **VHF: Monitor** Ch. 16 **Talk** n/a
Fax: n/a **Alternate Tel:** n/a
Email: n/a **Web:** n/a
Nearest Town: Oakland Beach *(0.25 mi.)* **Tourist Info:** (401) 732-1100

Navigational Information

Lat: 41°41.287' **Long:** 071°23.605' **Tide:** 3 ft. **Current:** 1 kt. **Chart:** 13224
Rep. Depths (*MLW*): Entry 6 ft. **Fuel Dock** 6 ft. **Max Slip/Moor** 6 ft./-
Access: NE corner of Greenwich Bay past flag at Warwick CC

Marina Facilities *(In Season/Off Season)*

Fuel: Gasoline
Slips: 100 Total, 5 Transient **Max LOA:** 50 ft. **Max Beam:** 15 ft.
Rate *(per ft.)*: **Day** $2.00/1.5 **Week** $10.50 **Month** $80
Power: 30 amp Incl., **50 amp** n/a, **100 amp** n/a, **200 amp** n/a
Cable TV: No **Dockside Phone:** No
Dock Type: Floating, Long Fingers, Pilings, Wood
Moorings: 0 Total, 0 Transient **Launch:** n/a
Rate: Day n/a **Week** n/a **Month** n/a
Heads: 2 Toilet(s), 2 Shower(s)
Internet: No **Laundry:** None
Pump-Out: OnSite, Self Service, 1 Central **Fee:** Free **Closed Heads:** Yes

Marina Operations

Owner/Manager: John Williams **Dockmaster:** Same
In-Season: year round, 8am-8pm **Off-Season:** n/a
After-Hours Arrival: Tie up at Gas Dock
Reservations: Yes **Credit Cards:** Visa/MC, Dscvr, Amex
Discounts: None
Pets: Welcome **Handicap Access:** No

Marina Services and Boat Supplies

Services - Docking Assistance **Communication -** FedEx, DHL, UPS, Express Mail **Supplies - OnSite:** Ice *(Cube)* **Under 1 mi:** Bait/Tackle *(Oakland Beach 490-2631)*, Propane *(UHaul 737-8536)* **3+ mi:** West Marine *(884-0900, 5 mi.)*

Boatyard Services

Near: Launching Ramp. **Nearest Yard:** Brewer's Greenwich Bay Marinas (401) 739-3871

Restaurants and Accommodations

Near: Restaurant *(Iggy's Doughboy & Chowder House 737-9459, $4-20, Market Price for seafood)*, *(Timmy's Landing 738-4777, L $7-15, D 13-25, Docks, carryout)*, *(Corner Pizza 921-3551, L $4-$15, D $4-$15, Del.)*, Pizzeria *(Three Filippous 77-378-10)* **Under 1 mi:** Restaurant *(Top of the Bay 921-3663, L $8-13, D $9-25)*, *(Carousel Grill 92-134-30 , L&D $7-23, 11:30-10pm)*, *(Marley's on the Beach 736-0400, $7-10, Kids' $5)*, Pizzeria *(Mikey B's 921-5899)* **1-3 mi:** Restaurant *(On the Dock Grill 681-4170)*, Fast Food *(McDs, BK)* **3+ mi:** Hotel *(Hampton 739-8888, $$129- $149, 4.5 mi.)*, *(Radisson 739-3000, $125-$269, 4.5 mi.)*, *(Best Western 634-1780, $70+, 4.5 mi.)*, *(Crown Plaza 732-6000, 4.8 mi.)*

Recreation and Entertainment

OnSite: Picnic Area, Grills, Fishing Charter *(Alibi 737-BOAT)* **Near:** Beach *(Oakland Beach)*, Playground *(Oakland beach)*, Hike/Bike Trails, Park *(Oakland Beach)* **Under 1 mi:** Boat Rentals *(Brewer 739-3871)*, Special Events *(Carnival & fireworks MemDay, July 3; Car shows Tues Nite)* **1-3 mi:** Tennis Courts *(Warwick Parks & Rec 739-2651)*, Golf Course *(Seaview CC 739-6311)*, Fitness Center *(WOW 739-9002)*, Bowling *(Meadowbrook 737-5402)*, Video Rental *(Redbox)*, Museum *(Art 737-0010)*, Sightseeing *(Aldrich Mansion 739-6850)*, Galleries *(Compliments 739-9300)*

Provisioning and General Services

Near: Fishmonger *(JJ MacLean 732-6693)*, Lobster Pound *(Harborlight Marina by dinghy)*, Catholic Church, Protestant Church **Under 1 mi:** Convenience Store *(7-Eleven 739-8608)*, Delicatessen *(Oakland Beach Market)*, Bank/ATM **1-3 mi:** Market *(Dave's 738-8300)*, Supermarket *(Stop and Shop)*, Gourmet Shop, Health Food *(Trader Joe's 821-5368)*, Liquor Store *(Haxtons 739-8030)*, Bakery *(Antonio's 738-3727)*, Green Grocer *(Morris Farm 738-1036)*, Post Office, Library *(Warwick 739-5440 Free internet)*, Beauty Salon *(West Shore 738-8332)*, Dry Cleaners *(Meadowbrook 739-7385)*, Laundry *(DP's 732-1773)*, Pharmacy *(CVS 737-2305)*, Hardware Store *(Salks 739-1027)*, Florist *(Ashley's 737-0331)*, Retail Shops *(Buttonwoods Plaza)*, Copies Etc. *(Copy World 739-7400)*

Transportation

OnCall: Rental Car *(Enterprise 732-5261)*, Taxi *(Bay 461-0780)*, Airport Limo *(Good Tymes 737-4954)* **Near:** Local Bus *(RIPTA)* **3+ mi:** InterCity Bus *(Peter Pan at T.F. Green, 5 mi.)* **Airport:** T.F. Green Int'l *(5 mi.)*

Medical Services

911 Service **1-3 mi:** Doctor *(Fleisig 885-0406)*, Dentist *(Dunn 739-5700)*, Chiropractor *(Hudyncia 732-4400)*, Optician *(Warwick 738-6277)*, Veterinarian *(West Shore 738-3447)* **Hospital:** Kent 736-4285 *(6 mi.)*

PHOTOS ON DVD: 17

Setting -- On the western shore of Warwick Cove, just past Timmy's Restaurant & Landing, the WCM's 100 slips are anchored by a low-slung, gray-clapboard dock house. The gas dock, a well-known landmark, is often lined with dinghies and kids hanging out enjoying ice cream. The decidedly working-class marina berths an eclectic range of aging yachts, liveaboards and sportfishers. - many owned by local anglers. Oakland Beach has an unmistakable summer, beachy, tourist feel which is reflected in the casual, kick-off-your-shoes eateries and seasonal businesses.

Marina Notes -- One of the area's older marinas, current owner took the helm in 1994. Bare bones facility with no boatyard services. Bathhouse: Basic full baths.Tile floor with fiberglass shower stalls and sink vanities. Convenient location to the docks. Note: Entrance to Warwick Cove can be difficult to spot from a distance; close attention to the channel is absolutely necessary. Area to the west is shallow - sunken barge off Oakland beach three feet below at mlw.

Notable -- Warwick Cove Marina's close proximity to Oakland Beach makes it an interesting destination. A very short dinghy ride nets ice cream at the gas docks, dinner at Timmy's or a day at the beach - or just walk across the peninsula. Hopping in the 1930s, the area is making a comeback. The beach has several coves protected by jetties - favorite spots for good bass fishing. Warm and shallow, with fine pebbly sand, it might be better for picnics on the great swaths of grass than for swimming. Marley's, The Carousel Grill and Twisted Pizza have recently opened near the beach. Iggy's Doughboy & Chowder, a huge local favorite for take-out or eat in, often sports long lines (worth the wait). Most of the basics are within an easy walk - but it can be crowded on weekends.

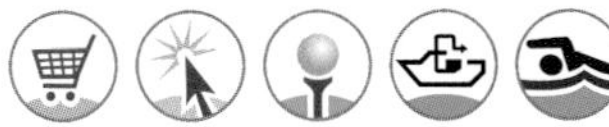

Navigational Information
Lat: 41°41.878' **Long:** 071°23.331' **Tide:** 5 ft. **Current:** 1 kt. **Chart:** 13221
Rep. Depths (*MLW*): Entry 6 ft. **Fuel Dock** n/a **Max Slip/Moor** 6 ft./-
Access: Greenwich Bay to the head of Warwick Cove

Marina Facilities *(In Season/Off Season)*
Fuel: No
Slips: 200 Total, 10 Transient **Max LOA:** 45 ft. **Max Beam:** 16 ft.
Rate *(per ft.)*: **Day** $2.00 **Week** $14 **Month** $60
Power: 30 amp $5, **50 amp** $10, **100 amp** n/a, **200 amp** n/a
Cable TV: No **Dockside Phone:** No
Dock Type: Floating, Long Fingers, Wood
Moorings: 4 Total, 0 Transient **Launch:** n/a, Dinghy Dock
Rate: Day n/a **Week** n/a **Month** n/a
Heads: 2 Toilet(s), 2 Shower(s)
Internet: Yes *(Wi-Fi, Free)* **Laundry:** None
Pump-Out: OnSite, Self Service, 1 Central **Fee:** $5 **Closed Heads:** Yes

Marina Operations
Owner/Manager: Kristin Cataldi **Dockmaster:** Same
In-Season: Year-Round, 8am-4:30pm **Off-Season:** n/a
After-Hours Arrival: Call ahead
Reservations: Yes, Required **Credit Cards:** Visa/MC
Discounts: Sea Tow **Dockage:** n/a **Fuel:** n/a **Repair:** n/a
Pets: Welcome **Handicap Access:** No

Bay Marina

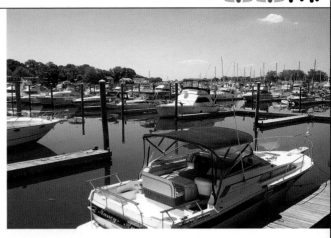

1800 West Shore Road; Warwick, RI 02889

Tel: (401) 739-6435 **VHF: Monitor** n/a **Talk** n/a
Fax: (401) 732-3436 **Alternate Tel:** n/a
Email: baymarina@aol.com **Web:** n/a
Nearest Town: Warwick *(4 mi.)* **Tourist Info:** (401) 732-1100

Marina Services and Boat Supplies
Services - Dock Carts **Communication -** Pay Phone (1), FedEx, DHL, UPS **Supplies - OnSite:** Ships' Store **Under 1 mi:** Bait/Tackle *(Oakland 490-2631)*, Propane *(U-Haul/Rhode Island Rentals 738-3855)* **3+ mi:** West Marine *(884-0900, 6 mi)*

Boatyard Services
OnSite: Travelift *(40T)*, Crane, Engine mechanic *(gas, diesel)*, Hull Repairs, Bottom Cleaning, Brightwork, Compound, Wash & Wax, Propeller Repairs, Painting **OnCall:** Air Conditioning, Inflatable Repairs, Upholstery, Metal Fabrication **Near:** Launching Ramp. **Dealer for:** Crusader Marine Engines, Onan generators, Cummin Engines. **Yard Rates:** $95/hr., Haul & Launch $8/ft. *(blocking $2/ft.)*, Power Wash $2/ft., Bottom Paint $9/ft. **Storage:** On-Land $32.50/ft.

Restaurants and Accommodations
Near: Restaurant *(Timmy's 738-4777, L $5-$10, D $13-$25, By dinghy)*, *(Rocky Point Pub 738-0500, L $5-$10, D $5-$15, Local Favorite)* **Under 1 mi:** Restaurant *(Islander 738-9861, L $5-11, D $7-18, Kids' $4)*, *(On the Docks Grill 681-4170)*, Pizzeria *(George's 738-5776)*, *(Mickey B's 921-5899)* **1-3 mi:** Restaurant *(Iggy's Doughboys & Chowder House 737-9459, $5-20, seafood market price)*, Fast Food *(McDs, BK)*, Hotel *(3 Royal Waterfront Suites 323-3290, $129-199)* **3+ mi:** Hotel *(Hampton 739-8888, $80+, 4 mi.)*, *(Holiday Inn 736-5000, $99+, 4 mi.)*

Recreation and Entertainment
OnSite: Picnic Area, Grills **Near:** Beach *(Oakland Beach)*, Playground, Jogging Paths *(Oakland Beach)*, Park *(Oakland Beach)* **Under 1 mi:** Tennis Courts *(Hendrickson H.S.)*, Golf Course *(Seaview Country Club 739-6311)*, Bowling *(Meadowbrook 737-5402)*, Fishing Charter, Video Rental *(Redbox)* **1-3 mi:** Fitness Center *(Work Out World 739-9002)* **3+ mi:** Movie Theater *(Showcase 738-3674, 6 mi.)*, Museum *(Warwick Museum Of Art 737-0010, 6 mi.)*

Provisioning and General Services
Near: Delicatessen *(Michael's 739-7299)*, Green Grocer, Bank/ATM **Under 1 mi:** Convenience Store *(7-Eleven 739-8608)*, Wine/Beer, Liquor Store *(Haxtons 737-6737)*, Fishmonger *(Mar 738-2424)*, Barber Shop *(West Shore 738-9117)*, Dry Cleaners *(Theresa's 739-9089)*, Laundry *(DP's 732-1773)* **1-3 mi:** Supermarket *(Stop & Shop 732-4616)*, Bakery *(Antonio's 738-3727)*, Catholic Church, Protestant Church, Library *(Warwick 739-5440)*, Beauty Salon *(Best Cuts 732-1342)*, Pharmacy *(CVS 737-2305)*, Hardware Store *(Salks Hardware & Marine 739-1027)*

Transportation
OnCall: Rental Car *(Enterprise 732-3795)*, Taxi *(Best 781-0706; Bay 461-0780)*, Airport Limo *(Good Tymes 738-4954)* **3+ mi:** Bikes *(Casters Bicycle Center 739-0393, 4 mi.)*, Rail *(Amtrak 800-USA-RAIL, 10 mi.)* **Airport:** TF Green *(4 mi.)*

Medical Services
911 Service **Under 1 mi:** Holistic Services *(West Shore 734-9355)* **1-3 mi:** Doctor *(Fleisig 885-0406)*, Dentist *(Dunn 739-5700)*, Chiropractor *(Hudyncia 732-4400)*, Optician *(Glucksman 739-1336)*, Veterinarian *(West Shore 738-3447)* **Hospital:** Kent County 737-7000 *(5 mi.)*

Setting -- Secluded in the eastern arm of busy Warwick Cove, this simple, family-oriented facility is the last marina to port in a quiet area well out of the summer hubbub. While not fancy, the grounds are neat and well-trimmed, and the older docks and pedestals are in good condition. The two-story, white clapboard office building houses a small but well-stocked store, the bathhouse and helpful staff. A comfortable picnic patio with grills sports long water views.

Marina Notes -- Locally owned marina in a close-knit community. Full-service boatyard. Dealer & service center for Crusader Marine Engines, Onan generators, Cummins Engines. Usually accommodates transients when others are at capacity. 100-foot wide channel with 5 ft at MLW. Good place to leave the boat for an extended period - last harbor in the cove means no passing wakes, and transportation is easy. Bathhouse: Basic, commercial, tiled floors, fiberglass shower stalls. Note: Transient Moorings, sprinkled throughout the Cove beginning at Harbor Light Marina, may be available from the Harbormaster, 738-2000.

Notable -- Warwick Cove is dominated by Oakland Beach, a state park with lifeguards, restrooms, concessions and summer throngs. From Bay Marina, it's closer to dinghy than to drive. One of Rhode Island's best-known restaurants, Timmy's on the Bay, is a short dinghy trip and has a courtesy dock. A major bus hub is a short walk, which makes exploring or shopping easy. Founded as a working man's resort in the 1880's, Oakland Beach hosted a small midway until the 1970s. Most of the attractions were lost to storms, except the Carousel which ended up at an Oregon museum that dispersed the animals to other carousels. Today, volunteers are re-building the carousel from scratch - carving the horses, painting the murals- and will house it in a screwpile lighthouse.

PHOTOS ON DVD: 11

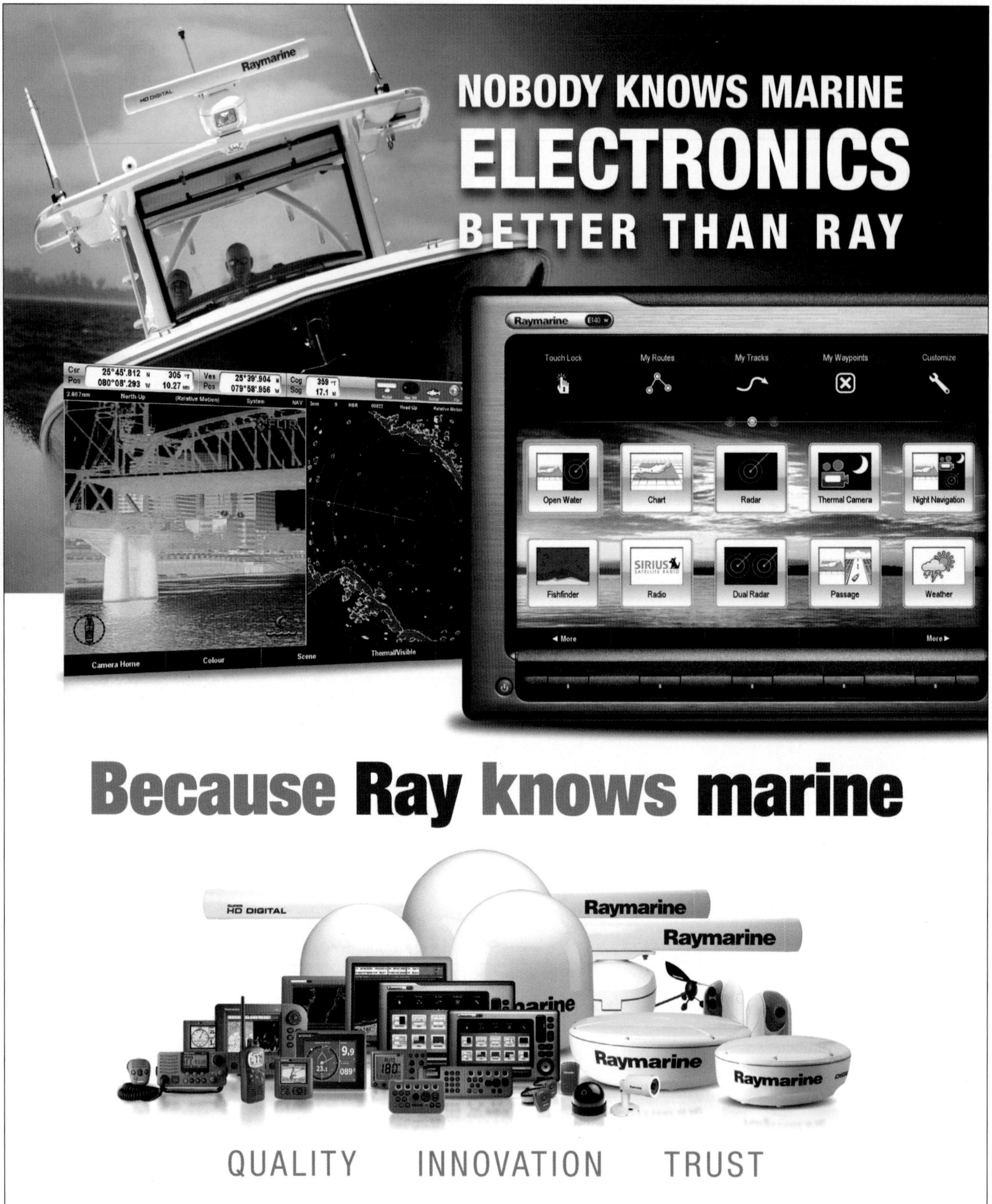

NOBODY KNOWS MARINE ELECTRONICS BETTER THAN RAY

Because Ray knows marine

QUALITY INNOVATION TRUST

Watch all that Ray Knows at Raymarine.com

Raymarine®
A FLIR COMPANY

Alphabetical Listing of Marinas, Harbors and Cities

L

M

N

O

P

Boaters' Resources Index

In an effort to defray some of the costs of researching and publishing the data intensive *Atlantic Cruising Club's Guides to Marinas*, Jerawyn Publishing has invited a select group of companies to place full page advertisements in this volume. We believe they offer products and services that are of interest to readers/users of ACC's *Guides*. We hope that you share our high regard for these companies and will support them. ***Please note:*** *To insure total editorial objectivity, ACC does not solicit or accept advertising or any other form of remuneration from the marinas that it covers in its Guides.*

Acknowledgments

The publisher, editors and authors extend their appreciation to everyone who contributed to this guide, which was more than three years in development. Hundreds of people have helped in various ways. We particularly want to thank the facilities owners, managers and dockmasters who provided enormous quantities of detailed information on their marina and boatyard operations (and reviewed ACC's interpretation along the way) despite their inability to control the final outcome.

The authors also owe a debt of gratitude to the tourism and government agencies and individuals who provided invaluable assistance and critical resources throughout the research process. Many at the Chambers of Commerce, Tourism Offices, Convention and Visitor's Bureaus and state governments shared their local knowledge providing invaluable assistance in the research and fact-checking of this volume.

A few people helped above and beyond, and we want to extend a very special and heartfelt thank you to: Molly Demma & Simon Mitchell, The St. John River Society, Fredericton, NB; William P. DeSousa-Mauk, DeMa Public Relations, Hyannis, MA; Pat Wamback, Nova Scotia Tourism, Culture, and Heritage Halifax, NS; Charlene Williams, Nancy Marshall Communications, Augusta, ME; Annie Everson, Newport CVB, RI.

Without the assistance of the following people, listed by province/state and then alphabetically by geographic regions, this Guide would not be as complete, as thorough or as accurate as it is:

NOVA SCOTIA

Emily Kimber, Destination Halifax; Kaitlyn Touesnard, Pat Wamback, Randy Brooks & Kristen Pickett, Nova Scotia Tourism, Culture, and Heritage; Liz Morine, Destination Southwest Nova Scotia; Jill Cruikshank, Region of Queens. Lodgings & Services: Rodd Grand Hotel, Yarmouth; Oak Island Resort, Western Shore; Chocolate Lake Hotel, Halifax; Digby Pines Resort, Digby; Bay Ferries Ltd.– "Princess of Acadia."

NEW BRUNSWICK

Brenda M. Cline, Deer Island Tourism Association; Holly Kirkpatrick, David Seabrook & Jocelyn Chen, Fredericton Tourism; Rob MacPherson, Natalie Parsons, Grand Manan Tourism Association; Melissa Bochar, New Brunswick Tourism; Diane Rioux, St. Andrews by the Sea Chamber of Commerce; Molly Demma & Simon Mitchell, The St. John River Society; Sally Cummings, Tourism Saint John. Lodgings & Services: Hilton Saint John, Delta Saint John; Lord Beaverbrook Crowne Plaza, Fredericton; Fairmont Algonquin, St. Andrews; Quoddy Loop Ferries; East Coast Ferries, Deer Island.

MAINE

Jessica Donahue & Kerrie Tripp, Greater Bangor CVB; Dee Virtue, Bangor Region Chamber of Commerce; Janet Dutson, Belfast Area Chamber of Commerce; Sue Walsh, Blue Hill Peninsula Chamber of Commerce; Kathy Coogan, Bucksport Bay Chamber of Commerce; Dan Bookham, Camden Rockport, Lincolnville Chamber of Commerce; Denise McCormick, The Cranberry Islands; Tony Cameron, Bar Harbor Chamber of Commerce; Lois Flynn, Campobello Island Tourism Welcome Center; Kathie Kull, Camden-Rockport-Lincolnville Chamber of Commerce; Downeast & Acadia Regional Tourism, Cherryfield; Hilda Lewis, Chamber of Commerce for Eastport; Jim Littlefield, East Penobscot Bay Association; Penny Weinstein, City of Ellsworth; Rose Whitehouse & Nancy Marshall, Communications for the State of Maine; Carolann Ouellette, Maine Office of Tourism; John Lawrence, Mount Desert Chamber of Commerce; Shari Closter, Penobscot Bay Regional Chamber of Commerce; Leanne Ouimet, Greater Portland Convention & Visitor's Bureau; Jim Close, Schoodic Chamber of Commerce; Kristin Hutchins, Southwest Harbor/Tremont Chamber of Commerce; Martha Sullivan, Sullivan Communications PR. Lodgings & Services: Motel East, Eastport, ME; Pleasant Bay B&B, Addison, ME; Seawall Motel, Southwest Harbor; Jasper's, Ellsworth; Inn on the Harbor, Stonington; Spring Fountain Motel, Bucksport; Best Western White House Inn, Bangor; Admirals Ocean Inn, Belfast; Schooner Bay Motor Inn, Rockport; Tugboat Inn, Boothbay Harbor; Casco Bay Lines, Portland; Chebeague Transportation, Great Chebeague Island, Casco Bay; Cranberry Cove Ferry, Southwest Harbor; Maine State Ferry Service, Rockland – Swan's Island, Vinalhaven, North Haven & Islesboro.

NEW HAMPSHIRE & MASSACHUSETTS

Adrienne Davis Brody, ADB Marketing; Larry Meehan & Stacy Shreffler, Greater Boston CVB; Amanda Fancy, North of Boston CVB; Frank Webber, Judy Caulkett, Colleen Magrath, Cape Ann Chamber of Commerce; Kristen Mitchell & Michele Pecoraro, Cape Cod Chamber of Commerce; Timothy R. Carroll & Diane Deblase, Town of Chilmark; Kathryn Balistrieri, Cuttyhunk Historical Society; Bill Desousa-Mauk, DeMa Public Relations, Hyannis; JoAnn Power, Lynn Area Chamber of Commerce; Ann Marie Casey & Katherine Koch, Marblehead Chamber of Commerce; Nancy Gardella, Martha's Vineyard Chamber of Commerce; Lawrel Strauch Spera, Nantucket Island Chamber of Commerce; Ann Marie Lopes, New Bedford Economic Development Office; Laurie Contrino, Greater Newburyport Chamber of Commerce; Paula Fisher & Paul Cripps, Plymouth County CVB; Tricia Ellis & Paula Fisher, See Plymouth; Mark Cary & Bridgette Desmond, Portsmouth, NH Chamber of Commerce; Discover Quincy; Arthur Motta, Southeastern Massachusetts CVB; Eric Gaynor, Winthrop Chamber of Commerce. Lodgings & Services: Annabelle B & B, Sandwich; Belfry Inn, Sandwich; The Bistro, Provincetown.

RHODE ISLAND

Evan Smith, Kathryn Farrington & Annie Everson, Newport CVB; Karla P. Driscoll, North Kingstown Chamber of Commerce; Kristen L. Adamo, Alissa Bateman & Jessica Caparco, Providence Warwick CVB; Kimberly Charlet, South County Tourism Council.

About the Author & Contributors

AUTHOR

Beth Adams-Smith

Beth and her husband, Richard, have been cruising the U.S. East Coast for several decades; other cruising adventures have taken them to Bermuda, the Bahamas, the Caribbean's Leeward and Windward Islands, Tahiti and the Society Islands, Pacific Northwest, Whitsunday Islands, Tonga, Baja, Belize and numerous cruising grounds throughout the Mediterranean – including Corsica, Greece, Croatia, and Turkey. Along the way, they've visited more than 2,500 marinas on North America's East and West coasts as cruisers, authors and editors, including the marinas in this *Guide*.

The primary writer/editor of the Atlantic Cruising Club's *Guides to Marinas*, Beth is also a digital media producer and has spearheaded the design and co-managed the development of Jerawyn Publishing's proprietary Datastract™ database management and digital publishing software starting with the first iteration in 1997 — including a library of over 30,000 nautical and travel images. She is also honchoing the redesign, rebuild, and on-going development of the new AtlanticCruisingClub.com. The website has served boaters since 1999, and, despite numerous upgrades, needed a gut renovation to handle the enhanced marina search capabilities, massive photo files, and library of new content.

In addition to her work on the ACC *Guides* (this is her 8th volume!), Beth writes cruising, destination, green boating, and healthy living articles for print magazines and their websites and for AtlanticCrusingClub.com, blogs as the "Wandering Mariner" focusing on holistic approaches to crew lifestyle and vessel management, cruising, destinations, waterborne and water-oriented travel and also blogs on Travegans.com — for travelers and boaters choosing a plant-based diet. She has produced numerous documentaries, multiple media, and database projects on holistic living, ecology, peacemaking, food, and complementary medicine. Beth holds a Doctorate in Technology and Media and a Masters in Health Education — both from Columbia University, a Bachelors in Broadcast Journalism from Boston University, and is a Certified Health Education Specialist. She is a member of the American Society of Journalists & Authors, Society of American Travel Writers and Boating Writers International.

CONTRIBUTING WRITERS

George Boase *(Rhode Island)*

George's boating experience began at 5-years-old on the Illinois, Green, Mississippi and Missouri rivers. He moved to Michigan and to boating on the Great Lakes. A career change brought him to Rhode Island where his passion for sailing blossomed on Narragansett Bay where he also added blue water experience. For the past 27 years, he has been sailing the northeast coast of the US from Maine to Long Island.

George is a well-respected ghost-writer and specializes in POD books for both back-table sales and promotions as well as published books. He also works with corporate clients on mission statements, business plans, RFPs and other white papers as well as short, concise SEO content for travel, lodging and business reviews. He has just finished writing "Anchoring with Style made Plain and Simple," and, as a member of Boating Writers International, continues to write magazine articles on yachting and blogging on "TheCruisingSailor.com" where the focus is on making yachting affordable for the average person. Currently George and his wife are preparing a new boat to begin life aboard and become full time cruisers in late 2011.

Peter Quandt *(Massachusetts)*

Peter is a lifelong sailor and power boater. Now primarily a Buzzards Bay sailor, he grew up sailing on Long Island's Great South Bay and Long Island Sound. At 15, he built two of his first wooden sailboats, including the spars and all the rigging. Though primarily a sailboat racer, Peter does kick back occasionally to cruise the Caribbean's Windward Islands.

Though boating is primarily an avocation, he has worked in the marine industry as a sailing instructor and manager of the Bahamas site of Offshore Sailing School, as a sail-maker, and as a salesman for boats and marine equipment. He speaks multiple languages, thanks to various extended periods of his career spent in France and Italy, where he sailed out of Anzio. Peter has written for a wide variety of audiences, including Department of State testimony before Congress, intelligence analysis for the CIA and the Pentagon, as well as somewhat lighter material for boating magazines.

Brian Mehler *(Southern Maine)*

Brian grew up in Freeport spending a great deal of his time in and around the water. After graduating from Villanova, he was a freelance writer and photo journalist focusing on the Maine Coast (as well as India and Nepal) and provided invaluable local knowledge to the research and photography of the southern Maine chapters. He is now a Masters candidate in the department of Communication, Culture and Technology at Georgetown University.

Order Form

Please ask for the *Guides* at your local book store or chandler or order directly from www.AtlanticCruisingClub.com

☐ **Please register me as a member of the Atlantic Cruising Club so that I can benefit from even greater discounts and email specials.**

☐ **Please send me the following *Atlantic Cruising Club's Guides to Marinas*:**

For Discounts, log onto www.AtlanticCruisingClub.com

Complimentary 6-month Silver Membership for purchasers of any ACC Guide to Marinas

_____ ***Atlantic Cruising Club's Guide to New England & Canadian Maritime Marinas — 8th Ed.***; *US $39.95*
Expanded Coverage & Totally Revised — in Full Color
Halifax, NS to Wickford, RI *(Including Bay of Fundy, St. Johns River, Buzzards & Narragansett Bays, Martha's Vineyard & Nantucket)*

_____ ***Atlantic Cruising Club's Guide to Long Island Sound Marinas***; *US $24.95*
Block Island, RI to Cape May, NJ *(Including Connecticut River, New York Harbor, Long Island's South Shore Inlets & New Jersey Inlets)*

_____ ***Atlantic Cruising Club's Guide to Chesapeake Bay Marinas***; *US $32.95*
C&D Canal, DE to Hampton Roads, VA *(Including Delmarva Atlantic Coast and Potomac, Choptank, Rappahannock and James Rivers)*

_____ ***Atlantic Cruising Club's Guide to Mid-Atlantic/ICW Marinas — in Full Color***; *US $39.95*
Hampton, VA to St. Mary's, GA *(Including Intracoastal Waterway, James, Pamlico & Neuse Rivers, N.C. Sounds & Outer Banks)*

_____ ***Atlantic Cruising Club's Guide to Florida's East Coast Marinas***; *US $29.95*
Fernandina, FL to Key West, FL *(Including St. Johns River, the Intracoastal Waterway and the Florida Keys)*

_____ ***Atlantic Cruising Club's Guide to Florida's West Coast Marinas — in Full Color***; *US $34.95 (January 2012)*
Everglades City, FL to Pensacola, FL *(Including Caloosahatchee River, Okeechobee Waterway and the Gulf Coast Intracoastal Waterway)*

_____ ***Atlantic Cruising Club's Guide to Pacific Northwest Marinas***; *US $29.95*
Campbell River, BC to Brookings, OR *(Including Gulf and San Juan Islands, Puget Sound, Strait of Juan de Fuca and the Hood Canal)*

__________ *Sub-Total*

__________ *Tax (New York State Residents only add 6.75%)*

__________ *Shipping & Handling (USPS — add $4.00 for first book and $2.00 for each subsequent book)*

Final Total

In Development: ***Atlantic Cruising Club's Guide to East Coast Mega-Yacht Marinas — in Full Color***
Halifax, Nova Scotia to Pensacola, Florida *(Facilities that accommodate yachts with LOAs 100 feet and over)*

Please charge the following credit card: Amex ☐ MasterCard ☐ Visa ☐ Discover ☐ Check Enclosed ☐

Number: __________ *Three/Four-Digit Security Number:* __________

Expiration Date: __________ *Signature:* __________

Name: __________ *Email:* __________

Address: __________ *City:* __________ *State or Province:* _____ *Zip:* __________

Home Phone: __________ *Office Phone:* __________ *Fax:* __________

Boat Name: __________ *Length:* __________ *Manufacturer:* __________

Boat Type: Sail Mono-Hull ☐ Sail Multi-Hull ☐ Power ☐ Power Multi-Hull ☐ Trawler ☐ Megayacht ☐

Home Port: __________ *Cruising Grounds:* __________

Please mail, fax. email, or call-in your order to: **Atlantic Cruising Club at Jerawyn Publishing, Inc.** PO Box 978; Rye, New York 10580
Tel: (914) 967-0994 or (888) 967-0994; Fax: (914) 206-6016; Email: Orders@AtlanticCruisingClub.com; Website: www.Atlantic CruisingClub.com